What a Young Man Should Know About Sex

WHAT A YOUNG MAN SHOULD KNOW ABOUT SEX

REVISED EDITION

Answers to Personal Problems

*by John F. Knight, M.B.B.S.**

*A standard medical degree in British countries

PACIFIC PRESS PUBLISHING ASSOCIATION
Mountain View, California
Omaha, Nebraska Oshawa, Ontario

Library of Congress Catalog Card No. 76-48572

Cover and page 207 by D. Tank; other color photos by Russell Gibbs
Cover design by Lauren Smith

Contents

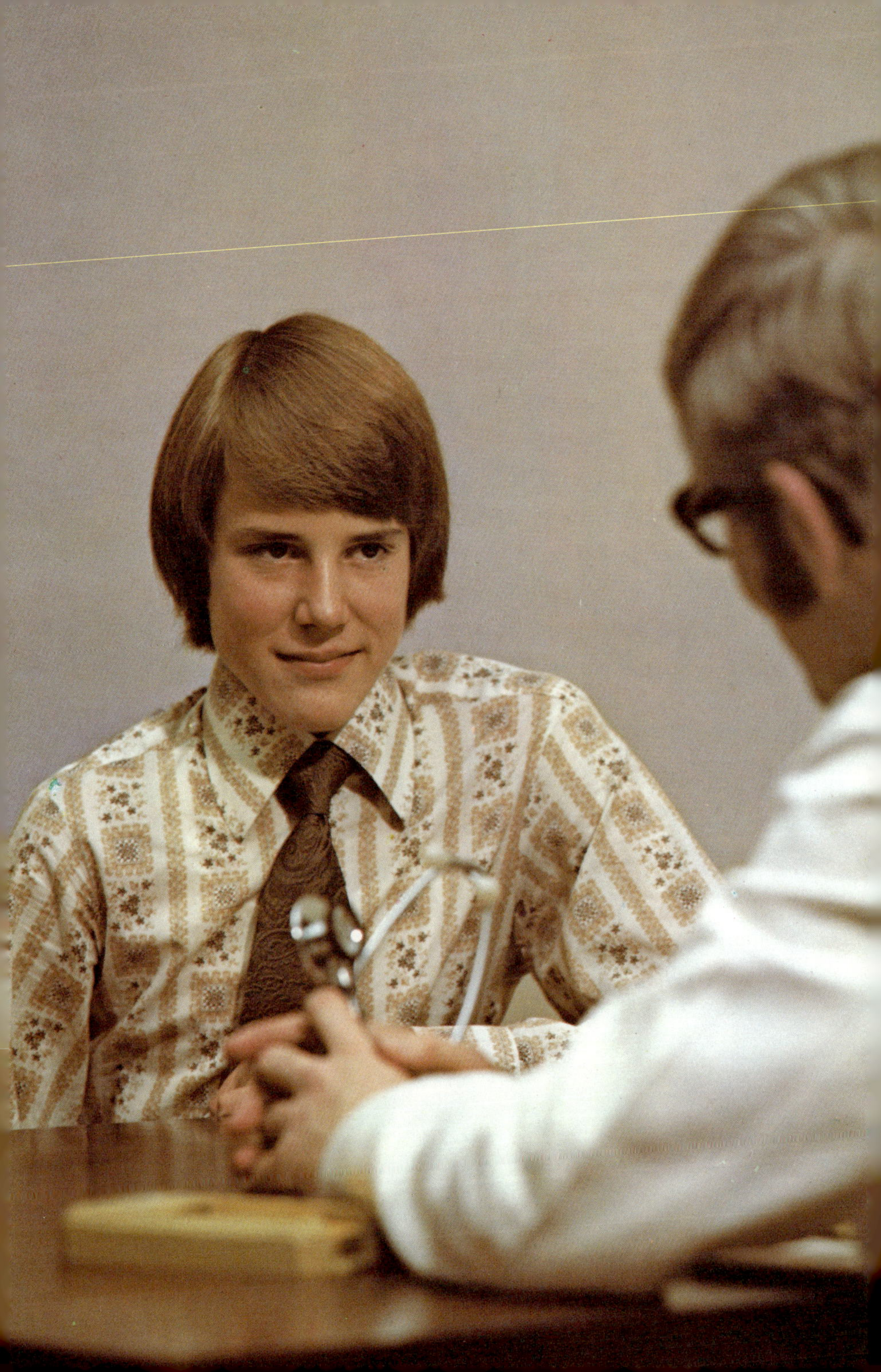

1

Hi There!

Hi there!

How d'you do!

I hear we're writing a book.

I've heard the same thing.

What's it all about? You know more of the finer points than I do.

It's to be a very important book for the up-and-coming members of the male species.

You mean a book for teen-age boys?

That's the general theme. And it contains some very important information.

About what?

The basic aim is to give this general age group a few of the fundamental facts about life.

Don't tell me it's another "All-about-the-birdies-and-bees" routine.

No, it isn't. But that, of course, is a pretty important piece of information every teen-ager is keen to know more about. We're surely touching on the delicate subject of "sex and all that." Indeed, this will form an important part of our book.

But let me say from the start, we're trying to get away from the round-and-round-the-mulberry-bush way it has been presented over the past fifty years.

Hooray for that!

We're living in the latter part of the twentieth century. Most of the kids today will see the year 2000 come and go (if the world is still intact by then). What was good information for Mom and Grandma just isn't acceptable to today's fellows.

You mean the idea is to present factual data in straight and sensible language, the kind teen-agers understand?

Exactly! And therefore, we don't even plan to discuss the birds or the bees as such. And we certainly won't be setting out those delicate little pictures the older-type books seemed to love so much.

Like two happy birds nesting together, or a farmyard scene, and strange pictures of frogs and all that?

You read me loud and clear. Out! Teen-age boys want facts today, and they want them clear and concise.

And that is what our little volume is going to present?

Yes, right from the shoulder!

In language everyone can understand?

For sure! We're cutting back the small-fry talk, but it's not our intention to make it an indecipherable textbook you need a university degree to follow, either. Only well-known technical words will be used in the appropriate spots. But these, too, will be kept to a minimum, so that no dictionary will be required.

I'm glad about that. I hate carting massive tomes everywhere I go so I can follow what's being said.

You'll have no problem. And neither will our readers. Any off-beat words will be self-explanatory. There'll be a few sensible, simple line illustrations to get our points across. A few technical and medical terms are inevitable, but I go for the straightforward, simple approach.

Now, you started off by saying something about sex–and all that.

Right. Every fellow in his teens knows a fair bit about sex by the time he reaches this ripe old age. However, I've found that even though he can recite the anatomy right off (and perhaps do a creditable job with art work too!), there are basic gaps he's still not too sure about.

So you plan to fill in the gaps?

More than that. Just to make sure he's getting the right idea, we'll start at the beginning, and explain with accurate information and illustrations. If the reader knows all about the bits we're explaining, he can skip across to the next section until he catches up to where his knowledge needs filling in.

However, I think he'll probably stick with it all right from the start.

I believe so, too. After all, there will be continuity from the very first page. If he misses vital points there, reading won't be quite so smooth when he flips over a chapter or so.

Sex—A Part of Life

Sex, then, plays an important part in this book. Right?

"Sex" is a harsh-sounding word. I suppose it covers a large range of subjects. I'd prefer to describe it as an introduction to boy-girl relationships. It'll cover the basics of the way we're all built, certainly. But it'll go on and discuss many of the social aspects of living with ourselves, and with each other. There are many facts that never occur to us when we're young, but which become problems as the years roll by, and we develop, and have to take our place in society.

Of course, getting back to "sex," the mere word can mean

different things to different people.

Quite so. Basically, life consists of two sexes, male and female. That's one definition of the word. Go on a bit, and it may relate to the relationship between male and female. This can be on a simple, uncomplicated level.

Or it can be projected a bit further.

Absolutely. The casual relationship sooner or later drifts on to a more intimate one, so that with marriage, the full relationship of sexual union is experienced. Sex then reaches its most meaningful relationship. It achieves fulfillment. The gradual progression from the simple to the complex is one of the wonders of life.

Of course, as far as the popular media is concerned, "sex" usually means one thing and one thing only.

Little doubt about that. And in the minds of plenty of our youthful readers, it probably has a similar interpretation. Just the same, this isn't to be criticized. With the pressures of the world at large continually pressing onto formative minds, there's little wonder the majority form the early impressions they do. One of the purposes of our little volume is to try and fix sex into its right perspective.

You mean that if you read the popular press, a lopsided impression is often gained?

That is so. Sex is merely one aspect of living, and if it can be fitted into a sensible mental slot, then we're getting progress. This important age group has many problems related to their sex, but not concerning sex (as we've described it).

Many are still at school, in college, attending university, doing apprenticeship courses, and so forth. All manner of complex difficulties are regularly arising. It's our intention to take up some of the more common ones and try to find sensible, simple answers.

Then you won't be too theoretical?

Look, I believe practical solutions are essential. Every problem has a correct answer. It may not always be 100 percent successful, but at least a reasonable answer to a problem is better than floundering in the dark and having no sense of direction or security—or having no solution at all. On the other hand, of course, many problems have straightforward answers. I don't know them all, but I feel I have a good idea of many of them.

How come?

There are several reasons. To start with, I've four growing teen-agers myself. On the home front, I've been bombarded with so many questions over the past few years that I sometimes believe I've heard the whole book firsthand!

That seems a reasonable starting point. Incidentally, are the four all boys or all girls?

Fortunately it's fifty-fifty. Girl-boy-girl-boy in that order. (I might even give you the magic formula for this sometime!)

Great! It could even make us millionaires overnight!

Second, I'm rather heavily involved with the popular press. In fact, as you know, I write several regular columns that seem to be read by a lot of people in the age spectrum we're talking about. The tremendous amount of mail these columns generate never ceases to amaze me. In fact, it arrives by the bagful—literally.

What are these letters about?

I'm sure they cover nearly every imaginable topic that young people could dream up. One thing is certain. I believe about 95 percent of the letters are genuine requests. They all bear names and addresses, and the majority are personally signed. This is pretty good evidence of good faith (as they say). Each one presents a personal problem of the writer.

Do you find many questions are repeated?

Do I ever! Indeed, extremely large numbers of questions

are asked over and over again. Sometimes almost identical language is used. But as the writers might live 3000 miles apart, it's not likely to be the same person, or folk even remotely connected. The simple fact of life is this: growing youth (and indeed people everywhere) experience identical problems as they journey through life.

As a point of interest, do you answer all these letters?

It varies a good deal. Many are answered. In fact, as so many "typical" letters are received, printed answers to many of these have been carefully worked out. But many of them still receive personal, "tailor-made" replies.

So this huge volume of mail, in a sense, will form the basic framework for the type of information you intend to give?

It will help. It at least lets us know the questions most people are asking right now. A large number of these will be incorporated in the pages that follow.

Any other way of assessing common problems?

Every day I see many people in my consulting rooms. This is the direct link with people having problems. If they weren't experiencing difficulties, they wouldn't be coming to see me in the first place. Over the years it has been my custom to make brief notes of the frequency of various complaints people come with.

So this also will form part of the book?

In a sense it will. It alerts us to the current everyday problems, as related to youth. There is no point in outlining masses of problems that aren't in existence! That would be foolish and of interest to no one. Better have the queries that most folk are asking right at this moment.

So you feel a pretty wide spectrum of up-to-date problems can be given?

All I can say is that I believe so. If we can do this, then I believe this book will have achieved a definite purpose in life.

2

Strange Facts About Boys

What Happens at Puberty

Now suppose we get down to some of the fundamentals.

No doubt most male readers (whatever their age) have a pretty good idea of how they're constructed.

Most likely. However, there's a bit more to it than the obvious outward appearances. I think it's worth spending a bit of time in these preliminary pages in setting out a little detail of the inner workings of the sexes.

Seeing this is a book predominantly designed for boys, let's start with them. We'll talk about the girls later.

Let's begin with the obviously "all-male" external parts.

Right. These are technically called the penis and the scrotum.

The penis is the elongated structure located at the upper junction of the legs at the front. During childhood (as every male recalls), it is quite small and rather inconspicuous and insignificant. But with advancing years of adolescence, under the control of body chemicals called hormones, the penis (and also the scrotum) increases in size.

It gradually elongates, becomes larger in circumference, and generally increases in overall size.

There is no hard-and-fast norm for the fully developed adult penis. Under normal, relaxed circumstances, it may measure anywhere from three to seven inches in length. Some men may dispute this, claiming other figures (in both directions). However, as long as it can satisfactorily perform the functions for which it was designed, that's all that really matters.

I usually tell patients who have a hang-up about the size and shape of their penis that it really isn't very important. "It's performance that counts," I explain. If you're anatomically intact, that is the chief concern.

Don't you think many males equate the size of the penis with masculinity?

There is absolutely no doubt about that. It's probably part of the forceful drive of the male of the species that so much attention is paid to this segment of the anatomy. But, I have to admit that the average male most certainly does think about it a great deal!

Sex Drive

Don't you think sexual drive is extremely forceful?

It is, and it matches the drive to survive, to satisfy hunger and thirst. That's another reason why so much importance is attached to this organ of procreation.

Don't some persons have an abnormally undersized penis?

True, but these are in the minority by far. There is a condition called micro-penis (which doctors rarely see), in which there is marked underdevelopment of this organ.

Didn't you run into an odd situation regarding this sort of case once? I vaguely recall that you told me about it.

Yes. In fact, I'm still hearing about it! In one of my daily newspaper columns which is a question-and-answer feature, I made brief mention of a letter I'd received from a father who was concerned about his son whom he felt was "underdeveloped."

My reply indicated that suitable treatment was often available for such cases, and that much could probably be done. What I imagined, of course, was that there was probably some inherent hormonal lack which if corrected could produce a relatively normal adult.

What happened?

What happened was that I was completely deluged with mail. Letters arrived by the hundred. This kept up for weeks and months. In fact, a year later I was still receiving correspondence.

It seemed every reader had applied this piece of information to himself, or his offspring, or some relative. Here, it seemed, was the universal panacea for their sex problems—both actual and future. The idea behind these letters seemed to be, "If I (my son, my relative) can be made more of a man, let's do it!"

What did you tell all these hopefuls?

We had a special letter printed. This outlined the truth of the matter. It pointed out that there was no universal "betterment elixir" for normal people. There was certainly specialized therapy for individuals who were anatomically and physiologically underdeveloped. But not for normal males who were probably not as well endowed (for want of a better term) as some others.

Male Hygiene

Normally the penis hangs limply down over the scrotum. Right?

Yes. It is quite flaccid for the major part of the time.

The organ consists of a slightly enlarged, tapered end part, or head, which is termed the glans penis. Behind this is the trunk, which is attached to the lower pelvic part of the body. In some, the glans is covered by the foreskin; in others this has been removed.

Isn't there a minor war going on at the present over the desirability of circumcision?

This seems to be so. Until recent times, it was almost standard procedure for male babies to be "circumcised" a few days after birth. In fact, in Australia it was almost routine, although of course the consent of the parents was usually first obtained.

Many factors in support of it have been put forward over the years. It's claimed that circumcision allows the glans to be kept clean.

Doesn't unpleasant material accumulate there easily?

True. A creamy material called *smegma* often gathers between the glans and the foreskin. Indeed, if it is not washed away very regularly (and particularly in warm weather), it can produce an unpleasant odor. It can also initiate irritation between the two surfaces. This can cause redness and even distinct pain in the general area.

This area should be carefully washed every day, don't you feel?

Of course. We wash the rest of the body each day (clean our teeth two or three times a day) and perform many other duties in a routine fashion. But many young men (and older men as well) who have not been circumcised seem to neglect this important part of the system.

It is relatively simple to pull the skin back gently over the glans and give it a thorough washing. After this, the foreskin automatically returns to its former position, or it can be returned manually.

Any debris and secretions can be gently removed this safe, simple way. This minor problem arises, of course, only in those who are not circumcised. With males who have had the foreskin removed, there is no room for this material to accumulate.

If the glans is not cleaned of this material, wouldn't that open the way to infection and pain and later discomfort?

Precisely. Germs may multiply in the secretions, and an uncomfortable condition called balanitis set up.

I've heard that cancer of the penis is not so common with circumcised males.

According to one stalwart supporter of circumcision: "Cancer of the penis virtually never occurs in a man who was circumcised at infancy."[1]

But others state that cancer of the penis is very rare in any case. Maybe it is so, although in 1967 there were 218 fatalities from the disease! (U.S. statistics.) Maybe they would have been still alive today (and performing economically worthwhile work) if they had been circumcised at birth!

Is this the only sort of cancer involved?

It is believed that cancer of the prostate gland (which is part of the urogenital system in males) is also less common in those who have been circumcised. A study which compared death from prostatic cancer among uncircumcised Swedes with Jews (who are routinely circumcised) seemed to indicate that cancer was far less frequent among the circumcised.[2]

Are wives affected in any way by circumcision or uncircumcision?

It seems that cancer of the cervix (or "neck" of the womb in women)—a very common cause of death—is far less common with Jewish women. That is, in those whose husbands have been circumcised.

Also, an irritating disorder of the vagina (the female genital tract) termed moniliasis, is more common when husbands have not been circumcised.

Some Medical Problems

What about males who have only a small aperture?

Yes, this is called *phimosis*. As time goes on, a certain number of uncircumcised males develop a condition where the opening at the far end of the foreskin is too small to allow the skin to be drawn back over the head of the penis. It's believed that about one uncircumcised male in ten will develop phimosis. If it does occur, infection can readily commence underneath. Pain, distension, and discharge can quickly follow. This in turn can make urination painful and indeed quite difficult.

Operations to relieve this (when adult life has been reached) can be extremely uncomfortable. Almost painless circumcision in infancy, the protagonists declare, is well worthwhile, for it will forever prevent such complications in later life.

Surely there must be some good points for not being circumcised.

Most definitely! It's claimed the uncircumcised adult male enjoys a far better sex life. The glans, being protected from external damage, is more sensitive, and is more responsive to sexual stimulation or intercourse. On the other hand, others hotly deny this. Drs. Masters and Johnson who carried out extensive tests in the United States recently, say that there is no difference in this respect between the two groups.[3]

Many doctors now believe that as we were born with foreskin, therefore it must be there to serve some useful purpose, even though we may not be fully aware what all these reasons are. They regard circumsion as nothing short of a barbaric act which is carried out more for traditional reasons than for any true, significant, scientifically explainable purpose.

What's the present situation in other countries, say in

Australia and New Zealand?

Recently, an official stand was made by the Australian Pediatric Society—the important group who care for babies. They stated that in their opinion circumcision should not be carried out as a routine measure. And that is that!

Does everyone follow this decision?

Not really. Just now, it's about fifty-fifty. Many mothers still desire their babies to be circumcised. No doubt they reason that if the father had it, the small son should likewise have it. Others take an intelligent interest in the "fors" and "againsts." Doctors likewise still seem divided. Maybe the position will change with the passage of time. In many European countries, few (if any) male babies have the operation performed.

We haven't made a lot of progress about our description of the male sex organs, have we?

Probably not. But I think it's worthwhile discussing some of the points about the organs as we come to them. After all, our readers are certain to hear gossip about these structures as they pass through life and wonder what it's all about. There is no harm in discovering the facts (the points for and the points against) at this early stage.

What do you personally instruct your patients in the circumcision business?

I have no axe to grind either way. I discuss the points in favor of circumcision, plus the points against it and then let the parents make up their own minds.

Do you try to force opinions?

No. It's not worth it.

However, there is one aspect I do stress. I feel that if there is more than one male offspring in the home, then there should be uniformity.

There is nothing worse than children of the same sex "being different.'' It can be mentally traumatic. It can make one feel inferior and, I feel, prove to be psychologically damaging. Boys *do* exchange more than notes!

This topic has often come to my notice over the years. Although it is impossible for entire schools to have anatomical uniformity, it certainly is possible within the home.

That will be enough for this chapter. We'll continue our discussion about the structure of the male organs in the next chapter.

REFERENCES:

1. Marvin S. Elger, MD, ''The Case for Circumcision,'' *Today's Health*, vol. 50, no. 4 (April 1972).
2. *Ibid.*
3. *Ibid.*

3

Production Line That Never Sleeps

In the second chapter we made a tentative start on our description of the external male organs of procreation.

That's a fine-sounding term. It sounds nice and euphonious.

Shouldn't offend a soul. Just remember, even though our volume is primarily designed for Bill, and Jim, and Harry, and his fellows to read, Uncle Joe, and Dad, and Grandad Tom might be taking a look inside the covers too.

That's correct. Therefore we must use language that will suit all.

Of course it's highly probable we'll have a smattering of female readers too.

They should be content to settle for the counterpart to this volume. It's entitled: What a Young Woman Should Know About Sex. With variations, it sets out the female equivalent of the material we're presenting here for boys.

We spoke briefly of the male penis. Its general features were described. In other words, how it looks to the casual observer under normal moments of inactivity. Now let's hear what is contained inside the penis.

It is an extremely intricate organ. The interior is composed mainly of a very loose, spongy material. This extends from the glans (the head, remember), along the body of the organ.

What's the significance of this spongy material?

Just this. At normal times only a small volume of blood is circulating in the penis. But at other times, particularly under the stimulation of sexual pleasure (whether this be physical or merely mental), a copious amount of blood surges into this spongy material.

As this occurs, the normally limp structure quite quickly becomes enlarged. As this happens, instead of hanging in a loose, downward direction, it points forward, and later in an upward direction. The more blood that enters the spongy mass, the firmer and more erect it becomes.

Is this the mechanics of what is called "erection"?

Yes. It is quite interesting to note that the direction in which it automatically points is very similar to the normal direction of the female vagina.

Designed this way by nature, of course.

Of course. Apart from its function of eliminating waste products from the system by way of the urine, the penis is also one of the organs of reproduction.

But before it can function in this capacity, it is essential for it to enter and traverse the female genital tract, the vagina.

In its limp state, this is mechanically impossible. But when it becomes enlarged, turgid, and erect, it becomes quite simple for the act to take place. Therefore this erection system has been designed to facilitate this function.

The Glands and Passages

What about the canal that traverses the penis?

This is called the urethra. It comes to the surface at the tip of the glans. To this point, it courses along the length of the

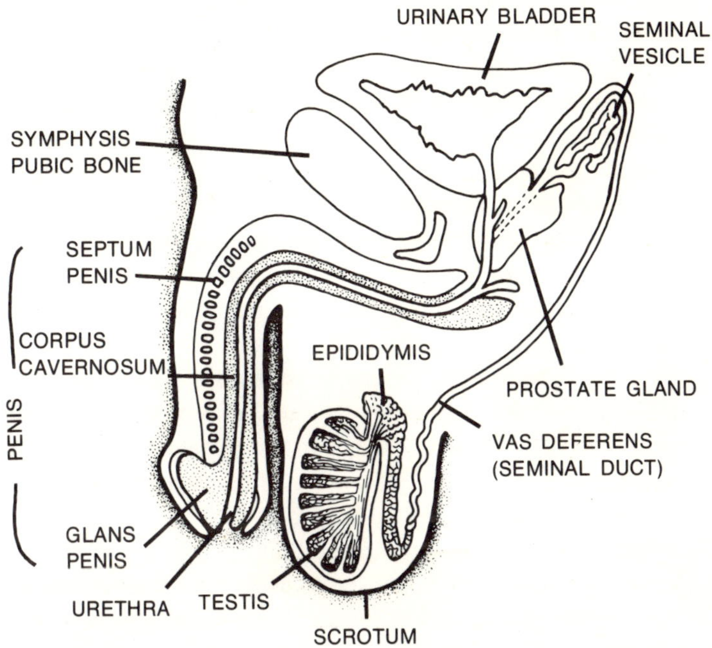

MALE ORGANS OF REPRODUCTION

This is a diagrammatic section of the external and internal reproductive male organs.

The penis normally hangs loosely downward. It is traversed by the narrow canal called the urethra. This transmits urine from the bladder to the exterior. But it also transports male cells (sperms) during intercourse.

It is formed of an inner spongy material that becomes engorged with blood during sexual stimulation (corpus cavernosum).

The loose baglike structure below and behind is called the scrotum. It houses the testes where the male cells are formed. The sperms travel via the epididymis, and later the vas deferens, up into the body to be stored in the seminal vesicles until they are discharged at intercourse.

Upon discharge they travel via the urethra to the exterior.

penis from the urinary bladder inside the abdomen.

The bladder is a large storehouse where the urine (containing excess fluids and waste products from the body) accumulates. The blood is continually filtering through the two kidneys (one on either side), and material not needed by the system is conveyed via fluid down two tubes into the bladder. Here it is stored until it can be conveniently voided. Therefore, in this context, the urethra is a simple tube which is part of the urinary system.

How does this fit in with its reproductive function?

Just below the bladder the urethra is joined by another tube which comes from another storehouse called the seminal vesicle.

In the seminal vesicles are housed masses of male cells called sperms. These are the male cells of reproduction. The spermatic fluid patiently waits in its storehouse until the moment it is required. This is usually when sexual intercourse occurs. We'll tell you more about that later on.

The interesting point to note is that the urethra, in effect, serves two functions. It transports urine from the bladder to the exterior. But at other times, it conveys male cells to the exterior from the seminal vesicles as well.

Don't the two functions get a bit mixed up every now and again?

Fortunately not. By an intricate and delicately balanced set of valves, only one function operates at any given time. When the tract is being used by the male cells, the urine is locked off. And vice versa.

Now let's get back to the other part of the external male apparatus. We've discussed the penis. The scrotum is the other obvious part.

The scrotum is merely a loose pouchlike structure that houses two organs called the testes. Without much effort

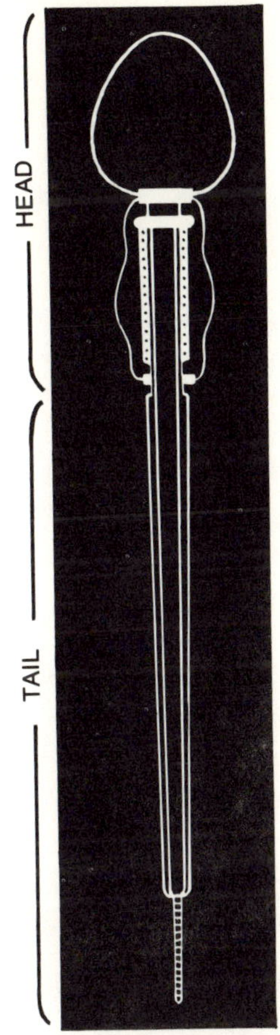

FIGURE 1

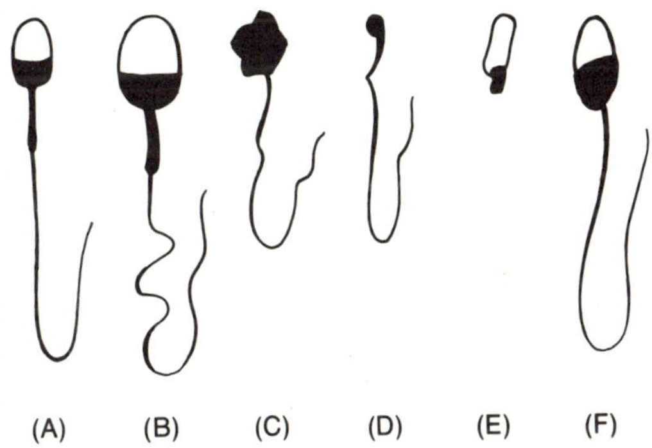

FIGURE 2

THE MALE REPRODUCTIVE CELL

This is the "spermatozoon" (or "sperm" for short), the male cell of the reproduction.

Produced continuously by the testes, enormous numbers are manufactured. Indeed, in one single emission up to 700 million male cells are released (and it takes only **one** to produce a pregnancy!).

Figure 1 shows the normal shape of the male sperm. It has a head and a tail portion. It is essential that the tail move freely to help propel it along.

In Figure 2, diagram (a) is the normal sperm. Diagrams (b) to (f) are "abnormal" sperms. These are not likely to reproduce. If a large number of these are normally present in the seminal fluid, problems and difficulties in becoming pregnant may occur.

these can readily be felt. The testes are two extremely delicate and important organs.

What's their chief purpose?

They have two functions. First, they are the factory for the production of the male cells of reproduction. One of these cells is technically referred to by doctors as a spermatozoon.

However, lazy humans, being what they are, invariably shorten this long word to sperm. Therefore we'll call the male cell a sperm also.

Each testis (on either side of the scrotum) is composed of many microscopic tubes which are in continuity. By a process that is going on nonstop, night and day, and referred to as spermatogenesis, male sperms are being manufactured. As they come off the production line, they pass into tubes that gradually increase in size.

The part of the tube nearest to the testis is called the epididymis. This leads into a larger one called the vas deferens (or seminal duct).

Is this the tube that leads into the body itself?

Yes, the vas (as it's commonly known) runs from the scrotum into the lower part of the body (which is called the pelvis), up into the smallish storehouse we spoke of earlier, the seminal vesicle.

So sperms are manufactured in the testis. From here they pass into the epididymis, thence into the vas, then into the body, to be stored in the seminal vesicles. Right?

Correct.

What Does a Sperm Do?

What does a sperm actually look like, and can it move of its own accord? I wonder just how it can climb uphill, so to speak, which it must do to get from point of manufacture to point of storage.

First of all, the sperm is a very minute, microscopic substance. It can be seen under the microscope, but only by use of the big powerful electron microscope (which magnifies anything up to 80,000 times) can the details of structure be worked out.

Basically, the sperm consists of a head, a middle piece, and a tail.

The head contains the life-bearing part or nucleus. This part also contains the vital chromosomes and genes which transmit the various hereditary characteristics. I'm sure you've all heard about your genes (for better or for worse!).

What does the tail do?

The function of the tail is for propulsion. With the sperm the tail moves with a wavelike action that passes from the front to the back of the cell. In this manner it can actively move itself along!

A bit like a tadpole?

Somewhat, though similar only in the matter of self-propulsion.

Do the testes produce many sperms?

The production rate is little short of phenomenal. In one single emission (for example, at the end point of sexual intercourse when ejaculation takes place) about two to four ml of seminal fluid are released. (That's roughly half a teaspoon.) This contains the astronomical number of up to 700 million sperms! Imagine that!

We're talking millionaire language now!

True enough. The actual cell numbers vary a good deal and are affected by various factors. Yet, the average count is around 200 million, the experts claim. And just think. Only *one* sperm is required to produce a pregnancy!

How rapidly can a sperm move?

Under normal circumstances they move along at the rate of

one to three cm a minute. For such minute objects this is really moving.

What happens when the sperms reach the seminal vesicle?

Here they are stored until they are required. But as the male cells travel upward to the vesicle, fluid is added to make their journey from this point on more simple.

Many glands are located in the tubes and passageways. They produce liquid, and this, too, is stored in the vesicles. The entire product is referred to as seminal fluid. In actual fact, the sperm is nourished from special nutrients contained in this fluid.

There is a passage leading from the vesicles to the exterior?

Yes. As we were saying earlier, a small canal leads from the vesicles, through the large prostate gland (which is situated under the bladder), and enters the canal called the urethra. This canal is the common duct that can transport to the exterior either urine (from the bladder) or sperms from the vesicles.

By a simple yet very efficient system of valves, backflows of urine or sperms are not possible. When urine is being voided, the canal leading to the vesicles shuts off, and vice versa. It is all very mechanical, very efficient, well designed. Accidents just don't happen as a rule.

Problems With Sperm

What happens if sperm production slackens off? I believe this can occur sometimes.

Normally, sperm production continues unabated right from the days of puberty (ie, 12 to 17—it varies with each developing lad) through until later life. Some of the reported ages at which males have been known to reproduce are incredible.

However, some males, for reasons not clearly understood, have below-normal sperm production. This can be worked out by performing "sperm counts." They are often ordered from the pathologist by doctors whose patients may be experiencing difficulty in reproducing.

It is now well known that if the sperm count falls from the average norm of 200 million to fewer than 60 million, possible troubles are in store.

Also if the "motility" factor of the sperms is impaired, problems could also be encountered. This means the sperms have lost their power of movement. In other words, they're unable to "swim" to their objective.

Finally, some men produce odd-shaped "deformed" sperms. If 20 percent or more are deformed, then problems of conception are a distinct possibility too.

This seems incredible when one considers that one solitary sperm is all that is needed to produce a new life.

Maybe it does, but these are the facts.

I've heard that certain diseases, such as mumps, can upset the sperm-producing process. What are the facts with this?

It is quite true. Mumps is produced by a virus. Generally, it is confined to the salivary glands around the neck region. But sometimes, for reasons not fully understood, it can race down to the testes. Here a very painful and indeed serious complication called orchitis can occur.

What happens?

The testes swell. Indeed, they can assume enormous proportions. I've seen them swell to the size of a large orange or grapefruit. The organ becomes extremely tender. This may persist for many days or even weeks.

Unfortunately, there is no specific therapy that is of much value. Certainly no antibiotic or drug will kill the mumps virus. Maybe we'll have the answer in capsule form someday; but right now we have none.

It's really a matter of the system's built-in defense mechanism building up to the point where it can overcome the invaders and kill them off.

This can react adversely on sperm production?

Unfortunately, yes. In some instances it can play such havoc as to destroy entirely the sperm-producing activity of the testes!

It either does this, or in some other way blocks the release of the sperms from the point of manufacture. In any case, many instances have occurred where there are absolutely no male cells in the spermatic fluid.

The outcome of this then is quite obvious.

Definitely. No sperms means the chance of a pregnancy being induced is also nil.

It can be a very sad state of affairs. Usually this fact is not realized until a married couple consistently fail to reproduce. Then, with careful investigation, the unhappy truth reveals itself.

Can other reasons cause a lack of sperm production?

There seem to be other causes for the condition of no sperms in the seminal fluid. Azospermia is the word the doctors talk about when this condition occurs. The causes are little understood. But one thing seems pretty certain: a cure for the dilemma is not readily forthcoming.

As a point of interest, what do these childless couples do if they subsequently desire a family? And after all, this is one of the purposes of married life.

The problem often becomes quite acute. Many of them adopt one or more babies.

Others decide that the relatively new idea of artificial insemination is both desirable and practical. I have seen this work very smoothly in several instances. Everyone thereafter is happy. But this may need a definite personality type to accept the idea readily. Many males (being proud and unrelenting) will not even consider the idea. They feel it is a slur on their manliness. Personally, I do not believe it is, but it is hard to alter personalities.

Again, others just accept the fact, put up with the situation, and live a life without children. Unfortunately, a certain proportion of such married couples split up and go their separate ways. As far as the male is concerned, of course, there is always the chance that the problem will recur should he decide to remarry, if a divorce has been granted.

Earlier you stated that the testes have two chief functions. The first is to produce the male cell, or sperm. What then is its second function? I am sure this must be relevant to our discussion.

It is very relevant. Indeed, it plays a phenomenally important part in the life of the male. In fact, from the moment a male is born, until he finally dies, even from old age, its effect is felt. It is far-reaching, essential, vitally important.

Enough of the sales patter; I'll believe you. What is it?

It lies in the production of a key chemical. It's commonly termed the male hormone. By name, it is called testosterone.

With the spate of new words we're tossing around, I believe it's worthwhile taking a break here. It's so easy to read words and then forget them ten seconds later.

It's always handy having an enlarged vocabulary. When it comes to anatomical and chemical data, it never goes amiss. It'll remain with you the rest of your life if you firmly implant it on your mind right now.

Then after that we'll press on with the next chapter, and go into the male hormone story in fuller detail?

Right.

4

When the Hormones Start Jangling

Commencing around the age of puberty—anywhere from the age of twelve (or even earlier) to sixteen or seventeen (it varies a little with different individuals)—the interstitial cells manufacture testosterone.

Unlike the sperms which are channeled into a definite tubular passageway, the testosterone flows directly into the bloodstream. (For this reason, the testis is sometimes referred to as an endocrine gland, or a gland of internal secretion. This means it pumps its product directly into the bloodstream and doesn't depend on pipes to take it to its destination as do some other glands.)

Testosterone is the all-male hormone. But strange to say, the testis also produces minute amounts of female hormone! (Even real he-men have a bit of this in their systems!) This is called estrogen. Of course, in women, the main hormone is estrogen, but females also produce a minute amount of male hormone! It all sounds a bit crazy, but it's a fact.

Is the production of testosterone constant at all times?

Not really. It starts to zero in at puberty. Then it remains at a high rate of production for many years. In older age groups, it tapers off. However, the time of this occurrence can vary greatly with different individuals.

Can anything upset hormonal production?

It's believed that severe malnutrition can depress production. A deficiency in the diet of the very valuable vitamin B complex is also believed to have an effect. However, with the normal all-round diet that most of us enjoy, these deficiencies are not likely to occur.

What Hormones Do

What happens when hormonal production begins?

Here is when the most outstanding changes occur in the growing male. It's during this age segment that a boy becomes a man. He is converted in a relatively short span of time from a gangling youth to a real he-man.

As the testosterone courses through the system, vital and far-reaching effects are produced.

Such as–?

First, the organs of reproduction start to give evidence of new growth. The penis elongates and enlarges in size. This becomes quite obvious. Inside, the other accessory organs of reproduction enlarge also. (The epididymis, the seminal vesicles, the prostate, all grow.) Then the so-called "secondary sex characteristics" become evident.

What does that include?

The skin covering the scrotum thickens and becomes ridged, and the whole organ enlarges.

Possibly most outstanding is the sudden growth of hair in key parts. Facial hair puts in an appearance, and before long junior (of yesterday) finds that he has a beard growing on his face. (I'll talk more of this later.) Hair commences to grow in the armpits, on the body (such as on the chest), and above the external genital organs.

The way the supra-pubic hair grows is quite interesting,

and is pointed out in every book on physiology you'll ever pick up. In the male it grows such that the upper margin is convex upward. In contradistinction, the upper line of supra-pubic hair growth in the female is the reverse—or rather, it is usually in a straight line. Don't ask me the significance of all this. It's just "one of those things" (and quite unimportant, too, it seems!). I doubt if it has ever been used in a court of law (or anywhere else) as a point of proof of one's sex!

What are some of the other secondary sex characteristics?

As every maturing teen-ager knows so well, the voice starts to play up. It cracks and finally it "breaks." Instead of speaking in a high-pitched tone, it drops several notches. Within a year or two (or maybe more), a full, deep, resonant, and usually very pleasing tone of voice develops. No longer will you be eligible as top soprano in the school choir. More likely you'll be selected as a baritone or bass for the local community concert or play. Once broken, this, too, is forever.

Doesn't the system become more muscular?

Certainly it does. Testosterone is an amazing muscle-producer. The body fills out, muscle development takes place, and the typical manly stance and build that we associate with maturing years takes shape.

In other words, you metamorphose into a man in every sense of the word. And once you've arrived, there you stay—for the remainder of your natural life.

Of course, all this is related to the process of sperm production as well, isn't it?

Yes. It's intimately tied in with the production of the male cells of reproduction. This means sperms commence to be produced. From the testes they find their way through the tubes to be stored in the seminal vesicles.

Of course, the key point about all this is one that seldom hits home for quite a while.

When sperm production starts, you are then perfectly capable of procreating. In short, you can induce pregnancy in a woman who has developed to the same degree.

I am sure that many fourteen-, fifteen-, sixteen-, and seventeen-year-olds do not comprehend the full significance of this fact. But a fact it is, and one that must be remembered, and treated with due respect.

How Nature Copes

What happens if sperm production causes the vesicles to fill? What then, seeing that most males in this age group are not married or engaging in sexual intercourse?

Nature takes care of this situation. As the vesicles fill up with seminal fluid, it is quite common to experience erotic dreams at night. The end point of this is a natural, normal nocturnal emission. The vesicles spontaneously contract, and the seminal fluid is released from the system via the urethra. It comes from the small aperture at the glans end of the penis. It's commonly called a "wet dream."

Lots of young men seem to develop phobias and guilt complexes about this.

True enough. Some who have experienced strict or religious upbringing may believe they are doing something wrong or wicked themselves and are causing these emissions.

Nothing, of course, could be further from the truth. This is a pure, natural situation. It is not harmful, it will not cause any bodily harm, it will not weaken the system or impair the intellect.

My advice is to ignore it completely. Rest assured that you are perfectly normal. It does not require a visit to the doctor or any other active measure. Don't even mention it to your close friends. I believe personal matters such as this are best kept to yourself. However, I feel it's worth making a few comments at this stage about emissions in general.

What are your thoughts?

Quite often these emissions are associated with sex-oriented dreams. It is common for the male to imagine he is indulging in actual intercourse, even though he is in fact asleep and has never engaged in physical contact with a female. It is just one of those unexplainable things that happen.

It indicates that tremenduous psychological development is going on in the young man's system. His brain is developing under the influence of testosterone. Suddenly the boy-girl relationship hits home base. He realizes he is fast becoming a man.

Sex, in all its attraction, in all its vibrant vitality, suddenly bursts forth. It doesn't take long to recognize it.

With the mass media yelling at him from every angle; with all the wiles of a sex-oriented community at every turn, it's so easy to become caught up in the mad hedonistic world of sex.

The result, of course, is that his erotic nocturnal excursions into fantasyland can become very real and meaningful. It's easy to gain a sense of deep satisfaction from these emissions. Therefore, at this stage, many endeavor to repeat the performance of the dreams of the previous evening. It doesn't take long to discover that artificial stimulation of the glans penis will produce a recognizably similar result.

Masturbation

So bad habits are developed?

That's one way of describing it. In simple terms, the habit of masturbation can gain a foothold.

Isn't the glans penis one of the most sensitive parts of the system?

It certainly is. Millions of tiny nerve-end organs are present there. During erection, these become even more sensitive than ever, and respond violently to stimulation. Of course, the reason for this is to make sexual intercourse successful.

But all this is best left to the appropriate time. It's designed for marriage, when the full implications and delights of sexual unity can be achieved. Why spoil it all by futile, wasteful indulgence of an artificial nature beforehand?

We'll be talking more about this later on. Right now we make mention of it only, and throw the thought into your mental slipstream. Just be "on guard." Don't commence foolish habits that you might regret later on. What can begin as simple, unimportant "fun habits" now, may develop into more serious ones later on. It's worth more than a passing thought.

Beards—And Such

Earlier you said you would mention hair when it relates to growing youth. What did you have in mind?

I'm constantly receiving letters from young fellows who aren't as happy as they'd like to be.

How come?

Merely because they haven't started to sprout facial hair! Of course, to those of us who've been shaving for more years than we'd like to think about, it's long since ceased to be of importance. In fact, I'm sure we'd be quite happy to be rid of our facial growth forever!

But not so with the up-and-coming teen-agers?

That's just it. They don't feel they're part of the in group. All humans are endowed with the herd instinct. They like to be "one of the mob." Being different is like being knocked.

You stick out in the crowd, become noticed.

This is probably OK when you're in the big league. But when you're only struggling to retain a toehold in current society, it's different. You aim at being identical—as far as possible.

Some schools require school uniforms. For sure, every kid around town hates the sight of his uniform. But deep down, he's really happy with it. It's a leveler. It brings everyone to the same standard. Joe's dad might own half the town, live in a mansion, run three cars and a yacht, and have a heated swimming pool. But just so long as Joe and you and Tom and Harry wear the same gray school gear, that makes you pretty well equal. Psychologically it operates this way.

Forgetting school gear for a moment, let's get back to hair. You know–the sort we sprout on our jowls.

When the hormones start jangling, facial hairs (as well as hair in other typical spots) appear. Some fellows, naturally, "mature" a bit before others. Facial hair growth becomes apparent much earlier with them than with others.

Therefore they can sprout a beard before their contemporaries do.

Right. But seeing it's a sign of manliness, so to speak, it suddenly becomes the "in thing." The bearded have the edge on the nonbearded. They imagine themselves as more grown up, more manly, more virile, more sporty.

Therefore, the rest of the fellows wish they had a beard too?

For sure. Indeed, the plaintive letters that my mailbag regularly disgorges never cease to impress on me the force of this.

"All the other fellows have beards, but I can't even grow *one* hair on my face." "I urgently need your help. How can I make hair grow on my face?" "I'm thinking of killing myself, [leaving home, committing suicide, changing schools, etc., etc., etc.] because my friends make fun of me, as I'm not yet shaving."

These are all typical examples I'm forever receiving.

What's the answer?

Of course the problem is generally self-curative. As soon as a bit more testosterone is produced by the system, hair *must* grow. It's merely a matter of time. Of course there are some rare hormone-deficient situations where the testes are not performing properly, and hair will not grow. But these are the exception and are quite uncommon. (They usually wind up in a specialized endocrine clinic attached to one of the major hospitals, and there, results of treatment are often excellent.) But for the average man-about-town, no treatment is required.

Does the reverse ever occur?

Definitely! As I said before, whatever we have in this world, we seem to want something different. I often receive letters from fellows who've been too well endowed with hair. Besides having an enormous and fast-growing black beard, they may have hair thickly located all over the body.

They too are looking for the magical potion that will either reduce hair growth or check it altogether!

What do you tell them?

I usually tell them about the hairless characters. I suggest that the reverse might not be as big a delight as they currently suppose. If you push home this idea, and build up the virility aspect a bit, most are content and believe they're modern-day Samsons after all!

How do you feel about current male hair fashions? Right now close clipping seems to be something that belongs to a bygone era.

Long hair, it seems, is here to stay for some time with the male of the species.

There are only two considerations I feel worthy of mention.

What are they?

First, irrespective of hair length, I cannot stand lack of hygiene or dirt where it ought not be. Water and soap are still cheaply available. Common sense in keeping the system clean at all times is imperative. There is no excuse for sloppy lack of this detail. Uncleanliness breeds disease and reduces the system's ability to conquer germs. I make no apology for this comment, and I don't care when this book is read. Cleanliness and sensible attention to hygiene will always pay dividends.

What's the second point?

The inherent dangers in long hair are worth more than passing mention.

If you've left school or college, and are engaged in industry, take all precautions to guard against your hair getting caught in machinery. So many fellows have had their hair (plus scalp) ripped off by machines that can't see, feel, or understand, that it's no longer funny.

Wear suitable headgear if this is the workroom recommendation. Most machines are fitted with special protective guards. But my experience indicates that in spite of this, accidents are common. It's OK when it's the other fellow's head. But when it's *yours,* it's different.

From the voice of experience, common sense, taking care, adhering to admonition, will help you keep your hair on. It's more comfortable that way.

5

All About Girls

When should parents come clean and tell their kids the facts of life?

That's a good question. I've no doubts on the answer. It's not ten or twelve, or fourteen years, or anything like that.

In fact, it starts from the day they chauffeur junior home from the hospital.

You mean his education starts with birth?

No doubt. If he's brought up in an environment right from babyhood where everything (sex matters and all) are treated normally, naturally, in a matter-of-fact way, there'll be no "difficult day" (as many parents regard it) on which they must "tell their children the facts of life."

There is no doubt that kids start asking questions at an early age.

Certainly! And what better opportunity than on these occasions to give forthright, honest, unembarrassed replies? With advancing years, more intelligent questions may be expected. If there has been good rapport between parent and child right through, the questions and answers will flow simply, evenly, in an unembarrassed way right along.

Youngsters have minds like sponges. They soak up enormous amounts of information. Probably much of it is never used. But a considerable amount is stored away in their subconscious. It's much like a computer. Facts are silently packed away, remaining there until, one day, fragments are pieced with other fragments, and answers to questions automatically rattle out. In my opinion, the sex story goes like that. By answering questions sensibly right from the start, a fairly comprehensive picture of the total is formed.

The developing mind can accept the story and relate it to life in general. Sure, as time progresses, a mass of other information will be churned into the memory banks—much of it hysterical, untruthful, and useless. This all spins around in the computer too. But this is all part of the process of learning. I think parents have the edge in that they can feed data in at a far earlier age than other agencies. Therefore, the future welfare of their kids is largely in their hands.

Don't you think that much of the sex education of young folk comes from hearsay?

Definitely. Kids get down to the nitty-gritty of sex pretty early. A close friend of mine who is a schoolteacher believes that by the time a kid enters high school he is very well versed in most theoretical elements of sex.

Do you believe this is true?

I think he's quite close to the mark. They may not have had the practical experience we term sex, but they are familiar with general principles.

Every now and again some anxious mother presents me with some of the erotic art work produced by one of her children. Of course it's usually pictures of the opposite sex. But the anatomical detail is accurate in most cases.

Which all goes to show that kids know a considerable amount at quite an early age.

Do you condone so-called "filthy talk" among school children?

The term "filthy" is relative, I think. Often discussions between children on sex topics is confined to their actual knowledge of the subject. As age increases, particularly when their built-in hormonal system starts operating, psychological changes are inevitable. They have no choice but to take an interest in sex. If they didn't, they would not be normal human beings.

A healthy attitude, and one in which there is freedom to discuss sex among themselves (as well as with their seniors), I feel is essential.

Discussion about sex isn't equated with "filth" merely because sexual matters are under discussion. To believe anything else would be a very narrow attitude. Open discussion in a frank manner is to be encouraged. This in itself is a hedge against pornography, and I certainly do not encourage the latter. When sex is on a level with other subjects, regarded as something normal, then "adulterated sex," pornography and all that, will not be sought out so vigorously.

The Female Anatomy

I go along with you, and feel the upcoming generation is fairly well clued in on sex. Just the same, to get things into perspective, it's our intention to give a brief rundown on the female system, just as we explained the anatomy and physiology of the male.

I'm in full agreement. It's certainly worth having the basics of both sexes in mind. That way a fuller appreciation and understanding of boy-girl relationships is easier.

Let's begin with the genital structure of the normal female.

Externally this is collectively referred to as the vulva. It includes all the parts that can be seen from the front.

Above, in front of the pubic bones (these are the bones that form the front part of the bony pelvis), is a swelling called the mons veneris. At puberty, hair commences to grow here, and later it is fully covered.

Below this and on either side are large rounded folds called the labia majora (or large lips). This is the female counterpart of the male scrotum. Normally, in the erect position with the legs together, the labia come together and form a general protection to the inner structures.

Isn't there a gland located in the labia?

Yes, and a very important one too. In the lower inner part of this fold on either side, is located a gland referred to as Bartholin's gland. It manufactures a thick, clear, sticky fluid, and this is directed via a narrow canal which opens at the vaginal inlet. Its purpose is to provide lubrication to facilitate intercourse.

In fact, under sexual stimulation, the gland frequently pours forth copious amounts of fluid, and this can certainly make the mechanics of penetration much simpler than would otherwise be the case.

What's the next structure?

It's termed the labia minora (or smaller lips), or sometimes it's called the nymphae.

This consists of two smaller folds of tissue, usually concealed by the labia majora. The folds are more prominent toward the front where they unite on either side of another important structure called the clitoris.

It's the clitoris that evokes so much interest throughout life. In fact, this is the female counterpart of the penis in the male.

The clitoris is a small, elongated structure, rounded at its end. It is made up of erectile tissue, and the glans, as in the penis, is extremely sensitive.

Indeed, the clitoris carries masses of nerve-end organs, and it is highly responsive to stimulation. It plays an enormously important part later on in married life, and it can be said without doubt that the physical side of marriage can rise or fall on an appreciation of this tiny structure and its significance. It is not visible when the person is standing. It is protected by the labia on either side.

The clitoris plays an integral part in intercourse. Stimulation causes general bodily excitation. The tiny organ becomes tensely filled with blood (similar to the penis). This helps prepare the system for penetration by the male penis, reflexly activates Bartholin's gland to produce its helpful secretions, and plays a key part in the final impulsive sensation known as orgasm.

Despite the fact that every female is similarly endowed with identical anatomical features, some women journey through married life quite unaware that such an organ exists. They often bitterly claim that they're "frigid."

Do you believe such a state as frigidity exists?

Basically, no! Frigidity is all in the mind. It merely reflects the sad fact that the person has never fully understood her basic anatomy, what's present, and why. I repeat, every woman has the fundamentals to guarantee perfect physical compatibility in marriage.

If she is unlucky and is married to a man who is either ignorant or merely concerned about his own lustful sensations, then the experience we refer to as orgasm might never come her way.

Instead of being something to enjoy, sex can develop into a rather uninteresting, mechanical performance.

"What's in it for me?" I have heard unhappily married women ask time and again. "*He* gets all the kicks. I'm just there, getting no enjoyment, no satisfaction whatsoever. Am

I supposed to?'' These incredible words are poured into doctors' ears every day of the week, time and again.

The answer, of course, is that sex is for *both* married partners to share and enjoy equally. If each takes the time, has the interest, and makes a slight effort, rapturous, long-lasting enjoyment is for both. There is absolutely no doubt about this. Never forget it. It can make the bonds of a happy marriage union so tight they'll never drift apart.

The Entrance to the Womb

Isn't the outlet of the bladder fairly close to the clitoris?

About an inch below the clitoris is a tiny aperature which is the external outlet of the uretha. This is the canal that conveys urine from the bladder to the exterior.

Behind this is located the vaginal orifice, the portal of entry to the female genital tract.

Aren't there all manner of myths about the covering to the vagina?

There certainly are. They alone might easily fill a book. But we'll spare our readers all that, and give a few of the basic facts only.

The covering is called the hymen. Its shape and extent varies enormously with different women.

Indeed, in some it may be represented merely by a thin rim about the vaginal entrance. It can vary from something like this, to the point where it completely covers the orifice. However, it seldom goes that far. In most virgins it is represented by an irregularly shaped, serrated-edged piece of thin tissue of varying dimensions. It is really a structural remnant, and serves no real purpose in adult life.

However, myth and fiction and old wives' tales have cloaked the hymen with all manner of strange beliefs. It's claimed to be a sign of virginity. There is no doubt that an intact hymen is usually broken down completely at first intercourse.

But conversely, the fact that there is virtually no hymen in place doesn't necessarily mean a lack of virginity. The range of normality is extremely wide.

Can't certain menstrual procedures affect the hymen?

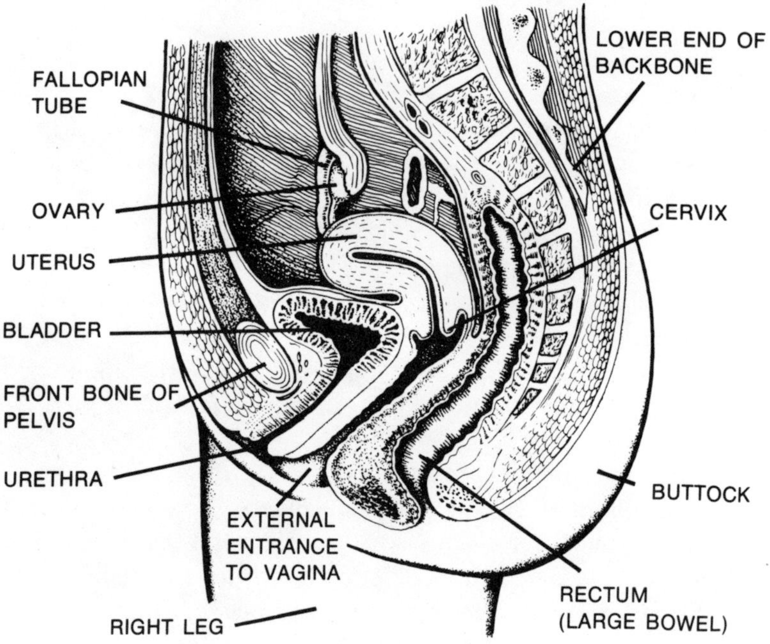

THE FEMALE PELVIS

This is a section through the female pelvis, and the chief organs of reproduction are being viewed from the left side.

The vaginal canal sits between the canal from the bladder, called the urethra (in front), and the part of the bowel called the rectum. At the upper end the uterus juts into the vagina. On either side of the uterus lie the Fallopian tubes, and the ovaries are located at the far end of each tube.

reply. But
u *yourself*
high moral
e to those
inally link
ith yours.
having to
e is prob-
al caliber

ircle, the
me later

e to the

the ex-

ans.
llopian

ternal
s. It is
ucous
folds.
d to
also
is of
of a
and

an increasing u
at the time of the m
ese to the external absorb
absorbent piece of material
vagina.
rst indication of the menstrual
ed at regular intervals. They
ak up the blood that is being
he regular monthly use of these
the remnants of the hymen in a
ntercourse does.
s composed of tougher material,
quently hear from young women
n inserting tampons, particularly
ecome fully accustomed to their
s due to a rigid hymen. This can
simple surgical procedure, and all's

ttach great significance to an intact

've had to carry out gynecological
European women. On occasion this
amination of the pelvic organs and
uterus (womb). In many instances the
parents) require a written certificate
the procedure, certifying its essential
lings. An intact hymen, it seems, is still
indisputable sign of premarital purity.
cur when the hymen is broken?
eed a good deal. Indeed, in some cultures
ched to this fact on the nuptial night!
y of ascertaining a woman's virginity?
eems, desires to marry a virgin. I am asked

,ı many times a week, every week.
,mically, it is not possible to give a defini
.nswer I do give is this: Live a life of which
,an be proud. Encourage friends who have simila
standards, and associate with them in preferen
whose standards are lower. In this manner you'll
up with a person whose outlook on life equates
You'll automatically find the right partner, withou
worry about physical points of proof. After all, the
ably a young lady seeking a young man of high mo
too.

If you're in a position that comes within her c
chances of a happy, successful marriage union at s
date are extremely high.

The Internal Genital Organs

So far we've got as far as the external entranc vagina.

Correct. The structures we've discussed compris ternal genital organs.

From here, we progress to the internal genital oı

These comprise the vagina, the uterus (or womb), f tubes, and ovaries.

Tell us more about the vagina.

This is the female genital tract that runs from the e opening upward and backward until it reaches the uter composed of firm tissue and lined by moist, pink n membrane. This is usually thrown into small, irregula

This, it seems, has many functions. The folds t increase male stimulation during intercourse. But the allow the whole structure to expand enormously. Thi utmost importance during pregnancy and at the tim confinement. Without this elastic capacity, tearing

Certainly. These days, there is an increasing use of internally worn tampons by women at the time of the monthly menstrual cycle. Many prefer these to the external absorbent pad. The tampon is a highly absorbent piece of material shaped to fit snugly inside the vagina.

It is simply slipped in at the first indication of the menstrual flow. The tampons are replaced at regular intervals. They effectively, unobtrusively soak up the blood that is being shed at this time. However, the regular monthly use of these can mechanically break down the remnants of the hymen in a manner similar to the way intercourse does.

Of course, if the hymen is composed of tougher material, this may not occur. We frequently hear from young women who encounter difficulty in inserting tampons, particularly early, before they have become fully accustomed to their anatomy. Occasionally it's due to a rigid hymen. This can usually be rectified with a simple surgical procedure, and all's well once more.

Don't some societies attach great significance to an intact hymen?

Yes. Several times I've had to carry out gynecological procedures on migrant European women. On occasion this has necessitated an examination of the pelvic organs and possibly surgery to the uterus (womb). In many instances the relatives (usually the parents) require a written certificate stating the nature of the procedure, certifying its essential character and the findings. An intact hymen, it seems, is still held by them to be an indisputable sign of premarital purity.

Does bleeding occur when the hymen is broken?

It can certainly bleed a good deal. Indeed, in some cultures great import is attached to this fact on the nuptial night!

Is there any way of ascertaining a woman's virginity?

Every male, it seems, desires to marry a virgin. I am asked

this question many times a week, every week.

Anatomically, it is not possible to give a definite reply. But the answer I do give is this: Live a life of which you *yourself* can be proud. Encourage friends who have similar high moral standards, and associate with them in preference to those whose standards are lower. In this manner you'll finally link up with a person whose outlook on life equates with yours. You'll automatically find the right partner, without having to worry about physical points of proof. After all, there is probably a young lady seeking a young man of high moral caliber too.

If you're in a position that comes within her circle, the chances of a happy, successful marriage union at some later date are extremely high.

The Internal Genital Organs

So far we've got as far as the external entrance to the vagina.

Correct. The structures we've discussed comprise the external genital organs.

From here, we progress to the internal genital organs.

These comprise the vagina, the uterus (or womb), fallopian tubes, and ovaries.

Tell us more about the vagina.

This is the female genital tract that runs from the external opening upward and backward until it reaches the uterus. It is composed of firm tissue and lined by moist, pink mucous membrane. This is usually thrown into small, irregular folds.

This, it seems, has many functions. The folds tend to increase male stimulation during intercourse. But they also allow the whole structure to expand enormously. This is of utmost importance during pregnancy and at the time of a confinement. Without this elastic capacity, tearing and

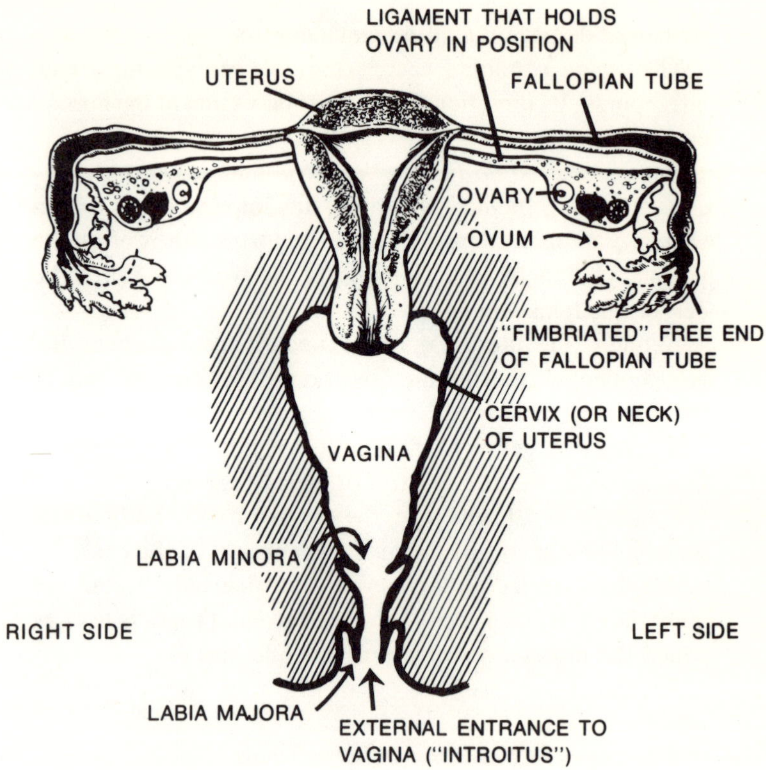

FEMALE ORGANS OF REPRODUCTION

This is a diagrammatic view of the female reproductive organs as they are located when viewed directly from the front. (Compare this picture with the "Sectional" one on a previous page.)

Once more it shows the continuity of the pathway from the exterior into the vagina, up into the womb (uterus) via the cervical canal, then out into the Fallopian tubes at the uppermost corners of the uterus. At the far end of the tubes are "fimbriated" tentacles that are in close relationship to the ovaries where the microscopic eggs (ova) are produced.

On the left side, an ovum has just been released by the ovary, and the dotted line shows the track it will follow. The free waving tentacles of the tube help sweep the ovum into the tube itself.

Pregnancy may occur in the tube if a male cell is encountered here.

structural damage would be inevitable.

The vagina, of course, accepts the male penis during sexual intercourse. Its direction therefore equates that of the normal erect penis.

Doesn't the womb fit into the picture somewhere?

Yes. In fact, the uterus (womb) juts into the upper dome-shaped part of the vaginal canal. It forms the roof of the vagina, you might say. This part of the womb is called the cervix (meaning "neck").

Actually the uterus is approximately pear-shaped, the large upper part (corpus uteri or "body") forming the bulk of the organ.

It gives way below to the "neck," technically referred to by doctors as the cervix uteri or merely cervix.

A narrow canal runs from the cervix into the body of the womb. The opening at the outer, lower part of the cervix is called the external os (or merely "outside hole"), and the inner part where it opens out into the womb proper is usually called the internal os (or simply "inside hole").

The canal traverses the entire length of the neck of the womb.

Isn't the cervix a rather important part?

Yes. In fact, with women, it's one of the most important parts of the body. It would rank about number one spot for the formation of cancer. No doubt you've all heard or read about the pap smear test that many women have done.

During this examination (which is carried out as a routine measure in doctors' offices), a very thin smear of cells is removed from the cervix. These are then applied to a glass slide, fixed in an alcohol solution, then dispatched to the pathologist's laboratory.

When prepared further with special stains, the slide is then placed under a powerful microscope and checked out

by the pathologist. In this way, very early stages of cancer can be detected. Typical cancer cells can actually be seen, and these, if present, are extremely important.

What happens if a pap smear gives a positive finding?

The pathologist alerts the physician. An operation called a cone biopsy is then promptly carried out.

A cone of tissue is removed from the cervix. In early stages of cervical cancer, this is frequently adequate to remove the early growth completely.

The cone is again examined by the pathologist. He can state with reasonable accuracy whether or not the entire growth has been removed. If he is satisfied, no further action is required.

What if he is not happy with the result?

Then it requires a further, more extensive operation for the patient.

Are these operations often life-saving?

Very definitely. The earlier cancer is detected, the earlier correct treatment is started, the greater are the chances of future survival.

Smear tests are an excellent way to discover premature cancer of the cervix, and are no doubt proving their worth many times over.

What's the shape of the cervix?

In women who have not reproduced, it is elongated and conical. However, after childbirth, it tends to flatten out. Tears often occur at the external os also.

What's the uterus (womb) like inside?

The womb is an interesting structure. It's basically there as an incubator. If a pregnancy occurs, it houses the fertilized egg. Thereafter it protects and nourishes the developing baby for the ensuing nine months, until birth takes place.

Each month, the lining of the womb prepares for an anticipated fertilized egg. Of course, this usually does not take place. So the lining (called the endometrium) is shed over a period of three to six days. From the practical point of view, this is represented by a blood discharge and is referred to as the menstrual period.

From one menstrual period to the next is usually an interval of twenty-eight days. However, this can vary a great deal.

Variations from twenty days up to forty days and even beyond are frequently reported. However, most women have a twenty-eight day cycle, and can almost set their calendars by the promptness of its arrival.

Where do the tubes fit into the picture?

There is a small cavity inside the uterus, but under normal conditions the walls are almost in apposition. At the uppermost part of the uterus the fallopian tubes enter, one on the right side and another on the left side. The tubes are each about four inches in length. They run outward and backward on either side. They are quite narrow, and not unlike a thin pencil.

A fine canal, lined by specialized cells, is continuous from the cavity of the uterus, and runs the entire length of each tube.

What are these lining cells like?

Each cell possesses a small projecting hair, called a cilium. The cells collectively are referred to as ciliated epithelium.

These microscopic hairs tend to wave in a given direction, and in fact set up currents that move toward the cavity of the uterus.

The basic function of the tubes is to transport the female *ovum* or egg from the ovary (where it is manufactured) down into the uterus.

Doesn't fertilization occur in the tube?

It can. If a male cell (sperm—remember we spoke of them

earlier) is present in the tube at the same time as the female ovum, then the two will unite, and fertilization is said to have occurred.

In other words, the woman becomes pregnant?

Right.

How does an ovum get into one of the tubes?

At the far outer end each tube widens out into a series of fingerlike tentacles. This is the so-called fimbriated end. These are in very close proximity to the ovary. Indeed, they no doubt play a part in helping to sweep the egg into the tube when it is released by the ovary.

Where does the ovary sit?

In a small depression very close to the fimbriated ends of the tube. There is one present on each side. They are almond-shaped structures usually whitish in color.

The ovaries hold the female key to reproduction. Indeed, at birth, a female baby's ovary contains somewhere between 250,000 and 500,000 potential eggs. Admittedly, a huge number of these never develop or just disintegrate, but even so, it can be seen that an enormous oversupply is present.

The ovary is the female equivalent of the male testis where the cells of reproduction are formed. Nature is particularly bounteous and makes sure that there is an enormous reserve in hand to guarantee that reproduction will be successful in due course.

However, besides producing ova, the ovaries also have further extremely important functions.

But I think we'll leave that until the next chapter, for it encompasses a wide field.

6

More About the "Other" Sex

Let's consider further the mystical intricacies of the female.

Good idea. It's an intriguing topic, and I'm quite sure our young male readers will agree! Without doubt the bodily changes that occur in maturing women are a constant source of delight and wonderment to the male counterpart!

Of course there are definite reasons underlying these changes.

Certainly. In the male we discovered that a clearly defined hormonal system was responsible for his development.

Similarly, potent chemicals cause female development. These are produced in the organ we were just discussing, the ovary.

Just as the male testis produces sperms, the cells of reproduction, along with the male hormone testosterone, so the ovary manufactures an unending succession of ova or eggs. But besides this, it is responsible for two sets of hormones. These have extensive and far-reaching consequences.

What happens to the ovary in the first few years of life?

Very little. In fact, until the age of puberty, there is no

activity there at all. But suddenly all this changes. In the age range between ten and fifteen years the ovary becomes charged with life and vitality. It awakes out of its sleepy torpor and starts to function.

The first outward indication of this vigor and vitality is the commencement of menstruation. This time is clinically referred to as the menarche. Although this is the time the first menstrual bleed takes place, it is often some time before the monthly cyclical program gets into regular swing. But it's usually merely a matter of time.

What goes on in the ovary to spark all this off?

As we mentioned earlier, the female ovary contains huge numbers of potential eggs. By the time puberty arrives, many of these have disintegrated. But a tremendous number have survived. In fact, between 100,000 and 200,000 primitive eggs (or follicles as they're called) are present.

Suddenly one of these microscopic structures begins to change. Nobody knows why any particular one is chosen. It's just "one of those things." It rapidly increases in size, and gradually works its way to the surface of the ovary.

What then?

It suddenly breaks through the outer lining of the ovary, and the ovum or egg is released into the pelvic cavity. What a prospect it faces! There is a vast uncharted sea for it to traverse. However, it is not as hopeless as it may sound.

Remember, the fingerlike fimbriated ends of the fallopian tubes are close by. As soon as the ovum is released, they begin to wave about in a most excited fashion. They set up currents and directional eddies that channel the egg into the free end of the tube. Once here, the sweeping cilia, the hairlike structures on the lining cells of the tubes, continue to carry the ovum downward toward the waiting uterus.

Then whether or not male sperms are present determines

the possibility that a pregnancy may or may not take place.

Precisely. Fertilization will take place if a male cell is encountered in the outer part of the tube. In any case, fertilization or not, the egg rolls onward until it reaches the inner part of the uterus.

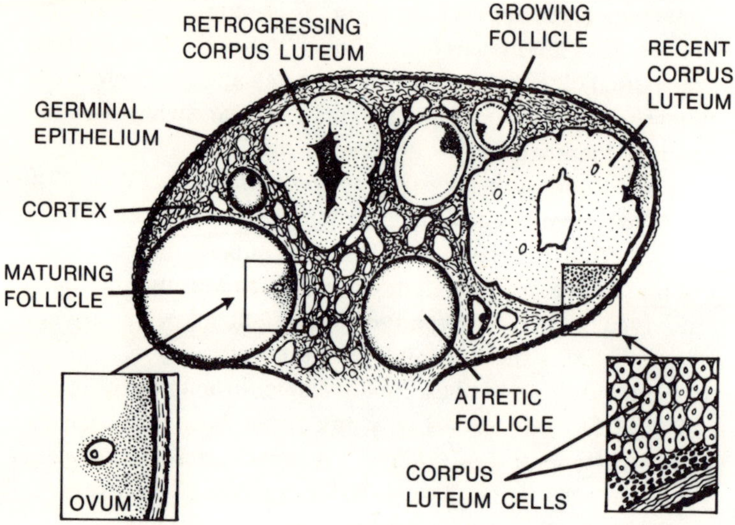

THE WONDERFUL OVARY

Incredible activity occurs within the ovary, and the above composite diagram shows the various phases leading from the formation of an egg (or ovum) to the situations immediately following its release.

The ovary houses thousands of potential eggs, called primordial follicles. Each month one develops, or matures. As it does so, it gradually enlarges, and comes near to the surface of the ovary. The tiny egg itself is finally released from the surface of the ovary and finds its way into a fallopian tube.

The space left by the ovum fills in and is then known as the corpus luteum. This then becomes an important hormone-producing structure.

With the passage of time, the corpus luteum becomes smaller and smaller and finally ceases to produce any hormone at all. Then, little by little, another primordial follicle commences to enlarge and to produce a subsequent ovum.

There are between 100,000 and 200,000 potential eggs in each ovary—or maybe more. The reproductive potential of the ovaries is enormous.

However, let's turn for a moment to the ovary. Things are really racing on apace here.

As soon as an ovum is released, the space that it occupied becomes filled with material. Within a very short space of time an organ referred to as the corpus luteum develops. In a miraculous manner, this then commences to produce its own chemical, a substance called progesterone. This is a very powerful substance. It pours forth into the bloodstream. In turn it exerts an influence on other parts of the system, chiefly the uterus itself, the breasts, and also the other sexual organs.

Its chief activity, as we'll see later on, is to have the uterus prepared for the reception of a fertilized ovum. In other words, it is mainly concerned with helping the system reproduce satisfactorily.

But of course in the majority of cases, pregnancy has not occurred. So what then?

The corpus luteum continues to pour out its hormones for 12 to 14 days. If pregnancy has not taken place, it decides to quit. Production ceases, and the corpus luteum shrivels away and is lost forever.

As this occurs, the lining of the womb (called the endometrium) gradually starts to crumble. A soft trickle of blood commences. This increases day by day, until finally the entire lining is shed in the form of the bleeding of menstruation.

But it's a case of "never say die"?

Certainly. Under the influence of another hormone which is also produced by the ovary, called estradiol, another follicle commences to develop. Little by little, as the days progress, it enlarges, until on about the fourteenth day from the previous commencement of menstruation, another ovum is ready to be released! And so the entire process is repeated.

However, apart from this cyclical function, these hormones also exert other profound changes on the system.

As we said earlier, until the age of 10 to 15 years, little activity takes place in the ovaries. But when the spark of new life triggers off in this age segment, quite apart from the menstrual system getting into full swing, other marked factors come into play too.

Other Changes

What are these?

They're collectively described as the *secondary sex characteristics* of the female.

Outwardly, the obvious signs of maturity commence. One of the most noticeable is the relocation of the fat deposits of the body. The typical female curves become well established. There is chest development as the breasts fill out and become a firm part of the figure; there is the growth of hair under the arms and in the genital region.

What about internal structures?

There are marked changes occurring here too. The vagina elongates and enlarges and the lining thickens. Likewise the uterus becomes firmer and more muscular. The tubes increase in development also. In fact, the entire system prepares for reproduction. Adulthood is approaching, and the system is getting geared for all eventualities.

Before long, the typical female development is complete. Menstruation becomes well established and regular. By now, the female system is quite able to reproduce.

As with the male, this is often not fully appreciated by developing women. The fact that they can produce babies of their own at fourteen, fifteen, or sixteen often does not occur to them.

What about psychological changes? How do these fit into the general picture?

They are taking place just as surely as physical development is occurring. Indeed, the growth of mental maturity is often obvious at this time of life. Suddenly girls realize that the small brothers of their best friends are no longer the abhorrent beasts they'd often imagined. Instead, boy meets girl, and the spark of sexual attraction begins.

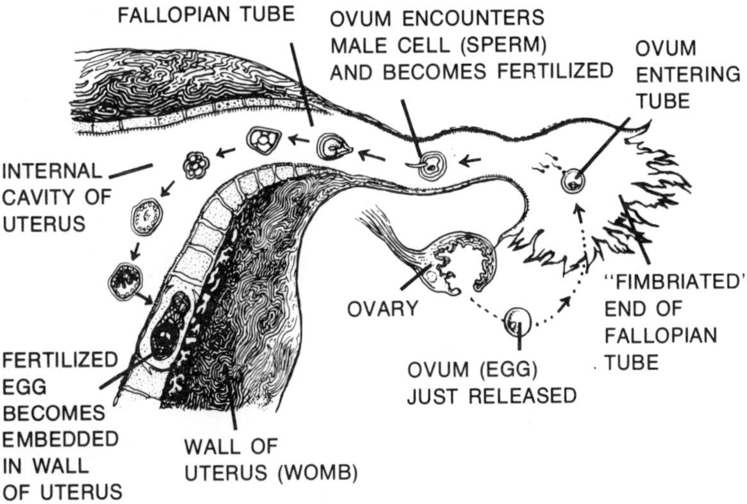

WHEN "OVULATION" OCCURS

This shows diagrammatically what happens at "ovulation," the time when the microscopic egg (ovum) is released by the ovary where it is manufactured.

Immediately it is released and is swept toward the fingerlike ends of the fallopian tube. These assist the egg to enter the free end of the tube. Here special "ciliated epithelium" lining cells (which contain waving hairlike structures), plus normal movements of the tube wall, help propel the egg along its length.

Fertilization can occur in the tube if a male cell is encountered here. The egg (whether fertilized or not) proceeds along the tube until it reaches the womb (uterus). A fertilized egg becomes embedded immediately in the wall of the womb. But if this has not occurred, the egg plus the lining of the womb is shed, and a normal menstrual period occurs.

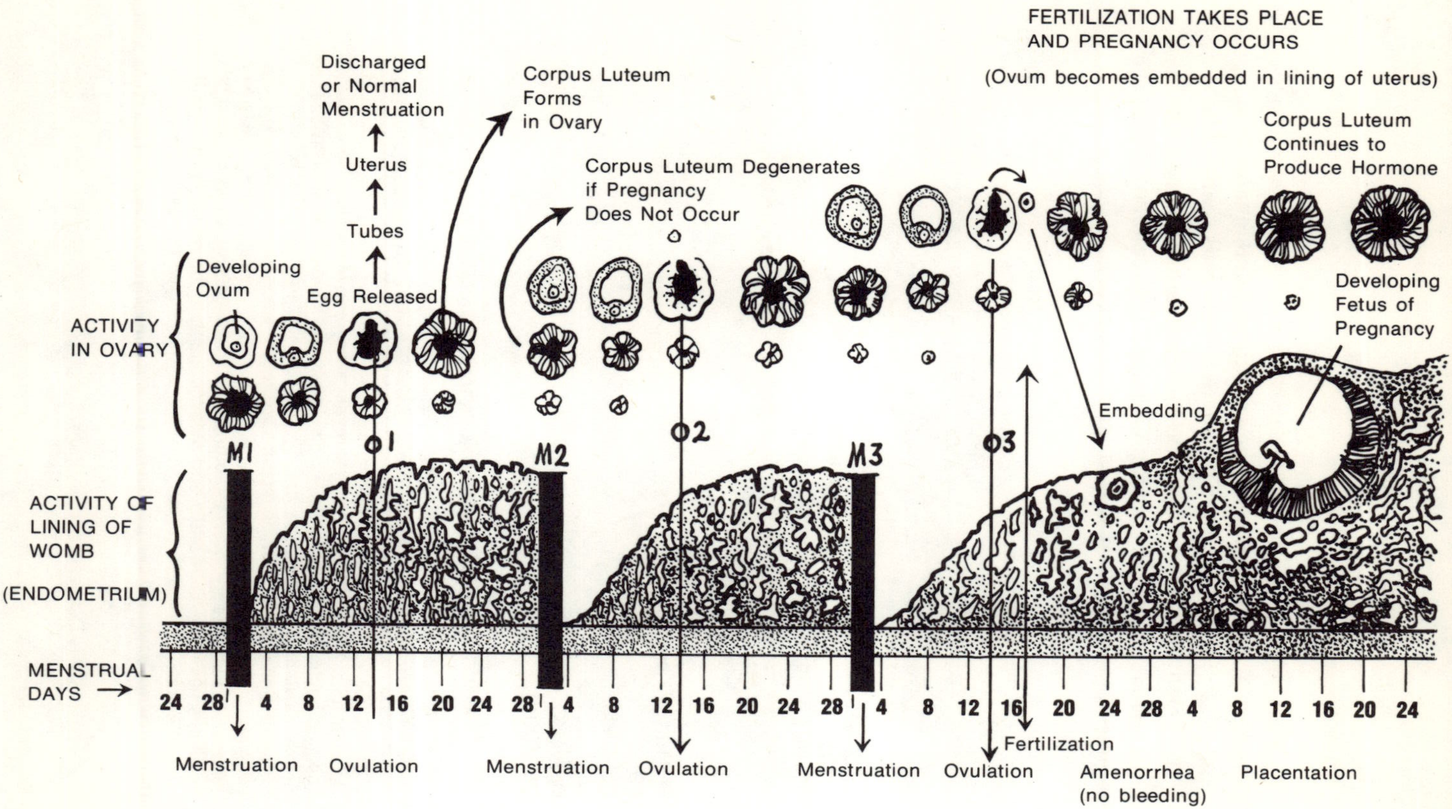
FERTILIZATION TAKES PLACE
AND PREGNANCY OCCURS
(Ovum becomes embedded in lining of uterus)
Discharged or Normal Menstruation
Uterus
Tubes
Corpus Luteum Forms in Ovary
Corpus Luteum Degenerates if Pregnancy Does Not Occur
Corpus Luteum Continues to Produce Hormone
Developing Ovum
Egg Released
Developing Fetus of Pregnancy
ACTIVITY IN OVARY
Embedding
M1
O1
M2
O2
M3
O3
ACTIVITY OF LINING OF WOMB
(ENDOMETRIUM)
MENSTRUAL DAYS →
24 28 4 8 12 16 20 24 28 4 8 12 16 20 24 28 4 8 12 16 20 24 28 4 8 12 16 20 24
Fertilization
Menstruation
Ovulation
Menstruation
Ovulation
Menstruation
Ovulation
Amenorrhea (no bleeding)
Placentation

Knowing When

Is there any way of knowing when ovulation takes place each month?

There are many ways of determining this, although most of these are fraught with problems. Unless the individual is extremely enthusiastic and takes several checks on a regular basis, it can be very difficult.

Isn't the temperature frequently used as a guide?

Yes. It's known that the body temperature rises when ovulation occurs. Prior to ovulation the body temperature taken before rising or performing any activity is around 36.3° to 36.8° C (97.3° to 98.2°F). When ovulation occurs, this suddenly jumps by 0.3° to 0.5° C (0.5° to 1.0°F).

OVULATION AND MENSTRUATION

This series of diagrams shows the relationship between ovulation and the menstrual cycle over three successive menstrual months.

The state of the ovary is seen in the little diagrams in the upper part of the picture. The state of the endometrium, or lining of the womb, is seen in the lower part.

The dark bands labeled M1, M2, M3 indicate that menstruation is taking place. At this time the unfertilized ovum, together with the inner lining of the womb (endometrium), is shed from the womb entirely. It lasts from three to six days.

The figures under the diagrams indicate the menstrual days (day 1 = the day menstruation commences, ie, when period bleeding starts.)

Soon after menstruation, the lining of the womb commences to build up again, just in case pregnancy occurs. During this time a primordial follicle in the ovary matures. About the fourteenth day it ruptures and leaves the ovary to enter the tube. This day is called "ovulation."

The space where the ovum was located in the ovary becomes the corpus luteum, and produces a hormone that further builds up the lining of the womb. But if pregnancy has not occurred about the twenty-eighth day, the lining (and unwanted ovum) is shed in another normal period bleed.

The entire process repeats monthly.

However, if fertilization occurs (right-hand side of diagram), the fertilized egg becomes firmly embedded in the endometrial lining of the uterus, and pregnancy is under way. The lining becomes very thick, and a copious blood supply is established. This month the lining is not shed as previously. The uterine lining at this point becomes the "placenta" later on.

Some enthusiastic married couples use this information as a form of birth control. By avoiding intercourse several days on either side of ovulation, the chances of pregnancy, of course, are theoretically impossible.

They—or rather the wife (often at the insistence of the husband, I might add)—take the morning "basal" temperature, and plot this on special graph paper against the days of the menstrual month. When the temperature shoots up, it often indicates that ovulation has occurred.

Conversely, some couples experiencing difficulty in conceiving, also use the system. It indicates when pregnancy is most likely to occur.

Are there other helpful signs in addition to the temperature variations?

Often, yes. Some women notice a distinct discomfort in the lower pelvic (or abdominal) region. Indeed, in some instances this has been so marked as to be misdiagnosed as an attack of appendicitis!

Other women notice a thin, stringy vaginal discharge at the time of ovulation. Sometimes a check of this material will indicate an alteration in its chemical composition. Test kits are available that help perform these tests.

Those who are keen to use the method are usually advised to follow some of the well-prepared textbooks which clearly set out the system in full detail.

Don't some religious faiths follow this system avidly?

Yes. Some religions do not go along with other widely practiced methods of birth control (such as using The Pill, contraceptive devices, or chemical and occlusive schemes). But they do permit the use of "natural" methods of family planning.

Therefore, this system has a rather large following. The adherents refer to it as the "ovulation method" of birth control. It's sometimes loosely referred to as the "rhythm method," but any mention of this is likely to bring hot protests from the users who claim that such a term is quite erroneous.

At The Other End Of Life

Supposing we project time a little, and take a quick look at what happens at the other end of the time spectrum. Just as the years of puberty see the commencement of menstruation and general body development, what finally occurs when these days draw to a close?

During the age forty-five to fifty years, the time of the menopause takes place. This has various names. Some refer to it as the climacteric, or the change of life. But names don't mean too much. It's merely a technical expression of an age group and the set of circumstances that occurs then.

What happens?

There is a reversal of the events of puberty.

The ovaries gradually cease to function. They become smaller, the follicles disappear and are replaced by fibrous tissue. Hormonal production gradually fades away. Menstruation gradually ceases. It may stop quite abruptly. Or more commonly, the length of time between successive periods lengthens, until finally many months separate them. Ultimately, they cease altogether.

What about pregnancy?

This becomes something from a bygone era. By the time the late forties come around, pregnancy isn't likely.

But we often hear about women having "menopausal" babies.

True, some do. But with advancing years, even if pregnancy does occur, in many cases the uterine lining is quite inadequate to sustain a fetal life. Therefore a miscarriage is quite likely to occur.

What's the latest age at which pregnancy can be carried on to full term?

No doubt everyone has heard of some anomaly. However, we stick to our authority which declares: "Pregnancy after forty-seven years is rare, and parturition over the age of fifty-two years has not been proved."[1]

What happens when the hormones of the system are gradually withdrawn? You said production persists pretty well continuously throughout the life of the male. Surely the female counterpart must suffer some symptoms if she's suddenly deprived of these vital factors?

True enough. In fact, many women passing through this stage of life develop problems.

Many undergo bouts of depression, nervousness, irritability, and similar symptoms. Others notice hot flashes, a full feeling in the head; some start to worry for no apparent reason. It's well established that many of these symptoms are an overreaction to the belief that their days of usefulness are at an end.

What then?

Fortunately, such is not the case. The sooner these women realize that their sexual activity may be just as meaningful and just as enjoyable as before (or even more enjoyable than before, particularly with the fear of further unwanted pregnancies out of the way forever), the sooner they are back on the road to happiness.

Is treatment available to them?

Definitely. Once, doctors used to feed them on sedatives and tranquilizers. However, more enlightened physicians nowadays tend to give hormonal replacement therapy for a limited period of time.

This artificially supplies what nature provided in the premenopausal days. Development of these artificial hormones is excellent. Indeed, they can bring new life, added spark, and vitality to women who are temporarily down and out.

Don't you think the home environment can play a part too?

Very definitely. Consideration and attention by the other members of the family toward the mother will do much to make her passage through these difficult days less of a hazardous problem. Often it is the younger members of the family who are sometimes still at home while their mother is enduring her difficulties.

I always try to enlist their support. It can mean such a great deal to mothers in distress.

REFERENCE:

1. *Samson Wright's Applied Physiology,* 11th ed., rev. C.A. Keele and E. Neil, eds. (London: Oxford University Press).

7

Dating Can Be Fun

What say we now become a bit practical? To date we've concentrated on the structure, nature, and development of the system. Certainly we've covered both sexes. It's essential to have a fairly detailed knowledge of this data. But the crux of the whole situation is how this applies to life in general.

What you say is quite correct. Theoretical knowledge is great. But to a certain point only. Until it can be translated into meaningful results, it isn't of much use to anyone.

Then let's apply some of our knowledge to life in general.

I'll go along with that idea.

Probably the greatest impact that hits any person in the age group under discussion is the final full realization and appreciation of the opposite sex.

These days kids are geared from a very early age to a knowledge that opposites attract. Television and the other mass media see to this. But for many years, it's an *observed* as opposed to an *experienced* situation. It's not until the adolescent years that one suddenly merges into the other.

There is absolutely no doubt that the impact is an exhilarating experience. It can definitely be an excursion into fantasy!

HONDA

You're getting a bit carried away, aren't you? But I do agree that the sudden awareness that occurs with advancing years can be an unforgettable and certainly a happy event.

In some young people it occurs at an early age. For others, it comes some years later. There seems no particular age at which the boy-girl impact hits home.

But wouldn't you agree that many simple relationships established at the early end of the age spectrum are of little consequence, and occur without much awareness of what's actually involved?

Certainly. But they are important, nonetheless. They pave the way, so to speak, for a fuller relationship later on. Simple relationships, at any age, are all part of the general growing up structure.

Merely conversing with the opposite sex is significant. It equals communication. As we know so well, many growing kids experience a terrifying difficulty in communicating—with their own sex, to say nothing of the opposite sex. Therefore, communications from an early age will certainly promote a more normal transition in later years.

What Is Dating?

What are your views on dating?

That's an interesting question. I guess everyone has a personal opinion on this topic.

First, just what does it mean? Does it mean sitting with your favorite schoolmate on the way home from school in the bus? Does it mean holding hands at the local church social, and later taking the girl back home to her front door? Does it mean racing off on weekends to the beach as a twosome, having a sporty day out together, and then returning home toward evening? Or does it get down to the more serious aspects? Such as an evening out together as an intimate twosome, a drive home in the car via a scheduled lane or parking lot, and a few hours' session of heavy petting and what not?

It looks as though you're asking all the questions now. So go right ahead. They're pretty practical ones. You answer them!

I was afraid you'd say that!

Dating, in the full meaning of the word in the current vernacular, embraces all of these, I feel. More specifically, it concerns a relationship between an individual boy and an individual girl. He takes her somewhere. In essence, it is a special arrangement between two persons who have found a mutual level of attraction. It can be on a simple plane. It may be on a more complex one.

Generally it starts on the former level. Depending on what happens and how the friendship matures, it may gradually (or rapidly) develop into a more mature, personal relationship.

Dating is a perfectly normal situation that takes place between couples.

Of course, the ultimate end point of dating (or whatever term you care to use) is one thing and one thing only.

Definitely. Dating is merely a prelude to the final selection of a life partner. It's a phase through which youth journey, and a very vital one at that. They gain experience in many aspects of living. They come to know other people, sample temperaments, pinpoint personality types, and begin to understand basic character types.

Throughout the experience of dating, people come to know other people on a deeper level of understanding. I believe the information collected subconsciously during the dating years is of utmost importance in the ultimate formation of a settled life pattern.

The majority of people have numerous dates over the years

with numerous people. This, too, is important. It gives the subconscious increased masses of data which is carefully stored in the brain's memory bank. It inevitably increases a person's expertise to cope with human beings as such throughout life.

It gives a person experience, you might say.

Precisely. It takes the human system some years before it has adequate yardsticks of comparison. Most things are relative in this world.

Although something may appear good at first inspection, it may not necessarily appear that way when critically compared with other similar items. But unless there are built-in items against which to compare, how then may a sensible, satisfactory answer be arrived at?

This is exactly what time and experience produce. Yardsticks of comparison. And all this takes place during the dating years of life.

It seems as though you're advocating lots of dates for everyone in this world before a final selection is made.

I believe the more dates that take place and possibly the more persons involved, the better acquainted two people become. The more experienced the people concerned become, theoretically, the better equipped they should be to make sensible choices when the question of marriage finally crops up.

Do you think this idea would hold up under critical analysis?

I'm not certain, but I feel it should, although there are endless variations. After all, we can point to any one of a dozen couples whose premarital romance encompassed their two selves and nobody else. They lived happily ever after.

Conversely, we can all name a large number of people who played the field in their youth, gained lots of this valuable experience we've discussed, and yet floundered in marriage before many years elapsed.

All this indicates that there are no hard and fast rules in the preselection preamble to a happy marriage. I'm merely suggesting that moving around in these happy days is an idea that shouldn't be knocked.

Lots of friends, lots of dates, going out in groups, going out as a couple, are all part of the mating routine. The greater the general activity, the more experience one has with his fellowman, the better equipped he should ultimately become when he finally decides on the selection of the girl to be his wife. This is the basic point I'm trying to drive home. Exceptions there will be, for sure. But we're trying to talk in general terms that affect most people most commonly.

The Basics of Dating

What are some of the basic ingredients of "dating"?

In this world in which young people are becoming more sophisticated at a progressively earlier age, and particularly with girls maturing at a younger age, dating probably begins early.

To start, it may be a simple arrangement. Probably it's an after-school clandestine meeting, or some simple day-time incident. Most probably it's a bit awkward at first, much depending on the personality of the individuals concerned.

As a general rule, members of all-boy families with little home relationship with girls, often find initial approaches a bit difficult. But this is generally transient, and not very meaningful. With initial successes, plus advancing years and experience, this soon fades. But it's worth mentioning, for many shy young fellows firmly believe they are abnormal when they watch with envious admiration as their friends flit around with gay abandon, while they themselves haven't the courage to make the first tentative advance.

Don't you think coeducational schools are a good leveler of the boy-girl society?

Definitely. Indeed, this may be one of the biggest single factors in bringing everyone to the same general social level. It certainly forces relationships and plays a big part in solving early problems which are otherwise common. The kids automatically mix. They're thrown into one another's company. They learn how to communicate with each other on a friendly, unembarrassed level. Maybe it removes a bit of the golden aura of the opposite sex, but this isn't really important. There's always a lot left in the storehouse!

A little success in the early stage certainly adds encouragement. Very quickly, even a teen-ager unsure of himself, fumbling and bumbling, will gain poise and expertise in his relations with the opposite sex. Nothing breeds success like success. Boy-girl relations are no exception.

What about the physical side of dating?

Without fail, this moves in at a very early stage. As we've discussed in earlier chapters, this is the age group when tremendous chemical changes are occurring in both sexes. Hormones are being produced at an increasingly rapid rate. As the characteristics of adulthood appear, so an adult-type mental outlook gradually takes over.

Instinctively, a tremendous interest in the opposite sex automatically occurs. There is an involuntary attraction which is hard to resist. The childish dislike of the opposite sex that seems to dominate the first dozen years of life is suddenly replaced by an awakening of a new type of interest.

What sets off as a mental communication is soon translated into a physical experience. A sudden appreciation of body contact takes place. Simple actions such as handholding gradually (or rapidly) progress as desires become more deep-rooted. Increasing physical contact produces a sensuous nervous system reaction. In short, it feels good to be in touch.

The Psychological Pressures of Dating

What's the end point of all this?

Without question, there is little hope of holding back the emotional pressures of physical contact once they become unleashed. The more two personalities become involved, the greater becomes the desire to be together on a physical as well as a mental plane.

And at this point problems can start to mount!

Too true. As simple relations wind on, they become more complex. The more one has, the more one wants. The developing system is crying out to be wanted, to be loved, to be possessed. Left unchecked, simple manifestations of admiration gradually proceed onward to more significant ones. The trivial pastime of handholding ceases to produce much charm. A greater degree of personal contact provides a greater degree of attraction.

So petting quickly begins. Simple petting, unless closely watched, will inevitably lead on to heavy petting. Textbooks are not needed to make an expert in this direction. It all happens casually, naturally, often automatically.

Why not set out exactly what can occur?

The entire system is provided with an intricate, intertwining, interconnected nervous network. Certain areas seem more endowed than others, and are more responsive to certain stimuli.

It is well known that, in women, definite parts of the body are extremely sensitive to touch. The nipples and area surrounding them as well as the general breast area are quite sensitive to touch. So is the lower abdominal region. This increases in sensitivity as the lower areas are approached. The suprapubic parts just above and below the hairline, the inner side of the thighs, and all parts of the genital region are extremely sensitive to gentle touch.

Above all else, the clitoris, the tiny organ just above the entrance to the vagina, is extremely tender and receptive to gentle manipulation. Other parts of the body are also quite receptive. Stroking the back, playing with the ears and lower part of the neck produces erotic overtones in many women. The lips, under emotional stress, are also hypersensitive as most young fellows discover at a relatively early age.

Heavy Petting

So now back to heavy petting.

Simple physical contact often arouses the desire to investigate further. So exploring hands tend to wander off automatically in the general directions mentioned above. Gentle, passive stroking can suddenly produce dramatic changes in both partners.

For the male, the obvious effect that his overtures are having in itself produces a sensuous feeling. For the female the physical effect of such approaches arouses her sensual inner desires. It produces a satisfying feeling of being wanted, or being desired (and what woman doesn't hope to be wanted by someone?).

The effect of this physical stimulation is to whip up the built-in hormonal system to a high pitch of frenzy. The male has probably been already excited on numerous occasions by erotic "wet dreams" which we've talked about before. Despite his purity of thought and high ideals, these nocturnal excursions into fantasy often cause him to picture himself as indulging in sexual activity.

The immediate problem, of course, is that fantasy can

readily become the real. Heavy petting is the quickest known method of exciting a compelling, surging desire to indulge in sexual intercourse that is very hard to withstand.

Indeed, many psychologists believe that once a certain point has been reached, it becomes impossible to stop the steady, heady train of events that leads inexorably on to complete fulfillment of desire, which is found only in sexual union. Once this point has been reached, it's so simple, so natural, so automatic, to carry on just a little bit farther.

If you're one of the legion who believe they have a special something about them that can withstand the temptations of heavy petting, forget it right now. You can't. You're human, like everyone else.

What, then, is the advice?

I think it's pretty straightforward. Lovemaking to the point of sexual union is for marriage, not before. Why spoil the pleasures of a happy, united life with one partner for the transient emotional strain of illicit physical attraction with all its resulting problems?

Intercourse is that special something which sets marriage apart. Why cheapen it beforehand? Why reduce the chances of ultimate marital success by giving way to selfish indulgence in this unplanned manner.

No doubt you hope ultimately to marry. Will you be looking for a virgin? Or would you be contented with secondhand goods that have been the subject of heavy petting sessions by an unknown number of romeos before you?

There is little doubt you'll be seeking out the former. What, then, do you propose to offer her in return? Secondhand material that's done the rounds of town? Or a person who has saved himself for the girl of his choice, looking forward to ultimate happiness on the days, weeks, months, years that follow the nuptial night?

Marriage is a two-way deal. It's give and take on both sides for a lifetime. But those who stay together longest are more likely to be the ones that begin on the right footing.

One marriage in every four in the United States ends in divorce or separation or failure, and the proportion is rising. Figures in other countries are not very far behind. Probed to the basic causes, sex plays a king-sized part in a large number, probably the majority of these.

"Sleeping around" (as it seems to be called) premaritally is often the way people become accustomed to this sort of routine even after marriage. It's hard to change habits that are started in younger days. It's a point worth remembering. I've seen the end results of this so often.

Unwanted Pregnancies

You suggested earlier that lovemaking out of wedlock can produce all manner of problems. Would you like to enlarge on this a little?

Certainly. Probably the greatest single problem is the chance of an unplanned (and certainly unwanted) pregnancy. True, I know all about the universal availability of The Pill and other contraceptive devices and systems. But so often, the girl is not prepared for the situation—which means she's a sure prospect for becoming pregnant.

I'm well aware that lots of unmarried women regularly take The Pill. They play around and lead what they describe as a free life. (This term is purely relative. When I see them a few years later, I really wonder if their momentary definition has been of much value to them in the long term!) It's worth noting and well worth remembering that any couple from the age of puberty onward is capable of reproducing.

Indeed, the chances of pregnancy in the fifteen- and sixteen-year age group and onward is exceptionally high. The entire system is geared to this end. It is extremely receptive, and physiologically is in peak condition. My record files bulge with problems like this. Lots of couples seem to believe that complete penetration and absolute union is necessary before pregnancy can occur.

Let me assure you that even a minor degree of penetration can produce a pregnancy. With all those millions of sperms flooding the general vaginal area, just remember that it takes only one to make the ultimate journey and link up with the female ovum to produce a pregnancy. The odds are really stacked against you.

Add to this, of course, the fact that women are far more responsive to lovemaking and general physical stimulation at the time of "ovulation." This is when the microscopic ovum (or egg) is released by the ovary. Their hormonal system is ready to react in a most responsive manner at this time.

The effect of all this, of course, is that pregnancy is far more likely than if intercourse occurs at some other time of the menstrual cycle.

Other Problems

Apart from the pregnancy angle, what other hidden dangers are there?

It's well established that venereal disease is more rampant in people who "sleep around."

Indeed, these diseases which are more commonly referred to as "VD" are becoming a major community problem once more. As a matter of fact, we are devoting a special chapter to this specific topic to alert our male readers to the inherent dangers.

I know you'll tell me bluntly that you (and your girl) don't sleep around. You're for each other, just a cozy twosome. That's fine, but who knows what the future holds? What's great today may not be so wonderful tomorrow or next week or next year. Particularly with younger couples, mental attitudes alter.

Partners who appeal to one another right now may completely lose this appeal in a couple of years' time.

Education, work, outside pressures, mental maturity, your own experience can radically alter your views. Therefore, tonight's partner in a heavy petting session could quite easily be somebody else's in twelve months' time. Unless, of course, you've finally determined in your hearts that you're for one another forever—and proved the point by becoming legally united in marriage. I assure you, this is the only meaningful guarantee.

Once you've contracted VD you have more than a simple infection to get rid of. It can take weeks and often months before you're certain that you are cured. Even then, there is always the horrid underlying fear that something may have occurred which could impair your future happiness. It certainly does nothing to elevate one's mental level and personal pride.

Psychological Reactions

What about inner psychological reactions?

There's little doubt that sex out of marriage can be mentally damaging. The person likely to suffer most is the girl.

Generally the male is the aggressor, and the female is the more passive partner. It's the male role to protect his partner, not to take unfair advantage of her whenever the opportunity offers. He should try to protect her both physically as well as mentally.

Females are more likely to have a deep guilt sense than the male for out-of-wedlock sexual activities. It's quite easy for these to reflect back and ultimately produce emotional strains and stresses. Tension, stress, anxiety, depression are some of the common results that can readily occur.

Indeed, this can strike back over a period of many years and play a serious part in life. It can lead to continued unhappiness and mental unrest. Even if marriage finally occurs, many girls harbor the thoughts of their single days with something less than pride. Indeed, it can remain like a dark blot on the page of a memory book.

These are not idle meanderings. They are the words older women actually use when describing to me some of their problems in later life.

Do you think premarital sex can interfere with the satisfactory consummation of marriage later on?

According to many of my correspondents, the answer is Yes. It is extremely common to receive very touching letters from women. The theme runs along these lines:

"Before we were married, Jim and I really had a ball. We made love several times a week, and received complete and satisfying fulfillment. But then we married, and somehow things got off the rails.

"In a fairly short time, we seemed to get less and less out of the relationship. Sex didn't give much enjoyment anymore. Instead of something to be enjoyed to the full, it developed into a meaningless routine. Satisfaction seldom came my way. Jim started to lose interest.

"As this side of our marriage slowly started to fall to bits, we gradually started finding fault with each other. First it was with little things. But gradually this increased. Tensions mounted. Arguments increased. Life became unattractive, dull, and uninteresting."

This would be a typical letter written by a woman who believed she was madly in love premaritally.

What is the final upshot of this sort of predicament?

It varies a great deal. Some press on and try to right their problems themselves. Others seek expert guidance from marriage counselors, ministers, or their own doctor.

Some couples feel it's not worth the effort, and either separate tentatively or permanently. Many of these, of course, wind up in the divorce courts and have their marriages finally terminated.

Getting Your Values Right

The obvious question here of course is this: Do you think it was really the act of premarital sex that caused the final marriage disharmony? Or was the union on a purely physical level? After a period of time, with a fuller realization of their own diverging basic interests and capabilities and characters, the marriage may have been doomed from the start.

This is a hard question to answer honestly. Maybe there is no definite answer. There is little doubt that any marriage based purely on physical attraction is headed for disaster before the ink dries on the marriage certificate.

But I am quite sure that couples who have tasted sex in all its full vigor before marriage are more likely to dive into marriage than a couple seeking mental as well as physical fulfillment after marriage. I think it's a case of having your values right. Set yourself a goal. Try to picture the qualities in the girl you hope will eventually become your wife. To make doubly sure, write them down. Revise the list often and carefully.

Then, to be fair, why not write another list of the type of qualities and attributes such a girl would be worthy of. When you complete list number two, that is, a word picture of the sort of person you should try to emulate, recognize that it is yourself; you have described what you wish yourself to be. If you don't come up to the qualities itemized, you're certainly not worthy of the girl you hope to marry.

But this can be altered. Try to achieve the high level set, and day by day you will gradually come nearer to the picture. For many of the reasons already listed I don't think you'll be seeking a girl who sleeps around.

And deep down, she will not be looking for you if this happens to be your personality type.

Do you think a careful appraisal along these lines will give a better-than-average chance of a happy marriage that's destined to survive?

I believe so. Indeed, it's a reasonable approach. No doubt many variations and additions could be made—and possibly deletions also. But it will certainly yield a solid starting point for a happy, problem-free marital union.

In this permissive society it seems increasingly popular to live together before marriage, to sleep around (as you succinctly put it), and what not.

I'm well aware of all this. But because the crowd does something, that does not make it morally right.

Let's be frank. The basic moral code of society (our society, even uncivilized society, practically every society) still adheres to sex in its rightful place— *after marriage*.

Whether you have any religious inclination or not, you must recognize the fact that civil laws are merely the application of God-given moral codes that have been in use by man for thousands of years.

These are spiritually condoned, and are not meant to be changed willy-nilly by the whims of fashion. Therefore, there is good reason why our national moral ethics should be maintained on a never-ending basis.

8

Marriage Is Better Still!

In the last chapter we suggested that the best and most fulfilling time to enjoy the delights of complete sexual union is after marriage.

Correct. Sex has a twofold purpose. The first and obvious one is that it's part of the system of reproduction. Without it the human race would soon die out. Indeed, it would never have reached today's stage at all!

But the second feature is also extremely important. It represents the full expression of affection between two partners. Indeed, it may readily become the most forceful binding tie of life. But there are well-established bonus extras as well. Without doubt it is one of the best tranquilizers yet devised by medical science. It can relieve anxiety and tension, soothe jangled, jaded nerves. It is a top-quality sedative, as well as a key restorative.

It is an excellent judge of human frailties. Indeed, there is no better way to settle disputes. Both partners end up mentally refreshed, inwardly happy and physically satisfied.

It's good for bad tempers, frayed spirits, tattered overwrought "nerves" with which this modern rough-and-tumble world abounds.

My! This reads a bit like an advertisement for some magical new pill!

I agree. But didn't you know that the best medicines of all come from nature? Generally speaking, they're free!

Your description "magical" is nearer the truth than you possibly realized. The benefits and advantages of a happy, well-adjusted marriage are legion. Indeed, when one visualizes the impact sex has upon life over a period of many years, it becomes more and more apparent that it's something very special. Something that should be reserved for the special part of life when two personalities are permanently linked.

This is how and when its full value comes to the fore.

This is another point in favor of reserving it for the time after the wedding certificate has been signed, sealed, and delivered. I am quite certain that the temporary delights which may occur with spasmodic premarital lovemaking have no real benefits of any lasting value. It's the warmth and affection and belonging that grow over a period of time that deepen the significance of it all.

Even Within Marriage

But we often hear of marriages falling apart even though the couple tried to carry out the general principles you've outlined.

That I cannot deny. But I must emphasize that lovemaking, family unity, and all that are something more than a regular mechanical action. When they deteriorate to that level (and I must admit that this is quite common), cracks have already started to appear in the marriage. The red lights are flashing good and strong. It's imperative that the couple concerned take stock and try to discover just how their marriage is getting off the rails.

Don't you think that couples expect to be expert lovers from the moment they are married? You know, the old fairy tale ending: "And the prince and the princess rode off into the sunset, and they lived happily ever after." Don't you think many couples enter marriage with the same idea ingrained into their minds?

That's for sure. Although they've probably both been trained over a period of many years for some profession or business or technical calling and have studied hard for a long time to become proficient, few ever consider that marriage is a serious undertaking and can likewise require training and effort.

Unfortunately there is no school of romance. You don't attend formal classes where the basics of a successful marriage are taught; where the difficulties and pitfalls are pointed out before they occur, and where trained personnel can outline some of the hazards that lie ahead. Maybe such schools will start one of these days, although I have my doubts.

Before marriage a few couples have the good sense to visit either a trusted, experienced friend or their minister or their own doctor if he is the family-physician type who will take the time to discuss problems in detail.

Here they at least get a smattering of possible events of the future. But these would be in the minority by far. I'd say that one couple in twenty might follow this line.

Premarital Advice

Do you think it's a good idea for a couple to buy a quality marriage manual and study this beforehand?

It certainly helps. Indeed, every course of any value has its own set of textbooks. The matrimonial course is about the only vital one that hasn't any set classes or timetable or essential reading list. Over the past few years some authors have produced excellent books which provide quality advice for people intending to marry. They cover most of the important aspects of marriage in depth.

Some of these are very intricate, and I feel they are too heavy for the average reader. But others are not so complex and are easy to read, simple to follow, and cover a wide number of essential topics.

I usually suggest to youngsters seeking marital advice to purchase one of these manuals and read it in general terms. "And when you've finished it all, shut up the book and let nature take its course," I finally suggest!

With a sound basic knowledge of the fundamentals, this, coupled with a person's own instinct, guided by God's will, will certainly make a happy start to marriage, I have found.

The Intimate Side

In the earlier chapters we talked about the anatomy and physiology of the male and female. We discussed the built-in chemical factories where hormones are produced, and we learned a little of their functions and their amazing powers. We've also documented the dangers of premarital sex and all that. However, let's be a bit more explicit. Although our readers probably know a great deal about the intimate side of sex, why not go over the topic in a little detail? After all, as you've said, this is the important, final physical end point of lovemaking, and as such is vitally important.

That's a reasonable suggestion. The reproductive system of the body is geared to cope adequately with physical union. In fact, it's made so easy that no great effort is really required. It's designed so that everything can happen so naturally, so automatically, with ease and facility that makes the most modern machine or architecture look clumsy.

In the last chapter we discussed in some detail the popular

pastime of petting. Although we don't condone heavy petting as a safe or satisfactory premarital exercise, the situation changes enormously after marriage. When unity can be a complete, satisfying, and ongoing proposition, it is different. Indeed, this is the time for which heavy petting should be reserved.

But once that marriage document has been officially executed, so many couples rush headlong into the delights of their newfound situation that they immediately generate problems of another nature. Enthusiasm is great, but unbridled postmarital expressions of selfish desire can undermine what should be a delightful experience.

In simple terms, you're saying that the esthetics of the chase should be continued after marriage?

Precisely. We've already described the so-called erotic areas of the female body. The nipple and breast regions, the suprapubic regions, inner parts of the thighs, vulval areas, and above all the clitoris are extremely sensitive to delicate touch.

Understanding, thoughtful husbands will be aware of these facts. Therefore, before embarking on the gratification of his own sensual pleasures, a husband will make every effort to share these delights with his wife.

Gentle stimulation of these areas will heighten her interest in what usually follows so naturally and so pleasurably. It will also make the final act one of deep significance, one that will draw the partners together in a vicelike grip of affection.

I always tell married couples that time spent in loveplay (as it is popularly called) is never wasted. The rewards are deep and lasting. It imparts to the wife the feeling that she is wanted, that she is an integral part of her husband's life, and that it means a lot if he is prepared to spend time attending to her inner needs as well as his own.

Is this a time-consuming activity?

It varies with the individual. Some women react instinctively and immediately. Others take time. It may vary from five minutes to half an hour or even longer. There is no hard-and-fast set of rules.

What's the indication that success is being achieved?

Apart from the obvious expression of satisfaction, the tiny glands at the vaginal entrance (called Bartholin's Glands) commence activity. They produce a fluid aimed at lubricating the vaginal entrance and also the whole vaginal tract. Indeed, when this occurs, it's the female counterpart of erection of the penis in the male.

Just as the wife is being stimulated into a full appreciation of her husband, the mere actions being performed tend to heighten his own sensuous feelings and desires.

At this point the wife indicates that she is in a receptive mood. Her thighs tend to fall apart; often she will assist her husband in directing the erect penis toward and into the vaginal entrance. It only requires gentle upward, inward pressure for the penis to penetrate the well-lubricated vaginal passageway in a gentle motion.

When the full length of the passage has been traversed, it's virtually automatic for the penis to be partially withdrawn, to be thrust gently upward and inward again.

These actions continue. All this time, the wife assists with the movements made by her husband, frequently pushing forward and then relaxing back again in time with his own thrusts.

During this venture, the glands continue producing the lubricating fluid. The glans (head) of the penis, the most sensitive part, moves against the corrugated lining of the vagina. Stimulation increases and finally reaches a crescendo which is termed the *orgasm*.

At this instant there is a release of seminal fluid from the seminal vesicles, the sperm storehouses located near the bladder. This material surges through the urethra, the tiny internal tube that leads to the exterior.

With several forceful, automatic movements over which there is absolutely no human control, ejaculation (as it is called) occurs.

At this instant, the erect penis is usually fully extended in the vaginal tract. A large amount of fluid is deposited high up in the vagina, very close to the *cervix,* or neck of the uterus (womb).

By this time major changes have come over the male. He is usually hot, flushed, may be perspiring, and is breathing in short deep gasps as the seminal fluid pours from the end of the penis. But once this vital end point has been reached, he is immediately overcome with a desire to relax. The penis rapidly loses its erectile power, and soon becomes limp and flaccid once more.

Indeed, the soporific effect of ejaculation is quite marked. With the release of the tension that has built up during the love-play incidents, an overwhelming feeling of deep satisfaction is the usual climactic aftermath. Most males thereafter have an intense desire to go to sleep. Indeed, this may be an excellent idea, and when undertaken under appropriate circumstances is certainly a sedative of the most natural and most successful type.

The Wife's Role

Does the female have such a marked end point to stimulation?

The answer is Yes, although many females claim they have never experienced the full satisfaction of true orgasm. Large numbers do achieve a climax which is a sensuous feeling that encompasses the entire body. The joyful feeling of exhilaration builds up during actual physical union, and in the successfully completed instance culminates in a sensation of delightful ecstacy.

As deep penetration progresses, she gives herself fully to her role. She too becomes flushed, breathes rapidly, and increases the rate of her body movements. Ultimately the end point of orgasm surges through the system. Sometimes the husband must continue the rythmic motions for a time after his own orgasm in order to bring his wife to her climax. He will gladly do this and share in her ecstacy. After this, a warm feeling pervades her entire being, and she relaxes in a happy state of complete satisfaction.

Is this the picture in every instance?

This is the picture as it should be. But unfortunately it is often marred by many outside influences. Many males seem so intent on satisfying their own basic sexual urges that they fail to understand the inner needs of their partners.

It's just as vital for the wife to enjoy complete satisfaction as it is for the husband. Indeed, when aroused and not satisfied, a letdown feeling of unreality will pervade the entire system. If this is repeated on a regular basis, many wives will finally shun lovemaking, believing it holds no joy for them.

Sensible husbands are attuned to the needs of their partners. The gentle actions that are the forerunner of successful lovemaking are constantly in their minds. They will go to considerable efforts to satisfy their wives in all respects. I believe these are the instances where marriages remain alive and active and vital for many years.

The experience does not develop into a one-sided affair with the husband on the receiving end of the deal permanently. It is a 50-50 arrangement, and both partners are alive to the needs of the other. Being alert to this aspect of giving, one will automatically receive a taste of life at its best. It's an ongoing affair. It can proceed year after year, with an ever-growing and increasing amount of deep, satisfying affection, intricately woven into the entire pattern of living.

Over the years I have discussed intimate marriage problems with many couples of all ages. One factor stands out clearly in nearly every instance: So long as each partner makes a genuine effort to appreciate and fulfill the needs and desires of his partner, the chances of a split are greatly diminished. But on the other hand, once the needs of the other are forgotten, then problems start to loom.

"My marriage is going on the rocks," is a sad complaint I hear every week in my metropolitan consulting rooms. "How can I save it? What should I do?"

It may be the wife who comes along; it may be the husband.

Problems in Marriage

What's your usual advice?

I like to consult with each partner individually. I try to dig down and find just where the problems are occurring. Often the superficial reasons offered are things such as, "Money . . . the car . . . the kids . . . the house . . . work . . . holidays . . . in-laws," and so on and so on. But generally these are merely a front for something more deep-seated.

We talk around these generalities for a while. Finally, when I gently ask, "What's the chief problem in your sex life?" the person looks up in startled surprise, but obviously delighted that the sensitive nerve has been tapped without having to bring up the dreaded subject himself or herself. More often than not, therein lies the problem.

"My husband worries only about himself. He couldn't care less about the way I feel. Self-gratification is his only wish in life."

Or maybe a husband will complain: "My wife's frigid. She's totally unresponsive. It's like sleeping with a block of ice [with a fish, in a refrigerator, etc. The list is very long, but the meaning is the same]."

What is the answer to problems like this?

To begin with, I tell them that 90 percent of problems like this can be solved. Provided each is willing to take a renewed interest in the other, we can hope for a reasonable chance of success.

Then it's a case of reestablishing the feelings that must have drawn them together in the first place. (They must have had these feelings, otherwise they would never have married.)

Together we go over the basics of the lovemaking game. Little by little, those who have forgotten are reminded of how it should all be done. For those who are still ignorant (and there are plenty of these people around despite their senior years), we discuss tactfully ways and means of wooing the partner, of bringing mutual joy, satisfaction, and happiness.

What are the results like?

For those who are willing to try—and those who are genuinely aware of their own failings—the results must be good. And they certainly are. Of course, those looking for a simple "out" will continue to use any old excuse. But in the main, married couples (particularly those with children) are seeking a way to remain together as a happy, workable unit.

Deep down they don't want to split up. If their problems can be solved, if they can find the path back to satisfying joy and happiness, sexual security and enjoyment, then they're almost there.

Never underestimate the positive power of the sex drive. It's just as powerful as the will to survive, the drive to succeed, and the other instinctive drives that keep the human race afloat.

For the population of a basically Christian nation, I believe that many of the Scriptural references recommending sharing, of being kind, or giving and receiving, apply to this facet of family living just as much as to the broader aspects of life.

To Sum Up

What's your final summing up in this chapter for our readers?

It's just this. I reiterate:

- Sexual experimenting is definitely for the important time of life after you have married.
- Don't cheapen it beforehand. You've a tremendous number of years ahead of you; don't complicate these with unnecessary problems.
- A happy, united sex life after marriage can do much to smooth away the cares, harrowing problems, and difficulties which you will face. Indeed, you'll need every ounce of help you can get. And often. Reserve it all for those important days.
- Bear in mind that sharing in life can produce a very satisfying result.
- Don't try to be on the winning side every time. Giving is all-important.
- Never forget that the more you give in life, the more you'll gather in return. Of this, there is absolutely no doubt.

I hope you get the general message. I trust you'll remember it and try to put it into practice.

9

Study Your Way to Success Unlimited

We've spent a lot of time discussing aspects of growing up, physically and mentally developing, the part sex plays in these years, and some of the problems associated with this. Now let's switch to some of the other very important aspects of life that crop up in the teens.

A good idea. Growing up is only one aspect. During this period a person must decide how he plans to spend the remainder of his life. It's not all fun and games, as all our readers either know already or will discover in the very near future.

Earning a living is a prominent goal of every male. It's important that a woman should have a means of support as well. There is no guarantee she will marry, and indeed, so many males seem doomed to an early demise these days, that a profession or knowledge of some money-earning vocation is imperative, I believe, for all women too.

However, we're mainly concerned with males in this book. Every male must have an ultimate money-earning objective in his sights. The earlier he realizes this, the better for him.

Wrapped up with this is the idea of education. In our

Western-type economy, more and more emphasis is being placed on education.

It seems that nearly every worthwhile job requires a certain level of educational attainment. Degrees, diplomas, and certificates are now prerequisites for nearly all callings today. The situation will progress farther in this direction as time advances.

Therefore, in a nutshell, every person must get a decent education if he hopes to enjoy a reasonable level of living in this world–is that it?

Precisely. Whether we go along with the system or not, this is one of the hard, cold facts of life as we know it.

Therefore, like it or not, nearly every male is destined to undergo a certain amount of formal training. When school is completed, some form of specific training should follow on.

There are many different forms, from university level, to college, technical, and allied institutions. Or the apprentice system may be the one of choice.

But being caught up in the web of one system or another is inevitable. Nearly everyone but the deadbeat drop-out is going to become so involved. So the purpose of this chapter is to offer a few suggestions as to how this system may be entered into with a reasonable degree of enjoyment and success.

How to Handle Study Problems

You mean it is a short summary of "How to Pass Exams More Proficiently," or "The ABC of Flying Through School"?

In essence, yes. But we can only offer suggestions. The rest—the hard work, of course—is still up to the student.

How do you propose dealing with this vast subject?

I'd like to approach it fairly simply under three chief headings. These will be:

1. The Environment.
2. The Physical Aspects.
3. The Study Routine.

Let's make a start then.

1. The Environment.

Let's have a look at these aspects:

A. Single room.
B. Quietness.
C. Lighting.
D. Temperature.
E. The chair.

That's a formidable start. Still, nothing like having a proper series of subheadings. I see you start off with a single room.

A. Single room.

That's right.

Ideally, every student from as early in secondary school as possible should have a room to himself. I believe it is nearly impossible for anyone to study properly when there are diverging interests to capture his attention. Such conditions are inevitable when you share a room with one or more.

I fully appreciate that it is often impossible to have a room to oneself, particularly when there are several children in the family. But it's the ideal to strive for. Many parents will go to great efforts to secure this for their children.

Often if a single room is not possible, it may be possible to subdivide an existing larger room by partitions that, in effect, screen off the various children's study-sleeping quarters.

Of course, if there is the thought of continuing education, particularly at university level, the demanding study hours, together with the avalanche of books and notes required, make a single room almost mandatory.

It's worth keeping in mind, and striving to achieve if at all possible. I believe it is number one point in favor of doing well in the study routine.

I see you have noted quietness as the second item on the list.

B. Quietness.

Knowledge, of course, is secured through various channels. Such as via the eyes when we read; via the ears when we listen to lecturers, teachers, recording gadgets, or repeat work out loud ourselves. Knowledge comes through actions when we actually talk aloud, either to ourselves or into recording devices for later re-hearing. These are also mental pictures which we conjure up in the conscious parts of our minds.

When we actively endeavor to feed material into our brains, all our senses must be attuned to this end. The more extraneous noises and outside diversions that occur, the greater is the competition. If a radio is blaring in the background, or if a television set is in the foreground (with its associated pictures and noises), the less chance the information you are trying to store into your mental memory bank has of getting there, let alone of staying there.

Children fighting in the background, yelling infants, screeching brakes from passing traffic, the roar of trucks on the highway outside, loud conversations are some of the competitors for our mental attention.

For sure, many of these cannot be avoided. You can't move out of your house merely because you live on a busy highway. You can't lessen the number of children in the family! But if there is any choice in selecting methods of reducing these competitors, seek them out and try to avail yourself of any way of improving them.

The key point is this: Go for quietness. You'll study more effectively with a peaceful environment. The material will sink in faster and stay there awaiting recall for a far greater time.

This is the reason why some students find it better to go to bed early and rise early before the household begins to make its morning din. It's worth more than a passing thought.

I see you attach a good deal of importance to lighting.

C. Lighting.

I certainly do. Indeed, unless a student has adequate and satisfactory lighting in his study room, he is headed for big problems. Ideally, daylight is the best form of lighting. The source should be coming from behind and to one side of the student so that it falls on his work, preferably without shadow.

A source of light directly in front is often a cause of eye problems. It can initiate strain, headaches, and considerable discomfort if used continually.

Since most study must be accomplished after sunset, a daylight-type fluorescent light is ideal. This is very nearly as good as daylight. Failing this, a frosted incandescent light comes next, but it is a poor substitute. A clear nonfrosted globe comes last.

Protect your eyes from direct vision into the source of illumination.

An eyeshade will often assist if the light source is incorrect, and particularly if it is causing obvious bother. Today a wide range of lights is available, and it is quite simple to select something suitable for a modest cost.

I see you have a heading devoted to temperature.

D. Temperature.

Yes, in fact I attribute a lot of importance to temperature. There is little doubt that, when one is at a too-comfortable temperature and the surroundings are peaceful and cozily warm, the chances of effective study reduce markedly. For this reason, wintertime is the ideal time in which to study with best results.

But this, of course, is not always possible. Study generally does encompass, sooner or later, a year-round cycle. Therefore, you must be geared to study, whatever the temperature is like outside.

Try to keep the room cool. I'm not advocating air conditioning, although this is the universal ideal.

In summer months keep rooms well ventilated. Brick houses are usually cooler during the morning and early afternoon. They tend to stay hot most of the night. This may be a point for going to bed early and rising to study in the early mornings.

In winter, don't overheat the rooms to a point where efficient study is not possible. I still believe that a blanket wrapped around the legs is far superior to a focal point of heat (eg, fire, radiator, or similar heat-producing apparatus). Your mind seems more mentally efficient if it's kept cool.

We're all aware of the extreme lethargy that overtakes most people on a hot afternoon (and particularly after a good lunch). This is disastrous to study!

Now what's this suggestion about "the chair"? Sounds a bit like a formal gathering of the board of directors!

E. The chair.

It has nothing to do with a directors' meeting. However, the person who takes care of his chair at the student level could well become a chairman of a board of directors in later life. It has happened before this. I mean it is essential to have a decent sort of chair to sit on! This may seem quite obvious, but it's incredible to see the odd, bizarre collection of chairs students sit on. Just remember that you'll spend untold hours

sitting on this one chair. It must be comfortable. Preferably go for a nonluxury sort. A simple, straight-back design is preferable, with either a thin cushion or reasonable upholstering on the seat.

It must be adjusted to the right height. Using a standard desk, the seat, too, will be a standard height. It must be suitable for many hours' writing as well as leaning back for meditation, mental revision, etc.

Also included under this heading are the other vital aspects of the study room.

Ideally, have a suitable desk. This need not be elaborate. Indeed, many students have made their own desks. Drawers, either shelves or cupboards, are also needed, varying a bit according to the nature of material you study from.

Bookcases and shelves in the room are usually necessary. It's preferable to have your study gear self-contained in your own room if at all possible, rather than having to run around to various locations in the house to find material. This only breaks the line of thought.

The Physical Aspects

I notice your second big heading encompasses the physical aspects of study. Just what does this include?

I'd like to set this aspect out in the following manner:

2. The Physical Aspects.

A. General health.

B. Diet.

C. Exercising.

D. Sleep.

E. Hygiene.

F. Circadian rhythm.

G. Programming.

This seems to cover an enormous variety of material. I

believe it's all very important. Let's start with general health.

A. General health.

I must emphasize from the very start the importance of general health. No student can expect to do well in his work unless he is in tip-top physical condition.

Imagine trying to run a machine effectively and efficiently if the gears are not oiled, if they are badly worn, filled with dirt and grime, not cleaned properly or regularly. The operator would soon be in king-sized trouble.

Similarly, your body is merely a machine (in one sense). But by looking after it carefully, you can guarantee that it will remain in good repair and operate smoothly. Neglect it, and you'll very soon run into difficulties. It will not operate correctly. Problem after problem will loom, and disaster upon disaster will occur.

In the next few pages we'll outline a few of the important issues that will help you keep in good physical (and mental) condition.

But if there is any disability, it should be referred to a doctor for correction without delay.

At this point I make special reference to visual defects. It is essential that your eyesight be in good order. So much work is done by the eyes in carrying information to the brain. The eyes must be in top working order. If there is any doubt as to their good health and efficiency, get a referral to a competent eye specialist without delay.

"Refractive errors" (that is, errors in the lens system of the eyes, through which the light reaches the sensitive retina at the back of the eye) are very common in growing children and young adults. The majority of these can be corrected. Eyeglasses may be required. Proper correction will allow greater efficiency in study.

Left unchecked, defects in eyesight can cause eyestrain,

quick fatigue of the eyes, and headaches. General fatigue and a disinclination to study are natural events that follow on from this. These are barriers to efficient study.

What do you have to say about diet?

B. Diet.

When I was a student attending university, the train I traveled on each day passed a large wall in an industrial suburb. On it was painted in faded letters: "What you eat today, walks and talks tomorrow."

It might not sound very subtle or original, but it made a lasting impression on my youthful mind at the time. In essence, it said, food is vital to life. In fact, it is *YOU*. Therefore, taking some interest in what you consume each day is of more than passing importance.

The diet of a student should encompass a natural balance of the essentials to good health. This embraces a balance of protein, carbohydrates (starches and sugars), fats, vitamins, minerals, roughage, and fluid.

Left to his own devices, a person often naturally tends to eat a reasonable balance of these foods. However, in our general economy, there is a vast tendency today for carbohydrate foods to be emphasized. Certainly these are "energy-giving" foods and are often proclaimed as such by the advertisers! But excess amounts of them are bad. They tend to give little lasting satisfaction to hunger; they tend to produce poor teeth (and encourage dental caries, or decay), and they certainly predispose to overweight.

We in the so called "advanced" countries are slowly digging our graves with our teeth. In other words, we're eating ourselves to death. Therefore, in general, go sparingly on the high-carbohydrate foods. By emphasizing the other essential nutrients you will automatically take on adequate starches to see you through.

Could you give an indication of the high-starch foods?

In summary, the commonest high-starch foods are potatoes—in all forms, such as boiled, baked, mashed potatoes, potato sticks and chips, "French fries" (as in fish-and-chips); bread—in all forms, such as toast, sandwiches, etc.; and sweets—in all forms, such as chocolates, jams, carbonated drinks, desserts, and cakes.

There is another way to classify the chief carbohydrates that I like to mention. It goes like this:

SUGARS:

(1) Refined sugars: granulated, cubes, powdered.

(2) Concentrated sweets: honey, molasses, syrups, jellies, jam, preserves, marmalade, candies, sweets, chocolates.

(3) Fruits: dried fruits, stewed fruits with added sugar, some fresh fruits such as grapes and bananas.

STARCHY FOODS:

(1) Cooked cereals: such as rolled oats, oatmeal, wheat cereals, rice, green corn.

(2) Ready-to-serve cereals: such as cornflakes, wheat flakes, puffed grain.

(3) Flours: wheat, rye, barley, cornstarch, arrowroot, cornmeal, tapioca, sago.

(4) Foods made from flour: macaroni, spaghetti, noodles, breads, pastries, cakes.

(5) Legumes: dried peas and beans. Also potatoes and other root vegetables.

Are you suggesting that our readers completely go off this formidable list of foods?

Certainly not. Reasonable amounts of starches are essential to good health. I wish to emphasize the importance of being aware of the types of food that will most likely be eaten to excess and often to the detriment of other sensible foods.

Every day in my consulting rooms I see adolescents and

SPECIAL
PLUMS
49¢ lb

adults whose daily luncheon consists of a bottle of a sugary carbonated drink, a hamburger (or fish and chips), and nothing else. The nutritive value of this is not very great.

A check on other meals for the day will indicate that they, too, are an unbalanced low-nutrition mass, composed largely of starchy foods. A sensible balance of the essential nutrients of all sections is vital to the student.

Would you care to outline, as a general suggestion, the type of foods a student should try to include in his daily menu?

Here is an excellent guide. It has been worked out by a panel of experts in nutrition, and I believe it applies to everyone who is endeavoring to maintain good health.

Include these foods in your daily diet:

- 3 cups of milk
- 2-3 ounces (65 g) of protein. (Meat, fish, poultry, or suitable equivalents for persons preferring vegetarian foods. See note below.)
- 1 egg two or three times a week
- 1 serving legumes, additional protein, or cheese
- 1 serving whole-grain cereal
- 3 slices whole-grain bread
- 4 servings vegetables, including:
  - 1-2 of potato
  - 1-2 of green or yellow vegetable
  - 1 of other vegetable
- 2 servings fruit, including:
  - 1 of citrus fruit (or other fruit containing vitamin C)
  - 1 of any other fruit
- 2 tablespoonfuls butter (or polyunsaturated margarine)
- 6-8 glasses of water

(Note: Generally speaking, 1 cup of undiluted evaporated milk equals 2 cups of fresh milk. 1 pound (.45 kg) dried milk equals 4.75 quarts (4.5 litres) fresh skim milk.)

Today, increasing numbers of students and adults are turning to an all-vegetarian menu. Basically, this eliminates the use of flesh foods, and concentrates on fruits, nuts, vegetables, and grains. Therefore, there is an emphasis on such items as eggs, milk, cheese, cereal grains, and legumes, and an abstinence from meat, fish, and poultry.

Many athletes and those requiring top physical fitness, often stick to such a dietetic routine. The result of their care is often amply rewarded in the success of their enterprises. It is worth giving careful thought to this type of diet.

What are your views on exercising for the student?

C. Exercising.

Regular daily exercising is vital to good health, and for this reason every student should make some effort to program this into his daily routine.

Very briefly, exercise keeps the muscle systems "in tone." In turn, this keeps the blood actively circulating through the system. Therefore all parts get adequate supplies of vital oxygen plus foods that are needed to keep the system in good running repair.

Exercising also assists respiration. The more you breathe, and the more deeply, the more oxygen the system takes aboard. At the same time, exhaling rids the system of many of the impurities that otherwise accumulate in the system.

The form of exercise probably doesn't matter too much, but it is imperative that everyone, especially students, have some regular vigorous exercise which induces deep breathing.

Many find simple walking adequate. This is certainly an easy line to follow, costs nothing (apart from a little time and effort), but produces excellent results. Others prefer the more strenuous lines, such as running and jogging on a regular daily basis. There are all manner of variations of these simple basic forms, such as cycling, swimming and surfing, or skiing. Or playing any of the more organized sports, like baseball, football, soccer, tennis, and basketball.

However, most students should have an exercise routine worked out, one that adapts to their own personal life-style. Organized sports are often difficult when you are endeavoring to adhere to a study program. Therefore they are often impractical. The simpler forms mentioned can be done at any time that suits the student. Slightly more sophisticated routines are found in the Canadian Air Force's "Five BX System" and similar programs.

They are all excellent. The chief essential is to adhere to whatever routine you decide to adopt. Then carry it out regularly. You'll study so much more efficiently and effectively if you do.

Sleep. What do you have to say about this?

D. Sleep.

Every person has his own particular ideas about the amount of sleep that is required. My advice to every student is this: Go for eight hours a night, every night!

I make no apologies, and believe that regular sleep is vital to efficient study, efficient memory, and mental acumen. Often eight hours is not possible on a night-by-night schedule. The next best thing is to try to catch up every few nights, or at most on a weekly basis. You cannot go week in and week out cutting down on sleep. If you think you can, and keep tempting fate, your mental sharpness will gradually suffer. Your powers of concentration and recall will decline.

I am well aware that Einstein and other "greats" in the past have existed (and apparently prospered) on three or four hours a night. If you believe you are in the same category, leave experimenting until after the vital examinations are over. Right now, it's more likely you're Mr. Average Student, and as such you'll do better on the norm. That means eight hours per night, or as near to it as possible.

During the hours of sleep the entire system comes to rest. The body has a chance to rehabilitate itself. Worn-out cells are repaired. Mental brightness is restored, vitality replenished. At the same time, the system's built-in computer system has a chance to assimilate the mass of material that has been fed into it during the previous wakeful hours.

How often have you fed a problem into this mighty system one evening, not knowing the answer, only to awaken bright and fresh next morning with the answer automatically staring you in the face? It's no miracle. It was merely your wonderful brain cells operating subconsciously while you were getting much-needed physical repose. Keen students are well aware of the way their minds operate. They make full use of it whenever possible (and that is every day).

This subheading labeled "Hygiene" interests me. Tell me more.

E. Hygiene.

Often we relate hygiene to the simple art of being clean. That is one important aspect, and I throw it in for good measure. These days more and more seem intent on remaining as dirty and grubby as possible. Keeping physically clean is important to good health. Bathe regularly. Wash the skin well with hot water, and use plenty of soap. Do this often.

Don't forget the hair. The scalp loves water and soap. It loves feeling clean. Being clogged up with body oils that are left to accumulate on the surface (together with dust and grit and grime from the environment) attracts germs and vermin. Yes, real living vermin!

In our affluent society? For sure. I see lots of undergrads from the large university not far from my rooms. I am ap-

palled by the sloppy dress, the squalor that many of these students seem to wallow in.

Social standing seems no bar. I endeavor to understand the swingers and fashion in general. But fashion never condones utter filth and lack of personal physical hygiene. If you want to succeed as a student, just pay regular attention to this very important aspect of daily living.

The simple measures of cleaning the teeth regularly (like morning and night at least), cleaning and cutting the nails, having a haircut from time to time, shaving regularly (even if you do go for the hirsute style), using an underarm deodorant, wearing clean clothing are also important.

Why? Because so many aspiring to success in life seem to forget that these aspects of life still exist. Successful students usually do not forget. Maybe that's an added reason why they make the grade so often.

But there are other aspects of hygiene I'd like to mention. How does your room look? What is your desk like? What about the shelves, bookcases, and drawers? Are they one conglomerate mess of papers, books, clippings, rulers, and stationery in an unkempt mess from which it is impossible to extricate anything without a minor revolution?

What about your briefcase? Is it half full of yesterday's lunch wraps, apple cores, notes, dirty handkerchiefs, and what not? And your bed? Neat and tidy, or one great mess too?

A student's mind is reflected in his room. An orderly mind inevitably produces an orderly desk, drawers, shelves, wardrobe, and bed.

It's worth bearing in mind. Often this comes automatically. Sloppy upbringing and training will produce sloppiness here too. It will also produce sloppy exam papers that don't exactly bring the highest marks.

I see you have a heading labeled "Circadian rhythm." This sounds exciting.

F. Circadian rhythm.

Exciting it is too.

The body has built into it a series of systems. We refer to these as circadian rhythms. It comes from the Latin *circa* which means "about," and *dies* which means "day." Roughly speaking, the systems encompass a space of twenty-four hours.

One example of this is the body's temperature. About 6 am the body temperature is at its lowest level. As the day progresses, the temperature rises. It reaches a peak between two and five in the afternoon.

Certain key glands in the body follow a similar rhythm. In turn, their secretions affect other parts of the system, and further rhythms flow out from this. Researchers have discovered that, in the average person, intellectual proficiency is at its lowest level around 4 am. From this point, mental acuity gradually improves. It reaches its zenith later in the day. This varies from person to person. Some find that they are at their peak of efficiency about midmorning and again in the evening. Others find a gradual buildup so that they are at maximum efficiency from, say, 7 to 10 pm.

Circadian rhythm has two important effects in life. One involves persons who travel overseas in modern jet aircraft a good deal. They frequently arrive at their destination and have to make key decisions at a time when their internal time clock is telling them that they should be sound asleep in bed.

For this reason, travelers overseas are now cautioned to play it cool after arrival. Indeed, scheduling their flights so they arrive in the evening (and to a good night's sleep) is often recommended. On no account should a traveler make any important decision within twenty-four hours of arrival. Nor should he try to drive a car in a busy city for at least a day.

From the student's point of view, the importance of recognizing circadian rhythm should be obvious. Your system is automatically and naturally geared to a maximum peak for mental acuity. Take advantage of this. Program your activities so that you are doing your key study when your mental efficiency is at its upper level. As I said earlier, it may be convenient for some to study early in the morning. However, in most cases, nature is against this. Therefore it's worth trying to reorganize physical factors to bring them into alignment with natural factors. It could make you that much more efficient in the long run.

I see you have a heading labeled "Programming." Just how important is this to the student?

G. Programming.

I believe it is of vital importance. Indeed, without it he's doomed to failure from the start.

"Programming" is the "in thing" right now. It smacks of the computer world. Indeed, the first computer to be made was the human brain. These brain computers have now been operating efficiently for some thousands of years. So the concept of computerization is not entirely new.

Sensible students will program their activities on a well balanced, clearly considered system. In fact, it is worth spending several hours working out the general principles of *your* personal program. This is best calculated at the beginning of a new term or semester.

On a piece of paper jot down the list of items that you hope to accomplish during the term. These will be in general terms, of course. But in general principle, you can certainly work this out fairly simply. At school you may be given a weekly timetable of actual classes to attend. This will form the general basis of the program. But apart from this there will be many items to consider. The amount of work to be achieved at home each night and on weekends; the set work; the "extra" work you hope to accomplish (if you're going for that extra grade).

Then there will be the factors we've outlined briefly before. There must be a given time slot for exercising, for eating adequate meals, for sleep, for personal and general hygiene. Into this you must phase the circadian rhythm factor.

Successful students often work out a "type program" for the day, varying this according to the specific requirements of any one day.

At this stage you're probably groaning and saying all this is not possible. But in practice it *is* possible. Successful students are those who recognize the importance of this early, and stick to it. Of course, variations will have to be made, but the general idea holds true. It is a sound way of approaching work. This is so whether you're a student or in business or a profession. If you can master the art of programming your life now, when you're still young, the chances of unlimited success for the remainder of your life are very good. Once

---

WHAT IS YOUR "IDEAL" WEIGHT?

On the next page is a comprehensive range of "ideal" weights. You will notice that from birth to seventeen years weight is related to age and height (Table A) and that weight in the fifteen-to-seventeen-year bracket is extremely variable. After this age group weight is related to height only. Consideration is given to sex (male or female) and whether you are of small, medium, or large physique. As many countries are switching to "metric" measuring systems, the tables are given in both.

A

AVERAGE HEIGHT AND WEIGHT FOR CHILDREN

Age	BOYS					GIRLS				
	Height			Weight		Height			Weight	
Years	Ft.	In.	Cm.	Lb.	Kg.	Ft.	In.	Cm.	Lb.	Kg.
Birth	1	8	50.8	7 1/2	3.4	1	8	50.8	7 1/2	3.4
1/2	2	2	66.0	17	7.7	2	2	66.0	16	7.2
1	2	5	73.6	21	9.5	2	5	73.6	20	9.1
2	2	9	83.8	26	11.8	2	9	83.8	25	11.3
3	3	0	91.4	31	14.0	3	0	91.4	30	13.6
4	3	3	99.0	34	15.4	3	3	99.0	33	15.0
5	3	6	106.6	39	17.7	3	5	104.1	38	17.2
6	3	9	114.2	46	20.9	3	8	111.7	45	20.4
7	3	11	119.3	51	23.1	3	11	119.3	49	22.2
8	4	2	127.0	57	25.9	4	2	127.0	56	25.4
9	4	4	132.0	63	28.6	4	4	132.0	62	28.1
10	4	6	137.1	69	31.3	4	6	137.1	69	31.3
11	4	8	142.2	77	34.9	4	8	142.2	77	34.9
12	4	10	147.3	83	37.7	4	10	147.3	86	39.0
13	5	0	152.4	92	41.7	5	0	152.4	98	45.5
14	5	2	157.5	107	48.5	5	2	157.5	107	48.5
15*	5	4	162.6	116	52.6	5	3	160.0	115	52.2
16*	5	6	167.6	128	58.0	5	4	162.6	118	53.5
17*	5	7	170.2	134	60.8	5	4	162.6	118	53.5

*Weight at ages 15, 16, and 17 is extremely variable.

"IDEAL" WEIGHT FOR ADULTS AGES OF 25 AND OVER#

B

Height (With Shoes)			"Ideal" Weight in Pounds and Kilograms for WOMEN (For weight without shoes or clothing, subtract 2-3 pounds)					
			Small Frame		Medium Frame		Large Frame	
Ft.	In.	Cm.	lb.	Kg.	lb.	Kg.	lb.	Kg.
5	0	152.4	105-113	47.6-51.3	112-120	50.8-54.4	119-129	54.0-58.5
5	1	154.9	107-115	48.5-52.2	114-122	51.7-55.3	121-131	54.9-59.4
5	2	157.5	110-118	49.9-53.5	117-125	53.1-56.7	124-135	56.3-61.2
5	3	160.0	113-121	51.3-54.9	120-128	54.4-58.1	127-138	57.6-62.6
5	4	162.6	116-125	52.6-56.7	124-132	56.3-59.9	131-142	59.4-64.4
5	5	165.1	119-128	54.0-58.1	127-135	57.6-61.2	133-145	60.3-65.8
5	6	167.6	123-132	55.8-59.9	130-140	58.9-63.5	138-150	62.6-68.0
5	7	170.2	126-136	57.2-61.7	134-144	60.8-65.3	142-154	64.4-69.9
5	8	172.7	129-139	58.5-63.1	137-147	62.2-66.7	145-158	65.8-71.7
5	9	175.3	133-143	60.3-64.9	141-151	64.0-68.5	149-162	67.6-73.5
5	10	177.8	136-147	61.7-66.7	145-155	65.8-70.3	152-166	69.0-75.3
5	11	180.3	139-150	63.1-68.0	148-158	67.1-71.7	155-169	70.3-76.7
6	0	182.9	141-153	64.0-69.4	151-163	68.5-73.9	160-174	72.6-78.9

C

Height (With Shoes)			"Ideal" Weight in Pounds and Kilograms for MEN (For weight without shoes or clothing, subtract 5-6 pounds)					
			Small Frame		Medium Frame		Large Frame	
Ft.	In.	Cm.	lb.	Kg.	lb.	Kg.	lb.	Kg.
5	2	157.5	116-125	52.6-56.7	124-133	56.3-60.3	131-142	59.4-64.4
5	3	160.0	119-128	54.0-58.1	127-136	57.6-61.7	133-144	60.3-65.3
5	4	162.6	122-132	55.3-59.9	130-140	58.9-63.5	137-149	62.1-67.6
5	5	165.1	126-136	57.1-61.7	134-144	60.8-65.3	141-153	63.9-69.4
5	6	167.6	129-139	58.5-63.1	137-147	62.2-66.7	145-157	65.8-71.2
5	7	170.2	133-143	60.3-64.9	141-151	64.0-68.5	149-162	67.6-73.5
5	8	172.7	136-147	61.7-66.7	145-156	65.8-70.8	153-166	69.4-75.3
5	9	175.3	140-151	63.5-68.5	149-160	67.6-72.6	157-170	71.2-77.1
5	10	177.8	144-155	65.3-70.3	153-164	69.4-74.4	161-175	73.0-79.4
5	11	180.3	148-159	67.1-72.1	157-168	71.2-76.2	165-180	74.8-81.7
6	0	182.9	152-164	69.0-74.4	161-173	73.0-78.5	169-185	76.7-83.9
6	1	185.4	157-169	71.2-76.7	166-178	75.3-80.7	174-190	78.9-86.2
6	2	188.0	163-175	73.9-79.4	171-184	77.6-83.5	179-196	81.2-88.9
6	3	190.5	168-180	76.2-81.7	176-189	79.8-85.7	184-202	83.5-91.6

#For ages 18 to 25 - approximate "ideal" weights can be calculated by subtracting 1.0 lb. (0.5 Kg.) for each year of age less than 25 years.

(Courtesy of the Metropolitan Life Insurance Company)

learned, the principles are never forgotten. You thenceforth use them automatically.

Once the general "type program" has been organized, day-to-day minor rearrangements will become essential. It's a handy idea to carry around a small notebook with you. On this jot down the items you must accomplish during the day. Then as the day proceeds, and you accomplish these items, strike them off the program for that day. Items not achieved go on to the next day's list and are programmed into that day. Similarly, they are struck off when accomplished.

In short, this really represents a series of goals being achieved. A person without a goal (or series of goals) is like a ship without a rudder. He never arrives anywhere, for he doesn't know where he is going.

If *he* doesn't know, how can his computer possibly know? He must fail. Conversely, if he knows, his computer knows, and there is no doubt he will successfully arrive at his goal. On time, intact, successful.

I notice that the third item under your general list of headings is about the study routine.

Yes. This is the final topic about which students must have a thorough knowledge. It's no meager item either. For this reason we plan to devote a special chapter solely to it.

So if you care to turn over to the next chapter, you will discover some of the ideas that will guarantee you more success than you believed possible.

Just using your own brain, your own inbuilt capabilities, some careful planning, a lot of common sense, and a system.

We hope you'll keep reading on. This could be vital to every student reading this book who is looking for success. And doesn't that include every student?

10

Operate Your Own Computer System -- For Free!

This is really a continuation of the previous chapter. So if you happen to be starting this book at this point, may we suggest that you flip back to the start of the preceding chapter. In this way you'll get better continuity, and it will mean more to you.

I agree. This really forms the third big section on how to achieve success through a sensible approach to study. We've already been over the key points of the part the environment plays. In other words, how our surroundings silently assist us in relaying data to our built-in computer system for storage and later retrieval—plus some of the essential physical elements associated with studying; how to keep fit and capable of maintaining peak mental keenness, you might say.

So now we come to perhaps the most vital key to achieving success at school, or at college, or university, or technical classes, or whatever or wherever. You see, it doesn't really matter what field you are studying or where you are carrying this out; certain basic patterns must be adhered to if you hope for success.

That's very true. What makes a brilliant student stand out

from the rest is the fact he's already realized and mastered the essentials to study. Without being told in so many words, he's automatically discovered for himself the way it's done.

I think you've entitled this section "The Study Routine."

That is so. And now I would like to give you a few subheadings to the general topic. This will make an understanding of the entire scheme so much easier to follow. Here it is:

3. The Study Routine.

A. Read generally.

B. Summarize.

C. Revise at once.

D. Revise regularly.

That seems a logical layout. Now let's get down to the hard facts. Point A. Read generally.

A. Read generally.

Whatever the topic under consideration, a general overall idea of what it's about is imperative. It is quite useless trying to understand scattered fragments without appreciating the whole picture. It's like going into an art gallery and looking at a segment of an entire picture. Just imagine if nine tenths of the picture were covered over with a mask, and you could see the remaining one tenth, perhaps a small fragment down at one corner. How much appreciation would you have for the whole picture? Absolutely none, I can assure you.

But stand back and take in the *entire* picture at a single sweeping glance, and the situation alters at once. You can visualize the magnitude of the work. In a flash you can see what the artist had in mind. You actually live with him and vitally become part of the scene depicted. You become involved. In so doing, your interest is aroused. The subject jumps to life. An intelligent awareness and vital interest is created at once.

The same applies to your study. Having a general overall

idea of the subject makes it so much more vital, living, real. Later on, when the material is broken down into smaller segments, you can see at a glance how each fits into the main picture.

Going back to our art gallery scene, if we were later taken into the room and only one tenth of the picture was on display, in a flash we would recognize it as part of the completed picture. Then it would mean something to us. How different from the first visit when the same piece was on display without our prior knowledge of the entire picture!

It doesn't matter what the subject under consideration happens to be. The same principle holds true. Go for a general understanding of the topic. Read it through as quickly as you can. Get the wide canvas in your mind. This way the specialized segments will unquestionably fit in better—both for now and later.

If you have any doubts on the value of this, just try it and see. Or better still, try understanding some topic piecemeal. I assure you, it is virtually impossible.

That's fine. So far so good. We've generally been over the topic under consideration. What now?

Let me put it this way:

B. Summarize.

(1) Chief headings.

(2) Subheadings.

(3) Sub-subheadings.

Now, don't be alarmed at this devious system of letterings and subheadings and what not. It is not nearly so complex as it might seem at first glance. In fact, a little later on we'll set the entire picture out on a single page to show how simple it is in operation. But right now, let's delve a little deeper into the way the system works.

(1) Chief Headings. After you have the general concept of

the topic under review, it's wise then to break the entire bulk down into a digestible form. It is impossible for the mind to retain a mass of written material just like that.

It is true that there are geniuses blessed with a "photographic memory." But they are the minority. The rest of us (which equals 99.9 percent of the population or perhaps even more) have to get it into the memory banks by sheer hard work.

That means reducing the mass of material into forms which can be programmed into the mind computer in pieces that are manageable.

Without doubt, the most efficient way to accomplish this is to summarize the entire mass of data. Most topics can be broken down into major groups of information. These can be called the "chief headings."

As you may have already noted, we have dealt with our topics in the preceding chapter and in this chapter under three key headings:

1. The Environment.
2. The Physical Aspects.
3. The Study Routine.

In other words, the entire mass of material that has formed these two chapters is basically wrapped up in these three simple chief headings.

There is absolutely no doubt that you can similarly reduce the work you are studying into a few simple major heads. For sure, you'll end up with a heap of summarized topics. But each set will hold the key to a vast storehouse of vital data.

Examinations, as you know quite well, are merely a testing of your ability at recalling material you have been taught at some time or other during school terms or university or college semesters.

Pick any subject you like, and the same principle holds

true. Therefore, the art of studying basically means the art of inserting material into your memory banks, plus the art of recall at will.

Right now we're mainly concerned with injecting the material "in." Later on we'll discuss the just-as-vital process of extracting it when you need it most of all.

(2) Subheadings. Now, just as it is possible to divide the material to be learned into a few broad headings, so it is possible to subdivide the material under each of these heads into smaller, more specific headings. Each subheading will generally incorporate varying aspects of the general proposition under consideration.

There may be a few or several subheadings. It will depend on and vary with the nature of the topic. When using this system for the first few times, I find that it is far better to "overdo" it than to "underdo" it.

It's fairly simple to make quite long lists of subheadings. However, after some experience, you'll find you will be making fewer subheadings. Experience brings greater efficiency.

(3) Sub-subheadings. We're still at it, I'm afraid. Now under this part you actually enumerate the key *facts* of the case.

If it's history you're doing, or geography (or any similar subject), it's the same.

First organize the general heads of your facts. But finally it comes down to the point of listing the facts themselves.

Be as brief as you can be. Abbreviate. Often you can use your own homemade shorthand system.

(My own personal system was to use red for major impact, then green for secondary impact, and finally blue for lesser impact still. Years after leaving university, I still use these three key colors.)

A little later on we'll give you a sample summary sheet so that any points not made clear here will become apparent then.

Now we've learned to summarize the information. I see that the next point on the agenda is devoted to revision.

C. Revise at once.

True. At this stage you've a complete composite picture of the entire subject. You've broken this down into component parts. As you've been doing this, a threefold operation has been going on. As you've been making the summary, you have been concurrently reading and writing, and most likely saying some of the information over to yourself either out loud or in your mind.

Therefore, we might summarize this situation as follows:

(1) Mental pictures.

(2) Visual pictures.

(3) Oral and auditory pictures.

Now let's take these bit by bit.

Right. Let's take a look at the mental pictures.

(1) Mental pictures. As you are reading your work, the information is projected into your mind as some sort of picture. They may be actual pictures or word pictures. But there is a picture of some sort, for sure.

Therefore, the summary is being indelibly written into your mind computer ("programmed" if you prefer) by this means. Pictures are being fed into your memory bank.

Once the impulses are there, they are there for keeps. Of this there is no doubt. (I'll tell you more about this later on to show just how efficient the system happens to be.)

What about the visual pictures?

(2) Visual pictures. The fact that you are actually applying words to paper in a condensed summarized fashion means that you are literally making word pictures. This further

reinforces what is already in your mind in the form of mental pictures.

Now what about the oral and auditory pictures?

(3) Oral and auditory pictures. By using your eyes you visualize the information that is transmitted to paper. Simultaneously, you might elect to talk some of this out loud, or in any event, you'll probably say much of this over to yourself aloud. Therefore, the previous impulses already programmed into the mind computer are once more being reinforced by two additional methods. Impulses race into it via the sense of sight and sound (or hearing).

Now, as we said a little earlier, the next step after making the summary is to *revise at once*. In so doing, we are experiencing the first attempt at retrieving from our computer some of the data just fed into its memory banks.

Upon completion of the summary, read it through. Use the underlining system if you so desire (or alternatively, you can leave this till the next revision).

Then close your eyes. Mentally recall the major headings you have composed. Then, one by one, endeavor to recall the chief subheads under each main head. Then, finally, try to recall the key points under each of these subheadings!

Actually this may be done in a few short minutes. If you find a little difficulty, you might prefer to take a sheet of scrap paper. Then actually write down the points in order.

Once more, you are using the same senses in recalling attempts as you used when feeding the data into the computer system.

All this may sound a little detailed, and maybe a trifle clumsy to the beginner. However, after a little experimenting, the system really swings into action.

The mere fact is that you are using a repetitive system for feeding in your work and a similar system for retrieving your work, and this calls for considerable facility in a very short time.

Very soon you will discover that as soon as you commence the retrieval "mental triggers" spark into action. You'll discover that once you have the first word picture, or mental image, this will automatically trigger off the succession of word pictures that bring the entire summary into focus. In other words, you recall your work. You remember it. Let me make this clear. The ability to recall clearly is often the chief factor which marks the brilliant student. You might question this, and ask how it applies to, say, mathematical problems. It's not really hard to adapt. Mathematics, after all, is merely a "summation of sums." The keen student can recall examples of the sets of sums he is trying to unravel at any given time. Therefore, once more, it's basically "remembering" or "recalling" or "retrieving" data fed into the memory banks at a previous time and reapplying them to the immediate problem. You'll find that this system works for all problems, irrespective of nature or size.

The last item on your little summary a few pages earlier was entitled "Revise regularly."

D. Revise regularly.

Let's consider this under the following subheadings:

(1) Revise daily.

(2) Revise weekly.

(3) Revise monthly.

Sounds a bit ominous to me. Let's start with point (1).

(1) Revise daily. Once you have revised your work immediately after making the initial summary, you can then put your work away. You'll either go on with the next topic or go to bed or go for a short walk or a jog or a run or have a glass of water. (No sweets or soda pop, remember. Perhaps an orange or an apple if you're starving.)

Then the ideal situation is to pull your summary from its folder at some stage the following day and revise it briefly. You may decide to try the "retrieval system" at once. Mentally (or using pencil and paper) you'll once more repeat the little routine of the previous night. Endeavor to recall as much of the summary as you can without looking at the written summary.

At the end, if you're stumped, check with the original. After a short time, you'll find yourself becoming more and more adept at retrieving the data from your memory bank.

If it's mathematics or some similar "problem" topic being covered, try to work out a few problems quickly, utilizing the systems you learned the previous day.

Conversely, if you find the going very tough, and you are not making headway, once more refer to the summary. Talk it out aloud. Get the information refreshed in your mind via seeing, mentally recalling, hearing, and again writing on a piece of paper.

When this little routine is over, reinsert the summary sheet into the appropriate folder or file where it can be readily found for another day.

Next you suggest we "Revise weekly."

(2) Revise weekly. Ideally, try to revise on a weekly basis for a week or two. There is usually no need to spend great lengths of time on these brief reviews. Indeed, only a minute or two per summary (and after a while, much less) is all that is required to go over the topic under review completely.

(3) Revise monthly. The same applies to long-term reviews. Endeavor to program time to go over previous work every month (or, later on, every two to three months, or once a term or semester).

I fully appreciate that time is in short supply, that work increases in volume and detail, and that it might *seem* impossible to get over it in this desired manner. But if you faithfully, regularly, stick to the general nature of the system, I assure you that it can be done.

In fact, a couple of hours spent each weekend merely revising past work in a fashion as suggested will markedly refresh your memory and might even make you a "brilliant" student.

You said earlier that you would present a complete summary of the past two chapters as an example of the thoughts you have in mind.

Exactly. The following is a summary of the material already presented. It sets out fairly clearly the points made. This is the general pattern of any summary. It doesn't matter what the material happens to be, the principles hold fast.

Never forget: Once you have mastered the art of summarizing, committing to memory, and discovering the art of retrieving data from your memory banks, you'll use the system every day for the rest of your life. There is absolutely no doubt about that. And forever, others will be wondering how you do it. You need never tell them. Just let them go away thinking how smart you really are. Which of course is the truth!

A Summary of These Two Chapters

Successful ways to more efficient study.

1. *The environment.*
   - A. Single room.
   - B. Quietness.
   - C. Lighting.
   - D. Temperature.
   - E. The chair.
2. *The Physical Aspects.*
   - A. General health.

B. Diet.
C. Exercising.
D. Sleep.
E. Hygiene.
F. Circadian rhythm.
G. Programming.

3. The Study Routine.

A. Read generally.
B. Summarize.
(1) Chief headings.
(2) Subheadings.
(3) Sub-subheadings (Actual data. Use shorthand.)
C. Revise at once.
(1) Mental pictures.
(2) Visual pictures.
(3) Oral and auditory pictures.
D. Revise regularly.
(1) Revise daily.
(2) Revise weekly.
(3) Revise monthly.

You say this system can be applied to any fact of study or work or living?

Indeed, it can. You've only to sit and meditate for a few moments to realize the vast potential the system holds. It is certainly worth becoming proficient in, I can assure you from personal experience over a large number of years.

I think you have a few other ideas to put forward here.

Yes. One is a little story that amused me when it occurred. I still think about it, and it still interests me. I feel that it pushes home the basic value of the system that has just been outlined in a very simple way.

Several years ago my small four-year-old (at the time) daughter named Sandra had a mania for jigsaw puzzles.

Indeed, the speed and accuracy with which she pieced together the irregular designs amazed me. No doubt fifty thousand other children in the country were just as proficient, but I didn't have the firsthand opportunity of witnessing their prowess. Hence the family story.

At first Sandra's jigsaws came singly and in big pieces, and with a picture to match. It didn't take long for her to learn to piece the segments together. The first once or twice she merely placed the pieces over the original picture. But as that became old hat, she did them without the picture.

Very soon this too became redundant and of no interest. So she turned the picture upside down, and merely relied on the shapes, and pieced these together, finally arranging them so as to get a faceless blank "picture" composed of the irregular saw marks of the puzzle makers.

It didn't take long for this also to become a game without any sting left in it. So one day she grabbed several sets of jigsaws and threw them into one big plastic bag, shook them well, and threw them on to the floor. She proceeded to turn them all face downward, and bit by bit pieced together half a dozen faceless pictures in half a dozen separate areas.

This quite amazed me. But over the next few days she became incredibly adept at this. Indeed, she would then set the clock up and say, "Time me." Thereupon we had to see how quickly she could piece together the faceless, upside-down puzzles.

Every now and again, to make it a bit more exciting, we would surreptitiously remove some pieces, and replace them with some foreign strays from another pack, just to pep the game up a little. These finally were tossed out by her computer as "irrelevant data" and discarded.

I hope this little story (perhaps meaningless in itself) drives a point home.

These shapes had become so indelibly ground into Sandra's mental computer that she knew instinctively exactly where they fitted into the entire whole of the finished picture. There was no doubt. She had revised the summary so often, so many times, reviewed, and re-reviewed, that the process was automatic. No thinking was needed. It was an instantaneous process.

To her, the "summary, revise, revise" routine was built-in.

To complete the story, I should say she has since been grabbed up by IBM as the nation's most spectacular walking computer. But to date this has not materialized. She is just a normal student, still plodding along, but still using, automatically, the ideas we've already expounded.

I love these little personal stories. It seems to bring us back to earth once more and make it all sound so very human! Now tell me about the "summarizing books" scheme you had in mind.

Often, as time goes by and the volume of work increases, the summary method outlined earlier can become quite prohibitive merely because of the time and volume factors. But the same general principles can still be effectively used.

Two ideas are worth mentioning.

Summarized (again), they may be termed:

(1) Book Summaries.

(2) Card Summaries.

Both are very effective and efficient.

Let's hear about the first scheme.

(1) Book Summaries.

Frequently it's essential to learn the contents of an entire book. It is usually a textbook on some topic, and this is usually the level of work when you reach university.

Making detailed summaries is often a huge job, and therefore the mechanics may have to be varied. An excellent method is as follows:

Use the colored-pencil system once more.

Select any color system you prefer. Red is a very prominent color, so reserve this for the main points.

Then use green, say, for the next important sequence of thought, and, say, blue for the lesser points.

It's then a case of going through the work in a similar manner. Go through a whole chapter rapidly to start.

Then select the key thoughts in the chapter and underline key words in bright red.

Underline the next key points in green. And the next key points in blue.

Then you can number the red key points sequentially, eg one, two, three, four (with a circle around each for greater prominence).

You can similarly mark the lesser subheadings or, if you prefer, merely make a mark beside them. This way they will stand out fairly prominently.

When this has been completed, you can make a very brief summary in the margin, using very abbreviated simple words that sum up the key thoughts of the material in question.

Often, in this manner, you can form a summary in half a dozen words of a page of printed book.

Alternatively, you can insert a piece of paper into your book that is roughly the same size as the pages of the text and have a summary of the entire chapter(s) written on it in a fashion similar to our first method, only in greater brevity.

However, once this has been done, the old system of "revise at once" then "revise regularly" comes into play again.

Sorry. But there is just no way of escaping this routine. It is the *only* way.

Use all the old ploys once more. Write down the summary if you have the time. Talk it out loud. Picture it in the mind's eye. All the methods play a part in the final effort of retrieval.

Now let's hear about the second system you mentioned.

(2) Card Summaries.

This consists of having a series of small cards about the size of an envelope. Each card is headed with a key chapter of your book. Then on the card is written the essential points of the chapter.

Indeed, it finally reads like the type of summary we initially set out. But here a vastly greater amount of work is condensed onto the card. There will be three to five major points. Then there will be a few subheads and more sub-subheads again.

But what previously took maybe two to three notebook pages is now condensed onto one small card.

Alternatively, a small notebook, roughly the same size, may be used, a single page equaling a card. In this fashion an enormous amount of work can be compressed into a short stack of cards. In fact, an entire textbook can be pulled into manageable proportions in this manner.

If it seems incredible, just try it and see how you make out. It certainly needs expertise and practice.

However, if you've been using the general summary system, say through secondary school, you'll automatically graduate to the card system when you hit advanced education.

The beauty of the card system is that you can take your cards with you anywhere you go. If you have ten minutes to spare, you can whip them out and go through an enormous amount of work. Do not laugh at this scheme. It has helped so many students to attain advanced degrees that it is not funny. It is practical, simple, workable, and a real winner.

11

The Simple Art of Developing Talent

The obvious question following on from the last chapter would inevitably be "How can I pass my examinations and gain the best results?"

True, true. In fact, in due course we plan to make some suggestions on that very important topic. After all, the basic reason for attending school, college, university, or any place of learning is finally to pass the prescribed course.

But passing exams is irrevocably bound up with another very important facet of life. For this reason I'd prefer that we deal with the wider spectrum first.

What exactly is that?

Putting it very simply and in terms everybody understands, it reads: "Goals in life."

Mm. I like the sound of that.

We all do. Whether we recognize the word as such or not, this is the end point, not merely of study, but of life itself. Our entire existence is made up of a successive series of goals.

There is a general broad overall goal to life. Then there are goals for the various age segments of life. Broken down further, there are goals for each year, thence for each part of the year, such as each term or semester if you're still studying. Or weekly and daily goals in the very short term.

A little while ago you said that not having a goal in life was akin to a ship without a rudder.

I'd like to repeat and reemphasize this fact right here.

Unless there is some aim to our daily lives, we are like bits of driftwood floating about on an endless ocean. There is nowhere to go, for there is no set course. When this is missing, it doesn't matter how competent the skipper is. If he has no destination, how can he possibly arrive?

But let's replace this with a person who has a definite idea of where he is heading. Then the picture changes dramatically. Every energy in his being may then be directed to a central, focal point. Life has renewed zest and meaning. Every action is aimed at getting him closer to his mark, nearer to his goal in life.

The Importance of Study

How important is this in trying to pass examinations? This brings the point in question a bit nearer home and makes it of more practical value to our male readers who are still trying to slog their way through secondary and college levels.

It is of undoubted importance. Usually the goal of passing an examination is a transitory one. It is part of the journey, usually to a more important goal.

Getting through secondary school is often merely the prelude to getting to something better. It may be the door to college education of some kind. Indeed, it is certainly a milestone on the way to an eventual meal ticket. Irrespective of our attitude to life, having a meal ticket is pretty important in this hard, cold, rugged world!

The way our economy is geared it is becoming increasingly important to have a reasonable level of educational attainment for even fairly menial types of employment. This then sets the really worthwhile levels of attainment so much higher.

Passing Examinations

Supposing the key goal in the present time segment of our male reader's life is to pass a series of examinations. What is your advice to him?

First, this must be his burning ambition right now. He has decided to undertake this particular course of study for a given reason. The reason may be to go on to a higher course of study once he has passed these examinations. Or he may be striving for a particular scholarship or to gain entry into a competitive educational institution or to secure employment in a particular company. In any event, passing these examinations must be to him the most important thing in life at the time. In short, it is his current goal in life.

I cannot overemphasize the importance that is to be put on the mental image of this goal. Not only must the student have it in mind, but he must be firmly convinced in his mind that this is really for him. If he can accept this, and let it become part of his thinking, he will be on his way to achieving his goals.

Right. Assuming he has the right frame of mind, given that he believes unquestioningly that he must succeed in this goal, that he must pass these vital examinations, what then?

The next fact is that, if he is afire with zeal, he will then get to work with enthusiasm. He will be prepared to spend long hours in close and constant study to achieve this goal. He will work out the most effective method of applying himself so that he gains the greatest possible mileage from his efforts. In short, he will most probably utilize a system similar to the one we have outlined in the previous pages.

This man knows that his brain is a computer. He is aware that it's largely up to him to program his machine correctly. And if he does this in a competent, methodical, sincere fashion, he also knows that the retrieval system will work wonderfully well when he requires it.

In short, he'll actively utilize "the system"?

There is no question about that. Environment, physical aspects of studying, the study routine will all be his conquests. He will know the routine by heart. He will automatically adhere to it. In fact, it becomes such a part of his life that it goes into action the moment he walks into his study room.

One Aspect You May Have Overlooked

Now what about providing a few more thoughts on an actual examination itself? To date we've discussed revision in the general sense of the term. This encompasses retrieving data for oneself. But the true test is applying this to an actual examination situation.

That is true. Of course if the system breaks down when the pressure of an exam is on, then it's virtually useless. However, the system will *not* break down if a few additional ideas are kept well in mind.

The first one is a simple, well-known quotation from the Scriptures. I use this one, for I cannot think of a more succinct way of phrasing it. It says: "As he [a man] thinketh . . . , so is he." In short, if you think success, then just as surely success will come your way.

Nobody can tell me that this is old-fashioned and written for a bygone era. I *know* it is written for men and women living right now.

I gather you are a firm believer in the Scriptures?

My answer is a very definite Yes. To me the Scriptures are the most up-to-date set of rules I have yet encountered.

Maybe lots of people are a bit scared of the Scriptures merely because they cannot understand the terminology which the Bible freely uses. There's little doubt the King James Version may be rather difficult for modern young people.

I agree entirely. Then how do you overcome this problem?

I go for one of the newer translations. There are plenty of versions written in today's language. Don't forget, Christ spoke in words that were current in *His* time. King James had the Bible translated into words that were current in *his* time. Therefore it seems logical to me to use a translation that uses terminology that is currently in common use right *now*.

The purists will say that some of the finer shades of meaning might be lost. But it's the overall evidence that we're seeking—the meat of the text, you might say.

What's your favorite version then?

I must confess I read and enjoy them *all*. (Yes, even the King James Version.)

In some of these modern versions so many issues seem to jump right out of the pages with new meaning. Indeed, the way they emphasize the importance of having goals in life, and making every effort to achieve them is little short of amazing.

The Bible constantly reinforces the fact that if we earnestly seek an achievement in life, with the help of God, we *shall* succeed.

Then in your opinion there is no doubt that success is attainable if one's own efforts are compounded with divine assistance?

Exactly! Just take a look at some of the incredible promises that the Scriptures hold.

I find that the book of Psalms contains promises that will encourage anyone having the faith to accept God and believe in His power. Here are just a few quotations from *The Living Bible, Paraphrased:*

"For the Lord watches over all the plans and paths of godly men." Psalm 1:6.

"I cried out to the Lord, and he heard me." Psalm 3:4.

"He will listen to me and answer when I call to him." Psalm 4:3.

"God is my shield; he will defend me." Psalm 7:10.

"All those who know your mercy, Lord, will count on you for help. For you have never yet forsaken those who trust in you." Psalm 9:10.

"I am pleading for your help, O Lord; for I have been honest and have done what is right, and you must listen to my earnest cry. Publicly acquit me, Lord, for you are always fair." Psalm 17:1, 2.

"He hears me from highest heaven and sends great victories." Psalm 20:6.

"Your words are a flashlight to light the path ahead of me, and keep me from stumbling." Psalm 119:105.

How do these quotations appeal to you? I personally believe they are the greatest set of promises a person could hope to come by. In fact, the book of Psalms is just bulging at the seams with hundreds of similar promises. Indeed, some are even more personal and explicit than those I've quoted!

And if you care to turn over a few more pages to the book of Proverbs, you'll find a bit more advice for the student (and in fact for anyone seeking to achieve goals).

"Hard work means prosperity; only a fool idles away his time," Solomon says in Proverbs 12:11.

"A wise man thinks ahead; a fool doesn't, and even brags about it!" Proverbs 13:16.

"Commit your work to the Lord, then it will succeed," we are promised in Proverbs 16:3.

So you see, it is merely a matter of hard work, physical and mental application of sensible, well-thought-out plans, plus an unwavering faith in God's ability to assist you, and you *cannot* fail.

I've read in some books where the writers refer to "higher intelligences" helping the mind to operate efficiently and assisting in the retrieval of material and in bringing ideas to fruition.

Oh, yes. It goes by all manner of names. But call it what you like, nearly all thinking men accept the fact there is some deeper intelligence in the universe that is ready to assist our mental processes. I prefer to accept what I've been given in the Scriptures. Maybe it suits my simple, unquestioning mind better.

Then, as an added bonus, I've proved the worth of this acceptance so many times during the course of my life that I have no desire to replace it with anything else. Ever!

Then you seem quite convinced about the supremacy of a divine power in this world?

Most certainly. I'd be a fool not to, and an ungrateful one at that. Indeed, if I were foolish enough to pride myself on being intrinsically bright and efficient in my own power, I think I would reap a little punishment very promptly.

"Pride disgusts the Lord. Take my word for it—*proud men shall be punished,*" I read in Proverbs 16:5. Therefore, I'm sure words such as these keep me in line!

At this point you might care to offer a short summary of your belief in how success can come to our examination candidate.

First, there must be a definite goal in mind. And there must be an unquestioned, burning ambition to achieve that goal.

Second, the student must diligently strive to this end. He must work hard and apply himself to the gathering and storing of knowledge on the chosen topic.

Third, he will seek guidance and direction from a higher power. In short, he will seek the help of God to assist in achieving the goal.

These are the basics for success in any examination (or interview or situation where skill and dexterity are needed).

The Examination

Now, let's get involved with the actual examination itself. Let's suppose that it is a written paper. An important feature from the very start of any exam is this: R-E-L-A-X!

Take it easy for the first few moments. Nobody is going to eat you alive. The paper is set, and nothing you can do at the moment of entering the exam room will alter the questions you're about to look at.

Sit down; make yourself comfortable; close your eyes; take a few deep breaths; look skyward if you so desire for the Scriptures advise: "Each morning I will look to you in heaven and lay my requests before you, praying earnestly." Psalm 5:3.

Now carefully read the examination paper. Take it slowly. Read it through once. Then read it through a second time. Take your pen and underline the key instructions. If you have three hours to answer six questions, that equals thirty minutes per question. Write this down clearly. If you have to answer six questions out of eight from three different sections (or whatever), similarly underline this, preferably in red.

You must *not* make simple errors. Thousands do—and fail. Although they knew the work they didn't follow the instructions properly! Incredible but true! (Then most likely they'll blame the examiners for being unkind and unfair!)

Select the questions (if there is a choice) you feel most competent to answer.

Check your watch and mark when you commence each question, and when you must finish each one. Leave a little time for general reviewing at the end if possible. (And it *is* possible if you program your examination routine correctly.)

In answering the questions, what are the key points?

Basically the same as before. Every question will involve retrieval from the computer system. Therefore, use the method you've been using all along. Jot down a summary on a piece of paper.

Just as surely as you take your time, seek spiritual guidance and relax, so that the material will come flowing from the memory banks that have been so routinely and thoroughly programmed. Of this there is no question.

If you are finding difficulty, close your eyes for a few moments, and again try to relax, or think of another question for a little while. Just as surely as you do this, then return to the original problem, so the data will ultimately come through.

Write down the key summary points as fast as you can as they come out crisp and fresh. Do not lose time or waste a single minute!

When you think you have them all (and one will trigger off the next in most instances), you may then care to rearrange them if you feel the order is not right.

Then it is an extremely good idea to write this summary on the opening page of your answer. Don't forget, examiners are human beings just like you and me. They've probably ten thousand similar answers to read through before their task is completed. If they see that your answer is orderly, that you obviously know what you are talking about, that your mind is tidy (as evidenced by the first page clearly set out), then you're ten up on the other 9,999 papers yet to come. The examiners are already viewing you with respect. And in examinations that means a whole lot!

If you're really smart, you will try to write in a legible hand too. Who likes getting eyestrain trying to decipher illegible scrawls? Be human. Be fair. This way your answers will appeal even more to the examiner. After all, he is the one man you are endeavoring to impress at this precise moment.

Write your answers in accordance with the summary on the opening page. Use major headings, subheadings and possibly sub-subheadings as we've been through earlier.

Underline the headings to make them jump right out of the page.

Make free use of numbers, letters, etc.

Use plenty of space.There's usually an abundance of paper, so don't fear the cost! (For once you're not directly paying for each single sheet!)

Keep a close check on the time.

It's often wise to subdivide your time per question into so many minutes for each chief heading of your answer. For example, if you have thirty minutes to answer the question, and there are three major headings to cover, that equals roughly ten minutes per section. Better still, make it eight minutes per heading, leaving six minutes to read over what you have written. Even if you take care, the pressure of exams can sometimes let you make foolish statements which could be incorrect! A brief runover to complete the question will assure you that this is not happening.

Supposing there are questions that defy an answer?

If you've done your homework systematically as we've already indicated, this should not happen. At some stage you must have studied the entire course. Nevertheless, do your best. Stick to the principles we've suggested. Even if you haven't revised the particular question for a long time, stick to the system.

Relax, close your eyes for a while, take it gently, don't hurry, don't panic (you're lost if you do), pray for guidance. Think.

In many cases, at least some part of the answer will come out of your memory banks—ultimately. Jot the bits and pieces down at once, and make the best of what does tumble out.

Finally, you'll come to the end of the paper. The gong will sound, and the ordeal is over.

Once more you can relax. Take another deep breath or two to clear your mind again. Give a silent "Thank You, God," and then leave the room.

Once outside, forget the whole deal. Postmortems are useless. The examination is in the past—forever. There is no point in arduously going over each question. It will not make a scrap of difference to what you have already written down.

If anything, it will make you unhappy that you didn't add this, delete that, and so on.

Leave the crowd. Go home and relax. Get some exercise, have a light meal, have a change of environment for the rest of the day. This way, the ordeal will quickly be forgotten. After all, you'll most likely need renewed vigor and mental acumen and a clear intellect for the next examination.

But postmortems? Forget them. Avoid them like the plague. Avoid the troublemongers and the depressed characters. Their moods are terribly contagious! Never forget this.

Working With What You Have

Earlier you indicated that there are many applications of this "Goals-in-life" point of view. Would you like to expand a little on this now?

Certainly! I believe that everything in life, as I've already stated, is merely a succession of planned goals. If they are planned carefully, so much the better. One very important application could be summarized: "How to develop talent."

There's little doubt that most people are born with some inherent ability, though it might take time to bubble to the surface. But sooner or later (and usually sooner) there is an indication. It might be playing a musical instrument—or acting or writing or a mechanical bent or a flair for figures and numbers or an obvious bent for electrical operations. In fact, the field is unlimited. Now, this has two important possible sequels.

Two? What are they?

Number one: If a person shows some obvious, above-average ability, it's often a good idea to encourage this, for it could be valuable in helping him select his final calling in life. Indeed, he'll automatically discover this special bent for himself in many cases and will tend to favor that particular choice. Indeed, this can sometimes show through from a very early age, even in primary school.

Don't laugh at that, for I've seen it occur very often. The world is half full of teen-age students who haven't a clue in the world what their lifework is to be. It's disastrous, but sadly true. Therefore, any obvious interest should be encouraged by anyone coming into contact with that person, right through from parents to teachers, including other members of the family and friends.

In other words, natural inclinations should help a person determine fairly clearly the line of work best suited to him.

Do you think most people are happy with their lot in life and the sort of work they do?

The answer is a very strong No! If they were, there wouldn't be so much industrial unrest and constant dispute. Job satisfaction seems to be something belonging to a bygone era.

Don't Be Like Harry

Personally, I can't think of anything worse than working at a job I don't like.

Neither can I, but millions do this every day of their working lives.

When I was a student at university, I boarded for a time with a lovely lady (a kind-hearted soul—she's still alive and keeps in touch, bless her) who resorted to this type of work to earn a living.

There was a chap at the same place called Harry. Every day, as regular as clockwork, at 7:30 am, Harry went off to work. And did he enjoy his work? No, sir! When he arrived at his place of work (which was a pickle manufacturing company), he donned a raincoat and big rubber boots. He then entered a room filled with onions.

For the next eight hours, Harry peeled onions. Hundreds of them. Thousands of them. By now perhaps several million of them! He cried all day long. His eyes were always red, swollen, painful-looking. Harry hated his job. There was certainly no job satisfaction, no love of the job, no anything (apart from an eternal odor of foul-smelling onions and sore eyes).

But Harry had no goal in life, no vision, no get-up-and-go, no ambitions, no zeal or zest. I am certain Harry, deep down, had some built-in talent. But he couldn't be bothered. Life wasn't treating him fairly (his words), and so what hope was there for him? Absolutely none, of course, and he proved the point.

The point I'm trying to make is that if you have an inherent liking for something, grab it with both hands. Encourage it to the hilt. Work at it, and your future lifework could develop from this initial prospect.

Performing work that gives you enjoyment is one of the

great satisfactions in life. Then you will be the opposite of poor old Harry.

You said there were two sequels to this.

Yes. In fact, the second is closely related to the first.

Besides recognizing the possible commencement of an inherent interest in something, the next important factor is to steer this interest through to something worthwhile.

So many good ideas and good intentions die on the vine before the harvest. It's almost a national tragedy. Therefore, any latent talent must be nurtured, watered, fertilized, and tended with gentle, loving care.

Jim's Story

Let's have another of your true-life stories.

Jim was an average sort of youngster. But from an early age his burning ambition in life was to be a writer. Now, that might sound very prosaic to you, but the fact remained that this was Jim's sole aim.

When he was in early primary school, he plagued his parents with regular issues of the "Daily News" (printed in awkward childish hand printing).

Next he acquired a printing press—a cheap prewar Japanese outfit consisting of big rubber type set on wooden blocks.

The "Daily News" immediately took on a more "professional" appearance, even if each page consisted of fewer than a dozen words!

Later a smaller "movable type" rubber printing set enhanced the appearance of the "Daily." Now each page consisted of about forty words, painstakingly set letter by letter! Indeed, it took a whole morning to set the type for one page.

During the war, this graduated to movable metal type. An old schoolteacher visited the home one day, read the "Daily

News,'' was impressed by the ingenuity of Master Jim, and handed him enough money to buy a font of real metal type! The ''Daily'' really took an upswing.

Came high school, and a weekly class newspaper enthralled classmates. Escapades, as unrealistic as imagination could dream up, regularly had the boys in Jim's class sitting on the edges of their seats.

By this time, city editors were being harassed by a succession of stories, articles, and other editorial matter on a wide variety of topics—mainly unprintable. But Jim pressed on. He'd carefully manufacture his stories, rewrite them as many as half a dozen times to bring them ''up to standard.'' But still the rejection slips mounted.

As high school continued, the class newspaper expanded and developed into a regular fifty-page affair. Then suddenly, one soft-hearted editor ran Jim's first story. This was like pouring gasoline onto a bonfire. The explosion really set in. Masses of copy—still mostly unprintable—poured forth from Jim's typewriter.

By now he'd taught himself the touch typing system, and could type out material at a reasonable speed from a second-hand typewriter. Bit by bit, more stories appeared in print, usually with his by-line. As every aspiring author knows so well, there is nothing like seeing one's own name in black ''by-line'' type! Jim was no exception.

Further stories and articles were published. Generally, they were followed by long faces from the rest of the family. His pious parents were not entirely in harmony with Jim's rather flamboyant, happy outlook on life, reflected in his fictional characters and thoughts expressed in article form.

But Jim had an overwhelming desire to be read by millions of people, not just a few thousand. Every paper that published another of his pieces was another rung up the ladder to success. Of that he had absolutely no doubt. "I'm sure I can influence the mob," he'd often say. "There's no doubt as to the power of the press. I won't rest till everyone in this country reads me on a regular basis."

More articles, more columns. Finally he hit the jackpot. A string of newspapers decided to run one of his features on a regular basis. Then several magazines picked up his material on a regular basis too. Some of the Sunday papers commenced featuring his work every weekend. Then came invitations to appear on television. This was soon followed by further invitations to script-write teleplays for television. Then requests for radio scripts, books, more articles, en masse. Indeed, Jim's dreams came true—more than he'd even dreamed possible.

From the childish editions of the "Daily News" as an eight-year-old, to a mass of regularly appearing articles in most major papers and magazines in the nation was quite a climb.

"But I *knew* it was merely a matter of time," Jim now says. "The goal was there. I was prepared to work hard, work long, and with my sights set this way, and with a belief that God would help me, how could I fail? It was just not possible *not* to succeed!"

So that's the story of Jim.

That's right. It's a true story, for I know this fellow quite well. To me, it's an example of what can happen when an obvious talent exists and an effort is made to develop such a talent. Jim wouldn't exchange his lot in life now at any price. He still bangs away at his typewriter all day and half the night. He has the ultimate in job satisfaction.

Although he's long since achieved his primary goal of being a writer with a nationwide reading audience, he has since set up several other goals as well. These, too, he is achieving one by one.

Goals For All

So much for Jim. But, how do you think this applies to Bill Brown and Sam Smith and Joe Jackson? In fact, how does it apply to the average man in the street?

It applies in exactly the same way. As I said earlier, everyone (and I mean everyone, even poor old Harry from the pickle factory) has some inherent ability. It's a matter of discovering this and piloting it through to ultimate success.

That success will come, with a bit of push, drive, application, incentive, and enthusiasm.

Do you think the eternal quest for cash comes into the picture a bit and could cloud the issue in some cases?

Undoubtedly yes. So many youngsters have their eyes on the pot of gold so much that it can surely cloud their long-distance vision.

What's the use of short-term returns if they are going to endanger the long-term financial rewards?

Getting a sensible goal that has long-term benefits is best. Striving to get a job at the legal age of leaving school merely for the sake of earning a few dollars is foolish thinking and unwise planning. Of course, in many instances, domestic economics makes this imperative.

But these days, with so many government-backed educational facilities available to those who apply themselves, the sphere has widened tremendously. Today, even youngsters from the poorest circumstances can achieve secondary and college training. It's really a matter of applying themselves if there is the desire and the inherent ability.

In summing up this section, I take it that you firmly believe that everyone has the ability to choose the right calling for his particular case and of developing latent abilities to the point where they can become a life calling?

Of this I have absolutely no doubts.

Indeed, there are several other related topics that could well be discussed right now. But what would you think of devoting another chapter to them?

That seems to be a reasonable idea. You can take a breather here, reader, and we'll have one as well.

But come right back, and we'll get on with a few other topics that could be vital to your future welfare and happiness. You might say it's how to get the best out of life.

12

Common Problems and How They're Solved

- **How to Gain Poise and Self-confidence**
- **How to Master the Art of Conversation**
- **Spare Time and What to Do With It**
- **How to Cope With Parents Who Are Wrong!**
- **Is Religion Out of Date?**
- **How to Cure Facial Pimples**

You've suggested that this chapter might be entitled "How to Get the Best out of Life!" Correct?

Yes, that's a pretty wide net. And some of the topics we plan for this chapter are certainly vital to everyday living. If anyone cares to give some thought to the propositions suggested he will definitely benefit, and life will become an exciting venture.

Indeed, the answer to many of the thoughts we intend putting up are projections from the last set of ideas in the preceding chapter.

Self-confidence

Let me open by posing a question: Many young fellows find they lack poise and self-confidence. Is there a simple solution for this?

This is a universal problem. Indeed, in the early teen years, tremendous internal systemic changes are going on. We've already mentioned many of them. The system is developing. Physically the body is maturing. Mentally, development is racing on apace too.

Indeed, the changes come on quite abruptly. So much so that many young men find themselves quite unable to cope. Thrown into the general turmoil is the problem of fighting on with ever-mounting school problems relating to study, grades, homework, and so on.

Pimples often crop up, and facial blemishes do anything but help build morale at this time. Often fellows find themselves either too fat or too skinny. This too upsets their mental equilibrium.

Then there is the inevitable boy-girl confrontation. In the early stages, and indeed often after some years' association, many growing males feel dreadfully ill at ease when associating with their female contemporaries.

The fact that Larry and Derek and others can swing along with apparent ease (and catch all the choice females in their trail) does nothing to help their personal self-esteem and confidence.

Do you believe there is an answer to this problem?

I most certainly do. In fact, it's exactly the same in general principle as the answers to the preceding problems outlined in earlier chapters. I reemphasize the tremendous value of having goals in life. Now, this applies to passing examinations for sure. Similarly it applies to developing talent and working on a system for a lifetime career.

But it also operates in the more personal matters of life, such as the very one under discussion. Young romeos with this problem in life must actively do two things.

First: They must recognize their inherent weakness. If they lack self-confidence—if they are shy, withdrawn, timid, scared to speak to girls (or to anyone for that matter, such as their employers or teachers)—this fact must be clearly noted. As we said earlier, there is no point in having the captain at the helm try to reach his destination unless he has clear-cut evidence as to where the destination happens to be.

Therefore, pinpointing the basic problem in terms precise and clear is hurdle number one to cross.

That's fine so far. Our man-of-the-hour now fully recognizes his difficulty. In fact, he's even written it down so that he'll have no doubts as to its precise nature. He has enumerated all aspects in clear-cut English. What next?

Number two. He must now set up his goal. This is the end point of his difficulties. Once he recognizes the problems, it is then a matter of stating forcefully to himself that he is determined that he will overcome these besetting difficulties. In fact, he then sets about working out a summary of the way in which he will achieve success. This is a system identical to the way knowledge is stored into the memory banks we discussed previously.

Ideally he will play it cool. Meditation is essential. Eyes closed, removing all irrelevant data from the mind, leaving it clear, fresh, and open, are important ingredients for success. Complete relaxation is necessary. Gradually, as he ponders the problems, various ideas will flash into his conscious mind. In fact, the longer and more carefully he considers the possibilities, the more there are to crowd into his mind.

He will have a pad and pencil at hand. As soon as the thoughts and ideas and word pictures come tumbling out, he'll be jotting them down as fast as he can. Ultimately, he'll have a formidable list of things to do that will completely change the entire outlook for him.

There is a second method which some people find even more successful.

This is to sleep on the problem. By giving it careful, meditative consideration at bedtime, then closing the eyes in sleep, the material is left to mull around in the hidden recesses of the mind to emerge with striking clarity the next morning. Generally in terms loud and clear!

Do you doubt the efficacy of the system? Then all I can say is you haven't tried it yet!

What sort of answers would a person expect?

They will vary with the individual. But supposing the person feels awkward with people (girls, seniors, etc.). Then it might be advisable for him to study up on a particular set of conversational topics. A brief rundown on the morning newspaper offers a huge amount of food for thought. He can soon become expert on some topic. Maybe a bit of personal research will be required. He can do the research and become the local authority on this or that aspect of news.

Or he can pick out some item of interest to the persons he desires to contact most of all. He should become well informed on these in a similar fashion, so that on the next encounter he will be able to engage fluently in a conversational aspect that will interest his audience.

The better you become at this (and it's really only a matter of practice) the more poised and full of self-confidence you'll feel next time. Nothing succeeds like success. Meeting people and engaging in conversation is no exception.

Very soon you'll discover that your fears were merely phantoms that really didn't exist. They existed only in your imagination.

Aids to Conversation

What about the art of conversation? Many fellows seem to have major problems in achieving this particular social grace.

In fact, the identical formula we've already outlined may be used for this as well. I must reemphasize (and I'll keep doing this until the subject has been exhausted, it's so vital) that the two-pronged attack is again essential. The person must be aware of the problem. For clarity this is best committed to paper to crystallize in his mind what he is then going to achieve.

At this point, once his terms of reference have become established, he then sets his goals. He determines that he will overcome the particular disability. He is 100 percent certain that he will very soon become one of the best, most interesting, most entertaining conversationalists in his social circle.

If he approaches this in the same way as that outlined earlier, he most certainly will succeed beyond his wildest dreams. Once more, success breeds success.

Take God into partnership, trust in Him, keep a hand in His hand, and failure cannot come your way after you try, try, and keep on trying. Just put the system to the test and see the wondrous results that come your way in a twinkling of an eye!

I often hear people say they have lots of spare time and never know what to do with it. Do you have a suitable answer for these people?

Sometimes I think I envy these people. But in truth, I guess I really feel sorry for them. My program is so jammed with commitments that I've barely time to complete my daily chores in twenty-four hours! I frequently wish I had less to do. But then, if that occurred, I'd start suffering the symptoms of job dissatisfaction too, no doubt!

The answer, of course, is that these people are just lazy.

I make no bones about it and offer no apologies. I have the utmost contempt for laziness. The world is too full of opportunity for people to have spare time on their hands.

As Proverbs 28:19 in *The Living Bible, Paraphrased,* so admirably states: "Hard work brings prosperity; playing around brings poverty." Those with time on their hands are playing around, wasting their lives, of value to nobody, not even themselves. They are headed for poverty in the spiritual sense, if not in the literal sense, but so often it is in both!

Goals

There is only one answer for these people. Set yourself a goal in life. Then you'll have something to work and strive for. Life will suddenly take on new meaning. You will find your time fully occupied with new vitality. Your every minute will be taken up. You'll be doing something of value. You'll reap a reward, even if it's just a feeling of mental satisfaction.

Most people who waste away their lives develop physical symptoms. We refer to them as "psychosomatic symptoms," but they are unpleasant enough.

Activity usually puts an end to these symptoms. Suddenly there isn't any more time to develop aches and pains here, there, and everywhere. The day is filled to overflowing. Each hour is planned. Every waking moment is filled. Life becomes vibrant, exciting, worthwhile.

Young men no longer have time to get into mischief. It gives added impetus to their moral codes and tends to keep their thinking and their actions clean and pure.

This is worth a lot in this world of dubious moral values. Crooks, thieves, dropouts and deadbeats, thugs, potential murderers, and hangers-on are usually bred from the race of fellows who have time on their hands, time with nothing to achieve. The devil finds work for idle hands and empty minds. Set your mind to work right away. Keep moving. Maintain a goal, and keep heading in the right direction. This way you'll keep a clear conscience, a level head, and a level eye.

Parental Discipline

While we are dealing with moral rectitude and training, lots of growing fellows believe their parents are wrong more often than they are right. How do you feel about this?

I'm like a few million other people around the place.

I've enjoyed the privilege of having once been a growing teen-ager myself. And currently I'm the parent of a set of teen-agers! Therefore, I'm in the enviable position of having a bit of both worlds, you might say. This can have a tremendous impact on one's views.

As an adolescent, I often believed my parents were hard and often wrong in their opinions and decisions. Well, that was some years ago. And in the interim I've grown gray hairs and often see my own children in identical situations to those I have been in. Now, of course, I tend to view the situations from an entirely different aspect. The fact is that the intervening years have endowed me with that precious, unpurchasable item called "experience."

Of course many of the answers I give my children may seem unjust, unfair, unreasonable to them. But with the knowledge I've gleaned over the years, I believe the suggestions and opinions I offer are in their best interest. If I didn't care one bit, I wouldn't offer any opinion whatsoever.

However, as a parent, I have a moral obligation to make an attempt to guide my children in what I believe are the right paths. "Discipline your son in his early years while there is hope. If you don't you will ruin your life,'' the wise man says in Proverbs 19:18. Looking back over my own early life, I see that my parents did right in their punishments. At the time I didn't always think they were justified or even fair.

But no doubt they were, and for sure some moral benefit accrued.

Now I have no spiteful recriminations. I am glad my parents were strict and a bit unrelenting. If anything, it tends to build a better moral character, and I trust a bit rubbed off in this manner. These of course are purely personal views.

Righting Wrongs

If a son feels that he has been wronged by his parents, what's the best line he could follow, in your opinion?

I believe he should wait till the heat of the moment has passed. There's little point in adding more fuel to a raging fire. Then, perhaps the next day, it's fair to go back to the parent and take the matter up in a quiet and reasonable atmosphere. If he feels the parent is wrong, and that he himself has been done an injustice, or the chastisement has been meted out on false premises, then this too should be revealed.

Parents are human and in the main do the best they can for their children. Of this there is little doubt in the vast majority of cases. Very often an amicable peace settlement can be arrived at. I must say that if this occurs, it usually brings the two parties much closer together than was the case beforehand. So there is a general, warming, beneficial net outcome.

Religion?

That seems a reasonable and practical approach. For sure, parents are not always right. Nor are they always wrong.

Do you think religion is out of date? These days, many seem to believe that it is old hat, and something relegated to musty churches and old ladies' meetings and the like.

I'm afraid I can't go along with that view. To me, *religion* may be out of date. But God lives on. Christ is alive today just as He was in the times the Scriptures were written, and when He was a man on earth living among men.

You've only to read some of the writings of the Scriptures to realize that these are as modern today as they were when they were originally handed down to mankind.

If you bother to give it any thought, our legal system is still reasonably up-to-date. (For sure, there are amendments pending, and always will be; but, in essence, the law as it stands is reasonable.)

This is based on God's law written thousands of years ago. The basic tenets are identical.

Therefore, God's message is certainly alive and very healthy and full of vitality. Every day these facts must come to mind as we automatically endeavor to live within the framework of our national legislation.

As I said earlier, modern Biblical translations written in modern idiom throw a new light on the Scriptures. Read any of the new versions if you have any doubt on the power and presence of God. Your mind will be altered within the first ten minutes. No doubts about that!

What is definitely out-of-date is the stuffy, fuddy-duddy approach *people* bring to religion. Everyone wants to grab God and have some sort of copyright over Him. Therefore, religions are still spreading and proliferating.

God belongs to no specific group. He belongs to everyone. You can't coop God up in a musty old church and claim sole rights to Him. These man-made manifestations are the things that are forcing the concept of religion's being out-of-date.

Not God. God is just as alive to the teens and the twenty-year-olds as He is to the elderly and infirm—equally as just, loving, forgiving, dynamic, available.

A Different Complexion

To change the subject, lots of young men get awfully self-conscious in the upper teen bracket because of facial pimples. Do you have any suggestion for these fellows?

Acne is a horrible condition and can make a depressed personality even more withdrawn and self-conscious. But don't despair if this is your unlucky problem in life. Today, treatment is at its best, and much can be done to relieve the situation. A reputable dermatologist should be consulted.

It is good to clean the face thoroughly with soap and hot water two to three times each day. More often if the skin feels greasy. Gently—very gently—squeeze out obvious blackheads. Sometimes hot towels must be applied if the blackheads are stubborn. Don't press too hard. Sometimes an epilator will assist in removing the debris, but use only methods approved by the dermatologist.

Then simple lotions or creams available from the doctor may be applied. It's best to avoid over-the-counter preparations, for these are usually so weak and ineffective that they seldom heal. This only aggravates the mental picture of failure. Therefore, if the situation is acute, consult a specialist.

Isn't diet important?

Yes, very important, some doctors claim. Reducing the intake of sweets, high-calorie foods (we listed all these in an earlier chapter), and particularly all items containing cocoa or chocolate will assist. Fatty foods, greasy fried preparations, nuts, and spicy fare are not recommended.

Eat a sensible all-round diet. (See chapter nine.) Try to avoid emotional upsets (particularly domestic feuds and girlfriend squabbles). It's believed that these can have a detrimental effect.

Factory work in a chemical-laden atmosphere often aggravates facial problems. The face is already alive with excessive amounts of grease, and adding more will only make the situation worse.

If all this fails, recourse to the antibiotics now gives almost universal relief. This must be given on a doctor's prescription and taken under his direct supervision. Fortunately, the results of this general line of medication are generally excellent.

13

Social Diseases Are on the Rampage

In these days of increasing tolerance and social permissiveness we hear more and more about the rising frequency of social problems.

Let's be more to the point. Let's call them "social diseases." After all, the incidence of sexually transmitted diseases is rising to serious levels. Not only is this the sad state of affairs in our land, but it's worldwide.

What exactly are these social diseases?

There is a long list of them. But for practical purposes the two chief ones are known as gonorrhea and syphilis.

The disorders are also given the general name of venereal disease (VD). The term harks back to ancient mythology, which named Venus as the goddess of love. Therefore, the intimacies associated with lovemaking (with an infected partner, let me stress) were essential prerequisites to infection. I'm afraid it doesn't say much for the goddess of love!

You were saying that the incidence of venereal disease is rising rapidly.

It certainly is. Soon after World War II, the diseases declined steadily. Indeed, so marked was the decline that the doctors began to think of them as something of a bygone era. No doubt it was associated with the impetus the war gave to the development and wide distribution of the antibiotics.

This seemed to be the cure-all for VD. Gonorrhea responded in a remarkable way. One single injection of penicillin produced almost instant cure. Syphilis also responded readily. The interminable queues that lined up for treatment outside the VD clinics at major public hospitals dwindled. Victims seeking therapy became fewer and fewer.

No doubt this brought about complacency among the public and doctors alike.

Apathy certainly gained the upper hand. However, little by little, the infecting organisms started to become resistant to penicillin and the other valuable antibiotics being used to check the diseases. Resistant strains therefore flourished, became established, and commenced to spread.

The situation now is that World Health Organization authorities believe that around 100 million people contract gonorrhea each year! Indeed, it's now second only to measles on the list of most common communicable diseases. But for every case reported, authorities believe that five, or more likely ten, cases go unreported.

The picture is much the same in regard to syphilis, although the figures are not quite so disastrously high. Nevertheless, syphilis is much more insidious; and, left unchecked, it can spell real trouble for the sufferer.

About 20 million persons are believed to suffer from syphilis. This represents a 90 percent increase over the past decade. But once more, many cases either go undiagnosed or unreported to the authorities. The true figure remains unknown.

There has been a similar increase in the other sexually transmitted diseases as well.

What Is The Cause?

What has caused this sudden explosion of VD?

Everyone is seeking the answer to this question. The two points already mentioned play a major part. But added to this is the fact that many kinds of modern methods of birth control are now readily available, and to virtually anyone requesting them.

Indeed, to quote a recent medical journal editorial: "In spite of the many uncertainties raised by moral, religious and scientific groups, The Pill, IUDs, foams, gels, and pessaries are openly purchased without embarrassment by users from all age groups and from all walks of life. They are offered by government health agencies to their citizens in overpopulated areas."

At this point the expert writer goes on to say: "Unless urgent measures are taken, any advantages gained by the widespread use of modern contraceptive methods could soon be counterbalanced by a worldwide acceleration in the prevalence of venereal disease."[1]

Let me quote a bit more from our expert: "Today there is a general permissiveness. Interpersonal relationships are superficial and fleeting. People travel widely, disseminating disease along their way. . . . The original source of infection is thus often impossible to trace, particularly as women may exhibit few symptoms of venereal disease. Resistance to antibiotics is firmly established, but it is still worse in the Far East and places like Vietnam. . . . Male homosexuality and unsupervised prostitution in both sexes provide further sources of infection."[2]

According to the experts, the situation is gradually going from bad to worse. It's gaining ground and getting out of hand.

What are the main medical problems with VD?

There are two aftereffects of infection.

First, there is the immediate result of an infection. This causes much discomfort in many instances. But perhaps more significant are the long-term effects. Both diseases can cause very serious consequences. As one writer declares: "The long-term debilitating effects caused by venereal infections are probably unequaled by any other one disease."[3]

Such results as sterility, disease of nearly any organ of the body and, in the case of syphilis, insanity many years after the initial infection are chronicled by the thousand in the books of medical history.

Gonorrhea

Let's take these two diseases separately and go into a little further detail. As gonorrhea appears to be the most prevalent, we will begin with this.

Gonorrhea is caused by a small microscopic organism that consists of two halves (a diplococcus). Officially the germs are known as *Neisseria gonorrhoeae.*

There is always a history of sexual intercourse. Anywhere from four to ten days later, the male notices a genital discharge and pain when he urinates. There is usually little doubt about an acute attack.

The discharge is often quite copious. It may be yellowish in color, but sometimes it has a greenish tinge. If the urethra is massaged a little, large quantities of this matter pour from the tip of the penis.

However, infections may also be very mild, and only minimal amounts of pus may be discharged. The patient may or may not feel a little off-color or exhibit swollen glands in the groin.

In the female the infection usually commences in the urethra, the vagina, or vaginal glands. It, too, is characterized by painful urination and a discharge of pus. It is very common for the infection to spread to adjacent organs. If you care to turn back to the illustrations of the female pelvis, you'll see how simply this can occur. There is a direct tract along which infections can spread.

Commonly the gonococcus (as it's called for short) races from the vaginal tract into the uterus, outward to the tubes, and into the pelvic cavity. Here it may infect the ovaries and spread to any other organ nearby.

Indeed, severe, rapid generalized infections can rapidly occur. Abdominal tenderness, pelvic pains, high fevers are some symptoms. The more serious manifestations are infections in the bloodstream (septicemia), the heart (endocarditis), and joints (arthritis).

The germ has a strong affinity for the lining of the eye, and serious cases of acute suppurative conjunctivitis and even blindness may take place. This is particularly serious when a baby is born to a woman suffering from gonorrhea. Infantile infections of the eyes have been responsible for many cases of blindness in innocent babies through no fault of their own. This is a tragedy for which there is no excuse.

What's the best routine to follow if a person becomes infected?

Immediate medical assistance must be sought. Indeed, in some countries it is legally mandatory, and penalties exist for those ignoring the law.

A person may consult his own family doctor if he so prefers. Here accurate diagnostic methods will firmly pinpoint the nature of the disease and will also give an indication as to which form of treatment is likely to give most effective results.

As it happens, gonorrhea may be associated with one or more of the other venereal infections. This will be checked out at the same time, and all infections will then be treated concurrently.

Although penicillin is still largely considered the drug of first choice, this may alter in time to come. There are, fortunately, several effective antibiotics that have a powerful effect on the gonococcus. The majority of cases can now be brought under control in a reasonable period of time.

It is imperative to continue treatment until a cure has been effected. Rely on your own doctor, and be guided entirely by his advice. It's essential that you come back for therapy as often as he suggests.

Are family doctors the only ones who can give treatment ?

No. There are very many places where treatment is readily and freely available. Practically every large public hospital has a special VD clinic. Smaller hospitals administer treatment at their outpatient clinics. Besides this, most large cities have special government-operated clinics, usually located at central points in the town. Here accurate diagnosis, treatment, and follow-up therapy are available free of cost.

Because of the seriousness and contagious nature of VD when it gets out of control, governments the world over attach considerable importance to attempts of eradicating every case that comes within their notice. In the interests of the people concerned, most government agencies make an earnest endeavor to track down all contacts and offer them suitable treatment as well. The source of the infection is sought, for the potential for infecting many others will remain unless a cure is effected here as well.

Governments are not interested in the moral issues involved in treatment. The patient is guaranteed freedom from publicity, and every case is treated privately and in strict confidence; therefore anyone suspecting that he could be infected has this assurance.

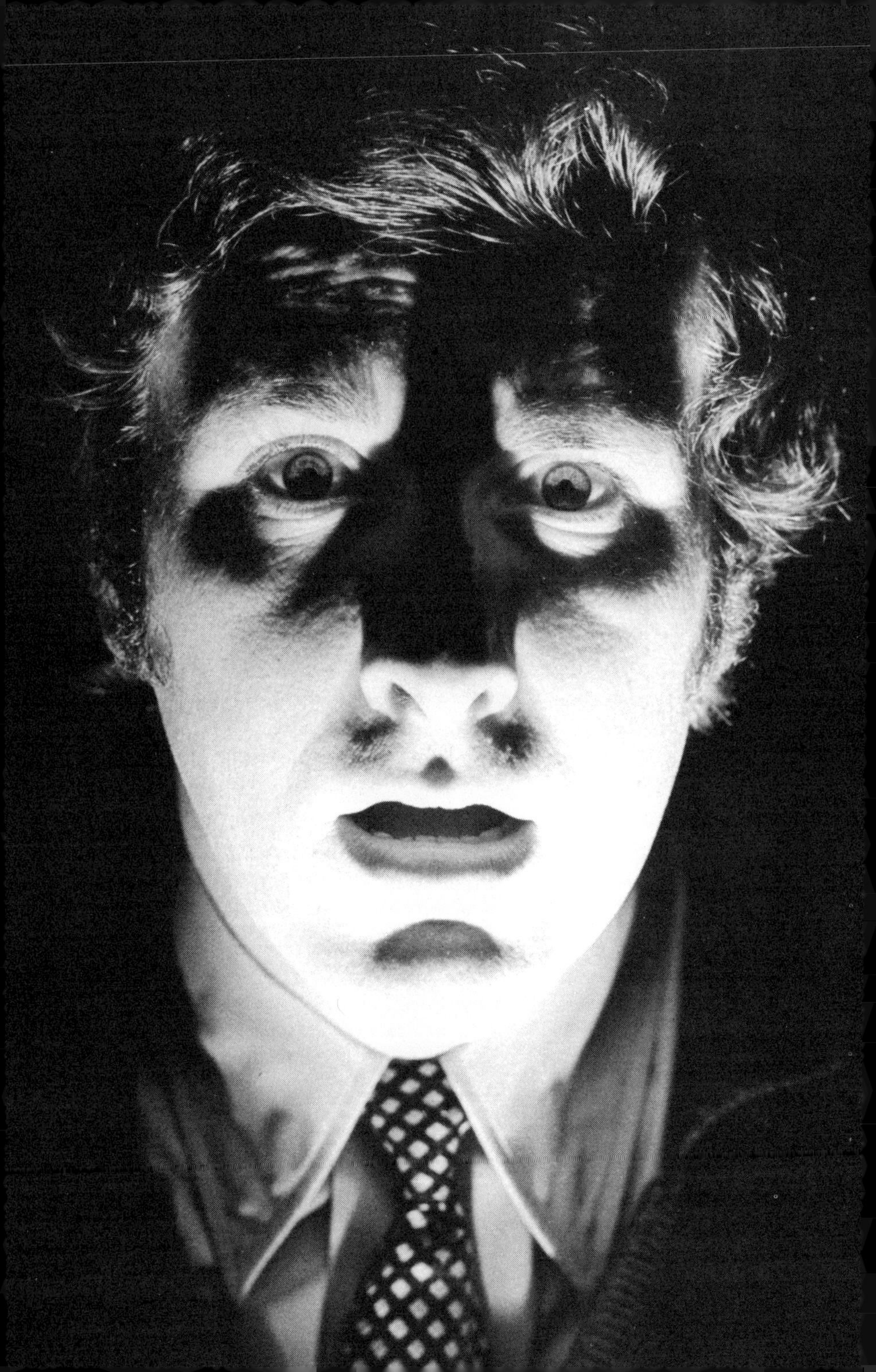

Syphilis

Now let's turn to the other common disease, syphilis.

This is caused by a germ called the *Treponema pallidum.* It is usually acquired by sexual intercourse. However, on rare occasions, it may be picked up by other means as well. The most tragic form is congenital syphilis where the infection is passed to a developing infant. The baby therefore inherits the disease.

How does an infected person become aware he has contracted the disease?

There are several different stages of syphilis, and the symptoms vary accordingly.

To start with, primary syphilis shows up anywhere from one to eight weeks after contact with an infected partner. (This is generally through sexual intercourse.)

It is characterized by a small sore called a chancre, usually about the genital region (eg, on the penis in males, about the vulva in females). In females it may be unnoticed, being deep inside the vaginal tract. The glands nearby tend to swell and may be tender.

At this stage, it is possible to make an accurate diagnosis. Material expressed from the sores and examined by a special method called dark field examination (making use of a special microscope) will often show the germ *T. pallidum.* It has the appearance of a madly wriggling corkscrew-shaped organism. Several such tests may be required in order to obtain positive results.

Other tests called quantitative complement fixation tests and flocculation tests (using blood samples) will progressively turn positive if the infection is syphilitic.

Then secondary syphilis occurs. The primary chancre (sore) will clear up. Indeed, many old-time claims of cure were fallacious because the lesion is destined to disappear whether or not treatment is given at this stage.

The secondary form is obvious and may be very widespread. It generally starts two or three weeks after the appearance of the primary sore. Usually there is a generalized swelling of the lymph glands in many parts of the body. A skin eruption may occur over any part, or all, of the body. The outstanding (and often diagnostic) feature about this is the lack of itch that accompanies it. Most simple dermatitic skin rashes are infuriatingly irritable. Syphilis rash is *not*.

There may be an inflammation reaction of the nose and upper air passageways, sore eyes, and maybe painful joints. Once more the telltale tests will show the germ in the skin eruptions. Blood tests may also indicate positive.

What happens after this?

Herein lies the great trap for the unwary. The latent stage sets in. The secondary stage clears up, and there is no obvious outward sign of the disease. But the germ is surely, quietly smoldering away in the general system. It is doing its diabolical work of destruction. Hardly an organ of the system is immune from its infamous attack.

Indeed, it's amazing how it can work under cover for so long and yet remain undetected unless special tests are carried out.

Finally the tertiary stage is reached. Indeed, it may take anywhere from two to twenty *years* for this to develop! There may be a widespread infiltration of any or many organs or systems. Alternatively, specific lesions called gummas may form, and these also can infiltrate any organ.

The skin or mucous membranes may be affected. Or bones and joints may be attacked, with resulting severe inflammation (such as periostitis, arthritis, synovitis and osteomyelitis).

The eye may be attacked, affecting any portion of the

entire organ. Lesions may attack any organ of the body. Even the heart is not immune. The heart itself, or the major blood vessels emanating from it, can be severely affected. Aortic aneurysms (rarely seen in modern times, but a distinct possibility ten to twenty years ago) occur when the aortic wall is attacked. A major bulge occurs in the wall, and if this bursts, it is virtually a death certificate in itself. Blood gushes everywhere, and the patient usually dies promptly from internal hemorrhaging and shock.

Another critical long-term aftereffect comes when the germ attacks the brain. Here, neurosyphilis can take place. A condition called tabes dorsalis may occur, and later on, a mental condition referred to as dementia paralytica may result.

At this stage the patient loses complete control of his mental powers and often of his physical well-being as well. In short, he becomes a vegetable, of no use to himself or others.

This is the terrifying picture of what was once a very common long-term outcome of syphilis. There is little doubt that a recurrence of these cases is destined for the future as the disease gains momentum.

How effective is treatment for syphilis?

As with gonorrhea, prompt medical supervision and adequate treatment yield good results. The patient must continue with therapy until he is cured.

Penicillin, despite the fact that it has been around for so many years, is still regarded as the drug of choice. But other antibiotics are often used as well. If there is any suggestion of syphilitic infection, it is absolutely imperative that immediate, efficient medical advice be sought. The best place is any of the government-run clinics where specialized attention is freely available.

The government is interested only in checking the rampant

spread of the disease. You are assured of absolute confidence at these clinics, and nobody will preach morals to you. (Although it might be a very good idea if some emphasis was placed on this aspect.)

What are the chances of recurrence?

Unfortunately, they are often quite high. Frequently, a patient has inadequate treatment, and a recurrence is merely a flare-up of an improperly treated disease. Perhaps more commonly, viewing the overall pattern of infection, the person who contracts VD the first time is the very one who'll go back for a second (and third and fourth) dose! It's incredible, but some people never learn.

"Sleeping around" (to use the current idiom) is one of the most notorious ways of contracting VD. Indeed, the rate of VD in persons not straying from their marital bed is virtually nil.

What advice do you have for our youthful readers?

Simply this. VD is an entirely preventable disease. By adhering to a high moral standard, you are guaranteed not to contract it. But live loosely, sleep around, and carry on with a wide range of people of questionable morals, and you could be headed for big trouble, both in the short term, and possibly in the long term.

Almost every week I see a patient who is trying to become pregnant, but cannot. Often, a check back will reveal that she has had a VD infection in earlier years. The tubes have sealed over. It may be only trivial, but quite enough to cause permanent sterility. Even though she may have strayed "only once," that is enough to bring on mental suffering that goes on for the remainder of her life. (For, as I've long since discovered, if there is one thing worse than a woman who produces too many children, it's the woman who cannot reproduce at all.)

Do not think that modern therapy permits you to live a life on the town at all times. It certainly can do a great deal in coping with infection. But by the time you're cured, much damage could already have occurred. Besides, who wants an interior that's been filled with these diabolical germs?

The Scriptures have never condoned the behavior of the adulterer or the fornicator. Why not be guided by this very sensible advice? Stick to it, and your problems in this department will never materialize.

Sex is for after marriage. By staying with one partner, you will have no problems after the wedding vows have been exchanged.

REFERENCE:
1. *Medical Journal of Australia* (1970), 2—759.
2. *Ibid.*
3. *Ibid.*

14

Artificial Sex

As we discovered in the early chapters of this book, sex plays an important part in adult life. Although its basic aim is to enable reproduction, it also forms an integral part of normal marriage. Right?

To recapitulate, sexual relations are a normal, vital, exciting part of the "after marriage" ritual. Those who hold Christian ideals believe that this is one of God's gifts to mankind. Not only is it of importance for momentary pleasures, but it plays a major part in uniting and unifying the husband-wife relationship. Does that capsulize it pretty well?

Well said. However, as with everything else in this world, abuses have crept in over the years. Bizarre aspects have cropped up; abnormal and unnatural forms have intruded into this aspect of living. It's important for our youthful reader to be aware of these.

In discussing these aspects, we should make it quite clear that we are not condoning them. Rather we recommend a great deal of caution. By being prepared and watchful, it is possible for one to avoid becoming involved in abnormal practices

Unnatural Sex

We are entitling this section "Unnatural Sex," for that in essence summarizes the situation.

The two chief headings to be discussed are these:

1. Masturbation.
2. Homosexuality.

Let's commence with the more common of the two, masturbation.

In simple terms, masturbation means the erotic artificial stimulation of the sexual organs often to the point of orgasm (climax), but usually without sexual contact.

It's practiced by both males and females, although the incidence among growing males is undoubtedly much higher. The very nature of the male anatomy seems to lend itself to this pastime, which is given various common names.

The male is very prone to erotic thoughts. Particularly in the second half of the teen years, the tremendous psychological and mental development changes that occur often bring an overabundant emphasis on sex.

The young man suddenly becomes aware that he is growing, that he is a male, that sexual development is going on apace. His penis, scrotum, and hair development (suprapubic, chest, face, armpits) become pronounced. This can occur quite suddenly.

Indeed, in a couple of years and even less, a puny, underdeveloped youngster can develop into adult manhood. His thoughts turn to the female form. As hormone production surges ahead, and as sperms fill his seminal vesicles, with nowhere to go, "wet dreams" often occur at night. These are usually associated with dreams which may involve erotic scenes, or actual sexual intercourse and sex play, often accompanied by very pleasurable sensations. It doesn't take long for boys to learn that they can artificially reproduce similar experiences quite simply by physical stimulation of their sex organs.

Indeed, commencing anywhere from the early teens (it varies with the personal development of the individual), an orgasm with ejaculation is possible. This means that the growing boy is quite capable of impregnating a female with sperms and initiating pregnancy. Similarly, it means that he is capable of recurring orgasms elicited by simple artificial means.

How widespread is masturbation in boys?

This subject has been researched by numerous authorities over the years. Many claim that 90 percent have practiced it in some form at some stage of their lives. They also claim that the other 10 percent (the abstainers) are liars!

Indeed, many regard this as an awakening of the awareness of their bodies and the things it can accomplish. Thus, they say, it is part of growing up.

What usually happens in the long term?

Generally speaking, it's believed to be a transitory phase and is practiced mainly by the younger age group. Usually it may persist for a short period of time, and then is abandoned as age progresses.

As a rule, when marriage takes place, masturbation is replaced by the more normal system of true sexual union. I am sure artificial sex was never meant to be, and certainly never designed to be perpetuated into the years of marriage.

Is masturbation considered to be physically harmful to the person practicing it?

This question cannot be answered with certainty. Definite proof is lacking, and little research has been done. The fact remains that it is unnatural and that it fosters an undue preoccupation with sex.

It is known that prostatic enlargement is a very common disorder of aging males. Indeed, prostatic hypertrophy is extremely widespread in the male community. The prostate, if you recall earlier chapters (have a look at the pictures to refresh your memory), is a smallish gland located just below the bladder. Through it passes the urethra, the small tube that conveys urine from the bladder storehouse to the exterior.

As the bladder increases in size, the prostate presses upward into the bladder (so reducing the capacity of that organ), and at the same time reduces the diameter of the urethra that passes through it. This can cause untold problems, and frequently leads on to surgical intervention.

Besides this, the prostate is a fairly common seat for cancer in older males. This serious condition usually commences as a simple *hypertrophy* or enlargement. Some doctors believe that masturbation practiced regularly can predispose to early (and more severe) prostatic hypertrophy (with its attendant risks and discomforts).

Therefore there seems at least one major point in favor of nonindulgence in the habit.

Agreed. Whether the concept is valid or not, we'll probably never know. But why play with fire? The long-range prospect seems to make it something of a risk.

Would you say the immediate problems also make the habit inadvisable?

Certainly. By experiencing these transient "pleasures" (if they can be called by this name, and even this is doubtful), it is very easy to quickly develop a sex-oriented outlook. Indeed, the more the habit is practiced, the greater amounts of time will be spent in erotic thoughts. There is nothing that will disturb a male's line of normal thought more than having his mind filled with sexually oriented material. If his mental machinery is geared to fit this line of thought, he'll gradually develop an impure, immoral outlook on life.

As we noted earlier, the Scriptures teach that "as he thinketh . . . , so is he." Let him fill his mind with impure thoughts, and that's the person he will inevitably become. Indeed, so preoccupied with sensuous thoughts do some young men become that their studies gradually start to fall behind. Their powers of normal concentration dwindle. Their entire outlook, all their waking hours can easily become filled with impure thoughts of the other sex.

For a student trying to make the grade, trying to achieve an education that will fit him for a decent position in the world, this is a most unsatisfactory position to be in.

I believe that sexually oriented activities are for after marriage. When engaged in with love and respect for the partner, sex means so much. Carried out in a carnal, erotically emotional capacity, it misses out. Save it for when it means most to you—and your wife.

Many doctors also believe that the constant stimulation of artificial sex play can reduce the sensitivity of the nerve-end organs located in the glans. This, they say, can reduce the pleasure that sex will ultimately have in store for them. Perhaps this is an added reason why abstinence is best.

Is this situation any different with females?

It is simple to stimulate the clitoris to the point where orgasm occurs. It may be carried out in a variety of ways. But the result is the same. A very pleasurable sensation takes place. But once again, this is purely transitory. There is no warmth, no affection, no intrinsic love involved. It is a means to an end, and in this respect, has a lot in common with the drug addict who is merely interested in the next "fix" for his personal gratification.

Girls who become involved in continually practicing masturbation likewise tend to become preoccupied with sex.

Eroticism fills their minds, often to the exclusion of the important aspects of life.

There is more to youthful living than self-abuse. Leave sex till the time when complete, normal, natural fulfillment is possible. Then it will mean so much more to you. One of the greatest things in life is the ability to share. In this respect, sex represents the ultimate. Sharing yourself with another, giving yourself to a person with whom you are deeply involved emotionally, in the full sense of the word, represents the maximum in true love. That comes after marriage.

Homosexuality

You mentioned that the other sexual abnormality was homosexuality.

This is a bizarre sex relationship, and researchers are still trying to discover the basic reason why it occurs. But that it does exist, and in rapidly increasing numbers, there is no doubt.

It means that instead of the normal heterosexual relationship between male and female, this is replaced by either a male-male or female-female relationship. Therefore, it is referred to as a homosexual relation. It is quite obvious that there are two possibilities:

A. Female-female homosexuality. This is often referred to as lesbianism.

B. Male-male homosexuality, which is generally referred to merely as homosexuality.

Tell us more about lesbianism.

This takes place when two females are sexually attracted to each other. It may occur in a variety of age brackets, and often the marital state is not necessarily a bar. Some females simply do not enjoy male company. They find members of their own sex far more pleasant to deal with, and they enjoy an erotic relationship with them.

A couple may carry on a clandestine relationship, just as illicit sexual relationships occur between unmarried boy-girl friendships. Frequently, especially in younger women, the precipitating factor may have been an unsatisfactory affair with a male. The girl may have been jilted or "used," or she may have met with some other unlucky incident that turned her off the male sex very strongly. Often at this juncture, probably a sympathetic, understanding female associate befriended her, and so a different, unwholesome, homosexual relationship gradually evolved.

In older women normal marriage and even reproduction may have taken place. A woman may finally find sex in the normal sense unpleasant, "vulgar," "painful," or any of the other multitude of ways such people describe their way of living at the time. She gradually finds herself attracted to another female who is usually able to administer affection, display feeling, and show kindness, tenderness and sympathy. So another abnormal relationship is established and flourishes.

Of course what many people cannot imagine is how two women could possibly indulge in "sex" as we understand it.

The answer is that they cannot. Their actions usually involve physical stimulation of each other's external genital organs.

In brief, one female will take the initiative and make up to her partner. With simple manipulation, she will physically stimulate (or masturbate) the other's clitoris to the point of maximum excitation. In this way her partner will achieve an orgasm. Then it's a reversal of the situation. The appeased partner will then similarly caress and physically arouse the other until she too achieves a climax.

Of course, there are all manner of side issues connected

with this. In some instances, there is a dominant personality. This person tends to assume the "male" role in the relationship, and the lesser person the female role. Therefore, in the sex relationship, all manner of artificial devices are used to maintain this type of effect.

But the basics are the same. The aim is to achieve artificial orgasm, using all the ploys and wiles, the love play, the skin stimulation, the breast stimulation that we have already discussed when describing normal sexual union.

Some couples go to extremes in their relationships. At times they will permanently live together. The dominant one will be the breadwinner and go out to work regularly, while the partner remains at home and carries out the usual domestic chores.

What is the situation with male homosexuality?

Basically, this is very similar. It involves males who find other males more attractive sexually than females.

The method most commonly attributed to males indulging in this form of sexual gratification is intercourse (if such a word can be used in this context) with their male partner via the back passage. Most normal people would regard this form of indulgence as less than attractive, and indeed downright repulsive. But many males do practice the method, and with apparent enjoyment and self-gratification.

A variety of other forms exist as well. Perhaps a common one is a mutual masturbation with a partner, simultaneously, or in sequence. This, too, is carried out in a variety of ways, most of which also seem most repulsive to the normal healthy young man.

The Case Against Homosexuality

How is homosexuality regarded in the community?

In some countries it has been legalized between consenting

male partners. However, most heterosexually inclined people regard homosexual activities with a very definite contempt. Moreover, the number of factors mitigating against the practice are enough to turn hopefuls and condoners against it with abhorrence.

What are some of these?

Perhaps the most outstanding aspect is that it's entirely immoral in a so-called Christian society. The Scriptures frequently speak out in crystal-clear tones against the practice. Indeed, at least one city was destroyed because its inhabitants practiced the vile habit. God rained down fire and brimstone on the city of Sodom to cleanse the spot from its foulness and wickedness. The word "sodomy" remains in our current vocabulary to this day as a memorial to their wickedness and sinful ways.

Many Bible students also believe that this was one reason why God poured down the great Flood. It was to re-create the world a better, purer place for man to live in. The degree of willfulness and sinning occurring in the days just prior to Noah's great triumph was of the most degrading nature.

However, these are really moral issues. Although I go along with them entirely, do you have supporting evidence that homosexuality as such is an adverse practice in the community?

Certainly. It is very well documented that venereal disease is rampant among practicing homosexuals. Indeed, in our last chapter we quoted expert reference to the fact that homosexuals are one important cause for the sudden upsurge of VD in the postwar era. In addition, some of the other more serious (but less frequent) forms of VD are readily transmitted by these people, the experts tell us.

Do you feel that we tend to criticize this type of person a bit unjustly? After all, we probably consider that we are normal and they are abnormal, when in fact they probably believe the reverse.

This could be so. In fact, increasing numbers of doctors and psychiatrists and social workers believe that homosexuals are in need of specialized treatment. It is believed that they suffer from some inherent defect, and instead of being thrown into jail for illegal acts, they should receive sensible medical remedial treatment, just as mental problems are treated these days.

After all, it is not very long ago that anyone with a psychiatric illness was considered "mad" and was promptly removed to an asylum and given scant attention. These days he is admitted to a psychiatric center for proper assessment, tests, and therapy. Times have changed. Perhaps this is how we should be attending to the homosexual misfit in the community.

It is probable that times will change even more. But this doesn't alter the fact that God specifically states His objection to these people as a class.

The sooner widespread efforts are made to help them adjust back to normal the better. In this way mankind will be doing a service to his fellowman. Simultaneously, he will be bringing those who have fallen by the wayside to a better understanding of what true living entails. What better and more satisfying work could there be for some type of social worker? We hope to see it occur in the not-too-distant future.

However, in the meantime, we would like to offer a special word of caution to young men. Homosexuals are always on the lookout for new recruits. They prefer young men. Some of these men are so warped mentally that they even go for youngsters in their early teens and younger.

Keep well away from adult men you do not know, and particularly those intimating they would like to be friendly.

They are potentially dangerous company for teen-age boys. Keep moving. Take every precaution.

There is little doubt that once entrapped in the snare, you could destroy your own life, and chances of academic progress, your physical vitality, and, above all, your Christian welfare.

15

When You Play With Fire, Wham!

What are your views on drugs and drug addiction?

I feel very strongly about them. Anybody who has developed a physiological dependence on certain chemicals could be said to be "addicted." In other words, his body has altered so that a continual supply of the product in question is needed to keep him feeling normal. If he is suddenly deprived of the supply, he develops withdrawal symptoms, and life becomes filled with misery and problems.

How do you view the present drug scene?

It seems to be deteriorating at a fairly rapid rate. But from the outset let's get our sights clear and get a proper understanding of the drugs that are the key troublemakers. They can be divided into several groups. I'll set it out this way for clarity:

1. Legally Approved and Acceptable Drugs.
   A. Tobacco.
   B. Alcoholic beverages.
2. Legally Disapproved Drugs (when not being taken under proper medical supervision).
   A. Narcotics.

B. Sedatives.

C. Stimulants.

D. Hallucinogens.

E. Hallucinogen intoxicants.

3. Legally Approved "Over-the-counter" Drugs.

Let's make a start with the first lot.

1. Legally Approved and Acceptable Drugs.

For some strange reason for which nobody has the perfect answer, drug addiction has the world in its grip.

Since the sixteenth century cigarette smoking has flourished in the Western world. Spanish explorers of America were the first to bring tobacco to Europe, and they introduced pipe smoking. English explorers introduced it to England about the same time. In 1590 sufficient quantities were being imported to encourage the queen to impose an import duty of 2d a pound. Tobacco has remained with us ever since, an ever-increasing source of public revenue, and an increasing hazard to public health.

Alcoholic beverages have been around since time immemorial. Ancient writings espouse the "value" of alcohol, and the Scriptures refer often to it.

These two drugs are used almost universally by people throughout the world. Both yield rich rewards for business concerns and governments alike. Collectively they represent the most flagrant example of mass legalized drug addiction. But chances of a reversal of this situation seem remote. It is so firmly entrenched in the social, business, and economic life of nations that it seems destined to remain for a long time.

Nevertheless, this doesn't mean that either vice is right. Mass use of a drug, irrespective of how much it is condoned, cannot make a poison nontoxic.

Let's take a closer look at tobacco.

A. Tobacco.

Today, the ever-increasing volume of carefully documented scientific data indicts cigarette smoking as a king-sized killer in modern communities. Among medical men, scientific workers, and researchers there is no doubt. Certainly the tobacco industry still debunks the findings with gay abandon, but the facts are indisputable. Cigarette smoking is a killer which is rapidly climbing to alarming proportions.

It's not practical to give masses of documented figures within the framework of this small book. So we'll select at random, say the United Kingdom, as a typical smoking Western country.

It is estimated that over 20,000 deaths in men between the ages of thirty-five and sixty-four are caused every year by smoking. The figure is rising annually.

The Risks

What are some of the specific hazards of smoking?

First, there is the absolute danger of shortening the life-span. The more a person smokes the greater are his chances of dying from diseases attributable solely to this cause. For example, cigarette smokers are about twice as likely to die in middle age as are nonsmokers, and they may have a risk similar to that of nonsmokers ten years older.

Another way of looking at this is that a thirty-five-year-old man who is an average smoker will have a life-span five and a half years shorter than the contemporary nonsmoker!

Life is sweet to most of us. The thought of an untimely demise is horrifying, even though we relegate it to some hazy distant future. A realization of how smoking can alter this is unnerving.

What is the present situation regarding smoking and lung cancer?

Lung cancer has now been produced in animals which have inhaled tobacco smoke. To quote the experts, "Expert committees in many countries are all agreed that cigarette smoking is the cause of cancer of the lung."[1] In addition, there is a clear relationship between the number of cigarettes smoked and the frequency of lung cancer.

What's the situation about filter tips, ceasing the smoking habit, and pipes and cigars?

A filter tip certainly reduces the hazard, but it does not completely eliminate it, by a long shot. If a smoker ceases, his chances of contracting lung cancer are reduced appreciably. Pipes and cigars are believed to play only a small part in causing lung cancer; they produce other maladies. Cigarettes are the coffin nails.

The experts estimate that 50,000 people will die each year from lung cancer in England and Wales by the 1980s. But if cigarette smoking were to stop, this would drop to 5000!

Rebuttals?

We regularly hear (mainly from the manufacturers) that the findings presented by the clinicians are false. Often very convincing material is offered in support of their claims.

Too true. However, "certain objections to the conclusion that cigarette smoking is a cause of lung cancer when examined are found to be without substance."[2]

What about the other chest disorders we hear mention of from time to time?

Yes. These encompass chiefly the well-known diseases of the chest, *chronic bronchitis* and *emphysema*. These are major problems and major causes of death. It is well documented that the intensity of these diseases is directly related to smoking and also to the number of cigarettes smoked. On many occasions it has been noted that lung improvement follows almost immediately if the habit is checked.

What is the current position regarding smoking and the heart?

Cigarette smoking is a major hazard to the heart and blood vessels. Liability to coronary heart disease is about twice as great in smokers as in nonsmokers. This, too, is related to the number of cigarettes smoked and the age at which smoking commenced.

Once more, risk of these diseases declines if smoking is stopped. Heart attacks are not always fatal. But if an attack occurs, the smoker runs a far graver risk than the nonsmoker.

In conclusion, the experts believe that "cigarette smoking is an important factor in causing coronary heart disease and that the general avoidance of cigarettes would greatly diminish the number of deaths from this condition."[3]

Other Scourges

There seems to be general acceptance of the fact that smoking during pregnancy is also harmful both to the mother as well as to the unborn child.

Quite definitely. Mothers who smoke are far more likely to have miscarriages. They tend to have smaller babies at birth (and that means the baby has a diminished chance at birth compared to his contemporary). Still births and death in the first few days of life are also more likely.

The list gets more formidable and terrifying the longer we probe the depths. What other scourges lie in store for the hapless fellow who chooses to follow his time-consuming, money-devouring form of entertainment?

Oh, there are still plenty of hidden witches in the cupboard! Such as cancers of the mouth, larynx, and esophagus being more frequent in the smoker, as well as increased risk of cancer of the bladder and pancreas too. There is also an increased risk of developing tuberculosis of the lungs and a delay in healing of stomach and duodenal ulcers.

Researchers have found that smokers are more *accident prone*. Fires traced back to smoking cause considerable loss in monetary terms, but more tragically cause many deaths. (In one year 100 people died in this way in Great Britain.)

Smoking can increase the risk of some forms of blindness. It is also related to liver diseases (because heavy drinkers nearly always smoke). Smokers have more disease of the teeth and gums. They are not nearly as physically fit as nonsmoking contemporaries.

Weight Problems

Isn't it true that smoking helps to control weight?

Don't think you can effectively and safely keep your weight down by smoking. "Those who give up smoking often put on a lot of weight, but this does not counteract the benefits to health otherwise produced," a panel of British experts has stated categorically.

Of course, most sensible persons will acknowledge that they're far better off not smoking.

Agreed. Yet in many instances even the most sensible person (in most respects) cannot bring himself to the point of actually quitting the habit once it has become firmly established. Often the inherent satisfaction gained from smoking seems to outweigh the mental torment a smoker knows looms so ominously.

Social pressure is another point. It's still the "in thing" to smoke, although this is gradually being shot to pieces. Many doctors now do not smoke, and other enlightened groups (often those having a direct relationship with smoking patients and their disastrous aftermath) do not either. But probably the main reason is that it's very hard to remove the habit once it has become firmly established.

How to Stop

What are some of the methods?

Most are really a projection of the general methods we've been talking about in earlier parts of this book. Making cessation of smoking your personal goal in life is one good method. This, combined with positive thinking, plus a firm sincere request for help from God, can quickly give success to your efforts.

But you have to be on the level. There can be nothing wishy-washy about this. Otherwise your efforts are doomed to failure before they begin. It is imperative that you keep telling yourself you *have* overcome the smoking habit. You *have* accomplished your goal. This is because you choose *not* to smoke. Bit by bit, this reinforces the fact that you have conquered the habit. And you will.

Many people find it helpful to follow a few simple hints. Such as drinking plenty of fluids. This helps remove from the system the toxins of your previous years of smoking.

Getting lots of exercise assists too. This brings more oxygen into the system and again helps eradicate the toxic byproducts of constant smoking.

Lots of pure fruit juices often quell the craving for another cigarette. Besides, these are healthful, are high in vitamin content, and the additional fluid further rids toxins from the system.

Going easy on highly seasoned foods, salty meats, salted nuts can also assist. In fact, many find a vegetarian diet most conducive to giving up the smoking habit. Reducing (or entirely eliminating) the daily coffee and tea routine also seems to help. Plenty of lukewarm-to-cool showers tone up the system and help check the withdrawal symptoms that reducing smoking often produces.

Group Therapy

It's often good to have a "buddy" who is experiencing the same problem as yourself. You can then dialogue back and forth. There is nothing like encouraging one another, comparing notes, etc., to gain the conquest.

Often the first week is the most rugged. But after that, things settle down, and indeed, the will to smoke, or even the desire, can be completely eliminated.

How do you feel about systems such as the "5-Day Plan" and related schemes?

There is little doubt that they are among the most effective ways yet designed. In the United States (and in many other countries) these are conducted by the Seventh-day Adventist Church as a nonprofit community service.

Cost of attending is minimal. The course runs for a couple of hours for five consecutive nights. Here, groups anywhere from half a dozen to a hundred or more receive formal lectures and demonstrations by doctors and others who present an easy-to-follow course of instruction.

The results often reach as high as 85 percent success rates at the end of the course. Even after six to twelve months, as many as 40 to 50 percent are still off the smokes. Independent surveys have frequently claimed this to be the most effective method currently available for persons with a genuine desire to quit the habit.

You said the Royal College of Physicians in London recently issued some suggestions to people who are trying to reduce (but can't quite quit) the habit.

Yes, indeed. This college has produced the most amazing documentation on the smoking system available anywhere.

In fact, we have drawn heavily on their data for this chapter, and we give them due acknowledgment right here.

We'll quote their suggestions verbatim:

"Those who continue to smoke should be encouraged to:

- Smoke fewer cigarettes
- Inhale less
- Smoke less of each cigarette
- Take the cigarette out of the mouth between puffs
- Take fewer puffs from each cigarette
- Smoke brands with low nicotine and tar content."[4]

I might add that the college recommends that children be taught from an early age the hazards associated with smoking and that every effort be made to deter them from starting the habit.

Let me hear the stories of Harold and Harry.

Harold

Harold had been an air force pilot during World War II. He'd been shot down over Germany, and for five years he eked out an existence as a POW. His less fortunate companions died. But due to his athletic build and general good health, plus an indomitable will to win, Harold lived on.

Harold was a nonsmoker. That is, until the rigors of POW life bit deep and hard. Then, to appease his appetite (for food was scant at all times, and nonexistent on many occasions) he took to the weed.

"We received supplies every now and again, and we could buy the stuff from the guards," he told me. "I was a fool to start, but when there is no end and no hope in sight, you say to yourself, 'So what?' "

Came liberation day. Harold came home, a confirmed and heavy smoker by this time.

Twenty-five years drifted by. I saw Harold intermittently for minor ills in my metropolitan consulting rooms.

Then suddenly he arrived, unannounced, one evening.

"I've a foul pain in my chest," he said, pointing to the region over the heart.

I tapped Harold's chest, checked his blood pressure, listened to his heart sounds.

"We'll check you out, old boy," I said.

"Go easy on this 'old' bit. I'm only mid-fifties!" Harold complained.

Harold went through the usual routines. His blood pressure was up; his heart showed signs of vessel narrowing. He was a candidate for definite heart trouble and certainly a starter for a dreaded "coronary."

"What's the score?" Harold demanded a few days later.

"Not good," I said without looking up.

"What do you mean?" from Harold. For once I detected a note of alarm in his voice. For a former air force pilot who sustained five years of hell in a prison camp this was saying something.

"How many cigarettes a day do you smoke?" I then asked.

"Fifty to seventy," Harold replied.

By now he owned and operated a substantial printing plant.

"Right. Now you can take your pick. From now on it's either *no* cigarettes per day—or else a wooden overcoat within five years. I'm being kind. I'm giving you the choice!"

I looked at Harold with a serious face. He looked back, pale around the gills.

"Thanks," he muttered. "You're on the level?"

"On the level!"

At that he left. Four weeks passed before I saw him again.

"Hi, doc," was his cheery greeting. "What swings?"

This wasn't the usual overburdened Harold I'd known over the past couple of decades.

"How are the cigarettes?" I asked as an opener.

"What cigarettes?" asked Harold, with a cheeky grin.

"You know, the fifty to seventy a day?"

"I don't know what you're talking about," he cut in. "Haven't felt better in my entire life. Now I'm really starting to live. Live, with a great big capital L."

I could hardly believe my ears.

"I don't like wooden overcoats. They're so uncomfortable."

"When did all this happen?" I asked, still surprised at the new man facing me.

"The moment I walked out of your office four weeks ago! 'Why be a fool?' I said to myself. 'A corpse isn't any good to man or beast.' Just came back to say thanks. All the lovely money I'm saving is just nobody's business either!"

Now, well over a year later, Harold still hasn't smoked, and he *never* will. He made a goal. He stuck to it. Positive thinking, positive power, common sense.

He looks years younger, he feels improved in health, he is working harder than ever, enjoying it more than ever. Heart pains have vanished. Blood pressure is normal. I've a feeling Harold will be around for many years to come.

Harry

Tremendous. Now what about Harry?

Old Harry was old in every sense of the word. He would have been eighty-four or eighty-five, I've forgotten which. Harry was a neighbor as well as a friend. For years he had been a confirmed reader of my medical newspaper column in one of the evening dailies. One day I did my thing about the futility of smoking, and how anyone so doing needed his head examined.

"Are you on the square about the smokes?" Harry asked

the next day when he confronted me on the issue.

"On the square, Harry," I replied in the same idiom.

"I've been an absolute fool. Here, I've been smoking since I was twelve years of age. What a king-sized nut! Why—I think I'll give it away right now."

"Great, Harry. Good luck," I said as he wandered off.

A week later he was back again, panting and wheezing as was his custom. My, his battered old lungs had taken it hard over those seventy-two years of being a human chimney.

"I've done it, I've done it!" he exclaimed as he came into my office.

"Done what, Harry?" I queried. I had momentarily forgotten the old man's resolution of the previous week.

"The cigarettes, doc. I've stopped smoking. Imagine that! After seventy-two years!"

Indeed, I was more than amazed. I was flabbergasted. To think that an old man of this vintage, a real antique, could master the habit after so many years!

"I'll check back in a month," he said as he shuffled off again.

Four weeks later, Harry was still off the smokes. Two months, six months, a year. Still no more smoking! In fact, Harry didn't smoke for another eighteen months in all.

The reason the record wasn't maintained further is that he peacefully passed to his rest one evening about that time.

But he had achieved a major victory.

He'd set a goal. He'd thought positively. He'd succeeded.

When I hear youngsters saying "I couldn't possibly give up smoking," I think of Harold and Harry. I think to myself, if those two fellows could knock the smoking habit just like that, well—*anyone* can.

B. Alcoholic beverages:

Let's press on with the next key topic in our discussion on legally approved and socially acceptable drugs.

Why such a diabolical drug should remain on the statute books of legality always puzzles me. I suppose the habit of indulging is so well established that any government trying to reeducate the masses would immediately be thrown out of office. Or maybe because it would then mean most lawmakers would automatically become lawbreakers!

Not long ago a medical news magazine came to my desk. It had been distributed worldwide to doctors and was an up-to-date appraisal of the world position in regard to alcoholism.

It stated: "Alcoholism abounds with paradoxes. It is a far more common and serious problem than other forms of drug dependence in developed countries. It [alcohol] is a notably toxic, habit-forming drug.

"There are a third of a million alcoholics in Britain, and several million in the United States. Alcoholism is a major public health hazard of epidemic proportions. Yet nobody knows precisely its cause, much less how to prevent and treat it."[5]

If alcohol is such a dangerous product, why then is it so popular?

Like smoking, I guess it's part of human nature. If it makes a person feel calmer, happier, or more joyful, then human beings will gravitate toward it.

It is strange that the human mind is more intent on the short-term effects of everything. How often it neglects the more important long-term damage!

The Partygoers

Of course you only have to be on the fringe of a party where the liquor is flowing freely to see the effect the product has upon those taking part. It's a prime "tongue loosener," to say the least. It is said to reduce tensions and increase the temporary feeling of well-being and exhilaration.

That it does this at the time, there can be no denying. But I often witness the selfsame gay party-timers the following morning. And, oh! What a dreadful sight they are to behold! Hangovers, headaches; bleary, bloodshot eyeballs. Ugh! The sight is enough to make any sane person sign the pledge in a real hurry.

Some years ago I worked in a small country town. Christmastime is the traditional party time everywhere, and here it was no exception. Very early in my medical experience I learned that the day after Christmas was a busy one for the local medical practitioner.

Thereafter I found it essential to have a large supply of my favorite (*their* favorite) hangover concoction ready on the double! Business was brisk all day through.

Although I'd resolved many years prior to this that drinking wasn't for me (or for any doctor for that matter), my resolutions were doubled when I witnessed the sorry stream of sad characters who passed through my office doors the "day after the night before."

The Road Toll

To what extent does alcohol feature in road accidents?

According to the experts, it is very significant. Indeed, many medical investigators claim that the majority of accidents have alcohol involved along the line somewhere.

Alcohol impairs the intellect, reduces driving ability and reaction time, and interferes with judgment. Reflex activity is reduced and visual perception is impaired.

And the problem involves more and more teen-agers.

"A Department of Health, Education, and Welfare (HEW)

report on alcohol and health made public July 11 [1974] indicated that alcohol abuse among high school students had risen sharply. The study . . . also contained the finding that heavy drinkers ran far greater risk of getting certain kinds of cancer—of the mouth, throat region, esophagus, and liver—than nondrinkers.

"According to Dr. Morris E. Chafetz, . . . alcoholism and related problems cost the nation [U.S.] more than $25 billion a year in lost work, medical expenses and motor vehicle accidents. . . .

"The report showed that one of every seven male high school seniors admitted getting drunk at least once a week; 34 percent of all high school seniors admitted being drunk at least four times a year. Chafetz labeled these statistics signs of 'early alcoholism.' "[6]

These figures are quoted merely to give an indication of the widespread nature of addiction to alcohol in the community in general and to show some of the civic and social disadvantages it presents.

How do you view the breathalizer tests that are now commonplace in many parts of the world?

All I can say is that I hope it helps to reduce the terrible road carnage. At least it is creating a new awareness of the relationship that alcohol has to general road safety, and it points up the dangers and hidden hazards it has for drivers in particular.

However, so often the person at the wheel is not the person who suffers most in road smashes. It is frequently the innocent person who meets disaster. But the test is bringing to justice those who are often responsible for road problems.

Finally

What is your summary of the alcohol situation?

The best advice I can offer is "Don't start!" Most of our readers, I trust, have not yet come to the point of decision on this issue. Sensible young men will heed the advice and admonition of the experts. They will not become involved in a habit which rapidly becomes highly addictive.

By shunning the problem before it becomes one, you will have the upper hand right from the start. Resist the social pressures. Nobody is making you take that first fateful glass.

Plenty of successful men and women do not drink. You do not have to be "one of the crowd" to make your mark in this world. Indeed, those with the strength to stand by their beliefs are often the men with the inherent stamina to make the grade in other facets of life too.

Don't be a sucker for the old line, "Join the fun. Look, everyone else is doing it." Everyone else is *not*. The real smart cookies prefer to keep their mental acumen intact, come what may; their consciousness unimpaired; their reflexes at peak capacity, and their senses where they should be. Believe me, it's worth it!

And for the record—as a doctor I do not smoke, I do not drink. I never have and never will. I'm too intent on making the most of this world to have time for such stupid, time-consuming, money-consuming, intellect-and-health-impairing pastimes!

REFERENCES:

1. "Smoking and Health Now," a report of the Royal College of Physicians (1971).
2. *Ibid.*
3. *Ibid.*
4. *Ibid.*
5. *Medical Journal of Australia,* July 25, 1970.
6. *Facts on File,* 1974, p. 699.

16

The Teen-age Blockbusters!

Now let's get on to the next major heading in the drug situation.

2. Legally Disapproved Drugs (when not being taken under proper medical supervision).

Yes. A very large number of drugs come under this heading. There are five chief chemical types involved here.

The point is this. A certain number of these are very valuable aids to normal medical treatment. Indeed, without them, patients would be at a serious disadvantage, and the normal routine of medicine would be severely hampered.

Certain drugs are given for the relief of intense pain (such as after a major operation) and for sedation. These are administered to patients under medical advice and are given usually in minimal doses for a very restricted period of time. Under these circumstances their use is legal and of definite benefit to mankind.

Drugs for "Kicks"

But when these same drugs fall into unscrupulous hands and are taken not for their medicinal benefit, but for the "kicks," that's when problems set in and escalate. Addiction can rapidly be acquired in many instances.

Doses are often out of all proportion to accepted medicinal norms. Irresponsible use such as this is definitely illegal and to be firmly condemned.

Do all these drugs have medicinal uses?

Certainly not. Indeed, several have been entirely banned for use of any kind. The use or even possession of some attracts stiff fines and/or prison terms.

Heroin, morphine, and cocaine are "hard" drugs. Amphetamines and marijuana are "soft" drugs. Any person who uses, manufactures, sells, or has any of these drugs in his possession without proper authority is liable to a prison sentence and/or a stiff fine.

If an offender has in his possession prohibited drugs in excess of certain amounts, he could be regarded as a pusher. This is an extremely grave offense, and a long prison sentence could result. The possession of certain other drugs can bring long prison sentences and heavy fines also. Many countries of the world go along in general principle with this type of legislation.

Is it possible to know which drug is which? In other words, which drugs produce serious consequences, and which aren't so serious?

Yes, and for this reason we're including a specially prepared table. This sets out the main groups of drugs. It outlines their medical use (if one exists), and gives an indication of the chances of producing addiction. It also sets out their immediate effects, along with the possible long-term effects.

(Refer to the table near the end of this chapter.)

It's a well recognized fact of life that more and more teen-agers are becoming involved in the drug culture. How widespread do you think this is?

According to the experts who spend their time poring over facts and figures, "one-third of all United States schools have a 'serious' drug problem."

How do young people get hold of drugs?

It's quite simple. They're readily available everywhere. In fact, sooner or later, nearly every growing teen-ager in this country will be offered drugs in one form or another.

How does the system operate?

Most commonly, it goes something like this: Someone approaches you, probably a school pal. "Look here," says School Pal, "I've got some caps." (Displays some brightly colored capsules or tablets with obvious pride.) "What about having one? I did. Made me feel great. Gives you a real lift. It'll make you feel great too."

You hesitate.

"It won't hurt you. Look at me. *I'm* all right. You know me. I'm your friend. Go on. Give it a try. I can get some more after this. No problem at all!"

It is as simple as that. Or alternatively, someone might approach you at a party, on the street, at the beach, at a swimming pool, in public transport, at a picnic, or at a sports event. There will be the same general line of talk. Capsules, or tablets, or maybe the idea of an injection.

There is talk of this "making you feel wonderful, able to study better, think clearer, having a marvelous sensation." It's always a positive story, one full of attraction and appeal.

How to Avoid the Traps

What is the best line of attack once you've been approached?

Sensible persons will immediately be suspicious. Drug taking is a foolhardy experiment. Once the first fateful step has been taken, it inevitably leads from one point to another in a general downhill direction. Those who have watched countless people reach the bottom rung of the ladder advise caution.

Teen-agers should resist any approach with drugs by a "friend" or friendliness by an unknown person. Under no circumstances take any pill, capsule, or injection from anyone unauthorized to dispense them. If the possibility opens to you, shun it promptly. Don't stop and talk. Keep moving. Be especially careful at the types of functions mentioned.

What drugs would a young person most likely be offered?

It will vary enormously. It varies from town to town, state to state, country to country. It depends on the current availability of drugs at any given time in any given place.

The amphetamines are still popular. In many countries these have now been totally banned. But there are still supplies fairly widely distributed. This is the well-known Speed (or "uppers").

For many years, the amphetamines were widely prescribed as an appetite depressant and were so used to help overweight people lose excess pounds. Just how many people became psychologically addicted to the powerful drug in this way is still unknown.

The barbiturates ("downers") group are used in medicine as nerve settlers. These are often offered by the drug peddlers but are not very popular.

What about marijuana?

Marijuana is extremely popular. It goes by various colloquial names. Grass and pot are two of the common ones.

Hashish is a clear resin that's derived from the hemp plant, but it's said to be up to ten times more potent. Actually, the word "hashish" is Arabic for "assassin." Once it was believed it gave the user a violent desire to kill. This is not true, but the name persists.

Keep Off the "Grass"!

Marijuana comes from a plant that grows almost anywhere. But supplies are generally illegally imported. The drug is widely distributed and readily available.

Pot imparts no physical disease to the user, and for this reason there has been widespread agitation over the past few years to have it legalized.

It has no therapeutic use in modern medicine. It contains a variety of properties common to stimulants, sedatives, tranquilizers, hallucinogens, and narcotics.

Its effect on driving performance indicates that its deleterious effects are very similar to those found when drivers have had a moderate intake of alcohol.[1]

In the social setting the fifth dimension is the one that gives greatest appeal. Subjective effects occur, such as alteration in time (it seems longer), space perception, euphoria (a feeling of exhilaration), relaxation, a sense of well-being and disinhibition, dulling of attention, fragmentation of thought, an altered sense of identity, exaggerated laughter and increased suggestibility, the feeling of a heightened artistic ability (but without any objective evidence of the fulfillment of greater talent).

The experts are quite convinced that "cannabis [marijuana] is a potent drug having as wide a capacity as alcohol to alter mood, judgment, and functional ability." Other authorities are quite definite that "cannabis is a dangerous drug."[2]

Another appealing factor, of course, is that smoking a drug seems so simple, so easy. It does not appear on the surface to be nearly as serious as injecting something into the body with a needle.

A major fear with marijuana is that its long-term effects are at present quite unknown. Many experts believe there could be serious repercussions, and only time will unravel this aspect.

What about LSD (short for lysergic acid diethylamide)?

This potent chemical was developed by a Swiss chemical researcher seeking a new cure for migraine headaches.

He hit upon "acid" and enjoyed a fantastic trip home from work that night on his bicycle. In a moment he realized he'd unleashed a genie.

LSD is an extremely potent drug. It gives a distorted picture of the outside world, but its use is very widespread. It is readily available.

Hard Drugs

What are the "hard drugs"?

These are the really serious ones and the most dangerous. They include narcotics.

The key danger is that the body soon comes to depend on their use. This rapidly develops. However, if it is decided to discontinue them, withdrawal symptoms set in.

These symptoms are terribly severe. Therefore, people on hard drugs tend to seek more and more supplies. Addicts go to any lengths to secure supplies.

The drugs are usually given by injection, either by the person himself or by an accomplice. Heroin is the greatest worry. It was used medically at one time, but now it is completely banned. It is believed that nobody can resist becoming addicted to heroin if it is given for any length of time.[2]

Other drugs in this category are also used. Pethidine, morphine, methadone, and others closely related are taken by the addict. These are often legally used by doctors to alleviate severe pain. They are given under proper medical supervision for short periods only.

What does it feel like to have a shot of heroin?

According to those who have been through the mill, the initial sensation (or "flash," as it's termed) is a remarkably pleasurable one.

However, the rub is that a gradually increasing amount is needed each time to experience the same initial impact.

As the amount increases, so does the cost, and the tolerance to the drug. Some addicts resort to crime to raise the necessary funds to support their habit.

Marijuana Use

If marijuana causes no outward sign of disease, why the concern about it?

There are many reasons. The person who takes the drug is almost invariably from a home in which problems exist. Quite often he takes it "in spite of everyone and everything." It is often his way of showing his rebellion to the world, his friends, or his parents.

Many surveys carried out with students attending universities indicate the same findings. Usually the marijuana user is involved with other drugs as well. Alcohol and tobacco are almost constant. But marijuana may lead on to a desire for more potent chemicals, and herein lies the real danger.

Of course, once this becomes established, the chances of rehabilitation diminish greatly. Many drug takers come from homes where parental unity was lacking. Supplies usually come from a friend in the early stage.

Most persons using the drug realize they are doing something which is illegal, but this does not worry them. Many are quite gifted intellectually and attain good grades at university, and indeed are open-minded and extroverts.

What happens when the hard stuff is started?

Inevitable disaster at this stage is just around the corner.

Indeed, if heroin is the drug of choice, it is merely a matter of time before ultimate destruction is in store.

Results of Heroin

Indeed, a recent count showed that in New York alone, 300 addicts died from heroin poisoning in one year. Since then, the figure has probably climbed steeply. In the United Kingdom, there are 1400 known heroin addicts.

The addict soon loses interest in his usual surroundings, family and friends, hobbies or work, and his own appearance. He associates with kindred spirits. His one and only delight is the next fix. Infections run high, for the addict ceases to care about sterility of the instruments used for the injections. Often incorrect doses are given, and this in itself has caused many deaths.

The addict will resort to any measure to obtain supplies. Crime, theft, even violence are parts of this routine to guarantee continuity of the drugs.

What is being done for addicts?

Various governmental agencies are doing their best. But the drug addict is happy in living the way he does. He is not interested in seeking help, for help is not what he personally desires.

Those endeavoring to eradicate the problem face a mountainous, almost impossible, task. Many private bodies endeavor to rehabilitate known addicts who come to their notice, but they cannot hope to cope with the problem.

Education the Answer

What is the answer then?

There is only one answer. Every teen-ager should be aware of the inherent dangers in taking drugs. Under no circumstances get on the road. It's a one-way ticket to doom.

Class of Chemical	Drug	Medical Use	Potential Physical Dependence	Potential for Psychologic[al] Dependence
NARCOTICS	Heroin	Illegal to use	Yes	Yes
	Morphine	To relieve pain	Yes	Yes
	Codeine	To relieve pain,diarrhea, or severe cough	Yes	Yes
	Paragoric	To relieve cough	Yes	Yes
	Pethidine	To relieve pain	Yes	Yes
	Methadone	To relieve pain	Yes	Yes
SEDATIVES	Barbiturates and Tranquilizers	To induce sleep, sedation, treatment of epilepsy and high blood pressure	Yes	Yes
	Bromides	Limited use for sedation and to induce sleep	Yes	Yes
	Alcohol	Limited medical use	Yes	Yes
	Glue	No medical use	Unknown	Yes
	Nicotine	No medical use	Yes (with very high intake)	Yes
STIMULANTS	Amphetamines	Strictly limited medical use	No	Yes
	Cocaine	Local anesthetic	No	Yes
	Caffeine	Mild stimulant	No	Yes
	APC	To reduce mild pain and fever	No	Yes
HALLUCINOGENS	STP	No medical use	No	Yes
	LSD	Minimal psychiatric use	No	Yes
	DMT	No medical use	No	Yes
	Mescaline	No medical use	No	Yes
	Psilocybin	No medical use	No	Yes
HALLUCINOGEN INTOXICANT	Marijuana	No present medical use	No	Yes

mediate Effects	Long-term Effects
rcotics reduce physical and psychological sensitivity, sulting in a loss of contact with reality. Sense of euphoria d reduced fear, tension and anxiety. Reduced physical tivity, drowsiness or sleep. Pinpoint pupils; constipation, usea, and vomiting in some individuals. High doses may use unconsciousness, coma, and sometimes death.	Withdrawal symptoms range from mild yawning, perspiration—tremors, loss of appetite and insomnia—to severe diarrhea, vomiting, muscle pain, and weight loss. Self-injection with unsterile syringes can lead to hepatitis, multiple abscesses, and septicemia. The commonest cause of death among individuals using narcotics is an overdose of the drug. With tolerance the drug dependent will require larger and larger doses to achieve effect. This becomes expensive, and addicts of long standing often turn to crime to maintain their habits.
nall doses reduce tensions, anxiety, and inhibitions, re-ting in a feeling of relaxation, drowsiness, or stupor. rger doses may produce slurred speech, staggering it, sluggish reactions, erratic emotionality, and ulti-ately sleep.	Convulsions, which may follow withdrawal, can be fatal—cause of many accidental deaths and suicides.
	Bromides accumulate in the body causing symptoms such as constant headache, irritability, and confusion.
	Continued heavy use may lead to DT, irreversible brain damage, heart damage, and cirrhosis of the liver.
ove effects also apply to glue sniffing; sniffers may also ffer from nausea, inflamed nostrils, lips, and eyes.	With continued glue sniffing, red and white blood cells are reduced. May be degenerative changes in heart muscle, central nervous system, and liver.
	Long-term heavy smoking may result in lung cancer, chronic bronchitis, and other respiratory complaints. Long-term abuse of nicotine may lead to high blood pressure and heart disease.
creased blood pressure and pulse rate. Decreased igue; elation and self-confidence and an increase in tivity. Dilated pupils, tremors, talkativeness, disorienta-n, hallucinations, and increased perspiration and urina-n. Severe depression frequently follows as the effect of stimulant wears off.	A high degree of tolerance develops, and self-administered dosage increases greatly. Psychiatric disturbance may occur.
evation of mood suppression of hunger, decreased igue. If administered intravenously, may cause a peak of nsation. May also cause sensory hallucinations, eg, im-inary insects crawling under the skin.	The mucous membranes around the nose may become damaged from continued inhalation of the drug. Also digestive disorders, emaciation, sleeplessness, and sensory hallucinations.
ually well tolerated in small amounts. It generally in-eases alertness and combats mild fatigue. May cause omnia, rapid pulse, and increased urination.	Caffeine is harmful to people with heart damage.
erdose of APC may cause gastric upset.	Continual abuse of APC may result in anemia, kidney damage, and stomach ulcers.
usions and hallucinations (eg, colored lights, ychedelic patterns, geometric designs, music, voices, nsations of warmth). May be an increased awareness of lor and colored objects, a seeming awareness of internal jans and processes of the body. Depersonalisation; re-ious and mystical experiences; increased suggestibil-; enhanced recall or memory; abrupt and frequent anges of mood. Panic states of severe anxiety (freak-ts) sometimes occur. Physical effects include pupil dila-n and sweating.	Little known about the long-term effects. Chromosomal damage has been reported by some scientists, but the evidence is still in the balance. May precipitate psychosis, attempted suicide, depression, and "flashback" experience.
tial stimulation which fades into relaxation accompanied euphoria, talkativeness, laughter, sensations of floating, seemingly increased esthetic appreciation and in-eased ability to communicate. There may be striking llucinations and illusions such as the slowing down of ie. This initial response may be followed by drowsiness sleep. Physical effects are decreased muscular coordi-tion, clumsiness, dry mouth, dizziness, bloodshot eyes, nger, occasionally nausea and vomiting, increased uri-ion, and sometimes diarrhea.	Little is known about long-term effects of marijuana. Consistent usage may lead to generalized fatigue, extended patterns of sleep, and general apathy. Recent research suggests the active principle is hallucinogenic and may have long-term ill effects if used heavily.

Read all you can about the problem. Discuss it with your friends. Fortify yourself and be prepared to recognize it the moment you see it on your doorstep. Do not get involved. Saying Yes the first time could be the start on the track to eternal physical and mental ruin.

Can you suggest further reading on this subject for those interested?

Yes. An excellent book devoted entirely to this topic is *The Creeping Madness.* Write to Narcotics Education, Inc., PO Box 4390, Washington, DC 20012, for information about this book and other material available on this vital topic.

In your original summary on the different types of drugs available you mentioned a third and final heading–on drugs anyone can buy. What is this all about?

3. Legally Approved Over-the-counter Drugs.

I feel quite strongly about this topic. To round off and complete the drug picture, it deserves special reference.

Pharmacies are stocked with an ever-proliferating assortment of medicines. Of course a great number are essential. These are chiefly the ones medically prescribed by the doctor for treating specific illness. These are usually available on presentation of a prescription. We're not knocking them.

But a mass of others are readily available as well "over-the-counter." Unfortunately, many of these are widely advertised in the mass media. In short, the public is regularly brainwashed on the so-called values of many of these products. Huge numbers of people are influenced by this type of publicity.

In our medicine-oriented community everyone is looking for a cure for his problems. Since many of these are closely bound up with physical sensations, the answer is often believed to come in the form of a pill or potion and from a chemist's bottle.

The Great Swallow

Therefore, the general populace consumes vast quantities of patent medicines. Pain-killers, nerve settlers, tonics, restoratives, sedatives by the truckload are swallowed by the unsuspecting public.

What would the most common ones be?

Most likely aspirin in multiple and varied forms. The APC preparations are quite popular. These, of course, consist of A for aspirin (a pain-killer), P for paracetamol (also a pain-killer and temperature reducer—it makes you perspire more, like aspirin), and C for caffeine (sometimes codeine). Caffeine gives a "kick," is a nerve stimulant; codeine is a pain-killer and can also cause constipation.

Hordes of people swallow vast quantities of these highly advertised pills regularly, irrespective of whether there is any medical indication for their use or not. It's customary in thousands of families for the adults to take one or two APCs regularly after breakfast. They then repeat this several times during the day.

Are there any dangers associated with this?

Very definitely. They are an irritant to the stomach lining. Many cases of stomach ulcers (to the point of severe sudden hemorrhaging) have been directly traced to indiscriminate use of APC preparations.

The constant "kick" the caffeine imparts can overtax the nervous system, cause sleeplessness (and the need for sedatives on a regular basis), plus nervousness, irritability, and a snappy disposition.

Doesn't this cause kidney damage too?

I was coming to the most lethal aspect. Analgesic nephropathy is now a widely recognized serious kidney disease. It is caused by the regular ingestion of excessive amounts of these analgesics.

It will cause recurring severe urinary tract infections and general ill health. Indeed, if left, it can ultimately kill.

How can the condition be treated?

It is quite simple. Merely by completely ceasing to take these drugs, the patient will gradually return to normal health.

"Tonics"

What's the value of some of the other freely purchasable "over-the-counter" drugs?

In my opinion, very little. Tonics often have alcohol as a basic ingredient, and this is usually the reason why an increased appetite often follows their use. Basically, a great many are quite useless. The amount of vitamins they sometimes contain would be more simply and cheaply obtained from eating a sensible, all-round, normal meal!

Sedatives, tranquilizers, and many other across-the-counter lines cannot be condemned too much. I believe most should be swept into the ocean and into eternal oblivion. But just think of the disservice we'd be doing the unlucky fish ingesting them there!

Although it's often hotly refuted by many, a good number of people become "addicted" (in a sense) to these harmful products.

What then is the cure for people with medical problems?

See a doctor if you believe you have some internal illness that warrants medical assistance. Be guided by his advice. Take medication if prescribed, but only the minimum amount for the absolute minimum length of time.

Many people would do far better living a sensible sort of life. Then the multiplicity of minor problems for which they seek patent medicines would never occur.

Getting adequate amounts of fresh air; getting plenty of

oxygen into their systems (deep breathing); getting plenty of sunshine; getting sensible amounts of sleep each day; thinking positive thoughts of success (surely, in relation to your health, there is nothing better); drinking plenty of cool, refreshing water; eating simple foods; going lightly on masses of rich, starchy food—all these help.

Have you noticed that all these commodities are available to everyone? Most of them for free!

I am certain God gave us these simple, readily available things to maintain good health and vigorous, long-lasting vitality.

Why not use them more often? You'll not only feel fitter, keep fitter, but you'll save a fortune over the years, and leave your contemporaries far behind in the race for better health.

REFERENCES:

1. *Medical Journal of Australia,* December 18, 1971, p. 1261.
2. *Ibid.*
3. *Ibid.,* December 4, 1971.

17

Parting Advice

So we finally come to the last chapter of our discussion together.

I'm going to miss our conversations. It will seem as though something is lacking in the daily routine!

But I can keep in touch with the facts through some other publications such as "Listen" and "Life and Health" and good books. Right?

Yes, *Listen* is published by the same company that prints this book. It comes out monthly and is written especially for the benefit of young people. And for those who would like to have a good reference set, the three-volume *You and Your Health* set is unsurpassed.

We're not trying to sales-talk you, but merely mention it if you happened to like this book.

Also if you have sisters (or possibly a girl friend) you think would appreciate the type of information in this book, there is the girl's counterpart written in a similar vein. It's called: *What a Young Woman Should Know About Sex.* It is the same price as this volume and is also readily available from the publishers.

The girl's book is written from the girl's point of view, and we believe it should prove helpful to her in a balanced acquisition of many fields of knowledge.

The two books are sold separately, but they are also issued in sets of two. Our publishers feel they fill a definite need in the community, and families with both boys and girls might find it a good idea to obtain the two volumes at the one time.

At what age do you think young people should start reading these books?

I don't think it matters. Often, the younger children are when they commence browsing through the pages, the better.

The body, how it's made, how it operates, is all so fundamental. It's so natural. Even children in early primary school are well acquainted with the basics of physiology. Therefore their minds are receptive to accepting this information if it is logically presented to them.

At the same time additional data can be fed into their minds which makes them ready for the more serious aspects of living that come along later.

Although these books have been designed primarily for the secondary school age group, they are quite suitable also for general perusal for younger (and I might say older) persons too.

You know, although we believe we are a well-informed nation as a whole, enormous numbers of people are still quite ignorant on many aspects of living.

I go along with that. I have a patient who has five children. About a year ago she came along to me pregnant for the sixth time!

She wasn't belligerent about it (as many sixth-timers might have been), but just a little perplexed at how she would cope with number 6.

As tactfully as I could, I suggested that after the baby was born, she might consider going on to The Pill or utilizing some other active "family-planning" system.

"The Pill?" she asked in obvious surprise. "What's that?"

This dear lady had never heard of The Pill!

In this era of mass publicity, when the facts of life are so blatantly beamed at us so regularly, here was a normal, healthy, mentally reasonable woman living in close proximity to a large city who didn't know about The Pill!

Which proves a point. If she didn't know, how many others don't?

Maybe many people have a shell of outer sophistication and knowledge, but deep down are not so wise at all.

We believe all youngsters and adolescents and even adults should read the type of books we are discussing, to make certain they personally have a reasonable working knowledge of all important facets of life.

It can make life so much more enjoyable. It can assist in avoiding the pitfalls. I am sure it can lead to better health, greater vitality, a clearer intellect, longer years, and greater happiness.

Do you have one or two short pieces of "parting advice" for our readers?

I'd suggest everyone should aim to get the facts of life (in all aspects) securely fixed in mind as soon as possible.

Endeavor to live a good, sensible, morally clean life, and your chances of success in general will escalate.

Also, set a major goal in life. Back this up with a series of lesser goals. Review these often and regularly.

Think positive thoughts of success.

Take God into partnership with you. Do not be afraid of asking for divine aid. Don't think others will scoff and laugh at you if you do. Keep one hand in touch with the "Supreme Intelligence."

This way you are undoubtedly assured of success unlimited. The world before you is tremendous. If you stick to simple tested and tried principles, it can be *yours*.

Our best wishes go with you for the rest of your life.

ZUM GELEIT

Am 20. September 1959 jährt sich zum zehnten Male der Tag, an dem mit der Bildung der Bundesregierung die Bundesrepublik Deutschland handlungsfähig wurde. Wenig mehr als vier Jahre nach dem Zusammenbruch der nationalsozialistischen Gewaltherrschaft haben die Westmächte damit die von ihnen im Jahre 1945 übernommene Oberste Staatsgewalt wieder in deutsche Hände gelegt.

Unter dem Zwang der weltpolitischen Verhältnisse mußte die staatliche Neuordnung auf den größeren Teil des Gebietes des Deutschen Reiches beschränkt bleiben. Der Eiserne Vorhang, das Symbol der Spaltung der Welt, durchschneidet das Reichsgebiet. Freiheit und demokratische Ordnung sind den Deutschen außerhalb der Bundesrepublik bis heute versagt worden.

Die Bundesregierung legt zum zehnjährigen Bestehen der Bundesrepublik Deutschland dieses Buch der Öffentlichkeit im Inland und Ausland vor. Es gibt Kunde davon, was der Fleiß und Arbeitswille des ganzen deutschen Volkes in den Gemeinden und Ländern auf allen Gebieten der Wirtschaft und des sozialen und kulturellen Lebens geleistet haben, um Deutschland einen ehrenvollen Platz als einem Glied mit gleichen Pflichten und gleichen Rechten in der Gemeinschaft der Völker zurückzugewinnen. In diesem Werk ist aber auch nachzulesen, wie die Bundesregierung in sorgfältiger und geduldiger Beobachtung der internationalen Situation und ihrer Fortentwicklung Schritt um Schritt das zerstörte Vertrauen der Welt zu Deutschland wiederherstellen und die innere und äußere Stellung der Bundesrepublik auf allen Gebieten festigen konnte.

Der große und berechtigte Stolz auf das Erreichte ist nicht ungetrübt. Das freie, gesicherte Leben der Deutschen in der Bundesrepublik ist überschattet von dem ungelösten Problem der Wiedervereinigung. Das Land Berlin ist bedroht, ein Drittel des deutschen Volkes der Bestimmung über das eigene Schicksal beraubt. Die friedliche Wiedervereinigung in Freiheit ist das Ziel der Deutschen diesseits und jenseits des Eisernen Vorhangs.

ZUM GELEIT

Am 20. September 1959 jährt sich zum zehnten Mal der Tag, an dem mit der Bildung der Bundesregierung die Bundesrepublik Deutschland handlungsfähig wurde. Wenig mehr als vier Jahre nach dem Zusammenbruch der nationalsozialistischen Gewaltherrschaft haben die Westmächte damit die von ihnen im Jahre 1945 übernommene Oberste Staatsgewalt wieder in deutsche Hände gelegt.

Unter dem Zwang der weltpolitischen Verhältnisse mußte die staatliche Neuordnung auf den größeren Teil des Gebietes des Deutschen Reiches beschränkt bleiben. Der Eiserne Vorhang, das Symbol der Spaltung der Welt, durchschneidet das Reichsgebiet; Freiheit und demokratische Ordnung sind den Deutschen außerhalb der Bundesrepublik bis heute versagt worden.

Die Bundesregierung legt zum zehnjährigen Bestehen der Bundesrepublik Deutschland dieses Buch der Öffentlichkeit im Inland und Ausland vor. Es gibt Kunde davon, was der Fleiß und Arbeitswille des ganzen deutschen Volkes in den Gemeinden und Ländern auf allen Gebieten der Wirtschaft und des sozialen und kulturellen Lebens geleistet haben, um Deutschland einen ehrenvollen Platz als einem Glied mit gleichen Pflichten und gleichen Rechten in der Gemeinschaft der Völker zurückzugewinnen. In diesem Werk ist aber auch nachzulesen, wie die Bundesregierung in sorgfältiger und geduldiger Beobachtung der internationalen Situation und ihrer Fortentwicklung Schritt um Schritt das zerstörte Vertrauen der Welt zu Deutschland wiederherstellen und die innere und äußere Stellung der Bundesrepublik auf allen Gebieten festigen konnte.

Der große und berechtigte Stolz auf das Erreichte ist nicht ungetrübt. Das freie, gesicherte Leben der Deutschen in der Bundesrepublik ist überschattet von dem ungelösten Problem der Wiedervereinigung. Das Land Berlin ist bedroht, ein Drittel des deutschen Volkes der Bestimmung über das eigene Schicksal beraubt. Die friedliche Wiedervereinigung in Freiheit ist das Ziel der Deutschen diesseits und jenseits des Eisernen Vorhangs.

DEUTSCHLAND HEUTE

Germania est omnis divisa
in partes sex

(vide p. 21 sq.)

VORWORT

Die Regierung der Bundesrepublik Deutschland hat in diesem Buch den Ablauf der Jahre seit der Katastrophe des Jahres 1945 festgehalten. Sie wendet sich damit an das deutsche Volk, dessen schwere Arbeit, gelenkt durch planvolle Führung, in wenigen Jahren einen so staunenswerten Aufschwung ermöglicht hat.

Die Bundesregierung wendet sich aber zugleich an das Ausland, das diesem schnellen Aufstieg verständlicherweise zweifelnd und vielfach besorgt gegenübersteht. Durch eine nüchterne Darstellung der Tatsachen soll dem ausländischen Leser die Möglichkeit geboten werden, die einzelnen Stufen dieses Weges nachzuprüfen nnd mitzuerleben. Dadurch wird sich die Einsicht vertiefen, daß es in diesem wunderbaren Geschehen kein „deutsches Wunder" gibt, sondern nur das harte Ringen eines ganzen Volkes: zuerst um die schlichte Behauptung seiner Existenz; sodann um internationale Kreditwürdigkeit, moralische Geltung in der Welt — und um Vertrauen von Mensch zu Mensch, von Volk zu Volk.

Der ausländische Leser wird auch die offenen Fragen, die ungelösten Probleme mit gleicher Offenheit dargelegt finden. Er wird sehen, daß manches Ziel nicht erreicht wurde, vor allem das am heißesten begehrte: die Wiedervereinigung. Er wird empfinden, was dieses Werk zum Ausdruck bringen möchte: daß Deutschland weder auf sich allein gestellt sein möchte noch sein kann, sondern daß es jetzt und in Zukunft der Freien Welt bedarf, in deren Gemeinschaft es sich seit 1945 als ein gleichberechtigtes Glied aufs neue eingefügt hat.

Felix von Eckardt
Bundespressechef

VORBEMERKUNG

Das „*Deutschlandbuch der Bundesregierung*" ist von 1953 bis 1957 in zusammen fünfzehn Auflagen in sechs Sprachen erschienen. Diese neue Ausgabe wird zunächst in deutscher, englischer, französischer und spanischer Sprache veröffentlicht. Sie ist auf den neuesten Stand gebracht und vor allem, den vielfachen Wünschen von Benutzern entsprechend, erheblich erweitert worden. Das trifft in besonderem Maße für den Sozialteil zu. Der Umfang hat sich gegenüber der ersten Auflage mehr als verdoppelt.

Es ist deshalb nicht damit zu rechnen, daß dieses viel benutzte Buch noch zahlreiche „Leser" findet, sondern es will in seiner neuen Gestalt *vor allem ein Nachschlagewerk* sein. Daher wurden die für das Verständnis notwendigen Überschneidungen und Wiederholungen absichtlich beibehalten. Um so ausführlicher mußte das Register gestaltet, und es mußte vornehmlich auf Ausländer abgestellt werden, die den größten Teil der Benutzer ausmachen.

Um der ausländischen Leser willen wurden auch Abkürzungen fast ausnahmslos ebenso wie die im Schriftdeutschen üblichen langen Sätze aufgelöst. Ich danke den Autoren dafür, daß sie nicht nur den Veränderungen zugestimmt haben, die zur inhaltlichen Abstimmung der Beiträge notwendig waren, sondern auch den teilweise weitgehenden Eingriffen in ihren Stil.

Gegenstand des Buches ist die Entwicklung der Teile des Deutschen Reiches seit 1945. Da auf vielen Gebieten zuverlässige Unterlagen nur aus der Bundesrepublik zur Verfügung stehen, und weil eine noch eingehendere Darstellung der Verhältnisse in den übrigen Teilen des deutschen Staatsgebietes den Umfang eines Bandes gesprengt haben würde, repräsentiert die Bundesrepublik in diesem Werk, wie es der politischen Wirklichkeit entspricht, weitgehend auch die übrigen Teile Deutschlands.

Das Deutschlandbuch ist eine Gemeinschaftsarbeit, an der fast sämtliche Ressorts des Bundes und viele private Mitarbeiter beteiligt sind. Die Autoren sind auf den Seiten 838 und 839 genannt. Es ist dem Redactor ein Bedürfnis, außer ihnen auch den zahlreichen nicht genannten Persönlichkeiten zu danken, die durch einzelne Hinweise und Auskünfte die Darstellung in hohem Maße bereichert haben.

Der Druck dieses Buches wurde am 11. August 1959 abgeschlossen — an dem Tage, an dem vor vierzig Jahren die Weimarer Reichsverfassung mit der Unterschrift FRIEDRICH EBERTs in Kraft trat.

HELMUT ARNTZ

INHALTSVERZEICHNIS

Wirtschaft

Soziales Leben

Kultur

LECTORI BENEVOLENTI

Das Statistische Bundesamt hat außer den Tabellen alle im Text enthaltenen Zahlen geprüft und die letzten statistischen Ergebnisse eingetragen. Soweit als möglich beziehen sich die Zahlen auf das Jahr 1958 beziehungsweise den 1. 1. 1959. Wo ältere Zahlen angegeben sind — wie zum Beispiel die der Volkszählung 1950 — liegen keine neuen statistischen Unterlagen vor. Auf die Zeit vor 1945 konnte nur zurückgegriffen werden, wo das Verständnis der Gegenwart es erheischte.

Die Bundesregierung hat die Absicht, diese *zeitgeschichtliche Dokumentation über Deutschland* auf dem neuesten Stand zu halten. Der Redactor bittet daher alle Benutzer darum, *Anregungen, Verbesserungen und Ergänzungen* zu seinen Händen dem Presse- und Informationsamt der Bundesregierung, Bonn, Welckerstraße 11, mitzuteilen.

GRUNDLAGEN

LANDSCHAFT, KLIMA, BODENSCHÄTZE

Deutschland in den Grenzen von 1937 nimmt nach seiner Oberfläche etwa den zehnten Teil Europas (ohne das europäische Rußland) ein, dessen drittgrößtes Land es ist. Ein größeres Staatsgebiet haben Frankreich und Spanien. In der Zahl der Einwohner wird Deutschland nur vom europäischen Teil der Sowjetunion übertroffen.

Deutschlands Nachbarländer sind im Westen (von Norden nach Süden) die Niederlande, Belgien, Luxemburg und Frankreich, im Süden die Schweiz und Österreich, im Osten die Tschechoslowakei, Polen, die Freie Stadt Danzig und Litauen, das seit 1940 der Sowjetunion einverleibt ist; im Norden Dänemark. Deutschland liegt zwischen dem 47. und 55. Grad nördlicher Breite sowie dem 6. und 23. Grad östlicher Länge. Die Nordgrenze Schleswig-Holsteins liegt also ungefähr auf der Breite Moskaus, Kamtschatkas und Labradors, die Südgrenze Bayerns auf der von Rostow, Charbin, Quebec oder Seattle.

Von der Nord- und Ostsee im Norden bis zu den Alpen im Süden, vom Rheinischen Schiefergebirge im Westen bis zur Ostpreußischen Seenplatte und dem Schlesischen Bergland im Osten gliedert Deutschland sich geographisch in fünf Großlandschaften:

das Norddeutsche Tiefland,
die Mittelgebirgsschwelle,
das West- und Süddeutsche Stufen- und Bergland,
das Süddeutsche Alpenvorland und
das Bayerische Alpenland.

Das Norddeutsche Tiefland südlich der Nord- und Ostseeküste mit den vorgelagerten Inseln ist die Fortsetzung des flandrischen Tieflandes und geht, sich allmählich verbreiternd, in das osteuropäische über. Es erreicht nur vereinzelt Höhen von 200 bis wenig über 300 m. Durch seenreiche, hügelige Geest- und Lehmplatten, dic im Nordwesten von Heiden und Mooren durchsetzt sind, und durch breite feuchte Niederungen ist es reich gegliedert. Fruchtbare Lößgefilde lagern sich vor dem Fuß der Mittelgebirgsschwelle, in die klimatisch begünstigte Tieflandbuchten südwärts tief eingreifen: die Kölner, Münsterer, Sächsisch-Thüringische und Schlesische Bucht. Im

Norden des Tieflandes hat Deutschland Anteil an den Marschen der Nordseeküste, die bis zum Geest-Steilrand reichen, sowie an der Ostseeküste. Diese ist im Westen durch Förden reich gegliedert; im Osten nimmt sie den Charakter einer Ausgleichsküste an. Die wichtigsten Inseln in der Ostsee sind Rügen, Usedom und Wollin, in der Nordsee die Ostfriesischen (unter anderen Borkum, Norderney) und Nordfriesischen Inseln (mit Helgoland, Amrum, Föhr, Sylt und den Halligen).

Die Mittelgebirgsschwelle ist von großer Mannigfaltigkeit. In ihr lassen sich mehrere geologisch-tektonische Zonen unterscheiden. Zur vorwiegend aus devonischen und unterkarbonischen Gesteinen aufgebauten Außenzone gehören unter anderen das Rheinische Schiefergebirge (Hauptteile: Hunsrück, Eifel, Hohes Venn, Taunus [880 m], Westerwald, Rothaargebirge) und, weiter ostwärts, die paläozoische Gebirgsinsel des Harz, die sich im Granitgebiet des Brocken bis 1.142 m heraushebt. Zur sogenannten saxo-thuringischen Zone rechnen der kristalline Teil des Odenwalds und Spessarts, der Thüringer Wald (982 m) und schließlich die Keilscholle des Erzgebirges (1.243 m). Die höchsten Erhebungen liegen allerdings in der „Zentralzone", dem Oberrheinischen Gebirgssystem (Vogesen und Schwarzwald, 1.493 m) sowie den Sudeten, die im Riesengebirge eine Höhe von 1.603 m (Schneekoppe) erreichen.

Zum West- und Süddeutschen Stufen- und Bergland gehören die Oberrheinische Tiefebene mit ihren Randgebirgen (Schwarzwald, Odenwald und Haardt), das Schwäbisch-Fränkische Stufenland mit der hochgelegenen Alb und der Bayerische Wald. Die höchste Erhebung liegt hier im südlichen Schwarzwald (Feldberg 1.495 m).

Das den Alpen breit vorgelagerte Süddeutsche Alpenvorland, die Schwäbisch-Bayerische Hochebene mit ihren flachwelligen Hügeln und ebenen Schotterflächen, hat eine mittlere Höhe von 500 m. Über tertiären Sedimenten liegen hier mehr oder weniger mächtig die von den in das Vorland hinausgequollenen diluvialen Alpengletschern und ihren Schmelzwassern abgelagerten Bildungen, das heißt Moränen und Schotter. Dazu kommt in den nördlichen Randzonen auch Löß.

Der Alpenanteil umfaßt nur einen schmalen Ausschnitt dieses jungen Faltengebirgs-Systems, dessen Bau im einzelnen sehr verwickelt ist. Auf eine Voralpenzone aus Sandsteinen folgen die zu den nördlichen Kalkalpen gehörenden Ketten, darunter die zwischen Oberrhein und Lech gelegenen Allgäuer Hochalpen (Großer Krottenkopf 2.657 m, Mädelegabel 2.645 m, Hochvogel 2.593 m), die reich an Wäldern und Wiesen sind, die sogenannten

Bayerischen Alpen zwischen Fernpaß und Inn mit dem wilden Wettersteingebirge (Zugspitze 2.963 m) und den zahlreichen, malerischen Gebirgsseen (Walchensee, Kochelsee, Tegernsee), und schließlich eindrucksvolle Glieder der Salzburger Kalkalpen im Berchtesgadener Ländchen (Watzmann 2.713 m, Königssee).

GEOGRAPHISCHE ANGABEN

Rhein (abwärts Konstanz)	865 km
Oder (bis Swinemünde)	761 km
Elbe	761 km
Donau (bis Passau)	647 km
Mittellandkanal (von der Ems bis zur Elbe)	325 km
Mittellandkanal (innerhalb der Bundesrepublik)	259 km
Zugspitztunnel	4.400 m
Zugspitze	2.963 m
Watzmann	2.713 m
Brocken (Harz)	1.142 m
Schneekoppe (Riesengebirge)	1.603 m
Großer Arber (Bayerischer Wald)	1.456 m
Fichtelberg (Erzgebirge)	1.214 m
Saaletalsperre (Bleiloch)	215 Mill. cbm
Edertalsperre (Edersee)	202 Mill. cbm
Bodensee (Gesamtfläche)	539 qkm
Bodensee (deutscher Anteil)	305 qkm
Insel Rügen	926 qkm
Insel Usedom	445 qkm
Insel Wollin	248 qkm
Insel Fehmarn	185 qkm

Quelle: Bundesanstalt für Landeskunde.

*

Das Gebiet des Deutschen Reiches ist aus Gründen, die in den folgenden Kapiteln dargelegt werden, derzeit kein Staatsgebiet unter einheitlicher Regierung. Die *Bundesrepublik Deutschland*, im Westen Deutschlands gelegen, umfaßt mit ihren zehn westlichen Ländern von Norden nach Süden Teile aller fünf Großlandschaften. Im Norddeutschen Tiefland liegen die Länder *Schleswig-Holstein*, *Hamburg*, *Bremen*, der größte Teil *Niedersachsens* und ein Teil *Nordrhein-Westfalens*. Die beiden letztgenannten setzen sich in die Mittelgebirgsschwelle fort, der auch die Länder *Rheinland-Pfalz*, *Saarland* und *Hessen* angehören, soweit diese nicht in das West- und Süddeutsche Stufen- und Bergland hineinreichen. In diesem und dem Süddeutschen Alpenvorland liegen die Länder *Baden-Württemberg* und *Bayern*. Am Alpenland hat allein Bayern Anteil.

EUROPA IN DEN GRENZEN VON 1937

Berlin, die Hauptstadt des Deutschen Reiches, liegt mit seinen beiden Teilen, *Berlin(West)*, das nach dem Grundgesetz ein Land der Bundesrepublik ist, und *Ostberlin*, jenseits der Elbe im Übergang vom westlichen zum östlichen Teil des Norddeutschen Tieflandes.

Die sogenannte *Deutsche Demokratische Republik* (DDR; früher: Sowjetische Besatzungszone) begrenzt die Bundesrepublik im Osten. Sie liegt im Mittelstück des Norddeutschen Tieflands; mit ihrem Südteil ragt sie in die

DAS GEBIET DES DEUTSCHEN REICHES
in den Grenzen vom 31. Dezember 1937 nach dem Stand vom 31. Dezember 1958[1]

[1] Die punktierten Linien im Gebiet der Bundesrepublik geben die Grenzen der 1945 gebildeten Besatzungszonen an.

BERLIN
(Berlin [West]
und Ostberlin)

Mittelgebirgsschwelle hinein. Ihr schließen sich ostwärts von Oder und Neiße, im Norden von der Ostsee, im Süden von den Sudeten flankiert, die zur Zeit unter fremder Verwaltung stehenden *Ostgebiete des Deutschen Reiches* (Stand vom 31. 12. 1937) an. Zu ihnen gehört neben Ostpommern,

Ostbrandenburg und Schlesien auch Ostpreußen, das nach dem Ersten Weltkrieg durch eine Landverbindung Polens zur Ostsee und zur Freien Stadt Danzig, den „Polnischen Korridor", vom übrigen Reichsgebiet getrennt wurde.

*

Deutschlands Klima ist durch seine Lage in der gemäßigten Zone mit ihrem häufigen Wetterwechsel bestimmt. Winde aus vorwiegend westlichen Richtungen und Niederschläge zu allen Jahreszeiten sind für dieses Klima charakteristisch. Die jährlichen Niederschlagsmengen betragen im Norddeutschen Flachland unter 500 bis über 700 mm, in den deutschen Mittelgebirgen um 700 bis über 1.000 mm und in den deutschen Alpen bis über 2.000 mm. Vom Nordwesten nach Osten und Südosten fortschreitend macht sich ein allmählicher Übergang vom mehr ozeanischen zum stärker festländischen Klima bemerkbar. Die Tagesschwankungen wie auch die jahreszeitlichen Temperaturunterschiede sind in Deutschland nirgendwo extrem. Die Durchschnittstemperaturen des Januars – des im statistischen Mittel kältesten Monats im Jahr – liegen im Flachland um +1,5° bis −3°C; in den Gebirgen erreichen sie je nach der Höhenlage bis unter −6°C. Im Hochsommer betragen die mittleren Julitemperaturen im Norddeutschen Tiefland 16 bis 19°C, in geschützten Tälern des Berglandes bis zu 20°C. Die durchschnittliche Jahrestemperatur liegt bei 9°C. Die wärmsten Temperaturen kommen in der Oberrheinischen Tiefebene vor. Die höheren deutschen Gebirge vom Harz bis zu den Alpen tragen mindestens von Januar bis März eine Schneedecke, die in schneereichen Wintern in über 500 m Meereshöhe einen Meter, über 1.000 m zwei Meter mächtig werden kann.

Der Süden Deutschlands gehört durch die Donau teilweise zum Einzugsgebiet des Schwarzen Meeres. Alle übrigen Landschaften werden durch Rhein, Ems, Weser und Elbe zur Nordsee und durch Oder und Weichsel zur Ostsee entwässert.

*

Das Bild der Landschaft wird weitgehend durch den *Wald* geprägt. Etwa 7 Millionen Hektar oder 28,7% der Gesamtfläche der Bundesrepublik sind mit Wald bestanden. Bei Kriegsende machte die Waldfläche in den Ostgebieten des Deutschen Reiches und in der sogenannten DDR je 2,95 Millionen Hektar aus.

In der Bundesrepublik entfallen auf den Staatswald etwa 31% und den Kommunalwald etwa 27%. In Privatbesitz sind etwa 42%. Landwirtschaft und Forstwirtschaft sind eng miteinander verflochten: von insgesamt 2.011.992 land- und forstwirtschaftlichen Betrieben mit einer Betriebsfläche

(Gesamtfläche) von 21.979.000 Hektar haben 701.231 Waldbesitz von zusammen 6,9 Millionen Hektar.

Nach den Holzarten entfallen auf die Eiche 11%, auf die Buche und anderes Laubholz 25%, auf Kiefer und Lärche 24% und auf die Fichte 40%. In Gebirgsregionen herrscht heute die Fichte; sandige Böden sind weitgehend mit Kiefern und Lärchen bestanden. Der Nadelwald hat durch die Forstwirtschaft seinen Umfang in den letzten hundertfünfzig Jahren stark vergrößert. Von Natur aus war im Westen einst, vornehmlich in den Mittellagen, der Laubwald – besonders die Buche – vorherrschend.

Die Forstwirtschaft Deutschlands ist seit über hundert Jahren hochentwickelt und wird intensiv betrieben. Unterschiede von Standort und Klima, und dadurch bedingt der Wechsel der Holzarten auf kleinem Raum, ergeben eine große Vielseitigkeit. Die gesunde Mischung der Besitzarten trägt zur Vielgestaltigkeit bei.

*

Deutschland ist in erster Linie *ein Industriestaat*, der sich auf die Be- und Verarbeitung der einheimischen Rohstoffe und eingeführter Grundstoffe stützt. Als Kohlenproduzent gehört Deutschland zur Spitzengruppe. Hauptindustriezweige sind nach wie vor Eisen- und Metallwarenindustrie sowie Maschinen- und Fahrzeugherstellung, die elektrotechnische Industrie, Textilindustrie und Bekleidungsgewerbe, Feinmechanik und Optik, Leder- und Papierindustrie, Papierherstellung und graphisches Gewerbe, Glas-, Porzellan- und Spielzeugfabrikation und eine sehr vielseitige Ernährungsindustrie. Neben der Industrie hat ein starkes *Handwerk* sich erhalten und weiterentwickelt. *Die Landwirtschaft* findet nur teilweise günstige natürliche Bedingungen; angebaut werden vor allem Roggen, Weizen, Gerste, Kartoffeln, Zuckerrüben und Gemüse. Örtlich sind Wein- und Obstbau von großer Bedeutung. Außerdem sind Kulturen von Hülsenfrüchten, Hanf, Flachs und Ölsaaten zu nennen. Viehzucht und Milchwirtschaft sind hoch entwickelt, bedürfen aber der Einfuhr von Kraftfutter. Waldwirtschaft und Fischerei sind weitere wichtige Erwerbsquellen. *Das Verkehrsnetz* gehört zu den besten und dichtesten Verkehrseinrichtungen Europas.

*

Mit *Bodenschätzen* ist Deutschland durchschnittlich bedacht. Im Norddeutschen Tiefland haben die Erdöllager im Nordwesten Bedeutung. Mit einer Jahresförderung von 4,4 Millionen t (1958) decken sie nahezu die Hälfte des Inlandbedarfs an Rohöl. Bis 1960 soll die Produktion bis auf

4,5 Millionen t gesteigert werden. Die Vorräte im Emsland, nördlich von Hannover und an der Küste Schleswig-Holsteins werden auf 59 Millionen t geschätzt.

Im Süden des Tieflandes am Fuß der Mittelgebirge (westlich von Köln, in Mitteldeutschland und in der Lausitz, in geringem Umfang auch in der Hessischen Senke und in Bayern) finden sich große Braunkohlenlager bis zu 100 m Mächtigkeit. Sie können meist im Tagebau abgebaut werden. Die Vorkommen im Bundesgebiet, soweit Abbau über Tage möglich ist, werden mit 5 Milliarden t angenommen. Das wäre ein Vorrat für etwa 70 Jahre. Gefördert wurden in der Bundesrepublik 1958: 93 Millionen t. Weit wichtiger noch sind die Steinkohlenvorkommen des Aachener Reviers, des Ruhrgebiets, des Saarreviers, der Zwickauer Mulde, des Waldenburger Reviers und Oberschlesiens. Die Vorkommen des Ruhrgebiets werden auf 50 Milliarden t geschätzt. Sie würden, wenn der heutige Verbrauch anhielte, über 400 Jahre reichen. Die Flöze gehen oft in eine Tiefe bis zu 1.000 m. Gefördert wurden 1958: 149 Millionen t Steinkohle im Bundesgebiet (einschließlich Saarlands) sowie angeblich 76 Millionen t in dem zur Zeit unter polnischer Verwaltung stehenden schlesischen Revier.

An der Gewinnung von Energie (Strom und Gas) im Bundesgebiet ist die Kohle mit etwa 84% in überragendem Ausmaß beteiligt. 42% der Stromerzeugung in Kraftwerken für die öffentliche Versorgung werden aus Steinkohlen und 37% aus Braunkohlen gewonnen. Der Steinkohlenverbrauch in Elektrizitäts- und Gaswerken beträgt fast ein Drittel des Gesamtverbrauchs.

Von entscheidender Bedeutung für die Landwirtschaft sind die Kalisalze. Die Vorkommen werden auf 2 Milliarden t Reinkali geschätzt. Das Deutsche Reich war vor dem Ersten Weltkrieg mit 96% der Weltgewinnung an Kalisalzen führend. Der Bundesrepublik sind nur noch die Vorkommen in Niedersachsen, Hessen und Baden verblieben. Die Förderung von über 16 Millionen t (2,0 Millionen t K_2O-Inhalt) im Jahre 1958 macht ein Viertel der Welterzeugung aus. Die Eisenerzvorkommen an Lahn, Sieg, Dill, im Jura und im Harzvorland (Salzgitter-Gebiet) enthalten etwa 3 Milliarden t; aber ihr Erz ist meist nicht hochwertig. Die Förderung von 18 Millionen t (4,7 Millionen t Fe-Inhalt) im Jahre 1958 deckt den eigenen Bedarf nur zu etwa 40%. Bei der Blei- und Zinkerzeugung ist die Eigenversorgung etwas günstiger.

Die beachtlichen Wasserkräfte werden besonders in Süddeutschland weitgehend der Licht- und Kraftgewinnung nutzbar gemacht. Die Stromerzeugung aus Wasserkraft betrug im Jahre 1957 fast 11,5 Milliarden Kilowattstunden.

FLÄCHE UND BEVÖLKERUNG

Im Jahre 1939 lebten im Gebiet der Bundesrepublik (einschließlich Saarlands) 58% der Reichsbevölkerung, die 69 Millionen betrug; hier entstanden etwa 59% des deutschen Sozialprodukts. Der Anteil der Landwirtschaft war in diesen Gebieten jedoch wesentlich geringer. Die Bevölkerung dieses Gebietes hat von 1939 bis Ende 1958 um mehr als 12 Millionen zugenommen, so daß die Bevölkerungsdichte je Quadratkilometer (km^2) von 173 auf 212 Einwohner angestiegen ist.

In der gleichen Zeit hat die Einwohnerzahl je Quadratkilometer landwirtschaftlicher Nutzfläche im Bundesgebiet eine Steigerung um 34% (von 273 auf 365 Personen) und gegenüber dem Deutschen Reich eine Steigerung um 50% (von 243 auf 365 Personen) erfahren. Der Selbstversorgungsgrad war von 80% vor dem Kriege auf 66% im Jahre 1950 abgesunken. Inzwischen liegt er fast wieder auf der Vorkriegshöhe.

*

Die Bundesrepublik[1] hat eine Fläche von 247.971 Quadratkilometern. Ihre längste Ausdehnung von Norden nach Süden mißt 832 Kilometer, von Osten nach Westen 453 Kilometer. Das Deutsche Reich umfaßt in seinen Grenzen von 1937: 470.700 Quadratkilometer und mißt fast 1.200 Kilometer von Osten nach Westen. Auf die Ostgebiete des Deutschen Reiches, die zur Zeit unter fremder Verwaltung stehen, entfallen rund 114.000, auf die mitteldeutschen Provinzen (die sogenannte DDR einschließlich Ostberlins) 108.000 Quadratkilometer. Berlin(West) mißt 481 Quadratkilometer.

Durch Maßnahmen der Siegermächte nach der Kapitulation der Wehrmacht, die am 8.5.1945 den Zweiten Weltkrieg beendete, ist das Gebiet des Deutschen Reiches gegenwärtig in sechs Teile zerstückelt:

1. Die 1949 aus der Britischen, Amerikanischen und Französischen Besatzungszone gebildete *Bundesrepublik Deutschland*, der am 1.1.1957 *Saarland* sich (zunächst politisch) anschloß.

1939: 40,25 Millionen Einwohner; 247.971 Quadratkilometer.

2. *Berlin(West)*, das zwar ein Land der Bundesrepublik ist, in dem aber die Anwendung des Grundgesetzes derzeit noch gewissen Beschränkungen unterliegt.

1939: 2,75 Millionen Einwohner; 481 Quadratkilometer.

[1] Ohne Berlin(West).

3. Die ursprüngliche Sowjetische Besatzungszone (die *sogenannte „Deutsche Demokratische Republik“*).

1939: 15,1 Millionen Einwohner; 107.431 Quadratkilometer.

4. *Ostberlin*, das zwar praktisch zur sogenannten DDR gehört, aber mit Rücksicht auf die internationalen Abmachungen, die den Viermächtestatus von Berlin betreffen, nach außen eine gewisse Sonderstellung hat.

1939: 1,59 Millionen Einwohner; 403 Quadratkilometer.

5. *Die Gebiete östlich der Oder und Neiße* (ohne den Nordteil Ostpreußens), die nach dem Potsdamer Abkommen vom 2. 8. 1945 „bis zur endgültigen Festlegung der Westgrenze Polens ... unter die Verwaltung des polnischen Staates“ gestellt worden sind, von Polen aber — nach der Austreibung der deutschen Bevölkerung — als ein Teil seines Staatsgebietes behandelt werden.

1939: 8,46 Millionen Einwohner; 101.092 Quadratkilometer.

6. *Das nördliche Ostpreußen.* Dieses Gebiet steht nach den Bestimmungen des Potsdamer Abkommens unter sowjetischer Verwaltung, ohne indessen seit 1945 zur Sowjetischen Besatzungszone zu gehören, und wird von der Sowjetunion — nach der Austreibung der deutschen Bevölkerung — als ein Teil ihres Staatsgebietes behandelt.

1939: 1,16 Millionen Einwohner; 13.204 Quadratkilometer.

DEUTSCHES REICHSGEBIET
in den Grenzen vom 31. 12. 1937[1]

Aufteilung nach dem Vorkriegsstand des Jahres 1939	Bevölkerung %	Fläche %	Einwohner je qkm
Bundesrepublik mit Berlin(West)	*62,0*	*25,8*	173
sogenannte „Deutsche Demokratische Republik“ mit Ostberlin	*24,1*	*23,0*	154
Ostgebiete des Deutschen Reiches unter fremder Verwaltung	*13,9*	*24,3*	84
Reichsgebiet	*100*	*100*	147

[1] Nach den Ergebnissen der Volkszählung vom 17. 5. 1939.

Quelle: Statistisches Bundesamt.

*

Die Bevölkerung der Bundesrepublik[1], deren Gebiet vor rund 150 Jahren 13,5 Millionen Einwohner zählte, hat Anfang 1955 die 50 Millionen

[1] Einschließlich Saarlands, ohne Berlin(West).

ALTER UND FAMILIENSTAND DER BEVÖLKERUNG DER BUNDESREPUBLIK DEUTSCHLAND[1]

Endgültiges Ergebnis der Volkszählung vom 13. September 1950

Bevölkerung der USA 1950 (zum Vergleich) Altersjahre

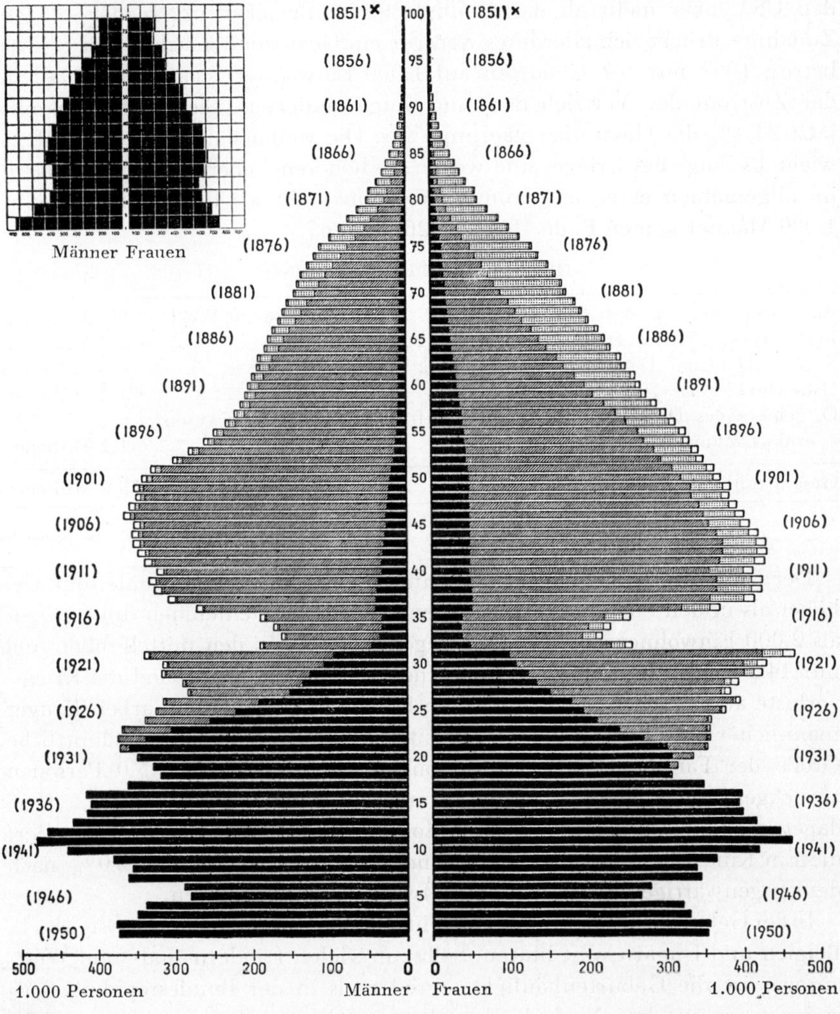

Ledige
Verheiratete
Verwitwete
Geschiedene

[1] Ohne Ausländer in IRO-Lagern. × Die in Klammern ( ) angegebenen Geburtsjahre sind nur als Hinweis zu werten, da Alters- und Geburtsjahre am 13. September nicht genau übereinstimmen.

Quelle: Statistisches Bundesamt.

überschritten und zählt heute bereits 52,5 Milionen Einwohner. Die Bundesrepublik hat also zwar dieselbe Flächenausdehnung wie der Staat Oregon in den USA, aber mehr als das dreißigfache an Bevölkerung. In der starken Zunahme drückt sich allerdings weniger ein Geburtenüberschuß aus (dieser betrug 1957 nur 5,7 Geburten auf 1.000 Einwohner), sondern vor allem der Zustrom der Vertriebenen und Zugewanderten. Sie machen bereits jetzt 24,4% der Gesamtbevölkerung[1] aus. Die weibliche Bevölkerung überwiegt als Folge des Krieges und wegen des höheren Lebensalters, das Frauen im allgemeinen erreichen, immer noch um mehr als drei Millionen. Auf 1.000 Männer kamen Ende 1958: 1.126 Frauen[2].

DIE DEUTSCHE BEVÖLKERUNG

Bundesrepublik (einschl. Saarlands, 31. 12. 1958; ohne Berlin[West])	52,5 Millionen
Berlin(West) (31. 12. 1958)	2,2 Millionen
Sogen. ,,Deutsche Demokratische Republik" (31.12.1957)	16,3 Millionen
Ostberlin (31. 12. 1957)	1,1 Millionen
Ostgebiete des Deutschen Reiches unter fremder Verwaltung (nicht exakt nachprüfbar)	1,1 Millionen
Gesamtzahl (teilweise geschätzt)	73,2 Millionen

Quelle: Statistisches Bundesamt.

Der Geburtenzuwachs ist in der Bundesrepublik auf dem Lande sehr viel höher als in den Städten. Die Geburtenziffer in den Gemeinden mit weniger als 2.000 Einwohnern beträgt 20,1 gegenüber 17,2 in den mittelgroßen und nur 14,2 in den Großstädten. Durch den Geburtenzuwachs sind die Kriegsverluste ausgeglichen; er hat aber die Einbußen vor allem an arbeitsfähiger männlicher Bevölkerung nicht zu beseitigen vermocht. Die durchschnittliche Größe der Familie (1871: 4,6 Personen) war bis 1956 auf 3,0 Personen zurückgegangen. Von den Haushaltungen bestanden 1933: 8,4%, 1956 dagegen 18,2% aus einer einzigen Person. Seit fast einem Jahrzehnt dominiert die Ein-Kind-Ehe. Drei und mehr Kinder hatten um 1860 rund 70%, nach dem gegenwärtigen Stand nur noch etwa 30% aller Familien.

In der Geburtenstatistik der Welt steht die Bundesrepublik neben Österreich, Belgien und Ungarn weit hinten. Selbst in vielen Ländern Süd- und Westeuropas ist die Geburtenhäufigkeit größer als in der Bundesrepublik, teilweise — so in den Niederlanden, Frankreich und Italien — sogar sehr

[1] Ohne Saarland.

[2] Von 52.492.500 Bundesbürgern am 31.12.1958 waren 27.807.500 weiblichen Geschlechts.

BEVÖLKERUNGSSTAND UND -VERÄNDERUNG [1]

Bevölkerungsstand [1]

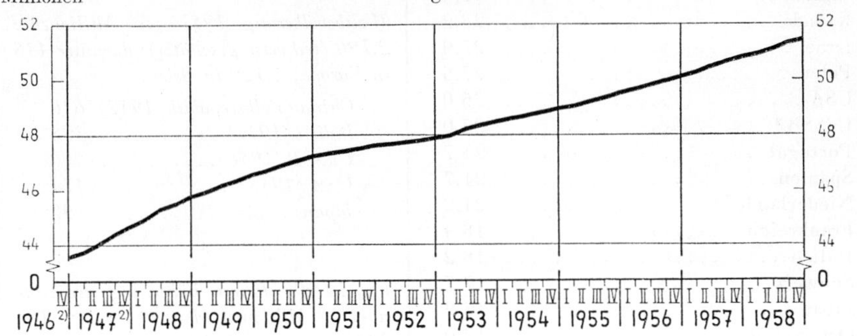

Bevölkerungszunahme
Geburten- und Wanderungsüberschuß

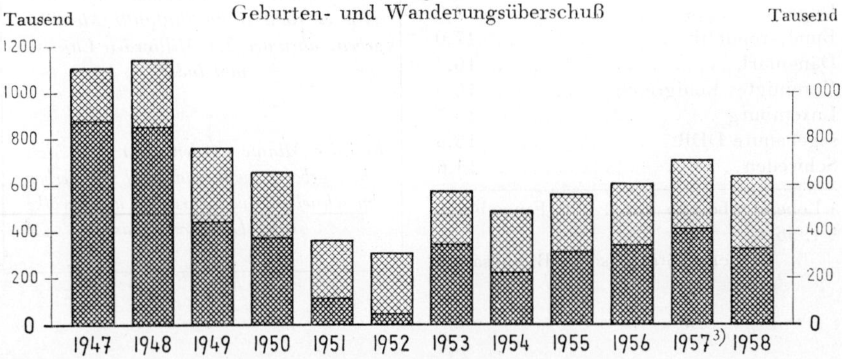

Zuzüge aus Berlin und der sogenannten DDR
sowie aus den deutschen Ostgebieten [4]

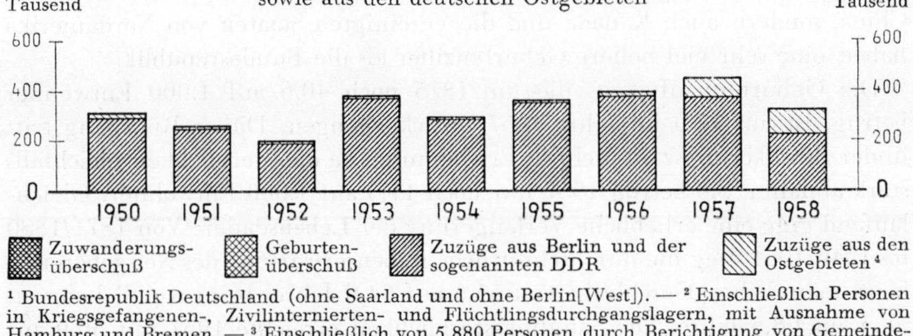

[1] Bundesrepublik Deutschland (ohne Saarland und ohne Berlin[West]). — [2] Einschließlich Personen in Kriegsgefangenen-, Zivilinternierten- und Flüchtlingsdurchgangslagern, mit Ausnahme von Hamburg und Bremen. — [3] Einschließlich von 5.880 Personen durch Berichtigung von Gemeindeergebnissen. — [4] Ostgebiete des Deutschen Reiches, zur Zeit unter fremder Verwaltung (Gebietsstand 31. 12. 1937).

Quelle: Statistisches Bundesamt.

GEBURTEN 1957[1]

China	41,5
Kanada	28,2
Israel	27,9
Polen	27,5
USA	25,0
UdSSR[2]	25,0
Portugal	23,7
Spanien	21,7
Niederlande	21,2
Frankreich	18,4
Italien	18,2
Schweiz	17,7
Japan	17,2
Österreich	17,0
Belgien	17,0
Ungarn	17,0
Bundesrepublik	17,0
Dänemark	16,7
Vereinigtes Königreich	16,5
Luxemburg	15,7
sogenannte DDR	15,6
Schweden	14,6

[1] Lebendgeborene auf 1.000 Einwohner.
[2] 1956.

Quelle: Statistisches Bundesamt.

Weltbevölkerung 1957 (in Millionen): 2.790 (teilweise geschätzt); darunter 438 in Europa, 1.529 in Asien.

China (Volksrepublik, 1957)	*640*
Indien (1957)	*388*
UdSSR (1956)	*200*
USA (1958)	*174*
Japan	*92*

*

Vor 10.000 Jahren haben auf der Erde rund 10 Millionen Menschen gelebt. Um 800 waren es 600 Millionen, um 1850: 1.250 Millionen. Um das Jahr 2000 wird es rund 6.000.000.000 Menschen geben, darunter 2,5 Milliarden Chinesen und Inder.

*

In jeder Minute werden etwa 170 Menschen geboren, während rund 90 sterben. Am schnellsten vermehrt sich die Bevölkerung Lateinamerikas.

erheblich; bei einigen ist auch die Sterblichkeit geringer. Noch ausgeprägter ist der Unterschied gegenüber wichtigen überseeischen Ländern. Nicht nur China, sondern auch Kanada und die Vereinigten Staaten von Nordamerika haben eine sehr viel höhere Geburtenziffer als die Bundesrepublik.

Die Geburtenhäufigkeit, die um 1875 noch 40,6 auf 1.000 Einwohner betrug, ist auf 17,0 im Jahre 1957 zurückgegangen. Dieser Rückgang tritt in der Bevölkerungszahl nicht in Erscheinung, da die Sterblichkeit gleichfalls stark abnahm. Sie betrug 1957 nur noch 11,3 auf 1.000 Einwohner. Gleichlaufend ging eine erhebliche Verlängerung der Lebensdauer: Von 1871/1880 bis 1949/1951 stieg die durchschnittliche Lebenserwartung des Neugeborenen beim männlichen Geschlecht von 35,6 auf 64,6 Jahre, beim weiblichen von 38,5 auf 68,5 Jahre. Die Säuglingssterblichkeit erreichte 1957 mit 36,9 auf je 1.000 Lebendgeborene ihren bisher niedrigsten Stand.

DIE NATÜRLICHE BEVÖLKERUNGSBEWEGUNG 1957
(westeuropäische Vergleichszahlen)

	Lebend-geburten	Sterbe-fälle	Geburten-überschuß	Lebend-geburten	Sterbe-fälle	Geburten-überschuß
	auf 1.000 Einwohner			Bundesrepublik = 100		
Bundesrepublik Deutschland ...	17,0	11,3	5,7	100	100	100
Frankreich	18,4	12,0	6,4	108,2	106,2	112,3
Verein. Königreich	16,5	11,5	5,0	97,1	101,8	87,7
Italien	18,2	10,0	8,2	107,1	88,5	143,9
Niederlande	21,2	7,5	13,7	124,7	66,4	240,4
Österreich	17,0	12,8	4,2	100,0	113,3	73,7
Schweden	14,6	9,9	4,7	85,9	87,6	82,5
Schweiz	17,7	10,0	7,7	104,1	88,5	135,1

Quelle: Statistisches Bundesamt.

Die *Überalterung im Bevölkerungsaufbau* ist so stark, daß der Anteil der über 65jährigen heute rund 10% der gesamten Bevölkerung ausmacht gegenüber rund 7,3% im Jahre 1939 und rund 5% in der Zeit vor dem Ersten Weltkrieg. Die Bevölkerungsstruktur der Bundesrepublik muß nicht nur gegenüber früheren Jahren, sondern auch gegenüber den Nachbarländern *als ungünstig bezeichnet werden.*

*

Gegenüber dem Zustrom spielt die *Auswanderung* zahlenmäßig keine bedeutende Rolle. Sie geht zu über 97% nach Übersee. Von 1946 bis 1956 sind rund 262.300 Personen nach den USA, 170.100 nach Kanada und 42.800 nach Australien ausgewandert.

Etwa 1% der Bevölkerung der Bundesrepublik sind Ausländer. Eine nationale Minderheit bilden nur die Dänen im Land Schleswig-Holstein.

*

Am 30. 6. 1958 wurden in der Bundesrepublik 24.526 selbständige politische *Gemeinden* ermittelt. Von den zweiundfünfzig Großstädten liegen

DIE DEUTSCHE BEVÖLKERUNG LEBT ZU

24,1 % in Gemeinden unter 2.000 Einwohnern (86,2% aller Gemeinden)	12,6 Millionen
45,4 % in Klein- und Mittelstädten	23,6 Millionen
30,6 % in Großstädten	15,9 Millionen
Gesamt (30. 6. 1958; einschließlich Saarlands, ohne Berlin[West]) ..	52,1 Millionen

BEVÖLKERUNG NACH DER STELLUNG IM BERUF

Gebiet	Zeit	Selbständige	Mithelfende Familienang.	Beamte	Angestellte	Arbeiter	Selbständige Berufslose
Erwerbspersonen in Prozent aller Erwerbspersonen							
Deutsches Reich	1882[1]	25,6	10,0		7,0a	57,4	—
	1907[1]	18,8	15,0		13,1a	53,1	—
Bundesgebiet	1950[2]	14,8	14,4	4,0	16,0	50,9	—
Berufszugehörige[3] in Prozent der Gesamtbevölkerung							
Deutsches Reich	1882[1]	36,9	4,3		6,8a	47,3	4,7
	1907[2]	25,1	7,0		12,6a	47,1	8,1
Bundesgebiet	1950[2]	14,5	7,1	4,7	15,1	42,6	18,0

[1] Gebietsstand 31.12.1937. — [2] Gebietsstand 13.9.1950 (Datum der Volkszählung). — [3] Erwerbspersonen einschl. der Selbständigen Berufslosen mit ihren Angehörigen ohne Hauptberuf. — a Einschließlich Soldaten. Quelle: Statistisches Bundesamt.

dreiundzwanzig allein im Land Nordrhein-Westfalen. Weltstädte sind nur Berlin(West) mit 2,2 Millionen, Hamburg mit 1,8 Millionen und München mit 1,0 Millionen Einwohnern. Die Bundeshauptstadt Bonn hatte am 30. 6. 1958: 142.000 Einwohner.

*

BEVÖLKERUNG NACH DER ERWERBSTÄTIGKEIT[1]

	Erwerbspersonen			Selbständige Berufslose			Angehörige ohne Hauptberuf		
	insges.	männl.	weibl.	insges.	männl.	weibl.	insges.	männl.	weibl.
Deutsches Reich[2]									
1882	42,3	61,1	24,3	3,1	3,0	3,1	54,6	35,9	72,6
1907	45,6	61,4	30,3	5,6	5,3	5,8	48,8	33,3	63,9
1925	51,2	67,9	35,4	6,1	5,6	6,7	42,7	26,5	57,9
1939[3]	51,6	67,6	36,1	9,2	8,8	9,6	39,2	23,6	54,3
Bundesrepublik Deutschland[4]									
1939[3]	51,7	67,7	36,2	8,5	8,4	8,6	39,8	23,9	55,2
1950	46,3	63,2	31,4	12,0	10,3	13,5	41,7	26,5	55,1

[1] In Prozent der Gesamtbevölkerung. — [2] Gebietsstand 1937. — [3] Einschließlich der Soldaten und des Arbeitsdienstes. — [4] Gebietsstand 13. 9. 1950.

Quelle: Statistisches Bundesamt.

BEVÖLKERUNG DER BUNDESREPUBLIK DEUTSCHLAND NACH DER ERWERBSTÄTIGKEIT
am 17. Mai 1939 und 13. September 1950

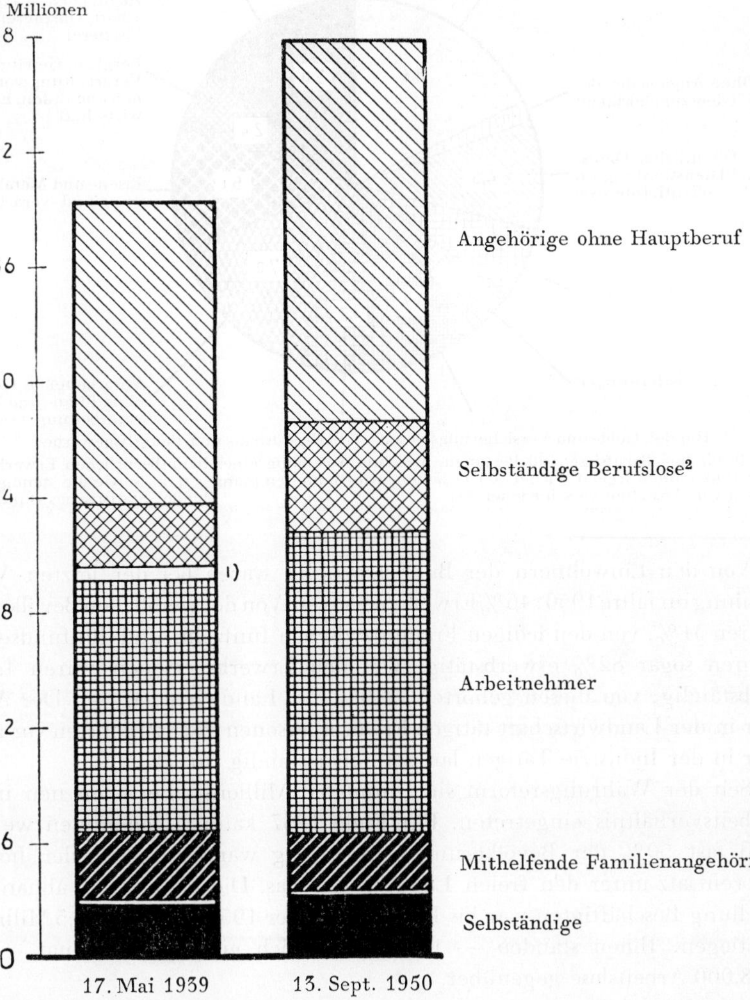

[1] Ihrer Dienstpflicht genügende Soldaten, Arbeitsmänner und Arbeitsmaiden. — [2] Selbständige Berufslose sind Personen, die ohne Ausübung einer hauptberuflichen Erwerbstätigkeit Einkommen irgendwelcher Art beziehen, wie Rentenempfänger u. ä., sowie die ständigen Insassen von Anstalten verschiedener Art.

Quelle: Statistisches Bundesamt.

DIE BEVÖLKERUNG DER BUNDESREPUBLIK DEUTSCHLAND NACH WIRTSCHAFTSABTEILUNGEN AM 13. SEPTEMBER 1950

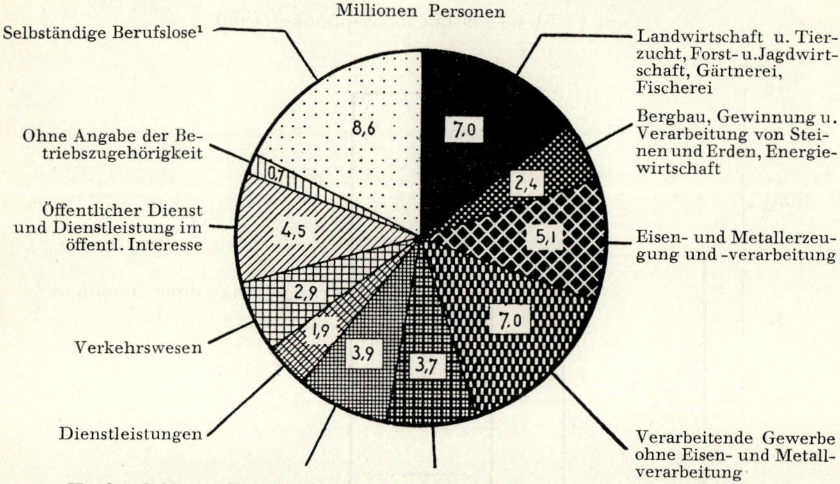

[1] Selbständige Berufslose sind Personen, die ohne Ausübung einer hauptberuflichen Erwerbstätigkeit Einkommen irgendwelcher Art beziehen, wie Rentenempfänger u. ä., sowie die ständigen Insassen von Anstalten verschiedener Art.

Quelle: Statistisches Bundesamt.

Von den Einwohnern der Bundesrepublik waren bei der letzten Volkszählung im Jahre 1950: 46% Erwerbspersonen. Von der weiblichen Bevölkerung waren 31%, von den ledigen Frauen zwischen fünfzehn und fünfundsechzig Jahren sogar 82% erwerbstätig. Von den Erwerbspersonen waren 14,8% selbständig; von diesen gehörten 24,5% der Landwirtschaft an. Der Anteil der in der Landwirtschaft tätigen Erwerbspersonen geht zugunsten vor allem der in der Industrie Tätigen langsam aber ständig zurück.

Seit der Währungsreform sind rund 6,6 Millionen Personen neu in ein Arbeitsverhältnis eingetreten. Für Ende 1957 kann angenommen werden, daß fast 50% der Bevölkerung erwerbstätig waren; das ist der höchste Prozentsatz unter den freien Ländern Europas. Die Zahl der in abhängiger Stellung Beschäftigten war bis Ende September 1958 auf über 19,3 Millionen gestiegen. Ihnen standen — im jahreszeitlich günstigsten Monat — nur 328.000 Arbeitslose gegenüber.

OPFER DER KRIEGE

I. DIE TOTEN[1]

Mein Volk, vergiß es nicht:
Es trägt ein jeder Toter
des *Bruders* Angesicht.

Zweimal innerhalb einer Generation hat der Tod eine Ernte gehalten, deren Folgen vor allem in den geburtenschwachen Ländern West- und Mitteleuropas lange Zeit sichtbar bleiben werden. Dieser Verlust hat nicht nur die einzelne Familie, sondern *das gefährdete Abendland als Ganzes* betroffen. Daß die Schwächung im Kampf gegeneinander erfolgte, muß als besonders tragisch empfunden werden.

Der *Erste Weltkrieg* (1914–1918) forderte vom deutschen Volk 1.936.897 Tote und 100.000 Vermißte. Die Verluste der Streitkräfte der übrigen Welt betrugen 7,2 Millionen, die der Zivilbevölkerung 500.000 Tote.

Der *Zweite Weltkrieg* (1939–1945) führte auf beiden Seiten zu noch ungleich höheren Zahlen an Toten und Vermißten. Nach wiederholt durch das Statistische Bundesamt durchgeführten vergleichenden Schätzungen belaufen die Zahlen für die deutschen Reichsangehörigen und Volksdeutschen sich auf über 7 Millionen. Sie verteilen sich im einzelnen auf:

Verluste der Wehrmacht des Reichsgebiets[2] 1939–1945 (einschließlich der seit 1939 als verstorben anzunehmenden Vermißten und Kriegsgefangenen)	3.760.000 Tote
Verluste der Wehrmacht an Volksdeutschen (ohne Österreich) 1939–1945	432.000 Tote
Verluste der deutschen Zivilbevölkerung (Wohnbevölkerung der späteren vier Besatzungszonen) durch Feindeinwirkung (vor allem Luftkrieg)[3]	430.000 Tote
Verluste der deutschen Zivilbevölkerung der Ostprovinzen des Reiches durch Vertreibung (einschl. der Luftkriegstoten[4]) 1944–1946	1.223.600 Tote
Zu übertragen:	5.845.600 Tote

[1] Die Zahlen beruhen zumeist auf Schätzungen nach den neuesten Quellen.

[2] Reichsgebiet = innerhalb der Grenzen vom 31. 12. 1937.

[3] Nicht eingerechnet sind die im Osten verschleppten deutschen Zivilpersonen (darüber siehe unten Seite 72).

[4] Der Angriff auf die mit Flüchtlingen überfüllte Stadt Dresden am 13. 2. 1945 forderte allein etwa 250.000 Tote.

Übertrag:	5.845.600 Tote
Verluste der „Volksdeutschen" (deutsche Siedlungsgebiete im Ausland[1]) durch Vertreibung 1944—1946	1.020.000 Tote
Verluste der Deutschen (einschließlich der deutschen Juden[2]) durch politische, rassische und religiöse Verfolgung 1939—1945	300.000 Tote
Insgesamt:	7.165.600 Tote

Das österreichische Volk, dessen Soldaten zur deutschen Wehrmacht gehörten, und das italienische Volk büßten zusammen 560.000 Tote und 190.000 Vermißte ein. Die Gesamtverluste der westlichen Alliierten werden auf 1,53 Millionen, die der ost- und südosteuropäischen Länder (ohne die Sowjetunion) auf 9 Millionen geschätzt. Diese letzte Zahl enthält nur eine Million gefallene Soldaten. Die hohen Verluste der Zivilbevölkerung beruhen vor allem auf der Politik der *Judenvernichtung* des Dritten Reiches. Für Polen werden 2.350.000, für Rumänien 220.000, für die Tschechoslowakei 243.000 und für Ungarn 180.000 umgekommene Juden geschätzt[3].

Die Verluste der sowjetischen Wehrmacht wurden auf 13,6 Millionen, die der Zivilbevölkerung auf 6,7 Millionen geschätzt. Diese Zahlen sind ebenso unsicher wie die aus der übrigen Welt, insbesondere Ostasien. Sie belaufen sich auf 7,6 Millionen gefallene Soldaten, 6 Millionen umgekommene Zivilisten und 3 Millionen Vermißte, die als tot anzusehen sind.

Die Zahlen, die auf diese Weise gewonnen werden, dürften freilich im ganzen der Wirklichkeit nahekommen. Danach forderte der Zweite Weltkrieg über 50 Millionen Tote.

In beiden Weltkriegen standen 170.000.000 Menschen[4] unter den Waffen (60.200.000 bzw. 110.000.000 Einberufene, davon 13.250.000 bzw. 20.000.000 Deutsche); von ihnen fielen mehr als 36.000.000 (9.240.000 und 26.850.000). In der gleichen Zeit hatte die Zivilbevölkerung über 25.300.000 Tote (500.000 und 24.840.000). 4.000.000 Soldaten und Zivilisten, von denen mehr als die Hälfte als tot anzunehmen ist, sind noch vermißt.

[1] Über die Verluste der nach Sibirien umgesiedelten Wolgadeutschen und anderen geschlossenen Volksgruppen deutschen Ursprungs in der Sowjetunion liegen keine Schätzungen vor.

[2] Die Zahl der umgekommenen *deutschen* Juden (Reichsgebiet) beläuft sich auf 170.000.

[3] Einzelheiten bei G. Reitlinger. The final solution, London 1953, der eine Gesamtzahl von 4,2 bis 4,8 Millionen umgekommener Juden errechnet.

[4] Die erste Zahl bezieht sich jeweils auf den Ersten, die zweite auf den Zweiten Weltkrieg.

II. DIE KRIEGS- UND ZIVILGEFANGENEN UND HEIMKEHRER

Seit Beendigung der Kampfhandlungen des Zweiten Weltkrieges sind über vierzehn Jahre vergangen. Seit 1945 haben das Deutsche Rote Kreuz und die kirchlichen Wohlfahrtsverbände, seit 1949 auch die Bundesregierung, sich des Problems der Vermißten und Gefangenen mit Nachdruck angenommen. Dennoch ist es nicht möglich gewesen, das Schicksal von mehr als 1.200.000 vermißten deutschen Wehrmachtangehörigen und von über 77.000 in Kriegsgefangenschaft geratenen Deutschen aufzuklären.

Bis zur Bildung der Bundesregierung wurden die Angelegenheiten der Kriegsgefangenen nicht zentral bearbeitet. Als Grundlage für eine systematische Nachforschung und Schicksalsklärung führte das Bundesministerium für Vertriebene daher im März 1950 im gesamten Bundesgebiet mit Berlin(West) eine *Registrierung der Kriegsgefangenen und Vermißten* durch.

Auf Vorstellung der Bundesregierung beschloß die Generalversammlung der Vereinten Nationen, den Versuch einer Lösung des Kriegsgefangenenproblems zu unternehmen. Ihrer zu diesem Zweck im Dezember 1950 gebildeten Kommission wurde von einer deutschen Delegation laufend umfassendes dokumentarisches Material vorgelegt. Zuletzt wurden im August 1954 namentliche Unterlagen über 1.156.663 auf dem östlichen Kriegsschauplatz vermißte Angehörige der ehemaligen deutschen Wehrmacht und über 118.507 Kriegsgefangene übergeben, die in den drei Gewahrsamsländern Sowjetunion, Tschechoslowakei und Polen als gefangen bekundet waren. Die westlichen Gewahrsamsländer haben sich damit einverstanden erklärt, durch Bereitstellung ihrer Unterlagen zur Aufklärung des Schicksals der Wehrmachtvermißten und der verschollenen Kriegsgefangenen beizutragen. Die östlichen Gewahrsamsländer dagegen sind auf diese Appelle bisher nicht eingegangen.

Erst anläßlich des Besuches des Bundeskanzlers in Moskau im September 1955 gelang es, von der Regierung der UdSSR die Zusicherung der Entlassung der restlichen deutschen Kriegsgefangenen zu erhalten. Bis zum Januar 1956 sind rund 10.000 deutsche Kriegsgefangene aus der Sowjetunion heimgekehrt. Nach Abschluß dieser letzten großen Entlassungsaktion verblieb in östlichen und westlichen Gewahrsamsländern nur noch eine geringe Anzahl von deutschen Kriegsgefangenen. Zum überwiegenden Teil sind sie wegen angeblicher Kriegsverbrechen zu langen Freiheitsstrafen verurteilt. Die übrigen früher bekundeten Gefangenen müssen zum ganz überwiegenden Teil als verstorben anzusehen sein. Auch weiterhin bleibt das

Schicksal der im Zusammenhang mit den Kriegsereignissen *vermißten und verschollenen Deutschen* zu klären. Hierbei handelt es sich um rund

1.156.000 Wehrmachtvermißte,
77.800 verschollene Kriegsgefangene,
800.000 zahlenmäßig ermittelte Zivilverschleppte und
über 3.000.000 Zivilpersonen aus den Vertreibungsgebieten, über deren Schicksal keine Nachricht vorliegt.

*

Seit Dezember 1949 wurden aus östlichem und westlichem Gewahrsam insgesamt rund 140.000 deutsche Kriegsgefangene in das Bundesgebiet und nach Berlin(West) entlassen. Der größte Teil dieser Heimkehrer braucht eine besondere Fürsorge mit dem Ziele einer schnellen Wiedereingliederung in das bürgerliche Leben.

Auf Grund des *Gesetzes über Hilfsmaßnahmen für Heimkehrer* wird jedem Heimkehrer ein Entlassungsgeld von 200 DM und bei Bedürftigkeit eine Übergangsbeihilfe von 300 DM gewährt, daneben Krankenhilfe, bevorzugte Arbeits- und Wohnungszuteilung und weitere soziale Hilfe, sowie außer den gesetzlichen Leistungen eine Begrüßungsgabe der Bundesregierung in Höhe von 100 DM. Die Angehörigen der noch nicht heimgekehrten Kriegsgefangenen erhalten bei Bedürftigkeit eine laufende Unterhaltsbeihilfe nach dem *Gesetz über die Unterhaltsbeihilfe für Angehörige von Kriegsgefangenen* sowie Erziehungsbeihilfen für die Ausbildung der Kinder.

Ehemalige Kriegsgefangene und Deutsche, die im ursächlichen Zusammenhang mit den Kriegsereignissen von einer ausländischen Macht verschleppt oder festgehalten worden sind, erhalten auf Grund des *Kriegsgefangenen-Entschädigungsgesetzes*, wenn sie am 3.2.1954 im Bundesgebiet oder im Lande Berlin ständigen Aufenthalt hatten, eine Entschädigung je nach der Länge des Gewahrsams über den 1.1.1947 hinaus. Im Rahmen dieses Gesetzes wurden bisher insgesamt 1.839.374 Entschädigungsanträge bearbeitet und hierfür 1.084 Millionen DM aufgewendet.

Auf Grund des gleichen Gesetzes werden Darlehen für den Aufbau der Existenz und zur Beschaffung von Wohnraum sowie Beihilfen zur Anschaffung von Hausrat gewährt. Bisher wurden insgesamt Darlehen in Höhe von 157,3 Millionen DM und Beihilfen in Höhe von 15,8 Millionen DM bewilligt.

*

Um die Lage der noch in den westlichen Gewahrsamsländern befindlichen Gefangenen zu erleichtern, werden sie laufend mit Geldsendungen zur

Verbesserung ihrer Verpflegung unterstützt. Daneben erhalten sie Gebrauchsartikel und Bekleidung. Ferner wird in Zusammenarbeit mit den Spitzenverbänden der freien Wohlfahrtspflege den Angehörigen durch Gewährung von Beihilfen die Möglichkeit zu Besuchen bei den Gefangenen gegeben. Durch Finanzierung von Fernunterrichtskursen werden sie auf einen späteren Beruf vorbereitet. Daneben können sie durch Fachbücher und Fachzeitschriften, die ihnen zur Verfügung gestellt werden, ihre beruflichen Kenntnisse auffrischen und erweitern oder sich in ihrer Freizeit mit Arbeiten, die ihrer persönlichen Neigung entsprechen, beschäftigen.

Die Gefangenen in den östlichen Gewahrsamsländern werden, soweit ihre Betreuung durch das Gewahrsamsland zugelassen ist, mit Hilfe der Wohlfahrtsverbände in monatlichen Paketsendungen mit Lebensmitteln, Unterwäsche, warmer Bekleidung und Gebrauchsartikeln aller Art versorgt.

Zur Verbesserung der Lage bedürftiger Angehöriger von Kriegsgefangenen wurde das *Gesetz über die Unterhaltsbeihilfe für Angehörige von Kriegsgefangenen* vom 13.6.1950 geschaffen. Es sichert diesem Personenkreis die gleichen Leistungen zu, wie sie im Bundesversorgungsgesetz für Kriegshinterbliebene vorgesehen sind. Bisher wurden für diesen Zweck rund 65 Millionen DM aufgewendet.

III. DIE KRIEGSBESCHÄDIGTEN UND HINTERBLIEBENEN

Als nach der Kapitulation die Zentralbehörden des Reiches beseitigt wurden, hörte auch die Reichsversorgung zu bestehen auf. Das bedeutete, daß es für die Millionen Opfer zweier Weltkriege, die Versehrten, Witwen, Eltern und Waisen, von einem Tag zum anderen niemand mehr gab, der sie betreute. Seit dem *Militärpensionsgesetz* vom 27.6.1871 war die Versorgung der Kriegsbeschädigten und ihrer Hinterbliebenen immer eine zentrale Aufgabe des Reiches gewesen. Die Auflösung der Versorgungsbehörden brachte Not und Verzweiflung über diejenigen, die dem Vaterland mit der eigenen Gesundheit oder mit dem Ernährer ihren Zoll entrichtet hatten. Zeitweise war durch die Militärbehörden jede Versorgung untersagt.

Die Gemeinden und Kreise, auf denen zunächst die Erhaltung des Staatswesens überhaupt beruhte, konnten nur Almosen geben und Katastrophen verhüten. Erst als die Länder gebildet worden waren, konnten neue gesetzliche Bestimmungen erlassen werden. Trotz gutem Willen gelangten die Länder weder zu einer allgemeingültigen Regelung noch zu Gesetzen, die alle berechtigten Ansprüche befriedigten.

In der Britischen Zone galten ab 1.8.1946 die Sozialversicherungsdirektiven Nr. 11, 19 und 24, auf Grund derer Renten nach den Vorschriften der sozialen Rentenversicherung gewährt wurden. Die US-Zone schuf mit Wirkung vom 1.2.1947 ein besonderes „Gesetz über Leistungen an Körperbeschädigte“, das die Grundsätze der Unfallversicherung zugrunde legte. Dem entsprach ab 1.8.1947 in der Britischen Zone in etwa die Direktive Nr. 27. In der Französischen Zone dagegen fanden teilweise weiterhin das alte Reichsversorgungsgesetz von 1920 und das Wehrmachtfürsorge- und -versorgungsgesetz von 1938, in Rheinland-Pfalz und Württemberg-Hohenzollern dagegen seit 1949 jeweils ein eigenes Versorgungsgesetz Anwendung. Sieben verschiedene Regelungen galten in den elf westdeutschen Ländern.

ANERKANNTE VERSORGUNGSBERECHTIGTE
in der Bundesrepublik Deutschland und in Berlin (West)

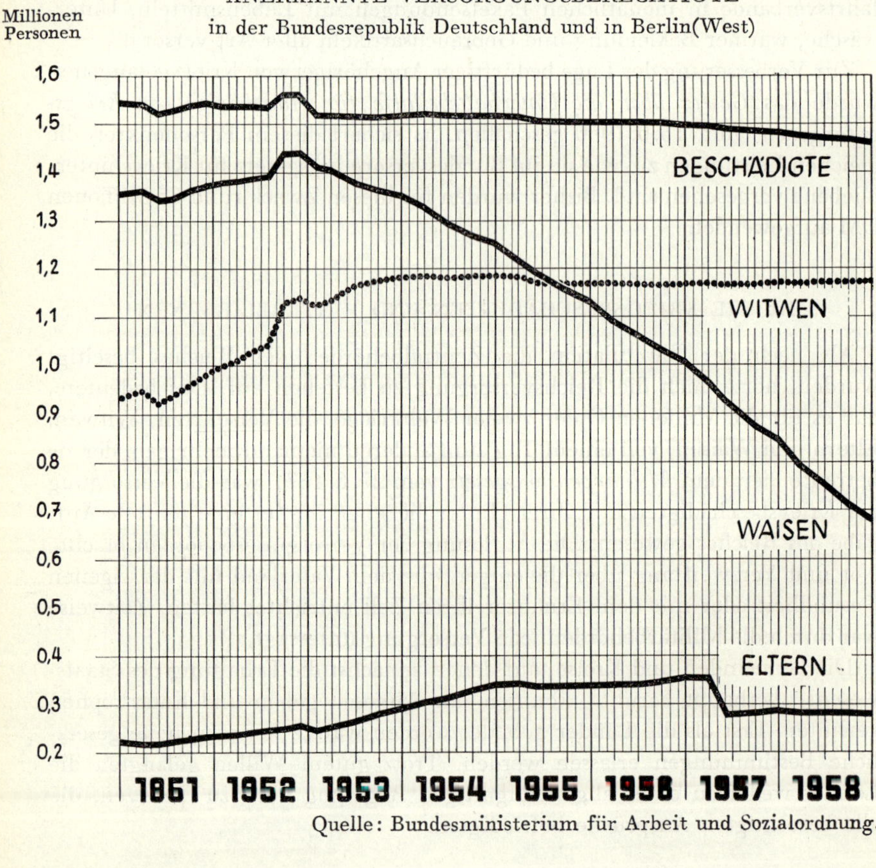

Quelle: Bundesministerium für Arbeit und Sozialordnung.

Die Bundesregierung hatte bereits in ihrer ersten Erklärung vor dem Bundestag sich verpflichtet, das Los der Kriegsopfer durch ein *Bundesversorgungsgesetz* (BVG) zu erleichtern. Dieses Gesetz, das erste große Sozialgesetz der Bundesrepublik, wurde am 21. 12. 1950 verkündet. Es erstreckte sich auch auf das Land Berlin. Fast jede deutsche Familie wird durch das BVG irgendwie angesprochen. Welche Bedeutung dem Gesetz zukommt, ergibt sich aus dem Schaubild auf Seite 36.

Das zweite Schaubild gibt einen Überblick über die Gliederung der Beschädigten nach dem Grade der Minderung der Erwerbsfähigkeit im gleichen zeitlichen Abstand vom Ende der beiden Weltkriege.

Die höheren Anteile nach dem Zweiten Weltkrieg sind nicht nur durch die Art und die Mittel der Kriegführung bedingt. In diesen Zahlen sind auch die Kriegsbeschädigten des Ersten Weltkrieges enthalten, soweit sie im Bundesgebiet oder im Land Berlin am 30. 11. 1951 noch Versorgung erhalten haben.

Der Finanzkraft des Bundes waren im Zeitpunkt des Inkrafttretens des Bundesversorgungsgesetzes angesichts der Notlage weiter Volkskreise Grenzen

DEUTSCHE KRIEGSBESCHÄDIGTE
Tausend

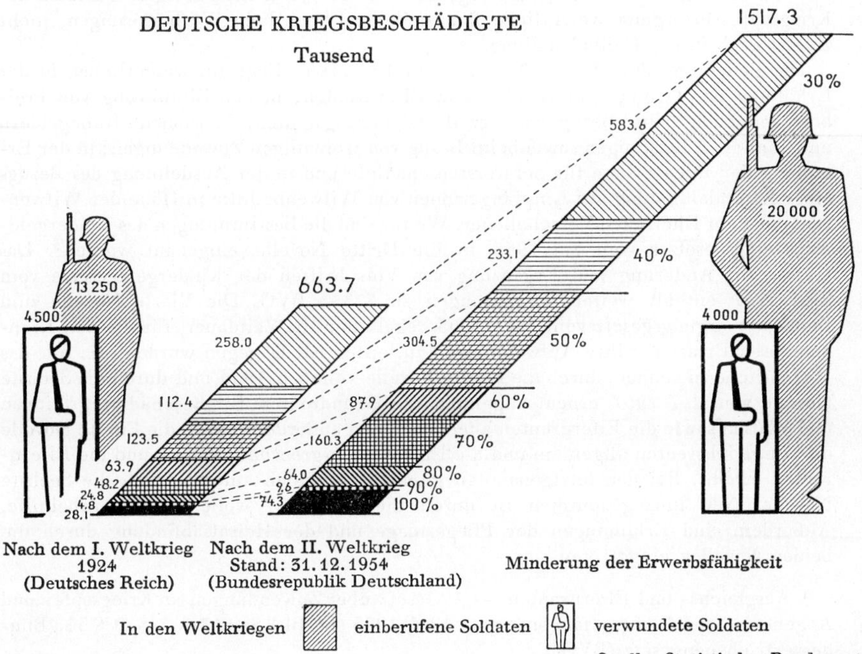

Quelle: Statistisches Bundesamt.

für die Erfüllung der Wünsche der Kriegsopfer gezogen. Daher ist die Kriegsopferversorgung eines der umstrittenen sozialen Probleme der Bundesrepublik geblieben, zumal die Entwicklung in der Zeit nach dem Inkrafttreten des Bundesversorgungsgesetzes die Löhne und Preise in der Weltwirtschaft in Bewegung gebracht hatte und hiervon auch die Bundesrepublik nicht verschont geblieben ist. Diese Entwicklung hatte nicht nur eine Minderung der Kaufkraft der Renten an sich zur Folge, sondern auch eine Erhöhung des sonstigen Einkommens der im Erwerbsleben stehenden Kriegsopfer und damit eine Minderung der vom sonstigen Einkommen der Versorgungsberechtigten abhängigen Ausgleichsrente.

Die Erste Novelle zum Bundesversorgungsgesetz vom 19.3.1952 brachte eine Erhöhung der Einkommensgrenzen, die für die Bemessung der Renten[1] maßgeblich sind. Einen weiteren Ausgleich für die gesunkene Kaufkraft der Renten in der zurückliegenden Zeit stellte die zusätzliche Zuwendung in Höhe einer Monatsrente an alle Empfänger von Versorgungsbezügen dar[2]. Diese Maßnahmen bedeuteten nur Zwischenlösungen, bis am 7.8.1953 die Zweite Novelle zum Bundesversorgungsgesetz erlassen werden konnte. Sie brachte außer der Erhöhung der Ausgleichs- und Elternrenten und der dafür maßgebenden Einkommensgrenzen um 20 % auf allen übrigen Gebieten der Kriegsopferversorgung wesentliche finanzielle und rechtliche Verbesserungen, nicht zuletzt auch in der Heilbehandlung.

Die Bedeutung der Dritten Novelle vom 19.1.1955 liegt im wesentlichen in der Erhöhung der Grund-, Ausgleichs- und Elternrenten; in der Einführung von Freibeträgen auch beim Bezug von Sozialversicherungsrenten, Pensionen, Ruhegeldern und ähnlichen Leistungen sowie beim Bezug von freiwilligen Zuwendungen; in der Erhöhung der Pflegezulage für Schwerstbeschädigte und in der Ausdehnung des Bezugs einer Kapitalabfindung auf Empfängerinnen von Witwenbeihilfe in Höhe der Witwenrente und auf Ehefrauen Verschollener. Weiter sind die Bestimmungen des Kindergeld-Anpassungsgesetzes vom 7.1.1955 in die Dritte Novelle eingebaut worden[3]. Das Gesetz zur Änderung und Ergänzung von Vorschriften der Kindergeldgesetze vom 27.7.1957 enthält weitere Ergänzungen zu § 34a BVG. Die Vierte Novelle zum Bundesversorgungsgesetz vom 3.11.1955 regelt nur die Zeitdauer, für die den Krankenkassen Ersatz für ihre Aufwendungen zu leisten ist. Dagegen wurden, um nur das Wesentliche zu nennen, durch die Fünfte Novelle vom 6.6.1956 und durch die Sechste Novelle vom 1.7.1957 erneut allgemein die Grundrenten für Beschädigte, Witwen und Waisen sowie die Elternrenten angehoben und außerdem durch die Fünfte Novelle die Ausgleichsrenten allgemein und die Einkommensgrenzen für diese und die Elternrenten erhöht. Bei den letztgenannten geschah dies noch einmal durch die Sechste Novelle. Neu hinzugekommen ist durch die Sechste Novelle die Elternbeihilfe. Außerdem sind Erhöhungen der Pflegezulage und der Heiratsabfindung durch die beiden Novellen eingetreten.

[1] Ausgleichs- und Elternrenten. — [2] Gesetz über Zuwendungen an Kriegsopfer und Angehörige von Kriegsgefangenen vom 12.1.1953 (BGBl I Seite 10). — [3] § 34a Bundesvertriebenengesetz (BVG).

Die hohen Beträge, die für die Versorgung der Kriegsopfer aufzubringen sind, müssen während einer sehr langen Zeit zur Verfügung stehen. Dieser Tatsache mußte der Gesetzgeber vor allem Rechnung tragen. Die finanzielle Folge des Krieges wird noch fortdauern, wenn längst eine neue Generation aufgewachsen ist. Heute noch, mehr als vierzig Jahre nach dem Ende des Ersten Weltkrieges, lebt allein in der Bundesrepublik noch rund eine halbe Million Kriegsopfer, deren Versorgungsberechtigung auf den Ersten Weltkrieg zurückgeht.

Nach dem Stand vom 31. 12. 1958 werden noch 3.602.654 Versorgungsberechtigte gezählt. Die Zahl der noch nicht erledigten Versorgungsanträge betrug am 31. 12. 1958: 94.436.

AUFGLIEDERUNG DER VERSORGUNGSBERECHTIGTEN

Beschädigte insgesamt		1.461.409
Darunter nach dem Grad der Beschädigung:		
30 %	556.516	
40 %	223.815	
50 %	290.136	
60 %	89.787	
70 %	147.485	
80 %	68.648	
90 %	11.954	
100 %	73.068	
Witwen und Witwer		1.174.429
Halbwaisen		654.190
Vollwaisen		32.278
Elternteile		169.106
Elternpaare		111.242
Insgesamt		3.602.654

Quelle: Bundesministerium für Arbeit und Sozialordnung.

Zu den Beschädigten sind noch rund 400.000 Versehrte zu zählen, deren Beschädigung unter 25% liegt. Diese erhalten keine Renten, können aber jederzeit durch Verschlimmerung ihres Leidens in die Versorgung durch eine Rente einbezogen werden.

Nach dem Stand vom 30. 9. 1958 wurden im Bundesgebiet und im Land Berlin 519.259 Kriegsbeschädigte orthopädisch versorgt, davon 101.755 aus dem Ersten und 417.504 aus dem Zweiten Weltkrieg. Von ihnen waren 128.410 einseitig Beinamputierte und 10.294 Doppelt-Beinamputierte, 41.873 einseitig Armamputierte, 904 Doppelt-Armamputierte und 109 dreifach und 31 vierfach Amputierte, außerdem 30.297 sonstige Amputierte; ferner 1.212 Querschnittsgelähmte und 6.514 Kriegsblinde, davon 924 mit sonstigen zusätzlichen schweren Beschädigungen, zum Beispiel 123 Blinde ohne Hände. Am 31. 3. 1958 wurden 64.828 Hirnverletzte gezählt.

Das Deutsche Reich gab für die Beschädigten und Hinterbliebenen 1929: 1,3 Milliarden RM und zwanzig Jahre nach dem Ende des Ersten Weltkrieges (1938) noch 900 Millionen RM aus. Das Bild änderte sich nach dem Zweiten Weltkrieg entscheidend. Zwar wurden 1948 — beim Wiedererstehen einer Versorgung — auch nur etwas über 900 Millionen DM ausgegeben; jedoch 1949 waren es bereits 1,9 Milliarden. 1950[1], nachdem das Bundesversorgungsgesetz in Kraft getreten war, stieg diese Summe auf 2,24 Milliarden. Sie erhöhte sich 1951 [einschließlich von Berlin(West)] auf 3,02 Milliarden, 1952 auf 3,04 Milliarden. Im Haushaltsjahr 1953 wurden 2,99 Milliarden, 1954: 2,89 Milliarden, 1955: 3,45 Milliarden, 1956: 3,94 Milliarden und 1957: 3,60 Milliarden für Versorgungsleistungen aufgewendet[1].

Wenn man die Leistung des Bundes für die Kriegsopfer während der mutmaßlichen Laufzeit des Gesetzes mit einem *Durchschnitt von 2,5 Milliarden DM jährlich* annimmt, ergibt sich ein Betrag, der *höher liegt als das gesamte Aufkommen, das aus dem Lastenausgleich erwartet wird.* Daraus ergibt sich die Verantwortungsfreudigkeit, mit der dieses nahezu einstimmig angenommene und bis in die jüngste Zeit durch wiederholte Novellen ergänzte Gesetz geschaffen worden ist.

Das Ziel des Bundesversorgungsgesetzes und der Novellen mußte bestehen in der sozialen Sicherstellung aller Anspruchsberechtigten, in der Gewährung materieller Leistungen, die den voll Erwerbsunfähigen das Existenzminimum sichern, und in der weitgehenden Unabhängigkeit aller unverschuldet in einen sozialen Notstand geratenen Anspruchsberechtigten von Leistungen der öffentlichen Fürsorge. Als Kernstück der Versorgung stellt das Gesetz heraus, daß dem Beschädigten alle Maßnahmen der Heilfürsorge zuteil werden, die zur Wiederherstellung seiner Gesundheit und Leistungsfähigkeit dienen; einschließlich orthopädischer Versorgung nach modernen Gesichtspunkten. Auf dem Gebiet der Berufsfürsorge sichert das Gesetz dem Beschädigten außerdem einen Anspruch auf alle Maßnahmen, die zur Erlangung und Wiedergewinnung seiner beruflichen Leistungsfähigkeit führen und ihn befähigen, am Arbeitsplatz und im Wettbewerb mit nicht Beschädigten sich zu behaupten.

[1] In den im Text genannten Ausgaben von 1950 bis 1958 sind Sach- beziehungsweise Personalausgaben und sonstige Verwaltungskosten nicht enthalten.

VERSCHOLLEN, VERSCHLEPPT, VERTRIEBEN, AUF DER FLUCHT . . .

Das Recht auf die Heimat und Selbstbestimmung.

„Die Bundesregierung ist Sachwalterin und Treuhänderin der Vertriebenen und hat deren Anspruch auf die Heimat stets vertreten. Sie wird sich auch in Zukunft dafür einsetzen, daß das Recht auf die Heimat gewahrt und das Selbstbestimmungsrecht gesichert wird.

Die Bundesregierung hat bewiesen, daß sie entsprechend der Regierungserklärung vom 20.10.1953 zwar bereit ist, für die Verständigung wirtschaftliche und finanzielle Opfer zu bringen, eine *Verzichtpolitik* jedoch ablehnt. Die wirtschaftliche und soziale Eingliederung der Vertriebenen im Bereich der Bundesrepublik schmälert nicht den Rechtsanspruch auf die Heimat.

Es gilt, mit Hilfe unserer Stellung und Wertung in der Freien Welt nicht nur unsere Freiheit zu erhalten, sondern sie auch zu unseren unter Zwangsherrschaft lebenden Brüdern und Schwestern zu bringen. Die Wiedervereinigung darf nicht zu einer Ausweitung der bolschewistischen Macht oder zu einer Preisgabe von Grundrechten der Vertriebenen führen."

(Aus einem Aufruf von Bundeskanzler Dr. KONRAD ADENAUER an die Vertriebenen und Flüchtlinge im August 1957.)

I. VERTREIBUNG, EINGLIEDERUNG, LASTENAUSGLEICH

Die Vertreibung

Das Potsdamer Abkommen vom 2.8.1945 zwischen den Vereinigten Staaten, dem Vereinigten Königreich und der Sowjetunion sagt in Artikel 13 zu der Massenaustreibung deutscher Menschen aus dem Osten: „Die drei Regierungen haben die Frage unter allen Gesichtspunkten beraten und erkennen an, daß die Überführung nach Deutschland der deutschen Bevölkerung oder von Bestandteilen derselben, die in Polen, der Tschechoslowakei und Ungarn zurückgeblieben sind, durchgeführt werden muß. Sie stimmen darin überein, daß jede derartige Überführung, die stattfinden wird, in ordnungsgemäßer und humaner Weise erfolgen soll. Da der Zustrom einer großen Zahl Deutscher nach Deutschland die Lasten vergrößern würde, die bereits auf den Besatzungsbehörden ruhen, halten sie es für wünschenswert, daß der Alliierte Kontrollrat in Deutschland zunächst das Problem unter besonderer Berücksichtigung der Frage einer gerechten Verteilung dieser Deutschen

BEVÖLKERUNGSBEWEGUNG NACH WESTDEUTSCHLAND 1945—1956

(Stand: 30. 6. 1956)

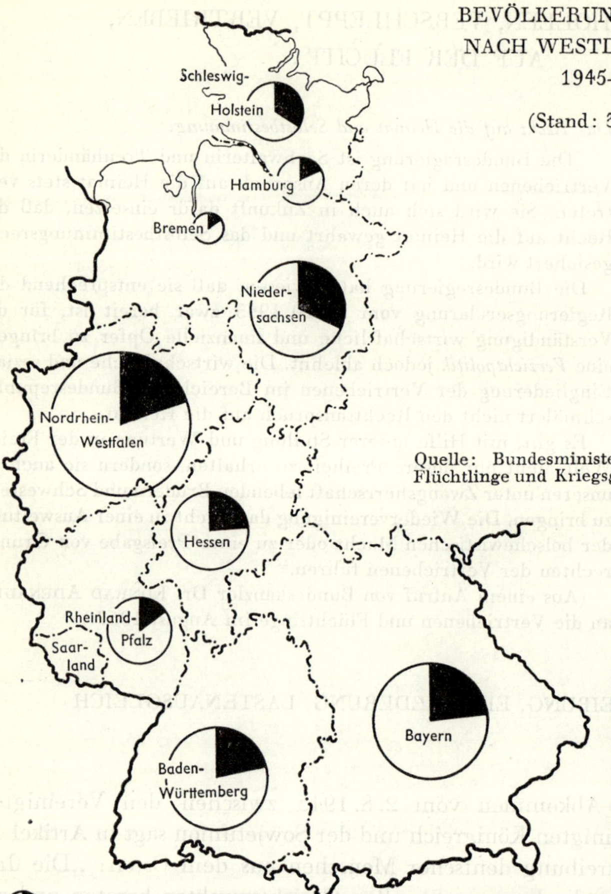

Quelle: Bundesministerium für Vertriebene, Flüchtlinge und Kriegsgeschädigte.

Vertriebene *und Zugewanderte* in % der Gesamtbevölkerung am 31. 12. 1958

Schleswig-Holstein	34,5
Hamburg	22,4
Niedersachsen	33,0
Bremen	22,9
Nordrh.-Westfalen	22,9
Hessen	25,8
Rheinland-Pfalz	13,5
Baden-Württbg.	23,9
Bayern	22,8
Bundesrepublik (ohne Saarland und Berlin[West])	24,4

= Anteil der Vertriebenen und Zugewanderten an der Bevölkerung der Länder der Bundesrepublik (ohne Saarland und Berlin[West]) am 30. 6. 1956

Die den Pfeilen im Schaubild auf Seite 43 beigegebenen Zahlen bedeuten:

A. Vertriebene aus den Deutschen Ostgebieten:
1. Pommern 2. Ostpreußen 3. Brandenburg 4. Schlesien

B. Vertriebene aus dem Ausland:
5. Danzig 6. Memelland 7. Estland, Lettland, Litauen 8. Polen 9. Sowjetunion 10. Tschechoslowakei 11. Rumänien 12. Ungarn 13. Jugoslawien 14. Übriges Europa und Übersee

C. Flüchtlinge und Zugewanderte aus:
15. Sowjetische Besatzungszone (spätere sogenannte DDR) und Berlin

D. Vertriebene aus den Deutschen Ostgebieten und dem Ausland, die in die Sowjetische Besatzungszone (die spätere sogenannte DDR) gelangt sind:
16. Vertriebene in der Sowjetischen Besatzungszone.

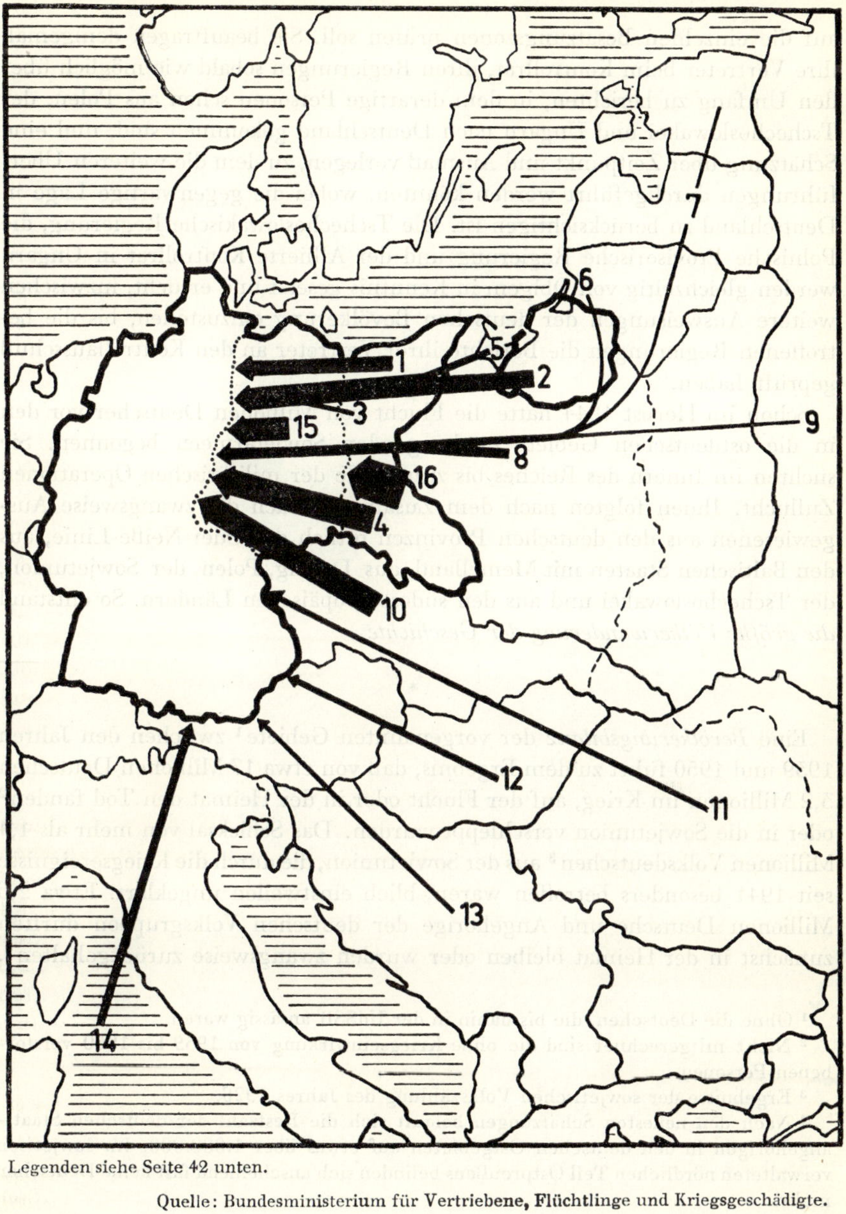

Legenden siehe Seite 42 unten.

Quelle: Bundesministerium für Vertriebene, Flüchtlinge und Kriegsgeschädigte.

auf die einzelnen Besatzungszonen prüfen soll. Sie beauftragen demgemäß ihre Vertreter beim Kontrollrat, ihren Regierungen sobald wie möglich über den Umfang zu berichten, in dem derartige Personen schon aus Polen, der Tschechoslowakei und Ungarn nach Deutschland gekommen sind, und eine Schätzung über Zeitpunkt und Ausmaß vorlegen, zu dem die weiteren Überführungen durchgeführt werden könnten, wobei die gegenwärtige Lage in Deutschland zu berücksichtigen ist. Die Tschechoslowakische Regierung, die Polnische Provisorische Regierung und der Alliierte Kontrollrat in Ungarn werden gleichzeitig von Obigem in Kenntnis gesetzt und ersucht, inzwischen weitere Ausweisungen der deutschen Bevölkerung einzustellen, bis die betroffenen Regierungen die Berichte ihrer Vertreter an den Kontrollausschuß geprüft haben.“

Schon im Herbst 1944 hatte die Flucht von Millionen Deutscher vor den in die ostdeutschen Gebiete eindringenden Sowjetarmeen begonnen. Sie suchten im Innern des Reiches bis zum Ende der militärischen Operationen Zuflucht. Ihnen folgten nach dem Zusammenbruch die zwangsweise Ausgewiesenen aus den deutschen Provinzen östlich der Oder-Neiße-Linie, aus den Baltischen Staaten mit Memelland, aus Danzig, Polen, der Sowjetunion, der Tschechoslowakei und aus den südosteuropäischen Ländern. So entstand *die größte Völkerwanderung der Geschichte*.

*

Eine *Bevölkerungsbilanz* der vorgenannten Gebiete[1] zwischen den Jahren 1939 und 1950 führt zu dem Ergebnis, daß von etwa 17 Millionen Deutschen 3,2 Millionen im Krieg, auf der Flucht oder in der Heimat den Tod fanden[2] oder in die Sowjetunion verschleppt wurden. Das Schicksal von mehr als 1,4 Millionen Volksdeutschen[3] aus der Sowjetunion, die durch die Kriegsereignisse seit 1941 besonders betroffen waren, blieb einstweilen ungeklärt. Etwa 2,6 Millionen Deutsche und Angehörige der deutschen Volksgruppen durften zunächst in der Heimat bleiben oder wurden zwangsweise zurückgehalten[4].

[1] Ohne die Deutschen, die bis dahin in der UdSSR ansässig waren.

[2] Nicht mitgerechnet sind die ohne Kriegseinwirkung von 1939 bis 1950 verstorbenen Personen.

[3] Ergebnisse der sowjetischen Volkszählung des Jahres 1926.

[4] Nach den neuesten Schätzungen beläuft sich die Restzahl der deutschen Staatsangehörigen in den deutschen Ostgebieten auf etwas über 1.000.000. Im sowjetisch verwalteten nördlichen Teil Ostpreußens befinden sich anscheinend fast keine Deutschen mehr.

VERTRIEBENE UND ZUGEWANDERTE[1] im Bundesgebiet am 13.9.1950[2]

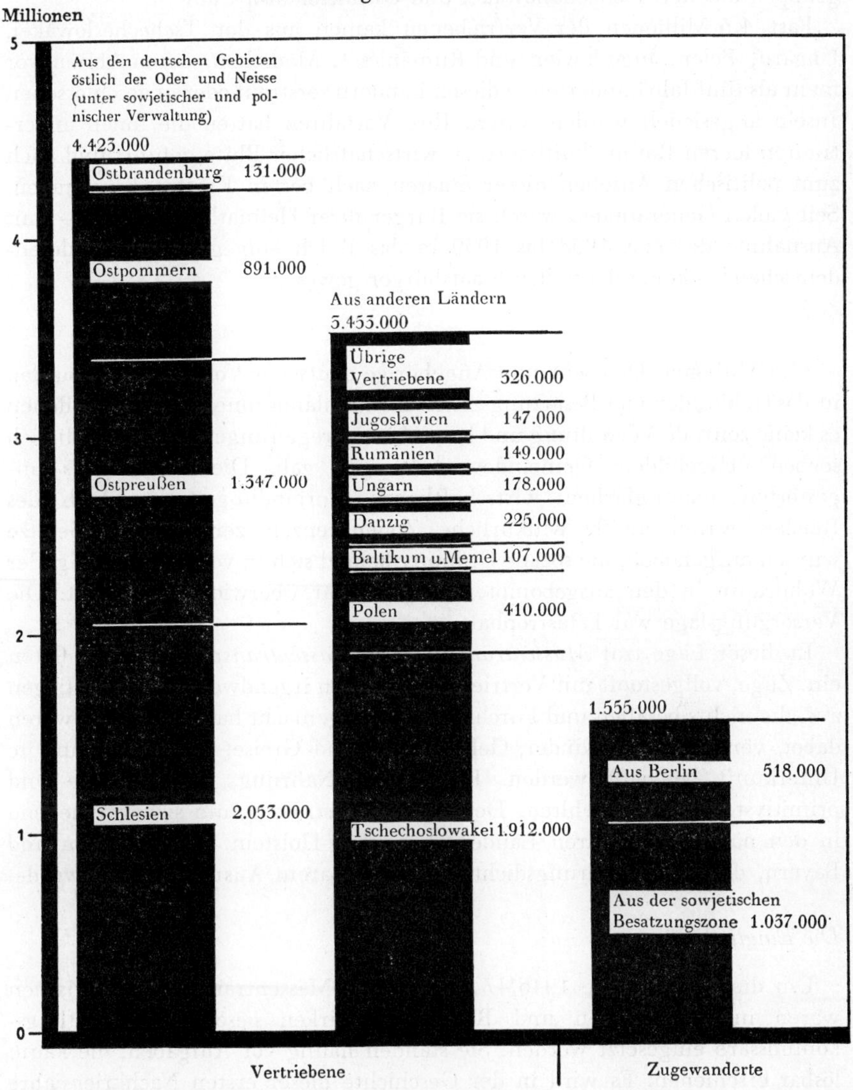

[1] Zugewanderte siehe Tabelle 1 Anm. 2. [2] Nach dem Wohnsitz am 1.9.1939.

Quelle: Bundesministerium für Vertriebene, Flüchtlinge und Kriegsgeschädigte.

Österreich nahm etwa 0,3 Millionen geflüchtete Angehörige deutscher Volksgruppen aus der Tschechoslowakei und Ostmitteleuropa auf.

Fast 4,5 Millionen der Vertriebenen kamen aus der Tschechoslowakei, Ungarn, Polen, Jugoslawien und Rumänien[1]; Menschen, deren Ahnen vor mehr als fünf Jahrhunderten in diesen Ländern zerstreut oder in geschlossenen Inseln angesiedelt worden waren. Ihre Vorfahren hatten die ihnen anvertrauten leeren Räume kultiviert, zu wirtschaftlicher Blüte geführt und auch zum politischen Ansehen dieser Staaten nach besten Kräften beigetragen. Seit vielen Generationen waren sie Bürger ihrer Heimatländer, aber — mit Ausnahme der erst 1938 bis 1939 in das Reich eingegliederten Sudetendeutschen — keine deutschen Staatsbürger gewesen.

*

11,8 Millionen Deutsche und Angehörige deutscher Volksgruppen wurden in das Gebiet der vier Besatzungszonen Deutschlands hineingepreßt, in denen es keine zentrale Verwaltung und keine Länderregierungen, sondern lediglich soeben neugebildete Gemeindeverwaltungen gab. Die bisher stets ungestörten mannigfachen wirtschaftlichen Verbindungen innerhalb des Reiches waren durch willkürliche Zonengrenzen zerschnitten. Gesetze wurden aufgehoben, die soziale Ordnung befand sich in voller Auflösung, der Wohnraum in den ausgebombten Städten war überwiegend zerstört. Die Versorgungslage war katastrophal.

In dieser Lage traf *Massentransport auf Massentransport* aus dem Osten ein. Züge, vollgestopft mit Vertriebenen, hielten irgendwo. Menschen stiegen aus, die nichts besaßen und Furchtbares durchgemacht hatten. Kranke waren dabei, verhungernde Kinder, Gebrechliche und Greise. Für sie alle mußte Unterkunft beschafft werden. Bekleidung, Nahrung, Medikamente und primitivster Hausrat fehlten. Der Flüchtlingsstrom staute sich vorwiegend in den nächsterreichbaren Ländern Schleswig-Holstein, Niedersachsen und Bayern, deren Bevölkerungsdichte in untragbarem Ausmaß erhöht wurde.

Die Eingliederung

Um die Jahreswende 1946/47 endeten die Massentransporte. Inzwischen waren in den Kreisen und Regierungsbezirken besondere Flüchtlingskommissare eingesetzt worden. Sie standen häufig vor Aufgaben, die kaum lösbar erschienen. Es wird in der Geschichte dieser ersten Nachkriegsjahre

[1] Nach dem Stand des Jahres 1950.

immer als eine nicht nur organisatorisch, sondern vor allem auch sittlich hohe Leistung fortleben, in welcher Weise der überwiegende Teil der einheimischen Bevölkerung und der Vertriebenen es verstanden hat, eine Katastrophe zu verhindern. Dabei wurden organisierte Selbsthilfebestrebungen der Vertriebenen durch die Besatzungsmächte, die jeden Zusammenschluß verboten, unmöglich gemacht.

Erst allmählich formten sich aus dem Chaos der ersten Monate nach der Kapitulation größere Verwaltungseinheiten, die sich mit der Not und der Verteilung der Vertriebenen beschäftigten. Zuerst entstanden in der Amerikanischen Zone die *Landesflüchtlingsverwaltungen.* Nach Errichtung des Süddeutschen Länderrats in Stuttgart und der Landesregierungen der Britischen Zone erhielten sie gewisse Vollmachten. 1947 konstituierte sich die Arbeitsgemeinschaft der Flüchtlingsverwaltungen in den beiden angelsächsischen Besatzungszonen, die nun in ständigem Kontakt standen und ihre Maßnahmen miteinander abstimmten.

Im Frühjahr 1947 wurde das erste gemeinsame Flüchtlingsgesetz für die Länder der Amerikanischen Zone erlassen. Ähnliche Gesetze für die Länder der Britischen Zone folgten. Sie brachten neben der Regelung sozialer und wirtschaftlicher Fragen die Anerkennung der völligen *Gleichberechtigung* der Vertriebenen mit der einheimischen Bevölkerung.

Seit 1948 wirkten Vertriebene als Abgeordnete politischer Parteien im erweiterten Wirtschaftsrat der Doppelzone. Sie gründeten einen Vertriebenen-Ausschuß, in dem sie sich besonders für die Eingliederung ihrer Leidensgenossen und die Vorbereitung eines Lastenausgleichs einsetzten.

Ende 1948 beschloß der Wirtschaftsrat, ein eigenes *Amt für die Fragen der Heimatvertriebenen* zu schaffen. Im März 1949 wurde die Arbeitsgemeinschaft der Flüchtlingsverwaltungen in dieses Amt überführt, das alle Maßnahmen zugunsten der Vertriebenen zu koordinieren suchte. Hauptleistungen dieser Periode sind das Flüchtlingssiedlungsgesetz, die Einbeziehung der Vertriebenen in die Marshallplanhilfe, das Soforthilfegesetz und die Aufklärung des Auslandes über Umfang, Art und Folgen der Vertreibung.

*

Als im Jahr 1948 die Vorbereitungen zur *Währungsreform* in Gang kamen, wurde von deutscher Seite vorgeschlagen, die Währungsumstellung mit dem *Lastenausgleich* zu verbinden. Den Vertriebenen sollte dadurch frühzeitig die Möglichkeit gegeben werden, mit den aus dem Lastenausgleich fließenden Mitteln sich eine neue Existenz zu gründen und eine quotale Entschädigung für ihre Vermögensverluste zu erhalten. Es ist heute unbestritten daß dieser deutsche Vorschlag den psychologischen Augenblick erkannt hatte, in dem ein wirkungsvoller Lastenausgleich am leichtesten durchzuführen gewesen wäre. Leider waren die Besatzungsmächte der Meinung, das Vertriebenenproblem und somit auch der Lastenausgleich gingen nur Deutschland an, während die Währungsreform eine alliierte Angelegenheit sei. Deshalb wurde zunächst das an der Kernfrage des Lastenausgleichs vorbeigehende Soforthilfegesetz geschaffen, um den schlimmsten Notstand zu überbrücken. Der Lastenausgleich mußte einem späteren Gesetz überlassen werden.

*

Das Grundgesetz der Bundesrepublik vom Mai 1949 bestätigte in Artikel 116 die rechtliche Gleichstellung der Vertriebenen mit den Einheimischen und schuf die Grundlage für weitere Eingliederungsmaßnahmen.

Aus dem Amt für Fragen der Heimatvertriebenen entstand das Bundesministerium für Vertriebene, dem im April 1954 auch die Betreuung der Kriegssachgeschädigten und Evakuierten, die bis dahin beim Bundesministerium des Innern lag, übertragen wurde. Seit diesem Zeitpunkt führt es die Bezeichnung „Bundesministerium für Vertriebene, Flüchtlinge und Kriegsgeschädigte".

Die praktische Wirksamkeit des Ministeriums ist durch den föderalistischen Aufbau des Bundes begrenzt. Nach wie vor ist es Sache der Länder, die Vertriebenen zu betreuen und die von den Landesregierungen und der Bundesregierung beschlossenen Gesetze durchzuführen. Der Leitgedanke der neuen Gesetzgebung war, den Vertriebenen nicht etwa ein Sonderrecht einzuräumen oder sie auf irgendeine Art zu beschäftigen, sondern sie in das Wirtschafts- und Sozialgefüge der Bundesrepublik einzugliedern. Ihnen sollten zum Aufbau einer neuen Existenz annähernd gleiche Startbedingungen wie den Einheimischen zur Verfügung stehen. Zugleich sollten die Lasten, die durch die Vertriebenen entstanden waren, in gerechter Weise verteilt werden.

Um die Vertriebenen zweckmäßig einzugliedern, waren zwei Voraussetzungen vordringlich: Man mußte sie entweder an geeignete *Arbeitsplätze* bringen und dort für menschenwürdige Unterkunft sorgen; oder es waren neue Arbeitsplätze am begründeten Wohnort zu schaffen. Die langwährende Untätigkeit vieler Vertriebenen in den Hauptflüchtlingsländern bedeutete ebenso wie das Leben in den Lagern eine soziale Gefahr. Daher mußten die Hauptflüchtlingsländer Schleswig-Holstein, Niedersachsen und Bayern entlastet werden, was nur im Wege der gelenkten Umsiedlung geschehen konnte.

Professor Dr. THEODOR HEUSS,
erster Bundespräsident
der Bundesrepublik Deutschland
(12.9.1949—14.9.1959)

Dr. h. c. HEINRICH LÜBKE,
Bundesminister für Ernährung,
Landwirtschaft und Forsten,
gewählter Bundespräsident der
Bundesrepublik Deutschland
(ab 15. 9. 1959)

Hohe Gäste aus aller Welt am Sitz der Bundesregierung

Ihre Majestäten der König und die Königin der Hellenen, der Doyen des Diplomatischen Korps mit dem Kgl. Dänischen Botschafter, der Großherzoglich Luxemburgische Ministerpräsident und der Großherzoglich Luxemburgische Botschafter, der Ministerpräsident des Vereinigten Königreichs, der Generalsekretär der NATO, der Italienische Staatspräsident und seine Gattin, der Kgl. Niederländische Außenminister, der Staatspräsident von Brasilien, Sir WINSTON und Lady CHURCHILL, der Portugiesische Außenminister und seine Gattin, der Kgl. Dänische Ministerpräsident — mit dem Präsidenten, dem Kanzler, dem Außen- und dem Wirtschaftsminister der Bundesrepublik. — Links oben: Bundespräsident Professor HEUSS in Washington als Gast des Präsidenten der USA, DWIGHT D. EISENHOWER

Tabelle 1

VERTRIEBENE[1] UND ZUGEWANDERTE[2]
Stand: 13.9.1950 und 30.9.1958

Land	Stand: 13.9.1950				Stand: 30.9.1958			
	Vertriebene		Zugewanderte		Vertriebene		Zugewanderte	
	1.000 Personen	% der Wohnbevölkerung	1.000 Personen	% der Wohnbevölkerung	1.000 Personen	% der Wohnbevölkerung	1.000 Personen	% der Wohnbevölkerung
Schleswig-Holstein	857	*33,0*	134	*5,2*	640	*28,2*	144	*6,4*
Hamburg	116	*7,2*	68	*4,2*	246	*13,6*	154	*8,6*
Niedersachsen	1.851	*27,2*	369	*5,4*	1.670	*25,6*	475	*7,3*
Bremen	48	*8,6*	21	*3,8*	103	*15,2*	51	*7,5*
Nordrhein-Westfalen	1.332	*10,1*	379	*2,9*	2.430	*15,8*	1.058	*6,9*
Hessen	721	*16,7*	166	*3,8*	860	*18,5*	330	*7,1*
Rheinland-Pfalz	152	*5,1*	47	*1,5*	296	*8,8*	151	*4,5*
Baden-Württemberg	862	*13,4*	144	*2,2*	1.326	*17,9*	433	*5,9*
Bayern	1.937	*21,1*	228	*2,5*	1.768	*19,1*	340	*3,7*
Bundesgebiet ohne Berlin(West)[3]	7.876	*16,5*	1.555	*3,3*	9.339	*18,2*	3.136	*6,1*
außerdem: Berlin(West)	148	*6,9*	80	*3,7*	185	*8,3*	.	.

[1] Als *Vertriebene* werden alle Deutschen angesehen, die am 1.9.1939 in den zur Zeit unter fremder Verwaltung stehenden Ostgebieten des Deutschen Reiches (Gebietsstand 31.12.1937) oder im Ausland gewohnt haben, einschließlich ihrer nach 1939 geborenen Kinder.

[2] Als *Zugewanderte* gelten alle Deutschen, die am 1.9.1939 in Berlin oder der sogenannten DDR gewohnt haben, einschließlich ihrer nach 1939 geborenen Kinder; in Berlin (West) nur Deutsche, die 1939 in der sogenannten DDR gewohnt haben.

[3] Die Zahl der Vertriebenen in der sogenannten DDR wird auf rund vier Millionen geschätzt.

Quelle: Statistisches Bundesamt.

Seit dem Spätherbst 1949 bis zum 31. 12. 1958 wurden rund 941.000 Vertriebene und Flüchtlinge umgesiedelt. Damit ist das 1.050.000 Personen umfassende Umsiedlungsprogramm der Bundesregierung zu 89,6% erfüllt.

*

Insgesamt sind seit dem 1. 9. 1939 über 3,1 Millionen Zugewanderte aus der Sowjetischen Besatzungszone registriert worden; sie machen 6,1% der

Tabelle 2

VERTRIEBENE[1] UND ZUGEWANDERTE[2]

(Bundesgebiet ohne Saarland)

Entwicklung 1946—1958

Stichtag	Wohnbevölkerung[3]	darunter			
		Vertriebene		Zugewanderte	
	1.000	1.000	%	1.000	%
13. 9. 1950	47.696	7.876	*16,5*	1.555	*3,3*
31. 12. 1951	47.597	8.120	*17,1*	1.758	*3,7*
31. 12. 1952	47.899	8.258	*17,2*	1.896	*4,0*
31. 12. 1953	48.468	8.451	*17,4*	2.153	*4,4*
31. 12. 1954	48.954	8.576	*17,5*	2.378	*4,9*
31. 12. 1955	49.508	8.756	*17,7*	2.611	*5,3*
31. 12. 1956	50.111[4]	8.889[4]	*17,7*	2.807	*5,6*
31. 12. 1957	50.813	9.148	*18,0*	3.029	*6,0*
30. 9. 1958	51.304	9.339	*18,2*	3.136	*6,1*

[1] Siehe Anmerkung 1 zu Tabelle 1.

[2] Siehe Anmerkung 2 zu Tabelle 1.

[3] Jeweiliger Gebietsstand.

[4] Diese und die folgenden Zahlen für Wohnbevölkerung und Vertriebene sind auf der Grundlage der Wohnungszählung vom 25. 9. 1956 aufgebaut.

Quelle: Statistisches Bundesamt.

Tabelle 3

DIE WOHNPARTEIEN IN NORMAL- UND NOTWOHNUNGEN

Bundesgebiet ohne Saarland

a) Gesamtbevölkerung und Vertriebene am 13. 9. 1950 und 25. 9. 1956

Art der Unterbringung	Wohnparteien					
	insgesamt		Vertriebene		Nichtvertriebene	
	Anzahl	%	Anzahl	%	Anzahl	%
	Stand: 13. 9. 1950					
Wohnungsinhaber in Normalwohnungen	9.417.227	*61,2*	581.284	*22,4*	8.835.943	*69,0*
Untermieter in Normalwohnungen	5.216.646	*33,9*	1.728.936	*66,6*	3.487.710	*27,3*
Wohnparteien in Unterkünften außerhalb von Normalwohnungen	761.982	*4,9*	284.698	*11,0*	477.284	*3,7*
Insgesamt	15.395.855	*100*	2.594.918	*100*	12.800.937	*100*
In % aller Wohnparteien	*100* %	—	*16,9* %	—	*83,1* %	—

Tabelle 3 (Fortsetzung)

DIE WOHNPARTEIEN IN NORMAL- UND NOTWOHNUNGEN

Bundesgebiet ohne Saarland

a) Gesamtbevölkerung und Vertriebene am 13. 9. 1950 und 25. 9. 1956

Art der Unterbringung	Wohnparteien					
	insgesamt		Vertriebene		Nichtvertriebene	
	Anzahl	%	Anzahl	%	Anzahl	%
	Stand: 25. 9. 1956					
Wohnungsinhaber in Normalwohnungen	12.663.584	*76,4*	1.808.949	*62,9*	10.854.635	*79,3*
Untermieter in Normalwohnungen	3.300.106	*19,9*	875.441	*30,5*	2.424.665	*17,7*
Wohnparteien in Unterkünften außerhalb von Normalwohnungen	605.306	*3,7*	188.900	*6,6*	416.406	*3,0*
Insgesamt	16.568.996	*100*	2.873.290	*100*	13.695.706	*100*
In % aller Wohnparteien	*100 %*	—	*17,3 %*	—	*82,7 %*	—

b) die Nicht-Vertriebenen nach Personengruppen (Geschädigte und Nichtgeschädigte) am 25. 9. 1956

Art der Unterbringung	Wohnparteien							
	Flüchtlinge aus der sogenannten DDR		Zugewanderte (ohne Flüchtlinge aus der sogen. DDR)		Sonstige Wohnungsgeschädigte		Nicht-Wohnungsgeschädigte	
	Anzahl	%	Anzahl	%	Anzahl	%	Anzahl	%
Wohnungsinhaber in Normalwohnungen	110.600	*69,9*	254.501	*54,9*	1.576.691	*74,5*	8.912.843	*81.4*
Untermieter in Normalwohnungen	37.894	*23,9*	174.224	*37,5*	434.725	*20,5*	1.777.822	*16,2*
Wohnparteien in Unterkünften außerhalb von Normalwohnungen	9.742	*6,2*	35.136	*7,6*	105.985	*5,0*	265.543	*2,4*
Insgesamt	158.236	*100*	463.861	*100*	2.117.401	*100*	10.956.208	*100*
In % aller Wohnparteien	*1,0 %*	—	*2,8 %*	—	*12,8 %*	—	*66,1 %*	—

Quelle: Statistisches Bundesamt.

Gesamtbevölkerung aus. Es gilt, sie ebenso wie die 9,3 Millionen Vertriebenen zu versorgen und einzugliedern[1]. Auch aus diesem Grunde gehört der *Wohnungsbau* zu den dringendsten Aufgaben der Bundesrepublik. Die Wohnungszählung 1950 wies aus, daß von 2,6 Millionen Vertriebenen-Haushaltungen (damals 7,5 Millionen Personen) nur 22% eine Normalwohnung innehatten, während rund 67% Untermieter in Normalwohnungen waren und die restlichen 11% in Lagern, Baracken und sonstigen Notunterkünften hausen mußten. Nach den Ergebnissen der Wohnungserhebung vom Herbst 1956 konnten (trotz der Vermehrung der Vertriebenenhaushalte auf 2,9 Millionen = 8,5 Millionen Personen) bereits 63% der Haushalte mit 6,1 Millionen Personen als Eigentümer oder Hauptmieter von Normalwohnungen untergebracht werden, während 30% zur Untermiete wohnten. Nur rund 7% lebten noch in Lagern und sonstigen Notunterkünften. Diese Ergebnisse der Wohnungszählung bedeuten, daß jeder zweite Vertriebenenhaushalt in den letzten sechs Jahren eine Wohnung erhalten konnte[2].

Der Gesamtbetrag der Förderungsmittel des Lastenausgleichs für den Wohnungsbau beläuft sich bis Mitte 1958 auf mehr als 8 Milliarden DM. In den letzten Jahren betrug er 30% der Gesamtleistungen der öffentlichen Hand für den Wohnungsbau. An dem mit öffentlichen Mitteln geförderten Wohnungsbau wurden im Durchschnitt der Jahre 1952 bis Juni 1958 die Vertriebenen mit fast 39%, einschließlich der Zugewanderten mit mehr als 43%, beteiligt.

Obwohl die Bundesrepublik mit ihrer jährlichen Bauleistung an der Spitze der europäischen Länder steht, ist der Fehlbedarf an Wohnungen für Vertriebene und Flüchtlinge noch immer größer als der anderer Bevölkerungskreise. Er wird auf über 1.000.000 Wohnungen veranschlagt.

Seit 1953 verschärfte die Wohnungsnot sich durch die verstärkte Zuwanderung aus der sogenannten DDR und neuerdings auch durch die Aussiedler. Für die Unterbringung der seit Frühjahr 1953 bis zum Frühjahr 1958 Zugewanderten und Aussiedler in Wohnungen hat der Bund 2,3 Milliarden DM bereitgestellt.

Um die beschleunigte Auflösung der Wohnlager zu ermöglichen, wurden im gleichen Zeitraum vom Bund 180 Millionen DM, und zwar zu zwei Dritteln aus Lastenausgleichsmitteln und einem Drittel aus Haushaltsmitteln, bereitgestellt. Für die Auflösung von Lagern im Rahmen der Räumung von Kasernen gab der Bund zusätzlich weitere 45 Millionen DM.

[1] Siehe die Tabellen 1 und 2 auf den Seiten 49 und 50.
[2] Siehe Tabelle 3 auf den Seiten 50 und 51.

Der Wohnungsbau im Rahmen der Umsiedlung von Vertriebenen, Flüchtlingen, Evakuierten und heimatlosen Ausländern aus überbelegten Ländern der Bundesrepublik in arbeitsintensive Länder (siehe oben) wird vom Bund mit 1.565 Millionen DM gefördert werden. Hiervon entfallen zwei Drittel auf Lastenausgleichs- und ein Drittel auf Haushaltsmittel. In gleicher Weise fördert der Bund die Wohnraumversorgung der Evakuierten, die außerhalb der allgemeinen Umsiedlungsmaßnahmen in das Land ihres Ausgangsortes zurückgeführt wurden.

Die Wohnungspolitik des Bundes hat das Ziel, die Geschädigten des Krieges auch durch den Wohnungsbau zu *Eigentum* zu bringen. An der Gesamtzahl der Eigentümer-Haushaltungen in Normalwohnungen waren 1956 beteiligt:

die Vertriebenen mit	6,3%
die Flüchtlinge aus der sogenannten DDR mit	0,3%
die Zugewanderten (ohne Flüchtlinge aus der sogenannten DDR) mit	0,6%
die einheimischen Geschädigten mit	7,0%
die Nichtgeschädigten mit	85,8%

*

Eine schwere Aufgabe ist die *Wiederansiedlung* der ursprünglich über 300.000 ehemals selbständigen *bäuerlichen Familien*. Als gesetzliche Grundlage für die Eingliederung dieses Personenkreises wurden schon 1946 von den Länderregierungen Bodenreformgesetze, von der Verwaltung des Vereinigten Wirtschaftsgebietes am 10. 8. 1949 das Flüchtlingsgesetz, am 19. 5. 1955 schließlich vom Bundestag das Bundesvertriebenengesetz — mit seinem Titel „Landwirtschaft" — erlassen.

Tabelle 4 SIEDLUNGSERFOLGE IN DEN JAHREN 1949 BIS 1958

Zahl	Stellenzahl	Fläche in ha
1949/50 (18 Monate)	10.670	101.608
1951	12.544	84.365
1952	11.870	62.784
1953	8.693	43.372
1954	13.234	51.465
1955	13.728	40.314
1956	12.361	41.528
1957	11.762	35.209
1958 (6 Monate)	4.244	13.891
1949—1958 I. Halbjahr..............	99.106	474.536

Quelle: Bundesministerium für Vertriebene, Flüchtlinge und Kriegsgeschädigte.

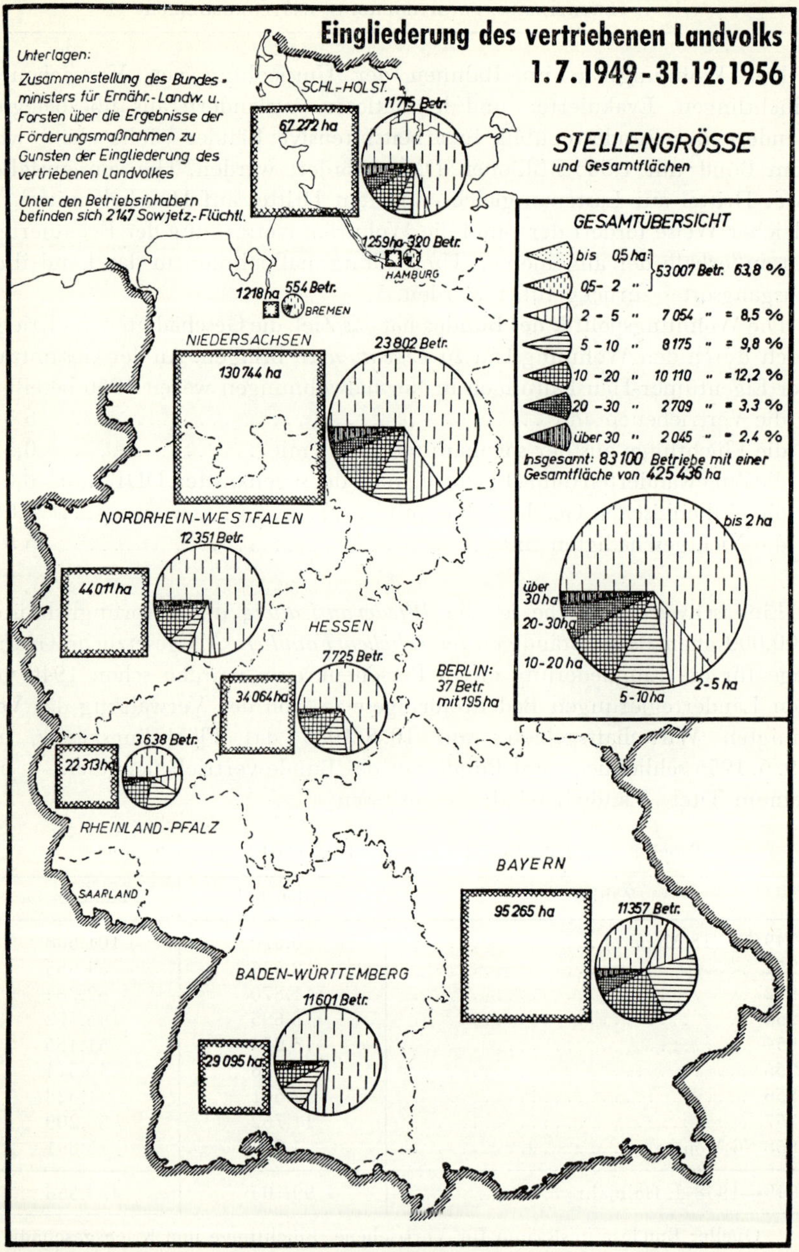
Eingliederung des vertriebenen Landvolks
1.7.1949 - 31.12.1956
STELLENGRÖSSE
und Gesamtflächen
Unterlagen:
Zusammenstellung des Bundesministers für Ernähr.- Landw. u. Forsten über die Ergebnisse der Förderungsmaßnahmen zu Gunsten der Eingliederung des vertriebenen Landvolkes
Unter den Betriebsinhabern befinden sich 2147 Sowjetz.-Flüchtl.
SCHL.-HOLST.
67 272 ha
11 715 Betr.
1259 ha 320 Betr.
HAMBURG
1218 ha
554 Betr.
BREMEN
NIEDERSACHSEN
130 744 ha
23 802 Betr.
NORDRHEIN-WESTFALEN
12 351 Betr.
44 011 ha
HESSEN
7725 Betr.
34 064 ha
BERLIN:
37 Betr.
mit 195 ha
3638 Betr.
22 313 ha
RHEINLAND-PFALZ
SAARLAND
BAYERN
95 265 ha
11 357 Betr.
BADEN-WÜRTTEMBERG
11 601 Betr.
29 095 ha
GESAMTÜBERSICHT
bis 0,5 ha
0,5- 2 "
53 007 Betr. 63,8 %
2 - 5 " 7 054 " = 8,5 %
5 - 10 " 8 175 " = 9,8 %
10 - 20 " 10 110 " = 12,2 %
20 - 30 " 2 709 " = 3,3 %
über 30 " 2 045 " = 2,4 %
Insgesamt: 83 100 Betriebe mit einer Gesamtfläche von 425 436 ha
bis 2 ha
über 30 ha
20-30 ha
10-20 ha
5-10 ha
2-5 ha

Bis zum 30.6.1958 konnten insgesamt 99.106 landwirtschaftliche Vollbauern- und Nebenerwerbsbetriebe mit zusammen 474.536 Hektar Betriebsfläche auf der Grundlage der angeführten gesetzlichen Bestimmungen an Flüchtlinge übergeben werden[1]. Aus öffentlichen Mitteln wurden dafür insgesamt 2.602.512.322 DM bereitgestellt, davon etwa 2.444.133.000 DM als Darlehen und 158.379.000 DM als Beihilfen. Ein erheblicher Teil dieser Mittel entstammt dem Lastenausgleich, der Rest den Haushalten von Bund und Ländern.

Die Zahl der Siedlungswilligen beläuft sich heute noch auf über 100.000 vertriebene Bauernfamilien. Nach dem beschlossenen Siedlungsprogramm 1958 sind 11.719 Stellen für diese Bewerber vorgesehen.

Die Vertriebenen eingliedern heißt, ihnen *Arbeitsplätze* von Dauer und entsprechend ihrer Qualifikation zu schaffen. Noch im Herbst 1950 betrug ihr Anteil an den Arbeitslosen im Bundesgebiet 34%. Dieser Anteil konnte bis September 1958 auf 19,5% gesenkt werden. An dem Rückgang der Arbeitslosigkeit der Vertriebenen insgesamt, der von Ende September 1953 bis zum 30.9.1958: 199.540 Köpfe betrug, waren die drei Hauptflüchtlingsländer (Schleswig-Holstein, Niedersachsen, Bayern) mit rund 74% beteiligt. Ende September 1953 hatten sie zusammen rund 190.000 Arbeitslose, Ende September 1958 rund 42.000.

Neben der Umsiedlung, durch welche die Vertriebenen in vom Arbeitsmarkt her gesehen günstigere Gebiete gelangten, wurden die Bemühungen zur Schaffung von Dauer-Arbeitsplätzen vor allem in den Hauptflüchtlingsländern mit Nachdruck fortgesetzt. Als besonders wirksam haben sich dabei die von der Bundesregierung durchgeführten Maßnahmen wie das 300-Millionen-DM-Schwerpunktprogramm des Jahres 1950, die Programme für die Sanierung der Notstandsgebiete, das Zonenrandprogramm und die Darlehen der Soforthilfe beziehungsweise des Lastenausgleichs zur Schaffung von Dauerarbeitsplätzen erwiesen. Die Bundesregierung erließ am 31.3.1954 Richtlinien für die Berücksichtigung bevorzugter Bewerber bei der Vergabe öffentlicher Aufträge. Nach ihnen sind vertriebene und geflüchtete Unternehmer sowie Personen und Unternehmen aus den Gebieten, die als notleidende Gebiete anerkannt sind, bei der Vergabe öffentlicher Aufträge besonders zu bedenken.

Ein großer Teil der wieder beschäftigten Vertriebenen hat allerdings, wie die Tabelle 5 zeigt, auf die frühere *wirtschaftliche Selbständigkeit* verzichten müssen. Während vor der Vertreibung rund 33% selbständig waren oder

[1] Siehe Tabelle 4, Seite 53.

EINHEIMISCHE UND VERTRIEBENE BEVÖLKERUNG

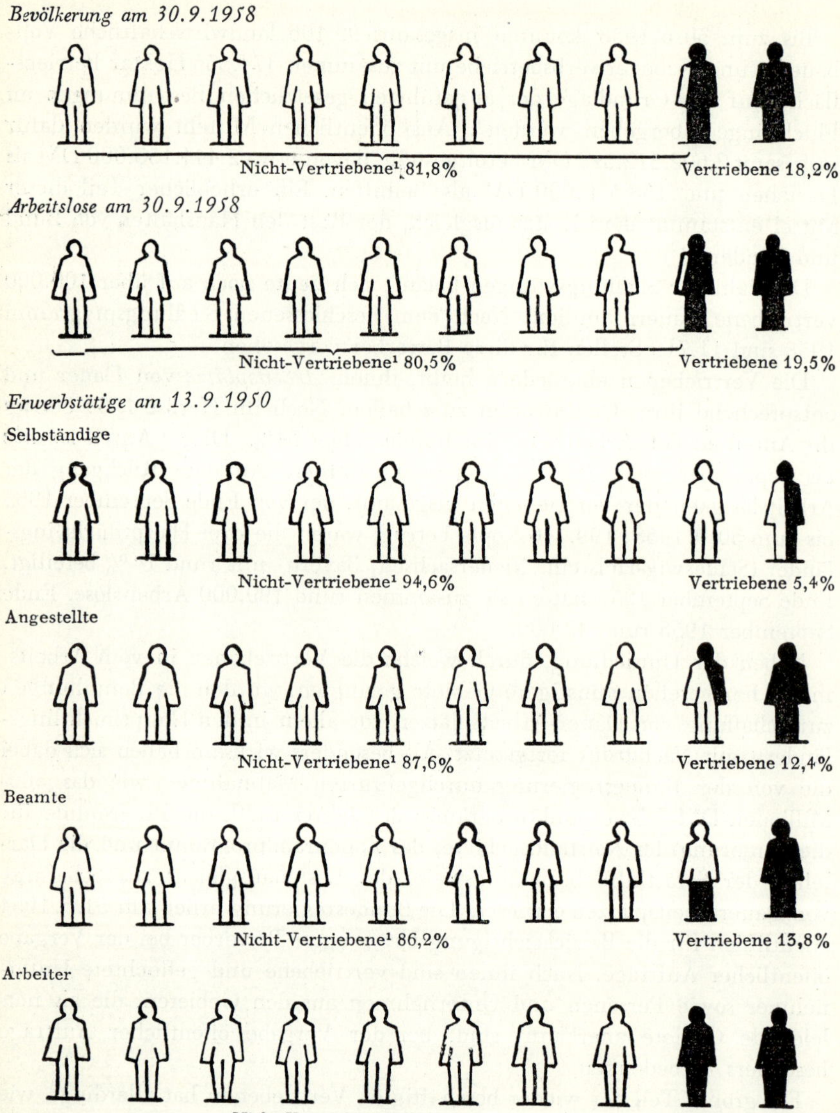

[1] Unter der nicht-vertriebenen Bevölkerung sind auch die Zugewanderten (Flüchtlinge) aus der sogenannten DDR angegeben.

Quelle: Bundesministerium für Vertriebene, Flüchtlinge und Kriegsgeschädigte.

in der Familie mithalfen, ist dieser Anteil auf 8% abgesunken. Der Anteil der Unselbständigen ist nach den Ergebnissen der Erhebung von 1954/1955 entsprechend von 67% auf 92% gestiegen. Von denjenigen, die in nichtselbständiger Tätigkeit arbeiten, sind etwa 20% nicht mehr in ihren früheren Berufen tätig. Vor allem die Land- und Forstwirtschaft hat an Bedeutung erheblich abgenommen: der Anteil der darin erwerbstätigen Vertriebenen ist von 29,0% auf 6,8% zurückgegangen. Demgegenüber ist der Anteil der industriellen und handwerklichen Berufe an den Erwerbstätigen von 28,2% auf 50,3% gestiegen. Ein Zeichen des starken Arbeitswillens der Vertriebenen ist die Tatsache, daß sie überwiegend Stellen angenommen haben, die weniger lohnend sind und deshalb von der einheimischen Bevölkerung mehr gemieden werden. Man schätzt, daß bisher etwa 40% erträglich in einen Beruf eingegliedert wurden, etwa 40% sich noch im Anfangsstadium der beruflichen Eingliederung befinden und etwa 20% der Vertriebenen noch keine Aussicht auf eine solche haben.

Die Gesamtzahl der *Industrieunternehmen* von Vertriebenen und Zugewanderten im Bundesgebiet wurde im September 1957 mit 10.400 (davon 6.600 Vertriebenenbetriebe) festgestellt. Die Zahl der Inhaber von *Handwerksbetrieben* betrug am 1.1.1958: 62.000 (einschließlich der Handwerksbetriebe Zugewanderter). Der Neugründung dieser Unternehmen ist eine beträchtliche Erhöhung des Sozialproduktes gefolgt.

Die gewerbliche Wirtschaft und die freiberufliche Tätigkeit der Vertriebenen wurde von der Bundesregierung und den Ländern durch Kredite und Bürgschaften nachhaltig gefördert. Bis zum 31.3.1958 wurden aus öffentlichen Programmen Kredite in einer Summe von rund 1,6 Milliarden DM gewährt. Davon entfallen auf das ERP-Sondervermögen 156 Millionen DM, auf den Lastenausgleichsfonds 851 Millionen DM für Aufbaudarlehen und 81 Millionen DM Arbeitsplatzdarlehen; ferner 42 Millionen DM auf Liquiditätskredite. Durch den Einsatz dieser Kredite ist es gelungen, annähernd 200.000 Vertriebene wieder in eine selbständige Existenz in Gewerbe, Handel und in freien Berufen zu bringen.

Im März 1951 überreichte der amerikanische Bankier H. C. SONNE, der Leiter einer ECA-Kommission für Flüchtlingsfragen, dem Bundeskanzler einen Bericht mit Vorschlägen über die Eingliederung der Vertriebenen. Diese Vorschläge sind aus Gründen, die nicht in der Zuständigkeit der Bundesregierung lagen, nicht zur Durchführung gelangt.

*

Aus der Erkenntnis, daß ein eigenes Finanzierungsinstitut notwendig ist, um dem besonderen Kreditbedarf der Vertriebenen zu dienen, wurde am

Tabelle 5

DIE VERTRIEBENEN

(Antragsteller A und B) nach Bevölkerungsgruppen, die erwerbstätigen Vertriebenen nach Berufsabteilungen und Stellung im Beruf im Vertreibungs- und Erhebungszeitpunkt (Stand 1954/55)

Bevölkerungsgruppen Erwerbstätige nach Berufsabteilungen Stellung im Beruf	Antragsteller A und B			
	im Vertreibungszeitpunkt		im Erhebungszeitpunkt	
	1.000	%	1.000	%
Bevölkerungsgruppen:				
Erwerbstätige	3.129,0	*55,0*	2.694,4	*47,3*
Erwerbslose	—	—	279,1	*4,9*
Selbständige Berufslose	273,8	*4,8*	1.209,2	*21,2*
Angehörige ohne Beruf	2.288,1	*40,2*	1.508,1	*26,5*
Insgesamt	5.690,9	*100*	5.690,9	*100*
Erwerbstätige nach Berufsabteilungen:				
1 Berufe des Pflanzenbaues und der Tierwirtschaft	908,4	*29,0*	183,1	*6,8*
2/3 Industrielle u. handwerkliche Berufe	883,9	*28,3*	1.355,0	*50,3*
4 Technische Berufe	83,0	*2,7*	83,1	*3,1*
5 Handels- und Verkehrsberufe	514,9	*16,5*	436,5	*16,2*
6 Berufe der Haushalts-, Gesundheits- und Volkspflege	180,6	*5,8*	214,7	*8,0*
7 Berufe des Verwaltungs- und Rechtswesens	337,9	*10,8*	234,5	*8,7*
8 Berufe des Geistes- und Kulturlebens	90,1	*2,9*	70,4	*2,6*
9 Berufstätige mit unbestimmtem Beruf	130,2	*4,2*	117,1	*4,3*
Erwerbstätige insgesamt	3.129,0	*100*	2.694,4	*100*
Erwerbstätige nach der Stellung im Beruf:				
Selbständige	573,0	*18,3*	169,6	*6,3*
Mithelfende Familienangehörige	470,4	*15,0*	35,7	*1,3*
Beamte	241,7	*7,7*	148,2	*5,5*
Angestellte	668,2	*21,4*	538,7	*20,0*
Arbeiter	1.175,7	*37,6*	1.802,3	*66,9*
Erwerbstätige insgesamt	3.129,0	*100*	2.694,4	*100*

Quelle: Statistisches Bundesamt, Statistik der Bundesrepublik Deutschland, Band 211.

12.5.1950 eine Vertriebenen-Bank mit einem Grundkapital von 5 Millionen DM errichtet. Das Kapital wurde aus Gegenwertmitteln des Marshall-Plans gegeben. Diese Bank, die als Refinanzierungsinstitut wirkt, entwickelte sich so günstig, daß ihre Bilanzsumme 1952 bereits 800 Millionen ausmachte. Infolge der engen Zusammenarbeit der Bank mit dem Hauptamt für Soforthilfe erschien es zweckmäßig, ihren Aufgabenkreis auch auf die Kriegssachgeschädigten und andere durch die Soforthilfe oder den Lastenausgleich begünstigte Personenkreise auszudehnen. Seit der Verabschiedung des Lastenausgleichsgesetzes ist der Bank die Aufgabe zugefallen, neben ihren bisherigen Geschäften alle im Rahmen des Lastenausgleichs zu vergebenden Kredite zu verwalten. Sie ist im Jahre 1954 unter Erhöhung des Grundkapitals auf 25 Millionen DM in eine Anstalt des öffentlichen Rechts unter der Firma „*Lastenausgleichsbank*" (Bank für Vertriebene und Geschädigte) umgewandelt worden. Ihre Bilanzsumme betrug zum 31.12.1957 über 5,7 Milliarden DM.

*

Durch ein Gesetz zu Artikel 131 des Grundgesetzes wurden die „Rechtsverhältnisse der verdrängten Personen des öffentlichen Dienstes" geregelt. Durch Gesetz sollte diese Gruppe wieder in ein festes Rechtsverhältnis gebracht werden und damit auch einen klaren Versorgungsanspruch erhalten. Die Dienstherren des öffentlichen Rechtes sind verpflichtet, 20% ihrer Planstellen mit verdrängten Personen des öffentlichen Dienstes zu besetzen. Für die Berufsangehörigen der ehemaligen Wehrmacht wurden im gleichen Zusammenhang Sonderbestimmungen getroffen. Im Zuge einer fortschreitenden Besserung der wirtschaftlichen Lage sollen gewisse Rechte noch erweitert und dem Beamtengesetz des Bundes angeglichen werden.

*

Das Gesetz über die Angelegenheiten der Vertriebenen und Flüchtlinge — kurz *Bundesvertriebenengesetz* genannt — ist durch den Bundestag am 10.5. 1953 verabschiedet worden. Dieses Gesetz gehört zu den wichtigsten, grundsätzlichen Regelungen, die für die Vertriebenen geschaffen worden sind. Es hat den Personenkreis rechtlich definiert. Die anerkannten Flüchtlinge aus der sogenannten DDR werden in gewissem Umfange den Vertriebenen gleichgestellt. Außerdem bringt das Gesetz Rahmenbestimmungen zur Durchführung der Umsiedlung, der Eingliederung und der Kulturarbeit.

*

BEVÖLKERUNGSVERGLEICH

Südafrikanische Union (1958) . . . . 14,4 Mill.

Vertriebene in Deutschland (vier Besatzungszonen) . 13,5 Mill.

Tschechoslowakei (1958) 13,5 Mill.

9,4 Millionen Vertriebene und 3,2 Millionen Zugewanderte in der Bundesrepublik; (ohne Saarland und Berlin); zusammen 12,6 Mill.

Niederlande (1958) . . 11,2 Mill.

Australien (1957) . . . 9,6 Mill.

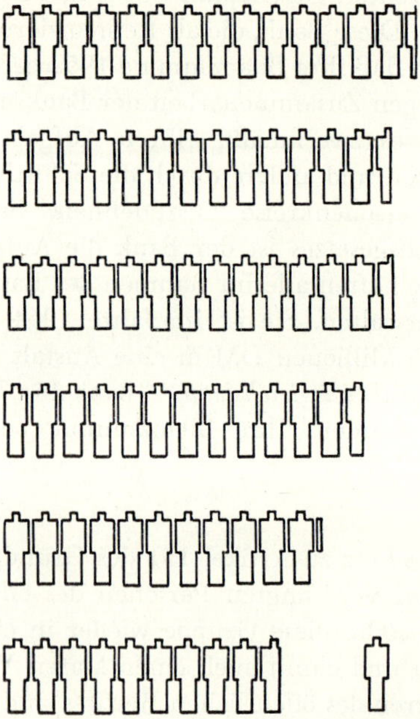

= 1.000.000

Quelle: Statistisches Bundesamt.

Um die Größenordnung der Probleme, die der Bundesregierung gestellt sind, ermessen zu können, muß man sich gegenwärtig halten, daß die Zahl der Vertriebenen und Zugewanderten in der Bundesrepublik die Einwohnerzahlen Australiens oder der Niederlande inzwischen hinter sich gelassen hat. Vor dem Zweiten Weltkrieg lebten im heutigen Bundesgebiet einschließlich Saarlands und von Berlin (West) 42.997.600 Einwohner. Am 30. 9. 1958 waren es — trotz schwersten Kriegsverlusten — 54.568.600. Einschließlich von Berlin (West) sind auf einem Raum, der 52,8 % des früheren Reichsgebietes umschließt, 78,7 % der Bevölkerung Deutschlands aus dem Jahre 1939 zusammengedrängt.

Durch die Vertriebenen und Zugewanderten ist die Bevölkerung des Bundesgebietes auf 220 Personen je Quadratkilometer angestiegen. Kein anderes Land Europas — außer den Niederlanden und den Stadtstaaten[1] — hat eine

[1] Vatikanstaat, Monaco usw.

vergleichbare Bevölkerungsdichte bei ähnlicher Wirtschaftsgrundlage. Belgien liegt zwar als Heimatland noch etwas darüber, hat aber Kolonien als ergänzenden Wirtschaftsraum. Die Zahl von 220 Menschen gewinnt erst Farbe, wenn man bedenkt, daß Frankreich auf den Quadratkilometer achtzig Einwohner hat; die USA haben sogar nur zweiundzwanzig, also etwa ein Zehntel der deutschen Bevölkerungsdichte, und die Sowjetunion mit neun Menschen nur den vierundzwanzigsten Teil aufzuweisen[1].

Der Lastenausgleich

Als Zeichen des deutschen Willens zur Selbsthilfe bis zur höchstmöglichen Grenze wurde schon bald nach Bildung der Bundesregierung das *Lastenausgleichsgesetz* (LAG) in Angriff genommen. Unzählige schwierige Fragen wurden in Kommissionen und Besprechungen geklärt. Die berechtigten Forderungen der Vertriebenen und der übrigen Geschädigten mußten mit den wirtschaftlichen Möglichkeiten in Einklang gebracht werden. Ende 1950 wurde der Regierungsentwurf den gesetzgebenden Körperschaften zugeleitet und am 18.8.1952 das Lastenausgleichsgesetz verabschiedet. Es löst die Leistungen aus dem Soforthilfegesetz ab, in dessen Laufzeit annähernd 6,0 Milliarden DM für die Vertriebenen und Kriegssachgeschädigten für verschiedene Zwecke ausgeschüttet wurden. Bis zum 31.3.1958 betrugen die Leistungen des Lastenausgleichsfonds für Vertriebene, Flüchtlinge aus der sogenannten DDR und Kriegssachgeschädigte insgesamt rund 24,5 Milliarden DM.

Das Lastenausgleichsgesetz belastet das abgabepflichtige Vermögen nach dem Stand vom 21.6.1948, dem Tag der Währungsreform, grundsätzlich mit 50% seines Einheitswertes. Die Vermögensabgabe, die verzinst werden muß, ist bis zum 31.3.1979 in Vierteljahresbeträgen zu entrichten. Diese sind nach der Art des der Abgabe unterliegenden Vermögens gestaffelt. Das Lastenausgleichsgesetz kennt als weitere Abgaben die Hypothekengewinnabgabe und die Kreditgewinnabgabe. Die Beiträge fließen in den Lastenausgleichsfonds, einen Spezialfonds außerhalb des Bundeshaushalts. Außer dem Fonds werden die Leistungen des Lastenausgleichs auch aus im Gesetz vorgesehenen Beiträgen von Bund und Ländern gespeist. Lastenausgleichsberechtigt sind Vertriebene, Kriegssachgeschädigte und, in begrenztem Umfange, Sparergeschädigte, sowie über den Härtefonds des Lastenausgleichs

[1] Vergleiche die Tabelle unter der Europakarte am Ende des Buches.

gewisse in einer besonderen Rechtsverordnung genannte Personenkreise, von denen die anerkannten Sowjetzonenflüchtlinge (C-Ausweis) die stärkste Gruppe sind. Das Gesamtaufkommen des Lastenausgleichs betrug im Rechnungsjahr 1957 rund 3,7 Milliarden DM. Das Kernstück der Leistungen stellt die *Hauptentschädigung* dar. Durch sie werden die Verluste quotal abgegolten, die durch Vertreibung und Kriegssachschäden entstanden sind, insbesondere Verluste an Wirtschaftsgütern, die zum land- und forstwirtschaftlichen Vermögen, zum Grundvermögen oder zum Betriebsvermögen gehörten.

Die Höhe der Hauptentschädigung wurde durch die am 2.8.1957 in Kraft getretene 8. Novelle bestimmt. Für die Verluste an Hausrat wird durch die *Hausratentschädigung* pauschaler Ersatz geleistet. Der Eingliederung der Geschädigten in den Wirtschaftsprozeß dienen die *Aufbaudarlehen* und die *Arbeitsplatzdarlehen*. Aufbaudarlehen werden gewährt zur Schaffung und Sicherung gewerblicher und ländlicher sowie freiberuflicher Existenzen, zum Wiederaufbau von zerstörtem oder beschädigtem Grundbesitz, sowie zum Wohnungsbau insbesondere am gesicherten Arbeitsplatz. Der Wohnungsbau wird ferner gefördert durch die aus der Hypothekengewinnabgabe fließende *Wohnraumhilfe*. Eine wichtige Leistung des Lastenausgleichs ist die *Ausbildungshilfe*, die für geschädigte Jugendliche gewährt wird. Soziale Funktionen in weitem Umfange erfüllt die *Unterhaltshilfe*, die Geschädigte erhalten, wenn sie infolge Alters oder Erwerbsunfähigkeit nicht imstande sind, den notwendigen Lebensbedarf für sich und ihre unterhaltsberechtigten Angehörigen zu beschaffen. Eine Aufstockung der Unterhaltshilfe erfolgt durch die *Entschädigungsrente* bei den Geschädigten, die einen Anspruch auf Hauptentschädigung besitzen. Zu erwähnen bleibt noch die Förderung von Heimen und Einrichtungen der freien und öffentlichen Wohlfahrtspflege durch Mittel des Lastenausgleichs.

Aus den Mitteln des Lastenausgleichs, aber auf Grund eines besonderen Währungsausgleichsgesetzes für Sparguthaben Vertriebener, wird eine Entschädigung für die genannten *Sparguthaben* gezahlt. Sie entspricht in ihrer Höhe der Währungsumstellung und dem Altsparergesetz.

Die *Feststellung der Vertreibungsschäden und der Kriegssachschäden* wird auf Grund eines besonderen, das Lastenausgleichsgesetz ergänzenden Gesetzes, des Feststellungsgesetzes in der Fassung vom 14.8.1952, durchgeführt.

Soziale Betreuung

Bei der Neugestaltung des sozialen Rechts konnte das Bundesministerium für Vertriebene erreichen, daß durch Flucht oder Vertreibung entstandene Schädigungen im Gesetz über die Versorgung der Opfer des Krieges berücksichtigt und erworbene sozialversicherungsrechtliche Ansprüche und Anwartschaften im Fremdrenten- und Auslandsrentengesetz gesichert wurden. Gesetzliche Maßnahmen wirkten der besonders unter der Vertriebenen- und

Flüchtlingsjugend herrschenden Berufsnot und Arbeitslosigkeit entgegen und leiteten Bemühungen um die berufliche Eingliederung der älteren Angestellten ein.

Die Notstände der *Zuwanderer* aus der sogenannten DDR sowie der *Aussiedler*, welche durch die seit 1955 verstärkte Aktion des Deutschen Roten Kreuzes zur Zusammenführung von Familien aus den Vertreibungsgebieten im Bundesgebiet eintreffen, erfordern besondere Hilfsmaßnahmen durch Bund, Länder und Gemeinden. Kinder und Jugendliche aus dem Kreise der Aussiedler beherrschen ohne Verschulden ihre deutsche Muttersprache großenteils nicht mehr. Für sie wurden bisher durch die Länder und Verbände der freien Wohlfahrtspflege rund 265 geschlossene Fördereinrichtungen mit zur Zeit rund 10.500 Plätzen geschaffen. Ihre Kapazität soll in Zukunft noch

Tabelle 6

DIE EMPFÄNGER VON LAUFENDER FÜRSORGE UND UNTERHALTSHILFE IM BUNDESGEBIET NACH LEISTUNGSARTEN UND GESCHÄDIGTENGRUPPEN (PERSONENKREISE)[1]

Art der Leistungen	Empfänger der Leistungen (Parteien)						
	Parteien insgesamt	davon					
		Vertriebene		Zugewanderte		Einheimische	
		Anzahl	% Sp. 1	Anzahl	% Sp. 1	Anzahl	% Sp. 1
	1	2	3	4	5	6	7
Laufende Unterstützungen der offenen Fürsorge (Sept. 1957)[2]	510.735	116.220	*22,7*	21.710	*4,3*	372.805	*73,0*
Unterhaltshilfe (30.9.1957)	782.680	585.502	*74,8*	—	—	197.178	*25,2*
Beihilfe zum Lebensunterhalt aus dem Härtefonds (30.9.1957)	6.343	—	—	5.950	*93,8*	393	*6,2*
Hilfsbedürftige zusammen[3]	1.299.758	701.722	*54,0*	27.660	*2,1*	570.376	*43,9*
Personenkreis in % (1.7.1957)	*100*	—	*17,9*	—	*5,8*	—	*76,3*

[1] Zahlenangaben für das Bundesgebiet einschließlich von Berlin (West).
[2] Auf Grund der Zusatz-Statistik 1957.
[3] Einschließlich der Mehrfachzahlungen. Diese beziehen sich auf die Unterstützten des Lastenausgleichs, die zugleich in der Fürsorge unterstützt werden.

Quelle: Statistische Informationen des Bundesausgleichsamtes Nr. 173 vom 10.12.1957: „Kriegsschadenrente und Beihilfen zum Lebensunterhalt bis zum 30.9.1957."

erweitert werden. Die schulische und berufliche Ausbildung der jugendlichen Vertriebenen, Flüchtlinge und Evakuierten wird durch Ausbildungsbeihilfen erleichtert. Ein durch die Bundesregierung geschaffener ,,Garantiefonds" soll den Beginn der Berufsausbildung beschleunigen und Härten beseitigen.

Die soziale Betreuung der Vertriebenen, Flüchtlinge und Kriegsgeschädigten durch die Verbände der freien Wohlfahrtspflege, die Organisationen der Vertriebenen und auch das Deutsche Müttergenesungswerk ist auf die sich ständig wandelnden Situationen der Not eingestellt. Aus dem Ausland ist insbesondere das Kinderhilfswerk der Vereinten Nationen (UNICEF) zu erwähnen, das in den Jahren 1949 bis 1953 Medikamente, medizinische Geräte und Rohstoffe im Werte von 11,5 Millionen DM zur Verfügung gestellt hat. Die Textilrohstoffe wurden in deutschen Betrieben zu Bekleidungsstücken verarbeitet. Eine große Hilfe stellte auch die fünfzigprozentige Fahrpreisermäßigung dar, welche die Deutsche Bundesbahn von 1949 bis 1953 den Heimatvertriebenen für bestimmte Reisen gewährte.

Der Aufwand für die Geschädigtengruppen in der offenen und geschlossenen Fürsorge von 1950 bis 1957 sowie über die Zahl der in der offenen Fürsorge laufend unterstützten Parteien und Personen nach Geschädigtengruppen geht aus den Tabellen hervor, die in dem Beitrag über die ,,Soziale Sicherung" enthalten sind. Die älteren Vertriebenen erhalten zur Entlastung der kommunalen Fürsorge Unterhaltshilfe usw. aus dem Lastenausgleich. In der vorstehenden Tabelle 6 wird deshalb eine Zusammenstellung über die Gesamtzahl der hilfsbedürftigen Vertriebenen und Zugewanderten (Parteien) gebracht, die Ende 1957 aus beiden Quellen laufend Unterstützungen erhielten.

Das Kulturerbe

Neben der wirtschaftlichen Eingliederung gewann die kulturelle Betreuung der Vertriebenen an Intensität und Bedeutung. Außer ihrer Arbeitskraft und ihren Fertigkeiten haben die Vertriebenen ihr großes ostdeutsches Kulturerbe mit sich getragen. Es gilt, dieses Erbe zu bewahren und zu entfalten, ja, im Bewußtsein aller Deutschen und Europäer lebendig zu erhalten. In den auf stammesmäßiger Grundlage gebildeten Kulturwerken haben sich führende kulturtragende Kräfte aus dem deutschen Osten gesammelt. Ihre Arbeit findet eine organische Ergänzung in einer Reihe von kulturellen Institutionen für spezielle Arbeitsgebiete. Neben anderen seien hier nur

Hohe Gäste aus aller Welt am Sitz der Bundesregierung

Der Indische Ministerpräsident, der Präsident der Republik Indonesien, SKM. der Negus von Äthiopien, der Präsident des Kgl. Afghanischen Parlaments, der Türkische Ministerpräsident, der Präsident von Liberia und seine Gattin, der Wirtschaftsminister des Königreichs Saudi-Arabien, die Wirtschaftsminister der Vereinigten Arabischen Republik, der Kaiserlich Japanische Arbeitsminister — mit dem Präsidenten, dem Kanzler und dem Wirtschaftsminister der Bundesrepublik Deutschland

Der Deutsche Bundesra
tagt im Bonner
Bundeshaus

Sitzung des
Deutschen
Bundestags

genannt: die *Künstlergilde*, die der Förderung der kulturell-schöpferischen Kräfte dient; die *Kommission für Volkskunde der Heimatvertriebenen*; eine Reihe Historischer Kommissionen; das *Institut für Kultur- und Sozialforschung* und andere mehr. Vorwiegend koordinierende und repräsentativen Aufgaben obliegen dem *Ostdeutschen Kulturrat* und dem *Kulturwerk der vertriebenen Deutschen*. Vielbeachtete Veranstaltungen, Ausstellungen und Publikationen beweisen, daß die hier aufgewendete durchaus gegenwartsnahe Arbeit Gewicht und Wirkung hat und auch der geistigen Fundierung des Heimatrechts förderlich ist. Schließlich seien auch die Bemühungen um eine Intensivierung der *Ostkunde im Unterricht* erwähnt, die sich als eines der wirksamsten Mittel für die Erhaltung eines gesamtdeutschen Bewußtseins erwiesen hat.

II. DIE ZUGEWANDERTEN AUS DER SOGENANNTEN DDR

Die gleichen Probleme wie für die Vertriebenen bestehen für die *Zugewanderten*[1]. Der Anteil derer, welche die Zone wegen Gefahr für Leib, Leben und Freiheit verlassen mußten, war in den Jahren 1952 und 1953 sehr hoch. Neben verhältnismäßig wenig alten und nicht mehr arbeitsfähigen Personen kommen viele Jugendliche und Angehörige mittlerer Jahrgänge über die Zonengrenzen, weil sie nicht in der Volkspolizei dienen oder sich den allgemeinen Zwangsmaßnahmen — das gilt vor allem für die Bauern — nicht unterwerfen wollen. Die Abwanderung ist so stark, daß die Bevölkerungsziffer der sogenannten DDR[2] nach deren Angaben seit 1946 von 18,4 Millionen auf 17,4 Millionen[3] gesunken ist.

Von 1949 bis zum 31.12.1958 haben in Berlin(West) 1.196.547 und in Gießen und Uelzen zusammen 991.888 Deutsche aus der sogenannten DDR die Aufnahme beantragt. An diesen Zahlen wird deutlich, daß Berlin das Tor zum Westen ist. Das trat im Jahre 1953 am eindrucksvollsten hervor; damals standen 297.040 Antragstellern in Berlin nur 34.350 Antragsteller in Gießen und Uelzen gegenüber. 257.306 Personen wurden im Jahre 1953 aus Berlin in das Bundesgebiet ausgeflogen, darunter 39.748 alleinstehende Personen unter vierundzwanzig Jahren. Insgesamt wurden bis zum 31.12.1958: 788.848 Flüchtlinge ausgeflogen; darunter 174.927 alleinstehende Personen unter vierundzwanzig Jahren.

[1] *Zugewanderte*: siehe Anmerkung 2 auf Seite 49.

[2] Mit Ostberlin.

[3] Nach dem Stand vom 31.12.1957.

Die Flüchtlinge aus der sogenannten DDR sind offenkundig Opfer des Kalten Krieges. Die materiellen Lasten können daher auf lange Sicht nicht nur von der Bundesrepublik getragen werden. Die Zuwanderer müssen, wenn sie in Berlin eintreffen, ausgestattet und zum größten Teil nach Westdeutschland ausgeflogen werden, weil Berlin (West) sie nicht zusätzlich unterbringen und ernähren kann. Jeder nicht arbeitsfähige Zuwanderer aus der sogenannten DDR kostet nach den Wohlfahrtssätzen 1.000 DM im Jahr. Für die Unterbringung der im Jahre 1957 eingetroffenen Flüchtlinge und Aussiedler in Wohnungen sind im Bundeshaushalt über 800 Millionen DM eingesetzt. Der Fehlbetrag, um den für rund 350.000 Personen erforderlichen Wohnraum zu erstellen, muß aus anderen Finanzierungsquellen aufgebracht werden.

III. DIE AUSSIEDLER

Der Zustrom aus der sogenannten DDR hat eine menschlich nicht minder ergreifende Aktion weniger sichtbar werden lassen: die Bemühungen um die Zusammenführung von Familien, die durch die Vertreibung der Jahre 1944 bis 1948 voneinander getrennt worden waren.

Bei der Austreibung der Millionen Deutschen aus den Ostgebieten des Reiches und den deutschen Siedlungsgebieten in Ost- und Südosteuropa blieben Hunderttausende zurück. Sie traf für Jahre das Los entrechteter Menschen. Das Gewaltsame und die Zufälligkeiten im Ablauf der äußeren Geschehnisse führten dazu, daß zu Tausenden nächste Familienangehörige von einander getrennt wurden.

Diese humanitär schwerwiegenden und vor allem den Einzelnen treffenden Folgen der politischen Ereignisse lösten schon 1948/49 Bemühungen des Internationalen Roten Kreuzes um Familienzusammenführung aus. Verhandlungen der Alliierten mit polnischen und tschechoslowakischen Regierungsstellen ermöglichten in den Jahren 1950 bis 1952 die Durchführung einer Familienzusammenführung. Sie erlaubte fast 60.000 Deutschen, sich mit ihren in den vier Besatzungszonen lebenden Angehörigen wieder zusammenzufinden[1].

Spätere Absprachen unter der gleichen Zielsetzung, so die mit Jugoslawien im Jahre 1951 über die Übernahme der dort lebenden Deutschen, vor allem aber die Vereinbarungen zwischen dem Deutschen und dem Polnischen

[1] Davon kamen 10.000 Deutsche im Rahmen der „Operation Link" in das Bundesgebiet.

Roten Kreuz in den Jahren 1954, 1955 und 1956 über die Familienzusammenführung, ließen die Zahl der als sogenannte *Aussiedler* aus diesen Gebieten kommenden Deutschen im Laufe der Jahre mehr und mehr ansteigen. Gleichartige Bemühungen der Rot-Kreuz-Gesellschaften erstreckten sich etwa ab 1956 auf die zahlreichen noch in der Tschechoslowakei, in Ungarn und in Rumänien getrennt lebenden Familienangehörigen. Diesen Bemühungen ist jedoch ein Ergebnis, welches das Problem menschlich befriedigend löst, bisher versagt geblieben. Nur in Einzelfällen sind auch aus diesen Ländern Ausreisen in größerem Umfang genehmigt worden.

*

Nach Errichtung der Botschaft der Bundesrepublik Deutschland in Moskau im Frühjahr 1956 mehrten sich die Meldungen von deutschen Staatsangehörigen, die sich noch in der Sowjetunion befinden und ihre Rückführung nach Deutschland anstreben. Eine deutsche Delegation, die sich vom Sommer 1957 bis zum April 1958 in der Sowjetunion aufhielt, konnte am 8.4.1958 mit der Regierung der UdSSR eine Vereinbarung über die Rückführung dieser Deutschen abschließen. Danach haben alle in der Sowjetunion befindlichen Deutschen, die am 21.6.1941 die deutsche Staatsangehörigkeit besaßen, ein Recht auf Ausreise. Zu diesem Personenkreis gehören vor allem die Memeldeutschen, die Ostpreußen und die ehemaligen Volksdeutschen, die aus Bessarabien, den baltischen Staaten und anderen Gebieten in den Jahren 1939/41 nach Deutschland umgesiedelt, hier eingebürgert und nach Kriegsende wieder in die Sowjetunion verbracht wurden.

Bei den Deutschen in der Sowjetunion, die erst nach dem 21.6.1941 die deutsche Staatsangehörigkeit erworben haben — dies ist die zahlenmäßig stärkste Gruppe — hat sich die Regierung der UdSSR lediglich zum Prinzip der Zusammenführung von infolge des letzten Krieges getrennten Familien bekannt; allerdings mit der ausdrücklichen Einschränkung, daß sie dabei auf der Grundlage ihrer Gesetzgebung verfahren wird.

Insgesamt sind infolge all dieser Bemühungen in den Jahren *von 1950 bis 1958: 366.820 Deutsche* aus den eingangs aufgeführten Gebieten in das Bundesgebiet übernommen worden.

Der größte Teil der Aussiedler (75,2%) kommt aus den deutschen Ostgebieten, die seit 1945 von Polen verwaltet werden, aus Danzig und dem eigentlichen polnischen Staatsgebiet. Die polnischen Behörden haben, besonders in den Jahren 1957 und 1958, durch eine Liberalisierung des Ausweisverfahrens dieses Ergebnis ermöglicht. Sie gestatteten allein 1957: 98.290 und 1958: 117.550 Personen die Ausreise nach Westdeutschland.

Tabelle 7

AUSSIEDLER 1950 BIS 1958

Herkunftsland	Zahl
Derzeitiger polnischer Verwaltungsbereich	275.930
Jugoslawien	53.700
Tschechoslowakei	19.760
Derzeitiger sowjetischer Verwaltungsbereich	8.020
Ungarn	3.890
Rumänien	3.080
Sonstige Länder	2.440

Quelle: Bundesministerium für Vertriebene, Flüchtlinge und Kriegsgeschädigte.

Tabelle 8

HERKUNFTSGEBIETE DER AUSSIEDLER 1958[1]
(einschließlich der über das freie Ausland übernommenen Vertriebenen)

Herkunftsgebiet	%
Nieder- und Oberschlesien	*60,8*
Ost- und Westpreußen	*10,9*
Pommern	*6,0*
Ostbrandenburg	*0,1*
Deutsche Ostgebiete unter polnischer oder sowjetischer Verwaltung	*77,8*
Freie Stadt Danzig	*4,1*
Polen (einschließlich der nach 1918 an Polen gefallenen deutschen Gebiete)	*7,0*
Sowjetunion (einschließlich der baltischen Staaten und des Memelgebietes)	*3,1*
Jugoslawien	*3,6*
Ungarn	*0,9*
Rumänien	*1,0*
Sonstige Länder	*0,5*
Aussiedler	*98,0*
In andere Staaten verschlagene und von dort (insbesondere aus Österreich) übernommene Personen	*2,0*
132.233 Personen	*100*

[1] Einschließlich sonstiger zunächst in andere Staaten verschlagener und von dort übernommener Personen.

Quelle: Bundesministerium für Vertriebene, Flüchtlinge und Kriegsgeschädigte.

Tabelle 9

ZUGÄNGE ÜBER DIE GRENZDURCHGANGSLAGER FRIEDLAND, PIDING UND SCHALDING

Herkunftsland (bzw. Aufenthalt nach der Vertreibung)	Zugänge in den Grenzdurchgangslagern in den Jahren									
	1950	1951	1952	1953	1954	1955	1956	1957	1958	Summe Sp. 1-9
	1	2	3	4	5	6	7	8	9	10
	Aussiedler									
Ostgebiete des Deutschen Reiches (zur Zeit unter polnischer Verwaltung), Danzig und Polen	31.761	10.791	194	147	662	860	15.674	98.290	117.550	275.929
Sowjetisch verwaltetes Gebiet (baltische Staaten, Memelgebiet und UdSSR)	—	1.721	63	—	18	154	1.016	923	4.122	8.017
Tschechoslowakei	13.308	3.524	146	63	128	184	954	762	692	19.761
Jugoslawien	179	3.668	3.407	7.972	9.481	11.839	7.314	5.130	4.708	53.698
Bulgarien	—	1	—	—	6	11	2	3	3	26
Rumänien	13	1.031	26	15	8	44	176	384	1.383	3.080
Ungarn	3	157	30	15	43	98	160	2.193	1.194	3.893
Albanien	—	—	—	—	—	—	—	—	2	2
China	392	124	181	84	44	12	6	5	6	854
Ungeklärte Fälle	1.509	50	1	—	—	—	—	—	—	1.560
Zusammen	47.165	21.067	4.048	8.296	10.390	13.202	25.302	107.690	129.660	366.820
	Aus dem sonstigen freien Ausland aufgenommene Vertriebene									
Österreich	57	1.519	6.845	5.699	4.240	1.987	5.583	5.822	2.080	33.832
Frankreich	80	1.240	1.617	1.044	572	386	253	130	160	5.482
Vereinigtes Königreich	5	107	124	91	29	26	11	31	32	456
Sonstige Länder	190	832	735	280	191	187	196	273	301	3.185
Zusammen	332	3.698	9.321	7.114	5.032	2.586	6.043	6.256	2.573	42.955

Gesamtzugänge: 409.775

Quelle: Bundesministerium für Vertriebene, Flüchtlinge und Kriegsgeschädigte.

Seit Abschluß der erwähnten deutsch-sowjetischen Vereinbarung — also seit Anfang April 1958 — sind in steigendem Umfang Entlassungen von Deutschen aus der Sowjetunion erfolgt. Vom 1.4. bis 31.12.1958 trafen insgesamt 4.136 Deutsche aus der Sowjetunion in der Bundesrepublik und in Berlin(West) ein. Die höchste Monatsziffer wurde im Dezember mit 1.107 Entlassungen erreicht. Es handelte sich fast ausschließlich um Memeldeutsche, Ostpreußen und Umsiedler aus den Jahren 1939 bis 1941.

Um die geordnete Unterbringung der laufend eintreffenden Aussiedler im Bundesgebiet sicherzustellen, werden sie zunächst in Grenzdurchgangslagern aufgefangen. Nach einem Verteilungsschlüssel, der auf die jeweiligen Aufnahmemöglichkeiten abgestellt ist, werden sie von dort auf die einzelnen Bundesländer verteilt. Hierbei werden in erster Linie bestehende verwandtschaftliche Bindungen, sodann sonstige Gesichtspunkte, die der späteren Eingliederung förderlich sind, nach Möglichkeit berücksichtigt. An der Spitze standen 1958 die Länder Nordrhein-Westfalen, Baden-Württemberg und Bayern. Ihre Schlüsselanteile betrugen 32,7, 15,5 und 12,9%.

Die meisten Aussiedler (1958 über 90%) passieren das Grenzdurchgangslager Friedland bei Göttingen in Niedersachsen. Hier enden auch die polnischen Aussiedlertransporte, die über Stettin in das Bundesgebiet geleitet werden und meistens eine Belegung um 500 Personen aufweisen. Die Aussiedler aus dem Südosten reisen dagegen über die bayerischen Grenzdurchgangslager Schalding und Piding in das Bundesgebiet ein. Über diese drei Lager sind seit dem Jahr 1950 rund 410.000 Vertriebene aus dem Osten und dem sonstigen Ausland aufgenommen worden. In den Jahren 1952 bis 1955 lag der Zugang relativ konstant um 15.000 Personen im Jahr. 1957 waren es rund 114.000, im Jahr 1958: 132.000 Personen.[1]

Die Eingliederung all dieser Menschen in das Wirtschaftsleben stellt Bund, Länder und Gemeinden vor erhebliche Aufgaben. Sie sind umso größer, als seit Jahren ein noch größerer Strom von Menschen aus Mitteldeutschland (1958: 204.000 Personen) im Bundesgebiet unterzubringen ist. Trotz erheblichen Bemühungen um den Bau von Wohnungen ist es unvermeidlich, daß steigend mit den Jahren (1958: über 60%) die Eingetroffenen zunächst für längere Zeit in Lagern der Länder und Gemeinden oder in Notunterkünften eine vorläufige Bleibe finden müssen, bis familiengerechte Wohnungen zur Verfügung gestellt werden können. Mit diesen Maßnahmen gehen mannigfaltige Bemühungen einher, diese Menschen in den Arbeitsprozeß einzugliedern, Lücken der schulischen und beruflichen Ausbildung

[1] Vergleiche die Tabellen 7, 8 und 9 auf den Seiten 68 und 69.

BEVÖLKERUNGSGEWINN UND -VERLUST

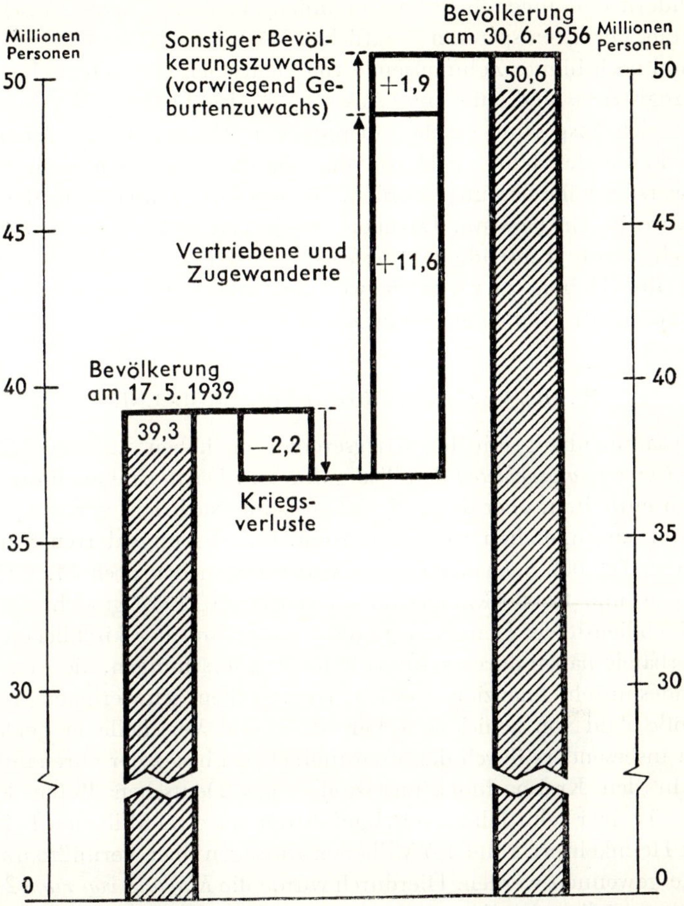

Quelle: Statistisches Bundesamt.

zu schließen und über die Fürsorge und Hilfen der caritativen und freien Wohlfahrtsverbände, wie auch über die „Friedlandhilfe", Notstände in Einzelfällen zu mildern. Zu den materiellen Sorgen tritt das Problem, im Bundesgebiet auch psychologisch den Boden dafür zu bereiten, daß diese Menschen, die über ein Jahrzehnt abgeschlossen unter einem anderen System und unter schwierigen Bedingungen leben mußten, eine besondere

Betreuung von Mensch zu Mensch erfahren. Hinzu kommt die Notwendigkeit, den Kindern und Jugendlichen unter ihnen einen schulischen Abschluß zu vermitteln, der ihren späteren beruflichen Werdegang sichert.

Obwohl noch immer Zehntausende von Deutschen beim Deutschen Roten Kreuz registriert sind, die eine Ausreise in das Bundesgebiet anstreben, zeichnet sich insgesamt gesehen bereits ein Abklingen der Aussiedlung ab. Im Laufe der Jahre, gebietsmäßig allerdings unterschieden, konnten die schwersten Fälle bereinigt werden. Diese positive Entwicklung der letzten zehn Jahre ist ein Gewinn. Darüber darf jedoch nicht übersehen werden, daß noch heute Tausende zwangsläufig zu der Entscheidung getrieben werden, ihre Heimat zu verlassen, weil sie ihnen mit ihren unerträglichen Verhältnissen zur Fremde geworden ist.

IV. DIE VERMISSTEN UND VERSCHOLLENEN

Im Zusammenhang mit den Kriegsereignissen haben *3.200.000 Deutsche aus den Vertreibungsgebieten* den Tod gefunden. Darin sind auch diejenigen Personen enthalten, über deren Schicksal keine Nachricht vorliegt, die aber als verstorben angesehen werden müssen. Für die ungeklärten Schicksale liegen über 760.000 Suchanträge vor. Außerdem suchen noch 14.000 Kinder ihre Eltern, und 12.000 Kinder werden von ihren Eltern gesucht.

Die Suchdienste des Deutschen Roten Kreuzes und der kirchlichen Wohlfahrtsverbände haben durch systematische Nachforschungen, die weitgehend aus Bundesmitteln finanziert werden, trotz großen Schwierigkeiten bereits eine große Zahl von Schicksalen Vermißter und Verschollener geklärt. So konnten insbesondere durch den unermüdlichen Einsatz der ehrenamtlichen Helfer in den Kreisnachforschungsstellen des Deutschen Roten Kreuzes durch die in über zehn Jahren durchgeführten fast zwei Millionen Befragungen von Heimkehrern rund 1,3 Millionen Aussagen über Vermißte und Verschollene gewonnen werden. Hierdurch wurde die *Klärung von rund 245.000 Schicksalen* möglich. Die jetzt begonnene und abschließende Befragung mit Bildlisten aller Vermißten wird sich über mehrere Jahre hinziehen und das höchstmögliche Maß an Aufklärung weiterer Schicksale bringen.

Während durch die amtliche Registrierung der Wehrmachtvermißten und Kriegsgefangenen im März 1950 die Voraussetzungen dafür geschaffen wurden, daß umfangreiche Namenslisten dieser beiden Personengruppen erstellt werden konnten, wird die Nachforschung nach Zivilverschleppten und Zivilvermißten durch das Fehlen von nur einigermaßen vollständigen

Registrierunterlagen immer noch sehr behindert. Von den etwa 800.000 zahlenmäßig ermittelten verschleppten Zivilpersonen konnte bisher nur ein Teil auch namentlich festgestellt werden.

Außer den als verschleppt erkannten Zivilpersonen ist das Schicksal eines erheblichen Teiles der früheren deutschen Einwohner der östlichen Vertreibungsgebiete noch ungeklärt. Obgleich der Kirchliche Suchdienst mit seinen zwölf Heimatortskarteien bereits über vierzehn Millionen Menschen aus diesem Personenkreis namentlich erfassen konnte, werden immer noch über drei Millionen Zivilpersonen aus diesen Gebieten vermißt. Die Durchführung der vom Deutschen Bundestag beschlossenen und von der Bundesregierung eingeleiteten „Gesamterhebung der deutschen Bevölkerungsverluste in den Vertreibungsgebieten" wird für weitere Nachforschungen eine entscheidende Hilfe sein. Rund 2,5 Millionen im Bundesgebiet lebende Vertriebene haben inzwischen in einer umfassenden Befragung wichtige Hinweise und Meldungen abgegeben. Schon die bisherigen Ergebnisse lassen erwarten, daß durch diese Maßnahme eine sehr hohe Zahl der ungewissen Schicksale geklärt werden wird.

Der Kindersuchdienst konnte bisher *rund 145.000 Kinder* mit ihren Eltern oder anderen Angehörigen zusammenführen.

V. DIE EVAKUIERTEN

Als „Vertriebene innerhalb des Bundesgebietes" hat man die *Evakuierten* bezeichnet, die im Kriege ausgebombt oder aus Sicherheitsgründen in weniger gefährdete Gegenden verbracht wurden. Über den zahlenmäßigen Umfang der Evakuierungen liegen genaue Angaben nicht vor; doch spiegelt sich das Ausmaß im Absinken der Einwohnerzahlen der Großstädte. So hatte zum Beispiel die Stadt Köln im Jahre 1939 eine Einwohnerzahl von 777.200, im März 1945 von etwa 40.000[1]. Am 20.10.1946 war die Einwohnerzahl der Stadt Köln bereits wieder auf 491.380 gestiegen und betrug am 1.7.1957: 727.455, also fast soviel wie im Jahre 1939.

Die „Statistische und Soziologische Arbeitsgruppe für Flüchtlingsfragen" hat nach Kriegsende eine *Gesamtzahl von rund vier Millionen Evakuierten* errechnet. Erschöpfende Zahlenangaben darüber, wieviele Evakuierte von 1945 bis 1950 in ihre Heimat zurückgekehrt sind, liegen nicht vor. Einen gewissen Anhaltspunkt geben jedoch die Ergebnisse der Statistik der Wohnraumvergabe. Die Rückführung der Evakuierten wurde durch eine im

[1] Statistisches Jahrbuch der Stadt Köln 1950.

Jahre 1951 erfolgte Befragung, die vom Bundesministerium für Wohnungsbau veranlaßt wurde, vorbereitet. Auf Grund dieser Erhebung haben damals etwa 305.000 Evakuierte den Wunsch geäußert, in ihre Heimat zurückzukehren.

Das *Bundesevakuiertengesetz* in der Fassung vom 5.10.1957 bringt für das gesamte Bundesgebiet und Berlin (West) eine einheitliche Regelung der Rückführung der Evakuierten und ihrer Eingliederung in das Berufs- und Wirtschaftsleben. Danach ist betreuungsberechtigter Evakuierter, wer in der Zeit vom 26.8.1939 bis 31.12.1946 seinen Heimatort aus kriegsbedingten Gründen verlassen hat und sich im Zeitpunkt des Inkrafttretens des Gesetzes (18.7.1953) noch außerhalb seines Heimatortes befand. Auf Grund seiner Erklärung, in den Ausgangsort zurückkehren zu wollen, wird er an seinem Heimatort registriert und damit als Evakuierter im Sinne des Gesetzes anerkannt. Er hat einen Rechtsanspruch auf Rückführung in seine Heimat. Evakuierte, deren Ausgangsort außerhalb des Bundesgebietes liegt, können einen Ersatz-Ausgangsort im Bundesgebiet erhalten. Die Kosten der Rückführung trägt die öffentliche Hand. Die Reihenfolge wird durch soziale und wirtschaftliche Gesichtspunkte bestimmt.

Bis zum 30.9.1958 haben sich rund 502.000 Evakuierte für die Rückführung gemeldet. Davon wurden bis zu diesem Zeitpunkt 458.000 Personen als anerkannte Evakuierte registriert.

*

Die Evakuierten stellen nur einen Teil der durch die Kriegsereignisse im Bundesgebiet unmittelbar Betroffenen dar. Öffentliches und privates Eigentum jeder Art war durch den Luftkrieg und die sonstigen Kriegseinwirkungen weithin zerstört und vernichtet. Es stand von vornherein fest, daß eine Behebung der Sachschäden ohne staatliche Hilfe nicht möglich sein würde. Die gesetzlichen Grundlagen für die Regelung der Leistungen zur Abgeltung der erfolgten Kriegssachschäden wurden durch das Soforthilfe- und später das Lastenausgleichsgesetz, also im gleichen Gesetzesrahmen wie für die Vertriebenen, geschaffen.

Kriegsschaden liegt nach dem Lastenausgleichsgesetz dann vor, wenn der Schaden unmittelbar durch Kriegshandlungen oder durch Beschädigung, Zerstörung oder Wegnahme von Sachen auf Grund behördlicher Maßnahmen, die im Zusammenhang mit den kriegerischen Ereignissen getroffen worden sind, in der Zeit vom 26.8.1939 bis zum 31.7.1945 entstanden ist[1]. Es handelt sich dabei in erster Linie um Schäden durch den Luftkrieg.

[1] § 15 LAG.

Entschädigt werden grundsätzlich nur die im Bundesgebiet und in Berlin-(West) entstandenen Kriegsschäden. Eine Reihe von Sonderbestimmungen sieht jedoch die Abgeltung von Schäden in den deutschen Ostgebieten (Ostschäden), in Ostberlin, dem deutschen Zollanschlußgebiet (Walsertal) und für die Bewohner von Helgoland (hier auch für Sachschäden nach dem 31.7.1945) vor. Von besonderer Bedeutung für die Kriegssachgeschädigten im Bundesgebiet und Berlin (West) ist das im Zusammenhang mit dem Lastenausgleichsgesetz ergangene Altsparergesetz vom 17.7.1953. Es bringt über die 1948 erfolgte Geldumstellung hinaus eine Entschädigung von Altspareinlagen bei den einheimischen Instituten nach dem Stand vom 1.1.1940 bis zu einer Aufwertungsquote von 20%. Von den Sparkassen sind bereits im Wege der Vorfinanzierung die anerkannten Altspareinlagen bis zu je 100 DM zur Auszahlung freigegeben worden.

Organisationen und Verbände

Am 14.12.1958 haben die beiden großen Verbände der Vertriebenen („Verband der Landsmannschaften" und „Bund der vertriebenen Deutschen") sich zu dem „*Bund der Vertriebenen — Vereinigte Landsmannschaften und Landesverbände*" zusammengeschlossen. Der Zweck des Bundes ist nach seinen Satzungen:

„Der Bund bekennt sich zur Charta der Heimatvertriebenen vom 5.8.1950. Er hat die Aufgabe,

1. sich für die Verwirklichung des Selbstbestimmungsrechtes, des Rechts auf die angestammte Heimat, der allgemeinen Menschenrechte und für eine gerechte Ordnung zwischen den Staaten und Völkern Europas einzusetzen;
2. die ihrer Heimat beraubten Deutschen sozial und wirtschaftlich zu fördern;
3. ihre Rechte zu vertreten, im Rahmen der Gesetze auch vor Gerichten;
4. ihre Forderungen gegenüber Regierung, gesetzgebenden Körperschaften und der Öffentlichkeit in allen Angelegenheiten zu vertreten, die mit dem Verlust der Heimat zusammenhängen;
5. das heimatliche Kulturgut zu erhalten, zu pflegen und zu vertiefen und zu verbreiten.

Der Bund ist überparteilich und überkonfessionell. Er kann Organisationen beitreten, deren Ziele seinem Zweck dienen."

Auch die beiden großen Organisationen der Flüchtlinge „*Gesamtverband der Sowjetzonenflüchtlinge*" und „*Vereinigte Landsmannschaften Mitteldeutschlands*" (*VLM*) haben eine Zusammenarbeit vereinbart.

Die Interessen der einheimischen Geschädigten werden durch zwei anerkannte Organisationen vertreten, den „*Zentralverband der Fliegergeschädigten, Evakuierten und Währungsgeschädigten*" (ZVF) und den „*Zentralverband der deutschen Haus- und Grundbesitzer e. V.*" Neben diesen Gruppen haben sich berufsständische Organisationen für Landwirte, die vertriebene Wirtschaft sowie die vertriebenen Beamten und Behördenangestellten gebildet. Die vertriebene Jugend hat sich in der „*Deutschen Jugend des Ostens*" organisiert, deren Mitglieder in beachtlichem Maße auch einheimische Jugendliche sind. Innerhalb der Kirchen sind schon 1945 besondere Organisationen begründet worden, und zwar der „*Konvent der zerstreuten evangelischen Ostkirchen*" und der „*Ostkirchenausschuß*" (Kirchlicher Hilfsausschuß für die Ostvertriebenen) sowie die „*Dienststelle des Beauftragten der Fuldaer Bischofskonferenz für die Heimatvertriebenen-Seelsorge*", die „*Katholische Arbeitsstelle* (*Nord*) *für Heimatvertriebene*" und die „*Katholische Arbeitsstelle* (*Süd*) *für Heimatvertriebene*", ebenso konfessionelle Jugendverbände.

Die Vertriebenen haben auch in den politischen Parteien eine Heimat gefunden. Diese sowie die Wohlfahrtsverbände haben schon sehr frühzeitig Betreuungsstellen errichtet.

Von besonderer Bedeutung ist die am 5. 8. 1950 in Stuttgart-Bad Cannstatt verkündete *Charta der deutschen Heimatvertriebenen.* In ihr erklären die Millionen von deutschen Vertriebenen, daß sie auf Rache und Vergeltung verzichten, die Einigung Europas bejahen und das Recht auf die Heimat als menschliches Grundrecht anerkannt und verwirklicht wissen wollen.

Seit im April 1950 das Internationale Arbeitsamt sich das erste Mal mit der übermäßigen Bevölkerungsdichte beschäftigte, die durch den Zustrom der Vertriebenen nach Westdeutschland entstanden ist, haben zahlreiche internationale Konferenzen nach Lösungen dieses Problems gesucht.

Inzwischen hat sich die Erkenntnis verbreitet, daß *Auswanderung keine fühlbare Hilfe* bringen kann. Länder, die bereit sind, Auswanderer aufzunehmen, legen Wert auf junge Kräfte und Facharbeiter. Infolge ihrer Bevölkerungsstruktur kann aber die Bundesrepublik gerade auf solche Kräfte nicht verzichten. Außerdem könnte es sich jährlich nur um durchschnittlich rund 60.000 Auswanderer handeln. Diese Zahl, zusammen mit den für die Auswanderung erforderlichen Kosten, steht in keinem Verhältnis zu der Gesamtzahl von *fast 12,5 Millionen Vertriebenen und Zugewanderten*, welche die Bundesrepublik aufzunehmen hatte, und den rund 550.000, die alljährlich neu in die Bundesrepublik kommen.

HEIMATLOSE AUSLÄNDER UND NICHTDEUTSCHE POLITISCHE FLÜCHTLINGE

Seit der französischen Revolution ist der Flüchtlingsstrom über die Grenzen der Länder Europas nicht abgerissen. Aus den verschiedensten mitunter gegensätzlichen politischen Gründen trieb er fast jedes Jahr Ungezählte aus ihrer angestammten Heimat. Nicht nur territoriale Veränderungen zwangen Optanten, ihre Heimat zu verlassen; auch akute Gegensätze zwischen Regierung und Volk, geglückte und mißglückte Revolutionen vermehrten die Zahl der Flüchtlinge. Zu ihnen traten mit dem Zwanzigsten Jahrhundert die rassisch und religiös Verfolgten. Die Zahl der Geflüchteten, Vertriebenen, Heimatlosen, Entwurzelten und Enterbten stieg nach dem Ersten und besonders während des Zweiten Weltkrieges zu ungeheuren Ausmaßen. Schon das Neunzehnte Jahrhundert war keineswegs von der Sünde politischer Intoleranz frei. Es wurde abgelöst durch das Zeitalter der industriellen und agrarischen Massengesellschaften, in denen Unmenschlichkeit und Brutalität zu Mitteln autoritärer und totalitärer Machtstaatspolitik werden konnten.

Im Frühjahr 1945 befanden sich auf dem Boden des zerfallenden Deutschen Reiches acht bis neun Millionen Ausländer aus allen europäischen Staaten, mit denen das Reich Krieg geführt, oder die es besetzt hatte. Diese schlecht ernährten und gekleideten Menschenmassen waren überwiegend in Lagern zusammengefaßt. Sie setzten sich aus Kriegsgefangenen, nationalen politischen Häftlingen und Arbeitskräften zusammen, die freiwillig oder gezwungen ihre Heimat verlassen hatten und in der deutschen Kriegswirtschaft tätig waren. Zu dieser Hauptgruppe kamen mehrere Hunderttausend wehrfähige Männer verschiedenster Volkszugehörigkeit, die als Freiwillige in der Wehrmacht gegen die Sowjetunion und damit gegen den Bolschewismus für ihre Freiheit gekämpft hatten. Schließlich gehörten dazu Menschen aller Altersklassen und sozialen Schichten, ja ganze Klein-Völker, die vor den sowjetischen Armeen flüchtend mit den zurückgehenden deutschen Truppen ihre Heimat aus politischen, religiösen oder anderen weltanschaulichen Gründen verlassen hatten.

Durch die unmittelbaren und mittelbaren Folgen des Ersten Weltkriegs waren mehr als fünf Millionen Menschen aus ihrer Heimat vertrieben oder zwangsumgesiedelt worden. Diese hohe Zahl verdoppelte sich fast im Verlauf des Zweiten Weltkriegs und nach seinem Ende. Unter diesen Ausländern befanden sich rund fünf Millionen Polen, 1,8 Millionen Franzosen, je 100.000 Belgier und Niederländer, etwa 60.000 Norweger und Dänen, rund 600.000

Angehörige der verschiedenen Balkanvölker, 2,5 Millionen Russen, Ukrainer, Weißruthenen und Angehörige anderer Völker aus der Sowjetunion, 750.000 Tschechen und Slowaken, außerdem fast 100.000 Esten, Letten und Litauer.

Dieses furchtbare Ergebnis des Zweiten Weltkrieges wird nur durch die Millionenzahlen der deutschen Staatsangehörigen und Volksdeutschen übertroffen, die ihre durch Jahrhunderte angestammte Heimat enterbt und entrechtet im Grauen der Flucht oder Vertreibung verlassen mußten.

*

Die siegreichen Alliierten nannten die entwurzelten Menschen „*Displaced Persons*“ (DPs). Um ihnen zu helfen, gründeten sie 1943 die „*United Nations Relief and Rehabilitation Administration*“ (UNRRA). Diese Organisation hatte die Betreuung, vor allem aber die Rückführung der DPs in ihre Heimat zur Aufgabe. Bei der Gründung der UNRRA entstanden Meinungsverschiedenheiten über die Frage, welchen Ländern und welchem Personenkreis in Europa ihre Hilfe zugute kommen sollte. Der damalige amerikanische Standpunkt, daß die ehemaligen Feindländer und alle Flüchtlinge deutscher Staatszugehörigkeit ausgeschlossen sein sollten, setzte sich durch. Diese Entscheidung wurde außerordentlich bedeutungsvoll, weil sie von der Nachfolge-Organisation der UNRRA, der 1947 gegründeten „*International Refugee Organization*“ (IRO), übernommen wurde.

Die UNRRA, unterstützt von den vier Besatzungsmächten und internationalen (meist überseeischen) Wohlfahrtsorganisationen, betrieb neben der materiellen Unterstützung als ihr Hauptziel die Rückführung der Heimatlosen in ihre Heimatländer und ihre Ansiedlung überwiegend in Übersee, soweit die DPs nicht in ihre Heimat zurückkehren wollten oder konnten.

Als die UNRRA 1947 ihre Tätigkeit beendete, hatte sie *sieben Millionen Menschen* aus Deutschland repatriiert oder neu angesiedelt, und zwar 2,1 Millionen nach der Sowjetunion, 874.500 nach Polen, 1,6 Millionen nach Frankreich und 2,4 Millionen nach dreizehn anderen Ländern.

Die Rücksiedlungsaktionen in die Heimatländer waren allerdings praktisch bereits 1946 beendet. Die sich schnell ausbreitende Macht des Kommunismus in Osteuropa lähmte nicht nur die Rückkehrwilligkeit bei vielen DPs und beendete die Zwangsrückführungen, sondern sie leitete dazu neue Fluchtbewegungen von Ost nach West ein.

Von den Esten, Letten und Litauern kehrten beispielsweise nur 2 %, von den Mitgliedern der westlichen polnischen Befreiungsarmee nur 30 % in ihre Heimat zurück. Neue Flüchtlinge trafen dagegen fortlaufend aus der Sowjetunion, seit 1947/48 auch aus Polen, der Tschechoslowakei und späterhin auch aus Rumänien und besonders Ungarn ein. Der Volksaufstand in Ungarn Ende 1956 zwang erneut rund 170.000 Menschen aller Altersklassen, in einer Massenbewegung ihre Heimat zu verlassen. Rund 14.500 von ihnen fanden in der Bundesrepublik Aufnahme. Auch die Fluchtbewegung aus Jugoslawien versiegte niemals ganz und lebte seit 1956 wieder verstärkt auf.

Außer den ungarischen Flüchtlingen, die nach den Oktoberereignissen des Jahres 1956 in die Bundesrepublik kamen, sind seit dem 1. 1. 1953 bis zum 31. 12. 1957 rund 7.000 Ausländer, vornehmlich aus den Ostblockstaaten, in die Bundesrepublik eingeströmt, die im Anerkennungsverfahren als politische Flüchtlinge anerkannt wurden.

*

Am 31. 1. 1952 stellte auch die Nachfolge-Organisation der UNRRA, die IRO, ihre Tätigkeit ein. In sechs Jahren hatte sie 274.501 Heimatlosen nach den USA, 136.249 nach Australien, 83.431 nach Kanada, 70.051 nach Israel und 55.451 nach Großbritannien zur Auswanderung verholfen. So großartig diese Leistung, an der dreizehn Länder des freien Westens sich beteiligten, auch war, so mußten doch andererseits erhebliche Härten in Kauf genommen werden. Die sehr strengen Einwanderungsbestimmungen einiger überseeischer Staaten bezüglich Vorstrafen, bisheriger politischer Betätigung, Gesundheitszustand und Arbeitsfähigkeit zwangen viele Auswanderungswillige, gegen ihren Willen in der Bundesrepublik zu bleiben. Durch diese Bestimmungen wurden Sippen und Familien zerrissen, und es blieb in der Bundesrepublik eine meist in Lagern wohnende Gruppe von Menschen verschiedener Volkszugehörigkeit zurück, die mehrere tausend Köpfe groß, der deutschen Sprache nicht mächtig, teils arbeitsunfähig, teilweise aber auch arbeitsunwillig war. Diese Menschen, mit ihrem Schicksal natürlich zutiefst unzufrieden, wurden durch den Lageraufenthalt und die Hoffnungslosigkeit ihres Daseins außerordentlich zermürbt, verloren weitgehend alle Aktivität und setzten ihrer wirtschaftlichen und sozialen Eingliederung mitunter sogar passiven Widerstand entgegen.

Die Politik der UNRRA und IRO sowie anderer internationaler Hilfsverbände hatte in der deutschen Bevölkerung, die vom eigenen Vertriebenen-Problem zutiefst berührt war, zeitweilig Ressentiments ausgelöst, die in manchen Fällen durch die Haltung ausländischer Flüchtlinge verstärkt wurden. Trotzdem setzte in der deutschen Öffentlichkeit sich zunehmend die Auffassung durch, daß für diese Opfer des Krieges und der Nachkriegsentwicklung die gesamte Freie Welt die Verantwortung trifft, und daß diese Verantwortung in einem angemessenen Umfang moralisch wie materiell auch vom deutschen Volk mitgetragen werden muß.

Bis Ende Januar 1952 brachte daher die deutsche Verwaltung einen Betrag von *über 2,5 Milliarden DM* für die soziale Betreuung beziehungsweise als Auswanderungsbeihilfe für diesen Personenkreis auf.

Am 1. 1. 1953 wurden die heimatlosen Ausländer von der IRO *in deutsche Betreuung* übernommen. Zum Zeitpunkt der Übergabe befanden sich insgesamt 277.350 nichtdeutsche Flüchtlinge im Bundesgebiet, davon 111.950 in Lagern. Das *Gesetz über die Rechtsstellung heimatloser Ausländer im Bundesgebiet* vom 25. 4. 1951, das der Bundestag mit Ausnahme der Kommunisten einstimmig annahm, legte die Rechtsstellung dieses Personenkreises fest und glich sie weitgehend der deutscher Staatsbürger an. Die Rechtssicherung durch diese gesetzgeberische Maßnahme ist als vorbildlich von der ganzen Welt anerkannt worden. In einigen Punkten geht sie erheblich über das hinaus, was den heimatlosen Ausländern durch die spätere Genfer Flüchtlings-Konvention vom 28. 7. 1951 gewährleistet wurde.

Weitere Vergünstigungen für die nichtdeutschen Flüchtlinge brachten das Bundesversorgungsgesetz vom 1. 10. 1950, das Bundesergänzungsgesetz zur Entschädigung der Opfer der nationalsozialistischen Verfolgung vom 1. 10. 1953 und das Gesetz über die Fremdrenten und Auslandsrenten vom 7. 8. 1953.

Bereits 1952 stellte die Bundesregierung 90 Millionen DM für Wohnungsbau und 45 Millionen DM für soziale Fürsorge für die heimatlosen Ausländer zur Verfügung. Von 1953 bis 1957 wurden jährlich im Durchschnitt 45 Millionen DM seitens der Bundesregierung neben den Mitteln, die Länder und Gemeinden oder caritative Verbände und Organisationen direkt oder indirekt aufbringen, zur Verfügung gestellt.

Der *Flüchtlingshilfefonds der Vereinten Nationen* hat erstmals im Jahre 1955 Beihilfen gewährt. Die Bundesrepublik Deutschland erhielt 1955: 420.000 Dollar, 1956: 464.000 Dollar, 1957: 550.000 Dollar als Hilfe zugewiesen.

Zu den damit teilfinanzierten Vorhaben zur wirtschaftlichen und sozialen Eingliederung nichtdeutscher Flüchtlinge traten deutsche öffentliche und private Mittel in Höhe von: 1955: 6 Millionen, 1956: 6,5 Millionen und 1957: 7 Millionen DM. Diese deutschen Mittel traten zusätzlich zu den bereits genannten pro Jahr ausgeworfenen 45 Millionen DM für soziale Fürsorgeleistungen hinzu. Zum Flüchtlingshilfefonds der Vereinten Nationen hat die Bundesrepublik in den Jahren 1955 und 1956 jährlich 100.000 DM, im Jahre 1957: 840.000 DM zugesteuert.

Die bisher angeführten Zahlen enthalten nicht die Leistungen der Bundesrepublik zu Gunsten der seit November 1956 in die Bundesrepublik aufgenommenen 14.500 ungarischen Flüchtlinge. Um diesen besonderen Personenkreis nach Deutschland zu transportieren und ihn in jeder Hinsicht aufzunehmen und einzugliedern, hat die Bundesrepublik sich keinerlei internationaler Hilfe bedient. Infolgedessen hatte sie auch dem Hohen Kommissar für seine Intervention zu Gunsten der ungarischen Flüchtlinge keinen Beitrag geleistst.

Im Anschluß an die Ereignisse des Oktobers 1956 in Ungarn hat die Bundesrepublik folgende Ausgaben getätigt:

an das Deutsche Rote Kreuz	1 Million DM
Getreidespenden für Ungarn	10 Millionen DM
Fürsorge und Lageraufenthalt	17 Millionen DM
Betreuung von Studenten und Schülern	400.000 DM
zusammen	28.400.000 DM

Die durch Wohlfahrtsorganisationen in der Bundesrepublik gesammelten Spenden betragen:

in bar	13 Millionen DM
in Sachwerten	27 Millionen DM
zusammen	40 Millionen DM

Im Haushaltsjahr 1957/58 wurden für diesen beschränkten Personenkreis veranschlagt:

für individuelle Fürsorge	20 Millionen DM
Aufwendungen zur Unterbringung — Wohnungsbeschaffung	10 Millionen DM
in den Haushalten der Länder	6 Millionen DM
zusammen	36 Millionen DM

Im Jahr 1955 wurde beim Bundesministerium für Vertriebene erstmals ein besonderer Titel in Höhe von 100.000 DM zur besonderen Unterstützung von Organisationen der heimatlosen Ausländer und nichtdeutschen politischen Flüchtlinge, die sich *kulturelle und soziale Aufgaben* gestellt haben, eingerichtet. Dieser Haushaltstitel wurde ab 1956 auf 300.000 DM erhöht.

1957 erhielten insgesamt einundfünfzig kulturelle und soziale Einrichtungen, Organisationen, wirtschaftliche Anstalten, Kirchen sowie Zeitschriften der heimatlosen Ausländer und nichtdeutschen politischen Flüchtlinge aus diesem Titel Unterstützung.

Die Bundesregierung ließ sich dabei die religiöse Betreuung der heimatlosen Ausländer durch Sicherstellung des Lebensunterhalts der Seelsorger, vornehmlich der orthodoxen Kirchen und mohammedanischen Religionsgemeinschaften, besonders angelegen sein.

Bedeutende Unterstützung erhält das *Ungarische Realgymnasium* mit Internat auf Burg Kastl/Oberpfalz durch das Land Bayern und die Bundesregierung.

Es sind dort bereits die vier Oberklassen zusammengezogen. Im Sommer 1959 wird die geschlossene neunklassige höhere Lehranstalt mit 400 Schülern, darunter rund fünfzig Mädchen, vereint sein.

Am 1.7.1957 befanden sich in der Bundesrepublik insgesamt[1] 208.500 heimatlose Ausländer und nichtdeutsche politische Flüchtlinge. Unter diesen waren die Polen mit rund 70.000 vor den Jugoslawen und Balten mit je rund 20.000 am zahlreichsten. Ihnen folgen die Ungarn.

68.000 heimatlose Ausländer und nichtdeutsche Flüchtlinge haben in Bayern, 52.000 in Nordrhein-Westfalen, 27.000 in Baden-Württemberg und 24.000 in Niedersachsen Aufnahme gefunden.

11,6% dieses Personenkreises = 24.289 lebten Ende 1957 noch in Lagern, Heimen und ähnlichen Einrichtungen. Mit hohem Einsatz von Bundes- und Landesmitteln unter Hinzuziehung von Mitteln aus dem bereits erwähnten Programm der Lagerräumung der Vereinten Nationen (UNRRF) und Mitteln des Lastenausgleichs wurden 1958 dreiundvierzig Lager mit rund 9.000 Personen geräumt. Die Lagerräumung hat zum Ziel, diesen Personenkreis möglichst in der Nähe des ständigen Arbeitsplatzes in endgültige Wohnungen zu bringen, um damit die gesellschaftliche und wirtschaftliche Eingliederung zu vollenden. Die übrigen Lager sollen bis 1962 planmäßig aufgelöst werden. Nur 4.549 arbeitsfähige Personen waren Ende 1957 noch arbeitslos. Ihre Vermittlung scheiterte bisher an mangelnder Einsatzfähigkeit und allzu geringen deutschen Sprachkenntnissen.

Abgesehen von allen anderen Aufwendungen wurden durch die Lastenausgleichsbank bis zum 31.12.1958 in 1.725 Fällen Darlehen in Höhe von rund 11,5 Millionen DM für die Begründung selbständiger Existenzen und für 1.685 Wohnungseinheiten Darlehen in Höhe von sechs Millionen DM für die Errichtung von Eigentumswohnungen gewährt. Bei einer durchschnittlichen Kopfzahl von vier Personen je Familie bedeutet das die Beschaffung von Wohnraum für nahezu siebentausend Personen.

Die Bundesregierung wird gemeinsam mit den Regierungen der Länder alles tun, um die *wirtschaftliche und soziale Eingliederung* der heimatlosen Ausländer und nichtdeutschen politischen Flüchtlinge fortzusetzen und möglichst zu vollenden. *Nicht* geplant ist jedoch, diesen Personenkreis *zu assimilieren oder einzudeutschen.* Jede Gruppe der Emigranten soll, soweit sie selbst dazu den Willen hat und ihn deutlich durch eigene Leistungen bekundet, ihre kulturelle Eigenständigkeit bewahren können. Mit dieser Politik soll — abgesehen vom Selbstzweck — auch beispielhaft gezeigt werden, wie die kommende europäische Gemeinschaft auf der gegenseitigen Achtung der Eigenständigkeit der Völker aufgebaut sein sollte.

[1] Die Staatenlosen und Personen mit jetziger oder früherer Staatsangehörigkeit eines Ostblockstaates einbegriffen; ohne Rücksicht darauf, ob diese Personen erst nach dem Zweiten Weltkrieg oder bereits vorher nach Deutschland gekommen sind.

AUS DEUTSCHER GESCHICHTE

Die Bewohner Deutschlands gehören zum germanischen Zweig der indogermanischen Sprachfamilie. Durch die Berührung mit den Römern werden die *Germanen* zuerst geschichtlich faßbar. Der obergermanisch-rhätische Limes wird von 90 bis 160 n. Chr. als feste Grenze zum römischen Herrschaftsbereich, im wesentlichen durch den Lauf des Rheins und der Donau bestimmt, errichtet; hundert Jahre darauf fällt er unter dem Druck der Westgermanen. Der Hunneneinbruch im 4. Jahrhundert löst die entscheidenden Wellen der germanischen Völkerwanderung aus: germanische Reiche entstehen in Italien, Gallien, Britannien, Spanien, Nordafrika. Angeln, Sachsen und Friesen lassen sich seit der Mitte des 5. Jahrhunderts in Britannien nieder. Den abwandernden Germanen folgen slawische Stämme nach Ostdeutschland. Als Ergebnis der Völkerwanderung finden die nachmals deutschen Stämme der Bayern, Alemannen (Schwaben), Thüringer, (Nieder-)Sachsen und Friesen sich weitgehend in ihren heutigen Sitzen. Die Franken, die schon im 3. Jahrhundert den Niederrhein überschritten hatten, greifen weit nach Westen aus.

102 v. Chr.: Kimbern und Teutonen in Italien

58 v. Chr.: CAESAR besiegt die Sueben unter ARIOVIST

9 n. Chr.: drei römische Legionen im Teutoburger Wald vernichtet

98 „Germania" des TACITUS'

375 Hunneneinfall in Europa

CHLODWIG I., König der merowingischen *Franken*, begründet um 500 ein Reich vom Rhein bis zur Garonne. Der Frankenname verbleibt allerdings später bei dem wesentlich romanischen Frankreich. „*Deutsch*" ist kein Stammesname. Es gehört zu althochdeutsch *diet* „Volk" und bezeichnet seit etwa 600 die einheimische, „völkische"

466—511 CHLODWIG I., Begründer des Fränkischen Reiches

732 Sieg des fränkischen Hausmeiers KARL MARTELL über die Mauren bei Poitiers: Europa wird dem christlichen Glauben erhalten

754 Tod des HL. BONIFATIUS

Sprache (*lingua theudisca*) im Gegensatz zur lateinischen. Seit etwa 600 entwickeln sich sprachliche Gemeinsamkeiten, welche die germanischen Stämme im heutigen West- und Süddeutschland von ihren Stammesverwandten im Norden abheben. So bildet sich auch von der Sprache her ein „*deutsches*" Volk aus. Sein stammhaftes Gefüge prägt den deutschen Staat bis zur Gegenwart in wesentlichen Zügen.

*

768—814 KARL DER GROSSE. Unterwerfung der Bayern und Sachsen durch die Franken

843 Teilungsvertrag von Verdun (870 Mersen, 880 Ribémont)

919—1024 das sächsische Kaiserhaus. Erste ostdeutsche Besiedlung unter Kaiser HEINRICH I. (919—936)

936—973 Kaiser OTTO I., DER GROSSE. Die Herzöge werden unterworfen, die Bischöfe Reichsfürsten

1138—1254 das staufische Kaiserhaus

Seit 1150 Minnesang

1193—1280 ALBERT DER GROSSE (ALBERTUS MAGNUS)

1198—1228 WALTHER VON DER VOGELWEIDE, der größte Lyriker deutscher Sprache im Mittelalter

Um 1205: WOLFRAM VON ESCHENBACH, der bedeutendste Epiker des Mittelalters, schreibt den „Parzival"

Im Jahre 800 wird der Frankenkönig KARL durch den Papst in Rom zum Kaiser gekrönt. Damit wird das „*regnum teutonicorum*" zum weltlichen Arm der Kirche. Durch die Teilungen unter KARLS Nachfolgern werden nördlich der Alpen aus dem karolingischen Großreich ein im wesentlichen romanisch bestimmtes Westreich (das spätere Frankreich) und ein deutsches Ostreich geschaffen. Bei diesem verbleibt auch Italien. Im Hochmittelalter (vom 9. bis zum Ausgang des 12. Jahrhunderts) hat das „*Heilige Römische Reich Deutscher Nation*" eine Friedensordnung über den Völkern Mitteleuropas aufgerichtet. Seit der Erneuerung der langobardischen Königswürde KARLS DES GROSSEN durch OTTO I. DEN GROSSEN (951) und dem Erwerb der burgundischen Krone durch KONRAD II. (1032) vereint der deutsche Herrscher drei Königskronen. Polen, Böhmen und Ungarn erkennen unter HEINRICH III. (1039—1056) die Oberherrschaft des Kaisers an. Unter den Stauferkaisern erlebt das Reich eine kulturelle Blütezeit und unter FRIEDRICH I. BARBAROSSA mit dem

1212—1250 Kaiser FRIEDRICH II.

1226 Kaiser FRIEDRICH II. belehnt den Deutschen Orden mit dem Land der heidnischen Preußen. Christianisierung, Staatengründung und Besiedlung im Anschluß an die deutsche Ostsiedlung in den Landschaften jenseits der Elbe (12. bis 13. Jahrhundert)

1241 Mongolenschlacht bei Liegnitz

1254—1273 Interregnum

1309 der Hochmeister des Deutschen Ordens verlegt seinen Sitz von Venedig nach der Marienburg in Westpreußen

1348 Gründung der ersten deutschen Universität in Prag (1386 Universität Heidelberg)

1358 Städtebund der Hanse unter Führung Lübecks

1415 FRIEDRICH VON HOHENZOLLERN wird durch Kaiser SIGISMUND mit der Mark Brandenburg belehnt

1438—1740 (1806) das habsburgische Kaiserhaus

1450 JOHANN GUTENBERG erfindet den Buchdruck

1465—1536 ERASMUS

1471—1528 ALBRECHT DÜRER

1483—1546 MARTIN LUTHER: Reformator, Bibelübersetzer und Begründer der neuhochdeutschen Schriftsprache

1497—1543 HANS HOLBEIN DER JÜNGERE

1521 Wormser Reichstag

1530 Confessio Augustana

ritterlichen Zeitalter auch eine Epoche neuen politischen Glanzes.

Unter FRIEDRICH II. werden zu Beginn des 13. Jahrhunderts wichtige Regalien an die geistlichen und weltlichen Fürsten übertragen. Verfassungsmäßig wird damit die Entwicklung der *Territorialhoheit* eingeleitet. Das Interregnum bedeutet den Übergang zur Wahlaristokratie: sieben Kurfürsten wählen den Kaiser. Die politische Kraft des Königtums ist vom Ende des 13. Jahrhunderts ab auf die Territorialgewalten übergegangen, in der gleichen Zeit also, in der Frankreich, England und Spanien sich zu nationalen Einheitsstaaten entwickeln.

Der Einfluß der Dynastien (Habsburger, Luxemburger, Wittelsbacher usw.) beruhte auf ihrer Hausmacht. Mit der Krönung RUDOLFS VON HABSBURG (1273) geht die Königswürde auf die *Habsburger* über, in deren Händen sie von 1438 bis zur Auflösung des Reiches (1806) zumeist verblieben ist. Mit der Erhebung MAXIMILIANS I. zum römischen König (1493) tritt das Reich wieder aktiv in die abendländische Politik ein; vom 15. bis zum ausgehenden 16. Jahrhundert übernimmt es die Führung der europäischen Wirtschaft. Der Vorstoß der Türken bis vor Wien (1529), die Kriege zwischem dem Reich und Frankreich, das heißt den Häusern Habsburg und Valois, LUTHERS *Reformation* und wenig später die Gegenreformation bestimmen eine Entwicklung, aus der die Fürsten mit weiterem Machtzuwachs hervorgehen. Die Religionsparteien beziehen seit etwa 1580 ihre Stellungen;

1555 Augsburger Religionsfrieden: *cuius regio eius religio*

1618—1648 Dreißigjähriger Krieg (1648 Friede von Münster und Osnabrück)

die Reichsverfassung ist lahmgelegt. Der *Dreißigjährige Krieg*, in dem Deutschland Kriegsschauplatz Europas ist, vermag die religiöse Spaltung trotz unsäglichen Verwüstungen nicht zu beheben. Die Niederlande, durch die Herrschaft der spanischen Habsburger seit 1556 dem Reich entfremdet, und die Schweiz scheiden 1648 endgültig aus dem Reichsverband aus. Das Reich ist in eine Mosaiklandschaft von Mittel-, Klein- und Kleinststaaten zerfallen und wirtschaftlich gelähmt. Trotzdem bleiben auch nach 1648 Kaiser und Reich selbstverständliche und gültige Ordnungselemente.

*

1646—1716 GOTTFRIED WILHELM LEIBNIZ

um 1650 das deutsche Barock. Der Pietismus. Die Aufklärung

1685—1750 JOHANN SEBASTIAN BACH

1687—1753 BALTHASAR NEUMANN

1724—1804 IMMANUEL KANT

1740—1786 König FRIEDRICH II., DER GROSSE, von Preußen

1749—1832 JOHANN WOLFGANG VON GOETHE

Seit 1750 zweite (klassische) Blütezeit der deutschen Dichtung (KLOPSTOCK, LESSING, HERDER usw.). Das Rokoko

1759—1805 FRIEDRICH VON SCHILLER

1770—1827 LUDWIG VAN BEETHOVEN

Aus der Abwehr der Türken im Osten (1683) und der Angriffe LUDWIGS XIV. im Westen geht die habsburgische Großmacht im Süden, aus den Kämpfen um die Vormachtstellung im Nordosten und Norden gegen Polen, Rußland und Schweden die brandenburgisch-preußische Macht um 1700 hervor. 1701 wird der brandenburgische Kurfürst zum König „in Preußen" gekrönt. Seit 1740 wird *Preußen* ebenfalls Großmacht.

Der seit Jahrhunderten wirksame Gegensatz zwischen dem Kaiser und den Reichsständen wird für mehr als hundert Jahre durch den österreichisch-preußischen Gegensatz abgelöst. Im Schutz dieser Auseinandersetzung wächst Rußland weit nach Europa hinein (Teilungen Polens von 1772 bis 1795). Aus den innerdeutschen Spannungen entfaltet sich eine geistige Blütezeit, die alle Gebiete der Philosophie, der

Dichtung, der Musik und der bildenden Künste ergreift.

Die Französische Revolution bedeutet nicht nur das Ende der seit dem 17. Jahrhundert aufgerichteten absolutistischen Staatsform, sondern mit der Idee des Nationalstaats auch das Erlöschen der Reichsidee. Österreich und Preußen erliegen beide dem Ansturm Napoleons. Nach der Gründung des Rheinbundes legt am 6. 8. 1806 der Römisch-Deutsche Kaiser FRANZ II. die Krone des „Heiligen Römischen Reiches Deutscher Nation" nieder.

Der Wiener Kongreß vermag die politische Einheit Deutschlands nicht wiederherzustellen. Die Wiener Bundesakte von 1815 ist nur Dokument eines losen Zusammenschlusses von fünfunddreißig Fürsten und vier Freien Reichsstädten. Von 1830 bis 1848 ringt das Bürgertum um die unerfüllte deutsche Einheit. 1848 tritt ein deutsches Parlament in der Frankfurter Paulskirche zusammen. Im Gegensatz zwischen Großdeutschen (mit Österreich) und Kleindeutschen (unter der Führung Preußens) zeigt sich die Ausweglosigkeit des Versuchs, das Reich neu zu gründen: der König von Preußen lehnt 1849 die ihm angetragene Kaiserkrone ab. Der preußisch-österreichische Gegensatz wird 1866 mit der Waffe ausgetragen. Seit diesem Jahr gehört Österreich, das durch fünf Jahrhunderte deutsche Kaiser stellte, dem deutschen Staat nicht mehr an.

Der Norddeutsche Bund unter Führung Preußens schließt 1867 Bündnisse mit den süddeutschen Staaten. Im Krieg zwischen Frankreich und dem Norddeutschen Bund

1806 Das „Heilige Römische Reich" hört zu bestehen auf

1808 die preußischen Reformen des FREIHERRN VOM STEIN

1813 der Freiheitskrieg gegen NAPOLEON unter Führung Preußens beginnt (Völkerschlacht bei Leipzig)

1815—1898 OTTO VON BISMARCK, der Eiserne Kanzler

1818—1883 KARL MARX

1837 die Personalunion zwischen Hannover und dem Vereinigten Königreich wird gelöst

1866 „Bruderkrieg" zwischen Preußen und Österreich (mit Süddeutschland)

(1870) erfüllen die Süddeutschen Staaten ihre Bündnispflicht. Durch ihren Beitritt zum Bund vollzieht sich die Reichsgründung BISMARCKS. Der König von Preußen, bisher Präsidium des Norddeutschen Bundes, wird 1871 Deutscher Kaiser.

Das neue Deutsche Reich bringt von 1871 bis 1914 großen wirtschaftlichen Aufstieg, vor allem auf dem Gebiet der industriellen Produktion. Der Lebensstandard seiner Bevölkerung ist beachtlich. Wissenschaftliche, technische und kulturelle Leistungen verschaffen dem Reich hohes Ansehen in der Welt. Es wird getragen von Namen wie ROBERT KOCH, WILHELM CONRAD RÖNTGEN, MAX PLANCK, ALBERT EINSTEIN und anderen. Seit 1881 schafft Deutschland als erster Staat eine vorbildliche Sozialgesetzgebung.

Der Erste Weltkrieg läßt deutlich werden, wie tief das Reich in die kontinental- und weltpolitischen Auseinandersetzungen verstrickt ist. Aber die deutsche Einheit bleibt erhalten, als das Reich nach der militärischen Niederlage unter bedeutenden Gebietsverlusten zur Republik wird. Die Weimarer Verfassung vom 11. 8. 1919 schafft eine demokratisch-parlamentarische Ordnung.

1914—1918 der Erste Weltkrieg

1919 Diktatfrieden von Versailles

Gemäß den siebenundzwanzig Punkten des amerikanischen Präsidenten WILSON und nach dem Willen der Siegermächte sollte Europa nach 1918 auf der Grundlage des Selbstbestimmungsrechts der Völker neu geordnet werden. Dieser Grundsatz wird in den Friedensverträgen nicht befolgt. Im Osten wird nur in einem kleinen Teil der unter fremde Verwaltung ge-

1922 Rapallo-Vertrag mit der Sowjetunion

1925 Locarno-Vertrag mit den westlichen Nachbarn. GUSTAV STRESEMANN und ARISTIDE BRIAND bemühen sich um die Annäherung Deutschlands und Frankreichs

stellten Gebiete eine Volksabstimmung angeordnet. In jedem Fall entscheidet die Bevölkerung sich mit großer Mehrheit für das Verbleiben im Deutschen Reich.

Danzig und das Memelland, deren Bevölkerung ebenfalls im Reichsverband bleiben wollte, erhalten ein internationales Statut. Dessen ungeachtet wird das Memelland 1923 durch einen Gewaltstreich Litauen einverleibt.

Während der Weltwirtschaftskrise nach 1929 nimmt die innere Schwäche der „Weimarer Republik" rasch zu. Sechsunddreißig Parteien werben schließlich um die Gunst der Wähler. Die Zahl der Arbeitslosen steigt um die Jahreswende 1932/1933 auf mehr als sechs Millionen. Diese Situation ermöglicht es einem Demagogen, ADOLF HITLER, Führer der stärksten Partei zu werden. Als solcher wird er 1933 nach demokratischen Spielregeln zum Reichskanzler ernannt. Durch seine und seiner Mitarbeiter Skrupellosigkeit und den Druck der hinter ihm stehenden Massen gelingt es ihm, sämtliche Verfassungsorgane auszuschalten und die Republik in eine formlose Despotie zu verwandeln.

1933 Beginn der nationalsozialistischen Gewaltherrschaft

1938 mit dem Anschluß Österreichs beginnen die Annexionen HITLERS

1939—1945 der Zweite Weltkrieg

Als Folge der nationalsozialistischen Politik bricht 1939 der Zweite Weltkrieg aus. Er endet 1945 mit der militärischen Niederlage Deutschlands. Die Siegermächte übernehmen die oberste Gewalt („*supreme authority*").

Das deutsche Reichsgebiet in seinen Grenzen von 1937 wird im Juni 1945 in vier Besatzungszonen aufgeteilt. Die östlichen Provinzen werden abgetrennt und nach der Austreibung des größten Teils der deutschen Bevölkerung „bis zum Friedensschluß" fremder Verwaltung unterstellt. Im Westen wird das „Saargebiet" mit einer Million deutschsprachiger Bevölkerung unter Gewährung teilweiser politischer Autonomie wirtschaftlich an Frankreich angegliedert.

Die Darstellung der weiteren Entwicklung ist der Gegenstand dieses Buches.

FORTBESTAND DES REICHES

Der bedingungslosen Kapitulation der Deutschen Wehrmacht am 8. 5. 1945 folgte am 23. 5. 1945 in Flensburg die Gefangensetzung des „amtierenden Reichsoberhauptes“, des Großadmirals DÖNITZ, und der „geschäftsführenden Reichsregierung“ durch britische Militärpolizei. Mindestens von diesem Zeitpunkt ab gab es weder eine Deutsche Reichsregierung noch Reichszentralbehörden. Diese Situation führte zu der Vier-Mächte-Erklärung „in Anbetracht der Niederlage Deutschlands und der Übernahme der obersten Regierungsgewalt hinsichtlich Deutschlands“, der sogenannten „*Berliner Erklärung*“ vom 5. 6. 1945. Mit dieser Erklärung, die sie förmlich verlautbarten, *übernahmen die vier Siegermächte die oberste Regierungsgewalt* (*supreme authority*) einschließlich der Befugnisse aller zentralen und nachgeordneten Behörden *in Deutschland*. Diese Erklärung wurde im Potsdamer Abkommen vom 2. 8. 1945 wiederholt. Die souveräne Gewalt übte zunächst der Oberste Befehlshaber der Alliierten Expeditions-Streitkräfte aus. Später lag die Hoheitsgewalt bei den vier Oberbefehlshabern, bei jedem von ihnen für den Bereich seiner Besatzungszone, und bei allen vier gemeinschaftlich, als dem „*Alliierten Kontrollrat*“, in den Angelegenheiten, die „Deutschland als Ganzes“ betrafen[1]. Die Abgrenzung der *Besatzungszonen* erfolgte durch eine weitere Feststellung, die ebenfalls vom 5. 6. 1945 datiert. Der Kontrollrat hatte seinen Sitz in Berlin. Die deutsche Reichshauptstadt wurde von den Vier Mächten besetzt und durch eine interalliierte Behörde (Kommandantur) verwaltet („*Vier-Mächte-Status*“ *von Berlin*).

Die Besatzungsmächte errichteten in Deutschland einen Verwaltungsapparat, der, zentral gelenkt, bis in das letzte Dorf reichte. Das deutsche öffentliche Leben befand sich in einem solchen Zustand der Erschütterung, daß erhebliche Zeit vergehen mußte, bis eigenständig gebildete deutsche Organe sich entfalten und Verwaltungsfunktionen und Regierungstätigkeit ausüben konnten. In dieser Zeit hat sich die *Gemeindeselbstverwaltung als staatserhaltendes Element* erwiesen.

Nach den Weisungen der Militärregierungen und entsprechend den zunächst beschränkten Mitwirkungsmöglichkeiten der deutschen Bevölkerung begann der *Wiederaufbau* der öffentlichen Verwaltung und die Einrichtung einer nach demokratischen Prinzipien gestalteten staatlichen Ordnung in

[1] Vergleiche Feststellung über das Kontrollverfahren in Deutschland vom 5. 6. 1945, bestätigt durch das Potsdamer Abkommen vom 2. 8. 1945 und ergänzt durch die Proklamation betreffend Aufstellung des Kontrollrats vom 30. 8. 1945.

allen Zonen *schrittweise von unten nach oben*. Hierbei gingen jedoch die Militärregierungen in den einzelnen Besatzungszonen recht unterschiedlich vor, sowohl was die Schnelligkeit, als auch was die Art und Weise des Aufbaues betraf.

In der *Amerikanischen Zone* wurden zahlreiche Verwaltungsfunktionen schon in den ersten Monaten nach dem Zusammenbruch auf deutsche Stellen übertragen. Die Militärregierung beschränkte sich jedoch in dieser Periode nicht auf die Überwachung, sondern sie nahm weitgehend Einfluß auf die Verwaltungstätigkeit selbst.

Bereits am 28. 5. 1945 setzte die Militärregierung für das Land Bayern eine *Regierung* ein, die erste Landesregierung nach dem Zusammenbruch der nationalsozialistischen Herrschaft. Die offizielle Bildung der *Länder* erfolgte durch Proklamation Nr. 2 der Amerikanischen Militärregierung vom 19. 9. 1945. Es wurden die Länder *Bayern*, *Württemberg-Baden* und *Hessen* gebildet; später wurde auch das Land *Bremen* der Amerikanischen Zone zugeschlagen. Die Bildung der Vertretungskörperschaften wurde von unten nach oben vollzogen. Am 15. 11. 1945 übertrug die Militärregierung den Gemeinden und Kreisen die Verwaltung ihrer Angelegenheiten. Im Dezember 1945 erfolgte die gesetzliche Neuregelung des Gemeinderechts. Die ersten politischen Wahlen nach Kriegsende waren die Wahlen zu den Vertretungskörperschaften in den Landgemeinden: am 20. 1. 1946 in Hessen, am 27. 1. 1946 in Bayern und Württemberg-Baden. Nachdem eine Reform des Kreisrechts durchgeführt worden war, folgten am 28. 4. beziehungsweise 25. 5. 1946 die Wahlen der Kreistage und der Stadtvertretungen. Um die Mitte des Jahres 1946 fand auf Weisung der Militärregierung die Wahl von verfassunggebenden Landesversammlungen statt. Ende 1946 (in Bremen 1947) wurden die *Landesverfassungen* verabschiedet und bestätigt. In Gemäßheit neuer Wahlgesetze wurden die ersten *Landesparlamente* (Landtage, in Bremen die Bürgerschaft) gewählt, so daß nunmehr Landesregierungen auf parlamentarischer Grundlage gebildet werden konnten. Die neu gebildeten Länder hatten *Staatscharakter*. Sie übernahmen sämtliche den Deutschen überlassenen Staatsaufgaben; auch solche, die früher dem Reich zugekommen waren.

In der *Britischen Zone* nahm zunächst die Britische Militärregierung die Befugnisse der Reichszentralgewalt wahr. Eine Normalisierung der Verwaltung vollzog sich auch hier zuerst in der Gemeindestufe. Aber selbst hier nahm die Militärregierung starken Einfluß auf Einzelheiten der Verwaltung; sie ernannte Bürgermeister und beratende Beiräte (Stadtausschüsse) aus Vertretern der neu konstituierten politischen Parteien.

Am 1. 4. 1946 wurde für den Gesamtbereich der Zone die *Revidierte Deutsche Gemeindeordnung* erlassen. Nach britischem Muster führte sie das Prinzip der „Doppelköpfigkeit der Verwaltung" in die Kommunalverfassung ein. Der *Staat Preußen*, der faktisch schon im Mai 1945 untergegangen war, wurde durch Gesetz des Kontrollrats und durch ergänzende Bestimmungen der Britischen Militärregierung für aufgelöst erklärt. So wurde der Weg frei für eine *territoriale Neugliederung* der Besatzungszone. In der zweiten Hälfte des Jahres 1946 wurden die Länder *Schleswig-Holstein*, *Niedersachsen* und *Nordrhein-Westfalen* gebildet. Die Freie und Hansestadt *Hamburg* erhielt den Status eines Landes. Die ersten Landtage wurden noch durch die Militärregierung eingesetzt. Die ersten Gemeindewahlen fanden am 15. 9. 1946, die Wahlen zu den Landtagen im Laufe des Jahres 1947 statt. Die Ausarbeitung von Verfassungsurkunden wurde als nicht vordringlich angesehen und bis zur Konstituierung der Bundesrepublik zurückgestellt (Schleswig-Holstein 1949, Nordrhein-Westfalen 1950, Niedersachsen 1951, Hamburg 1952).

In der *Französischen Zone* wurden ebenfalls um die Mitte des Jahres 1946 drei Länder gebildet: *Rheinland-Pfalz*, *Baden* und *Württemberg-Hohenzollern*[1]. Auch hier vollzog der Aufbau der Verwaltung sich stufenweise von unten nach oben, zurückhaltender als im amerikanischen, aber doch rascher als im britischen Besatzungsgebiet.

Am 15. 9. 1946 fanden erste Gemeindewahlen, am 13. 10. 1946 Wahlen zu den Kreisversammlungen statt. Nach dem Ergebnis dieser Wahlen wurden *verfassunggebende Versammlungen* gebildet. Am 18. 5. 1947 fanden die Volksabstimmungen statt, durch die die *Landesverfassungen* bestätigt wurden. Gleichzeitig wurden die Landtage gewählt. So war auch hier die Grundlage für die normale Entwicklung eines demokratischen Verfassungslebens gelegt.

In der *Sowjetischen Besatzungszone* wurden von Ende 1946 bis Anfang 1947 fünf Länder gebildet: *Thüringen*, *Sachsen*, *Sachsen-Anhalt*, *Brandenburg* und *Mecklenburg*[2]. Die Entwicklung vollzog sich zunächst in Formen, die der Erwartung Raum ließen, daß sie sich ähnlich wie in den Ländern der drei westlichen Besatzungszonen gestalten würde. Das erwies sich aber bald als ein Irrtum.

Die Landesverfassungen wurden nach einem von der Sozialistischen Einheitspartei (SED) ausgearbeiteten Muster gestaltet. Trotz Verwendung überkommener demokratischer Begriffe wurde der beherrschende Einfluß der SED als der kommunistischen „Staatspartei" durch Manipulierung der Wahlen gesichert. Die Länder hatten keinen Staatscharakter; sie waren in der politischen Wirklichkeit Verwaltungseinheiten, die durch die in Berlin errichteten und von der Sowjetischen Militär-Administration abhängigen „Deutschen Zentralverwaltungen" gelenkt wurden. *In steigendem Maße setzten die sowjetischen Auffassungen sich durch* und begannen alle Bereiche des privaten und öffentlichen Lebens zu durchdringen. Eine Darstellung dieser Entwicklung, die zu der tragischen *Spaltung Deutschlands* in „West" und „Ost" führte („Eiserner Vorhang"), findet sich an anderer Stelle dieses Buches[3].

[1] Im Jahre 1952 schlossen sich die Länder Baden und Württemberg-Hohenzollern mit dem Land Württemberg-Baden zum Land *Baden-Württemberg* zusammen.

[2] Für die weitere Entwicklung ist Seite 145—159 zu vergleichen.

[3] Siehe Seite 174—176 und 190—195.

Der Gedanke an einen wieder zu konstituierenden deutschen Gesamtstaat ist nach dem Zusammenbruch in keinem deutschen Land aufgegeben worden. Da in den Jahren 1945 bis 1947 die Zeit hierfür noch nicht reif war, gewann zunächst die Frage der Bildung von *zentralen Organen über der Landesebene* Bedeutung. Sie wurde in den westlichen Besatzungszonen unter dem Einfluß und mit der Hilfe der Besatzungsmächte, wenn auch nicht einheitlich, in Angriff genommen.

Den Anfang machte die *Britische Zone* im März 1946 mit der Bildung des „Zonenbeirats" mit dem Sitz in Hamburg. Ihm gehörten Vertreter der politischen Parteien, der Landesregierungen und der Gewerkschaften an. Seine Aufgabe war es, die Militärregierung zu beraten. Später wurden Zonenzentralämter mit den Zuständigkeiten etwa der früheren Reichsministerien gebildet. Da das Verhältnis der Länder zueinander in der *US-Zone* von vornherein föderalistisch gestaltet war, wurden hier Zentraleinrichtungen nur mit koordinierenden Aufgaben geschaffen. Hervorzuheben ist der „Länderrat", ein permanenter Rat der Ministerpräsidenten, der seinen Sitz in Stuttgart hatte. In der *Französischen Zone* wurden erst wesentlich später (1947) und nur für wenige ausgewählte Sachgebiete Generaldirektionen als zentrale Verwaltungsstellen zugelassen.

Im Hinblick auf die katastrophalen wirtschaftlichen Verhältnisse in Deutschland machten am 20. 7. 1946 die USA den Vorschlag, die vier Besatzungszonen *in wirtschaftlicher Hinsicht als Einheit* zu behandeln. Dieser Vorschlag hatte den Wortlaut und den Geist des Potsdamer Abkommens für sich (Teil III Abschnitt B Ziffer 14: „Während der Besatzungszeit ist Deutschland als eine wirtschaftliche Einheit zu betrachten"). Frankreich und die Sowjetunion lehnten dennoch ab. Darauf unterzeichneten am 29. 5. 1947 die Britische und die Amerikanische Militärregierung für ihre beiden Zonen das *Abkommen über die Einrichtung eines Wirtschaftsrates für das „Vereinigte Wirtschaftsgebiet"*. Gleichzeitig wurde die Organisation der Zweizonenverwaltung durch Besatzungsrecht festgelegt. Eine Ausweitung der ‚Bizone' zur ‚Trizone', die auch die unter französischer Besatzungshoheit stehenden deutschen Länder umfaßte, ist erst später, gleichzeitig mit der Errichtung der Bundesrepublik Deutschland im Herbst 1949, erfolgt.

Die Verfassung des *Wirtschaftsrates*, der seinen Sitz in Frankfurt hatte, wurde mehrfach umgestaltet. Neben dem Wirtschaftsparlament, dessen Vertreter von den Landtagen der acht Länder der Doppelzone gewählt wurden, stand ein *Länderrat* als zweite Kammer. An der Spitze der fünf Verwaltungen (für Wirtschaft, Ernährung und Landwirtschaft, Finanzen, Verkehr und Post) standen *Direktoren.* Die Aufgabe der Koordinierung lag bei einem *Oberdirektor*. Bei diesen institutionellen Einrichtungen handelte es sich deutlich um den Versuch, die deutsche Gesamtverfassung vorzuformen; ein Versuch, der materiell auf die Wirtschaftsverfassung und gebietsmäßig auf die „Bizone" beschränkt war. Allerdings bedurften die vom Wirtschaftsrat beschlossenen Gesetze noch der Zustimmung des *Bipartite Board* der Amerikanischen und Britischen Militärregierung. In der Zeit seines Bestehens (bis zur Konstituierung der Bundesorgane im Herbst 1949) hat der Wirtschaftsrat rund 150 Gesetze verabschiedet. Sie betrafen bedeutsame Fragen der Wirtschaft, der Finanzen, des Verkehrs und der Landwirtschaft und galten später als Bundesrecht weiter.

Nachdem die Versuche deutscher Stellen, eine gesamtdeutsche Repräsentation zu schaffen, an den politischen Forderungen gescheitert waren[1], die von den Regierungen der Länder der Sowjetischen Besatzungszone gestellt wurden, und nachdem auch der Kontrollrat in Berlin als das Gemeinschaftsorgan der Besatzungsmächte im März 1948 durch den demonstrativen Auszug des Vertreters der Sowjetunion *de facto* funktionsunfähig geworden war, konzentrierten die Bemühungen der drei westlichen Alliierten sich darauf, einen handlungsfähigen deutschen Staat wenigstens in Westdeutschland ins Leben zu rufen. Nach Maßgabe der „*Londoner Beschlüsse*" vom 2. 6. 1948 übergaben die Militärgouverneure den in Frankfurt versammelten Regierungschefs der elf westdeutschen Länder am 1. 7. 1948 drei Schriftstücke, die sogenannten „*Frankfurter Dokumente*". Dokument I enthielt den Vorschlag zur Einberufung einer verfassunggebenden Versammlung für das Gebiet dieser Länder spätestens zum 1. 9. 1948. Dokument II ließ Anregungen für eine Änderung der innerdeutschen Ländergrenzen zu. Dokument III endlich enthielt Leitsätze für ein von den Drei Mächten noch zu erlassendes Besatzungsstatut.

Die Richtlinien für den Inhalt der künftigen staatlichen Grundordnung forderten „eine demokratische Verfassung ..., die für die beteiligten Länder eine Regierungsform des föderalistischen Typs schafft, welche am besten geeignet ist, die gegenwärtig zerrissene *deutsche Einheit* schließlich wieder herzustellen, und welche die Rechte der beteiligten Länder schützt, eine angemessene Zentralinstanz schafft und Garantien der individuellen Rechte und Freiheiten enthält".

Am 8. und 21. 7. 1948 wurden diese Vorschläge von den Regierungschefs der westdeutschen Länder allein und am 26. 7. 1948 gemeinsam mit den Militärgouverneuren beraten. Dabei wurde Einigung über die Grundlagen des westdeutschen Zusammen

[1] Vergleiche die Konferenz der Regierungschefs der Länder der vier Zonen vom 6. bis 8. 6. 1947 in München.

schlusses erzielt. Die Ministerpräsidenten setzten zur Vorbereitung der Arbeiten an der Verfassung einen Ausschuß von Sachkennern ein, der vom 10. bis 23. 8. 1948 auf der Insel Herrenchiemsee in Bayern tagte. Der Verfassungsentwurf von Herrenchiemsee diente dem ,,Parlamentarischen Rat" als eine wertvolle Arbeitsunterlage

Die 65 Abgeordneten des *Parlamentarischen Rates* (dazu fünf Abgeordnete von Berlin[West] mit beratender Stimme) wurden von den Landtagen der beteiligten elf Länder gewählt. Sie waren von Weisungen unabhängig. Die politischen Parteien waren wie folgt vertreten: CDU/CSU siebenundzwanzig, SPD siebenundzwanzig, FDP fünf, Zentrum, DP und Kommunisten je zwei Sitze[1]. Der Parlamentarische Rat trat termingemäß am 1. 9. 1948 in Bonn am Rhein zusammen. Er wählte Dr. KONRAD ADENAUER zu seinem Präsidenten. Nach schwierigen Beratungen, in die sich auch die Militärgouverneure mehrfach einschalteten, verabschiedete der Parlamentarische Rat am 8. 5. 1949 das *Grundgesetz für die Bundesrepublik Deutschland.* Dieses trat nach Genehmigung durch die Militärgouverneure und Annahme durch die Volksvertretungen der Länder am 23. 5. 1949 in Kraft. Am 14. 8. 1949 wurde vom deutschen Volk in den drei Westzonen der erste *Deutsche Bundestag* gewählt. Nach Maßgabe der Bestimmungen des Grundgesetzes wurden im September 1949 der *Bundespräsident* und der *Bundeskanzler* gewählt und die *Bundesregierung* gebildet. Auch der *Bundesrat* konstituierte sich und wählte seinen Präsidenten. Mit der Bildung der obersten Verfassungsorgane waren die Voraussetzungen für die praktische Anwendbarkeit der Vorschriften des Grundgesetzes gegeben. *Die Bundesrepublik Deutschland war handlungsfähig.*

Am 21. 9. 1949 trat auch das schon unter dem 10. 4. 1949 im Text bekanntgegebene *Besatzungsstatut* in Kraft. Durch dieses wurde das Verhältnis der Bundesrepublik zu den drei Besatzungsmächten, die nunmehr durch ihre ,,*Hohen Kommissare*" repräsentiert wurden, erstmals rechtsförmlich festgelegt. Das Besatzungsstatut war noch ,,in Ausübung der von den Regierungen Frankreichs, der Vereinigten Staaten und des Vereinigten Königreiches *beibehaltenen obersten Gewalt*" verkündet worden. Dennoch bedeutete es den *Abschluß der ersten Phase der Besatzungsherrschaft.* Die Bundesrepublik erhielt weitgehende eigene Entscheidungsbefugnisse. Die wirtschaftlichen und politischen Beziehungen zwischen der Bundesrepublik und den drei Westmächten festigten sich rasch[2].

[1] Die Abkürzungen der Parteinamen sind Seite 300 ff. erklärt.
[2] Die einzelnen Marksteine auf diesem Wege siehe Seite 168 ff.

Dementsprechend hat auch das Besatzungsverhältnis bald einen Wandel erfahren. Die Revision des Besatzungsstatuts vom 6. 3. 1951 brachte eine Einschränkung und Abschwächung der alliierten Kontrollbefugnisse. Den Abschluß dieser Entwicklung bildete der *Vertrag über die Beziehungen zwischen der Bundesrepublik Deutschland und den Drei Mächten* (sogenannter „Deutschland-Vertrag") vom 26. 5. 1952 in der Fassung des in Paris unterzeichneten *Protokolls über die Beendigung des Besatzungsregimes in der Bundesrepublik Deutschland vom* 23. 10. 1954. Durch diese Regelungen ist der größte Teil der den Besatzungsmächten zustehenden oder von ihnen ausgeübten Rechte erloschen. Das Besatzungsstatut wurde durch Proklamation vom 5. 5. 1955 aufgehoben. An die Stelle der Hohen Kommission sind *Botschaften* der Drei Mächte getreten. *Die Bundesrepublik erhielt die volle Macht eines souveränen Staates.* Vorbehalten blieben jedoch den Drei Mächten ihre bisherigen Rechte und Verantwortlichkeiten in bezug auf Berlin, Deutschland als Ganzes und eine friedensvertragliche Regelung. Bis zum Abschluß des Friedensvertrages wirken die Unterzeichnerstaaten des Pariser Vertragswerkes nach ihrer feierlichen Erklärung zusammen, um mit friedlichen Mitteln ihr gemeinsames Ziel zu verwirklichen: „Ein *wiedervereinigtes Deutschland*, das eine freiheitlich-demokratische Verfassung, ähnlich wie die Bundesrepublik, besitzt und in die europäische politische Gemeinschaft integriert ist." Aus der Eigenart der Deutschland-Frage ist es erklärlich, daß die Drei Mächte auch ihre Rechte hinsichtlich der Vierten Besatzungsmacht sich vorbehalten haben.

*

* *

1945 mochte es dem deutschen Volke scheinen, als sei mit der militärischen Niederlage, mit dem totalen Zusammenbruch der öffentlichen Ordnung und mit der Besetzung des gesamten Staatsgebietes durch die Siegermächte auch der Staat der Deutschen untergegangen. Die *Vernichtung des deutschen Staates* gehörte aber nicht zu den Kriegszielen der alliierten Mächte. So verlautbarten sie auch in Übereinstimmung mit früheren Erklärungen (Konferenz von Moskau 1943, Jalta-Konferenz vom Februar 1945) in ihrer schon oben erwähnten Berliner Erklärung vom 5. 6. 1945: „Die Übernahme zu den vorstehend genannten Zwecken der besagten Regierungsgewalt und Befugnisse bewirkt *nicht die Annektierung Deutschlands.*" Die Übernahme der obersten Regierungsgewalt, das heißt die treuhänderische Wahrnehmung der zentralen deutschen Hoheitsbefugnisse durch die Besatzungsmächte, war

Bundespräsident Professor THEODOR HEUSS mit dem Regierenden Bürgermeister von Berlin, WILLY BRANDT

Bundeskanzler Dr. KONRAD ADENAUER mit dem Führer der parlamentarischen Opposition, ERICH OLLENHAUER (SPD)
↓

Unten links: Bundestagspräsident Dr. EUGEN GERSTENMAIER (rechts) mit dem Bundesminister für Wirtschaft, Vizekanzler Professor LUDWIG ERHARD

Von links nach rechts: der Präsident des Bundesrats WILHELM KAISEN, Bürgermeister von Bremen, mit dem Präsidenten des Bundesverfassungsgerichts, Dr. GEBHARD MÜLLER, und dem Bundesminister des Auswärtigen, Dr. HEINRICH VON BRENTANO, auf der Bremer Schaffermahlzeit
↓

Vertriebene 1945: ohne Habe im zerstörten Vaterland

Vertriebene 1959:
im eigenen Heim

auch nicht als eine Dauerlösung, sondern nur als eine Zwischenphase gedacht. Die Oberbefehlshaber sollten diese oberste Gewalt lediglich zeitlich begrenzt ausüben; nämlich „*während der Zeit*, in der Deutschland die sich aus der bedingungslosen Kapitulation ergebenden grundlegenden Forderungen erfüllt" (so die oben erwähnte Erklärung vom 5. 6. 1945). Nach Durchführung des Zweckes der Besetzung sollte es wieder *Sache des deutschen Volkes selbst* sein, „sein Leben auf einer demokratischen und friedlichen Grundlage aufzubauen" (so das Potsdamer Abkommen vom 2. 8. 1945).

Im Hinblick auf die *Eigenart der Lage Deutschlands nach dem Zusammenbruch*, die in der Geschichte der großen Staaten keine Parallele hat, kann es nicht Wunder nehmen, daß die „*Deutschland-Frage*" nicht nur politisch, sondern auch in juristischer Hinsicht zu einem Problem ersten Ranges wurde. Sowohl die deutsche Rechtslehre und Rechtsprechung, als auch die überwiegenden Stimmen der Rechtswissenschaft und hohe Gerichte im Ausland stimmten jedoch bald, unbeschadet der vielfach abweichenden Begründungen, in der Kernfrage überein, daß der deutsche Staat über den Schicksalstag des 8. 5. 1945 hinaus Bestand behalten hat. *Rechtssubjekt des Völkerrechts und damit Mitglied der Staatengemeinschaft ist Deutschland auch in der Phase der Besetzung geblieben. Eingeschränkt war nur seine völkerrechtliche Handlungsfähigkeit.*

Von diesem Aspekt her erhält auch die Aufforderung der Drei Mächte vom Juli 1948 an die Regierungschefs der westdeutschen Länder, eine Bundesverfassung zu schaffen und eine deutsche Regierung zu bilden, ihre richtige Deutung. Sie bedeutete die Erklärung, daß — jedenfalls nach Auffassung der westlichen Alliierten — die *Notstandslage*, welche die Besatzungsmächte nach der Kapitulation der Wehrmacht und der Ausschaltung der früheren Reichsregierung zur Übernahme der obersten Gewalt veranlaßt hatte, nunmehr beendet sei, und daß die Besatzungszwecke im wesentlichen erfüllt seien. Damit konnten die neu gebildeten Verfassungsorgane in einem kontinuierlichen Prozeß, der bis zum 5. 5. 1955 mittags 12 Uhr währen sollte, wieder *in die vorübergehend okkupierte deutsche Hoheitsgewalt hineinwachsen*. Durch die Konstituierung der Bundesrepublik Deutschland ist mithin *kein neuer Staat* geschaffen worden, sondern es ist das vor 1945 bestehende Reich, allerdings in einer durch die politische Entwicklung seit 1945 erzwungenen räumlichen Begrenzung, wiederhergestellt worden. Daß die Normalisierung der staatlichen Verhältnisse zur großen Enttäuschung des deutsches Volkes auf die drei westlichen Zonen beschränkt werden mußte, lag darin begründet, daß eine Gesamtlösung nur im Einvernehmen aller Vier Besatzungsmächte hätte getroffen werden können. Die Vierte Besatzungsmacht hat sich aber einer freiheitlichen demokratischen Lösung der gesamtdeutschen Frage auf der Grundlage der Selbstbestimmung des deutschen Volkes bisher beharrlich versagt.

Die Bundesrepublik ist die legitime Gestalt des Deutschen Reiches. Sie ist identisch mit dem deutschen Staat, wie er 1867 in der Gestalt und unter dem Namen des Norddeutschen Bundes, 1871 als Deutsches Reich und 1919, in einem tiefgreifenden Wandel der Verfassung, in der Weimarer Republik in Erscheinung getreten ist. Allerdings kann die deutsche Staatsgewalt, repräsentiert durch die Verfassungsorgane der Bundesrepublik, zur Zeit nur in einem Teil des deutschen Gebietes geltend gemacht werden.

*

Politisch freilich ist dieser Anspruch der Bundesrepublik nicht unbestritten. Auf dem Territorium des Reiches ist noch ein Gebilde entstanden, das sich als „Staat" bezeichnet: die „Deutsche Demokratische Republik" der Sowjetischen Besatzungszone. Auch sie erhebt Anspruch darauf, Deutschland, zum mindesten einen gleichberechtigt neben der Bundesrepublik bestehenden souveränen deutschen „Teilstaat", darzustellen (sogenannte „Zwei-Staaten-Theorie"). Diesem Anspruch gegenüber braucht nicht so sehr Gewicht darauf gelegt zu werden, daß von der deutschen Bevölkerung etwa drei Viertel in der Bundesrepublik leben und nur ein Viertel in der sogenannten DDR. Völkerrechtlich ist entscheidend, *daß nur die Regierung der Bundesrepublik eine demokratische Grundlage in freien Wahlen hat*, während die von der kommunistischen Einheitspartei beherrschte sogenannte DDR eine rechtswidrige und usurpierte sowjetische Herrschaftsform auf deutschem Boden ist. Die Regierung der sogenannten DDR entbehrt der Legitimität. Hieraus folgt, daß nur die im Rahmen einer rechtsstaatlichen Verfassung hierzu berufenen Organe der Bundesrepublik in der Gemeinschaft der freien Völker der Welt als die Repräsentanten des deutschen Staates auftreten und für das deutsche Volk in internationalen Angelegenheiten verbindlich sprechen und handeln können.

Die maßgebenden Bundesorgane haben von Anfang an die *Identität des Bundes mit dem Reich* betont. Sie haben dementsprechend der von der Sowjetunion gelenkten Regierung der sogenannten DDR das Recht bestritten, für ganz Deutschland zu sprechen oder zu handeln (zum Beispiel in der Frage der Anerkennung der „Oder-Neiße-Grenze"). Zu der Erklärung der Regierung der Sowjetunion vom 25.3.1954, daß sie die

,,DDR" als einen ,,souveränen Staat" anerkenne, hat der *Deutsche Bundestag* am 7.4.1954 einstimmig folgenden Beschluß gefaßt: ,,Der Deutsche Bundestag erklärt, daß das deutsche Volk sich niemals mit der Spaltung Deutschlands abfinden und die Existenz zweier deutscher Staaten hinnehmen wird. Er wiederholt die Feststellung, daß das kommunistische Regime in der sowjetisch besetzten Zone Deutschlands nur durch Gewalt existiert und keine Vertretung des deutschen Volkes ist. Die Bundesregierung als die einzige demokratisch und frei gewählte deutsche Regierung ist allein berechtigt, für alle Deutschen zu sprechen. An dieser oft bekundeten Stellungnahme hat sich durch die Erklärung der Regierung der Sowjetunion vom 25.3.1954 nichts geändert."

*

Für die Bundesrepublik bestand bisher kein Anlaß — und auch die neuesten Noten der Sowjetunion vom 27.11.1958 betreffend Berlin und vom 10.1. 1959 betreffend den Entwurf eines Friedensvertrages mit Deutschland geben hierzu keine Veranlassung —, diese rechtlich einwandfrei begründete und in politischer Hinsicht unabdingbare These preiszugeben. Es ist offenkundig, daß vielmehr das deutsche Volk sich selbst preisgäbe, würde es in einer von der Sowjetunion propagierten ,,Konföderation" der Bundesrepublik mit der sogenannten DDR eine Wiedervereinigung unter sowjetischem Vorzeichen, das heißt eine ,,Wiedervereinigung in Unfreiheit", hinnehmen.

Die Bundesregierung ist sich der weitreichenden innenpolitischen und internationalen Auswirkungen bewußt, die aus der von ihr vertretenen Auffassung von der Identität der Bundesrepublik mit dem Deutschen Reich sich ergeben. So hat sie den Beweis erbracht, daß sie im Rahmen ihrer wirtschaftlichen Leistungsfähigkeit gewillt ist, auch die vor dem Bestehen der Bundesrepublik vom Reich eingegangenen Verpflichtungen zu erfüllen. Das bezieht sich nicht nur auf die Einhaltung der in *internationalen Verträgen des Reiches* begründeten Verpflichtungen und auf die Anerkennung der *Auslandsschulden des Reiches*, sondern zum Beispiel auch auf den vielbeachteten großen Komplex der sogenannten *Wiedergutmachungsfragen*.

BUND UND LÄNDER

Die Bundesrepublik Deutschland ist, wie ihr Name sagt, ein *föderativer Staat.* Schon die Präambel des Grundgesetzes hebt ausdrücklich hervor, daß diese Verfassung „*das deutsche Volk in den Ländern* Baden, Bayern, Bremen, Hamburg, Hessen, Niedersachsen, Nordrhein-Westfalen, Rheinland-Pfalz, Schleswig-Holstein, Württemberg-Baden und Württemberg-Hohenzollern" beschlossen hat. Auch in Artikel 23, der den vorläufigen Geltungsbereich des Grundgesetzes umschreibt, werden die vorstehend genannten Länder nochmals aufgezählt, und es wird hier zusätzlich das Land Berlin genannt.

Nach dem gegenwärtigen Stand (1959) sind jedoch einige Veränderungen und Vorbehalte zu berücksichtigen. Entsprechend der in Artikel 118 GG vorgesehenen besonderen Regelung schlossen sich am 25. 4. 1952 die drei Länder Baden, Württemberg-Baden und Württemberg-Hohenzollern nach Durchführung einer Volksabstimmung (16. 12. 1951) zu dem *Bundesland Baden-Württemberg* zusammen.

Mit Wirkung vom 1. 1. 1957 ist *Saarland*, nachdem es seinen Beitritt gemäß Artikel 23 GG erklärt hatte, ein Land der Bundesrepublik geworden. Das Bundesgesetz über die „Eingliederung des Saarlandes" vom 23. 12. 1956 sieht jedoch entsprechend den Vereinbarungen des zwischen der Bundesrepublik Deutschland und der Französischen Republik abgeschlossenen Vertrages zur Regelung der Saarfrage vom 27. 10. 1956 eine „*Übergangszeit*" vor, die auf drei Jahre bemessen ist. Während dieser Übergangszeit bilden Saarland und Frankreich weiterhin ein einheitliches Zoll- und Währungsgebiet nach Maßgabe besonderer Bestimmungen.

Hinsichtlich des Landes *Berlin (West)* besteht noch ein Vorbehalt der Drei Mächte. Berlin darf nicht „durch den Bund regiert" werden. Dennoch besteht kein Zweifel, daß Berlin in staatsrechtlicher Hinsicht ein *Land der Bundesrepublik* ist. Das Grundgesetz gilt in und für Berlin, soweit nicht die Vorbehalte der Drei Mächte seine Anwendbarkeit noch beschränken. Bundesorgane dürfen zur Zeit noch nicht unmittelbare Bundesgewalt über Berlin ausüben, soweit die Drei Mächte dies nicht für einzelne Bereiche zugelassen haben. Demgemäß ist das Land Berlin im Bundestag und im Bundesrat nur durch Abgeordnete und Vertreter ohne Stimmrecht vertreten.

Die Bundesrepublik besteht somit aus elf Bundesländern, wobei das Land Berlin unter Berücksichtigung des Vorbehalts der Drei Mächte als „elftes Bundesland" zu bezeichnen ist (vergleiche die nachfolgende Übersicht).

DIE LÄNDER DER BUNDESREPUBLIK

Land	Hauptstadt	Fläche[1]		Bevölkerung am 31. 12. 1958[2]	Bevölkerungszunahme 1939—1958		Bevölkerungsdichte	
		qkm	q-Meile	1.000		%	Einwohner je qkm	Einwohner je q-Meile
Schleswig-Holstein	Kiel	15.688	6.057	2.275,8	686,8	*43,2*	145	376
Hamburg		747	288	1.807,6	95,7	*5,6*	2.419	6.276
Niedersachsen	Hannover	47.372	18.290	6.515,6	1.975,9	*43,5*	138	356
Bremen		404	156	677,5	114,6	*20,4*	1.678	4.343
Nordrhein-Westfalen	Düsseldorf	33.958	13.111	15.458,6	3.524,2	*29,5*	455	1.179
Hessen	Wiesbaden	21.108	8.150	4.651,5	1.172,4	*33,7*	220	571
Rheinland-Pfalz	Mainz	19.828	7.656	3.354,7	394,7	*13,3*	169	438
Baden-Württemberg	Stuttgart	35.750	13.803	7.433,0	1.956,6	*35,7*	208	539
Bayern	München	70.549	27.239	9.278,0	2.193,9	*31,0*	132	341
Saarland	Saarbrücken	2.567	991	1.040,2	130,6	*14,4*	405	1.050
Bundesgebiet ohne Berlin(West)		247.971	95.742	52.492,5	12.245,4	*30,4*	212	548
Berlin(West)		481	186	2.226,0	— 524,5	*— 19,1*	4.628	11.968
Bundesrepublik	Bonn	248.452	95.927	54.718,5	11.720,9	*27,3*	220	570

[1] Letzte verfügbare Fläche. — [2] Fortgeschriebene Bevölkerung; Grundlage: Wohnungsstatistik vom 25.9.1956.

Quelle: Statistisches Bundesamt.

Artikel 29 GG sieht eine *Neugliederung der Länder* nach landsmannschaftlicher Verbundenheit, geschichtlichen und kulturellen Zusammenhängen, wirtschaftlicher Zweckmäßigkeit und sozialem Gefüge vor. Die Neugliederung soll Länder schaffen, die nach Größe und Leistungsfähigkeit die ihnen obliegenden Aufgaben wirksam erfüllen können. Sie soll durch Bundesgesetz erfolgen, das in jedem betroffenen Gebietsteil zum Volksentscheid zu stellen ist. Das Nähere ist in Artikel 29 und im Bundesgesetz über Volksbegehren und Volksentscheid bei Neugliederung des Bundesgebietes vom 23. 12. 1955 nebst Durchführungsverordnung vom 29. 12. 1955 geregelt. Im Jahr 1955 hat ein von der Bundesregierung eingesetzter Sachverständigenausschuß, dem Reichskanzler a. D. HANS LUTHER vorstand, ein umfassendes Gutachten zum Neugliederungsproblem erstattet (LUTHER-*Gutachten*). Die Entwicklung dieser Frage bleibt abzuwarten.

Der bundesstaatliche Aufbau der Bundesrepublik ist kein künstliches Produkt. Er hat seine Wurzeln in der deutschen Geschichte. Zwar sprechen die Urkunden schon seit nahezu tausend Jahren von einem deutschen „*Reich*"; dieses ist aber niemals ein Einheitsstaat gewesen. Etwa seit der Mitte des 13. Jahrhunderts bildeten sich auf dem Boden des „Heiligen Römischen Reiches Deutscher Nation" verhältnismäßig unabhängige Territorialstaaten, deren tatsächliche Souveränität im Westfälischen Frieden von 1648 bestätigt wurde. Das Deutsche Reich der folgenden Jahrhunderte war nur noch ein loser *Staatenbund*, dessen Mitglieder die Oberhoheit der habsburgischen Kaiser in Wien formal anerkannten. Der deutsche Rechtsgelehrte SAMUEL VON PUFENDORF hat dieses Reich in einer berühmten Schrift von 1667 als ein „unregelmäßiges Gebilde, einem Monstrum vergleichbar" bezeichnet. 1806 löste sich dieses Schattenreich auch *de jure* auf.

Die fünfunddreißig Fürsten und vier Freien Städte auf dem deutschen Territorium schlossen sich auf dem Wiener Kongreß zu einem „völkerrechtlichen Verein der deutschen souveränen Fürsten und Freien Städte", dem *Deutschen Bund*, zusammen[1]. Dieser *Staatenbund* hatte bis 1866 Bestand. Die Politik Preußens unter OTTO VON BISMARCK als Ministerpräsidenten und Außen-

[1] Deutsche Bundesakte von 1815 und Wiener Schlußakte von 1820.

minister führte 1867 zur Gründung des *Norddeutschen Bundes* und 1871 durch Hinzutritt der drei süddeutschen Staaten (die beiden Königreiche Bayern und Württemberg und das Großherzogtum Baden) und des Großherzogtums Hessen zur Bildung des Deutschen Kaiserreichs. Das neue *Deutsche Reich* war ein echter *Bundesstaat*, nicht nur ein Staatenbund. Zentrales Verfassungsorgan war der *Bundesrat*. Er repräsentierte die Gesamtheit der verbündeten Fürsten und war Träger der Reichsgewalt. Auch an der Verwaltung des Reiches war er maßgeblich beteiligt. Wenn Preußen von den einundsechzig Stimmen im Bundesrat auch nur siebzehn besaß, so war seine Vormachtstellung dennoch verfassungsrechtlich und politisch gesichert. Das Präsidium des Bundes führte der jeweilige König von Preußen als Deutscher Kaiser. Reichsgesetze konnten nur durch übereinstimmende Mehrheitsbeschlüsse des Reichstags und des Bundesrats zustandekommen.

Durch die Revolution von 1918 wurden zwar die monarchischen Spitzen beseitigt; aber die bundesstaatliche Struktur des Reiches blieb, wenn auch in einer abgewandelten Form, erhalten. In der republikanischen und demokratischen *Weimarer Verfassung* von 1919 wurden die Gliedstaaten als „Länder" bezeichnet. Während das Reichsgebiet des Kaiserreichs noch zweiundzwanzig Staaten und drei Freie Städte umfaßte, verringerte die Zahl der Länder in der Weimarer Republik sich auf siebzehn und schließlich durch den Anschluß kleinerer Länder an Bayern und Preußen auf vierzehn. Zentrales Verfassungsorgan war nunmehr der *Reichstag* als die Repräsentation des Staatsvolkes. Zur Vertretung der Länder bei der Gesetzgebung und Verwaltung des Reichs war der *Reichsrat* gebildet worden. Die Länder waren in ihm entsprechend ihrer Bevölkerungszahl vertreten; jedoch war die Vormachtstellung Preußens beseitigt worden. Der Reichsrat hatte nur schwache Befugnisse. In der Gesetzgebung besaß er nur ein aufschiebendes Veto.

Dem nationalsozialistischen Regime, das 1933 an die Macht kam, erschien die föderative Verfassung als ein Anachronismus. Die Landesregierungen wurden bereits 1933 „gleichgeschaltet". Ihre Leitung wurde „Reichsstatthaltern" übertragen. 1934 wurden die Landtage aufgelöst. Die Hoheitsrechte der Länder wurden auf das Reich übertragen. So war der Weg frei für den Ausbau des *zentralistischen Einheitsstaates* nationalsozialistischer Prägung, der 1945 mit dem Zusammenbruch des „Dritten Reiches" sein Ende fand.

*

Wenn die Schöpfer der Verfassung der Bundesrepublik 1948/1949 bewußt zum *föderativen Prinzip* zurückkehrten, so entsprach das wohl den Weisungen der Besatzungsmächte, aber zugleich auch dem Wunsch des größten Teils der deutschen Bevölkerung in den Ländern der drei westlichen Besatzungszonen. Der Bundesstaatsgedanke bedeutet nicht nur ein formales Prinzip. Artikel 28 Absatz 1 GG bestimmt, daß die verfassungsmäßige Ordnung in den Ländern den Grundsätzen des republikanischen, demokratischen und sozialen Rechtsstaats im Sinne des Grundgesetzes entsprechen muß. *Es besteht ein Höchstmaß an verfassungsrechtlicher Homogenität zwischen den Gliedstaaten und dem Gesamtstaat.* So ist es verständlich, wenn das Grundgesetz festlegt, daß der föderative Aufbau der Bundesrepublik auch durch ein verfassungänderndes Gesetz nicht aufgehoben werden darf[1].

Die Anhänger des Einheitsstaates wenden ein, daß die Bundesrepublik mit ihrer föderativen Verfassung eine Sonderstellung innerhalb der westeuropäischen Staatenwelt einnehme, wenn man von der Schweiz und Österreich absehe. Dem ist jedoch entgegenzuhalten, daß auch die Vereinigten Staaten von Nordamerika und mehrere lateinamerikanische Republiken Bundesstaaten sind, und daß die föderative staatliche Struktur sich dort durchaus bewährt hat. Von anderen wird hervorgehoben, daß im Hinblick auf die europäische Integration und die Entwicklung schließlich zu einem europäischen Bundesstaat die innerstaatliche föderalistische Struktur und Aufteilung der Kompetenzen zwischen dem Bund und den Ländern ein Nachteil sein könnte. Es würde eine Überorganisation sein, wenn die bundesstaatlich gegliederte Bundesrepublik Deutschland ihrerseits als Gliedstaat einer bundesstaatlich organisierten europäischen Gemeinschaft in Erscheinung treten würde. Der Entwicklung mag es überlassen bleiben, in welcher Form die europäische Gemeinschaft dereinst Gestalt gewinnen wird, und welche Einflüsse sich daraus auf die Struktur der Gliedstaaten ergeben werden. — Für die gesamtdeutsche Situation bleibt hervorzuheben, daß im sowjetisch besetzten Teil Deutschlands das föderalistische Prinzip gänzlich preisgegeben worden ist. Im Jahre 1952 wurden dort die Landesregierungen und die Landtage aufgehoben; das Gebiet der Länder wurde in vierzehn Bezirke eingeteilt, die der Zentralregierung unmittelbar unterstehen. Die „Länder" stellten bis zu ihrer völligen Beseitigung Ende 1958 nur noch Selbstverwaltungskörper höherer Ordnung dar. Demgemäß wurde im Dezember 1958 die neben der „Volkskammer" formal noch bestehende „Länderkammer" aufgelöst. Dieser weitere Ausbau des zentralistischen diktatorischen Apparats der Führung der SED entlarvt auch den von der Sowjetunion und ihren Statthaltern in der sogenannten DDR propagierten Plan einer angeblichen „Konföderation" der „zwei deutschen Staaten" (sogenannte „Zwei-Staaten-Theorie", vergleiche oben Seite 98). Abgesehen davon, daß die Bundesrepublik einen zweiten deutschen Staat nicht kennt und nicht anerkennt, liegt klar zu Tage, daß sich schlechthin Unvereinbares — nämlich das auf Unrecht gegründete zentralistische System der Diktatur in der sogenannten DDR und die freiheitliche demokratische Grundordnung des Rechtsstaats der Bundesrepublik — nicht mischen und nicht verbinden läßt. Mit echten bundesstaatlichen Vorstellungen hat der polemische Begriff der „Konföderation" nichts zu tun.

[1] Vergleiche Art. 79 Abs. 3 GG.

Das Grundgesetz der Bundesrepublik trägt dem föderativen Aufbau institutionell dadurch Rechnung, daß es neben dem Bundestag als dem unmittelbaren Repräsentationsorgan des Staatsvolkes, dem Bundespräsidenten als dem Staatsoberhaupt und der vom Bundeskanzler geleiteten Bundesregierung den *Bundesrat* geschaffen hat. *Durch den Bundesrat wirken die Länder bei der Gesetzgebung und Verwaltung des Bundes mit*[1]. Der Bundesrat ist in seiner Zusammensetzung und in seinen Kompetenzen durchaus anders ausgestaltet als der Reichsrat der Weimarer Verfassung und der Bundesrat der Verfassung des Kaiserreichs. Er besteht aus Mitgliedern der Regierungen der Länder. Abgestuft nach der Einwohnerzahl haben die Länder drei, vier oder fünf Stimmen[2]. So gehören dem Bundesrat zur Zeit (1959) einundvierzig stimmberechtigte Mitglieder an, dazu vier Mitglieder des Landes Berlin ohne Stimmrecht. Die Stimmen eines Landes können nur einheitlich abgegeben werden. Die Entscheidung über die Stimmabgabe wird in den einzelnen *Landeskabinetten* getroffen.

In gewissem Sinne kann man den Bundesrat als eine *zweite Kammer* auffassen, wie sie in allen Bundesstaaten zu finden ist. Ein wesentlicher Unterschied liegt aber darin, daß die Mitglieder des Bundesrates nicht das Recht der persönlichen Entscheidung haben wie beispielsweise die Mitglieder des Senats in den USA, die überdies nicht delegiert, sondern in den einzelnen Staaten gewählt werden.

Es entspricht der geschilderten Konstruktion des Bundesrates, daß als Präsidenten dieser Kammer die Ministerpräsidenten (Regierenden Bürgermeister) der *Länder* amtieren, und zwar in jährlichem Wechsel. Die Bundesregierung ist gehalten, den Bundesrat über die Führung der Geschäfte und damit sowohl über die innerpolitische als auch über die außenpolitische Lage der Bundesrepublik auf dem Laufenden zu halten[3]. Die Bedeutung, die dem Bundesrat institutionell zukommt, erhellt auch daraus, daß die Befugnisse des Bundespräsidenten im Falle seiner Verhinderung oder bei vorzeitiger Erledigung des Amtes durch den Präsidenten des Bundesrates wahrgenommen werden[4]. Bundesrat und Bundestag wählen je zur Hälfte die Mitglieder des Bundesverfassungsgerichts[5], das als der „Hüter der Verfassung" im Streitfall auch zur Wahrung der bundesstaatlichen Garantien des Grundgesetzes berufen ist. Im Fall der vorsätzlichen Verletzung des Grundgesetzes durch den Bundespräsidenten ist der Bundesrat ebenso wie der Bundestag befugt, Anklage vor dem Bundesverfassungsgericht zu erheben[6]. Für den Fall, daß in einer be-

[1] Art. 50 GG. — [2] Art. 51 GG. — [3] Art. 53 Satz 3 GG. — [4] Art. 57 GG.
[5] Art. 94 GG. — [6] Art. 61 GG.

sonderen Konfliktslage zwischen der Bundesregierung und dem Bundestag der normale Gesetzgebungsweg blockiert ist, hat das Grundgesetz, allerdings unter engen Voraussetzungen, einen „Reserveweg der Gesetzgebung" eröffnet, der über den *Bundesrat* als die andere am Gesetzgebungsverfahren beteiligte Kammer führt[1].

Der Bundesrat hat das Recht der *Gesetzesinitiative*; er macht jedoch hiervon in der Praxis verhältnismäßig wenig Gebrauch. Im *Gesetzgebungsverfahren* muß jede von der Bundesregierung eingebrachte Gesetzesvorlage den Bundesrat passieren, ehe sie dem Bundestag zugeleitet wird („Erster Durchgang"). Der Bundesrat nimmt zu diesen Vorlagen in der knappen Frist von drei Wochen in der Regel umfassend Stellung[2]. Hat der Bundestag das Gesetz beschlossen, so muß es nochmals dem Bundesrat im „Zweiten Durchgang" vorgelegt werden, bevor es vom Bundespräsidenten ausgefertigt und verkündet werden kann.

Bundesgesetze, die in das *Finanzwesen* der Länder eingreifen, insbesondere also Steuergesetze[3], ferner Bundesgesetze, welche die Länder als eigene Angelegenheiten oder im Auftrag des Bundes ausführen, oder welche die *Einrichtung von Behörden* der Länder oder das *Verwaltungsverfahren* von Landesbehörden betreffen[4], können ohne die Zustimmung des Bundesrates keine Gesetzeskraft erlangen. In diesen Fällen bedarf es übereinstimmender Beschlüsse von Bundestag und Bundesrat wie bei einem echten Zweikammersystem (*absolutes Veto* des Bundesrates). Bei allen anderen Gesetzen kann der Bundesrat lediglich Einspruch erheben. Er legt damit ein *aufschiebendes Veto* ein, das vom Bundestag mit qualifizierter Mehrheit überstimmt werden kann[5]. Um im Gesetzgebungsverfahren ein Kompromiß zwischen den beiden Kammern zu ermöglichen, ist nach dem Beispiel der USA die Institution eines *Vermittlungsausschusses* geschaffen worden. Der Vermittlungsausschuß setzt sich aus je elf Mitgliedern des Bundestages und des Bundesrates zusammen. Die Sitzungen sind nicht öffentlich. Auch die Mitglieder des Bundesrates sind in diesem Gremium an Weisungen nicht gebunden[6]. Diese im deutschen Verfassungsleben neue Einrichtung hat sich durchaus bewährt. Von 142 Gesetzen, die bisher Gegenstand des Vermittlungsverfahrens waren, sind nur sieben endgültig gescheitert.

*

[1] Art. 68, 81 GG. — [2] Art. 76 Abs. 2 GG. — [3] Vergleiche zum Beispiel Art. 105 Abs. 3, Art. 106 Abs. 4 und Abs. 5, Art. 107 GG. — [4] Art. 84 Abs. 1, Art. 85 Abs. 1 GG. — [5] Art. 77 Abs. 3 GG. — [6] Zu Einzelheiten vergleiche Art. 77 Abs.2 GG und die Geschäftsordnung des Vermittlungsausschusses.

Da die Bundesgesetze durch die Länder grundsätzlich als eigene Angelegenheit ausgeführt werden[1], ist die *Stellung der Länder in der Exekutive* besonders stark. Die Sachbereiche der Bundeseigenverwaltung und der Bundesauftragsverwaltung sind eng umgrenzt und müssen jeweils im Grundgesetz ausdrücklich bezeichnet sein[2]. Führen die Länder Bundesgesetze als eigene Angelegenheit aus, so hat der Bund im Rahmen der *Bundesaufsicht* nur enge Befugnisse einer Rechtskontrolle. Zum Schutze ihrer verfassungsrechtlichen Befugnisse können die Länder, ebenso aber auch der Bundesrat, wenn er als Bundesorgan sich in seinen Kompetenzen verletzt wähnt, das Bundesverfassungsgericht anrufen[3].

Die Gegner einer föderativen Verfassung wenden ein, daß diese geeignet sei, die Gesetzgebung und Verwaltung des Gesamtstaates ungebührlich zu komplizieren. Diese Gefahr ist nicht ohne weiteres von der Hand zu weisen. Bei einem zentralistischen Staatsaufbau würde jedoch die andere, weit größere Gefahr auftauchen, daß manche Landesteile sich von der Zentralregierung vernachlässigt oder gar vergewaltigt fühlen könnten. Die praktischen Erfahrungen seit 1949 haben bewiesen, daß die bundesstaatliche Verfassung sich nicht als Hemmschuh für den politischen und wirtschaftlichen Fortschritt erweist. Es hat sich immer wieder gezeigt, daß der Bundesrat als das Kernstück der föderativen Anlage dieser Verfassung sehr wohl die Interessen des Gesamtstaates vor denen der Länder zu berücksichtigen weiß; ungeachtet der Tatsache, daß einige Landesregierungen von Parteien getragen werden, die im Bundestag in Opposition zur gegenwärtigen Bundesregierung stehen.

Es versteht sich von selbst, daß die Länder, die im Bundesrat an der Bildung des Gesamtstaatswillens (Bundeswillens) beteiligt sind, bestrebt bleiben, an dieser zentralen Stelle auch ihre eigenen Interessen zur Geltung zu bringen. Soweit das Allgemeininteresse des Bundes nicht entgegensteht, ist das ihr gutes Recht, ja sogar ihre Pflicht. Ein Land wie Nordrhein-Westfalen, in dem Bergbau und Schwerindustrie vorherrschend sind, wird sich in wirtschaftspolitischen Fragen oft anders entscheiden als ein Land der Verarbeitungsindustrie, wie etwa Hessen, ein Agrarland anders als die drei „Stadtstaaten" Berlin(West), Hamburg und Bremen. Es gibt aber auch Fragen, die alle Länder gemeinsam angehen. In solchen Fällen bringt der Bundesrat die übereinstimmenden Interessen der Länder gegenüber dem Bundestag und der Bundesregierung zu Gehör.

[1] Art. 83 GG. — [2] Art. 85, 86, 87, 87b, 120a GG. — [3] Vergleiche zum Beispiel Art. 84 Abs. 4, Art. 93 Abs. 1 GG.

Innerhalb der Bundesregierung besteht ein besonderes *Ministerium für Angelegenheiten des Bundesrates und der Länder*. Ihm obliegt die Aufgabe, den Bundesrat und die Länder über die Arbeit und die Absichten der Bundesregierung zu unterrichten und umgekehrt die Wünsche und die Auffassungen des Bundesrates und der Länder dem Bundeskabinett zu übermitteln. So können Interessengegensätze zwischen dem Gesamtstaat und den Gliedstaaten frühzeitig erkannt und im Rahmen des Möglichen ausgeglichen werden. Es ist von entscheidender Bedeutung, daß das Gesamtverhältnis zwischen dem Bund und den Ländern von dem beide Seiten in gleichem Maße verpflichtenden *Prinzip der Bundestreue* bestimmt bleibt. Nach der Rechtsprechung des Bundesverfassungsgerichts gehört der Verfassungsgrundsatz der Bundestreue zu den dem Grundgesetz *immanenten Verfassungsnormen*, die das Verhältnis von Bund und Ländern betreffen. Die *Pflicht zu bundesfreundlichem Verhalten* bedeutet sowohl für den Bund als auch für die Länder eine Schranke, wenn sie von ihren Zuständigkeiten Gebrauch machen. Tatsächlich haben der Bund und die Länder trotz manchen Gegensätzen in Einzelfragen, die freimütig ausgetragen wurden, in der schweren Zeit des Aufbaues der gesamtstaatlichen Ordnung seit 1949 *ohne schwere Konflikte* zusammengewirkt.

DIE LÄNDER AUS EIGENER SICHT

Alle Länder der Bundesrepublik Deutschland verkörpern ein eigenes Wesen und Gewicht, das im Grunde unabhängig ist von ihrer Größe und von ihrer Einwohnerzahl. Neben dem Flächenumfang, der Bevölkerungszahl und der Bevölkerungsdichte spielen die besonderen wirtschaftlichen und kulturellen Schwerpunkte und nicht zuletzt auch die historischen Überlieferungen eine große Rolle bei der Beurteilung der einzelnen Länder.

DIE LÄNDER DER BUNDESREPUBLIK DEUTSCHLAND
Stand: 31.12.1958

a) Nach der Bodenfläche		b) Nach der Zahl der Einwohner		c) Nach der Bevölkerungsdichte	
Land	qkm	Land	Einwohner 1.000	Land	Einwohner je qkm
Bayern	70.549	Nordrhein-Westf.	15.459	Berlin(West)	4.628
Niedersachsen	47.372	Bayern	9.278	Hamburg	2.419
Baden-Württ.	35.750	Baden-Württ.	7.433	Bremen	1.678
Nordrhein-Westf.	33.958	Niedersachsen	6.516	Nordrhein-Westf.	455
Hessen	21.108	Hessen	4.652	Saarland	405
Rheinland-Pfalz	19.828	Rheinland-Pfalz	3.355	Hessen	220
Schleswig-Holstein	15.688	Schleswig-Holstein	2.276	Baden-Württemberg	208
Saarland	2.567	Berlin(West)	2.226	Rheinland-Pfalz	169
Hamburg	747	Hamburg	1.807	Schleswig-Holstein	145
Berlin(West)	481	Saarland	1.040	Niedersachsen	138
Bremen	404	Bremen	678	Bayern	132

Quelle: Statistisches Bundesamt.

Dem Bundesland Berlin(West) ist ein eigenes Kapitel dieses Buches vorbehalten. Die übrigen Länder werden hier in der Reihenfolge ihrer territorialen Größe behandelt.

*

* *

Nach der Statistik des Fremdenverkehrs ist *Bayern* das meistbesuchte deutsche Land. Das wirkliche Wesen der bayerischen Landschaft und der bayerischen Menschen ist dem Fremden allzu oft verdeckt durch das Klischee verstaubter Witzblätter und kitschiger Heimatfilme. Viele Sommergäste, die zum Urlaub an die Seen und in die Gebirgstäler Oberbayerns fahren, lernen Bayern als ein romantisches, aber industriell etwas zurückgebliebenes Land kennen. Sie erhalten nur ein einseitiges und unvollkommenes Bild.

Bessere Kenner der Geschichte wissen wohl, was Bayern im deutschen Kulturraum bedeutet, seit St. Kilian, St. Emmeran und St. Korbinian in Würzburg, Regensburg und Freising wirkten. Sie wissen, daß die Klöster von Tegernsee, Benediktbeuren und Wessobrunn seit frühester Zeit Pflegestätten der Wissenschaft, der Kunst und der Dichtung waren. Die heiterfrommen Bauwerke des Barock und des Rokoko, vor allem die strahlenden Kirchen des fränkischen Baumeisters Balthasar Neumann und die Wieskirche (Kloster Steingaden bei Schongau) des Altbayern Dominikus Zimmermann dürfen als der schönste Ausdruck bayerischen Wesens gelten. Neben den Ruinen und modernen Neubauten der bombengeschädigten Großstädte Nürnberg und Augsburg wird der Gast die stolzen Denkmäler ihres weltweiten mittelalterlichen Ruhmes auffinden, und die Landeshauptstadt und Millionenstadt München wird er nicht nur als den Ort des weltberühmten Hofbräuhauses schätzen, sondern auch als einen Mittelpunkt deutscher Kunst und Wissenschaft. An den Münchner Hochschulen (Universität, Technische Hochschule, Akademien) befinden sich mehr als 20.000 Studierende.

Von allen Ländern des gegenwärtigen Deutschlands hat Bayern als einziges seine geschichtlichen Grenzen bewahrt. Seit mehr als 150 Jahren sind in diesen Grenzen die Franken, Schwaben und Altbayern zum „bayerischen Volk" zusammengewachsen. Freilich hört man auch sagen, es gebe eigentlich gar kein bayerisches Volk — bayerisch mit y! —, sondern allenfalls ein baierisches. Aber seit in den Jahren 1806 bis 1816 das neue Königreich Bayern entstand, ist dort über gegensätzliche Stammeseigentümlichkeiten hinweg ein Staatsvolk mit einem so ausgeprägten Staatsgefühl entstanden, wie es kaum in einem anderen Bundesland lebendig ist. Nirgendwo sonst in Deutschland gibt es Gletscher und ewigen Schnee, und selbst in den nordbayerischen Landesteilen, die der Oberbayer als „Flachland" ansieht, überragen die ovalen Kuppen des Bayerischen Waldes und des Fichtelgebirges die höchsten Gipfel der meisten anderen deutschen Länder noch um ein gutes Stück.

Anders als typische Hochgebirgsländer hat sich jedoch Bayern niemals von der übrigen Welt abkapseln können. Älteste europäische Verkehrsstraßen führen durch den Freistaat. Den ersten Unterbau für manche moderne Autostraße legten römische Legionäre. Die Nibelungen folgten auf ihrem sagenhaften Zug vom Rhein her dem bayerischen Oberlauf der Donau. Bayern war für die ewige deutsche Sehnsucht nach dem Süden von jeher die letzte Etappe vor der Bezwingung der gefährlichen Alpenpässe. Geographisch im Mittelpunkt des „Abendlandes" gelegen und — abgesehen von den

Alpen — ohne natürliche Grenzen, war Bayern wie wenige andere Länder und Staaten unmittelbar und mitleidend in das europäische Schicksal einbezogen. Jedes Jahrhundert brachte ihm eine unübersehbare Fülle neuer Menschen, Einflüsse und Ereignisse. Wenige Völker und Staaten der Alten Welt sind in ihrer folkloristischen, sozialen und kulturellen Zusammensetzung so vielfältig gegliedert wie Bayern. Es wurde dadurch ein Land fruchtbarer Synthese, eine Eigenschaft, die sich auch nach 1945 bei der Eingliederung der mehr als zwei Millionen Vertriebenen und Flüchtlinge aus dem Osten bewähren mußte.

Um für die so vermehrte Bevölkerung genügend Lebensraum und Existenzmöglichkeiten zu schaffen, mußte die Entwicklung der gewerblichen Wirtschaft kräftig vorangetrieben werden. Das alte Bauernland wurde auch zum Industrieland. Zwar fehlen Kohlen und Erze für den Ausbau einer Schwerindustrie; aber die Suche nach anderen Bodenschätzen war erfolgreich. Im Alpenvorland und im Innviertel werden jetzt Öl- und Erdgasquellen ausgebeutet. Daß Bayern bei der friedlichen Nutzung der Atomkräfte den ersten Versuchsreaktor und das erste Atomkraftwerk errichtete, mag für die technische und wirtschaftliche Entwicklung ebenso entscheidend werden wie einst der bahnbrechende Ausbau der Wasserkräfte, der neue Energiequellen erschloß und insbesondere der bayerischen Elektroindustrie eine führende Stellung in Deutschland sicherte. Aber aller großindustriellen Entwicklung zum Trotz haben die Bayern ihre Freude an bäuerlicher und handwerklicher Leistung bewahrt. Mittlere und kleinere Fabriken und Gewerbebetriebe überwiegen.

Bei allen Wandlungen und tiefgreifenden Umschichtungen, die für die letzten hundert Jahre und mehr noch für die letzten vierzehn Jahre kennzeichnend sind, ist für die bayerische Bevölkerungsstruktur eine harmonische Ausgeglichenheit bestimmend. Auch das Zahlenverhältnis der Konfessionen hat sich durch die Völkerwanderung der Kriegs- und Nachkriegsjahre kaum merklich geändert. Wie in den Jahren vor dem Kriege waren bei der Volkszählung 1950 ungefähr 72% katholisch und rund 27% evangelisch. Innere Vielfalt und maßvolle Ausgeglichenheit bestimmen auch das kulturelle und politische Leben unter dem weißblauen Himmel. Sie haben Bayern zum Hort des Föderalismus in der jungen Bundesrepublik gemacht. Oftmals als liebenswürdig-lächerliche bayerische Marotte bekrittelt, erscheint den Bayern dieser Föderalismus immer mehr als einzig möglicher Weg, um die Gefahren der Technik und der gesellschaftlichen Umschichtungen in Freiheit zu meistern.

*

Vom äußersten Süden der Bundesrepublik führt der Weg zum Norden. Zwischen der reich gegliederten Nordseeküste und dem letzten größeren Mittelgebirgszug, dem Harz, zwischen der Zonengrenze und den Niederlanden, liegt *Niedersachsen*, ein „junges Land mit altem Namen". Ein junges Land, weil es erst 1946 aus den Ländern Braunschweig, Oldenburg, Schaumburg-Lippe und Hannover (das von 1866 bis 1945 preußische Provinz war) gebildet worden ist. Ein Land mit altem Namen und großer Überlieferung, weil die Sachsen nach dem Ende des Karolingischen Reiches im Jahre 918 mit HEINRICH I. den Deutschen König stellten, und weil es seit dem Ende des Mittelalters einen niedersächsischen Wehrkreis im Gefüge des alten Reiches gab. Die Jahrhunderte lange territoriale und dynastische Zersplitterung des niedersächsischen Raumes hat das niederdeutsch-niedersächsische Stammesbewußtsein und die plattdeutsche Mundart nicht zu beseitigen vermocht. Neben Bayern ist Niedersachsen also ein Land mit lebendiger Tradition und starkem Selbstbewußtsein. Ein niedersächsisches Staatsgefühl bildet sich dagegen erst allmählich heraus.

Die Grenzlage gegenüber der sogenannten DDR gehört neben anderen Faktoren, wie den ungünstigen Wasserverhältnissen und dem hohen Anteil an Vertriebenen und Flüchtlingen, zu den schweren Belastungen, die auf Niedersachsen ruhen. 564 km lang dehnt sich die Zonengrenze an der Elbe und, wo sie den Strom verläßt, an einem mit Wachtürmen bewehrten Stacheldrahtverhau. Die Zonengrenzstadt Helmstedt ist in der ganzen Welt bekannt geworden. Einst blühende Wirtschafts- und Kulturräume wurden durch diese widernatürliche Grenze zerrissen. Trotzdem fühlt sich Niedersachsen von seiner geschichtlichen Aufgabe her und im Interesse der Menschen diesseits und jenseits der Zonengrenze als ein „Land der Mitte". Die Landeshauptstadt Hannover mit mehr als einer halben Million Einwohnern liegt am Schnittpunkt der beiden großen Verkehrslinien, die vom äußersten Norden zum Süden und von Paris bis Moskau das europäische Festland durchqueren. Die lange und reich gegliederte Nordseeküste verbindet über die Hansestädte Hamburg und Bremen, die beide Niedersachsen als Hinterland schätzen, und über zahlreiche niedersächsische Häfen den deutschen Raum mit den Schiffahrtnationen der Welt und mit den Kontinenten jenseits der Meere.

Auch Niedersachsen hat nach 1945 mehr als zwei Millionen Flüchtlinge und Vertriebene aufnehmen müssen. Seine Einwohnerzahl verzeichnet im Vergleich zu 1939 mit 43,5% (1958) den größten Anstieg aller Bundesländer. Im Regierungsbezirk Lüneburg betrug die Zunahme sogar 69%.

Die Flucht in die Freiheit: aus der sogenannten DDR nach Berlin(West).

Im provisorischen Flüchtlingslager Berlin-Papestraße

Das Notaufnahmelager Berlin-Marienfelde

General Dr. Speidel, Befehlshaber der Alliierten Landstreitkräfte in Zentraleuropa, in Fontainebleau

General Norstad, Oberster Alliierter Befehlshaber in Europa, und General Heusinger, Generalinspekteur der Bundeswehr, bei der Übergabe der ersten Verbände der Bundeswehr an SHAPE am 8. 7. 1957

Paris, Palais Chaillot Aufnahme der Bundesrepublik in di NATO

Ein Land, das immer noch vorwiegend agrarischen Charakter gehabt hatte, mußte große Anstrengungen unternehmen, um durch industrielle, soziale und kulturelle Maßnahmen der neuen Bevölkerungsstruktur gerecht zu werden. Entgegen allen Erwartungen dürfte in den Wirren der Nachkriegsjahre nicht zuletzt gerade dieser Zwang dazu beigetragen haben, daß in Niedersachsen auch ein gemäßigtes politisches Klima der Mitte und des Ausgleichs entstehen konnte. Die konfessionellen Verhältnisse liegen fast umgekehrt wie bei Bayern: 77% Evangelische leben zusammen mit 19% Katholiken.

Mit Genugtuung verzeichnet der im Frühjahr 1959 erschienene Vierjahresbericht der Landesregierung, daß Niedersachsen auf einigen der Notstandsgebiete, die sich aus der Nachkriegsbelastung ergaben, vorbildlich vorangekommen ist. Genannt seien die Seßhaftmachung von Landarbeitern, die bäuerliche Eingliederung vertriebener Landwirte ohne irgendwelche bodenreformerische Zwangsmaßnahmen, die landeskulturelle Erschließung des weiten moorigen Emslandes im deutsch-niederländischen Grenzgebiet, die Ingangsetzung eines langfristigen Küstenplanes zur Überwindung der schwierigen Wasserverhältnisse im weiten Bereich der Nordseeküste und der Flußmündungen, die Durchführung eines regionalen Förderungsprogramms zum Abbau des west-östlichen Wirtschaftsgefälles zwischen Rhein und Elbe, die Verbesserung und erhebliche Ausweitung von Hafenanlagen, die Erschließung des Hinterlandes durch eine Rohölleitung von Wilhelmshaven zum rheinischen Industriegebiet, die industrielle Erschließung weiter Gebiete besonders im mittleren und südlichen Niedersachsen: in den Räumen Hannover, Braunschweig, Salzgitter (Eisenerze), Wolfsburg — und die auch im europäischen Maßstab einzigartigen Ergebnisse der Deutschen Industriemesse Hannover.

Trotz so starker Betonung des wirtschaftlich-industriellen Bereichs ist festzuhalten, daß immer noch 72% der Gesamtbevölkerung Niedersachsens in Landkreisen wohnen. Als Zuchtgebiet für Pferde, Rinder und Schweine, als Land der Rüben-, Kartoffel- und Getreidezüchter, als Standort des größten geschlossenen deutschen Obstbaugebietes (an der Niederelbe) und als Lieferant landwirtschaftlicher Qualitätserzeugnisse hat Niedersachsen den guten Ruf seiner Landwirtschaft weiter befestigen können. Eine solche Wirtschafts- und Wohnstruktur stellt auch der Kulturpolitik besondere Aufgaben. Das Gewicht beim Aufbau der zerstörten oder der Bevölkerungszahl nicht mehr entsprechenden Schulen verschiebt sich daher immer mehr auf das Landschulwesen. Die „kulturelle Aufrüstung" des flachen Landes durch Volkshochschulen, Wandertheater, Heimatvereine und in letzter Zeit auch durch Dorfgemeinschaftshäuser erfaßt immer weitere Bereiche. Angesichts der ideologischen Gefahren, die von der Weltanschauung des Ostens drohen, ist Niedersachsen besonders stolz auf sein reich gegliedertes öffentliches Schulwesen, auf seine Berufs- und Fachschulen, seine Ingenieurschulen, Technischen Hochschulen (in Hannover und Braunschweig), die Tierärztliche Hochschule in Hannover, die Bergakademie in Clausthal, die Hochschule für Sozialwissenschaften in Wilhelmshaven, auf seine zahlreichen Pädagogischen Akademien und die weltberühmte Universität in Göttingen.

*

Im Südwesten der Bundesrepublik, begrenzt von der Schweiz und Frankreich, liegt das Land *Baden-Württemberg*. Es ist, von Saarland abgesehen, das jüngste Bundesland. Erst durch eine Volksabstimmung vom 9. 12. 1951 wurde es aus den Ländern Baden, Württemberg-Baden und Württemberg-Hohenzollern am 25. 4. 1952 gebildet. Diese waren dadurch entstanden, daß die alten Länder Baden und Württemberg auf Grund einer Vereinbarung der amerikanischen und französischen Besatzungsmacht im Jahre 1945 entlang der Autobahn Karlsruhe—Stuttgart—Ulm geteilt wurden. Die Verfassung des neuen Landes Baden-Württemberg trat am 19. 11. 1953 in Kraft. Gewisse badische Kreise erstreben eine Revision des gegenwärtigen Zustandes.

Im Jahrhundert der Hohenstaufen-Kaiser war der deutsche Südwesten Mitte und Herz des Reiches gewesen. Nach dem Zerfall der staufischen Kaisermacht wurde das Gebiet in eine Vielzahl größerer und kleiner, ja kleinster Territorien unter weltlichem und geistlichem Regime aufgesplittert. Zahlreiche Städte, mehr als anderswo in deutschen Landen, wußten als Reichsstädte ihre unmittelbare Freiheit unter Kaiser und Reich zu wahren. Stärkere Bedeutung gewannen freilich die größeren weltlichen Herrschaftsgebiete. In den Fürstenstädten Heidelberg (1386), Freiburg (1457) und Tübingen (1477) wurden Universitäten errichtet, die das geistige Antlitz des Landes auch heute noch prägen. Die Gegensätze von Stadt und Land wurden leichter als anderswo überbrückt. Auch die aktive Teilhabe der Bürger am Staatsleben reicht bis ins späte Mittelalter zurück. In der Grafschaft Württemberg (1457), im Breisgau und in anderen Gebieten Schwäbisch-Österreichs übten die Untertanen schon früh landständische Rechte aus. Als die Gebiete unter NAPOLEON durch das Königreich Württemberg, das Großherzogtum Baden und die hohenzollerischen Fürstentümer eine stärkere

Zusammenfassung erfahren hatten, zog der Lebensstil der konstitutionellen Monarchie in diese Länder ein. Württembergs „demokratische" und Badens „liberale" Stimmen drangen aus den Landtagen in Stuttgart und Karlsruhe über die Landesgrenzen hinaus und wurden in ganz Deutschland gehört. Auf der Grundlage dieser demokratisch-parlamentarischen Freiheit erwuchsen die Technische Hochschule in Karlsruhe (1825), die älteste in Deutschland, und kurz darauf die Technische Hochschule in Stuttgart (1829).

Technik und Industrie hielten also früh ihren Einzug in dieses Land. Sie breiteten sich neben einer immer noch bedeutenden und gesunden Landwirtschaft über das ganze Gebiet aus. Die Struktur der baden-württembergischen Wirtschaft ist als außerordentlich günstig zu bezeichnen. Ein von der Bundesregierung eingesetzter Sachverständigenausschuß, der über die Neugliederung des Bundesgebietes ein Gutachten erstatten sollte, kam 1955 zu dem Gesamturteil: „Für die Ergänzung der verschiedenen Wirtschaftszweige untereinander, für die Zusammenfassung als Ganzes und für seine Gliederung im einzelnen kann Baden-Württemberg als ein Muster wirtschaftlicher Zweckmäßigkeit bezeichnet werden."

Die Landwirtschaft zeichnet sich durch die Vielseitigkeit ihrer Produktion aus. Ihr Leistungsniveau wurde durch die Industrialisierung günstig beeinflußt. Es ist das Land der landwirtschaftlichen Kleinbetriebe und der Sonderkulturen. Von 387.000 Betrieben bewirtschaften 269.000 eine Fläche bis unter 5 ha. Auch das Handwerk hat trotz der starken Industrialisierung sich weiter entfalten können. Baden-Württemberg weist unter den Bundesländern mit 19,2 Betrieben und 84,8 Beschäftigten je 1.000 Einwohner die größte Handwerksdichte auf. Das Handwerk dient als Ausbildungsstätte des beruflichen Nachwuchses für die gewerbliche Produktion. Seine Leistungsfähigkeit kommt daher auch unmittelbar dem industriellen Fortschritt zugute. Nach Nordrhein-Westfalen ist Baden-Württemberg sowohl noch der absoluten Beschäftigtenzahl als auch nach dem Grad der Industrialisierung das zweitstärkste Industrieland der Bundesrepublik. Da einheimische Rohstoffe und Bodenschätze nur vereinzelt zur Verfügung stehen, hat sich in langen Jahrzehnten eine überwiegend arbeitsintensive Verarbeitungs- und Veredelungsindustrie entwickelt, die wegen ihrer Mannigfaltigkeit und Spezialisierung stark zum Export orientiert ist. Im Jahre 1958 betrug der Auslandsumsatz fünf Milliarden DM. Im Einklang mit der Aufwärtsentwicklung von Industrie und Handwerk steht das hohe Leistungsniveau des Handels und des Verkehrsgewerbes.

Die Landschaft von Baden-Württemberg ist am nachhaltigsten durch Rhein und Donau und ihre Zuflüsse geformt worden. Sie kennt nichts Gigantisches und Trennendes, wie Hochgebirge und Meer, sondern zeigt in buntem Wechsel von Höhen und Tälern immer neue, aber doch verwandte Bilder, den Mutterboden des schwäbisch-alemannischen und fränkischen Volkstums. Ohne schroffe Gegensätze von Ständen und Klassen lebt das Volk in einem milden sozialen Klima, geprägt auch durch den Ausgleich von Stadt und Land, und mit einem wachen demokratischen Bewußtsein in glücklich-harmonischer Ausgeglichenheit, die sich auch im Gleichgewicht der Konfessionen ausdrückt. Bundespräsident Professor Dr. THEODOR HEUSS konnte von seiner Heimat sagen: „Dies Land mit seiner Überlieferung, Modell der deutschen Möglichkeiten, steht heute in dem Auftrag zum rechten Beispiel."

*

Es wird immer eine geschichtliche Merkwürdigkeit bleiben, daß im niederrheinisch-westfälischen Raum, einer der ältesten Kulturlandschaften Deutschlands, bis zum Jahre 1946 nie eine eigenständige Staatsgründung erfolgt ist. Seine Existenz verdankt das Land *Nordrhein-Westfalen* zwei Verordnungen der ehemaligen britischen Besatzungsmacht: vom 23.8.1946 „betreffend Auflösung der Provinzen des ehemaligen Landes Preußen in der Britischen Zone und ihre Neubildung als selbständige Länder" und der Verordnung Nr. 77 vom 21.1.1947, durch die ein halbes Jahr später das ehemalige Land Lippe-Detmold mit diesem neuen Land unter dem Namen Nordrhein-Westfalen verschmolzen wurde.

Geistes- und kulturgeschichtlich gehören „Nordrhein" und „Westfalen" zusammen. Diese Tatsache ergibt sich eindrucksvoll aus der jahrhundertelangen Geschichte der beiden Landschaften. Die Menschen dieses niederrheinisch-westfälischen Raumes haben in den letzten hundert Jahren jenes Gebiet dicht besiedelt und entwickelt, das heute das wirtschaftliche Herz der Bundesrepublik darstellt, das Ruhrgebiet. Es ist darüber hinaus als das größte Industriegebiet Europas bekannt. Dieser Struktur entsprechend hat Nordrhein-Westfalen an der industriellen Gütererzeugung der Bundesrepublik einen bedeutenden Anteil. Von der Rohstofferzeugung des gesamten Bundesgebietes entfallen bei Kohle auf Nordrhein-Westfalen allein 95% und bei Eisen 84%. Von der gesamten industriellen Produktion bringt das Land rund 40% hervor. Die Wirtschaftskraft Nordrhein-Westfalens ergibt sich am deutlichsten aus der Größe seines Volkseinkommens. Mit etwa 56 Milliarden DM im Jahre 1957 erreicht es einen Anteil von 34% am westdeutschen Sozialprodukt. Innerhalb der nordrhein-westfälischen Wirtschaft tritt die Industrie stärker in Erscheinung als in den meisten anderen Bundesländern. Auf sie entfällt mehr als die Hälfte des Volkseinkommens. Die übrigen Wirtschaftsbereiche folgen erst im weiten Abstand: der Handel mit einem Anteil von 13%, das Baugewerbe mit 7%, der Verkehr mit 6% und die Land- und Forstwirtschaft mit 4%. Von den mehr als sechs Millionen Beschäftigten der Wirtschaft sind allein 2,8 Millionen in der Industrie tätig.

Das Entstehen der starken industriellen Ballung in Nordrhein-Westfalen ist auf die ungewöhnlich günstige Verbindung der wichtigsten standortbildenden Faktoren zurückzuführen: Rohstoffvorkommen, günstige Transportwege, große Energiequellen. Ausschlaggebend vor allem für das Entstehen der eisenschaffenden Industrie waren die Vorkommen von Steinkohle an der Ruhr und bei Aachen, ferner die Erzlager im Siegerland und im Sauerland sowie die Wasserstraßen. Mittelbar wurden dadurch auch die Textilbetriebe standortmäßig begünstigt; sie zogen die in der Schwerindustrie nur wenig verwendbaren weiblichen Arbeitskräfte an sich. Aus der gewerblichen Wirtschaft Nordrhein-Westfalens heben sich der Kohlenbergbau, die Eisen- und Stahlgewinnung, der Maschinenbau, die Eisen-, Stahl-, Blech- und Metallwarenindustrie, die chemische sowie die Textilindustrie als wichtige Zweige heraus. Diese sechs Gruppen zusammen machen 60% der nordrhein-westfälischen Industrieproduktion aus. Nordrhein-Westfalen bestreitet als wichtigstes Ausfuhrland der Bundesrepublik rund 40% ihres Exportvolumens. Es ist außerdem das verkehrsreichste Land.

Im Lande leben rund 3,5 Millionen Flüchtlinge und Vertriebene. Das ist zwar nicht prozentual, aber absolut die größte Flüchtlings- und Vertriebenenzahl in einem deutschen Bundesland. Daraus läßt sich ermessen, eine wie schwierige Aufgabe es war, für diese Menschen sowie für Evakuierte und Bombengeschädigte ausreichend Wohnungen zu beschaffen. Seit der Währungsreform des Jahres 1948 wurden in Nordrhein-Westfalen innerhalb von zehn Jahren rund 1,6 Millionen Wohnungen gebaut. Aber das Programm ist damit noch nicht erfüllt. Um wieder einigermaßen normale Verhältnisse auf dem Wohnungsmarkt zu erreichen, muß das Land auch in den folgenden vier Jahren allein im öffentlich geförderten sozialen Wohnungsbau rund 100.000 Wohnungen im Jahresdurchschnitt neu errichten.

Nordrhein-Westfalen ist ein Land mit überwiegend katholischer Bevölkerung. Das Schulwesen des Landes ist in ausgeprägter Form auf der Grundlage des „Elternrechts“ gegliedert. Neben dem Volksschulwesen und den höheren Lehranstalten gibt es ein vielfältiges System von Berufs- und

Berufsfachschulen, Abendgymnasien und Volkshochschulen. Ein Institut in Oberhausen führt begabte, bereits im Beruf stehende junge Menschen auf dem sogenannten „zweiten Bildungsweg", wie auch in anderen Bundesländern, zur Hochschulreife. Weitere solche Institute sind in Essen und in der Landeshauptstadt Düsseldorf geplant. Besondere Förderung genießt auch der technische Nachwuchs auf der Technischen Hochschule in Aachen, der alten Kaiserstadt, und an zahlreichen Ingenieurschulen. Universitäten gibt es in der berühmten Domstadt Köln und in Münster und Bonn. Schwerpunktprogramme der gegenwärtigen Landesregierung beschäftigen sich mit dem Schulbau, der Förderung des Gesundheitswesens und dem Straßenbau.

*

Das Bundesland *Hessen* wurde 1945 aus den früheren preußischen Provinzen Kurhessen (Kassel) und Nassau (Wiesbaden), aus den Provinzen Starkenburg und Oberhessen sowie den rechtsrheinischen Teilen der Provinz Rheinhessen des ehemaligen Volksstaates Hessen (Darmstadt) gebildet. Das linksrheinische Rheinhessen (Mainz) und der Regierungsbezirk Montabaur fielen bei dieser Neugliederung an das neue Land Rheinland-Pfalz.

Auch das Land Hessen versteht sich geographisch und verkehrswirtschaftlich als Brücke und Mitte. In der Tat: es verbindet den Norden mit dem Süden der Bundesrepublik, den Westen Europas mit Berlin, Mitteldeutschland und dem Osten. Symbolisiert wird diese Verkehrslage durch die imposante Autobahn-Verkehrsspinne des sogenannten Frankfurter Kreuzes und den Frankfurter Rhein-Main-Flughafen, der sich zum bedeutendsten deutschen Schnittpunkt des inner- und außereuropäischen Luftverkehrs entwickelt hat. Die gesamte Grenzlänge des Landes beträgt 1.413 km. Die höchste Erhebung des Landes ist die Wasserkuppe in der Rhön mit 950 m. Landeshauptstadt ist Wiesbaden. Die größte Stadt ist Frankfurt mit fast 650.000 Einwohnern. In großer Mannigfaltigkeit reihen die hessischen Landschaften sich aneinander; vom Hohen Meißner bis zum Rheinstrom, von der Weser bis zum Neckar; von den herben, aber reizvollen Erhebungen des Vogelbergs und der Rhön zu den waldreichen Mittelgebirgen des Taunus, Odenwalds und Spessarts. Wie die Bilder eines bunten Teppichmusters wechseln die Landschaften. Dicht beieinander liegen geballte Industriebezirke, reiches Bauernland, arme Berggegenden und dazwischen liebliche und teils berühmte Heilbäder und Luftkurorte, hineingestreut zahlreiche Burgen und Schlösser. Hessen ist, gemessen an der Größe des Landes, das wald- und bäderreichste Land der Bundesrepublik.

Für beide Konfessionen ist Hessen ein bedeutungsvolles Land. Hier hat BONIFATIUS gewirkt, im Dom zu Fulda liegt er begraben. Einige Landschaften tragen den Stempel klarster Katholizität, gekrönt von eindrucksvollen Domen. Hier hat aber auch PHILIPP DER GROSSMÜTIGE die Reformation betrieben. Das berühmte Religionsgespräch, das MARTIN LUTHER und HULDRYCH ZWINGLI an einen Tisch brachte, fand im Marburger Schloß statt. 64,% der Einwohner gehören den evangelischen Kirchen an, 32% der katholischen Konfession.

Hessen gliedert sich in drei Wirtschaftsräume. Der bedeutendste und zugleich bevölkerungsreichste ist das südhessische Rhein-Main-Gebiet mit der Handels- und Bankenmetropole Frankfurt, den Städten Offenbach, Wiesbaden und Darmstadt unter Einschluß von Taunus und Odenwald. Industrie und Verkehrsdichte prägen das Antlitz dieser Landschaft. Mittelhessens Lahn-Dill-Gebiet mit der Industriestadt Wetzlar und der Stadt Gießen im Herzen von Hessen schließen sich nach Norden an. Industrie und Landwirtschaft bilden hier in ungefähr gleichem Maße die Erwerbsquellen. Nordhessen als dritter Wirtschaftsraum ist vorwiegend bäuerlich orientiert. Die ackerbauliche Nutzung, charakterisiert durch Klein- und Mittelbetriebe und zahlreiche landwirtschaftliche Nebenerwerbsquellen, herrscht hier ebenso vor wie auf den guten Böden der Wetterau und des Limburger Beckens in Mittelhessen. Ein berühmtes Gemüse-, Obst- und Weinbaugebiet ist der Rheingau und das Land um die Bergstraße.

An Bodenschätzen besitzt Hessen Braunkohle (Nordhessen), Eisenerze (Mittelhessen), Kali, Erdöl und Erdgas. Besonders die Kali- und Erdgasvorkommen sind, gemessen an den Förderziffern der Bundesrepublik, von großer Bedeutung. Auch Nordhessen kennt mit Kassel, Fulda, Hersfeld und Eschwege industrielle Schwerpunkte von Gewicht. Dieses Gebiet ist aber durch die nahe Zonengrenze, die in einer Länge von 268 km Hessens östliche Landesgrenze bildet, seines natürlichen Hinterlandes beraubt. Die Folgen sind sehr fühlbar.

Mehr als zwei Drittel (71%) des gesamten industriellen Umsatzes werden bei insgesamt 6.677 Industriebetrieben (ohne Bauindustrie) von 542 Betrieben mit 200 und mehr Beschäftigten erzeugt. Vertriebene und Flüchtlinge haben bisher nicht ansässige Wirtschaftszweige, wie Rauchwarenhandel und Glasindustrie, nach Hessen gebracht. Auch das Verlagswesen hat sich stark entwickelt. Hessen ist das Land mit der verhältnismäßig höchsten Industrieausfuhr in der Bundesrepublik. Hessen hat 77.000 Handwerksbetriebe. Typisch ist der Kleinbetrieb.

Einen sichtbaren Aufschwung erlebte das hessische Hochschulwesen mit den Universitäten Frankfurt und Marburg und der Technischen Hochschule in Darmstadt. Auch die Justus-Liebig-Universität in Gießen wurde wieder eröffnet. Hessen ist unter allen Bundesländern das einzige mit voller Schulgeld- und Lernmittelfreiheit.

*

Erst 1945, durch Verfügung der Besatzungsmächte, entstand das Land *Rheinland-Pfalz*. Aber bei der Betrachtung des rheinland-pfälzischen Raumes wird eine zweitausend Jahre alte Geschichte lebendig.

Nachdem das Römische Reich nach der Eroberung Galliens festen Fuß auf dem linken Rheinufer gefaßt hatte, gehörte der größte Teil des Gebietes vier Jahrhunderte lang fest zum Verband des römischen Staatswesens, und zwar als die beiden Provinzen Germania inferior und Germania superior. Die Grenze zwischen beiden Provinzen verlief am Vingstbach zwischen Brohl und Niederbreisig. Die gleiche Grenze hatte bezeichnenderweise als kirchliche und staatliche Grenzlinie zwischen den Räumen der Kurfürstentümer Trier und Köln bis in das 19. Jahrhundert hinein Bedeutung. Noch heute ist sie als Dialektgrenze spürbar. Das Gebiet um die mittlere Mosel mit dem Raum um die Stadt Trier gehörte zur Provinz Belgica. Zugleich war das Gegenufer der Provinzgrenze am Rhein der Ausgangspunkt des Limes.

In der Zeit nach der Völkerwanderung wurde das gesamte Rheingebiet dem Fränkischen Reiche eingegliedert. Dabei wurden die alten römischen Zentren die Keimzellen der kirchlichen und staatlichen Organisation. Hier sind insbesondere die Städte Trier, Mainz, Speyer und Worms als Mittelpunkte zu nennen. Noch heute legen die alten Dome davon Zeugnis ab. Das Bild, das das Gebiet des heutigen Landes Rheinland-Pfalz im späten Mittelalter und in den ersten Jahrhunderten der Neuzeit bis zur Französischen Revolution bot, wird bestimmt durch die Entwicklung der Territorialgewalten. Im wesentlichen beherrschten die drei Kurstaaten Trier, Mainz und Pfalz den mittelrheinischen Raum. Ungeachtet interner Gegensätzlichkeiten traten die drei mittelrheinischen Kurfürstentümer als Folge ihrer übereinstimmenden äußeren Interessen nach außen vielfach geschlossen auf. In der napoleonischen Aera haben die linksrheinischen Teile des Landes zu Frankreich gehört. Nach dem Wiener Kongreß fiel das Gebiet des heutigen Landes an Preußen, Bayern und Hessen-Darmstadt.

Fast in seiner gesamten Ausdehnung ist Rheinland-Pfalz ein Land der Mittelgebirge. Vom Rhein und seinen Nebenflüssen Mosel, Saar, Ahr, Nahe und Lahn hat es die entscheidenden Lebensimpulse empfangen. Von diesen Flüssen wird es auch räumlich gegliedert. Drei natürliche landschaftliche Einheiten zeichnen sich ab: das Rheinische Schiefergebirge, das Saar-Nahe-Hügelland mit dem Pfälzer Bergland und im nördlichen Teil die Oberrheinische Tiefebene. Fast zwei Drittel des Landes nimmt das Rheinische Schiefergebirge ein, das sich nahezu mit den Regierungsbezirken Trier, Koblenz und Montabaur deckt. Unruhiger und kleinräumiger ist die Oberfläche des Saar-Nahe-Hügellandes und des Pfälzer Berglandes. Als kleinste geographische Einheit zieht sich die zum Oberrheinischen Tiefland gehörende Speyer-Wormser Rheinebene in zehn bis zwanzig Kilometer Breite vom Bienwald an der elsässischen Grenze bis oberhalb von Oppenheim hin. 58% der Bevölkerung bekennen sich zur katholischen und 41% zur evangelischen Konfession. Die konfessionellen Verhältnisse in den einzelnen Gebieten des Landes spiegeln noch weitgehend das Bild der territorialen Grenzen aus der Zeit zwischen der Reformation und der Französischen Revolution.

Rheinland-Pfalz ist stark landwirtschaftlich bestimmt. Dennoch entbehrt es im Verhältnis der einzelnen Wirtschaftsgebiete zueinander nicht einer gewissen Ausgeglichenheit. Mittel- und Kleinbetriebe herrschen in allen Wirtschaftszweigen vor. Neben einer extensiven Landwirtschaft in den ausgedehnten Mittelgebirgslagen steht die intensive Nutzung des Bodens in den Ebenen und Flußniederungen. Hier sind die Intensivkulturen des Landes mit dem Anbau von Gemüse, Obst, Tabak, Hopfen, Zuckerrüben und Braugerste zu finden. Die Flußlandschaft des Rhein-Mosel-Nahe-Ahr-Raumes stellt zusammen mit der Pfalz ein großes geschlossenes Weinbaugebiet dar, das mit etwa 50.000 ha Fläche 75% der gesamten Weinerzeugung des Bundesgebietes hervorbringt. Einen starken Anteil an der Gesamtnutzung hat der Wald, der fast überall 40% der Fläche erreicht oder übersteigt. Der starke Anteil der Landwirtschaft an dem wirtschaftlichen Gesamtgefüge des Landes kommt in einem Anteil der Erwerbstätigen von 31% zum Ausdruck. Die bedeutende Stellung des Obstbaues wird durch den Produktionswert von 90 Millionen DM im Jahr unterstrichen. Rund 20% des landwirtschaftlichen Reinertrages bei nur 5,1% Flächenanteil entfallen auf den Weinbau.

Innerhalb der gewerblichen Wirtschaft ist das Kräfteverhältnis zwischen Industrie, Handwerk und Handel ausgeglichen. Die wirtschaftlichen Kernräume sind: die Oberrheinische Tiefebene (mit Ludwigshafen); der westliche Teil des Pfälzer Waldes (mit Pirmasens und Zweibrücken); die Kaiserslauterner Senke; das Mainzer Becken als Zentrum des deutschen Weinhandels; die Flußlandschaft an der Nahe; das Trierer Becken; das Koblenz-Neuwieder

Becken von Niederlahnstein bis zur Remagener Pforte; das obere Siegtal im Kreis Altenkirchen, das durch seine Erzvorkommen eine beachtliche Schwerindustrie entwickelt hat. Ein wichtiger wirtschaftlicher Faktor ist der Fremdenverkehr. Das Land ist als Reise-, Bäder- und Weinland weit über die Grenzen hinaus bekannt geworden. Wie nur wenige Länder ist es ausgezeichnet mit mannigfaltigen Naturschönheiten, mit einzigartiger Burgenromantik, mit weltbekannten kunsthistorischen Sehenswürdigkeiten aus zwei Jahrtausenden, mit zahlreichen heilenden Quellen und mit weltberühmten Weinen. Der bei Adenau gelegene Nürburgring zieht alljährlich Hunderttausende an, die sich für den Motor-Rennsport begeistern. Die Weinstraße, die sich am Haardt-Gebirge entlang zieht, lockt besonders im Frühling und Herbst viele Reisende an. Das Klima ist so mild, daß die zahlreichen Mandelbäume Früchte tragen, was in Deutschlands Breitengraden eine Seltenheit ist.

Als Grenzland im Westen kommt dem Lande Rheinland-Pfalz eine besondere Rolle zu. Der Südteil grenzt an Frankreich, der westliche und nordwestliche Teil an Luxemburg und Belgien. Die familiären und kulturellen Beziehungen über die politischen Grenzen hinweg ermöglichen einen Kontakt mit den Nachbarn, der den Bestrebungen eines Vereinigten Europas förderlich ist.

Der Johannes-Gutenberg-Universität in Mainz ist das Auslands- und Dolmetscherinstitut in Germersheim angeschlossen. Daneben hat das Land eine Theologische Fakultät des Bischöflichen Stuhles in Trier. An bedeutenden Bildungsstätten sind weiterhin zu nennen die Hochschule für Verwaltungswissenschaften in Speyer, mehrere Pädagogische Akademien, Fachschulen für Musik, Kunst- und Bautechnik, Keramik, Textil, Handwerk und Gewerbe.

*

Schleswig-Holstein ist das nördlichste Land der Bundesrepublik, eine Brücke zu den skandinavischen Staaten, auf der jütischen Halbinsel als südlicher Nachbar von Dänemark zwischen Elbe, Nord- und Ostsee gelegen. Die Landeshauptstadt ist Kiel, dessen Universität ein Institut für Weltwirtschaft angegliedert ist. Die Bevölkerung gehört überwiegend (88%) der evangelischen Konfession und dem niedersächsischen Stammes- und Sprachbereich an. Geschichtlich gesehen siedelten im Süden die nordelbischen Sachsen, die Stämme der Holsten, Stormarn und Dithmarscher, im Westen die Friesen und im nördlichen Teil nach Abzug der Angeln die Jüten. Schleswig-Holstein ist also nicht nur Grenzland, sondern zugleich Völkerbrücke zwischen Nord- und Südgermanen.

Nach dem Niederbruch des Reiches im Jahre 1945 wurde Schleswig-Holstein zum ersten Male in seiner Geschichte ein selbständiges staatliches Gebilde. Vorher hatte sich das Ringen um Schleswig, zeitweise auch um Holstein, wie ein roter Faden durch die Geschichte deutsch-dänischer Nachbarschaft gezogen. Von 1460 bis 1848 lebten die beiden Herzogtümer Schleswig und Holstein mit dem dänischen Königreich unter einem Herrscher aus dem Hause Oldenburg in Personalunion. 1866 wurde Schleswig-Holstein eine preußische Provinz. Nach dem Ersten Weltkrieg kam der nördlichste Streifen des Landesteils Schleswig, hart nördlich Flensburg, auf Grund einer Volksabstimmung an Dänemark. Zu beiden Seiten der Grenze gibt es aber auch heute noch völkische Minderheiten. Ihr Rechtsstatus ist durch deutsch-dänische Verhandlungen im Jahre 1955 festgelegt worden. Beide Minderheiten haben volle kulturelle Freiheit und politische Vertretung in den nationalen Parlamenten.

Schleswig-Holstein wurde, neben Niedersachsen, das Land mit dem höchsten Anteil an Vertriebenen und Flüchtlingen, als das Reich zusammenbrach. 1,5 Millionen Einheimische mußten in den ersten Nachkriegsjahren 1,2 Millionen Menschen aus Mittel- und Ostdeutschland aufnehmen. Da auch die Industrie nur gering entwickelt war, galt Schleswig-Holstein damals als das ,,Armenhaus der Bundesrepublik". Durch planmäßige Umsiedlung der Vertriebenen konnte ihre Zahl um mehr als ein Drittel verringert werden. Durch zielbewußten Aufbau einer industriellen Erzeugung, durch beträchtliche, wenn auch im Laufe der Jahre abnehmende Finanzhilfen des Bundes und der Länder und durch Sondermaßnahmen des Bundes ist der Notstand jetzt im wesentlichen behoben. Die Verantwortlichen im Lande verweisen mit Stolz darauf, daß der Fleiß und der Aufbauwille einer von Natur aus zähen Bevölkerung jede Hilfe nachweislich reich gelohnt haben, ss daß dieses fremder Hilfe noch immer bedürftige Land kein ,,Faß ohne Boden" war.

Die Wirtschaft des nördlichsten Bundeslandes ist überwiegend auf die Erzeugung und Veredelung von Bodenprodukten — Landwirtschaft, Erdöl, Steine und Erden — und auf die Schiffahrt ausgerichtet. Die Erdölindustrie hat besonders im Landesteil Holstein ein reiches Betätigungsfeld gefunden. Außer den eigenen Funden (400.000 t im Jahre 1958) wird ein im Bau befindlicher Ölhafen bei Brunsbüttelkoog künftig Import-Rohöl aufnehmen, so daß in dem DEA-Werk bei Heide in Dithmarschen eine Kapazität von 1,5 Millionen t jährlich verarbeitet werden kann. In der Werftindustrie herrschen die bundeseigenen Kieler Howaldtswerke vor, die im Jahre 1958 unter den europäischen Werftbetrieben an erster Stelle standen. Hier wurde unter anderem der 65.000 t-Tanker „Olympia-Challenger" des griechischen Reeders ONASSIS gebaut, der größte Schiffsneubau Europas. Neben weiteren Großwerften in Flensburg, Rendsburg und der alten Hansestadt Lübeck gibt es noch eine ansehnliche Zahl mittlerer und kleinerer Werftbetriebe.

Schleswig-Holsteins verkehrspolitische Sonderstellung beruht auf der Tatsache, daß sich hier die Schiffahrtslinien zwischen Nord- und Ostsee mit dem Bahn- und Straßenverkehr zwischen Mittel- und Nordeuropa kreuzen. Der Nordostsee-Kanal, der das Land in seiner ganzen Breite durchschneidet, hatte im Jahre 1958 über 70.000 Durchfahrten. Die Vertiefung des Kanalbettes auf 12 m und die Modernisierung der Schleusen wird die Voraussetzungen dafür schaffen, daß auch neuzeitliche Großschiffe diese 98 km lange Wasserstraße ohne Schwierigkeiten passieren können. Knotenpunkt dieses Verkehrs ist die Stadt Rendsburg. Die Kreuzungsschwierigkeiten des Kanal- und Landverkehrs sollen durch einen Kanaltunnel behoben werden. Der Nordsüdverkehr auf der Europa-Straße 3 wird entlastet durch den Verkehr auf der sogenannten „Vogelfluglinie". In einigen Jahren wird eine neue Fährstrecke von der Nordküste der Ostseeinsel Fehmarn bis zur Südküste der dänischen Insel Laaland erheblichen Zeitgewinn bringen.

Grundlage des schleswig-holsteinischen Wirtschaftslebens ist jedoch weiterhin die Landwirtschaft. 76% der Bodenfläche werden durch sie genutzt. Nur 8% sind mit Wald bestanden. Der Nachteil eines relativ kurzen Sommers wird durch den klimatischen Vorteil eines milden Seeklimas ausgeglichen. Aufzucht von Fleischvieh und Milchwirtschaft, Gemüsebau, Obstkulturen und (bei Hamburg) Baumschulen bilden das Rückgrat der agrarischen Struktur. Die Milchwirtschaft gehört zu den ertragreichsten des Bundesgebietes. Die Milchveredelungsbetriebe haben sich ihre Absatzmärkte weit über die Landesgrenzen hinaus erschlossen.

An den Küsten mit ihren zahlreichen bekannten Seebädern gibt es einen regen Fischereibetrieb mit Räuchereien und Fischkonservenfabriken. Das Schwergewicht des Fischfangs liegt in der Kutterfischerei. Zentrum des Fischabsatzes ist der Kieler Seefischmarkt, Heimathafen der Fischdampferflotte und zugleich der einzige Großumschlagplatz für Süßwasserfische im Bundesgebiet.

Die „Holsteinische Schweiz", ein fruchtbares und landschaftlich reizvolles Hügelland mit Wäldern und Seen, ist ein beliebtes Erholungsgebiet. Der förden- und hafenreichen Ostseeküste steht im Westen das Wattenmeer und das fruchtbare Marschenland der Nordseeküste gegenüber. Im Kampf mit dem „Blanken Hans" wird hier durch Entwässerungs- und Eindeichungsarbeiten immer neuer wertvoller Boden gewonnen.

Saarland konnte erst am 1.1.1957 staatsrechtlich in den Verband der Bundesrepublik aufgenommen werden. Die wirtschaftliche Rückgliederung soll auf Grund des deutsch-französischen Saarvertrages am 31.12.1959 vollendet sein. Diesem Schlußstrich unter jahrzehntelange deutsch-französische Auseinandersetzungen um das Gebiet an der Saar waren 1935 und 1955 Volksabstimmungen vorausgegangen, bei denen die Bevölkerung sich für die Zugehörigkeit zum deutschen Volks- und Staatsverband ausgesprochen hatte.

Das Volk an der Saar ist überwiegend katholischer Konfession (73%). Die Übervölkerung des Gebietes wird besonders deutlich in dem stark industrialisierten Saartal zwischen Dillingen und der Hauptstadt Saarbrücken und im Kohlenrevier. Die Erzeugung von Rohstahl, die eisenverarbeitende Industrie, die Energiewirtschaft, Kohle und Chemie machen das Land zu einem Kerngebiet der europäischen Montan-Industrie. Der Außenhandel war bisher stark nach Frankreich orientiert. Die „Universität des Saarlandes" in Saarbrücken wurde nach dem letzten Kriege gegründet. Sie hat Deutsch und Französisch als gleichberechtigte Lehr- und Prüfungssprachen.

*

Die *Freie und Hansestadt Hamburg* ist, ähnlich wie Bremen und wie früher einmal Lübeck, ein Stadtstaat. Ihre Privilegien und Reichsunmittelbarkeit gehen bis auf Kaiser BARBAROSSA zurück. Stets haben es die hamburgischen Bürger, ihr Rat oder ihr Senat (Landesregierung) verstanden, Unabhängigkeit und Freiheit zu erhalten. So ist Hamburg zweierlei in einem: Bundesland und Einheitsgemeinde. Allerdings besitzen einige Ortsteile am Stadtrand oder in den Marschen (Altes Land, Vierlande, Walddörfer) noch dörflichen Charakter.

Für die Geschichte Hamburgs wie für seine gegenwärtige Existenz besitzt der große Hafen entscheidende Bedeutung. Er übt eine deutsche Funktion aus, auf die sich die Freie und Hansestadt weitgehend spezialisiert hat. Aus diesem Grunde hat der Zweite Weltkrieg Hamburg noch vernichtender getroffen als der Erste: durch Zerschlagung und Blockierung fast sämtlicher Hafenbecken infolge der Luftangriffe, durch Versenkung von fast dreitausend Schiffen im Elbstrom und in den Hafenzugängen, durch weitgehende Zerstörung der Werften und Docks und durch die Ablieferung sämtlicher seegehenden Schiffe mit Ausnahme weniger Einheiten, die nur für die Küstenschiffahrt verwendbar waren. In anderen Bundesländern blieben wesentliche Produktionsstätten und wesentliche Rohstoffquellen greifbar.

Die Hamburger, deren Wohnungen zu 53% total zerstört waren, mußten hinsichtlich ihres Schiffbaus, ihrer Schiffahrt und ihres Handels auf dem Nullpunkt beginnen. Sie haben es mit Unverdrossenheit und Unbeirrbarkeit getan und sich durch keinerlei äußere Einwirkungen von ihrer gesamtdeutschen Aufgabe abbringen lassen. Hamburg hätte nach 1945 die Landeshauptstadt eines neuen Landes Nordmark (einschließlich Schleswig-Holsteins) werden können. Damit wäre es die Hauptstadt eines Agrarlandes geworden. Es richtete stattdessen alle seine Energien auf die Wiederherstellung seines Hafens, seiner Werften und seines Exporthandels.

Der Eiserne Vorhang hat die Hälfte des natürlichen Hamburger Hinterlandes abgeschnitten. Hamburg ist so zu einer doppelten Grenzstadt geworden, deren Seegrenze wesentlich weiter entfernt liegt (135 km) als der Eiserne Vorhang (30 km). Trotzdem gelang es den gemeinsamen Anstrengungen des Senats und der Bürgerschaft, die früheren engen Kontakte zu allen überseeischen Ländern wiederherzustellen. 1958 wurde der Hamburger Hafen von 19.000 Schiffen angelaufen. Mehr als 220 Liniendienste verbinden den Hamburger Hafen mit sämtlichen wichtigen Häfen aller Küsten und Kontinente. Als ein wesentlicher Aktivposten beim Wiederaufbau der Schiffahrts- und Handelsstadt erwiesen sich das Vertrauen und das Ansehen, das die alte Hansestadt und ihre Kaufleute in Übersee besaßen. Dieser moralische Kredit war die beste Voraussetzung für den neuen materiellen Kredit, den die Elb-Hanseaten in der Welt erringen konnten. Durch die Halbierung des Hinterlandes sind allerdings die Standortbedingungen für Hamburg ungünstiger geworden. Seine Hafenwirtschaft ist krisenempfindlicher als die Wirtschaft anderer Bundesländer. Während es anderen Häfen, beispielsweise Bremen oder den Häfen der Benelux-Staaten, gelang, ihren Güterumschlag im Verhältnis zur Vorkriegszeit auf mehr als 220% zu steigern, mußte sich Hamburg mit 120% des Vorkriegsumschlags begnügen. Nicht zuletzt ist daran auch die Strangulierung seiner wichtigsten Binnenwasserstraße, der Elbe, schuldig, durch die Hamburg auch zum natürlichen Hafen von Prag bestimmt ist. Zum Ausgleich war Hamburg genötigt, seine Industrie weiter auszubauen und dadurch als Stadt zum größten Industriestandort des Bundesgebiets zu werden.

Wenn auch die Hamburgische Universität zu den jüngeren Hochschulen der Bundesrepublik gehört, war die Hansestadt doch stets auch die Stätte eines reichen kulturellen Lebens. Schon bevor ein deutscher Fürstenhof dazu überging, eine ständige Hofoper ins Leben zu rufen, gelang es bürgerlichen Mäzenen Hamburgs, einen Opernhof mit Repertoire-Programm zu schaffen. Auch das Hamburgische Nationaltheater, durch dessen Inszenierungen GOTTHOLD EPHRAIM LESSING zur Aufzeichnung seiner „Hamburgischen Dramaturgie" veranlaßt wurde, besaß zu Lebzeiten GOETHES bereits führenden Rang. Hamburgs Kaufleute setzten ihren Stolz darein, wertvolle völkerkundliche Museumsstücke aus der ganzen Welt zusammenzutragen und sie in den hamburgischen Museen für die Wissenschaft und für die Öffentlichkeit zugänglich zu machen. Die hansische Eigenstaatlichkeit führte auch auf staatsrechtlichem Gebiet dazu, daß zu Zeiten schwacher Reichsgewalt, gemeinsam mit Bremen und Lübeck, internationale Beziehungen auf der Basis eigener Handels-, Freundschafts- und Friedensverträge entwickelt wurden, deren Pflege mehreren hundert hansestädtischen Konsulaten übertragen war. Begünstigt durch die Standortbedingungen konnte Hamburg Sonderleistungen auf dem Gebiet des Versicherungsrechts, des Seerechts, der Tropenmedizin und der überseeischen Sprachforschung entfalten. Hamburgs Universität entwickelte sich bezeichnenderweise aus der Stiftung eines früheren Kolonialinstituts. Eine Musikhochschule und eine Kunsthochschule runden das Bild der kulturellen Einrichtungen ab.

Die in Jahrhunderten geübte Selbstverantwortung freier Bürger drückt sich auch im parlamentarischen Stil Hamburgs aus. Es ist ein Stil der Versachlichung, der wesentlich mitgetragen wird von den Behörden-Deputationen. In ihnen können die ehrenamtlich wirkenden Deputierten als Vertrauensträger der Bevölkerung auch auf die Exekutive einwirken. In diesen Deputationen können keine Reden zum Fenster hinaus gehalten werden. Hier wird traditionsbewußt mit Argumenten operiert, an denen auch die Plenarsitzung des Landesparlaments, das den Namen Bürgerschaft trägt, nicht vorbei kann. So lebt die stadtstaatliche Demokratie in Hamburg eigenwillig und selbstbewußt, weltoffenen Blicks und doch auf den sicheren Fundamenten ihrer Geschichte.

*

Auch die *Freie Hansestadt Bremen* ist ein Stadtstaat. Daß sie trotz ihrer geringen Größe und Bevölkerungszahl innerhalb des föderativen Aufbaues der Bundesrepublik ein selbständiges Land ist, hat ebenso starke historische wie aktuelle politische Gründe.

Die bremische Eigenstaatlichkeit reicht bis ins hohe Mittelalter zurück. Unter KARL DEM GROSSEN Amtssitz eines Bischofs, wurde Bremen rasch zu einem Mittelpunkt der nordischen Christenheit. Früh waren Handel und Schiffahrt Schwerpunkte seiner wirtschaftlichen Betätigung. Seine Reichsunmittelbarkeit wurde zwar erst gegen Ende des Dreißigjährigen Krieges vom Kaiser verbrieft; aber seine bürgerliche Eigenständigkeit war schon seit dem Dreizehnten Jahrhundert so stark, daß der Einfluß des Erzbischofs auf die Geschicke der Stadt nur noch wenig bedeuten konnte.

Zum Lande Bremen gehört auch die Stadt Bremerhaven, die 1827 als Anlegeplatz für Hochseeschiffe gegründet wurde. Das war die Voraussetzung für die Aufgabe Bremens, durch Seeschiffahrt und Handel das Reich mit den übrigen Ländern und Kontinenten zu verbinden. In der Neuzeit erfordert das eine Fülle komplizierter Maßnahmen. Dazu gehört für Bremen die ständige Ausbaggerung der Unterweser und der Anschluß an Bahnen, Straßen und Kanäle; nicht zuletzt auch ein System besonderer Verkehrstarife. So liegt der Schwerpunkt des Landes Bremen, ebenso wie der Hamburgs, auf der Wahrnehmung der maritimen Interessen der Bundesrepublik. Diese Aufgabe ist ihm durch die geschichtliche Entwicklung und seine geographische Lage zugewachsen. Darin besteht, heute wie in der Vergangenheit, der entscheidende Grund für Bremens Eigenstaatlichkeit.

Stimmgewicht und Einflußmöglichkeiten, die der bremische Stadtstaat nach dem Grundgesetz im Bundesrat und im Gesamtstaat hat, stehen in keinem Verhältnis zu der Einwohnerzahl und dem geringen Umfang des Territoriums. Diese Erscheinung ist für einen Bundesstaat typisch. Sie läßt erwarten, daß der Schwerpunkt der Betätigung des Stadtstaates innerhalb des Gesamtstaates bei den maritimen Aufgaben verbleibt. Der Bremer Senat hat das allezeit erkannt und sich demgemäß bei den Fragen, die Bremen nicht unmittelbar angehen, weiser Zurückhaltung befleißigt.

Der durch die Europäische Wirtschaftsgemeinschaft noch verschärfte Wettbewerb, in dem Bremen als Seehafen und Welthandelsplatz zu anderen großen Häfen steht, fordert die Konzentration aller öffentlichen finanziellen und wirtschaftlichen Kräfte auf diese Aufgabe. Die Eingliederung der Stadt in ein anderes, größeres Bundesland würde dem abträglich sein. Das Grundgesetz hat daher die traditionell überkommene Reichsunmittelbarkeit Bremens auch für den neuen Gesamtstaat anerkannt. Bremens Wirtschaft ist zur See orientiert. Sein Handel ist überwiegend Außenhandel, wobei Import und Export sich die Waage halten. Neben den bremischen Reedereien stehen die Werften und die dazu gehörige Hilfsindustrie. Schließlich verarbeiten die bremischen Industrien in großem Umfang über See herangebrachte Rohstoffe, so die Tabakindustrie, die Kaffeeröstereien, Mühlen, Wollwäscherei und Wollkämmerei. Ein bedeutender Wirtschaftszweig ist die Hochseefischerei. Sie wird mit einem gesamtdeutschen Anteil zu über 50% von Bremerhaven aus betrieben.

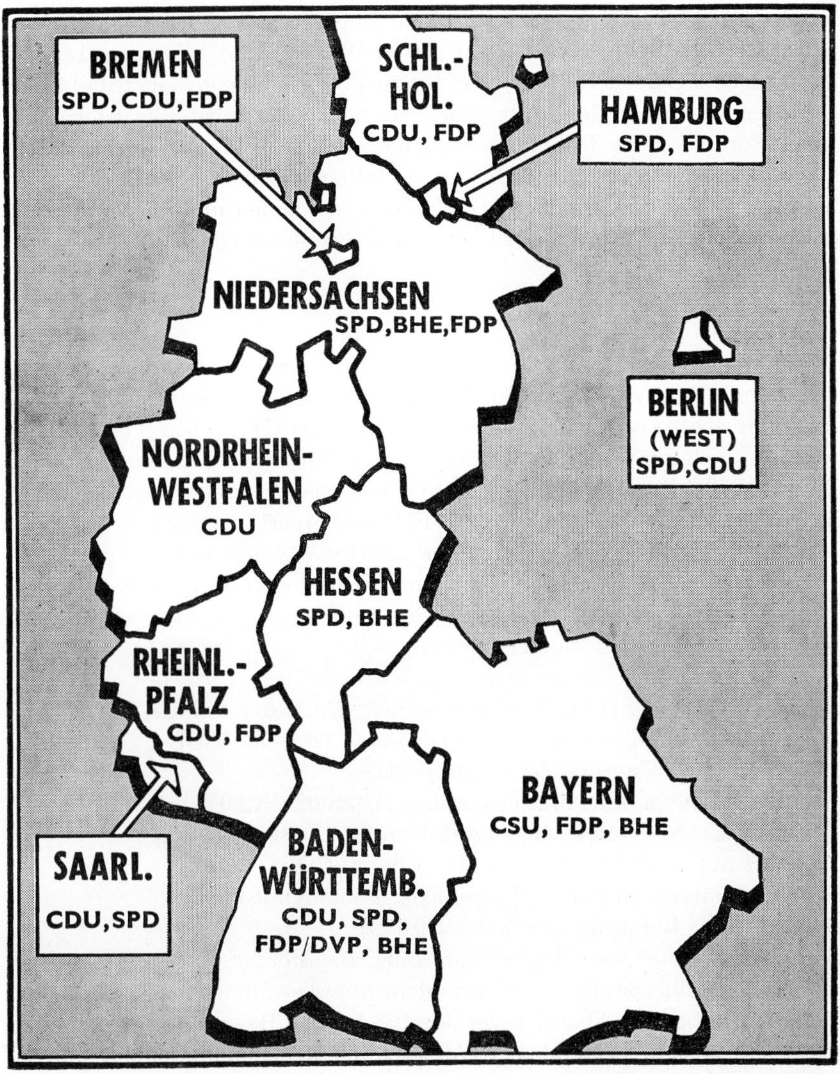

Im Stadtstaat Bremen haben sich in langer Tradition eigentümliche staatsrechtliche Verhältnisse entwickelt. Sie haben ihren Niederschlag auch in der neuen Bremischen Landesverfassung gefunden. Diese weist trotz durchaus neuzeitlichem demokratischem Gepräge gegenüber anderen deutschen Ländern Besonderheiten auf, deren Wurzeln in die Zeit von 1848/49 zurückgehen. Damals vollzog sich in Bremen der Übergang vom aristokratisch regierten Stadtstaat des Mittelalters zur republikanischen Staatsform der Gegenwart. So ist die Teilnahme der Bürger an der Ausübung der staatlichen Gewalt in eigentümlichen Formen erhalten geblieben. Derartige Verhältnisse scheinen heute nur noch in einem so kleinen und überschaubaren Staatswesen wie dem der Freien Hansestadt Bremen möglich.

*
* *

Die Regierungsverhältnisse in Bonn wurden seit 1949 durch die unangefochtene Führung der Christlich-Demokratischen Union (CDU/CSU) bestimmt. Die Koalition der CDU/CSU mit der Deutschen Partei (DP), zeitweise auch mit den Freien Demokraten (FDP) und dem Gesamtdeutschen Block (GB/BHE), stand immer einer Opposition gegenüber, die im wesentlichen von den Sozialdemokraten (SPD) verkörpert wurde. Im Gegensatz hierzu haben sich *in den Ländern und Hansestädten die mannigfachsten Regierungskoalitionen* gebildet. Nach dem Stande vom Juli 1959 steht die Regierung in:

Bayern unter Ministerpräsident SEIDEL (CSU);
Niedersachsen unter Ministerpräsident KOPF (SPD);
Baden-Württemberg unter Ministerpräsident KIESINGER (CDU);
Nordrhein-Westfalen unter Ministerpräsident MEYERS (CDU);
Hessen unter Ministerpräsident ZINN (SPD);
Rheinland-Pfalz unter Ministerpräsident ALTMEIER (CDU);
Schleswig-Holstein unter Ministerpräsident v. HASSEL (CDU);
Saarland unter Ministerpräsident Dr. RÖDER (CDU);
Hamburg unter dem Ersten Bürgermeister BRAUER (SPD);
Bremen unter Bürgermeister KAISEN (SPD);
Berlin(West) unter dem Regierenden Bürgermeister BRANDT (SPD).

Aus dem Blickpunkt einer verantwortungsbewußten Staatspolitik hat dieses bunte Bild der Koalitionsverhältnisse bei den Regierungen der Länder sicherlich zu dem erstaunlichen Aufschwung der Bundesrepublik und zu ihrem erfreulichen politischen und sozialen Klima beigetragen. Die Opposition kann auf diese Weise ihren Beitrag zur deutschen Politik nicht nur im Bundestag leisten, sondern in den Ländern und im Bundesrat aktiv an der Gestaltung der Dinge mitwirken.

BERLIN

Geschichtlicher Rückblick

Berlin, die Stadt in der Mitte des europäischen Kontinents, hat ein bewegtes und bewegendes Schicksal erfahren. Im Wandel der Zeiten haben Höhen und Tiefen in reichem Maße das Gesicht dieser Stadt und ihrer Menschen geprägt. Berlin ist heute mehr als je zuvor der Spiegel unserer Zeit. Als Stadt wird Berlin erstmals im Jahre 1230 erwähnt. 1470 wurde es ständige Residenz der Kurfürsten von Brandenburg sowie Sitz der Behörden und des Kammergerichts. Daraus entwickelten sich intensive Beziehungen zu Mitteldeutschland, dem Zentrum der Reformation. Schwere Schäden verursachten der Dreißigjährige Krieg und die Pestjahre um 1600. Berlin erhielt neue Auftriebe, nachdem Kurfürst FRIEDRICH-WILHELM (der Große Kurfürst, † 1688) das Fundament zum Brandenburgisch-Preußischen Staat gelegt hatte. Unter FRIEDRICH DEM GROSSEN, seinem Enkel, erlangte die Stadt die Bedeutung einer europäischen Metropole. 1866 wurde Berlin Hauptstadt des Norddeutschen Bundes und 1871 nach der Reichsgründung durch BISMARCK mit damals 826.000 Einwohnern die Hauptstadt Deutschlands. Seither zog Berlin die schöpferischen Kräfte aus allen Landen an; die Stadt wurde in zunehmendem Maße politischer, wirtschaftlicher und kultureller Mittelpunkt Deutschlands und eines der geistigen Zentren Europas. Am 27.4.1920 wurde aus Berlin und seinen Vororten (acht Stadtgemeinden, neunundfünfzig Landgemeinden und siebenundzwanzig Gutsbezirken) Groß-Berlin gebildet. Die Einwohnerzahl erhöhte sich auf 3,8 Millionen (1939); sie hatte 1943 fast 4,5 Millionen erreicht.

Berlin in der Stunde Null

Um die Entwicklung Berlins in den letzten Jahren zu zeichnen, beginnt man am besten mit dem Augenblick, der in der Geschichte des deutschen Volkes als die „Stunde Null" bezeichnet wird. Das war für Deutschland der 8.5.1945, als die Deutsche Wehrmacht bedingungslos kapitulierte. Für die Hauptstadt Berlin begann die Stunde Null allerdings schon am 2.5.1945 zu schlagen, als es den Truppen der Roten Armee gelang, die militärische Eroberung der Stadt abzuschließen.

In der Stunde Null war Berlin eine tote Stadt. Schon in den letzten Jahren des Krieges hatte sie infolge der sich steigernden amerikanischen und britischen Luftangriffe gewaltige Zerstörungen erfahren. Der zwanzig Tage dauernde Endkampf übertraf an Tod und Vernichtung alles bisher Geschehene.

Als am 2.5.1945 die Kämpfe in und um Berlin ihr Ende fanden, machte der Trümmerschutt in der Reichshauptstadt ein Sechstel der Trümmermassen in allen anderen deutschen Städten zusammen aus. In Berlin waren mehr Häuser zerstört als München je gezählt hat. In einem Zeitraum von zwei Monaten, in dem die Sowjetische Besatzungsmacht unumschränkte Herrscherin des Gebiets und der Bevölkerung von Berlin war, gelang es ihr, die wichtigsten Posten der ersten Berliner Nachkriegsverwaltung mit kommunistischen Vertrauensleuten zu besetzen. Darüber hinaus wurde durch brutale und radikale Maßnahmen des Siegers das wirtschaftliche Leben der Stadt im Zustand der Leichenstarre gehalten. Im Sommer 1945 waren 80% der Berliner Wirtschaftskapazität im Werte von etwa 3,5 bis 4 Milliarden Mark demontiert worden. Die Geld- und Kresitinstitute wurden geschlossen, die Geldbestände der öffentlichen Hand als Beutegut eingezogen. Auch der einzelne Einwohner der Stadt stand vor dem Nichts — über drei Millionen Menschen hungerten in dem Ruinenfeld.

Auf Grund von Abkommen, die noch während des Krieges zwischen den Alliierten Mächten geschlossen worden waren, übernahmen am 4.7.1945 amerikanische und britische, am 12.7.1945 auch französische Truppen die ihnen zugewiesenen Stadtteile als Besatzungssektoren. Gleichzeitig begann die aus den vier Stadtkommandanten bestehende Alliierte Kommandantur ihre Tätigkeit. Dabei gelang es dem Sowjetischen Kommandanten, mindestens für den Anfang die von ihm in die neugeschaffene Berliner Verwaltung eingeschleusten kommunistischen Personen in ihren Funktionen zu halten.

Berlin wird Viersektorenstadt

Das nunmehr zur Viersektorenstadt gewordene Berlin wurde Sitz des Alliierten Kontrollrates, der eine Art oberster alliierter Regierungsinstanz für ganz Deutschland darstellte und auch der für das Besatzungsgebiet Berlin eingesetzten Alliierten Kommandantur übergeordnet war. Am 20.10.1946 wurden die ersten und nach dem Kriege einzigen gesamtberliner Wahlen zur Stadtverordnetenversammlung abgehalten. Als antifaschistische Parteien waren die Sozialdemokratische Partei, die Christlich-Demokratische Union, die Liberal-Demokratische Partei und die Sozialistische Einheitspartei zugelassen. Die SED war in der Sowjetzone und im Sowjetsektor Berlins am 22.4.1946 gegründet worden, während die Sozialdemokraten in den Westsektoren von Berlin die Zwangsvereinigung ihrer Partei mit der kommunistischen abgelehnt hatten. Das Ergebnis dieser ersten Nachkriegswahlen war eine für die Sowjetische Besatzungsmacht unerwartet vernichtende Niederlage der SED; sie erhielt nur 26 von 130 Sitzen. Die Bevölkerung hatte den Vertrauensleuten der Sowjets das Vertrauen versagt. Die Berliner hatten damit ihrem Willen Ausdruck verliehen, die Diktatur des HITLER-Regimes nicht durch eine Diktatur kommunistischer Prägung ersetzen zu lassen, sondern ihr Gemeinschaftsleben künftig nach den Prinzipien demokratisch-rechtsstaatlicher Ordnung selbst zu gestalten. Diese Erkenntnis hat die verantwortlichen Politiker der Sowjetunion veranlaßt, nunmehr in verstärktem Maße die Zusammenarbeit im Kontrollrat und in der Kommandantur zu stören. Die Funktionsfähigkeit dieser die oberste Gewalt in Berlin ausübenden Gremien — deren Beschlüsse einstimmig gefaßt werden mußten — wurde durch ständige sowjetische Vetos gelähmt. Zugleich wurden die Kommunisten beauftragt, die innenpolitische demokratische Entwicklung in Berlin durch Störaktionen zu hemmen mit dem Ziel, sie schließlich völlig zu unterbinden.

Die Blockade

Gemeinsame Besprechungen der Finanz- und Wirtschaftsberater der Besatzungsmächte über eine einheitliche Währungsreform in Groß-Berlin führten am 22.6.1948 zu keinem Ergebnis, da der Vertreter der Sowjetunion auf einer in Berlin und in der Sowjetzone gleichen Währung bestand. Ein entsprechender sowjetischer Währungsbefehl wurde von den Westmächten für ungültig erklärt. In Berlin(West) wurde am 24. Juni die DM-West als gesetzliches Zahlungsmittel eingeführt, nachdem am Tage zuvor im sowjetisch besetzten Machtbereich die DM-Ost zum alleinigen Zahlungsmittel erklärt worden war.

Am 24.6.1948 begann die Blockade Berlins. Mit der Sperrung der Verkehrswege zu Lande und zu Wasser versuchten die Sowjets, die Versorgung der drei Westsektoren zu unterbinden und die Menschen in diesem Teil der Stadt zur politischen Kapitulation zu zwingen. Der Absicht der Machthaber im Kreml, die Bevölkerung von Berlin(West) durch Hunger und Kälte in die Knie zu zwingen und die Drei westlichen Alliierten aus der Stadt zu verdrängen, wurde schon vierundzwanzig Stunden später durch die Landung der ersten amerikanischen Transportmaschinen mit Lebensmittel für die Einwohner Westberlins auf dem mitten im Herzen der Stadt gelegenen Flugplatz Tempelhof entgegengetreten. Am 26.6.1948 wurde die Luftbrücke nach

Berlin offiziell eröffnet. Damit war der Kampf um Berlin in ein entscheidendes Stadium getreten. Ein neues Kapitel in der Berliner Nachkriegsgeschichte hatte begonnen. Das Leben in Berlin(West) war während der Blockade beherrscht von Hunger und Kälte, von Stromsperren und Gaskontingentierungen, von Lockungen und Drohungen der Kommunisten jenseits des Brandenburger Tores — und vom ständig stärker werdenden Dröhnen der Luftbrückenflugzeuge. Die sich aus diesen Verhältnissen ergebenden Erschwernisse und Entbehrungen in allen Bereichen des täglichen Lebens wurden ertragen, weil die Westberliner von dem Willen beseelt waren, sich das Recht auf Selbstbestimmung ihrer staatlichen Ordnung zu erhalten. — In der Nacht zum 12.5.1949 wurde die Blockade von Berlin(West) aufgehoben. Die Luftbrücke wurde jedoch mit dem Ziel, eine größere Menge lebenswichtiger Güter in der Stadt als Vorrat zu lagern, bis zum 6.10.1949 weitergeführt. An diesem Tage wurde ein in der Geschichte der Luftfahrt einzigartiges Unternehmen beendet. In der Zeit vom 25.6.1948 bis zum 6.10.1949 wurden in 277.728 Flügen 2.110.235 t Güter aller Art — davon 67% Kohlen, 24% Lebensmittel und 9% Rohmaterialien, Zeitungspapier, Medikamente und anderes — nach Berlin(West) geflogen. Im gemeinsamen Ringen um die Erhaltung der freiheitlichen Existenz der Stadt waren ehemalige Gegner zu Freunden geworden. Die Westmächte und die Berliner hatten sich in der Verteidigung gemeinsamer Ideale zusammengefunden und die Bedrohung erfolgreich abgewehrt.

Die Spaltung Berlins

Am 6.9.1948 stürmten kommunistische Demonstranten das im sowjetischen Sektor gelegene Stadthaus und besetzten den Sitzungssaal der aus den Wahlen vom 20.10.1946 hervorgegangenen Stadtverordnetenversammlung. Die sowjetische Besatzungsmacht und die ihr unterstehende Polizei weigerten sich, die Unabhängigkeit des Stadtparlaments zu schützen. Da die nach demokratischen Grundsätzen frei gewählten Stadtverordneten nicht gewillt waren, unter dem Druck der Kommunisten weiter in Ostberlin zu tagen, verlegten sie ihren Sitz nach Berlin(West). Am 30. November wurde in Ostberlin ein neuer, von Kommunisten beherrschter Magistrat ohne demokratische Legitimation eingesetzt; er amtiert noch heute, ohne jemals durch demokratische Wahlen bestätigt worden zu sein. Der rechtmäßig gewählte Magistrat wurde dadurch gezwungen, am 1. Dezember seine Amtsgeschäfte — ohne die der SED angehörenden Mitglieder — im Rathaus Schöneberg in Berlin(West) aufzunehmen.

Damit war die Spaltung Berlins in einen freien und einen unfreien Teil endgültig vollzogen. Eine organisch gewachsene und zusammengewachsene Stadt war gewaltsam durch eine widernatürliche Grenze, durch rund 150 Schlagbäume und zahlreiche Straßensperren in zwei Verwaltungen, in zwei Versorgungssysteme, in zwei völlig verschiedene Lebenssphären zerrissen: in den freien Teil Berlins, 480 Quadratkilometer groß, mit rund 2,2 Millionen Einwohnern, mit 110,6 Kilometer Zonengrenze und 45,1 Kilometer Sektorengrenzen, und den Ostsektor von Berlin, 400 Quadratkilometer groß, mit rund 1,2 Millionen Einwohnern, die gegen ihren Willen von einem kommunistischen Gewaltregime beherrscht wurden und noch immer beherrscht werden.

Das Volk von Berlin wuchs in den Jahren seiner schwersten Schicksalskrise zu einer Gemeinschaft zusammen, die umfassender als irgendeine Kräftegruppierung ist. Die während der Blockade fest begründete Zusammenarbeit zwischen den Westmächten und Berlin vertiefte sich in der Erkenntnis, daß es im Ringen um Berlin nicht nur darum geht, Freiheit und Selbstbestimmungsrecht für 2,2 Millionen Menschen zu erhalten, sondern vor allem auch darum, die Prinzipien zu verteidigen, die allen freien Völkern unveräußerliche Grundwerte ihrer Existenz bedeuten.

Zwei Welten

Berlin(West) ist nach der 1950 in Kraft gesetzten „Verfassung von Berlin" Stadt und Land zugleich. Der Senat, die Regierung des Landes Berlin, setzt sich aus dem Regierenden Bürgermeister, seinem Vertreter und elf Senatoren zusammen. Nach den Wahlen vom 7.12.1958 sind im Abgeordnetenhaus (Parlament) von Berlin(West) achtundsiebzig Sozialdemokraten und fünfundfünfzig Christliche Demokraten vertreten. An diesen Wahlen beteiligten sich 92,9% der wahlberechtigten Einwohner. Das Ergebnis war ein gewaltiges Bekenntnis der Berliner Bevölkerung für die Freiheit und für die Demokratie. Die kommunistische SED erhielt nur 1,9% der Stimmen. Wahlbeteiligung und Wahlergebnis sind zu einem in der ganzen Welt beachteten Volksentscheid gegen die sowjetischen Berlin-Forderungen geworden.

Die Spaltung der Stadt wird von den Machthabern in Ostberlin systematisch vertieft. Die beiden widernatürlich und gewaltsam getrennten Stadtteile entwickeln sich immer weiter auseinander. Ostberlin wird — wie die sogenannte DDR — in verstärktem Maße in ein System der Abhängigkeiten zum Ostblock und zur Sowjetunion gebracht. Die Machthaber im Ostsektor ließen 1952 das Telephonnetz zerschneiden. Seither ist ein Telephongespräch von einem Haus diesseits zu einem Partner im gegenüberliegenden Haus jenseits einer Straße, die die Sektorengrenze darstellt, nur noch über eine Stadt in Westdeutschland oder im Ausland, also beispielsweise über München oder über Rom und Leipzig nach Ostberlin, möglich.

Berlin ist zu einem Brenn- und Kristallisationspunkt zwischen West und Ost geworden. Die Stadt liegt im Schnittpunkt zweier gegensätzlicher Welten. An keinem Ort berühren und begegnen sich Freiheit und Unfreiheit so eng, nirgendwo prallen die beiden großen Kräftegruppierungen, die in unserer Zeit die Welt beherrschen, so hart aufeinander wie in Berlin. Hier ist der Kontrast am stärksten. Niemand, der nach Berlin kommt, wird sich dem nachhaltigen Eindruck und der Erkenntnis entziehen können, daß neben den eigenen Sorgen die der siebzehn Millionen Deutschen in der sogenannten DDR und darüber hinaus die Nöte aller freiheitsliebenden Völker jenseits des Eisernen Vorhanges nicht vergessen werden dürfen.

Der Volksaufstand vom 17. Juni 1953

In Ostberlin und in der sogenannten DDR, im sogenannten Arbeiter- und Bauernstaat, wurde die brutale Ausbeutung der menschlichen Arbeitskraft in immer stärkerem Maße vorangetrieben. Der „Ministerrat" der sogenannten DDR beschloß am 28.5.1953 weitere Erhöhungen der Arbeitsnormen. Die Unruhe unter der Bevölkerung, besonders in der Arbeiterschaft, führte am 17.6.1953 zu offener Empörung in Ostberlin. Der Volksaufstand griff sofort auf die sogenannte DDR über und wurde zu einer machtvollen Demonstration gegen das kommunistische Regime. Ein waffenloses Volk hatte sich gegen seine Unterdrücker erhoben. Die „Regierung" in der sogenannten DDR konnte sich nur mit Hilfe der sowjetischen Besatzungstruppen an der Macht halten. Der Aufstand der Deutschen in Ostberlin und in der sogenannten DDR für ein freies, menschenwürdiges Dasein wurde von den Panzerdivisionen der Sowjetarmee blutig niedergeschlagen. Das gleiche Schicksal erlitt das ungarische Volk rund drei Jahre später.

Insel der Freiheit

Weit über zwei Millionen Menschen haben seit Anfang 1949 in Westberlin und im Bundesgebiet offiziell um Asyl gebeten. Die tatsächliche Zahl der Flüchtlinge seit 1945 ist jedoch weit größer, sie wird auf 3,2 Millionen geschätzt. Noch heute verlassen Tag für Tag Hunderte Deutsche Heim und Herd, Haus und Hof, Verwandte und Freunde, um dem physischen und dem psychischen Zwang, um der materiellen und der geistigen Kollektivierung durch ein totalitäres System zu entfliehen. Es sind Landflüchtige im eigenen Land. Frauen, Männer, Jugendliche und Kinder, sie wählen die Flucht in eine ungewisse Zukunft, in einen völligen Neuanfang ihrer Existenz als ihr Schicksal. In der Mitte des Zwanzigsten Jahrhunderts und in der Mitte Europas entfliehen an jedem Tag Hunderte dem kommunistischen Terror. Von 1949 bis Ende 1958 war der freie Teil Berlins für 1.270.472 offiziell registrierte Flüchtlinge die rettende Insel. Rund 180.000 von ihnen blieben in Westberlin und wurden hier in Arbeit und Lohn gebracht. Die anderen wurden in den westlichen Teil der Bundesrepublik Deutschland abgeflogen und fanden in den Bundesländern eine neue Heimat.

Berlin gehört zur Bundesrepublik

Als im Jahre 1949 die Länder der Amerikanischen, der Britischen und der Französischen Besatzungszone im Begriff waren, sich zur Bundesrepublik Deutschland zusammenzuschließen, war der Oberbürgermeister von Berlin-(West), Ernst Reuter, sich der Tatsache bewußt, daß der freie Teil Berlins auf die Dauer nur dann existieren konnte, wenn er sich an den freien Teil Deutschlands so eng wie möglich — staatsrechtlich und wirtschaftlich — anschloß. Deshalb schaltete sich Ernst Reuter bei den Besprechungen zwischen den Drei westlichen Besatzungsmächten und den Regierungen der westdeutschen Länder nachhaltig ein. Seine Forderung stieß bei den deutschen Verhandlungspartnern auf volles Verständnis und führte mit dazu, daß nach der ausdrücklichen Bestimmung des Grundgesetzes vom 23.5.1949 und nach der Verfassung von Berlin vom 1.9.1950 Berlin ein Land der Bundesrepublik Deutschland ist. Allerdings erfuhr die Zugehörigkeit von Berlin(West) zur Bundesrepublik auf Grund besatzungsrechtlicher Vorbehalte gewisse Beschränkungen. Diese Beschränkungen wirken sich noch heute dahingehend aus, daß die Berliner Bundestagsabgeordneten und die Berliner Bundesmitglieder bei der Plenarabstimmung über Bundesgesetze nicht stimmberechtigt sind, und daß Bundesgesetze nach einem bestimmten Verfahren durch Beschluß des Abgeordnetenhauses von Berlin formal übernommen werden müssen, wozu Berlin in der Regel verpflichtet ist.

Unabhängig von diesen Beschränkungen ist jedoch im Laufe der vergangenen zehn Jahre die wirtschaftliche und staatsrechtliche Bindung Berlins an den Bund immer stärker geworden. Dies zeigt sich auch darin, daß Berlin am Verfassungsleben der Bundesrepublik wie die übrigen zehn deutschen Länder im vollen Umfange teilnimmt. Berlin hat zweiundzwanzig Abgeordnete im Deutschen Bundestag, die allerdings zur Zeit noch nicht von der Bevölkerung Berlins unmittelbar gewählt, sondern in mittelbarer Wahl durch das Abgeordnetenhaus bestimmt werden. Die zweiundzwanzig Berliner Abgeordneten haben jedoch in vollem Umfange die Rechte und Pflichten eines Mitgliedes des Deutschen Bundestages. Ebenso entsendet der Senat von Berlin vier Mitglieder in den Bundesrat. Als Regierungschef eines Landes der Bundesrepublik ist im Zuge des turnusmäßigen Wechsels des Präsidenten des Bundesrates im Geschäftsjahr 1957/58 der Regierende Bürgermeister von Berlin, WILLY BRANDT, Präsident des Bundesrates gewesen und hat in dieser Eigenschaft den auf Reisen abwesenden Bundespräsidenten vertreten.

Die staatsrechtliche Bedeutung der von den Besatzungsmächten ausgesprochenen Vorbehalte hinsichtlich der Zugehörigkeit Berlins zum Bundesgebiet war eine zeitlang auch innerhalb der deutschen Juristen bestritten. Erfreulicherweise hat — wenigstens für den Bereich der deutschen Rechtsauffassung — das Bundesverfassungsgericht in Karlsruhe in seiner Entscheidung vom 21.5.1957 die Frage der staatsrechtlichen Stellung Berlins einwandfrei in dem Sinne geklärt, daß Berlin ein Land der Bundesrepublik Deutschland ist. Das Festhalten an dieser Entscheidung und die konsequente Weiterführung der von ERNST REUTER eingeleiteten Politik erscheint gerade heute, da nach zehn Jahren der Osten die Freiheit Berlins aufs neue bedroht, von weittragender Bedeutung. Ein einstimmiger Beschluß des Deutschen Bundestages vom 6.2.1957 besagt: „*Berlin ist die Hauptstadt Deutschlands.*"

Der Wiederaufbau

Die Reichshauptstadt Berlin war nicht nur Sitz der Reichsregierung und ihrer Behörden, sondern auch der Zentralen der großen Organisationen und Verbände. Die Erträge, die Berlin früher aus vielfältigen Dienstleistungen erzielte, stellten vor dem Kriege die Hälfte seiner Existenzgrundlage dar. Nicht nur der Verlust der Hauptstadtfunktionen, der viele ältere Angestellte arbeitslos werden ließ, sondern auch die zunehmende Überalterung der Berliner Bevölkerung verursachen besondere Schwierigkeiten. Berlin (West) hatte im Jahresdurchschnitt 1950 nach Aufhebung der Blockade etwa 300.000 Arbeitslose, das waren rund 32% der unselbständigen Erwerbspersonen. Im Bundesgebiet waren es zur gleichen Zeit 10,4%. Trotz den hemmenden Einflüssen — es mußten zusätzliche Arbeitsplätze für die ständig neu hinzukommenden Flüchtlinge geschaffen werden — konnte die Arbeitslosenzahl systematisch herabgesetzt werden. Sie hatte im September 1958 mit knapp 60.000 (6,4%) ihren bisher tiefsten Stand erreicht (westliches Deutschland:

PRODUKTIONSINDEX
ohne Bau und Energieerzeugung (1936 = 100)

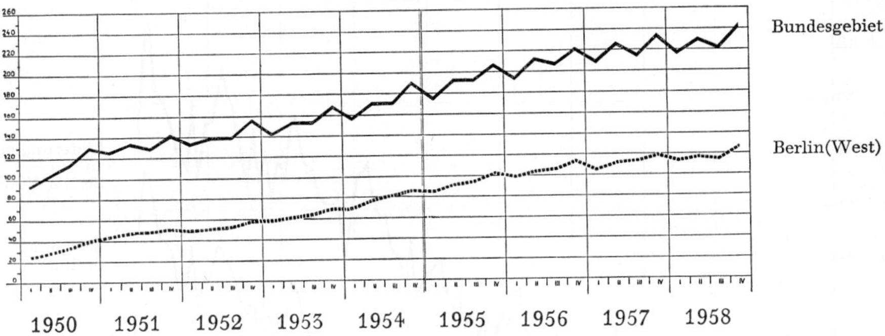

1,7%). Die Zahl der festen Arbeitsplätze konnte seit 1950 um über 300.000 erhöht werden. Ende 1958 wurden in Berlin(West) in allen Zweigen der Wirtschaft rund 870.000 feste Arbeitsplätze gezählt. Berlin(West) ist mit fast 300.000 Arbeitnehmern die größte Industriestadt Deutschlands. Der stärkste Zweig ist die Elektroindustrie. An zweiter Stelle steht die Nahrungs- und Genußmittelindustrie, ihr folgen die Bekleidungsindustrie und die Maschinenbauindustrie. Der Umsatz der Industrie von Berlin(West) betrug im Jahre 1958: 7.100 Millionen DM. Die gesamten Warenlieferungen von Berlin(West) nach Westdeutschland erreichten 1958 einen Wert von 4,4 Milliarden DM.

INDUSTRIESTRUKTUR[1]

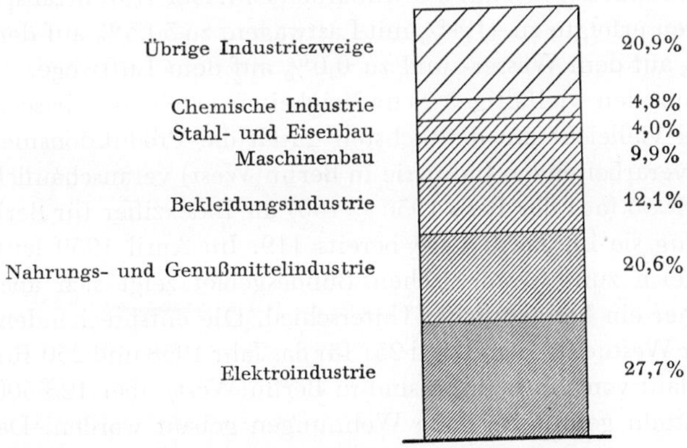

[1] Umsätze techn. Einheiten 1958 (einschließlich Verbr. Steuer)

DER HANDEL WESTDEUTSCHLANDS MIT BERLIN(WEST) SEIT AUFHEBUNG DER BLOCKADE

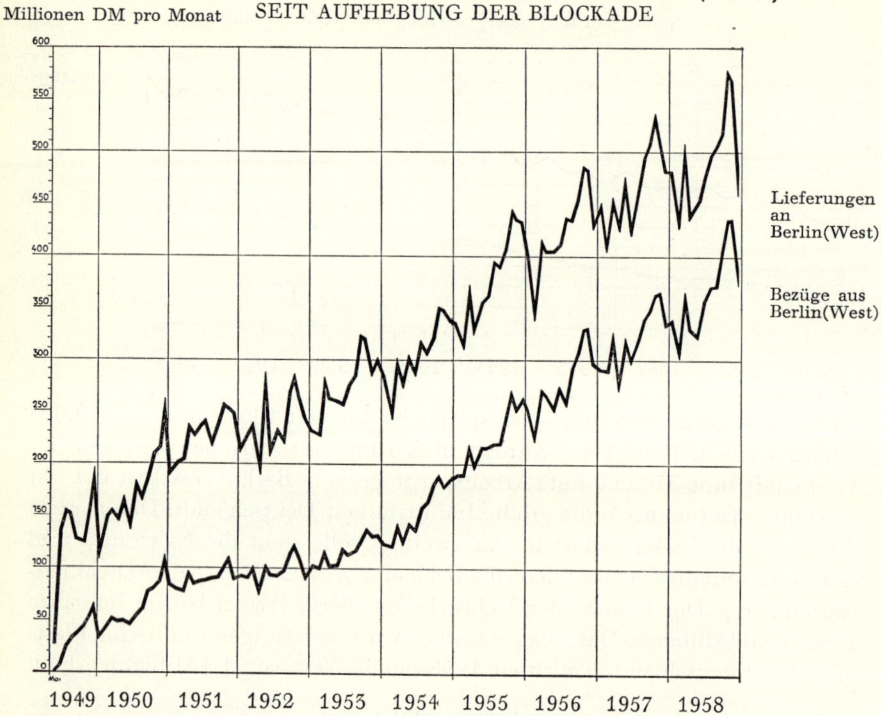

Die Bezüge beliefen sich auf 5,9 Milliarden DM. Der Warentransport in beiden Richtungen erfolgte zu 41,4% mit Lastwagen, zu 30,3% auf dem Schienen-, zu 27,9% auf dem Wasser- und zu 0,0% auf dem Luftwege.

Der trotz den vielfältigen Schwierigkeiten erreichte wirtschaftliche Aufstieg wird vielleicht am deutlichsten durch die Produktionsmengen-Indexziffer der verarbeitenden Industrie in Berlin(West) veranschaulicht. Während im Jahre 1950 (auf der Basis 1936 = 100) die Indexziffer für Berlin(West) 32 war, betrug sie im Jahre 1958 bereits 119. Im April 1959 lautete sie 130. Im Vergleich zum westdeutschen Bundesgebiet zeigt sich aber auch hier noch immer ein beträchtlicher Unterschied. Die entsprechenden Vergleichszahlen für Westdeutschland sind 237 für das Jahr 1958 und 250 für April 1959.

Im Verlauf von zehn Jahren sind in Berlin(West) über 128.500 mit öffentlichen Mitteln geförderte neue Wohnungen gebaut worden. Das entspricht dem Neubau einer Großstadt von fast einer halben Million Einwohnern.

Einer der markantesten Punkte des Wiederaufbaues in Berlin(West) ist das Hansaviertel, das im Kriege fast völlig zerstört worden war. Dort sind jetzt 1.262 moderne und gesunde Wohnungen entstanden, die von Architekten aus vierzehn Nationen entworfen wurden. In die großzügige Neugestaltung Berlins wurden viele Parks und Grünflächen eingeplant, die das Stadtbild nicht nur verschönern, sondern vor allem auch der Großstadtbevölkerung gesunde Wohnverhältnisse bieten. 28,5 Millionen Quadratmeter Grünflächen wurden in Berlin(West) bis Ende 1958 neu angelegt beziehungsweise wiederhergestellt. Aber nicht nur Wohnungen und Grünflächen gehören zum Wiederaufbauprogramm. Schulen, Kirchen, Sportplätze und -hallen, Kinder- und Altersheime, kulturelle Bauten und viele andere mehr wurden nach modernen Gesichtspunkten und neuzeitlichen architektonischen Erkenntnissen wieder aufgebaut beziehungsweise neu errichtet. Das gleiche gilt für Verkehrsbauten jeglicher Art. Seit 1953 wird mit finanzieller Unterstützung durch die Bundesrepublik das U-Bahnnetz in Berlin(West) mit dem Ziel erweitert, die jetzige Länge dieses Verkehrsnetzes von achtundfünfzig Kilometern zu verdoppeln. 1956 ist mit dem Bau eines kreuzungsfreien Schnellstraßenringes begonnen worden, der die Stadt in einer Breite von insgesamt siebenundzwanzig Metern durchzieht und in jeder Richtung aus drei 3,5 Meter breiten Fahrspuren besteht. Der städtebauliche Wiederaufbau von Berlin-(West) schließt in der Planung das Gebiet des Ostsektors ein, der noch heute in weiten Teilen ein Ruinenfeld darstellt. Die Neugestaltung wird unter dem Gesichtspunkt durchgeführt, Berlin zur voll funktionsfähigen Hauptstadt Deutschlands auszubauen.

Der Wiederaufbau von Berlin(West) mußte unter den erschwerenden Bedingungen der Insellage, des völligen Abgeschnittenseins vom natürlichen Hinterland, durchgeführt werden. Die Versorgung der über 2,2 Millionen Menschen mit lebenswichtigen Nahrungsmitteln und Gütern aller Art vollzieht sich über die schmalen Lebensadern, die Berlin(West) mit der Bundesrepublik Deutschland verbinden; es sind vier Autostraßen, vier Eisenbahnlinien, drei Luftkorridore und zwei Wasserwege. So wird beispielsweise die für Säuglinge und Kleinkinder lebensnotwendige Frischmilch Tag für Tag mit großen Kühlwagen über die Interzonenstraßen über mehrere hundert Kilometer aus Schleswig-Holstein, aus Niedersachsen oder aus Bayern nach Berlin gebracht.

Die Lage von Berlin(West) macht eine finanzielle Unterstützung durch die Bundesrepublik Deutschland unerläßlich. Diese besteht aus der sogenannten Bundeshilfe an den Etat der Stadt, aus wirtschaftlichen und steuerlichen

Förderungsmaßnahmen usw. Berlin(West) führt — wie jedes andere Bundesland — die dem Bund zustehenden Steuern ab, und die Bundesrepublik hat laut Gesetz ganz oder teilweise Zahlungen für Sozial- und Versicherungsrenten, Entschädigungs- und Versorgungsleistungen übernommen.

Die Nettozuwendungen, die Berlin(West) beispielsweise im Jahre 1958 vom Bund erhielt, erreichten eine Höhe von 1.600 Millionen DM. Die Nachteile beim Bezug von Rohstoffen und beim Absatz der Produkte werden durch Vorteile ausgeglichen, durch niedrigere Steuern, billige Kredite und Garantien für etwaige politische Risiken. Die umfangreichen Investitionsvorhaben, die nach wie vor ständig und seit dem November 1958 verstärkt eingehen, zeigen ebenso wie die gestiegenen Auftragseingänge aus dem In- und Ausland ein hohes Maß an Vertrauen in die freiheitliche Zukunft Berlins. Das wirtschaftliche und das soziale Gleichgewicht der Stadt könnte jedoch ohne die finanziellen Zuwenduugen aus der Bundesrepublik Deutschland und weitere Förderungsmaßnahmen durch das westliche Ausland nicht gesichert werden.

Berlin will Frieden und Freiheit

Die Forderung der Regierung der Sowjetunion, Westberlin in eine sogenannte ,,Freie Stadt" umzuwandeln, wurde mit der Bedingung verknüpft, in das Leben dieser ,,Freien Stadt Westberlin" dürfe sich kein Staat einmischen. Eine Verwirklichung dieser Absicht würde die Herauslösung von Berlin(West) aus den vielfältigen politischen, rechtlichen, wirtschaftlichen und finanziellen Verflechtungen mit Westdeutschland und der Freien Welt bedeuten. Damit wäre der Stadt die Lebensgrundlage entzogen, — das wäre gleichbedeutend mit dem Verlust der Freiheit. Die Schutzmächte, als solche werden die Truppen der westlichen Alliierten von den Berlinern empfunden, sollen die Stadt verlassen, die dann jeglichen Schutzes beraubt wäre, aber weiterhin von sowjetischen Divisionen umgeben bliebe. Berlin(West) würde verarmen und in wirtschaftliche Abhängigkeit von der die Stadt umgebenden sogenannten DDR und den Ländern des Ostblocks geraten.

Das wäre das Ende der ,,Freien Stadt Westberlin". Sie würde in kurzer Zeit mit allen politischen, wirtschaftlichen und sonstigen Konsequenzen vom System des Kommunismus aufgesogen werden. In der Erkenntnis dieser Konsequenzen haben die Berliner mit der Wahlbeteiligung und dem Wahlergebnis vom 7.12.1958 ihre Antwort auf die sowjetischen Forderungen erteilt; sie haben unmißverständlich ,,nein" gesagt.

Zu den erfreulichen Erfahrungen seit dem 27.11.1958 — dem Tag, an dem die Sowjetunion in ihren Noten die Änderung des Status' von Berlin forderte — gehört nicht nur die Feststellung, daß die Berliner nicht geschwankt und keinen Augenblick daran gedacht haben, sich von dem als richtig erkannten Wege abbringen zu lassen, sondern auch die Tatsache, daß Berlin sich in dieser kritischen Phase fest auf seine Freunde verlassen konnte. Der Dank der Einwohner dieser Stadt gilt daher besonders der Bundesrepublik, die Berlin als einen unlösbaren Bestandteil des freien Teiles Deutschlands betrachtet, und den Regierungen und den Völkern der Westmächte, die sich in so eindrucksvoller Weise zu ihren in und für Berlin übernommenen Pflichten und Rechten bekannt haben.

Bereits am 12.9.1944 wurde im „Londoner Protokoll" der „Europäischen Beratenden Kommission" von den Regierungen des Vereinigten Königreichs, der Sowjetunion und der USA festgelegt, daß Deutschland in Besatzungszonen „und in ein Berliner Gebiet", das dem Gebiet von Groß-Berlin nach dem Gesetz über die Bildung einer neuen Stadtgemeinde Berlin vom 27.4.1920 entspricht, aufgeteilt werden sollte. Das „Berliner Gebiet", so heißt es in diesem Protokoll, wird „gemeinsam von den bewaffneten Streitkräften der USA, des Vereinigten Königreichs und der Sowjetunion besetzt". In einem Zusatzprotokoll vom 14.9.1944 ist die von diesen Mächten gemeinsam zu leitende Verwaltung dieses Gebietes festgelegt. Ein weiteres Ergänzungsprotokoll bestimmt die gleichberechtigte Beteiligung Frankreichs an der „gemeinsamen Verwaltung von Groß-Berlin". Weitere Abkommen, die den Viermächte-Status von Berlin eindeutig bestätigen, sind am 1.5.1945 sowie am 20.6. 1949 abgeschlossen worden. Im letzteren verpflichtete sich die Sowjetunion, das normale Funktionieren der Verkehrs- und Nachrichtenverbindungen zwischen Berlin und den Westzonen Deutschlands zu gewährleisten. Darüber hinaus haben die Vier Mächte „ihre gemeinsame Verantwortung für die Regelung der deutschen Frage" in dem Gipfelkonferenz-Abkommen vom 23.7.1955 anerkannt.

Das Vorgehen der Sowjetunion stellt den Versuch dar, eindeutige völkerrechtliche Abmachungen zu brechen. Die Westmächte haben die einseitige Aufkündigung dieser Verträge abgelehnt, und die unmittelbar betroffenen Menschen, die Berliner, haben die Forderungen der Sowjetunion genau so unmißverständlich zurückgewiesen.

In der Berlin-Frage hat sich weitgehend die Überzeugung durchgesetzt, daß den unberechtigten und gegen den Willen der Völker gerichteten Machtansprüchen des kommunistischen Systems Einhalt geboten werden muß. Der Weg von Kompromissen ohne Rechtsgrundlage würde nicht nur allgemein das Vertrauen in die westliche Solidarität, sondern eine in ihren Folgen nicht abzusehende Schwächung des demokratischen Prinzips bedeuten und darüber hinaus einen Zustand ständiger Unruhe in Mitteleuropa hervorrufen.

Das Berlin-Problem ist nicht Ursache, sondern Folge der widernatürlichen Teilung Deutschlands. Daher kann es weder durch eine isolierte, noch durch Scheinlösungen überwunden werden.

Das Berliner und das deutsche Problem sind nur Teile der großen Auseinandersetzung, die in unserer Zeit zwischen der freiheitlich-demokratischen und der kommunistischen Welt ausgetragen wird. Der Streit um Berlin ist von der kommunistischen Propaganda künstlich erzeugt worden. Die sogenannte Berlin-Krise soll aber nicht nur dazu dienen, allein an dieser Stelle eine Veränderung der Verhältnisse zu Gunsten der einen und zu Ungunsten der anderen Seite zu erzwingen. Berlin soll zugleich als Hebel dienen, um gesamteuropäische und weltpolitische Entwicklungen im Interesse der sowjetischen Politik zu beeinflussen.

Eine gerechte Lösung des Berlin-Problems und der deutschen Frage kann es nur im Sinne des Selbstbestimmungsrechtes der Völker geben. Daher verlangen die Berliner, daß der gegenwärtige Status ihrer Stadt, verbunden mit der Anwesenheit der Schutzmächte, so lange erhalten bleibt, bis sich neue Bedingungen in diesem Sinne ergeben.

Mit dem Blick auf das freie Berlin verbindet sich für ungezählte Menschen jenseits des Eisernen Vorhanges die Hoffnung, einst selbst ein Leben in Freiheit wiederzugewinnen. Freiheit und Sicherheit für Berlin bedeuten daher mehr, als den Schutz eines relativ kleinen Gebietes und seiner 2,2 Millionen Einwohner. In der weltumspannenden politisch-ideologischen Auseinandersetzung unserer Zeit geht es um die entscheidende Frage der gesellschaftlichen und der politischen Ordnung, um die Möglichkeiten der individuellen Lebensgestaltung. Es geht ganz einfach um Freiheit oder Unfreiheit mit allen Konsequenzen. In diesem Ringen der beiden großen Kräftegruppen nimmt Berlin nicht nur geographisch eine Sonderstellung ein. Dieser Stadt fällt vor allem auch die symbolische Bedeutung einer Schlüsselstellung zu. Die geschichtliche Entwicklung in der jüngsten Vergangenheit hat Berlin für die westliche Welt mit dem Begriff der Freiheit identifiziert. Diese Stadt verkörpert die Grundlagen der westlichen Politik.

Noch immer ist die Hauptstadt Deutschlands wie das Land gespalten. Im Ringen um die Freiheit Berlins und um die Wiedervereinigung Deutschlands geht es nicht allein um einen legitimen Anspruch des Deutschen Volkes, sondern um ein gemeinsames Interesse all derer, denen an der Ordnung in Europa zur Sicherung des Friedens in der Welt gelegen ist.

DER EISERNE VORHANG

— hier als willkürliche Grenze zur Bundesrepublik von den Machthabern der sogenannten DDR errichtet —

— durchschneidet Deutschland von Norden nach Süden

HAUPT-
STADT
BERLIN

Das Brandenburger Tor, 1788—1791 durch K. G. LANGHANS errichtet (Quadriga von J. G. SCHADOW)

Schloß Bellevue (1785 unter FRIEDRICH DEM GROSSEN erbaut), der Berliner Amtssitz des Bundespräsidenten

Der Kurfürstendamm mit der Ruine der KAISER-WILHELM-Gedächtnis-Kirche (erbaut von F. SCHWICHTER, 1891—1895)

HAUPT-
STADT
BERLIN

Sommerferien an den Havelseen im Westen von Berlin

Blick von der Siegessäule auf das Hansaviertel

Teilstück der 580 Meter langen „Nordbogenbrücke“ über die Spree für den „Stadtring Berlin der Bundesautobahnen“

Das Rathaus der Stadt Breslau
(14. bis 16. Jahrhundert)

Das Rathaus der Stadt Eßlingen am Neckar
(15. Jahrh.; nach 1586 die Vorderseite aufgestock

Das Rathaus der Stadt Osnabrück (1487—1512)

DIE SOGENANNTE „DEUTSCHE DEMOKRATISCHE REPUBLIK"

I. VON DER SOWJETISCHEN BESATZUNGSZONE ZUM SATELLITENSTATUS

Nach dem Ende des Zweiten Weltkrieges im Jahre 1945 wurde Deutschland durch die vier Siegermächte in Besatzungszonen aufgeteilt. Diese zunächst als vorübergehend gedachte Maßnahme hat infolge der Spannungen zwischen den drei Westmächten und der Sowjetunion zur *Spaltung Deutschlands* geführt.

Im Potsdamer Abkommen von 1945 behandelten die Siegermächte Deutschland noch als Ganzes. Wenig später begann die Verschiedenartigkeit der weltpolitischen Zielsetzungen der in der Kriegskoalition vertretenen Regierungen sich in der Behandlung der deutschen Frage auszuwirken. Der Gegensatz zwischen den drei Westmächten auf der einen und der Sowjetunion auf der anderen Seite führte schließlich zur Spaltung der Welt in zwei sich gegenüberstehende Blöcke. Der beide Seiten trennende

DIE SOGENANNTE DDR

	Fläche	Bevölkerung			Bevölkerungsdichte		
		17. 5. 1939	31. 8. 1950	31. 12. 1958	1939	1950	1958
	qkm[1]	Millionen			Einwohner je qm		
Sogenannte DDR .	107.431	15,2	17,2	16,2	141	160	151
Ost-Berlin	403	1,6	1,2	1,1	3.941	2.951	2.730
Insgesamt	107.834[2]	16,7	18,4	17,3	155	171	160

[1] Gebietsstand vom 1.1.1958. Quelle: Statistisches Bundesamt.

Eiserne Vorhang verläuft durch Deutschland. Die Spaltung Deutschlands ist ein ursächlicher Teil der Ost-West-Spannung, welche die ganze Welt in Unruhe hält. Kein Versuch, den Ost-West-Konflikt zu lösen, kann an der deutschen Frage vorbeigehen. Jede Bemühung um eine solche Entspannung wird als ein Schritt zur Beendigung der Spaltung Deutschlands von den Menschen in der Bundesrepublik und in der sogenannten DDR, der ehemaligen Sowjetischen Besatzungszone Deutschlands, begrüßt. Denn es geht bei der Wiedervereinigung Deutschlands in erster Linie um die *Beendigung der Unfreiheit*, in der siebzehn Millionen Mitteldeutsche durch das kommunistische Regime von Ostberlin gehalten werden.

*

Die Grenzen der 1945 gebildeten Sowjetischen Besatzungszone waren durch Zufälligkeiten bestimmt. Die Ostgrenze wird durch die Gebiete festgelegt, die zur Entschädigung Polens für die Gebietsabtretungen an die Sowjetunion unter polnische Verwaltung gestellt wurden (sogenannte Oder-Neiße-Grenze). Nach Westen sind im wesentlichen die Grenzen der Länder oder Provinzen Mecklenburg, Brandenburg, Sachsen, Anhalt und Thüringen gewählt worden. Dies entsprach den Abmachungen der Konferenz von Jalta, aber nicht der Lage zur Zeit der Einstellung der Kampfhandlungen. Damals waren große Teile der vorgenannten Gebiete von amerikanischen Truppen besetzt. Sie wurden 1945 freiwillig geräumt und den Sowjets übergeben.

BEVÖLKERUNG NACH GEMEINDE-GRÖSSENKLASSEN [1]
Stand am 31. 12. 1957

Gemeinden mit ...Einwohner	% der Bevölkerung
unter 5.000	*41,4*
5.000 – 50.000	*52,2*
50.000 – 100.000	*5,6*
über 100.000	*20,7*

[1] Sogenannte DDR einschließlich Ostberlins.

Quelle: Statistisches Bundesamt.

*

Die Sowjetische Militäradministration (SMA) hatte zur politischen Willensbildung zunächst vier Parteien zugelassen: die Kommunistische Partei Deutschlands (KPD), die Sozialdemokratische Partei Deutschlands (SPD), die Christlich-Demokratische Union (CDU) und die Liberal-Demokratische Partei (LDP). Die SPD durfte jedoch bereits bei den ersten Wahlen keine Listen aufstellen, da sie Ostern 1946 mit der KPD zur *Sozialistischen Einheitspartei Deutschlands* (SED) vereinigt worden war. Außer der SED, CDU und LDP wurden sogenannte „*antifaschistisch-demokratische Massenorganisationen*" wie die Vereinigung der gegenseitigen Bauernhilfe (VdgB), die Freie Deutsche Jugend (FDJ), der Freie Deutsche Gewerkschaftsbund (FDGB), der Demokratische Frauenbund Deutschlands (DFD) und der Kulturbund zur demokratischen Erneuerung Deutschlands zur Listenaufstellung zugelassen.

Die Funktionen innerhalb der Einheitspartei SED wurden zuerst paritätisch besetzt, gingen im Laufe der Zeit aber in steigendem Maße an „linientreue" Kommunisten über. Dadurch glaubten die Sowjets, ihre Ziele auf parlamentarischer Ebene durchsetzen zu können, zumal das politische Gewicht der SED durch die ebenfalls auf ihre „Anregungen" hin ins Leben gerufenen „antifaschistisch-demokratischen Massenorganisationen" vergrößert werden sollte.

Unter dem Vorzeichen „*freier und demokratischer Wahlen*" fanden im September 1946 Gemeindewahlen in der Sowjetzone statt. Während die SED in allen 11.623 Gemeinden zugelassen war, durften die LDP und CDU nur in 1.182 beziehungsweise 2.082 Gemeinden Kandidaten aufstellen. Trotzdem ergab sich ein Ergebnis von nur 52,4% für die SED gegenüber 39,9% für die CDU und LDP zusammen. Die „Massenorganisationen" erhielten nicht einmal 1% der Stimmen.

Für die Wahlpropaganda zu den Land- und Kreistagswahlen am 20. 10. 1946 hatte die Sowjetische Militäradministration beispielsweise 900 t Papier allein für die SED zugeteilt, für die CDU und LDP nur 9 t. Von den 520 gewählten Abgeordneten entfielen auf die SED 249, CDU 133, LDP 122. Die VdgB mit 15 Sitzen und der Kulturbund mit einem Sitz ergänzten das Wahlergebnis zugunsten der SED auf 50,96% gegen 49,04% für CDU und LDP zusammen.

Nach diesen Wahlen erkannte die SED, daß es ihr mit Hilfe auch scheinbar ordnungsgemäßer Wahlen nicht möglich sein würde, die erforderliche parlamentarische Mehrheit zur Durchführung ihrer Deutschlandpolitik zu erlangen. So wurde auf außerparlamentarischem Wege die sogenannte *Volkskongreßbewegung* inszeniert. Jede legale politische Opposition gegen die SED wurde gewaltsam ausgeschaltet. Dem ersten Volkskongreß am 6./7.12. 1947 folgte der zweite am 17./18. 3. 1948, der sich selbst zu einem „Deutschen Volksrat" erklärte und auf Befehl Moskaus den Entwurf für eine „*gesamtdeutsche Verfassung*" ausarbeitete. Der dritte Volkskongreß fand am 15./16. 9. 1949 statt.

Am 5. 10. 1949 bildete der „Deutsche Volksrat" auf Weisung der Sowjetischen Militäradministration sich zu einer „Provisorischen Volkskammer" um, die eine „Provisorische Regierung" mit OTTO GROTEWOHL (SED) *als Ministerpräsidenten* und dem Generalsekretär der SED, WALTER ULBRICHT, *als stellvertretendem Ministerpräsidenten* ernannte. Auf dem gleichen „demokratischen" Wege wurde aus den Landtagen und Länderregierungen die „Provisorische Länderkammer" mit vierunddreißig Vertretern gebildet. Beide Kammern bestellten den SED-Vorsitzenden WILHELM PIECK *zum „Staatspräsidenten"*. Diesen kommunistisch beherrschten „Volksvertretungen" übertrug die Sowjetische Militäradministration formal die bisher von ihr ausgeübten Gesetzgebungs- und Verwaltungsfunktionen.

Mit General TSCHUIKOW und seinem politischen Berater SEMJONOW an der Spitze wurde die *Sowjetische Kontroll-Kommission* (SKK) die Nachfolgerin der Sowjetischen Militäradministration. Moskau entsandte außerdem Botschafter

PUSCHKIN als „Chef der Diplomatischen Mission der UdSSR" nach Berlin, um den von Moskau eingesetzten Staat äußerlich als souverän darzustellen. Mit einem Telegramm STALINS vom 13.10.1949 wurde die von der Volkskammer verabschiedete Verfassung der sogenannten *„Deutschen Demokratischen Republik"* sanktioniert.

Auf Grund eines Abkommens zwischen der Sowjetunion und der Regierung der sogenannten DDR vom August 1953 wurden die diplomatischen Vertretungen der sogenannten DDR und der Staaten des Ostblocks gegenseitig zu Botschaften beziehungsweise Gesandtschaften erhoben. Demzufolge wurde der Hohe Kommissar SEMJONOW im September zum Botschafter der Sowjetunion in der sogenannten DDR ernannt.

Am 27.3.1954 beschloß der Ministerrat der sogenannten DDR eine Erklärung über die Herstellung der *Souveränität der sogenannten DDR*, in der er eine entsprechende Erklärung der Sowjetregierung vom 25.3.1954 bestätigte und sich zu den Verpflichtungen aus dem Potsdamer Abkommen sowie aus dem Aufenthalt sowjetischer Truppen in der sogenannten DDR bekannte.

Die Sowjetregierung verkündete am 6.8.1954 die Aufhebung aller seit 1945 seitens der sowjetischen Besatzungsmacht erlassenen Anordnungen und Befehle und erklärte sich zur Einhaltung der Verpflichtungen bereit, die sich aus dem Potsdamer Abkommen der Vier Mächte ergeben.

Die am 17.10.1954 abgehaltenen Scheinwahlen zur Volkskammer und zu den Bezirkstagen ergaben bei fast überall erzwungener offener Stimmenabgabe nach Bekanntgabe der Regierung 99,46% Ja-Stimmen zur Einheitsliste der durch die SED gelenkten „Nationalen Front".

Auch die am 16.11.1958 abgehaltenen Wahlen zur Volkskammer und zu den Bezirkstagen unterschieden sich in nichts von den voraufgegangenen. Für den Wahlvorschlag der von der SED gelenkten „Nationalen Front" stimmten bei einer Wahlbeteiligung von rund 98% nach Angaben der Machthaber 99,8% der Wähler.

*

Der „17. Juni"

Die wahre Einstellung der mitteldeutschen Bevölkerung zur Regierung der sogenannten „Deutschen Demokratischen Republik" zeigte sich am 17.6.1953, als lediglich der Einsatz der sowjetischen Militärmacht das kommunistische Regime vor seiner Beseitigung durch die aufständischen Massen rettete. Noch wenige Tage vorher hatte die SED sich genötigt gesehen, einen „Neuen Kurs" zu erklären, um der bis zum Siedepunkt gelangten Mißstimmung in der Bevölkerung Herr zu werden. Als jedoch am 16.6.1953 die Bauarbeiter Ostberlins wegen der heraufgesetzten Normen einen Demonstrationsmarsch wagten, stellte die Ostberliner Bevölkerung sich sogleich auf ihre Seite. Am folgenden Tage bewies der Aufstand in 350 Städten und Orten Mitteldeutschlands, daß alle taktischen Winkelzüge der herrschenden „Sozialistischen Einheitspartei" als Stimmungsmanöver durchschaut waren. Die achtjährige Diktatur hatte die Diktatoren als unglaubwürdig entlarvt (siehe oben Seite 136).

Trotzdem gab die SED nach dem Aufstand vor, die Volkserhebung sei das Werk amerikanischer Agenten und faschistischer Provokateure gewesen.

Die seit der Verkündung des „*Neuen Kurses*" getroffenen Maßnahmen wurden vom Zentralkomitee auf seiner fünfzehnten Tagung im Juli 1953 als „erste Schritte auf dem Wege der Verwirklichung des neuen Kurses der Partei und der Regierung, der eine für die Dauer geltende politische Linie der Partei ist", ausgegeben. Als wesentlicher Bestandteil des „Neuen Kurses" täuschte die SED die Aufgabe des Produktionsmittel-Primats zugunsten der gesteigerten Produktion von Konsumgütern vor. Im Juni 1955 erklärte der Parteisekretär ULBRICHT jedoch auf der 24. Tagung des Zentralkomitees: „Manche von Euch werden sich wundern, daß ich die Bezeichnung ‚Neuer Kurs' nicht gebrauche. Die Bezeichnung der Korrekturen, die wir auf einigen Gebieten im Herbst 1953 vorgenommen haben, als ‚Neuer Kurs' hat einige Genossen veranlaßt, falsche Theorien über die vorrangige Entwicklung der Konsumgüterindustrie zu verbreiten. Wir haben damals einige ökonomische Überspitzungen korrigiert." Der „Neue Kurs" sollte also nur als Werbeslogan die Massen vom Aufbegehren gegen das Pankower Regime abhalten. Als die SED mit Hilfe der Besatzungsmacht wieder fest im Sattel saß, nahm sie auf allen Gebieten die Zügel von neuem fest in die Hand. Der „*Aufbau des Sozialismus*", das heißt die Erweiterung der staatskapitalistischen Wirtschaft, und die „*Festigung der Arbeiter- und Bauernmacht*", das heißt die weitere Durchdringung des gesamten öffentlichen Lebens mit kommunistischen Kadern, blieben weiterhin Hauptziele der SED.

*

In ihrer völligen außenpolitischen Abhängigkeit von der Sowjetunion, in ihrer unerschütterten Ergebenheit gegenüber der KPdSU und in ihrer unverändert streng bolschewistischen Innenpolitik ist die SED im Unterschied zu den kommunistischen Parteien anderer Satellitenstaaten nach wie vor ein Bannerträger des Stalinismus. Der „Neue Kurs" des Jahres 1953 hatte den im Sommer 1952 verkündeten „Aufbau des Sozialismus" (eine Phase stärker ausgeprägter „Diktatur des Proletariats") nur kurz unterbrochen. Das Jahr 1957/58 brachte eine weitere Verschärfung der innenpolitischen Situation: eine rasch voranschreitende Kollektivierung der Landwirtschaft, die Wiederherstellung der absoluten Vorherrschaft der SED auf allen Gebieten des kulturellen Lebens, die Verschärfung des Kirchenkampfes und vor allem die Isolierung der mitteldeutschen Bevölkerung von der Bundesrepublik. Auf dem Fünften Parteitag der SED im Juli 1958 wurde eine neue Entwicklungsphase des Bolschewisierungsprozesses verkündet: „*Die Vollendung des Sozialismus in der DDR.*"

Die Aufrüstung in der sogenannten DDR

Bereits 1948 setzte auf Anordnung der sowjetischen Besatzungsmacht in Mitteldeutschland die Aufrüstung ein. Unter der Bezeichnung von Polizeitruppen wurden bewaffnete Formationen aufgestellt, aus deren Ausbildung und Organisation auf außerpolizeiliche, militärische Verwendungsmöglichkeiten geschlossen werden konnte. Diese sogenannten „Grenzpolizeibereitschaften" wurden 1952 in „Kasernierte Volkspolizei" (KVP) umbenannt. Diese gliederte sich in Verbände des Heeres, der Luftwaffe und der Marine. Mitte 1957 hatte sie eine Gesamtstärke von rund 120.000 Mann. Die militärische Ausbildung dieser Truppen ist von einer ausgesprochen politisch-ideologischen Schulung durchdrungen. Ihr liegt die Erziehung zum Haß zugrunde, wie sie in einem Aufsatz der Halbmonatszeitschrift der politischen Verwaltung der KVP zum Ausdruck kommt:

„Die Angehörigen der Volkspolizei sind durchdrungen vom Haß gegen die amerikanischen, englischen und französischen Imperialisten, die die Bevölkerung der doppelten Versklavung unterwerfen wollen . . . Sie sind erfüllt von unverbrüchlicher Freundschaft zur Sowjetunion und ihrer Armee, unserer Befreierin."

Dennoch sind die Truppenteile durchaus nicht als politisch völlig zuverlässig zu betrachten.

Die unverhüllte Aufrüstung erhielt mit einer Änderung der Verfassung im Herbst 1955 ihre formale Grundlage. Im Januar 1956 wurde die KVP in „*Nationale Volksarmee*" (NVA) umbenannt. Sie ist, dem Warschauer Vertrag gemäß, dem gemeinsamen Oberkommando der Ostblockstaaten unterstellt. Die bis dahin ausschließlich khakifarbenen Uniformen der KVP wurden bewußt denjenigen der alten deutschen Wehrmacht angeglichen. Dadurch trachtet die SED auch nach außen hin die deutsche Wehrtradition für sich in Anspruch zu nehmen. Die NVA blieb bei einer Stärke von zwei Panzer- und fünf Infanteriedivisionen, erweiterte also nicht den Rahmen der vormaligen KVP.

In der sogenannten DDR besteht keine allgemeine Wehrpflicht. Ihre Einführung erscheint aus vielerlei Gründen ebenso unmöglich wie eine weitere wesentliche Verstärkung der bewaffneten Streitkräfte. Sowohl wegen des Mangels an Arbeitskräften als auch aus politischen Gründen wird die sogenannte DDR auf absehbare Zeit keine Veränderungen vornehmen können. Die Mittel des Systems, sich genügend „Freiwillige" für ihre militärischen Verbände zu erpressen, reichen bislang aus.

Neben den erklärtermaßen militärischen Verbänden bestehen in der sogenannten DDR jedoch noch verschiedene Polizeiformationen. Mit rund 46.000 Mann Grenzpolizei, 8.500 Mann Transportpolizei und 30.500 Mann Bereitschaftspolizei (unter anderem die ehemaligen Wacheinheiten des Staats-Sicherheits-Dienstes), also insgesamt 85.000 Mann, ergänzen sie die Volksarmee wesentlich. Diese Verbände und die NVA haben mindestens 50.000 nach 1946 ausgebildete Reservisten.

Die militante Form des sogenannten Arbeiter- und Bauernstaates kommt jedoch ganz besonders in den militärähnlichen Verbänden und in der vormilitärischen Erziehung der einzig zugelassenen Jugendorganisation, der Freien Deutschen Jugend (FDJ), zum Ausdruck. Nach dem Volksaufstand im Juni 1953 wurden sogenannte „*Kampfgruppen*" der SED ins Leben gerufen. Sie sind vornehmlich aus SED-Mitgliedern der Belegschaften großer Betriebe, der Universitäten, Verwaltungen und Maschinentraktoren-Stationen aufgestellt, angeblich zum Schutz der Betriebe vor „westlichen Agenten, Provokateuren und Saboteuren". Ihre Stärke beträgt nominell etwa 300.000 Mann; ihre militärische Ausbildung obliegt jetzt zum Teil der NVA.

Seit 1952 gehört zum Dienst der FDJ, der Staatsjugendorganisation, die Ausbildung an Waffen. Mit Gewehren ausgerüstete Marschformationen der FDJ, Mädchen genau wie Jungen, gehören seitdem zu den normalen Bildern des mitteldeutschen Alltags. Um auch ältere Jahrgänge und sportbegeisterte Menschen einer vormilitärischen Ausbildung zu unterziehen, wurde 1952 die „*Gesellschaft für Sport und Technik*" durch eine Regierungsverordnung gegründet. In ihr werden Erwachsene und Jugendliche im Segelfliegen, Fallschirmspringen, im Gelände-, Motor- und Wassersport und in der Nachrichtentechnik ausgebildet. Diese Organisation zählt etwa 625.000 Mitglieder.

Der ständige Einfluß der politisch-ideologischen Schulung in allen militärischen und paramilitärischen Verbänden darf nicht unterschätzt werden.

Dennoch straft die ungebrochene Haltung der mitteldeutschen Bevölkerung und die Tatsache der hohen Fluchtziffern von Jugendlichen und Angehörigen der bewaffneten Verbände die Propaganda der SED Lügen, die unaufhörlich von der begeisterten Bereitschaft zur Verteidigung der „Errungenschaften der DDR" spricht.

II. MITTELDEUTSCHE WIRTSCHAFT – HEUTE

Die wirtschaftliche Entwicklung in der sogenannten DDR verlief nach Kriegsende völlig unterschiedlich zu der in der Bundesrepublik. Diese Entwicklung wurde entscheidend beeinflußt

- durch die im Vergleich zur Bundesrepublik weitaus umfangreicheren Demontagen in der Industrie und an Verkehrseinrichtungen;
- durch die sehr erheblichen Reparationsentnahmen aus der laufenden Produktion durch die Sowjetunion, die sich über einen Zeitraum von acht Jahren erstreckten;
- durch die sehr weitgehenden Enteignungs- und Verstaatlichungsmaßnahmen der neuen Machthaber in der Industrie, im Handel und im Verkehr sowie durch die Inangriffnahme der Kollektivierung der Landwirtschaft;
- durch Einführung eines Systems totaler staatlicher Wirtschaftsplanung und Wirtschaftslenkung;
- durch die Spaltung des vorher einheitlichen deutschen Wirtschaftskörpers.

Es wurde nicht etwa versucht, die als Kriegsfolge von den neuen Machthabern vorgefundene ungünstige Ausgangsposition für einen Neuanfang durch engen wirtschaftlichen Kontakt zu dem abgetrennten westlichen Teil Deutschlands auszugleichen. Vielmehr verfolgten die von Kommunisten beherrschten Behörden der sogenannten DDR in Übereinstimmung mit der Sowjetischen Besatzungsmacht eine Politik, welche die Aufrechterhaltung auch der wirtschaftlichen Spaltung Deutschlands zum Ziele hatte. Ihre gänzliche Hinwendung zu den politischen und wirtschaftspolitischen Grundsätzen der Sowjetunion liefert dafür immer neue Beweise.

Die Umstellung der mitteldeutschen Wirtschaft auf die Interessen der Sowjetunion begann sogleich nach Kriegsende. Die durch rigorose Demontagen und Entnahmen aus der laufenden Produktion gekennzeichnete sowjetische Besatzungspolitik wurde von den kommunistischen Machthabern im östlichen Teil Deutschlands nicht nur widerspruchslos hingenommen, sondern auch aktiv gefördert. Bereits in den Jahren vom Kriegsende (1945) bis 1950 wurde die mitteldeutsche Industrieproduktion weitgehend auf die Lieferanforderungen der Sowjetunion ausgerichtet. Die Umstellung der mitteldeutschen Wirtschaft auf sowjetische Interessen wurde durch die Ziele des für die Jahre 1951 bis 1955 aufgestellten Ersten Fünfjahrplans weiter vorangetrieben.

Neben der Ausweitung der Produktion in allen Industriezweigen gehörte es zu den Hauptzielen in dieser Planperiode, durch den Aufbau eigener Grundstoffindustrien und eines produktionsstarken Schwermaschinenbaus die nach der Beendigung der sowjetischen Demontagen und der Spaltung Deutschlands evident gewordenen strukturellen Mißverhältnisse zu überwinden. In dieser Zielsetzung kam unmißverständlich zum Ausdruck, daß die kommunistischen Machthaber in Mitteldeutschland ihre Politik des Ausscherens aus der gesamtdeutschen Wirtschaftsverflechtung fortzusetzen gewillt waren, und daß sie weiterhin die auf lange Sicht berechnete wirtschaftliche Verselbständigung des von ihnen beherrschten deutschen Gebietes gegenüber der westdeutschen Wirtschaft anstrebten. Die für ihre Wirtschaft erforderliche Komplettierung von außen suchen sie nicht bei ihren Landsleuten, sondern im östlichen Ausland.

Die Produktionsziele des Ersten Fünfjahrplans sind nicht in allen Bereichen erfüllt worden, obwohl amtlich bekanntgegeben wurde, daß die industrielle Bruttoproduktion zwischen 1950 und 1955 auf mehr als das Doppelte angestiegen sei. Nicht erreicht wurden die Planziele in den wichtigsten Bereichen der Grundstofferzeugung: bei Braunkohle, Eisenerz, Walzstahl, Elektroenergie, Soda, Ätznatron und Kalziumkarbid. Die Grundstofferzeugung, die sich verdoppeln sollte, stieg planwidrig nur um 79% an. Damit wurde ein wesentliches Ziel des Ersten Fünfjahrplans, nämlich die Beseitigung des Mißverhältnisses der Produktion zwischen der Grundstoff- und der Verarbeitungsindustrie, nicht erreicht. Diese Planziele im Grundstoffbereich gingen offensichtlich über das Leistungsvermögen der noch unter den Nachwirkungen der sowjetischen Besatzungspolitik leidenden Wirtschaft Mitteldeutschlands hinaus.

Diese Erkenntnis mag ausschlaggebend dafür gewesen sein, daß in den Planzielen des für die Jahre 1956 bis 1960 aufgestellten Zweiten Fünfjahrplans gewisse Änderungen in der Grundkonzeption sich als notwendig erwiesen. Auffälligerweise liegen die Steigerungsraten in einigen Bereichen der Grundstoffindustrie bedeutend niedriger als im Bereich der Investitionsgüter: Erzbergbau und Hüttenwesen sollen nur um 26%, dagegen zum

Beispiel der Werkzeugmaschinenbau um 196% gesteigert werden. Im Durchschnitt soll die Grundstofferzeugung um etwa 45%, der Maschinenbau jedoch um 75% ansteigen.

In diesen Planzahlen kommt die Absicht der weiteren wirtschaftlichen Verflechtung mit den Ländern des Sowjetblocks zum Ausdruck. Die in Mitteldeutschland fehlenden Grundstoffe sollen nicht durch weiteren Ausbau entsprechender Produktionskapazitäten, sondern durch Importe, vor allem aus der Sowjetunion, beschafft werden, während der erhöhte Produktionsausstoß im Maschinenbau in großem Umfange für den Export in die Länder des Sowjetblocks bereitgestellt werden soll. Die geplante Industrialisierung in den Ländern des Sowjetblocks soll in erster Linie mit den Maschinenlieferungen aus Mitteldeutschland durchgeführt werden. In der Zunahme der Zusammenarbeit der im sogenannten „Rat für gegenseitige Wirtschaftshilfe" zusammengefaßten Länder des Sowjetblocks zeichnet sich der Beginn einer internationalen Arbeitsteilung zwischen diesen Ländern mit totaler staatlicher Wirtschaftsplanung ab. Das reibungslose Funktionieren dieser Arbeitsteilung dürfte jedoch auch in Zukunft nicht unerheblich durch die zum Teil recht divergierenden Interessen der einzelnen Länder getrübt werden.

Der Außenhandel der sogenannten Deutschen Demokratischen Republik ist seit Jahren überwiegend ostwärts orientiert. Die mitteldeutschen Behörden exportieren nicht nach dem ‚kapitalistischen Ausland", um sich Bezugsmöglichkeiten für Waren offenzuhalten, die auch im Bereich des Sowjetblocks nicht zu haben oder knapp sind, sondern um sich damit auch politische Verbindungen zu schaffen.

DER AUSSENHANDEL[1]
DER SOGENANNTEN DEUTSCHEN DEMOKRATISCHEN REPUBLIK IM JAHRE 1958
Millionen Rubel

	Export		Import	
	Wert	%	Wert	%
Länder des Sowjetblocks . . .	5.788	*76,6*	4.779	*71,2*
davon: Sowjetunion	(3.355	*44,8*)	(2.773	*41,3*)
Westliche Länder	923	*12,2*	1.176	*17,5*
Bundesrepublik (Interzonenhandel)	845	*11,2*	761	*11,3*
Insgesamt	7.556	*100*	6.716	*100*

[1] Einschließlich des Interzonenhandels.

Auch in der Planperiode des Zweiten Fünfjahrplans gilt in der sogenannten DDR — wie in allen kommunistisch beherrschten Ländern — das „ökonomische Gesetz des Produktionsmittelprimats", das heißt der Vorrang der Erzeugung von Grundstoffen und Investitionsgütern. Die bisherige Entwicklung zeigt die nachstehende Tabelle.

DIE PRODUKTIONSSTEIGERUNGEN IN DER SOGENANNTEN DDR
1950 = 100

Jahr	Grundstoffe und metallverarb. Industrie	Konsumgüterindustrie (ohne Lebensmittel)
1951	121	120
1952	143	132
1953	164	142
1954	182	158
1955	197	166
1956	214	170
1957	230	184

Quelle: Statistisches Jahrbuch der DDR, 1957.

Die Versorgung der Bevölkerung mit industriellen Gebrauchsgütern ist entsprechend der verhältnismäßig geringen Steigerung in der Konsumgüterindustrie seit Jahren vernachlässigt.

Der Anteil der *Privatbetriebe* an der gesamten industriellen Bruttoproduktion betrug im Jahre 1955: 14,7%; Ende 1958 nur noch 11,5%.

Hier wird die mit den umfangreichen Enteignungsmaßnahmen ab Sommer 1946 beginnende Tendenz der fortschreitenden „*Sozialisierung*" deutlich. Neben der entschädigungslosen Enteignung dienten steuerliche und strafrechtliche Mittel zur Verwirklichung der klassenkämpferischen Ziele der Wirtschaftspolitik der SED. Allerdings ist die SED sich des Wertes der noch vorhandenen Privatbetriebe für die Produktionsleistung einzelner Wirtschaftszweige bewußt und hält aus wirtschaftlichen Gründen mit einer radikalen Enteignung der restlichen Privatbetriebe zurück. Die gegenwärtig angewandte Methode zur Überführung von Privatbetrieben in Staatseigentum besteht darin, durch staatliche Kapitalbeteiligung oder die Beteiligung von volkseigenen Betrieben an Privatbetrieben die völlige Kontrolle und Lenkung des privaten Wirtschaftssektors herbeizuführen. Die Beteiligung erfolgt in Form einer Kommanditgesellschaft. Dabei wird der ehemalige Privatunternehmer persönlich haftender Gesellschafter und bezieht ein lohnsteuerpflichtiges Gehalt. Gegenüber den übrigen Privatunternehmen werden den neuen Gesellschaften steuerliche Vergünstigungen und bessere Materialversorgung gewährt; sie sind den örtlichen volkseigenen Betrieben gleichgestellt. Auf diese Weise hofft der Staat, die Privatunternehmer von der Flucht in die Bundesrepublik abzuhalten und sich die unternehmerischen Fähigkeiten innerhalb der von Mißerfolgen gekennzeichneten Planwirtschaft

ANTEIL DER PRODUKTION DER PRIVATBETRIEBE AN DER GESAMTPRODUKTION BESTIMMTER INDUSTRIEZWEIGE
%

	1950	1957
Bergbau	1	0
Metallurgie	1	0
Chemie	11	7
Baumaterialien	25	17
Maschinenbau	17	9
Elektrotechnik	13	6
Feinmechanik und Optik	20	9
Holzbe- und -verarbeitung	60	31
Textilindustrie	35	21
Bekleidung, Leder, Schuhe, Rauchwaren	53	34
Zellstoff, Papier, Polygraphie	30	18
Nahrungs- und Genußmittel	33	12

Quelle: Bundesministerium für Gesamtdeutsche Fragen.

zu erhalten. Ende April 1959 hatten von den rund 11.600 privaten Industriebetrieben 6.000 eine staatliche Beteiligung aufgenommen oder beantragt.

*

Der durchschnittliche Nominallohn liegt in der sogenannten DDR um 10%, die reale Kaufkraft mittlerer Einkommen um rund 33% niedriger als in der Bundesrepublik. Dies bedeutet, daß bei den niedrigen Einkommen die Mitarbeit der Frau erforderlich ist.

Erst im Jahre 1958 — also dreizehn Jahre nach Kriegsende — wurde in der sogenannten DDR die Rationierung der Lebensmittel aufgehoben. Die Preise für die hochwertigen Lebensmittel liegen durchweg höher als in der Bundesrepublik.

Die durchschnittliche steuerliche Belastung der mitteldeutschen Bevölkerung wird nicht unerheblich durch die Tatsache beeinflußt, daß auf hundert Personen im arbeitsfähigen Alter im Jahre 1957: 26,8 Personen im rentenfähigen Alter entfielen (Bundesrepublik 1957: 20,1).

*

Die Politik der SED auf dem Gebiet der *Landwirtschaft* war von Anfang an auf die Vernichtung des freien selbständigen Bauerntums gerichtet, das nach LENIN die „Wurzel des Kapitalismus" ist, um damit die Kollektivierung einzuleiten. Die im September 1945 in der Sowjetischen Besatzungszone unter der irreführenden Bezeichnung „Bodenreform" durchgeführte Umwandlung der mitteldeutschen Agrarstruktur nach Sowjetischem Muster war eine eindeutig politische Angelegenheit und hatte den Zweck, das stärkste Element des Widerstandes gegen den Kommunismus, das Bauerntum, zu zerschlagen. Damit sollte ein Landproletariat geschaffen werden, mit dem sich die Ziele des Kommunismus' leichter verwirklichen ließen. Das entschädigungslos enteignete Land von rund 11.600 Gutsbesitzern und Bauern mit mehr als 100 Hektar Besitz wurde dazu benutzt, 210.000 sogenannte Neubauernstellen zu schaffen und eine Landaufbesserung weiterer 80.000 Kleinstbauern vorzunehmen. Die Zerschlagung dieser leistungsfähigen Betriebe in unproduktive Wirtschaften ist bis heute einer der Gründe für die mangelhafte Versorgung der sogenannten DDR mit Lebensmitteln. Der Ende 1948 proklamierte „Klassenkampf auf dem Lande" hatte zum Ergebnis, daß von den früher in Mitteldeutschland existierenden rund 83.000 Betrieben von mehr als zwanzig Hektar Größe nur noch etwa 20.000 vor-

ZUM ERWERB BESTIMMTER LEBENSMITTEL UND BEKLEIDUNGSSTÜCKE ERFORDERLICHE ARBEITSZEIT IN DER SOGENANNTEN DDR UND IN DER BUNDESREPUBLIK[1]

Warenart	Mengen-Einheit	Bundesrepublik	Sogenannte DDR
		Stunden/Minuten	
Roggenbrot	kg	0/22	0/11
Zucker	kg	0/35	0/47
Schweinebauch	kg	2/03	3/22
Rindfleisch (Kochfleisch)	kg	2/20	2/57
Butter	kg	3/19	4/58
Milch	Liter	0/12	0/21
Eier	12 Stck.	1/08	1/57
Kartoffeln	5 kg	1/28	0/18
Herren-Straßenanzug (Kammgarn, Zellwolle)	1 Stck.	58/29	63/42
Damenkleid (Kunstseide)	1 Stck.	12/44	34/16
Herren-Straßenschuhe (Boxcalf)	1 Paar	16/33	42/54
Damen-Straßenschuhe (Boxcalf)	1 Paar	15/08	35/09
Herren-Sporthemd (Popeline)	1 Stck.	6/33	18/16
Damen-Strümpfe (Perlon)	1 Paar	1/36	4/08
Damen-Pullover (langer Ärmel, wollhaltig)	1 Stck.	10/03	20/18

[1] Monatsdurchschnitt, errechnet nach den Netto-Stundenlöhnen, bei einer Arbeitszeit von 45 Wochenstunden für einen Industriearbeiter. Stand: Ende 1958.

Quelle: Bundesministerium für Gesamtdeutsche Fragen.

DIE FORTSCHRITTE DES „SOZIALISTISCHEN SEKTORS" IN DER LANDWIRTSCHAFT
(in Prozenten der gesamten landwirtschaftlichen Nutzfläche)
Stand: Jeweils 15. Juni

Eigentumsform	Einheit	1939	1950	1955	1956	1957	1958
Gesamte landw. Nutzfläche	Mill. ha	6,590	6,528	6,482	6,480	6,465	6,448
	%	100	100	100	100	100	100
Sozialistischer Sektor	%	—	5,7	27,3	30,6	32,9	38,0
davon:							
Volkseigene Güter	%	—	2,7	4,4	4,4	4,6	5,8
Öffentliche landwirtschaftliche Betriebe (ÖLB)	%	—	3,0	4,4	3,6	4,2	2,8
Landwirtschaftliche Produktionsgenossenschaften (LPG)	%	—	—	18,5	22,8	24,1	29,4
Privater Sektor	%	100	94,3	72,7	69,4	67,1	62,0
davon:							
Betriebe bis unter 5 ha	%	9,2	14,6	14,8	14,8	14,8	14,5
Betriebe von 5—20 ha	%	31,8	55,3	44,7	42,7	41,2	37,6
Betriebe von 20—50 ha	%	22,4	20,2	11,9	10,8	10,1	9,0
Betriebe über 50 ha	%	36,6	4,2	1,3	1,1	1,0	0,9

Quelle: Bundesministerium für Gesamtdeutsche Fragen.

handen sind. Ihr Anteil an der Gesamtzahl der landwirtschaftlichen Betriebe in der sogenannten DDR beträgt nur noch 2,6%. Dabei ist die Anzahl der Betriebe in der Größe zwischen 50 und 100 Hektar mit wenig über 900 fast bis zur Bedeutungslosigkeit gesunken.

DIE PREISE AUSGEWÄHLTER LEBENSMITTEL NACH DEM STAND VOM FEBRUAR 1959
(in DM je kg)

Warenart	Sogenannte DDR DM-Ost	Bundesrepublik DM-West
Butter	9,80	7,02
Margarine (Sorte I)	3,00	2,04
Vollmilch (Liter)	0,68	0,43
Schweinefleisch (Kotelett)	8,20	6,13
Rindfleisch (Schmorfleisch)	9,60	5,43
Jagdwurst	6,80	5,81
Eier, Stück	0,32	0,20
Zucker (Raffinade)	1,54	1,24

Quelle: Bundesministerium für Gesamtdeutsche Fragen.

Das endgültige Ziel der Landwirtschaft der SED ist die totale Vernichtung der privaten Bauernwirtschaften und der Aufbau der Kolchoswirtschaft. Die Leistungsschwäche der durch die Bodenreform geschaffenen Kleinbetriebe wurde von der SED ausgenutzt, um die Abhängigkeit der Kleinbauern vom Staat durch die Einrichtung von staatlichen Maschinen-Traktoren-Stationen (MTS) zu erhöhen. Durch Zuweisung nahezu der gesamten Neuproduktion von landwirtschaftlichen Maschinen und Traktoren an die MTS nehmen diese eine entscheidende Vormachtstellung auf dem Lande ein. Mit rund 600 MTS-Stationen und mehr als 2.000 MTS-Stützpunkten ist dieses Kollektivierungs-Instrument ausschlaggebend für die Arbeit in der Landwirtschaft der sogenannten DDR.

Mit der Bildung landwirtschaftlicher Produktionsgenossenschaften seit Juli 1952 ist der eigentliche Kolchosierungsprozeß eingeleitet worden. Durch den Eintritt in die landwirtschaftliche Produktionsgenossenschaft, der auf angeblich freiwilliger Entscheidung beruht, tatsächlich aber meist auf Zwang und Druck hin erfolgt, verliert der Bauer seine Selbständigkeit und wird, obwohl er dem Buchstaben nach weiter Eigentümer seines Grundes und Bodens bleibt, praktisch zum wirtschaftlich und sozial abhängigen Kolchosarbeiter degradiert.

Von 1952 bis Ende Mai 1959 sind auf Grund der allgemeinen Lage in der mitteldeutschen Landwirtschaft fast 127.000 Personen aus der bäuerlichen Bevölkerung der sogenannten DDR in die Bundesrepublik geflohen. Davon waren mehr als 36.000 selbständige Bauern.

DIE DEUTSCHEN OSTGEBIETE UNTER FREMDER VERWALTUNG

Fast ein Viertel des deutschen Staatsgebietes in den Grenzen von 1937 kam am Ende des Zweiten Weltkrieges unter fremde Verwaltung. Auf der Konferenz von Jalta (3.2. bis 11.2.1945) hatten die Alliierten beschlossen, Polen für die durch die Sowjetunion annektierten ostpolnischen Gebiete durch eine Verlegung der polnischen Grenze nach Westen und Norden zu entschädigen, ohne daß Vereinbarungen über den Umfang der von Deutschland abzutrennenden Gebiete getroffen wurden. Nach der Niederwerfung Deutschlands wurden auf der Potsdamer Konferenz (17.7. bis 2.8.1945) die ostwärts der „Oder-Neiße-Linie" gelegenen Gebiete des Deutschen Reiches bis zur endgültigen Regelung durch den Friedensvertrag der polnischen Verwaltung unterstellt. Der nördliche Teil Ostpreußens mit Königsberg wurde — ebenfalls vorbehaltlich der endgültigen Regelung durch den Friedensvertrag — der Sowjetunion zugesprochen.

OSTGEBIETE DES DEUTSCHEN REICHES UNTER FREMDER VERWALTUNG

Verwaltungsbezirk	Hauptstadt	Fläche am 1.1.1943	Einwohner am 17.5.1939[1]
		qkm	Anzahl
Provinz Ostpreußen	Königsberg	36.996	2.488.122
darunter unter polnischer Verwaltung		23.792	1.330.680
Provinz Pommern soweit östlich der Oder-Neiße-Linie	Stettin	31.301	1.895.230
Provinz Mark Brandenburg mit Landkreis Rothenburg (Oberlausitz), soweit östlich der Oder-Neiße-Linie	—	11.627	659.737
Provinz Niederschlesien ohne Landkreis Rothenburg (Oberlausitz), jedoch mit Stadtkreis und Landkreis Zittau, soweit östlich der Oder-Neiße-Linie	Breslau	24.640	3.048.480
Provinz Oberschlesien	—	9.733	1.529.258
Ostgebiete des Deutschen Reiches insgesamt	—	114.296	9.620.827
in % des Deutschen Reiches (Gebietsstand: 31.12.1937)	—	24,3	13,9

[1] Datum der letzten Volkszählung vor dem Zweiten Weltkrieg.

Quelle: Statistisches Bundesamt.

ÜBECK, einst die Königin der niederdeutschen Hansestädte, heute durch den Eisernen Vorhang ihres Hinter-
ınds beraubt: Salzspeicher an der Trave aus dem 16. Jahrhundert und das Holstentor, das 1478 vollendet wurde

lick in die Mengstraße — eine der Straßen um die hoch-
otische Marienkirche (13. bis 14. Jahrhundert), in denen
die Häuser der Patrizierfamilien standen

Das Geburtshaus des Dichters THOMAS MANN
in der Mengstraße

Zunftzeichen des Brauers, Küfers und Böttchers vor der Brauerei Krone (Gebäude von 1486) in Lüneburg

links oben:
Im Kurpark von Bad Pyrmont

Der Rießersee bei Garmisch-Partenkirchen — bekannt durch Rodel- und Bobmeisterschaften

Getreideernte — noch mit dem „Hafermotor“

Strohgedeckter Bauernhof an der Este im Alten Land unweit von Hamburg

Mosellandschaft bei Kinheim (nördlich von Traben-Trarbach)

DIE SOGENANNTE „DEUTSCHE DEMOKRATISCHE REPUBLIK“

Pavillon im Zwinger zu Dresden (1714—1722) von DANIEL PÖPPELMANN

Das alte Rathaus in Leipzig, 1556 vom Bürgermeister HIERONYMUS LOTTER erbaut

Schloß Sanssouci bei Potsdam, 1745—1747 unter FRIEDRICH DEM GROSSEN von GEORG WENZESLAUS VON KNOBELSDORFF erbaut

Als die sowjetischen Truppen in den ersten Monaten des Jahres 1945 die jenseits der Oder und Lausitzer Neiße gelegenen deutschen Ostgebiete besetzten, befanden sich dort noch fast 3,5 Millionen Deutsche. Im Laufe des Sommers 1945 kehrte mehr als eine Million Flüchtlinge in die von Sowjettruppen besetzten Ostgebiete zurück. Die deutsche Bevölkerung zum Zeitpunkt des Potsdamer Abkommens betrug also rund 4,5 Millionen. Der Großteil davon wurde in den Jahren 1945 bis 1947 ausgewiesen.

Den vorrückenden Sowjettruppen waren bereits im Februar 1945 „Bevollmächtigte der polnischen Regierung" in die eroberten deutschen Ostgebiete gefolgt. Diese bereiteten noch vor Abschluß der Kampfhandlungen — und damit bereits einige Monate vor der Potsdamer Konferenz — den Aufbau einer polnischen Verwaltung vor und lösten in den Monaten April und Mai 1945 die sowjetrussischen Militärbehörden ab. Das Gebiet der Freien Stadt Danzig wurde schon am 30.3.1945 in den polnischen Staatsverband einverleibt. Im Sommer 1945 wurden die deutschen Ostgebiete territorial neugegliedert: die neuerrichteten Wojewodschaften decken sich nicht mehr mit den preußischen Provinzen. Ganz offenkundig war angestrebt, die historischen Grenzen und Zusammenhänge in den deutschen Ostgebieten zu verwischen. Dieses Ziel verfolgte auch eine Neugliederung der Verwaltung im Sommer 1950, als die deutschen Ostgebiete auf zehn nach Hauptstädten benannte Wojewodschaften aufgeteilt wurden. Von ihnen bestehen nur noch fünf (Stettin, Köslin, Grünberg, Breslau und Oppeln) ausschließlich aus Gebietsteilen des Deutschen Reiches in den Grenzen von 1937.

DIE NEUGLIEDERUNG DER DEUTSCHEN OSTGEBIETE

Verwaltungsbezirk	Unter fremder Verwaltung
Provinz Ostpreußen	
sowjetisch verwaltet	„Oblast Kaliningrad"
polnisch verwaltet	zu den Wojewodschaften Allenstein, Danzig und Bialystok
Östlicher Teil der Provinz Pommern	zu den Wojewodschaften Stettin und Köslin, Teile zu Posen und Danzig
Östlicher Teil der Provinz Mark Brandenburg	zu den Wojewodschaften Grünberg und Stettin
Provinz Nieder- und Oberschlesien mit den östlichen Teilen des Stadt- und Landkreises Zittau	zu den Wojewodschaften Breslau, Oppeln und Kattowitz

Quelle: Statistisches Bundesamt.

Ungeachtet des vorläufigen Charakters der Übertragung der Verwaltung wurde noch vor der deutschen Kapitulation (Mai 1945) die Bezeichnung „Wiedergewonnene Gebiete" eingeführt. Für sie wurde im Herbst 1945 ein besonderes Ministerium unter Leitung von WLADYSLAW GOMULKA, des Sekretärs der kommunistischen Polnischen Arbeiterpartei, eingerichtet. Ihm unterstand auch das Staatliche Repatriierungsamt, das für die Ausweisung der Deutschen und die Ansiedlung von Polen zuständig war. Am 12.1.1949 wurde das „Gesetz über die Eingliederung der wiedergewonnenen Gebiete in den polnischen Staatsverband" beschlossen, das die Sonderstellung der deutschen Ostgebiete aufhob.

Während die herkömmliche Kreiseinteilung, von regionalen Änderungen abgesehen, für einen Teil der Kreise beibehalten blieb, wurde die ländliche Gemeindeeinteilung bereits 1946 aufgehoben und die untere Verwaltung nach dem in Polen üblichen System der umfassenderen Landgemeinde (*gmina*) aufgebaut. Seit 1950 ist die kommunale Selbstverwaltung an die staatlichen Organe in Form der „Nationalräte" übergegangen.

Zu den ersten umfassenden Maßnahmen der polnischen Verwaltung gehörte die Ausmerzung der deutschen Ortsnamen. Bis 1950 wurden mehr als 30.000 deutsche Orts- und Flurnamen durch polnische Bezeichnungen ersetzt.

*

Mit den Sowjettruppen trafen noch vor dem Waffenstillstand erste Gruppen von Polen in den deutschen Ostgebieten ein, die sich dort eigenmächtig ansiedelten. Im Jahr 1946 setzte eine gelenkte Ansiedlung von „Repatrianten" aus den von der Sowjetunion annektierten ostpolnischen Gebieten (1,9 Millionen) ein, und in den nachfolgenden Jahren wurden in den deutschen Ostgebieten vor allem Umsiedler aus Zentralpolen (3,8 Millionen) und polnische Rückwanderer aus Westeuropa und Übersee (0,1 Millionen) angesiedelt. Besonders infolge der erheblichen, herkunftsmäßig bedingten Unterschiede zwischen diesen Bevölkerungsgruppen ist die angestrebte „Integration" der deutschen Ostgebiete in den polnischen Staats- und Volkskörper noch nicht zustande gekommen. Wenn die jenseits von Oder und Neiße verbliebenen Deutschen und die sogenannten „Autochthonen" (deren Volkstumszugehörigkeit nicht eindeutig zu definieren ist) hinzugerechnet werden, beträgt der Bevölkerungsstand in den deutschen Ostgebieten (1958) etwa 7 Millionen Einwohner gegenüber 9,6 Millionen vor dem Kriege. Dabei ist die im Rahmen der Gesamtplanung des Ostblocks vorgenommene Industrialisierung zu berücksichtigen, die einerseits eine permanente Landflucht bewirkt und andererseits zu einer ständigen Bevölkerungszunahme in den Großstädten, teilweise über den Vorkriegsstand hinaus, geführt hat. Das flache Land weist, allen Bemühungen der staatlichen Werbung zum Trotz, eine erhebliche Unterbesiedlung auf, von der besonders Ostpreußen und Pommern betroffen sind. Hier beträgt die Bevölkerungsdichte teilweise nicht einmal die Hälfte jener der Vorkriegszeit. Auch die kleineren Städte weisen einen beträchtlichen Bevölkerungsschwund auf. Zahlreiche Kleinstädte haben den Stadtcharakter verloren und sind in Dorfgemeinden umgewandelt worden.

BEVÖLKERUNGSSTAND IN DEN STÄDTEN (AUSWAHL)

Name	Fremde Bezeichnung	Einwohner in 1.000	
		17.5.1939	31.12.1957
Breslau	Wrocław	630	396
Stettin	Szczecin	383	244
Hindenburg	Zabrze	126	185
Gleiwitz	Gliwice	117	129
Beuthen	Bytom	101	179
Elbing	Elblacg	86	72
Liegnitz	Legnica	84	53
Waldenburg	Wałbrzych	64	111
Oppeln	Opole	53	57
Allenstein	Olsztyn	50	62
Stolp	Słupsk	50	51
Landsberg (Warthe)	Gorzów Wielkopolski	48	48
Kolberg	Kołobrzeg	37	14
Glogau	Glogów	33	7
Swinemünde	Świnoujście	30	18
Braunsberg	Braniewo	21	15
Arnswalde	Choszczno	13	6
Goldap	Gołdap	14	10
Greifenhagen	Gryfino	17	5

Mit der Ansiedlung polnischer Bevölkerung ging ein tiefgreifender Strukturwandel einher. Er wurde um so bedeutsamer, seitdem Polen mit dem „Aufbau der Volksdemokratie" sich nach dem sowjetischen Modell richtet. Die Kollektivierung der Landwirtschaft und die Errichtung umfangreicher Staatslandwirtschaften haben das Bild des Dorfes und der bäuerlichen Gesellschaft grundlegend geändert. Die Kollektivierung wurde zwar seit dem politischen Umschwung im Herbst 1956 weitgehend aufgehoben;

aber ein gesunder Bauernstand kann sich nicht entwickeln. Beträchtlich ist der auch durch den Mangel an Arbeitskräften bedingte Rückgang der landwirtschaftlichen Produktion gegenüber der Erzeugung in der Vorkriegszeit. Die Hektarerträge liegen noch unter den ohnehin nicht hohen gesamtpolnischen Durchschnittserträgen. An die Stelle des früher in den deutschen Ostgebieten üblichen Fruchtwechsels ist vielerorts die von den polnischen Neusiedlern ausgeübte Bestellungsart des extensiven Dreifelderwechsels (mit Brachland) getreten. Ein besonderes Problem sind die nach der Vertreibung der Deutschen einsetzende Versteppung und Verwaldung des Landes und die starke Zunahme der brachliegenden Flächen. Nach privaten Schätzungen ist die landwirtschaftliche Nutzfläche in den deutschen Ostgebieten um mindestens ein Viertel gegenüber dem Vorkriegsstand zurückgegangen. Aus begreiflichen Gründen gibt es keine amtlichen Angaben über den Umfang der unbewirtschafteten Flächen; jedoch Einzelmitteilungen in der Presse und vor allem die Propaganda für die „Brachland-Aktionen" sind aufschlußreich.

*

Die *Lage der Wirtschaft* war in den einzelnen ostdeutschen Gebieten bei Kriegsende recht unterschiedlich. Nach globalen Angaben waren 40% der Industriebauten und 70% der industriellen Ausrüstung zerstört. Dagegen ist geltend gemacht worden, daß es polnischerseits üblich ist, als Kriegsfolgen auch Schäden zu bezeichnen, die aus dem Verfall in den ersten Nachkriegsjahren stammen. Das an industriellen Anlagen und Kapazitäten reiche Oberschlesien war von Kampfhandlungen wenig berührt worden, und die dort beheimatete deutsche Bevölkerung hatte kaum eine Fluchtmöglichkeit gehabt. Andere Standorte der Industrie (zum Beispiel Breslau, Danzig, Stettin) hingegen waren durch Kriegsereignisse schwer zerstört, weitgehend entvölkert und außerdem durch die von der sowjetischen Besatzungsmacht vorgenommenen Plünderungen, Brandstiftungen und Demontagen beträchtlich in Mitleidenschaft gezogen. In der weiteren Entwicklung wurde der mit dem Ostblock koordinierten Schwerindustrie mit ihren Hauptstandorten in Oberschlesien der Vorrang gegeben. Aus diesem Grund blieben zahlreiche Mittel- und Kleinbetriebe der verarbeitenden Industrie ungenutzt oder vernachlässigt — eine Parallele zur Entwicklung des Städtewesens in den deutschen Ostgebieten unter polnischer Verwaltung.

Die stark ausgebaute Schwerindustrie und die Erzeugung von Produktionsmitteln liegen in verschiedenen Zweigen (Kohle, Hüttenwesen, chemische Industrie, Zement, Energiewirtschaft) über dem Vorkriegsstand, so daß die

Hälfte der polnischen Exportgüter aus den deutschen Ostgebieten stammt (die an sich nur 29% zum gesamten Wert der polnischen Industrieproduktion beisteuern). Nur in geringfügigem Umfang — wie letztlich auch aus diesen Zahlen zu schließen ist — sind die kriegszerstörten oder stillgelegten Anlagen der Leicht- und Konsumgüterindustrie wieder in Gang gesetzt worden. Ihre Benachteiligung bei der Zuweisung staatlicher Investitionen — die gesamte Wirtschaft ist, von einigen kleinen Betrieben abgesehen, verstaatlicht — ist augenfällig.

Ein hervorstechendes Merkmal für die Entwicklung in den deutschen Ostgebieten seit 1945 ist die Vernachlässigung des Wohnungswesens. Obwohl 40% der Häuser in den Städten und 25% der landwirtschaftlichen Gebäude durch die Kriegs- und Nachkriegswirren zerstört worden waren, hat es in den deutschen Ostgebieten unter polnischer Verwaltung keinen nennenswerten Wohnungsbau gegeben. Im Gegenteil, verschiedene Kleinstädte, vor allem in Pommern, wurden im Rahmen von „Ziegel-Aktionen" rücksichtslos für den Wiederaufbau von Warschau ausgeschlachtet. Da es auch an jeder Reparaturtätigkeit des sozialisierten Hausbesitzes fehlt, sind die Gebäude in den Städten und Dörfern dem Verfall preisgegeben.

Eine Fülle deutscher Kulturdenkmäler ist den Kampfhandlungen und den mutwilligen Zerstörungen der Nachkriegszeit zum Opfer gefallen. Insbesondere wurden zahlreiche Schlösser und Adelssitze abgetragen oder in ihrem kriegszerstörten Zustand belassen. Dagegen widmete die polnische Denkmalpflege sich interessiert den Bauwerken der Renaissance und ließ auch zahlreiche Kunstdenkmäler aus dem deutschen Mittelalter wiederherstellen oder doch wenigstens sichern.

In den ersten Nachkriegsjahren war die in den Ostgebieten verbliebene deutsche Bevölkerung schutzlos den täglich wiederkehrenden Übergriffen der Miliz oder einzelner Polen und der systematischen Entrechtung seitens der polnischen Verwaltung ausgesetzt. Als nach Abschluß der Massenausweisungen der Mangel an Arbeitskräften die kommunistischen Planungen beeinträchtigte, änderte sich allmählich die Situation der Deutschen in den Gebieten jenseits von Oder und Neiße — wie in den meisten anderen ostmitteleuropäischen Vertreibungsgebieten —, und die Deutschen erhielten gewisse Rechte wieder. Sie sind jedoch ständig Polonisierungsbestrebungen unterworfen, die sich besonders an die Inhaber polnisch klingender Familiennamen und an die sogenannten „Autochthonen" richten. Seit 1949 dürfen Ehen zwischen Deutschen und Polen geschlossen werden. Seit 1951 besitzen alle in den Ostgebieten verbliebenen Deutschen die Möglichkeit, ohne besondere Voraussetzungen die polnische Staatsangehörigkeit zu erwerben. Seit 1950 wurden etwa 100 deutsche Schulen in Pommern, Ostbrandenburg und Schlesien eingerichtet. Eine ganze Reihe von ihnen wurde jedoch in jüngster Zeit wieder geschlossen. Das deutschsprachige Schulwesen und die bis 1958 in Breslau erscheinende Tageszeitung „Arbeiterstimme" sind nicht Einrichtungen der deutschen Volksgruppe, sondern stehen als Werkzeuge der Regierung vorwiegend im Dienste polnischer Kulturpolitik und kommunistischer Propaganda. Deutsches Kulturleben organisierte sich in der „Deutschen sozial-kulturellen Gesellschaft".

*

Der nördliche Teil Ostpreußens nimmt unter den deutschen Ostgebieten eine Sonderstellung ein. Im Potsdamer Abkommen vom 2. 8. 1945 hatten die Alliierten vereinbart, daß die Westgrenze der UdSSR „vorbehaltlich der endgültigen Bestimmung der territorialen Fragen bei der Friedensregelung" in Ostpreußen auf der Linie nördlich Braunsberg-Goldap verlaufen sollte. Ohne Rücksicht auf den provisorischen Charakter dieser Absprache gliederte die Sowjetunion das ihr zugesprochene Gebiet als „Oblast Kaliningrad" in die Russische Sozialistische Föderative Sowjetrepublik ein und machte es somit zu einem Bestandteil der UdSSR. Das Memelland wurde von Ostpreußen abgetrennt und der Litauischen Unionsrepublik zugeschlagen. Die im Memelland noch ansässige deutsche Bevölkerung erhielt 1948 die sowjetische Staatsangehörigkeit. Damit wurde sie von der Aussiedlung ausgeschlossen, die in den Jahren 1947 bis 1949 die gesamte deutsche Bevölkerung im nördlichen Ostpreußen bis auf winzige Reste erfaßte. Die russische Bevölkerung beträgt etwa 600.000 Menschen (gegenüber 1,1 Millionen Deutschen in der Vorkriegszeit) und besteht vorwiegend aus Umsiedlern aus den nord- und zentralrussischen Gebieten. Verwaltung, Landwirtschaft und Industrie sind ausschließlich nach sowjetischem Muster organisiert. Das hermetisch von dem südlichen Teil Ostpreußens abgeschlossene Gebiet hat für die UdSSR vor allem eine militärische Bedeutung. Der Wiederaufbau des von schweren Kriegs- und Demontageschäden getroffenen Landes steht dahinter zurück. Im internationalen Handelsverkehr hat der Königsberger Hafen seine traditionelle Funktion verloren.

*

* *

Die Bundesrepublik Deutschland vertritt die Auffassung, daß die Frage der deutschen Ostgrenze nur in einem Friedensvertrag mit der legitimierten gesamtdeutschen Regierung geregelt werden kann, und daß für den völkerrechtlichen Gebietsstand Deutschlands die Grenzen des Deutschen Reiches am 31.12.1937 maßgeblich sind. Sie geht davon aus, daß die Frage der deutschen Ostgebiete bisher durch keinen für Deutschland verbindlichen Akt geregelt ist. Der zwischen den Behörden der sogenannten DDR und Polen abgeschlossene Grenzvertrag vom 6.7.1950 wird als ungültig angesehen, da das Regime der sogenannten DDR keine Legitimation besitzt, Fragen zu regeln, die Gesamtdeutschland angehen. Die Westmächte betonten anläßlich der erwähnten Vereinbarungen zwischen der sogenannten DDR und Polen sowie im Notenwechsel des Jahres 1952, daß auf der Potsdamer Konferenz die endgültige Festlegung der deutschen Grenzen ausdrücklich dem künftigen Friedensvertrag vorbehalten worden sei.

Die Politik der Bundesregierung macht das Prinzip des Selbstbestimmungsrechtes der Nationen geltend und tritt für das Recht auf Heimat ein. Gleichzeitig jedoch geht sie davon aus, daß eine Lösung der Frage der deutschen Ostgebiete nur auf dem Verhandlungswege denkbar ist. Sie weiß sich dabei einig mit den Vertriebenen, die in der ,,Charta der deutschen Heimatvertriebenen" vom 5.8.1950 den *Verzicht auf Rache und Vergeltung* als ihr ,,Grundgesetz und als unumgängliche Voraussetzung für die Herbeiführung eines freien und geeinten Europas" proklamiert haben.

POLITIK

DIE AUSSENPOLITIK DER BUNDESREGIERUNG

EIN ÜBERBLICK ÜBER WEGSTRECKEN UND ZIELE

I. VOM BESATZUNGSSTATUT ZUR SOUVERÄNITÄT (1949 BIS 1955)

A. DIE BEMÜHUNGEN UM DEN ALLMÄHLICHEN ABBAU DES BESATZUNGSSTATUTS (1949 BIS 1951)

1. Bei Amtsübernahme der Bundesregierung im September 1949 war das auf Grund der Washingtoner Beschlüsse vom April 1949 erlassene *Besatzungsstatut* in vollem Umfang in Kraft. Dies bedeutete für die Bundesrepublik:
   - völkerrechtliche Handlungsunfähigkeit;
   - keine diplomatischen oder konsularischen Beziehungen zu fremden Staaten;
   - keine Mitgliedschaft in internationalen Organisationen;
   - Bevormundung durch die Besatzungsmächte auf innenpolitischem Gebiet;
   - Überwachung der innerdeutschen Verwaltung;
   - Vetorecht der Alliierten gegenüber der deutschen Gesetzgebung;
   - schärfste Kontrolle der deutschen Wirtschaft, insbesondere der Produktion, der Währung und der Forschung:
     - Verbot beziehungsweise Beschränkung wichtigster Industriezweige (Schiffahrt, Maschinenbau, chemische Industrie, Beschränkung der Stahlproduktion auf 5,6 Millionen Tonnen pro Jahr), Demontage nicht nur der kriegsindustriellen Werke, sondern auch des sogenannten „überflüssigen Potentials";
   - Generalklausel der Alliierten, die zur Zurücknahme sämtlicher an deutsche Instanzen abgetretene Rechten berechtigte.
2. Diese Fesseln werden erstmalig durch das von dem Bundeskanzler mit den drei Alliierten Hohen Kommissaren am 22. 11. 1949 geschlossene *Petersberger Abkommen* gelockert.
   Einzelergebnisse:
   - Rettung wesentlicher Industriezweige vor der Demontage (August-Thyssen-Hütte, Borsig Werke Berlin, Teile von Salzgitter usw.);
   - Genehmigung konsularischer Beziehungen zum Ausland;

Berechtigung zur Mitarbeit in internationalen Organisationen;
Ankündigung vorbereitender Arbeiten zur Beendigung des Kriegszustandes.

Als Gegenleistung für diese Konzessionen:
Beitritt der Bundesrepublik zum *Ruhrstatut.*

3. Durch die *New Yorker Konferenz* im September 1950 erfährt das Besatzungsregime in den folgenden Monaten eine erneute Auflockerung.
Einzelergebnisse:
Anerkennung des alleinigen Rechtes der Bundesregierung, für das gesamte Deutschland zu sprechen;
Recht zur Errichtung diplomatischer Vertretungen im Ausland;
Genehmigung zur Errichtung von Bereitschaftspolizeien der Länder;
grundsätzliche Anerkennung des Bedürfnisses der Bundesrepublik nach Sicherheit durch Gewährung einer Sicherheitsgarantie für das Bundesgebiet und die Westsektoren Berlins und die Zusage der Verstärkung der alliierten Sicherheitstruppen;
Beschleunigung der Arbeiten zur Beendigung des Kriegszustandes;
Erleichterungen auf dem Gebiet der wissenschaftlichen Forschung;
große wirtschaftliche Erleichterungen:
Aufhebung der Beschränkungen auf dem Gebiet des Schiffbaus und der Schiffahrt;
Zulassung der Produktion von künstlichem Gummi und synthetischem Benzin;
Erleichterung auf allen Gebieten der chemischen Produktion.
Am 6. 3. 1951 tritt ein *revidiertes Besatzungsstatut* in Kraft.
(Die weitere Entwicklung siehe I. C 1. und 2.)

B. BEGINN DER EINGLIEDERUNG DER BUNDESREPUBLIK DEUTSCHLAND IN DIE FREIE WELT

1. Nach Entstehung der Bundesrepublik war es eine der dringlichsten Aufgaben der Regierung, Deutschland aus der Isolierung herauszuführen, in die es durch das nationalsozialistische Regime und den Krieg geraten war. Zur Anknüpfung normaler internationaler Beziehungen wird der *Wiederaufbau des Auswärtigen Dienstes* mit besonderer Dringlichkeit in Angriff genommen.

Zeitplan:

Bereits das Petersberger Abkommen vom 22. 11. 1949 ermöglicht der Bundesrepublik die Errichtung konsularischer Vertretungen im Ausland.

Im November 1949 werden im Amtsbereich des Bundeskanzleramts die „Verbindungsstelle zur Alliierten Hohen Kommission (AHK)" und das „Organisationsbüro für konsularische und wirtschaftliche Vertretungen im Ausland" gebildet.

Im Juni 1950 wird die „Dienststelle für Auswärtige Angelegenheiten" im Bundeskanzleramt, welche die Verbindungsstelle zur AHK und das Organisationsbüro zusammenfaßt, geschaffen.

Die im September 1950 auf der NewYorker Konferenz eingeleitete Revision des Besatzungsstatuts sieht das Recht zur Errichtung diplomatischer Vertretungen im Ausland vor.

Am 16. 3. 1951 wird die „Dienststelle für Auswärtige Angelegenheiten" in ein selbständiges Ministerium, das „Auswärtige Amt", umgewandelt. Bundeskanzler Dr. ADENAUER übernimmt gleichzeitig das Amt des Bundesministers des Auswärtigen (bis 7. 6. 1955).

Am 22. 5. 1950 wird das Generalkonsulat London als erste Auslandsvertretung der Bundesrepublik eröffnet. Anschließend wird der Ausbau der Auslandsvertretungen rasch fortgesetzt. Er erreicht bis 1. 6. 1959 folgenden Stand:

Botschaften	57
Gesandtschaften	10
Handelsvertretung (Helsinki)	1
Sonstige Vertretungen (Vereinte Nationen, Europarat, OEEC, NATO, EWG und EAG sowie Genf)	6
Generalkonsulate	33
Konsulate	56
Wahlkonsulate	149
Wahl-Vizekonzulate	8

Übersicht über die Vertretungen der Bundesrepublik im Ausland siehe unten III. A.

2. Durch die Lockerung der alliierten Bestimmungen über die auswärtigen Beziehungen der Bundesrepublik ist es der Bundesregierung möglich, innerhalb der *europäischen Organisationen* und auf Konferenzen aktiv am europäischen Einigungswerk mitzuwirken.

Zeitplan:

Am 25. 10. 1949 tritt die Bundesrepublik der OEEC (*Organisation für europäische wirtschaftliche Zusammenarbeit*) bei;

am 13. 7. 1950 wird die Bundesrepublik assoziiertes Mitglied des *Europarats* in Straßburg. Am 2. 5. 1951 erfolgt ihre Anerkennung als Vollmitglied;

am 18. 4. 1951 wird der Vertrag über die Gründung einer *Europäischen Gemeinschaft für Kohle und Stahl*, der Deutschland, Frankreich, Italien,

Belgien, die Niederlande und Luxemburg angehören, in Paris unterzeichnet. Damit ist erstmalig eine europäische überstaatliche Gemeinschaft geschaffen.

Hauptaufgaben der „Montan-Gemeinschaft":

Schaffung eines Gemeinsamen Marktes für Kohle und Stahl unter Beseitigung aller Zölle, aller mengenmäßigen Beschränkungen und aller diskriminierenden Maßnahmen hinsichtlich der Preise und Lieferungsbedingungen, ferner Sicherung einer geordneten Versorgung der Mitgliedstaaten mit Kohle und Stahl;

Hebung des allgemeinen Lebensstandards durch Produktionserweiterung.

Seit März 1952 ist die Bundesrepublik in Paris an den Arbeiten zur Schaffung eines *Gemeinsamen Europäischen Agrarmarktes* beteiligt. Diese Arbeiten werden seit dem 6. 3. 1955 im Rahmen der OEEC weitergeführt.

Am 27. 5. 1952 unterzeichnet der Bundeskanzler in Paris den Vertrag über die Gründung der *Europäischen Verteidigungsgemeinschaft* (EVG), deren Mitgliedstaaten die sechs Mitglieder der Montan-Gemeinschaft sein sollen.

Die Bundesrepublik ist Mitglied der *Europäischen Verkehrsminister-Konferenz* seit deren Gründung am 17. 10. 1953.

Unter deutscher Mitarbeit entsteht in den Jahren 1951 und 1952 in einer von den Staaten der Montan-Gemeinschaft beschickten *ad hoc*-Versammlung der Verfassungsentwurf einer *Europäischen Politischen Gemeinschaft*, die, aufbauend auf den Verträgen über die Gründung einer Montangemeinschaft und über die Gründung einer Europäischen Verteidigungsgemeinschaft, den Weg zu einer möglichst umfassenden europäischen Gemeinschaft ebnen soll (Fortgang siehe II. C).

3. Die Bundesregierung bemüht sich besonders um die Regelung der Fragen der *Wiedergutmachung* und der *Schuldenregelung*.

a) Am 27. 9. 1951 erklärt der Bundeskanzler vor dem Bundestag die Bereitschaft der Regierung, das von dem Naziregime begangene Unrecht an den Juden in Form materieller Hilfe im Rahmen des Möglichen wiedergutzumachen.

Am 21. 3. 1952 beginnen in Den Haag Wiedergutmachungs-Verhandlungen mit Vertretern des Staates Israel und der Conference on Jewish Material Claims against Germany.

Nach Unterzeichnung des *Wiedergutmachungs-Abkommens* durch den Bundeskanzler und den israelischen Außenminister SHAREDT (Luxemburg, 10. 9. 1952) tritt das Abkommen am 27. 3. 1953 in Kraft.

Dem Staat Israel werden 3 Milliarden DM zur Erstattung der Eingliederungskosten zur Verfügung gestellt, die Israel durch die Aufnahme jüdischer Flüchtlinge, die infolge nationalsozialistischer Maßnahmen ihre Heimat verlassen mußten, erwachsen sind. Außerdem stellt die Bundesregierung 450 Millionen DM zur Unterstützung in Not befindlicher jüdischer Opfer des Nationalsozialismus', die außerhalb Israels wohnen, zur Verfügung.

b) Im Interesse der Wiederherstellung des deutschen Auslandskredites und der Wiederaufnahme normaler Beziehungen zwischen Schuldnern und Gläubigern werden 1951 Besprechungen über deutsche öffentliche und private Auslandsschulden aus der Vor- und Nachkriegszeit eingeleitet. Diese Besprechungen führen am 27. 2. 1953 in London zur Unterzeichnung des *Abkommens über deutsche Auslandsschulden*.

C. WEITERE KLÄRUNG DER BEZIEHUNGEN DER BUNDESREPUBLIK DEUTSCHLAND ZU DEN DREI MÄCHTEN

1. Nachdem im Dezember 1950 auf der Brüsseler Konferenz eine *deutsche Beteiligung an der Verteidigung des Westens* beschlossen worden war, erklärt der Bundeskanzler, daß eine solche Beteiligung stattfinden könne, wenn das Besatzungsstatut durch ein System freiwillig abgeschlossener Verträge ersetzt werde. Auf Grund dieser Forderung finden seit Mai 1951 Verhandlungen statt. Sie führen am 26. 5. 1952 in Bonn zur Unterzeichnung des *Deutschland-Vertrags* durch den Bundeskanzler und die Außenminister Frankreichs, des Vereinigten Königreichs und der USA.

   Das Vertragswerk

   beendet das Besatzungsregime,

   legt grundsätzlich die Wiederherstellung der deutschen Souveränität fest,

   setzt an die Stelle der Besatzungskosten einen Verteidigungsbeitrag,

   bindet die Westalliierten vertraglich, die Wiedervereinigung Deutschlands zu fördern.

2. Das Inkrafttreten des Montan-Vertrags am 23. 7. 1952 führt in der Bundesrepublik zu folgender weiteren *Lockerung der Besatzungsfessel*:

Aufhebung des Ruhrstatuts;
Abschaffung der Kohle- und Stahl-Kontrollgruppen;
Fortfall sämtlicher anderen alliierten Eingriffsrechte in die deutsche Kohle- und Stahlwirtschaft, insbesondere der Beschränkung der Stahlerzeugung.

3. Die Bemühungen um eine Klärung des deutschen Verhältnisses zu den Drei Westalliierten und um eine Förderung der europäischen Verteidigungsanstrengungen erfahren einen vorübergehenden harten Rückschlag durch die am 30. 8. 1954 erfolgte *Ablehnung der EVG durch die französische Nationalversammlung*. Infolge dieser Entscheidung müssen auch die Arbeiten für die Schaffung einer Europäischen Politischen Gemeinschaft eingestellt werden.

4. Das so entstandene Vakuum wird jedoch rasch ausgefüllt. Die neuen Verhandlungen im September und Oktober 1954 in London und anschließend in Paris führen nicht nur zu einer *Revision des Deutschland-Vertrags* zugunsten der Bundesrepublik, sondern auch zur Fertigstellung eines neuen Plans für die Verteidigungsanstrengungen Westeuropas.
Das am 23. 10. 1954 in Paris unterzeichnete Vertragswerk überläßt die Regelung der Verteidigung teils nationaler Zuständigkeit, teils dem nunmehr als „Westeuropäische Union" bezeichneten System des Brüsseler Vertrags von 1948 (Belgien, Frankreich, Luxemburg, Niederlande, Vereinigtes Königreich, vermehrt um die Bundesrepublik und Italien) und dem der NATO (Belgien, Dänemark, Frankreich, Griechenland, Island, Italien, Kanada, Luxemburg, Niederlande, Norwegen, Portugal, Türkei, USA, Vereinigtes Königreich, vermehrt um die Bundesrepublik).
Grundlegende Idee des Vertragswerks:
Rein defensiver Charakter;
uneingeschränkte Gleichberechtigung aller Mitgliedstaaten;
enge Bindung des Vereinigten Königreichs an den Kontinent.
Die *Westeuropäische Union* (WEU)
ist ein automatisch wirkendes Verteidigungsbündnis;
beschränkt die Truppenstärke und Rüstung nationaler Streitkräfte.
Der *Nordatlantik-Vertrag* (NATO)
ist ein Verteidigungsbündnis mit gleicher Beistandspflicht;
führt militärisch-technische Integration nationaler Streitkräfte im mitteleuropäischen Befehlsbereich durch;
fördert allgemeine politische Zusammenarbeit im atlantischen Bereich.

Am 27.2.1955 werden die Pariser Verträge durch die Bundesregierung ratifiziert. Sie treten am 5.5.1955 in Kraft. *Damit ist das Besatzungsregime beendet, die Bundesrepublik souverän.*

D. DIE BEMÜHUNGEN UM DIE WIEDERVEREINIGUNG

Seit ihrem Bestehen hat die Bundesregierung in der Regelung ihrer Beziehungen zu den Drei Westmächten und in dem Abbau politischer Gegensätze zu ihren westlichen Nachbarn durch eine Vertiefung der europäischen Zusammenarbeit die erste Voraussetzung dafür erblickt, daß sie erfolgreiche Bemühungen um die *Wiedervereinigung Deutschlands* einleiten konnte. Je fester sich ihr Verhältnis zu den Nachbarländern gestaltete, desto mehr konnte sie sich unmittelbar in die internationalen Auseinandersetzungen über die deutsche Frage einschalten.

Die Bundesregierung ging dabei von dem Gedanken aus, daß die Wiedervereinigung Deutschlands nur mit friedlichen Mitteln und unter freiheitlichen Vorzeichen erfolgen darf. Daher wurde der Kernpunkt ihrer Forderungen die *Abhaltung völlig freier Wahlen in ganz Deutschland.*

Zeitplan:

1. Note an die Alliierte Hohe Kommission vom 9.3.1951, in der die Vier Besatzungsmächte ersucht werden, die Abhaltung freier Wahlen zu ermöglichen.
2. Regierungserklärung vom 27.9.1951 vor dem Bundestag: vierzehn Punkte zur Sicherung der Wahlfreiheit und Vorschlag einer Untersuchungskommission der Vereinten Nationen (UNO).
3. Note der Bundesregierung an die Alliierte Hohe Kommission vom 4.10.1951 mit dem Ersuchen, die UNO um Einsetzung einer Untersuchungskommission zu bitten.
4. Erklärung der deutschen Vertreter Dr. von Brentano, Dr. Schäfer und Professor Reuter vor der politischen Kommission der UNO in Paris zur Unterstützung des Ansuchens der Bundesregierung auf Einsetzung einer Untersuchungskommission (8.12.1951).
5. Beschluß der Vollversammlung der UNO vom 20.12.1951 über Einsetzung einer Untersuchungskommission, bestehend aus Vertretern der Niederlande, Islands, Brasiliens, Pakistans und Polens. Die polnische Regierung lehnt die Beteiligung ab.
6. Der Bundestag beschließt am 6.2.1952 mit großer Mehrheit ein Gesetz über die Grundsätze für die freien Wahlen einer verfassunggebenden deutschen Nationalversammlung.
7. Besuch der UNO-Kommission in der Bundesrepublik und in Berlin (West) vom 16. bis 25.3.1952. Die sogenannte DDR verweigert Einlaß und Zusammenarbeit.

8. Fast gleichzeitig, am 10.3.1952, übermittelt die Sowjetregierung den Regierungen der Drei Westmächte eine Note, die Vorschläge für einen Friedensvertrag enthält. Darin heißt es: „Es versteht sich, daß ein solcher Friedensvertrag unter unmittelbarer Beteiligung Deutschlands, vertreten durch eine gesamtdeutsche Regierung, ausgearbeitet werden muß".

9. Die Regierungen der Drei Westmächte weisen in ihrer Note vom 25.3.1952 darauf hin, daß die Sowjetnote der Voraussetzung für die Durchführung freier Wahlen nicht genügend Rechnung trägt. Gleichzeitig fordern sie die Bündnisfreiheit einer gesamtdeutschen Regierung.
Der Notenwechsel zwischen der Sowjetregierung und den Drei Westmächten wird im Frühjahr und Sommer 1952 längere Zeit fortgesetzt, ohne zu einem Ergebnis zu führen.

10. Der Bundeskanzler richtet am 29.5.1953 ein Memorandum an Präsident EISENHOWER, in dem in acht Leitsätzen die Forderungen der Bundesregierung nach Durchführung freier Wahlen in Gesamtdeutschland, nach Bildung einer freien gesamtdeutschen Regierung und nach politischer Entscheidungsfreiheit dieser gesamtdeutschen Regierung enthalten sind.

11. Am 17.6.1953 bricht sich die Empörung der Bevölkerung der sogenannten DDR über die Verweigerung der Freiheitsrechte durch die Sowjetunion und die „Zonenregierung" in einem elementaren Volksaufstand Bahn. Der Bundeskanzler weist die Regierungschefs der Drei Westmächte erneut auf die Notwendigkeit hin, die unhaltbaren Zustände in der sogenannten DDR zu beseitigen.

12. Die Regierungen der Drei Westmächte schlagen am 15.7.1953 der Regierung der Sowjetunion vor, ein Treffen der Außenminister der Vier Mächte durchzuführen, das sich mit der Frage der Herbeiführung der Wiedervereinigung Deutschlands befassen soll. Nach längerem Notenwechsel kommen die Vier Mächte überein, am 25.1.1954 in Berlin eine Viermächte-Konferenz durchzuführen.

13. Vom 25.1. bis 18.2.1954 findet in Berlin die Viermächte-Konferenz über Deutschland statt. Der britische Außenminister EDEN unterbreitet für die Drei Westmächte Vorschläge für die Wiedervereinigung Deutschlands (sogenannter EDEN-Plan). Die Wiedervereinigung soll in den folgenden Stadien vollzogen werden:
   Freie Wahlen in ganz Deutschland;
   Einberufung einer aus diesen Wahlen hervorgehenden Nationalversammlung;
   Ausarbeitung einer Verfassung und Vorbereitung der Friedensvertrags-Verhandlungen;
   Annahme der Verfassung und Bildung einer gesamtdeutschen Regierung, die für die Aushandlung des Friedensvertrages zuständig ist;
   Unterzeichnung und Inkrafttreten des Friedensvertrags.
Diese Vorschläge haben die Zustimmung der Bundesregierung gefunden. Die Sowjetunion lehnt diese Vorschläge ab.

14. Der Bundestag nimmt am 25.2.1954 eine Entschließung an, in der es heißt:
   „Der Deutsche Bundestag bedauert auf das Tiefste, daß die Berliner Konferenz keine Lösung der Deutschland-Frage gebracht hat.

Aus den Stellungnahmen des Sowjetischen Außenministers geht eindeutig hervor, daß die Sowjetunion heute nicht willens ist, die Wiedervereinigung Deutschlands in Freiheit zuzulassen."

15. Am 25.3.1954 proklamiert die Sowjetregierung die Souveränität der Regierung der sogenannten DDR. Diese Souveränität wird weder von der Bundesregierung noch von den Westmächten anerkannt.
16. Das Bemühen der Bundesregierung ist in der Folgezeit darauf gerichtet, daß kein Staat, der zum Zeitpunkt der Souveränitätserklärung für die sogenannten DDR diplomatische oder konsularische Beziehungen zur Bundesregierung unterhält, bei der Regierung der sogenannten DDR diplomatisch vertreten ist.
17. In der Schlußakte der Londoner Konferenz, die nach dem Scheitern der EVG stattfand, erklären die Drei Westmächte am 3.10.1954, die Regierung der Bundesrepublik Deutschland sei allein berechtigt, für Deutschland zu sprechen. Die Drei Westmächte erklären unter anderem, daß:

    „sie die Regierung der Bundesrepublik Deutschland als die einzige deutsche Regierung betrachten, die frei und rechtmäßig gebildet wurde und daher berechtigt ist, für Deutschland als Vertreter des deutschen Volkes in internationalen Angelegenheiten zu sprechen;
    die Schaffung eines völlig freien vereinigten Deutschlands durch friedliche Mittel ein grundsätzliches Ziel ihrer Politik bleibt;
    sie die anderen Mitgliedstaaten der NATO auffordern werden, sich dieser Erklärung anzuschließen."

18. Das Pariser Protokoll über die Beendigung des Besatzungsregimes in Deutschland vom 23.10.1954 enthält den „Vertrag über die Beziehungen zwischen der Bundesrepublik und den Drei Mächten". Darin wird in Artikel 7, Absatz 1 und 2, festgelegt:

    „Die Unterzeichnerstaaten sind darüber einig, daß ein wesentliches Ziel ihrer gemeinsamen Politik eine zwischen Deutschland und seinen ehemaligen Gegnern frei vereinbarte *friedensvertragliche Regelung für ganz Deutschland* ist, welche die Grundlage für einen dauerhaften Frieden bieten soll. Sie sind weiterhin darüber einig, daß die endgültige Festlegung der Grenzen Deutschlands bis zu dieser Regelung aufgeschoben werden muß.
    Bis zum Abschluß der friedensvertraglichen Regelung werden die Unterzeichnerstaaten zusammenwirken, um mit friedlichen Mitteln ihr gemeinsames Ziel zu erwirken: ein wiedervereinigtes Deutschland, das eine freiheitlich-demokratische Verfassung, ähnlich wie die Bundesrepublik, besitzt und in die europäische Gemeinschaft integriert ist."

19. Sämtliche NATO-Mächte schließen sich in Paris am 23.10.1954 ihrerseits dem Grundgedanken der Londoner Schlußakte an: die friedliche Wiedervereinigung Deutschlands stellt ein gemeinsames Ziel dar, das auf dem Wege einer friedensvertraglichen Regelung für Gesamtdeutschland erreicht werden soll.
20. Am 9.12.1954 richtet die Sowjetunion eine Note an die Drei Westmächte und bietet die Zulassung freier Wahlen an, sofern vorher der militärische Status von Gesamtdeutschland geregelt werde. Dieses Angebot erneuert die Sowjetregierung am 15.1.1955. Sie droht aber gleichzeitig an, daß bei Annahme der Pariser Verträge eine neue Lage entstehen werde.

20. Als die Bundesrepublik am 5. 5. 1955 souverän wird und die Pariser Vertragswerke in Kraft treten, hat die Politik der Bundesregierung in der Frage der Wiedervereinigung die ausdrückliche Zusage der Unterstützung durch alle Mächte der westlichen Verteidigungsallianz erfahren.

II. DIE AUSSENPOLITIK DER BUNDESREPUBLIK SEIT DER SOUVERÄNITÄTSERKLÄRUNG (1955 BIS 1959)

Der 5. 5. 1955 bedeutet einen wichtigen Einschnitt in der Außenpolitik der Bundesrepublik. Sie ist nunmehr in die Lage versetzt, selbständig an die Lösung wichtiger außenpolitischer Probleme heranzutreten. Die neue Lage läßt es als zweckmäßig erscheinen, die Personalunion in der Leitung der Ämter des Bundeskanzlers und des Außenministers aufzuheben. Am 7. 6. 1955 tritt Dr. HEINRICH VON BRENTANO als Außenminister an die Stelle von Dr. ADENAUER, der weiterhin Bundeskanzler bleibt.

A. AUSSENWIRTSCHAFT

Im Rahmen der Bemühungen um den Wiedergewinn der Stellung, die Deutschland früher in Europa und in der Welt einnahm, kommt der *Ausweitung des Außenhandels* eine entscheidende Bedeutung zu. Mit einer Bevölkerung von rund 54 Millionen Menschen[1] — davon rund 12 Millionen Vertriebene und Flüchtlinge — ist die Bundesrepublik nur bei stärkstem Export von arbeits-intensiven Investitions- und Konsumgütern lebensfähig. Schon vor dem Kriege, als Deutschlands Abhängigkeit von der Einfuhr dank den agrarischen Überschußgebieten in Mittel- und Ostdeutschland geringer war als heute, nahm das Deutsche Reich im *Welthandel* hinter den Vereinigten Staaten und dem Vereinigten Königreich zeitweilig *den dritten Platz* ein.

In den ersten Nachkriegsjahren ist der deutsche Außenhandel erheblich gedrosselt. Erst mit der Währungsreform des Jahres 1948 und dem Einsatz der Marshallplanhilfe beginnt ein rascher Aufstieg, der mit fortschreitender staatlicher Konsolidierung der Bundesrepublik zu überraschenden Erfolgen führt.

Im Vordergrund der deutschen Handelspolitik steht zunächst der Abschluß zahlreicher bilateraler Handels- und Verrechnungsabkommen. Diese ermöglichen eine schnelle Ausweitung der Handelsbeziehungen. Bis 1951 weist der

[1] Einschließlich von Berlin(West).

deutsche Außenhandel einen Passivsaldo auf. Seit 1952 ist die deutsche Handelsbilanz bei anhaltend steigendem Gesamtvolumen des Güteraustauschs aktiv. Die Ausfuhr steigt von nur 4 Milliarden DM im Jahre 1949 auf 37 Milliarden DM im Jahre 1958. Einem Einfuhrüberschuß im Jahre 1949 von fast 4 Milliarden DM steht 1958 ein Ausfuhrüberschuß von fast 6 Milliarden DM gegenüber. Die Bundesrepublik hat mit einem Anteil von rund 7% an der Welteinfuhr und rund 9% an der Weltausfuhr im Jahre 1957 den traditionellen dritten Platz des Deutschen Reiches im Welthandel zurückgewonnen.

Der *Umsatz des Außenhandels* (Einfuhr und Ausfuhr zusammen) entwickelt sich wie folgt:

Jahr	Milliarden	
	DM	$
1949	11,982	2,849
1950	19,736	4,684
1951	29,302	6,976
1952	33,112	7,891
1953	34,536	8,231
1954	41,372	9,862
1955	50,189	11,960
1956	58,825	14,021
1957	67,664	16,127
1958	68,103	16,215

In der Zusammensetzung des deutschen Außenhandels nach Warengruppen spiegelt sich die Struktur der deutschen Wirtschaft. Der Anteil der *industriellen Fertigwaren* an der deutschen Ausfuhr steigt von 64,8% (1950) auf 82,2% (1958). Auf der Einfuhrseite sind es die Güter der *Ernährungswirtschaft*, die mit 30,2% (1958) den ersten Platz einnehmen. Ihnen folgen industrielle Fertigwaren (27,3%) und industrielle Rohstoffe (24,7%).

B. KLÄRUNG VON TERRITORIALEN FRAGEN UND REGELUNG DER BILATERALEN BEZIEHUNGEN ZU DEN WESTLICHEN NACHBARSTAATEN UND DER ÜBRIGEN WELT

Die Bundesregierung setzte nach dem 5. 5. 1955 die Bemühungen zielbewußt fort, ihr Verhältnis zu den westlichen Nachbarstaaten weiter zu klären. Dabei stand das Interesse an einer Klärung der *bilateralen Fragen*, die sich aus der Besetzung Deutschlands nach dem Kriege ergeben hatten, im Vordergrund.

Bereits 1951 war es gelungen, durch den Abschluß des Kehler Hafenabkommens das Gebiet des Hafens von *Kehl*, der aus der französischen Besatzungszone ausgegliedert und der Verwaltung des französischen Departements Bas-Rhin unterstellt worden war, mit Wirkung vom 1.1.1952 in die deutsche Hoheitsgewalt zurückzuführen.

Am 1.3.1952 wurde die Insel *Helgoland* durch die britische Besatzungsmacht an die Bundesrepublik zurückgegeben.

Demgegenüber bedurfte die Klärung anderer Fragen, die ebenfalls das Verhältnis zu den deutschen Nachbarn betrafen, längerer Verhandlungen. Ihr Erfolg ist weitgehend nur durch die Politik der europäischen Zusammenarbeit ermöglicht worden.

1. *Bundesrepublik — Frankreich:*

Die Entwicklung der deutsch-französischen Beziehungen wurde in erster Linie durch die Frage des „Saargebiets" bestimmt, das nach 1945 politisch von Deutschland abgetrennt und wirtschaftlich an Frankreich angeschlossen worden ist. Beide Regierungen streben zunächst eine Lösung der *Saarfrage* im Rahmen des Aufbaus einer europäischen Staatengemeinschaft an. Jedoch fordert die Bundesrepublik, daß diese Lösung die Wiederherstellung der politischen Freiheiten an der Saar voraussetze.

Zeitplan:

Am 18.4.1951 wird bei der Unterzeichnung des Vertrags über die Montan-Gemeinschaft festgelegt, daß die endgültige Regelung der Saarfrage dem Friedensvertrag oder einem gleichartigen Vertrag vorbehalten werden muß.

Am 30.11.1952 werden bei den Wahlen zum Saarländischen Landtag die „deutschen" Parteien nicht zugelassen. Die Bundesregierung gibt daraufhin zu erkennen, daß sie den neu gewählten Landtag nicht als frei gewählte Vertretung ansehen kann.

In den Jahren 1953 und 1954 werden die Bemühungen fortgesetzt, um den deutsch-französischen Gegensatz in der Saarfrage im Rahmen der Europäischen Politischen Gemeinschaft zu einem Ausgleich zu bringen.

Das Vorhaben scheitert am 30.8.1954, als die französische Nationalversammlung das Projekt der EVG ablehnt.

Am 23.10.1954 wird nach neuen deutsch-französischen Verhandlungen in Paris ein Abkommen abgeschlossen. Es sieht einen provisorischen Status der

Saar im Rahmen der gleichzeitig gegründeten Westeuropäischen Union und die Annahme dieses Statuts durch ein Referendum der Saarbevölkerung vor.
Das Abkommen tritt am 5.5.1955 in Kraft.
Am 23.10.1955 lehnt die Saarbevölkerung nach dreimonatigem Wahlkampf, an dem sich auch die bisher verbotenen „deutschen" Parteien beteiligen, mit über zwei Dritteln Mehrheit das „Saarstatut" ab.
Das Abstimmungsergebnis führt nicht, wie befürchtet wurde, zu neuen deutsch-französischen Spannungen. Beide Regierungen stimmen darin überein, daß dem eindeutigen Wunsche der Bevölkerung auf Rückkehr nach Deutschland Rechnung getragen und das französische Wirtschaftsinteresse berücksichtigt werden müsse.

Im Februar 1956 werden demgemäß Verhandlungen eingeleitet. Sie führen am 27. 10. 1956 zu einem Vertrag, der neben den gleichzeitig behandelten Fragen der Moselkanalisierung und der Schiffbarmachung des Oberrheins die Saarfrage endgültig regelt.
Der Vertrag legt im einzelnen fest:
Die Eingliederung der Saar in die Bundesrepublik erfolgt in Etappen;
die politische Eingliederung vollzieht sich am 1. 1. 1957;
die Einbeziehung der Saar in das Wirtschaftsgebiet der Bundesrepublik erfolgt nach einer Übergangszeit von höchstens drei Jahren;
am Ende der Übergangszeit tritt das Saarland auch in das deutsche Währungs- und Zollgebiet ein.

Am 1.1.1957 kehrt die Saar nach Deutschland zurück.

Mit der endgültigen Regelung des Saarproblems und der mit ihm zusammenhängenden Fragen ist das deutsch-französische Verhältnis von allen Belastungen befreit worden. Die engen Beziehungen zwischen der Bundesrepublik und Frankreich erleiden durch die innerpolitischen Veränderungen keine Beeinträchtigung, die sich 1958 in Frankreich vollziehen. Das kommt vor allem bei den Begegnungen des Bundeskanzlers mit General DE GAULLE in Colombey-les-deux-Eglises (September 1958), Bad Kreuznach (November 1958) und Marly (5. 3. 1959) sowie bei dem Staatsbesuch des Französischen Ministerpräsidenten DEBRE in Bonn im Mai 1959 zum Ausdruck.

2. Die Bundesregierung sucht ferner das Problem der auf Grund des Pariser Protokolls vom 22. 3. 1949 *unter vorläufige Auftragsverwaltung gestellten westlichen Grenzgebiete* im Wege zweiseitiger Verhandlungen zu lösen. Verhandlungen hierüber hat sie mit Belgien, den Niederlanden und Luxemburg eingeleitet.

a) *Bundesrepublik — Belgien*

Die am 14. 11. 1955 begonnenen deutsch-belgischen Verhandlungen führen am 24. 9. 1956 in Brüssel zur Unterzeichnung eines Grenzabkommens. Es löst die beide Länder interessierenden Grenzfragen und führt zur Rückkehr der vorübergehend unter belgischer Auftragsverwaltung befindlichen Gebietsteile in den deutschen Staatsverband. Am 13. 8. 1958 werden von den Außenministern beider Staaten die Ratifikationsurkunden dieses Vertrages ausgetauscht. Am 28. 8. 1958 tritt er in Kraft. Damit ist eine endgültige Entspannung des deutsch-belgischen Verhältnisses herbeigeführt.

b) *Bundesrepublik — Niederlande*

Nach dem Besuch des niederländischen Außenministers LUNS in Bonn am 1. 3. 1957 beginnen deutsch-niederländische Verhandlungen. Sie sollen zu einer Bereinigung aller Fragen führen, die für beide Länder von Wichtigkeit sind. Nach Besprechungen des Bundesaußenministers mit seinem niederländischen Kollegen am 23. 6. 1958 kommen die zeitweise unterbrochenen Verhandlungen Anfang 1959 erneut in Gang.

c) *Bundesrepublik — Luxemburg*

Ähnliche Besprechungen werden Anfang Juli 1957 mit Luxemburg eingeleitet. Eine gemischte deutsch-luxemburgische Kommission hat am 27. 5. 1959 in Bad Ems die Prüfung der zwischen der Bundesrepublik und Luxemburg schwebenden Fragen abgeschlossen. Das Verhandlungsergebnis wird als Abkommen den beiden Parlamenten vorgelegt werden.

3. In weiteren Verhandlungen werden auch die Beziehungen der Bundesrepublik zu Dänemark und Österreich geklärt.

a) *Bundesrepublik — Dänemark*

Bereits im Frühjahr 1955 werden mit der dänischen Regierung Verhandlungen über die *Rechte der beiderseitigen Minderheiten* geführt. Diese Verhandlungen finden am 29. 3. 1955 ihren Abschluß mit einer deutsch-dänischen Erklärung, welche die Rechte der Minderheiten in den beiderseitigen Grenzgebieten genauer umreißt.

b) *Bundesrepublik — Österreich*

Längere Zeit nehmen die deutsch-österreichischen Besprechungen über eine Klärung derjenigen Probleme in Anspruch, die sich aus dem im

Mai 1955 erfolgten Abschluß des österreichischen Staatsvertrags ergeben. Vor allem das schwierige *Problem des deutschen Vermögens in Österreich* ist der Anlaß zu eingehenden Erörterungen in der Öffentlichkeit beider Länder.

Im November 1955 kommen beide Regierungen überein, eine gemischte Kommission einzusetzen.

Am 15. 6. 1956 wird nach langen Unterhandlungen eine befriedigende Lösung herbeigeführt. Die Ratifikationsurkunden des Vertrages werden bei einem Besuch des österreichischen Außenministers FIGL am 15. 6. 1958 in Bonn ausgetauscht. Mit Inkrafttreten dieses Vertrages ist auch diese letzte Hypothek auf dem deutsch-österreichischen Verhältnis beseitigt.

Es ist somit gelungen, weitgehend alle konkreten Probleme zu lösen, die sich aus dem Zweiten Weltkrieg und aus der Zeit der Besetzung Deutschlands nach 1945 für die Beziehungen der Bundesrepublik zu ihren westlichen Nachbarländern ergeben haben. Die Bundesregierung stellt mit Bedauern fest, daß mit den Nachbarstaaten der östlichen Hemisphäre noch keine vergleichbare Bereinigung eingeleitet werden konnte.

4. *Bundesrepublik — Vereinigtes Königreich*

Durch die gemeinsame Partnerschaft im Atlantikpakt und der Westeuropäischen Union sind enge Bindungen zwischen der Bundesrepublik und dem Vereinigten Königreich gegeben. Sie werden auch auf bilateraler Ebene rasch vertieft. Der gegenseitige Gedankenaustausch hat 1958 einen besonders hohen Stand vertrauensvoller Zusammenarbeit angenommen. Die Besuche des Bundeskanzlers in London vom 16. bis 19. 4. 1958 und des britischen Premierministers MACMILLAN am 8. und 9. 10. 1958 in Bonn sowie der Staatsbesuch des Bundespräsidenten vom 20. bis 23. 10. 1958 in London sind ein beredtes Zeugnis dafür.

5. *Das Verhältnis zu den Vereinten Nationen*

Die Bundesrepublik ist seit ihrem Bestehen bemüht, in der Welt als Repräsentantin des gesamten deutschen Volkes aufzutreten und freundschaftliche Beziehungen zu allen Völkern herzustellen.

Sie ist zwar noch nicht Vollmitglied der Vereinten Nationen; jedoch ist sie Mitglied in elf Sonderorganisationen der Vereinten Nationen. In folgenden Sonderorganisationen wurde die Bundesrepublik in die Führungsausschüsse berufen:

1954 in der Internationalen Arbeitsorganisation (ILO)
1954 in der UNESCO
1957 in der Weltgesundheitsorganisation (WHO)
1957 im Weltpostverein (UPU)
1958 im Weltkinderhilfswerk (UNICEF)
1959 in der Welternährungsorganisation (FAO)

6. *Nicht gebundene Welt und Entwicklungsländer*
Besondere Bedeutung mißt die Bundesrepublik dem Ausbau freundschaftlicher Beziehungen zu den Ländern Afrikas und Asiens bei. Sie glaubt dabei nicht nur in ihrem eigenen, nationalen Interesse, sondern darüber hinaus auch im wohlverstandenen Interesse der gesamten Freien Welt zu handeln. Bei mancher Gelegenheit konnte in den vergangenen Jahren die Bundesrepublik, deren Ansehen in Asien und Afrika nicht durch Vorurteile gegen den „Kolonialismus" belastet ist, vermittelnd wirken.
Die Bundesrepublik ist sich in diesem Zusammenhang ihrer *Verpflichtung* bewußt, zu der *wirtschaftlichen und sozialen Entwicklung* der asiatischen und afrikanischen Staaten beizutragen.

Einzelergebnisse:

a) Seit 1949 besteht zur Ermöglichung der Ausfuhr von industriellen Ausrüstungsgütern und anderem Investitionsmaterial ein System von *Bürgschaften und Garantien des Bundes* (Hermes, Kreditanstalt für Wiederaufbau). Nach § 17 des Bundeshaushaltsgesetzes 1959 sind außerdem Bürgschaften des Bundes in Höhe von zwei Milliarden DM vorgesehen. Auf diese Weise unterstützt die Bundesregierung den Abschluß langfristiger Lieferverträge auf kommerzieller Basis.

b) Seit 1956 führt die Bundesrepublik mit jährlich 50 Millionen DM eigene *bilaterale Maßnahmen zur Förderung der Entwicklungsländer* durch. Im Haushalt 1959 wurde zudem eine Bindungsermächtigung für den gleichen Zweck in Höhe von 70 Millionen DM gegeben.
Diese, *auf der Grundlage gleichberechtigter Partnerschaft* durchgeführten Maßnahmen umfassen folgende Vorhaben:
Volkswirtschaftliche Vorplanungen, Beratungsdienste, Aufbau von Gewerbeschulen und Lehrwerkstätten, Anlage von Muster- und Demonstrationseinrichtungen, Förderung des Gesundheitswesens, Ausbildung von Fachkräften.

Mit mehr als vierzig Regierungen sind bisher Vereinbarungen über bestimmte Förderungsmaßnahmen abgeschlossen worden, so unter anderem mit Indien, Pakistan, Iran, der Vereinigten Arabischen Republik, Irak, der Türkei, Griechenland usw. Im Rahmen dieser Absprachen wurden acht volkswirtschaftliche Vorplanungen durchgeführt, zehn Beratungsdienste aufgebaut und zwölf Gewerbeschulen, Lehrwerkstätten und Musteranlagen im Ausland errichtet. Etwa zweihundert qualifizierte Sachverständige sind zur Erfüllung dieser Aufgaben ins Ausland entsandt worden. Das Fachausbildungsprogramm in der Bundesrepublik umfaßt etwa zweitausend Personen.

C. FORTFÜHRUNG DER EUROPÄISCHEN ZUSAMMENARBEIT

Hand in Hand mit den Bemühungen um eine Klärung der bilateralen Beziehungen zu den westlichen Nachbarstaaten und der nicht gebundenen Welt laufen die Bemühungen um eine Vertiefung der *europäischen Zusammenarbeit.* Sie werden seit Inkrafttreten der Pariser Verträge noch intensiver fortgesetzt.

Zeitplan:

1. Anfang Juni 1955 ergreifen die Staaten der Europäischen Gemeinschaft für Kohle und Stahl eine neue Initiative, um den Bereich der europäischen wirtschaftlichen Zusammenarbeit zu erweitern. Am 1. und 2.6.1955 versammeln sich Vertreter der sechs Montanunion-Staaten in Messina. Sie beschließen, daß

   „auf dem Wege zur Schaffung eines geeinten Europas weitergegangen werden muß: durch Entwicklung gemeinsamer Institutionen, durch Fortschreiten der Verschmelzung der nationalen Wirtschaften, durch Errichtung eines Gemeinsamen Marktes und durch fortschreitende Harmonisierung ihrer sozialen Politik".

   In Ausführung dieses Beschlusses wird eine Konferenz von Regierungsvertretern nach Brüssel einberufen, um die Vorschläge für die Errichtung eines Gemeinsamen Marktes und für den Aufbau einer Europäischen Atom-Gemeinschaft in Vertragsform zu bringen.

2. Am 5.7.1955 übermittelt die Bundesregierung dem Europarat die Anerkennung der Europäischen Konvention und des Europäischen Gerichtshofes für Menschenrechte und Grundfreiheiten. Damit ist der Schutz des Individuums in der Bundesrepublik gegen die Verletzung seiner Grund- und Menschenrechte über die innerdeutschen Garantien hinaus einer europäischen Instanz unterworfen.

3. Nach einer Arbeitstagung der Außenminister der sechs Montanunion-Staaten in Paris im Februar 1956 nimmt die Außenministerkonferenz von Venedig am 29. und 30.5.1956 den durch die Brüsseler Regierungssachverständigen aufgestellten

Bericht über die Schaffung eines Europäischen Gemeinsamen Marktes und einer Europäischen Atomgemeinschaft als Verhandlungsgrundlage an. Die Konferenz beschließt die Einsetzung einer Regierungskonferenz zur Ausarbeitung von Vertragsentwürfen über den Gemeinsamen Markt und die Europäische Atomgemeinschaft.

4. Die Unterzeichnung beider Verträge erfolgt in Rom am 28. 3. 1957. Die Verträge sehen vor:

   Gemeinsamer Markt:

   Grundgedanke ist der etappenweise Abbau der Binnenzölle der sechs Staaten, die einen gemeinsamen Außentarif aufstellen. Nach Ablauf einer Übergangszeit von zwölf (höchstens fünfzehn) Jahren wird damit ein einheitlicher *europäischer Markt ohne innere Handelsschranken* bestehen.

   Europäische Atomgemeinschaft (jetzt EAG genannt): wird eine Organisation der sechs Staaten sein, die
   a) gemeinsame Anlagen errichtet,
   b) die wissenschaftliche Forschung koordiniert,
   c) die Mitgliedsländer mit Kernbrennstoffen versorgt.

5. Am 1.1.1958 tritt der Vertrag in Kraft, der die *Europäische Wirtschaftsgemeinschaft* (EWG) begründet. Im Laufe des Jahres 1958 werden die Institutionen der EWG zunächst in Brüssel errichtet. Der Staatssekretär des Auswärtigen Amts, Professor Dr. WALTER HALLSTEIN, wird Präsident der Europäischen Wirtschaftskommission. Am 1.1.1959 beginnen in den sechs Teilnehmer-Staaten am Gemeinsamen Markt die ersten Maßnahmen zum Abbau der Handelsschranken.

6. Die Kommission der *Europäischen Atomgemeinschaft* (EAG) hat ebenfalls am 1.1.1958 in Brüssel ihre Tätigkeit aufgenommen.

7. Von Anfang an hat die Absicht bestanden, den „Gemeinsamen Markt der Sechs" durch eine *Freihandelszone*, die elf Mitgliedstaaten der OEEC umfassen soll, zu ergänzen. Die Verhandlungen über die Freihandelszone werden 1958 im Rahmen der OEEC weitergeführt. Dabei bemüht die Bundesregierung sich stets um eine vermittelnde Haltung.

D. DAS ATLANTISCHE BÜNDNIS UND DIE ABRÜSTUNG

Das Bestreben der Bundesregierung, die europäische Zusammenarbeit auf wirtschaftlichem und politischem Gebiet zu erweitern, wurde durch gleichzeitige Bemühungen gefördert, die auf eine Sicherstellung der *Verteidigungsfähigkeit des Freien Europas* abzielen.

Zeitplan:

1. Am 7.5.1955 wird die konstituierende Sitzung des Rates der Westeuropäischen Union in Paris durchgeführt.

2. Am 9.5.1955 ist die Bundesrepublik erstmalig auf einer Sitzung des Atlantikpaktrates vertreten.

3. Am 4.5.1956 unterbreitet die Bundesregierung Anregungen, die der Vertiefung der Zusammenarbeit des NATO-Rates auch auf nicht-militärischem, das heißt auf politischem, wirtschaftlichem und kulturellem Gebiet dienen sollen. Die Vorschläge werden bei der Planung der weiteren Tätigkeit der Nordatlantikpakt-Organisation weitgehend berücksichtigt.

4. Auf deutsche Initiative tritt am 15.9.1956 der Ministerrat der WEU zusammen, um gewisse politische Probleme, die sich aus der Umrüstung von konventionellen auf atomare Waffen ergeben können, zu prüfen. Die Mitgliedstaaten der Westeuropäischen Union tragen in ihren Beratungen dem Wunsch der Bundesregierung Rechnung, daß eine etwaige Umrüstung nicht die europäische Verteidigungskraft in Frage stellen darf.

5. Am 26.2. und 18.3.1957 tritt der Ministerrat der Westeuropäischen Union zusammen. Auf Vorschlag der Bundesregierung ersucht der Ministerrat den NATO-Rat um eine generelle Überprüfung der NATO-Verteidigung und ihrer wirtschaftlichen Grundlagen. Das deutsche Drängen auf eine Klärung dieser Frage ist ausgelöst durch die Besorgnis über die Ankündigung der Britischen Regierung, einen erheblichen Teil der britischen Streitkräfte vom europäischen Festland zurückzuziehen.

6. Am 18.3.1957 tritt in London der Abrüstungsausschuß der Vereinten Nationen (Mitglieder: USA, Vereinigtes Königreich, Frankreich, Kanada, Sowjetunion) zusammen. Die Bundesregierung ist bestrebt, im Rahmen ihrer Möglichkeiten die Bemühungen zu unterstützen, die auf eine Regelung des Abrüstungsproblems abzielen.

7. Am 2. und 3.5.1957 tagt der NATO-Rat in Bonn.

8. Auf einer Debatte über die Frage der atomaren Abrüstung, die der Deutsche Bundestag am 10.5.1957 durchführt, erklärt Bundesverteidigungsminister STRAUSS im Namen der Bundesregierung zur Abrüstungsfrage:

   „Die Bundesregierung ist — das sei hier neuerdings und nochmals betont — jederzeit bereit, allen internationalen Vereinbarungen zuzustimmen — ohne für sich besondere Forderungen zu stellen und damit die Verhandlungen zu erschweren —, auf die sich die Großmächte einigen."

   Und zur Frage der atomaren Rüstung:

   „Die Bundesregierung hat die Ausrüstung der Bundeswehr mit Atomwaffen bisher weder verlangt, noch ist sie ihr angeboten oder aufgedrängt worden. Es ist ihr ausgesprochener Wunsch, daß durch den Abschluß eines Abrüstungsabkommens dieses Problem sich von selbst erledigt. Unser Land hat als einziger Staat der Welt auf die Herstellung von Massenvernichtungsmitteln verzichtet..."

9. Am gleichen Tag nimmt der Bundestag ohne Gegenstimmen in der Frage der atomaren Abrüstung folgende Entschließung an:

„Der Deutsche Bundestag ist der Überzeugung, daß im Zeitalter der Atomwaffen jeder Krieg das Leben und die Gesundheit der gesamten Bevölkerung gefährdet und zur Selbstvernichtung der Menschheit führen kann. Er ersucht daher die Bundesregierung, auf die mit uns verbündeten Staaten der Freien Welt und die Sowjetunion einzuwirken, daß

a) durch internationale Vereinbarungen die unverzügliche Einstellung weiterer Atombombenversuche erreicht wird,

b) eine allgemeine Abrüstung und ein damit verbundenes generelles Verbot für Atomwaffen durchgeführt werden.

Der Bundestag hält es für eine wesentliche Aufgabe der deutschen Politik, dazu beizutragen, daß im Zusammenleben der Völker humanitäre Gesichtspunkte und die Ehrfurcht vor dem Leben endlich wieder die ihnen gebührende Geltung erhalten. Er befürwortet daher alle Maßnahmen zu einer Entspannung, welche die Anwendung dieser Grundsätze ermöglichen."

Die Entschließung ist von der Bundesregierung den an den Arbeiten der Abrüstungskommission beteiligten Mächten zur Kenntnis gebracht worden.

10. Die Zusammenarbeit innerhalb der NATO hat im Laufe der letzten Jahre zu verstärkter politischer Konsultation und weitgehender Interdependenz auf dem Gebiet der Rüstung geführt. In Übereinstimmung mit der militärischen Gesamtplanung der NATO vollzieht sich der weitere Aufbau der *Bundeswehr*. In diesem Zusammenhang wird auch eine Ausrüstung der Bundeswehr mit modernsten Waffen zur Diskussion gestellt. Hierzu beschließt der Bundestag nach langer Debatte gegen die Stimmen der Opposition am 25.3.1958:

„In Übereinstimmung mit den Erfordernissen dieses Verteidigungssystems und angesichts der Aufrüstung des möglichen Gegners müssen die Streitkräfte der Bundesrepublik mit den modernsten Waffen so ausgerüstet werden, daß sie den von der Bundesrepublik übernommenen Verpflichtungen im Rahmen der NATO zu genügen vermögen und den notwendigen Beitrag zur Sicherung des Friedens wirksam leisten können."

Diese Bemühungen sollen *bis zum Zustandekommen eines allgemeinen Abrüstungsabkommens* fortgesetzt werden.

11. Am 18.7.1958 stellt der Bundeskanzler in Beantwortung eines Schreibens, das der Sowjetische Ministerpräsident zu der Frage einer Einstellung von Kernwaffenversuchen am 4.4.1958 an ihn gerichtet hat, folgendes fest: „Die Bundesregierung

wünscht nichts sehnlicher, als daß es im Interesse einer internationalen Entspannung bald gelingen möge, zu einem Abkommen zu gelangen, das eine umfassende, allgemeine und kontrollierte Abrüstung vorsieht. Hierzu würde auch die Einstellung der Versuche mit Kernwaffen gehören."

12. In diesem Sinne begrüßt die Bundesregierung die Fortschritte, die sich 1958 auf dem Gebiet der Abrüstung abzeichnen, so zum Beispiel den erfolgreichen Abschluß der Sachverständigen-Konferenz zur Einstellung der Kernwaffenversuche in Genf und den günstigen Beginn der gegenwärtig noch tagenden politischen Konferenz zum gleichen Thema. Die Bundesregierung ist sich bewußt, daß das wichtigste nationale Anliegen, die *Wiedervereinigung* der Nation herbeizuführen, *nur in einem Klima der Entspannung* möglich sein wird. Eine solche Entspannung könnte durch erste Abrüstungsmaßnahmen eingeleitet werden, denen dann Zug um Zug Schritte auf dem Wege der allgemeinen Abrüstung und der Wiedervereinigung Deutschlands folgen sollten.

E. BEZIEHUNGEN DER BUNDESREPUBLIK ZUR SOWJETUNION

Nachdem die Bundesrepublik die Souveränität erhalten hatte und die Bereinigung der deutschen Beziehungen zu den Westmächten und den westlichen Nachbarn Deutschlands zusehends Fortschritte machte, zeichnete sich die Möglichkeit ab, auch die *Beziehungen zur Sowjetunion auf eine neue Grundlage* zu stellen.

1. Am 7.6.1955 sieht die Sowjetregierung sich veranlaßt, der Bundesregierung vorzuschlagen, zwischen beiden Ländern Beziehungen aufzunehmen. Sie lädt den Bundeskanzler zu einem Besuch nach Moskau ein. Die Bundesregierung sagt am 30.6.1955 zu.
2. Vom 9. bis 13.9.1955 weilt eine deutsche Delegation unter Leitung des Bundeskanzlers in Moskau. Es finden Besprechungen statt über die Frage der Wiedervereinigung Deutschlands, die Frage der Rückkehr der in der Sowjetunion verbliebenen Kriegsgefangenen und der an der Ausreise aus der Sowjetunion verhinderten Deutschen.
   Insbesondere die Wiedervereinigungsfrage wird eingehend erörtert (vergleiche Teil II. F). Nachdem sich die Sowjetregierung bereit erklärt hat, die Rückführung der Kriegsgefangenen und der Zivilpersonen deutscher Staatsangehörigkeit unverzüglich einzuleiten und vollständig durchzuführen, kommen beide Delegationen überein, diplomatische Beziehungen zwischen der Bundesrepublik und der Sowjetunion aufzunehmen und Botschafter auszutauschen.
3. Die diplomatischen Beziehungen werden Anfang 1956 nach Rückkehr der deutschen Kriegsgefangenen aus der Sowjetunion aufgenommen. Am 7.1.1956 überreicht der Sowjetische Botschafter in Bonn, am 12.3.1956 der Deutsche Botschafter in Moskau sein Beglaubigungsschreiben.

Auch nach Herstellung diplomatischer Beziehungen tritt in dem deutsch-sowjetischen Verhältnis keine Entspannung ein. Die Fortdauer der Spannungen ist durch die sowjetische Einstellung in der Frage der Wiedervereinigung und durch die Tatsache begründet, daß es nicht gelingt, die Frage der in der Sowjetunion zurückgehaltenen deutschen Zivilpersonen befriedigend zu klären.

4. Die Vorgänge in Ungarn und Polen im Zuge der Ostblockkrise im Oktober und November 1956 werden von der Bundesregierung mit größter Aufmerksamkeit verfolgt. Die Bundesregierung läßt keinen Zweifel darüber, daß sie in der Beurteilung des ungarischen Freiheitskampfes und der Unterdrückung dieses Freiheitskampfes durch die Sowjetunion mit der Freien Welt einig geht.

5. Der Sowjetische Ministerpräsident schlägt am 5.2.1957 in einer Botschaft an den Bundeskanzler die Einleitung deutsch-sowjetischer Verhandlungen vor, die auf die Frage eines Handelsvertrags, den Abschluß einer Konvention über kulturelle und wissenschaftlich-technische Zusammenarbeit und den Abschluß einer Konsularkonvention eingehen sollen.

6. In seiner Antwort vom 22.2.1957 fordert der Bundeskanzler, daß sich die Verhandlungen ausdrücklich auch auf die Frage der in der Sowjetunion noch zurückgehaltenen Deutschen erstrecken sollen.

7. Nach weiterem Meinungsaustausch kommen beide Regierungen im Juli überein, Verhandlungen über die Frage der Handelsbeziehungen und über die Frage der in der Sowjetunion noch zurückgehaltenen Deutschen zu beginnen. Die Verhandlungen werden am 22.7.1957 eingeleitet. Sie geraten jedoch bald ins Stocken; denn die sowjetische Regierungsdelegation bezeichnet den Punkt der Tagesordnung, der die Repatriierung betrifft, ohne Debatte als erledigt.

8. Am 16.8.1957 werden die Verhandlungen vorübergehend unterbrochen. Sie kommen auf der Grundlage der alten Tagesordnung am 15.11.1957 wieder in Fluß, nachdem beide Seiten in mehrfachem Noten- und Briefwechsel die auseinandergehenden Standpunkte angeglichen haben.

9. Am 8.4.1958 werden die deutsch-sowjetischen Regierungsverhandlungen in Moskau erfolgreich abgeschlossen. Auf dem Gebiet des Handels werden ein dreijähriges „Langfristiges Abkommen über den Waren- und Zahlungsverkehr“ und ein „kleiner“ Handelsvertrag — das „Abkommen über allgemeine Fragen des Handels und der Seeschiffahrt“ — abgeschlossen. Die konsularischen Beziehungen werden mit dem Abschluß eines Konsularvertrages auf eine rechtliche Grundlage gestellt. Die Einrichtung von Konsulaten bleibt zusätzlichen Verhandlungen vorbehalten.
Die Vereinbarungen auf dem Gebiet der Repatriierung sind im Schlußkommuniqué vom 8.4.1958 und in mündlichen Erklärungen enthalten, die vereinbarungsgemäß zwischen den Leitern der beiden Delegationen in der Schlußsitzung am 8.4.1958 ausgetauscht werden. Die Repatriierung sieht im wesentlichen die Möglichkeit der Rückkehr nach Deutschland für diejenigen Personen vor, die sich auf dem Territorium der UdSSR befinden und am 21.6.1941 die deutsche Staatsangehörigkeit besaßen.

10. Die Unterzeichnung der Verträge erfolgt am 25. 4. 1958 in Bonn durch den Bundesaußenminister und den Ersten Stellvertretenden Ministerpräsidenten der Sowjetunion MIKOJAN. In dem gemeinsamen Schlußkommuniqué vom 28. 4. 1958 wird vereinbart, daß noch im Laufe des Jahres 1958 Verhandlungen mit dem Ziele geführt werden sollen, die kulturellen und technisch-wissenschaftlichen Beziehungen auf eine festere Grundlage zu stellen.

11. Gleichwohl leitet die Sowjetregierung am 10. 11. 1958 eine politische Aktion mit dem Ziel der Einbeziehung von Berlin (West) in den sowjetischen Machtbereich ein. Mit ihrer Note vom 27. 11. 1958 schlägt sie eine Neufestsetzung des Status' von Berlin (West) vor. Dieser würde in seiner Konsequenz zur völligen Abhängigkeit von der sogenannten DDR führen. Sie setzt damit die deutsch-sowjetischen Beziehungen der bisher schwersten Belastung aus (vergleiche Teil F).

12. Trotzdem werden die Bemühungen um die Herstellung von Kontakten von deutscher Seite weiterhin gefördert. In Übereinstimmung mit dem am 25. 4. 1958 unterzeichneten „Langfristigen Waren- und Zahlungsabkommen" werden am 6. 12. 1958 Verhandlungen über das Warenprotokoll 1959 in Bonn aufgenommen.

13. Am 10. 12. 1958 beginnen gemäß der im Schlußkommuniqué vom 28. 4. 1958 getroffenen Übereinkunft in Bonn Verhandlungen über den kulturellen und technisch-wissenschaftlichen Austausch zwischen der Bundesrepublik Deutschland und der Sowjetunion. Sie werden am 25. 5. 1959 durch eine Vereinbarunge abgschlossen. Diese ist am 30. 5. 1959 in Kraft getreten.

F. WIEDERVEREINIGUNG DEUTSCHLANDS UND EUROPÄISCHE SICHERHEIT

Je mehr die Stellung der Bundesrepublik sich festigte, desto mehr konnte die Bundesregierung ihre außenpolitischen Bestrebungen auf ihr Hauptziel, die *Wiedervereinigung Deutschlands*, konzentrieren. Bei dem internationalen Meinungsaustausch, der seit 1955 in dieser Frage geführt wurde, zeigte sich, daß eine fruchtbringende Erörterung der Wiedervereinigungsfrage nur dann möglich ist, wenn gleichzeitig die Fragen der *Europäischen Sicherheit* und dor *Abrustung* berücksichtigt werden (vergleiche auch II. D).

Zeitplan:

1. Die Regierungschefs Frankreichs, des Vereinigten Königreichs, der Sowjetunion und der USA stellen auf der ersten Genfer Konferenz am 23. 7. 1955 fest:

   „In Anerkennung ihrer gemeinsamen Verantwortung für die Regelung der deutschen Frage und die Wiedervereinigung Deutschlands haben die Regierungschefs sich darüber geeinigt, daß die Regelung der Deutschland-Frage und die Wiedervereinigung Deutschlands im Wege freier Wahlen im Einklang mit den nationalen Interessen des deutschen Volkes und dem Interesse der europäischen Sicherheit erfolgen muß."

   Den Außenministern der Vier Mächte wird die Direktive erteilt, im Oktober 1955 erneut in Genf zusammenzutreten, um diese Frage zu prüfen (sogenannte Genfer Direktive).

2. Vom 9. bis 13. 9. 1955 weilt der Bundeskanzler in Moskau. In dem Briefwechsel, der zur Bestätigung des bei dieser Gelegenheit erzielten deutsch-sowjetischen Übereinkommens vorgenommen wird, erklärt der Sowjetische Ministerpräsident:

   „. . . daß die Herstellung und Entwicklung normaler Beziehungen zwischen der Sowjetunion und der Bundesrepublik Deutschland zur Lösung der ungelösten Fragen beitragen wird, die das gesamte deutsche Volk betreffen, und somit zur Lösung des nationalen Hauptproblems des gesamten deutschen Volkes — der Wiederherstellung der Einheit des deutschen demokratischen Staates — verhelfen wird . . ."

   Der Bundeskanzler notifiziert im Zusammenhang mit der Aufnahme diplomatischer Beziehungen zwischen beiden Ländern dem Sowjetischen Ministerpräsidenten die Vorbehalte, daß die *endgültige Festsetzung der Grenzen Deutschlands dem Friedensvertrag vorbehalten bleiben* muß; ferner, daß die Aufnahme diplomatischer Beziehungen mit der Regierung der Sowjetunion *keine Änderung des Rechtsstandpunktes der Bundesregierung* bedeutet „in Bezug auf ihre Befugnisse zur Vertretung des deutschen Volkes in internationalen Angelegenheiten und in Bezug auf die politischen Verhältnisse in denjenigen deutschen Gebieten, die sich gegenwärtig außerhalb ihrer effektiven Hoheitsgewalt befinden" (s. S. 220).

3. Auf der Genfer Außenministerkonferenz wiederholen die Drei Westmächte am 28.10.1955 die Vorschläge, die der britische Außenminister EDEN auf der Berliner Außenministerkonferenz zur Frage der Wiedervereinigung vorgelegt hatte. Außerdem erklären die Westmächte sich bereit, der Sowjetregierung für den Fall der Wiedervereinigung Deutschlands besondere Garantien zu geben.

Außenminister MOLOTOW lehnt diese Vorschläge ab. Unter Mißachtung der am 23.7.1955 erteilten Direktive der vier Regierungschefs geht er auf die Frage freier Wahlen in Gesamtdeutschland nicht ein. Er fordert direkte Verhandlungen zwischen der Bundesrepublik und der sogenannten DDR über die Frage der Wiedervereinigung.

4. Das Ministerkomitee des Europarates erklärt am 13.12.1955, daß die Wiedervereinigung Deutschlands auf der Grundlage freier Wahlen unerläßlich ist.
5. Am 2.9.1956 ergreift die Bundesregierung eine neue Initiative und unterbreitet der Sowjetunion ein Memorandum, in dem die deutsche Forderung auf Wiedervereinigung erneut eingehend dargelegt wird. Die Bundesregierung schlägt einen Meinungsaustausch vor, der eine Einigung der Vier Mächte über die Wiedervereinigung erleichtern würde.
6. Die sowjetische Antwort vom 22.10.1956 geht über die deutschen Vorschläge hinweg und wiederholt die sowjetische These von der *Existenz zweier deutscher Staaten*.
7. Am 6.3.1957 tritt in Washington auf deutsche Anregung erstmalig eine aus Vertretern der Bundesrepublik, Frankreichs, des Vereinigten Königreichs und der USA bestehende Arbeitsgruppe zusammen, um neue Grundlagen für eine gemeinsame Politik der Drei Westmächte und der Bundesrepublik in den Fragen der Wiedervereinigung und der europäischen Sicherheit zu erarbeiten.
8. Bei den Verhandlungen des seit dem 18.3.1957 in London tagenden Abrüstungsunterausschusses der Vereinten Nationen wird auch die Frage der Schaffung europäischer Sicherheits- und Inspektionszonen erörtert.
9. Am 20.5.1957 richtet die Bundesregierung in Beantwortung der sowjetischen Note vom 22.10.1956 ein neues Memorandum an die Sowjetregierung und unterstreicht die Notwendigkeit einer baldigen Wiedervereinigung Deutschlands auf Grund freier Wahlen.
10. Das Kommuniqué, das in Washington am 28.5.1957 nach dem Besuch des Bundeskanzlers bei dem Präsidenten der USA veröffentlicht wird, hält die Erklärung Präsident EISENHOWERS fest, daß die Vereinigten Staaten „auf dem Gebiet der Abrüstung nichts unternehmen werden, was geeignet wäre, die Wiedervereinigung Deutschlands zu erschweren".
    Der Bundeskanzler erklärt seinerseits, daß die Bundesregierung den Zeitpunkt einer neuen Vierer-Konferenz über die Wiedervereinigung Deutschlands für gekommen hält, wenn ein einleitendes Abkommen über die Abrüstung abgeschlossen ist.
11. Am 29.7.1957 unterzeichnen der Bundesaußenminister und die Botschafter der USA, des Vereinigten Königreichs und Frankreichs in Berlin die „Berliner Erklärung". Darin werden die Grundlagen der westlichen Deutschland-Politik nochmals festgehalten und die innere Verbindung der Probleme der Wiedervereinigung und der Abrüstung unterstrichen.
12. Die Sowjetregierung weist am 2.8.1957 die Berliner Erklärung zur Wiedervereinigung zurück und bezeichnet den Vorschlag der sogenannten DDR zur Schaffung einer *Konföderation der beiden deutschen Staaten* als einzig reale Möglichkeit.
13. In ihrem Abrüstungsvorschlag vom 29.8.1957 weisen die Westmächte erneut auf den Zusammenhang zwischen der Lösung politischer Fragen (Deutschlandproblem) und der Maßnahmen zur Abrüstung hin.

14. Die diplomatischen Beziehungen zwischen der Bundesrepublik und Jugoslawien werden am 19.10.1957 infolge der Anerkennung der sogenannten DDR durch Jugoslawien abgebrochen.
15. Ein Memorandum der Sowjetunion vom 29.2.1958 nennt den Abschluß eines Friedensvertrages mit Deutschland als Thema einer Gipfelkonferenz, schließt aber die Frage der Wiedervereinigung als Verhandlungsgegenstand aus.
16. Erklärung der Bundesregierung vom 15.3.1958, daß die Wiedervereinigung Gegenstand von Verhandlungen einer Gipfelkonferenz sein müsse.
17. Einstimmige Entschließung des Bundestages am 20.7.1958 über die Bildung eines Viermächte-Gremiums zur Erarbeitung von Vorschlägen zur Lösung der deutschen Frage. Noten entsprechenden Inhalts werden am 9.9.1958 zusammen mit einem Aide-Mémoire den Vier Mächten zugestellt.
18. Die „Regierung" der sogenannten DDR schlägt am 4.9.1958 in Noten an die Vier Mächte und die Bundesrepublik die Bildung einer Viermächte-Kommission unter Hinzuziehung der beiden deutschen Staaten vor. Die Sowjetunion unterstützt diesen Schritt am 18.9.1958 und lehnt die von der Bundesrepublik vorgeschlagene Bildung eines Viermächte-Gremiums ab.

G. DIE BERLIN-KRISE

1. Der Parteisekretär der SED, ULBRICHT, erklärt am 27.10.1958 in Ostberlin, ganz Berlin gehöre zum Hoheitsgebiet der sogenannten DDR.
2. Parteisekretär und Ministerpräsident CHRUSCHTSCHEW fordert am 10.11.1958 in einer Rede im Moskauer Sportpalast den Verzicht der Vier Mächte auf ihren Sonderstatus in Berlin. Die Sowjetunion ihrerseits werde die ihr verbliebenen Funktionen in Berlin der sogenannten DDR übertragen.
3. Note der Sowjetunion vom 27.11.1958 an die Drei Westmächte und die Bundesrepublik, *Aufkündigung des Viermächte-Status' von Berlin*, Aufforderung, binnen sechs Monaten einen neuen Status auf der Basis einer entmilitarisierten „Freien Stadt" zu vereinbaren. Andernfalls werde die Sowjetunion einseitig ihre Berlinrechte an die sogenannte DDR abtreten.
4. Dezembertagung des Atlantikpakt-Rates in Paris. Das sowjetische Sechs-Monate-Ultimatum und die sowjetischen Berlin-Vorschläge werden zurückgewiesen. Bereitschaft zu Verhandlungen über die Deutschland-Frage und über die damit zusammenhängenden Probleme der „Europäischen Sicherheit" und „Abrüstung". Dieser Standpunkt wird der Sowjetregierung durch Noten der drei Westmächte und der Bundesregierung zur Kenntnis gebracht.
5. Note der Sowjetregierung vom 10.1.1959 an die Teilnehmerstaaten des Krieges gegen Deutschland, an die Bundesrepublik und die sogenannte DDR betreffend *Vorschlag eines Friedensvertrags mit Deutschland.*

6. Zusammentritt einer Viermächte-Arbeitsgruppe (USA, Vereinigtes Königreich, Frankreich und Bundesrepublik) am 5. 2. 1959 in Washington zur Erarbeitung der westlichen Antwortnoten auf den sowjetischen Vorschlag vom 10. 1. 1959 und zur Ausarbeitung eines Fragebogens über die Einstellung der Westmächte zu den Problemen „Wiedervereinigung", „Sicherheit" und „Berlin".
7. In Beantwortung sowjetischer Noten vom 10.1.1959 schlagen die Drei Westmächte und die Bundesrepublik am 16.2.1959 der Sowjetunion die Abhaltung einer Vier-Mächte-Außenministerkonferenz vor.
8. Tagung der Viermächte-Arbeitsgruppe in Paris vom 9. bis 20.3.1959 zur Erarbeitung eines gemeinsamen westlichen Standpunktes für die bevorstehenden Ost-West-Konferenzen.
9. In Noten vom 30.3.1959 erklärt sich die Sowjetunion mit einer Außenministerkonferenz ab 11.5.1959 in Genf einverstanden.
10. Konferenz der Außenminister der Vereinigten Staaten, des Vereinigten Königreichs und Frankreichs in Washington vom 31.3. bis 1.4.1959. Gleichzeitig Konferenz der drei westlichen Außenminister mit dem Außenminister der Bundesrepublik in Washington.
11. Ministerratstagung der NATO vom 2. bis 4.4.1959 in Washington.
12. Tagung der Viermächte-Arbeitsgruppe in London vom 13. bis 23.4.1959.
13. Konferenz der Außenminister der Drei Westmächte und der Bundesrepublik in Paris am 29. und 30.4.1959.
14. Beginn der Genfer Konferenz der Außenminister der Vereinigten Staaten, der Sowjetunion, Frankreichs und des Vereinigten Königreichs am 11. 5. 1959 zur Vorbereitung einer später vorgesehenen Gipfelkonferenz.
15. Am 14. 5. 1959 legen die westlichen Delegationen in Genf ihren gemeinsamen „Friedensplan" vor, der in vier Stufen eine Regelung des Problems der deutschen Wiedervereinigung und der Europäischen Sicherheit vorsieht. Der Plan enthält ferner einige Vorschläge, die bisher im Rahmen der allgemeinen Abrüstung behandelt wurden. Bis zur Wiedervereinigung Deutschlands wird als Zwischenlösung für Berlin die Bildung einer von den Vier Mächten garantierten, wiedervereinigten Stadt Gesamt-Berlin vorgeschlagen. Als Endstufe der parallel in Angriff zu nehmenden Lösung der deutschen Frage und des Sicherheitsproblems ist eine endgültige Friedensregelung mit einer gesamtdeutschen Regierung vorgesehen.
16. Am 19.6.1959 vertagt die Konferenz sich auf den 13.7.1959.

III. ÜBERSICHTEN

A. VERTRETUNGEN DER BUNDESREPUBLIK IM AUSLAND

1. Botschaften:

Accra
Addis Abeba
Ankara
Asunción
Athen
Bagdad
Bangkok
Beirut
Bern
Bogotá
Brüssel
Buenos Aires
Canberra
Carácas
Ciudad Trujillo
Colombo
Conakry
Den Haag
Djakarta
Djidda
Habana
Heiliger Stuhl
Kabul
Kairo
Karachi
Kopenhagen
Kuala Lumpur
La Paz
Lima
Lissabon
London
Luxemburg
Madrid
Manila
Mexiko
Monrovia
Montevideo
Moskau
New Delhi
Oslo
Ottawa
Paris
Pretoria
Quito
Rabat
Reykjavik
Rio de Janeiro
Rom
San José
San Salvador
Santiago de Chile
Seoul
Stockholm
Teheran
Tokyo
Tunis
Washington
Wien

2. Gesandtschaften:

Amman
Dublin
Khartum
Managua
Panama
Port-au-Prince
Rangun
Saigon
Taizz
Tripolis
Wellington
Helsinki (Handelsvertretung)

3. Sonstige Vertretungen:

Vertretung bei der UNO (New York)
Vertretung beim Europarat (Straßburg)
Vertretung bei der OEEC (Paris)
Vertretung bei der NATO (Paris)
Vertretung bei der EWG und EAG (Brüssel)
Vertretung bei den Internationalen Organisationen (Genf)

4. Generalkonsulate:

Algier
Amsterdam
Antwerpen
Barcelona
Basel
Bombay
Chicago
Damaskus
Genf
Genua
Göteborg
Hongkong
Istanbul
Kalkutta
Léopoldville
Los Angeles
Lüttich
Mailand
Marseille
Montreal
Nairobi
New Orleans
New York
Osaka-Kobe
Rotterdam
Salisbury
Salzburg
San Francisco
São Paulo
Singapore
Sydney
Valparaiso
Zürich

5. Konsulate:

Alexandrien
Apenrade
Atlanta
Belo Horizonte
Bergen
Bilbao
Bordeaux
Boston
Bregenz
Casablanca
Cleveland
Concepción
Curitiba
Dacca
Dakar
Detroit
Edinburgh
Edmonton
Graz
Guayaquil
Houston
Innsbruck
Iskenderun
Izmir
Johannesburg
Kansas City
Kapstadt
Kingston
Lagos
Lille
Linz
Liverpool
Lourenço Marques
Luanda
Lyon
Maastricht
Madras
Malmö
Melbourne
Nancy
Neapel
Nicosia
Palermo
Philadelphia
Porto
Porto Alegre
Posadas
Recife
Rosario
Saloniki
Seattle
Toronto
Vancouver
Windhuk
Winnipeg
Zagreb

6. Wahlkonsulate:

Aalborg
Aalesund
Aarhus
Aberdeen
Abidjan
Aden
Antofagasta
Arendal
Arequipa
Bahia Blanca
Bari
Barranquilla
Beira
Belfast
Blantyre/Limbe
Blumenau
Bristol
Bucaramanga
Bulawayo
Cádiz
Callao
Cardiff
Cartagena (Kolumbien)
Cartagena (Spanien)
Catania
Cienfuegos
Colón
Córdoba
Cork
Cuzco
Dallas
Dar es Salaam
Djibouti
Dover
Durban
East London
Elisabethville
Encarnación
Enschede
Florianópolis
Formosa (Argentinien)
Fortaleza
Frederikshavn
Fúnchal
Gent
Grimsby
Groningen
Guadalajara
Hälsingborg
Halifax
Halmstad
Harstad
Haugesund
Heraklion/Kreta
Honolulu
Huelva
Hull
Ica
Ijui
Iquitos
Jönköping
Khorramshahr
Kirkenes
Kitchener
Korsör
Kristiansand S.
Kristiansund N.
Las Palmas de Gran Canaria
Lerwick
Limerick
Linköping
Livorno
Lugano
Luleå
Málaga
Manizales
Maracaibo
Matadi
Mendóza
Messina
Miami
Mombasa
Narvik
Newcastle upon Tyne
Nizza
Norfolk
Nyköbing
Odense
Oruro
Osorno
Ostende
Pacasmayo
Paramaribo
Patras
Piura
Plymouth
Ponta Delgada
Port Elisabeth
Port of Spain
Port Said
Porto Amélia
Potosi
Prince Rupert
Puebla

Puerto La Cruz
Puerto Montt
Resistencia
Rio Grande
Rönne
Rolándia
Salta
Salvador (Brasilien)
San Carlos de Bariloche
San Juan de Puerto Rico
San Ramón
Sandefjord
Santa Cruz (Bolivien)
Santa Cruz de Tenerife
Santa Fé
Santa Marta
Santander
Santiago de Cuba
Santos
Sassari
Sevilla
Southampton
Stanleyville
Stavanger
St. Gallen
Sucre
Sundsvall
Suva
Svendborg
Tarragona
Temuco
Thorshavn
Toulouse
Trelleborg
Tromsö
Trondheim
Tucumán
Turin
Uddevalla
Västervik
Valdivia
Valetta/Malta
Vejle
Veracruz/Tampico
Vigo
Volos
Willemstad

7. *Wahl-Vizekonsulate:*

Akureyri
Campo Grande
Granada
Hella
Jujuy
Nuevitas
Seydisfjördur
Vestmannaeyjar

B. ÜBERSICHT ÜBER OFFIZIELLE BESUCHE WICHTIGER PERSÖNLICHKEITEN

Die Eingliederung Deutschlands in das internationale Geschehen wird unter anderem durch zahlreiche Staatsbesuche und offizielle Reisen dokumentiert.

1. *Staatsbesuche des Bundespräsidenten*

Besuch in Griechenland	14. 5. — 22. 5.1956
Besuch in der Türkei	5. 5. — 13. 5.1957
Besuch in Italien	18.11. — 26.11.1957
Besuch beim Heiligen Stuhl	27.11. — 28.11.1957
Besuch in Kanada	28. 5. — 3. 6.1958
Besuch in den USA	4. 6. — 23. 6.1958
Besuch im Vereinigten Königreich	20.10. — 23.10.1958

2. *Wichtige Auslandsreisen und Staatsbesuche des Bundeskanzlers*

Besuch in Paris	11. 4. — 19. 4.1951
Besuch in Rom	14. 6. — 23. 6.1951
Besuch in Paris	20.11. — 23.11.1951
Besuch in London	3.12. — 8.12.1951
Besuch in Paris	28.12. — 31.12.1951
Besuch in London	14. 2. — 19. 2.1952
Besuch in Paris	18. 3. — 21. 3.1952
Besuch in Paris	22. 7. — 25. 7.1952

Besuch in Luxemburg	8. 9. — 12. 9.1952
Besuch in Rom	22. 2. — 28. 2.1953
Besuch in den USA	1. 4. — 19. 4.1953
Besuch in Paris	22. 6. — 23. 6.1953
Besuch in Den Haag	26.11. — 28.11.1953
Besuch in Paris	11.12. — 14.12.1953
Besuch in Athen	9. 3. — 17. 3.1954
Besuch in Ankara	18. 3. — 25. 3.1954
Besuch in Brüssel	18. 8. — 22. 8.1954
Besuch in London	27. 9. — 3.10.1954
Besuch in Paris	19.10. — 20.10.1954
Besuch in den USA	26.10. — 3.11.1954
Besuch in Paris	7. 5. — 12. 5.1955
Besuch in den USA	12. 6. — 19. 6.1955
Besuch in Moskau	8. 9. — 14. 9.1955
Besuch in Luxemburg	5.10.1955
Besuch in Luxemburg	4. 6. — 5. 6.1956
Besuch in den USA	8. 6. — 15. 6.1956
Besuch in Brüssel	24. 9. — 26. 9.1956
Besuch in Paris	6.11.1956
Besuch in Paris	18. 2. — 20. 2.1957
Besuch in Rom	23. 3. — 27. 3.1957
Besuch in Teheran	27. 3. — 2. 4.1957
Besuch in Washington	23. 5. — 30. 5.1957
Besuch in Wien	13. 6. — 15. 6.1957
Besuch in London	16. 4. — 19. 4.1958
Besuch in Colombey-les-Deux-Eglises	14. 9. — 15. 9.1958
Besuch in Paris	3. 3. — 5. 3.1959
Besuch in Washington	27. 5. — 29. 5.1959

3. *Offizielle Reisen des Bundesaußenministers*

Der Bundesminister des Auswärtigen, Dr. VON BRENTANO, reiste nach folgenden Staaten:

USA	27. 9. — 4.10.1955
Niederlande	7. 3. — 8. 3.1956
Vereinigtes Königreich	30. 4. — 3. 5.1956
Griechenland	14. 5. — 22. 5.1956
Dänemark	24. 5. — 26. 5.1956
Norwegen	27. 5. — 29. 5.1956
Österreich	9. 1. — 11. 1.1957
USA	2. 3. — 13. 3.1957
Australien	17. 3. — 25. 3.1957
Indien	28. 3. — 29. 3.1957
Türkei	5. 5. — 8. 5.1957
USA	25. 5. — 30. 5.1957

Österreich	13. 6. — 15. 6. 1957
Italien und Vatikan	18. 11. — 28. 11. 1957
Vereinigtes Königreich	4. 12. — 7. 12. 1957
Portugal	31. 3. — 2. 4. 1958
Spanien	3. 4. — 10. 4. 1958
Kanada	28. 5. — 3. 6. 1958
USA	4. 6. — 7. 6. 1958
Frankreich	3. 3. — 5. 3. 1959

4. *Besuche wichtiger ausländischer Persönlichkeiten und Staatsmänner in der Bundesrepublik*

Der Außenminister der Vereinigten Staaten von Nordamerika DEAN G. ACHESON	13. 11. 1949
Der Französische Außenminister ROBERT SCHUMAN	13. 1. — 15. 1. 1950
Der Königlich Niederländische Außenminister Dr. D. STIKKER	22. 2. 1950
Der Königlich Dänische Außenminister O. B. KRAFT	19. 3. 1951
Der Königlich Britische Außenminister MORRISON	19. 5. 1951
Der Oberbefehlshaber der Atlantikpakt-Streitkräfte General DWIGHT D. EISENHOWER	2. 5. 1952
Die Außenminister DEAN G. ACHESON, A. EDEN und R. SCHUMAN	24. 5. — 26. 5. 1952
Der Oberbefehlshaber der Atlantikpakt-Streitkräfte General RIDGWAY	2. 9. 1952
Der Ministerpräsident und Minister des Auswärtigen der Italienischen Republik ALCIDE DE GASPERI	21. 9. — 24. 9. 1952
Der Außenminister der Vereinigten Staaten von Nordamerika JOHN FOSTER DULLES	5. 2. — 6. 2. 1953
S. K. H. der Vizekönig des Yemen	18. 2. — 4. 3. 1953
Der Königlich Norwegische Minister des Auswärtigen HALVARD MANTHEY LANGE	1. 5. — 5. 5. 1953
Der Österreichische Außenminister Dr. KARL GRUBER	18. 5. — 21. 5. 1953
Seine Kaiserliche Hoheit der Kronprinz von Japan	31. 7. — 5. 8. 1953
Der Australische Außenminister The Rt. HON. R. G. CASEY	7. 10. — 9. 10. 1953
Der Königlich Griechische Koordinationsminister SPYROS MARKEZINIS	9. 11. — 11. 11. 1953
Der Königlich Niederländische Minister des Auswärtigen Dr. J. W. BEYEN	15. 11. — 18. 11. 1953
Das Präsidium der Hohen Behörde der Montan-Union	9. 12. 1953
Der Premierminister von Kanada LOUIS STEPHEN ST. LAURENT	10. 2. — 12. 2. 1954
Der Königlich Britische Schatzkanzler R. A. BUTLER	7. 5. — 9. 5. 1954
Der Spanische Landwirtschaftsminister CAVESTANY	16. 5. — 21. 5. 1954

Der Argentinische Minister des Auswärtigen Dr. JERÓNIMO REMORINO und der Argentinische Minister für wirtschaftliche Angelegenheiten Dr. ALFREDO GÓMEZ MORALES	26. 5. — 31. 5. 1954
Der Königlich Griechische Ministerpräsident Marschall ALEXANDER PAPAGOS in Begleitung des Außenministers STEPHANOPOULOS und des Koordinationsministers TH. KAPSALIS	30. 6. — 6. 7. 1954
I.K.H. Prinzessin MARGARET von Großbritannien	12. 7. 1954
Der Südafrikanische Transportminister O. SAUER	3. 9. — 5. 9. 1954
Der Wirtschaftsminister der Republik Chile JORGE SILVA GUERRA und der Minister für Land- und Siedlungsfragen MARIO MONTERO SCHMIDT	8. 9. — 15. 9. 1954
Der Türkische Ministerpräsident ADNAN MENDERES und der Türkische Außenminister Prof. FUAD KÖPRÜLÜ	2. 10. — 9. 10. 1954
Der Kaiserlich Japanische Ministerpräsident SHIGERU YOSHIDA	12. 10. — 15. 10. 1954
Seine Kaiserliche Majestät HAILE SELASSIE I, Kaiser von Äthiopien	8. 11. — 14. 11. 1954
Der ehemalige Präsident der Vereinigten Staaten von Nordamerika HERBERT HOOVER	22. 11. — 27. 11. 1954
Der Italienische Haushaltsminister Prof. Dr. EZIO VANONI	13. 12. — 15. 12. 1954
Der Ceylonesische Ministerpräsident und Minister für Verteidigung und Auswärtige Angelegenheiten Sir JOHN KOTELAWALA	14. 2. — 16. 2. 1955
Seine Kaiserliche Majestät Mohammed REZA SCHAH PAHLAVI Schahinschah von Iran und Ihre Majestät Kaiserin SORAYA	23. 2. — 5. 3. 1955
Der Portugiesische Wirtschaftsminister Dr. ULISSES CRUZ DE AGUIAR CORTES	5. 3. — 12. 3. 1955
Der Königlich Dänische Ministerpräsident und Außenminister H. C. HANSEN	28. 3. — 30. 3. 1955
Der Präsident der spanischen Syndikate JOSÉ SOLIS RUIZ	20. 5. — 28. 5. 1955
Der Ministerpräsident des Königreichs Thailand Feldmarschall P. PIBULSONGGRAM	26. 5. — 28. 5. 1955
Die Gattin des Peruanischen Staatspräsidenten Frau MARIA DELGADO DE ODRIA	14. 6. — 16. 6. 1955
Der Generalsekretär der Nordatlantikpakt-Organisation Lord ISMAY	4. 7. — 5. 7. 1955
Der Königlich Griechische Koordinationsminister PAPALIGOURAS und der Königlich Griechische Finanzminister EVTAXIAS	18. 9. — 25. 9. 1955
Der Präsident der Hohen Behörde der Europäischen Gemeinschaft für Kohle und Stahl RENÉ MAYER	23. 9. 1955
Der Mexikanische Wirtschaftsminister Lic. GILBERTO LOYO	2. 10. — 13. 10. 1955

19. 9.1950	Abkommen über die Gründung einer Europäischen Zahlungsunion (EZU) nebst Protokoll über die vorläufige Anwendung des Abkommens	1. 7.1950
4.11.1950	Konvention zum Schutze der Menschenrechte und Grundfreiheiten	5.12.1952
18. 4.1951	Vertrag über die Gründung einer Europäischen Gemeinschaft für Kohle und Stahl	23. 7.1952
21. 4.1951	Protokoll von Torquay zum Allgemeinen Zoll- und Handelsabkommen	1. 9.1951
30. 6.1952	Europäisches Rundfunkabkommen	3. 7.1953
11. 7.1952	Weltpostvertrag nebst Schlußniederschrift und anhängenden Bestimmungen über Luftpostbriefsendungen nebst Schlußniederschrift	21. 3.1955
27. 2.1953	Abkommen über deutsche Auslandsschulden	4. 9.1953
17.10.1953	Abkommen über die Errichtung einer Europäischen Konferenz der Verkehrminister	17.10.1953
19.10.1953	Satzung des Zwischenstaatlichen Komitees für Europäische Auswanderung	8.11.1954
11.12.1953	Europäische Konvention über die Gleichwertigkeit der Reifezeugnisse	3. 3.1955
23.10.1954	Protokoll zur Beendigung des Besatzungsregimes in der Bundesrepublik Deutschland	5. 5.1955
23.10.1954	Abgeänderte Fassung des Vertrags über die Beziehungen zwischen der Bundesrepublik Deutschland und den Drei Mächten vom 26.5.1952	5. 5.1955
23.10.1954	Abgeänderte Fassung des Vertrages über die Rechte und Pflichten ausländischer Streitkräfte und ihrer Mitglieder in der Bundesrepublik Deutschland vom 26.5.1952	5. 5.1955
23.10.1954	Abgeänderte Fassung des Vertrages zur Regelung aus Krieg und Besatzung entstandener Fragen vom 26.5.1952	5. 5.1955
23.10.1954	Vertrag über den Aufenthalt ausländischer Streitkräfte in der Bundesrepublik Deutschland	5. 5.1955
23.10.1954	Protokoll zur Änderung und Ergänzung des Brüsseler Vertrags vom 17.3.1948	6. 5.1955
27.10.1956	Vertrag zwischen der Bundesrepublik Deutschland, der Französischen Republik und dem Großherzogtum Luxemburg über die Schiffbarmachung der Mosel	31.12.1956
28. 3.1957	Vertrag zur Gründung der Europäischen Wirtschaftsgemeinschaft. In Kraft getreten am	1. 1.1958
28. 3.1957	Vertrag zur Gründung der Europäischen Atomgemeinschaft. In Kraft getreten am	1. 1.1958

2. *Wichtige bilaterale Verträge:*

Datum des Abkommens	
19.10.1951	Abkommen zwischen dem dazu ermächtigten Land Baden und dem Port Autonome de Strasbourg über die *Organisation einer gemeinsamen Verwaltung des Hafens von Kehl* nebst Anlagen.
10. 9.1952	Deutsch-israelisches Abkommen über *Leistungen der Bundesrepublik Deutschland an Israel.* Das Abkommen ist am 27.3. 1953 in Kraft getreten.
10. 9.1952	Deutsch-israelisches Abkommen über *deutsches Vermögen in Israel.*
27. 2.1953	Deutsch-italienische Vereinbarung über die *Wiederaufnahme der Tätigkeit deutscher Institute in Italien.*
27. 2.1953	Deutsch-britisches Abkommen über die Regelung der *Ansprüche* des Vereinigten Königreichs *aus der Deutschland geleisteten Nachkriegs-Wirtschaftshilfe.* Das Abkommen ist am 16.9.1953 in Kraft getreten.
23.10.1954	Deutsch-französisches *Kulturabkommen* nebst Briefwechsel. Das Abkommen nebst Briefwechsel ist am 28.7.1955 in Kraft getreten.
23.10.1954	Deutsch-französisches Abkommen über das Statut der Saar. Das Abkommen ist am 5.5.1955 in Kraft getreten.
29.10.1954	Deutsch-amerikanischer *Freundschafts-, Handels- und Schiffahrtsvertrag.* Der Vertrag ist am 14.7.1956 in Kraft getreten.
30. 6.1955	Deutsch-amerikanisches Abkommen über *gegenseitige Verteidigungshilfe.* Das Abkommen ist am 27.12.1955 in Kraft getreten.
13. 9.1955	Deutsch-sowjetisches Übereinkommen über die *Aufnahme diplomatischer Beziehungen.* Das Übereinkommen ist am 25.9.1955 in Kraft getreten.
20.12.1955	Deutsch-italienische Vereinbarung über die *Anwerbung und Vermittlung von italienischen Arbeitskräften* nach der Bundesrepublik Deutschland. Die Vereinbarung ist am 20.12. 1955 in Kraft getreten.
10. 3.1956	Deutsch-jugoslawische Vereinbarung über die Regelung von Ansprüchen auf *Entschädigung für nicht realisierbare Restitutionen* und von Ansprüchen gegen die deutsche Verrechnungskasse. Die Vereinbarung ist am 10.3.1956 in Kraft getreten.
10. 3.1956	Deutsch-jugoslawischer Vertrag über *wirtschaftliche Zusammenarbeit.* Der Vertrag ist am 22.1.1957 in Kraft getreten.

24. 9.1956 Vertrag zwischen der Bundesrepublik Deutschland und dem Königreich Belgien über eine *Berichtigung der deutsch-belgischen Grenze* und andere die Beziehungen zwischen beiden Ländern betreffende Fragen. Der Vertrag ist am 28.8.1958 in Kraft getreten.

27.10.1956 Vertrag zwischen der Bundesrepublik Deutschland und der Französischen Republik zur *Regelung der Saarfrage.* Der Vertrag ist am 1.1.1957 in Kraft getreten.

15. 6.1957 Vertrag zwischen der Bundesrepublik Deutschland und der Republik Österreich zur *Regelung vermögensrechtlicher Beziehungen.* Der Vertrag ist am 10.6.1958 in Kraft getreten.

8. 5.1957 Kulturabkommen zwischen der Bundesrepublik und der Türkischen Republik. Das Abkommen ist am 9.6.1958 in Kraft getreten.

26. 2.1958 Regierungsabkommen zwischen der Bundesrepublik und Indien über die Prolongierung der Zahlungen für das Stahlwerk Rourkela. Das Abkommen eröffnet einen Kredit von rund 660 Millionen DM für Indien.

25. 4.1958 Langfristiges Abkommen über den Waren- und Zahlungsverkehr zwischen der Bundesrepublik und der Sowjetunion (in Kraft getreten). Abkommen über allgemeine Fragen des Handels und der Seeschiffahrt zwischen der Bundesrepublik Deutschland und der Sowjetunion (am 24.4.1959 in Kraft getreten). Konsularvertrag zwischen der Bundesrepublik Deutschland und der Sowjetunion (am 24.5.1959 in Kraft getreten).

7. 5.1958 Wirtschaftsvereinbarungen zwischen der Bundesrepublik und der Vereinigten Arabischen Republik über Bundesbürgschaften für langfristige deutsche Lieferungen und Programm für deutsche technische Hilfeleistungen in Höhe von 350 Millionen DM.

6. 1.1959 Zweites Kredithilfeabkommen zwischen der Bundesrepublik und Indien zur Durchführung des Zweiten indischen Fünfjahresplanes über 168 Millionen DM.

25. 3.1959 Paraphierung einer Vereinbarung zwischen der Bundesrepublik und der Sowjetunion über den kulturellen, wissenschaftlichen und technischen Austausch. Unterzeichnet und damit in Kraft getreten am 30.5.1959.

18. 3.1959 Unterzeichnung eines deutsch-griechischen Regierungsabkommens über wirtschaftliche und technische Zusammenarbeit.

25. 4.1959 Unterzeichnung eines deutsch-äthiopischen Abkommens über technische und wirtschaftliche Zusammenarbeit.

DER DEUTSCHE STAAT GESTERN, HEUTE UND MORGEN

In dem chaotischen Zusammenbruch des Frühjahrs 1945 ging jener deutsche Staat von *gestern* unter, der für viele seiner Nachbarn und zeitweilig für die ganze Welt ein Alpdruck gewesen war. Erst nach Jahren konnte ein neues Staatswesen aufgebaut werden. Mit der Konstituierung der Bundesrepublik im Jahre 1949 wurde der erste Schritt getan; seine Souveränität erhielt der deutsche Staat von *heute* aber erst im Mai 1955 bei Inkrafttreten der bereits im Mai 1952 unterzeichneten, dann im Oktober 1954 umgestalteten Pariser Verträge („Vertrag über die Beziehungen zwischen der Bundesrepublik Deutschland und den Drei Mächten" und Zusatzverträge). Noch immer ist dieser Staat auf ein Rumpfgebiet beschränkt und seiner eigentlichen Hauptstadt beraubt, noch immer macht die politische Teilung Deutschlands gewisse Einschränkungen seiner Souveränität nötig, noch immer hat dieser Staat schwer an den Folgen des verlorenen Krieges zu tragen; aber es ist ihm trotz diesen großen Belastungen gelungen, sich wieder einen geachteten Platz in der Staatengemeinschaft zu erwerben. Der deutsche Staat von *morgen* wird erst nach Lösung der entscheidenden politischen Fragen, nach der Wiederherstellung der Einheit Deutschlands und der Unterzeichnung eines echten Friedensvertrages, aufgebaut werden können.

Als am 11. 11. 1918 der durch die militärische Niederlage Deutschlands herbeigeführte Waffenstillstand von Compiègne den Ersten Weltkrieg beendete, war ihm zwei Tage zuvor eine Revolution voraufgegangen, die den deutschen Staat aus einem Kaiserreich in eine demokratische Republik verwandelt hatte. Als die deutschen Heere am 8. 5. 1945 kapitulierten, ging diesem Ende der Feindseligkeiten keine politische Umwälzung voraus. Kein vernünftiger Mensch in Deutschland und in der Welt aber konnte ernstlich daran zweifeln, daß dieser militärische Zusammenbruch zugleich *das Schicksal eines politischen Regimes* besiegelte und notwendigerweise zu einer tiefgreifenden Strukturwandlung des deutschen Staates führen mußte. Die Formen, in denen diese Strukturwandlung sich vollzog, waren neuartig und ohne Vorbild. Kaum jemals ist in der neueren Geschichte ein großes Volk infolge eines verlorenen Krieges *seiner politischen Selbstbestimmung und seiner eigenen Regierungsgewalt so vollständig beraubt* worden wie das deutsche Volk nach 1945. Die Formel von der „*bedingungslosen Kapitulation*", welche die Alliierten 1943 auf der Konferenz von Casablanca in ihr Kriegsprogramm aufgenommen hatten, ging nunmehr in Erfüllung und wurde zu Konsequenzen hingeführt, die keine noch so einfallsreiche Phantasie auf dem Gebiete völkerrechtlicher Gestaltungsformen sich hatte vorstellen können.

Ein Regime von regionalen und lokalen Militärregierungen wurde errichtet, das mit unerbittlicher Entschlossenheit das in *Jalta* am 11.2.1945 beschlossene *Besatzungsziel* — die „Vernichtung des deutschen Militarismus und des Nazitums" — in Angriff nahm. Die Koordinierung dieser Besatzungspolitik wurde einem *Viermächte-Kontrollrat* übertragen.

Am 5. 6. 1945 regelten die vier Besatzungsmächte das Regime dieser Militärverwaltungen durch eine Reihe von Deklarationen. An ihrer Spitze stand die Erklärung, daß es „in Deutschland keine zentrale Regierung oder Behörde gebe, die fähig wäre, die Verantwortung für die Aufrechterhaltung der Ordnung, die Verwaltung des Landes und die Ausführung der Forderungen der siegreichen Mächte zu übernehmen", und daß daher die „Regierungen des Vereinigten Königreichs, der Vereinigten Staaten von Nordamerika, der Union der Sozialistischen Sowjetrepubliken und die Provisorische Regierung der Französischen Republik die *oberste Regierungsgewalt in Deutschland* (*supreme authority*) einschließlich aller Befugnisse der deutschen Regierung, des Oberkommandos der Wehrmacht und der Regierungen, Verwaltungen oder Behörden der Länder, Städte und Gemeinden" übernähmen. Zugleich wurde Deutschland „innerhalb seiner Grenzen, wie sie am 31.12.1937 bestanden, für Besatzungszwecke in *vier Zonen* aufgeteilt".

Das von den Regierungschefs der USA, der Sowjetunion und des Vereinigten Königreichs vereinbarte *Potsdamer Abkommen* vom 2. 8. 1945 bestätigte diese Regelung. Es wurde hinzugefügt, daß bis auf weiteres keine zentrale deutsche Regierung errichtet, Deutschland jedoch während der Besatzungszeit als eine wirtschaftliche Einheit betrachtet werden sollte. In den wirtschaftlichen Bestimmungen dieses Potsdamer Abkommens fanden sich deutliche Spuren des MORGENTHAU-*Planes*. Diesen Plan — der nie verwirklicht worden ist — hatten die Alliierten schon auf der Konferenz von Quebec am 15. 9. 1944 erörtert. Er zielte auf die Umwandlung Deutschlands in ein Land ab, das sich in erster Linie von Ackerbau und Weidewirtschaft ernähren sollte.

Erst spät ist in Deutschland der Wortlaut jener *Direktive des amerikanischen Generalstabs an den Oberbefehlshaber der US-Besatzungstruppen* in Deutschland vom April 1945 bekannt geworden, die ganz vom Geist des MORGENTHAU-Planes getragen war und in diesem Geiste Anweisungen für die amerikanische Besatzungspolitik in Deutschland gab[1]:

[1] Diese Direktive ist hier im Wortlaut *auszugsweise* wiedergegeben.

„Es muß den Deutschen klargemacht werden, daß Deutschlands rücksichtslose Kriegsführung und der fanatische Widerstand der Nazis die deutsche Wirtschaft zerstört und Chaos und Leiden unvermeidlich gemacht haben, und daß sie nicht der Verantwortung für das entgehen können, was sie selbst auf sich geladen haben. Deutschland wird nicht besetzt zum Zweck seiner Befreiung, sondern als ein *besiegter Feindstaat.* Ihr Ziel ist nicht die Unterdrückung, sondern die Besetzung Deutschlands, um gewisse wichtige alliierte Absichten zu verwirklichen. Bei der Durchführung der Besetzung und Verwaltung müssen Sie gerecht, aber fest und unnahbar sein. Die Verbrüderung (*fraternization*) mit deutschen Beamten in Ihrer Zone werden Sie streng unterbinden. Das Hauptziel der Alliierten ist es, Deutschland daran zu hindern, je wieder eine Bedrohung des Weltfriedens zu werden . . .

Abgesehen von den für diese Zwecke (der industriellen Abrüstung) erforderlichen Maßnahmen werden Sie *keine Schritte* unternehmen, die a) zur wirtschaftlichen Wiederaufrüstung führen oder b) geeignet sind, die deutsche Wirtschaft zu erhalten oder zu stärken . . .

Sie werden Schätzungen darüber anstellen, welche Zuschüsse notwendig sind, um Hungersnot und die Ausbreitung von Krankheiten und zivilen Unruhen zu vermeiden, welche *die Besatzungsstreitkräfte gefährden* könnten. Als Grundlage für diese Schätzungen soll ein Programm dienen, durch das die Deutschen selbst für ihre Versorgung aus eigener Arbeit und eigenen Hilfsquellen verantwortlich gemacht werden. Sie werden alle durchführbaren wirtschaftlichen und polizeilichen Maßnahmen ergreifen, um sicherzustellen, daß die deutschen Hilfsquellen voll ausgenutzt werden und der Verbrauch auf dem Mindestmaß gehalten wird. Sie werden nichts unternehmen, was geeignet wäre, den Mindestlebensstandard in Deutschland auf einem höheren Niveau zu erhalten als in irgendeinem benachbarten Mitgliedsstaat der Vereinten Nationen."

*

Es bedurfte immerhin mehrerer Jahre, um deutlich werden zu lassen, daß eine *Besatzungspolitik mit diesen Zielen weder sinnvoll noch durchführbar* war. Gerade die mit der Durchführung dieser Besatzungspolitik beauftragten alliierten Befehlshaber selbst haben erkannt, daß die Zielsetzung verfehlt war. Sie mußten sich bald davon überzeugen, daß man ein Millionenvolk *nicht durch eine autoritäre Militärbürokratie zu demokratischer Lebensführung „umerziehen"* kann, und daß die Drosselung des wirtschaftlichen Lebens nur zu einer unerträglichen Belastung der heimatlichen Steuerzahler führen mußte. Je länger der Kontakt mit der deutschen Bevölkerung dauerte und je intensiver er wurde, desto mehr wuchs auch die Einsicht in die schweren *seelischen Konflikte und Probleme*, die das Leben in einer totalitären Diktatur für jeden Einzelnen mit sich gebracht hatte, und die sich einer Erfassung durch die schematischen Kategorien einer moralisierenden Säuberungspolitik entziehen mußten. Solche Einsichten, die sich mit einer wachsenden Ernüchterung in der Beurteilung des sowjetischen Bündnispartners verbanden, führten zu einer zunächst langsamen, später rascher fortschreitenden *Auflockerung der Besatzungspolitik* — freilich erst in einem Augenblick, in dem man dem Wirtschaftspotential des künftigen deutschen Partners in der Abwehrfront gegen den Kommunismus durch umfangreiche und wirtschaftlich unsinnige Demontagen schweren Schaden zugefügt und sein Solidaritätsbewußtsein auf eine harte Probe gestellt hatte. Das wirtschaftliche Hilfsprogramm des MARSHALL-*Planes* trat an die Stelle der MORGENTHAU-Politik. Die schematischen politischen Säuberungsverfahren wurden allmählich abgebaut und die Bildung eigenständiger deutscher Orts- und Landesbehörden und schließlich auch einer deutschen Bundesregierung gefördert. Am Ende dieses ersten, sowohl für die Alliierten wie für die Deutschen wenig erfreulichen Abschnittes der Besatzungspolitik stand die *Konstituierung der Bundesrepublik* im Herbst 1949 und die Inkraftsetzung eines neuen *Besatzungsstatuts*, in dem die drei westlichen Besatzungsmächte sich gewisse Selbstbeschränkungen in der Ausübung ihrer Regierungs- und Verwaltungsbefugnisse auferlegten. Schon beim Erlaß dieses Besatzungsstatuts waren die Besatzungsmächte sich darüber im klaren, daß auch dieses Statut nur eine Übergangslösung darstellen konnte, und nahmen seine Überprüfung nach Ablauf eines Jahres in Aussicht. Diese fand im März 1951 ihren Niederschlag in einer Revision des Besatzungsstatuts, die den deutschen Behörden eine neuerliche Erweiterung ihrer Befugnisse einräumte. Ein Auswärtiges Amt sowie diplomatische und konsularische Vertretungen im Ausland wurden errichtet, fremde Diplomaten in Bonn akkreditiert. Die Bundesrepublik trat dem Europa-Rat in Straßburg bei und schloß mit fünf weiteren europäischen Ländern den Vertrag über die Gründung einer Europäischen Gemeinschaft für Kohle und Stahl. Der Kriegszustand mit den Westmächten, der bis dahin formell fortbestanden hatte, wurde durch ausdrückliche Erklärungen beendet.

*

Auf dieser Grundlage hat der deutsche Staat von 1945 bis Mai 1955 gearbeitet. Aber die nächste Phase seiner Entwicklung begann sich schon kurze Zeit nach der Errichtung der Bundesrepublik abzuzeichnen.

Während die Oppositionsparteien die sofortige Aufnahme von Viermächte-Besprechungen forderten und darin den richtigen Weg zur Wiedergewinnung der deutschen Einheit in Freiheit sahen — eine Auffassung, die sie auch nach dem wenig verheißungsvollen Verlauf der Berliner Konferenz (25. 1. bis 18. 2. 1954) nicht preisgaben —, hat die Politik der Bundesregierung und der hinter ihr stehenden Parteien zunächst ihren Ausdruck in den *Verträgen* gefunden, *die am 26.5.1952 in Bonn und am 27.5.1952 in Paris unterzeichnet und am 19.3.1953 durch den Deutschen Bundestag gebilligt wurden.* Nach längeren Auseinandersetzungen über die Frage der Verfassungsmäßigkeit der Verträge nahm der Bundestag mit einer Zweidrittelmehrheit und mit Zustimmung des Bundesrates (das heißt unter Beachtung der für eine Verfassungsänderung vorgeschriebenen Erfordernisse) ein Gesetz zur Ergänzung des Grundgesetzes an, das nach seiner Präambel der „Klarstellung von Zweifeln über die Auslegung des Grundgesetzes" dienen sollte. Dieses Gesetz erklärte die Verteidigung, einschließlich der Wehrpflicht für Männer vom vollendeten achtzehnten Lebensjahr an, sowie den Schutz der Zivilbevölkerung zu einer ausschließlichen Zuständigkeit des Bundes. Nach dem Inkrafttreten dieses Gesetzes vollzog der Bundespräsident unverzüglich die Ratifikation der Verträge. Die Ratifikationsurkunde wurde am 30. 3. 1954 in Bonn und Paris hinterlegt.

Indessen blieb der entsprechende Schritt des französischen Vertragspartners, der für die völkerrechtliche Verbindlichkeit der Verträge erforderlich war, aus. Nach einer langen Zeit der Ungewißheit verwarf die Nationalversammlung in Paris am 30. 8. 1954 den EVG-Vertrag[1]. Wenngleich diese Ablehnung sich nicht auf den „*Deutschlandvertrag*" erstreckte, so konnte doch auch dieser wegen des zwischen den beiden Verträgen bestehenden rechtlichen „Junktims" nicht in Kraft gesetzt werden.

Die durch diesen Beschluß heraufgeführte Krise der westlichen Verteidigungsgemeinschaft konnte jedoch überraschend schnell überwunden werden. Auf den Konferenzen von London (Neunmächte-Konferenz vom 28. 9. bis 3. 10. 1954) und Paris (21. bis 23. 10. 1954) wurde eine Einigung auf neuer Grundlage erzielt. Die Eingliederung der Bundesrepublik in die Verteidigung des Westens wurde auf andere Weise ins Auge gefaßt: in der Form des unmittelbaren Beitritts der Bundesrepublik zum Nordatlantikpakt und zu dem gleichzeitig umgestalteten und erweiterten Brüsseler Vertrag von 1948 (dem ursprünglich nur Frankreich, Großbritannien und die Benelux-Staaten angehörten, und der nunmehr Italien und der Bundesrepublik

[1] Einzelheiten siehe Seite 274.

zum Beitritt geöffnet wurde). Zugleich wurde der Deutschlandvertrag aus seiner rechtlichen Verbindung mit den Verteidigungsabkommen befreit und inhaltlich in bedeutsamer Weise umgestaltet.

Am 27.2.1955 hat der Deutsche Bundestag das neue Pariser Vertragswerk gebilligt, am 18.3.1955 passierte es den Bundesrat und konnte am 24.3.1955 vom Bundespräsidenten unterzeichnet und im Bundesgesetzblatt verkündet werden. Nachdem die französische Nationalversammlung am 23./27. und 29.12.1954 und der Rat der Republik am 27.3.1955 das Vertragswerk gebilligt hatten, waren die letzten Hindernisse beseitigt. Die Hinterlegung der Ratifikationsurkunden in Washington, Brüssel und Bonn ist am 20.4. und 5.5.1955 erfolgt.

Seit dem 5.5.1955 ist das Pariser Vertragswerk in Kraft.

*

Die durch die Verträge eingeleitete neue Phase der staatlichen Entwicklung der Bundesrepublik stand unter dem doppelten Zeichen der vollständigen Liquidation des Besatzungsregimes und ihrer engen politisch-militärischen Verbindung mit der nordatlantischen Staatengruppe.

Daß das Besatzungsregime irgendwann einmal sein Ende finden mußte, lag auf der Hand. Wenn es eine völkerrechtliche Grundlage hatte, so konnte diese nur in der Befugnis der Siegermächte gelegen haben, das besiegte Land bis zum Abschluß eines Friedensvertrages unter ihrer Kontrolle zu halten. Die besondere und im Völkerrecht unbekannte Form der Besetzung, der Deutschland unterworfen wurde, und die mit der vorübergehenden Übernahme der obersten Regierungsgewalt („*supreme authority*") verbunden war, ließ sich, wenn überhaupt, nur aus der Tatsache rechtfertigen, daß Deutschland 1945 keine handlungsfähige Regierung mehr besaß. Eine Kontrollbesetzung zwischen Kriegsende und Friedensschluß kann jedoch, wenn der Friedensschluß in eine ungewisse Zukunft rückt, nicht für unbegrenzte Zeit aufrechterhalten werden. Und eine *handlungsfähige deutsche Regierungsgewalt* existierte in Westdeutschland seit langem. Die Alliierten hatten selbst daran mitgeholfen, sie zu organisieren und mit den erforderlichen Machtmitteln auszustatten. Die Gründe für die Aufrechterhaltung eines Besatzungsregimes und zumal dieser besonders umfassenden und intensiven Besatzungsherrschaft, wie sie in Deutschland bestand, waren demnach längst fragwürdig geworden. Es bedurfte jedoch eines weiteren politischen Anstoßes, um die Verhandlungen in Gang zu setzen. Ihn gab der Entschluß, Deutschland an der westlichen Verteidigung zu beteiligen. Zugleich mit diesem Beschluß erklärten die Drei Westmächte auf der *Brüsseler Konferenz* im Dezember 1950 ihre Bereitschaft, mit der Bundesregierung Vertragsverhandlungen aufzunehmen.

Von Anfang an war damit klar, daß die Verhandlungen politisch an die Bedingung einer *deutschen Beteiligung an der westlichen Verteidigung* geknüpft waren. Die Form dieser Beteiligung blieb zunächst offen. Auf der Washingtoner Konferenz im September 1951 hatten die drei westlichen Außenminister sich darauf geeinigt, daß sie in der Form einer Teilnahme an der *Europäischen Verteidigungsgemeinschaft* verwirklicht werden sollte.

Mit den Pariser Vereinbarungen vom 23. 10. 1954 wurde dieser Plan aufgegeben und durch den Beschluß ersetzt, nationale deutsche Streitkräfte zuzulassen; sie sollten jedoch in gleicher Weise wie die Streitkräfte anderer Mitgliedsstaaten der NATO dem Atlantischen Oberkommando unterstellt werden.

*

Das politische Ergebnis der vertraglichen Vereinbarungen konnte vorerst *nicht die volle, uneingeschränkte und unbelastete Souveränität* der Bundesrepublik sein. Wie die internationale Lage mit ihren weltpolitischen Gegensätzen zwischen Ost und West sich entwickelt hatte, würde dieses Ergebnis die Vierte Besatzungsmacht in Deutschland herausgefordert haben. Die Drei westlichen Besatzungsmächte ließen von vornherein keinen Zweifel daran, daß sie nicht die Absicht hatten, den Konflikt mit der Sowjetunion in der deutschen Frage auf die Spitze zu treiben. Die Bundesregierung akzeptierte diesen Standpunkt; denn auch sie war nicht daran interessiert, die Viermächte-Basis der Besetzung Deutschlands aus dem Jahre 1945 vollständig zu vernichten. Diese Basis war schließlich das letzte Bindeglied geworden, das Ost- und Westdeutschland, Berlin und das „Saargebiet“ noch zusammenhielt. Auf dieser Basis beruht die Verantwortung, welche die Drei Westmächte heute noch im Hinblick auf die Verhältnisse in der sogenannten DDR in den deutschen Ostgebieten jenseits der Oder-Neiße-Linie und in Ostberlin geltend machen. Auf dieser Basis beruht den Sowjets gegenüber ihre Verantwortlichkeit für die friedliche Wiedervereinigung Deutschlands. Durch diese Überlegung war die Konstruktion des ursprünglichen Vertrages von 1952 bestimmt. Diese Grundgedanken liegen, wenn auch noch stärker als 1952 auf das unbedingt Notwendige reduziert, auch der neuen Vertragsfassung von 1954 zugrunde.

Form und Inhalt des sogenannten „Deutschlandvertrages“ und seiner Zusatzverträge wurden in starkem Maße durch die besonderen Gegebenheiten des gespaltenen Deutschlands bestimmt. Daher konnten auch drei wesentliche Momente der heutigen Lage Deutschlands durch dieses Vertragswerk nicht geändert werden:

1. Die Drei Westmächte sahen sich gezwungen, auch weiterhin Truppen in beträchtlicher Zahl auf deutschem Boden zu belassen.
2. Die politische Teilung konnte durch die Verträge selbst nicht behoben werden. Das Schicksal der Gebiete östlich der Oder-Neiße-Linie blieb ungeklärt.
3. Der Abschluß eines echten, endgültigen Friedensvertrags blieb weiterhin aufgeschoben.

Diese harten und jeder wirklichen Konsolidierung der Lage entgegenstehenden Tatsachen ließen sich durch keine Übereinkunft zwischen den Drei Westmächten und der Bundesrepublik aus der Welt schaffen.

Von diesem Blickpunkt her gesehen hatten die Verträge vor allem drei Aufgaben zu bewältigen:

1. Das aus einer kriegerischen Besetzung (*occupatio bellica*) hervorgegangene und nur in den Formen seiner Ausübung gemilderte Besatzungsregime mußte beendet werden. Aufgabe der vertraglichen Regelung war es daher, das *Besatzungsstatut aufzuheben*, das bisherige Besatzungsregime mit allen seinen Organen zu beseitigen und der Bundesrepublik volle Freiheit in ihren inneren und auswärtigen Angelegenheiten zu geben, soweit die internationale Lage dies erlaubte.
2. Da es im gemeinsamen Interesse der Bundesrepublik und der Drei Westmächte unumgänglich ist, daß weiterhin alliierte Streitkräfte in beträchtlicher Zahl im Bundesgebiet stationiert bleiben, bedurften die *Rechtsstellung dieser Streitkräfte* und die Fragen ihrer materiellen Versorgung und ihrer Unterbringung einer Neuregelung auf vertraglicher Grundlage. Diese Regelung ist 1952 zunächst in der Form eines Zusatzvertrags zum Deutschlandvertrag, des sogenannten „*Truppenvertrages*“, erfolgt.
3. Eine militärische Besetzung, die einem verlorenen Kriege nachfolgt, dient in der Regel den Siegermächten als Instrument zur Durchsetzung ihrer Kriegsziele; sie soll die Verwirklichung dieser Ziele im Friedensvertrag oder womöglich darüber hinaus bei der Erfüllung des Friedensvertrags verbürgen. Die Umwandlung des bisherigen Besatzungsregimes in eine Truppenstationierung zum Zwecke der gemeinsamen Verteidigung beraubt die Westalliierten in gewissem Umfang dieses Instruments zur Durchsetzung ihrer Kriegsziele. Der Verzicht auf dieses Instrument war nur um den Preis gewisser vertraglicher Zusicherungen zu erlangen. Es mußten daher bestimmte, aus Krieg und Besatzung entstandene Fragen

geregelt werden, die *unter normalen Umständen in einem Friedensvertrag* zu regeln sind.

Der „Deutschlandvertrag" (Vertrag über die Beziehungen zwischen der Bundesrepublik Deutschland und den Drei Mächten) mit seinen Zusatzverträgen[1] ist daher zwar *kein separater Friedensvertrag* zwischen den Drei Westmächten und der Bundesrepublik; aber er ist immerhin ein *vorläufiger Kriegsabschlußvertrag*, der seiner Funktion nach einen vorübergehenden Ersatz für einen solchen Friedensvertrag bieten soll.

Die Bundesrepublik hat durch den Deutschlandvertrag wieder die *volle Macht eines souveränen Staates über ihre inneren und äußeren Angelegenheiten* erhalten. Die drei Westmächte haben lediglich im Hinblick auf die internationale Lage die bisher von ihnen ausgeübten oder innegehabten Rechte in bezug auf Berlin und auf Deutschland als Ganzes einschließlich der Wiedervereinigung Deutschlands und einer Friedensvertragsregelung behalten (Artikel 2). Die Bundesregierung hat sich verpflichtet, ihre Politik in Einklang mit den Prinzipien der Satzung der Vereinten Nationen und mit den im Statut des Europarates aufgestellten Zielen zu halten (Artikel 3 Absatz 1). Sie ist damit einverstanden, daß vom Inkrafttreten der Abmachungen über den deutschen Verteidigungsbeitrag an Streitkräfte der gleichen Nationalität und Effektivstärke wie zur Zeit dieses Inkrafttretens in der Bundesrepublik stationiert werden dürfen (Artikel 4). Die Rechtsgrundlage für den Aufenthalt dieser Streitkräfte ist nicht mehr ein Vorbehaltsrecht, sondern eine besondere vertragliche Vereinbarung. Zu diesem Zwecke ist in Paris am 23. 10. 1954 ein besonderer „Vertrag über den Aufenthalt ausländischer Streitkräfte in der Bundesrepublik Deutschland" abgeschlossen worden.

Die Bundesrepublik und die Drei Mächte sind sich darüber einig, daß wesentliches Ziel ihrer gemeinsamen Politik eine zwischen Deutschland und seinen ehemaligen Gegnern frei vereinbarte *friedensvertragliche Regelung für ganz Deutschland* ist, welche die Grundlage für einen dauerhaften Frieden bilden soll. Sie sind sich darüber einig, daß die endgültige Festlegung der Grenzen Deutschlands bis zu dieser Regelung aufgeschoben werden muß. Bis dahin werden sie zusammenwirken, um mit friedlichen Mitteln ihr gemeinsames Ziel zu verwirklichen: ein *wiedervereinigtes Deutschland*, das

[1] Das sind: der „Vertrag über die Rechte und Pflichten ausländischer Streitkräfte und ihrer Mitglieder in der Bundesrepublik Deutschland"; das „Abkommen über die steuerliche Behandlung der Streitkräfte und ihrer Mitglieder"; der „Finanzvertrag" und der „Vertrag zur Regelung aus Krieg und Besatzung entstandener Fragen".

eine freiheitlich-demokratische Verfassung, ähnlich wie die Bundesrepublik, besitzt und in die europäische Gemeinschaft integriert ist (Artikel 7). Ein Schiedsgericht wird für alle Streitigkeiten zuständig sein, die sich aus den Bestimmungen dieser Verträge ergeben. Nur solche Streitigkeiten, die sich aus der Ausübung der Vorbehaltsrechte ergeben, unterliegen nicht der Gerichtsbarkeit dieses Schiedsgerichts oder eines anderen Gerichts (Artikel 9).

Die im ursprünglichen Vertragstext von 1952 vorgesehenen Notstandsbefugnisse der Drei Mächte in besonderen Fällen sind in der Pariser Fassung des Vertragstextes von 1954 fortgefallen. Die Drei Mächte behalten nur solange ihre bisherigen Rechte zum Schutze der Sicherheit ihrer Streitkräfte, bis die deutschen Behörden durch entsprechende gesetzliche Vollmachten selbst in den Stand gesetzt sind, wirksame Maßnahmen zum Schutze der Sicherheit der ausländischen Streitkräfte zu treffen (Artikel 5 Absatz 2). Die dazu erforderliche deutsche Gesetzgebung ist in Bearbeitung.

Die Tatsache, daß der Deutschlandvertrag noch nach seiner Unterzeichnung jahrelang ein bloßes Projekt blieb und nicht in Kraft gesetzt werden konnte, hat sich letztlich günstig ausgewirkt; denn auf der Pariser Konferenz vom Oktober 1954 wurde eine Revision des Vertragstextes vorgenommen, die im ganzen eine wesentliche Verbesserung darstellt. Der Gedanke, daß der deutsche Staat wieder souverän sein müsse, und daß ihm keine Beschränkungen mehr auferlegt werden dürften, die nicht durch die internationale Lage zwingend geboten sind, kam nunmehr klar und eindeutig zum Ausdruck.

Mit der Ratifizierung des Pariser Vertragswerkes, der Bildung der Westeuropäischen Union und dem Beitritt Deutschlands zum Nordatlantikpakt war das Ende der Besatzungszeit erreicht und damit ein unerfreulicher Abschnitt der Nachkriegsentwicklung abgeschlossen.

*

Die Wiedererlangung der Souveränität leitete eine *neue Phase* in der Entwicklung zum deutschen Staat von heute ein. Die Bundesrepublik war nunmehr wieder in die Lage versetzt, eine selbständige Politik zur vollständigen Wiederherstellung des deutschen Staatswesens und seiner internationalen Geltung zu treiben. In enger Zusammenarbeit mit ihren westlichen Verbündeten war die Politik der Bundesregierung daher vor allem auf folgende Ziele gerichtet:

1. Aufnahme der Bundesrepublik als echten Partner in die Gemeinschaft der freien Völker der Welt.

2. Wiederherstellung der staatlichen Einheit Deutschlands auf dem Boden einer freiheitlichen Staats- und Sozialordnung.
3. Sicherung der Bundesrepublik gegen alle äußeren Gefahren.
4. Abschluß eines Friedensvertrages, der das Verhältnis des deutschen Volkes zu seinen Nachbarn dauerhaft und gerecht ordnet.
5. Förderung des Weltfriedens durch Zusammenarbeit und Freundschaft mit möglichst vielen Nationen der Welt im Geiste der Grundsätze und Ideale, die in der Charta der Vereinten Nationen ihren Ausdruck gefunden haben.

*

Die Bundesregierung hat bei ihrem Bemühen um Verwirklichung dieser Ziele auf vielen Gebieten erfreuliche Erfolge gehabt, sie hat jedoch auch auf sehr wesentlichen Gebieten immer neue Enttäuschungen erleiden müssen.

Auf dem Gebiet der *europäischen Integration*, die mit der Preisgabe des Gedankens der europäischen Verteidigungsgemeinschaft einen gewissen Rückschlag erlitten hatte, konnten in den folgenden Jahren wieder bedeutende Fortschritte erzielt werden. Die Europäische Gemeinschaft für Kohle und Stahl, die als erster Schritt zur europäischen Integration geschaffen worden war, hatte inzwischen erste Erfolge zu verzeichnen. In konsequenter Weiterentwicklung der ihr zugrunde liegenden Ideen wurden die Verträge zur Gründung der Europäischen Wirtschaftsgemeinschaft (EWG) und der Europäischen Atomgemeinschaft (EAG) ausgearbeitet[1]. Mit dem Inkrafttreten dieser Verträge am 1.1.1958 war der Wille der sechs beteiligten Staaten, sich zu einer engeren wirtschaftlichen Gemeinschaft zusammenzuschließen, erneut eindrucksvoll unter Beweis gestellt und zugleich eine tragfähige Grundlage für die politische Einigung Europas geschaffen worden.

Die Zusammenarbeit der Bundesregierung mit den übrigen Mächten der *Nordatlantikpakt-Organisation* wurde in dieser Phase immer enger und bedeutungsvoller. Mit zunehmendem Aufbau der Bundeswehr intensivierte sich auch die deutsche Mitarbeit in den militärischen Stäben und Einrichtungen der NATO. Über das militärische Gebiet hinaus wurde diese Zusammenarbeit auf den politischen, wirtschaftlichen und kulturellen Bereich ausgedehnt.

*

Auch auf dem Gebiet der *Wiederherstellung der staatlichen Einheit Deutschlands* konnte durch die Rückgliederung von Saarland ein wichtiger Fortschritt erzielt werden. Die *Regelung der Saarfrage* hat bewiesen, daß es

[1] Unterzeichnung in Rom am 25.3.1957.

möglich ist, heiß umstrittene Territorialfragen auf friedlichem Wege einer gerechten und ausgewogenen Lösung zuzuführen, wenn nur auf beiden Seiten der ernste Wille vorhanden ist, das Selbstbestimmungsrecht der Völker zu achten und strittige Fragen im Geiste der Grundsätze und Ideale der Charta der Vereinten Nationen zu lösen. Mit der Ablehnung des Saarstatuts am 23.10.1955 hatte die Bevölkerung von Saarland zugleich ihre nationale Verbundenheit mit Deutschland zum Ausdruck gebracht. Die französische Regierung zeigte sich in Anerkennung des Selbstbestimmungsrechts der Völker bereit, aus dem Abstimmungsergebnis die politischen Folgerungen zu ziehen. Am 27.10.1956 konnte als Ergebnis langer Verhandlungen und nach erheblichen Opfern auf beiden Seiten der Vertrag zwischen der Bundesrepublik Deutschland und der Französischen Republik unterzeichnet und die politische Eingliederung von Saarland in die Bundesrepublik herbeigeführt werden. Damit war es endlich gelungen, die seit dem Kriegsende bestehenden Meinungsverschiedenheiten zwischen Deutschland und Frankreich im Geiste einer wahrhaft europäischen Politik zu überbrücken. Die politische Eingliederung von Saarland vollzog sich am 1.1.1957 unter Berücksichtigung der von der Bundesrepublik stets vertretenen Auffassung, daß Saarland nie aufgehört habe, ein Teil des deutschen Staatswesens in den Grenzen von 1937 zu sein.

*

So erfolgreich die Verhandlungen mit Frankreich über die Regelung der Saarfrage verliefen, so enttäuschend waren die Resultate der Bemühungen der Bundesrepublik um die *Befreiung der sowjetischen Besatzungszone.*

Als die Drei Westmächte im Sommer 1948 daran gingen, nur einen Teil des früheren Deutschlands zusammenzufassen, hofften sie, daß ihre Bemühungen um die Wiederherstellung einer zentralen deutschen Staatsgewalt auch beispielgebend auf die Sowjetunion wirken würden. Die Sowjetunion hatte sich bisher geweigert, ihre Besatzungszone mit den drei westlichen Besatzungszonen zu vereinigen. Viele Monate hatten die Drei Westmächte versucht, die sowjetische Zustimmung zur Einsetzung einer gesamtdeutschen Regierung zu erhalten und die Wiedervereinigung Deutschlands herbeizuführen. Weil die Sowjetunion immer neue Einwände erhob, entschlossen sich die Drei westlichen Besatzungsmächte, den Anfang mit einer Wiederherstellung der deutschen Staatsgewalt in ihren eigenen drei Zonen zu machen. Die Sowjetunion hat sich diesem Vorgehen zur großen Enttäuschung des *gesamten* deutschen Volkes nicht angeschlossen, sondern die von ihr besetzte Zone nach Einsetzung eines von Moskau abhängigen kommunistischen Regimes unter dem Namen „Deutsche Demokratische Republik" verselbständigt, obgleich die Bevölkerung dieses Gebiets weder damals den Willen zur Eigenstaatlichkeit hatte noch heute besitzt. Damit war die Spaltung Deutschlands vollzogen.

Die Wiedervereinigung mit dem unter sowjetischer Besatzung stehenden Gebiet Mitteldeutschlands, der sogenannten DDR, bildete seit dem Augenblick der Wiedererlangung der Souveränität das zentrale Thema der politischen Bemühungen der Bundesregierung. Bei Durchführung dieser Politik mußte die Bundesregierung einerseits darum bemüht sein, die Verbindung zum Westen zu erhalten und zu intensivieren; andererseits mußte sie versuchen, die Sowjetunion davon zu überzeugen, daß auch den sowjetischen Interessen gedient sei, wenn die Ungerechtigkeit der Teilung Deutschlands beendet würde.

Zwischen der Bundesregierung und den Drei Westmächten bestand und besteht über die Notwendigkeit der Wiedervereinigung Deutschlands und über die Wege, sie zu erreichen, völlige Übereinstimmung. Die Drei Westmächte sind wie die Bundesregierung davon überzeugt, daß es sich bei der Wiedervereinigungsfrage um ein brennendes Problem handelt, das nicht nur die Deutschen angeht, sondern alle diejenigen, die Frieden und Sicherheit in Europa und in der ganzen Welt wollen. Sie haben dies in den vergangenen Jahren wiederholt — und zum Teil in feierlicher Form — dargetan. Die in der *Nordatlantikpakt-Organisation* zusammengeschlossenen vierzehn Staaten haben sich mit den Erklärungen der Drei Westmächte identifiziert.

Das große Ziel der deutschen Politik, die Wiederherstellung der staatlichen Einheit Deutschlands, kann jedoch nur dann verwirklicht werden, wenn es zu einer *übereinstimmenden* Entscheidung der *Vier* Mächte kommt, die 1945 die Verantwortung für die Zukunft Deutschlands übernommen haben.

Leider erwiesen sich bisher alle Hoffnungen als trügerisch, auch die *Sowjetunion* als *vierte* für die Wiedervereinigung Deutschlands verantwortliche Macht werde endlich zu der Erkenntnis gelangen, daß kein dauerhafter Frieden und keine echte Sicherheit in Europa und in der Welt möglich sei, solange sie darauf beharre, dem deutschen Volk die Einheit zu versagen.

Zwar einigten sich die in Genf vom 18. bis 23.7.1955 versammelten Regierungschefs der vier Großmächte auf eine *Direktive* an ihre Außenminister, in der diese beauftragt wurden, in einer zweiten Genfer Konferenz im Oktober 1955 die Frage der Wiedervereinigung Deutschlands in Verbindung mit dem Sicherheitsproblem zu erörtern (siehe Seite 190). Das Ergebnis der zweiten Genfer Konferenz (27.10. bis 16.11.1957) brachte dem deutschen Volk aber bittere Enttäuschung: Um dem Auftrag der vier Regierungschefs nachzukommen und ihrer in der Direktive ausdrücklich bestätigten gemeinsamen Verantwortung für die Wiedervereinigung Deutschlands zu genügen, unterbreiteten die drei westlichen Außenminister, in vollem Einverständnis mit der Bundesregierung handelnd, dem sowjetischen Außenminister MOLOTOW detaillierte Vorschläge für die gleichzeitige Lösung der deutschen Frage und der durch sie bedingten Sicherheitsfragen. Diese Vorschläge boten der Sowjetunion sehr weitgehende Sicherheitsgarantien für den Fall der deutschen Wiedervereinigung an. Auch der Sowjetische Außenminister legte der Konferenz zwei Vorschläge für ein europäisches Sicherheitssystem vor, die aber beide von der Aufrechterhaltung der Teilung Deutschlands ausgingen und das Ziel verfolgten, die westliche Verteidigungsorganisation aufzulösen. Die Sowjetunion ließ keinen Zweifel daran, daß sie die Zustimmung zur Wiedervereinigung Deutschlands nicht aus Besorgnis um ihre Sicherheit verweigerte. Sie machte sich vielmehr die von den kommunistischen Führern der sogenannten DDR in aller Deutlichkeit erhobene Forderung zu eigen, daß die dort zur Zeit herrschende wirtschaftliche Ordnung auf Gesamtdeutschland ausgedehnt werden müsse. Die Sowjetunion hat damit zu erkennen gegeben, daß sie die Bolschewisierung ganz Deutschlands erstrebt und die Teilung Deutschlands solange aufrecht erhalten will, als sie dieses Ziel nicht zu erreichen vermag.

Der enttäuschende Ausgang der Genfer Außenministerkonferenz hat die Bundesregierung nicht davon abhalten können, ihre Bemühungen um einen Fortschritt in der Lösung der Wiedervereinigungsfrage energisch fortzusetzen.

Zwischen den beiden Konferenzen hatte die Bundesregierung auf Einladung der Sowjetischen Regierung sich bereit gefunden, eine vom Bundeskanzler geführte Delegation nach Moskau zu entsenden. Die Verhandlungen (9. bis 13. 9. 1955) ergaben das beiderseitige Einverständnis über die Aufnahme diplomatischer Beziehungen. Zur Wahrung des Rechtsstandpunktes der Bundesregierung wurde der Regierung der Sowjetunion jedoch folgender *Vorbehalt* notifiziert: „. . . 1. Die Aufnahme der diplomatischen Beziehungen zwischen der Regierung der Bundesrepublik Deutschland und der Regierung der UdSSR stellt keine Anerkennung des derzeitigen beiderseitigen territorialen Besitzstandes dar. Die endgültige Festsetzung der Grenzen Deutschlands bleibt dem Friedensvertrag vorbehalten.

2. Die Aufnahme diplomatischer Beziehungen mit der Regierung der Sowjetunion bedeutet keine Änderung des Rechtsstandpunktes der Bundes-

regierung in bezug auf ihre Befugnisse zur Vertretung des deutschen Volkes in internationalen Angelegenheiten und in bezug auf die politischen Verhältnisse in denjenigen deutschen Gebieten, die sich gegenwärtig außerhalb ihrer effektiven Hoheitsgewalt befinden" (siehe Seite 191).

Die Aufnahme diplomatischer Beziehungen zur Sowjetunion, die in Durchführung der Moskauer Vereinbarungen Anfang 1956 verwirklicht wurde, eröffnete der Bundesregierung die Möglichkeit, auch mit der Regierung der Sowjetunion, der vierten der für die Wiedervereinigung Deutschlands völkerrechtlich verantwortlichen Mächte, in einen direkten Gedankenaustausch zu treten. Am 7.9.1956 übergab der deutsche Botschafter in Moskau der Sowjetischen Regierung ein Memorandum der Bundesregierung zur Frage der Wiederherstellung der deutschen Einheit. Kernstück des Memorandums war das Anerbieten, mit der Sowjetunion ein europäisches Sicherheitssystem zu diskutieren, das der Sowjetunion die Möglichkeit geben sollte, der Wiedervereinigung zuzustimmen, ohne sich bedroht zu fühlen. Die sowjetische Antwortnote wurde am 22.10.1956 übergeben. Hinsichtlich des Weges zur Wiedervereinigung erklärte sie, daß die Genfer Direktive überholt und gesamtdeutsche Wahlen zum gegenwärtigen Zeitpunkt nicht möglich seien; demgegenüber bezeichnete sie Verhandlungen zwischen der Bundesrepublik und der sogenannten Deutschen Demokratischen Republik als unumgänglich notwendig. Trotz dem wenig konzilianten Ton der Note setzte die Bundesregierung den unmittelbaren Meinungsaustausch mit der Sowjetunion über die Wiedervereinigung fort. In ihrem Memorandum vom 20.5.1957 bezeichnete sie die Wiedervereinigung als Grundfrage der deutsch-sowjetischen Beziehungen. Sie forderte, daß die Sowjetunion konstruktive Vorschläge für die Wiedervereinigung mache, nachdem sie bisher alle Vorschläge der Bundesregierung als Verhandlungsgrundlage abgelehnt habe.

Um die Sowjetunion im Hinblick auf die Londoner Abrüstungsverhandlungen mit Nachdruck auf die überragende Bedeutung der Deutschlandfrage hinzuweisen, wurden die Grundsätze und Ziele der westlichen Wiedervereinigungspolitik erneut in der „*Berliner Erklärung*" präzisiert, die von den vier Regierungen (Frankreich, Vereinigtes Königreich, USA, Bundesrepublik) am 29.7.1957 in Berlin unterzeichnet wurde.

Ein Erfolg war allen diesen Appellen und Anfragen leider nicht beschieden. Die sowjetische Regierung beharrte vielmehr — wie ihre unmittelbar vor den Bundestagswahlen überreichte Note vom 7.9.1957 und alle späteren Äußerungen zeigten — *auf ihrer unnachgiebigen Haltung.*

Als die Sowjetunion kurz vor der Jahreswende 1957 die Einberufung einer *Gipfelkonferenz* anregte, war die Bundesregierung daher bestrebt, auch die Frage der Wiedervereinigung Deutschlands auf die Tagesordnung zu bringen. Sie begrüßte es freudig, daß Präsident EISENHOWER in einem Schreiben an Ministerpräsident BULGANIN am 12. 1. 1958 unter Hinweis auf die bestehenden Viermächte-Verpflichtungen die Einbeziehung der deutschen Frage in die Tagesordnung der Gipfelkonferenz vorschlug. Leider lehnte die Sowjetunion nicht nur die Behandlung der deutschen Frage auf der Gipfelkonferenz ab, sondern sie leugnete auch die noch auf der Genfer Gipfelkonferenz 1955 feierlich anerkannte Verantwortung der Vier Mächte für die Wiedervereinigung.

Eine einstimmig gefaßte Bundestagsentschließung vom 2. 7. 1958, der sich am 18. 7. 1958 auch der Deutsche Bundesrat anschloß, brachte ein neues Element in die Diskussion der Wiedervereinigungsfrage. Der Bundestag regte die Bildung eines *Viermächte-Gremiums* an, dessen Aufgabe es sein sollte, „gemeinsame Vorschläge zur deutschen Frage" zu erarbeiten. Die Bundesregierung machte sich diesen Vorschlag des Bundestages zu eigen und notifizierte ihn am 9. 9. 1958 den Vier Mächten. Während die Westmächte dem Vorschlag der Bundesregierung zustimmten, erklärte die Sowjetunion sich zwar zur Diskussion eines Friedensvertrages in einer Viermächte-Kommission bereit, nicht jedoch zu Verhandlungen über die Wiedervereinigung, die ausschließlich zur Kompetentz der „beiden deutschen Staaten" gehöre. Die Bundesregierung wandte sich in ihrer an die Sowjetunion gerichteten Note vom 17. 11. 1958 gegen eine negative Begrenzung des Verhandlungsgegenstandes und gab erneut der Hoffnung Ausdruck, daß die Sowjetunion an der Verwirklichung des Vorschlags zur Bildung eines Viermächte-Gremiums mitwirken würde. Stattdessen unternahm die Sowjetunion in einer neuen Aktion, die diesmal die *Berlin-Frage* betraf, den Versuch, sich eines weiteren Teils der Viermächte-Verantwortlichkeit für Deutschland zu entledigen. Mit den Noten vom 27. 11. 1958 setzte sie die Bundesregierung und die Drei Westmächte davon in Kenntnis, daß sie die internationalen Abkommen, auf denen der Viermächte-Status Berlins beruht, als nicht mehr in Kraft befindlich betrachte. Gleichzeitig schlug die Sowjetunion zur Schaffung einer sogenannten „Freien Stadt Westberlin" den Westmächten innerhalb von sechs Monaten durchzuführende Verhandlungen vor, nach deren Scheitern „ein Gegenstand für Verhandlungen zwischen den ehemaligen Besatzungsmächten in der Berlin-Frage nicht mehr gegeben" sei.

Die Bundesregierung hat zusammen mit den anderen Teilnehmerstaaten der Pariser NATO-Konferenz vom 14. bis 18.12.1958 ihre Entschlossenheit zum Ausdruck gebracht, die Freiheit Berlins zu wahren und weder eine einseitige Aufhebung des Viermächte-Status noch eine Gefährdung der Verkehrswege von und nach Berlin hinzunehmen. Diese Haltung fand in den Noten der Drei Westmächte vom 31.12.1958 und der Bundesregierung vom 5.1.1959 ihren Ausdruck. Darin wurde gleichzeitig aber die Bereitschaft zur Erörterung der Berlin-Frage im Rahmen von Verhandlungen über die Lösung der deutschen Frage und der Frage der europäischen Sicherheit erklärt.

Unter gleichzeitiger Erwiderung auf diese Noten rückte die Sowjetunion mit den Noten vom 10.1.1959 erneut die Frage eines *Friedensvertrages* mit Deutschland in den Vordergrund. Sie legte mit diesen Noten einen Entwurf für einen Friedensvertrag vor, der — was die Wiedervereinigung betrifft — darauf abzielt, den Zustand der deutschen Spaltung zu legalisieren und außerdem vom deutschen Volk den Verzicht auf die deutschen Ostgebiete sowie den Verzicht auf Sicherheit zu verlangen.

Bedeutsamer als der Abschluß eines Friedensvertrages ist für das deutsche Volk die Wiederherstellung seiner staatlichen Einheit. Für diese entscheidende Schicksalsfrage des deutschen Volkes bringen die sowjetischen Vorschläge aber keine Lösung. Die Bevölkerung Mitteldeutschlands soll nach den sowjetischen Vorstellungen — entgegen ihrem Willen von der gemeinsamen Gestaltung eines freiheitlichen Staatswesens ausgeschlossen — nach wie vor unter dem Joch eines ihr aufgezwungenen kommunistischen Regimes leben. Der Wunsch des deutschen Volkes nach Wiedervereinigung in Freiheit soll unberücksichtigt bleiben.

So erweist sich auch der deutsche Staat von *heute*, dessen friedfertige, freiheitlich-demokratische Haltung im deutschen Volk fest verwurzelt ist, jener Staat, der wieder Ansehen und Vertrauen in der Welt genießt und dessen wirtschaftlicher Aufschwung weithin Anerkennung gefunden hat, nur als *Provisorium*. Erst der deutsche Staat von *morgen*, nach friedlicher Wiederherstellung der staatlichen Einheit Deutschlands auf dem Boden einer demokratisch gesicherten freiheitlichen Staats- und Sozialordnung errichtet, wird wieder als ein *Definitivum* anzusehen sein, in dem das gesamte deutsche Volk seine Kräfte vereinen kann, um in Zusammenarbeit und Freundschaft mit möglichst vielen Nationen mitzuwirken an der Ausgestaltung und Förderung des Weltfriedens.

WIEDERVEREINIGUNG IN FREIHEIT

Die Lage der Menschen in Mitteldeutschland

Die Teilung Deutschlands wird nicht selten als bloße geographische Trennung angesehen, durch die der eine — westliche — Teil zur Gemeinschaft der Freien Völker, der andere Teil — Mitteldeutschland — zum sowjetischen Herrschaftsbereich zählt. Daß diese Teilung mehr bedeutet als die Zugehörigkeit der beiden Gebiete zu verschiedenen Machtbereichen, auch mehr, als die übliche unkritische Unterscheidung in einen freien und einen unfreien Teil, ist jedem bewußt, der die spezifische Eigenart der bolschewistischen Diktatur zu beurteilen weiß.

Während die aus der Geschichte und der Gegenwart bekannten Diktaturen sich zumeist mehr oder weniger mit der Ausübung der absoluten Macht begnügen, wurzelt die bolschewistische Diktatur in der Ideologie des Marxismus-Leninismus. Diese Ideologie hat bekanntlich nicht nur die Weltrevolution zum Vorwurf. Als Kern enthält sie ein Geschichts- und Weltbild von gleichsam religiösem Charakter, zu dem die Menschheit insgesamt, zunächst jedoch vornehmlich die Bevölkerung im Herrschaftsbereich des Kommunismus, bekehrt werden soll. Der dialektische und historische Materialismus sieht den Menschen als durch die kapitalistische Epoche sich selbst entfremdet an. Der neu zu schaffende Mensch des Kommunismus' jedoch findet sich nach dieser Lehre selbst wieder, weil er jeden Egoismus aufgegeben hat und freiwillig zum absoluten Gemeinschaftswesen geworden ist. Der Mensch gilt nur insofern etwas, als er der Gemeinschaft nützt. Demgemäß erstrebt das bolschewistische Regime die totale Entprivatisierung des Lebens, die totale Beherrschung des einzelnen Menschen durch die „Gesellschaft" (zunächst den Staat), die Kollektivierung des gesamten Lebens. Die Freiwilligkeit der Entpersönlichung kann erst in der Zukunft erreicht werden; denn die geschichtlich gewachsenen Umwelt-Tatsachen wie Klassen, Privateigentum, Religion usw. stehen ihr noch entgegen. Der vorhandene Widerstand der Menschen muß deshalb mit der von der kommunistischen Minderheit — der Partei — eroberten Staatsgewalt unterdrückt und gebrochen werden, sei es durch Propaganda, suggestive Überredung oder Freiheitsentzug.

Die Verwirklichung dieser Theorie ist ein schrecklicher Prozeß. Er begann mit der Oktoberrevolution 1918 in Rußland. Nach dem letzten Krieg hat er sich bis in das Herz Europas ausgebreitet. Nach STALINS Tod weist er in Mitteldeutschland die derzeitig konsequenteste stalinistische Strenge auf. Durch diesen Prozeß, dem die mitteldeutsche Bevölkerung nun bereits seit vierzehn Jahren unterworfen ist, wird die gesamte Situation der sogenannten DDR gekennzeichnet. Es gibt praktisch kaum einen Lebensbereich, den die Kommunisten nicht in ihre Bemühungen zur Weltumwandlung einbezogen hätten.

Die Tatsache, daß er nur in seinem Nutzen für die Gesellschaft von Wert ist, erfährt der Mensch in vielfältiger Weise. Das beginnt spätestens bei der Berufswahl, die rigoros im Sinne des Plans entschieden wird, wenn Wunsch und Arbeitskräfte-Planung nicht übereinstimmen.

Der Lohn ist absoluter Leistungslohn, ohne Rücksicht auf Alter, Familienstand oder Berufserfahrung. Die festgesetzte Arbeitsnorm ist das zur Erfüllung des Plans Notwendige, die Erfüllung des Plans ist Gradmesser der Zugehörigkeit zur Gesellschaft. Plan-Übererfüller werden ausgezeichnet, Nichterfüller öffentlich gerügt oder gar bestraft.

Wer eine politisch nicht konforme Meinung vertritt, hat nicht mehr den politischen Prozeß zu erwarten, er gilt als kriminell. Das Strafmaß richtet sich nicht nach der persönlichen Verantwortlichkeit, sondern nach dem Gesichtspunkt, inwieweit der Täter der Gesellschaft noch schaden kann: Der jüngere Mensch wird härter bestraft, weil er noch Widerstand leisten könnte.

Überhaupt ist zur Rechtssituation eine ungeheure Diskrepanz zwischen Recht und Gesetz festzustellen. Grundlage des gesamten Rechtswesens ist die sogenannte „demokratische Gesetzlichkeit", die stillschweigend mit Recht gleichgesetzt wird. Die in der sogenannten DDR geschaffenen Gesetze und die erklärten Ziele der herrschenden Staatspartei, der SED, heben das in der Verfassung verbriefte Recht weitgehend auf.

Einige Beispiele:

In Artikel 9 der Verfassung der sogenannten DDR heißt es: „Alle Bürger haben das Recht, innerhalb der Schranken der für alle geltenden Gesetze ihre Meinung frei und öffentlich zu äußern — niemand darf benachteiligt werden, wenn er von diesem Recht Gebrauch macht."

Aber Hunderte sind zu hohen Strafen verurteilt worden, weil sie in Briefen an westdeutsche Verwandte kritische Bemerkungen über die Zustände in der sogenannten DDR gemacht hatten.

Artikel 14 der Verfassung der sogenannten DDR sagt: „Das Streikrecht der Gewerkschaften ist gewährleistet." — Wo blieb dieses Streikrecht am 16. und 17.6.1953? Hunderte von Arbeitern wurden zu langjährigen Zuchthausstrafen verurteilt, weil sie gewagt hatten, ihre Kollegen zur Arbeitsniederlegung aufzurufen. Und der damalige Justizminister FECHNER, der das Streikrecht zu verteidigen versuchte, mußte selbst für Jahre hinter Zuchthausmauern.

Artikel 35 der Verfassung lautet: „Jeder Bürger hat das Recht auf gleiche Bildung und auf freie Wahl seines Berufes." — In den „Richtlinien für die Zulassung zum Studium an den Universitäten und Hochschulen zum Studienjahr 1953/54" heißt es jedoch: „Bevorzugt werden zum Studium zugelassen:

1. Arbeiter und deren Kinder . . .
2. Werktätige Bauern oder deren Kinder . . ."

Artikel 3 der Verfassung lautet: „Die im öffentlichen Dienst Tätigen sind Diener der Gesamtheit und nicht einer Partei." Artikel 6: „Alle Bürger sind vor dem Gesetz gleichberechtigt." Artikel 127: „Die Richter sind in ihrer Rechtsprechung unabhängig und nur der Verfassung und dem Gesetz unterworfen." — Jede Lektüre von Publikationen der sogenannten DDR beweist, daß diese Verfassungsartikel bloßes Wortgeklingel sind.

Wie das klassenkämpferische Prinzip in der Wirtschaftsordnung der sogenannten DDR wirksam geworden ist, läßt der Abschnitt „Wirtschaft in der sogenannten DDR" deutlich werden.

Gemäß der herrschenden Staatsideologie ist das Recht der Person aufgehoben zugunsten eines universalen gesellschaftspolitischen Rechtes. Göttliches Recht, Naturrecht und praktisch auch die Menschenrechte werden vom System abgelehnt. Wer sich gegenüber den geltenden Gesetzen auf solches Recht beruft, begibt sich also in die Illegalität. Da die SED sich nicht nur mit diesen Gesetzen, sondern auch mit „Friede", „Fortschritt", „Wohl der Menschheit", identifiziert, bedeutet eine solche Illegalität in den Augen der Ideologen gleichzeitig das Bekenntnis zu „Krieg", „Reaktion", „Ausbeuterklasse".

Die Möglichkeit, durch Gespräche mit Gleichgesinnten die depressive menschliche Situation zu erleichtern, sucht das System durch ein ausgedehntes Netz gedungener und erpreßter Spitzel zu unterbinden. Die Atmosphäre des Mißtrauens schränkt den Verkehr der Menschen untereinander weitgehend ein. Das Schweigen-Müssen gehört zur Grundsituation des mitteldeutschen Menschen.

Selbst der intimste Bereich, die Freiheit des Denkens, welche die Würde der Person begründet, kann sich — innerlich bewahrt und nach außen getarnt — dem Einfluß des Systems nicht immer ganz entziehen. Propaganda und Schulung, vom Kindergarten bis zum Einfluß auf nicht Organisierte durch Hausagitationen, Transparente, Plakate, ideologische Infiltration bei jeglichem Kulturgenuß — all dies wirkt auf die Menschen ein. Man ist bemüht, den Andersdenkenden unentwegt in die Zwangslage zu bringen, Aussagen zu machen, die seiner eigentlichen Überzeugung ganz und gar nicht entsprechen. Diese Methoden der moralischen Korrumpierung zwingen den Menschen in äußerste Gewissensnot. Das moralische Rückgrat soll gebrochen werden, bis schließlich die Kapitulation vor dem System erfolgt.

Daß das kommunistische Regime von der *Beeinflussung der Jugend* sich am meisten verspricht, ist klar. Hier liegen nicht Traditionen und die Kenntnis freiheitlicher Zustände als Bewußtseinshemmungen im Wege. Vom Kindergarten bis zur Abschlußklasse der Oberschule ist der Jugendliche pausenlos und praktisch in allen Schulfächern durch den Lehrplan einer weltanschaulichen Beeinflussung ausgesetzt, die den Auffassungen des Elternhauses widerspricht und unter Ausnutzung der noch nicht ausgereiften Fähigkeit zur Kritik eine erbarmungslose geistige und seelische Verkümmerung des Jugendlichen zum Ziel hat. Ein wesentliches Grundmotiv sowjetkommunistischer Pädagogik ist der Haß gegen den Andersdenkenden, den Gegner des Bolschewismus.

In der Entschließung des V. Pädagogischen Kongresses im Jahre 1956 heißt es: „So glühend wie die Liebe zu Deutschland, die wir in unseren Kindern zu entzünden im Stande sind, so heiß wird der Haß unserer Jugend gegen alle Feinde des deutschen Volkes sein und so stark ihre Bereitschaft und ihr Wille, den Staat der deutschen Arbeiter und Bauern, die Deutsche Demokratische Republik, gegen jeden Angriff, gegen jede Schädigung zu verteidigen."

Zu welchen Ergebnissen diese Art „Erziehung" führt, zeigt folgendes Beispiel: In der „Deutschen Lehrerzeitung", dem offiziellen Organ der Lehrerschaft in der sogenannten DDR, berichtet eine Erzieherin, wie sie den Kindern das berüchtigte „Gesetz zum Schutze des Friedens" erläutert: „Ich sage zu den Kindern: ‚Seht, viele Schulen wurden durch den Krieg zerstört!' Die Kinder bringen eine Fülle von Beispielen. Ich erzähle, wie Lehrer und Kinder am Aufbau der neuen Schule mitarbeiten, wie sie sich mit allen Kräften mühen, und wie dann, als sie neu erbaut dasteht, andere versuchen, sie wieder zu zerstören. ‚Das sind die Kriegshetzer', fallen mir die Kinder ins Wort. ‚ADENAUER hat selbst eine Fabrik, in der Kriegsmaterial hergestellt wird, deshalb will er den Krieg', weiß Karla zu erzählen. ‚Man muß sie einsperren', verlangen die Kinder, Ja, einige gehen in ihrem Haß gegen das Böse, das zerstören will, was wir aufbauen, noch weiter. ‚Man muß sie töten', fordern sie . . . Der Kinderkreis ist eine einzige Empörung, kleine Fäuste werden geballt, und temperamentvoll verlangt Wolfgang, man solle die bösen Menschen totschlagen.

Trotz einem unerhörten Druck hat das System es nicht vermocht, den inneren Widerstand der Bevölkerung zu brechen. Die Monotonie der Propagandaparolen, die Plumpheit der Schulungsmethoden, die Widernatürlichkeit der bolschewistischen Ideologie selbst erzeugen aus sich heraus jene Abwehrkräfte, die einen endgültigen und durchschlagenden Erfolg des kommunistischen Regimes unmöglich machen. Den Parolen wird jede Aufmerksamkeit verweigert, die ständigen Aufforderungen rufen Stumpfheit hervor, die stete Abwehr schlägt in Unmut, in Opposition um. Die Freiwilligkeit und Spontaneität des Mitmachens, die das System mit allen Mitteln erreichen will, wird mit allen diesen Mitteln verhindert. Selbst bei der Jugend hat die SED keinen entscheidenden Erfolg erzielen können. Das im Sommer 1957 erlassene Verbot für Studenten und Oberschüler, in die Bundesrepublik zu reisen, die dauernden Klagen über die Mißerfolge der Freien Deutschen Jugend (FDJ), der hohe Prozentsatz der Jugendlichen und der Lehrer unter den mitteldeutschen Flüchtlingen sind ein beredtes Zeugnis der tatsächlichen Lage in der sogenannten DDR. Gerade die von der SED durch die großzügige Handhabung der Stipendien so umworbene Studentenschaft ist zu einem Herd der Unruhe und des Widerstandes geworden.

FLÜCHTLINGSZAHLEN SEIT 1952

Jahr	Flüchtlinge Personen	Jugendliche unter 25 Jahren	
		Personen	% der Gesamtzahl
1952	182.400	97.400	53,3
1953	331.400	161.200	48,7
1954	184.200	90.400	49,1
1955	252.900	132.600	52,5
1956	279.200	136.900	49,0
1957	261.600	136.600	52,2
1958	204.000	98.200	48,2

Quelle: Statistisches Bundesamt.

Ein wesentlicher Grund für die Erfolglosigkeit des SED-Regimes sind die verwandtschaftlichen Bindungen zwischen der mittel- und westdeutschen Bevölkerung. Jeder dritte Bewohner Westdeutschlands hat Verwandte in Mitteldeutschland. Das ist eine zusätzliche Erklärung dafür, warum die Bevölkerung der Bundesrepublik sich niemals mit einer Lösung abfinden könnte, welche die Mitteldeutschen in der Unfreiheit beläßt.

Der Stand der Bemühungen um die Wiedervereinigung

Aus der geschilderten Situation der Menschen in der sogenannten DDR ergibt sich, daß das Problem der Wiedervereinigung sehr viel tiefer greift als eine nur politische Frage. Wesentliches Motiv ist das Gefühl der Verantwortung für das Schicksal der *siebzehn Millionen mitteldeutscher Menschen.*

Ihre Not zu beenden, freiheitliche Zustände in Mitteldeutschland herzustellen, scheint nach allen Erfahrungen von nunmehr vierzehn Jahren nur möglich durch die Wiedervereinigung der getrennten Teile Deutschlands.

Daß menschliche Bande diese getrennten Teile eng verbinden, daß die sogenannte DDR nicht abgeschrieben ist, wird aus dem regen Besucherverkehr der Jahre 1953 bis 1957 deutlich. Sein Rückgang im Jahre 1958 um 75% gegenüber 1957 beruht auf drastischen Maßnahmen der Behörden der sogenannten DDR. Nur noch in dringenden Fällen (wie Todesfall und ähnliches) wird es gestattet, Verwandte im Bundesgebiet zu besuchen.

DER BESUCHERVERKEHR AUS DER SOGENANNTEN DDR IN DIE BUNDESREPUBLIK

1953	1.516.200
1954	2.554.900
1955	2.261.700
1956	2.431.600
1957	2.721.000
1958	690.000

Quelle: Bundesministerium für Gesamtdeutsche Fragen.

Der spontane Versand von Paketen mit Lebensmitteln, Kleidern, Bedarfsartikeln verschiedenster Art und Büchern macht deutlich, daß die westdeutsche Bevölkerung die Lage in der sogenannten DDR erkennt und zu persönlichen Opfern für das höchste Anliegen der Nation bereit ist.

DER PAKETVERSAND AUS DER BUNDESREPUBLIK IN DIE SOGENANNTE DDR UND NACH OSTBERLIN

	Pakete	Päckchen	Insgesamt
1953	14.303.000	17.273.000	31.576.000
1954	16.742.000	24.158.000	30.900.000
1955	14.268.000	21.069.000	35.337.000
1956	rd. 18.000.000	rd. 21.000.000	rd. 39.000.000
1957	20.122.000	20.912.000	41.034.000
1958		zusammen	39.300.000

Quelle: Bundesministerium für Gesamtdeutsche Fragen.

So hat die Wiedervereinigungs-Politik der Bundesregierung in der Haltung der westdeutschen Bevölkerung (und selbstverständlich auch in dem Willen der Mitteldeutschen) eine breite Grundlage. Die Bundesrepublik hat es vermocht, durch ihr glaubwürdiges Bekenntnis zur freiheitlichen Demokratie und zur Einheit der westlichen Völker die Regierungen befreundeter

Nationen zur tätigen Unterstützung ihrer Wiedervereinigungs-Politik zu gewinnen.

*

Die Bemühungen der Bundesregierung um die Wiederherstellung der Einheit Deutschlands seit 1949 sind in der vierten Auflage dieses Buches (1955) auf den Seiten 115 bis 121 eingehend geschildert worden. In ihrem zeitlichen Ablauf sind sie hier auf den Seiten 174 bis 176 und 190 bis 193 noch einmal festgehalten.

In Übereinstimmung mit den Regierungen der USA, des Vereinigten Königreichs und Frankreichs geht die Bundesregierung davon aus, daß die Vier ehemaligen Besatzungsmächte nicht aus ihrer Verantwortung für die deutsche Frage entlassen sind. Diese Politik findet in einhelligen Beschlüssen des Deutschen Bundestages volle Unterstützung. Sie führte auf der Konferenz der Vier Regierungschefs in Genf im Jahre 1955 zu dem Erfolg, daß auch der Sowjetische Ministerpräsident BULGANIN das Schlußkommuniqué unterzeichnete, in dem von der „gemeinsamen Verantwortung für die Regelung der deutschen Frage“ und von der Wiederherstellung Deutschlands durch freie Wahlen die Rede ist. Dieser Erfolg ist durch die seitherige sowjetische Politik in Frage gestellt worden, die auf die Anerkennung der sogenannten „Deutschen Demokratischen Republik“ ausgeht.

Während die Direktive der Genfer Konferenz der Vier Regierungschefs „in Anerkennung ihrer gemeinsamen Verantwortung für die Regelung der deutschen Frage“ noch eine Einigung darüber erklärte, „daß die Regelung der Deutschland-Frage und die Wiedervereinigung Deutschlands im Wege freier Wahlen im Einklang mit den nationalen Interessen des deutschen Volkes und dem Interesse der europäischen Sicherheit erfolgen muß“, werteten Ministerpräsident BULGANIN und Parteisekretär CHRUSTSCHEW auf der Schlußsitzung in Genf beziehungsweise auf der Rückreise durch die sogenannte DDR freie Wahlen als „mechanische Zusammenlegung der beiden Teile Deutschlands“. Außenminister MOLOTOW erklärte auf der Genfer Außenministerkonferenz im Oktober 1955, eine derartige „mechanische Verschmelzung der beiden Teile Deutschlands durch freie Wahlen“ könne zur „Verletzung der ureigensten Interessen der Werktätigen der 'DDR, führen, was nicht akzeptiert werden kann“. Er wies auf den zwischen der Sowjetunion und der sogenannten DDR im September 1955 abgeschlossenen Vertrag hin, durch den die Sowjetunion die „Souveränität“ der 'DDR' anerkannt hatte.

Der Karlsplatz mit dem Lutherdenkmal in Eisenach
Die Albrechtsburg über Meißen

Schon bei den Feierlichkeiten anläßlich des fünften Jahrestages der sogenannten DDR hatte W. ULBRICHT im Jahre 1954 erklärt, die Wiedervereinigung werde erst dann erfolgen, „wenn die Aktionseinheit der Arbeiterklasse in ganz Deutschland hergestellt wird".

Seither lassen sich sämtliche Erklärungen und Handlungen der SED in der Wiedervereinigungsfrage gemäß den außenpolitischen Erklärungen der Sowjetunion auf zwei Grundsätze zurückführen: Die Spaltung Deutschlands soll vertieft werden, um die Anerkennung der sogenannten DDR als des zweiten deutschen Teilstaats innerdeutsch und international zu erzwingen. Eine Wiedervereinigung Deutschlands soll das System der sogenannten DDR auch auf das Gebiet Westdeutschlands ausdehnen.

Vorarbeiten für die Wiedervereinigung

Die seit vierzehn Jahren andauernde Teilung Deutschlands hat dazu geführt, daß die beiden großen Teilgebiete West- und Mitteldeutschland in ihrer politischen, kulturellen, wirtschaftlichen und sozialen Gestalt sich auseinander entwickelt haben. Die angestrebte totale Umwandlung der gesamten Verhältnisse in Mitteldeutschland gemäß den Zielen der bolschewistischen Ideologie durch das kommunistische Regime ist oben dargelegt worden. Wenn auch die mitteldeutsche Bevölkerung bis auf eine verschwindende Minderheit in ihrem Widerstand gegen die kommunistische Diktatur verharrt, hat doch die in ihrer Machtausübung ungehinderte SED auf den verschiedensten Sektoren des öffentlichen Lebens Tatsachen geschaffen, die den Verhältnissen in der Bundesrepublik diametral entgegengesetzt sind.

Diese Umstände werfen für den Tag der Wiedervereinigung zahlreiche Probleme auf. Von ihnen sind die *wirtschaftlichen Fragen* am deutlichsten erkennbar und in ihrer Auswirkung am besten abzuschätzen. Mit diesen Problemen hat sich seit 1952 der „*Forschungsbeirat für Fragen der Wiedervereinigung Deutschlands beim Bundesminister für Gesamtdeutsche Fragen*" befaßt und Ergebnisse seiner Tätigkeit der Öffentlichkeit vorgelegt.

Der Beirat geht davon aus, daß die Wiedervereinigung West- und Mitteldeutschlands sich auf friedlichem Wege vollzieht, und daß eine Neuregelung der in Betracht kommenden Fragen von einem in seinen Entschließungen freien gesamtdeutschen Gesetzgeber getroffen werden muß. Um die dann fälligen Entscheidungen zu erleichtern, ist der Forschungsbeirat bemüht, die in den verschiedenen Bereichen der Wirtschaft und des sozialen Lebens entstehenden Probleme wissenschaftlich zu analysieren und Vorschläge für ihre Lösung zu machen.

Im Rahmen dieser Arbeit hat der Beirat eine Reihe von Empfehlungen beschlossen. Danach soll die zentral gelenkte Zwangswirtschaft der sogenannten DDR in eine im Grundsatz marktwirtschaftliche Ordnung überführt werden. Weil bei der Wiedervereinigung die Kontinuität der Produktion, der Beschäftigung und der Versorgung der Bevölkerung ohne Störung aufrechterhalten werden muß, ist *die wirtschaftliche Wiedervereinigung als ein Prozeß und nicht als ein Ereignis* anzusehen, das an einem bestimmten Tage beendet ist. Die Schutzbedürftigkeit der gegenüber der westdeutschen schwächeren mitteldeutschen Wirtschaft nach der Wiedervereinigung ist unbestritten. Da die mitteldeutsche Wirtschaft ebenso wie die westdeutsche sich ständig weiter entwickelt, wird immer wieder die Abwandlung gefundener Lösungen erforderlich sein. Die Umwandlung der mitteldeutschen Wirtschaft wird nur dann rasch und ohne unverhältnismäßige Reibungen durchgeführt werden können, wenn Westdeutschland eine erhebliche Starthilfe gibt.

Im Bereich der *industriellen Wirtschaft* wird für die verschiedensten Sektoren die Vorbereitung von Krediten, die Übernahme von Bürgschaften, die Gewährung von Steuererleichterungen und nötigenfalls auch von Subventionen erforderlich sein. Für den möglichen Fall des Ausbleibens von Lieferungen aus den osteuropäischen Ländern ist rechtzeitig eine Hilfe der Bundesrepublik für die Versorgung mit Grundstoffen und Rohmaterial vorzubereiten. Nach dem gegenwärtigen Stande werden bei der Wiedervereinigung in vielen Produktionsbereichen Maßnahmen zur Modernisierung und Rationalisierung der bestehenden Anlagen erforderlich werden, die sehr hohe Zulieferungen an Investitionsgütern notwendig machen.

Die durch den Raubbau in den Kriegs- und Nachkriegsjahren stark beeinträchtigte Leistungsfähigkeit des mitteldeutschen *Waldes* muß durch sofortige radikale Schutzmaßnahmen sowie durch Holzzufuhren normalisiert werden.

Die mitteldeutsche *Textilindustrie* hat die aus dem Kriege überkommenen Anlagen zur Herstellung von Zellwolle weiter ausgebaut und zur Grundlage ihrer Rohstoffversorgung gemacht. Um die dadurch bedingte verminderte Qualität ihrer Erzeugnisse zu verbessern, müßte nach der Wiedervereinigung eine Erhöhung der Einfuhr von Wolle und Baumwolle gewährleistet werden.

Die „*volkseigenen Betriebe*" sind zu einem nicht geringen Teil früheren Privateigentümern unter Mißachtung rechtsstaatlicher Grundsätze entschädigungslos entzogen worden. Um sie marktwirtschaftlich funktionsfähig zu machen, sind gewisse Änderungen in ihrer rechtlichen Stellung und wirtschaftlichen Führung erforderlich. Die mit einer Regelung der Eigentumsfrage zusammenhängenden ungemein schwierigen rechtlichen und wirtschaftlichen Probleme lassen eine kurzfristige Lösung dieser Frage kaum zu. Die Lösung muß vielmehr dem definitiven gesamtdeutschen Gesetzgeber vorbehalten bleiben. Bis dahin werden Regelungen gelten müssen, die eine erfolgreiche Entwicklung dieser Betriebe gestatten und fördern, der Entscheidung über die Eigentumsfrage aber nicht vorgreifen. Auf jeden Fall müssen die früheren rechtmäßigen Eigentümer angemessen entschädigt werden.

*

Auf dem Gebiet der *Land- und Forstwirtschaft* gibt die zunehmende Sowjetisierung, besonders die Kollektivierung, Anlaß, die strukturellen Probleme in den Vordergrund der Überlegungen zu stellen. In diesem Zusammenhang spielen die durch die Bodenreform von 1945 geschaffenen Tatbestände eine entscheidende Rolle. Maßgebliche Gesichtspunkte dabei sind die Sicherung der Volksernährung, die Schaffung lebensfähiger Betriebe sowie die Wiederherstellung und Festigung des selbständigen bäuerlichen Besitzes. Eine endgültige Neuordnung der Eigentumsverhältnisse wird jedoch auch hier dem gesamtdeutschen Gesetzgeber vorbehalten bleiben müssen. Das rechtsstaatliche Prinzip der Entschädigung für entzogenes Eigentum, das seit 1945 in Mitteldeutschland in zahllosen Fällen verletzt worden ist, wird der Gesetzgeber zur Geltung zu bringen haben.

Im Interesse der Aufrechterhaltung und Förderung der landwirtschaftlichen Produktion wird eine schnelle zusätzliche Bereitstellung von Schleppern, Maschinengeräten sowie von hochwertigem Saat- und Pflanzgut und ausreichenden Mengen von Düngemitteln für notwendig erachtet. Die Maschinen-Traktoren-Stationen (MTS) sind ihrer politischen Funktion zu entkleiden, aus dem allgemeinen Haushalt und seinen Bindungen zu lösen, infolge ihrer Bedeutung für die Kontinuität der Arbeit in der mitteldeutschen Landwirtschaft jedoch für eine Übergangszeit beizubehalten. Die gegenwärtig von den Maschinen-Traktoren-Stationen wahrgenommene landtechnische Beratung soll nach der Wiedervereinigung im Rahmen des gesamten neuzuschaffenden Beratungswesens der Landwirtschaft Mitteldeutschlands erfolgen. Dieses erscheint angesichts der Umstellung von der landwirtschaftlichen Zwangswirtschaft auf die Marktwirtschaft besonders notwendig. Landhandel und Genossenschaften sollen alsbald funktionsfähig gemacht, die landwirtschaftlichen Berufsorganisationen wieder ins Leben gerufen werden.

Für die Wiederherstellung marktwirtschaftlicher Verhältnisse hat der private und genossenschaftliche *Handel* entscheidende Bedeutung. Er soll den bereits jetzt nicht voll funktionsfähigen staatlichen Handel so schnell wie möglich ablösen, dessen Privilegien sofort zu beseitigen sind. Der staatliche Großhandel soll nach der Wiedervereinigung liquidiert, die staatlichen Einzelhandelsgeschäfte sollen in nichtstaatliche umgewandelt werden. Westdeutsche und Westberliner Groß- und Einzelhandelsunternehmen sollen in einer begrenzten Übergangszeit weder ihren Sitz nach Mitteldeutschland verlegen noch dort Zweigniederlassungen gründen dürfen, um die Reaktivierung der mitteldeutschen Handelsunternehmen zu erleichtern. In diesem Zeitraum soll auch natürlichen und juristischen Personen, die ihren Wohnsitz oder Sitz außerhalb der jetzigen sogenannten DDR haben, die Neugründung von Handelsunternehmen in Mitteldeutschland untersagt sein.

Die Entwicklung des *Außenhandels* des früheren sowjetischen Besatzungsgebietes wird nach der Wiedervereinigung entscheidend davon abhängen, welche Regelungen für die internationalen Beziehungen aus der Zeit vor der Wiedervereinigung getroffen werden. Auf alle Fälle sind die staatlichen und sonstigen systembedingten Außenhandelsorgane der jetzigen sogenannten DDR aufzulösen und auch auf dem Gebiete des Außenhandels so rasch wie möglich marktwirtschaftliche Bedingungen herzustellen. Wegen der besonderen Verhältnisse des Außenhandels der sogenannten DDR können allerdings Fristen für die Beendigung der Tätigkeit der staatlichen Außenhandelsorgane nicht vorgesehen werden. Zwischen ihnen und inländischen Partnern bestehende Einzelkontrakte sollen je nach Zumutbarkeit weiter bestehen. Ihre Auflösung oder Änderung soll nicht erfolgen, soweit dadurch eine Gefährdung der Erfüllung der fortgeltenden Außenhandelsverpflichtungen eintreten würde. Bei weiter bestehenden Einzelkontrakten der staatlichen Organe des Außenhandels mit Partnern aus westlichen Ländern soll inländischen Lieferanten oder Beziehern mit Zustimmung des ausländischen Partners die Möglichkeit gegeben werden, in die Kontrakte einzutreten. Das staatliche Handelsorgan oder sein Rechtsnachfolger soll nötigenfalls eine subsidiäre Haftung übernehmen. Einzelkontrakte mit Partnern aus östlichen Ländern sind von den staatlichen Handelsorganen oder ihren allgemeinen Rechtsnachfolgern abzuwickeln. Bei der Wiedervereinigung wird besondere Aufmerksamkeit darauf gerichtet werden müssen, die von den beiden Teilen Deutschlands abgeschlossenen und nach der Wiedervereinigung fortgeltenden zwischenstaatlichen Handelsverträge und -vereinbarungen in ihrer Erfüllung zu sichern und zusammenzufassen.

Bereits in der Übergangszeit nach der Wiedervereinigung sollten die Mängel in der *Energieversorgung* Mitteldeutschlands so rasch wie möglich behoben werden. Hierzu sind in erster Linie zusätzliche Lieferungen an Steinkohle notwendig. Ferner sollten Ersatz-Investitionen in den Kraftwerken vorgenommen werden, um eine bessere Ausnützung des Wirkungsgrades der zur Stromerzeugung eingesetzten Kohle zu ermöglichen. Aber auch die Effizienz der Kraftübertragungsanlagen in den Betrieben könnte durch ihre Modernisierung wesentlich erhöht werden. Schließlich wäre die alte großräumige Verbundwirtschaft zwischen West- und Mitteldeutschland wieder herzustellen.

*

Um das mitteldeutsche *Eisenbahnnetz* wieder voll funktionsfähig zu machen, wird es notwendig sein, alle Hauptstrecken wieder vollständig zweigleisig auszubauen. Diesellokomotiven und Güterwagen sind in großem Umfang neu zu beschaffen. Die durch die Verwendung von Braunkohle ausgebrannten Schwellen müssen vordringlich erneuert werden.

Die Bedingungen über den Abschluß und Inhalt von *Arbeitsverträgen* müssen nach der Wiedervereinigung sofort von der allseitigen staatlichen Reglementierung befreit werden. Die Koalitionsfreiheit und das Recht zum Abschluß von Tarifverträgen, sowie die Freiheit zur Vereinbarung besserer als der gesetzlichen oder tariflichen Mindestbedingungen sind sogleich wieder herzustellen. Die endgültige Regelung der Arbeitsverhältnisse soll den Vereinbarungen der Tarifpartner und den Entscheidungen des gesamtdeutschen Gesetzgebers vorbehalten bleiben. Die Übergangsregelung soll an die gegenwärtig in Mitteldeutschland geltenden Bestimmungen anknüpfen und eine Mindestregelung sein. Sie soll die endgültige Regelung nicht präjudizieren.

Im Bereich des *Versicherungswesens* soll das bestehende staatliche Versicherungsmonopol bei voller Sicherung der Kontinuität des Versicherungsschutzes durch den Wettbewerb zwischen privaten und öffentlich-rechtlichen Versicherungsunternehmen ersetzt werden.

An die Stelle des zentralisierten, staatlich gelenkten *Bankapparates* der Deutschen Notenbank der sogenannten DDR sollen Banken treten, welche die mitteldeutsche Wirtschaft bei der Anpassung an die neuen Marktverhältnisse wirksam unterstützen können. Dabei wird die rasche Einführung eines wertbeständigen Zahlungsmittels von entscheidender Bedeutung sein.

Unverzüglich nach der Wiedervereinigung muß es gelingen, die außerordentlich hohe, insbesondere indirekte, steuerliche Belastung der mitteldeutschen Bevölkerung etwa der Höhe der westdeutschen Steuer anzupassen. Der damit verbundene Rückgang der Staatseinnahmen wird trotz der Verringerung mancher Ausgabeposten möglicherweise zu einem Defizit im Staatshaushalt führen. Dieses wird nicht ohne westdeutsche Hilfe ausgeglichen werden können.

Die hier aufgeführten Überlegungen und Vorschläge lassen deutlich die *Vielschichtigkeit der wirtschaftlichen Problematik der Wiedervereinigung* erkennen. Die Tätigkeit des Forschungsbeirats stellt eine wesentliche Grundlage für jene Maßnahmen dar, die von der Bundesrepublik im Hinblick auf die Wiedervereinigung ins Auge gefaßt werden müssen. Sie werden dem gesamtdeutschen Gesetzgeber seine Aufgabe erleichtern, *im wiedervereinigten Deutschland eine freiheitliche Ordnung* zu verwirklichen.

In der Phase der Festigung der inneren und äußeren Verhältnisse der Bundesrepublik hat das *Grundgesetz* von 1949 seine Bewährungsprobe voll bestanden. Als eine nur vorläufige Regelung konzipiert, die durch eine gesamtdeutsche Verfassung abgelöst werden soll[1], hat sich das Grundgesetz inzwischen zur *Voll-Verfassung* des freien Teils des Deutschen Reiches während der Übergangszeit herausgebildet. Es ist in den Jahren 1951 bis 1956 in einer Reihe von Bestimmungen ergänzt und geändert worden[2].

Das Grundgesetz stellt eine durchaus *eigenständige Lösung* einer modernen demokratischen Verfassung dar. Als eine republikanische und demokratische rechtsstaatliche Verfassung knüpft das Grundgesetz an die Tradition der deutschen „Paulskirchenverfassung" aus den Revolutionsjahren 1848/49 und an die Weimarer Reichsverfassung von 1919 an. Der Parlamentarische Rat hat sich aber bemüht, *die Fehler der Vergangenheit möglichst zu vermeiden.* Die starke Betonung der bundesstaatlichen Einrichtungen bedeutet eine entschiedene *Absage an Unitarismus und Zentralismus.* Sie bedeutet zugleich eine über die traditionelle Gewaltentrennung hinausgehende weitere *Verteilung der Macht im Staate.* Da bei der Bildung der Länder in den Jahren 1945 bis 1947 vielfach die zeitbedingten Interessen der Besatzungsmächte bestimmend waren, ist allerdings eine *Neugliederung des Bundesgebietes* vorbehalten[3].

Im *Bundesrat* besitzen die Länder ein Verfassungsorgan, durch das sie bei der Gesetzgebung und Verwaltung des Bundes mitwirken[4]. Bundestag und Bundesrat bilden eine Art Zweikammersystem. Sie unterscheiden sich aber durchaus von den entsprechenden Institutionen der BISMARCKschen Reichsverfassung von 1871 und der Weimarer Verfassung von 1919. Der Bundestag wird auf die Dauer von vier Jahren gewählt. Wenn er auch als die unmittelbar vom Volke gewählte Repräsentation[5] den Vorrang vor allen anderen Verfassungsorganen hat, ergibt sich doch eine gewisse Machtbeschränkung dieses Organs aus der starken Stellung, die dem *Bundeskanzler* als dem Chef der Bundesregierung eingeräumt worden ist. Der Bundeskanzler wird vom Bundestag mit absoluter Mehrheit gewählt; er kann nur durch ein „konstruktives" Mißtrauensvotum, das heißt durch die Wahl eines neuen Bundes-

[1] Vergleiche die Präambel und den Artikel 146 des Grundgesetzes (= GG). — [2] Vergleiche hierzu Art. 12, 17a, 45a, 45b, 59a, 65a, 73 Nr. 1, 79 Abs. 1 Satz 2, 87a, 87b, 96a, 106, 107, 120a, 143. — [3] Art. 29 GG. — [4] Art. 50 GG; siehe oben Seite 105. — [5] Art. 39 GG.

kanzlers, abberufen werden[1]. Der *Bundespräsident* wird von der *Bundesversammlung*, die aus den Abgeordneten des Bundestages und der gleichen Zahl eigens zu diesem Zweck von den Landtagen entsandter Vertreter (Wahlmänner) besteht, für die Dauer von fünf Jahren gewählt[2]. Er ist das Staatsoberhaupt. Seine Stellung ist im wesentlichen repräsentativer Natur. Dennoch kommen ihm bedeutsame Befugnisse der Mitwirkung bei der Bildung der Bundesregierung und überhaupt bei der staatlichen Willensbildung zu. Die Kompetenz, über Verfassungsstreitigkeiten zwischen den obersten Bundesorganen oder zwischen dem Bund und den Ländern zu entscheiden, die Gesetze auf ihre Verfassungsmäßigkeit zu überprüfen und in einer Reihe von weiteren Fällen als ,,*Hüter der Verfassung*" zu fungieren, obliegt dem *Bundesverfassungsgericht*[3], das seinen Sitz in Karlsruhe hat.

Der Grundgesetzgeber hat sich aber nicht mit der Festlegung und sorgfältigen Abgrenzung der Zuständigkeiten zwischen den Verfassungsorganen des Bundes und zwischen dem Bund und den Ländern begnügt. Er hat es für geboten erachtet, über das organisatorische Minimum einer bundesstaatlichen Verfassung hinaus, die *materiellen Werte* deutlich werden zu lassen, die der Verfassung zugrunde liegen und die Richtschnur allen staatlichen Handelns abgeben: ,,Die Würde des Menschen ist unantastbar. Sie zu achten und zu schützen ist Verpflichtung aller staatlichen Gewalt" (Artikel 1 Absatz 1). ,,Das Deutsche Volk bekennt sich zu unverletzlichen und unveräußerlichen Menschenrechten als Grundlage jeder menschlichen Gemeinschaft, des Friedens und der Gerechtigkeit in der Welt" (Artikel 1 Absatz 2). Die wesentlichen *Grundrechte* sind in einem Katalog zusammengefaßt und stehen an der Spitze der Verfassung[4]. Zu den immanenten Werten des Grundgesetzes gehört ferner das *Bekenntnis zum Sozialstaat*[5]. Auch der *Ausbau der rechtsstaatlichen Institutionen*, insbesondere des Rechtsschutzes, und die Sicherung der Unabhängigkeit der Rechtsprechung als der ,,Dritten Gewalt" sind hier zu nennen. Die Bundesrepublik ist jedoch eine ,,*wachsame Demokratie*": der eigentliche Kern ihres Wertsystems und die tragenden Prinzipien des Staatsaufbaues, auch die föderalistische Grundlage der Verfassung, sind für unabänderlich erklärt worden. Sie sind der Disposition auch des verfassungändernden Gesetzgebers entzogen[6]. Den Feinden der freiheitlichen demokratischen Grundordnung wird der Schutz der Grundrechte

[1] Art. 63 und 67 GG. — [2] Art. 54 GG. — [3] Art. 93 GG; Gesetz über das Bundesverfassungsgericht vom 12.3.1951 in der Fassung des Gesetzes vom 21.7.1956. — [4] Art. 1 bis 19 GG. — [5] Art. 20 Abs. 1 und 28 Abs. 1 GG. — [6] Art. 79 Abs. 3 GG.

versagt[1]. Politische Parteien, die nach ihren Zielen oder nach dem Verhalten ihrer Anhänger darauf ausgehen, die freiheitliche demokratische Grundordnung zu beeinträchtigen oder zu beseitigen oder den Bestand der Bundesrepublik zu gefährden, sind verfassungswidrig. Über die Frage der Verfassungswidrigkeit entscheidet das Bundesverfassungsgericht[2].

Nach dem Willen des Verfassunggebers soll das Grundgesetz zu gegebener Zeit durch eine Verfassung abgelöst werden, die vom *gesamten deutschen Volk* in freier Entscheidung beschlossen worden ist[3]. Neben dieser *gesamtdeutschen Tendenz* ist dem Grundgesetz aber auch eine *supranationale Tendenz* eigen. Die Bundesrepublik erstrebt, wie es in der Präambel heißt, das Ziel, „als gleichberechtigtes Glied in einem vereinten Europa dem Frieden der Welt zu dienen". Sie kann durch Gesetz Hoheitsrechte auf zwischenstaatliche Einrichtungen übertragen[4]. Sie kann zur Wahrung des Friedens sich einem *System gegenseitiger kollektiver Sicherheit* einordnen und wird hierbei in die *Beschränkungen ihrer Hoheitsrechte* einwilligen, die eine friedliche und dauerhafte Ordnung in Europa und zwischen den Völkern der Welt herbeiführen und sichern[5]. Die Bundesregierung hat seit ihrem Bestehen den Prozeß der europäischen Integration und Föderation, ungeachtet mancher Rückschläge in der Entwicklung, zielbewußt gefördert. Aus den vorstehend angezogenen Bestimmungen des Grundgesetzes wird deutlich, in welchem Maße alle demokratischen Parteien, die 1948/1949 an dem Akt der Verfassungsschöpfung mitwirkten, bestrebt waren, neue Wege der Verwirklichung *dauerhafter zwischenstaatlicher Beziehungen* zu beschreiten, ohne allerdings, solange die angestrebte größere Gemeinschaft des Europäischen Bundesstaates noch nicht Wirklichkeit geworden ist, den Aufbau und die Sicherung der eigenen staatlichen Existenz zu vernachlässigen. Die Konzeption des Grundgesetzes und ihr folgend die Politik der Bundesregierung sind eine deutliche *Absage an ein antiquiertes starres Souveränitätsdenken.*

[1] Art. 18 GG. — [2] Art. 21 Abs. 2 GG. Im einzelnen vergleiche hierzu den folgenden Beitrag „Die innere Sicherung des demokratischen Staates". — [3] Art. 146. — [4] Art. 24 Abs. 1 GG. — [5] Art. 24 Abs. 2 GG.

DIE INNERE SICHERUNG DES DEMOKRATISCHEN STAATES

Der Bestand des demokratischen Staates ist, wie die Geschichte lehrt, von inneren Gefahren bedroht. Die Demokratie ist auf der Freiheit der Bürger gegründet; die demokratische Verfassung muß daher gegen den Mißbrauch der Freiheit geschützt werden. So begleitet die Idee des *Verfassungsschutzes* das moderne freiheitliche Staatsdenken. Die immer reichere Entfaltung des demokratischen Staatslebens hat dabei zu einer entsprechenden Erweiterung und Vertiefung des Verfassungsschutzes geführt. Das eigentümliche Problem liegt darin, die richtige Grenze zu finden, innerhalb derer zwar der *Mißbrauch der Freiheit* bekämpft, nicht aber die Freiheit selbst als das unerläßliche Lebenselement der Demokratie preisgegeben wird.

Durch die leidvollen Erfahrungen in der Epoche der nationalsozialistischen Diktatur (1933—1945) ist dem deutschen Volk die Kostbarkeit des Gutes der Freiheit in einem besonderen Maß bewußt geworden. Im Grundgesetz der Bundesrepublik und einer Reihe von Bundesgesetzen ist daher ein reiches Maß an Garantien für die demokratische Staats- und Rechtsordnung unter gleichzeitiger Sicherung der Freiheit der Einzelpersönlichkeit entwickelt worden; teils im System der Verfassung selbst und damit im wesentlichen präventiver Natur (*institutioneller Verfassungsschutz*), teils gegen bereits zutage tretende Verletzungen (*repressiver Verfassungsschutz*). Beide Formen des Verfassungsschutzes wären auf die Dauer nicht wirksam, wenn es nicht gelänge, im Bewußtsein und im Herzen der Staatsbürger der Demokratie eine sichere Grundlage zu geben (*erzieherischer Verfassungsschutz*). Auch in den Verfassungen der Länder finden wir zahlreiche Bestimmungen, die der Sicherung des demokratischen Staates dienen.

I. DER INSTITUTIONELLE VERFASSUNGSSCHUTZ

Geschützt ist vor allem der Kerngehalt der staatlichen Ordnung. Das Grundgesetz (GG) bezeichnet ihn als die „*freiheitliche demokratische Grundordnung*"[1]. Welche Verfassungsgrundsätze darunter zu verstehen sind, hat der Gesetzgeber in § 88 des Strafgesetzbuches in der Fassung des Strafrechtsänderungsgesetzes vom 30.8.1951 näher umschrieben. Das Bundesverfassungsgericht hat in seinem Urteil vom 23.10.1952, das in dem Verfahren gegen die Sozialistische Reichspartei ergangen ist, die freiheitliche

[1] Vergleiche zum Beispiel Art. 18, Art. 21 Abs. 2, Art. 91 Abs. 1 GG.

demokratische Grundordnung als eine Ordnung bezeichnet, „die unter Ausschluß jeglicher Gewalt- und Willkürherrschaft eine rechtsstaatliche Herrschaftsordnung auf der Grundlage der Selbstbestimmung des Volkes nach dem Willen der jeweiligen Mehrheit und der Freiheit und Gleichheit darstellt". Zu den grundlegenden Prinzipien dieser Ordnung sind nach der Auffassung des Bundesverfassungsgerichts mindestens zu rechnen: die Achtung vor den im Grundgesetz konkretisierten Menschenrechten, vor allem vor dem Recht der Persönlichkeit auf Leben und freie Entfaltung, die Volkssouveränität, die Gewaltenteilung, die Verantwortlichkeit der Regierung, die Gesetzmäßigkeit der Verwaltung, die Unabhängigkeit der Gerichte, das Mehrparteienprinzip und die Chancengleichheit für alle politischen Parteien mit dem Recht auf verfassungsmäßige Bildung und Ausübung einer Opposition.

HITLER hat sich oft gerühmt, daß er mit Hilfe der von ihm gegründeten und befehligten NSDAP „legal" an die Macht gelangt sei. Wenn auch diese Behauptung bei näherer Prüfung nicht zutrifft — die Weimarer Reichsverfassung (WRV) von 1919 bot nach ihrer ganzen Anlage und nach ihrem inneren Gehalt keine Handhabe für einen Übergang von einer rechtsstaatlichen Demokratie zur Diktatur und Despotie —, so lag doch in diesem geschichtlichen Vorgang die nicht überhörbare Mahnung, die Möglichkeit einer solchen scheinbar legalen Zerstörung der Demokratie noch wirksamer auszuschalten, also in einer künftigen Verfassung *den institutionellen Verfassungsschutz zu erweitern und zu verstärken.*

Dieser Mahnung sind die Schöpfer des Grundgesetzes vor allem dadurch nachgekommen, daß der in Artikel 20[1] ausdrücklich verankerte Grundsatz der *Gewaltenteilung*, der eine Zusammenballung von staatlicher Macht an einer Stelle verhindern soll, weit stärker als früher zur Geltung gebracht worden ist. Hauptmerkmal der verfassungsmäßigen Ordnung des Grundgesetzes ist im ganzen eine überwiegende Schwächung der Stellung der staatlichen Exekutive zugunsten des Parlaments, eine erhöhte Kontrolle der Verwaltung (Verwaltungsgerichtsbarkeit auf der Grundlage einer „Generalklausel"), aber auch der Legislative (Verfassungsgerichtsbarkeit nach einem ausgedehnten enumerativen System) und dementsprechend eine *Stärkung der rechtsprechenden Gewalt* selbst in einem Maße, daß mitunter schon von der Gefahr eines „Justizstaates" gesprochen wurde.

1. Im Weimarer Verfassungssystem ist der wesentliche Ansatzpunkt für die Entwicklung zur nationalsozialistischen Diktatur die eigenartige Stellung

[1] Abs. 2 und Abs. 3.

einer auf die *Machtfülle des Reichspräsidenten* gestützten Reichsregierung gewesen (sogenannte „Präsidialregierung").

Der Reichspräsident, unmittelbar vom Volke gewählt, besaß die Befugnis, die Reichsregierung zu berufen und zu entlassen; er hatte das Recht, den Reichstag aufzulösen; er war Oberbefehlshaber der Wehrmacht und schließlich Träger der verfassungsmäßigen Notstandsvollmachten[1]. Von diesen Vollmachten war insbesondere in den Krisenjahren 1930 bis 1932 überwiegend aus wirtschaftlichen Gründen, aber auch zu dem Versuch der Bekämpfung der Parteiströmungen, welche die Bevölkerung in immer stärkerem Maß radikalisierten, in extensiver Weise Gebrauch gemacht worden. Einmal an die Regierung berufen, setzte HITLER die staatliche Machtfülle zugunsten seiner Partei und zur Unterdrückung aller anderen Parteien und geistigen und politischen Richtungen ein. Die nationalsozialistische Diktatur fand schon in den ersten Monaten nach der „Machtergreifung" ihre scheinbar legale Hauptstütze im „Ermächtigungsgesetz" vom 24.3.1933, in dem der Reichstag, unter dem Druck der Macht der NSDAP und das volle Ausmaß der Gefahr für den Bestand des Rechtsstaats noch nicht erkennend, der Regierung HITLER eine umfassende Ermächtigung gab, Reichsgesetze ohne Beteiligung des Parlaments zu erlassen. Diese Regierungsgesetze durften von der Reichsverfassung abweichen. Im „Neuaufbaugesetz" vom 30.1.1934 wurde diese Kompetenz sodann dahingehend erweitert, daß die Reichsregierung schlechthin neues Verfassungsrecht setzen konnte. Für die Diktatur bestand keine Schranke mehr.

Alle diese Möglichkeiten hat das Grundgesetz ausgeschaltet. Die Stellung des nicht mehr unmittelbar vom Volk, sondern von der Bundesversammlung[2] gewählten *Bundespräsidenten* wurde im ganzen schwächer ausgestaltet als die Stellung des früheren Reichspräsidenten. Der *Bundeskanzler*, vom Bundestag gewählt, ist diesem unmittelbar verantwortlich[3]. Ein der Generalklausel des Artikels 48 WRV auch nur annähernd vergleichbares Notstandsrecht wurde in die Verfassung bewußt nicht aufgenommen. Ein gewisser Ausgleich zugunsten der Exekutive ergibt sich allerdings aus der Einführung des sogenannten konstruktiven Mißtrauensvotums[4]. Der Bundestag kann den Bundeskanzler jederzeit mit absoluter Mehrheit abberufen; aber nur, wenn vorher eine Mehrheit für einen Nachfolger zustande gekommen ist. Durch diesen wirksamen Schutz gegen Regierungskrisen wurde die Stellung des Bundeskanzlers gegenüber dem Parlament sehr gefestigt; man kann

[1] Art. 48 WRV. — [2] Art. 54 GG. — [3] Art. 65 Abs. 1, Art. 67 GG.
[4] Art. 67 GG.

praktisch von einer Wahl der Regierung auf Zeit sprechen. Die Möglichkeit, im Wege der *Ermächtigung* die Befugnis zur Rechtsetzung vom Parlament auf die Regierung zu übertragen, wurde in Artikel 80 GG *in enge Grenzen* gewiesen. Als Rechtsetzungsakte der Exekutive sind im wesentlichen nur mehr gesetzesabhängige Ausführungs- und Durchführungsverordnungen verfassungsrechtlich zugelassen. Auch für den Fall des Staatsnotstands besteht normativ *keinerlei Generalvollmacht* für eine Rechtsetzung durch die Regierung bei Behinderung des Parlaments oder gar unter Ausschaltung des Parlaments. Lediglich für den speziellen Fall eines „Gesetzgebungsnotstands" sieht Artikel 81 GG einen *Reserveweg der Gesetzgebung* vor: Eine als dringlich bezeichnete Vorlage kann in einem durch zahlreiche Klauseln gesicherten besonderen Verfahren an Stelle des Bundestages, der sich diesem Gesetzgebungsakt versagt, von der Länderkammer, dem Bundesrat, zum Gesetz erhoben werden. Der Gesetzgebungsnotstand ist nicht nur zeitlich begrenzt; auch Änderungen oder Durchbrechungen des Grundgesetzes sind in diesem Verfahren ausdrücklich ausgeschlossen[1].

Eine *verstärkte Kontrolle durch die rechtsprechende Gewalt* stellt sicher, daß die Exekutive in ihren von der Verfassung gezogenen Grenzen bleibt. So hat das *Bundesverfassungsgericht* auch auf Verlangen des Bundestages die Verfassungsmäßigkeit der Maßnahmen der Bundesregierung und der anderen an der Exekutive beteiligten obersten Verfassungsorgane zu überprüfen[2]. Auch eine *Präsidentenanklage* ist vorgesehen[3]. Die Verwaltung in ihren verschiedenen Stufen unterliegt einer fast unbeschränkten *verwaltungsgerichtlichen Kontrolle*[4].

2. Die Funktion der Legislative wird von dem Bundestag ausgeübt. Die Mitwirkungsbefugnisse des Bundesrats (vergleiche oben Seite 105) bedeuten zugleich *Hemmung und Kontrolle*. Die Macht der Legislative wird aber auch dadurch beschränkt, daß ihr nicht nur im Grundgesetz selbst inhaltliche Schranken verschiedener Art gezogen werden, sondern daß sie vor allem auch einer erhöhten gerichtlichen Kontrolle unterworfen ist.

Die *inhaltlichen Schranken* bestehen zunächst darin, daß Verfassungsänderungen sehr erschwert worden sind. Nach Artikel 79 Absatz 1 GG sind Durchbrechungen der Verfassung im Einzelfall, ohne daß zugleich der Wort-

[1] Art. 81 Abs. 3 und 4 GG.

[2] Art. 93 Abs. 1 Nr. 1 in Verbindung mit den Bestimmungen des Gesetzes über das Bundesverfassungsgericht — BVerfGG — vom 12. 3. 1951.

[3] Art. 61 GG. — [4] Art. 19 Abs. 4 GG.

laut des Grundgesetzes geändert oder ergänzt wird, unzulässig. Änderungen oder Ergänzungen des Textes der Verfassung bedürfen einer Zweidrittelmehrheit nicht nur im Bundestag, sondern auch im Bundesrat. Die Änderung der wichtigsten Grundlagen der demokratischen Ordnung, wie namentlich des Prinzips der Gewaltenteilung, ferner eine Änderung des der Verfassung zugrunde liegenden föderalistischen Prinzips oder des in Artikel 1 GG niedergelegten Bekenntnisses zu den Menschenrechten ist in Artikel 79 Absatz 3 GG schlechthin verboten. Für die Gesetzgebung sind inhaltliche Schranken ferner in dem Katalog der Grundrechte aufgerichtet. Die Grundrechte sind bewußt nicht mehr, wie in der WRV von 1919, durch einen allgemeinen Vorbehalt zugunsten des einfachen Gesetzgebers geschwächt. Auch der Gesetzgeber darf ein Grundrecht „in keinem Fall in seinem Wesensgehalt" antasten[1]. In Artikel 1 Absatz 3 GG ist unabänderlich festgelegt worden, daß die Grundrechte Gesetzgebung, vollziehende Gewalt und Rechtsprechung als unmittelbar geltendes Recht binden.

Die *richterliche Kontrolle der Gesetzgebung* ist durch die ausdrückliche Anerkennung der richterlichen Prüfungszuständigkeit[2] gesichert. Während das „vorkonstitutionelle" Recht der Prüfung durch das jeweils zuständige Prozeßgericht unterliegt, ist die Prüfung der Verfassungsmäßigkeit der unter dem Grundgesetz verabschiedeten Gesetze bei dem Bundesverfassungsgericht konzentriert („*konkrete Normenkontrolle*" auf Vorlage durch das Prozeßgericht). Hinzu kommt als sehr bedeutsamer weiterer Schritt rechtsstaatlicher Gewährleistung die Einführung der sogenannten *abstrakten Normenkontrolle*, die losgelöst von einem anhängigen Rechtsstreit durch die in Artikel 93 Absatz 1 Nr. 2 GG genannten Verfassungsorgane eingeleitet werden kann.

3. Die vielfältigen Möglichkeiten richterlicher Kontrolle der Exekutive und Legislative erweisen die starke Stellung der Rechtsprechung namentlich in ihrer höchsten Form, der *Verfassungsgerichtsbarkeit*, so daß im vollen Sinn des Begriffs von der „*dritten Gewalt*" im Staat gesprochen werden kann. Die sachliche und persönliche Unabhängigkeit der Richter ist in Artikel 97 GG garantiert.

Da indes für den Bestand der Demokratie Gefahr auch entstehen könnte, wenn der Demokratie feindlich gesinnte Richter gegen die Grundsätze des Grundgesetzes oder gegen die verfassungsmäßige Ordnung eines Landes verstoßen sollten, steht mit

[1] Art. 19 Abs. 2 GG. — [2] Art. 100 Abs. 1 GG.

der Einführung der „*Richteranklage*"[1] die Rechtsprechung ihrerseits unter einer beschränkten Kontrolle des Parlaments, jedoch wiederum nur unter richterlicher Garantie (Zuständigkeit des Bundesverfassungsgerichts).

4. Zu dieser *Aufteilung der Staatsgewalt unter den obersten Verfassungsorganen des Bundes tritt hinzu die kaum minder bedeutsame Teilung der Macht zwischen dem Bund und den Ländern.* Auch die föderative Ordnung ist ein Schutz gegen Zusammenballung von Macht an einer Stelle; ja gerade hierin liegt mit ein starkes Argument zu ihrer Rechtfertigung. Die Teilung bezieht sich weniger auf den Sachbereich der Legislative als auf die Exekutive. Nach dem Grundsatz des Artikels 83 GG führen die Länder die Bundesgesetze als eigene Angelegenheit aus, soweit das Grundgesetz nichts anderes bestimmt oder zuläßt.[2] Die Kompetenzaufteilung zwischen Bund und Ländern ist auch verfassungsgerichtlich geschützt.[3] Für die innere Sicherung des demokratischen Staates ist von entscheidender Bedeutung die Bestimmung des Grundgesetzes, daß die verfassungsmäßige Ordnung in den Ländern den Grundsätzen des republikanischen, demokratischen und sozialen Rechtsstaats im Sinne des Grundgesetzes entsprechen muß (Festlegung des Grundsatzes der *verfassungsrechtlichen Homogenität*), und daß der Bund dies ausdrücklich gewährleistet. Diese Gewährleistung erstreckt sich nach Artikel 28 Absatz 3 GG auch auf das Recht der Selbstverwaltung der Gemeinden und Gemeindeverbände nach demokratischen Prinzipien.

5. Die der Erhaltung der demokratischen Staatsordnung dienenden Rechtsnormen der Verfassung greifen schließlich noch über die Träger staatlicher Hoheit hinaus auf die der staatlichen Willensbildung dienenden und ihr vorausliegenden *politischen Parteien.* Erstmals in der deutschen Verfassungsentwicklung wurden diese soziologischen Gebilde in das System der staatsrechtlichen Ordnung einbezogen; einerseits um ihre Freiheit zu gewährleisten, andererseits um ihrer Entwicklung im Interesse des Schutzes der Demokratie die unabdingbar notwendigen Grenzen zu ziehen. Die Gründung von politischen Parteien ist nach Artikel 21 Absatz 1 GG frei, ihre innere Ordnung muß aber demokratischen Grundsätzen entsprechen. Die näheren Vorschriften hierüber müssen in dem vom Grundgesetz vorgesehenen *Parteiengesetz* noch getroffen werden.

Zusammenfassend kann wohl gesagt werden, daß der *institutionelle Schutz der Verfassung* in der ausgewogenen Verteilung der staatlichen Kompetenzen

[1] Art. 98 GG. — [2] Vergleiche hierzu die Ausführungen in dem Abschnitt „Bund und Länder", oben Seite 106ff. — [3] Art. 93 Abs. 1 Nr. 3 und 4 GG.

auf verschiedene Verfassungsorgane, namentlich in der starken Stellung der „dritten Gewalt", *jedenfalls für normale Zeiten ernstliche Gefahren für die Demokratie ausschließen wird.* Für den Fall eines zivilen Notstandes ist die erhebliche Beschränkung der Notstandsbefugnisse der Bundesregierung ein Schwächemoment für die Exekutive, die gewappnet sein sollte, unter Umständen starken Angriffen auf die verfassungsmäßige Ordnung und den Bestand des demokratischen Staates schlagkräftig entgegenzutreten. Solange eine entsprechende Ergänzung der Verfassung noch nicht erfolgt ist, kann die Exekutive wirksam von den Mitteln des repressiven Verfassungsschutzes Gebrauch machen, die in einer Reihe von Einzelbestimmungen des Grundgesetzes und in der ergänzenden Gesetzgebung des Bundes gegeben sind.

II. DER REPRESSIVE VERFASSUNGSSCHUTZ

Im Gegensatz zur Weimarer Verfassung, die infolge ihrer übergroßen Toleranz auch gegenüber verfassungsfeindlichen Strömungen dem durch sie getragenen Staat keinen ausreichenden Schutz zu gewähren vermochte, haben das Grundgesetz und ergänzende Gesetze wirksame Bestimmungen zum Schutz gegen Angriffe auf die demokratische Freiheit geschaffen. Die Bundesrepublik hat darüber hinaus auch Behörden eingerichtet, die in der Lage sind, offen oder getarnt auftretende Verletzungen der verfassungsmäßigen Ordnung im Wege des *repressiven Verfassungsschutzes* mit Nachdruck zu bekämpfen.

1. Wohl die weitesttragende gesetzliche Vorschrift dieser Art ist der Artikel 91 GG. Er besagt, daß ein Land die Polizeikräfte anderer Länder anfordern, daß aber auch der Bund die Polizeikräfte aller Länder seinen Weisungen unterstellen kann, wenn dies zur Abwehr einer drohenden Gefahr für den Bestand oder die freiheitliche demokratische Grundordnung des Bundes oder eines Landes erforderlich ist.

Die Meisterung einer etwaigen revolutionären Lage erfordert bei der Größe des Bundesgebiets die Bereitstellung ausreichender, für einen Großeinsatz ausgerüsteter und geschulter Polizeiformationen. Als daher die New Yorker Außenministerkonferenz im September 1950 dem Bund und seinen Ländern die Aufstellung kasernierter und vollmotorisierter Polizeieinheiten in der Stärke von insgesamt 30.000 Mann gestattete, hat die Bundesregierung bereits im Oktober 1950 mit den Landesregierungen ein Verwaltungsabkommen über die Errichtung von *Bereitschaftspolizeien* der Länder in der Stärke von 10.000 Mann abgeschlossen. In dem Abkommen verpflichtete sich der Bund, auf seine Kosten die Bewaffnung und das Gerät, insbesondere die Nachrichtenmittel und Kraftfahrzeuge, für diese Einheiten zu beschaffen. Die Überwachung der Ausbildung der Verbände der Bereitschaftspolizei und der Vorbereitung ihres Einsatzes im Falle des Artikels 91 GG steht nach dem Abkommen dem Bund zu.

Da die Grenzlage des Bundesgebietes zum Machtblock der autoritären östlichen Staaten wegen der ständigen Einschleusung verfassungsfeindlicher Elemente und der starken Beunruhigung der Grenzbevölkerung durch Maßnahmen des „Kalten Krieges" eine besondere Gefährdung der demokratischen Ordnung und inneren Sicherheit des Bundesgebietes mit sich bringt, die nicht ernst genug zu nehmen ist, hat der Bund, gestützt auf den Artikel 87 Absatz 1 GG, durch das Gesetz vom 16.3.1951 über den Bundesgrenzschutz *Bundesgrenzschutzbehörden* geschaffen, die zunächst mit 10.000 Polizeibeamten ausgestattet wurden. Hiervon entfielen rund 1.000 Mann auf den *Bundespaßkontrolldienst*, der das Bundesgebiet durch die Ausübung der Paßnachschau gegen verbotene Grenzübertritte sichert. Da nach den New Yorker Beschlüssen noch weitere 10.000 Mann Polizeieinheiten aufgestellt werden konnten, beschloß der Bundestag am 19.6.1953, den Bundesgrenzschutz auf 20.000 Mann zu erhöhen. Der Bundesgrenzschutz ist eine Freiwilligentruppe. Er ist das wertvollste sonderpolizeiliche Sicherheitsinstrument des Bundes, das vielfältigen Anforderungen gerecht werden muß. Um bei der Aufstellung der Bundeswehr die im Bundesgrenzschutz gesammelten Erfahrungen auszunutzen, wurde der Bundesminister für Verteidigung durch das Zweite Gesetz über den Bundesgrenzschutz vom 30.5.1956 ermächtigt, aus den Verbänden des Bundesgrenzschutzes Verbände der Bundeswehr aufzustellen. Der Übertritt geschah auf freiwilliger Grundlage. Der im Bundesgrenzschutz verbleibende Teil (rund 50%) bildet den Grundstock für die Wiederauffüllung des Grenzschutzes auf 20.000 Mann. Die Angehörigen des Bundesgrenzschutzes sind ebenso kaserniert und vollmotorisiert ausgerüstet wie die Bereitschaftspolizeien der Länder. Sie sichern das Bundesgebiet gegen alle die Sicherheit der Grenzen gefährdenden Störungen der öffentlichen Ordnung im Grenzgebiet bis zu einer Tiefe von 30 km. Im Falle des Artikels 91 GG können sie auch im übrigen Bundesgebiet zur Abwehr einer drohenden Gefahr für den Bestand oder die freiheitliche demokratische Grundordnung des Bundes oder eines Landes eingesetzt werden.

Während die vorstehend dargelegten Maßnahmen letzten Endes die Meisterung einer etwaigen bereits in das Revolutionäre abgleitenden Lage zum Ziele haben, schaffen die Artikel 21 und 9 GG die Möglichkeit, zuzugreifen, bevor die Dinge so weit gekommen sind. Nach Artikel 21 Absatz 2 GG sind *Parteien*, die nach ihren Zielen oder nach dem Verhalten ihrer Anhänger darauf ausgehen, die freiheitliche demokratische Grundordnung zu beeinträchtigen oder zu beseitigen oder den Bestand der Bundesrepublik zu gefährden, *verfassungswidrig*. Die Entscheidung über die Verfassungswidrigkeit steht dem Bundesverfassungsgericht zu. Mit der Feststellung der Verfassungswidrigkeit verbindet das Bundesverfassungsgericht auf Grund des seine Zuständigkeit regelnden Bundesgesetzes vom 12.3.1951 die Auflösung der Partei — oder eines rechtlich oder organisatorisch selbständigen Teiles der Partei — und das Verbot, eine Ersatzorganisation zu schaffen. Das Gericht kann zugleich die Einziehung des Vermögens der Partei oder des selbständigen Teiles der Partei zugunsten des Bundes oder des Landes zu gemeinnützigen Zwecken aussprechen[1]. Vorsätzliche Zuwiderhandlungen gegen diese Entscheidungen oder gegen die zu ihrem Vollzug getroffenen Maßnahmen werden mit Gefängnis nicht unter sechs Monaten bestraft[2]. Von dem ihr zustehenden Antragsrecht hat die Bundesregierung bisher in zwei Fällen Gebrauch gemacht. Sie hat im November 1951 den Antrag aus Artikel 21 Absatz 2 GG gegen die neonazistische „Sozialistische Reichspartei" (SRP) und gegen die „Kommunistische Partei Deutschlands" (KPD) gestellt. Die Verfassungswidrigkeit und Auflösung der SRP hat das Bundesverfassungsgericht durch Urteil vom 23.10.1952 ausgesprochen. Das Verfahren gegen die KPD ist durch das Urteil vom 17.8.1956 abgeschlossen worden. Auch die KPD wurde in der Bundesrepublik für verfassungswidrig erklärt und aufgelöst. Das umfassend begründete Urteil hat weltweite Beachtung gefunden.

Drohen die Gefahren für den demokratischen Staat von *anderen Organisationen* als Parteien, dann ist Artikel 9 Absatz 2 GG einschlägig. Nach dieser Bestimmung sind Vereinigungen verboten, deren Zwecke oder deren Tätigkeit den Strafgesetzen zuwiderlaufen oder die sich gegen die verfassungsmäßige Ordnung oder gegen den Gedanken der Völkerverständigung richten. Dieses durch das Grundgesetz selbst ausgesprochene Verbot ist unmittelbar anwendbares Recht. Auch die Exekutivbehörden jedes Landes der Bundesrepublik können den Artikel 9 Absatz 2 GG auf Organisationen anwenden, die nur in diesem Land bestehen.

Verstoßen *Einzelpersonen* gegen die freiheitliche demokratische Grundordnung, dann können die durch sie herbeigeführten Gefahren durch Verwirkungsmaßnahmen und durch strafrechtliche Maßnahmen abgewendet werden. Wer die Freiheit der Meinungsäußerung, insbesondere die Presse-

[1] § 46 BVerfGG. [2] § 42 BVerfGG.

AUFBAU DER BUNDESREPUBLIK DEUTSCHLAND

DER BUNDESRAT

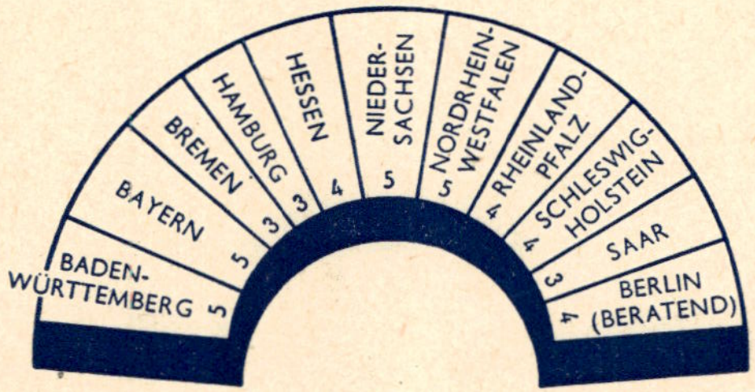

PRÄSIDENT: WILHELM KAISEN (SPD) BÜRGERMEISTER DER FREIEN HANSESTADT BREMEN[1]

Durch ihn nehmen die Länder an der Bundesgesetzgebung teil. Zweimalige Beratung der Gesetze, beschränktes Einspruchsrecht. Ohne feste Amtsperiode. Mitglieder werden von den Regierungsparteien der 10 Länder der Bundesrepublik ernannt und abberufen. Die Abstimmung geschieht, wie oben dargestellt, länderweise, nicht nach Parteien. Gesamtzahl 41. Dazu 4 beratende Stimmen von Berlin. Zur Zeit bestehen 14 Ausschüsse; darunter der Vermittlungsausschuß (je 11 Mitglieder von Bundestag und Bundesrat). Der Vorsitz wechselt jährlich unter den Chefs der Regierungen der Länder

[1] Ab 1. 11. 1959: Dr. Franz Josef Röder, Ministerpräsident des Saarlandes.

DER BUNDESTAG

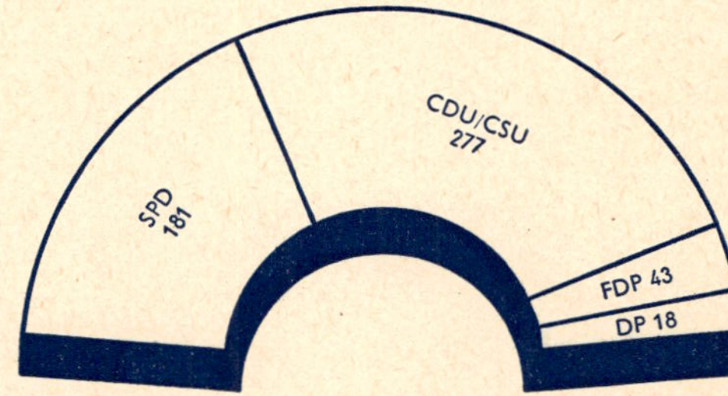

PRÄSIDENT: DR. EUGEN GERSTENMAIER (CDU)

Die Mitglieder werden von der Bevölkerung der Bundesrepublik auf 4 Jahre gewählt. Der Bundestag kann jedoch vom Bundespräsidenten auf Vorschlag des Bundeskanzlers innerhalb von 21 Tagen nach Verweigerung eines Vertrauensvotums für den Bundeskanzler aufgelöst werden, sofern er nicht einen neuen Bundeskanzler wählt. Zahl der stimmberechtigten Abgeordneten 497, dazu 22 nicht stimmberechtigte Abgeordnete aus Berlin (West)

freiheit, die Lehrfreiheit, die Versammlungsfreiheit, die Vereinigungsfreiheit, das Brief-, Post- und Fernmeldegeheimnis, das Eigentum oder das Asylrecht zum Kampfe gegen die freiheitliche demokratische Grundordnung mißbraucht, *verwirkt diese Grundrechte*. Das Bundesverfassungsgericht spricht die Verwirkung und ihr Ausmaß durch Urteil aus[1].

Als Verwirkungsmaßnahme gegen einzelne Personen kommt ferner die Entziehung der Versorgungsbezüge nach § 9 des Gesetzes zu Artikel 131 GG in Betracht. Diese Entziehung ist insbesondere dann geboten, wenn der Empfänger der Versorgungsbezüge durch aktive Förderung neonazistischer oder kommunistischer Tendenzen sich gegen die freiheitliche demokratische Grundordnung betätigt. Der Tatbestand muß in einem förmlichen Disziplinarverfahren festgestellt werden.

Wirksame Handhaben zur Bekämpfung verfassungsfeindlicher Bestrebungen bietet auch das *Strafrechtsänderungsgesetz* vom 30. 8. 1951. Durch dieses Gesetz wird nicht nur der Hoch- und Landesverrat wieder unter Strafe gestellt, sondern es ist darüber hinaus eine besondere Tatbestandsgruppe „Staatsgefährdung" geschaffen worden.

Die Bestimmungen über den *Hochverrat* schützen die verfassungsmäßige Ordnung, den Gebietsstand des Bundes und der Länder sowie die Person des Bundespräsidenten und die Ausübung seiner verfassungsmäßigen Befugnisse gegen jede Einwirkung mit Gewalt oder durch Drohung mit Gewalt. Die Bestimmungen über die *Staatsgefährdung* erklären sonstige Angriffe auf den Bestand der Bundesrepublik oder die Verfassungsgrundsätze für strafbar, sofern deren Beeinträchtigung oder Beseitigung angestrebt wird, sei es durch Mißbrauch oder Anmaßung von Hoheitsbefugnissen, sei es durch Einwirkung auf öffentliche Verkehrsanlagen, Fernmeldeanlagen oder Versorgungsbetriebe durch Aussperrung, Streik oder sonstige Störmaßnahmen. Als Staatsgefährdung wird auch eine Einwirkung auf die Angehörigen des öffentlichen Dienstes angesehen, die in der Absicht erfolgt, die pflichtgemäße Bereitschaft zum Schutze des Bestandes oder der Sicherheit der Bundesrepublik Deutschland oder der verfassungsmäßigen Ordnung des Bundes oder eines Landes zu untergraben. Als *Landesverrat* wird der Verrat von Staatsgeheimnissen in jeder Form bestraft.

Wichtig ist auch eine Bestimmung des Strafrechtsänderungsgesetzes, nach der gegen die Gründer, Rädelsführer und Hintermänner verfassungsfeindlicher Organisationen strafrechtlich eingeschritten werden kann. § 92 StGB erklärt den staatsgefährdenden Nachrichtendienst für strafbar. In § 93 wird das Herstellen, Vervielfältigen, Vertreiben, Beziehen oder Einführen verfassungsfeindlicher Schriften, Schallaufnahmen, Abbildungen oder Darstellungen unter Strafe gestellt.

[1] Art. 18 GG.

2. Für den repressiven Verfassungsschutz stehen der Bundesregierung mit wichtigen Zuständigkeiten ausgestattete Behörden zur Verfügung.

Durch das Gesetz über die Zusammenarbeit des Bundes und der Länder in Angelegenheiten des Verfassungsschutzes vom 27.9.1950 ist das *Bundesamt für Verfassungsschutz* mit Sitz in Köln errichtet worden. Das Amt hat keine Exekutivbefugnisse. Es hat jedoch die wichtige Aufgabe, Nachrichten über verfassungsfeindliche Bestrebungen zu sammeln und auszuwerten und für eine gegenseitige Unterrichtung des Bundesamtes und der *Landesämter für Verfassungsschutz* zu sorgen. Das Bundesamt hat die bei ihm anfallenden Erkenntnisse den zuständigen Behörden des Bundes und der Länder zur Herbeiführung aller nach dem Gesetz zulässigen Maßnahmen zu übermitteln. Diese Behörden prüfen selbständig und in eigener Verantwortung, ob die vom Bundesamt beschafften Unterlagen ausreichen, um das Verbot einer Organisation, den Antrag auf Erlaß eines Haftbefehls usw. zu begründen. Die Zusammenarbeit zwischen dem Bund und den Ländern in Angelegenheiten des Verfassungsschutzes erstreckt sich auf alle gesetzmäßigen Maßnahmen, die zur Abwehr verfassungsfeindlicher Bestrebungen ergriffen werden können. Erfolgt ein Angriff auf die verfassungsmäßige Ordnung des Bundes, dann kann die Bundesregierung den obersten Landesbehörden die für die Zusammenarbeit der Länder mit dem Bund auf dem Gebiete des Verfassungsschutzes erforderlichen Weisungen erteilen[1].

Das durch Gesetz vom 8.3.1951 errichtete *Bundeskriminalamt* dient dem kriminalistischen Erfahrungs- und Nachrichtenaustausch mit den *Landeskriminalämtern*. Das Bundeskriminalamt kann ausnahmsweise selbst exekutiv tätig werden, wenn eine zuständige Landesbehörde darum ersucht oder der Bundesminister des Innern die Verfolgung einer strafbaren Handlung aus schwerwiegenden Gründen anordnet. Solche Gründe können auch gegeben sein, wenn es sich um die Verfolgung von erheblichen Straftaten verfassungsfeindlichen Charakters handelt. Die Beamten des Bundeskriminalamts sind in diesem Fall Hilfsbeamte der Staatsanwaltschaft und befugt, im ganzen Bundesgebiet tätig zu sein und jede Unterstützung von örtlich zuständigen Polizeistellen zu verlangen. Das Bundeskriminalamt hat seinen Sitz in Wiesbaden; die Sicherungsgruppe des Bundeskriminalamts befindet sich in Bad Godesberg.

Die durch das Gesetz vom 12.9.1950 geschaffene *Behörde des Generalbundesanwalts beim Bundesgerichtshof* in Karlsruhe ist zuständig für die in erster Instanz beim Bundesgerichtshof zu erhebenden Anklagen des Hoch-

[1] § 5 des Gesetzes vom 27.9.1950.

verrats, der Staatsgefährdung und des Landesverrats, soweit sie nicht die Verfolgung dieser Strafsachen an die Landesstaatsanwaltschaften abgibt oder sie ihnen überläßt. Der Generalbundesanwalt ist an die Weisungen des Bundesministers der Justiz gebunden. Die Bundesregierung kann somit ihren Einfluß auf die Verfolgung staatsfeindlicher Bestrebungen durch Anklageerhebung geltend machen.

Zusammenfassend kann gesagt werden, daß für den repressiven Verfassungsschutz in der Bundesrepublik weitreichende gesetzliche Vorschriften und mit wirksamen Befugnissen ausgestattete Behörden zur Verfügung stehen. Daß die gesamte Tätigkeit des repressiven Verfassungsschutzes *streng auf gesetzlicher Grundlage* vor sich geht, gehört zum Wesen der Bundesrepublik als eines demokratischen Rechtsstaates.

III. DER ERZIEHERISCHE VERFASSUNGSSCHUTZ

Institutioneller und repressiver Verfassungsschutz sind erforderlich, um die aktiven verfassungsfeindlichen Kräfte abzuwehren. Ein demokratischer Staat ist aber erst dann wirklich gesichert, wenn er auf dem unerschütterlichen Vertrauen seiner Staatsbürger beruht. Auch die Demokratie bedarf der Gefühlskräfte. Gerade die freiheitliche Staatsform ist ohne die Kraft des Gefühls, das auch zu Opfern bereit ist, nicht zu halten. Ohne Verfassungstreue der Bevölkerung ist der demokratische Rechtsstaat existenzunfähig. Die Bundesregierung hat sich daher von Anfang an bemüht, auch das Verständnis der Bevölkerung für den demokratischen Staat, seine inneren Werte und seine Einrichtungen zu vertiefen.

Diese schwierige Aufgabe muß mit viel Behutsamkeit angefaßt werden. Die Bevölkerung und nicht zuletzt die Presse lehnen mit gutem Grund alles ab, was irgendwie den Anschein einer „Staatspropaganda“ erweckt. Da aber die Bevölkerung ständig von rechts- und linksradikaler Seite antidemokratischen Einflüssen ausgesetzt ist, würde es unverantwortlich sein, wenn die Bundesregierung darauf verzichten würde, die Bevölkerung durch Verbreitung des demokratischen Ideengutes und Vertiefung der staatsbürgerlichen Bildung zur Demokratie zu erziehen und dadurch gegen destruktive radikale Einflüsterungen immun zu machen.

Diese Aufgabe, mit allen geeigneten und in einem nicht-totalitären Staat vertretbaren Mitteln den demokratischen und überdies den europäischen Gedanken zu festigen und zu vertiefen, ist der im Jahre 1952 errichteten „*Bundeszentrale für Heimatdienst*“ mit Sitz in Bonn anvertraut worden.

Sie arbeitet auf überparteilicher Grundlage. Das zur Kontrolle der Überparteilichkeit und der Wirksamkeit ihrer Maßnahmen tätige siebzehnköpfige *Kuratorium* setzt sich wie ein Ausschuß des Bundestages aus Abgeordneten aller Parteien zusammen.

Der Name „Bundeszentrale für Heimatdienst" wurde in Anlehnung an die einstige *Reichszentrale für Heimatdienst* gewählt, die zu Ende des Ersten Weltkrieges als Informationsstelle der Reichsregierung zu ähnlichen Zwecken gegründet worden war. Auch damals hatte ein Beschluß des Reichstags vom 5.7.1920 festgelegt, daß die Aufklärung der Bevölkerung „nicht im Geiste einzelner politischer Parteien", sondern „vom Standpunkte des Staatsganzen" erfolgen sollte.

Die Länder haben in den *Landeszentralen für Heimatdienst* der Bundeszentrale entsprechende Einrichtungen geschaffen. Die Landeszentralen sind im Zusammenwirken mit der Bundeszentrale auf freiwilliger Basis übereingekommen, ihre Planungen und Aktionen zu koordinieren. Das Lehrmaterial und der Informationsstoff der Bundeszentrale steht den Landeszentralen unbeschränkt zur Verfügung.

Die Bundeszentrale und die Landeszentralen sind bestrebt, möglichst wenig in eigener Regie durchzuführen. Sie bemühen sich vielmehr um die freiwillige Mitarbeit aller Kräfte, die sich für die Sicherung und Vertiefung des demokratischen Gedankens und für die Vertiefung des Gedankens des europäischen Zusammenschlusses mitverantwortlich fühlen. Sie vergeben daher ihre Publikationsaufträge an freie Journalisten, Schriftsteller und Verleger im ganzen Bundesgebiet. Wer Initiative besitzt und gute Vorschläge macht, kann damit rechnen, daß ihn die Bundeszentrale oder die Landeszentralen für Heimatdienst unterstützen und fördern. Presse und Film, Rundfunk und Fernsehen sind angemessen beteiligt.

In enger Zusammenarbeit mit den Kultusministerien der Länder wird wertvolles *Material zur politischen Bildung* für Schüler, Studenten und Erwachsene ausgearbeitet. Die wegen ihrer sachlichen Qualität sehr geschätzten „*Informationen zur politischen Bildung*" erscheinen in einer Auflage von rund 800.000 Exemplaren.

Die Bundeszentrale und die Landeszentralen sind auch bemüht, mit *neuartigen psychologischen Methoden* den politisch indifferenten und uninteressierten Massenmenschen unserer Tage anzusprechen. Versuche auf diesem Wege sind zum Beispiel mancherlei *Preisausschreiben*, deren Themen unmittelbar oder mittelbar der staatsbürgerlichen Bildung dienen. Da der Durchschnittsmensch bekanntlich vom Optischen her leichter erreichbar und beeinflußbar ist, wird auch der *Film* für Zwecke der allgemeinen politischen Bildung eingeschaltet.

Große und kleine Verbände und Gruppen, die im Bewußtsein ihrer Verantwortung für das Ganze ihre Mitglieder zu loyalen und pflichtbewußten Staatsbürgern zu erziehen suchen, werden in ihren Bildungsvorhaben unterstützt. Die Kirchen, die Gewerkschaften und die Berufsverbände, aber auch weitere große Organisationen, haben an dieser Arbeit regen Anteil. Tagungen und Lehrgänge demokratischer und europäischer Vereinigungen werden von der Bundeszentrale auch finanziell gefördert.

Als ein besonders wirksames Mittel staatsbürgerlicher Bildung und politischer Information gibt die Bundeszentrale für Heimatdienst die Wochenzeitung „*Das Parlament*" heraus. „Das Parlament" berichtet in aufgelockerter Textgestaltung über die Sitzungen des Bundestages und des Bundesrates, aber auch über bedeutsame Entscheidungen, die in den Parlamenten der Länder fallen. In den sitzungsfreien Wochen des Bundestags werden *Sondernummern* über wichtige allgemein interessierende politische, wirtschaftspolitische und sozialpolitische und andere Themen herausgegeben, die oftmals weit über die Grenzen der Bundesrepublik hinaus Beachtung und Anklang finden. Die regelmäßige Beilage „*Aus Politik und Zeitgeschichte*" hat literarisch und wissenschaftlich hohen Rang. Die Überparteilichkeit der Zeitung wird von einem *Beirat*, der sich aus Abgeordneten der großen Parteien des Bundestages zusammensetzt, laufend überwacht.

Der Bundeszentrale für Heimatdienst ist das von der Bundesregierung im November 1957 gegründete *Ostkolleg*, das seinen Sitz in Köln hat, unterstellt. Das Ostkolleg hat die Aufgabe, durch die Veranstaltung von Studientagungen zur geistig-politischen Auseinandersetzung mit dem internationalen Kommunismus beizutragen.

Es ist eine alte Erfahrung, daß man *niemanden durch bloße Wissenserziehung für die Ideale der Demokratie gewinnen kann.* Sicherlich ist eine gewisse Summe von Grundkenntnissen erforderlich, um zum Beispiel das nicht einfache Funktionieren der modernen parlamentarischen Demokratie oder das planvolle Zusammenwirken von Bund und Ländern in dem in vieler Hinsicht verwickelt aufgebauten Bundesstaat zu erfassen. Noch wichtiger aber als das Wissen um die elementaren Tatsachen ist, daß im Schulleben, im Familienleben, im Vereinsleben schon dem jungen Menschen die demokratischen Spielregeln zur selbstverständlichen Gewohnheit, staatsbürgerliche Haltung und schlechthin die demokratischen Tugenden zum Leitbild und selbstverständlichen Wertmaßstab werden. Fairneß und Friedfertigkeit,

Mäßigung und Bescheidenheit, Aufgeschlossenheit für die Diskussion und Kompromißbereitschaft, Toleranz und darüber hinaus echte Nächstenliebe und das Gefühl der Selbstverantwortung kennzeichnen eine andere *Wertskala* als autoritätsgläubige Einordnung und blinder Gehorsam, Forschheit und Bereitschaft zu Händeln, Unduldsamkeit und die Verachtung jeden, auch des echten Kompromisses. Von hier aus ist es kein weiter Schritt zu der Einsicht, *daß der Gedanke der Demokratie immer nur dort auf fruchtbaren Boden gefallen ist, wo die Demokratie* nicht als eine bloße Form für den Ablauf des staatlichen Geschehens hingenommen, sondern wo sie *als eine echte Lebensform empfunden und gehandhabt wird*. Nur in einem Volke, das in diesem Geiste lebt, ist der demokratische Staat auf die Dauer auch von innen her wirklich gesichert.

DIE MILITÄRISCHE SICHERUNG

Am Ende des Zweiten Weltkrieges wäre kein Volk glücklicher gewesen als das deutsche, wenn seine völlige Entwaffnung den Anstoß dazu gegeben hätte, allgemein abzurüsten und alle Energien allein für die friedliche Ordnung der Menschheit einzusetzen. Auch die Erste Bundesregierung faßte später den Entschluß zur Politik der Wiederbewaffnung nur zögernd und gewiß nicht, weil sie etwa im Besitz bewaffneter Macht erst das Wesen des souveränen Staates gesehen hätte. Vielmehr sah die Bundesregierung mit Sorge die schwere Last, die jede Rüstung dem Staate aufbürdet, und die damit verbundenen Gefahren für die Sozialpolitik. Noch tiefer mag sie aus der globalen Spannung unserer Zeit heraus empfunden haben, was der ältere MOLTKE vor achtzig Jahren einem Zeitgenossen anvertraute: „Wer teilte nicht den innigen Wunsch, die schweren Militärlasten erleichtert zu sehen, welche vermöge seiner Weltstellung, in der Mitte der mächtigen Nachbarn, zu tragen Deutschland genötigt ist!" Und ebenso wie MOLTKE mußte die Bundesregierung auf die Erfüllung dieses Wunsches verzichten, weil die dazu vorauszusetzenden „glücklicheren Verhältnisse" erst dann eintreten können, „wenn alle Völker zu der Erkenntnis gelangen, daß jeder Krieg, auch der siegreiche, ein nationales Unglück ist"[1].

Die Siegermächte von 1945 vermochten jedenfalls solche glücklicheren Verhältnisse nicht zu gestalten. Gleichwohl gingen sie zunächst mit Eifer daran, das deutsche Leben zu „entmilitarisieren", das heißt alles Soldatische daraus zu verbannen.

Entmilitarisierung Deutschlands

Im Februar 1945 entschieden ROOSEVELT, CHURCHILL und STALIN in Jalta über das Schicksal, das die deutsche Wehrmacht erfahren sollte, wenn sie bedingungslos kapituliert haben würde. Sie verkündeten in dem gemeinsam unterzeichneten Schlußbericht der Konferenz: „Es ist unser unbeugsamer Wille, den deutschen Militarismus und Nationalsozialismus zu zerstören und dafür Sorge zu tragen, daß Deutschland nie wieder im Stande ist, den Weltfrieden zu stören. Wir sind entschlossen, alle deutschen Streitkräfte zu entwaffnen und aufzulösen; den deutschen Generalstab, der wiederholt die

[1] Brief MOLTKES an C. F. A. HAUSCHILD vom 28.2.1879 über die Möglichkeit der Abrüstung. Nachlaß MOLTKE Nr. XII 9.

Wiederaufrichtung des deutschen Militarismus zu Wege gebracht hat, für alle Zeiten zu zerschlagen; sämtliche deutschen militärischen Einrichtungen zu entfernen oder zu zerstören"[1]. Diesen Beschluß setzten die Alliierten mit den Direktiven in die Tat um, die sie in Potsdam dem von ihnen kraft gemeinsamer oberster Regierungsgewalt eingesetzten Alliierten Kontrollrat gaben. Bis Ende 1946 legte dieser Rat die Maßnahmen fest, die von den Zonenbefehlshabern zu ergreifen waren, um den „deutschen Militarismus" zu liquidieren. Grundlegend war die Proklamation Nr. 2 vom 20.9.1945. In ihr wurde bestimmt, daß alle militärischen Verbände, Dienststellen und Einrichtungen „vollständig und endgültig" aufzulösen seien, desgleichen alle militärischen Organisationen. Darüber hinaus wurde die Pflege soldatischer Tradition in jeder denkbaren Form verboten[2].

Ein Jahr später erklärte das Kontrollratsgesetz Nr. 34 alle in der Proklamation Nr. 2 aufgeführten militärischen Einrichtungen für ungesetzlich. „Wer irgendeine Bestimmung dieses Gesetzes verletzt oder zu verletzen sucht, setzt sich strafrechtlicher Verfolgung durch ein Gericht der Militärregierung und denjenigen Strafen, einschließlich der Todesstrafe, aus, die das Gericht verhängt"[3]. Vor Erlaß dieses Gesetzes hatte der Kontrollrat jede militärische Ausbildung verboten. Militärische Bauten durften nicht mehr errichtet werden[4]. Hinsichtlich des Sportwesens verfügte der Rat, daß es zu beschränken und zu entmilitarisieren sei. Munition und Waffen aller Art einschließlich von Jagdgewehren und Seitenwaffen waren abzuliefern. Militärische Literatur sollte beschlagnahmt und eingezogen werden. Militärische Denkmäler und Museen waren zu beseitigen[5].

[1] „Bericht über die Krimkonferenz", abgedruckt im Amtsblatt des Kontrollrates in Deutschland, Ergänzungsbl. Nr. 1, Berlin 1945, Seite 4f.

[2] Amtsblatt des Kontrollrates in Deutschland, Nr. 1, Seite 8ff.

[3] Gesetz Nr. 34 vom 30.8.1946 bezüglich der Auflösung der Wehrmacht, ebenda Nr. 10 vom 31.8.1946, Seite 172f.

[4] Gesetz Nr. 8 vom 30.11.1945 bezüglich der Ausschaltung und des Verbots der militärischen Ausbildung, a. a. O. Nr. 2, Seite 33 und Gesetz Nr. 23 vom 10.4.1946 bezüglich des Verbots militärischer Bauten in Deutschland, a. a. O. Nr. 6, Seite 136.

[5] Direktive Nr. 23 vom 17.12.1945 bezüglich der Beschränkung und Entmilitarisierung des Sportwesens in Deutschland, a. a. O. Nr. 3, Seite 49; Befehl Nr. 2 vom 7. 1. 1946 bezüglich der Einziehung und Ablieferung von Waffen und Munition, a. a. O. Nr. 6, Seite 130; Befehl Nr. 4 vom 13.5.1946 bezüglich der Einziehung von Literatur und Werken nationalsozialistischen und militärischen Charakters, a. a. O. Nr. 7, Seite 151f.; Direktive Nr. 30 vom 13.5.1946 bezüglich der Beseitigung deutscher Denkmäler und Museen militärischen und nationalsozialistischen Charakters, a. a. O. Nr. 7, Seite 154.

Gleichzeitig begann man, das deutsche Volk „umzuerziehen". Die Besatzungsmächte setzten kurzerhand das deutsche Soldatentum mit dem Nationalsozialismus gleich. Dabei hätte auf alliierter Seite spätestens am 20.7.1944, als die Widerstandsgruppe im Oberkommando der Wehrmacht und im Oberkommando des Heeres sich zum Handeln entschloß, erkannt werden müssen, daß soldatischer Auffassung in Deutschland die nationalsozialistische Gewaltherrschaft wesensfremd war. Aber durch den in der Leidenschaft des Krieges geborenen Plan der Umerziehung wurde der Soldat schlechthin zum Verbündeten der Partei und der von HITLER geführten Angriffskriege und begangenen Rechtsbrüche gemacht[1]. Die ehemaligen Soldaten und Beamten wurden in ihrer Gesamtheit diffamiert und ihrer materiellen Lebensgrundlagen beraubt. Millionen Soldaten wurden nach dem Waffenstillstand in Ost und West rechtswidrig in Gefangenschaft festgehalten — eine Maßnahme, die dem HITLER-Regime mit Recht als verbrecherisch vorgeworfen worden war — oder erwarteten ihre Aburteilung in Gefängnissen. In Nürnberg und an anderen Orten wurden Befehlshaber und andere Militärpersonen in zahlreichen Verfahren durch alliierte Militärgerichte verurteilt. Bestimmte Kategorien von Offizieren kamen in sogenannten automatischen Arrest und teilten damit das Schicksal der höheren Beamten verschiedenster Kategorien und der Leiter wirtschaftlicher und wissenschaftlicher Einrichtungen.

Immerhin gelang es der Verteidigung im großen Nürnberger Kriegsverbrecherprozeß bereits, die beantragte kollektive Verurteilung von „Generalstab und OKW" zu verhindern[2]. Kein geringerer als der frühere Chef des Generalstabs der USA, General MARSHALL, hatte diese Entscheidung durch seinen Rechenschaftsbericht an den Präsidenten der Vereinigten Staaten von Amerika vom 10.10.1945 gefördert[3]. Seine Stimme blieb im

[1] Siehe Anmerkung 3 auf dieser Seite.

[2] Unter dieser Bezeichnung hatte die alliierte Gerichtsbarkeit willkürlich eine Reihe höchster Befehlshaber zusammengefaßt, die tatsächlich niemals gemeinsam einen Führungsorganismus gebildet hatten.

[3] Siehe Baseler Nachrichten vom 6.11.1945. Immerhin ist der Zeitgeist aus den erläuternden Sätzen des Urteils erkennbar: „Wenn diese Offiziere auch nicht eine Gruppe nach dem Wortlaut des Statuts bildeten, so waren sie doch sicherlich eine rücksichtslose militärische Kaste. Der zeitgenössische deutsche Militarismus erlebte mit seinem jüngsten Verbündeten, dem Nationalsozialismus, eine kurze Blütezeit, wie er sie in der Vergangenheit kaum schöner gekannt hat . . ." (Der Prozeß gegen die Hauptkriegsverbrecher vor dem Internationalen Militärgerichtshof, Nürnberg 1947 bis 1949, Bd. I, Seite 313).

übrigen im Westen nicht die einzige, die sich schon damals im Widerspruch zur offiziellen Propaganda der Besatzungsmächte äußerte[1].

Das änderte jedoch zunächst nichts an dem von den Besatzungsmächten eingeschlagenen Weg, obwohl bereits offenbar wurde, daß der Friede keineswegs gesichert war. Auch das Zwischenspiel in der Britischen Zone, wo vier deutsche Armeekorps als ,,entwaffnete deutsche Wehrmacht" mit eigener Verwaltung unter britischem Oberbefehl bestehen geblieben waren, wurde auf sowjetischen Protest im Dezember 1945 mit der Auflösung dieser Truppenteile beendet. Sie hatten bis dahin zivile Aufgaben des Wiederaufbaues erledigt. Einzelentlassungen wurden bereits im Sommer vorgenommen[2]. Die inzwischen bekanntgewordenen politischen Hintergründe der britischen Maßnahme deuten auf die realistische Einschätzung der latenten sowjetischen Gefahr hin. Während die amerikanischen Streitkräfte bald nach der Kapitulation begannen, deutsche Kriegsgefangene zu entlassen — wobei allerdings rund 1.750.000 Kriegsgefangene als Arbeitskräfte an Frankreich übergeben wurden —, überführten die Sowjets die Masse der Gefangenen ins Innere Rußlands. Französische Werbebüros stellten in größerem Umfang Fremdenlegionäre ein. Andererseits wurden zuerst bei den britischen Streitkräften, später bei den amerikanischen und französischen, Arbeitseinheiten aus Freiwilligen auf deutschem Boden aufgestellt. Einheiten der ehemaligen deutschen Kriegsmarine wurden im Rahmen des deutschen Minenräumdienstes, der unter alliierter Kontrolle stand, zur Räumung der Schiffahrtsstraßen eingesetzt Alle diese Maßnahmen fanden im Rahmen der Liquidation des Zweiten Weltkrieges statt. Sie standen in keinem Zusammenhang mit der Jahre später — lange nach der Aufrüstung in der sogenannten DDR — einsetzenden Aufstellung militärischer Verbände in Westdeutschland.

[1] So nahm Feldmarschall MONTGOMERY in seiner Rede in Portsmouth am 26.9.1946 zum Problem des soldatischen Gehorsams Stellung: ,,Das schwierige Problem, strikten Gehorsam gegenüber Befehlen zu erreichen, kann in einem demokratischen Zeitalter nur durch Einschärfung von drei Prinzipien erreicht werden: 1. Die Nation ist etwas, was der Mühe wert ist; 2. Die Armee ist die notwendige Waffe der Nation; 3. Die Pflicht des Soldaten ist es, ohne zu fragen allen Befehlen zu gehorchen, die die Armee, das heißt die Nation, ihm gibt."

[2] Vergleiche HANS MEIER-WELCKER, Deutsches Heerwesen im Wandel der Zeit, Arolsen 1954, Seite 122. In Hamburg war monatelang der Wehrmachtstab-Nord unter General d. Pz. Tr. CRAMER tätig. Vergleiche hierzu die Stellenbesetzung des Stabes bei W. KEILIG, Das deutsche Heer 1939—45, Bad Nauheim, 1956ff., Seite 182, 1—10.

Erst nach Jahren fand die unmenschliche Behandlung der deutschen Soldaten ein Ende. Im Winter 1955/56 kehrten die letzten deutschen Kriegsgefangenen aus der Sowjetunion heim[1]. Dabei ließen die Sowjets die Frage nach dem Schicksal unzähliger Verschollener offen. In der Bundesrepublik stellte Bundeskanzler ADENAUER vor dem Deutschen Bundestag am 5. 4. 1951 unter lebhaftem Beifall der Abgeordneten der Mitte und von rechts fest: „Niemand darf die Berufssoldaten wegen ihrer früheren Tätigkeit tadeln ... Das Kapitel der Kollektivschuld der Militaristen neben den Aktivisten und Nutznießern des nationalsozialistischen Regimes muß ein für allemal beendet sein"[2].

Der Westen organisiert seine Verteidigung

Im Vertrauen darauf, daß das Kriegsbündnis mit den Sowjets den Frieden garantiere, begannen die Westmächte unmittelbar nach der deutschen Kapitulation Truppen aus dem Operationsgebiet abzuziehen und bald darauf große Teile von ihnen zu demobilisieren. Allein, die Sowjetunion hatte schon während des Krieges insgeheim Maßnahmen eingeleitet, die es ihr ermöglichen sollten, nach Kriegsende ihren Macht- und Einflußbereich weiterhin auszudehnen. CHURCHILL war darüber beunruhigt. Schon drei Tage nach Beginn der Waffenruhe in Europa fragte er den amerikanischen Präsidenten, was bezüglich der Sowjetunion geschehen solle, wenn der Abzug amerikanischer Streitkräfte fortgesetzt würde. CHURCHILL machte TRUMAN auf die sowjetische Haltung gegenüber Polen und den Balkanstaaten aufmerksam und verwies auf die Handvoll nicht-amerikanischer Divisionen in Westeuropa, denen zwei- bis dreihundert sowjetische gegenüberstanden. Hinsichtlich der Absichten der Sowjets formulierte der britische Premier in seinem Telegramm die berühmt gewordenen Sätze: „Ein eiserner Vorhang ist vor ihrer Front niedergegangen. Was dahinter vorgeht, wissen wir nicht." CHURCHILL forderte schließlich angesichts der verabredeten Aufgabe

[1] Im November 1955 befanden sich in westlichem Gewahrsam von 166 Inhaftierten noch 27 Soldaten (einschließlich der Angehörigen der Waffen-SS), die alle von Gerichten verurteilt worden waren. Seit 1950 waren 3.491 Deutsche aus Gefängnissen der Westmächte entlassen worden, das heißt 95 % der 1950 noch Inhaftierten.

[2] Zweite Beratung der Gesetzesvorlage zur Regelung der unter Artikel 131 GG fallenden Personen in der 130. Sitzung des Bundestages am 5. 4. 1951. Siehe Verhandlungen des Deutschen Bundestages, 1. Wahlperiode 1949, Stenographische Berichte, Band 6, Seite 4984 (C).

mitteldeutscher Gebiete eine Konferenz mit den Sowjets, um „zu einer Regelung zu kommen, ehe unsere Kraft geschwunden ist . . ."[1].

Die Potsdamer Konferenz führte indessen dazu, daß der Westen die Warnungen des bald gestürzten Premiers nicht beachtete. Die Sowjets hingegen bauten den Ostblock auf. In den Randzonen ihres Einflußgebietes kam es dabei zu offenen Auseinandersetzungen; so vor allem in Griechenland (1946/47). Während die Spannung zwischen Ost und West wuchs, schwand die Möglichkeit, die Organisation der Vereinten Nationen zu einem weltweiten System kollektiver Sicherheit zu entwickeln. Der Westen sah sich schließlich veranlaßt, seine Abwehr in der Form regionaler Zusammenschlüsse zu organisieren.

Außenminister BYRNES leitete mit seiner Stuttgarter Rede am 6. 9. 1946 einen neuen Abschnitt der amerikanischen Deutschlandpolitik ein. Im März 1947 verkündete der amerikanische Präsident in seiner Kongreßbotschaft die sogenannte *Truman-Doktrin.* Sie sah die Unterstützung derjenigen freien Staaten durch die USA vor, die sich der Unterwerfung durch bewaffnete Minderheiten oder durch Druck von außen widersetzen würden. Drei Monate später legte der inzwischen zum Außenminister der USA ernannte General MARSHALL seinen Wirtschaftsplan dar.

Am 2. 9. 1947 schlossen die Staaten des amerikanischen Kontinents mit Ausnahme von Nicaragua, Ekuador und Kanada im Vertrag von Rio de Janeiro sich zum sogenannten *Rio-Pakt* zusammen, einem Bündnis zur gemeinsamen Verteidigung.

In Europa gingen Großbritannien und Frankreich bereits im März 1947 das Bündnis von Dünkirchen ein. Dieses Abkommen wurde ein Jahr später durch den Beitritt der Benelux-Staaten in Brüssel zum „Vertrag über die wirtschaftliche, soziale und kulturelle Zusammenarbeit sowie über die kollektive Verteidigung" erweitert (*Brüsseler Vertrag* oder *Westunion*). Der Vertrag richtete sich hinsichtlich der gemeinsamen Verteidigung der Vertragspartner allerdings gegen eine mögliche deutsche Bedrohung. Er wurde für die Dauer von fünfzig Jahren abgeschlossen. Noch im Laufe des Jahres 1948 wurde ein gemeinsames Oberkommando für die Streitkräfte der fünf Paktstaaten unter Feldmarschall MONTGOMERY mit dem Sitz in Fontainebleau errichtet (*Uniforce*).

Die immer bedrohlicher werdende sowjetische Machtpolitik, die im Juni 1948 mit der Blockade Berlins einen Höhepunkt erreichte, veranlaßte die amerikanische Regierung, die westeuropäischen Abwehrbemühungen wirksam zu unterstützen. So nahm der Senat am 11. 6. 1948 nahezu einstimmig die sogenannte VANDENBERG-Entschließung an. Sie gestattete es der Regierung

[1] CHURCHILL an TRUMAN am 12. 5. 1945. Siehe CHURCHILL, Der Zweite Weltkrieg, Band 6, 2. Buch, deutsche Ausgabe, Stuttgart 1954, Seite 261 ff.

grundsätzlich, schon in Friedenszeiten militärische Bindungen außerhalb des amerikanischen Kontinents einzugehen und den freien Völkern militärische Hilfe zu leisten. Kanada schloß sich diesem Vorgehen an. Die Vereinigten Staaten führten im gleichen Monat die allgemeine Wehrpflicht wieder ein.

In den folgenden Monaten suchten die Westmächte die Form einer Organisation ihrer gemeinsamen Verteidigung. Aus einem lebhaften Gedankenaustausch ergab sich die neuartige internationale Organisation des *Nordatlantischen Verteidigungsvertrages* (NATO). Er wurde am 4. 4. 1949 von den Außenministern Belgiens, Dänemarks, Frankreichs, des Vereinigten Königreichs, Islands, Italiens, Kanadas, Luxemburgs, der Niederlande, Norwegens, Portugals und der USA unterzeichnet[1]. Die NATO ist eine Interessengemeinschaft souveräner Staaten. Sie haben sich gegenseitig verpflichtet, bei jedem bewaffneten Angriff gegen einen oder mehrere von ihnen im Gebiet zwischen Nordamerika und der Türkei, Grönland und Nordafrika dem Angegriffenen Unterstützung zukommen zu lassen, ,,indem jeder für sich und im Zusammenwirken mit den anderen Vertragsstaaten solche Maßnahmen unter Einschluß des Einsatzes bewaffneter Streitkräfte ergreift, die er für notwendig erachtet, um die Sicherheit des nordatlantischen Raums wieder herzustellen und zu erhalten''[2]. Im Gegensatz zum Brüsseler Vertrag war im Atlantikpakt nicht mehr von einem deutschen Angriff die Rede, sondern es wurde umgekehrt festgestellt, daß auch ein Angriff auf die Besatzungstruppen in Westdeutschland einem Angriff auf einen Mitgliedstaat gleichkomme[3]. Damit übernahmen die auf westdeutschem Boden und in Berlin(West) stationierten Truppen der NATO-Mitgliedstaaten praktisch den Schutz dieses Gebietes dort, wo sie stark genug waren, einen möglichen Angriff abzuwehren. Einer vollen Garantie der im Entstehen begriffenen Bundesrepublik entsprach dieser Schutz infolge der zahlenmäßigen Schwäche der alliierten Verbände freilich nicht.

Die NATO bildete regionale militärische Schwerpunkte der Abwehr, vornehmlich in Europa, dessen Front besonders gefährdet war. Damit wurde die NATO zum Kernstück des mit der Bildung weiterer Bündnissysteme in der Folgezeit entstehenden globalen westlichen Sicherheitssystems (SEATO, Balkanpakt, Bagdadpakt, WEU und andere).

[1] Griechenland und die Türkei traten der NATO 1951 bei, die Bundesrepublik im Jahre 1955 als fünfzehnter Mitgliedstaat.

[2] Vergleiche Artikel 5 des Nordatlantikvertrages.

[3] Vergleiche Artikel 6 des Nordatlantikvertrages.

Der Ruf nach deutschen Soldaten

In der westlichen Welt waren bereits im Herbst 1948 Stimmen zu vernehmen, die eine deutsche Beteiligung an der gemeinsamen Verteidigung forderten. Die öffentliche Meinung in den westlichen Besatzungszonen reagierte jedoch ablehnend. Das Kriegserlebnis, die Umerziehung, der zerschlagene und zerstörte Staat und das Wissen um die weiterentwickelten Massenvernichtungsmittel beeinflußten das Bewußtsein der deutschen Menschen vorerst stärker als es die Tatsache der sowjetischen Bedrohung vermochte. Aber auch Beobachter, die sich weniger vom Gefühl leiten ließen, kamen zu ablehnenden Auffassungen[1]. Ablehnend war auch weiterhin die öffentliche Meinung der westlichen Völker selbst, naturgemäß besonders solcher, die eine deutsche Besetzung erlebt hatten. Aber der Ruf nach deutschen Soldaten zum Schutz der besonders bedrohten europäischen Mittelfront war ergangen und wurde in dem Maße lauter, in dem die westliche Abwehrorganisation aufgebaut wurde. Nur zögernd gingen Teile der deutschen Bevölkerung darauf ein. Die große Mehrheit lehnte die Aufforderung, wieder Waffen zu tragen, mit der Parole „Ohne mich" ab.

Auch die Bundesregierung verhielt sich zunächst ablehnend[2]. Alsbald nach ihrer Bildung vereinbarte sie mit den Besatzungsmächten eine enge Zusammenarbeit bei der Entmilitarisierung des Bundesgebietes[3]. Als Bundeskanzler ADENAUER Anfang Dezember 1949 zur Frage einer Wiederaufrüstung im Interview mit dem Cleveland Plain Dealer Stellung nahm, kam es darüber zu einer Debatte im Bundestag.

Der Kanzler wiederholte dort seine Ausführungen, die darauf hinausliefen, daß er eine deutsche Nationalarmee entschieden ablehne. In der Niederschrift über das Interview, die er verlas, hieß es weiter, „daß unter keinen Umständen zugestimmt

[1] So schrieb die Süddeutsche Zeitung am 18.12.1948: „... Wir sind der Ansicht, daß auch eine bescheidene Armee eine schwere Gefahr für unsere politische Zukunft wäre. Nur Ländern mit gefestigten politischen Traditionen gelingt es, ihre Wehrmacht und deren Führer von Übergriffen auf den Bereich der Politik abzuhalten ...".

[2] Der Bundeskanzler hat dies wiederholt eindeutig zum Ausdruck gebracht, siehe zum Beispiel Neue Zeitung vom 5.12.1949, Frankfurter Rundschau vom 21.11.1949, Hamburger Echo vom 20.4.1950, Welt am Sonntag vom 6.8.1950.

[3] Siehe Petersberger Abkommen vom 22.11.1949. Darin gab die Bundesregierung ihrer „ernsten Entschlossenheit Ausdruck, die Entmilitarisierung des Bundesgebietes aufrechtzuerhalten und sich mit allen ihr zur Verfügung stehenden Mitteln zu bemühen, die Wiedererstehung bewaffneter Streitkräfte irgendwelcher Art zu verhindern" (Art. III des Abkommens).

werden könne, daß Deutsche als Söldner oder Landsknechte in fremde Heere eintreten. Auch wenn das Verlangen nach einem deutschen Beitrag zur Sicherheit Europas in einer unabdingbaren Weise von den Alliierten gestellt würde, käme die Aufstellung einer deutschen Wehrmacht nicht in Frage. Im äußersten Fall sei alsdann die Frage eines deutschen Kontingents im Rahmen der Armee einer europäischen Föderation zu überlegen"[1]. Für die SPD antwortete der Abgeordnete OLLENHAUER, seine Fraktion lehne es ab, „eine deutsche Wiederbewaffnung auch nur in Erwägung zu ziehen". Er fuhr fort: „Die Verantwortung für die Sicherung des Gebietes der Bundesrepublik liegt bei den Besatzungsmächten"[2].

Die westdeutsche Wiederbewaffnung wurde weiter diskutiert. CHURCHILL forderte sie im März 1950. Am 3.3.1950 sagte der französische General BILLOTTE vor dem anglo-amerikanischen Presseverband in Paris: „Wir wollen offen eingestehen, daß wir ohne die Deutschen nicht an der Elbe-Linie kämpfen können." Die Erwägungen richteten sich schließlich auf einen deutschen Beitrag innerhalb einer europäischen Vereinigung, wie es der Bundeskanzler in seinem Interview angedeutet hatte. Ähnlich hatte die SPD schon im Dezember 1948 erklärt: „Die Frage einer künftigen Wehrverfassung ist abhängig von der Rolle, die Deutschland in einer künftigen europäischen Gemeinschaft spielen wird. Eine Diskussion darüber kann nur unter dem Gesichtspunkt eines Systems internationaler kollektiver Sicherheit geführt werden"[3].

In den ersten Monaten des Jahres 1950 sah die Bundesregierung sich gezwungen, Schutzmaßnahmen gegen Übergriffe der im Entstehen begriffenen Volkspolizei der sogenannten DDR zu ergreifen. Deshalb forderte der Bundeskanzler von den Besatzungsmächten die sofortige Verstärkung der alliierten Truppen in der Bundesrepublik, die Garantie des westdeutschen Gebietes und am 28.4.1950 die Genehmigung zur Aufstellung einer mobilen Bundespolizeitruppe.

Am 24. Mai beauftragte er den General der Panzertruppen a. D. GRAF SCHWERIN mit der Ausarbeitung von Vorschlägen hinsichtlich der Bildung einer *Bundespolizei*. Nach Ausbruch des Korea-Konfliktes (25.6.1950) hielt die Bundesregierung Sofortmaßnahmen in der Bundesrepublik für dringlich.

Im Juli besprach GRAF SCHWERIN mit Vertretern des Bundeskanzleramtes, des Bundesministeriums des Innern und mit dem Oppositionsführer KURT SCHUMACHER die Polizeiverstärkung. Mehrfach fanden Gespräche mit dem amerikanischen Hohen

[1] 24. Plenarsitzung des Bundestages am 16.12.1949. Siehe Verhandlungen des Deutschen Bundestages, a. a. O., Band 1, Seite 735.

[2] a. a. O., Seite 735.

[3] Punkt 5 der Erklärung des SPD-Vorstandes vom 11.12.1948 in Bad Godesberg.

Kommissar statt. Schließlich genehmigte der Rat der Alliierten Hohen Kommissare am 28.7.1950 in einer Note an den Bundeskanzler eine gewisse Verstärkung der Länderpolizeien, sprach sich aber gegen eine Bundespolizei aus, wofür er lediglich Besprechungen mit Vertretern der Bundesregierung anregte. Um für die Behandlung von Detailfragen eine sachkundige deutsche Gegenstelle für solche Besprechungen zu haben, erhielt GRAF SCHWERIN den Auftrag, im Bundeskanzlerant ein kleines Büro mit einigen Mitarbeitern einzurichten (bezeichnet als Zentrale für Heimatdienst). Die Ereignisse in Korea und die sich verstärkenden europäischen Einigungsbestrebungen ließen den Gedanken eines deutschen Wehrbeitrages im Laufe des Sommers mehr in den Vordergrund treten. Er verband sich nun mit der Idee einer europäischen Union. Im August machte ANDRÉ PHILIP in der Beratenden Versammlung des Europarates den Vorschlag, eine Europa-Armee zu bilden. GEORGES BIDAULT schlug dort die Ernennung eines europäischen Kommissars für den Aufbau einer gemeinsamen Verteidigung vor, während PAUL REYNAUD für die Ernennung eines europäischen Kriegsministers eintrat. Die Versammlung nahm am 11. August die Resolution CHURCHILLS an, unverzüglich eine Europa-Armee unter deutscher Beteiligung aufzustellen.

Bundeskanzler ADENAUER richtete am 29.8.1950 an den geschäftsführenden Vorsitzenden der Alliierten Hohen Kommission das „*Memorandum über die Sicherung des Bundesgebietes nach innen und nach außen*" und bat um Übermittlung an die für Mitte September in New York einberufene Außenministerkonferenz der USA, des Vereinigten Königreichs und Frankreichs. In dem Memorandum wiederholte der Bundeskanzler „in dringendster Form" seine Bitte um Verstärkung der alliierten Truppen, indem er auf die gefährdete Lage der etwa fünf alliierten Divisionen in der Bundesrepublik hinwies. Er wiederholte ferner seine Forderung nach einer klaren Sicherheitsgarantie. Die Bundesregierung, so hieß es in dem Memorandum weiter, könne ihr Gebiet höchstens mit dem schwachen Zollgrenzdienst und den geringen Kommunal- und Länderpolizeien gegen Übergriffe in solchen Fällen schützen, in denen die Alliierten nicht bereit sein würden, ihre Streitkräfte einzusetzen. Daher wurde eine Schutzpolizei des Bundes vorgeschlagen. Schließlich wiederholte der Bundeskanzler seine Bereitschaft, „im Falle der Bildung einer westeuropäischen Armee einen Beitrag in Form eines deutschen Kontingents zu leisten", lehnte aber erneut die Aufstellung einer deutschen Nationalarmee betont ab.

Zwei Tage später stimmten die Mitglieder des Bundeskabinetts dem Memorandum zu mit Ausnahme des Bundesinnenministers HEINEMANN, der den Schritt des Bundeskanzlers ablehnte und seinen Rücktritt erklärte.

Die Drei Mächte beschlossen in New York, ihre Stationierungstruppen nicht mehr nur als Besatzungstruppen zu betrachten, sondern als Schutz der

Bundesrepublik und der Westsektoren Berlins. Sie erläuterten den Beschluß ausdrücklich dahingehend, ,,daß sie jeden Angriff auf die Bundesrepublik oder auf Berlin, von welcher Seite er auch kommen mag, also auch wenn er nur von der Volkspolizei ohne Intervention Sowjetrußlands unternommen würde, als einen gegen sie selbst gerichteten Angriff ansehen würden''. Die Mächte würden ferner die Effektivstärke ihrer auf dem Gebiet der Bundesrepublik stehenden Truppen ,,innerhalb kürzester Frist'' erhöhen.

Dagegen wurde eine Bundespolizei abgelehnt, jedoch einer einheitlich zu bildenden Polizei auf Länderbasis zugestimmt. Über den Einsatz deutschen Militärpotentials waren sich die Mächte nur hinsichtlich des Verbots einer deutschen Nationalarmee einig[1]. Die auf die Außenministerkonferenz folgende Tagung des Atlantikrates endete in dieser Hinsicht ebenfalls ohne Beschluß. Es wurde lediglich der Militärausschuß beauftragt, Empfehlungen über die Möglichkeiten eines deutschen Verteidigungsbeitrages auszuarbeiten.

Damit deutscherseits möglichen alliierten Anfragen eigene Forderungen entgegengesetzt werden konnten, berief GRAF SCHWERIN im Auftrag des Bundeskanzlers Anfang Oktober 1950 einen Ausschuß militärischer Sachverständiger zu einer Tagung ein. Der Ausschuß wurde von Generaloberst a. D. v. VIETINGHOFF geleitet und setzte sich aus einer Reihe höherer Offiziere, darunter den Generalen HEUSINGER und Dr. SPEIDEL, zusammen. Auf der Tagung erarbeiteten die Militär-Experten eine für die Bundesregierung bestimmte ,,*Denkschrift über die Aufstellung eines deutschen Kontingents im Rahmen einer internationalen Streitmacht zur Verteidigung Westeuropas*''. Die Denkschrift ging davon aus, daß der Anreiz für die Sowjetunion zu einer aggressiven Politik umso geringer wird, je stärker der Westen sich sichert. Ehe aber eine deutsche Wehrkraft zur Schließung der Lücke in Europa eingesetzt werden könne, müßten politische, militärische und psychologische Voraussetzungen geschaffen werden, wie Übertragung der Souveränität, Aufhebung der Kontrollratsgesetze, volle Gleichberechtigung deutscher Verbände, Verbot von Vorbereitungen zum Partisanenkampf und Revision von Urteilen über Kriegsverbrecher nach deutschem Recht. Ein deutsches Kontingent solle nur in Europa verwendet werden dürfen. Für die Aufstellungszeit müßten die alliierten Truppen so verstärkt werden, daß das Kontingent hinter ihrem Schutzschirm gebildet werden könne. Das Ziel müsse die Aufstellung von zwölf deutschen Divisionen sein, die im Verein mit zwölf bis

[1] Die New Yorker Beschlüsse wurden in dem Memorandum der Hohen Kommissare erläutert, das A. FRANÇOIS-PONCET am 23.9.1950 dem Bundeskanzler überreichte.

vierzehn alliierten Divisionen als gepanzerte Faust einen sowjetischen Angriff soweit ostwärts wie möglich aufhalten sollten, bis rückwärtige europäische und amerikanische Streitkräfte zum Gegenschlag heraneilen würden. Sofortmaßnahmen wären noch im Jahre 1950 einzuleiten. Das innere Gefüge der Truppe sollte grundlegend neu gestaltet werden. GRAF BAUDISSIN, der eben falls dem Ausschuß angehörte, umriß in der Denkschrift seine Reformideen.

Während die Regierungen und Völker der Westmächte sich über das ,,Wie" eines deutschen Beitrages zu einigen suchten, nahm die Diskussion um das ,,Ob" in der Bundesrepublik heftige Formen an. Wo in der deutschen Öffentlichkeit die Form eines Beitrages erwogen wurde, stand die Forderung nach deutscher *Gleichberechtigung* im Vordergrund.

Der Bundesvorsitzende des Deutschen Gewerkschaftsbundes, FETTE, erklärte im August 1950 vor der Auslandspresse in Bonn, daß die Verteidigung der Freiheit zwar notwendig, ein deutscher Verteidigungsbeitrag aber nur im Rahmen einer europäischen Armee unter völliger Gleichberechtigung möglich sei. Der Oppositionsführer SCHUMACHER ging auf der Pressekonferenz in Bonn am 23.8.1950 noch weiter, indem er ausführte: ,,Hier, wo wir untersuchen müssen, ob es eine Situation gibt, bei der eine deutsche militärische Leistung einen Sinn hat, sage ich: diese Situation tritt dann ein, wenn die Weltdemokratie, wenn vor allen Dingen die Vereinigten Staaten, Deutschland offensiv nach dem Osten verteidigen, das heißt, das ganze Deutschland vor den schwersten Zerstörungen des Krieges bewahren und Europa die Kriegsentscheidung mit allen Kräften östlich von Deutschland sucht. Das ist die erste und einzige Voraussetzung für unser Ja oder Nein zur deutschen Rüstung. Das große Können und das große Wollen der USA und der anderen Demokratien muß hier in Deutschland eindrucksvoll sichtbar werden; das heißt, es muß nicht nur eine theatralische Verstärkung durch eine oder zwei Panzerdivisionen kommen, sondern es muß die Konzentration des großen Teils der militärischen Kräfte der Weltdemokratie hier erfolgen. Andernfalls können wir unserem desillusionierten Volk nicht zumuten, zur Waffe zu greifen." SCHUMACHER lehnte dann eine nur teilweise Aufrüstung und unzulängliche Bewaffnung ab, weil Schwäche nur eine zusätzliche Gefährdung mit sich bringe. Er forderte: ,,Die militärische Offensivkraft muß bei der Kriegsentscheidung an Weichsel und Njemen liegen." Kurze Zeit später wandte SCHUMACHER den Begriff ,,Vorfeld-Verwendung" für die unzureichende Aufstellung deutscher Verbände an und setzte dem das klare Nein der SPD entgegen.

Am 16.9.1950 präzisierte er in Stuttgart die Voraussetzung für die Zustimmung seiner Partei: ,,Wir sind bereit, wieder Waffen zu tragen, wenn die westlichen Alliierten mit uns das gleiche Risiko und die gleiche Chance der Abwehr eines sowjetischen Angriffs übernehmen und sich mit größtmöglicher Macht an der Elbe etablieren."

*

EVG-Konzept gegen NATO-Lösung

Bei den New Yorker Konferenzen im September 1950 hatten die französischen Vertreter der vor allem von amerikanischer Seite angestrebten Eingliederung eines deutschen Kontingents in die NATO widersprochen. Am 24. Oktober unterbreitete der französische Ministerpräsident RENE PLEVEN der Nationalversammlung seinen Vorschlag, das Problem des deutschen Beitrags innerhalb der europäischen Gemeinschaft zu lösen. Im Namen seiner Regierung schlug PLEVEN vor, eine europäische Armee im Rahmen der politischen Institutionen des vereinten Europas zu schaffen. Diese Streitkräfte der europäischen Länder sollten keine Koalitionsarmee bilden, sondern „*une fusion complète des éléments humains et matériels*"[1]. Die Kontingente der Teilnehmerstaaten sollten in der Europa-Armee in den kleinstmöglichen Verbänden integriert werden, die bereits bestehenden nationalen Streitkräfte jedoch erst nach einer Übergangszeit, deren Dauer von einem Ministerrat im Einvernehmen mit der NATO bestimmt werden sollte. Auf dieser Basis, so sagte PLEVEN, beabsichtige seine Regierung Großbritannien und die freien Staaten Europas zur Beratung einzuladen. Trotz heftigen Widerspruchs vor allem von Links und Rechts nahm die Nationalversammlung den Plan am 25.10.1950 mit Mehrheit an. Sie verlangte jedoch, daß weder eine nationale deutsche Armee noch ein deutscher Generalstab zugelassen werde.

Bundeskanzler ADENAUER erklärte vor dem Bundestag am 8. November, daß die Bundesregierung grundsätzlich zur Mitarbeit bei der Beratung des PLEVEN-*Planes* bereit sei.

Vorbehalte, die gegen gewisse Formulierungen des Planes zu machen seien, habe der französische Hohe Kommissar in einer Unterredung am Vortage mit dem Bemerken entkräftet, daß jede Diskriminierung Deutschlands ausgeschlossen sei. Der Bundeskanzler stellte fest: „Wir betrachten den PLEVEN-Plan als einen wertvollen Beitrag zur Integration Europas[2]". Dagegen sagte SCHUMACHER, indem er die Mißbilligung seiner Fraktion zur Verhandlungsbereitschaft der Regierung begründete: „Der Geist des Planes PLEVEN ist nicht der Geist der Aussöhnung." Der Plan enthalte die Ungleichheit im Opfer und bringe nicht die von der SPD geforderte Konzentration wirklicher militärischer Macht. „Die große Auseinandersetzung", so führte der Oppositionsführer aus, „vollzieht sich ja nicht zwischen den Remilitarisierern schlechthin und irgendwelchen absoluten Pazifisten mit einer Friedensformel des garantierten Erfolges. Die große Auseinandersetzung vollzieht sich zwischen denjenigen, die unter

[1] Journal Officiel de la République Française, Débats parlementaires, Assemblée Nationale, Jg. 1950, Nr. 104, 234. Sitzung vom 24.10.1950.

[2] Verhandlungen des Deutschen Bundestages, a. a. O., Band 5, Seite 5565 (A).

heutigen Umständen ihr Wollen zur Remilitarisierung einfach durchdrücken wollen und denjenigen, die eine feste nationale und internationale Voraussetzung dafür verlangen, ohne deren Durchführung sie Nein sagen werden"[1].

Der Bundeskanzler hatte Ende Oktober 1950 den Bundestagsabgeordneten THEODOR BLANK mit der Führung der Verhandlungen mit der Alliierten Hohen Kommission über die Unterbringung zusätzlicher alliierter Truppen und der Bearbeitung allgemeiner Fragen der Sicherheit beauftragt.

Hierzu wurde durch Kabinettsbeschluß vom 23. 10. 1950 eine neue Dienststelle im Bundeskanzleramt mit Sitz in der Bonner Ermekeilkaserne gebildet[2]. Der geringe Personalbestand des Amtes BLANK erschwerte von Anfang an die erschöpfende Bearbeitung aller gestellten Planungsaufgaben. Gegenüber den Verhandlungspartnern, die über eingearbeitete Ministerien und Generalstäbe verfügten, war das Amt trotz mehrfachen Neueinstellungen im Nachteil.

Während die beratende Versammlung des Europarates am 24. November die Idee des PLEVEN-Planes mit großer Mehrheit guthieß, erhoben die NATO-Staaten Einwände gegen seine militärische Grundkonzeption. Vor allem lehnten sie die Forderung ab, daß der kleinste national-homogene Verband das Bataillon sein solle. Die Staaten einigten sich am 7. Dezember auf den sogenannten SPOFFORD-*Plan*, in dem die ursprünglichen amerikanischen Forderungen wieder stärker berücksichtigt waren. Die nationale Grundeinheit sollte nun die Kampfgruppe mit etwa 6.000 Mann sein. Am 18. Dezember forderte der NATO-Rat in Brüssel die Bundesregierung zu vorbereitenden Besprechungen mit den Hohen Kommissaren über militärtechnische Voraussetzungen eines deutschen Beitrags auf. Die Besprechungen begannen am 9. 1. 1951 auf dem Petersberg bei Bonn. Sie wurden auf deutscher Seite von BLANK und den Generalen HEUSINGER und SPEIDEL als militärischen Sachverständigen geführt. Die deutsche Delegation hatte Weisung, die *militärische Gleichberechtigung deutscher Streitkräfte* zu verlangen und für große national-homogene Verbände, integriert in der oberen

[1] Ebenda, Seite 3568ff.

[2] BLANK führte bis 1955 die Bezeichnung „*Der Beauftragte des Bundeskanzlers für die mit der Vermehrung der alliierten Truppen zusammenhängenden Fragen*". Seine Dienststelle nahm die Arbeit mit etwa 20 Personen auf. Sie wurde im Laufe des Jahres 1951 auf etwa 70, Ende 1951 auf rund 140 Personen und im Sommer 1952 erneut vergrößert. Im März 1953 betrug die Kopfstärke 708 Personen (davon 120 ständig in Paris). Nur rund 200 Angehörige der Dienststelle waren ehemalige Offiziere. Sie arbeiteten zum Teil auf Gutachter-Basis. GRAF SCHWERIN war kurz nach BLANKS Ernennung zurückgetreten. Seine Dienststelle wurde aufgelöst, einzelne Mitarbeiter wurden von BLANK übernommen.

GLIEDERUNG der DIENSTSTELLE BLANK im Sommer 1952

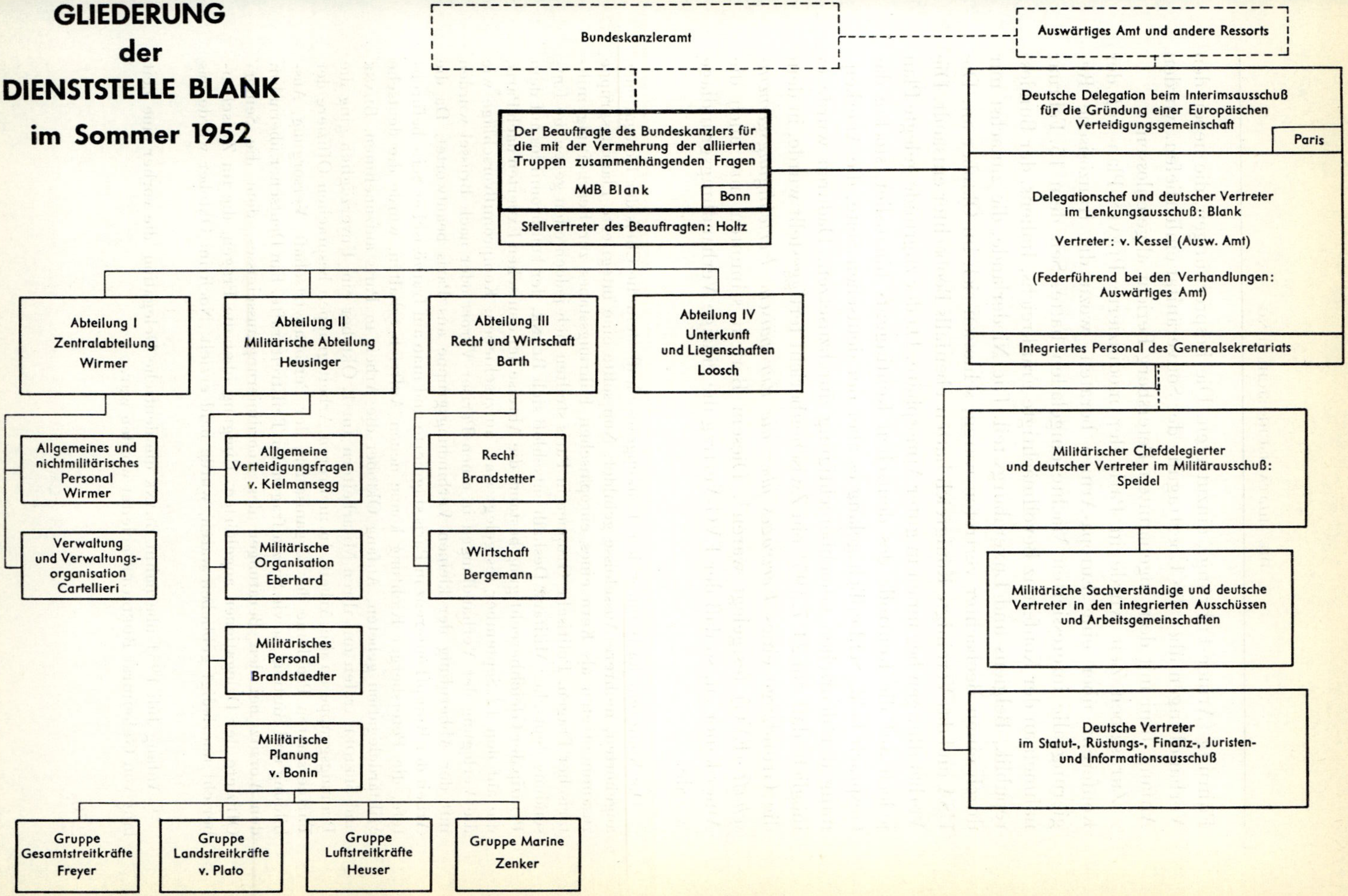
Bundeskanzleramt
Auswärtiges Amt und andere Ressorts
Der Beauftragte des Bundeskanzlers für die mit der Vermehrung der alliierten Truppen zusammenhängenden Fragen
MdB Blank
Bonn
Stellvertreter des Beauftragten: Holtz
Deutsche Delegation beim Interimsausschuß für die Gründung einer Europäischen Verteidigungsgemeinschaft
Paris
Delegationschef und deutscher Vertreter im Lenkungsausschuß: Blank
Vertreter: v. Kessel (Ausw. Amt)
(Federführend bei den Verhandlungen: Auswärtiges Amt)
Integriertes Personal des Generalsekretariats
Militärischer Chefdelegierter und deutscher Vertreter im Militärausschuß: Speidel
Militärische Sachverständige und deutsche Vertreter in den integrierten Ausschüssen und Arbeitsgemeinschaften
Deutsche Vertreter im Statut-, Rüstungs-, Finanz-, Juristen- und Informationsausschuß
Abteilung I Zentralabteilung Wirmer
Allgemeines und nichtmilitärisches Personal Wirmer
Verwaltung und Verwaltungsorganisation Cartellieri
Abteilung II Militärische Abteilung Heusinger
Allgemeine Verteidigungsfragen v. Kielmansegg
Militärische Organisation Eberhard
Militärisches Personal Brandstaedter
Militärische Planung v. Bonin
Gruppe Gesamtstreitkräfte Freyer
Gruppe Landstreitkräfte v. Plato
Gruppe Luftstreitkräfte Heuser
Gruppe Marine Zenker
Abteilung III Recht und Wirtschaft Barth
Recht Brandstetter
Wirtschaft Bergemann
Abteilung IV Unterkunft und Liegenschaften Loosch

Führung (Armee-Führung), einzutreten. Die Besprechungen, die neben den Verhandlungen über die Übertragung der Souveränität einherliefen, wurden Anfang Juni mit dem sogenannten Petersberg-Bericht abgeschlossen.

Zur selben Zeit wurde in Paris der modifizierte PLEVEN-Plan auf der Konferenz über eine Europa-Armee beraten, wozu die französische Regierung alle interessierten Mächte eingeladen hatte. Seit dem 15. Februar nahmen an der Konferenz Bevollmächtigte Frankreichs, Italiens, der Bundesrepublik, Belgiens und Luxemburgs teil. Die Niederlande, die zunächst nur durch einen Beobachter vertreten waren, schlossen sich im Oktober an. Die USA und das Vereinigte Königreich hatten ebenfalls Beobachter entsandt. Die Verhandlungen begannen in guter Atmosphäre. Da der zugrunde gelegte Plan jedoch auf die Kontrolle des deutschen Kontingents hinauslief, stockte das Gespräch bald. Schließlich gelang es aber der deutschen Seite, die Anerkennung der deutschen Gleichberechtigung durchzusetzen. Dadurch wurde es möglich, daß am 24.7.1951 ein Zwischenbericht fertiggestellt wurde, in dem die Grundzüge eines *Vertrages über die Europäische Verteidigungsgemeinschaft* (EVG) festgelegt waren[1]. Diesem Bericht stimmten nun auch die Amerikaner zu, so daß der EVG-Vertrag die einzige Verhandlungsgrundlage wurde.

Die Konferenz hatte unter dem Lenkungsausschuß, dem die Chefs der Delegationen angehörten, mehrere Ausschüsse gebildet. Nun sollte eine integrierte Planungsgruppe zusammentreten als Kern eines europäischen Führungsstabes zur Bearbeitung militärischer Fragen. Politische Gruppen in Paris stellten sich jedoch offen gegen die Entsendung deutscher Militärs. Deshalb entschloß sich BLANK, der kompromißlos auf dem Prinzip der Gleichberechtigung bestand, die Abreise der deutschen Experten nach Paris, die auf den 12. September festgelegt war, aufzuschieben. Kompromißvorschläge wie die Verlegung der Verhandlungen in einen Pariser Vorort oder nach Brüssel wurden mit der Abberufung der kleinen Verbindungsgruppe aus Paris beantwortet. Da die Arbeit der Rumpfkonferenz in Paris stagnierte und man auf französischer Seite befürchtete, die Petersberger Richtung könne neuen Auftrieb erhalten, wurde die deutsche Militärdelegation gebeten, Anfang Oktober die Arbeit in Paris aufzunehmen. BLANK und SPEIDEL trafen mit ihren Mitarbeitern am 1. Oktober ein. Unverzüglich ging die Planungsgruppe an die Arbeit. In mehreren Arbeitsgruppen besprachen Offiziere der Partnerstaaten Probleme der Organisation, der Personalwirtschaft, Versorgung, Ausbildung und Rüstung, sowie Spezialfragen der Teilstreitkräfte. Ein Deutscher übernahm den Vorsitz bei den Beratungen des Koordinierungsausschusses, dem die Senior-Offiziere der Delegationen angehörten. Einigung über die Fragen, die im Zwischenbericht unerledigt geblieben waren, wurde bald erzielt. Noch im Oktober wurde das

[1] Anfang Juli 1951 übernahm BLANK die deutsche Delegation, die vorher eine Zeit lang von Geheimrat ROEDIGER geleitet worden war.

groupement als Grundverband in Divisionsstärke für die ganze EVG bestimmt. Die auf Kampferfahrung gestützte Argumentation der deutschen Sachverständigen und die Zähigkeit der deutschen Delegierten auf politischer Ebene hatten erreicht, daß nicht deutsche Bataillone, sondern Divisionen der Gemeinschaft zur Verfügung gestellt werden sollten. Ein wesentliches Element der Diskriminierung des deutschen Partners war damit beseitigt.

Im Herbst 1951 wurden die EVG-Verhandlungen mit den *Verhandlungen über die Aufhebung des Besatzungsstatuts* gekoppelt. Ein weiteres Junktim neben der Verbindung von EVG und Montanunion beherrschte damit die Europapolitik. Auf der Pariser Außenministerkonferenz am 22.11.1951, an der erstmalig der deutsche Bundeskanzler und Außenminister teilnahm, verlangte DEAN ACHESON die Fertigstellung der Vertragsentwürfe zum EVG- und Deutschlandvertrag innerhalb von neunzig Tagen.

Neue Schwierigkeiten mußten auf Konferenzen der Außenminister überwunden werden. Die Benelux-Staaten wandten sich gegen starke Zentralorgane für die Gemeinschaft, wie Frankreich sie vorschlug. Desgleichen lehnten die kleineren Partner das gemeinsame Budget ab. Die Bundesrepublik und Frankreich dagegen trafen sich in dieser Verhandlungsphase in gemeinsamen Interessen. Die spätere starke Stellung des Ministerrates hingegen entsprang dem Verlangen der Benelux-Staaten. Italien nahm eine weniger entschiedene Haltung ein. Besondere Bedeutung erlangte das Problem der Beziehungen zwischen EVG und NATO. Darüber wurden zusätzliche Vertragsprotokolle entworfen, die gegenseitige Beistandsverpflichtungen und enge Zusammenarbeit zwischen dem Ministerrat der EVG und der NATO zum Inhalt hatten.

Der EVG-Vertrag mit Zusatzabkommen und Protokollen wurde am 9.5.1952 paraphiert und am 27. Mai im Uhrensaal des Quai d'Orsay feierlich unterzeichnet.

Im Vertrag verpflichteten die Signatarstaaten sich zum automatischen Beistand im Verteidigungsfalle. Die europäischen Streitkräfte sollten aus nationalhomogenen Divisionsverbänden (*groupements*) mehrerer Typen bestehen und vom Armeekorps aufwärts integriert sein; das heißt: jedes Korps sollte aus Divisionen verschiedener Nationalität bestehen. Die Stäbe vom Korps an aufwärts waren mit Befehlshabern und Personal verschiedener Nationalität zu besetzen. Das deutsche Kontingent sollte nach seiner Aufstellung zwölf Kampfverbände mit den entsprechenden Führungsstäben, Unterstützungstruppen, Versorgungseinheiten und Schulen, sowie eine taktische Luftwaffe, Marineverbände und Truppen der gemeinsamen Territorialorganisation umfassen. Insgesamt sollte die Bundesrepublik etwa 500.000 Mann aufstellen. Diese sollten nach dem Grundsatz der allgemeinen Wehrpflicht einberufen werden, wie in den übrigen Vertragsländern.

Für die Aufstellungszeit war für jeden Mitgliedstaat ein militärischer Bevollmächtigter vorgesehen, der zugleich der nationalen Regierung und dem Kommissariat, dem zentralen Exekutivorgan der Gemeinschaft, unterstand. Die EVG sollte gemeinsamen supranationalen Behörden unterstehen, die teilweise mit der Montanunion verbunden waren und mit ihr in die geplante *Europäische Politische Gemeinschaft* eingefügt werden sollten. Die einsatzbereiten europäischen Verteidigungsstreitkräfte waren dem NATO-Oberbefehlshaber zur Verfügung zu stellen.

Mit diesem Vertrag schien ein bedeutender Erfolg in der Sicherheitspolitik des Westens und auf dem Wege zur Vereinigung der europäischen Kernstaaten erzielt worden zu sein. Große Hoffnungen gründeten sich darauf. Freilich erwiesen das Abseitsstehen des Vereinigten Königreichs und andere ungelöste politische Fragen sich bald als schwere Hypothek bei dem Versuch, die EVG zu verwirklichen.

Zunächst versuchten die Regierungen die Zeit zwischen Unterzeichnung und Inkrafttreten durch Weiterarbeit in Paris zu nutzen. Die Delegationen wurden erheblich vergrößert und im Interimsausschuß nach verschiedenen Sachgebieten gegliedert. In einem der Vertragsprotokolle war dieser Ausschuß beauftragt worden, Empfehlungen für den kommenden Ministerrat der Gemeinschaft auszuarbeiten, über die dieser unmittelbar nach Inkrafttreten des Vertrages entscheiden sollte[1].

[1] Der Interimsausschuß, CICOCED (*Comité Intérimaire de la Conférence pour l'Organisation d'une Communauté Européenne de Défense*), gliederte sich in eine Reihe von Ausschüssen, Unterausschüssen und *ad hoc*-Ausschüssen, die dem Lenkungsausschuß unterstanden und im Laufe der Zeit vermehrt wurden. Präsident des Lenkungsausschusses war der Franzose Herve Alphand. Auf sechs großen Ausschüssen ruhte die Hauptlast der Arbeit: Militärausschuß (mit dem Koordinierungsausschuß und den Abteilungen Personal, Sicherheit, Organisation und Ausbildung, Versorgung, Fernmeldewesen, Taktische Studienkommission, Heer, Marine, Luftwaffe mit jeweils einer Anzahl Unterausschüssen); Statut-Ausschuß (mit Ausschüssen für Strafrecht, Zivilrecht, Öffentliche Dienste, Öffentliche Sicherheit und andere); Rüstungsausschuß (mit Ausschüssen zur Bearbeitung von Rüstungsfragen, Standardisierung, Patentwesen und andere); Finanzausschuß (Steuer-, Zoll- und andere Fragen); Juristenausschuß; Informations-Ausschuß. Daneben gab es mehrere gemischte Unterausschüsse (Militärische Strafgerichtsbarkeit, Zivilpersonalstatut, Besoldung) und *ad hoc*-Ausschüsse (für Organisation des Kommissariats, Außenhilfe, Zusammenarbeit mit der NATO). Zur Verfügung der Konferenz stand ein integriertes Allgemeines Verwaltungssekretariat. Die USA und das Vereinigte Königreich unterhielten ständige Beobachter beim Interimsausschuß, SHAPE richtete eine Verbindungsstelle ein.

Der deutsche Anteil am Interimsausschuß betrug im Februar 1953: 194 Personen (ständige Mitglieder und Inhaber von Planstellen in Heimatbehörden). Darunter waren rund 60 ehemalige Offiziere.

Schloß Meersburg am odensee aus dem 7. Jahrh. (erneuert im 16. Jahrh.). Von hier zog der letzte Staufer KONRADIN 1267 nach Italien

Blick von der Evangelischen Pfarrkirche in Freudenstadt (1601—1614) auf den Schwarzwald

Pfälzischer Adelssitz (jetzt Sektkellerei Schloß Wachenheim) aus der Barockzeit in Wachenheim an der Weinstraße

DEUTSCHE OSTGEBIETE UNTER POLNISCHER VERWALTUNG

Nachwinter im Isergebirge (Niederschlesien)

unten:
Die Hakenterrasse in Stettin mit Regierungsgebäuden und Landesmuseum, 1911 am Bollwerk (1550—1570) über der Oder errichtet

Die Donnersmarck-Hütte in Hindenburg (Oberschlesien), dem um 1300 gegründeten Zabrze, das 1915 umbenannt wurde

DEUTSCHE OSTGEBIETE UNTER POLNISCHER VERWALTUNG

Neiße (Oberschlesien), um 1200 gegründet und wenig später mit Magdeburger Stadtrecht ausgestattet

Im großen Remter der Marienburg (Westpreußen), dem 1274 gegründeten Schloß der Hochmeister des Deutschen Ordens

Glasschleifer bei der Arbeit

Hydraulische Presse in der Schmiede der Firma Friedrich Krupp, Essen

Spinnmaschine für Acetat-Seide — eine vollautomatische Anlage der Farbenfabriken Bayer, Leverkusen

Das Ratifizierungsverfahren kam auf Grund erheblicher Widerstände nur zögernd in Gang[1]. In den Parlamenten und in der öffentlichen Meinung vor allem Frankreichs und der Bundesrepublik erhoben sich starke Bedenken gegen den Vertrag.

Die ungelöste Saarfrage, das Verlangen nach Assoziierung des Vereinigten Königreichs und der nordischen Staaten, die Hoffnung, mit den Sowjets bei einer Viererkonferenz doch noch zur weltweiten Entspannung zu kommen, wodurch die EVG überhaupt hinfällig werden könnte, sowie militärische Probleme führten zu wechselnden außenpolitischen Aushilfen, ohne daß die Aussicht auf Verwirklichung des Projekts wuchs. An die Stelle des erhofften glatten Ablaufs der Ratifizierung trat die Politik der Junktims, Vorleistungen, Zusatzprotokolle und schließlich das Suchen nach Alternativlösungen. Die deutsche öffentliche Meinung blieb gespalten vor allem hinsichtlich der Auswirkung der Verträge auf die deutsche Wiedervereinigung.

Die Opposition lehnte das Vertragswerk ab, weil es ihren Vorstellungen über eine deutsche Sicherheitspolitik nicht entsprach[2]. Sie stimmte deshalb auch gegen die Erste Wehrergänzung des Grundgesetzes von 26. 2. 1954.

Immerhin stimmte der Bundestag im März 1953 als erstes Parlament den Verträgen zu. Frankreich, das sich in einer schwierigen innenpolitischen Lage befand und bei allen Entschlüssen die Besonderheit der Französischen Union mit ihren überseeischen Gebieten berücksichtigen mußte, verhielt sich abwartend.

[1] Die erste Lesung fand im Deutschen Bundestag am 9. und 10. 7. 1952 statt, die zweite im Dezember. In dritter Lesung wurden die Verträge am 19. 3. 1953 mit 224 gegen 166 Stimmen bei zwei Enthaltungen angenommen. Nachdem die Texte am 15. 5. 1953 den Bundesrat passiert hatten, und als auch das Bundesverfassungsgericht keine Einwände erhob, wurde das Ratifizierungsverfahren am 30. 3. 1954 abgeschlossen. Die Niederlande hinterlegten als erster Signatarstaat die Ratifizierungsurkunde am 25. 2 1954 in Paris. In Belgien stimmten Abgeordnetenkammer und Senat am 26. 11. 1953 beziehungsweise 12. 3. 1954 mit starker Mehrheit zu, ebenso die Luxemburgische Abgeordnetenkammer am 7. April; Italien und Frankreich hielten sich zurück.

[2] Bei der Debatte über die Wehrpolitik der Bundesregierung am 7. 2. 1952 sagte OLLENHAUER: ,,Das politische Problem, vor dem wir hier und heute stehen, ist die konkrete Frage, der niemand ausweichen kann, ob die von der Bundesregierung eingeschlagene Politik und die von ihr angewandten Mittel zu einer sinnvollen und vertretbaren Mitwirkung der Bundesrepublik an einer europäischen Verteidigung führen können. Wir Sozialdemokraten verneinen diese Frage.“ [Verhandlungen des deutschen Bundestages, Band 10, Seite 811 (A).] Am 25. 2. 1954 sagte OLLENHAUER im Bundestag zur Stellung der SPD hinsichtlich eines deutschen Beitrages in dem von ihr vorgeschlagenen Sicherheitssystem: ,,Die Sozialdemokratische Partei Deutschlands ist bereit, für die Erfüllung aller Verpflichtungen einzutreten, die sich aus der Mitgliedschaft eines vereinigten Deutschlands in einem solchen internationalen Sicherheitssystem ergeben“ (ebenda, Band 18, Seite 525).

Vielfach wurde die Auffassung vertreten, man dürfe die Geschlossenheit der französischen Armee nicht preisgeben. Die politischen Gegner der EVG wurden durch die sowjetische Entspannungspolitik in ihrem Widerstand gegen die EVG bestärkt und machten es den Befürwortern des Vertrages immer schwerer, diesen der parlamentarischen Behandlung zuzuleiten. In Reden und Aufsätzen appellierten die Gegner an das Gewissen der französischen Nation, indem sie vor der Gefahr eines wiedererstehenden deutschen Militarismus' warnten. Die französische Regierung legte dem Interimsausschuß am 11. 2. 1953 ergänzende Protokolle zum Vertrag vor. Aber deren Beratung und Annahme beschleunigten die Ratifizierung nicht. Auch die im April 1954 in feierlicher Form vollzogene Assoziierung des Vereinigten Königreichs förderte nicht den Ratifizierungswillen des französischen Parlaments; ebenso wenig die Ankündigung EDENS, das Vereinigte Königreich werde eine der britischen Divisionen in der Bundesrepublik der EVG unterstellen, noch das Versprechen EISENHOWERS, die amerikanischen Streitkräfte würden solange in Europa bleiben, als Gefahr drohe. Am 9. Juni verwarf der außenpolitische Ausschuß der Französischen Nationalversammlung den EVG-Vertrag. Erneut erwog die Regierung Änderungen und formulierte sie schließlich in einem Memorandum, das Ministerpräsident MENDES-FRANCE der nach Brüssel einberufenen Konferenz der EVG-Staaten am 19. 8. 1954 vorlegte. Die neuen Forderungen, die in der Erkenntnis gestellt wurden, daß der Vertrag keine Aussicht habe, in der ursprünglichen Form von der Nationalversammlung gebilligt zu werden, hatten die Aufhebung der politischen und militärischen Integration zum Ziel. MENDES-FRANCE beschwor seine Partner, der Abänderung zuzustimmen, andernfalls würde er gestürzt und von einer Volksfrontregierung abgelöst werden. Aber die in Brüssel versammelten Außenminister lehnten ab. Frankreich solle sich klar äußern zum Vertrag, wie er formuliert worden war. Am 22. August wurde die Konferenz trotz Vermittlungsversuchen von PAUL HENRI SPAAK abgebrochen.

Nun bestand nur noch die Hoffnung, daß die Zurückweisung der französischen Forderungen die Nationalversammlung zur Annahme des Vertrages bewegen würde. Aber am 30. 8. 1954 lehnten es die Abgeordneten der Nationalversammlung mit 319 gegen 264 Stimmen ab, den Vertrag weiter zu behandeln[1]. Die Nationalversammlung ging zur Tagesordnung über. Damit war die EVG-Konzeption gescheitert[2].

[1] In der Debatte hatte HERRIOT, der greise Präsident der Nationalversammlung und heftigste Gegner der EVG, ausgerufen: ,,*Pour moi, la Communauté européenne, laissez-moi vous le dire comme je le pense au seuil de ma vie, en résumant dans cette conviction tous les efforts qui j'ai pu faire: pour moi, pour nous, la Communauté européenne, c'est la fin de la France*" (Journal Officiel, a. a. O., Nr. 85 A. N., Seite 4467). Den Befürwortern der EVG hingegen, wie PAUL REYNAUD, blieb nur übrig zu resignieren. Er sagte nach der Abstimmung in den Lärm der Abgeordneten hinein, die sich gegenseitig ,,*à bas la Wehrmacht*" und ,,*à Moscou*" zuriefen, die Marseillaise und die Internationale anstimmten: ,,*Pour la première fois depuis qu'il y a un Parlement en France, un traité aura été repoussé sans que l'auteur de ce traité ni son signataire aient la parole pour le défendre*" (ebenda, Seite 4471).

[2] Der EVG-Interimsausschuß wurde im September bis auf einen kleinen Abwicklungsstab aufgelöst, der seine Tätigkeit im November 1954 einstellte.

Die Bundesrepublik wird Mitglied der NATO und WEU

Ungelöst wie im Jahre 1950 stellte sich von neuem das Problem des deutschen Verteidigungsbeitrages. Alsbald setzte in der Richtung der Petersberger Überlegungen vom Frühjahr 1951 eine starke Aktivität der interessierten Regierungen ein. Das Vereinigte Königreich übernahm die Vermittlerrolle. Schon am 11.9.1954 begab sich Außenminister EDEN auf eine Blitzreise in die Hauptstädte der ehemaligen EVG-Länder. Er regte die einfache Lösung an, die Idee der europäischen Integration zurückzustellen, den Deutschlandvertrag umgehend in Kraft zu setzen und die Bundesrepublik als souveränen Staat mit eigenen Streitkräften in die NATO aufzunehmen. Zusätzlich sollte der Brüsseler Vertrag auf die Bundesrepublik und Italien ausgedehnt werden. Dieser Plan war die Grundlage für die Neunmächtekonferenz, die am 28.9.1954 in London begann. EDEN ergriff als Vorsitzender die Initiative, indem er erklärte, das Vereinigte Königreich werde sich verpflichten, seine NATO-Divisionen und taktischen Fliegerverbände für die Dauer des Abkommens auf dem Kontinent zu belassen. Am 3. Oktober wurde die Londoner Akte unterzeichnet, in der die Regierungen der EVG-Staaten, der USA, des Vereinigten Königreichs und Kanadas überein kamen, im Sinne des britischen Planes zu verfahren. Es war der fünfundzwanzigste Todestag GUSTAV STRESEMANNS.

Drei Wochen später traten die Außenminister in Paris wieder zusammen, um die inzwischen auf der Grundlage der Londoner Akte ausgearbeiteten neuen Verträge zu paraphieren. Die Unterzeichnung fand am 23. Oktober statt, nachdem MENDES-FRANCE und ADENAUER sich über das Saarabkommen geeinigt hatten.

Das aus mehreren Teilen bestehende Pariser Vertragswerk löst das Problem des deutschen Verteidigungsbeitrages durch die Aufnahme der Bundesrepublik in die *Westeuropäische Union* (WEU), zu der der Brüsseler Vertrag erweitert wurde, und in die NATO. Im Vertrag über die WEU, der zwischen den Benelux-Staaten, der Bundesrepublik, Frankreich, dem Vereinigten Königreich und Italien abgeschlossen wurde, unterwirft die Bundesrepublik sich der freiwilligen Beschränkung ihrer Streitkräfte auf die Höchststärken, wie sie im Sonderabkommen zum EVG-Vertrag festgelegt worden waren[1]. Ferner nimmt die Bundesrepublik weitgehende Rüstungsbeschränkungen auf sich, verzichtet insbesondere auf die Herstellung von atomaren, biologischen und chemischen Waffen und erklärt sich bereit, „die Einhaltung

[1] Art. 1 des Protokolls Nr. II über die Streitkräfte der WEU.

dieser Verpflichtungen durch die zuständige Stelle der Organisation des Brüsseler Vertrages überwachen zu lassen"[1]. Diese Aufgabe fällt dem Amt für Rüstungskontrolle zu[2]. Allgemein vereinbaren die WEU-Mächte, „die Einheit Europas zu fördern und seiner fortschreitenden Integrierung Antrieb zu geben"[3].

Mit dem Beitritt zum Nordatlantikvertrag verpflichtete sich die Bundesrepublik, „sich jeglicher Handlung zu enthalten, die mit dem rein defensiven Charakter dieses Vertrages unvereinbar ist"[4]. Die Bundesregierung verpflichtete sich darüber hinaus, „die Wiedervereinigung Deutschlands oder die Änderung der gegenwärtigen Grenzen der Bundesrepublik Deutschland niemals mit gewaltsamen Mitteln herbeizuführen und alle zwischen der Bundesrepublik und anderen Staaten gegebenenfalls entstehenden Streitfragen mit friedlichen Mitteln zu lösen"[5]. Auf Grund ihrer Mitgliedschaft stellt die Bundesrepublik ihre Feldstreitkräfte der NATO in vollem Umfang zur Verfügung. Der Alliierte Oberbefehlshaber Europa hat gegenüber diesen Verbänden (*assigned forces*) die gleichen Befugnisse wie gegenüber den anderen Kontingenten. Die Integration erfolgt grundsätzlich auf der Ebene der Heeresgruppe und der taktischen Luftflotte, kann aber auch auf unteren Ebenen herbeigeführt werden. Im übrigen gewährt die Bundesregierung dem NATO-Rat genau so Einblick in ihre personellen und materiellen Planungen wie die anderen Partner und fügt sich in den Rahmen der *strategischen und logistischen Planungen* der alliierten Kommandobehörden der NATO[6]. Die Verträge sichern die deutsche Gleichberechtigung in der NATO und in der WEU.

In der parlamentarischen Behandlung ging diesmal Frankreich voran. Genau vier Monate nachdem die Nationalversammlung den EVG-Vertrag verworfen hatte, am 30. 12. 1954, stimmte sie den Pariser Verträgen zu und verwirklichte damit im Grunde, was Frankreich mit der EVG hatte verhindern wollen. Freilich war auch die Opposition gegen die deutsche

[1] Protokoll Nr. III über die Rüstungskontrolle. 1958 wurde durch den Rat der WEU der Herstellungsverzicht erstmalig gelockert (Genehmigung für die Fertigung von Panzerabwehrraketen und zum Bau eines Marineschulschiffes bis zu 5.000 t).

[2] Protokoll Nr. IV.

[3] Art. II des Protokolls zur Änderung und Ergänzung des Brüsseler Vertrages.

[4] Protokoll zum Nordatlantikvertrag über den Beitritt der Bundesrepublik Deutschland.

[5] Anlage A.

[6] Entschließung zur Durchführung von Abschnitt IV der Schlußakte der Londoner Konferenz, sowie Text des Nordatlantikvertrages.

Wiederbewaffnung in der neuen Form diesseits und jenseits des Rheines kaum geringer geworden.

Die Fraktion der SPD forderte bei der dritten Beratung der Pariser Verträge im Bundestag, daß diese erst in Kraft treten sollten, wenn erneute Verhandlungen zwischen den Vier Besatzungsmächten Deutschlands mit dem Ziel der Wiedervereinigung in Freiheit ergebnislos verlaufen sein würden. OLLENHAUER führte unter anderem aus: „Es ist kein Gegenstand der Diskussion, jedenfalls nicht auf unserer Seite, daß wir das Recht und die Notwendigkeit der Verteidigung der Freiheit und der Demokratie auch mit militärischen Mitteln anerkennen." Der Oppositionsführer begründete dann die Ablehnung durch seine Fraktion: „Wer in diesem Stadium und in dieser Lage die Ratifizierung der Verträge vor neue Verhandlungen über die Wiedervereinigung setzt, wenn auch nur vor einen Versuch, zu solchen neuen Verhandlungen zu kommen, der dokumentiert damit, daß er unter allen Umständen der definitiven Eingliederung der Bundesrepublik in das Nordatlantikpakt-System den Vorzug vor der Wiedervereinigung gibt"[1].

Der Bundestag nahm die Verträge jedoch mit Mehrheit an. Bis zum Mai 1955 hatten alle Vertragspartner die Ratifikationsurkunden hinterlegt. Am 5. 5. 1955 trat das Vertragswerk in Kraft. Am 8. Mai wurde die Bundesrepublik in die NATO aufgenommen. Die WEU konstituierte sich in Paris. Seit dem 9. 5. 1955, dem zehnten Jahrestag der bedingungslosen militärischen Kapitulation Deutschlands, wehen am Sitz der NATO in Paris und vor dem europäischen Hauptquartier der NATO bei Marly-le-Roi die Fahnen der Bundesrepublik.

Vorarbeit für das deutsche Kontingent

Bis zum Inkrafttreten der Verträge hatte die Bundesregierung keine Maßnahmen hinsichtlich der Aufstellung des deutschen Kontingents ergriffen. Nur die Planung war in der Dienststelle BLANK bearbeitet worden. Sie mußte nach dem 30. 8. 1954 neu gestaltet werden, weil zahlreiche Aufgaben, die nach der EVG-Konzeption in integrierte Zuständigkeit hätten fallen sollen, nun national zu bearbeiten waren. Es galt aus dem Nichts Feldstreitkräfte des Heeres, der Luftwaffe und der Marine zu schaffen in einer Gesamtstärke von etwa einer halben Million Soldaten, zuzüglich bodenständiger Verteidigungstruppen und Einheiten der militärischen Territorialorganisation. Der Beginn der Aufstellung war abhängig vom Zeitpunkt und Inhalt der einzubringenden Wehrgesetze. Die Aufstellungsplanung mußte andererseits mit den am Aufstellungstag gültigen NATO-Planungen

[1] Verhandlungen des Deutschen Bundestages, a. a. O., Band 23, Seite 3894ff.

übereinstimmen. Damit hingen wiederum die Fragen der Unterbringung und der Dislozierung zusammen; ebenso die Anlieferung der ersten Waffen aus dem Ausland, die dem technischen Entwicklungsstand der Aufstellungszeit entsprechen mußten. Erst wenn diese voneinander abhängigen Voraussetzungen geschaffen waren, konnten die ersten Soldaten eingestellt werden.

Die Wehrgesetzgebung

Nach Auffassung der Bundesregierung hätte ein umfassendes Soldatengesetz nicht rasch genug verabschiedet werden können. Daher brachte sie als Vorausmaßnahme ein *Freiwilligen-Gesetz* ein, dessen parlamentarische Beratung weniger Zeit beanspruchte[1]. Das Gesetz, dessen Gültigkeit bis zum 31. 3. 1956 befristet war, wurde am 16. 7. 1955 vom Bundestag gegen die Stimmen der sozialdemokratischen Fraktion verabschiedet und am 23. Juli verkündet. Es bestimmte, daß zur Vorbereitung des Aufbaus der Streitkräfte bis zu 6.000 Freiwillige als Soldaten für Lehrgänge, NATO-Stäbe, zur Vorbereitung der Materialübernahme und der bodenständigen militärischen Einrichtungen, sowie für militärfachliche ministerielle Aufgaben eingestellt werden konnten.

Zur gleichen Zeit erließ der Bundespräsident die erste Anordnung über Uniformen und Dienstgradabzeichen der Streitkräfte, sowie über die Ernennung und Entlassung der freiwilligen Soldaten. Am 23. Juli trat ferner das *Gesetz über die Einrichtung des Personalgutachterausschusses* in Kraft. Ihm fiel die Aufgabe zu, die für die Einstellung vorgeschlagenen Offiziere vom Oberst an aufwärts auf ihre persönliche Eignung zu überprüfen und Richtlinien vorzuschlagen, nach denen die persönliche Eignung der übrigen Soldaten zu prüfen sein würde. Der Personalgutachterausschuß nahm im August seine Tätigkeit auf[2]. Im Oktober wurde die vorläufige Besoldungsordnung

[1] Für die parlamentarische Behandlung von Wehrfragen sind zuständig: *Im Bundestag*: Der „Bundestagsausschuß für Fragen der Europäischen Sicherheit", der seine Arbeit am 3. 9. 1952 aufgenommen hat. Der Ausschuß wurde am 16. 12. 1955 Verfassungsorgan mit Untersuchungsvollmacht für die parlamentarische Kontrolle der Streitkräfte und am 10. 1. 1956 umbenannt in „Bundestagsausschuß für Verteidigung". Ihm gehören 29 Abgeordnete als ordentliche Mitglieder an. Vorsitzender ist der Abgeordnete Dr. RICHARD JAEGER (CDU/CSU), stellvertretender Vorsitzender der Abgeordnete HANS MERTEN (SPD) [vor ihm FRITZ ERLER (SPD)]. *Im Bundesrat*: Der „Bundesratsausschuß für Verteidigung", in dem jedes Bundesland eine Stimme hat.

[2] Der Gedanke, in das Einstellungsverfahren für höhere Offiziere ein Gremium vertrauenswürdiger Personen einzuschalten, war schon bei den ersten Sitzungen des Bundestagsausschusses für Fragen der europäischen Sicherheit gutgeheißen worden. Der PGA setzte sich aus 37 Persönlichkeiten zusammen, die auf Vorschlag der Bundesregierung vom Bundespräsidenten berufen wurden. Der Ausschuß hat seine Arbeiten im Herbst 1957 nahezu abschließen können.

GLIEDERUNG
des
BUNDESMINISTERIUMS FÜR VERTEIDIGUNG
Ende 1955
(Bei Beginn der Aufstellung der Bundeswehr)

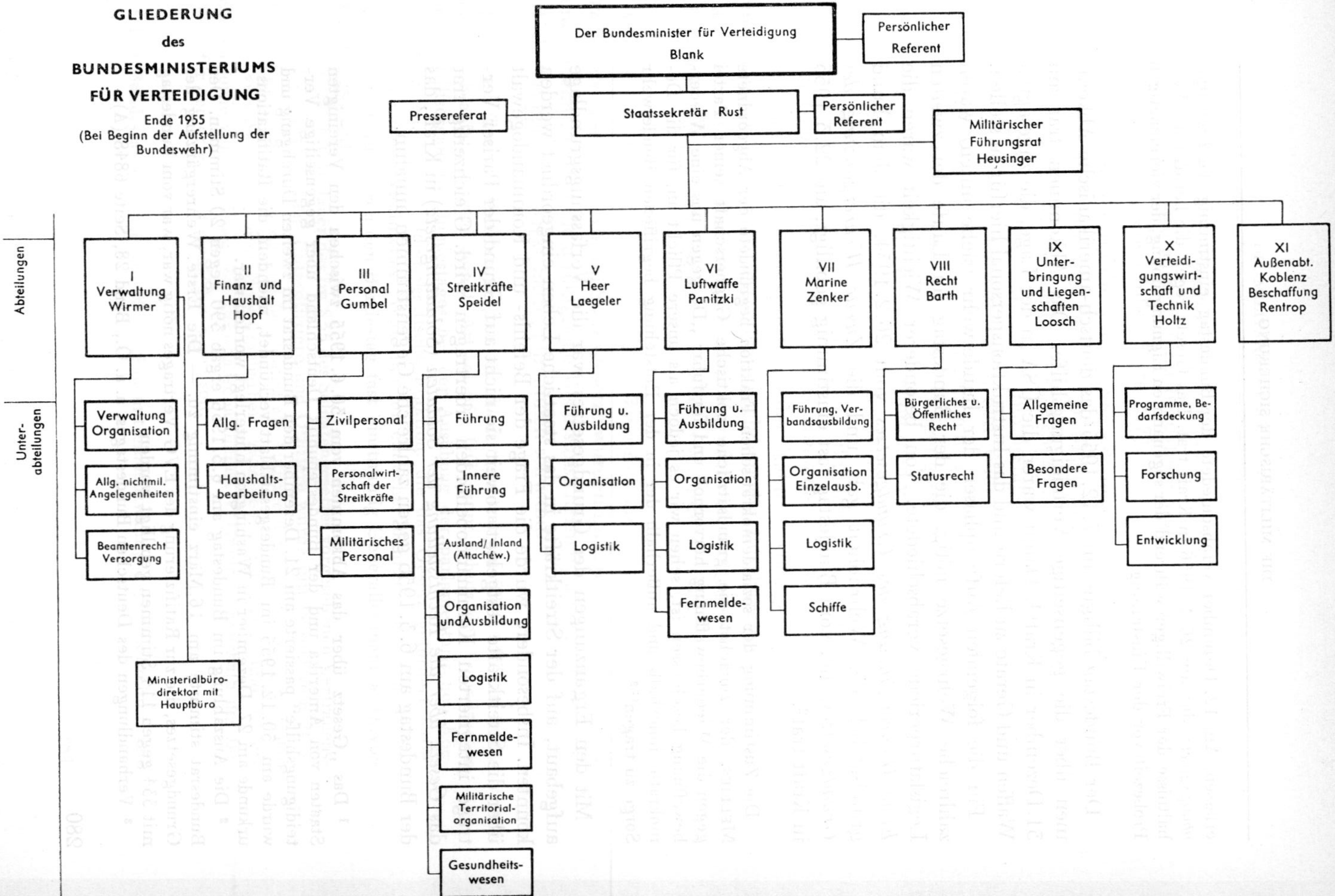

Der Bundesminister für Verteidigung
Blank
Persönlicher Referent
Pressereferat
Staatssekretär Rust
Persönlicher Referent
Militärischer Führungsrat Heusinger
Abteilungen
Unter-abteilungen
I Verwaltung Wirmer
II Finanz und Haushalt Hopf
III Personal Gumbel
IV Streitkräfte Speidel
V Heer Laegeler
VI Luftwaffe Panitzki
VII Marine Zenker
VIII Recht Barth
IX Unter-bringung und Liegen-schaften Loosch
X Verteidi-gungswirt-schaft und Technik Holtz
XI Außenabt. Koblenz Beschaffung Rentrop
Verwaltung Organisation
Allg. nichtmil. Angelegenheiten
Beamtenrecht Versorgung
Ministerialbüro-direktor mit Hauptbüro
Allg. Fragen
Haushalts-bearbeitung
Zivilpersonal
Personalwirt-schaft der Streitkräfte
Militärisches Personal
Führung
Innere Führung
Ausland/ Inland (Attachéw.)
Organisation undAusbildung
Logistik
Fernmelde-wesen
Militärische Territorial-organisation
Gesundheits-wesen
Führung u. Ausbildung
Organisation
Logistik
Führung u. Ausbildung
Organisation
Logistik
Fernmelde-wesen
Führung, Ver-bandsausbildung
Organisation Einzelausb.
Logistik
Schiffe
Bürgerliches u. Öffentliches Recht
Statusrecht
Allgemeine Fragen
Besondere Fragen
Programme, Be-darfsdeckung
Forschung
Entwicklung

ERGEBNISSE DER SCHLUSSABSTIMMUNGEN ÜBER DIE WICHTIGSTEN WEHRVORLAGEN IM DEUTSCHEN BUNDESTAG

Gesetzesvorlage	Datum der Schlußabstimmung	Abgegebene Stimmen	Ja	Nein	Enthaltungen	Stellungnahme der Fraktion der SPD
EVG-Vertrag	19. 3. 1953	392	224	166	2	Ablehnung mit 128 Stimmen
1. Wehrergänzung des Grundgesetzes	26. 2. 1954	478	334	144	—	Ablehnung mit 144 Stimmen
Beitritt zum Brüsseler Pakt und zur NATO	27. 2. 1955	473	314	157	2	Ablehnung mit 150 Stimmen
Personalgutachterausschußgesetz	15. 7. 1955	Gegen einige Gegenstimmen und bei Enthaltungen angenommen				Zustimmung
Freiwilligengesetz	16. 7. 1955	Gegen zahlreiche Gegenstimmen angenommen				Ablehnung
Eignungsübungsgesetz	15. 12. 1955	Einstimmig angenommen				Zustimmung
Soldatengesetz	6. 3. 1956	Gegen zahlreiche Gegenstimmen angenommen				Ablehnung
2. Wehrergänzung des Grundgesetzes	6. 3. 1956	390 Ja- und 20 Nein-Stimmen				Zustimmung
Wehrpflichtgesetz	7. 7. 1956	455	269	166	20	Ablehnung mit 141 Stimmen
Gesetz über die Dauer des Wehrdienstes	5. 12. 1956	Mit Mehrheit angenommen				Ablehnung
Wehrbeschwerdeordnung	14. 12. 1956	Einstimmig angenommen				Zustimmung
Wehrdisziplinarordnung	21. 2. 1957	Angenommen				Zustimmung
Wehrstrafgesetz	20. 3. 1957	Gegen zahlreiche Gegenstimmen angenommen				Ablehnung
Gesetz über den Wehrbeauftragten des Bundestages	11. 4. 1957	Angenommen				Ablehnung
Soldatenversorgungsgesetz	12. 4. 1957	Einstimmig angenommen				Zustimmung
Ordensgesetz	28. 6. 1957	Bei einigen Enthaltungen mit Mehrheit angenommen				Ablehnung

Quelle: Bundesministerium für Verteidigung.

Die bereits 1955 ausgearbeitete und im Frühjahr 1956 eingebrachte Vorlage eines *Organisationsgesetzes* wurde bisher nicht beraten. Erst mit diesem Gesetz wird der Bundestag die Spitzengliederung der Bundeswehr und die Organisation des Bundesministeriums für Verteidigung endgültig festlegen. Dieses Recht hat die Legislative in den §§ 7 des Freiwilligengesetzes und 66 des Soldatengesetzes sich vorbehalten. Jede vorherige Organisationsform der Bundeswehr hat nur provisorischen Charakter.

Die Aufgabe der Bundeswehr

Der politische Entschluß, sich freiwillig in die gemeinsame Abwehr der freien Völker des Westens einzuordnen, entsprang der Erkenntnis, daß die Bundesrepublik in ihrer geographischen Lage weder personell noch materiell in der Lage ist, sich allein gegen einen Angriff aus dem Osten zu verteidigen. Die Bejahung der demokratischen Verfassung und der Wille zum Frieden weckten den *Willen zur Selbstverteidigung*. In dem Maße, wie die Bundeswehr die gefährliche Lücke in der westlichen Verteidigungsfront allmählich ausfüllt, wird der Schutz der Bundesrepublik dadurch erhöht, daß die auf ihrem Boden stationierten Streitkräfte der NATO-Staaten und deren Verbände in den Nachbarländern ihrerseits dem aktiven Schutz der Bundesrepublik dienen. Das politisch-strategische Ziel der NATO ist es, das Risiko eines Angriffs auf die Gemeinschaft so groß zu machen, daß er sinnlos wird. Um dieses Ziel zu erreichen, bedarf es einer Verteidigungskonzeption, bei der davon ausgegangen werden muß, daß der Angreifer den Vorteil des ersten Schlages besitzen wird, weil die NATO selbst niemals einen Angriffskrieg führen kann. Es kommt also darauf an, daß sie den ersten Schlag übersteht, um danach zurückschlagen zu können. Die strategische Konzeption beruht auf Grund dieser Überlegung auf dem Gedanken von „*Schild und Schwert*". Der Schild hat den ersten Schlag abzuwehren. Er muß daher eine hohe Abwehrkraft besitzen. Das Schwert dagegen muß vor allem mit nuklearen Waffen ausgerüstet sein, die mit Fernbombern oder Raketen unverzüglich auf die Angriffsbasen im Hinterland des Aggressors wirken können, von denen aus die Schwerpunkte seiner Offensive gespeist werden. In dieser Konzeption liegt die Abwehraufgabe des deutschen Kontingents naturgemäß in der Stärkung des Schildes, und zwar durch starke Heeresverbände und taktische Luftstreitkräfte zu deren Unterstützung, sowie durch Marine- und Marinefliegerverbände zur Abriegelung der Ostsee und damit zum vorgeschobenen Schutz der lebenswichtigen Nachschublinien von Amerika nach

Europa. Aus dieser Aufgabe ergibt sich von selbst, daß das Heer wesentlich stärker sein muß als die anderen Teilstreitkräfte; denn diese haben in den Kontingenten der Verbündeten ihren Rückhalt. So wird zum Beispiel der Verzicht auf strategische Fliegerverbände, der für eine reine Nationalarmee untragbar wäre, dadurch gerechtfertigt, daß die Schwertaufgabe in erster Linie bei den Luftflotten der Angelsachsen, insbesondere bei dem amerikanischen strategischen Bomberkommando, liegt.

Auf diese Aufgabe der Bundeswehr wurden die Zeit- und Aufbaupläne abgestellt. Ihr tieferer Sinn, durch Abschreckung den Frieden zu erhalten, kann jedoch nur dann die geschichtliche Entwicklung wirksam beeinflussen, wenn die erforderliche hohe Abwehrkraft tatsächlich erreicht wird.

Der Aufbau der Bundeswehr

Die Streitkräfte der Bundesrepublik tragen seit der Verkündung des Soldatengesetzes den Namen *Bundeswehr*. Ihre Aufstellung lag in den Händen des Sicherheitsbeauftragten BLANK, der im Juni 1955 zum Bundesminister für Verteidigung ernannt wurde.

Seine bisherige Dienststelle wurde so zum Ministerium erweitert und gegliedert, daß sie den neuen Führungsaufgaben gewachsen sein konnte[1]. Anfang Oktober 1955 gab BLANK die Aufstellungsweisung Nr. 1 heraus, die den 1. 1. 1956 als Zeitpunkt für die Bildung der ersten Einheiten (*physical start*) des Heeres, der Luftwaffe und der Marine bestimmte. In Anderna ch (Heer), Nörvenich (Luftwaffe) und Wilhelmshaven

[1] Im Juni 1955 wurde die militärische Abteilung unter Generalleutnant HEUSINGER in sieben Unterabteilungen gegliedert (für Personalwesen, Allgemeine Verteidigungsfragen, Versorgungsangelegenheiten [Logistik], Gesamtstreitkräfte, Heer, Luftwaffe und Marine).

Im November 1955 wurde das Bundesministerium für Verteidigung in elf Abteilungen umgegliedert:

I (Verwaltung)	VII (Marine)
II (Finanzen und Haushalt)	VIII (Rechtswesen)
III (Personalbearbeitung der Zivilverwaltung und der Streitkräfte)	IX (Unterbringung und Liegenschaften)
IV (Streitkräfte)	X (Verteidigungswirtschaft und Technik)
V (Heer)	
VI (Luftwaffe)	XI (Außenstelle Koblenz)

Später wurde ein militärischer Führungsrat unter dem Vorsitz von Generalleutnant HEUSINGER gebildet, während Generalleutnant Dr. SPEIDEL die Abt. IV übernahm.

Im Frühjahr 1956 wurde aus Teilen der Abteilungen X und XI eine zwölfte Abteilung für technische Entwicklungsfragen eingerichtet.

(Marine) waren demnach insgesamt sieben Lehrkompanien aus den nach dem Freiwilligengesetz verfügbaren 6.000 Freiwilligen aufzustellen.

Am 10. Oktober wurden Prüfgruppen für die Prüfung der Bewerber nach den Richtlinien des Personalgutachterausschusses sowie in fachlicher Hinsicht gebildet. Wenige Wochen später, am 12.11.1955, dem 200. Geburtstag SCHARNHORST, händigte der Bundesminister für Verteidigung den ersten freiwilligen Soldaten die Ernennungsurkunden aus. Am 1. Dezember traten die Vorkommandos der Lehrkompanien in den drei für sie bestimmten Standorten zusammen. Die Kompanien wurden am 1. 1. 1956 aufgestellt.

Gleichzeitig begann die Entsendung deutscher militärischer Vertreter in die Organe der NATO und der WEU. Die Stellen der nationalen militärischen Vertreter beim Oberkommando der alliierten Streitkräfte in Europa (SHAPE) und beim Ausschuß der militärischen Vertreter in Washington wurden besetzt. Andere Offiziere übernahmen Funktionen in den integrierten Generalstäben von SHAPE und AFCENT (Oberkommando der allierten Streitkräfte in Mitteleuropa, Fontainebleau)[1]. Zum Studium und Sammeln neuer Erfahrungen gingen weitere Offiziere zur NATO-Verteidigungsakademie nach Paris und zu Lehrgängen aller Waffengattungen nach den Vereinigten Staaten. Die Entsendung von Militärattachés wurde vorbereitet[2].

Am 20. 1. 1956 begrüßte der Bundeskanzler rund 1.500 freiwillige Soldaten auf dem Andernacher Kasernenhof. Dieser Tag wurde später zum „*Geburtstag der Bundeswehr*" bestimmt.

Die Übernahme von 9.572 Freiwilligen aus dem Bundesgrenzschutz im Juli 1956 und des Bundesgrenzschutzes See bedeutete eine wesentliche Verstärkung der Bundeswehr; aber die Einstellung weiterer Freiwilliger verzögerte sich von da an erheblich. Es mangelte vor allem an der nötigen Anzahl von Unterkünften. Die politische Forderung, das vorgesehene Aufstellungstempo einzuhalten, konnte trotz dem Drängen der Alliierten nicht erfüllt werden.

Gleichzeitig verstärkte sich die Abneigung der Bundestagsfraktionen und der Länderregierungen, die Dienstzeit der Wehrpflichtigen auf mindestens 18 Monate festzusetzen. Die Opposition verlangte, die Bundeswehr solle sich auch künftig aus Berufssoldaten und längerdienenden Freiwilligen ergänzen.

Zum neuen Verteidigungsminister wurde der bisherige Bundesminister für Atomfragen, FRANZ JOSEF STRAUSS, am 18. 10. 1956 ernannt. Am 7. 11. 1956

[1] Anfang 1959 waren in integrierten Stäben 142 deutsche Offiziere und 165 Unteroffiziere und Mannschaften tätig. Am 1. 1. 1959 trat Generalleutnant FOERTSCH die wichtige Stelle des Stellvertretenden Stabschefs und Leiters der Abteilung „*Plans and Policy*" bei SHAPE an.

[2] Anfang 1959 waren 26 Militärattachés (Heer, Marine und Luftwaffe) in 14 Ländern tätig.

gab STRAUSS vor der Presse einen neuen Zeitplan bekannt. Die Verpflichtung, letztlich eine halbe Million Soldaten aufzustellen, sei kein Dogma, sondern ein Anhaltspunkt für einen fairen und angemessenen Beitrag der Bundesrepublik zur gemeinsamen Verteidigung.

Am 1.4.1957 wurde die Bundeswehr durch rund 10.000 Wehrpflichtige verstärkt und erreichte im Juli eine Personalstärke von 100.000 Mann. Die ersten einsatzfähigen Verbände wurden der NATO am 1. April zur Verfügung gestellt (sogenannte „*assigned forces*"), indem Vizeadmiral RUGE dem Befehlshaber der Seestreitkräfte Europa Mitte, dem holländischen Admiral BOS, zwei Minensuchgeschwader übergab. Anfang Juli folgten drei Grenadierdivisionen und ein weiteres Minensuchgeschwader. Sie wurden am 5. Juli in Marburg vom Generalinspekteur der Bundeswehr, General HEUSINGER, dem Oberbefehlshaber Europa, General NORSTAD, übergeben. Die Heeresverbände unterstehen dem Befehlshaber der Landstreitkräfte Europa Mitte, General Dr. SPEIDEL, der seinen Dienst im Hauptquartier des Oberbefehlshabers Europa Mitte, General VALLUY, bereits am 3.4.1957 in Fontainebleau angetreten hatte.

Da mit der Verabschiedung des Organisationsgesetzes durch den Zweiten Bundestag nicht mehr zu rechnen war, erfolgte eine provisorische Neugliederung des Bundesministeriums für Verteidigung. Seit Juli 1957 ist der Generalinspekteur der Bundeswehr der oberste Soldat in der Bundesrepublik. Er steht unter dem Staatssekräter an der Spitze des generalstabsmäßig gegliederten Führungsstabes der Bundeswehr und hat Weisungsrecht gegenüber den Inspekteuren des Heeres, der Luftwaffe, der Marine und des Sanitäts- und Gesundheitswesens [1]. Die Führungsstäbe und die Inspektion des Sanitäts- und Gesundheitswesens sind neben den zivilen Abteilungen und der Personalabteilung in das Bundesministerium für Verteidigung eingegliedert. Mehrere Ämter wurden dem Ministerium nachgeordnet. Diese klare „Joint-Lösung", schränkt in Deutschland erstmalig die früher übliche Selbständigkeit der Teilstreitkräfte dadurch ein, daß die Führungsverantwortung in einer Hand

[1] Generalinspekteur der Bundeswehr wurde General HEUSINGER. Er hatte die Abteilung IV, aus der der Führungsstab der Bundeswehr gebildet wurde, am 1.3.1957 von General Dr. SPEIDEL übernommen. Chef des Stabes beim Generalinspekteur ist Brigadegeneral PANITZKI (Luftwaffe). Generalleutnant RÖTTIGER, seit dem 24.9.1956 Leiter der Abteilung V, wurde zum Inspekteur des Heeres ernannt; Generalleutnant KAMMHUBER, seit 6.6.1956 Leiter der Abteilung VI, zum Inspekteur der Luftwaffe; Vizeadmiral RUGE, seit 6.3.1956 Leiter der Abteilung VII, zum Inspekteur der Marine. Generalarzt Dr. JOEDICKE wurde im August 1957 zum Inspekteur des Sanitäts- und Gesundheitswesens ernannt.

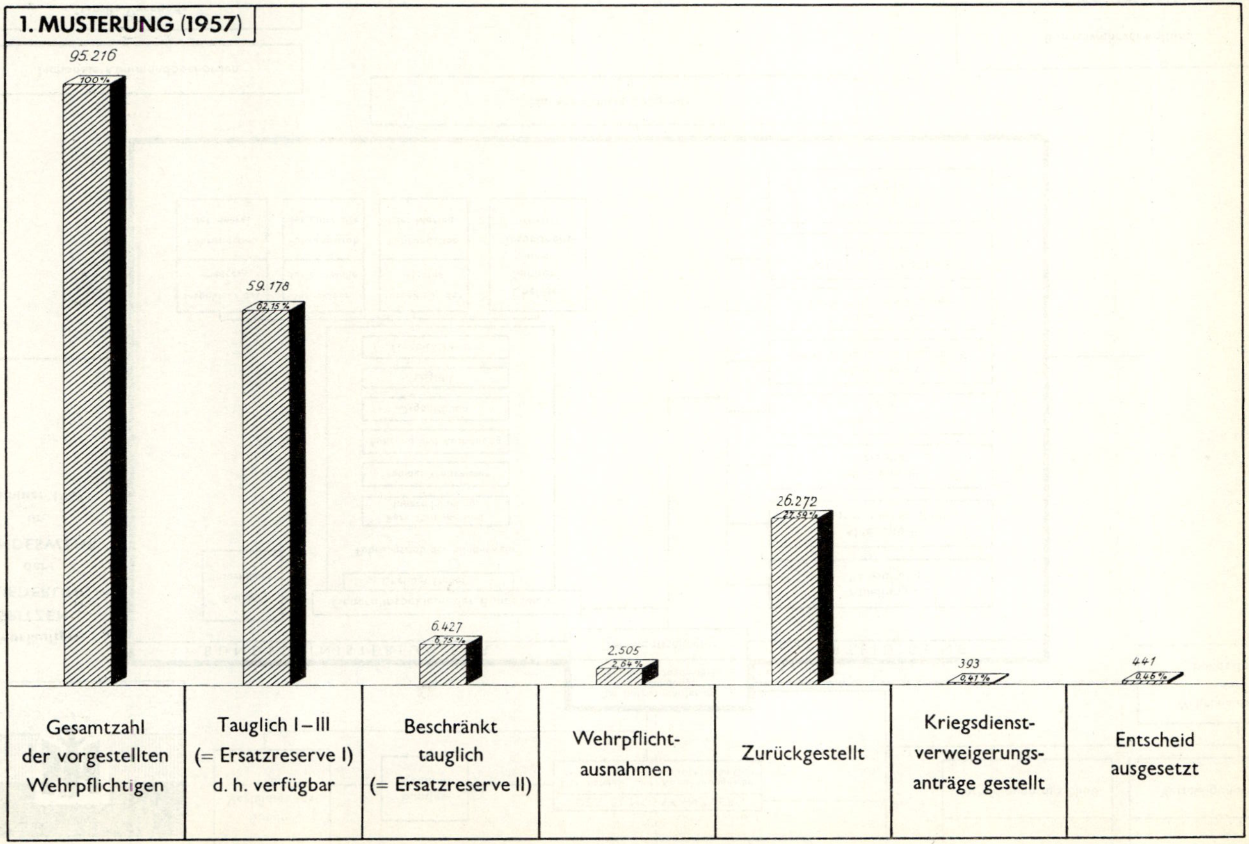
1. MUSTERUNG (1957)
95.216
100 %
59.178
62,15 %
6.427
6,75 %
2.505
2,64 %
26.272
27,59 %
393
0,41 %
441
0,46 %
Gesamtzahl der vorgestellten Wehrpflichtigen
Tauglich I–III (= Ersatzreserve I) d. h. verfügbar
Beschränkt tauglich (= Ersatzreserve II)
Wehrpflicht-ausnahmen
Zurückgestellt
Kriegsdienst-verweigerungs-anträge gestellt
Entscheid ausgesetzt

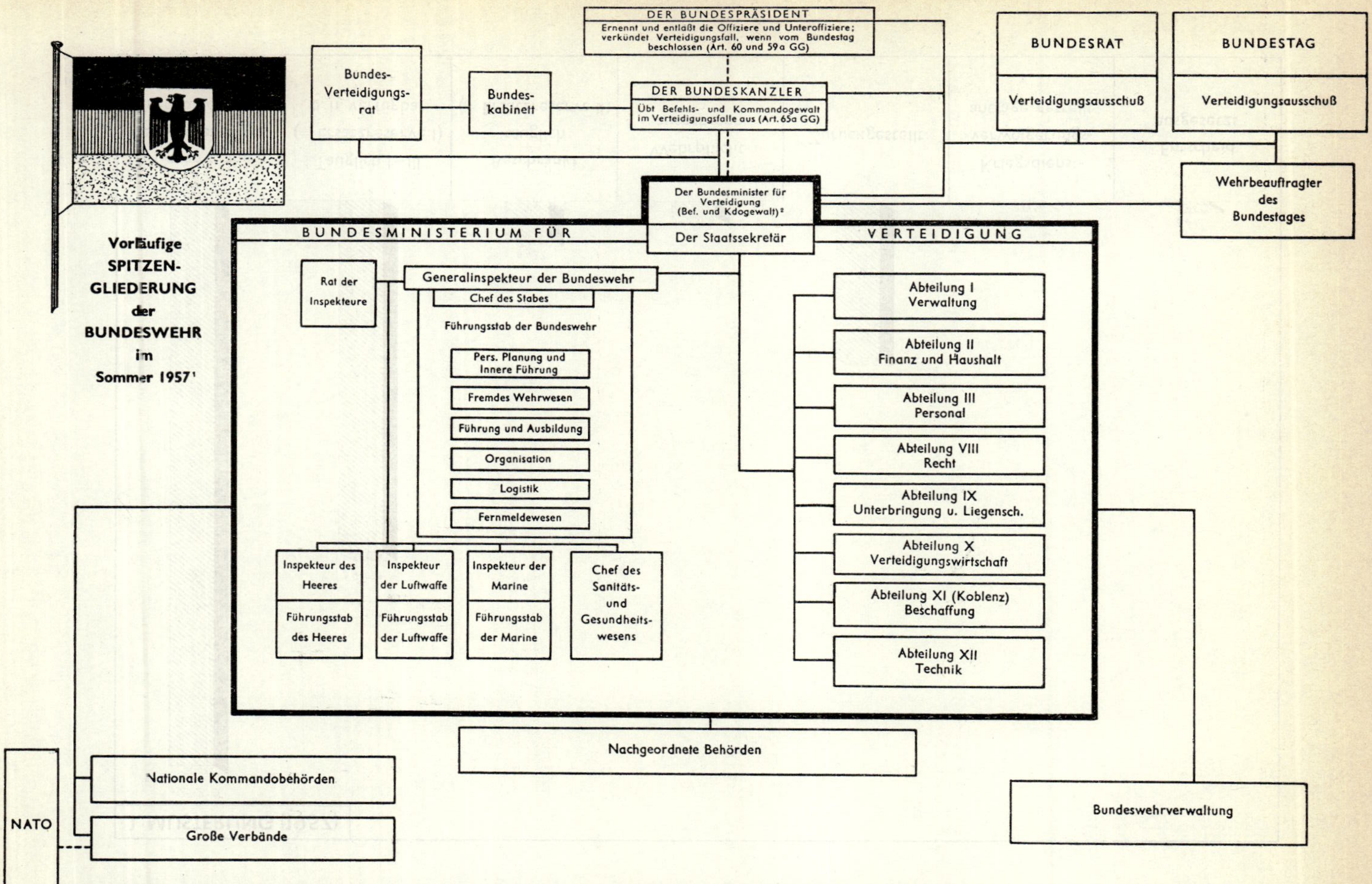

[1] Die endgültige Organisation wird vom Bundestag bestimmt.

[2] Der Bundesminister für Verteidigung übt die Befehls- und Kommandogewalt im Frieden aus (Art. 65a GG).

Ein Zahnrad für Schneckengetriebe wird bearbeitet (DEMAG, Duisburg)

Die Continental-Gummiwerke in Hannover

Die Westfalenhütte in Dortmund

Anolon-Betrieb im Werk Uerdingen —

Polymerisationskessel im Werk Leverkusen —

der Farbenfabriken BAYER

Ausländische Praktikanten bei der Ausbildung in deutschen Industriebetrieben

Die Raststätte
Düsseldorf-Nord
an der Autobahn
Köln—Hannover

Das Autobahn-Rasthaus
Hannover—Garbsen

Die 12 km lange
MALAKOFF-Brücke
der Autobahn
Stuttgart—Ulm

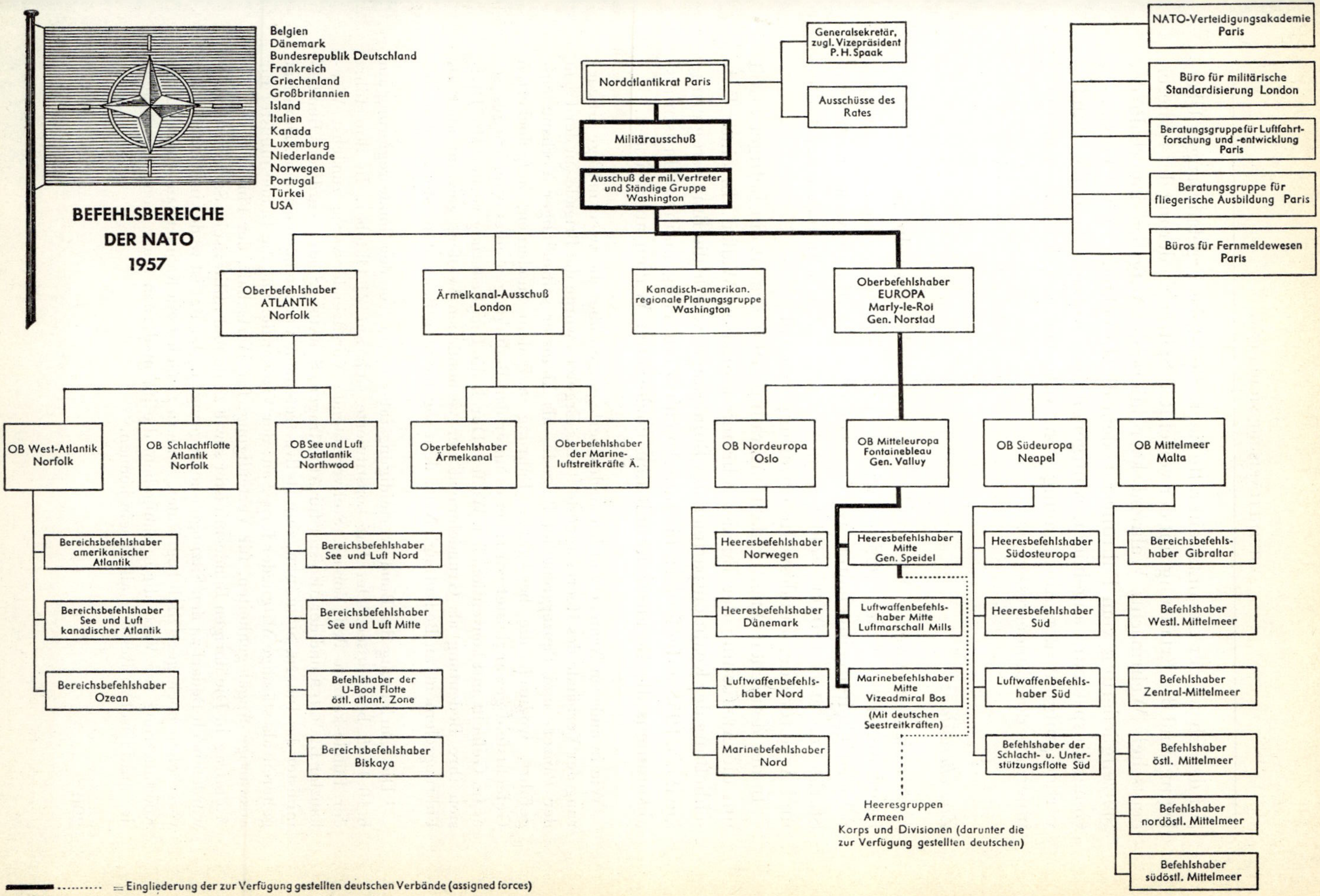
BEFEHLSBEREICHE
DER NATO
1957
Belgien
Dänemark
Bundesrepublik Deutschland
Frankreich
Griechenland
Großbritannien
Island
Italien
Kanada
Luxemburg
Niederlande
Norwegen
Portugal
Türkei
USA
Nordatlantikrat Paris
Generalsekretär, zugl. Vizepräsident P. H. Spaak
Ausschüsse des Rates
Militärausschuß
Ausschuß der mil. Vertreter und Ständige Gruppe Washington
NATO-Verteidigungsakademie Paris
Büro für militärische Standardisierung London
Beratungsgruppe für Luftfahrtforschung und -entwicklung Paris
Beratungsgruppe für fliegerische Ausbildung Paris
Büros für Fernmeldewesen Paris
Oberbefehlshaber ATLANTIK Norfolk
Ärmelkanal-Ausschuß London
Kanadisch-amerikan. regionale Planungsgruppe Washington
Oberbefehlshaber EUROPA Marly-le-Roi Gen. Norstad
OB West-Atlantik Norfolk
OB Schlachtflotte Atlantik Norfolk
OB See und Luft Ostatlantik Northwood
Oberbefehlshaber Ärmelkanal
Oberbefehlshaber der Marine-luftstreitkräfte Ä.
OB Nordeuropa Oslo
OB Mitteleuropa Fontainebleau Gen. Valluy
OB Südeuropa Neapel
OB Mittelmeer Malta
Bereichsbefehlshaber amerikanischer Atlantik
Bereichsbefehlshaber See und Luft kanadischer Atlantik
Bereichsbefehlshaber Ozean
Bereichsbefehlshaber See und Luft Nord
Bereichsbefehlshaber See und Luft Mitte
Befehlshaber der U-Boot Flotte östl. atlant. Zone
Bereichsbefehlshaber Biskaya
Heeresbefehlshaber Norwegen
Heeresbefehlshaber Dänemark
Luftwaffenbefehlshaber Nord
Marinebefehlshaber Nord
Heeresbefehlshaber Mitte Gen. Speidel
Luftwaffenbefehlshaber Mitte Luftmarschall Mills
Marinebefehlshaber Mitte Vizeadmiral Bos
(Mit deutschen Seestreitkräften)
Heeresbefehlshaber Südosteuropa
Heeresbefehlshaber Süd
Luftwaffenbefehlshaber Süd
Befehlshaber der Schlacht- u. Unterstützungsflotte Süd
Bereichsbefehlshaber Gibraltar
Befehlshaber Westl. Mittelmeer
Befehlshaber Zentral-Mittelmeer
Befehlshaber östl. Mittelmeer
Befehlshaber nordöstl. Mittelmeer
Befehlshaber südöstl. Mittelmeer
Heeresgruppen
Armeen
Korps und Divisionen (darunter die zur Verfügung gestellten deutschen)
= Eingliederung der zur Verfügung gestellten deutschen Verbände (assigned forces)

auf der Ebene der Gesamtstreitkräfte liegt. Sie ist das Ergebnis langer Überlegung und der Erfahrung mit der verfehlten Spitzengliederung der früheren deutschen Wehrmacht. Während koordinierende Aufgaben innerhalb der Spitzengliederung vom Führungsrat, dem die Inspekteure unter Vorsitz des Generalinspekteurs angehören, wahrgenommen werden, dient der Bundesverteidigungsrat der Abstimmung von Aufgaben der Landesverteidigung innerhalb der Bundesressorts[1].

Zwischenbilanz

Um die Jahreswende 1958/59 begann für die Bundeswehr die zweite Aufbauphase. Der Ende 1956 entwickelte Zeitplan hatte trotz vielfältigen Schwierigkeiten eingehalten werden können. Die Bundeswehr hatte eine Stärke von etwa 180.000 Soldaten und rund 50.000 Beamten, Angestellten und Arbeitern der Bundeswehrverwaltung erreicht.

In der deutschen Öffentlichkeit entbrannte 1958 erneut ein heftiger Streit um die Ausrüstung der Bundeswehr mit atomaren Waffen. In einer Entschließung der Koalitionsparteien des Bundestages wurde die Bundesregierung am 25.3.1958 aufgefordert, bis zum Abschluß eines allgemeinen Abrüstungsabkommens die Bundeswehr mit den modernsten Waffen auszurüsten.

Wie in anderen Armeen wurden auch Überlegungen über die zweckmäßige Gliederung der Verbände des Heeres angestellt. Als Ergebnis wurde die Brigade (in der Form der Panzer- und Panzergrenadier-Brigade) als kleinster selbständiger Verband eingeführt, wodurch die bewegliche Führung auf dem modernen, aufgelockerten Gefechtsfeld gewährleistet wird; sei es unter den Bedingungen eines Atomkrieges, sei es im Gefecht mit konventionellen Waffen. Durch die Umgliederung verliert die Division ihre Bedeutung als Grundelement der verbundenen Waffen, gewinnt aber als Führungselement an Bedeutung. Nach dem sogenannten Baukastensystem können bis

[1] Die Einrichtung des Bundesverteidigungsrates wurde von der Bundesregierung am 6.10.1955 beschlossen. Der Rat konstituierte sich am 21. Oktober. In ihm führt der Bundeskanzler den Vorsitz. Stellvertretende Vorsitzende waren zunächst Vizekanzler Blücher und der Minister für Atomfragen, Strauss. Später wurde der Bundesminister des Innern, Schröder, zum stellvertretenden Vorsitzenden ernannt. Dem Rat gehören als ständige Mitglieder ferner an: der Vizekanzler und die Bundesminister für auswärtige Angelegenheiten, für Verteidigung, für Wirtschaft, der Finanzen und für Atomfragen. Die übrigen Bundesminister sowie zivile und militärische Sachverständige werden nach Bedarf zu den Sitzungen herangezogen. Der Rat ist weder im Grundgesetz vorgesehen noch gesetzlich begründet, sondern zunächst ein Kabinettsausschuß für die Koordinierung von Verteidigungsaufgaben, die im modernen Staat nicht mehr Sache des militärischen Ressorts allein sein können.

zu fünf Brigaden in einer Division zusammengefaßt werden. Die neue Brigadegliederung wurde im Herbst 1958 erstmals praktisch erprobt.

Die Luftwaffe begann 1958 mit der Aufstellung fliegender Verbände und bereitete die Bildung von Flugabwehrraketen-Batterien vor. Daneben wurde der Aufbau der konventionellen Flugabwehr fortgesetzt. Anfang 1959 unterstanden der NATO-Führung drei Jagdbomber- und ein Transportgeschwader.

Die Marine vergrößerte ihren Anteil an der Verteidigung zur See durch weitere Verbände in der Nord- und Ostsee. Sie verfügte Ende 1958 über 103 Kriegs- und 11 Hilfsschiffe.

Auch die Territoriale Verteidigung wurde ausgebaut. Ihr Zweck ist es, die Operationsfreiheit der verbündeten Streitkräfte und die Sicherheit im rückwärtigen Gebiet der Bundesrepublik im Verteidigungsfall zu gewährleisten. Da jedoch der Schwerpunkt der Aufstellung bei den deutschen NATO-Verbänden liegt, werden die Einheiten der Territorialen Verteidigung, die

GLIEDERUNG DES BUNDESMINISTERIUMS FUR VERTEIDIGUNG *

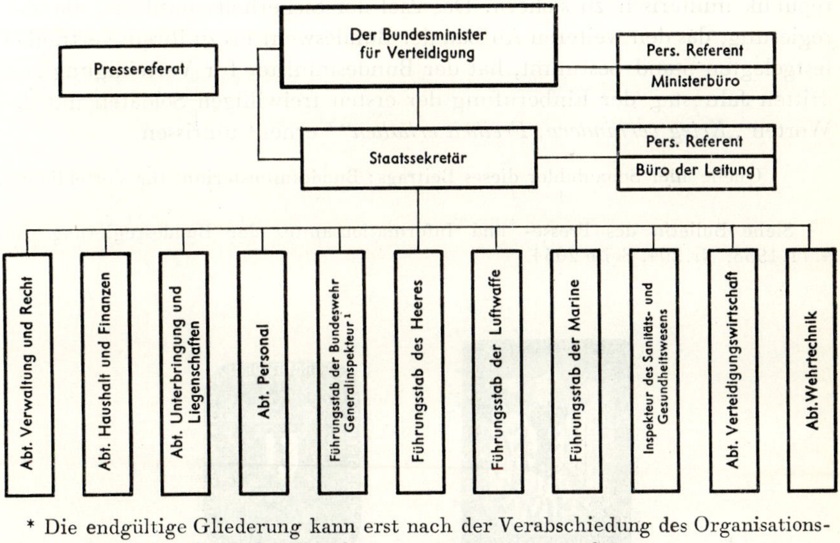

* Die endgültige Gliederung kann erst nach der Verabschiedung des Organisationsgesetzes durch den Deutschen Bundestag vorgenommen werden.

[1] Der Generalinspekteur der Bundeswehr hat Weisungsbefugnis gegenüber den anderen militärischen Abteilungen des Bundesministeriums für Verteidigung.

unter nationaler Führung verbleibt, erst später im geplanten Umfang aufgestellt werden können.

Die Bundeswehrverwaltung hat eine Reihe wichtiger Dienststellen errichtet, darunter insbesondere das Bundesamt für Wehrtechnik und Beschaffung und das Bundeswehrersatzamt. Der Berufsförderung der Soldaten dienen 26 Bundeswehr-Fachschulen. Die Sprachausbildung obliegt der Sprachenschule der Bundeswehr. Ende 1958 waren etwa 30.000 Soldaten als Reserve verfügbar; rund 60.000 Wehrpflichtige waren bis dahin zur Ableistung ihres Grundwehrdienstes einberufen worden. Zum 1.9.1958 wurden etwa 450.000 Wehrpflichtige des Geburtsjahrganges 1938 durch die Bundesländer zur Erfassung aufgerufen. Ihre Musterung durch die Wehrersatzbehörden begann am 3.11.1958. Ende 1958 benutzte die Bundeswehr 294 Unterkunftsanlagen; 31 Neubauten von Kasernen waren fertiggestellt worden. Der Luftwaffe standen 16 Flugplätze zur Verfügung.

*

In den wenigen Zahlen dieser Zwischenbilanz spiegelt sich der Stand der Ausführung des politischen Auftrages, durch Stärkung der NATO die Bundesrepublik militärisch zu sichern. Das Ziel der Sicherheitspolitik der Bundesregierung, das den weiteren Aufbau der Bundeswehr bis zu ihrem vertraglich festgelegten Stand bestimmt, hat der Bundesminister für Verteidigung zum dritten Jahrestag der Einberufung der ersten freiwilligen Soldaten mit den Worten „*Krieg verhindern*, *Freiheit erhalten*“ [1] erneut umrissen.

Quelle aller Schaubilder dieses Beitrags: Bundesministerium für Verteidigung.

[1] Siehe Bulletin des Presse- und Informationsamtes der Bundesregierung vom 4.11.1958, Nr. 204, Seite 2034.

DIE ÖFFENTLICHE MEINUNG

In dem großen Zusammenbruch im Frühjahr 1945 mußte auch die Presse untergehen; denn sie war in besonderem Maß ein Instrument des „Dritten Reiches" geworden. Um *von der „Gleichschaltung" zu demokratischer Pressefreiheit* zu gelangen, bedurfte es nach der Auffassung der Alliierten eines völligen Neubeginns. Der Wiederaufbau begann bereits am vierten Tage nach dem Waffenstillstand, dem 12.5.1945, mit der *Nachrichten-Kontrollvorschrift Nr.1*. Sie machte die Herausgabe einer Zeitung von einer *Lizenz* der Alliierten Militärregierungen abhängig.

Bevor die Gründung einer deutschen Zeitung möglich war, wurde die Bevölkerung durch Nachrichtenblätter der Militärbehörden unterrichtet. Aus diesen Nachrichtenblättern entwickelten sich die von den Militärregierungen herausgegebenen ersten Tageszeitungen. Drei Blätter ragten bald als große politische Organe über die anderen hinaus: „Die Neue Zeitung" in der Amerikanischen, „Die Welt" in der Britischen und die „Tägliche Rundschau" in der Sowjetischen Besatzungszone. Die „Tägliche Rundschau", das Blatt der Sowjetischen Militäradministration, war die erste eigentliche Zeitung, die nach dem Zusammenbruch in Deutschland herausgegeben wurde. Ihr folgte bereits sechs Tage später eine zweite deutsche Tageszeitung mit sowjetischer Lizenz, die „Berliner Zeitung".

Im Gegensatz zu diesen beiden Organen des Kommunismus' riefen die Alliierten im Westen Deutschlands eine freie, unabhängige Presse ins Leben. Bereits vor der Kapitulation hatten die „Aachener Nachrichten" im Januar 1945 die Lizenz Nr.1 erhalten. Am 31.7.1945 erhielt die „Frankfurter Rundschau" als erstes Blatt, das wieder ausschließlich von Deutschen herausgegeben wurde, amerikanische Lizenz. Am 5.9.1945 folgte ihr die „Rhein-Neckar-Zeitung". Die Lizenzierung dieses in Heidelberg erscheinenden Blattes ist besonders bemerkenswert, weil sich unter seinen Lizenzträgern Professor THEODOR HEUSS befand. Auf diese Weise konnte der nachmalige Bundespräsident seine seit 1933 unterbrochene politische Tätigkeit wieder aufnehmen.

Der Wiederaufbau der deutschen Presse stand im Zeichen der Weltsituation von 1945. Diese Problematik wird schon darin sichtbar, daß unter den ersten Lizenzträgern sich in nicht geringer Zahl Angehörige der Kommunistischen Partei und Gesinnungsfreunde von ihnen befanden. Dagegen wurden Berufsjournalisten, auch wenn sie der nationalsozialistischen Ideologie nicht erlegen waren, zunächst von der Zeitungsarbeit ferngehalten.

Das äußere Bild der Presse war selbst in den drei westlichen Besatzungszonen nicht einheitlich. In der Amerikanischen Zone wurden „*überparteiliche Zeitungen*" lizenziert, indem in einer Gruppe von Lizenzträgern Personen verschiedener politischer Richtungen vereinigt wurden. In der Britischen Zone wurde die Neuordnung des Pressewesens erst im Frühjahr 1946 eingeleitet. Dort wurden überwiegend *parteigebundene Zeitungen* zugelassen, das heißt, die Parteien brachten ihnen genehme Personen als Lizenzträger in Vorschlag. Die Franzosen lizenzierten ebenfalls „überparteiliche" Blätter, ließen aber bereits im August 1946 auch drei Parteizeitungen zu, darunter ein Organ der Kommunistischen Partei. In Mainz erscheint noch heute „Die Freiheit" als offiziöses Organ der Sozialdemokratischen Partei Deutschlands. In der Amerikanischen Zone ist es den Parteien auch später nicht gelungen, parteieigene Blätter ins Leben zu rufen.

Seit 1946 wurde eine Vielzahl neuer Zeitungen und Zeitschriften gegründet. Bis zur Währungsreform hatten sie zwar nicht über Lesermangel, aber um so mehr über Papierknappheit zu klagen. Anfang 1949 erfolgte ein für den Wiederaufbau des Zeitungswesens entscheidender Schritt. Am 4.5.1949 wurde in der amerikanischen Besatzungszone mit der *Generallizenz Nr. 3* der Lizenzzwang für Zeitungen und andere Druckwerke aufgehoben. Die übrigen Zonen folgten. Jetzt konnte die stattliche Zahl der kleinen und mittleren Blätter aus dem Kreis der sogenannten *Heimatpresse*, die für das deutsche Pressebild immer charakteristisch gewesen ist, mit den alten Titeln wieder ins Leben gerufen werden.

Ehemals bekannte und alte Zeitungsriesen wie die „Frankfurter Zeitung", „Kölnische Zeitung", „Rheinisch-Westfälische Zeitung", „Deutsche Allgemeine Zeitung", „Vossische Zeitung", „Berliner Lokalanzeiger", „Hamburger Fremdenblatt" usw. kehrten allerdings nicht wieder. In den meisten Fällen wurde ihre Neugründung nicht versucht, in einzelnen Fällen scheiterte sie. Wiedergekehrt ist indessen, wenn auch erst 1952, die Berliner „*Morgenpost*". Dieses Blatt war einst mit der höchsten Auflage unter den deutschen Tageszeitungen das Lieblingsblatt des Berliner Kleinbürgertums.

Der Fortbestand langjähriger Tradition, hauptsächlich getragen von den mittleren und kleineren Blättern, drückt sich unter anderem darin aus, daß 55,2% der gegenwärtig erscheinenden Zeitungen aus der Zeit vor 1900 stammen. Zwei Blätter können ihre Gründung auf das 18. Jahrhundert zurückführen. Nach der Titelzahl entspricht die heutige deutsche Presse nicht ihrem einstigen Umfang. Hinsichtlich ihrer Auflage im Verhältnis zur Bevölkerungsziffer aber kann sie sich mit der Vergangenheit messen. Zur Zeit des Höchststandes der deutschen Tagespresse (1932) erschienen in Deutschland 4.703 Tageszeitungen mit einer Gesamtauflage von 25 Millionen.

Bereits 1939 waren sie auf 2.288 Blätter mit einer Gesamtauflage von 16 Millionen zusammengeschrumpft. Für das Jahr 1955 verzeichnet die Statistik für die Bundesrepublik mit Berlin(West) 1.464 Tageszeitungen, davon 690 Hauptausgaben und 774 Bezirksausgaben. In dem Vorhandensein vieler *Bezirksausgaben* und in der Unterhaltung von Gemeinschaftsredaktionen durch mehrere kleinere Zeitungen liegt ein charakteristischer Unterschied zu der Zeit vor 1933. Hieraus erklärt sich auch der zahlenmäßige Rückgang der Zeitungstitel. Die berechnete Druckauflage aller in der Bundesrepublik mit Berlin(West) erscheinenden Zeitungen beträgt 17,3 Millionen.

In dem vielgestaltigen Blätterwald gibt es einzelne Organe, die als kennzeichnend für das derzeitige deutsche Zeitungsbild gelten können. In Frankfurt am Main erscheint als eine der führenden politischen Zeitungen die „*Frankfurter Allgemeine*". In deutsche Hände übergegangen ist „*Die Welt*", Hamburg, die ebenfalls zu den führenden unabhängigen politischen Tageszeitungen zählt. Im Gegensatz zu dieser ursprünglich englischen Gründung ist das einstige Organ der amerikanischen Militärregierung „*Die Neue Zeitung*" eingestellt worden. Die Einstellung dieses Blattes, das mit seiner betonten Pflege der Information und Dokumentation einen eigenen Rang eingenommen hatte, wird von vielen Deutschen bedauert. Unter den sozialdemokratisch bestimmten Zeitungen kann die „*Frankfurter Rundschau*" als führend angesehen werden. Von den in Berlin herauskommenden politischen Tageszeitungen sind zu nennen „*Der Tagesspiegel*", das Abendblatt „*Der Kurier*", zu dessen Herausgebern Bundesminister Ernst Lemmer gehört, und der sozialdemokratische „*Telegraf*". Ein Blatt neuartigen Typs ist die in Hamburg täglich erscheinende „*Bildzeitung*", ein Boulevard-Blatt, das dem aktuellen Foto einen gleichrangigen Platz neben dem Wort einräumt und mit einem Verkaufspreis von 10 Pfennig eine Auflage von mehr als zwei Millionen erreichte. In München gelten die „*Süddeutsche Zeitung*" und der „*Münchner Merkur*" als repräsentative politische Organe.

Neben der Tagespresse haben sich einige *Wochenzeitungen* politischen Charakters entwickelt. Neuartig sind Wochenblätter wie „*Christ und Welt*" in Stuttgart und das „*Sonntagsblatt*" in Hamburg; beide nehmen aus evangelisch-christlicher Sicht heraus Stellung. Eine Wochenzeitung mit „christlich-abendländischer" Grundhaltung ist der in Köln erscheinende „*Rheinische Merkur*". Wie diese drei haben auch „*Die Zeit*" in Hamburg und — als sozialdemokratisches Organ — der „*Vorwärts*" in Bad Godesberg sich einen Namen als politische Wochenzeitungen für Politik, Kultur und Wirtschaft gemacht.

Zur Tages- und Wochenpresse kommen die Zeitschriften. Sie sind außerordentlich vielgestaltig. Es gibt in der Bundesrepublik mit Berlin(West) nach einer 1955 aufgestellten Statistik 5.630 Zeitschriften aller Gattungen mit einer bekanntgegebenen Druckauflage von 119,1 Millionen. Die größte Gruppe stellen mit 710 Titeln Industrie und Handel, dicht gefolgt von 646 Zeitschriften aus dem Gebiet von Kirche und Religion. Die Kirchenblätter stehen mit einer Auflage von über 16 Millionen an der Spitze der Zeitschriften und nehmen somit einen beachtlichen publizistischen Rang ein. Als charakteristisch für die deutsche Nachkriegssituation können die „Vertriebenen-Zeitschriften“ gelten. Ihre Auflage wird mit 1.280.000 angegeben.

Eine Strukturwandlung gegenüber der Vorkriegszeit hat die *Illustrierten-Presse* zu verzeichnen. Früher hatte Deutschland nur vereinzelte „Illustrierte“ von mehr als örtlicher Bedeutung. Heute erscheinen über zwanzig derartige Blätter mit einer Auflage von über 6 Millionen. Eine Millionenauflage hat auch die Gewerkschaftspresse, die damit ebenfalls ein sehr starkes Element der öffentlichen Meinungbildung darstellt und in dem Wochenblatt „*Welt der Arbeit*“ über ein repräsentatives Organ verfügt. Nicht zu übersehen sind die verbandsgebundenen Jugendzeitschriften und die Frauenzeitschriften. Mit einer Auflage von rund 1,8 Millionen beziehungsweise 4,3 Millionen sprechen sie die genannten Bevölkerungsgruppen an. Bei diesen Zeitschriften liegt keine erhebliche Wirkung in die Breite vor. Ihre politische Wirkung auf eine besonders interessierte Lesergruppe ist jedoch nicht zu unterschätzen.

*

Fast alle Zeitungen und Zeitschriften befinden sich *in Privathand*. Nur verhältnismäßig wenige dienen einer Partei oder einem Verband als offizielles Sprachrohr, wenn man von den periodisch erscheinenden „Mitteilungsblättern“ absieht. Sofern die Zeitungen nicht einer Partei, Gewerkschaft oder einem sonstigen Verband verpflichtet sind, ist ihre Gestaltung dem einzelnen Herausgeber überlassen. Es gibt also in der Bundesrepublik keine von der Regierung „gelenkte Meinung“.

*

Ein Organ der Selbstkontrolle haben die Berufsverbände der Zeitungsverleger, Zeitschriftenverleger und Journalisten sich 1957 im „*Deutschen Presserat*“ geschaffen. Der Presserat hat zur Aufgabe, negative Erscheinungen auf dem Gebiet der Presse aufzugreifen und erforderlichenfalls Empfohlungen für die Abstellung zu geben. Diese freiwillige Selbstkontrolle, die ihr Vorbild und linksbürgerliche Kreise. Mit Entschiedenheit tritt die SPD für die nationalen Interessen Deutschlands ein, und ebenso eindeutig hat sie sich von jeder Verbindung zu den Kommunisten distanziert. Die sozialdemokratische Fraktion des Bundestages steht seit 1949 in Opposition zur Bundesregierung. An den meisten Regierungen der Länder ist die SPD hingegen beteiligt und stellt einige Regierungschefs. Diese Tatsache ist für die Entscheidungen des Bundesrats von Bedeutung.

Die *Freie Demokratische Partei* (*FDP*) zeigt in ihren Landesverbänden keinen einheitlichen politischen Charakter, sondern es bestehen teilweise starke Spannungen zwischen mehr liberalen und mehr nationalen Flügeln. In Württemberg-Baden, wo sie den Namen *Demokratische Volkspartei* (*DVP*) trägt, ist sie eine liberaldemokratische Partei, deren Wählerschichten im freiheitlich gesonnenen Bürgertum und in der Tradition des Revolutionsjahres 1848 wurzeln.

Von der FDP spaltete sich 1956 die Freie Volkspartei (FVP) ab. Sie hat sich kurz darauf mit der Deutschen Partei zusammengeschlossen.

Die CDU/CSU hatte 1956 rund 350.000, die SPD 612.000 Mitglieder.

*

Die vierte der von den Besatzungsmächten lizenzierten Parteien war die *Kommunistische Partei Deutschlands* (*KPD*). Zunächst konnte sie in mehreren Landesregierungen sogar Ministerposten besetzen. Schon bald zeigte sich jedoch deutlich ihre völlige Abhängigkeit vom Weltkommunismus und ihre Verantwortung für das undemokratische Geschehen in der Sowjetischen Besatzungszone. Die Zahl der Mitglieder der KPD wurde 1946 auf 300.000 geschätzt, 1953 auf 80.000. In der gleichen Zeit ging die Zahl der KPD-Wähler von 1.360.000 auf 600.000 zurück. Bei den Bundestagswahlen 1953 wurden nur noch 2,2% der Stimmen für die KPD abgegeben. Auch mit Hilfe getarnter Organisationen ist es trotz großem Propagandaaufwand den Kommunisten nicht gelungen, die Beachtung der öffentlichen Meinung zu finden.

Das Urteil des Bundesverfassungsgerichts vom 17.8.1956, durch das die KPD verboten wurde, erging also nicht wegen eines bedrohlichen Ausmaßes kommunistischer Tätigkeit. Das Verbot mußte vielmehr ergehen, weil es das offene Ziel der KPD war, durch subversive Tätigkeit den demokratischen Staat zu beseitigen.

*

DIE ZUSAMMENSETZUNG DER PARLAMENTE DER LÄNDER DER BUNDESREPUBLIK NACH PARTEIEN

Land	CDU	CSU	SPD	FDP[1]	GB/BHE	DP	Sonstige[3]	Fraktionslose u. Unabhängige
Baden-Württemberg	56		36	21	7			
Bayern		83	61	13	19		28[2]	
Bremen	17		53	8		18		
Hamburg	41		69	10				
Hessen	24		44	20	7			1
Niedersachsen	51		65	8	13	20		
Nordrhein-Westfalen	104		81	15				
Rheinland-Pfalz	52		37	10			1	
Saarland	16	11	8	13				2
Schleswig-Holstein	33		26	3	5		2	
Berlin(West)	55		78					

[1] In Baden-Württemberg DVP, im Saarland DPS. — [2] Bayernpartei. — [3] Zentrum, Freie Demokratische Vereinigung, SSW (Südschlesw. Wählerverband, Schleswig-Holstein), Deutsche Reichspartei.

Der 1957 gewählte Dritte Bundestag besteht aus 519 Abgeordneten. Von ihnen sind 253 in den Wahlkreisen unmittelbar, die übrigen über Landeslisten gewählt worden. Jeder Wähler hatte wiederum zwei Stimmen, von denen er die erste einem Kandidaten seines Wahlkreises geben konnte. Die zweiten Stimmen wurden auf Landeslisten nach dem Höchstzahlverfahren von D'HONDT verteilt. Von der für jede Landesliste ermittelten Abgeordnetenzahl werden dabei diejenigen Sitze abgerechnet, welche die betreffende Partei in den Wahlkreisen des Landes erhalten hat. Die restlichen Sitze werden aus der Landesliste besetzt.

Da die alliierten Vorbehalte hinsichtlich Berlins zum Zeitpunkt der Wahl noch in Kraft waren, wurden nur 497 Abgeordnete im Bundesgebiet gewählt. Zu ihnen treten 22 Vertreter des Landes Berlin, die vom Berliner Abgeordnetenhaus gewählt sind. Auch bei den Wahlen von 1957 wurden nur Parteien berücksichtigt, die mindestens 5% der Stimmen im gesamten Wahlgebiet erhalten oder in mindestens drei Wahlkreisen einen Sitz errungen hatten. Diese Bestimmung galt nicht für Listen, die von Parteien nationaler Minderheiten eingereicht wurden.

WIRTSCHAFT

DER ARBEITSMARKT

Die günstige Entwicklung der Lage des Arbeitsmarktes in der Bundesrepublik wird am sinnfälligsten durch einen Vergleich der Zahlen der Bevölkerung, der abhängig Beschäftigten und der Arbeitslosen in den Jahren 1950 bis 1958. Hierbei ergibt sich, daß bereits im Jahre 1955 ein Beschäftigtenstand erreicht war, der als *Vollbeschäftigung* bezeichnet werden kann. Mit der Zunahme der Bevölkerung ist der Beschäftigtenstand laufend gestiegen. Die Quote der Beschäftigten erhöhte sich von 29,3% im Jahre 1950 auf 38,3% im Jahre 1958. Die Quote der Arbeitslosen sank von 8,2% am 30.9. 1950 auf 1,7% am 30.9.1958.

Im einzelnen wird die Entwicklung im Bundesgebiet (ohne Saarland und Berlin [West]) durch die folgende Tabelle veranschaulicht:

WOHNBEVÖLKERUNG, BESCHÄFTIGTE, ARBEITSLOSE

Wohnbevölkerung		Beschäftigte[1]	Arbeitslose		Empfänger der Arbeitslosenversicherung oder Arbeitslosenhilfe
Jahresdurchschnitt	Personen		Personen	Quote %	Personen
	1	2	3	4	5
1950	46.907.900	13.827.000	1.580.000	*10,3*	1.271.659
1951	47.412.900	14.556.000	1.432.000	*9,0*	1.193.176
1952	47.727.800	14.995.000	1.379.000	*8,4*	1.156.952
1953	48.172.400	15.583.000	1.259.000	*7,5*	1.067.439
1954	48.709.900	16.286.000	1.221.000	*7,0*	1.040.920
1955	49.203.000	17.175.000	928.000	*5,1*	786.646
1956	49.800.400	18.056.000	762.000	*4,0*	629.598
1957	50.464.900	18.611.000	662.000	*3,4*	540.754

[1] Arbeiter, Angestellte und Beamte.

Quelle: Bundesmininisterium für Arbeit und Sozialordnung.

Die Beschäftigungslage entwickelte sich in den einzelnen Bezirken und Ländern der Bundesrepublik unterschiedlich. Die Gebiete, in die nach Kriegsende der Flüchtlingsstrom überwiegend gelenkt worden war, hatten einen Bevölkerungszuwachs zu verzeichnen, auf den sie nach ihrer wirtschaftlichen Struktur nicht eingerichtet waren. Schwierigkeiten bestanden ferner in den *Zonenrandgebieten.* Es mußten besondere Maßnahmen getroffen werden, um die Arbeitslosigkeit in diesen Gebieten zu verringern und, soweit möglich, zu beseitigen. Diesem Zweck dienten in den letzten Jahren umfangreiche *Umsiedlungen.* Sie wurden auf freiwilliger Grundlage unter Wahrung der Freizügigkeit und der freien Wahl des Arbeitsplatzes durchgeführt. Bis zum März 1958 wurden in Gebiete mit günstigerer Wirtschaftslage umgesiedelt:

aus Schleswig-Holstein .... 389.180 Vertriebene
aus Niedersachsen............... 280.543 Vertriebene
aus Bayern .... 231.256 Vertriebene

Daneben wurde die Aufnahme auswärtiger Arbeit durch Gewährung von Trennungsbeihilfen, Übernahme von Reise- und Umzugskosten aus Bundesmitteln und aus Mitteln der Bundesanstalt für Arbeitsvermittlung und Arbeitslosenversicherung gefördert. Ferner wurden vom Bund, von der Bundesanstalt und von den Ländern beträchtliche Mittel zur Schaffung neuer Arbeitsplätze durch Ausweitung bestehender und Einrichtung neuer Arbeitsstätten zur Verfügung gestellt.

Durch finanzielle Förderung von Notstandsarbeiten wurden weitere Möglichkeiten der Beschäftigung von Arbeitslosen geschaffen. Die Arbeitslosigkeit konnte auf diese Weise in den wirtschaftlich schwächeren Teilen der Bundesrepublik gesenkt werden.

ZAHL DER ARBEITSLOSEN

	Jahresdurchschnitt					
	1953	1954	1955	1956	1957	30. 9. 58[1]
Schleswig-Holstein .	120.617	104.014	87.811	72.123	55.995	27.434
Niedersachsen	253.960	238.300	180.585	149.882	130.100	57.159
Bayern	328.208	301.276	230.389	199.706	191.681	78.310

[1] Die letzte Zahl zeigt den Stand im Scheitelpunkt der Saison.

Quelle: Bundesministerium für Arbeit und Sozialordnung.

Daß die Aufgabe des regionalen Kräfteausgleichs noch nicht endgültig gelöst ist, zeigt die Tatsache, daß im September 1958 die Quote der Arbeitslosen in einigen Arbeitsamtsbezirken der Länder Bayern und Niedersachsen noch 5% und mehr betrug. Auch in den einzelnen Wirtschaftsabteilungen verlief die wirtschaftliche Entwicklung unterschiedlich. Dies drückte sich in Schwankungen der Beschäftigungslage aus; vor allem im Steinkohlen- und Erzbergbau, in der Eisen- und Stahlerzeugung, dem Textil- und Bekleidungsgewerbe. Drohender Arbeitslosigkeit wurde durch betriebliche Maßnahmen (Verkürzung der Arbeitszeit) und staatliche Hilfe, wie Umvermittlung und Gewährung von Kurzarbeitergeld, begegnet, um Entlassungen zu vermeiden.

Von besonderer Bedeutung waren die *jahreszeitlichen Schwankungen* der Beschäftigungslage. Die günstige Entwicklung der Beschäftigung wurde jeweils in den Wintermonaten durch eine stark rückläufige Bewegung unterbrochen. So waren Ende Januar 1958: 1.432.000 Personen arbeitslos gemeldet. Von den Saison-Arbeitslosen waren im Winter 1956/57: 52%, im Winter 1957/58: 57% Angehörige des Baugewerbes. Die winterliche Arbeitslosigkeit im Baugewerbe in dem bisherigen Ausmaß stellt eine starke volkswirtschaftliche und soziale Belastung dar.

Die Bundesregierung hält eine befriedigende Lösung dieses Problems für notwendig. Sie wird mit den beteiligten Stellen und Organisationen die Bestrebungen fortsetzen, das ganzjährige, kontinuierliche Bauen zu fördern und dadurch die Arbeitslosigkeit der Bauarbeiter im Winter einzuschränken. Die bisherigen Verhandlungen und Erörterungen haben offensichtlich mit dazu beigetragen, daß die winterliche Arbeitspause im Jahre 1959 früher als sonst beendet wurde.

*

Der wirtschaftliche Aufschwung ist noch nicht allen Arbeitnehmern in gleicher Weise zu Gute gekommen. Für einige Personengruppen bestanden besondere Schwierigkeiten, sich in dem scharfen Wettbewerb des Arbeitslebens durchzusetzen. Zu diesen gehören vor allem die Personen, die durch eine gesundheitliche Schädigung in ihrer Erwerbsfähigkeit gemindert sind. Ihnen mußte in erster Linie geholfen werden. Das sollte durch das *Gesetz über die Beschäftigung Schwerbeschädigter* vom 16.6.1953 geschehen. Dieses Gesetz geht von dem Grundgedanken aus, daß Schwerbeschädigten in ihrem Fortkommen durch Maßnahmen, die ihre Unterbringung im Arbeitsprozeß sicherstellen, und durch einen besonderen Kündigungsschutz geholfen werden muß. Es begründet zu Gunsten Schwerbeschädigter eine Beschäftigungspflicht der Arbeitgeber und macht die Wirksamkeit von Kündigungen von der Zustimmung der Hauptfürsorgestellen abhängig. Ferner gewährt es einen Anspruch auf bezahlten zusätzlichen Urlaub. Zu den Schwerbeschädigten rechnen alle in ihrer Erwerbsfähigkeit um mindestens 50% geminderten Kriegsopfer, Arbeitsopfer und durch nationalsozialistische Verfolgungsmaßnahmen Beschädigte. Außerdem gehören Blinde zum Personenkreis der

Schwerbeschädigten. Personen, die in ihrer Erwerbsfähigkeit weniger als 50%, aber mindestens 30% gemindert sind, können den Schwerbeschädigten gleichgestellt werden. Alle Arbeitgeber, die über sieben und mehr Arbeitsplätze verfügen, müssen einen bestimmten Anteil ihrer Arbeitsplätze mit Schwerbeschädigten besetzen.

Mit Hilfe dieses Gesetzes konnte die Mehrzahl der Schwerbeschädigten auf angemessenen Arbeitsplätzen untergebracht werden. Die Zahl der arbeitslosen Schwerbeschädigten im Bundesgebiet ist von 35.257 im Juli 1953 auf 14.329 im Juli 1958 gesunken.

Da die Zahl der unbesetzten Pflichtplätze für Schwerbeschädigte infolge der günstigen wirtschaftlichen Entwicklung im Ansteigen ist, soll das Schwerbeschädigtengesetz durch eine Novelle der Entwicklung angepaßt werden.

Im Interesse der Personen, die in ihrer Erwerbsfähigkeit gemindert sind, aber nicht unter das Schwerbeschädigten-Gesetz fallen, wurde im Gesetz über Arbeitsvermittlung und Arbeitslosenversicherung in der Fassung vom 3.4.1957 bestimmt, daß die Bundesanstalt besondere Vorkehrungen zu treffen hat, um die Wiedereingliederung auch dieser Personen in den Arbeitsprozeß zu ermöglichen. Die Bundesanstalt hat Vorschriften zur Durchführung von Maßnahmen für die Arbeits- und Berufsförderung behinderter Personen erlassen. Diese Maßnahmen sollen Arbeitsuchende und Berufsanwärter, die infolge geistiger oder körperlicher Behinderung ihre Arbeitskraft nicht voll entfalten können, befähigen, die normalerweise in einem bestimmten Beruf oder Arbeitsbereich erzielten Leistungen annähernd zu erreichen.

*

Für Vertriebene, Flüchtlinge aus der sogenannten DDR, Spätheimkehrer, Evakuierte, Aussiedler, ehemalige politische Häftlinge aus dem Osten, Witwen und Ehefrauen von Kriegs- und Arbeitsopfern bestanden ebenfalls große Schwierigkeiten, den Anschluß an das Arbeitsleben zu gewinnen. Zu ihren Gunsten wurde in einer Reihe von gesetzlichen Bestimmungen der Bundesanstalt für Arbeitsvermittlung und Arbeitslosenversicherung die Verpflichtung zur bevorzugten Arbeitsvermittlung auferlegt. Die Bemühungen um die Arbeitsvermittlung der Vertriebenen haben dazu geführt, daß der Anteil der Vertriebenen an den Arbeitslosen sich ständig verringert hat. Er betrug am 30.9.1958: 19,5%. Auch bei anderen Personengruppen bestehen Unterbringungsschwierigkeiten im allgemeinen nur noch bei älteren Angehörigen (über 45 Jahre) bestimmter Berufe, vor allem den kaufmännischen, Verwaltungs- und auch technischen Angestellten. Mit den besonderen Schwierigkeiten der Unterbringung der Gruppe der *älteren Arbeitnehmer* hat die Bundesregierung sich eingehend beschäftigt. Zwar hat die Zahl der arbeitslosen älteren Angestellten seit 1950 sich ständig verringert (vergleiche die

ARBEITSLOSE ANGESTELLTE ÜBER 45 JAHRE

Zeitpunkt	Männlich	Weiblich
31. 10. 1950	80.149	22.256
31. 7. 1954	51.186	21.095
15. 10. 1955	36.556	21.439
15. 10. 1956	27.885	18.837
15. 10. 1957	24.912	15.676
15. 10. 1958	22.736	15.168

Quelle: Bundesministerium für Arbeit und Sozialordnung.

obenstehende Übersicht); sie ist aber immer noch in Anbetracht des günstigen Beschäftigtenstandes verhältnismäßig hoch. Auch scheint ihr Absinken sich zu verlangsamen.

Die Gründe der Zurückhaltung der Arbeitgeber gegenüber diesem Personenkreis sind nicht immer klar erkennbar. Es wirken offenbar verschiedene Umstände zusammen, wie mangelndes Vertrauen in die Fähigkeit zur Anpassung und Umstellung von älteren Arbeitnehmern (vor allem bei früher selbständig tätig gewesenen Personen), ungünstiger Altersaufbau in vielen Betrieben, Schwierigkeiten der Einbeziehung in die betrieblichen sozialen Leistungen, Scheu vor der Beschäftigung älterer qualifizierter Kräfte mit unterwertigen Arbeiten. Die Arbeitsvermittlung dieser Personen wird um so schwieriger, je länger die Arbeitslosigkeit andauert. Am 15. 10. 1958 wurden 4.201 arbeitslose männliche Angestellte gezählt, die zwei Jahre und länger arbeitslos waren.

Die Bundesregierung, die Bundesanstalt für Arbeitsvermittlung und Arbeitslosenversicherung und die Sozialpartner waren bemüht, unbegründeten Vorurteilen, die zum Teil bei den Arbeitgebern gegenüber der Einstellung älterer Arbeitnehmer bestehen, entgegenzutreten. Die Bundesregierung hat, um dadurch ein Beispiel zu geben, im Jahre 1957 allen Bundesbehörden vorgeschrieben, bei notwendigen Personalvermehrungen arbeitslose ältere Angestellte einzustellen. Daraufhin wurden bis zum Oktober 1958 etwa zweitausend arbeitslose ältere Angestellte bei Bundesbehörden eingestellt. Auch die Landesregierungen haben sich in ähnlicher Weise für die Beschäftigung arbeitsloser älterer Arbeitnehmer eingesetzt. In einigen Bezirken wurde in größerem Umfange von der im Gesetz über Arbeitsvermittlung und Arbeitslosenversicherung geschaffenen Möglichkeit Gebrauch gemacht, zusätzliche gemeinnützige Maßnahmen als Notstandsarbeiten zu fördern, die Arbeitsgelegenheiten für ältere Angestellte schaffen und im öffentlichen Interesse liegen. Das gilt insbesondere für solche, die kulturellen oder wissenschaftlichen Zwecken dienen. Diese Notstandsarbeiten verfolgen vor allem den Zweck, den arbeitslosen älteren Angestellten Gelegenheit zu geben, in einer geregelten Arbeit sich zu bewähren. In vielen Fällen sind diese Angestellten endgültig in ein Arbeitsverhältnis übernommen worden. Ferner ist die

Bundesanstalt für Arbeitsvermittlung und Arbeitslosenversicherung auf Grund einer entsprechenden gesetzlichen Ermächtigung bemüht, durch Gewährung von Beihilfen zur Eingliederung an Arbeitgeber die Unterbringung der arbeitslosen älteren Angestellten zu fördern. Die Bundesanstalt führte laufend Lehrgänge durch, in denen arbeitslose ältere Angestellte beruflich fortgebildet wurden.

Die Bundesanstalt hat weiter damit begonnen, eine kostenlose Arbeitsvermittlung für Angehörige künstlerischer Berufe einzurichten. Diese Personen waren bisher im wesentlichen auf die Inanspruchnahme privater, von der Bundesanstalt zugelassener, Künstlervermittler angewiesen.

*

Die *Verknappung der Arbeitskräfte*, die in einer Reihe von Wirtschaftsabteilungen und Berufen sich zeigte, erforderte einmal verstärkte Bemühungen um die Deckung des Kräftebedarfs und zwang zum anderen zur Auseinandersetzung mit Folgeerscheinungen der Mangellage; wie dem Problem der Ausleihung von Arbeitskräften, der Arbeitsvermittlung von Führungskräften, der Fluktuation und der Abwerbung von Arbeitskräften.

Der Bedarf an Arbeitskräften konnte einmal durch vermehrte *Einstellung weiblicher Arbeitskräfte* gedeckt werden. Die Zahl der weiblichen Arbeitskräfte stieg von September 1957 bis September 1958 um rund 166.000 auf 6.573.000.

DER ANSTIEG
DER FRAUENBESCHÄFTIGUNG

Jahresdurchschnitt	Weibliche Beschäftigte 1.000
1950	4.168
1952	4.658
1954	5.214
1956	5.982
1957	6.285

Quelle: Statistisches Bundesamt.

Um den beruflichen Fähigkeiten der Frauen besser gerecht zu werden, wurde ihrer stärkeren Beteiligung an qualifizierten Berufen besondere Aufmerksamkeit geschenkt. Es wurde mit Erfolg versucht, ihnen solche Berufe in erhöhtem Maße zugänglich zu machen, insbesondere auch auf technischem Gebiet. Auf diese Weise wird dem gegenwärtigen und künftigen Bedarf der Wirtschaft an gut vorgebildeten und geistig beweglichen Kräften, der mit zunehmender Technisierung steigt, Rechnung getragen und gleichzeitig die berufliche Situation der Frauen verbessert. Um weitere Möglichkeiten für die Verwendung von Frauen in technischen Berufen zu erschließen und geeignete Methoden der Anlernung zu entwickeln, wurden wissenschaftliche Untersuchungen veranlaßt.

Bei allen Bemühungen um die Förderung der Frauenarbeit wurde die Problematik der Erwerbstätigkeit von Müttern nicht außer acht gelassen.

Eine weitere Kräftereserve wurde dadurch erschlossen, daß Industriebetriebe in Gebieten errichtet oder erweitert wurden, in denen Arbeitskräfte ansässig sind, die durch besondere Umstände nicht in der Lage sind, auswärtige Arbeit anzunehmen. Durch Verlagerung von Betrieben in ländliche Bezirke wurde zugleich der Abwanderung landwirtschaftlicher Arbeitskräfte vorgebeugt, die auf diese Weise (als mithelfende Familienangehörige) der Landwirtschaft erhalten bleiben. Zur Behebung des Kräftemangels in der Landwirtschaft, im Baugewerbe und in der Baustoffindustrie wurden auf Grund einer deutsch-italienischen Vereinbarung vom 22. 12. 1955 italienische Arbeitskräfte angeworben. Im Jahre 1956 haben 15.608, im Jahre 1957: 14.795, im Jahre 1958: 19.240 italienische Arbeitskräfte im Bundesgebiet (ohne Saarland) gearbeitet. Auch andere ausländische Arbeitskräfte haben in den letzten Jahren Arbeit in der Bundesrepublik aufgenommen.

AUSLÄNDISCHE ARBEITNEHMER IN DER BUNDESREPUBLIK

31. 7. 1954	70.097
31. 7. 1955	76.843
31. 7. 1956	95.355
31. 7. 1957	104.603
1958	133.000

Quelle: Statistisches Bundesamt.

In einigen Bezirken hatten unter dem Druck des Mangels an Arbeitskräften unzulässige Methoden der Beschaffung von Arbeitskräften sich entwickelt. Vorübergehender, in seiner Dauer nicht übersehbarer Mehranfall an Arbeit veranlaßte eine Reihe von Betrieben, Arbeitskräfte von anderen Firmen auszuleihen. Diese Arbeitskräfte wurden nicht Stammkräfte des entleihenden Betriebes, nahmen an den sozialen Vergünstigungen, die in dem Betrieb gewährt wurden, nicht teil und unterlagen den meist kürzeren Kündigungsfristen des für die ausleihende Firma zuständigen Tarifvertrages. Solche Arbeitskräfte verursachten daher dem entleihenden Betrieb weniger Kosten als reguläre Arbeitskräfte und konnten schneller abgestoßen werden. Den Arbeitskräften war vielfach daran gelegen, auf diese Weise in eine Dauerbeschäftigung hineinzuwachsen. Bei den ausleihenden Firmen handelte es sich häufig um Baufirmen oder um Scheinfirmen, die sich ausschließlich mit dem Umsatz von Arbeitskräften beschäftigten und hierfür von den aufnehmenden Betrieben bezahlt wurden. Diesem Leiharbeiter-Unwesen wurde von den Behörden der Arbeitsverwaltung mit Entschiedenheit entgegengetreten. Die ausgeliehenen Arbeitskräfte sind nach und nach in ordnungsmäßige Arbeitsverhältnisse überführt worden. Die Frage kann damit praktisch als geklärt angesehen werden.

Die Bundesanstalt für Arbeitsvermittlung und Arbeitslosenversicherung hat mehr und mehr sich auch der Vermittlung von Führungskräften angenommen.

Der Mangel an Arbeitskräften führte zeitweilig auch zu unerwünschten Fluktuationserscheinungen. Insbesondere der Bergbau und die Land- und Hauswirtschaft sowie kleinere Betriebe hatten über die Abwanderung —

zum Teil unter Vertragsbruch — der Arbeitskräfte zu anderen Betrieben oder Wirtschaftszweigen zu klagen. Über die besonders starke Fluktuation im Bergbau wurden eingehende Untersuchungen angestellt. Die im Rahmen der Arbeitsmarktpolitik gegebenen Möglichkeiten wurden ausgeschöpft, um eine Beunruhigung des Arbeitsmarktes durch unerwünschte Fluktuation zu unterbinden.

*

Die *Nachwuchslage* war durch die seit 1954 rückläufige Entwicklung der Zahl der Schulabgänger gekennzeichnet, die noch bis 1960 anhalten wird. Die Zahl der von der Schule abgehenden Volksschüler, die im Jahre 1953/54 rund 820.000 betrug, ist im Jahre 1958 auf 543.919 zurückgegangen. Entsprechend rückläufig war auch die Zahl der Ausbildungsverhältnisse. Dem sinkenden Angebot von Kräften stand ein steigender Nachwuchsbedarf gegenüber.

Der Ausgleich zwischen Angebot und Nachfrage wurde auch durch die *Berufswünsche* der Jugendlichen erschwert. Angesichts der erweiterten Auswahlmöglichkeiten waren die Berufsanwärter in der Berufswahl vielfach unsicher und unschlüssig. Auch überwog zum Teil das materielle Interesse an einer sicheren und gut bezahlten Tätigkeit gegenüber den Gesichtspunkten der echten Neigung und Eignung. Der Zug zum Großbetrieb machte sich auch bei den Jugendlichen bemerkbar. Die Berufsberatung der Arbeitsverwaltung, die in starkem Maße (zu 90%) von den Schulabgängern in Anspruch genommen wurde, war somit vor schwierige Aufgaben gestellt. Sie war bemüht, durch Aufklärung über die zahlreichen Ausbildungsmöglichkeiten, die Berufserfordernisse und die voraussichtlichen Berufsaussichten auf die Berufswahl der Jugendlichen und die Besetzung der Ausbildungsplätze Einfluß zu nehmen. Dabei wurde der technischen Entwicklung besondere Beachtung geschenkt. Im Jahre 1957 konnte rund 6.000, im Jahre 1958 rund 15.000 bedürftigen Personen durch Gewährung einer *Ausbildungsbeihilfe* aus Mitteln der Bundesanstalt für Arbeitsvermittlung und Arbeitslosenversicherung eine ordnungsmäßige Ausbildung ermöglicht werden. Hierfür wurden im Jahre 1958: 20 Millionen DM bereitgestellt. Diese Beihilfen ergänzten wirksam die verschiedenen sonstigen Ausbildungsbeihilfen (zum Beispiel der öffentlichen Fürsorge, nach dem Bundesvertriebenengesetz und dem Lastenausgleichsgesetz). Die Bundesanstalt hat ferner den regionalen Ausgleich dadurch gefördert, daß sie Mittel für den *Bau von Jugendwohnheimen* zur Verfügung stellte. Mit Hilfe dieser Mittel in Höhe von 27,1 Millionen DM wurden seit 1953 etwa 300 Jugendwohnheime mit fast 20.000 Heimplätzen erstellt.

Eine befriedigende Regelung der Probleme des Arbeitsmarktes erforderte eine einheitliche, das ganze Bundesgebiet umfassende Arbeitsverwaltung und ein einheitliches Recht der Arbeitsvermittlung und Arbeitslosenversicherung. Es mußte den Grundsätzen des sozialen Rechtsstaates entsprechen und mit der internationalen Rechtsentwicklung in Einklang stehen. Die einheitliche Organisation der Arbeitsverwaltung wurde durch das *Gesetz über die Errichtung einer Bundesanstalt für Arbeitsvermittlung und Arbeitslosenversicherung* vom 10.3.1952, das einheitliche Recht der Arbeitsvermittlung und Arbeitslosenversicherung durch das *Gesetz zur Änderung und Ergänzung des Gesetzes über Arbeitsvermittlung und Arbeitslosenversicherung* vom 23.12.1956 geschaffen. Beide Gesetze knüpfen an die Rechtsentwicklung vor 1933 an und tragen der Entwicklung nach dem Zweiten Weltkrieg Rechnung. Sie beruhen auf dem sozialpolitischen Grundgedanken, daß Arbeitsvermittlung, Berufsberatung und Vermittlung von Lehrstellen öffentliche Aufgaben sind, die von einer als öffentlich-rechtliche Körperschaft errichteten Organisation der Selbstverwaltung der Arbeitgeber und Arbeitnehmer unter Mitwirkung der öffentlichen Körperschaften durchzuführen sind. Die *Bundesanstalt für Arbeitsvermittlung und Arbeitslosenversicherung* — eine Körperschaft des öffentlichen Rechts — gliedert sich in die Hauptstelle, die Landesarbeitsämter und Arbeitsämter.

Ihre Organe sind die Verwaltungsausschüsse der Arbeits- und Landesarbeitsämter, der Vorstand und Verwaltungsrat der Bundesanstalt. Sie setzen sich zu gleichen Teilen aus Vertretern der Arbeitgeber, Arbeitnehmer und der öffentlichen Körperschaften zusammen. Die Bundesanstalt ist Träger der Arbeitsvermittlung, Berufsberatung und der Arbeitslosenversicherung. Ihrer Befugnis zur alleinigen Durchführung der Arbeitsvermittlung und Berufsberatung entspricht auf der anderen Seite ihre Pflicht, zu Gunsten aller eine Arbeit, einen Rat oder eine Lehrstelle Suchenden, die sich an sie wenden, vermittelnd und beratend mit dem Ziel tätig zu werden, eine abhängige Tätigkeit oder Ausbildung zu beschaffen. Die Bundesanstalt hat sich zu bemühen, Arbeitgebern die benötigten Arbeitskräfte und Lehrlinge nachzuweisen. Sie kann zur Förderung der Arbeitsaufnahme besondere finanzielle Leistungen an die Arbeitsuchenden oder Arbeitgeber gewähren, wie zum Beispiel die Erstattung von Reise-, Umzugs- und Vorstellungskosten, Gewährung von Trennungsbeihilfen, Anlernzuschüssen oder Beihilfen zur Eingliederung und Ausbildung. Ferner kann sie berufliche Bildungsmaßnahmen durchführen und die Errichtung von Arbeiterwohnheimen und Jugendwohnheimen durch Darlehen oder Zuschüsse fördern. Die Vermittlung von Arbeits- und Lehrstellen und die Berufsberatung müssen unparteiisch, unentgeltlich sowie nach fachlichen und sozialen Gesichtspunkten erfolgen. Schließlich kann die Bundesanstalt Maßnahmen zur Arbeitsbeschaffung als Notstandsarbeiten fördern. — Für einzelne Berufe und Personengruppen kann die Bundesanstalt, wenn dies zweckmäßig ist (wie zum Beispiel in der Künstlervermittlung), auf Antrag Einrichtungen oder Personengruppen mit der Vermittlung von Arbeit und von Lehrstellen beauftragen, sofern der Antragsteller die Gewähr für eine ordnungsmäßige Ausführung des Auftrages bietet.

Auf dem Gebiet der *Arbeitslosenversicherung und Arbeitslosenhilfe* wurden durch das Gesetz von 1956 wesentliche Verbesserungen vorgenommen. Der Kreis der Personen, die arbeitslosenversicherungspflichtig sind, wurde insbesondere im Zusammenhang mit der Reform der Rentenversicherung erweitert. Die Wochensätze des Arbeitslosengeldes und der Unterstützung aus der Arbeitslosenhilfe sowie die Familienzuschläge für Angehörige wurden erhöht und die Entgeltgrenzen, nach denen die Beiträge und Leistungen höchstens zu bemessen sind, von 500 DM auf 750 DM monatlich heraufgesetzt. Der Erwerb der Anwartschaft und des Anspruches auf eine längere Bezugsdauer wurden erleichtert, die Wartezeit verkürzt, eine günstigere Anrechnung von Gelegenheitsverdiensten und eine Unfallversicherung für Arbeitslose eingeführt. Der Beitrag zur Arbeitslosenversicherung wurde auf 2% des Arbeitseinkommens gesenkt. Auch die Bestimmungen über die Berücksichtigung von Abfindungen und Entschädigungen, die im Zusammenhang mit der Beendigung einer Beschäftigung gewährt werden, wurden zu Gunsten der Empfänger von Leistungen geändert.

*

Die Übereinstimmung der Gesetzgebung und Verwaltungspraxis in der Bundesrepublik mit der internationalen Rechtsentwicklung auf dem Gebiet des Arbeitsmarktes und der Sozialpolitik wurde durch die Ratifikation einer Reihe von Übereinkommen der Internationalen Arbeitsorganisation (ILO) bestätigt. Zugleich wurde damit die Bereitschaft der Bundesrepublik zu einer internationalen Zusammenarbeit im Sinne dieser Übereinkommen bekundet. Ratifiziert wurden die Übereinkommen über Zwangs- oder Pflichtarbeit (29), über die Organisation der Arbeitsmarktverwaltung (88), über Büros für entgeltliche Arbeitsvermittlung (96), über Wanderarbeiter (97), über Mindestnormen der sozialen Sicherheit (102) und über die Abschaffung der Zwangsarbeit (105).

Die Bundesregierung wird in ihrer Arbeitsmarktpolitik auch weiterhin das Ziel verfolgen, einen hohen Stand der Beschäftigung zu erreichen und zu erhalten, bei dem es jedem Arbeitswilligen möglich ist, in freier Wahl einen Arbeitsplatz zu erlangen, der eine ausreichende Lebensgrundlage bietet.

LANDWIRTSCHAFT, FORSTEN, FISCHEREI

I. LANDWIRTSCHAFT UND ERNÄHRUNG

Rückblick

Mit dem Zusammenbruch stellten Millionen ausländischer Arbeitskräfte, die bislang auf dem Lande und in allen Zweigen der Ernährungswirtschaft gearbeitet hatten, verständlicherweise ihre Tätigkeit ein. Sie mußten aber weiterhin und sogar bevorzugt aus deutschen Beständen ernährt werden. Millionen eigener Arbeitskräfte waren in Gefangenschaft. Aus den Erträgen der westdeutschen Landwirtschaft waren zusätzlich acht Millionen Vertriebene zu ernähren. Durch den vor den westlichen Besatzungszonen heruntergehenden Eisernen Vorhang und durch die Abtrennung der Deutschen Ostgebiete wurden 48 % der landwirtschaftlichen Nutzfläche und 55 % des Ackerlandes, die das Deutsche Reich 1937 besaß, vom Westen abgetrennt. Auf Ost- und Mitteldeutschland, wo nur 27 % der Reichsbevölkerung verblieben, entfielen vor dem Krieg 54,9 % der Getreide-, 57,3 % der Kartoffel- und 66,7 % der Zuckerrübenernte.

Im Winter 1945/46 schwankte die Nahrungszuteilung in den Notbezirken um 700 bis 800 Kalorien — bisher wurden 2.000 als das Existenzminimum angesehen. Erst der Frühsommer 1948 brachte die Wende . . .

In dieser Zeit schwerster Ernährungslage konnten die deutschen Wohlfahrtsverbände etwa 160.000 t Lebensmittel aus dem Ausland verteilen. Drei Jahre hindurch wurden vom Roten Kreuz 120.000 Kinder aus Auslandsspenden ernährt und insgesamt 130 Millionen Portionen Essen ausgeteilt. Vom September 1948 ab wurde auch 150.000 Studenten eine tägliche Zusatzmahlzeit gewährt. Bis zur Beendigung der alliierten Finanzhilfe am 30.6.1950 war die Zahl der Verpflegten auf 5.123.000 Kinder und Jugendliche zwischen sechs und achtzehn Jahren und 250.000 Studenten gestiegen. Sie erhielten monatlich über 10.000 t hochwertige Lebensmittel mit einem Kostenaufwand von 15 Millionen Dollar je Monat.

Deutschland wird nicht vergessen, was diese Hilfe zu einer Zeit bedeutet hat, in der die Hand des Todes, der Seuchen, der Tuberkulose schwer auf dem unterernährten Volk lag.

Bevölkerung und Fläche

Die Gesamtfläche der Bundesrepublik beläuft sich auf 24,4 Millionen ha. Davon werden zur Zeit 14,2 Millionen ha (= 58,2 %) landwirtschaftlich genutzt. 7,0 Millionen ha (= 28,7 %) entfallen auf Wald und Forsten.

Tabelle 1

AUFGLIEDERUNG DER FLÄCHEN[1]

	Ø 1935/38	1958	Ø 1935/38	1958
	1.000 ha		%	
Wirtschaftsfläche nach den Hauptarten der Nutzung				
Landwirtschaftliche Nutzfläche	14.612	14.227	*59,5*	*58,2*
Wald, Forsten und Holzungen	6.952	7.007	*28,3*	*28,7*
Unkultivierte Moorflächen	298	190	*1,2*	*0,8*
Öd- und Unland	930	691	*3,8*	*2,8*
Gewässer	356	404	*1,5*	*1,7*
Alle sonstigen Flächen[2]	1.391	1.916	*5,7*	*7,8*
Insgesamt	24.540	24.435	*100*	*100*
Landwirtschaftliche Nutzfläche nach Kulturarten				
Ackerland	8.609	8.032	*58,9*	*56,5*
Gartenland	309	402	*2,1*	*2,8*
Geschlossene Obstanlagen	67	67	*0,5*	*0,5*
Rebland	81	75	*0,6*	*0,5*
Wiesen	3.624	3.616	*24,8*	*25,4*
Weiden und Hutungen	1.909	2.025	*13,1*	*14,2*
Baumschulen und Korbweiden-Anlagen	13	11	*0,1*	*0,1*
Zusammen	14.612	14.227	*100*	*100*
Ackerland nach Haupt-Fruchtgruppen				
Getreide	5.152	4.915	*59,8*	*61,2*
Hülsenfrüchte	100	36	*1,2*	*0,4*
Hackfrüchte	1.910	1.880	*22,2*	*23,4*
Gemüse und Gartengewächse	81	85	*0,9*	*1,1*
Handelsgewächse	89	76	*1,0*	*0,9*
Futterpflanzen	1.223	996	*14,2*	*12,4*
Zum Unterpflügen bestimmte Hauptfrüchte	8	5	*0,1*	*0,1*
Brache	46	41	*0,5*	*0,5*
Zusammen	8.609	8.032	*100*	*100*

[1] Bundesgebiet ohne Saarland und ohne Berlin (West). — [2] Gebäude und Hofflächen, Straßen und Wege, Eisenbahnen, Friedhöfe, öffentliche Parkanlagen und Sportplätze, Flug- und Übungsplätze.

Quelle: Statistisches Bundesamt.

Infolge der zunehmenden Ausdehnung der Wohnflächen, Industrieanlagen, Straßen usw. geht die landwirtschaftliche Nutzfläche etwas zurück. Zu einem Teil erfolgt ein Ausgleich durch Kultivierung bisher landwirtschaftlich nicht genutzter Flächen.

Durch die Abtrennung Westdeutschlands und vor allem durch den ungeheuren Zustrom von Flüchtlingen und Vertriebenen nach dem Kriege sowie die Notwendigkeit, Berlin(West) mit zu versorgen, hat das Verhältnis zwischen Bevölkerung und Fläche in der Bundesrepublik sich entscheidend verschoben. Im Durchschnitt der letzten Vorkriegsjahre belief sich die Bevölkerung im Gebiet der heutigen Bundesrepublik auf 38,5 Millionen, im Wirtschaftsjahr 1957/58 war die Zahl der zu versorgenden Personen in der Bundesrepublik einschließlich von Berlin(West) um 14,5 Millionen (= 37,6%) auf 53,0 Millionen angestiegen.

Tabelle 2

BEVÖLKERUNG UND FLÄCHE

Wirtschaftsjahr	Bevölkerung	Gesamtfläche	Landw. Nutzfläche	Einwohner je 100 ha Gesamtfläche	Einwohner je 100 ha l. Nutzfläche	Landw. Nutzfl. je Einwohner
	Mill.	Mill. ha	Mill. ha	Anzahl		ha
Reichsgebiet						
⌀ 1935/38	67,7	47,0	28,7	144	236	0,42
Bundesgebiet						
⌀ 1935/38 ohne Berlin(West)	38,5	24,5	14,6	157	263	0,38
⌀ 1935/38 mit Berlin(West)	41,2	24,5	14,6	167	282	0,35
1948/49 mit Berlin(West)	48,2	24,4	14,2	198	340	0,29
1957/58 mit Berlin(West)	53,0[1]	24,4	14,3	217	373	0,27

[1] Berichtigt.

Quelle: Berechnungen des Bundesministeriums für Ernährung, Landwirtschaft und Forsten auf Grund von Unterlagen des Statistischen Bundesamts.

Zusammensetzung der Bevölkerung

Wie in allen Industrieländern hat auch in Deutschland die Zahl der landwirtschaftlichen Bevölkerung sich laufend verringert. Noch stärker ist bei der gleichzeitigen raschen Zunahme der Gesamt-Bevölkerung der Rückgang des relativen Anteils. Die e Entwicklung hat nach dem Kriege in der Bundes-

Tabelle 3

ZUSAMMENSETZUNG DER BEVÖLKERUNG

Jahr[1]	Bevölkerung insgesamt	davon: Erwerbspersonen in der Land- und Forstwirtschaft und deren Angehörige ohne Hauptberuf		davon: übrige
	Millionen	Millionen	%	Millionen
Reichsgebiet (Gebietsstand von 1937)				
1882	40,2	16,0	*39,9*	24,1
1895	46,4	15,5	*33,5*	30,9
1907	55,6	15,0	*27,0*	40,6
1925	63,2	14,4	*22,8*	48,8
1933	66,0	13,7	*20,8*	52,3
1939	69,3	12,3	*17,7*	57,0
Bundesgebiet ohne Saarland und ohne Berlin (West)				
1939	39,3	7,1	*17,9*	32,3
1950	46,9[2]	7,0[3]	*15,0*[3]	39,9[3]
1958[4]	51,1	5,8[3]	*11,4*[3]	45,3[3]

[1] Stichtag der jeweiligen Volks- und Berufszählung. — [2] Berichtigt. — [3] Schätzung des Bundesministeriums für Ernährung, Landwirtschaft und Forsten. — [4] Stand: 30. 6. 1958.

Quelle: Statistisches Bundesamt.

Tabelle 4

WERTSCHÖPFUNG DER LANDWIRTSCHAFT UND DER ANDEREN WIRTSCHAFTSBEREICHE

Jahr	Netto-Inlandsprodukt zu Faktorkosten: insgesamt	davon: Landwirtschaft, Forstwirtschaft, Fischerei		davon: alle anderen Wirtschaftsbereiche		insgesamt	Landw., Forstw., Fischerei	alle anderen Wirtschaftsbereiche
	Mrd. DM	Mrd. DM	%	Mrd. DM	%	1950 = 100	1950 = 100	1950 = 100
1950	74,5	8,5	*11,4*	65,9	*88,5*	100	100	100
1951	91,1	10,3	*11,3*	80,9	*88,8*	122	121	123
1952	101,3	11,2	*11,1*	90,1	*88,9*	136	132	137
1953	108,8	11,2	*10,3*	97,6	*89,7*	146	132	148
1954	117,5	11,4	*9,7*	106,1	*90,3*	158	134	161
1955	135,0	12,1	*9,0*	122,8	*91,0*	181	142	186
1956	148,5	12,9	*8,7*	135,6	*91,3*	199	152	206
1957	160,8	14,3	*8,9*	146,5	*91,1*	216	168	222
1958	169,3	15,0[1]	*8,9*	154,3[1]	*91,1*	226	176	234

[1] Schätzung des Bundesministeriums für Ernährung, Landwirtschaft und Forsten.

Quelle: Statistisches Bundesamt.

republik infolge des Zustroms von Flüchtlingen und Vertriebenen sich verstärkt fortgesetzt.

Der Anteil der landwirtschaftlichen Bevölkerung[1] machte im Bundesgebiet vor dem Kriege 7,0 Millionen (= 17,9%) aus. Bis zum Jahre 1958 ist er auf schätzungsweise 5,8 Millionen (= 11,4%) zurückgegangen.

Wertschöpfung

Der Beitrag der Landwirtschaft[1] zum Volkseinkommen (Wertschöpfung) ist in der Nachkriegszeit mit der Gesamtentwicklung von Jahr zu Jahr gestiegen; im ganzen jedoch langsamer als der Anteil der übrigen Wirtschaftsbereiche zusammen. Der relative Anteil der Landwirtschaft[1] ist daher rückläufig. Diese Entwicklung ist kennzeichnend für eine wachsende Industriewirtschaft mit steigendem Lebensstandard.

Boden und Klima

Fast zwei Drittel des Bundesgebietes bestehen aus Gebirgs- und Mittelgebirgslagen. Vorherrschend sind Bodenarten mit mäßiger und geringer natürlicher Fruchtbarkeit. Westdeutschland hat im ganzen ein gemäßigtes und zu einem großen Teil ozeanisch beeinflußtes Klima. Die Niederschlagsmengen liegen im Jahr zwischen 500 und 2.000 mm. Der größte Teil der landwirtschaftlich genutzten Gebiete der Bundesrepublik hat Niederschlagsmengen zwischen 500 und 700 mm im Jahr. Im ganzen überwiegt die Wald- und Grünlandnutzung und der Anbau anspruchsloser und wenig wärmebedürftiger Pflanzen.

Die landwirtschaftlichen Betriebe

Die Landwirtschaft des Bundesgebiets beruht in der Hauptsache auf den bäuerlichen Betrieben. Unter ihnen überwiegen wiederum die klein- und mittelbäuerlichen Familienbetriebe. Daneben besteht eine große Zahl von Kleinbetrieben, deren Inhaber einen anderen Nebenberuf oder auch Hauptberuf haben. Der Anteil der größeren Betriebe ist im ganzen nicht nur der Zahl, sondern auch der Fläche nach sehr gering. Die durchschnittliche Größe der Betriebe über 0,5 ha landwirtschaftlicher Nutzfläche beträgt zur Zeit rund 7,6 ha landwirtschaftlicher Nutzfläche.

[1] Einschließlich der Forstwirtschaft und Fischerei.

Ein sehr großer Teil der landwirtschaftlichen Betriebe im Bundesgebiet ist zu klein, um ein ausreichendes Einkommen zu ermöglichen. Dazu kommen außerdem die Nachteile der sehr verbreiteten Flurzersplitterung und enger Hoflagen im Dorf, die eine rationelle Betriebsführung und die Ausnutzung der technischen Möglichkeiten beeinträchtigen und erschweren. Die Änderung dieser Verhältnisse macht von Jahr zu Jahr durch Selbsthilfe und staatliche Maßnahmen Fortschritte. Eine umfassende Verbesserung kann aber erst in einem längeren Zeitraum erreicht werden.

Tabelle 5

DIE LANDWIRTSCHAFTLICHEN BETRIEBE NACH GRÖSSENKLASSEN DER LANDWIRTSCHAFTLICHEN NUTZFLÄCHE

Jahr	0,5 bis unter 2 ha	2 bis unter 5 ha	5 bis unter 10 ha	10 bis unter 20 ha	20 bis unter 50 ha	50 bis unter 100 ha	100 ha und darüber	Insgesamt
Zahl der Betriebe in 1.000								
1939 ...	603,2	560,6	410,8	252,6	114,4	13,5	3,5	1.958,6
1949 ...	583,1	543,9	400,7	254,8	112,4	12,7	3,0	1.910,6
1955 ...	553,7	487,5	382,3	262,6	114,0	13,0	2,8	1.815,9
1958 ...	526,7	443,7	366,0	274,1	117,7	13,4	2,8	1.744,4
In % der Gesamtzahl								
1949 ...	*30,5*	*28,5*	*21,0*	*13,3*	*5,9*	*0,6*	*0,2*	*100*
1958 ...	*30,2*	*25,4*	*21,0*	*15,7*	*6,7*	*0,8*	*0,2*	*100*
Zu- oder Abnahme gegen 1949 in %								
1958 ...	*—9,7*	*—18,4*	*—8,6*	*+7,6*	*+4,7*	*+5,3*	*—7,8*	*—8,7*
Landwirtschaftliche Nutzfläche in 1.000 ha								
1939 ...	654	1.869	2.900	3.494	3.308	872	665	13.762
1949 ...	636	1.807	2.840	3.525	3.245	823	561	13.437
1955 ...	612	1.658	2.746	3.633	3.293	844	506	13.292
1958 ...	566	1.475	2.634	3.805	3.391	866	494	13.231
In % der gesamten landwirtschaftlichen Nutzfläche								
1949 ...	*4,7*	*13,5*	*21,1*	*26,2*	*24,2*	*6,1*	*4,2*	*100*
1958 ...	*4,3*	*11,2*	*19,9*	*28,8*	*25,6*	*6,5*	*3,7*	*100*
Zu- oder Abnahme gegen 1949 in %								
1958 ...	*—11,0*	*—18,3*	*—7,3*	*+8,0*	*+4,5*	*+5,3*	*—12,0*	*—1,5*

Quelle: Statistisches Bundesamt.

In der Zusammensetzung der Betriebe ist mit dem allgemeinen wirtschaftlichen Anstieg eine sehr beachtliche Entwicklung eingetreten. Die besseren Verdienstmöglichkeiten in nichtlandwirtschaftlichen Wirtschaftszweigen haben neben der Abwanderung von Arbeitskräften aus den landwirtschaftlichen Betrieben, die noch behandelt wird, auch zur Verkleinerung oder Aufgabe von Kleinbetrieben durch Verkauf oder Verpachtung der landwirtschaftlich genutzten Flächen geführt. Die abgegebenen Flächen scheiden zu einem Teil durch Verwendung für andere Zwecke ganz aus der landwirtschaftlichen Nutzung aus. Zum größten Teil werden sie jedoch von anderen landwirtschaftlichen Betrieben übernommen, die durch die Vergrößerung ihrer Flächen eine bessere Ausnutzung des Betriebes und damit eine Erhöhung ihres Einkommens erzielen. Somit geht die Zahl der kleinen Betriebe zurück, und die Zahl der mittel- und großbäuerlichen Betriebe steigt an.

Die Arbeitskräfte in der Landwirtschaft

Bei der überwiegend bäuerlichen Struktur der Landwirtschaft im Bundesgebiet werden die Arbeitskräfte zum größten Teil durch die bäuerlichen Familien gestellt. Im ganzen wird fast 80% des Arbeitsaufwandes in der Landwirtschaft der Bundesrepublik von Familienarbeitskräften geleistet und nur etwas über 20% von Lohnarbeitskräften. Die meisten Betriebe wirtschaften nur oder fast ganz mit familieneigenen Arbeitskräften, wobei die Mithilfe der Bauersfrau eine sehr große Rolle spielt. Der Bestand an

Tabelle 6

ARBEITSAUFWAND DER LANDWIRTSCHAFT IN VOLLARBEITSKRÄFTEN

Wirtschaftsjahr	Gesamtbestand an Vollarbeitskräften			Bestand je 100 ha landw. Nutzfläche		
	Familien-arbeits-kräfte	Lohn-arbeits-kräfte	zusammen	im Gesamt-durch-schnitt	davon in Betrieben bis 5 ha	davon in Betrieben ab 5 ha
	1.000				landw. Nutzfläche	
1938/39	2.896	820	3.716	27,9	52,1	21,3
1950/51	2.885	857	3.742	27,9	57,3	21,5
1951/52	2.793	797	3.590	26,8	54,8	20,7
1952/53	2.708	753	3.461	25,9	53,0	20,0
1953/54	2.601	719	3.320	24,9	51,1	19,3
1954/55	2.466	690	3.156	23,7	47,8	18,7
1955/56	2.324	669	2.993	22,5	44,8	18,0
1956/57	2.198	647	2.845	21,4	42,4	17,4
1957/58	2.101	614	2.715	20,5	40,6	16,8

Quelle: Bundesministerium für Ernährung, Landwirtschaft und Forsten.

LANDWIRTSCHAFTLICHE ARBEITSKRÄFTE IN VOLLARBEITSKRÄFTEN

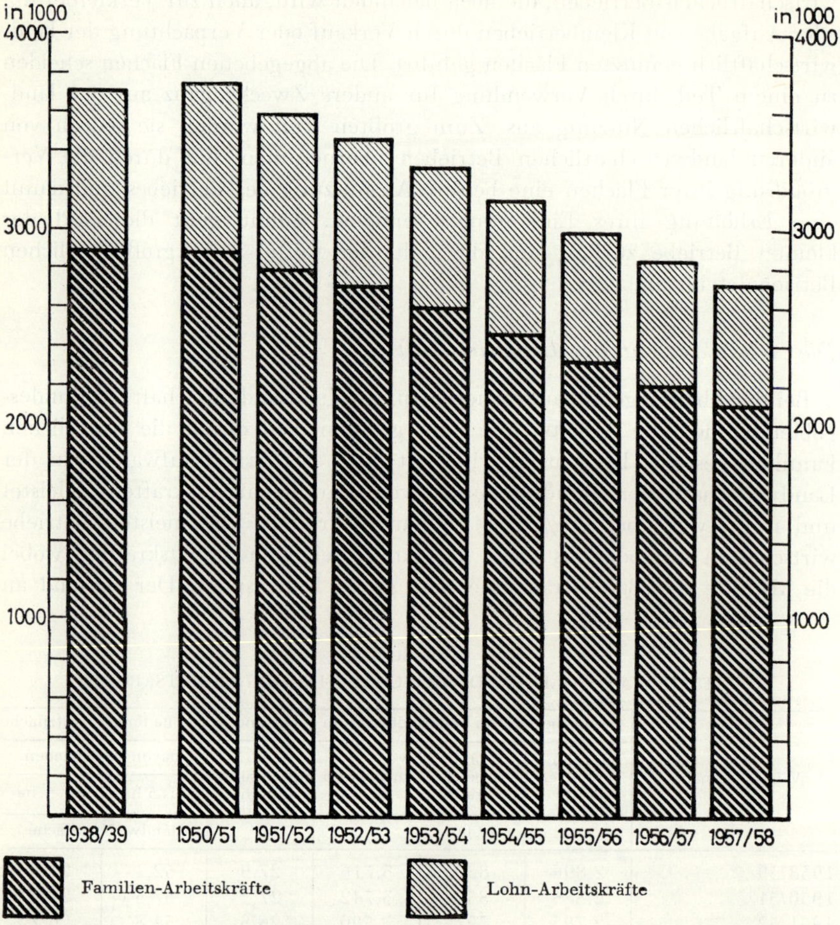

Quelle: Bundesministerium für Ernährung, Landwirtschaft und Forsten.

Arbeitskräften — bezogen auf die Flächeneinheit — nimmt im allgemeinen mit abnehmender Betriebsgröße erheblich zu. Infolge des sehr großen Anteils kleiner und mittlerer landwirtschaftlicher Betriebe ist der durchschnittliche Besatz mit Arbeitskräften in der Bundesrepublik im Vergleich zu Ländern mit anderer Betriebsstruktur verhältnismäßig hoch.

BESTAND AN SCHLEPPERN, MÄHDRESCHERN UND MELKMASCHINEN

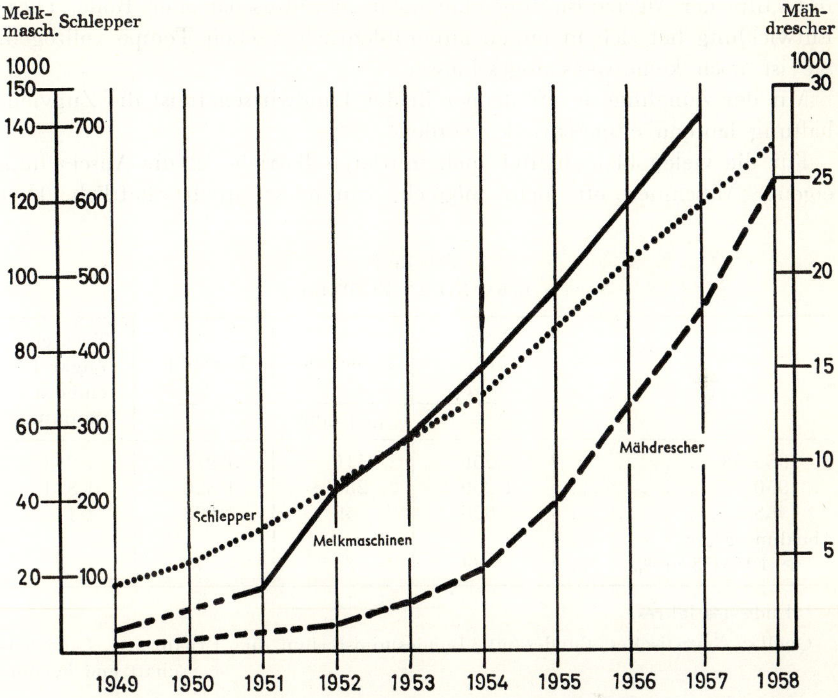

Quelle: Bundesministerium für Ernährung, Landwirtschaft und Forsten.

Die Abwanderung von Arbeitskräften aus der Landwirtschaft in andere Wirtschaftszweige, die in den ersten Nachkriegsjahren unterbrochen war, hat mit der rasch ansteigenden wirtschaftlichen Entwicklung nach der Währungsreform sich verstärkt fortgesetzt. Vom Wirtschaftsjahr 1950/51 bis zum Wirtschaftsjahr 1957/58 hat sich der Bestand an landwirtschaftlichen Arbeitskräften — ausgedrückt in Vollarbeitskräften — um rund eine Million (= 27%) verringert. An diesem Rückgang waren die Familienarbeitskräfte und die Lohnarbeitskräfte etwa gleich stark beteiligt.

Die Mechanisierung der Landwirtschaft

Die Abwanderung von Arbeitskräften hat die westdeutsche Landwirtschaft zu einer zunehmenden Mechanisierung gezwungen. Daneben spielt aber auch die Erleichterung der Arbeit und die Verkürzung der Arbeitszeit mit Hilfe der Mechanisierung eine nicht zu unterschätzende Rolle. Diese Entwicklung hat sich in einem außerordentlich raschen Tempo vollzogen. Sie ist noch keineswegs abgeschlossen.

Mit der Zunahme der Schlepper in der Landwirtschaft ist die Zugviehhaltung laufend eingeschränkt worden.

Für die vielen kleinen und auch mittleren Betriebe ist die Anschaffung eigener Maschinen oft nicht möglich, zumindest unwirtschaftlich. Hier

Tabelle 7
BESTAND AN ZUGVIEH

Jahr[1]	Pferde über 3 Jahre	Zugochsen	Zugkühe	Tierische Zugkrafteinheiten zusammen
	in 1.000			
∅ 1935/38	1.256	315	1.972	1.934
1950	1.200	280	1.820	1.824
1958	826	59	1.028	1.143
Abnahme gegen ∅ 1935/38 in %	*— 34*	*— 81*	*— 48*	*—41*

[1] Ende des Jahres.

Quelle: Statistisches Bundesamt / Bundesministerium für Ernährung, Landwirtschaft und Forsten.

Tabelle 8
VERBRAUCH VON HANDELSDÜNGER IN NÄHRSTOFFEN

Wirtschaftsjahr	Stickstoff	Phosphat	Kali	Stickstoff	Phosphat	Kali
	kg/ha landw. Nutzfläche			1938/39 = 100		
1938/39	23,6	28,3	43,4	100	100	100
1947/48	18,4	15,1	28,5	78	53	66
1950/51	25,6	29,6	46,7	109	105	108
1952/53	29,5	27,7	54,3	125	98	125
1954/55	31,7	36,3	60,2	134	128	139
1956/57	36,9	40,1	61,5	156	142	142
1957/58	39,7	41,6	69,2	168	147	159

Quelle: Bundesministerium für Ernährung, Landwirtschaft und Forsten.

spielt die Verwendung von Maschinen in gemeinschaftlichem Besitz oder von Lohnmaschinen eine wichtige Rolle.

Verbrauch von Handelsdünger

Die Anwendung von Handelsdünger zur Steigerung der Bodenerträge, die während des Krieges und besonders in den ersten Nachkriegsjahren sehr zurückgegangen war, ist seitdem wieder rasch und stark erhöht worden. Im Wirtschaftsjahr 1950/51 war der Vorkriegsstand erstmalig wieder überschritten worden.

Die staatlichen Maßnahmen zur Verbilligung des Handelsdüngers, die 1956 einsetzten, haben die Anwendung von Handelsdünger erheblich gefördert.

Tabelle 9

BRUTTO-BODENPRODUKTION IN GETREIDEEINHEITEN

Wirtschaftsjahr	Je ha landw. Nutzfläche	Insgesamt	1935/36 bis 1938/39 = 100
	dz	Mill. t	
1935/36—1938/39	28,2	41,1	100
1946/47	20,4	28,8	70
1947/48	16,4	23,2	56
1948/49	24,0	34,1	83
1949/50	26,0	36,9	90
1950/51	29,7	42,0	102
1951/52	31,4	44,4	108
1952/53	29,2	41,5	101
1953/54	32,0	45,5	111
1954/55	31,9	45,5	111
1955/56	32,0	45,6	111
1956/57	32,4	46,3	113
1957/58	32,9	46,9	114
1958/59	34,6	49,2	120

Quelle: Bundesministerium für Ernährung, Landwirtschaft und Forsten.

Die Bodenproduktion

Die landwirtschaftliche Nutzfläche in der Bundesrepublik beträgt 14,2 Millionen ha. Davon entfielen im Jahre 1958 rund 8,0 Millionen ha (= 56,5%) auf Ackerland und rund 5,6 Millionen ha (= 39,6%) auf Dauergrünland.

Tabelle 10

ANBAUFLÄCHEN, ERTRÄGE UND ERNTEN

Wirtschafts-jahr	Brot-getreide	Futter-getreide[1]	Getreide zusammen	Kartoffeln	Zuckerrüben
			Anbaufläche in 1.000 ha		
∅ 1935/38 .	2.861	2.291	5.152	1.162	130
1948 ...	2.441	1.762	4.203	1.151	157
1950 ...	2.444	1.960	4.404	1.141	193
1952 ...	2.622	2.039	4.661	1.147	222
1954 ...	2.707	2.063	4.770	1.190	254
1956 ...	2.699	2.170	4.869	1.135	269
1957 ...	2.751	2.123	4.874	1.119	259
1958 ...	2.869	2.046	4.915	1.061	284
			Erträge in dz je ha		
∅ 1935/38 .	21,9	23,0	22,4	185	327
1948 ...	19,8	17,6	18,8	205	300
1950 ...	23,7	22,5	23,2	245	393
1952 ...	25,1	24,1	24,6	208	318
1954 ...	26,5	26,3	26,4	225	392
1956 ...	27,4	26,5	27,0	236	326
1957 ...	28,5	26,6	27,7	235	415
1958 ...	26,5	26,7	26,6	214	419[2]
			Ernten in 1.000 t		
∅ 1935/38 .	6.258	5.278	11.536	21.492	4.253
1948 ...	4.828	3.097	7.925	23.547	4.720
1950 ...	5.792	4.414	10.206	27.959	7.579
1952 ...	6.582	4.903	11.485	23.854	7.066
1954 ...	7.168	5.422	12.590	26.769	9.950
1956 ...	7.384	5.749	13.133	26.756	8.776
1957 ...	7.838	5.646	13.484	26.289	10.750
1958 ...	7.611	5.472	13.083	22.664	12.500[2]

[1] Einschließlich von Körnermais. — [2] Vorläufige Ergebnisse.

Quelle: Statistisches Bundesamt.

Der Rest von rund 0,6 Millionen ha waren Gärten, Obstanlagen und Rebland. Der Anteil der einzelnen Nutzungsarten an der gesamten landwirtschaftlichen Fläche zeigt im allgemeinen keine großen Veränderungen von Jahr zu Jahr. Gegenüber der Vorkriegszeit ist eine Einschränkung der Ackerfläche und eine Ausdehnung des Dauergrünlandes erfolgt.

Weit über die Hälfte des Ackerlandes wird mit Getreide bestellt. Knapp ein Viertel entfällt auf den Anbau von Hackfrüchten (Kartoffeln und Rüben) und etwa ein Achtel auf Futterpflanzen.

Die Bodenproduktion war in den ersten Nachkriegsjahren sehr stark zurückgegangen. Den Tiefstand brachte die Ernte des Jahres 1947, die durch die lang anhaltende Dürre noch besonders beeinträchtigt wurde. Danach erfolgte ein rascher Wiederanstieg. Mit der Ernte des Jahres 1950 wurde die Vorkriegshöhe wieder überschritten. Die Ernte des Jahres 1958 erreichte ein Gesamtergebnis von 20% über Vorkriegshöhe.

Die Ernten der einzelnen pflanzlichen Erzeugnisse haben sich zum Teil unterschiedlich entwickelt. Im Vergleich mit der Vorkriegszeit ist der Anbau von Getreide und Kartoffeln etwas eingeschränkt worden, während der Anbau von Zuckerrüben auf etwa den doppelten Umfang ausgedehnt worden ist.

Die Viehwirtschaft

Die Viehwirtschaft ist die Haupteinnahmequelle der westdeutschen Landwirtschaft, insbesondere der klein- und mittelbäuerlichen Betriebe, die im allgemeinen einen starken Viehbesatz haben. Etwa drei Viertel der pflanzlichen Erzeugung in der Bundesrepublik werden verfüttert. Außerdem werden noch Futtermittel eingeführt.

Tabelle 11

VIEHBESTÄNDE

in 1.000 Stück

Anfang Dezember	Pferde		Rindvieh		Schweine		Schafe insgesamt	Hühner insgesamt
	insgesamt	davon unter 3 Jahre	insgesamt	davon Milchkühe	insgesamt	davon Zuchtsauen		
Ø 1935/38	1.542	285	12.114	5.990	12.494	1.027	1.889	51.124
1948...	1.618	389	10.569	5.263	6.755	830	2.492	25.173
1950...	1.570	370	11.149	5.734	11.890	1.113	1.643	48.064
1952...	1.360	194	11.641	5.822	12.979	1.006	1.544	51.343
1954...	1.172	100	11.521	5.777	14.525	1.259	1.226	55.092
1956...	1.025	81	11.815	5.641	14.408	1.248	1.146	53.868
1957...	967	84	11.948	5.572	15.418	1.365	1.127	55.977
1958...	907	81	12.066	5.561	14.654	1.265	1.106	57.305

Quelle: Statistisches Bundesamt.

Tabelle 12

KUHBESTAND[1] UND MILCHERZEUGUNG

Wirtschaftsjahr	Milchkuhbestand	Milcherzeugung		Milchkuhbestand	Milcherzeugung	
		je Kuh	insgesamt		je Kuh	insgesamt
	1.000 St.	kg	1.000 t	∅ 1935/38 = 100		
∅ 1935/38	6.040	2.480	15.000	100	100	100
1948/49	5.223	2.017	10.535	87	81	70
1950/51	5.706	2.560	14.610	95	103	97
1952/53	5.815	2.765	16.077	96	112	107
1954/55	5.791	2.910	16.848	96	117	112
1956/57	5.649	2.996	16.924	94	121	113
1957/58	5.607	3.169	17.770	93	127	118

[1] Jahresdurchschnittsbestand. Quelle: Statistisches Bundesamt.

Im Vergleich mit der Vorkriegszeit hat der Rindviehbestand etwa die gleiche Höhe wieder erreicht. Der Schweinebestand, der im Verlaufe des Krieges und in den ersten Nachkriegsjahren stark eingeschränkt worden war, hat den Vorkriegsstand überschritten. Der Pferdebestand geht infolge der Motorisierung laufend zurück.

Tabelle 13

RINDVIEH- UND SCHWEINEBESTAND[1] UND FLEISCHANFALL

Wirtschaftsjahr	Rindviehbestand und Fleischanfall				Schweinebestand und Fleischanfall			
	Rindviehbestand	Fleischanfall [2]	Rindviehbestand	Fleischanfall [2]	Schweinebestand	Fleischanfall	Schweinebestand	Fleischanfall
	1.000 St.	1.000 t	1935/38 = 100		1.000 St.	1.000 t	1935/38 = 100	
∅ 1935/38	12.114	681	100	100	11.144	1.012	100	100
1948/49	10.573	364	87	54	4.877	348	44	34
1950/51	11.150	567	92	83	9.116	880	82	87
1952/53	11.641	650	96	95	11.944	1.146	107	113
1954/55	11.520	751	95	110	11.747	1.239	105	122
1956/57	11.815	764	98	112	13.003	1.357	117	134
1957/58	11.948	850	99	125	14.100	1.464	127	145

[1] Schweinebestand Anfang Dezember (Mitte des Wirtschaftsjahres). Rindviehbestand Anfang Juni (Beginn des Wirtschaftsjahres: 1. Juli).

[2] Anfall von Rind- und Kalbfleisch zusammen.

Quelle: Berechnungen des Bundesministeriums für Ernährung, Landwirtschaft und Forsten auf Grund von Unterlagen des Statistischen Bundesamts.

Tabelle 14
HENNENBESTAND[1] UND EIERANFALL

Wirtschaftsjahr	Durchschn. Hennenbestand	Eiererzeugung		Durchschn. Hennenbestand	Eiererzeugung	
		je Henne	insgesamt		je Henne	insgesamt
	Mill. Stück	Stück	Mill. Stück	ø 1935/38 = 100		
ø 1935/38	44,4	108	4.810	100	100	100
1948/49	20,7	97	2.005	47	90	42
1950/51	41,6	120	4.990	94	101	104
1952/53	44,8	121	5.420	101	112	113
1954/55	48,4	127	6.150	109	118	128
1956/57	47,3	131	6.200	107	121	128
1957/58	48,9	134	6.550	110	124	136

[1] Jahresdurchschnittsbestand.

Quelle: Berechnungen des Bundesministeriums für Ernährung, Landwirtschaft und Forsten auf Grund von Unterlagen des Statistischen Bundesamts.

Die Leistungen des Viehbestandes sind infolge verbesserter Züchtung, Fütterung und Haltung durchweg gestiegen und haben die Vorkriegshöhe weit überschritten.

Die Nahrungsmittelproduktion

Die gesamte Nahrungsmittelproduktion der westdeutschen Landwirtschaft — umgerechnet auf Getreideeinheiten — besteht zur Zeit zu einem Viertel aus pflanzlichen Erzeugnissen und zu drei Vierteln aus tierischen Erzeugnissen. Im Verlauf der Kriegs- und ersten Nachkriegsjahre war die Nahrungsmittelproduktion bis zum Wirtschaftsjahr 1947/48 auf 58% des Durchschnitts der letzten Vorkriegsjahre gesunken. Dabei war der Rückgang der Produktion pflanzlicher Nahrungsmittel erheblich schwächer (auf 84%) und der Abfall der Produktion tierischer Erzeugnisse stärker (auf 50%). Seitdem ist die Nahrungsmittelproduktion fast von Jahr zu Jahr gestiegen. Dabei holte die Produktion tierischer Nahrungsmittel die Produktion der pflanzlichen Nahrungsmittel wieder ein. Im Wirtschaftsjahr 1950/51 erreichte die Nahrungsmittelproduktion wieder die Vorkriegshöhe. Für das Wirtschaftsjahr 1958/59 wird sie auf 136% des Durchschnitts der letzten Vorkriegsjahre veranschlagt.

Im Vergleich mit der Bodenproduktion ist die Nahrungsmittelproduktion stärker angestiegen. Diese Entwicklung ist in erster Linie auf die Verwendung motorischer Zugkraft an Stelle von Zugtieren zurückzuführen.

Das dadurch eingesparte Futter wird unmittelbar zur Nahrungsmittelproduktion verwendet. Bei der Erzeugung tierischer Nahrungsmittel wirkt sich außerdem die steigende Einfuhr von Futtermitteln aus.

Die Einfuhr von Gütern der Ernährungswirtschaft

Die Bundesrepublik ist für die Ernährung ihrer Bevölkerung in quantitativer wie in qualitativer Hinsicht auf Einfuhren von Nahrungs- und Futtermitteln angewiesen.

NAHRUNGSMITTELPRODUKTION

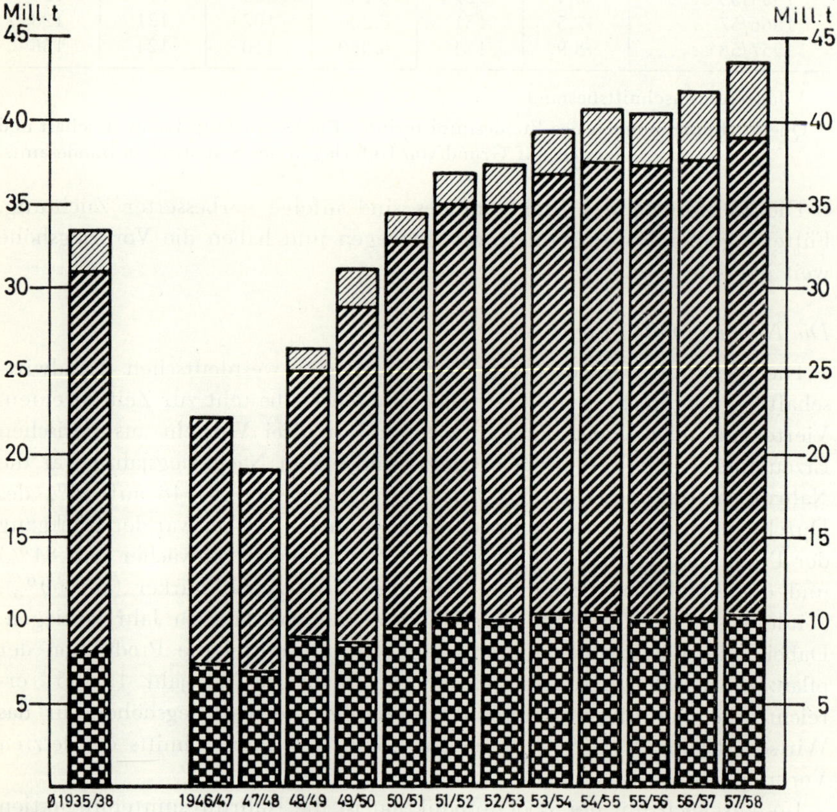

Quelle: Bundesministerium für Ernährung, Landwirtschaft und Forsten.

DIE FINANZIERUNG DER ERNÄHRUNGSWIRTSCHAFTLICHEN EINFUHR

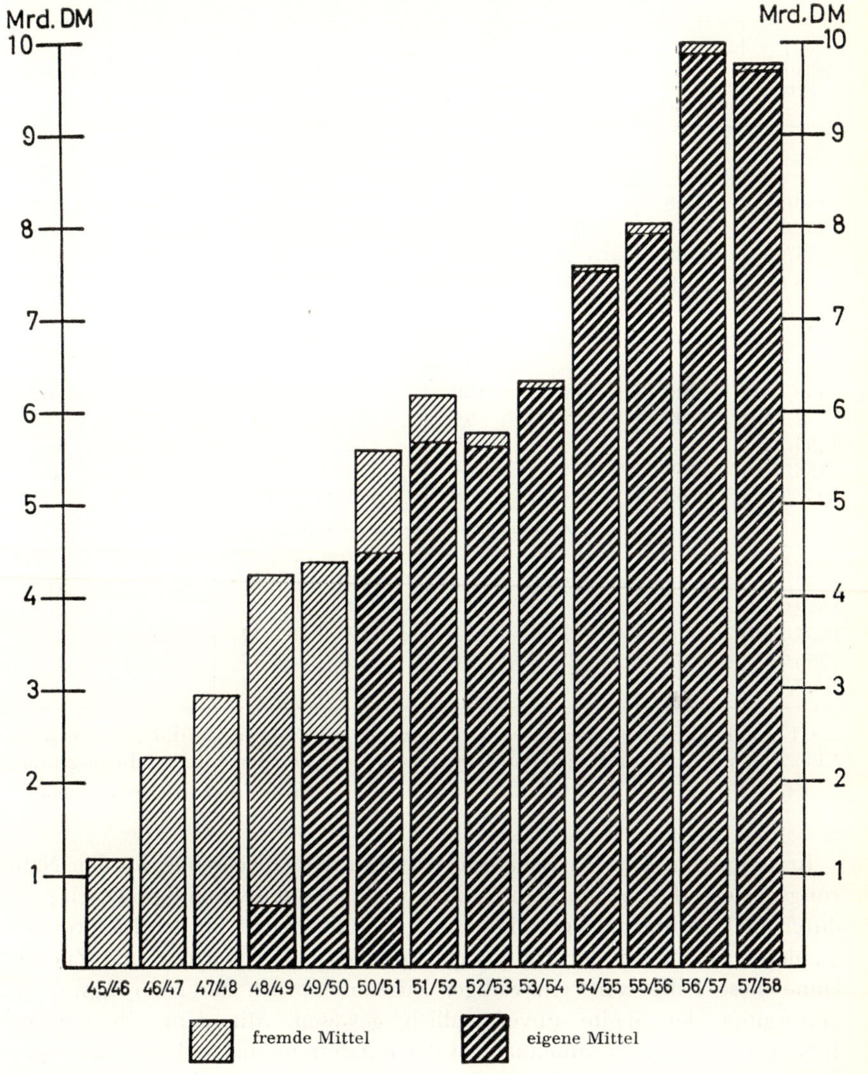

Quelle: Bundesministerium für Ernährung, Landwirtschaft und Forsten.

Tabelle 15

EINFUHR

Wirtschaftsjahr	Ernährungswirtschaft					Gewerbliche Wirtschaft	Insgesamt
	Nahrungsmittel			Genußmittel	zusammen		
	pflanzliche	tierische[1]	zusammen				
				Werte (in Milllionen DM)			
1950/51	3.608	1.506	5.114	477	5.591	7.989	13.580
1952/53	3.868	1.179	5.047	739	5.786	10.157	15.943
1954/55	4.565	1.712	6.277	1.299	7.576	14.453	22.029
1956/57	6.010	2.358	8.368	1.611	9.979	20.234	30.213
1957/58	5.853	2.229	8.083	1.681	9.764	21.597	31.360
				Meßziffern (1950/51 = 100)			
1950/51	100	100	100	100	100	100	100
1952/53	107	78	99	155	103	127	117
1954/55	127	114	123	272	136	181	162
1956/57	167	157	164	338	178	253	222
1957/58	162	148	158	352	175	270	231
				Zusammensetzung der Einfuhr (%)			
1950/51	*71*[2]	*29*[2]	*91*[3]	*9*[3]	*41*[4]	*59*[4]	*100*
1952/53	*77*	*23*	*87*	*13*	*36*	*64*	*100*
1954/55	*73*	*27*	*83*	*17*	*34*	*66*	*100*
1956/57	*72*	*28*	*84*	*16*	*33*	*67*	*100*
1957/58	*72*	*28*	*83*	*17*	*31*	*69*	*100*

[1] Einschließlich lebender Tiere. — [2] Bezogen auf Nahrungsmittel zusammen. — [3] Bezogen auf Ernährungswirtschaft zusammen. — [4] Bezogen auf Einfuhr insgesamt.

Quelle: Statistisches Bundesamt.

In den ersten drei Wirtschaftsjahren nach dem Kriegsende wurden Nahrungsmitteleinfuhren aus dem Ausland nach Westdeutschland praktisch ganz durch die USA und das Vereinigte Königreich finanziert. Bei den Lieferungen handelte es sich in der Hauptsache um Getreide, Ölsaaten und Zucker. Ohne diese Hilfe wäre ein völliger Zusammenbruch der Nahrungsmittelversorgung der Städte unvermeidlich gewesen. Mit dem allmählichen Ingangkommen eines Außenhandels der Bundesrepublik und dem Ansteigen der ernährungswirtschaftlichen Einfuhren trat die Auslandshilfe immer mehr zurück.

Der relative Anteil der Einfuhr von Gütern der Ernährungswirtschaft (einschließlich der Genußmittel) an dem Wert der Gesamteinfuhr der Bundesrepublik lag in den letzten Jahren bei etwa einem Drittel. Annähernd drei Viertel des Wertes der Einfuhr von Nahrungsmitteln (ohne Genußmittel) entfallen auf pflanzliche Erzeugnisse.

Die Zusammensetzung des Wertes der Einfuhren von Gütern der Ernährungswirtschaft nach ihrer Herkunft aus verschiedenen Ländergruppen zeigt von Jahr zu Jahr gewisse Schwankungen, im ganzen jedoch keine wesentliche Verschiebung.

Im Wirtschaftsjahr 1957/58 stammten vom Gesamtwert der Einfuhr von Gütern der Ernährungswirtschaft 27% aus den EWG-Ländern und 41% aus den Ländern der geplanten Freihandelszone.

Tabelle 16

HERKUNFT DER ERNÄHRUNGSWIRTSCHAFTLICHEN EINFUHR[1]

Wirtschafts-jahr	Ernährungswirtschaftliche Güter					
	insgesamt Mill. DM	darunter (in %)				
		Freie Dollar-Länder	EZU-Raum	EWG-Raum[2]	Frei-handels-zone[3]	übrige Verrechn.-Länder
1950/51	5.591	*26*	*62*	*30*	*45*	*12*
1951/52	6.174	*28*	*59*	*24*	*38*	*19*
1952/53	5.786	*28*	*57*	*26*	*42*	*15*
1953/54	6.313	*23*	*55*	*27*	*40*	*21*
1954/55	7.576	*22*	*56*	*24*	*38*	*22*
1955/56	8.034	*26*	*55*	*27*	*41*	*18*
1956/57	9.979	*31*	*50*	*23*	*36*	*19*
1957/58	9.764	*27*	*53*	*27*	*41*	*19*

[1] Nach Herstellungsländern. Zuordnung der Länder nach dem Stand vom Mai 1959.

[2] Mutterländer einschließlich der Übersee-Gebiete. — [3] Mutterländer.

Quelle: Berechnungen des Bundesministeriums für Ernährung, Landwirtschaft und Forsten auf Grund von Unterlagen des Statistischen Bundesamts.

Der Verbrauch von Nahrungsmitteln

Die Versorgung mit Nahrungsmitteln war in den ersten Jahren nach dem Zusammenbruch für den größten Teil der Bevölkerung Westdeutschlands völlig unzureichend. Die Verhältnisse dieser Zeit sind bereits in den früheren Ausgaben von „Deutschland heute“ behandelt worden[1].

[1] Vergleiche die vierte Auflage dieses Buches, 1955, Seite 201—211.

BEVÖLKERUNG UND NAHRUNGSMITTELVERBRAUCH

Durchschnitt 1935/38 = 100

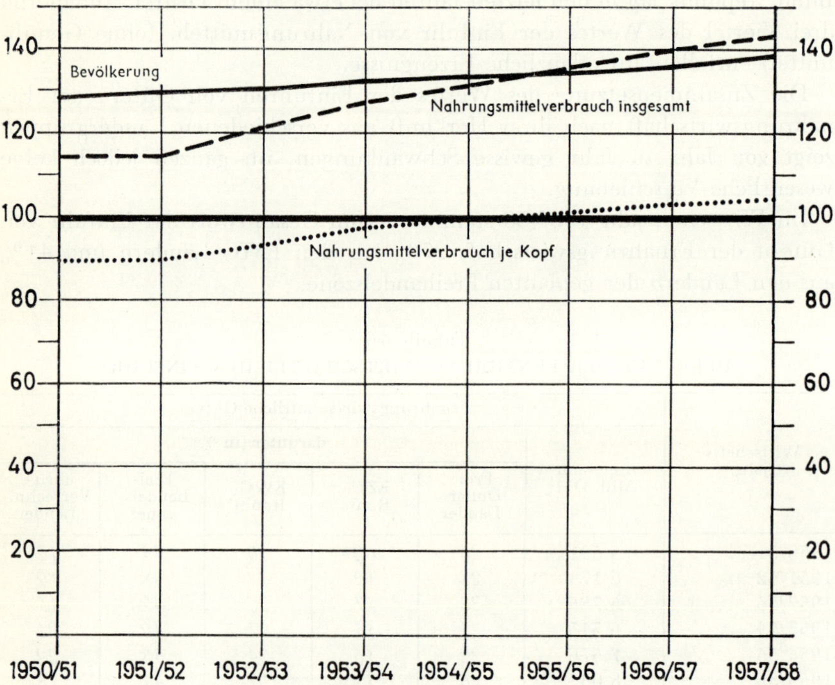

Quelle: Bundesministerium für Ernährung, Landwirtschaft und Forsten.

Mit der allmählichen Verbesserung der Versorgungslage durch die Steigerung der Erzeugung und Erhöhung der Einfuhren nach der Währungsreform wurde es zu Beginn des Jahres 1950 möglich, die Rationierung der Lebensmittel und damit die Zwangbewirtschaftung der landwirtschaftlichen Erzeugnisse aufzuheben. Der durchschnittliche Verbrauch von Nahrungsmitteln je Kopf der Gesamtbevölkerung hat jedoch erst im Wirtschaftsjahr 1955/56 die Vorkriegshöhe wieder erreicht und sie seitdem etwas überschritten. Erheblich stärker als der Durchschnittsverbrauch ist der gesamte Nahrungsverbrauch gegenüber der Vorkriegszeit infolge der außerordentlichen Zunahme der Bevölkerung durch den Zustrom von Flüchtlingen und Vertriebenen nach dem Krieg gestiegen.

Die Entwicklung des Verbrauchs bei den einzelnen Nahrungsmitteln ist zum Teil sehr unterschiedlich verlaufen. Sie läßt wesentliche Änderungen in der Zusammensetzung des Nahrungsverbrauchs und der Verzehrsgewohnheiten erkennen.

Der Verbrauch von Getreideerzeugnissen im ganzen und von Kartoffeln, der im Krieg und den ersten Nachkriegsjahren über Vorkriegshöhe gelegen hatte, geht seitdem laufend zurück. Der Zuckerverbrauch hat seit einigen

Tabelle 17

NAHRUNGSMITTELVERBRAUCH JE EINWOHNER UND JAHR[1]

kg

Erzeugnis	Ø 1935/38	1948/49	1956/57	1957/58	1957/58 ± % gegen 1935/38	1957/58 ± % gegen 1948/49
Getreideerzeugnisse insgesamt in Mehlwert	110,5	126,8	91,7	89,5	— *19,0*	— *29,4*
darunter:						
Weizenmehl	61,0	80,2	61,1	60,1	— *1,5*	— *25,1*
Roggenmehl	47,0	38,0	27,4	26,0	— *44,7*	— *31,6*
Hülsenfrüchte	2,3	3,2	1,7	1,5	— *34,8*	— *53,1*
Kartoffeln	176,0	224,0	152,0	150,0	— *14,8*	— *33,0*
Zucker (Weißzucker)	25,5	19,9	28,3	28,0	+ *9,8*	+ *14,1*
Gemüse	51,9	60,8	45,3	48,9	— *5,8*	— *19,6*
Frischobst	36,3	22,3	56,6	28,8	— *20,7*	+ *29,1*
Trockenobst	1,7	1,9	2,0	2,5	+ *47,1*	+ *31,6*
Südfrüchte	5,7	1,5	13,6	18,8	+*229,9*	+*1.153,3*
Fleisch (ohne Fett)	52,8	18,6	50,1	52,6	— *0,4*	+ *182,6*
darunter:						
Rindfleisch	14,8	6,8	15,6	16,0	+ *8,1*	+ *135,3*
Kalbfleisch	29,2	7,3	27,1	28,8	— *1,4*	+ *294,5*
Fische (Filetgewicht)	6,8	9,4	6,9	6,9	+ *1,5*	— *26,6*
Vollmilch[2]	128,4	71,0	127,3	127,8	— *0,5*	+ *80,0*
Käse	3,5	2,7	4,3	4,3	+ *22,9*	+ *59,3*
Eier und Eiprodukte	7,4	2,5	11,3	11,6	+ *56,8*	+ *364,0*
Fette insgesamt (Reinfett)	21,0	9,8	25,4	25,2	+ *20,0*	+ *157,1*
davon:						
Butter	6,7	3,7	5,9	6,1	— *9,0*	+ *64,9*
Schlachtfette	6,3	2,5	5,8	5,8	— *7,9*	+ *132,0*
pflanzl. Öle u. Fette	8,0	3,6	13,7	13,3	+ *66,3*	+ *269,4*

[1] Einschließlich von Berlin(West).

[2] Einschließlich von Sahne und Kondensmilch in Milchwert.

Quelle: Bundesministerium für Ernährung, Landwirtschaft und Forsten.

NAHRUNGSVERBRAUCH JE KOPF
Durchschnitt 1935/38 = 100

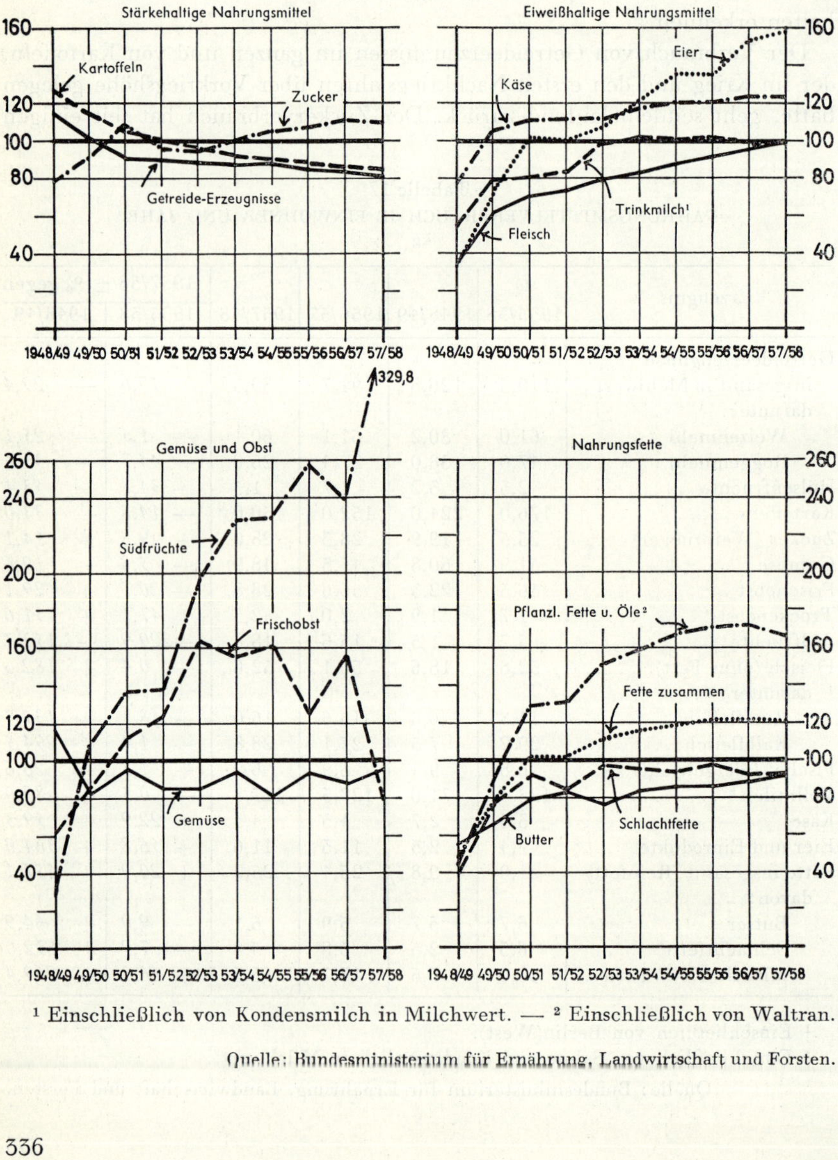

[1] Einschließlich von Kondensmilch in Milchwert. — [2] Einschließlich von Waltran.

Quelle: Bundesministerium für Ernährung, Landwirtschaft und Forsten.

Ernst-Reuter-Siedlung in Berlin: Häuser im Rahmen des Sozialen Wohnungsbaues

Die Hauptverwaltung der Deutschen Bundesbahn in Frankfurt am Main

HAUPTSTADT BERLIN

Zehngeschossiges Wohnhaus

Die Kongreßhalle

Jahren den Vorkriegsdurchschnitt überschritten und wird voraussichtlich noch weiterhin etwas ansteigen.

Der Verbrauch von Gemüse liegt etwas niedriger als vor dem Kriege. Dabei muß jedoch die Umstellung auf einen stärkeren Verzehr von sogenanntem Feingemüse berücksichtigt werden. Der Obstverbrauch ist im ganzen erheblich angestiegen, zeigt jedoch, bedingt durch die wechselnden Ernten, zum Teil beträchtliche Schwankungen. Der Verbrauch von Südfrüchten ist steil angestiegen.

Unter den eiweißhaltigen Nahrungsmitteln hat der Fleischverbrauch, der in den ersten Nachkriegsjahren besonders stark gesunken war, erst im Wirt-

NAHRUNGSVERBRAUCH AUS INLANDSERZEUGUNG UND AUS EINFUHR

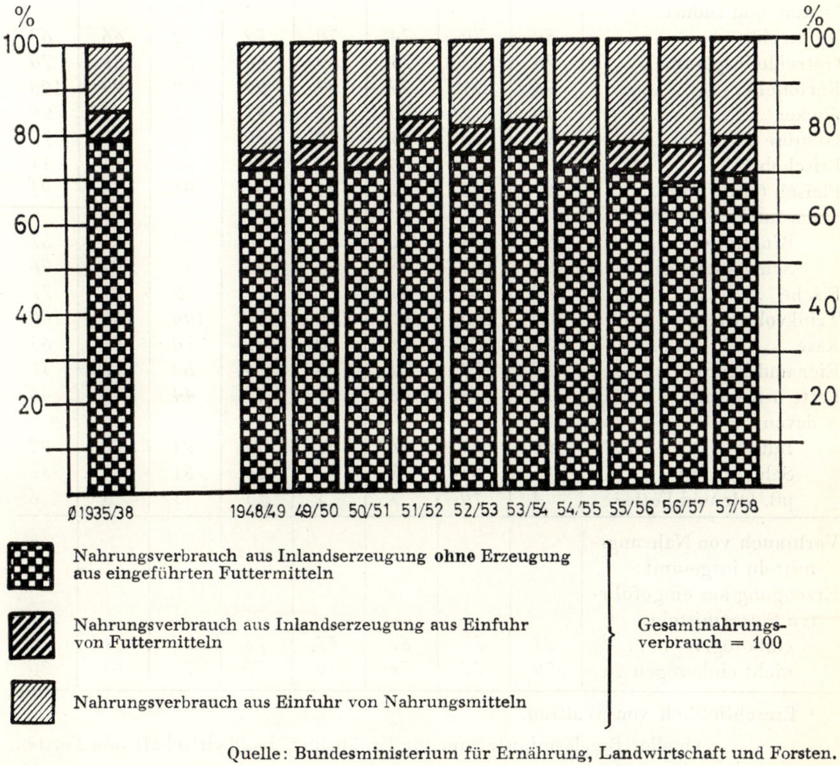

Quelle: Bundesministerium für Ernährung, Landwirtschaft und Forsten.

schaftsjahr 1957/58 die Vorkriegshöhe wieder erreicht; eine weitere Erhöhung ist anzunehmen. Der Verbrauch von Käse und von Eiern hat den Vorkriegsdurchschnitt schon verhältnismäßig hoch überschritten. Dabei ist der Eierverbrauch besonders stark angestiegen und dürfte sich noch weiter

Tabelle 18

ANTEIL DES VERBRAUCHS AUS INLANDSERZEUGUNG AM GESAMTVERBRAUCH WICHTIGER NAHRUNGS- UND FUTTERMITTEL

%

	1935/36 bis 1937/38	1948/49 bis 1950/51	1951/52 bis 1953/54	1954/55 bis 1956/57	1954/55	1955/56	1956/57	1957/58
Weizen	65	44	57	50	44	54	53	58
Roggen	89	90	95	95	87	98	99	98
Futter- und Industriegetreide	80	70	74	70	72	72	66	67
Getreide insgesamt	78	65	73	69	66	72	68	70
Kartoffeln	96	99	99	99	99	99	99	100
Zucker	50	57	80	77	85	81	68	90
Gemüse	91	90	85	79	79	81	77	77
Frischobst	98	87	86	79	88	68	81	55
Fleisch (ohne Fett)	93	92	95	90	93	91	88	91
darunter:								
Rindfleisch	97	88	92	84	90	84	80	87
Schweinefleisch	90	94	98	96	96	97	94	96
Fische	100	66	85	77	77	79	75	77
Trinkvollmilch	100	100	100	100	100	100	100	100
Käse	87	83	76	70	72	70	67	63
Eier und Eiprodukte	89	74	71	60	64	60	56	57
Fette insgesamt	58	48	46	43	43	44	43	46
davon:								
Butter	96	94	96	91	92	93	88	92
Schlachtfette	86	63	77	82	80	81	84	87
pfl. Öle und Fette [1]	4	10	7	5	5	5	5	6
Verbrauch von Nahrungsmitteln insgesamt:								
Erzeugung aus eingeführten Futtermitteln								
einbezogen	85	77	82	77	78	77	76	78
nicht einbezogen	79	72	76	70	72	71	68	70

[1] Einschließlich von Waltran.

Quelle: Bundesministerium für Ernährung, Landwirtschaft und Forsten.

ausdehnen. Der Verbrauch von Trinkmilch (einschließlich von Rahm und Kondensmilch) hat die Vorkriegshöhe wieder erreicht und zeigt seitdem keine weitere Erhöhung.

Der Verbrauch von Fetten insgesamt liegt seit 1954/55 um etwa 20% über dem Vorkriegsdurchschnitt. Diese Erhöhung ist allein auf eine starke Zunahme des Verzehrs von Margarine und sonstigen pflanzlichen Fetten zurückzuführen. Der Verbrauch von Butter und von Schlachtfetten hingegen liegt noch unter dem Vorkriegsdurchschnitt.

Diese Entwicklung in der Zusammensetzung der Ernährung in Westdeutschland nach dem Kriege entspricht in der Tendenz der in fast allen Industrieländern.

Anteil der Eigenerzeugung am Nahrungsverbrauch

Der Anteil des Verbrauchs aus Eigenerzeugung am Gesamtverbrauch von Nahrungsmitteln betrug im Durchschnitt der letzten Vorkriegsjahre für das Gebiet der heutigen Bundesrepublik ohne die Erzeugung aus eingeführten Futtermitteln 79%. In den zehn Wirtschaftsjahren von 1948/49 bis 1957/58 schwankte der Anteil zwischen 68 und 78%, ohne daß eine eindeutige Tendenz zu einer Zunahme oder Abnahme festzustellen wäre.

Bei den einzelnen Erzeugnissen liegen die Anteile zum Teil sehr verschieden und zeigen Abweichungen von der Gesamtentwicklung.

Maßnahmen zur Förderung der Land- und Ernährungswirtschaft — Marshallplanhilfe

Zu dem raschen Anstieg der landwirtschaftlichen Erzeugung in den ersten Jahren nach der Währungsreform hat die Bereitstellung von ERP-Gegenwertmitteln als Starthilfe entscheidend beigetragen. Die Mittel wurden in Form von Krediten an einzelne Landwirte vor allem zur Verbesserung der Produktionsgrundlagen und als Zuschüsse zu allgemeinen Förderungsmaßnahmen für den Ausbau des landwirtschaftlichen Schulwesens und der Wirtschaftsberatung, für Forschungsaufträge und ähnliche Zwecke gegeben. Auch für die Wiederaufnahme der Flurbereinigung wurden ERP-Mittel verwendet. Die Zuteilung der Mittel wird noch fortgesetzt. Bis zum Ende des Haushaltsjahres 1958 ist insgesamt über eine Milliarde DM aus ERP-Mitteln für die Landwirtschaft zur Verfügung gestellt worden.

Gesetze zur Marktordnung

Für die landwirtschaftlichen Grunderzeugnisse wurden 1950 und 1951 von der Bundesregierung vier Marktordnungsgesetze erlassen, und zwar das

Gesetz über den Verkehr mit Getreide und Futtermitteln;
Gesetz über den Verkehr mit Milch, Milcherzeugnissen und Fetten;
Gesetz über den Verkehr mit Zucker;
Gesetz über den Verkehr mit Vieh und Fleisch.

Die Gesetze stellen ein in sich geschlossenes System dar. Sie sollen dazu dienen, im Rahmen der Sozialen Marktwirtschaft der Landwirtschaft den Absatz ihrer Erzeugnisse und den Verbrauchern die Versorgung mit Nahrungsmitteln zu angemessenen Preisen weitgehend zu sichern. Für die Durchführung dieser Aufgaben bedient die Bundesregierung sich der Einfuhr- und Vorratsstellen.

Als Grundlage für die Verbesserung der Qualität der landwirtschaftlichen Erzeugnisse wurde im Jahre 1951 das Handelsklassengesetz geschaffen. Durch Steigerung der Güte der Waren soll der Absatz gefördert und zugleich dem Verbraucher Gewähr für die Qualität der Erzeugnisse gegeben werden.

Agrarprogramm der Bundesregierung von 1953

Die zunehmende handelspolitische Verflechtung und die Vorbereitung der westdeutschen Landwirtschaft auf einen größeren europäischen Agrarmarkt haben die Bundesregierung veranlaßt, in den Mittelpunkt ihres im Oktober 1953 verkündeten Agrarprogrammes eine wesentliche Verstärkung der Maßnahmen zur Erhöhung der Leistungs- und Wettbewerbsfähigkeit sowie zur Steigerung der Produktivität der Betriebe zu stellen. Da in vielen Mittel- und Kleinbetrieben den Bestrebungen zur Hebung der Produktivität ungünstige strukturelle Verhältnisse entgegenstehen, ist eine durchgreifende Verbesserung der Agrarstruktur eingeleitet worden. Es handelt sich dabei vor allem um die Zusammenlegung der zersplitterten Fluren, die Aufstockung zu kleiner Betriebe, die Aussiedlung aus zu enger Dorflage, die Modernisierung der Gebäude, die rechtzeitige Hofübergabe durch entsprechende Altersversorgung, die Eingliederung bäuerlicher Vertriebener und Flüchtlinge und wasserwirtschaftliche Maßnahmen.

Das Landwirtschaftsgesetz von 1955

Nach langen Vorarbeiten wurde im September 1955 das vom Bundestag einstimmig angenommene Landwirtschaftsgesetz erlassen. § 1 des Gesetzes lautet:

Um der Landwirtschaft die Teilnahme an der fortschreitenden Entwicklung der deutschen Volkswirtschaft und um der Bevölkerung die bestmögliche Versorgung mit Ernährungsgütern zu sichern, ist die Landwirtschaft mit den Mitteln der allgemeinen Wirtschafts- und Agrarpolitik — insbesondere der Handels-, Steuer-, Kredit- und Preispolitik — in den Stand zu setzen, die für sie bestehenden naturbedingten und wirtschaftlichen Nachteile gegenüber anderen Wirtschaftsbereichen auszugleichen und ihre Produktivität zu steigern. Damit soll gleichzeitig die soziale Lage der in der Landwirtschaft tätigen Menschen an die vergleichbarer Berufsgruppen angeglichen werden.

Das Gesetz bestimmt, daß die Bundesregierung jährlich dem Bundestag einen Bericht über die Lage der Landwirtschaft vorzulegen hat. Zu diesem sind vor allem die Buchführungsergebnisse landwirtschaftlicher Betriebe heranzuziehen, um die unterschiedlichen Verhältnisse in den verschiedenen Bodennutzungssystemen und Betriebsgrößen aufzuzeigen. Dabei soll gleichzeitig dargestellt werden, wie weit in den landwirtschaftlichen Betrieben ein Lohn, der den Löhnen vergleichbarer Berufsgruppen entspricht, ein Entgelt für die Tätigkeit des Betriebsleiters und eine angemessene Verzinsung des für den Betrieb notwendigen Kapitals erreicht worden sind. Zusammen mit diesem Bericht, dem sogenannten „Grünen Bericht", hat die Bundesregierung einen Plan, den sogenannten „Grünen Plan", vorzulegen, in dem sie Maßnahmen zur Verbesserung des Verhältnisses zwischen Aufwand und Ertrag vorschlägt.

Grüner Bericht und Grüner Plan

Die bis jetzt aufgestellten „Grünen Berichte" — im Februar 1959 wurde der vierte Bericht vorgelegt — lassen zum Teil sehr starke Unterschiede der Einkommensverhältnisse der Betriebe erkennen. Sie sind bedingt durch die natürlichen Gegebenheiten und die allgemeinen wirtschaftlichen Bedingungen, durch Bodennutzung und Betriebsgröße.

Bei den Maßnahmen der „Grünen Pläne" handelt es sich im allgemeinen nicht um grundsätzlich neue Maßnahmen, sondern mehr um eine Verstärkung in der einen oder anderen Richtung. In Anbetracht der Tatsache, daß ein großer Teil der landwirtschaftlichen Betriebe des Bundesgebiets durch ungünstige strukturelle Produktionsbedingungen benachteiligt ist, wird in den „Grünen Plänen" — vornehmlich seit dem vierten Plan —

besonderes Gewicht auf die Maßnahmen zur Verbesserung der Agrarstruktur durch Flurbereinigung, Aussiedlung aus enger Dorflage und Aufstockung zu kleiner Betriebe gelegt. Damit soll die deutsche Landwirtschaft gleichzeitig für einen schärferen Wettbewerb im Gemeinsamen Markt gestärkt werden.

II. FORST- UND HOLZWIRTSCHAFT

Der Krieg setzte auch dem Wald hart zu. Das Ende des Krieges brachte für Deutschland zunächst den Verlust von 2.950.000 ha wertvollen Waldbesitzes in den Gebieten östlich der Oder-Neiße-Linie. In den Forsten der sogenannten DDR (ebenfalls 2.950.000 ha) wurde bisher ein unverantwortlicher Raubbau getrieben.

Die Ernteerträge des Waldes reifen im Durchschnitt erst in sechzig bis einhundertzwanzig Jahren heran. Daher gilt für die Forstwirtschaft als Grundsatz die unbedingte Einhaltung der *Nachhaltigkeit der Nutzung*. Bereits seit 1935 wurde gegen diesen Grundsatz, ohne den eine geordnete Forstwirtschaft nicht denkbar ist, verstoßen. Im Zuge der Autarkiebestrebungen hatte man vom Forstwirtschaftsjahr (Fwj.) 1935 an den Einschlag auf 150% des Nachhalts-Hiebsatzes festgesetzt. Der Mehreinschlag betrug für das Gebiet der Bundesrepublik bis zum Jahr 1945 insgesamt etwa 110 Millionen Festmeter (fm.)

In den ersten Nachkriegsjahren traten neue große Forderungen an die Forstwirtschaft heran. Sie mußte

1. die einheimische Wirtschaft, an die gesteigerte Anforderungen für den Wiederaufbau herantraten, mit Nutzholz versorgen,
2. den Hausbrandbedarf wegen des Mangels an Kohlen vorwiegend mit Holz befriedigen und
3. umfangreiche Holzmengen in der Britischen und Französischen Besatzungszone für die sogenannten Direktoperationen und schließlich auch in der Amerikanischen Zone für erhöhte Exporte von Schnittholz nach dem Vereinigten Königreich bereitstellen.

Deutschland hatte 1938 je Kopf der Bevölkerung einen Holzbedarf von 1,03 fm. Die fehlenden Nutzholzmengen konnten im eigenen Land nicht voll aufgebracht werden. So bedurfte es zum Beispiel besonderer Anstrengungen, das für die Kohlenförderung notwendige Grubenholz zu beschaffen. Vor dem Krieg wurde es in der Hauptsache in den ausgedehnten Kiefernbeständen östlich der Elbe eingeschlagen. Ebenso schwierig war die Beschaffung des Bauholzes für die im Ruhrgebiet zu schaffenden Wohnungen für Bergarbeiter. Die fast ausschließliche Verwendung von Holz für *Hausbrandzwecke* führte 1945 bis 1949 zur Vergeudung wertvollen Nutzholzes, das für den Wiederaufbau verloren ging. In diesen Jahren sind insgesamt 85 Millionen fm Holz verbrannt worden. Davon wären mindestens zwei Drittel als Nutzholz verwertbar gewesen. Nicht minder schwer hat die deutsche Forstwirtschaft die Entnahme von 5.785.000 fm Nutzholz in der Britischen Zone und von 11.562.000 fm Nutzholz in der Französischen Zone getroffen. Dieses Holz wurde teils als Reparationsleistung, teils zur Devisenbeschaffung durch die Besatzungsmächte eingeschlagen. Der Einschlag wurde meist nicht nach den Grundsätzen einer geordneten Forstwirtschaft vorgenommen. Aus der Amerikanischen Besatzungszone mußten in den Jahren 1948 bis 1950: 1.147.000 cbm Schnittholz für Exportzwecke nach dem Vereinigten Königreich bereitgestellt werden; das entspricht rund 1.630.000 fm Rundholz.

Die negative Bilanz der Kriegs- und Nachkriegsjahre war zunächst:

1. eine ausgedehnte Borkenkäfer-Katastrophe in den Fichtengebieten. Ihr fielen mehr als 20 Millionen fm Nutzholz zum Opfer. Die räumliche Ordnung des Waldes wurde durch sie erheblich gestört;
2. eine Minderung des stehenden Vorratskapitals des Waldes an Holz um mehr als 200 Millionen fm;
3. eine dadurch bedingte erhebliche Reduzierung des Zuwachses;
4. ein starkes Anwachsen der Kahlflächen bis auf das Zehnfache der Normalfläche;
5. eine weitgehende Vernachlässigung der Wald- und Bestandspflege.

*

Die Normalisierung der Forstwirtschaft begann schrittweise. Zunächst wurde im Jahre 1948 in Verhandlungen mit den Besatzungsmächten der sogenannte *Long-term-Plan* aufgestellt. Nach diesem sollte innerhalb eines Übergangszeitraumes von fünf Jahren der damals im Wege einer *Zwangsumlage* angeordnete weit überhöhte Einschlag auf den Nachhalts-Hiebsatz zurückgeführt werden. Gleichlaufend hiermit wurde angestrebt, die für die Bedarfsdeckung der Wirtschaft fehlende Nutzholzmenge durch allmählich steigende Importe aus den Ländern mit Holzüberschuß zu beschaffen. Notwendige Voraussetzung hierfür war die Einstellung der Holzeinschläge durch

Tabelle 19
HIEBSATZ, EINSCHLAGSPROGRAMM UND ISTEINSCHLAG DER FORSTEN IN DER BUNDESREPUBLIK
(alle Besitzarten)

Forstwirtschaftsjahr (1.10. bis 30.9.)	Nachhaltiger Hiebsatz		Einschlagprogramm		Isteinschlag	
	insgesamt in 1.000 fm mit Rinde [1]	Festmeter je ha Holzbodenfläche [1,2]	1.000 fm mit Rinde [3]	1.000 fm mit Rinde [4]	Prozent des Einschlagprogramms [5]	Festmeter m. R. je ha Holzbodenfläche
1946 . . .	18.800	2,8		47.487	*106*	7,0
1947 . . .	18.800	2,8		51.260	*100*	7,5
1948 . . .	18.800	2,8		44.333	*102*	6,5
1949 . . .	18.800	2,8		35.784	*102*	5,2
1950 . . .	18.800	2,8	29.000	29.842	*102*	4,4
1951 . . .	18.800	2,8	25.708	29.735	*114*	4,4
1952 . . .	18.800	2,8	22.147	28.277	*126*	4,1
1953 . . .	20.700	3,1	21.940	25.262	*113*	3,7
1954 . . .	20.700	3,1	20.519	25.061	*120*	3,7
1955 . . .	21.400	3,2	21.395	29.101	*134*	4,3
1956 . . .	22.800	3,4	22.700	24.880	*108*	3,6
1957 . . .	23.000	3,4	22.924	26.286	*113*	3,9
1958 . . .	23.370	3,4	23.450			
1959 . . .	23.370	3,4	25.264			

[1] Bis 1957 ohne Saarland.

[2] Holzbodenflächen der Forsten aller Besitzgrößen und Besitzarten nach der Forsterhebung 1948 (mit Hamburg und Bremen) und der Forsterhebung 1953 im Saarland mit insgesamt 6.817.000 ha.

[3] Bis 1958 ohne Saarland.

[4] Einschließlich Besatzungseinschlag (Direktoperationen und deutscher Einschlag für Exportauflagen) in den Jahren 1946 bis 1949. Ohne den Einschlag der Privatforsten im Saarland.

[5] 1946 bis 1949 nur britisch-amerikanisches Besatzungsgebiet (Bizone); 1950 bis 1958 Bundesgebiet ohne Saarland.

Quelle: Bundesministerium für Ernährung, Landwirtschaft und Forsten.

die Besatzungsmächte in der Französischen und Britischen Zone und der Schnittholzexporte nach dem Vereinigten Königreich aus der Amerikanischen Zone.

Die Einfuhr von Nutzholz wurde erst nach der Währungsreform möglich. Die Holzumlagen, die seit 1936 angeordnet waren, kamen mit dem 30.9.1949 in Wegfall. Mit dem Beginn des Forstwirtschaftsjahres 1950[1]

[1] 1.10.1949 bis 30.9.1950.

Tabelle 20

DIE HOLZEINFUHR DER BUNDESREPUBLIK

Sorten	Forstwirtschaftsjahr (1.10. bis 30.9.)								
	1950	1951	1952	1953	1954	1955	1956	1957	1958
	1.000 Festmeter m. R.								
Stammholz	255	420	490	760	1.260	1.990	1.830	2.040	1.900
Grubenholz	45	90	680	560	650	1.500	1.390	1.140	1.200
Faserholz	550	1.050	1.410	970	1.490	2.190	2.020	1.710	1.400
Schnittholz und Schwellen....	920	1.200	2.390	3.130	3.070	5.250	4.010	4.410	4.500
Holzmasse, Zellstoff, Papier und Waren daraus.......	1.550	1.940	1.760	2.150	3.110	3.940	3.920	4.630	4.900
Sperrholz, Furniere, Faserplatten, Spanplatten und andere Halb- und Fertigwaren aus Holz einschließlich von Holzkohle ...	60	150	160	250	260	320	380	450	550
Nutzholz Summe	3.380	4.850	6.890	7.820	9.840	15.190	13.550	14.380	14.450
Brennholz und Abfälle	20	10	110	100	280	110	200	210	250
Im ganzen	3.400	4.860	7.000	7.920	10.120	15.300	13.750	14.590	14.700

Quelle: Bundesministerium für Ernährung, Landwirtschaft und Forsten.

wurde das jährliche Programm des Holzeinschlags mit den Landesforstverwaltungen als den Repräsentanten des gesamten Waldbesitzes der Länder frei vereinbart. Der Waldbesitz hat die so festgesetzten Einschlagsprogramme in allen darauf folgenden Jahren nicht nur erfüllt, sondern er hat trotz den Übernutzungen während der voraufgegangenen sechzehn Jahre zusätzliche Holzmengen in erheblichem Umfang der Wirtschaft zur Verfügung gestellt.

Grundlage des Einschlagsprogramms ist der *planmäßige periodische Nachhalts-Hiebsatz*, der auf der Grundlage des Zuwachses der Forsten basiert. Der Nachhalts-Hiebsatz steigt allmählich an und hat seinen Kulminationspunkt noch nicht erreicht. Er liegt augenblicklich unter der Zuwachsleistung, weil die jüngeren und mittelalten Altersklassen noch überwiegen und die während der Jahre 1935 bis 1950 erfolgten Eingriffe in das Holzvorratskapital des Waldes erst aufgefüllt werden müssen. Dann erst wird eine optimale Nutzung wieder möglich sein.

Die Bundesrepublik — ein Holzeinfuhrland

Deutschland ist trotz seinen reichen Waldbeständen seit vielen Jahrzehnten ein Holzeinfuhrland. Etwa ein Drittel seines Holzbedarfs mußte früher und muß auch heute wieder durch Importe gedeckt werden. Nach 1945 kam die *Holzeinfuhr* nur langsam in Gang. Von 1950 an zeigt sie rasch steigende Zahlen (Tabelle 20). Das Hauptkontingent der Einfuhren entfällt auf Nadelschnittholz, das vornehmlich aus Österreich, Schweden, Finnland und der Sowjetunion geliefert wird. Aber auch Nadelfaserholz, der wichtigste Rohstoff für die deutsche Zellstoff- und Papierindustrie, und Nadelgrubenholz werden in beachtlichen Mengen eingeführt. Sie kommen in der Hauptsache aus Finnland, Schweden und Österreich. Früher hat Deutschland große Holzmengen aus Rußland bezogen. Die Einfuhr von dort hat erst seit 1957 wieder einen bemerkenswerten Umfang. Im Handelsvertrag mit der Sowjetunion von 1957 entfallen auf das Holzkontingent verschiedener Sorten etwa 20% des Gesamtwertes.

In den letzten Jahren hat auch die Einfuhr von Laubstammholz aus Übersee zur Sperrholz- und Furnierherstellung ein bedeutendes Volumen erreicht. Dadurch wurde das heimische Buchenstammholz, das in seinen besseren Qualitäten bisher vornehmlich der Sperrholzerzeugung diente, weitgehend verdrängt.

Der *Export* von Rohholz aus der Bundesrepublik ist wegen der unzureichenden Eigenversorgung nur mit besonderer Genehmigung möglich und hat einen sehr beschränkten Umfang. Der Ausfuhr von Produkten der holzbe- und verarbeitenden Industrie kommt größere Bedeutung zu.

Die Preisentwicklung auf dem Holzmarkt

Die Preise für Rohholz waren abweichend vom allgemeinen Preisstopp bereits seit 1934 gebunden. Nach Aufhebung der Preisbestimmungen im Juli 1948 erwies es sich bald als notwendig, für das nur in beschränktem Umfang aus heimischer Erzeugung zur Verfügung stehende Rohholz Richt-

Tabelle 21

PREISINDEXZIFFERN[1] FÜR ROH- UND NADELSCHNITTHOLZ

Forstwirtschaftsjahr 1954 = 100

Erzeugnis	Forstwirtschaftsjahr (Oktober bis September)								
	1950	1951	1952	1953	1954	1955	1956	1957	1958
Rohholz aus Staatsforsten[2]	58	67	97	105	100	130	119	124	114
Nadelschnittholz[3]	71	82	120	110	100	123	119	117	116

[1] Bundesdurchschnitt (Bundesrepublik Deutschland ohne Saarland).

[2] Die Jahresdurchschnitte wurden besonders berechnet durch Wägung der Monatsmeßziffern für die einzelnen Güte- bzw. Stärkeklassen mit den monatlichen Verkaufsmengen des Forstwirtschaftsjahres 1954.

[3] Aus dem Index der Erzeugerpreise industrieller Produkte; Originalbasis 1950 = 100, umbasiert auf Forstwirtschaftsjahr 1954 = 100.

Quelle: Statistisches Bundesamt.

preise festzusetzen. Auch für das wichtigste Produkt der nächsten Ablaufstufe, das Schnittholz, wurden Richtpreise bekanntgegeben. Die endgültige Freigabe der Rohholzpreise erfolgte am 17.5.1952; die Schnittholzpreise waren bereits am 1.10.1951 freigegeben worden.

Der Aufhebung der Preisbindungen für Rohholz folgte eine sprunghafte Anpassung des innerdeutschen Preisniveaus an das des europäischen Holzmarktes. In den Jahren nach 1952 war die Preisbewegung zum Teil recht unausgeglichen. In den letzten drei Jahren, bedingt durch den stimulierenden Einfluß steigender Einfuhren, hat sich auf dem heimischen Holzmarkt eine allmähliche Beruhigung der Preisentwicklung mit rückläufiger Tendenz angebahnt. Damit folgt der in starkem Maße von Einfuhr abhängige deutsche Holzmarkt der auf dem Weltrohstoffmarkt seit mehr als einem Jahr zu beobachtenden Preisentwicklung, die durch fallende Frachtraten unterstützt wird. Auch Brennholz ist im Preis stärker zurückgegangen, da Hausbrandkohle ausreichend zur Verfügung steht und sich auch eine stärkere Umstellung auf Ölfeuerung und Elektrizität vollzieht.

In der *Sägeindustrie*, einer ausgesprochenen Mittelstandsindustrie mit überwiegend Familienbetrieben, hat sich im letzten Jahrzehnt neben einer Anpassung an die Rohholzgrundlage aus heimischer Erzeugung eine Strukturwandlung vollzogen. Um konkurrenzfähiger zu sein, hat eine große Zahl von Handels-Sägewerken ihrem Werk einen Verarbeitungsbetrieb angeschlossen. Als neuer Zweig der Holzbearbeitung hat sich die *Holzspanplatten-Industrie* günstig entwickelt. Ihre Produktion ist von 19.337 cbm im Forstwirtschaftsjahr 1951 auf 406.000 cbm im Forstwirtschaftsjahr 1958 gestiegen. Die zunehmende Verwendung von Holzplatten verschiedenster Art statt des früher gebräuchlichen Massivholzes hat eine tiefgreifende Umschichtung in der Holzwirtschaft zur Folge, die noch nicht zum Abschluß gekommen ist. Die Holzverwendung ist als Folge der Holzverknappung während und nach dem Krieg, die das Vordringen der Kunststoffe begünstigte, zurückgegangen. Holzveredelung und Holznormung, aber auch die seit einigen Jahren intensiv betriebene Werbung für den Rohstoff Holz, sollen dieser Entwicklung Einhalt gebieten oder verloren gegangene Verwendungsmöglichkeiten wieder zurückgewinnen.

*

Die *Forstpolitik* der Bundesregierung hat die Aufgabe, die überregionalen Ziele zu koordinieren und, soweit erforderlich, ihre Verwirklichung durch gesetzliche Bestimmungen sicherzustellen. Der Schwerpunkt der Forstpolitik liegt bei den Länderregierungen.

Soweit die forstliche Gesetzgebung beim Bund ressortiert, wurde das *Gesetz über forstliches Saat- und Pflanzgut* vom 25.9.1957 neu erlassen. Es enthält Bestimmungen über die Anerkennung von Waldbeständen, aus denen gewerbsmäßig forstliches Saatgut gesammelt werden darf, sowie über den Handel im Verkehr mit forstlichem Saat- und Pflanzgut.

Seit dem Zweiten Weltkrieg sind in den einzelnen Ländern Forstgesetze moderner Art entstanden. Sie enthalten nicht nur forstpolitische prohibitive Verbote zur Walderhaltung, sondern erstmals auch Bestimmungen, die der Sicherung der Leistungsfähigkeit und Ertragssteigerung des Waldes dienen.

Ein *Bundesforstgesetz* ist in Bearbeitung. Es soll die klassischen Forderungen an eine ordnungsgemäße Forstwirtschaft festlegen und eine unserer heutigen Auffassung entsprechende neue Regelung der gesetzlichen Zuständigkeit zwischen Bund und Ländern herbeiführen.

*

Eine der größten Aufgaben, denen die Forstwirtschaft sich nach dem Krieg gegenübergestellt sah, war die *Wiederaufforstung* der in den Kriegs- und ersten Nachkriegsjahren entstandenen *Kahlflächen.* In den Jahren 1949 bis 1957 wurden als Nachholarbeit insgesamt 700.000 ha wieder aufgeforstet. Dabei wurde der Begründung von Mischkulturen, soweit es die Umstände gestatteten, Rechnung getragen. Die *Aufforstung von Ödland* hatte in den Jahren 1949 bis 1958 einen Umfang von 65.873 ha. Noch heute gibt es in der Bundesrepublik fast 250.000 ha Ödland. Etwa die Hälfte davon ist aufforstungswürdig. Ein neues Problem bildet die Aufforstung der *Grenzertragsböden* aus bisher landwirtschaftlicher Nutzung. Die *Umwandlung des Niederwaldes*, der in der Bundesrepublik im Jahre 1945 noch 240.000 ha umfaßte, und des Mittelwaldes mit 95.000 ha ist weiter vorangetrieben worden. Die *Holzzucht außerhalb des Waldes* hat nach 1945 größere Ausdehnung gefunden. Im Vordergrund steht der Anbau der schnellwüchsigen Pappel.

Es ist ein Ziel der Forstpolitik, den *Zusammenschluß* kleiner Waldflächen zu größeren Wirtschaftseinheiten zu fördern und hierfür die gesetzlichen Grundlagen zu schaffen. Ansatzpunkte zur Verwirklichung dieses Zieles ergeben sich bei der Flurbereinigung und bei der Gründung von Waldwirtschafts-Gemeinschaften. Dabei soll jedem Eigentümer sein Wald erhalten bleiben und die gesunde Verbindung von Wald und Hof gefestigt werden.

Die *forstliche Wirtschaftsberatung* hat nach dem Kriege in größerem Umfang eingesetzt. Sie gilt entsprechend den starken Bindungen zur Landwirtschaft in erster Linie dem bäuerlichen Kleinwaldbesitz. Der Bund stellt für diesen Zweck zur Zeit jährlich 450.000 DM zur Verfügung. Er hat seit dem 15.10.1957 einen auf Bundesebene tätigen Berater für forsttechnische Fragen eingesetzt.

Naturschutz und Landschaftspflege gehören seit Jahrzehnten zu den besonderen Anliegen der Forstwirtschaft und werden mit namhaften Mitteln gefördert.

*

Forst- und Holzwirtschaft sind durch den Vertrag über die *Europäische Wirtschaftsgemeinschaft (EWG)* stark berührt. Sie stehen der durch ihn eingeleiteten Entwicklung des Abbaues der Kontingente und der Zollschranken positiv gegenüber. Die Bundesrepublik ist innerhalb der EWG nur mit 27,2% an der Gesamtwaldfläche beteiligt. Trotzdem steht sie mit 47% der Nadelholzproduktion und 52% der Nadelstammholzproduktion, dem wichtigsten Gebrauchssortiment, an erster Stelle. Mit jährlich mehr als 14 Millionen fm hat sie aber auch den größten Einfuhrbedarf.

*

Die Forstwirtschaft hatte noch bis vor wenigen Jahren ausreichend *Arbeitskräfte.* Gegenwärtig sind rund 30.000 ständige neben je etwa 40.000 regelmäßig Beschäftigten (mindestens 60 Arbeitstage im Jahr) und 40.000

nicht ständigen Arbeitskräften tätig. Jahrelange Vollbeschäftigung der gesamten Wirtschaft und der Sog der Großstadt, zum Teil aber auch die zögernde Angleichung der Löhne der Waldarbeiter an die vergleichbarer Industriearbeiter, führten dazu, daß seit einigen Jahren gebietsweise Mangel an Waldarbeitern auftritt. Neben einer rationellen Arbeitsgestaltung haben *Technisierung* und *Motorisierung* in den letzten Jahren in verstärktem Maße Eingang im Wald gefunden. Hier arbeitet mit Mitteln des Bundes und der Länder die *Technische Zentralstelle der deutschen Forstwirtschaft* (*TZF*). Darüber hinaus wird die Ausbildung der Waldarbeiter zu Facharbeitern in zum großen Teil neu errichteten oder erweiterten Waldarbeits-Schulen tatkräftig gefördert. Innerhalb des Bundesgebietes bestehen dreizehn Waldarbeits-Schulen.

Die *Bundesforschungsanstalt für Forst- und Holzwirtschaft* in Reinbek wurde seit Ende des Krieges reorganisiert und weiter ausgebaut. Dort kann im Rahmen der Universität Hamburg das *Studium der Holzwissenschaft* (Diplom-Holzwirt) und ein *Zusatzstudium für Weltforstwirtschaft* absolviert werden. Der Austausch mit dem Ausland und die Beratung der Entwicklungsländer spielten eine wichtige Rolle. Forstliche Experten, sowohl Wissenschaftler als auch Praktiker, wurden in den vergangenen Jahren in steigender Zahl auf Anforderung in außereuropäische Länder entsandt oder als Beauftragte der FAO verpflichtet. Sie haben mit dazu beigetragen, das frühere hohe Ansehen der deutschen Forstwirtschaft im Ausland wiederherzustellen.

*

Zur Forstwirtschaft gehört, wenn auch als materiell nicht bedeutender Nebenzweig, die *Jagd*. Sie erlebte in den ersten Nachkriegsjahren infolge der vollkommen ungeregelten Abschußverhältnisse, des übermäßigen Dranges von Angehörigen der Besatzung nach jagdlicher Betätigung und des Mangels auch nur der primitivsten Pflege des Wildstandes einen katastrophalen Niedergang. Während der Bestand aller sonstigen Wildarten erheblich reduziert wurde, nahm das Vorkommen des schwer zu bejagenden Schwarzwildes zu. Dadurch entstanden der Landwirtschaft teilweise sehr hohe Schäden an den für die Ernährung dringend benötigten Feldfrüchten. Erst der umfangreiche Einsatz deutscher Jagdkommandos konnte hier Abhilfe schaffen. Vom Jahre 1949 an wurde allmählich auch deutschen Jägern wieder die Ausübung der Jagd freigegeben. Die jagdlichen Verhältnisse normalisierten sich darauf rasch. Nach den mit den stationierten Truppen abgeschlossenen Verträgen liegt die Jagdhoheit seit Jahren wieder ganz in deutscher Hand. Für Angehörige der Stationierungstruppen bleiben ausreichende Abschußmöglichkeiten reserviert.

III. FISCHWIRTSCHAFT

Neben den Erträgen des Bodens gewannen die Erträge des Meeres seit Anfang des Jahrhunderts für die Ernährung der Bevölkerung Europas steigende Bedeutung. Auch die deutsche Seefischerei wurde zwischen den beiden Weltkriegen stark ausgebaut. Mit ihren Erträgen von rund 750.000 t stand sie 1938 an dritter Stelle in Europa. Von 1936 bis 1939 beteiligte sich Deutschland wieder am Walfang.

Der Zweite Weltkrieg brachte der deutschen Fischwirtschaft schwere Rückschläge sowohl bei der Fischdampferflotte selbst als auch an den Fischereihäfen und Verarbeitungsbetrieben.

Angesichts der katastrophalen Ernährungslage bemühten die Besatzungsmächte sich bald nach der Kapitulation, die Seefischerei wieder in Gang zu setzen. Die Standorte lagen überwiegend im Gebiet der Bundesrepublik (Bremerhaven, Cuxhaven, Hamburg, Kiel). Die USA und das Vereinigte Königreich stellten die ihnen zugesprochenen Beuteschiffe wieder zur Verfügung. Ende 1945 befanden sich bereits wieder 114 Fischdampfer und Heringslogger und über 1.500 Kutter in Fahrt. Der Einsatz der Fischereiflotte bereitete wegen des großen Mangels an Betriebsmitteln (Kohle, Treibstoff, Netze, Reparaturmaterial) ungewöhnliche Schwierigkeiten. Zudem war ein großer Teil der Fanggebiete minenverseucht.

Durch Verjüngung und Modernisierung der Fischdampferflotte gelang es, ab 1951 das Durchschnittsalter von 1938 zu unterschreiten. Seit 1945 stiegen

Tabelle 22

AUFTEILUNG DER FISCHEREIERTRÄGE NACH FANGGEBIETEN

Jahr	Fanggebiete insgesamt	Davon:				
		Nordsee[1]	Island	norweg. Küste[2]	Ostsee[3]	Sonstige Fanggebiete
	1.000 t	%	%	%	%	%
1938[4]	561	40,7	24,7	33,9	—	0,7
1948	381	59,9	10,5	15,6	14,0	—
1950	525	52,0	23,7	13,9	7,7	2,7
1952	638	51,1	25,1	14,5	5,4	3,9
1954	657	55,8	27,6	8,0	5,3	3,3
1956	695	46,5	15,3	14,0	5,9	18,3
1957	686	53,9	13,5	12,9	6,3	13,4

[1] Einschließlich des Kanals. — [2] Einschließlich der Barentsee und der Bäreninsel. — [3] Einschließlich des Kattegatts. — [4] Nur Fischdampfer.

Quelle: Statistisches Bundesamt.

Tabelle 23

FISCHVERSORGUNG[1]

1.000 t

Jahr	Anlandungen[2]	Einfuhr[3]	Ausfuhr[3]	Lieferungen an die sog. DDR und Ost-Berlin[3]	Verfügbar[3]	Davon für Futter	Davon für menschliche Ernährung
Ø1935/38	618	224	15	—	827	45	782
1948	381	287	—	.	668	10	658
1950	525	112	6	9	622	85	537
1952	638	96	22	12	700	122	578
1954	657	111	28	36	704	128	576
1956	695	127	44	33	745	127	618
1957	686	120	39	30	737	145	592

[1] Ohne Produktion der deutschen Binnenfischerei. — [2] Anlande-Gewicht auf Frischfisch-Basis. — [3] Be- und verarbeitete Fische nach dem jeweiligen Produktgewicht.

Quelle: Statistisches Bundesamt.

die Fischereierträge der Bundesrepublik von 80.000 t auf über 700.000 t. Sie haben damit die des Jahres 1938, auf das Bundesgebiet bezogen, überschritten. In der europäischen Seefischerei steht die Bundesrepublik wieder an dritter Stelle.

Der Wiederaufbau der Loggerflotte (Große Heringsfischerei) und der Kutterflotte machte gute Fortschritte. Für den Wiederaufbau der Fischereiflotte wurden von der Währungsreform bis zum Ende des Rechnungsjahres 1957 (31.3.1958) aus öffentlichen Mitteln Kredite in Höhe von rund 62 Millionen DM bereitgestellt und für rund 40 Millionen DM Bürgschaften geleistet. Bund und Küstenländer wendeten für die Förderung der Seefischerei auf den verschiedensten Gebieten rund 191 Millionen DM auf; davon nahezu 97 Millionen DM für Wiederinstandsetzung, Unterhaltung und Ausbau der Fischereihäfen.

Der Bund gab beträchtliche Mittel für die aus der ehemaligen Reichsanstalt für Fischerei hervorgegangene *Bundesforschungsanstalt für Fischerei*. Außerdem stellte er drei zivile Fischereischutzboote (Lazarett-, Werkstatt-, Funk- und Wetterschiffe) für die Betreuung der Fischereifahrzeuge auf See und ein Fischerei-Forschungsschiff in Dienst. Der Wiederaufbau der *Biologischen Anstalt für Meeresforschung Helgoland*, die zur Bundesforschungsanstalt für Fischerei gehört, auf der Insel Helgoland steht vor dem Abschluß.

HAUPTSTADT
BERLIN

Siebzehngeschossiges
Hochhaus für
Junggesellen

Zehngeschossiges
Wohnhaus —
beide im
Hansa-Viertel

Bauernhaus im Alten Land
(Niedersachsen)

Melktrupp

Kartoffel-
Vollernte-
Maschine

In der Fischwirtschaft sind mittelbar oder unmittelbar in rund 20.000 Betrieben etwa 110.000 Erwerbstätige beschäftigt, davon rund 12.700 auf der Fischereiflotte.

1945 konnten fast nur die Nordsee und die Küstengebiete der Ostsee befischt werden. Im Laufe der Jahre wurden wieder alle Fanggebiete der Vorkriegszeit aufgesucht und neue Fischgründe erschlossen. Das Schwergewicht der Fischerei liegt jedoch nach wie vor in der Nordsee. Bei den Anlandungen steht daher der Hering mit etwa 45% der Fischereierträge an erster Stelle.

Im Jahre 1938 standen für die Fischversorgung des Reichsgebietes aus eigenen Fangerträgen und Einfuhren über 900.000 t zur Verfügung. Der Verbrauch an Seefischen war auf 12 kg Frischgewicht je Kopf der Bevölkerung gestiegen. Außerdem wurden beträchtliche Mengen an Fischmehl, das ein wichtiges Futtermittel für die Landwirtschaft darstellt, erzeugt. Vor dem Kriege wurden bis zu 40% der Anlandungen und Einfuhren des Reiches von den Gebieten östlich des heutigen Eisernen Vorhanges verbraucht. 1957 gingen 5% der im Bundesgebiet für den menschlichen Verzehr zur Verfügung stehenden Mengen in das Gebiet der sogenannten DDR.

Die weitgehende Abhängigkeit der Seefischerei von der Natur und die leichte Verderblichkeit der Ware gestatten nur einen beschränkten Marktausgleich. Infolgedessen besteht häufig ein Mißverhältnis zwischen Angebot und Nachfrage, das immer wieder vorübergehende Absatzschwierigkeiten auslöst. Durch eine Reform der Markt- und Absatzmethoden soll dieses Problem aber in den nächsten Jahren gelöst werden.

Neben der deutschen Produktion sind Einfuhren zur Sicherstellung einer gleichmäßigeren Versorgung erforderlich. Sie bestehen vor allem aus Heringen, die nicht zu allen Zeiten des Jahres von der eigenen Fischereiflotte gefangen werden können. Seit 1950 bewegt sich der Fischverbrauch wieder zwischen 11 und 12 kg Frischgewicht je Kopf der Bevölkerung.

DIE ENTWICKLUNG DER WIRTSCHAFT

Die westdeutsche Wirtschaft nach dem Zusammenbruch

Der wirtschaftliche Zusammenbruch des Jahres 1945 war ebenso vollständig wie die militärische Niederlage. Die Industriezentren waren von Bomben schwer getroffen, Brücken zerstört, Straßen- und Bahnverbindungen unterbrochen. In vielen Städten gab es weder eine Kanalisation noch eine regelmäßige Versorgung mit Strom, Gas und Wasser. Millionen von Stadtbewohnern, die vor Bombenangriffen und Geschützfeuer auf das flache Land geflohen waren, strömten zurück. Sie fanden vielfach ihre Häuser ausgebrannt oder geplündert. Hunderttausende von Zwangsarbeitern zogen durch das Land. Millionen Deutscher aus den Gebieten jenseits der Oder und Neiße befanden sich auf dem Treck nach Westen. Zu ihnen gesellten sich Flüchtlinge aus der Sowjetischen Besatzungszone und heimkehrende Kriegsgefangene, soweit sie das Glück hatten, schnell entlassen zu werden.

Das Deutsche Reich hatte durch die Unterstellung der Ostgebiete unter fremde Verwaltung ein Viertel seines Gebietes und seiner landwirtschaftlichen Nutzfläche verloren. Bald trennte der Eiserne Vorhang auch die Sowjetische Zone ab. Das westliche Deutschland umfaßte nun noch die Amerikanische, Britische und Französische Zone, die von ihrer jeweiligen Militärbehörde nach verschiedenen Grundsätzen verwaltet wurden. Einigkeit aber bestand unter den alliierten Mächten in der Absicht, die *Industriekapazität Deutschlands auf etwa 65% des Standes von 1936* zu verringern, wie es im Ersten Industrieplan für Deutschland im März 1946 vorgesehen war.

Die Westzonen umfaßten nur 52% des Deutschen Reiches in seinen Grenzen von 1937. Bis zum Juni 1948 wuchs ihre Bevölkerung um rund 15%, und zwar fast ausschließlich infolge des Zustromes von Vertriebenen. Das deutsche Volk hätte sich gern durch seiner Hände Arbeit ernährt; bis zur Normalisierung der wirtschaftlichen Verhältnisse um die Mitte des Jahres 1948 — dem Zeitpunkt der Währungsreform — gab es jedoch nur geringe Möglichkeit für produktives Arbeiten. Zuerst waren vor allem die Trümmer der Katastrophe zu beseitigen.

*

Anfang 1947 wurden die Amerikanische und Britische Besatzungszone zu einem „Vereinigten Wirtschaftsgebiet" zusammengefaßt. Der wirtschaftliche Anschluß der Französischen Zone vollzog sich praktisch erst nach der Währungsreform.

Im August 1947 wurde der Zweite Industrieplan veröffentlicht. Er brachte wesentliche Erleichterungen; aber anderseits sah er die *Demontage* von 496 Fabriken in der Britischen, 236 in der Französischen und 185 in der Amerikanischen Zone vor. Die Mehrzahl der Deutschen war willens, den Schaden wieder gutzumachen, den Deutschland den Völkern Europas zugefügt hatte. Trotzdem war es schwer einzusehen, wie die demontierten Produktionseinrichtungen in anderen Ländern wieder aufgebaut werden könnten. In vielen Fällen besaßen die Maschinen nach ihrer Entfernung nur noch Schrottwert, und selbst dieser war von den Kosten des Ausbaus und Abtransports aufgezehrt. Umso stärker war das Gefühl der Dankbarkeit im deutschen Volke, als in den Vereinigten Staaten Stimmen laut wurden, die diesem sinnlosen Tun Einhalt geboten. Es sei nur an Namen wie HERBERT HOOVER, JAMES P. WARBURG und an die Arbeiten des HUMPHREY- und des HERTER-Ausschusses erinnert. Dennoch wurden *erst Ende April 1951 die Verladungen der letzten Demontage* durchgeführt.

Vom Tage der deutschen Kapitulation bis zum Juni 1948 schien die wirtschaftliche Lage hoffnungslos zu sein. Obwohl nur 12% der westdeutschen Industriekapazität durch Bombenschaden vernichtet und 8% der Demontage anheimgefallen waren, verblieb, gemessen am Umsatz des Jahres 1936, nur noch ein Potential von durchschnittlich 61%. Die alliierte *Joint Export Import Agency* (JEIA) regelte den Außenhandel. Sie führte Exporte durch, die zu 80% aus Rohstoffen, vor allem aus Kohle und Holz, bestanden, und sorgte für die dringendsten Einfuhren an Nahrungsmitteln. Die Herstellung bestimmter Güter war verboten, vieles andere durfte nur in begrenzter Menge erzeugt werden. Ein Teil dieser *Produktionsbeschränkungen* blieb noch bis 1951 wirksam.

Die deutsche Bevölkerung war vor allem deswegen entmutigt, weil sie in dieser Zeit nicht einmal den notdürftigen Lebensunterhalt bestreiten konnte. Das Geld bot keinen Gegenwert für die Arbeitsleistung. Was an Gütern produziert wurde, war für Geld nicht zu haben. Das Wirtschaften sank auf die primitive Stufe des Warentausches hinab. Wer in den Fabriken arbeitete, konnte Bezahlung in Ware verlangen. Wer aber zum Beispiel als Lehrer oder als Arzt tätig war, mußte aus seiner persönlichen Habe – sofern der Krieg sie ihm gelassen hatte – Besitzgüter gegen Lebensmittel, Tabak und Kohlen eintauschen. Die amtliche *Lebensmittelzuteilung* sah für den Normalverbraucher nicht ganz 1.000 Kalorien pro Tag vor. Sie deckte – ganz abgesehen von der veränderten Zusammensetzung und Minderwertigkeit der Nahrung – nur etwa 40% des physiologisch notwendigen Mindestbedarfs.

Für die Zuteilungsperiode vom 1. bis 31. 3. 1948, also für eine Zeit von viereinhalb Wochen kurz vor der Währungsreform, standen dem Normalverbraucher Lebensmittelmarken für folgende Mengen zur Verfügung:

8.250 g Brot	1.000 g Zucker
170 g Fett	125 g Kaffee-Ersatz
450 g Fleisch	9.000 g Kartoffeln
1.400 g Nährmittel	1 l Magermilch
62 g Käse	

Nach der Produktionsstatistik der Britischen Zone 1946/47 hätte jeder Einwohner alle vierzig Jahre einen Anzug, alle zehn Jahre ein Oberhemd, alle vier Jahre ein Paar Socken und alle drei Jahre ein Paar Schuhe erhalten können. Der ,,Normalverbraucher" bekam noch weniger, da bevorzugte Gruppen zuerst versorgt werden mußten. VICTOR GOLLANCZ sagte seinen britischen Landsleuten im Oktober 1947, daß im Vereinigten Wirtschaftsgebiet nur jede siebente Person im Jahr einen Teller, jede fünfte eine Zahnbürste, jede einhundertundfünfzigste eine Waschschüssel erhalten könne, daß nur jeder dritte Tote in einem Sarg begraben und nur jeder zweite Säugling mit Windeln in der Wiege liege.

Kein Wunder also, daß der Schwarzmarkt einen immer größeren Teil der Waren an sich zog und der Preisstop kaum mehr beachtet wurde. Die Bewirtschaftung war praktisch zusammengebrochen. An eine konstruktive Wirtschaftspolitik war nicht zu denken.

Angesichts dieser katastrophalen Versorgungslage bedeuteten die *Liebesgabensendungen aus dem Ausland*, die Hilfe der Wohltätigkeitsorganisationen und die amerikanischen und britischen Notstandseinfuhren für viele Deutsche die Rettung. Diese Zeichen der Nächstenliebe ermutigten das deutsche Volk und gaben ihm die Kraft, ganz von vorn zu beginnen.

Um die Mitte des Jahres 1948 hatte die westdeutsche Produktion erst einen Stand von 50% des Niveaus von 1936 erreicht. Alle anderen am Marshall-Plan teilnehmenden Länder konnten bis dahin weit größere Fortschritte erzielen und hatten — bis auf ganz wenige Ausnahmen — den Vorkriegsstand schon wieder überschritten.

Die Grundlagen der westdeutschen Wirtschaftspolitik seit 1948

In diesen schweren Jahren war die gedankliche Vorbereitung der wirtschaftlichen Normalisierung keineswegs unterblieben. Die politische Entwicklung nach dem Kriegsende hatte den Wunsch des deutschen Volkes nach einer demokratischen Verfassung gezeigt. Führende Wirtschaftswissenschaftler hatten schon seit Jahren, wenngleich ohne Beachtung in der breiten

Tabelle 1

INDEX DER INDUSTRIELLEN PRODUKTION[1] EUROPÄISCHER LÄNDER UND DER USA

Umbasiert auf 1936 = 100

Land	1938	1948	1949	1950
Bundesrepublik Deutschland[2]	119	60	89	111
Belgien	98	119	122	125
Dänemark	105	137	146	162
Frankreich[3]	99	107	117	120
Griechenland[3]	119	89	106	133
Vereinigtes Königreich[3]	101	128	136	146
Italien	115	117	125	145
Niederlande	122	139	156	177
Norwegen	110	146	160	180
Österreich	112	103	138	163
Schweden[4]	112	169	175	183
USA[4]	86	189	173	202

[1] Soweit nicht anders vermerkt: Industrie einschließlich Energiewirtschaft, ohne Bauwirtschaft. — [2] Ohne Saarland. — [3] Einschließlich Bauwirtschaft. — [4] Ohne Energiewirtschaft.

Quelle: Europäischer Wirtschaftsrat.

Öffentlichkeit zu finden, eine *neue Form der Wirtschaftsordnung* ausgearbeitet, die einem solchen *freiheitlichen und sozialen Gemeinwesen* gerecht werden konnte.

Deutsche Soziologen und Nationalökonomen, die auch in den schwersten Jahren mit ihren Fachkollegen im ausländischen Exil Verbindung hielten, schilderten die Unvereinbarkeit einer kollektivistischen Wirtschaftsplanung mit politischer und geistiger Freiheit und analysierten die Gründe des inneren Widerspruchs zwischen den Versprechungen der allumfassenden Wirtschaftslenkung und ihrem höchst fragwürdigen sozialen Erfolg. Damit waren die Ursachen des Versagens der Lenkungswirtschaft erkannt. Ebenso offenkundig aber waren die Mängel des uneingeschränkten Wirtschaftsliberalismus'. Der historische Liberalismus hatte die der Freiheit gleichrangigen Werte der Gerechtigkeit und des sozialen Schutzes vernachlässigt. Das Problem der Machtbeschränkung war ungelöst geblieben.

Auf dem Hintergrund der Erfahrungen mit dem Kollektivismus und dem Liberalismus entstand so die Konzeption der *Sozialen Marktwirtschaft*, die nicht lediglich durch die *Verbesserung des Lebensstandards* der breiten Massen soziale Erfolge aufweisen kann, sondern auch fähig ist, *den Ablauf des Wirtschaftsprozesses den politischen und sozialen Erfordernissen der Gegenwart anzupassen.*

Die Soziale Marktwirtschaft

Die Politik der Sozialen Marktwirtschaft stellt eine sinnvolle Verbindung von freier Selbstregulierung des Marktprozesses und einer äußeren, hauptsächlich sozial motivierten Steuerung des Wirtschaftsgeschehens dar. Sie bietet die Möglichkeit, soziale und gesellschaftspolitische Ziele im Rahmen der marktwirtschaftlichen Ordnung zu verwirklichen. Die Marktwirtschaft ist freiheitlich und eigentumsfreundlich, und damit ist sie das dem Lebensstil der westlichen Welt entsprechende Wirtschaftssystem. *Der Markt* mit seiner variablen Wert- und Preisrechnung und der durch ihn vollzogenen Koordination der Pläne aller Wirtschaftenden nimmt eine beherrschende Stellung ein. Seine Funktionsweise läßt die höchstmögliche materielle Ergiebigkeit erwarten. Zur Aufrechterhaltung dieser Vorzüge bedarf es – und hierin besteht der erste entscheidende Unterschied gegenüber der rein liberalen Wirtschaft – der ständigen *Sicherung des Wettbewerbs durch den Staat.* Nur unter der Bedingung eines intensiven Wettbewerbs kann die Produktivität nachhaltig gesteigert werden und dem Verbraucher zugute kommen.

Da aber das Ergebnis des ungesteuerten Marktgeschehens unter sozialen Gesichtspunkten nicht immer und überall befriedigt, sind Korrekturen notwendig und auch möglich. Das System der Marktwirtschaft verschließt sich nicht dem politischen, vor allem nicht dem sozialen Gestaltungswillen unserer Zeit. Die einzige Bedingung für eine reibungs- und widerspruchslose Verknüpfung von Marktfreiheit und staatlicher Steuerung besteht darin, daß diese Steuerung sich nur solcher Instrumente bedient, welche die Funktionszusammenhänge des Marktes nicht zerreißen. In dieser Bedingung liegt der zweite wichtige Unterschied zwischen der neuen Wirtschaftspolitik und dem zusammenhanglosen Interventionismus der Vergangenheit.

So verstanden ist also die Soziale Marktwirtschaft kein Mischsystem von Lenkungs- und Freiheitselementen, sondern ein tatsächlich neuer und selbständiger „*Dritter Weg*“. Die Betonung des Ordnungsgedankens in der Wirtschaftspolitik erfordert ein Abgehen von der früheren Auffassung, die Wirtschaft brauche lediglich in jedem ihrer Glieder gefördert zu werden, um das Gesamtwohl zu erreichen. Die Rücksichtnahme auf den Gesamtzusammenhang des Wirtschaftsgeschehens steht bei allen wirtschaftspolitischen

Eingriffen im Vordergrund. Die Ordnungsaufgabe fällt dem Staate zu, während die Dispositionsfreiheit der Wirtschaftenden innerhalb dieses Rahmens unangetastet bleibt.

Der Beginn des Aufbaus

Die Umstellung der Lenkungswirtschaft der Kriegs- und Nachkriegszeit auf diese neue Politik konnte erst mit der Währungsreform geschehen. Durch die drastische Sanierung des Geldwesens wurde der aus der Kriegsfinanzierung herrührende Geldüberhang von einem Tag zum andern beseitigt: alle Geldwerte und Forderungen wurden auf ein Zehntel, Bargeld und Bankguthaben sogar auf 6,5% reduziert. Das Ausmaß der Geldausstattung wurde so gewählt, daß die verfügbare Produktion zu Preisen umgesetzt werden konnte, die im Vergleich zum Ausland und zur Vorkriegszeit als normal anzusehen waren.

Gleichzeitig mit der Währungsreform wurden die seit langem geltenden Preisvorschriften und die Bewirtschaftungsmaßnahmen zum überwiegenden Teil aufgehoben. Das Gewicht dieser Entscheidung läßt sich nur ermessen, wenn man sich den chaotischen Zustand der westdeutschen Wirtschaft vergegenwärtigt. Die Freunde der Lenkungswirtschaft verwiesen immer wieder auf die Geringfügigkeit der Produktion und auf die Gefahr untragbarer Knappheitspreise, die eine Ausbeutung der arbeitenden Massen bedeuten würden. Außerdem verstieß die Abschaffung von Preisstop und Rationierung gegen den Sinn der Vorschriften der alliierten Kontrollinstanzen. Sie hatten angeordnet, daß vor jeder *Änderung* der Preisverordnungen eine Genehmigung einzuholen war. Niemand hatte mit der völligen *Aufhebung* dieser Vorschriften gerechnet. Die Kühnheit des Entschlusses, die meisten Preisvorschriften aufzuheben, gab aber den Weg frei für den beispiellosen Wiederaufstieg des westdeutschen Wirtschaftspotentials, das in den folgenden Jahren zu einem wertvollen Bestandteil der Weltwirtschaft werden sollte.

Bewährung der jungen Marktwirtschaft

LUDWIG ERHARD, der damalige Direktor der Verwaltung für Wirtschaft für das Gebiet der Amerikanischen und Britischen Zone, setzte sein ganzes Vertrauen in die ungeheuren Kräfte, die nun, vom äußeren Zwang befreit, sich entfalten konnten. Allein die Tatsache, daß jeder fortan frei und ungehindert produzieren, kaufen und verkaufen konnte, wonach der Konsument verlangte, und die Gewißheit, daß Arbeitsleistung und unternehmerische

Initiative wieder mit gutem, kaufkräftigem Geld entlohnt wurden, setzten Energien frei, von denen man geglaubt hatte, sie seien längst in Resignation erloschen.

Der erste Geldstoß aus der Freigabe der Bankguthaben wurde durch die Waren aufgefangen, die plötzlich aus den zurückgehaltenen Lagern zum Verkauf angeboten wurden. Alles kam nun darauf an, einem Volke, dem soeben erst die beglückende Freude des Kaufen-Könnens wiedergeschenkt worden war, die Enttäuschung schnell entleerter Vorräte zu ersparen. In einem unglaublich schnellen Umstellungsprozeß strebten die Arbeiter wieder in produktive Beschäftigung, lebten Handelsbeziehungen wieder auf, war der Fluß der Rohstoffe und Waren, unterstützt durch Auslandshilfe, wieder in Gang gekommen. Trotz den Engpässen, die jetzt deutlich hervortraten, schnellte die Produktion in einem halben Jahr von 50% auf 70% des Standes von 1936 empor, und da die Lebenshaltungskosten weit weniger anstiegen, war schon gegen Ende des Jahres 1948 der Erfolg der neuen Wirtschaftspolitik und das Vertrauen in das neue Geld als gesichert anzusehen.

Diese erste Entwicklungsphase war durch eine starke Expansion der Gütererzeugung bei noch stärkerer Ausdehnung der Geldschöpfung gekennzeichnet. Die Beherrschung des Preisauftriebs stellte deshalb das zentrale Problem der Wirtschaftspolitik dar. Schon in der nächsten Phase ab Anfang 1949 aber zeigte sich die Notwendigkeit, dem sich verlangsamenden Produktionsanstieg bewußt neue Antriebe zu verleihen. Zum ersten Mal erzwang die Marktlage einen Konkurrenzkampf der Produzenten. Wenngleich eine Anpassung der Produktion an die nun mit mehr Überlegung geäußerten Konsumentenwünsche durchaus vorteilhafte Wirkungen erwarten ließ, verlangte die durch den ununterbrochenen Zustrom von Flüchtlingen aus dem Osten erhöhte Arbeitslosigkeit gebieterisch nach stärkerer *Expansion*. Dringlich war vor allem die Investitionstätigkeit in der noch unter Preiskontrolle gehaltenen Grundstofferzeugung, wenn die Ausweitung der Produktion gesichert bleiben sollte. Die Kreditpolitik der Bank deutscher Länder verschloß sich diesen Forderungen nicht; sie mußte aber gleichzeitig auf die *Entwicklung der Zahlungsbilanz* achten. Die Abwertungswelle im Herbst 1949, die für die Bundesrepublik einen geringeren Exportvorteil bedeutete als für die meisten anderen Länder, und auch die Lockerung der Beschränkungen im Außenhandel ließen die Einfuhr schneller ansteigen als die Ausfuhr. So wünschenswert einerseits der schon in diesem frühen Stadium einsetzende Konkurrenzdruck des Auslandes war, so schwierig wurde andererseits die Vermehrung der eigenen Produktion.

Zu Anfang des Jahres 1950 wurde ein *Arbeitsbeschaffungs- und Wohnungsbauprogramm* eingeleitet, ergänzt durch eine Reihe von *Maßnahmen zur Förderung des Exports*. Diese Impulse trafen mit der darauf folgenden Korea-Hausse zusammen und wirkten umso stärker. Es waren aber schon um die Mitte des Jahres deutliche Zeichen dafür erkennbar geworden, daß auch ohne diese politisch bedingten Einflüsse eine weitere Aufwärtsentwicklung der Produktion möglich gewesen wäre, denn allein im zweiten Halbjahr 1950 wuchs die industrielle Erzeugung um rund 20%.

*

Die Nervosität, ausgelöst durch den Ausbruch des Korea-Krieges und noch verstärkt durch das Eingreifen chinesischer Truppen gegen Ende des Jahres,

BESCHÄFTIGUNG UND ARBEITSLOSIGKEIT[1]

Millionen Millionen

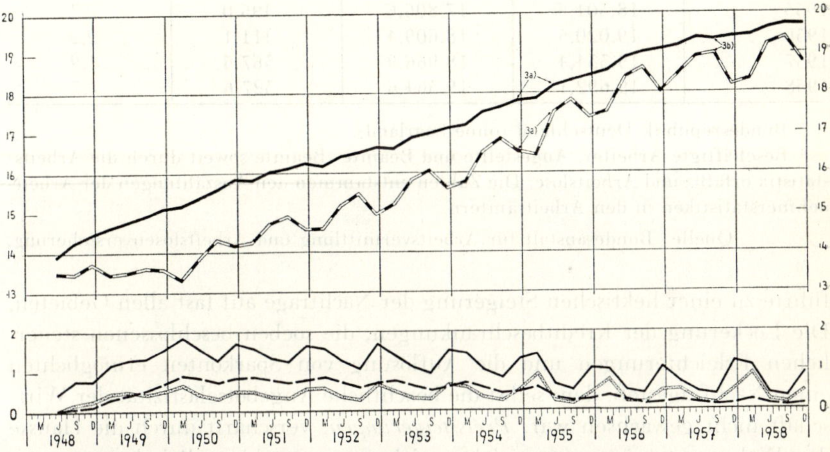

Unselbständige Erwerbspersonen[2] — Beschäftigte[3] — Arbeitslose[4]

Hauptunterstützungsempfänger[5] in der Arbeitslosenversicherung — Hauptunterstützungsempfänger[5] in der Arbeitslosenhilfe

[1] Bundesrepublik Deutschland (ohne Saarland). — [2] Beschäftigte Arbeiter, Angestellte, Beamte (soweit durch die Arbeitsstatistik erfaßt) und Arbeitslose. (Die Zahlen entstammen den Auszählungen der Arbeitnehmerkarteien in den Arbeitsämtern). — [3] Arbeiter, Angestellte und Beamte. — a) Beschäftigte geschätzt. — b) Vor der Zählung ist die Kartei der beschäftigten Arbeitnehmer im Abschnitt der älteren Arbeitnehmer bereinigt worden. Diese statistische Korrektur kann man nach angestellten Vergleichsrechnungen mit 120.000 bis 140.000 annehmen. Ein Vergleich mit früheren Ergebnissen ist aus diesem Grunde nur bedingt möglich. — [4] Ab 1953 ohne Heimarbeiter und ab 1955 einschließlich arbeitsloser Flüchtlinge in Durchgangslagern. — [5] Ab 1955 Stand am 15. des jeweiligen Berichtsmonats.

Quelle: Bundesanstalt für Arbeitsvermittlung und Arbeitslosenversicherung.

Tabelle 2

BESCHÄFTIGUNG UND ARBEITSLOSIGKEIT[1]

Stichtag 30. 9.	Unselbständige Erwerbspersonen[2] insgesamt	davon Beschäftigte	davon Arbeitslose	
	1.000			% aller Arbeitnehmer
1948	14.247,2	13.463,1	784,1	*5,5*
1949	14.918,1	13.604,4	1.313,7	*8,8*
1950	15.567,4	14.295,6	1.271,8	*8,2*
1951	16.119,6	14.884,7	1.235,0	*7,7*
1952	16.506,9	15.456,3	1.050,6	*6,4*
1953	16.985,6	16.044,4	941,2	*5,5*
1954	17.653,2	16.830,7	822,5	*4,7*
1955	18.301,6	17.806,6	495,0	*2,7*
1956	19.020,5	18.609,4	411,1	*2,2*
1957	19.334,4	18.966,9	367,5	*1,9*
1958	19.692,1	19.364,6	327,6	*1,7*

[1] Bundesrepublik Deutschland (ohne Saarland).

[2] Beschäftigte Arbeiter, Angestellte und Beamte (Beamte soweit durch die Arbeitsstatistik erfaßt) und Arbeitslose. Die Zahlen entstammen den Auszählungen der Arbeitnehmerstatistiken in den Arbeitsämtern.

Quelle: Bundesanstalt für Arbeitsvermittlung und Arbeitslosenversicherung.

führte zu einer hektischen Steigerung der Nachfrage auf fast allen Gebieten. Die Lockerung der Kreditbeschränkungen, die soeben beschlossenen steuerlichen Erleichterungen und die Auflösung von Sparkonten ermöglichten einen Nachfragestoß, dem selbst die beachtliche Angebotselastizität der Wirtschaft nicht gewachsen war. *Preissteigerungen*, verschärft durch die Hausse der Weltmarktpreise, waren daher nicht zu vermeiden. Bei dem sprunghaften Anstieg der Produktion von 111% im Monatsdurchschnitt 1950 auf 141% im vierten Vierteljahr 1951 (1936 = 100) zeigten sich bald *Engpässe in der Grundstoffversorgung*, die man durch Einfuhren zu überwinden versuchte, um den nachgelagerten Produktionsstufen die weitere Expansion zu erleichtern. Auch die Demontagen und Kapazitätsbeschränkungen waren immer noch spürbar.

In dieser Situation schien die Wirtschaftsordnung ernstlich gefährdet. Pläne zur Einschränkung der übertriebenen Nachfrage überstürzten sich. Aber die

MESSZIFFERN DER DURCHSCHNITTLICHEN BRUTTO-ARBEITSVERDIENSTE DER INDUSTRIEARBEITER[1]
1950 = 100

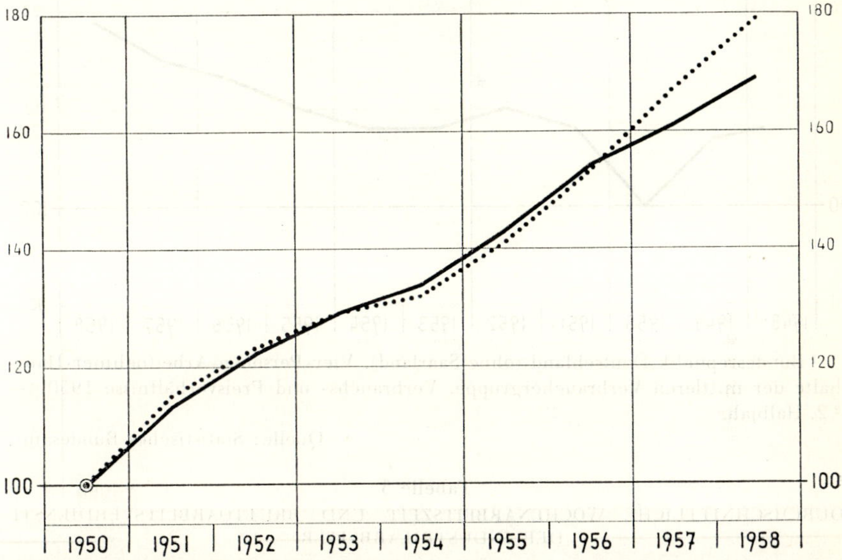

[1] Bundesrepublik Deutschland (ohne Saarland). — Ohne Bergbau.

Quelle: Statistisches Bundesamt.

Anregung, nunmehr auch den Grundstoffsektor aus der Preiskontrolle zu entlassen und ihm so die notwendigen Mittel zu schneller Ausweitung der Produktion zuzuführen, wurde nicht akzeptiert. Dagegen entschloß man sich nach monatelangen Beratungen zu einer *Investitionshilfe* für die Grundstoffindustrie. Die Mittel wurden von den sehr rentablen, verarbeitenden Industriezweigen und dem Handel durch eine Zwangsanleihe aufgebracht. Aus politischen Gründen mußten zwar wieder Vorschriften über die Verwendung einiger wichtiger Rohstoffe erlassen werden; doch wurden sie nur mit äußerster Zurückhaltung angewendet.

Von Mitte 1950 an übertraf die *Steigerung der Löhne* den Anstieg der Kosten für die Lebenshaltung. Die Verbesserung des Lebensstandards hielt an, vor allem bei den zwischen März 1950 und September 1951 neu in den

PREISINDEX FÜR DIE LEBENSHALTUNG[1]

1950 = 100

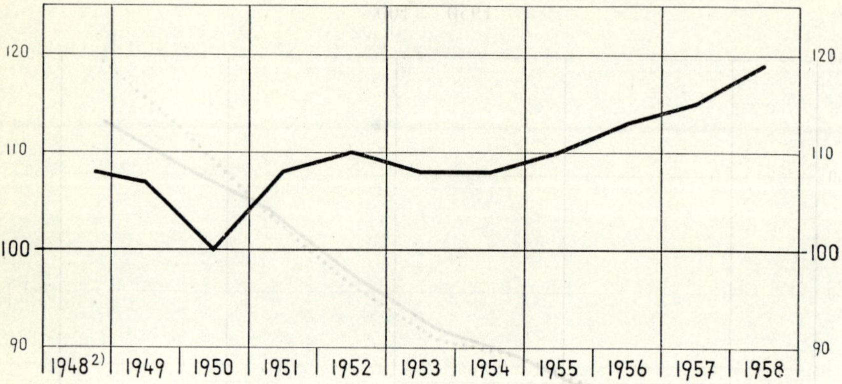

[1] Bundesrepublik Deutschland (ohne Saarland). Vier-Personen-Arbeitnehmer-Haushalte der mittleren Verbrauchergruppe. Verbrauchs- und Preisverhältnisse 1950. — [2] 2. Halbjahr.

Quelle: Statistisches Bundesamt.

Tabelle 3

DURCHSCHNITTLICHE WOCHENARBEITSZEIT UND BRUTTOARBEITSVERDIENSTE DER INDUSTRIEARBEITER[1]

Jahr	Durchschnittlich bezahlte Wochenarbeitszeit	Durchschnittlicher Bruttostunden- verdienst		Durchschnittlicher Bruttowochen- verdienst	
	Stunden	Pfennige	Zunahme gegenüber dem Vorjahr in %	DM	Zunahme gegenüber dem Vorjahr in %
1950	48,2	127,0	.	61,33	.
1951	47,6	145,7	*14,7*	69,41	*13,2*
1952	47,7	156,8	*7,6*	74,96	*8,0*
1953	48,1	163,6	*4,3*	78,88	*5,2*
1954	48,8	168,0	*2,7*	82,04	*4,0*
1955	49,0	179,1	*6,6*	87,98	*7,2*
1956	48,2	194,9	*8,8*	94,17	*7,0*
1957	46,5	212,5	*9,0*	98,75	*4,9*
1958	45,7	227,3	*7,0*	103,91	*5,2*

[1] Bundesrepublik Deutschland (ohne Saarland). — Ohne Bergbau.
[2] 1 DM = 100 Pfennige.

Quelle: Statistisches Bundesamt.

VERÄNDERUNG DES PRODUKTIONSNIVEAUS DER INDUSTRIE 1957 GEGENÜBER 1950 NACH INDUSTRIEGRUPPEN

Index der industriellen Nettoproduktion[1]; arbeitstäglich, 1950 = 100

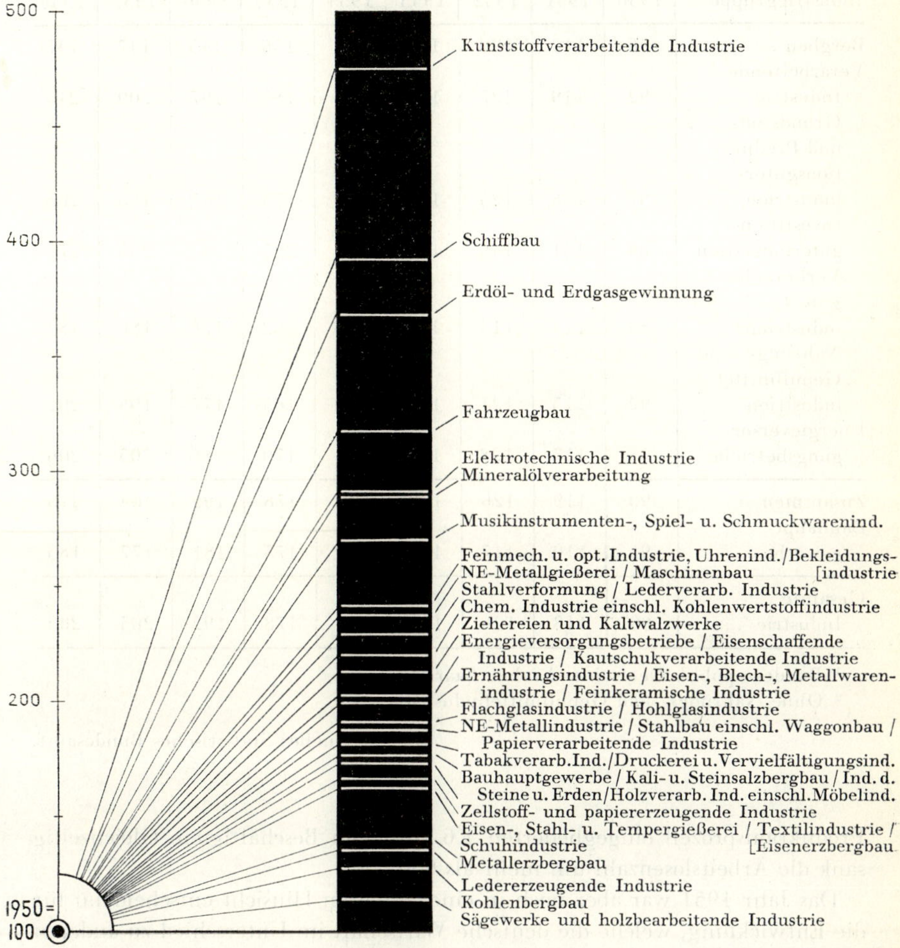

[1] Bundesrepublik Deutschland (ohne Saarland).

Quelle: Statistisches Bundesamt.

Tabelle 4

INDEX DER INDUSTRIELLEN NETTOPRODUKTION[1] NACH INDUSTRIEGRUPPEN

arbeitstäglich, 1950 = 100

Industriegruppe	1936	1951	1952	1953	1954	1955	1956	1957	1958
Bergbau	96	112	120	123	128	136	143	147	147
Verarbeitende Industrie	92	119	127	141	158	183	197	209	216
Grundstoff- und Produktionsgüterindustrien ...	97	118	123	132	151	175	187	198	203
Investitionsgüterindustrien	89	131	146	154	181	223	243	253	271
Verbrauchsgüterindustrien[2] ...	88	114	115	134	146	162	176	186	184
Nahrungs- und Genußmittelindustrien ...	92	113	121	142	150	165	177	195	202
Energieversorgungsbetriebe	55	117	128	134	151	170	189	203	206
Zusammen	90	119	126	139	155	178	192	204	210
Bauhauptgewerbe	91	110	117	139	153	173	181	177	183
Gesamte Industrie	90	118	126	139	155	178	192	203	209

[1] Bundesrepublik Deutschland (ohne Saarland).
[2] Ohne Nahrungs- und Genußmittelindustrien.

Quelle: Statistisches Bundesamt.

Produktionsprozeß eingegliederten 1,6 Millionen Beschäftigten. Gleichzeitig sank die Arbeitslosenzahl um mehr als 600.000.

Das Jahr 1951 war aber noch in einer anderen Hinsicht entscheidend für die Entwicklung, welche die deutsche Wirtschaft im Unterschied zu anderen Ländern Europas nehmen sollte: Westdeutschland hatte seinen Markt den Einfuhren geöffnet, indem es den Verpflichtungen des Europäischen Wirtschaftsrates (OEEC) zur *Liberalisierung* nachgekommen war. Der Nachfragesog in der Korea-Krise führte zu einem Defizit in der Zahlungsbilanz im Jahre

INDEX DER INDUSTRIELLEN NETTOPRODUKTION[1]

arbeitstäglich, 1950 = 100

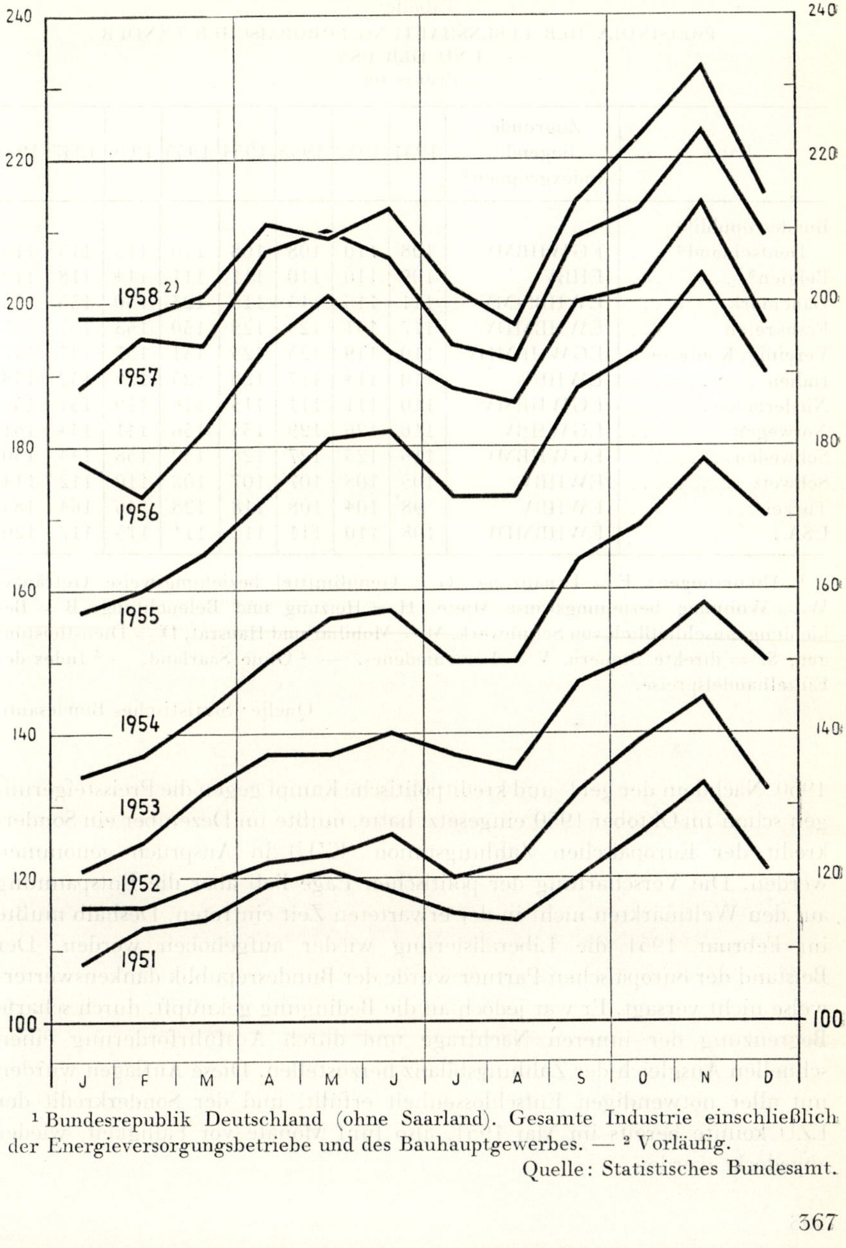

[1] Bundesrepublik Deutschland (ohne Saarland). Gesamte Industrie einschließlich der Energieversorgungsbetriebe und des Bauhauptgewerbes. — [2] Vorläufig.

Quelle: Statistisches Bundesamt.

Tabelle 5
PREISINDEX DER LEBENSHALTUNG EUROPÄISCHER LÄNDER UND DER USA
1950 = 100

Land	Zugrunde liegende Indexgruppen[1]	1951	1952	1953	1954	1955	1956	1957	1958
Bundesrepublik Deutschland[2] ...	EGWHBMV	108	110	108	108	110	113	115	119
Belgien[3]	EHBV	109	110	110	111	111	114	118	119
Dänemark	EWHBStMV	111	115	115	116	123	130	133	135
Frankreich	EWHBMDV	117	131	129	129	130	133	137	157
Vereinig. Königreich	EGWHBMDV	110	119	123	125	131	137	143	147
Italien	EWHBV	110	114	117	120	123	129	132	138
Niederlande	EGWHBMV	110	111	111	115	116	119	131	134
Norwegen	EGWHBV	116	126	129	135	136	141	144	151
Schweden.........	EGWHBMV	116	125	127	128	132	138	144	150
Schweiz	EWHBV	105	108	107	107	108	110	112	114
Türkei	EWHBV	98	104	108	118	128	146	164	184
USA	EWHBMDV	108	110	111	112	111	113	117	120

[1] Abkürzungen: E = Ernährung, G = Genußmittel beziehungsweise Getränke, W = Wohnung beziehungsweise Miete, H = Heizung und Beleuchtung, B = Bekleidung einschließlich von Schuhwerk, M = Mobiliar und Hausrat, D = Dienstleistungen, St = direkte Steuern, V = Verschiedenes. — [2] Ohne Saarland. — [3] Index der Einzelhandelspreise.

Quelle: Statistisches Bundesamt.

1950. Nachdem der geld- und kreditpolitische Kampf gegen die Preissteigerungen schon im Oktober 1950 eingesetzt hatte, mußte im Dezember ein Sonderkredit der Europäischen Zahlungsunion (EZU) in Anspruch genommen werden. Die Verschärfung der politischen Lage ließ aber die Entspannung auf den Weltmärkten nicht in der erwarteten Zeit eintreten. Deshalb mußte im Februar 1951 die Liberalisierung wieder aufgehoben werden. Der Beistand der europäischen Partner wurde der Bundesrepublik dankenswerterweise nicht versagt. Er war jedoch an die Bedingung geknüpft, durch scharfe Begrenzung der inneren Nachfrage und durch Ausfuhrförderung einen schnellen Ausgleich der Zahlungsbilanz herzustellen. Diese Auflagen wurden mit aller notwendigen Entschlossenheit erfüllt, und der Sonderkredit der EZU konnte bereits im Mai 1951, also fünf Monate vor Fälligkeit, wieder abgedeckt werden.

PREISINDEX DER LEBENSHALTUNG
EUROPÄISCHER LÄNDER UND DER USA

1950 = 100

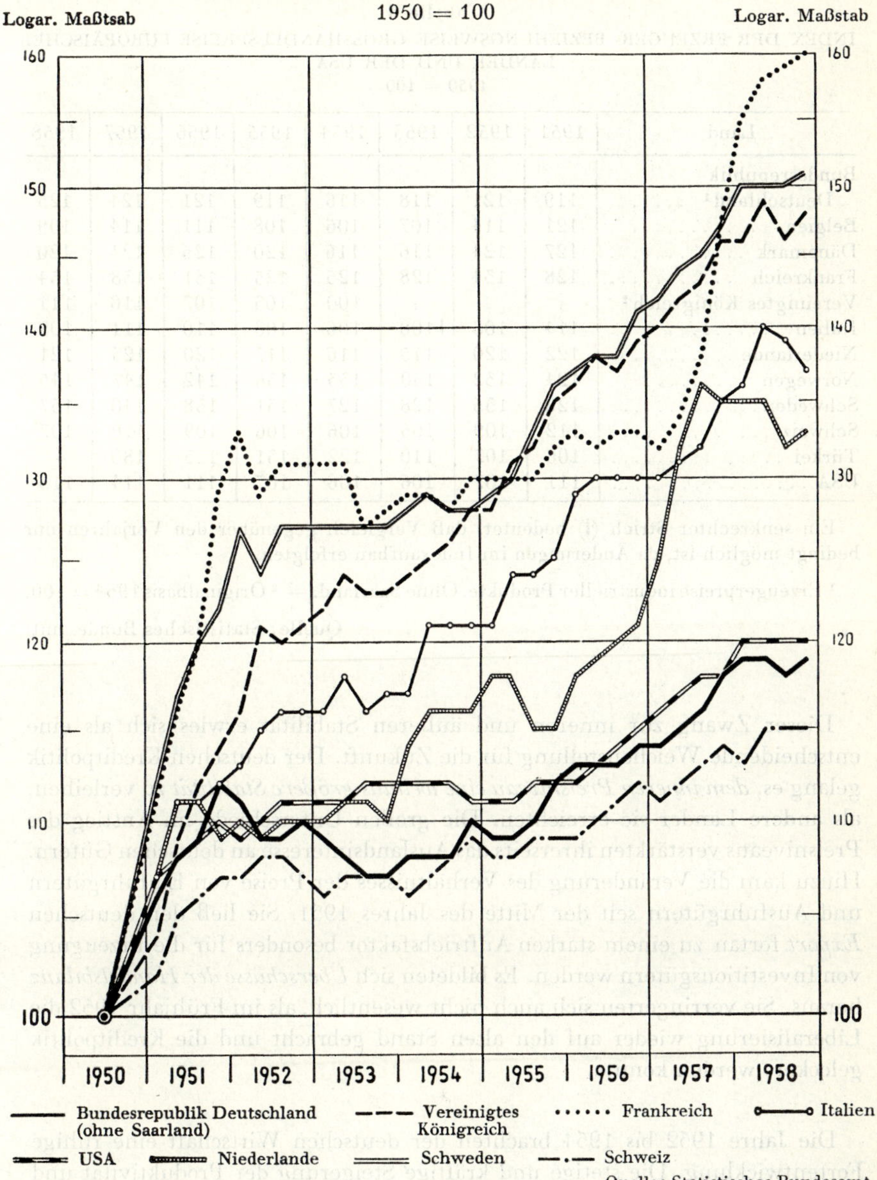

Quelle: Statistisches Bundesamt.

Tabelle 6
INDEX DER ERZEUGER- BEZIEHUNGSWEISE GROSSHANDELSPREISE EUROPÄISCHER LÄNDER UND DER USA
1950 = 100

Land	1951	1952	1953	1954	1955	1956	1957	1958
Bundesrepublik Deutschland[1]	119	121	118	116	119	121	124	125
Belgien	121	114	107	106	108	111	114	109
Dänemark	127	124	116	116	120	125	121	120
Frankreich	128	134	128	125	125	131	138	154
Vereinigtes Königreich[2]	.	.	.	100	103	107	110	111
Italien	114	108	| 108	106	108	110	111	108
Niederlande	122	120	115	116	117	120	123	121
Norwegen	124	132	130	133	136	142	147	145
Schweden	128	135	128	127	131	138	140	137
Schweiz	112	109	105	106	106	109	110	107
Türkei	106	107	110	122	131	153	180	—
USA	111	107	106	106	107	111	114	115

Ein senkrechter Strich (|) bedeutet, daß Vergleich gegenüber den Vorjahren nur bedingt möglich ist, da Änderungen im Indexaufbau erfolgten.

[1] Erzeugerpreise industrieller Produkte. Ohne Saarland. — [2] Originalbasis 1954 = 100.

Quelle: Statistisches Bundesamt.

Dieser Zwang zur inneren und äußeren Stabilität erwies sich als eine entscheidende Weichenstellung für die Zukunft. Der deutschen Kreditpolitik gelang es, *dem inneren Preisniveau eine weitaus größere Stabilität* zu verleihen, als andere Länder sie erreichten. Die großen Unterschiede im Anstieg des Preisniveaus verstärkten ihrerseits das Auslandsinteresse an deutschen Gütern. Hinzu kam die Veränderung des Verhältnisses der Preise von Einfuhrgütern und Ausfuhrgütern seit der Mitte des Jahres 1951. Sie ließ den deutschen *Export* fortan zu einem starken Auftriebsfaktor besonders für die Erzeugung von Investitionsgütern werden. Es bildeten sich *Überschüsse der Handelsbilanz* heraus. Sie verringerten sich auch nicht wesentlich, als im Frühjahr 1952 die Liberalisierung wieder auf den alten Stand gebracht und die Kreditpolitik gelockert werden konnte.

*

Die Jahre 1952 bis 1954 brachten der deutschen Wirtschaft eine ruhige Fortentwicklung. Die stetige und kräftige Steigerung der Produktivität und des Einkommens der breiten Massen führten bei leicht sinkendem Preisniveau zu einer beachtlichen Verbesserung des Lebensstandards. So kam die westdeutsche Bevölkerung zum ersten Mal nach dem Kriege wieder in den ungeschmälerten Genuß hohen Verbrauchs und einer Warenqualität, die besser als vor dem Kriege ist.

In diesen Jahren fand die Wirtschaftspolitik Zeit, sich den bis dahin ungelösten Fragen zuzuwenden. Der *Lastenausgleich* erhielt seine endgültige Gestalt, der *Verkehr* einen neuen gesetzlichen Rahmen. *Der Wohnungsbau* wurde durch breit angelegte Maßnahmen auf dem Kapitalmarkt gefördert. Die Bedienung der deutschen *Auslandsschulden* wurde nach erfolgreichen internationalern Verhandlungen wieder aufgenommen. Die ersten Schritte zur *Integration der europäischen Volkswirtschaften* wurden getan, und die *Konvertierbarkeit der Währungen* schien näher zu rücken. Alles dies bedeutete zum großen Teil noch ein Aufräumen der Trümmer, die der Krieg hinterlassen hatte; aber vieles geschah doch mit dem Blick in die Zukunft, von der das deutsche Volk eine friedliche und glückliche Zusammenarbeit mit der freien Welt erhoffte.

Die Mengenkonjunktur dieser Phase kam einem Idealzustand nahe, wie er jedem Wirtschaftspolitiker vorschwebt. Bis in das Jahr 1954 hinein hielt die allgemeine *Stabilität des Preisniveaus* an. Seit 1955 vollzog sich ein allmählicher Übergang zur ausgesprochenen *Hochkonjunktur*. Sie gab auch dem Preisniveau einen gewissen Auftrieb, wie es nach dem Erreichen der Vollbeschäftigung, den darauf folgenden Lohnerhöhungen und bei der den Importen vorauseilenden Ausfuhrentwicklung durchaus erklärlich ist.

Der wiederholte *Wechsel der Konjunktur* ist geradezu ein Kennzeichen der Nachkriegsgeschichte der deutschen Wirtschaft: Die Hausse des zweiten Halbjahres 1948 wandelte sich Anfang 1949 zu einem etwas gedämpfteren Wachstum. Unter den Einwirkungen der Korea-Krise weitete sich die Wirtschaft wieder stark aus. Nach einer Erholungspause in den Jahren 1952 bis 1954 setzte wieder eine starke Hochkonjunktur ein, die sich erst 1957 und 1958 entspannte. Für die Zukunft rechnet die deutsche Wirtschaft mit einem *ruhigen, aber stetigen Wachstum.*

Gestaltende Wirtschaftspolitik

Entsprechend der wirtschaftspolitischen Konzeption der Bundesregierung konnte es nicht ihre Aufgabe sein, etwa durch eine mehrjährige Vorausplanung die Wachstumsrate der Wirtschaft festzulegen und einzelnen

INDEX DER INDUSTRIELLEN PRODUKTION[1]
EUROPÄISCHER LÄNDER UND DER USA (1950 = 100)

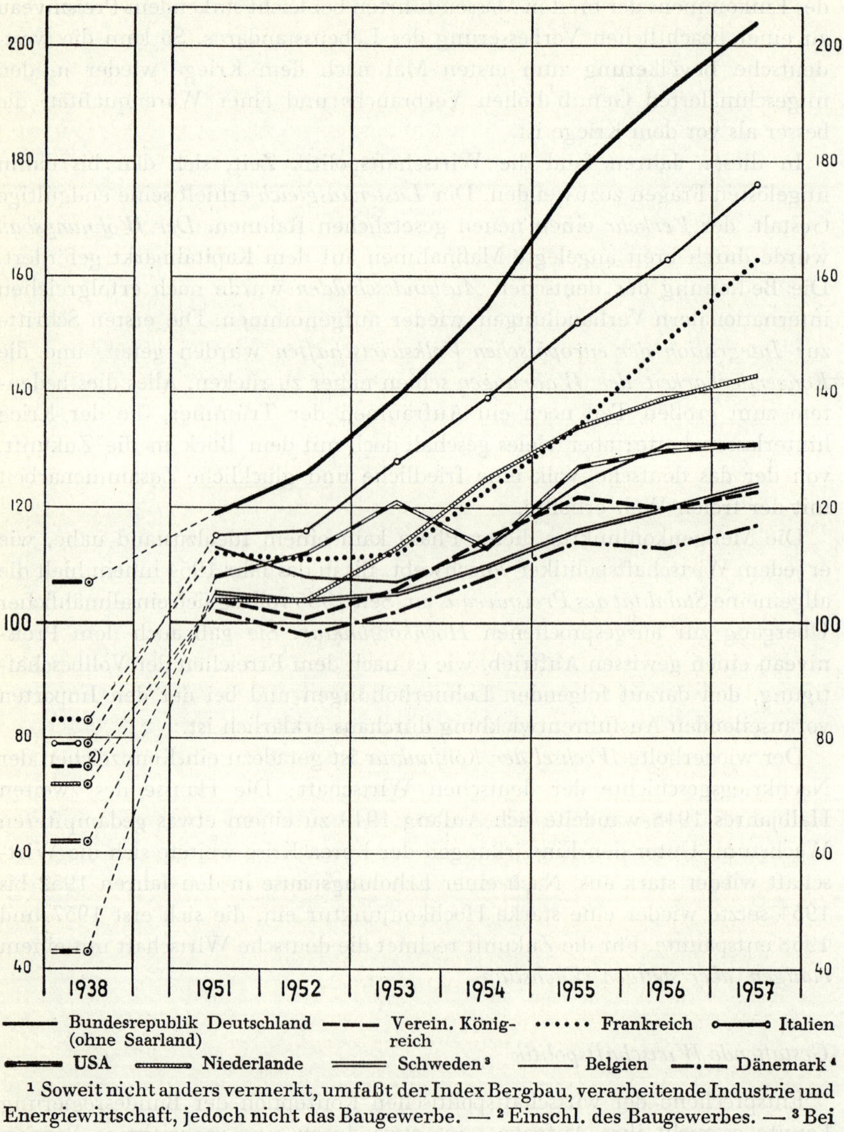

[1] Soweit nicht anders vermerkt, umfaßt der Index Bergbau, verarbeitende Industrie und Energiewirtschaft, jedoch nicht das Baugewerbe. — [2] Einschl. des Baugewerbes. — [3] Bei Bergbau nur Eisenerzbergbau, Energiewirtschaft ohne Gaswerke. — [4] Ohne Bergbau.

Quelle: Statistisches Bundesamt.

Tabelle 7

INDEX DER INDUSTRIELLEN PRODUKTION[1] EUROPÄISCHER LÄNDER UND DER USA

1950 = 100

Land	1938	1951	1952	1953	1954	1955	1956	1957	1958
Bundesrepublik Deutschland[2] .	107	119	126	139	155	178	192	204	210
Belgien	.	113	108	107	113	124	131	131	123
Dänemark[3]	.	102	98	102	108	114	I 117	123	123
Frankreich	83	112	111	112	123	134	149	162	172
Vereinigtes Königreich	75a)	104	101	106	115	I 121	122	123	122
Italien	79	113	116	128	I 139	152	163	176	180
Niederlande	72	104	104	113	125	134	140	143	143
Schweden	62	105	104	105	110	116	120	124	125
USA[4]	43	107	111	120	112	124	128	128	120

[1] Soweit nicht anders vermerkt, umfaßt der Index Bergbau, verarbeitende Industrie und Energiewirtschaft, jedoch nicht das Baugewerbe. — [2] Ohne Saarland. — [3] Ohne Bergbau. — [4] Ohne Energie-Erzeugung. — a) Einschließlich des Baugewerbes. — Zu I siehe Tabelle 6.

Quelle: Statistisches Bundesamt.

Wirtschaftsbereichen einen bestimmten Anteil an diesem Zuwachs zuzumessen. Ein sogenannter *Long Term Plan*, der im Zusammenhang mit der Verwendung der Marshall-Hilfe unter Mitwirkung alliierter Dienststellen erarbeitet worden war, wurde von der tatsächlichen Entwicklung der Produktion weit übertroffen. Es gab in Westdeutschland überhaupt keine Gesamtplanung im lenkungswirtschaftlichen Sinne. Die Überlegenheit einer mehr auf das Qualitative abzielenden Politik, die in erster Linie um die Herstellung einer marktwirtschaftlichen Ordnung bemüht ist und im übrigen der Wirtschaft mit indirekter Förderung diejenigen Hilfen und Anregungen gibt, deren sie nach den jeweiligen Umständen bedarf, ist von der praktischen Erfahrung der vergangenen Jahre eindeutig bestätigt worden.

So hat die Wirtschaftspolitik sich stets bemüht, dem *Wettbewerb* als dem allgemeinen Ordnungsprinzip Geltung zu verschaffen, wo immer dies möglich war. Nur in der ständigen Auseinandersetzung mit dem Konkurrenten ist es möglich, den wirtschaftlichen Fortschritt und die Produktivität anzuspornen und durch Preissenkung oder Qualitätsverbesserung dem Verbraucher zugute kommen zu lassen. Die gesetzlichen Grundlagen für eine staatliche Sicherung dieses Wettbewerbs fanden sich schon in Vorschriften der Besatzungsmächte. Sie fanden die Zustimmung der deutschen Wirtschaftspolitik; jedoch sollten sie möglichst bald durch eine den deutschen Verhältnissen besser angepaßte Gesetzgebung ersetzt werden. Obschon ein entsprechender Gesetzesentwurf seit 1949 vorlag, währten die Verhandlungen über diese schwierige Materie mehrere Jahre. Erst Mitte 1957 kam es daher zur Verabschiedung des Gesetzes gegen Wettbewerbsbeschränkungen. In diesem Gesetz ist auch die Behandlung der marktbeherrschenden Unternehmen geregelt.

Das Prinzip wettbewerblicher Marktverfassung ließ sich jedoch nicht in allen Zweigen der westdeutschen Wirtschaft mit der gleichen Konsequenz durchsetzen. So zeigte es sich, daß die *landwirtschaftliche Erzeugung* wie in vielen anderen Staaten eines besonderen Schutzes vor der Auslandskonkurrenz bedurfte, weil sie seit dem Ende des vergangenen Jahrhunderts den Kontakt mit dem Weltmarkt verloren hatte. Dieser Schutz erstreckt sich auf die wichtigsten landwirtschaftlichen Erzeugnisse und bedient sich der Einfuhrregulierung. Die Agrarpolitik verfolgt das Ziel, die inländischen Erzeugungsmöglichkeiten auszunutzen und das Einkommen der Landwirtschaft so zu heben, daß sie durch Rationalisierung und Strukturverbesserungen allmählich die Wettbewerbsfähigkeit wiedergewinnen kann.

Auch im *Verkehrswesen* tritt an die Stelle des Wettbewerbs eine weitgehend vom Staat festgelegte Abgrenzung der Aufgaben, die von den Verkehrsträgern, der Eisenbahn, dem Straßenverkehr und der Binnenschiffahrt, zu übernehmen sind.

In der *Wohnungswirtschaft* war es aus sozialen Rücksichten nicht möglich, die Wohnungsmieten überall dem Spiel von Angebot und Nachfrage zu überlassen. Um die Mieten auf einem mäßigen Niveau halten zu können, übernahm es der Staat, ausreichendes und billiges Kapital für den Wohnungsbau bereitzustellen.

Bei einigen Berufszweigen hat der Gesetzgeber den Zutritt zum Markt von gewissen Voraussetzungen abhängig gemacht. Handwerker und Einzelhändler müssen vor Errichtung eines Gewerbebetriebes berufliche Kenntnisse nachweisen. Ähnliches gilt für andere Berufe, deren gewissenhafte Ausübung aus Gründen der öffentlichen Sicherheit und Ordnung oder im Interesse der Volksgesundheit geboten erscheint.

Die Deutsche Bundesbahn, das Post- und Telegraphenwesen und einige Erwerbsunternehmen befinden sich in öffentlicher Hand. Während die erstgenannten nach gemeinwirtschaftlichen Grundsätzen arbeiten, verhalten sich die Erwerbsunternehmen in aller Regel wie private Firmen. Die

Beteiligungen des Staates entstanden bereits vor dem Kriege. Da die Soziale Marktwirtschaft eine saubere Trennung zwischen den Aufgaben des Staates und dem Tätigkeitsfeld der Wirtschaft verlangt, suchte man nach Möglichkeiten, diesen Besitz der öffentlichen Hand in privates Eigentum zu überführen. Eine Vermögensübertragung so großen Ausmaßes wirft jedoch Fragen auf, die nicht in kurzer Zeit gelöst werden können; besonders wenn mit dieser Privatisierung gleichzeitig der Grundstein für eine Vermögensbildung möglichst vieler Arbeiter und Angestellten gelegt werden soll.

Die staatspolitische Bedeutung einer breit gestreuten Eigentumsbildung war auch eines der bestimmenden Motive für die *Förderung des Mittelstandes*. Obschon der Kreis derjenigen, die sich zum Mittelstand zählen, nicht nach objektiven Merkmalen abgrenzbar ist, nimmt die mittelstandsfördernde Wirtschaftspolitik sich besonders der kleinen Gewerbetreibenden, des Handels und des Handwerks an. So wurden die Steuersenkungen in einer Weise ausgestaltet, daß sie bessere Möglichkeiten zur Bildung von Eigenkapital boten. Auch die Kreditprogramme des ERP-Sondervermögens und die Bürgschaften des Bundeshaushalts berücksichtigten die Bedürfnisse mittelständischer Unternehmen. Um die Kreditversorgung zu erleichtern, wurden mit Hilfe der Bundesregierung Kreditgarantie-Gemeinschaften gegründet. Große Beachtung wurde der Rationalisierung der Betriebsführung geschenkt; für diesen Zweck stellte der Bund Zuschüsse bereit. Es wurde auch nicht versäumt, die mittelständische Wirtschaft bei der Vergabe öffentlicher Aufträge in besonderem Maße zu berücksichtigen.

Eine neue Aufgabe erwächst der Wirtschaftspolitik mit der Eingliederung von *Saarland*. Um sie möglichst ohne wirtschaftliche Störungen verlaufen zu lassen, muß die Währungsumstellung und die Neuorientierung des Warenverkehrs sorgfältig vorbereitet werden. Ähnlich wie bei der Hilfe für die isolierte Berliner Wirtschaft wird die Bundesregierung auch der saarländischen Wirtschaft finanziell zur Seite stehen und für eine rasche Anpassung an den inzwischen erreichten Leistungsstand des übrigen Bundesgebietes sorgen. Die *Lohnbildung* ist in der Bundesrepublik völlig den Gewerkschaften und Arbeitgebern überlassen. Die zwischen ihnen ausgehandelten Löhne gelten durchweg auch für diejenigen Arbeitnehmer, die nicht Gewerkschaftsmitglieder sind. Ein großer Teil der Arbeiterschaft erhält eine Bezahlung, die über das in den Tarifvereinbarungen festgelegte Niveau hinausgeht. Viele Unternehmen, deren Produktivität es erlaubt, gewähren ihrer Belegschaft hohe freiwillige Sozialleistungen oder gar Gewinnbeteiligungen, die vereinzelt die Form eines Eigentumsanteils am Betrieb annehmen.

BEITRÄGE DER WIRTSCHAFTSBEREICHE[1] ZUM BRUTTOINLANDSPRODUKT

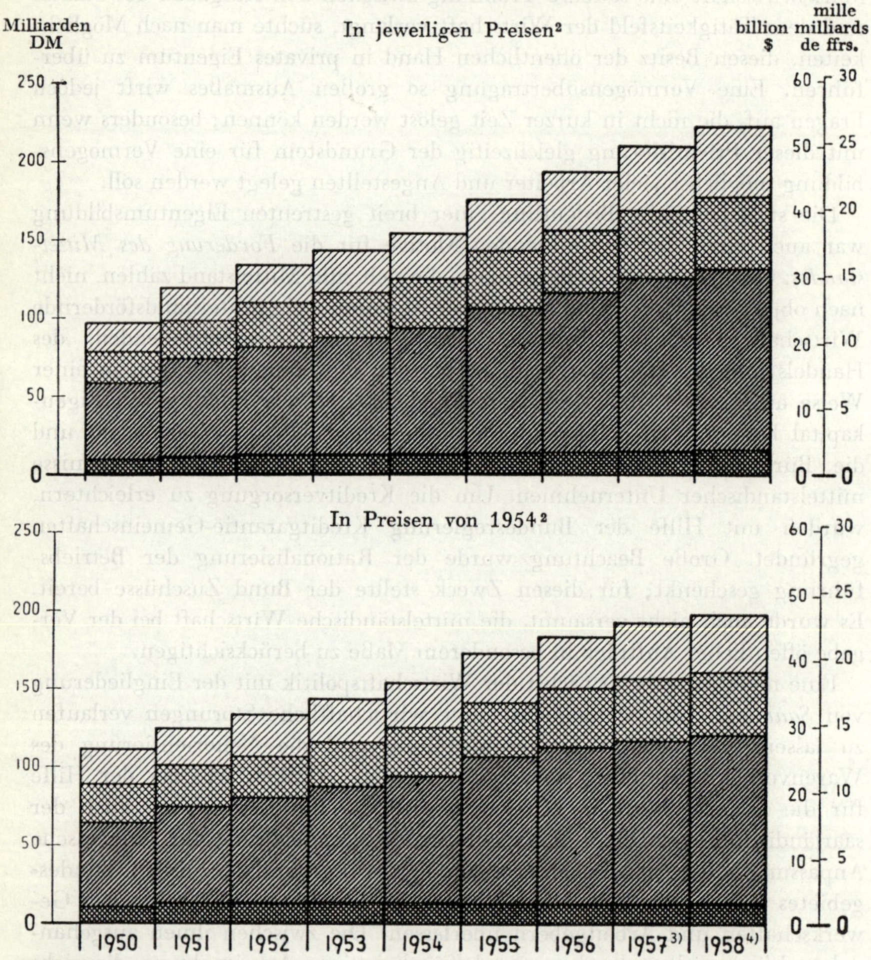

Landwirtschaft, Forstwirtschaft, Fischerei

Bergbau und Energiewirtschaft, Verarbeitendes Gewerbe, Baugewerbe

Handel und Verkehr (einschl. Nachrichtenübermittlung)

Banken und Privatversicherungen, Wohnungsvermietung, Staat, Sonstige Dienstleistungen

[1] Bundesrepublik Deutschland (ohne Saarland). — [2] Von Scheingewinnen bzw. -verlusten bereinigt. — [3] Vorläufige Ergebnisse. — [4] Erste vorläufige Ergebnisse.

Quelle: Statistisches Bundesamt.

VERWENDUNG DES BRUTTOSOZIALPRODUKTS[1]

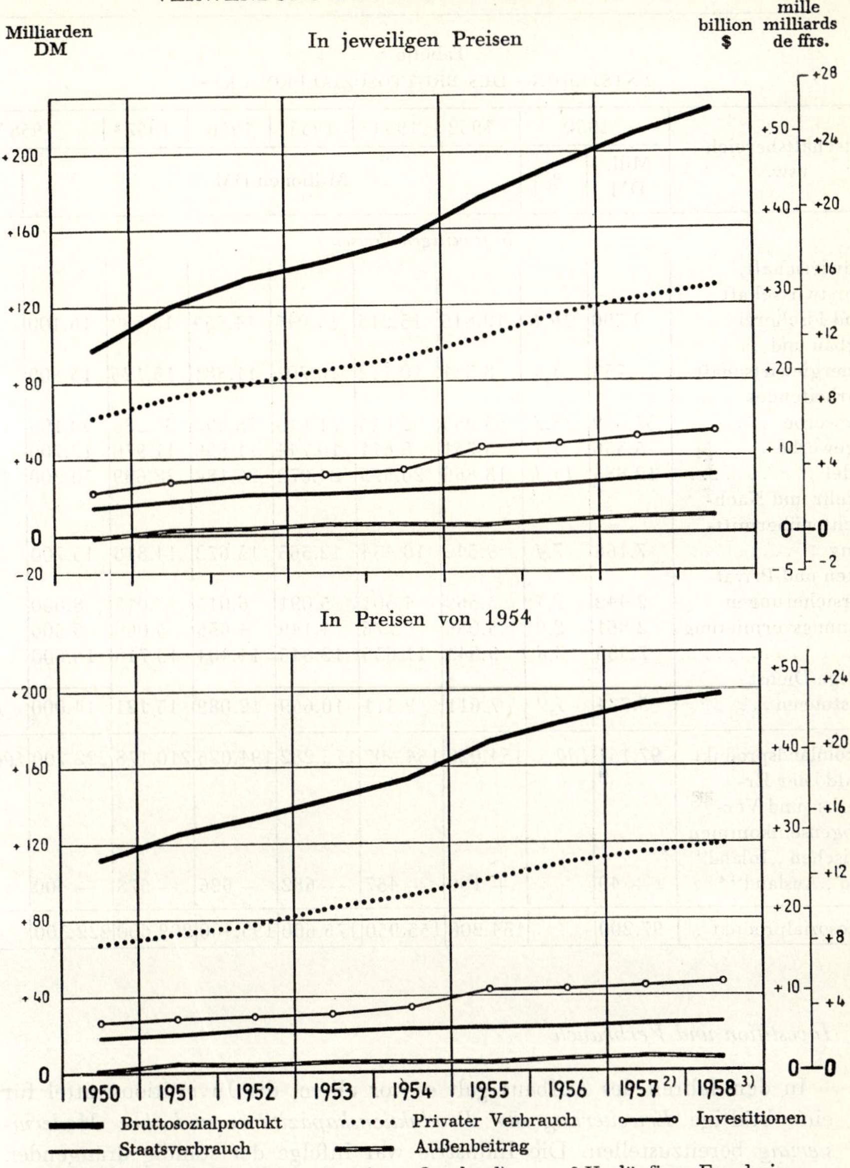

[1] Bundesrepublik Deutschland (ohne Saarland). — [2] Vorläufige Ergebnisse. — [3] Erste vorläufige Ergebnisse.

Quelle: Statistisches Bundesamt.

Tabelle 8

ENTSTEHUNG DES BRUTTOSOZIALPRODUKTS[1]

Wirtschaftsbereich usw.	1950		1952	1954	1955	1956	1957[2]	1958[3]	
	Mill. DM	%	Millionen DM						%
			in jeweiligen Preisen						
Landwirtschaft, Forstwirtschaft und Fischerei	9.790	*10,1*	12.815	13.215	14.045	14.554	15.362	16.100	*7,2*
Bergbau und Energiewirtschaft	5.733	*5,9*	8.351	10.112	10.701	11.881	13.125	13.800	*6,2*
Verarbeitendes Gewerbe	37.609	*38,7*	53.935	62.615	71.613	78.697	85.288	90.100	*40,5*
Baugewerbe	5.356	*5,5*	6.751	8.611	10.744	11.896	11.970	12.700	*5,7*
Handel	12.885	*13,3*	18.866	20.379	24.072	26.182	28.699	30.200	*13,6*
Verkehr und Nachrichtenübermittlung	7.168	*7,4*	9.342	10.454	12.363	13.672	14.816	15.700	*7,0*
Banken und Privatversicherungen ..	2.442	*2,5*	3.369	4.301	5.091	6.015	7.013	8.000	*3,6*
Wohnungsvermietung	2.861	*2,9*	3.036	3.776	4.149	4.636	5.066	5.500	*2,5*
Staat	7.533	*7,8*	9.944	11.633	12.845	14.404	15.718	16.600	*7,5*
Sonstige Dienstleistungen	5.774	*5,9*	7.611	9.311	10.659	12.089	13.121	14.000	*6,3*
Bruttoinlandsprodukt	97.151	*100*	134.020	154.407	176.282	194.026	210.178	222.700	*100*
∓ Saldo der Erwerbs- und Vermögenseinkommen zwischen „Inland" und „Ausland"[4] .	+ 49	.	+ 180	— 457	— 682	— 626	— 578	— 400	.
Bruttosozialprodukt .	97.200	.	134.200	153.950	175.600	193.400	209.600	222.300	.

Investition und Verbrauch

In den Jahren des Aufbaus galt es vor allem, die Investitionsmittel für eine kräftige *Erweiterung der Produktionskapazitäten und ihre Modernisierung* bereitzustellen. Die Industrie war infolge der ständig drängenden Nachfrage imstande, einen ungewöhnlichen und – unter sozialen Gesichtspunkten – unwillkommen hohen Teil ihres Finanzbedarfs aus Gewinnen

Tabelle 8 (Fortsetzung)
ENTSTEHUNG DES BRUTTOSOZIALPRODUKTS

Wirtschaftsbereich usw.	1950		1952	1954	1955	1956	1957[2]	1958[3]	
	Mill. DM	%	Millionen DM						%
			in Preisen von 1954						
Landwirtschaft, Forstwirtschaft und Fischerei	10.430	*9,3*	12.790	13.215	12.900	12.760	12.790	13.200	*6,7*
Bergbau und Energiewirtschaft	7.730	*6,9*	9.190	10.112	10.750	11.400	11.800	11.800	*6,0*
Verarbeitendes Gewerbe	40.520	*36,3*	51.430	62.615	73.890	78.580	83.170	85.800	*43,3*
Baugewerbe	6.080	*5,4*	6.730	8.611	9.820	10.440	9.900	10.200	*5,2*
Handel	15.670	*14,0*	17.590	20.379	22.540	24.550	26.320	27.100	*13,7*
Verkehr und Nachrichtenübermittlung	8.460	*7,6*	9.500	10.454	11.800	12.780	13.330	13.200	*6,7*
Banken und Privatversicherungen ..	2.680	*2,4*	3.500	4.301	4.770	5.220	5.690	6.100	*3,1*
Wohnungsvermietung	2.910	*2,6*	3.230	3.776	4.140	4.460	4.840	5.200	*2,6*
Staat	10.110	*9,0*	11.110	11.633	12.130	12.480	13.240	13.500	*6,8*
Sonstige Dienstleistungen	7.150	*6,4*	8.200	9.311	10.030	10.970	11.620	11.900	*6,0*
Bruttoinlandsprodukt	111.740	*100*	133.270	154.407	172.770	183.640	192.700	198.000	*100*
∓ Saldo der Erwerbs- und Vermögenseinkommen zwischen „Inland" und „Ausland"[4] .	+ 60	.	+ 180	— 457	— 670	— 590	— 450	— 300	.
Bruttosozialprodukt .	111.800	.	133.450	153.950	172.100	183.050	192.250	197.700	.

[1] Bundesrepublik Deutschland (ohne Saarland). — [2] Vorläufige Ergebnisse. — [3] Erste vorläufige Ergebnisse. — [4] Ein Minuszeichen (—) bedeutet, daß Ausländern mehr Erwerbs- und Vermögenseinkommen aus dem „Inland" zugeflossen sind als Inländern aus dem „Ausland", ein Pluszeichen (+) bedeutet das Umgekehrte.

Quelle: Statistisches Bundesamt.

zu decken. Dazu war sie aber auch gezwungen; denn die auf dem Kapitalmarkt gesammelten Sparbeträge flossen zum großen Teil dem Wohnungsbau zu. Ergänzend stellte der Staat aus Steuermitteln und aus dem ERP-Sondervermögen große Beträge sowohl dem Wohnungsbau wie für die Finanzierung

Tabelle 9
VERWENDUNG DES BRUTTOSOZIALPRODUKTS [1]

Verwendungsart	1950		1952	1954	1955	1956	1957 [2]	1958 [3]	
	Mill. DM	%	Millionen DM						%
			in jeweiligen Preisen						
Privater Verbrauch	61.845	*63,6*	79.111	92.328	102.340	114.460	123.000	130.000	*58,5*
Staatsverbrauch	14.350	*14,8*	21.060	22.350	23.920	25.470	28.000	30.000	*13,5*
laufende Käufe für zivile Zwecke	9.970	*10,3*	13.550	16.400	17.880	20.120	21.650	...	...
Verteidigungsaufwand [4]	4.380	*4,5*	7.510	5.950	6.040	5.350	6.350	...	...
Investitionen	22.176	*22,8*	30.592	33.929	45.076	46.890	50.300	53.400	*24,0*
Anlagen	18.455	*19,0*	25.470	32.205	39.770	44.300	46.100	49.200	*22,1*
Ausrüstungen	9.410	*9,7*	13.800	16.960	21.115	23.400	24.100	25.800	*11,6*
Bauten	9.045	*9,3*	11.670	15.245	18.655	20.900	22.000	23.400	*10,5*
Vorratsveränderungen	+3.721	*+3,8*	+5.122	+1.724	+5.306	+2.590	+4.200	+4.200	*+1,9*
Außenbeitrag	—1.171	*—1,2*	+3.437	+5.343	+4.264	+6.580	+8.300	+8.900	*+4,0*
Bruttosozialprodukt	97.200	*100*	134.200	153.950	175.600	193.400	209.600	222.300	*100*
			in Preisen von 1954						
Privater Verbrauch	67.030	*60,0*	77.600	92.328	101.050	109.890	114.930	118.800	*60,1*
Staatsverbrauch	18.050	*16,1*	22.050	22.350	22.850	23.080	24.660	25.700	*13,0*
Investitionen	26.400	*23,6*	29.450	33.929	43.400	43.480	45.030	46.800	*23,7*
Anlagen	22.200	*19,9*	24.650	32.205	38.200	41.020	41.130	42.900	*21,7*
Ausrüstungen	11.330	*10,1*	13.260	16.960	20.835	22.300	22.270	...	...
Bauten	10.870	*9,7*	11.390	15.245	17.365	18.720	18.860	...	...
Vorratsveränderungen	+4.200	*+3,8*	+4.800	+1.724	+5.200	+2.460	+3.900	+3.900	*+2,0*
Außenbeitrag	+ 320	*+0,3*	+4.350	+5.343	+4.800	+6.600	+7.630	+6.400	*+3,2*
Bruttosozialprodukt	111.800	*100*	133.450	153.950	172.100	183.050	192.250	197.700	*100*

[1] Bundesrepublik Deutschland (ohne Saarland). — [2] Vorläufige Ergebnisse. — [3] Erste vorläufige Ergebnisse. — [4] Bis 5. 5. 1955 Besatzungskosten.

Quelle: Statistisches Bundesamt.

der gewerblichen Wirtschaft bereit. Die Gewährung staatlicher Darlehen für Industrie und Gewerbe war stets mit einem besonderen wirtschaftspolitischen Zweck verbunden. Es handelte sich vor allem darum, strukturelle Verwerfungen zu beseitigen, die aus den Zerstörungen des Krieges und der Abtrennung Ost- und Mitteldeutschlands entstanden waren. Daher mußten die staatlichen Mittel eine hohe Anstoßwirkung haben. Sie wurden meist unter der Auflage vergeben, daß der gleiche Betrag und mehr aus privaten Mitteln hinzugelegt werden mußte. Auf diese Weise wurden die „*Engpässe*" sehr schnell überwunden und in Gebieten mit hoher Arbeitslosigkeit zahlreiche *Arbeitsplätze* geschaffen.

Die *Investitionsquote* der westdeutschen Volkswirtschaft überstieg in allen Jahren 21% des Bruttosozialprodukts. Anders hätte die gewaltige Produktionsleistung, die das Volkseinkommen von 1950 bis 1958 mehr als verdoppelte, sicher nicht realisiert werden können.

Der *Staatsverbrauch* nahm dagegen in den letzten Jahren einen immer geringeren Teil der volkswirtschaftlichen Leistung in Anspruch. Trotz mehrfachen Steuersenkungen erzielte der Fiskus wegen der Ausdehnung der

Tabelle 10

PRIVATER VERBRAUCH JE EINWOHNER[1]

Jahr	Privater Verbrauch je Einwohner			
	in jeweiligen Preisen		in Preisen von 1954	
	DM	Zunahme gegenüber dem Vorjahr in %	DM	Zunahme gegenüber dem Vorjahr in %
1950	1.318	.	1.429	.
1951	1.521	*15,4*	1.526	*6,8*
1952	1.657	*8,9*	1.625	*6,5*
1953	1.786	*7,8*	1.788	*10,0*
1954	1.895	*6,1*	1.895	*6,0*
1955	2.079	*9,7*	2.053	*8,3*
1956	2.298	*10,5*	2.207	*7,5*
1957[2]	2.437	*6,0*	2.277	*3,2*
1958[3]	2.543	*4,3*	2.323	*2,0*

[1] Bundesrepublik Deutschland (ohne Saarland). — [2] Vorläufige Ergebnisse. — [3] Erste vorläufige Ergebnisse.

Quelle: Statistisches Bundesamt.

PRIVATER VERBRAUCH JE EINWOHNER[1]

1950 = 100

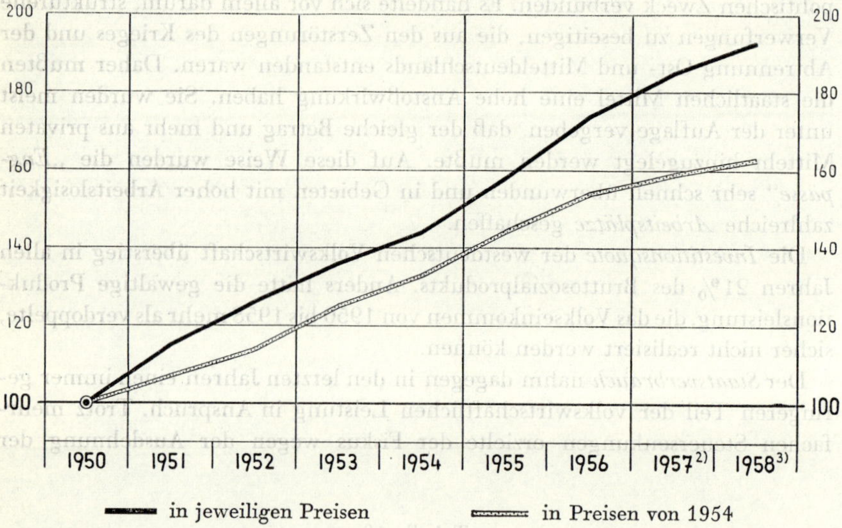

[1] Bundesrepublik Deutschland (ohne Saarland). — [2] Vorläufige Ergebnisse. — [3] Erste vorläufige Ergebnisse.

Quelle: Statistisches Bundesamt.

Wirtschaftskraft steigende Einnahmen, so daß die wachsenden staatlichen Bedürfnisse zufriedenstellend gedeckt werden konnten. Der mit 13 bis 15% gering erscheinende Anteil des Staatsverbrauchs am Bruttosozialprodukt darf jedoch nicht verwechselt werden mit der Belastung der Wirtschaft durch Steuern und Abgaben. Diese ist wesentlich höher; sie beanspruchte 1957 etwa ein Drittel des Bruttosozialprodukts. Daran läßt sich erkennen, in wie hohem Ausmaß der Staat eine Umverteilung des Volkseinkommens vornimmt.

Es war vor allem die hohe Investitionsquote, die den *privaten Verbrauch* der Bevölkerung auf kaum 60% des Bruttosozialprodukts beschränkte. Die verhältnismäßig große Konstanz dieses Anteils über mehrere Jahre hinweg bedeutet aber andererseits, daß der Lebensstandard mit dem allgemeinen Wirtschaftswachstum gestiegen ist. Tatsächlich läßt sich von 1950 bis 1958 eine Verdoppelung des privaten Verbrauchs von 62 Milliarden DM auf 130 Milliarden DM feststellen. Da die Preise sehr viel weniger gestiegen sind, ergibt sich eine reale Zunahme des privaten Verbrauchs von 77%. Sogar wenn

Tabelle 11

ZU- (+) BZW. ABNAHME (—) DES SOZIALPRODUKTS NACH VERWENDUNGSARTEN[1]

Verhältniszahlen

Verwendungsart	Zu- (+) beziehungsweise Abnahme (—) in %							
	1951	1952	1953	1954	1955	1956	1957[2]	1958[3]
	gegenüber							
	1950	1951	1952	1953	1954	1955	1956	1957[2]
	in jeweiligen Preisen							
Bruttosozialprodukt	+ *23,0*	+ *12,2*	+ *7,1*	+ *7,1*	+ *14,1*	+ *10,1*	+ *8,4*	+ *6,1*
Privater Verbrauch	+ *16,6*	+ *9,7*	+ *8,8*	+ *7,3*	+ *10,8*	+ *11,8*	+ *7,5*	+ *5,7*
Staatsverbrauch ...	+ *23,6*	+ *18,8*	+ *1,5*	+ *4,5*	+ *7,0*	+ *6,5*	+ *9,9*	+ *7,1*
Anlageinvestitionen	+ *20,6*	+ *14,4*	+ *12,5*	+ *12,3*	+ *23,5*	+ *11,4*	+ *4,1*	+ *6,7*
Einfuhr	+ *31,2*	+ *15,2*	+ *5,9*	+ *26,8*	+ *25,5*	+ *14,8*	+ *17,8*	+ *3,9*
Ausfuhr	+ *63,2*	+ *19,6*	+ *14,0*	+ *20,6*	+ *17,8*	+ *19,3*	+ *19,0*	+ *4,4*
	in Preisen von 1954							
Bruttosozialprodukt	+ *11,8*	+ *6,8*	+ *7,8*	+ *7,1*	+ *11,8*	+ *6,4*	+ *5,0*	+ *2,8*
Privater Verbrauch	+ *8,0*	+ *7,2*	+ *11,0*	+ *7,1*	+ *9,4*	+ *8,7*	+ *4,6*	+ *3,3*
Staatsverbrauch ...	+ *9,7*	+ *11,4*	— *1,4*	+ *2,8*	+ *2,2*	+ *1,0*	+ *6,8*	+ *4,2*
Anlageinvestitionen	+ *4,1*	+ *6,7*	+ *15,2*	+ *13,4*	+ *18,6*	+ *7,4*	+ *0,3*	+ *4,3*
Einfuhr	+ *5,3*	+ *20,3*	+ *19,5*	+ *30,3*	+ *21,4*	+ *12,0*	+ *18,8*	+ *8,6*
Ausfuhr	+ *36,2*	+ *14,1*	+ *20,3*	+ *23,8*	+ *16,1*	+ *15,3*	+ *18,3*	+ *4,9*

[1] Bundesrepublik Deutschland (ohne Saarland). — [2] Vorläufige Ergebnisse. — [3] Erste vorläufige Ergebnisse.

Quelle: Statistisches Bundesamt.

man noch berücksichtigt, daß wegen der Bevölkerungsvermehrung ein etwas geringerer Betrag auf den einzelnen Einwohner entfällt, bleibt ein realer Zuwachs von 63%, der die effektive *Verbesserung* des *Lebensstandards* kennzeichnet.

In den einzelnen Jahren waren die Zuwachsraten des privaten Verbrauchs je Einwohner natürlich verschieden. 1951 betrug der Zuwachs 15,4%, in den folgenden Jahren verminderte er sich auf 8,9%, 7,8% und 6,1%. Erst 1955 war wieder ein Anstieg auf 9,7%, 1956 auf 10,5%, 1957 allerdings mit nur 6% eine Abschwächung zu verzeichnen, die sich 1958 noch fortsetzte. In diesen letzten Jahren zeigt sich die Steigerung der Masseneinkommen, die stärker als die Preiserhöhung war und damit eine beträchtliche Erhöhung des Lebensstandards bedeutet.

*

DURCHSCHNITTLICHER BRUTTOSTUNDENVERDIENST
DER INDUSTRIEARBEITER[1]
Zunahme gegenüber dem Vorjahr in %

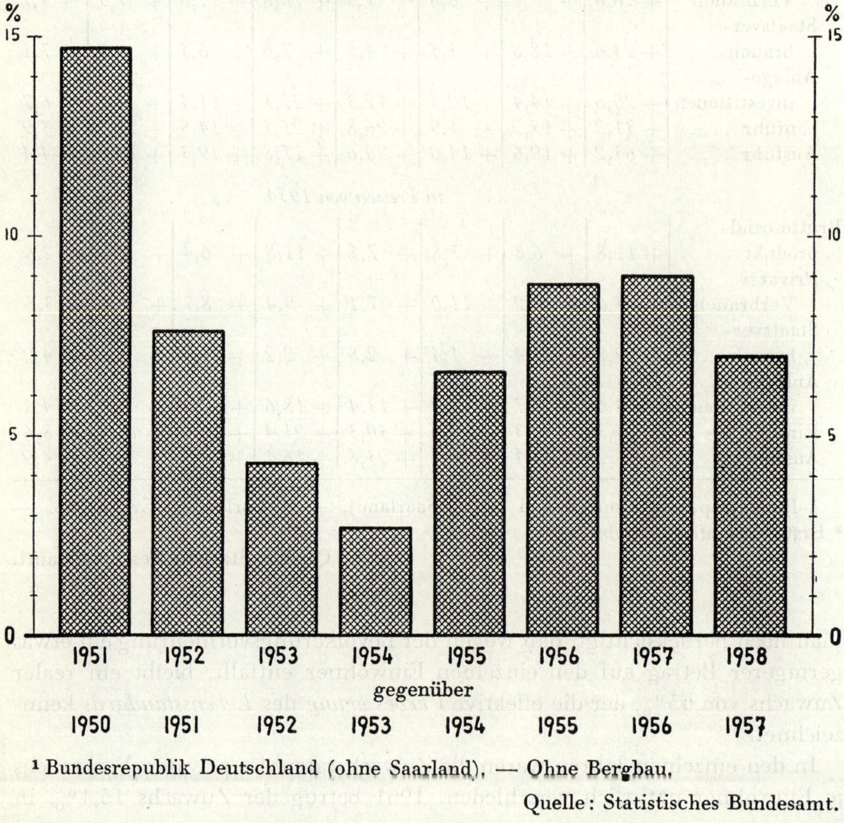

[1] Bundesrepublik Deutschland (ohne Saarland). — Ohne Bergbau.

Quelle: Statistisches Bundesamt.

Die *Produktivität der Arbeitsleistung* konnte durch die gewaltigen Investierungen sehr stark gesteigert werden. In der Industrie[1] betrug der Zuwachs der Produktivität in den Jahren 1950 bis 1957 mehr als 50%. Auch nach Erreichen der Vollbeschäftigung konnte zum Beispiel im Jahre 1957 noch eine Steigerung von 7,5% erreicht werden. Betrachtet man den Zeitraum der letzten acht Jahre, so stellt man fest, daß die Lohnaufbesserungen sich etwa im Rahmen der Produktivitätssteigerung hielten; doch gehen sie seit 1955 darüber hinaus. Nicht zuletzt darauf ist es zurückzuführen, daß die Preise seither leicht anziehen; denn die Produktionsausweitung stößt allmählich an eine Grenze, die angesichts der Vollbeschäftigung und der immer weiter gehenden Verkürzung der Arbeitszeit nur durch eine erneute Rationalisierungswelle überwunden werden kann.

[1] Ohne Energieversorgungsbetriebe und Bauhauptgewerbe.

INDEX DES PRODUKTIONSERGEBNISSES
JE ARBEITERSTUNDE IN DER INDUSTRIE[1]
1950 = 100

Zunahme gegenüber dem Vorjahr in %

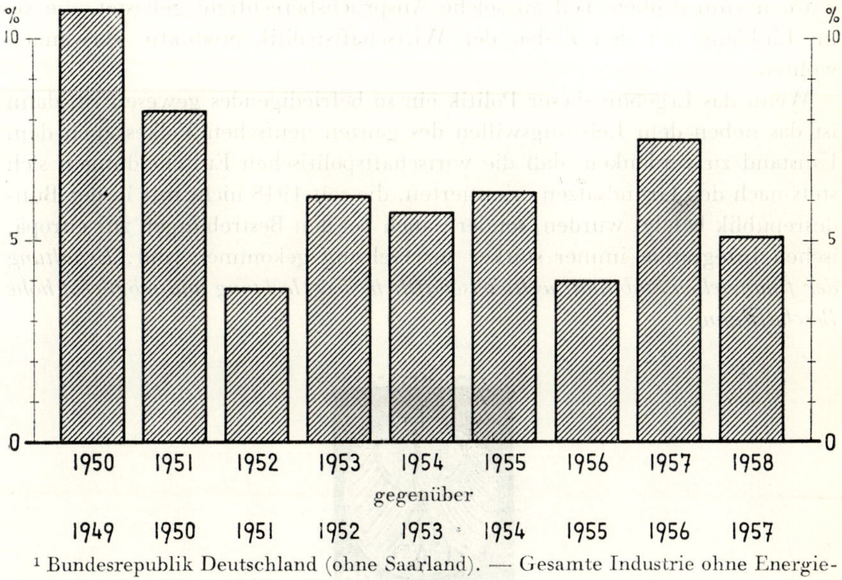

[1] Bundesrepublik Deutschland (ohne Saarland). — Gesamte Industrie ohne Energieversorgungsbetriebe und ohne Bauhauptgewerbe.

Quelle: Statistisches Bundesamt.

Umsichtige Wirtschaftspolitik

Die Wirtschaftspolitik der Bundesregierung hat ein vielfältiges Instrumentarium angewendet, um das wirtschaftliche Geschehen nach ihren Vorstellungen zu steuern und den äußeren Umständen anzupassen. Sie hat bei jeder bedeutenden Maßnahme versucht, eine Mehrzahl von Zielsetzungen miteinander zu verbinden. So wurden zum Beispiel Steuersenkungen, die in erster Linie als Entlastung der Wirtschaft gedacht waren, häufig derart ausgestaltet, daß sie die Kapitalbildung förderten oder auch denjenigen Unternehmen zugute kamen, die in Notstandsgebieten ansässig oder von Vertriebenen neu gegründet worden waren. Auch die landwirtschaftliche Rationalisierung, der Schiffbau und der Wohnungsbau sind auf diese Weise gefördert worden. Das ERP-Sondervermögen, das aus den Hilfeleistungen des Marshall-Plans angesammelt worden war, wurde stets so eingesetzt, daß es als eine Ergänzung der privaten Investitionen in solchen Bereichen diente, die infolge der Preisbindung ihrer Erzeugnisse und Leistungen oder aus anderen Gründen nicht in der Lage waren, ausreichendes Kapital vom freien Markt zu erlangen. Selbst die Zahlungen aus dem Lastenausgleich wurden zum großen Teil an solche Anspruchsberechtigte geleistet, die sie im Einklang mit den Zielen der Wirtschaftspolitik produktiv verwenden wollten.

Wenn das Ergebnis dieser Politik ein so befriedigendes gewesen ist, dann ist das neben dem Leistungswillen des ganzen deutschen Volkes auch dem Umstand zu verdanken, daß die wirtschaftspolitischen Entscheidungen sich stets nach den Grundsätzen orientierten, die seit 1948 nicht nur in der Bundesrepublik befolgt wurden, sondern auch bei den Bestrebungen zur europäischen Integration immer stärker zur Geltung gekommen sind: *Erhaltung der finanziellen Stabilität, weltwirtschaftliche Verflechtung und möglichst hohe Beschäftigung.*

DEUTSCHLAND IN DER WELTWIRTSCHAFT

Der Neubeginn

Unmittelbar nach dem Kriegsende gab es keinen deutschen Außenhandel im eigentlichen Sinne. Auf Weisung und für Rechnung der alliierten Dienststellen wurden Rohstoffe ausgeführt und Lebensmittel eingeführt. Erst allmählich wurden deutsche Stellen in das Außenhandelsverfahren eingeschaltet und industrielle Rohstoffe in das Einfuhrprogramm einbezogen. Die Rohstoffeinfuhren waren jedoch ausschließlich dazu bestimmt, in Exportwaren verarbeitet zu werden, damit die Einfuhren bezahlt werden konnten. Nicht „lebenswichtige" Güter waren von jeder Einfuhr ausgeschlossen. Die Außenhandelsstellen der Französischen Zone (OFICOMEX) und der Amerikanisch-Britischen Zone (OMGUS) vereinbarten die Preise und führten die Abrechnung durch. Während der Exportpreis in Dollar bezahlt werden mußte – was den europäischen Abnehmern nicht leicht fiel –, erhielt der deutsche Exporteur nur den im Inland geltenden Stoppreis vergütet. Erst nach dem Stimmungsumschwung im Ausland, dessen erstes Zeichen die Rede des amerikanischen Außenministers BYRNES in Stuttgart war (September 1946), und mit der Vereinigung der Britischen und Amerikanischen Zonen wurde der Plan gefaßt, die Westzonen innerhalb von drei Jahren außenwirtschaftlich selbständig zu machen. Die *Joint Export Import Agency* (JEIA) übernahm die Geschäftsführung und schaltete deutsche Kaufleute stärker in die Vertragsverhandlungen ein.

Der Tag der Währungsreform war auch für die Entwicklung des Außenhandels von entscheidender Bedeutung. Die JEIA-Periode ging schnell zu Ende, als ein Wechselkurs für die Deutsche Mark festgelegt wurde und verpflichtende Warenabkommen mit dem Ausland zustande kamen. Das Vereinigte Wirtschaftsgebiet kam in den Genuß der unbedingten Meistbegünstigung durch die Teilnehmerländer des Allgemeinen Abkommens über Handel und Zölle (GATT). Es nahm später auch an dem ersten multilateralen Zahlungsabkommen der CEEC, der Vorläuferin des Europäischen Wirtschaftsrates, und den folgenden Vereinbarungen über die sogenannten Ziehungsrechte teil. Nach der Konstituierung der Bundesrepublik wurde den deutschen Dienststellen der selbständige Abschluß von Handelsverträgen ermöglicht. Als im Jahr 1950 die Europäische Zahlungsunion gegründet wurde, trat die Bundesrepublik ihr als gleichberechtigtes Mitglied bei.

AUSSENHANDEL[1]

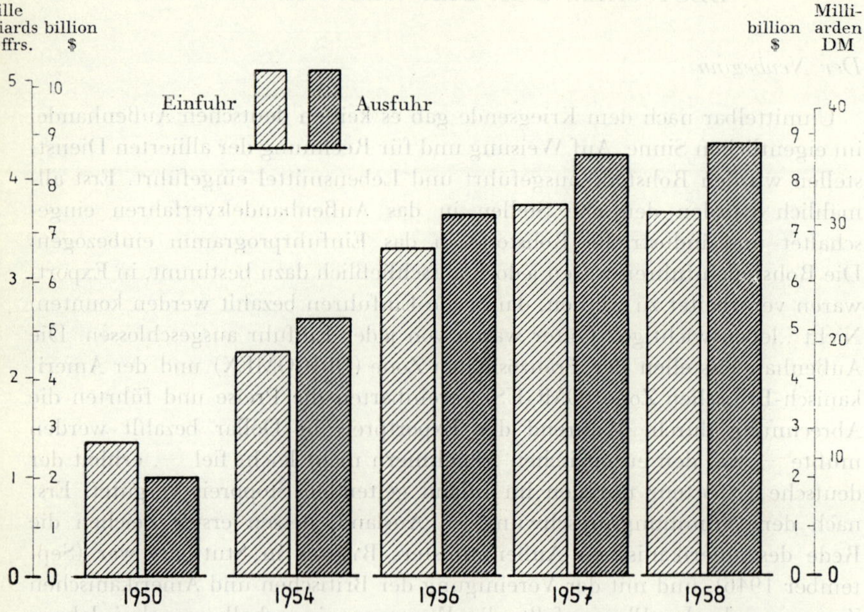

[1] Bundesrepublik Deutschland (ohne Saarland), einschließlich von Berlin(West).

Quelle: Statistisches Bundesamt.

Vor der Währungsreform konnte die Einfuhr nur zu etwa 40% von der Ausfuhr gedeckt werden. Der überwiegende Teil der Einfuhren wurde aus alliierten Mitteln bezahlt. In den Jahren ab 1950 nahm diese Auslandshilfe schnell ab, und schon im Jahr 1951 war die volle Bezahlung aller Einfuhren durch Ausfuhrerlöse gesichert.

Ausweitung und Struktur des Außenhandels

Die Einfuhrwerte der Bundesrepublik betrugen 1958 fast das dreifache des Jahres 1950, und die Ausfuhr stieg sogar auf mehr als das vierfache. Die Ursachen dieser außerordentlich schnellen Rückkehr Deutschlands zu den Weltmärkten lassen sich leicht aus den folgenden Tatsachen erkennen:

Die erste *Liberalisierung* der westdeutschen Einfuhr aus den Ländern des OEEC-Raumes wurde schon 1948 verfügt. Nach einer infolge der Korea-Krise notwendig gewordenen Unterbrechung im Jahre 1951 wurde die Liberalisierung Anfang 1952 auf 57% der privaten Einfuhren des Jahres 1949

Tabelle 1

EINFUHR[1] UND AUSFUHR

Jahr	Einfuhr			Ausfuhr	Einfuhr- (—) bzw. Ausfuhrüberschuß (+)	
	insgesamt	darunter: finanziert mit fremden Mitteln[2]			insgesamt	ohne Einfuhr aus fremden Mitteln
	Millionen DM		%	Millionen DM		
1950	11.373,9	2.018,4	*17,7*	8.362,2	— 3.011,8	— 993,4
1951	14.725,5	1.798,4	*12,2*	14.576,8	— 148,7	+ 1.649,7
1952	16.202,9	481,3	*3,0*	16.908,8	+ 705,9	+ 1.187,2
1953	16.010,4	264,8	*1,7*	18.525,6	+ 2.515,2	+ 2.780,0
1954	19.337,1	290,8	*1,5*	22.035,2	+ 2.698,1	+ 2.988,9
1955	24.472,4	129,7	*0,5*	25.716,8	+ 1.244,4	+ 1.374,0
1956	27.963,9	129,7	*0,5*	30.861,0	+ 2.897,2	+ 3.026,8
1957	31.696,9	101,6	*0,3*	35.968,0	+ 4.271,1	+ 4.372,8
1958	31.133,1	75,0	*0,2*	36.998,1	+ 5.864,9	+ 5.939,9

[1] Darunter sind die mit fremden Mitteln finanzierten Einfuhren gesondert nachgewiesen. — [2] Bundesrepublik Deutschland (ohne Saarland), einschließlich von Berlin (West). — [3] Marshallplan-Mittel (ERP), GARIOA und OK-Contributions. — Seit dem 31.12.1952 hat die Finanzierung aus fremden Mitteln sich im wesentlichen auf die Sonderhilfe für Berlin(West) beschränkt.

Quelle: Statistisches Bundesamt.

Tabelle 2

INDICES DER TATSÄCHLICHEN WERTE UND DES VOLUMENS DER EIN- UND AUSFUHR[1]

1950 = 100[2]

Jahr	Index			
	der tatsächlichen Werte		des Volumens[3]	
	Einfuhr	Ausfuhr	Einfuhr	Ausfuhr
1951	130	175	103	140
1952	143	202	124	153
1953	141	222	138	173
1954	170	264	169	211
1955	215	308	210	246
1956	246	370	236	286
1957	279	431	265	326
1958	274	443	283	338

[1] Bundesrepublik Deutschland (ohne Saarland), einschließlich von Berlin(West). — [2] Von Originalbasis 1954 = 100 umbasiert auf 1950 = 100. — [3] Mengen bewertet mit Durchschnittswerten von 1954.

Quelle: Statistisches Bundesamt.

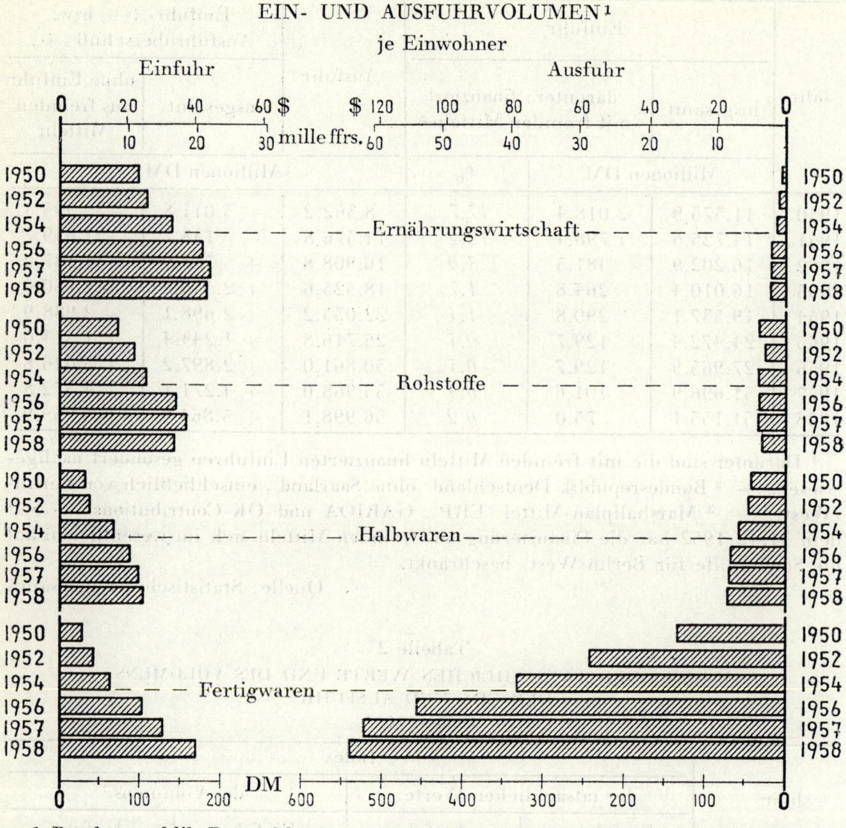

[1] Bundesrepublik Deutschland und Berlin(West). — Mengen bewertet mit Durchschnittswerten von 1954.

Quelle: Statistisches Bundesamt.

gebracht. Schrittweise wurde sie auf 91,2% der Rohstoffe und 98,2% der Fertigwaren erhöht (Stand 1. 1. 1959). Seit dem Frühjahr 1952 wurden auch gegenüber den nicht in der OEEC vertretenen Ländern Einfuhrfreilisten eröffnet. Im März 1954 stimmten diese Freilisten bis auf wenige Positionen mit den im OEEC-Raum gültigen Listen überein. Ganz ähnliche Regelungen wurden auch im Verkehr mit den Ländern getroffen, die nur durch ein Verrechnungsabkommen mit der Bundesrepublik verbunden sind. Auch hier ist also praktisch eine weitgehende Liberalisierung erreicht.

Für Einfuhren aus dem Dollar-Raum wurde im Februar 1954 ebenfalls eine Freiliste veröffentlicht. Bis zum Sommer 1958 ist das Ausmaß dieser *Dollar-Liberalisierung* in fünf Stufen auf rund 95%, gemessen an den privaten Einfuhren des Jahres 1953, gebracht worden. Diese Maßnahmen der Bundesrepublik verfolgten die Absicht, hinsichtlich des Liberalisierungsgrades möglichst bald zu einer völligen Gleichstellung der Einfuhren aus allen Währungsräumen zu gelangen. Der Übergang zahlreicher Länder zur freien Eintauschbarkeit der Währungen wird im Jahre 1959 eine weitere Angleichung notwendig machen.

Soweit noch Kontingente aufrecht erhalten werden müssen, werden sie als Mindestkontingente behandelt. Häufig werden mehr Lizenzen erteilt, als das Kontingent vorsieht. Selbst diese Kontingente werden nach Möglichkeit nicht bilateral ausgeschrieben, sondern sie stehen jedem Lieferland innerhalb eines Währungsraumes gleichermaßen offen.

Die Bundesrepublik hat auch den Bemühungen um den *Abbau der Zölle* sich nicht verschlossen. Die ersten Zollzugeständnisse wurden auf der GATT-Konferenz in Torquay im Jahre 1951 ausgehandelt und verwirklicht. Alljährlich fanden weitere Konferenzen dieser Art statt. Gewisse Schwierigkeiten tauchten allerdings auf, als diejenigen Länder, die traditionell einen geringen Zollschutz hatten, ihre Sätze nicht mehr weiter senken konnten und die Länder mit verhältnismäßig hohen Zöllen nicht zu einem weiteren Abbau bereit waren, ohne Zugeständnisse anderer zu erhalten. Trotzdem hat die Bundesrepublik von sich aus Zollsenkungen vorgenommen; denn sie hält jede Ermäßigung des Zollschutzes für sinnvoll und macht sie nicht unbedingt von Gegenleistungen anderer Länder abhängig. Eine individuelle Zollsenkung, die mehr als 700 Positionen betraf, wurde am 1. 4. 1955 angeordnet. Ihr folgten drei weitere autonome Zollsenkungen, und zwar aus konjunkturpolitischen Gründen. Die erste davon, im Juli 1956, schrieb für alle Erzeugnisse der gewerblichen Wirtschaft einen Höchstzoll von 21% des Wertes und darüber hinaus eine gestaffelte Senkung für bestimmte Waren vor, verbunden mit einer individuellen Zollsenkung für einige ernährungswirtschaftliche Güter. Dadurch wurden die GATT-Vereinbarungen des gleichen Jahres gleichsam vorweggenommen. Die vierte konjunkturpolitische Zollsenkung folgte im August 1957. Sie ermäßigte alle Zollsätze gewerblicher Güter mit Ausnahme weniger Schutzpositionen um 25%. Ab 1959 liegen die Zollsätze für 80% aller gewerblichen Güter nur noch bei 10% und darunter.

Die Öffnung der deutschen Grenzen für die Einfuhr war in den Jahren des Aufbaus, als ganz Europa einen „*Dollar drive*" begonnen hatte, von einer gewissen *Förderung der Ausfuhr* begleitet. Das Exportförderungsgesetz, das den Exporteuren körperschafts- und einkommensteuerliche Erleichterungen brachte, wurde jedoch schon am 31.12.1955 außer Kraft gesetzt; denn die Bundesrepublik hatte zusammen mit dem Vereinigten Königreich sich verpflichtet, alle Exportförderungsmaßnahmen möglichst schnell aufzuheben. Gegenwärtig besteht für die Exporteure noch die Möglichkeit, zur Absicherung bestimmter Risiken Garantien und Bürgschaften des Staates in Anspruch zu nehmen. Dabei wird jedoch streng darauf geachtet, daß der Exporteur einen Teil des Risikos selbst trägt. Die so versicherten Geschäfte betreffen zum weit überwiegenden Teil den Export in Entwicklungsländer. Hier kann es den Exporteuren nicht immer zugemutet werden, die nicht im rein Kaufmännischen liegenden Risiken und die häufig geforderte langfristige Finanzierung ganz ohne Hilfe zu tragen. Bis in das Jahr 1957 hinein konnten Exportwechsel zu einem den Auslandszinsen angeglichenen Zinssatz außerhalb der für die Banken geltenden Rediskontlimits von der Notenbank diskontiert werden. Diese Möglichkeit ist inzwischen gänzlich entfallen.

Damit hat die Bundesrepublik alle Maßnahmen, die als Exportförderung angesehen werden könnten, entweder aufgehoben oder doch auf ein gerechtfertigtes Maß zurückgeführt. Ihre Industrie sieht sich auf den Auslandsmärkten einer sehr scharfen und nicht immer auf echten Kostenvorteilen beruhenden Konkurrenz gegenüber. Sie muß aber in Zukunft diesen Konkurrenzkampf ohne die Hilfe des Staates bestehen.

*

Die *Gesamtentwicklung des deutschen Außenhandels* ließ die Bundesrepublik in der Einfuhr seit 1954, in der Ausfuhr seit 1955 den *dritten Platz im Welthandel* nach den USA und dem Vereinigten Königreich einnehmen. Damit erreichte sie wieder die Stellung im Welthandel, die Deutschland vor dem Kriege innehatte. In wie starkem Maße die wirtschaftliche Verflechtung der Bundesrepublik mit der Weltwirtschaft gegenüber der eigenen durchschnittlichen wirtschaftlichen Entwicklung zugenommen hat, zeigt der Anteil des Umsatzes im Außenhandel am Sozialprodukt:

	1936	1950	1958
Brutto-Sozialprodukt (Milliarden RM/DM)	47,9	99,0	222,3
Außenhandels-Umsatz absolut (Milliarden RM/DM) .	6,2	19,7	68,1
Anteil am Brutto-Sozialprodukt (%)	*12,9*	*19,9*	*30,6*

Tabelle 3

ANTEILE DER EIN- UND AUSFUHR EUROPÄISCHER LÄNDER UND DER USA AN DER WELTEIN- UND -AUSFUHR

%

Jahr	Welthandel [1]							
	insgesamt	darunter						
		Europa	darunter					USA
			Bundesrepublik Deutschland [2]	Belgien-Luxemburg	Frankreich [3]	Vereinigtes Königreich	Niederlande	
Einfuhr								
1929	100	56,3	9,1 [a]	2,8	6,5	15,3	3,1	12,3
1938	100	58,3	9,2 [a]	3,2	5,6	17,6	3,3	8,1
1950	100	43,1	4,6	3,3	5,2	12,1	3,5	16,3
1951	100	43,4	4,4	3,1	5,5	13,2	3,2	14,7
1952	100	42,3	4,8	3,1	5,5	11,8	2,8	14,7
1953	100	43,0	5,0	3,2	5,2	12,0	3,1	15,5
1954	100	44,8	5,8	3,2	5,5	11,5	3,6	13,8
1955	100	45,8	6,6	3,2	5,4	11,8	3,6	13,8
1956	100	45,8	6,8	3,3	5,8	10,7	3,8	13,8
1957	100	45,7	7,0	3,2	5,7	10,3	3,8	13,0
Ausfuhr								
1929	100	49,6	9,9 [a]	2,7	6,1	10,9	2,5	15,9
1938	100	48,5	9,6 [a]	3,3	4,0	10,5	2,6	13,9
1950	100	37,1	3,6	3,0	5,5	11,0	2,5	18,3
1951	100	37,8	4,6	3,5	5,5	9,7	2,6	19,9
1952	100	38,9	5,5	3,4	5,3	10,0	2,9	20,8
1953	100	38,6	6,0	3,1	5,2	9,9	2,9	21,3
1954	100	40,4	6,8	3,0	5,6	9,7	3,1	19,3
1955	100	41,5	7,3	3,3	5,9	9,7	3,2	18,3
1956	100	41,2	7,9	3,4	5,0	9,5	3,1	20,1
1957	100	41,8	8,5	3,2	5,1	9,3	3,1	20,5

[1] Welthandel ab 1950 ohne Außenhandel der Länder China, Bulgarien, Rumänien, Sowjetunion, Ungarn, Polen, Tschechoslowakei und der sogenannten DDR. — [2] Bundesrepublik Deutschland (ohne Saarland) einschließlich von Berlin(West); ohne den Warenverkehr mit der sogenannten DDR und Ostberlin. — [3] Ab 1950 einschließlich des Außenhandels von Saarland. — [a] Deutsches Reich (Gebietsstand: 31. 12. 1937).

Quelle: Statistisches Bundesamt.

Tabelle 4

EIN- UND AUSFUHR[1] NACH WARENGRUPPEN

Jahr	Einfuhr					Ausfuhr				
	insgesamt	Ernährungswirtschaft	Gewerbliche Wirtschaft			insgesamt	Ernährungswirtschaft	Gewerbliche Wirtschaft		
			zusammen	darunter				zusammen	darunter	
				Rohstoffe	Fertigwaren				Rohstoffe	Fertigwaren
Werte in Millionen RM beziehungsweise DM										
1936[2]	2.838	980	1.858	1.123	241	3.381	68	3.313	354	2.633
1950	11.374	5.013	6.360	3.368	1.429	8.362	196	8.166	1.168	5.422
1951	14.726	5.876	8.850	5.249	1.588	14.577	489	14.088	1.318	10.660
1952	16.203	6.065	10.138	5.635	2.146	16.909	379	16.529	1.281	12.704
1953	16.010	5.852	10.158	5.224	2.497	18.526	476	18.050	1.488	13.839
1954	19.337	7.151	12.186	5.502	3.208	22.035	515	21.521	1.694	16.943
1955	24.472	7.635	16.837	7.281	4.640	25.717	683	25.034	1.568	20.198
1956	27.964[a]	9.162	18.657	8.225	5.196	30.861[a]	834	29.945	1.715	24.412
1957	31.697[a]	9.975	21.569	9.376	6.452	35.968[a]	829	35.044	1.939	28.951
1958	31.133[a]	9.408	21.438	7.685	8.500	36.998[a]	882	35.998	1.710	30.398
Anteil der Warengruppen an der Gesamtein- beziehungsweise -ausfuhr in %										
1936[2]	*100*	*34,5*	*65,5*	*39,6*	*8,5*	*100*	*2,0*	*98,0*	*10,5*	*77,9*
1950	*100*	*44,1*	*55,9*	*29,6*	*12,6*	*100*	*2,3*	*97,7*	*14,0*	*64,8*
1951	*100*	*39,9*	*60,1*	*35,6*	*10,8*	*100*	*3,4*	*96,6*	*9,0*	*73,1*
1952	*100*	*37,4*	*62,6*	*34,8*	*13,2*	*100*	*2,2*	*97,8*	*7,6*	*75,1*
1953	*100*	*36,6*	*63,4*	*32,6*	*15,6*	*100*	*2,6*	*97,4*	*8,0*	*74,7*
1954	*100*	*37,0*	*63,0*	*28,5*	*16,6*	*100*	*2,3*	*97,7*	*7,7*	*76,9*
1955	*100*	*31,2*	*68,8*	*29,8*	*19,0*	*100*	*2,7*	*97,3*	*6,1*	*78,5*
1956	*100*[a]	*32,8*	*66,7*	*29,4*	*18,6*	*100*[a]	*2,7*	*97,0*	*5,6*	*79,1*
1957	*100*[a]	*31,5*	*68,0*	*29,6*	*20,4*	*100*[a]	*2,3*	*97,4*	*5,4*	*80,5*
1958	*100*[a]	*30,2*	*68,9*	*24,7*	*27,3*	*100*[a]	*2,4*	*97,3*	*4,6*	*82,2*

[1] Bundesrepublik Deutschland (ohne Saarland), einschließlich von Berlin(West). — [2] Geschätzt. — [a] Ab 1956 sind Rückwaren und Ersatzlieferungen nicht mehr in den einzelnen Warengruppen, sondern nur noch in der Gesamtein- und -ausfuhr enthalten.

Quelle: Statistisches Bundesamt.

Innerhalb des Außenhandels ergaben sich im Laufe der Jahre Verschiebungen, die für die Normalisierung der Struktur kennzeichnend sind. Der Anteil der ernährungswirtschaftlichen Einfuhren an der Gesamteinfuhr hat sich verringert. Er beträgt aber auch heute noch ein knappes Drittel. Die gewerbliche Einfuhr bestand anfänglich zu mehr als der Hälfte aus Rohstoffen, heute nur noch zu einem Drittel. Dagegen drängte die Einfuhr von Fertigerzeugnissen stärker in den Vordergrund. Sie erreichte 1958 einen Anteil von rund 27%. Daran zeigt sich eine so weitgehende *Verbesserung der Leistungsfähigkeit* der westdeutschen Wirtschaft, daß sie einerseits mit einem geringeren Rohstoffverbrauch auskommen kann, andererseits aber auch fähig und willens ist, mehr und mehr Fertigerzeugnisse aus dem Ausland aufzunehmen. Der zunehmende Austausch industrieller Fertigwaren ist ein überzeugender Beweis dafür, wie stark gerade die hochentwickelten Industrieländer sich gegenseitig ergänzen können.

In der Ausfuhr haben sich keine wesentlichen Verschiebungen zwischen ernährungswirtschaftlichen und gewerblichen Ausfuhren ergeben. Das liegt daran, daß die Exporte von Gütern der Ernährungswirtschaft – trotz steigendem Volumen – keinen bedeutenden Platz in der Gesamtausfuhr einnehmen. Innerhalb der gewerblichen Exporte war deutlich festzustellen, wie schnell der Anteil der Rohstoffe zurückging, als der Zwang zur Rohstoffausfuhr fortgefallen war. Dafür stieg der Anteil der Fertigwarenausfuhr stark an. Er hat mit rund 82% den Vorkriegsstand übertroffen.

Zweifellos hat die anhaltende Hochkonjunktur im Ausland, die weitgehend von Investitionen getragen ist, zu dieser Entwicklung entscheidend beigetragen. Aber auch die im Vergleich zum Ausland größere *Stabilität des deutschen Preisniveaus* hat die Auslandsaufträge anschwellen lassen. Nicht zuletzt aber ist die Tatsache von Bedeutung, daß die *Qualität der deutschen Erzeugnisse* und die Bereitwilligkeit der Industrie, hoch spezialisierte Maschinen und Ersatzteile für den individuellen Bedarf des Bestellers anzufertigen, im Ausland sehr geschätzt werden.

*

Die Bundesrepublik bezieht rund die Hälfte ihrer Einfuhren aus europäischen Ländern und verkauft zwei Drittel ihrer Ausfuhren an ihre europäischen Nachbarn. Aber auch die USA sind mit rund 14% an den Lieferungen beteiligt und nehmen etwa 7% der Ausfuhr auf. Die Vereinigten Staaten sind für die Bundesrepublik ein interessanter, aber auch schwieriger Markt. Sie bemüht sich, mehr und mehr dorthin zu liefern.

Es ist keineswegs die Absicht der Bundesrepublik, ihren Handel mit jedem einzelnen Handelspartner oder mit den Ländern eines jeden Währungsraumes genau auszugleichen. Die *Abkehr vom bilateralen Denken* wird in der Bundesrepublik ernst genommen. Nachdem im Raum der Europäischen Zahlungsunion (EZU) eine Teilkonvertibilität unter den Währungen der

AUSSENHANDEL[1] NACH WARENGRUPPEN

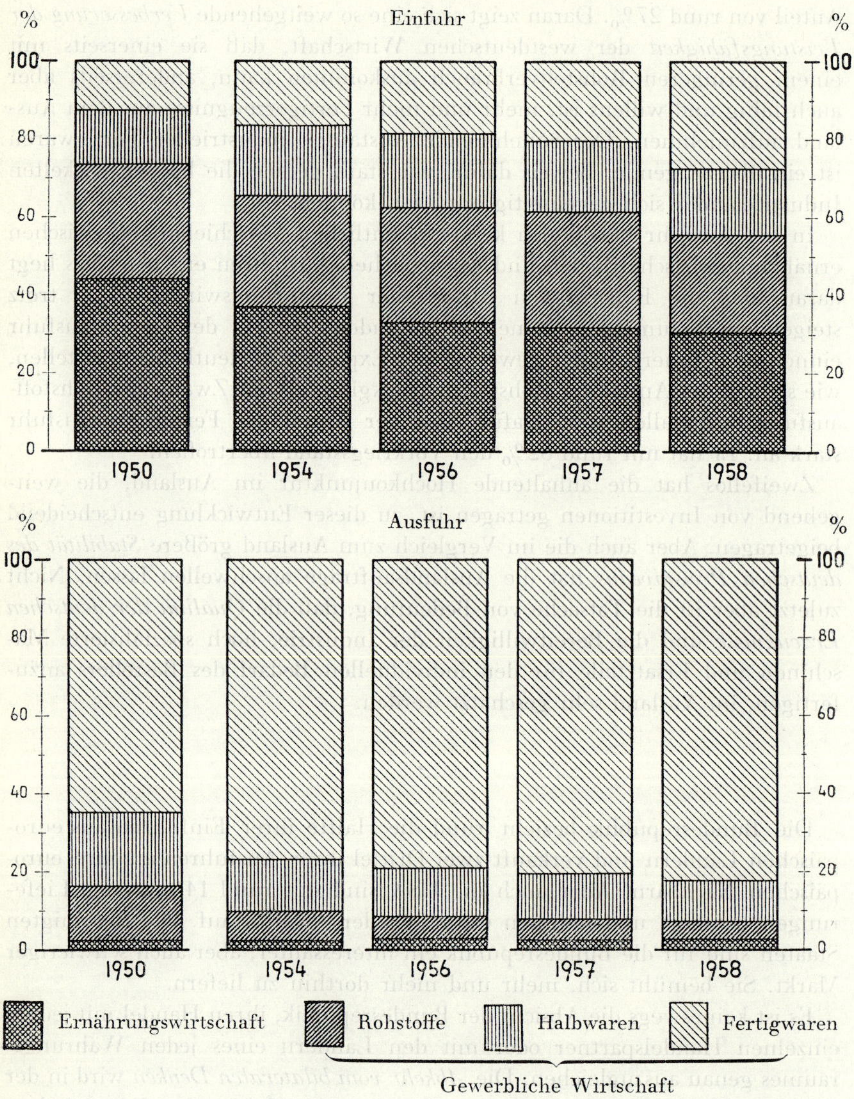

[1] Bundesrepublik Deutschland (ohne Saarland) einschließlich von Berlin (West).

Quelle: Statistisches Bundesamt.

Tabelle 5

EIN- UND AUSFUHR[1] NACH ERDTEILEN UND AUSGEWÄHLTEN LÄNDERN

% der Gesamtein- beziehungsweise -ausfuhr

Herstellungs- bzw. Verbrauchsland	Einfuhr					Ausfuhr				
	1954	1955	1956	1957	1958	1954	1955	1956	1957	1958
Europa	52,7	52,9	52,0	50,7	55,4	66,2	66,8	66,8	64,6	63,7
darunter:										
Belgien-Luxemburg	4,5	5,7	4,8	4,2	4,5	7,2	6,7	6,8	6,7	6,6
Frankreich[2]	5,0	5,9	4,8	4,9	5,1	5,4	5,7	6,3	6,3	5,8
Vereinigtes Königreich	4,4	3,5	4,1	3,6	4,4	3,9	4,0	4,1	3,9	3,9
Niederlande	7,9	7,2	7,2	7,1	8,0	9,3	9,4	9,3	9,0	8,1
Sowjetunion	0,5	0,6	0,8	1,3	1,2	0,2	0,4	0,9	0,7	0,8
Afrika	8,1	7,2	6,8	6,4	6,4	6,0	5,7	4,8	5,3	5,2
Amerika	26,0	26,7	28,9	31,3	27,2	16,3	15,6	16,0	16,5	16,7
darunter:										
Kanada	2,0	2,0	2,4	2,4	3,1	0,8	0,9	1,2	1,1	1,2
USA	11,5	13,1	14,2	17,8	13,5	5,6	6,3	6,7	6,9	7,1
Asien	10,7	10,6	9,6	9,0	9,2	9,4	9,7	10,5	11,7	12,5
Australien und Ozeanien	2,4	2,4	2,5	2,4	1,7	1,5	1,5	1,2	1,2	1,3
Eismeergebiete und nicht ermittelte Länder	—	0,0	0,0	0,0	0,0	0,0	0,0	0,0	0,0	0,0
Schiffsbedarf	0,1	0,1	0,1	0,1	0,1	0,6	0,7	0,7	0,7	0,5
Insgesamt	100	100	100	100	100	100	100	100	100	100

[1] Bundesrepublik Deutschland (ohne Saarland), einschließlich von Berlin(West).
[2] Einschließlich von Saarland.

Quelle: Statistisches Bundesamt.

Partnerländer erreicht war, indem die Verrechnung der Salden zu 75% in Gold und Dollars geschah, hatte die Bundesrepublik im April 1953 die sogenannte ,,liberalisierte Kapitalmark" eingeführt. Mit ihr wurden die Anlage- und Wertpapier-Investitionen von Ausländern in Westdeutschland getätigt. Ferner wurde die sogenannte ,,beschränkt konvertierbare D-Mark" (BEKO-Mark) geschaffen. Sie entsprach etwa dem transferablen englischen Pfund und eröffnete einer Reihe von Ländern mit Verrechnungsabkommen

Tabelle 6

EIN- UND AUSFUHR[1] NACH WÄHRUNGSRÄUMEN
(Millionen DM)

Währungsraum[2]	Einfuhr					Ausfuhr					Einfuhr- (—) bzw. Ausfuhr- (+) überschuß 1958
	1954	1955	1956	1957	1958	1954	1955	1956	1957	1958	
Länder des beschränkt konvertierbaren Währungsraumes .	16.123,2	19.258,0	20.930,4	22.605,9	23.300,3	19.202,4	22.194,5	26.586,6	30.763,7	31.781,0	+ 8.480,8
Länder des EZU-Raums	13.269,9	16.375,2	17.385,7	18.961,9	19.659,3	16.101,7	18.931,6	22.539,2	25.857,7	25.946,3	+ 6.287,1
Sterling-Mitgliedsländer der OEEC ...	2.319,1	3.289,8	3.537,7	3.659,9	3.943,7	1.728,9	1.876,4	2.223,7	2.533,1	2.632,0	— 1.311,7
Sterling-Nichtmitgliedsländer der OEEC	1.017,1	621,6	654,3	798,3	646,1	1.031,1	1.481,7	1.838,0	2.367,3	2.618,3	+ 1.972,2
Andere EZU-Länder (Mitgliedsländer der OEEC) ...	9.588,3	12.355,6	13.042,9	14.342,1	14.942,4	13.222,6	15.297,1	18.125,6	20.581,7	20.397,9	+ 5.455,4
Andere EZU-Länder (Nichtmitgliedsländer der OEEC) ...	345,3	108,1	150,9	161,6	127,1	119,1	276,4	351,9	375,6	298,2	+ 171,1
Länder, die nicht über die EZU abrechnen.....	2.853,2	2.882,8	3.544,7	3.644,0	3.641,0	3.100,6	3.262,8	4.047,4	4.906,0	5.834,7	+ 2.193,7

EIN- UND AUSFUHR NACH WÄHRUNGSRÄUMEN (Fortsetzung)
(Millionen DM)

DM-Abkommensländer . .	2.718,3	2.753,2	3.337,6	3.443,4	3.331,6	2.535,1	2.633,2	3.314,3	3.942,8	4.487,7	+ 1.156,1
Länder ohne Zahlungsabkommen . . .	134,9	129,6	207,1	200,6	309,4	565,5	629,6	733,1	963,2	1.347,1	+ 1.037,7
Länder des frei konvertierbaren Währungsraumes .	3.192,9	5.190,2	7.003,0	9.057,6	7.801,8	2.699,9	3.342,4	4.047,6	4.965,2	5.016,3	— 2.785,5
Eismeergebiete, nichtermittelte Länder, Schiffsbedarf	21,0	24,3	30,5	33,4	31,1	132,9	180,0	226,9	239,1	200,7	+ 169,6
Insgesamt	19.337,1	24.472,4	27.963,9	31.696,9	31.133,1	22.035,2	25.716,8	30.861,0	35.968,0	36.998,1	+ 5.864,9

[1] Bundesrepublik Deutschland (ohne Saarland), einschließlich von Berlin(West). — [2] Darstellung nach Einkaufs- und Käuferländern. — Die Zuordnung der Länder zu den einzelnen Währungsräumen richtet sich nach der überwiegenden Art der Abwicklung des Zahlungsverkehrs der Bundesrepublik nach dem Stande vom Mai 1958 für alle nachgewiesenen Berichtsjahre.

Quelle: Statistisches Bundesamt.

die Möglichkeit, ihre im Verkehr mit Westdeutschland erzielten Exporterlöse auch zum Einkauf in anderen Ländern zu verwenden. Damit konnte der Handel unter den Ländern mit „halbweicher" Währung wesentlich belebt werden.

Die einfache Verrechnung im EZU-Raum und die Liberalisierung erleichterten eine besonders intensive Verflechtung innerhalb dieses Währungsgebietes. Seit 1952 nahm die Bundesrepublik eine immer stärkere Gläubigerstellung gegenüber der Gesamtheit der EZU-Länder ein. Da die dort erzielten Überschüsse zum größeren Teil in harter Währung beglichen werden, kann das entstehende Defizit der Bundesrepublik gegenüber dem Dollarraum leicht abgedeckt werden. Dieser Passivsaldo gegenüber den Dollar-Ländern entstand nicht zuletzt aus dem Umstand, daß die Bundesrepublik auch dort frühzeitig fast den gleichen Liberalisierungsgrad anwandte wie im europäischen Raum.

Auch der Handelsverkehr mit den Ländern, mit denen die Bundesrepublik ein bilaterales oder beschränkt multilaterales Verrechnungsabkommen geschlossen hat, entwickelte sich recht lebhaft. Die Bundesrepublik war bemüht, möglichst viele dieser Länder in die beschränkt multilaterale Verrechnung einzubeziehen und so auch in diesem Raum den Austausch zu erleichtern.

Die Befreiung des Zahlungsverkehrs

Ende des Jahres 1958 gingen die meisten europäischen Länder dazu über, ihre Währungen frei gegeneinander eintauschbar zu machen. Die Bundesrepublik gehörte seit mehreren Jahren zu den eifrigsten Befürwortern der *Konvertibilität*, und sie begrüßt diesen Schritt vor allem, weil sie daraus einen sehr bedeutenden Nutzen für die Weltwirtschaft erhofft. Künftig wird im internationalen Handel nicht mehr nach Bezugsquellen mit ,,weicher" Währung einerseits und mit ,,harter" Währung andererseits unterschieden werden müssen. Ohne Rücksicht auf den Währungsraum wird dort eingekauft werden, wo die Ware am günstigsten angeboten wird. Jeder Einwohner der Bundesrepublik und jeder Ausländer kann jede beliebige Währung mit Deutscher Mark erwerben. In der ,,Härtung" ihrer Währung ist die Bundesrepublik den anderen Ländern vorausgeeilt. Während die meisten übrigen Mitglieder der nunmehr aufgelösten Europäischen Zahlungsunion das Recht des freien Umtausches nur den jeweiligen Ausländern zubilligten, hat die Bundesrepublik auch ihren eigenen Staatsangehörigen diese Freiheit gewährt. Die Konvertibilität erstreckt sich in der Bundesrepublik auch auf den internationalen Kapitalverkehr, und sogar die Einfuhr und Ausfuhr von Gold ist völlig unbehindert. Damit ist die seit dem Anfang der dreißiger Jahre bestehende Devisenbewirtschaftung fortgefallen und ein neuer Abschnitt in der Geschichte des Welthandels eingeleitet.

Hilfe für Entwicklungsländer

Eine Volkswirtschaft, die so eng mit den Märkten der westlichen Welt verbunden ist wie die deutsche, und die sich in einer so vorteilhaften außenwirtschaftlichen Situation befindet, muß sich auch verantwortlich fühlen für die in ihrer Industrialisierung und Einkommenshöhe noch zurückgebliebenen Völker. In Anerkennung dieser Verpflichtung bietet die Bundesrepublik ihre Hilfe an. Sie wird versuchen, die Lage dieser Länder auf verschiedenste Weise zu bessern. Seit langem gewährt sie *Möglichkeiten zur*

Aus enger Dorflage ausgesiedelte Höfe im Taunus

Dorfgemeinschaftshaus in Hessen

Mähdrescher bei der Arbeit

Im Hamburger Hafen

Das Hochsee-Fährschiff „Theodor Heuss“
der Deutschen Bundesbahn

Trans-Europ-Expreß: Ein Dieseltriebzug
der Deutschen Bundesbahn

Ein Güterzug der Deutschen Bundesbahn
an der Geislinger Steige auf der Strecke
Stuttgart—Ulm

	Stand der Leistungen am 31. 7. 58 Millionen DM	feststehende künftige Leistungen Millionen DM	mögliche künftige Leistungen Millionen DM
A. *Effektive Aufbringung öffentlicher und quasi-öffentlicher Mittel*			
I. *Mitgliedschaft in internationalen Organisationen*			
Weltbank	1.601	—	1.109
Technisches Hilfsprogramm der UN	10	—	—
Internationale Finanzkorporation	15	—	—
EWG-Entwicklungsfonds für die überseeischen assoziierten Gebiete	—	840	—
DM-Ziehungen von Entwicklungsländern beim Währungsfonds	72	—	—
insgesamt	1.698	840	1.109
II. *Bilaterale Maßnahmen zur Wirtschafts- und Entwicklungshilfe*			
Konsolidierungskredite aus der Umstellung des bilateralen Zahlungsverkehrs	202	10	—
Umschuldungsmaßnahmen zur Prolongation von Handelsschulden	218	410	—
Abwicklung von Transfer-Rückständen	130	—	—
Sondermaßnahmen	—	378	—
Langfristige Export-Finanzierung (90 % an Entwicklungsländer)	277	438	74
Technische Hilfe	108	53	—
insgesamt	1.035	1.369	74
B. *Öffentliche Sicherheits- und Gewährleistungen*			
Garantien und Bürgschaften im Ausfuhrgeschäft (85—90 % Entwicklungsländer) Plafond 9,5 Mrd. DM	7.550		1.950
C. *Besondere Positionen des privaten Kapitalexports*			
Auslandsinvestitionen	723	—	—
Beteiligung deutscher Banken an Weltbankanleihen	3	4	—
Privater Anteil an Umschuldungsmaßnahmen	600	—	—

Quelle: Tätigkeitsbericht der Bundesregierung, 1958.

technisch-wirtschaftlichen Beratung und erleichtert die *Finanzierung von Projekten zur Industrialisierung*. Sie wird aber auch Hilfe leisten, damit die Erzeugnisse der Entwicklungsländer den Anforderungen des Weltmarkts entsprechen. Weiter wird sie ihren Inlandsmarkt für Einfuhren aus diesen Ländern öffnen; denn nur so werden sie in die Lage versetzt, Kredite und sonstige Hilfen zurückzuzahlen.

Ein wichtiger Schritt zur Angleichung der Produktionsstruktur und des Industrialisierungsgrades wird der *Kapitalexport* sein. Deutsche Investitionen im Ausland sind heute ohne Beschränkungen möglich, sei es zur Gründung von Unternehmungen oder zum Erwerb von Beteiligungen. Seit Anfang 1952 bis Ende 1958 sind private Investitionen im Ausland in Höhe von 2,2 Milliarden DM getätigt worden. Davon entfielen 880 Millionen DM auf die Entwicklungsländer.

Weit bedeutender sind jedoch die finanziellen Leistungen, die außerhalb des privaten Kapitalexports von der Bundesrepublik für das Ausland und besonders zugunsten der Entwicklungsländer erbracht wurden, und zu denen sie sich für die kommenden Jahre verpflichtet hat. Zur Wiedergutmachung der im Kriege anderen Völkern zugefügten Schäden und zur Abdeckung der öffentlichen und privaten Auslandsschulden wurden bisher Zahlungen in einem Gesamtbetrag von 6,4 Milliarden DM geleistet. Darüber hinaus wurde den verschiedenen internationalen Organisationen und Hilfsfonds bis Mitte 1958 ein Betrag von 6,7 Milliarden DM zur Verfügung gestellt.

Speziell für die entwicklungsfähigen Länder sind die in der Übersicht auf Seite 401 zusammengestellten Leistungen zu nennen.

Die wirtschaftliche Integration Europas

Die Errichtung des Internationalen Währungsfonds (IMF) und das Allgemeine Abkommen über Handel und Zölle (GATT) sind die Anfänge der *Befreiung des Welthandels von Handelsbeschränkungen*. Die Statuten des Weltwährungsfonds, der nach den Verhandlungen von Bretton Woods 1944 gegründet wurde, sind beherrscht von dem Gedanken an eine geeinte Welt, die aus den Wirren des Krieges entstehen und eine stabile Währungsordnung erhalten sollte. Aus der Formulierung der Havanna Charter sollte eine entsprechende Vereinbarung über die Freiheit des Welthandels entstehen; doch kam es 1948 nur zu einer Teilregelung in Gestalt des GATT, einer weltumspannenden Absprache über den Abbau der mengenmäßigen Beschränkungen und die Herabsetzung von Zöllen. Der Umstand, daß die

Nachkriegsverhältnisse und die Praktiken vieler Länder mit dem Ziel der Vollbeschäftigung nicht geeignet waren, die geschaffenen Organisationen voll wirksam werden zu lassen, machte die Gründung besonderer europäischer Organisationen notwendig.

Dollarmangel und Devisenbewirtschaftung, Kontingentierungen und hohe Zollmauern waren das Ergebnis der Wirtschaftskrise, des Krieges und des Auseinanderlebens der Volkswirtschaften. Erst mit der Gründung des *Europäischen Wirtschaftsrates* (OEEC) im Jahre 1948 wurde, angeregt durch den Marshall-Plan, ein Instrument der Koordinierung der europäischen Volkswirtschaften geschaffen. Der im Marshall-Plan enthaltene Gedanke europäischer Selbsthilfe und gegenseitiger Abstimmung fand seinen Ausdruck in den Programmpunkten „Liberalisierung des Handels" und „Konvertibilität der Währungen". Damit waren nicht nur die Ziele, sondern auch die Methoden gekennzeichnet, mit denen man die Verbesserung des Lebensstandards anstreben wollte. Als 1950 die *Europäische Zahlungsunion* (EZU) gegründet wurde, schien auch das Instrument zur Bewältigung der Zahlungsprobleme gefunden.

Sowohl der Internationale Währungsfonds wie das GATT hatten in ihren Satzungen die nationalstaatliche Autonomie in der inneren Wirtschaftspolitik uneingeschränkt anerkannt. Solange aber in vielen Ländern mit der Vollbeschäftigung starke Inflationserscheinungen einhergingen, mußten die Erfolge im Abbau der Handelsbeschränkungen gering bleiben. Erst als die europäischen Staaten auf Grund der Erfahrungen, die sie in der Korea-Krise gemacht hatten, der Erhaltung der finanziellen Stabilität mehr und mehr Bedeutung zumaßen, konnte die OEEC mit der Liberalisierung erfolgreicher sein. Auch die seit langem geplante Zollunion der Benelux-Staaten konnte erst realisiert werden, nachdem ihre finanziellen Verhältnisse in bessere Übereinstimmung gebracht worden waren. Vor den gleichen Problemen steht man auch bei der Errichtung des Gemeinsamen Marktes der Europäischen Wirtschaftsgemeinschaft.

Die Bundesrepublik nimmt an allen diesen *Integrationsbestrebungen* regen Anteil. Sie tut es nicht nur, weil sie wirtschaftlich an einer möglichst weitgehenden Verflechtung mit den Weltmärkten interessiert sein muß, sondern weil sie politisch mit der freien Welt eng zusammenarbeiten will. Der SCHUMAN-Plan vom Mai 1950 fand daher die uneingeschränkte Befürwortung der Bundesrepublik, ebenso wie die Pläne zur Gründung einer Europäischen Politischen Gemeinschaft, der Europäischen Verteidigungsgemeinschaft und der Europäischen Wirtschaftsgemeinschaft.

Der Marshall-Plan, die OEEC und EZU

Die großzügige Hilfe der USA an die europäischen Länder hat den Anstoß zum Wiederaufbau der zerstörten Produktionsstätten gegeben und den Willen der europäischen Nationen zur Zusammenarbeit geweckt. Man kann zweifeln, welcher dieser beiden Impulse der stärkere war. Jedenfalls läßt sich rückblickend feststellen, daß es ohne die *Marshall-Hilfe* nicht so schnell zu einer europäischen Einigung gekommen wäre. Die mit der Durchführung des Marshall-Plans betraute Economic Cooperation Administration (ECA) wurde Anfang 1952 von der Mutual Security Agency (MSA) abgelöst, diese ein Jahr später in die Foreign Operations Administration (FOA) und schließlich Mitte 1955 in die International Cooperation Administration (ICA) überführt. Mit dieser Umorganisation trat der Marshall-Plan immer mehr aus dem Blickfeld des öffentlichen Interesses. Aber die *amerikanische Hilfe* wirkt auch heute noch in der Bundesrepublik fort. Im Londoner Schuldenabkommen von 1953 wurde bestimmt, daß ein Drittel der bis Mitte 1951 an die Bundesrepublik gelieferten Hilfseinfuhren im Werte von einer Milliarde Dollar als langfristiger Kredit betrachtet werden soll. Die anderen zwei Drittel, also zwei Milliarden Dollar, gelten als Schenkung. Auch die Hilfslieferungen nach der Jahresmitte 1951 gelten – bis auf einen Kredit in Höhe von 71 Millionen DM – als geschenkt. Die Erlöse aus dem Verkauf dieser Hilfslieferungen durch die Regierung sind in einem Sondervermögen angesammelt, das zu Investitionen in der Wirtschaft dient. Auf diese Weise laufen in der Bundesrepublik nach dem Stand vom 31.3.1958 Finanzierungsprogramme der verschiedensten Art in Höhe von 7.165 Millionen DM. Berücksichtigt man, daß solche Programme nach Maßgabe der Zins- und Tilgungsrückflüsse immer wieder neu anlaufen können, dann wird offensichtlich, welchen Vorteil die deutsche Volkswirtschaft auch heute noch aus der amerikanischen Hilfsaktion zieht.

Der *Europäische Wirtschaftsrat* (OEEC) stand seit seiner Gründung am 16.4.1948 im Mittelpunkt des eigentlichen Integrationsgeschehens. Diese Organisation war ein überaus wertvolles Instrument vertrauensvoller Zusammenarbeit der europäischen Regierungen. Es zeigte sich, daß hier, trotz dem Erfordernis der Einstimmigkeit, weitreichende Beschlüsse gefaßt werden konnten. Die OEEC bemüht sich, die Wirtschaftspolitik ihrer Mitglieder aufeinander abzustimmen. Das wird umso notwendiger, je mehr die Liberalisierung des Handels- und Kapitalverkehrs fortschreitet; denn die Freizügigkeit des wirtschaftlichen Austausches bringt Ungleichheiten zwischen den einzelnen Volkswirtschaften zum Vorschein. Ihre Beseitigung ist nur auf Grund einer engen Fühlungnahme der Regierungen und durch entschlossene Maßnahmen der Partnerländer möglich. Die Ungleichheiten äußerten sich vor allem in den extremen Gläubiger- und Schuldnerpositionen, die sich bei der Abrechnung in der EZU ergaben. Diese Schwierigkeiten harren noch einer dauerhaften Lösung. Angesichts der unterschiedlichen Entwicklung des Preisniveaus der Mitgliedsländer auch nach dem Übergang zur Konvertibilität im EWA dürfte sie in einer strafferen *Koordination des kredit- und konjunkturpolitischen Handelns* zu suchen sein.

Tabelle 7

ENTWICKLUNG DES KUMULATIVEN GESAMTSALDOS DER BUNDESREPUBLIK DEUTSCHLAND[1] GEGENÜBER DER EZU

Millionen Rechnungseinheiten

Jahr	Saldo am Jahresende
1950, 2. Halbjahr . .	— 356,7
1951	+ 43,3
1952	+ 377,9
1953	+ 821,2
1954	+ 995,7
1955	+ 1.600,5
1956	+ 2.600,4
1957	+ 4.026,0
1958	+ 4.581,1

[1] Ohne Saarland, einschließlich von Berlin(West).

Quelle: Statistisches Bundesamt.

Die Montan-Union

Der Wunsch nach schnellerem und vollständigerem wirtschaftlichen Zusammenschluß eines engeren Kreises europäischer Länder führte 1950 zu dem Vorschlag des damaligen französischen Außenministers Robert Schuman, die Kohle- und Stahlindustrie Belgiens, Frankreichs, Italiens, Luxemburgs, der Niederlande und der Bundesrepublik Deutschland zu einer *überstaatlichen* Gemeinschaft zusammenzuschließen. Der Vertrag über diese *Europäische Gemeinschaft für Kohle und Stahl* trat im Juli 1952 in Kraft. Die Vertragsstaaten gaben einen Teil ihrer nationalen Souveränität zugunsten dieser überstaatlichen Einrichtung auf und überführten ihre Kohle- und Stahlindustrie in einen echten gemeinsamen Markt. In diesem Markt sollte es beim Austausch der Erzeugnisse dieser Industrien keine wirtschaftlichen Grenzen, also weder Handelsbeschränkungen noch Zölle und sonstige Behinderungen, geben. Durch diese und andere Vorschriften sollte erreicht werden, daß die Produktion ausgeweitet, die Beschäftigung gesteigert und so der Lebensstandard jedes einzelnen der 165 Millionen Einwohner der sechs Partnerstaaten gehoben wird.

STEINKOHLENFÖRDERUNG DER LÄNDER DER EUROPÄISCHEN GEMEINSCHAFT FÜR KOHLE UND STAHL

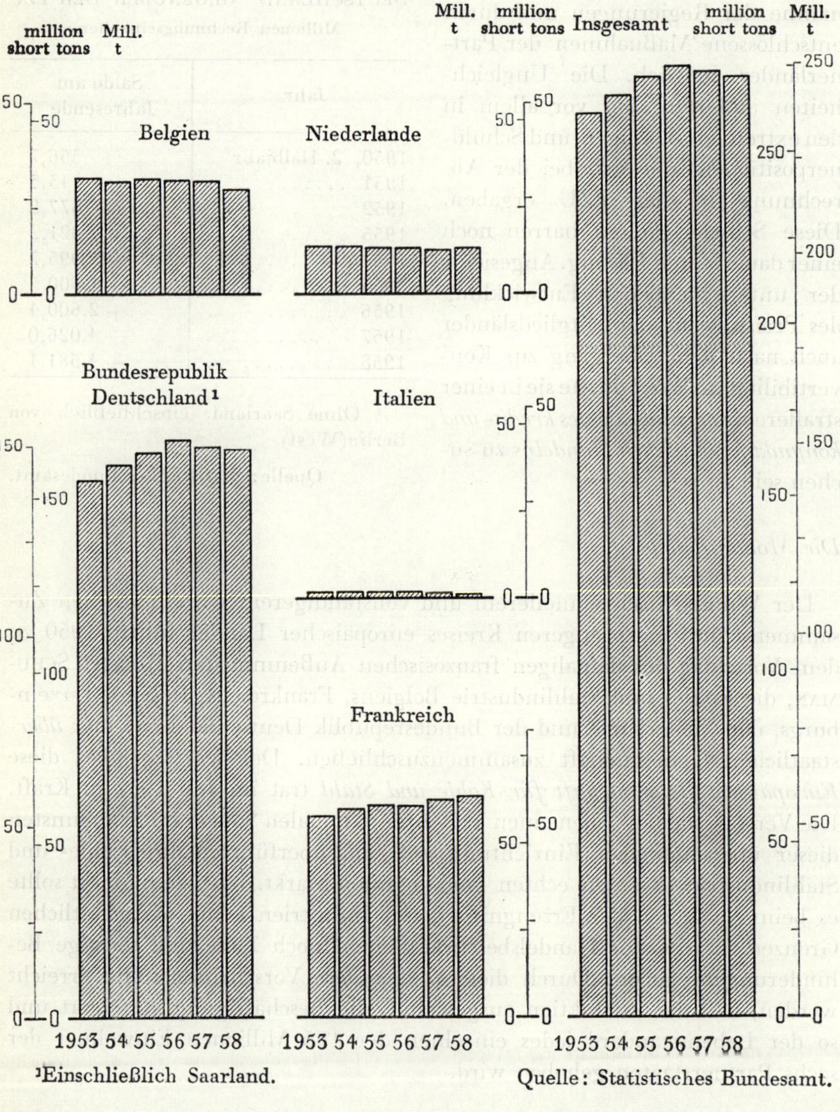

¹Einschließlich Saarland.

Quelle: Statistisches Bundesamt.

EISENERZFÖRDERUNG DER LÄNDER DER EUROPÄISCHEN GEMEINSCHAFT FÜR KOHLE UND STAHL

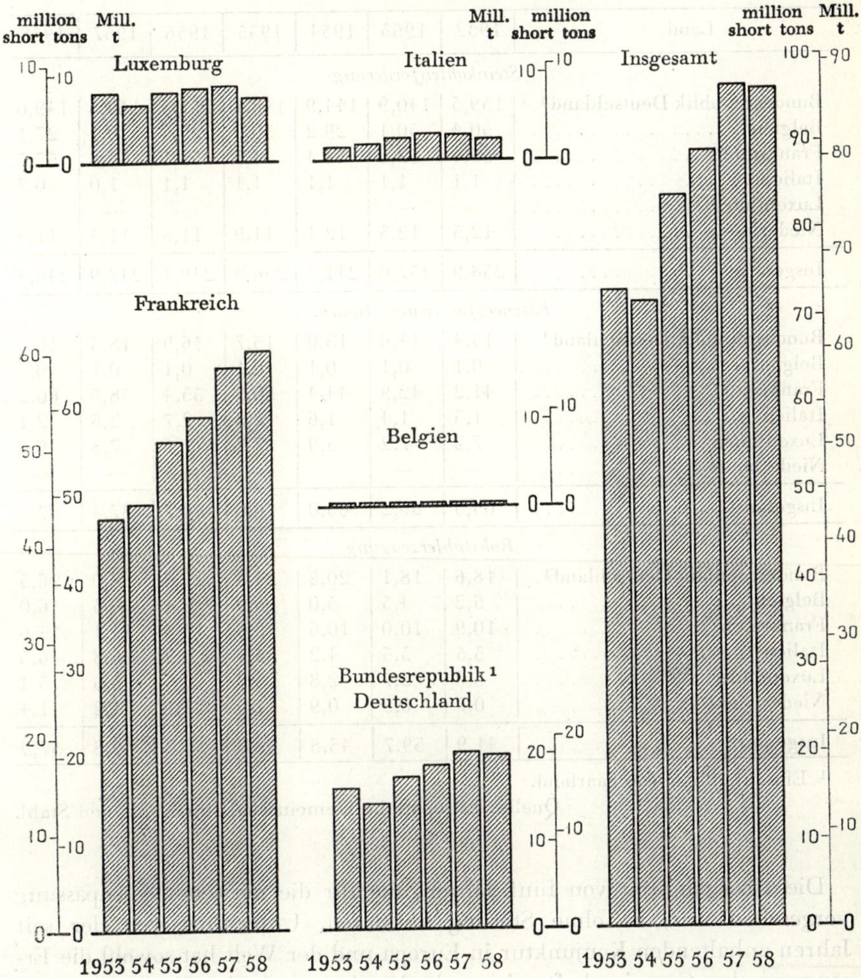

[1] Einschließlich von Saarland.

Quelle: Statistisches Bundesamt.

Tabelle 8

STEINKOHLENFÖRDERUNG, ROHEISEN- UND ROHSTAHLERZEUGUNG DER LÄNDER DER EUROPÄISCHEN GEMEINSCHAFT FÜR KOHLE UND STAHL

Millionen t

Land	1952	1953	1954	1955	1956	1957	1958
Steinkohlenförderung							
Bundesrepublik Deutschland[1]	139,5	140,9	144,9	148,1	151,5	149,6	149,0
Belgien	30,4	30,1	29,2	30,0	29,6	29,1	27,1
Frankreich	55,4	52,6	54,4	55,3	55,1	56,8	57,7
Italien	1,1	1,1	1,1	1,1	1,1	1,0	0,7
Luxemburg	—	—	—	—	—	—	—
Niederlande	12,5	12,3	12,1	11,9	11,8	11,4	11,9
Insgesamt	238,9	237,0	241,7	246,4	249,1	247,9	246,4
Eisenerzförderung (Roherz)							
Bundesrepublik Deutschland[1]	15,4	14,6	13,0	15,7	16,9	18,3	18,0
Belgien	0,1	0,1	0,1	0,1	0,1	0,1	0,1
Frankreich	41,2	42,9	44,4	50,9	53,4	58,5	60,2
Italien	1,3	1,4	1,6	2,2	2,7	2,6	2,1
Luxemburg	7,2	7,2	5,9	7,2	7,6	7,8	6,6
Niederlande	—	—	—	—	—	—	—
Insgesamt	65,3	66,2	65,0	76,0	80,7	87,4	87,1
Rohstahlerzeugung							
Bundesrepublik Deutschland[1]	18,6	18,1	20,2	24,5	26,6	28,0	26,3
Belgien	5,2	4,5	5,0	5,9	6,4	6,3	6,0
Frankreich	10,9	10,0	10,6	12,6	13,4	14,1	14,6
Italien	3,5	3,5	4,2	5,4	5,9	6,8	6,3
Luxemburg	3,0	2,7	2,8	3,2	3,5	3,5	3,4
Niederlande	0,7	0,9	0,9	1,0	1,1	1,2	1,4
Insgesamt	41,9	39,7	43,8	52,6	56,8	59,8	57,9

[1] Einschließlich von Saarland.

Quelle: Europäische Gemeinschaft für Kohle und Stahl.

Die Übergangszeit von fünf Jahren, die für die notwendige Anpassung vorgesehen war, ist ohne Störung verlaufen. Unterstützt von der seit Jahren anhaltenden Konjunktur in Europa und der Welt hat sowohl die Erzeugung der Gemeinschaft wie auch der Austausch der Erzeugnisse zugenommen. Die Wirksamkeit der völligen Aufhebung aller Handelshindernisse wird besonders daran erkennbar, daß der Austausch der Montan-Erzeugnisse stärker intensiviert werden konnte als der Austausch anderer

ROHSTAHLERZEUGUNG
DER LÄNDER DER EUROPÄISCHEN GEMEINSCHAFT
FÜR KOHLE UND STAHL

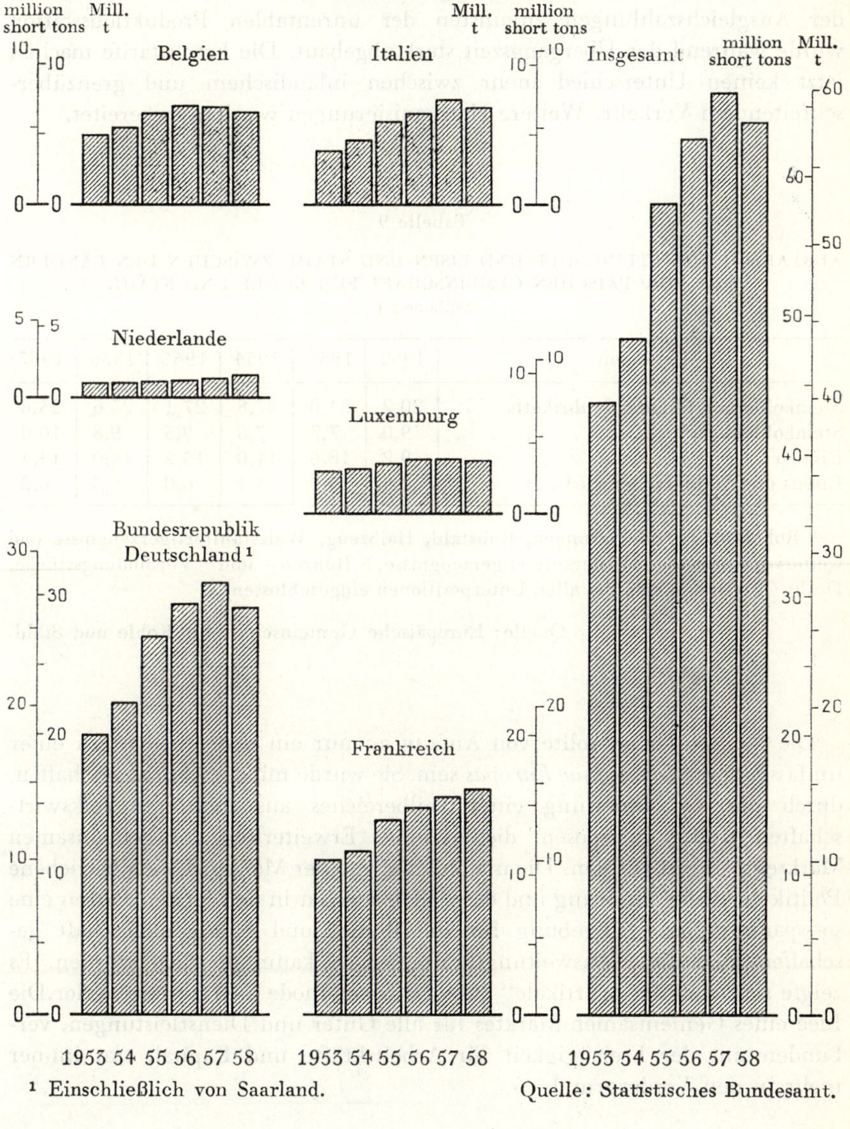

[1] Einschließlich von Saarland.

Quelle: Statistisches Bundesamt.

Waren. Die Beseitigung der wirtschaftlichen Grenzen hat zu einer Änderung der Lieferströme geführt; so konnten Frachtkosten erspart werden. Auch die Konkurrenz zwischen den Erzeugern ist intensiviert worden. Das System der Ausgleichszahlungen zugunsten der unrentablen Produktionsstätten wurde während der Übergangszeit stark abgebaut. Die Frachttarife machen jetzt keinen Unterschied mehr zwischen inländischem und grenzüberschreitendem Verkehr. Weitere Harmonisierungen werden vorbereitet.

Tabelle 9

AUSTAUSCH VON STEINKOHLE UND EISEN UND STAHL ZWISCHEN DEN LÄNDERN DER EUROPÄISCHEN GEMEINSCHAFT FÜR KOHLE UND STAHL

Millionen t

Erzeugnis	1952	1953	1954	1955	1956	1957
Steinkohle und Steinkohlenbriketts	20,2	24,0	27,8	27,1	23,6	23,6
Steinkohlenkoks....................	9,0	7,7	7,6	9,5	9,8	10,0
Eisenerz..........................	9,2	10,6	11,0	13,2	14,0	14,4
Eisen- und Stahlerzeugnisse [1]	2,4	3,0	4,4	6,0	5,5	6,2

[1] Roheisen, Ferrolegierungen, Rohstahl, Halbzeug, Walzstahlfertigerzeugnisse und weiterverarbeitete Walzstahlfertigerzeugnisse, Röhren und Verbindungsstücke, Draht (Edelstähle sind bei allen Unterpositionen eingeschlossen).

Quelle: Europäische Gemeinschaft für Kohle und Stahl.

Die Montan-Union sollte von Anfang an nur ein erster Schritt zu einer umfassenderen *Integration Europas* sein. Sie wurde mit der Absicht geschaffen, durch die Verschmelzung eines Teilbereiches aus mehreren Volkswirtschaften Kräfte auszulösen, die zu einer Erweiterung des gemeinsamen Marktes zwingen würden. Die unabhängig von der Montan-Union betriebene Politik der Liberalisierung und des Zollabbaus hat in den letzten Jahren eine so spannungslose Umgebung für die Kohle- und Stahlgemeinschaft geschaffen, daß diese Ausweitungskräfte jedoch kaum deutlich wurden. Es zeigte sich, daß die „vertikale" Integrationsmethode an Interesse verlor. Die Idee eines Gemeinsamen Marktes für alle Güter und Dienstleistungen, verbunden mit der Freizügigkeit für Arbeitskräfte und Kapital, trat immer mehr in den Vordergrund.

Übergangszeit auf die Gemeinschaft verlagert werden. In der Hand der nationalen Regierungen verbleibt jedoch die Beeinflussung des Konjunkturverlaufs, vor allem also die Geld- und Kreditpolitik. Hier wie auch hinsichtlich der Steuer- und Sozialsysteme ist eine enge Fühlungnahme der Regierungen miteinander vorgesehen. Man darf sich von ihr eine weitgehende Angleichung der Maßnahmen versprechen.

Bei den Vertragsverhandlungen hat die Bundesrepublik sich bemüht, die kommende Wirtschaftsgemeinschaft so weit wie möglich *nach liberalen Grundsätzen* auszugestalten. Natürlich waren in einigen Punkten Konzessionen notwendig, um den besonderen Wünschen der Partner entgegenzukommen. Im ganzen wird man aber sagen können, daß die Interessen sich in einem ausgewogenen Gefüge zusammengefunden haben und der Vertrag eine erfolgversprechende Grundlage der wirtschaftlichen Integration ist, an deren Ende vielleicht sogar die *politische Einheit Westeuropas* stehen wird.

Der Zusammenschluß der Europäischen Wirtschaftsgemeinschaft wird überall in der Bundesrepublik befürwortet. Nichtsdestoweniger ist Deutschland sehr stark interessiert an einer engen Verbindung der sechs EWG-Länder mit den anderen Mitgliedern der OEEC. Deshalb hat die Bundesregierung stets ihren Einfluß geltend gemacht, um schnell zu einem umfassenderen *Freihandelsraum* zu kommen. Mit einer europäischen Freihandelszone oder einer ähnlichen Konstruktion möchte sie die Gefahr einer Abkapselung der EWG von der übrigen Welt bannen und strebt daher großzügige Vereinbarungen an, die den Warenstrom in ganz Europa möglichst wenig behindern.

BAUEN UND AUFBAUEN

Im Gebiet der Bundesrepublik Deutschland waren durch den Luftkrieg und durch sonstige Kampfhandlungen über $2^1/_4$ Millionen Wohnungen, mehr als 20% des gesamten Wohnungsbestandes, bei Kriegsende total zerstört. Weitere 2,5 Millionen Wohnungen wiesen mehr oder weniger große Schäden auf, so daß sie nicht mehr oder erst nach Vornahme entsprechender Reparaturarbeiten bewohnbar waren. Im Vergleich zu dem hohen Zerstörungsgrad in Deutschland haben (nach einer Untersuchung der OEEC in Paris) Holland und Italien 4%, Frankreich 3%, Belgien und Großbritannien rund 2% ihres Wohnungsbestandes der Vorkriegszeit verloren. Die Kriegszerstörungen an Wohnraum in Deutschland gehen also weit über die in anderen Ländern hinaus.

*

Die Zerstörung erschöpfte sich nicht im Augenfälligen. Nicht nur die Häuser, Fabriken, Geschäfts- und Verwaltungsgebäude waren vernichtet, auch die unterirdischen Abwasserleitungen waren in den einzelnen Städten zu hunderten Malen zerschlagen und zerbrochen. Das gleiche galt von den Wasser- und Gasleitungen, Telephonkabeln und elektrischen Stromzuführungen. Sanitäre Anlagen und Wasserleitungen konnten deshalb nicht benutzt werden. Die Entnahme von Frischwasser war unmöglich; das Wasser mußte weit entfernt an einzelnen Pumpen mit Eimern geholt werden. Wichtige Teile der Gaswerke lagen in Trümmern. Aus den gleichen Gründen fuhren die Straßenbahnen nicht, und die Aufnahme des Eisenbahnbetriebes war unmöglich, denn die Brücken waren zerstört und die Gleisanlagen unbrauchbar. Die aus den Verlagerungsorten langsam zurückkehrenden Bewohner fanden ein Chaos in ihren Städten vor. Alle Voraussetzungen zu einem Gemeinschaftsleben fehlten.

Der durch den Krieg reduzierte Wohnraum reichte schon für die alteingesessene Bevölkerung bei weitem nicht mehr aus. Nach Kriegsende kam der Wohnungsbedarf von Millionen Vertriebener und Flüchtlinge hinzu, die in Westdeutschland Zuflucht fanden. Der Anteil der Vertriebenen und Zugewanderten an der Gesamtbevölkerung[1] betrug am 31. 12. 1958: 24,4% (12,6 Millionen Personen).

Wohl gingen sogleich nach dem Zusammenbruch ungezählte Einzelne daran, auszubessern, zu flicken und mit Notdächern zu versehen, was noch einigermaßen bewohnbar schien, wohl wurden Wohnlauben, Garagen, Keller, Baracken bis zur letzten

[1] Bundesrepublik ohne Saarland und Berlin(West).

Ecke belegt, wohl konnten sich die wenigen Glücklichen, die etwas zu tauschen hatten, über den schwarzen und den grauen Baumarkt mit Arbeitskräften und Baumaterialien versorgen und sogar Neubauten errichten — aber das alles besagte wenig gegenüber solchem Mangel. Zudem war dieser Baueinsatz, so vernünftig er schien, volkswirtschaftlich ein Unding. Die Trümmerräumung von Hand kostete ein Mehrfaches der maschinellen Räumung und war dazu keine echte Beseitigung; denn jeder hatte nur das Bestreben, sein Grundstück freizumachen. Auf 400 Millionen Kubikmeter hat man den Schutt geschätzt, der 1945 auf Deutschland lag, dabei noch siebzehn Milliarden ganze Ziegelsteine, die nun die „Bauherren" aus den Trümmern heraussuchten und von Hand sauber putzten.

Obgleich die westdeutschen Länder seit ihrer Gründung alles unternahmen, um die knappen und zwangsbewirtschafteten Baustoffe für die Reparatur und den Wiederaufbau von Wohnhäusern bereitzustellen, konnte in den Jahren 1945 bis 1947 von einem wirklichen Wiederaufbau lediglich auf dem flachen Lande die Rede sein. Die Landbevölkerung hatte die Möglichkeit, die Arbeitskräfte des Baugewerbes in den damaligen Hunger- und Notzeiten zu verpflegen. Sie konnte die notwendigen Baumaterialien unter der Hand durch Hergabe von Naturalien sich leichter beschaffen. Außerdem waren in den Dörfern die *Probleme der Neuplanung* leichter zu lösen als in den Städten. Ihr Wiederaufbau war daher bereits zu einem Zeitpunkt weitgehend durchgeführt, zu dem in den Städten mit ihren hohen Zerstörungsgraden Wiederaufbau und Neugestaltung erst angepackt werden konnten. Insgesamt wurde seit dem Zusammenbruch bis Ende 1948 etwa eine halbe Million Wohnungen gebaut.

Über 4,5 Millionen neue Wohnungen seit 1949

Erst als nach der Neuordnung des Geldwesens im Juni 1948 die Voraussetzungen für ein normales Wirtschaften wieder gegeben und die drückenden Sorgen um das tägliche Brot gewichen waren, konnte der Wohnungsbau auch in den Städten in größerem Stil in Angriff genommen werden. Schon 1949 wurden 215.000 Wohnungen überwiegend durch Wiederaufbau, Wiederherstellung, Um-, An- und Ausbau neu geschaffen, also etwa halb soviel wie in den vier Jahren 1945 bis 1948 zusammen. Als die Erste Bundesregierung im Herbst 1949 ihr Amt antrat, stand die drückende Wohnungsnot vieler Millionen und ihre Beseitigung als ungelöstes ernstes Problem vor ihr. Die Bundesregierung ist sich von Anbeginn an der Größe dieser Aufgabe bewußt gewesen. Schon in ihrer ersten programmatischen Regierungserklärung vom 20. 9. 1949 bezeichnete sie die Errichtung von neuen Wohnungen als eine ihrer vordringlichsten Aufgaben. Die Zweite Bundesregierung bekräftigte in ihrer Regierungserklärung diesen Standpunkt. War es in den ersten Jahren nach Gründung der Bundesrepublik vor allem darauf angekommen, so schnell wie möglich so viele Wohnungen wie möglich zu bauen, so verschob sich schon bald der Schwerpunkt der Betrachtungsweise von der quantitativen auf die qualitative Wertung. Trotz politischen Widerständen mannigfacher Art setzte sich die Erkenntnis durch, daß ein möglichst großer Teil der neugebauten Wohnungen in der Form von Eigenheimen, Kleinsiedlungen oder von Wohnungseigentum errichtet werden und den Bewohnern als *persönliches* Eigentum zugute kommen müsse.

Dementsprechend hieß es in der Regierungserklärung der Dritten Bundesregierung, die 1957 ihr Amt antrat, in diesem Zusammenhang: „Streuung von Besitz in weitem Umfang ist nötig, um einer möglichst großen Zahl von Staatsbürgern Selbstgefühl und das Gefühl der Zugehörigkeit zum Volksganzen zu geben.“

*

Als einer der ersten wichtigen gesetzgeberischen Akte des Ersten Deutschen Bundestages wurde bereits Anfang 1950 das *Erste Wohnungsbau-Gesetz* einstimmig angenommen. Es bestimmte die Wohnungsbauleistung für die folgenden sechs Jahre (1951 bis 1956). An seine Stelle trat von 1957 ab das *Zweite Wohnungsbau-Gesetz* (*Wohnungsbau- und Familienheim-Gesetz*). Es gab den bereits erwähnten wohnungspolitischen Zielen der Bundesregierung — dem Bau von Familienheimen und der vermehrten Eigentumsbildung — ihre gesetzliche Form. Die beiden Gesetze bilden seit der Gründung der Bundesrepublik die Grundlage der wohnungspolitischen Arbeit in Westdeutschland. *Ihr Schwergewicht liegt auf dem sozialen Wohnungsbau.*

Beide Wohnungsbau-Gesetze gehen von einer Dreiteilung des Wohnungsbaues aus und unterscheiden

1. den öffentlich geförderten sozialen Wohnungsbau,
2. den steuerbegünstigten Wohnungsbau und
3. den frei finanzierten Wohnungsbau.

Der *öffentlich geförderte soziale Wohnungsbau* ist in erster Linie für die breiten Schichten der Bevölkerung mit begrenztem Einkommen bestimmt. Die öffentliche Hand fördert die Finanzierung dieser Wohnungen durch Gewährung niedrig verzinslicher Darlehen oder durch Gewährung von Zinszuschüssen oder Miet- beziehungsweise Lastenbeihilfen. Die mit Hilfe dieser Mittel errichteten Wohnungen werden von den Wohnungsämtern

adukt im Verlauf der Bundesstraße 9 (Beseitigung einer gefährlichen Bahnunterführung) bei Remagen a. Rh.

Kleeblatt der Autobahnstrecken im Raum des „Frankfurter Kreuzes" (Schnittpunkt der Autobahnen Kassel—Mannheim und Köln—Würzburg)

Die Donau-Staustufe Jochenstein, das größte Lauf-Wasserkraftwerk Mitteleuropas

DEUTSCHE
BUNDES-
POST

Elektrischer Wertzeichengeber

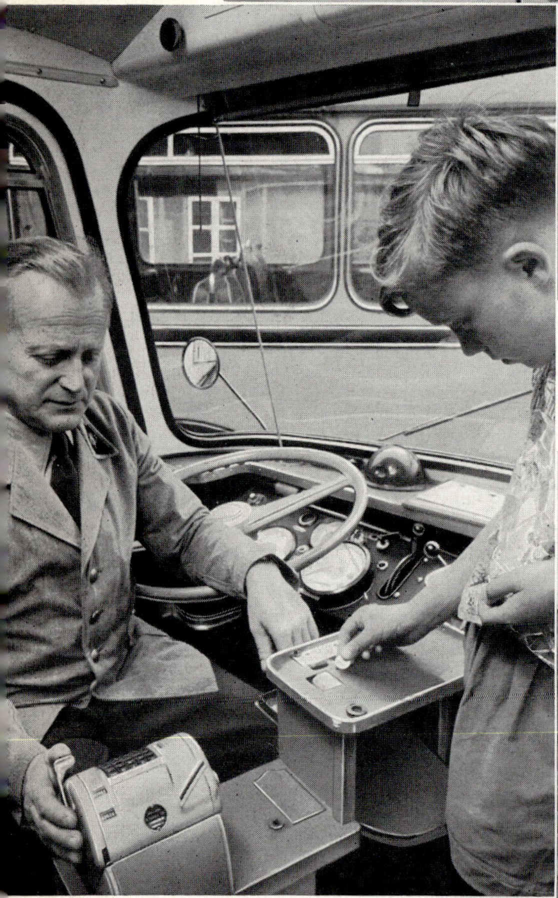

Der Kraftwagenführer bedient schnell durch moderne Fahrscheindrucker und Wechselkassen

Moped und Hausbriefkästen erleichtern dem Postboten die Arbeit

bewirtschaftet und unterliegen den Bestimmungen des Mieterschutzgesetzes. Die Größe dieser Wohnungen ist begrenzt, die Mieten sind relativ niedrig.

Nach dem Zweiten Wohnungsbaugesetz hat die staatliche Förderung des Wohnungsbaues das Ziel, *zugleich* mit der Beseitigung der Wohnungsnot weite Kreise des deutschen Volkes durch *Bildung von Einzeleigentum* mit dem Grund und Boden zu verbinden. Darum sind in dem Gesetz eine Reihe von Vorschriften enthalten, welche die Errichtung von Familienheimen begünstigen. Das Gesetz bestimmt Rangstufen, nach denen die zuständigen Stellen bei der Zuteilung der öffentlichen Darlehen zu verfahren haben. Die verfügbaren öffentlichen Mittel sollen in erster Linie solchen Bauherren von Familienheimen gewährt werden, die zu den Wohnungsuchenden mit geringem Einkommen zählen. Kinderreiche, Schwerkriegsbeschädigte und Kriegerwitwen mit Kindern genießen den gleichen Vorteil. An zweiter Stelle sind dann andere Bauherren von Familienheimen gleichberechtigt neben den Bauherren von Mietwohnungen zu berücksichtigen, die für Wohnungsuchende mit geringem Einkommen bestimmt sind.

Ferner ist in dem Gesetz festgelegt, daß die Durchschnittssätze der öffentlichen Darlehen beim Bau von Familienheimen um mindestens 10% höher zu bemessen sind als bei anderen Wohnungen. Besondere Vorschriften sorgen dafür, daß auch Bauherren mit geringem Einkommen die finanziellen Lasten tragen können, die der Bau eines eigenen Heimes nun einmal mit sich bringt. So können zugunsten solcher Bauherren die zuvor erwähnten Durchschnittssätze überschritten werden. Kinderreiche Bauherren erhalten nach der Kinderzahl bemessene sogenannte „Familien-Zusatzdarlehen". Schließlich ist die Gewährung von Zinszuschüssen, Annuitätsdarlehen oder Lastenbeihilfen möglich.

WOHNFLÄCHE JE WOHNUNG[1]

qm

[1] Ohne Wohnungen in Nichtwohnbauten. — [2] Vorläufig.

Quelle: Bundesministerium für den Wohnungsbau.

DIE WOHNUNGSGRÖSSE IM WOHNUNGSBAU

Fertiggestellte Wohnungen nach Wohnräumen einschließlich Küche

%

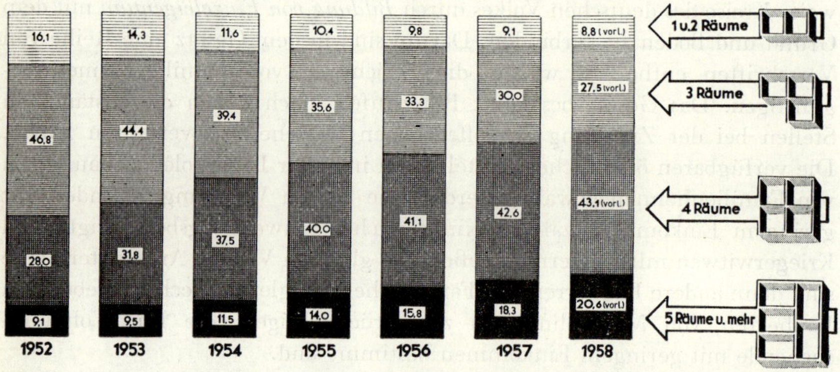

Quelle: Bundesministerium für den Wohnungsbau.

Die zahlreichen beachtlichen Vergünstigungen haben dazu geführt, daß in den Jahren 1957/58 — also seit dem Inkrafttreten des Familienheim-Gesetzes — etwa 120.000 Familienheime im Rahmen des sozialen Wohnungsbaues gefördert werden konnten. Im gesamten Wohnungsbau sind im Jahre 1958 *fast doppelt so viele Einfamilienhäuser gefördert worden wie 1953*. Daraus ergibt sich, eine wie große Bedeutung der Familienheimbau in den letzten Jahren für die Wohnungsversorgung der Bevölkerung der Bundesrepublik gewonnen hat.

Dem Ziel des Zweiten Wohnungsbau-Gesetzes — in zunehmendem Maße familiengerechte Wohnungen zu bauen — entspricht auch das Ansteigen der Wohnungsgrößen. Der Anteil der fertiggestellten Wohnungen mit vier und mehr Räumen (einschließlich der Küche), der 1952 noch bei nur rund 37% lag, betrug 1958 über 63%. Die durchschnittliche Wohnfläche lag 1958 bei nahezu 70 qm je Wohnung.

*

In seiner letzten Fassung sah das Erste Wohnungsbaugesetz vor, daß von 1951 bis 1956 insgesamt zwei Millionen Wohnungen des sozialen Wohnungsbaues für die breiten Schichten des Volkes gebaut werden sollten. Nach dem

Zweiten Wohnungsbau-Gesetz sollen von 1957 bis 1962 erneut 1,8 Millionen solcher Wohnungen errichtet werden. Seit 1949 bis 1958 sind etwa 2,75 Millionen Wohnungen entstanden, die den Bestimmungen über den sozialen Wohnungsbau entsprechen.

Der soziale Wohnungsbau repräsentiert damit etwas mehr als die Hälfte des gesamten Wohnungsbauvolumens der Bundesrepublik. Daneben haben vor allem der — bereits erwähnte — steuerbegünstigte und in geringerem Maße auch der frei finanzierte Wohnungsbau für die gesamte Wohnungsbauleistung entscheidende Bedeutung.

Der *steuerbegünstigte Wohnungsbau* ist ebenfalls in seiner Wohnfläche, wenn auch nicht so eng, begrenzt. Die Mietbildung ist zwar frei; jedoch kann auf Antrag des Mieters unter bestimmten Voraussetzungen die Miete auf die Kostenmiete herabgesetzt werden. Sofern diese Wohnungen nur Steuervergünstigungen, also keine unmittelbare öffentliche Hilfe, erhalten, sind sie von der Wohnraumbewirtschaftung freigestellt. Die Steuervergünstigungen bestehen darin, daß bei Erfüllung der gesetzlichen Voraussetzungen die Bauten für zehn Jahre von der gemeindlichen Grundsteuer befreit werden können. Weiter kann jeder, der zugunsten des Wohnungsbaues unverzinsliche Darlehen mit mindestens zehnjähriger Laufzeit und gleichbleibenden Tilgungsraten gibt, ein Viertel dieses Darlehensbetrages bei der Einkommensteuer absetzen. Voraussetzung ist allerdings, daß das Darlehen dem Wiederaufbau oder Eigentumsmaßnahmen (Eigenheime, Kleinsiedlungen und Wohnungseigentum) zugute kommt[1]. Außerdem können Bauherren Aufwendungen für ihren eigenen Wohnungsbau innerhalb von zwölf Jahren, gestaffelt bis zu 50% der Aufwendungen, im Wege der Sonderabschreibung bei der Einkommensteuer absetzen, ohne daß hier Beschränkungen hinsichtlich Wohnfläche und Miete bestehen[2].

Der *frei finanzierte Wohnungsbau* unterliegt keinerlei Bindungen; auf diese Kategorie entfallen allerdings nur wenige Prozente des gesamten Volumens des Wohnungsbaus.

Die — zuvor skizzierten — vielfältigen Förderungsmaßnahmen der Bundesregierung haben die Wohnungsbauleistung in der Bundesrepublik auf eine in früheren Jahrzehnten nie gekannte Höhe hinaufgetrieben. Die Zahl der bezugsfertigen Wohnungen betrug im Jahre 1949 noch 215.000. Ein Jahr später waren es schon 360.000. 1953 wurde erstmalig die Grenze von

[1] § 7 c des Einkommensteuer-Gesetzes.

[2] § 7 b des Einkommensteuer-Gesetzes. Die Vergünstigungen des § 7 b können auch im Rahmen des frei finanzierten Wohnungsbaus in Anspruch genommen werden.

FERTIGGESTELLTE WOHNUNGEN

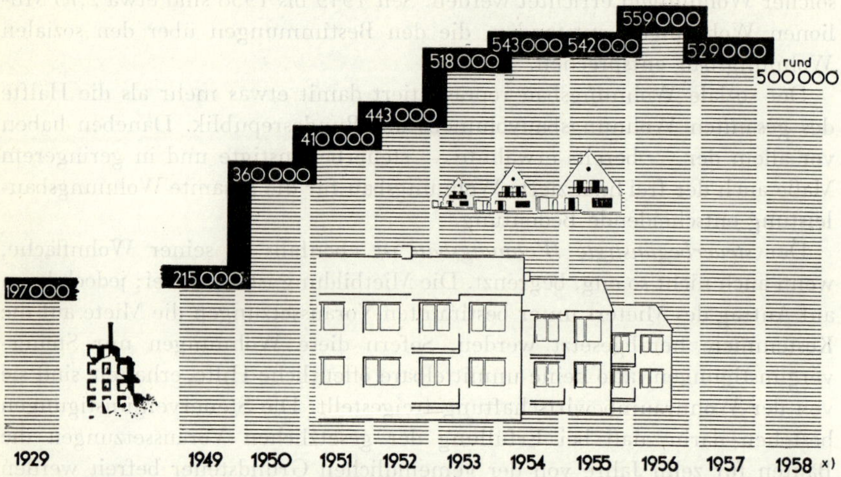

x Geschätzt. Quelle: Bundesministerium für den Wohnungsbau.

einer halben Million überschritten, und seitdem hat die Wohnungsbauleistung von Jahr zu Jahr sich auf diesem Niveau gehalten. Insgesamt wurden seit 1949 über 4,5 Millionen Wohnungen gebaut. *Fünfzehn bis sechzehn Millionen Menschen* haben somit in diesem Jahrzehnt wieder eine eigene, wenn auch nach Größe und Ausstattung oft nur bescheidene, Wohnung erhalten.

Die Ergebnisse des Wohnungsbaues in der Bundesrepublik werden besonders sichtbar, wenn man sie mit den *Leistungen früherer Jahre* vergleicht. In der Weimarer Republik wurden insgesamt etwa 2,5 Millionen Wohnungen gebaut. Trotzdem bestand schon vor dem Zweiten Weltkrieg ein fühlbarer Mangel an Wohnungen. Zu einem guten Teil war er durch die einseitige Inanspruchnahme der Bautätigkeit für die Rüstung hervorgerufen. Die höchste Produktion im alten Reichsgebiet wurde im Jahre 1929 mit 339.000 Wohnungen[1] erreicht; das bedeutete auf das Gebiet der Bundesrepublik umgerechnet nicht ganz 200.000 Wohnungen.

Was die Wohnungsbauleistung der Nachkriegszeit nicht nur für die physische, sondern vor allem auch für die *psychische und politische Gesundung des deutschen Volkes* bedeutet, kann nur ermessen, wer jemals den eigenen Herd und den Wohnraum mit Fremden teilen mußte. Die gesundheitlichen,

[1] 315.700 Wohnungen ohne das Gebiet von Saarland.

sittlichen und politischen Schäden, die durch das Zusammenpferchen großer Menschenmengen auf engem Raum in Massenunterkünften, die gemeinsame Benutzung der Koch- und Schlafstellen und Mangel an sanitären Anlagen entstehen können, sind nicht in Zahlenwerten auszudrücken. Ein hoher Wohnungsstandard hingegen bannt nicht nur diese Gefahren, sondern hebt zugleich das Leistungsvermögen und die Arbeitsbereitschaft der Menschen aller Berufe.

Immerhin gibt es trotz den hohen Bauergebnissen auch heute noch Wohnungsnot. Anfang 1959 fehlten im Bundesgebiet noch etwa anderthalb Millionen Wohnungen. Jahr für Jahr entsteht darüber hinaus durch den Zustrom von Flüchtlingen aus der sogenannten DDR und durch die Neugründung von Ehen zusätzlicher Wohnungsbedarf in einer Höhe von 150.000 bis 200.000 Wohnungen jährlich. Das heißt, daß in der Bundesrepublik — bei gleichbleibender jährlicher Bauleistung von rund einer halben Million Wohnungen — noch etwa fünf Jahre nötig sein werden, um zu einer ausgeglichenen Bedarfslage zu gelangen.

Schon heute muß die Bundesregierung die Vorbereitungen treffen, damit nach diesem Zeitpunkt *die Regeln der Marktwirtschaft auch im Wohnungswesen* wieder zur Geltung gelangen. Die gesetzgeberischen Arbeiten für dieses Ziel sind in Angriff genommen. Einer der Kernpunkte des vorbereiteten Gesetzes soll ein neues „*soziales Mietrecht*“ sein, das auch in Zukunft nach dem Abbau der Wohnungs-Zwangswirtschaft jedem Bürger eine ausreichende Wohnung rechtlich und wirtschaftlich sichern soll.

78 Milliarden DM Kapitalaufwand

Die Wohnungsbauleistung, die in Deutschland im letzten Jahrzehnt erbracht wurde, hat dem Steuerzahler erhebliche Opfer abgefordert. Mehr als sechsundzwanzig Milliarden des investierten Kapitals kamen von der öffentlichen Hand. Im einzelnen flossen die Mittel zum Bau dieser viereinhalb Millionen Wohnungen aus drei Quellen:

1. Vom *Kapitalmarkt*, das sind die Sparkassen, Pfandbriefinstitute, private und soziale Versicherungsträger sowie die Bausparkassen;
2. von der *öffentlichen Hand*, das sind die Haushalte des Bundes, der Länder und der Gemeinden und die Mittel des Lastenausgleichs einschließlich der Aufbaudarlehen;
3. aus *sonstigen Quellen* verschiedener Art, wie echtes Eigenkapital, Arbeitgeberdarlehen und -zuschüsse, Selbsthilfe, Mieterdarlehen und -zuschüsse und anderes mehr.

Insgesamt wurden in den Jahren von 1949 bis 1958 etwa 78 Milliarden DM im Wohnungsbau investiert. In den ersten Jahren war der Anteil der öffentlichen Mittel höher als der Finanzierungsbeitrag, den der Kapitalmarkt aufbringen konnte. Nach dem — durch die Korea-Krise verursachten — Tiefpunkt im Jahre 1951 hat jedoch die Spartätigkeit in der Bundesrepublik einen kräftigen Aufschwung genommen, weil das Vertrauen in die Stabilität der deutschen Währung sich festigen konnte. Infolgedessen ist der Anteil der Kapitalmarkt-Mittel an der gesamten Finanzierung des Wohnungsbaues ständig gestiegen. 1958 stammten rund 5,3 der insgesamt aufgebrachten etwa 12 Milliarden DM vom Kapitalmarkt.

Diese Entwicklung kommt den Plänen der Bundesregierung entgegen, deren Ziel es ist, mehr und mehr die private Initiative im Wohnungsbau zum Zuge zu bringen und dementsprechend auch dem Wohnungsbau soweit wie möglich private Finanzierungsquellen zu erschließen. Dadurch soll der Steuerzahler allmählich von der Aufbringung dieser Milliarden-Beträge entlastet werden. Aus diesem Grunde ist schon im Zweiten Wohnungsbaugesetz vorgeschrieben worden, daß die für den allgemeinen sozialen Wohnungsbau bestimmten Haushaltsmittel des Bundes ab 1958 jährlich um zehn Prozent verringert werden.

Mit diesen Darlegungen über den Wohnungsbau ist jedoch nur *ein* Aspekt der deutschen Wiederaufbauleistung umrissen. In einem zivilisierten

FINANZIERUNG DES WOHNUNGSBAUES

Milliarden DM

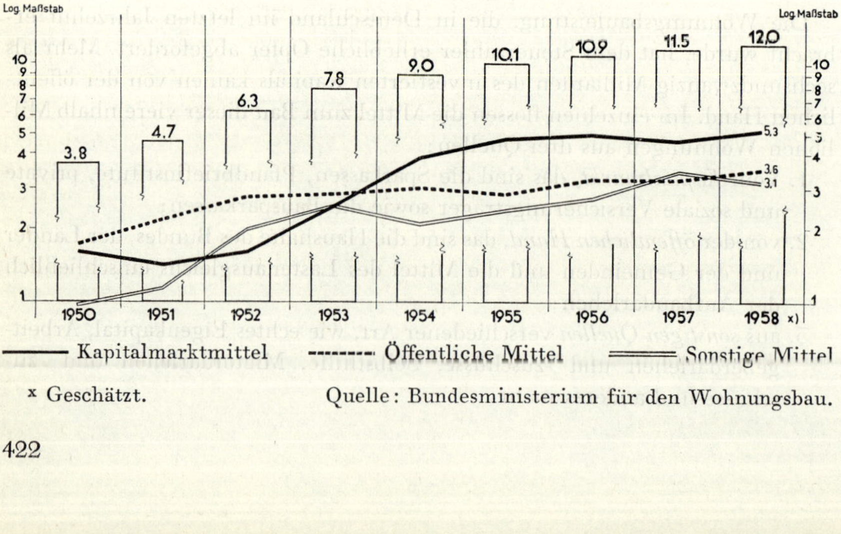

Kapitalmarktmittel — Öffentliche Mittel — Sonstige Mittel

x Geschätzt. Quelle: Bundesministerium für den Wohnungsbau.

Siedlung des sozialen Wohnungsbaus in Geisenheim

Staat vermag *die Wohnung ihre Funktion nur noch in Verbindung mit öffentlichen und gewerblichen Bauten* zu erfüllen. Deshalb ist die Bautätigkeit auch auf diesen Gebieten, sobald die Umstände es erlaubten, mit großen Projekten angelaufen. Die Forderungen, die dabei an die Planenden und Ausführenden gestellt wurden, sind so vielfältig, daß ein summarischer Überblick sie nur unvollkommen aufzeigen kann.

Die weitgehenden Zerstörungen an *Verkehrsbauten*, wie Bahnhöfe und Straßenanlagen, wurden in vielen Fällen Anlaß zu wesentlichen Verbesserungen. Besonders ins Gewicht fiel die Wiederherstellung der Autobahnen und der Reichs- (jetzt Bundes-) Straßen. Aber auch ein Teil der westdeutschen Großstädte besitzt heute nicht nur instandgesetzte, sondern unter Wahrnehmung aller Verbesserungsmöglichkeiten modernisierte Straßenzüge. In vielen Fällen erlaubte die Zerstörung eine Verbreiterung der Straßen und die Herstellung von kürzeren Verbindungen und Durchbrüchen, die den Verkehr flüssiger ablaufen lassen. Dennoch sind gerade in den Großstädten noch umfangreiche Bauaufgaben übriggeblieben, deren Lösung notgedrungen zunächst vertagt werden mußte. Wie in der ganzen Welt, gibt es auch in den deutschen Städten Wohnviertel, deren Zustand mit den Begriffen einer modernen Sozialhygiene nicht mehr vereinbar ist, so daß sie eine menschenwürdige Unterbringung ihrer Bewohner nicht mehr gestatten. Gerade solche

Gewerkschaftsschule in Lohr am Main

Altstadtquartiere haben häufig die Zerstörungen des Krieges überdauert. Entscheidendes zur Besserung dieser Verhältnisse kann jedoch erst geschehen, wenn die Wohnungsnot völlig überwunden ist. Die Wiederaufnahme der „*Altstadtsanierung*", die in den Dreißiger Jahren bereits einmal angelaufen war, wird deshalb in Deutschland die Aufgabe des nächsten Jahrzehnts sein.

Wer die im Wiederaufbau begriffenen Städte der Bundesrepublik aufsucht, erkennt zugleich, daß die Innenstädte, die im wesentlichen den Geschäftsbetrieb auf sich konzentrieren, ein Bild *außergewöhnlicher Aktivität der gewerblichen Wirtschaft* zeigen. Nach anfänglicher Beschränkung auf erdgeschossige Ladenbauten sind in den letzten Jahren auch viele tiefe Lücken durch gewerbliche Bauten, Büro- und Geschäftshäuser, geschlossen worden. Die unterschiedliche Zweckbestimmung der Bauaufgaben ergibt ein ungewöhnlich vielfältiges Bild des Wiederaufbaus. Von großer Bedeutung sind die auf- und neugebauten *Schulen*, nicht nur ihrem zahlenmäßigen Umfang nach, sondern wegen der Einarbeitung der neuen sozialen und pädagogischen Erkenntnisse in diese Bauten. In ähnlicher Weise ist das bei der Wiederherstellung und dem Bau von *Krankenhäusern* geschehen, die im Aufbauprogramm der Städte ebenfalls einen breiten Raum einnehmen. Ihre Erneuerung hat in zahlreichen Kurorten zu einer Erweiterung und Verbesserung der Sanatorien und sonstigen Kuranlagen geführt. Trotzdem ist es in beiden Bereichen noch nicht gelungen, den Fehlbestand durch Neubauten zu überwinden.

Nicht vergessen werden dürfen die der öffentlichen Obhut unterstellten Bauten für kulturelle Einrichtungen, Theater, Konzerthallen, Ausstellungsbauten usw. Fast jede Großstadt hat es inzwischen fertiggebracht, mindestens ein großes *Theater* wieder in Betrieb zu nehmen, und zwar durchaus nicht behelfsmäßig. Neben diesen Bauten sind die notwendigen Erneuerungen der Kraftwerke, Marktanlagen, Verwaltungsgebäude usw. hervorzuheben. Mit der Neuordnung des Geldwesens erhielten zugleich die Geldinstitute, Banken und Versicherungen die Möglichkeit, durch Neubauten den nötigen Büroraum, häufig in repräsentativer Gestalt, zu schaffen. Zahlreiche große öffentliche Verwaltungsgebäude haben ebenso wie die der Wirtschaft wesentlich zur Neugestaltung der Stadtbilder beigetragen.

Trotz diesen Leistungen bestimmt die *Initiative des deutschen Bürgers*, der jede gebotene Möglichkeit der Instandsetzung seines Hausbesitzes ausgeschöpft hat, das Gesamtbild der Innenstädte. Sein Vorgehen schuf die Voraussetzung dafür, daß durch den intensiven Aufbauwillen der gewerblichen Wirtschaft der jetzige Bestand an Büro- und Geschäftshäusern erreicht wurde.

Dank den intensiven *Bemühungen der Wohlfahrtsverbände*, der Arbeiterwohlfahrt, Caritas und Inneren Mission, wurde eine stattliche Zahl von Heimplätzen für Jugendliche in Heimen für Jungarbeiter und Angestellte geschaffen. Die auf diese Weise begründeten Wohnmöglichkeiten müssen zu der Zahl der selbständigen Wohnungen hinzugerechnet werden. Das gilt ebenso von den vielen Altersheimen, die von den gleichen Verbänden wiederhergestellt oder neu geschaffen werden konnten. Auch diese Heime konnten nur durch Zuhilfenahme öffentlicher Mittel in erheblichem Umfang errichtet werden.

*

Einen besonderen Platz nimmt die Wiederherstellung der *Sakralbauten* beider Konfessionen ein. Soweit ihr Zustand es erlaubte, sind Kirchen wiederaufgebaut worden. In vielen Fällen aber wurden Neubauten vollendet, die freilich in ihrer Gestalt heute wesentlich kleiner in Erscheinung treten als manche ihrer Vorgänger. In diesem Zusammenhang muß auch die umfangreiche *Tätigkeit der Denkmalpflege* genannt werden. Sie hat manches wertvolle historische Bauwerk vor dem völligen Verfall gerettet und den systematischen Wiederaufbau oder wenigstens die Sicherung der Gebäude ermöglicht.

Mit weitgehender Unterstützung durch die Mittel des Marshall-Planes konnten im Zusammenwirken der zuständigen Wirtschaftskreise bedeutsame *Hotelbauten* verwirklich werden. Das intensive Wiederanlaufen des Wirtschaftslebens machte die Lösung der Hotelfrage besonders brennend; nicht nur in Bezug auf die Schaffung von Übernachtungsmöglichkeiten, sondern weitgehend auch auf die Wiederherstellung oder den Neubau von Gaststätten und Caféhäusern verschiedenster Art. Dieser Bereich hat eine sehr intensive Belebung erfahren. Mit ähnlichem Eifer hat sich der Wiederaufbau der *Lichtspielhäuser* vollzogen, deren Zahl in vielen Großstädten die Vorkriegsziffern überschritten hat. Bei all diesen Bauten handelt es sich nicht um einfache Wiederherstellungen. Fast durchweg tritt das Bemühen zutage, die gegebenen Verbesserungsmöglichkeiten auszuschöpfen. Infolgedessen sind heute viele Gaststätten, Lichtspielhäuser und Hotels auf einen modernen Stand gebracht worden, der vor ausländischer Kritik um so eher bestehen kann, als auch die Erfahrungen und Errungenschaften des Auslandes nutzbar gemacht worden sind.

In den Randbezirken der Großstädte und an anderen verkehrsgünstig gelegenen Stellen hat sich ein weitgehender *Wiederaufbau von Industrieanlagen* vollzogen. Auch hier war das Augenmerk der Unternehmer auf die Anwendung neuester Techniken gerichtet. Hand in Hand damit ging die Schaffung und *Wiederherstellung bedeutsamer Verkehrsbauten.* In großer Zahl sind Straßen-, Fluß- und Eisenbahnbrücken geschaffen worden, um das unterbrochene Verkehrsnetz nicht nur wieder anzuknüpfen, sondern es planmäßig zu verdichten. Hafen- und Flugplatzanlagen sowie Bauten der Bundesbahn und Bundespost von bedeutsamem Umfang vervollständigen das Bild. Die Vielfältigkeit, mit der sich der Aufbauwille bisher hat auswirken können, zeigt die Intensität der Wiederbelebung der Wirtschaft. Dankbar bekennt das deutsche Volk, daß dieser Wiederaufbau keine so raschen Fortschritte hätte machen können ohne die helfende Hand kirchlicher Organisationen und privater Spender im Ausland, deren Tätigkeit auf dem weiten Trümmerfeld buchstäblich die ersten Steine ins Rollen brachte, und ohne die lange und tief wirkende Unterstützung durch den Marshall-Plan.

Durch die Jahrhunderte haben die Baumeister mit ihren Werken das Gesicht Deutschlands geformt. Nicht nur in der Pracht der Dome und Paläste, sondern auch im bürgerlichen und ländlichen Wohnhaus, in der Dorfkirche und dem Fabrikbau prägte diese Gestaltung sich sichtbar aus. So bedeutet jeder Neubau zugleich Arbeit an der äußeren Gestalt des neuen Deutschlands.

ÖFFENTLICHE FINANZEN

Die Aufgabe: Sicherung der inneren Stabilität

In der Entwicklung der öffentlichen Finanzen spiegelt sich der Weg wider, den die Bundesrepublik seit der Währungsreform zurückgelegt hat. Viele finanzwirtschaftliche Probleme sind gelöst worden, neue Aufgaben harren noch künftiger Lösung. In dem vergangenen Jahrzehnt wurden Leistungen vollbracht, die einmalig waren. Sie stellten aber auch an die deutsche Volkswirtschaft finanzielle Anforderungen, für die es einen Vergleich aus früheren Zeiten nicht gibt.

Voraussetzung dieser Leistung war die Währungsreform im Jahre 1948 (20.6.1948). Sie war die Grundlage für die Ordnung der öffentlichen Finanzen. Was vorher geschah, war nur ein Versuch, soziale Notstände zu beseitigen. Die vorausgehende Nachkriegshilfe der Besatzungsmächte konnte die Not zwar mildern, aber nicht beheben. Erst als nach der Währungsreform wieder ein Rechnen mit festen Größen möglich war, traten zugleich geordnete Lebensverhältnisse ein.

Alle Inflationen haben von der mangelnden Ordnung der öffentlichen Haushalte ihren Ausgang genommen. Aus dieser Erfahrung war in den Jahren des Wiederaufbaus leitender Grundsatz der deutschen Finanzpolitik: *Wahrung der inneren Stabilität von Währung und Finanzen.* Alle finanzpolitischen Maßnahmen wurden auf dieses Ziel ausgerichtet und ihm untergeordnet. Um das Gleichgewicht von Einnahme und Ausgabe zu sichern und volkswirtschaftlich ein Optimum an Nutzen zu erreichen, wurden für die Erfüllung der Aufgaben der öffentlichen Haushalte strenge Maßstäbe angelegt. Aus dem grundlegenden Wandel der Zusammenhänge zwischen Staat und Wirtschaft und aus der Dynamik der Verflechtung aller Teile der Volkswirtschaft ergab sich von selbst, daß der Staat bei dieser Aufgabe von der Wirtschaft wirksam unterstützt wurde. Nur so konnten die Maßnahmen, die den Wiederaufbau in Gang bringen sollten, zur vollen Wirksamkeit gelangen. Zugleich sollte durch sie die Eigenverantwortung der Wirtschaft gestärkt werden, um den staatlichen Einfluß auf ein Maß beschränken zu können, das die Gesamtentwicklung beider Teile förderte. Durch sinnvolle Koordinierung der Erfüllung der Aufgaben zwischen den einzelnen Trägern der Finanzverantwortung — Bund, Ländern, Gemeinden und Trägern der Sozialversicherung — und auch durch zeitliche Ordnung der Nachkriegsaufgaben mußte der öffentliche Finanzbedarf mit der volkswirtschaftlichen Leistungsfähigkeit in Einklang gebracht werden. Dann erst konnte die ungeheure Steuerlast der ersten Nachkriegsjahre erleichtert werden.

Bund und Länder

Das Schwergewicht der staatlichen Aufgaben lag nach der Währungsreform zunächst bei den *Ländern*. Erst das am 23. 5. 1949 in Kraft getretene *Grundgesetz* schuf die verfassungsrechtliche Grundlage der Bundesrepublik. Es regelte auch die Finanzverantwortung zwischen Bund und Ländern. Neben den eigenen zentralen Aufgaben des Bundes (Auswärtiger Dienst, Bundesfinanzverwaltung, Wasserstraßen, Schiffahrt und andere) wurden ihm mit Wirkung vom 1.4.1950[1] die bisher von den Ländern getragenen Kriegsfolgelasten, die Zuschüsse zur Sozialversicherung und die Arbeitslosenhilfe übertragen. Den Ländern und ihren Gemeinden sind somit die „klassischen" Staatsaufgaben verblieben. Dies sind in erster Linie die Rechtspflege, Innere Sicherheit und Ordnung, Schulwesen, Wohlfahrts- und Fürsorgewesen, Gesundheitswesen und Straßenbau. Sie werden teils im staatlichen, teils im kommunalen Bereich durchgeführt. Die Hansestädte und Berlin(West) haben insofern eine Sonderstellung, als bei ihnen staatlicher und kommunaler Haushalt im wesentlichen eine Einheit darstellen. Soweit die Länder ihren Gemeinden Aufgaben zur Durchführung übertragen haben, sind sie an den Lasten durch besondere Finanzzuweisungen beteiligt. Hierbei kann es sich um allgemeine oder zweckgebundene Zuweisungen handeln. Umgekehrt tragen bei einzelnen Aufgaben, wie zum Beispiel bei den Personalausgaben der Volksschulen, auch die Gemeinden durch Zuweisungen an das Land anteilig zu den Kosten bei.

Von den Einnahmequellen der Länder gingen im Jahre 1950 zum Ausgleich der vom Bund übernommenen Lasten die Zölle, Verbrauchsteuern (mit Ausnahme der Biersteuer), die Umsatz- und Beförderungsteuer auf den Bund über. Den Ländern verblieben die Einkommen- und Körperschaftsteuer, Vermögensteuer, Kraftfahrzeugsteuer und verschiedene Verkehrsteuern. An den vom Bund übernommenen Soziallasten und an den Besatzungskosten wurden die Länder zunächst in Form von Interessenquoten in Höhe von 10 bis 25% der Ausgaben beteiligt. Da diese Ausgaben aber zwangsläufig stiegen, wurden, um die Lastenbeteiligung der Länder elastischer ihrer unterschiedlichen Steuerkraft anzupassen, nur die von den Stadt- und

[1] Erstes Überleitungsgesetz vom 28.11.1950.

Landkreisen getragenen Interessenquoten von 15% an der Kriegsfolgenhilfe aufrechterhalten. An die Stelle der übrigen Interessenquoten trat bereits im folgenden Rechnungsjahr (1951) eine Beteiligung des Bundes an der Einkommen- und Körperschaftsteuer, der sogenannte „*Bundesanteil*". Soweit bei einzelnen Ländern noch Zahlungsrückstände und schwebende Schulden aus den Vorjahren bestanden, die sich aus den bisher von ihnen getragenen Kriegsfolgelasten ergeben hatten, wurden sie im Rechnungsjahr 1952 durch eine Umschuldungsaktion (250 Millionen DM) mit Hilfe des Bundes und der leistungsstärkeren Länder bereinigt.

Die durch das Grundgesetz eingeführte *Verteilung der Lasten zwischen Bund und Ländern* war als vorläufig gedacht und sollte später durch eine endgültige Regelung ersetzt werden. Sie hat aber bis zum Jahre 1955 bestanden. Die Höhe der Beteiligung des Bundes an der Einkommen- und Körperschaftsteuer war jährlich neu festzusetzen. Das führte im Laufe dieser Jahre zu ständig neuen Auseinandersetzungen zwischen Bund und Ländern. Der Bund wollte infolge des starken Ansteigens seiner Ausgaben, insbesondere in Erwartung steigender Verteidigungsausgaben, den Anteil erhöhen, um die Erfüllung seiner Aufgaben zu sichern. Die Länder aber glaubten, diese Erhöhung nicht zubilligen zu können. Der Bundesanteil betrug im Rechnungsjahr 1951: 27%. Er stieg in den beiden folgenden Jahren auf 37 beziehungsweise 38%. Auch für das Rechnungsjahr 1954 wurde er nachträglich auf 38% festgesetzt.

Abschließend wurde die Steuerverteilung zwischen Bund und Ländern erst im Rahmen der *Finanzreform* durch das Finanzverfassungsgesetz vom 23.12.1955 geregelt. Es brachte eine Neufassung der Artikel 106 und 107 des Grundgesetzes. Prinzipiell wurde an der bisherigen, oben bereits erwähnten Steuerverteilung zwischen Bund und Ländern festgehalten. Der Katalog der Bundessteuern wurde aber durch die Ergänzungsabgabe zur Einkommen- und Körperschaftsteuer erweitert. Diese Steuer kann der Bund bei starkem Anwachsen seines Steuerbedarfs ohne Zustimmung des Bundesrats erheben — eine Bestimmung, die bisher noch nicht verwirklicht worden ist. Das Kernstück der Reform war die Neufestsetzung des Beteiligungsverhältnisses an der Einkommen- und Körperschaftsteuer. Ihr Aufkommen steht nunmehr Bund und Ländern gemeinsam zu. Die Anteile sind durch den neuen Artikel 106 GG unmittelbar festgesetzt. Für die Rechnungsjahre 1955 bis 1957 war der Bund mit $33^1/_3$%, ab 1958 ist er mit 35% am Aufkommen beteiligt. Damit haben die jährlichen Auseinandersetzungen um die Höhe des Bundesanteils zunächst ein Ende gefunden. Das Grundgesetz sieht aber vor, daß diese Regelung der Anteile später innerhalb von zwei Jahren (frühestens am 1.4.1958) geändert werden kann, falls die Finanzgewichte zwischen Bund und Ländern (einschließlich ihrer Gemeinden) sich so erheblich verschoben haben, daß ihre Haushaltslage gefährdet ist und ihnen erhebliche Fehlbeträge entstanden sind. Der Bund soll dann die Belange der Länder weitgehend berücksichtigen. Das Beteiligungsverhältnis kann zu Gunsten der Länder auch dann geändert werden, wenn ihnen zusätzliche Aufgaben auferlegt oder Einnahmen entzogen werden. Die endgültige Regelung der Steuerverteilung zwischen Bund und Ländern hat seit 1955 eine wesentlich ruhigere Entwicklung ihrer finanziellen Beziehungen als in früheren Jahren gewährleistet.

Im Rahmen der Finanzreform wurde auch die *Finanzverantwortung zwischen Bund und Ländern* neu geordnet[1]. Bund und Länder tragen nunmehr die Ausgaben selbst, die aus der Wahrnehmung ihrer Aufgaben sich ergeben. Soweit der Bund den Ländern Bundesaufgaben zuweist, trägt er die Zweckaufwendungen, während die persönlichen und sächlichen Verwaltungsausgaben von den Ländern übernommen werden. Bei den Gemeinschaftsaufgaben (Aufgaben, die von den Ländern unter Mitwirkung des Bundes erfüllt werden) ist der Bund an den Sachausgaben entsprechend beteiligt. Bei neuen Aufgaben wird jeweils sachlich geprüft, auf welcher Ebene sie zweckmäßig und wirtschaftlich am besten erfüllt werden. Die Regel wird dabei sein, daß im Zweifel die Erfüllung staatlicher Aufgaben Sache der Länder ist. Das Ziel dieser „Flurbereinigung" des bundesstaatlichen Gesamthaushalts war, die Bedürfnisse beider Ebenen so aufeinander abzustimmen, daß eine Überlastung der Steuerpflichtigen vermieden wird und die Einheitlichkeit der Lebensverhältnisse gewahrt bleibt. Auf Grund dieser grundsätzlichen Regelung wurde auch die bisherige Lastenverteilung geändert. Die Erstattung von Verwaltungskosten (zum Beispiel die Beteiligung des Bundes an den Kosten der Steuerverwaltung) fiel nunmehr fort. Bei der Kriegsfolgenhilfe, für die der Bund die Finanzverantwortung trägt, während die Durchführung in der Hand der Länder und ihrer Gemeinden liegt, trat an die Stelle der erwähnten Beteiligung der Länder mit einer Interessenquote eine degressive Pauschalierung der Bundesleistungen. Andererseits wurde bei anderen Bereichen der sozialen Kriegsfolgelasten, für die eine Pauschalierung nicht in Frage kam, die Verantwortung der Länder durch Erhöhung ihrer Interessenquoten verstärkt.

*

[1] Art. 106 Abs. 4 Ziffer 1 GG und Finanzanpassungsgesetz vom 23.12.1955.

Der dritte Baustein der Finanzreform, der allerdings nicht das Verhältnis „Bund und Länder", sondern das Verhältnis der Länder untereinander berührt, war die *Neuordnung des Finanzausgleichs*. Der frühere Finanzausgleich hatte seine Aufgabe, die Unterschiede der Steuerkraft zwischen den steuerstarken und steuerschwachen Ländern zu mildern, nicht voll erfüllt. Infolgedessen wurden, um seine Intensität zu stärken und eine gleichmäßigere Erfüllung der Aufgaben durch die Länder zu sichern, die Ausgleichszahlungen erheblich erhöht. Auch sein Vollzug wurde wesentlich vereinfacht. Die Ausgleichsbeträge haben im Rechnungsjahr 1957 insgesamt 793,3 Millionen DM betragen[1]. Sie verteilten sich auf folgende Länder:

Ausgleichspflichtige Länder	Millionen DM	Ausgleichsberechtigte Länder	Millionen DM
Nordrhein-Westfalen	354,9	Bayern	139,0
Baden-Württemberg	174,1	Niedersachsen	208,0
Hessen	46,3	Rheinland-Pfalz	173,1
Hamburg	199,4	Schleswig-Holstein	273,2
Bremen	18,6		

Vom Rechnungsjahr 1958 ab sind die Ausgleichsleistungen weiter angehoben, da durch den Einbau der Abgabe „Notopfer Berlin" in die Körperschaftsteuer ohne eine Änderung des Länder-Finanzausgleichs die Finanzausstattung der leistungsfähigeren Länder sich günstiger gestaltet haben würde. Der gesamte Ausgleichsbetrag wird nach der neuen Regelung rund 937 Millionen DM erreichen.

Außerhalb des horizontalen Finanzausgleichs wurde 1956 ein *Sonderlastenausgleich* zwischen Bund und Ländern *für die Verteilung der Entschädigungslasten* (Wiedergutmachung) nach dem Bundesentschädigungsgesetz vom 29.6.1956 eingeführt. Diese Lasten werden nunmehr je zur Hälfte vom Bund und der Gesamtheit der Länder [ohne Berlin(West)] getragen. Für die vom Lande Berlin zu leistenden Entschädigungen ist eine Sonderregelung getroffen. Danach haben der Bund 60%, die Gesamtheit der Länder 25% und das Land Berlin 15% aufzubringen (vergleiche Seite 465).

*

Eine Sonderstellung hat in allen Jahren *Berlin(West)* eingenommen. Zur Aufrechterhaltung seiner inneren Widerstandskraft und zur Entlastung seiner

[1] Vierte VO zur Durchführung des Länderfinanzausgleichs-Gesetzes vom 17.1.1959.

wirtschaftlichen Lage waren besondere finanzielle Hilfsmaßnahmen notwendig. Bereits 1948 hatte Berlin aus Haushaltsmitteln des Vereinigten Wirtschaftsgebietes Kredite in Höhe von 218 Millionen DM erhalten. Ab 1949 wurden die Zuwendungen an Berlin erheblich erhöht. Zu ihrer Deckung wurde das „*Notopfer Berlin*" als besondere Abgabe von Arbeitnehmern, Veranlagten, Körperschaften und auf Postsendungen eingeführt. Diese Abgabe war zunächst kurz befristet; sie ist aber bis zum Jahre 1956 laufend erhoben worden. Mit Wirkung vom 1.10.1956 wurde sie nur noch von den Körperschaften entrichtet und ist nunmehr im Rahmen der Steuerreform 1958 als Sonderabgabe endgültig fortgefallen. Ihr Aufkommen wurde in die Körperschaftsteuer eingebaut. Eine feste Grundlage erhielten die finanziellen Beziehungen zwischen dem Bund und Berlin(West) durch das Dritte Überleitungsgesetz vom 4.1.1952. Der Bund übernahm die Bundeseinnahmen (Steuern) und die Bundesausgaben, insbesondere also die sozialen Kriegsfolgelasten und Besatzungskosten in Berlin, auf seinen Haushalt. Dadurch stellte er Berlin den übrigen Ländern der Bundesrepublik gleich. Diese Maßnahme bedeutete eine weitgehende Entlastung des Berliner Haushalts. Zur Deckung des Fehlbetrags in seinem Haushalt erhielt Berlin nunmehr einen laufenden allgemeinen Bundeszuschuß. Dieser wurde im Jahre 1956 durch spezielle Zuschüsse und Darlehen zum Aufbauplan Berlin, für den sozialen Wohnungsbau, für Untergrundbahn-Bauten und andere dringliche Maßnahmen erweitert. Diese *Bundeshilfe* für das Land Berlin — durch das Dritte Überleitungsgesetz in der Fassung vom 11.5.1956 neu geordnet — ist so bemessen worden, daß das Land Berlin „befähigt ist, die durch seine besondere Lage bedingten Ausgaben zur wirtschaftlichen und sozialen Sicherung seiner Bevölkerung zu leisten und seine Aufgaben als Hauptstadt eines geeinten Deutschlands zu erfüllen". Auch nach Fortfall des Notopfers Berlin werden diese Leistungen weiter aufrecht erhalten. Bis zum Ende des Rechnungsjahres 1958 haben die Bundesleistungen für Berlin *netto rund zehn Milliarden DM* erreicht.

*

Auch *Saarland*, das politisch vom 1.1.1957 ab auf Grund des Saarvertrages in die Bundesrepublik eingegliedert wurde, hat gegenüber den übrigen Ländern der Bundesrepublik eine Sonderstellung; denn seine finanzwirtschaftliche Eingliederung konnte noch nicht vollständig vollzogen werden. Nur Bahn und Post sind bereits ab 1.1.1957 auf den Bund übergegangen. Die Stellung von Saarland entspricht etwa der Stellung der Bundesländer, die diese vor der Überleitung der Bundeseinnahmen und -ausgaben auf den

Bund im Jahre 1950 hatten. Während der Übergangszeit sind Saarland aus währungspolitischen Gründen alle Steuereinnahmen verblieben. Andererseits hat es alle Ausgaben (einschließlich der Ausgaben, die im Bundesgebiet vom Bund getragen werden) selbst zu leisten. Bundeszuschüsse werden für diese Aufgaben nicht gewährt. Der Bund hat aber die Möglichkeit, durch allgemeine Finanzzuschüsse Fehlbeträge des Landeshaushalts auszugleichen und durch wirtschaftsfördernde Maßnahmen während der Übergangszeit die spätere Eingliederung vorzubereiten. Im Rechnungsjahr 1956 hat die Finanzhilfe 175 Millionen DM betragen. Für das Rechnungsjahr 1957 wurde ein Haushaltzuschuß in Höhe von 29 Millionen DM gegeben. Weitere Mittel sind für Beteiligungen an den Saarbergwerken verausgabt worden. Für das Rechnungsjahr 1958 hat der Bundeshaushalt eine Finanzhilfe in Höhe von 65 Millionen DM und 85 Millionen DM für Beteiligungen an den Saarbergwerken verausgabt. Im Rechnungsjahr 1959 wird sich im Vollzug der Rückgliederung von Saarland für den Bundeshaushalt durch die Übernahme französischer Darlehensforderungen gegenüber Saarland und den Saarbergwerken sowie durch eine Zahlung von 578 Millionen DM an Frankreich anläßlich der Einführung der Deutschen Mark in Saarland einmalig eine höhere Belastung ergeben.

*

*   *

Die Regelung der Finanzbeziehungen zwischen Bund und Ländern hat in den letzten Jahren wesentlich dazu beigetragen, die gleichmäßige Erfüllung der Aufgaben besser als früher zu sichern. Trotzdem haben die Länder zur Entlastung ihrer Haushalte neue Forderungen an den Bund gestellt. Sie betreffen in erster Linie die Übernahme bisheriger Länderlasten. Insbesondere richten diese Wünsche sich auf eine höhere Beteiligung des Bundes an den Lasten der Wiedergutmachung in Berlin. Sie werden aber im Hinblick auf die Finanzlage des Bundes kaum zu erfüllen sein.

Die finanzielle Verflechtung der Haushalte untereinander ist nach der „Flurbereinigung" eng geblieben, zumal der Bund zur Durchführung seiner Aufgaben sich weitgehend der Länder bedient. Die vom Bundeshaushalt an die Länderhaushalte fließenden Summen decken etwa ein Fünftel des Finanzbedarfs der Länder. Die Überweisungen, Darlehen und Zuschüsse einschließlich der Bundeshilfe für Berlin haben 1957 rund sechs Milliarden DM erreicht. 1958 sind sie weiter verstärkt worden.

Tabelle 1
DIE HAUSHALTSEINNAHMEN UND -AUSGABEN DER LÄNDER
1951 BIS 1958 (EINSCHLIESSLICH VON BERLIN[WEST])
Millionen DM[1]

Einnahme- bzw. Ausgabeart	Rechnungsjahr						
	1951	1952	1953	1954	1955	1956	1957
A. Haushalts-einnahmen							
Landessteuern, Anteil an der Einkommen- und Körperschaftsteuer	7.427	8.439	9.173	9.709	10.795	12.955	13.991
Gemeindesteuern (Hansestädte und Berlin[West])	437	537	584	657	681	787	834
Zuweisungen und Zuschüsse vom Bund	1.092	1.368	1.291	1.572	1.673	2.338	3.419
Umlagen und Beiträge von Gemeinden	265	311	361	434	473	523	553
Sonstige laufende Einnahmen	2.691	3.044	2.717	2.845	3.317	3.353	3.440
Schuldenaufnahme vom Bund	330	624	779	814	800	1.074	1.326
Kreditmarktmittel[2]	1.249	1.228	1.527	1.164	1.281	1.386	1.731
Übrige Einnahmen[3]	249	344	443	630	629	730	843
Rein-Einnahmen insgesamt	13.739	15.894	16.874	17.826	19.648	23.147	26.135

Anmerkungen siehe Seite 435.

Steuerliche Entlastung der Wirtschaft

Die Steuerpolitik der Bundesregierung war darauf ausgerichtet, die durch Kontrollratsgesetze eingeführten außerordentlich hohen Steuerbelastungen nach und nach abzubauen. Diese Maßnahmen konnten nur Schritt für Schritt durchgeführt werden. Sie mußten den wachsenden Anforderungen, die an die öffentlichen Haushalte gestellt wurden, angepaßt werden; denn zu große Steuerausfälle hätten die Stabilität der Finanzen gefährdet. Daß die Maßnahmen zunächst nicht, wie oft gefordert wurde, durch eine Neugestaltung des Steuersystems durchgeführt wurden, war vor allem in der

DIE HAUSHALTSEINNAHMEN UND -AUSGABEN DER LÄNDER (Fortsetzung)
1951 BIS 1958 (EINSCHLIESSLICH VON BERLIN[WEST])
Millionen DM[1]

Einnahme- bzw. Ausgabeart	Rechnungsjahr						
	1951	1952	1953	1954	1955	1956	1957
B. Haushaltsausgaben							
Persönliche und sächliche Verwaltungsausgaben	4.051	4.328	4.758	5.432	5.958	6.656	7.309
Versorgung	716	835	936	1.060	1.172	1.346	1.457
Kriegsfolge- und Sozialleistungen.........	806	1.061	837	719	974	1.070	1.110
Wiedergutmachung	.	.	186	254	528	1.184	1.677
Schuldendienst	630	652	846	966	1.181	1.220	1.238
Zuweisungen							
a) Allgemeine Finanzzuweisungen an Gemeinden (Gemeindeverbände)	833	875	891	924	1.002	1.103	1.346
b) Spezielle Zuweisungen an Gemeinden (Gemeindeverbände)	605	710	765	671	796	888	887
c) An Bund und Lastenausgleichfonds	92	222	736	670	853	968	1.043
Sonstige laufende Ausgaben.............	2.060	2.165	2.203	2.388	2.480	2.745	3.261
Darlehen und Investitionszuschüsse[4]							
a) für den Wohnungsbau............	2.616 (a und b)	2.234	2.242	2.314	2.122	2.798	2.664
b) sonstige Bauten (einschl. Grunderwerb) ..		888	1.193	1.185	1.318	1.831	2.123
Bauten	464	594	633	687	947	1.068	1.036
Übrige Ausgaben[5]	443	433	433	409	441	487	591
Rein-Ausgaben insgesamt	13.317	14.997	16.658	17.678	19.771	23.364	25.746

1 Abweichungen in den Summen durch Runden der Zahlen. — 2 Einschließlich der Aufnahme von Schulden bei Trägern der Sozialversicherung und beim Lastenausgleichfonds. — 3 Schuldentilgung, Entnahme aus Rücklagen, Vermögensveräußerung, vermögenswirksame Einnahmen und Abführungen des Erwerbsvermögens. — 4 Einschließlich der Darlehen und Zuschüsse an Gemeinden. — 5 Rücklagenbildung, einmalige und außerordentliche Beschaffungen, vermögenswirksame Ausgaben für das Erwerbsvermögen.

Quelle: Bundesministerium der Finanzen.

unübersichtlichen Lage der Finanzen begründet. Begünstigt wurden die seit der Währungsreform eingeleiteten steuerpolitischen Maßnahmen aber dadurch, daß die außerordentlich schnelle Entwicklung der volkswirtschaftlichen Leistungen dazu beitrug, die Steuerermäßigungen und damit verbundene Steuerausfälle durch ein steigendes Steueraufkommen weitgehend zu kompensieren.

Ihr besonderes Augenmerk wandte die Bundesregierung vor allem der *Einkommensteuer* zu, bei der die Belastungen infolge der sehr hohen Tarifsätze und übermäßigen Progression als besonders drückend empfunden wurden. Diese Tarife waren in den Jahren vor der Währungsreform entschuldbar, weil sie den Kaufkraftüberhang abschöpfen sollten. Später aber hemmten sie den Leistungswillen außerordentlich. Zunächst fanden die Bestrebungen der Bundesregierung, hier Entlastungen eintreten zu lassen, nicht die Zustimmung der Besatzungsmächte. Um die Eigeninitiative der Unternehmungen zu heben und die Investitionstätigkeit nach der Währungsreform wieder anzuregen, half man sich deshalb mit der Einführung von Sondervergünstigungen. Diese trugen schon im Anfangsstadium wesentlich zum Aufschwung der Wirtschaft bei. 1950 wurde erstmalig nach der Währungsreform der Tarif der Einkommensteuer gesenkt. Auch verschiedene Verbrauchsteuern (auf Zucker, Bier und Zigarren) wurden ermäßigt, um Erzeugung und Absatz zu beleben.

Dieser 1950 eingeschlagene Weg wurde anläßlich der Koreakrise durch eine Erhöhung der Umsatz- und Körperschaftsteuer unterbrochen. Im übrigen konnte er in den folgenden Jahren konsequent weiter verfolgt werden. Weitere Tarifsenkungen folgten 1953 im Rahmen der *Kleinen Steuerreform* unter gleichzeitigem Abbau verschiedener Sondervergünstigungen bei der Einkommensteuer; auch mit der Absicht, die steuerlichen Wirkungen auf die Preise zu mildern und die Entwicklung der Konjunktur in diesen Jahren zu beleben. Die Tarifsenkung betrug durchschnittlich 15%. Der Satz der Körperschaftsteuer wurde für die Gewinnausschüttung der Kapitalgesellschaften auf 30% ermäßigt, während der allgemeine Steuersatz noch auf 60% belassen wurde. Bereits im folgenden Jahre setzte die Bundesregierung zielbewußt ihre Steuerpolitik fort. Die *Große Steuerreform 1956* und ergänzende Maßnahmen im Jahre 1956 sowie die Übergangsregelung der Ehegattenbesteuerung 1957 und der Fortfall des Notopfers Berlin (1955 für Postsendungen und 1956 für natürliche Personen) brachten weitere Erleichterungen der Steuerlast. Der allgemeine Körperschaftsteuersatz wurde auf 45% gesenkt. Bei der Einkommensteuer traten neben den Tarifermäßigungen zusätzliche Erleichterungen durch Erhöhung der Freibeträge, der Pauschbeträge für Werbungskosten usw. ein. Zwar wurde ein Teil der Sondervergünstigungen abgebaut; andere aber wurden neu oder wieder, wenn auch vorübergehend, eingeführt. Bei der Gewerbesteuer wurde versucht, insbesondere die mittelständische Wirtschaft durch Anheben der Freibeträge und Beitragsstufen zu entlasten.

Einen vorläufigen Abschluß hat die Neuordnung der Einkommen- und Körperschaftsteuer durch die *Steuerreform 1958* gefunden.[1] Diese Reform stand in engem Zusammenhang mit dem Problem der *Ehegattenbesteuerung*. Das Bundesverfassungsgericht hatte durch Beschluß vom 17.1.1957 die bisherige Form der Zusammen-Veranlagung der Ehegatten, bei der infolge der Tarifprogression sich aus der Eheschließung eine steuerliche Mehrbelastung ergab, für verfassungswidrig erklärt. Diese Mehrbelastung wird nunmehr (mit Wirkung vom 1.1.1958) durch das sogenannte „Splitting" vermieden. Die Regelung geht von dem Grundsatz aus, daß beide Ehepartner — auch wenn nur einer der Ehepartner Einkommen bezieht — das Einkommen gemeinsam erworben haben. Das gemeinsame Einkommen wird bei dem Splittingverfahren in zwei gleiche Teile zerlegt und jeder von ihnen der Steuer unterworfen. Die Halbierung des Einkommens führt bei der Zusammenveranlagung zu einem für die Steuerpflichtigen wesentlich günstigeren Ergebnis; zugleich aber wird der Grundsatz der steuerlichen Gleichstellung aller Ehen gesichert. Daß daneben auch die getrennte Besteuerung auf Antrag möglich ist, sei in diesem Zusammenhang erwähnt. In Verbindung mit der Besteuerung der Ehegatten wurde der Einkommensteuertarif neu geordnet. Durch Vorschaltung einer Proportionalstufe (20% bis 8.000 DM bei Ledigen und bis 16.000 DM bei Verheirateten) mit indirekter Progression durch höhere Freibeträge (allgemeiner Freibetrag, Kinderfreibeträge und andere) sind auch die Bedürfnisse des Mittelstandes und der kinderreichen Familien berücksichtigt worden. Außerdem wurden im Rahmen der Reform auch andere Vorschriften (wie zum Beispiel die Abschreibungssätze und die Vorschriften über sogenannte Kapitalansammlungs-Verträge) geändert. Im ganzen gesehen hat sich durch diese Reform eine erhebliche Senkung der Steuerbelastung ergeben. Einige Härten, die im Lohnsteuerabzugs-Verfahren aufgetreten sind, müssen demnächst beseitigt werden. Die Senkung beläuft sich auf durchschnittlich 12%. Rund 2,8 Millionen Einkommenbezieher sind von der Einkommensteuer freigestellt

[1] Gesetz zur Änderung steuerlicher Vorschriften auf dem Gebiet der Steuern vom Einkommen und Ertrag und des Verfahrensrechts vom 18.7.1958.

worden. Gegenwärtig haben rund 10,3 Millionen, das ist fast die Hälfte der Empfänger von Einkommen, keine Einkommensteuer mehr zu zahlen.

Zugleich mit der Neuordnung der Einkommensteuer und in engem Zusammenhang mit verschiedenen Maßnahmen zur Förderung des Kapitalmarktes wurde ferner der Tarif der Körperschaftsteuer geändert. Der Satz der Körperschaftsteuer für nicht ausgeschüttete Gewinne wurde, unter Einrechnung des Satzes für das wegfallende Notopfer Berlin der Körperschaften, an den Spitzensatz der Einkommensteuer angenähert. Er beträgt nunmehr 51%. Die Doppelbesteuerung für ausgeschüttete Gewinne durch die Körperschaft- und Einkommensteuer wurde dadurch gemildert, daß der Steuersatz von bisher 30% auf 15% herabgesetzt wurde. Die frühere Ermäßigung auf 30% hatte nicht ausgereicht, den Aktienmarkt neu zu beleben. Den wirtschaftlichen Notwendigkeiten kleinerer Kapitalgesellschaften (sogenannter ,,personenbezogener" Kapitalgesellschaften) wird durch die Einführung eines Staffeltarifs und eines niedrigeren Steuersatzes (49%, bei Ausschüttungen 26,5%) Rechnung zu tragen versucht. Die Sonderabgabe ,,Notopfer Berlin", die für die Körperschaften noch bestand, ist durch das Reformgesetz 1958 aufgehoben, aber, wie erwähnt, in die Sätze der Körperschaftsteuer mit eingerechnet.

Einen Überblick über die Entlastung der Steuerzahler seit dem Jahre 1949 gibt das folgende Zahlenbeispiel. Es zeigt die Lohnsteuerbelastung einer vierköpfigen Familie von Arbeitnehmern bei einem Monatsgehalt von 400 DM, 600 DM und 1.000 DM auf Grund der Steuertabellen der einzelnen Jahre[1].

Tabelle 2

LOHNSTEUERBELASTUNG EINER FAMILIE VON ARBEITNEHMERN

Jahr	Lohnsteuer bei einem Arbeitslohn von		
	400 DM	600 DM	1.000 DM
1949	21,75 DM	75,25 DM	252,50 DM
1950/52	16,25 ,,	59,55 ,,	203,75 ,,
1953	11,75 ,,	50,00 ,,	178,80 ,,
1954	10,00 ,,	45,40 ,,	165,05 ,,
1955/56	4,90 ,,	35,80 ,,	124,75 ,,
1957	0,00 ,,	14,00 ,,	92,90 ,,
1958	0,00 ,,	1,00 ,,	81,00 ,,

[1] Ohne Berücksichtigung der persönlichen Verhältnisse und damit der weiteren Ermäßigungen durch Anrechnung erhöhter Werbungskosten, Sonderausgaben und außergewöhnlicher Belastungen.

Quelle: Bundesministerium der Finanzen.

Der allgemeine Steuersatz der *Umsatzsteuer* war im Jahre 1951 infolge erhöhter Soziallasten und der Anforderungen für einen deutschen Verteidigungsbeitrag von 3 auf 4% erhöht worden. Unter dem Leitgedanken einer stärkeren Besteuerung des Verbrauchs wurden im Rahmen der Steuerreform 1955 und 1956 auch für einzelne Umsatzbereiche Erleichterungen eingeführt. Insbesondere sollten der gewerbliche Mittelstand und die Landwirtschaft in ihrer wirtschaftlichen Entwicklung gestärkt werden. Hier sind zu nennen die Befreiung der Lieferung von Milcherzeugnissen, Senkung des Satzes für Frischmilchlieferungen, Erhöhung der Freigrenze für freie Berufe, Einführung eines Freibetrages von 8.000 DM bei Umsätzen bis zu 80.000 DM sowie die Steuerbefreiung der Landwirtschaft. Eine Reform der Umsatzsteuer hat die Bundesregierung mit dem Ziele in Aussicht gestellt, die Mängel des gegenwärtigen Systems, das heißt seine kumulative Wirkung (Allphasen-Umsatzsteuer) zu verringern oder zu beseitigen.

Auch bei den *Zöllen* und *Verbrauchsteuern* wurden die Steuersätze in diesen Jahren nach und nach gesenkt: 1952 bei der Schaumweinsteuer, 1953 bei der Tabak-, Kaffee- und Teesteuer, 1956 bei der Zucker- und Zündwarensteuer, 1955 und 1956 die Zolltarife im Rahmen der konjunkturpolitischen Maßnahmen der Bundesregierung. Dagegen wurden aus verkehrspolitischen Gründen[1] die Sätze der Kraftfahrzeugsteuer, der Beförderungsteuer sowie der Mineralölsteuer erhöht. Zum Ausgleich der Einnahmeausfälle, die durch die Zollsenkung im Rahmen des EWG-Vertrages entstanden wären, sind am 23.12.1958 die Kaffee- und Teesteuern angehoben worden.

Die finanziellen Auswirkungen der in den Jahren 1953 bis 1958 durchgeführten Änderungen des Steuerrechts waren erheblich. Bezogen auf einen Zeitraum von zwölf Monaten, dürften die Steuersenkungen insgesamt 10,5 Milliarden DM ausmachen. Das heißt: kumuliert auf das Jahr 1958 bezogen, wäre das Steueraufkommen um diesen Betrag höher gewesen. Auf die Steuern vom Einkommen und Vermögen entfallen von diesem Betrage allein etwa 9 Milliarden DM. Die Mindereinnahmen durch die Steuerreform 1958 sind für Bund und Länder mit rund 2,2 Milliarden DM veranschlagt worden. Als Ganzes gesehen haben die Maßnahmen somit eine wesentliche Entlastung der Volkswirtschaft mit sich gebracht. Etwas mehr als die Hälfte der Mindereinnahmen entfällt auf den Bundeshaushalt.

Durch die in diesen Jahren eingeleiteten Reformen hat die Wirtschaftsentwicklung sich weitgehend belebt. Es trat gleichsam eine Wechselwirkung ein: das Anwachsen der volkswirtschaftlichen Leistung ergab steigende

[1] Verkehrsfinanzgesetz vom 6.4.1955.

Tabelle 3 **KASSENMÄSSIGE STEUEREINNAHMEN IM BUNDESGEBIET (EINSCHLIESSLICH VON BERLIN[WEST])**

Millionen DM[1]

Steuerarten	Rechnungsjahr							
	1951	1952	1953	1954	1955	1956	1957	1958[2]
A. *Bundes- und Ländersteuern*	23.528	27.627	29.650	31.664	35.223	39.361	41.021	43.949
davon:								
1. *Besitz- u. Verkehrsteuern* . . .	10.381	13.140	14.446	15.231	15.994	18.811	19.592	21.266
darunter:								
Einkommen- u. Körperschaftsteuer	8.437	10.926	11.562	12.173	12.363	15.038	16.085	17.451
Notopfer Berlin	645	815	1.006	1.136	1.310	1.085	544	148
Vermögensteuer .	151	181	572	523	613	762	827	946
Kraftfahrzeugsteuer	420	479	543	615	766	871	993	1.110
2. *Umsatz- u. Umsatzausgleichsteuer*	7.473	8.422	8.978	9.959	11.497	12.276	12.702	13.163
3. *Zölle u. Verbrauchsteuern* . . .	5.674	6.065	6.226	6.474	7.732	8.274	8.727	9.520
darunter:								
Zölle	852	1.122	1.319	1.551	1.849	2.014	2.002	2.255
Tabaksteuer	2.363	2.360	2.281	2.346	2.625	2.816	2.960	3.124
Kaffeesteuer	452	561	441	305	368	412	461	498
Zuckersteuer . . .	419	337	362	379	380	170	164	155
Biersteuer	293	334	373	396	455	496	579	606
Aus dem Branntweinmonopol. . . .	542	527	551	516	611	710	788	888
Mineralölsteuer . .	553	634	716	810	1.256	1.510	1.613	1.822
B. *Gemeindesteuern* . .	3.736	4.361	4.826	5.292	5.627	6.331	7.059	7.615[3]
darunter:								
Grundsteuer A, B	1.217	1.235	1.299	1.350	1.379	1.415	1.473	1.535[3]
Gewerbesteuer[3]	2.178	2.753	3.127	3.509	3.779	4.423	5.074	5.552[3]
C. *Sonderabgaben* . . .	2.129	2.013	2.243	2.422	2.805	2.200	2.359	2.427
davon:								
Lastenausgleichs- (Soforthilfe-) Abgaben	2.059	1.802	2.037	2.235	2.754	2.180	2.036	2.213
Kohlenabgabe . .	70	211	205	187	51	20	323	214
Steuereinnahmen insgesamt	29.394	34.001	36.718	39.378	43.656	47.892	50.440	53.991

[1] Abweichungen in den Summen durch Runden der Zahlen. — [2] Einschließlich der Lohnsummensteuer. — [3] Vorläufiges Ergebnis

Quelle: Bundesministerium der Finanzen / Statistisches Bundesamt.

Steuereinnahmen, so daß wiederum trotz den steigenden Anforderungen an die Finanzen neue Maßnahmen zur Steuerentlastung ins Auge gefaßt werden konnten. Zeitweilig stieg das Steueraufkommen sogar schneller als die Ausgaben, was zur Folge hatte, daß die Haushalte mit Überschüssen abschlossen; besonders, weil die Verteidigungsausgaben die in der Planung vorgesehenen Beträge zunächst nicht erreichten. Die steuerliche Gesamtbelastung des Sozialprodukts ist im Verlauf der verschiedenen Reformen zurückgegangen, wie die folgende Übersicht zeigt:

Tabelle 4
STEUERBELASTUNG DES SOZIALPRODUKTS

Rechnungsjahr	Steuereinnahmen[1]	
	Milliarden DM	in % des Sozialprodukts
1950	21,6	*21,4*
1951	29,4	*23,6*
1952	34,0	*24,4*
1953	36,7	*24,6*
1954	39,4	*24,6*
1955	43,7	*23,9*
1956	47,9	*23,8*
1957	50,4	*23,1*
1958[2]	54,0	*23,3*

[1] Bundes- und Ländersteuern, Gemeindesteuern und Sonderabgaben. — [2] Gemeindesteuern mit vorläufigem Ergebnis.
Quelle: Bundesministerium der Finanzen.

Daß die Entlastung sich nicht stärker auswirkte, war durch den progressiven Tarif der Einkommensteuer bedingt. Die in der Zwischenzeit gestiegenen steuerpflichtigen Einkommen sind in höhere Steuerstufen hineingewachsen, so daß die Senkung der Tarife teilweise kompensiert wurde.

Trotz den erheblichen Minderungen der Steuerbelastung ist die Bundesrepublik im internationalen Vergleich nach wie vor das mit Steuern und Sozialabgaben am stärksten belastete Land geblieben. In Prozenten des Bruttosozialprodukts zu Marktpreisen betrug die Belastung im Jahre 1956 in der Bundesrepublik 31,6%, in Luxemburg 30,9%, in den Niederlanden 29,2%, in Frankreich 28,8%, in Italien 27,7%, in Belgien 23,5%, im Vereinigten Königreich 29,4% und in den USA 25,9%.

Der öffentliche Finanzbedarf

Der öffentliche Finanzbedarf ist in diesen Jahren erheblich gestiegen. Sein Anwachsen war eine natürliche Folge der großen Anforderungen, die sich aus den wirtschaftlichen und sozialen Notständen ergaben. Der Wiederaufbau der Finanzwirtschaft bedurfte einer Anlaufzeit, ehe das gesamte Ausmaß der künftigen Leistungen übersehen werden konnte. Erst nachdem im Jahre 1950 die Aufgaben- und Lastenverteilung zwischen Bund und Ländern geregelt war und die Kriegsfolgelasten auf den Bund übergegangen waren,

Tabelle 5
DIE AUSGABEN UND EINNAHMEN DER ÖFFENTLICHEN HAUSHALTE
1951 BIS 1958
(Bund, Länder, Hansestädte, Berlin[West], Gemeinden, Gemeindeverbände und Soforthilfe- bzw. Lastenausgleichfonds)
Milliarden DM[1]

Ausgabe- bzw. Einnahmeart	Rechnungsjahr							
	1951[2]	1952[2]	1953[2]	1954[2]	1955[2]	1956[2]	1957[2]	1958[3]
A. Ausgaben								
Sozialleistungen ...	8,22[4]	9,33	11,56	11,67	12,24	13,52	14,81	15,4
Wiedergutmachung	0,13	0,29	0,45	0,59	0,87	1,48	1,94	1,8
Schuldendienst	0,96	1,01	1,81	2,39	2,45	2,87	3,26	3,5
Persönliche und sächliche Verwaltungsausgaben	7,44	8,38	9,55	10,34	11,05	12,47	13,77	15,1
Pensionen.........	1,28	1,50	1,69	1,82	1,98	2,24	2,36	2,5
Subventionen......	0,76	0,74	0,22	0,24	0,35	1,05	1,58	1,2
Allgemeine Haushalts- und Zweckausgaben[5] .	3,33	2,90	3,72	3,87	4,26	4,82	6,02	6,8
Investitionen	6,64	8,37	9,44	10,77	11,88	13,60	14,78	15,5
Verteidigungs-(Besatzungs-)Lasten	7,89	7,89	5,52	5,89	6,11	7,33	7,55	8,8
Rückstellung des Besatzungskostenüberhanges	—	—	1,86	2,16	—	—	—	—
Reiner Finanzbedarf	36,66	40,41	45,82	49,75	51,19	59,37	65,94	70,6

Anmerkungen siehe Seite 443.

war eine vorläufige Ordnung hergestellt. Der Umfang dieser Lasten erforderte zudem zwangsläufig eine gewisse Rangfolge, nach der sie erfüllt werden konnten. Zunächst mußten die Aufgaben geordnet werden, deren Regelung aus sozialen Gründen nicht hinausgeschoben werden konnte: Kriegsopferversorgung, Lastenausgleich, Versorgung der unter Artikel 131 GG fallenden Personen, Wiedergutmachung, Förderung des Wohnungsbaus usw. Dann erst konnten die Probleme der inneren und äußeren Kriegsfolgelasten gelöst werden. Ihre finanzwirtschaftliche Größenordnung ließ sich in den ersten Jahren noch nicht abschätzen. Eine frühzeitige Regelung hätte daher zu wenig befriedigenden und auch nicht tragbaren Lösungen geführt.

*

DIE AUSGABEN UND EINNAHMEN DER ÖFFENTLICHEN HAUSHALTE (Fortsetzung)
1951 bis 1958

Ausgabe- bzw. Einnahmeart.	Rechnungsjahr							
	1951[2]	1952[2]	1953[2]	1954[2]	1955[2]	1956[2]	1957[2]	1958[3]
B. Einnahmen								
Steuern und Zölle . .	29,45	34,24	36,63	39,43	43,68	47,93	50,44	54,0
Gebühren, Beiträge und dergleichen. .	3,86	4,12	4,55	4,97	5,40	5,89	6,36	6,7
Ablieferung des Erwerbsvermögens .	0,73	0,87	0,95	1,12	1,43	1,04	0,97	1,2
Schuldenaufnahme, Vermögensveräußerung und Darlehensrückflüsse	1,41	3,01	4,34	4,00	4,11	3,97	5,49	6,4
Sonstige allgemeine Deckungsmittel[6] .	0,66	0,16	0,29	0,27	0,50	0,17	0,28	0,2
Einnahmen insgesamt	36,11	42,40	46,77	49,79	55,12	58,98	63,45	68,5
C. Abschluß								
Mehreinnahmen (+) Mehrausgaben(—)	—0,55	+1,99	+0,95	+0,04	+3,93	—0,38	—2,49	—2,1
Saldo der Rücklagen des Gesamthaushalts [Zuführung (—), Entnahme (+)]	—0,21	—0,12	—0,13	—0,08	—0,05	—0,10	+0,25	+1,7
Gesamtabschluß (ohne Deckung von Fehlbeträgen aus Vorjahren), Mehreinnahmen (+), Mehrausgaben (—)	—0,76	+1,87	+0,82	—0,04	+3,88	—0,48	—1,64	—0,4

[1] Abweichungen in den Summen durch Runden der Zahlen. — [2] Ergebnisse der Finanzstatistik; 1957: vorläufig. — [3] Schätzung. — [4] Ohne Ausgaben des Landes Berlin, jedoch einschließlich der Bundesausgaben in Berlin(West). — [5] Einschließlich des Saldos des Verrechnungsverkehrs (soweit nicht bei Sozialleistungen und Wiedergutmachung enthalten). — [6] Einschließlich der Einnahmen aus Münzprägung und Saldo der Finanzzuweisungen und Umlagen.

Quelle: Bundesministerium der Finanzen / Statistisches Bundesamt.

Tabelle 6

FINANZBEDARF UND SOZIALPRODUKT

1950 bis 1958

Kalender- bzw. Rechnungsjahr	Bruttosozialprodukt [1]	Ausgaben	
	Milliarden DM		%
1950 [2]	97,2	27,3	*28,1*
1951	124,2	36,7	*29,5*
1952	139,3	40,4	*29,0*
1953	149,5	44,0 [3]	*29,4*
1954	160,3	47,6 [3]	*29,7*
1955	183,0	51,2	*28,0*
1956	201,7	59,4	*29,4*
1957 [4]	218,7	65,9	*30,1*
1958 [4]	232,0	70,6 [5]	*30,4*

[1] Bundesgebiet einschließlich von Berlin(West). — [2] Ohne Berlin(West). — [3] Ohne Rückstellungen des Besatzungskostenüberhanges. — [4] Vorläufiges Ergebnis. — [5] Schätzung.

Quelle: Bundesministerium der Finanzen.

Seit der Währungsreform haben sich die Ausgaben der öffentlichen Verwaltung — Bund, Lastenausgleich, Länder, Gemeinden und Gemeindeverbände ohne Sozialversicherung — verdreifacht. Sie stiegen von 23,4 Milliarden DM (1949) auf rund 66 Milliarden DM im Rechnungsjahr 1957. Für das Rechnungsjahr 1958 wird ein weiteres Anwachsen des Finanzbedarfs auf rund 71 Milliarden DM erwartet. Es wird sich in erster Linie infolge der erhöhten Ausgaben des Bundeshaushalts ergeben. Ein Vergleich mit der Entwicklung des deutschen Sozialprodukts zeigt aber, daß der Finanzbedarf sich im Rahmen der volkswirtschaftlichen Leistungssteigerung gehalten hat. Sein Anteil am Bruttosozialprodukt hat sich seit 1949 nur wenig verändert; er betrug durchschnittlich 29 bis 30%. Verglichen mit den Vorkriegsverhältnissen ist er relativ hoch. Doch ist dies eine Erscheinung, die sich nicht auf die Bundesrepublik allein beschränkt, sondern in allen Teilen der Freien Welt zu beobachten ist. Der Staat beansprucht heute einen größeren Teil der volkswirtschaftlichen Leistung als früher, da seine Aufgaben mit der Integration der menschlichen Beziehungen umfassender geworden sind. Für die Bundesrepublik trifft dies in besonderem Maße zu; denn ihre Finanzentwicklung ist vorwiegend von den Lasten bestimmt, die sich aus der Liquidation des Krieges ergeben haben. Mehr als die Hälfte der

Tabelle 7

DIE VERTEILUNG DER GESAMTEN AUSGABEN AUF VERWALTUNGSEBENEN
1951 bis 1958

Rechnungsjahr	Ausgaben[1] Milliarden DM	Davon entfallen in Prozenten auf:			
		Bund	Lastenausgleich [2]	Länder [3]	Gemeinden und Gemeindeverbände
1951	36,7	*48,8*	*6,6*	*26,5*	*18,1*
1952	40,4	*48,9*	*4,5*	*27,4*	*19,2*
1953	45,8	*47,7*	*5,3*	*27,7*	*19,3*
1954	49,8	*45,7*	*6,9*	*27,4*	*20,0*
1955	51,2	*42,9*	*5,0*	*30,0*	*22,1*
1956	59,4	*45,2*	*4,2*	*29,7*	*20,9*
1957 [4]	65,9	*46,8*	*3,9*	*28,3*	*20,9*
1958 [5]	70,6	*46,6*	*4,1*	*28,3*	*21,0*

[1] Von Doppelzählungen bereinigte Ausgaben (Reiner Finanzbedarf). — [2] 1951 bis 31. 8. 1952: Soforthilfefonds. — [3] Einschließlich der Hansestädte und von Berlin-(West). — [4] Vorläufiges Ergebnis. — [5] Schätzung nach Teilergebnissen.

Quelle: Bundesministerium der Finanzen / Statistisches Bundesamt.

Ausgaben des öffentlichen Gesamthaushalts entfiel in den ersten Jahren auf diese Ausgaben. Erst seit 1955 ist eine merkliche relative Abnahme zu beobachten. Im Bundeshaushalt gaben sie den Ausschlag: im Rechnungsjahr 1950 betrug ihr Anteil rund 86%. Auch im Rechnungsjahr 1957 haben sie noch mehr als 40% des Finanzbedarfs erfordert.

Annähernd 50% der gesamten Ausgaben entfallen auf Bund und Lastenausgleich, rund 30% auf die Länderhaushalte (einschließlich der Hansestädte und von Berlin[West]) und rund 20% auf die Gemeinden und Gemeindeverbände.

Der Bundeshaushalt

Die stärksten Impulse der Entwicklung der öffentlichen Finanzen gingen vom *Bundeshaushalt* aus. Infolge seiner engen Verflechtung mit den Finanzen der Länder und Gemeinden wurde auch deren Entwicklung davon mitbeeinflußt. Freilich waren hier auch andere Faktoren mitbestimmend, wie zum Beispiel die Höhe der persönlichen Verwaltungskosten und des

DER FINANZBEDARF DER ÖFFENTLICHEN VERWALTUNG
1949 bis 1958
Bund / Lastenausgleich / Länder / Gemeinden

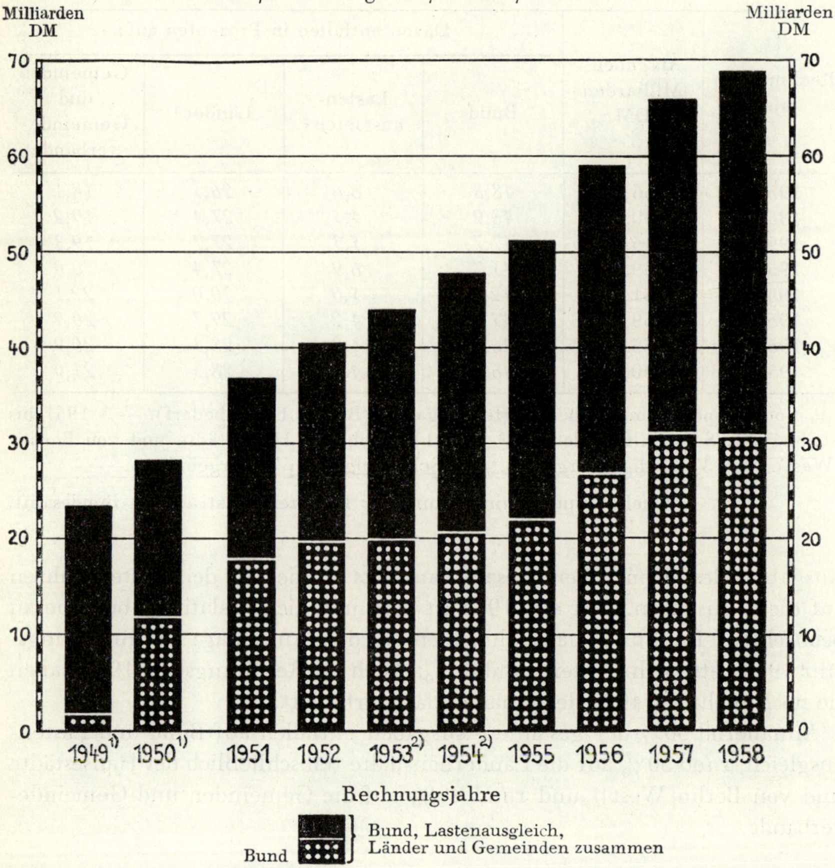

[1] Ohne Berlin(West). — [2] Ohne Besatzungskosten-Rückstellungen.

Quelle: Bundesministerium der Finanzen.

Sachaufwands für die staatlichen und regionalen Aufgaben (Schulen, Rechtspflege, Polizei, gemeindliche Anstalten, Straßenunterhaltung usw.) sowie die Höhe des Schuldendienstes.

Im Rechnungsjahr 1950 betrugen die Ausgaben des Bundes erst 14,7 Milliarden DM, ohne die vorverfügten (durchlaufenden) Mittel 12,4 Milliarden

Tabelle 8

KRIEGSFOLGELASTEN[1]

1950 bis 1958

Rechnungsjahr	Kriegsfolgelasten insgesamt		davon entfallen auf den Bund		
	Milliarden DM	in % der Ausgaben	Milliarden DM	in % der Spalte 2	in % der Ausgaben des Bundes
1950[3]	16,9	57,9	11,6	68,8	86,2
1951[3]	20,6	56,6	15,7	76,3	83,3
1952	22,4	54,4	17,1	76,5	83,5
1953	22,0	47,3	15,6	71,2	69,5
1954	23,2	46,0	15,8	68,2	67,3
1955	21,4	41,2	14,7	68,7	64,5
1956	20,5	34,1	13,5	65,6	48,7
1957[4]	21,0	31,4	13,9	66,4	43,9
1958[4]	20,3	28,5	13,5	66,7	40,4

[1] Besatzungs- und Besatzungsfolgekosten, Soziale Kriegsfolgelasten (einschließlich des Lastenausgleichs und der Wiedergutmachung), Arbeitslosenhilfe, Fremdrenten, Wirtschaftsförderung, Wohnungsbau, Kriegsschäden-Beseitigung; einschließlich des Verwaltungsaufwands. — [2] Bund, Länder und Gemeinden (Gemeindeverbände). — [3] Ohne Berlin(West). — [4] Vorläufige Ergebnisse.

Quelle: Bundesministerium der Finanzen.

DM. Infolge steigender Ausgaben für Besatzung und Sozialleistungen, sowie Erweiterung der Finanzhilfe Berlin durch Übernahme von bisher vom Berliner Landeshaushalt getragenen Soziallasten auf den Bundeshaushalt, stiegen die Ausgaben im Rechnungsjahr 1951 auf 20,9 beziehungsweise 18,8 Milliarden DM. Bis zum Rechnungsjahr 1955 ergab sich eine relativ gleichmäßige Zunahme der Ausgaben. Erst 1956 sind die Ausgaben mit 33,3 beziehungsweise 28,4 Milliarden DM erneut erheblich gewachsen. Das im Haushaltsplan 1956 veranschlagte Ausgabensoll — 35,0 Milliarden DM einschließlich der den Haushalt durchlaufenden Mittel und 32,7 Milliarden DM ohne diese, in erster Linie Lastenausgleichsabgaben — wurde allerdings nicht erreicht, da die Verteidigungsausgaben hinter den veranschlagten Summen zurückblieben.

Das Rechnungsjahr 1956 ist aber ein Wendepunkt in der Entwicklung der Bundesfinanzen, wie ein Vergleich mit den beiden folgenden Rechnungsjahren zeigt. 1956 sind die Ausgaben um 4,0 Milliarden DM gestiegen und

Tabelle 9

DIE HAUSHALTSEINNAHMEN UND -AUSGABEN DES BUNDES 1951 BIS 1959

Millionen DM[1]

Einnahme- bzw. Ausgabeart	Rechnungsjahr								
	1951	1952	1953	1954	1955	1956	1957	1958	1959
	Rechnungsmäßiges Ist-Ergebnis								Haushalts-Soll
A. Haushaltseinnahmen									
1. Steuern/Bundesanteil[2]									
a) Bundessteuern und Zölle	13.838	15.349	15.984	17.344	20.314	21.407	21.678	22.857	23.225
b) Bundesanteil an der Einkommen- und Körperschaftsteuer	2.278	3.926	4.390	4.630	4.120	5.013	5.366	6.108	6.475
c) Interessenquoten der Länder	82	26	—	—	—	—	—	—	
2. Wirtschaftliche Unternehmen und Münzwesen[3]	573	333	388	458	315	405	407	439	430
3. Anleihen[4]	37	934	1.147	475	—	0	169	179	4.162
4. Verwaltungseinnahmen									
a) Abschöpfungsbeträge	162	142	267	415	403	383	368	425	390
b) Sonstige Verwaltungseinnahmen ..	506	610	660	691	945	1.146	5.132[7]	4.380[8]	2.362[9]
5. *Haushaltseinnahmen im engeren Sinne*	17.476	21.319	22.836	24.013	26.097	28.354	33.121	34.387	37.704
6. Durchlaufende Posten, Doppelzählungen[5]	2.083	1.783	4.473	3.950	6.664	4.927	3.912	6.060	2.085
7. Gesamteinnahmen	19.559	23.102	27.309	27.963	32.761	33.281	37.033	40.446	39.789

[1] Abweichungen in den Summen durch Runden der Zahlen. — [2] Ohne Kohlenabgabe. Interessenquoten der Länder: Restbeträge. — [3] Ohne Bundesvermögen. — [4] Einschließlich der Schuldbuchverpflichtungen. — [5] Unter anderen: Lastenausgleichsabgaben und ihre Abführung an den Lastenausgleichfonds (LAF); Beitrag an den ordentlichen beziehungsweise außerordentlichen Haushalt. — [6] Einschließlich der Rückstellungen (1953: 1.863, 1954: 2.157 Millionen DM). — [7] Einschließlich der Entnahme aus Rückstellung (1.020 Millionen DM) und Zuführung aus dem Einnahmen-Mehr 1955 (2.981 Millionen DM). — [8] Einschließlich der Entnahme aus Rückstellung (1.811 Millionen DM) und Zuführung der Minderausgabe 1957 in Höhe von 744 Millionen DM. — [9] Einschließlich der Entnahme aus Rückstellung (1.200 Millionen DM). Quelle: Bundesministerium der Finanzen.

DIE HAUSHALTSEINNAHMEN UND -AUSGABEN DES BUNDES 1951 BIS 1959 (Fortsetzung)
Millionen DM[1]

	1951	1952	1953	1954	1955	1956	1957	1958	1959
B. Haushaltsausgaben									
1. Verteidigungslasten	7.915	7.892	7.385[6]	8.050[6]	6.105	7.329	7.547	8.824	11.772
2. Sozialleistungen .	6.877	7.641	8.857	8.778	9.814	10.905	11.824	11.694	11.750
3. a) Finanzhilfe Berlin	550	662	682	833	929	895	957	1.128	1.130
b) Rückgliederung von Saarland	—	—	—	—	—	224	131	175	1.011
4. Subventionen, Vorratshaltung . .	733	693	177	227	302	1.035	1.601	1.240	1.167
5. Wohnungsbau und Siedlung . . .	326	601	1.082	831	873	1.055	1.443	1.772	1.820
6. Andere wichtige Förderungsmaßnahmen									
a) Bundesbahn . .	—	60	150	488	515	758	1.046	981	865
b) Sonstige	213	553	262	396	451	915	1.093	946	1.122
7. Schuldendienst . .	255	257	876	939	642	1.079	1.188	1.141	2.240
8. Wiedergutmachung									
a) Leistungen nach dem Bundesentschädigungsgesetz . .	—	—	—	24	131	565	893	808	1.300
b) Israel	—	80	238	331	250	250	247	253	250
c) Sonstige Rückerstattungen .	—	10	19	44	106	148	138	129	404
9. Wirtschaftliche Unternehmen und Münzwesen[3]	111	62	39	31	119	56	60	27	48
10. Übrige Ausgaben	1.842	2.800	3.691	3.262	2.787	3.142	4.228	5.269	5.672
11. Minderausgaben	—	—	—	—	—	—	—	—	–2.846
12. Haushaltsausgaben im engeren Sinne	18.822	21.311	23.456	24.234	23.024	28.554	32.396	34.388	37.704
13. Durchlaufende Posten, Doppelzählungen[5]	2.045	1.786	4.494	3.956	6.664	4.927	3.893	6.059	2.085
14. Gesamtausgaben	20.868	23.097	27.950	28.189	29.688	33.281	36.288	40.446	39.789
C. Mehreinnahmen (+), *Mehrausgaben* (—) .	—1.309	+6	—641	—227	+3.072	±0	+744	±0	±0

haben auch 1957 und 1958 nochmals erheblich zugenommen (vergleiche die Übersicht). Die Entwicklung ergab sich nicht zum wenigsten durch die relativ hohen Ausgabenbeschlüsse, die der Bundestag 1956 und 1957 gefaßt hatte (unter anderen Erhöhung der Sozialleistungen, Grüner Plan). Diese Ausgabebewilligungen waren mit eine Folge der hohen *Kassenüberschüsse* der Jahre 1953 bis 1955, die durch das Zurückbleiben der Verteidigungsausgaben gegenüber den Voranschlägen entstanden waren. Die Kassenbestände des Bundes hatten Ende September 1956 mit 7 Milliarden DM ihren Höchststand erreicht. Da es sich bei den Mehrbewilligungen vorwiegend um künftig wiederkehrende Ausgaben handelt, bedeutet die Ausgabensteigerung zugleich eine Vorbelastung künftiger Haushaltsjahre.

Zur Deckung der Mehrausgaben standen 1957 die Rückstellungen (insgesamt 4,02 Milliarden DM) aus Vorjahren und die kassenmäßige Mehreinnahme aus dem Rechnungsjahre 1955 zur Verfügung. Da aber im Rechnungsjahr 1957 die für den Aufbau der Bundeswehr veranschlagten Ausgaben nicht voll verausgabt wurden und andere Ausgaben nicht die bewilligten Summen erreichten, kamen die Rückstellungen nicht in voller Höhe zum Einsatz. Die Aufnahme einer Anleihe konnte ebenfalls zunächst zurückgestellt werden. Auch 1958 ist die Entwicklung des Haushalts noch relativ günstig verlaufen. Das Deckungsproblem wird daher erst 1959 erneut in den Vordergrund treten. Der Haushalt 1959 ist mit einem Gesamtvolumen der Ausgaben von 39,8 Milliarden DM (einschließlich der vorverfügten Mittel) um rund 1.000 Millionen DM höher als der Haushaltsplan 1958 (mit 38,7 Milliarden DM). Zur Deckung wird außer den restlichen Mitteln der Rückstellung aber eine Anleihe von rund 4,2 Milliarden DM (einschließlich eines Sonderkredits der Deutschen Bundesbank zur Einführung der DM im Saarland [vergleiche Seite 433]) benötigt werden.

Die Schwerpunkte: Verteidigungs- und Sozialleistungen

Verteidigungslasten und Sozialleistungen haben die Entwicklung des Bundeshaushalts sehr wesentlich mitgestaltet. Sie bilden die strukturellen Schwerpunkte, von denen seit 1950 der Ausgabenbedarf abhängig war und auch künftig bestimmt werden wird. In den letzten beiden Jahren haben auch die Ausgaben zur Wirtschaftsförderung stärker an Gewicht gewonnen.

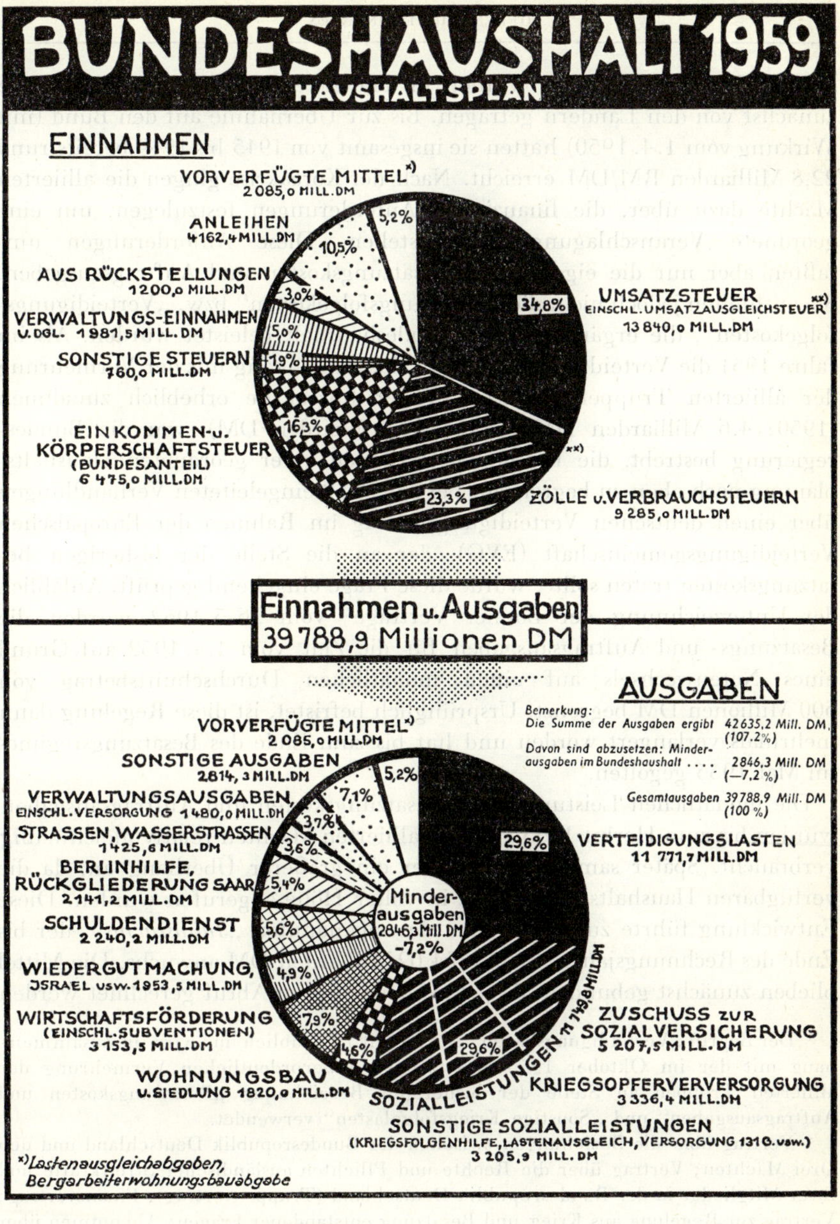
BUNDESHAUSHALT 1959
HAUSHALTSPLAN
EINNAHMEN
VORVERFÜGTE MITTEL*)
2 085,0 MILL.DM
5,2%
ANLEIHEN
4162,4 MILL.DM
10,5%
AUS RÜCKSTELLUNGEN
1200,0 MILL.DM
3,0%
VERWALTUNGS-EINNAHMEN
U.DGL. 1981,5 MILL.DM
5,0%
SONSTIGE STEUERN
760,0 MILL.DM
1,9%
34,8%
UMSATZSTEUER
EINSCHL. UMSATZAUSGLEICHSTEUER**)
13 840,0 MILL.DM
16,3%
EINKOMMEN- u. KÖRPERSCHAFTSTEUER
(BUNDESANTEIL)
6 475,0 MILL.DM
**)
23,3%
ZÖLLE u. VERBRAUCHSTEUERN
9 285,0 MILL.DM
Einnahmen u. Ausgaben
39 788,9 Millionen DM
AUSGABEN
Bemerkung:
Die Summe der Ausgaben ergibt 42 635,2 Mill. DM (107,2%)
Davon sind abzusetzen: Minderausgaben im Bundeshaushalt .... 2846,3 Mill. DM (—7,2%)
Gesamtausgaben 39 788,9 Mill. DM (100%)
VORVERFÜGTE MITTEL*)
2 085,0 MILL.DM
5,2%
SONSTIGE AUSGABEN
2814,3 MILL.DM
7,1%
VERWALTUNGSAUSGABEN,
EINSCHL. VERSORGUNG 1480,0 MILL.DM
3,7%
STRASSEN, WASSERSTRASSEN
1425,6 MILL.DM
3,6%
BERLINHILFE, RÜCKGLIEDERUNG SAAR
2 141,2 MILL.DM
5,4%
SCHULDENDIENST
2 240,2 MILL.DM
5,6%
Minderausgaben
2846,3 Mill. DM
-7,2%
29,6%
VERTEIDIGUNGSLASTEN
11 771,7 MILL.DM
WIEDERGUTMACHUNG,
ISRAEL USW. 1953,5 MILL.DM
4,9%
WIRTSCHAFTSFÖRDERUNG
(EINSCHL. SUBVENTIONEN)
3 153,5 MILL.DM
7,9%
4,6%
29,6%
SOZIALLEISTUNGEN 11 749,8 MILL.DM
ZUSCHUSS ZUR SOZIALVERSICHERUNG
5 207,5 MILL.DM
WOHNUNGSBAU
U. SIEDLUNG 1820,0 MILL.DM
KRIEGSOPFERVERVERSORGUNG
3 336,4 MILL.DM
SONSTIGE SOZIALLEISTUNGEN
(KRIEGSFOLGENHILFE, LASTENAUSGLEICH, VERSORGUNG 131 G. usw.)
3 205,9 MILL.DM
*) Lastenausgleichsabgaben,
Bergarbeiterwohnungsbauabgabe

Die *Verteidigungslasten*[1] wurden in den ersten Jahren nach Kriegsende zunächst von den Ländern getragen. Bis zur Übernahme auf den Bund (mit Wirkung vom 1.4.1950) hatten sie insgesamt von 1945 bis 1949 bereits rund 22,8 Milliarden RM/DM erreicht. Nach der Koreakrise gingen die alliierten Mächte dazu über, die finanziellen Anforderungen festzulegen, um eine geordnete Veranschlagung sicherzustellen. Diese Anforderungen umfaßten aber nur die eigentlichen Besatzungskosten und Auftragsausgaben. Sie enthielten jedoch nicht die ,,Besatzungsfolgekosten" bzw. ,,Verteidigungsfolgekosten", die ergänzend vom Bundeshaushalt geleistet wurden. Als im Jahre 1951 die Verteidigungslasten im Zusammenhang mit der Vermehrung der alliierten Truppen im Verlauf der Koreakrise erheblich zunahmen (1950: 4,6 Milliarden DM, 1951: 7,9 Milliarden DM), war die Bundesregierung bestrebt, die Lasten aus Gründen einer geordneten Haushaltsplanung nach oben zu begrenzen. Bei den 1952 eingeleiteten Verhandlungen über einen deutschen Verteidigungsbeitrag im Rahmen der Europäischen Verteidigungsgemeinschaft (EVG), der an die Stelle der bisherigen Besatzungskosten treten sollte, wurde diese Frage eingehend geprüft. Anläßlich der Unterzeichnung der Bonner Verträge[2] vom 26.5.1952 wurden die Besatzungs- und Auftragsausgaben für die Zeit vom 1.4.1952 auf Grund eines Notenwechsels auf einen monatlichen Durchschnittsbetrag von 600 Millionen DM begrenzt. Ursprünglich befristet, ist diese Regelung dann mehrmals verlängert worden und hat bis zum Ende des Besatzungsregimes im Mai 1955 gegolten.

Die monatlichen Leistungen für Besatzungskosten und Auftragsausgaben wurden bis zum Herbst 1953 von den alliierten Mächten relativ gleichmäßig verbraucht. Später sammelte sich aber ein größerer Überhang an, da die verfügbaren Haushaltsmittel nicht in voller Höhe abgerufen wurden. Diese Entwicklung führte zum Entstehen des sogenannten ,,*Juliusturms*", der bis Ende des Rechnungsjahres 1954 auf 4,02 Milliarden DM anwuchs. Die Mittel blieben zunächst gebunden, da jederzeit mit ihrem Abruf gerechnet werden

[1] Der Begriff ,,Verteidigungslasten" ist erst seit 1951 üblich und wird im Zusammenhang mit der im Oktober 1950 einsetzenden außerordentlichen Vermehrung der alliierten Truppen an Stelle der bisherigen Bezeichnung ,,Besatzungskosten und Auftragsausgaben" und ,,Sonstige Kriegsfolgelasten" verwendet.

[2] Vertrag über die Beziehungen zwischen der Bundesrepublik Deutschland und den Drei Mächten; Vertrag über die Rechte und Pflichten ausländischer Streitkräfte und ihrer Mitglieder in der Bundesrepublik Deutschland (Truppenvertrag); Finanzvertrag; Vertrag zur Regelung aus Krieg und Besatzung entstandener Fragen; Abkommen über die steuerliche Behandlung der Streitkräfte und ihrer Mitglieder.

mußte, und wurden einem Sonderkonto der Bank Deutscher Länder (Deutsche Bundesbank) zugeführt. Die weitere Entwicklung der Verteidigungslasten in den Jahren 1955 und 1956 verlief aber anders als erwartet. Die Überhänge an Besatzungskosten, die den Besatzungsmächten auch noch nach dem 5.5.1955 zur Verfügung standen, wurden infolge verzögerter Aufrüstung aus laufenden Haushaltsmitteln gedeckt. Infolgedessen konnten nunmehr, wie erwähnt, die zunächst gebundenen Rückstellungen aufgelöst und zum Teil bereits im Bundeshaushalt 1957 zum allgemeinen Haushaltsausgleich verwandt werden. Die restlichen Beträge werden 1958 und 1959 verbraucht sein.

Das Besatzungsregime endete im Mai 1955 durch den Beitritt der Bundesrepublik zur NATO und zur WEU[1]. Die Bundesrepublik wurde nunmehr auch in finanzieller Hinsicht den Mitgliedstaaten der NATO gleichgestellt. Zugleich entfiel die Leistung der Besatzungskosten. An ihre Stelle traten *Stationierungskosten* als Beitrag der Bundesrepublik für den Unterhalt der im Geltungsbereich des Grundgesetzes stationierten nichtdeutschen Streitkräfte. Nach dem Finanzvertrag (Artikel 4) hatte die Bundesrepublik für die ersten zwölf Monate nach Inkrafttreten der Verträge (5.5.1955) einen Gesamtbetrag von 3,2 Milliarden DM zur Verfügung zu stellen[2]. Mit dem 6.5.1956 endete also die Pflicht, einen Beitrag zu den Stationierungskosten zu leisten. Gleichzeitig begann der Aufbau der eigenen Streitkräfte. Da dieser Aufbau aber eine wesentlich längere Anlaufzeit benötigte, als die ursprüngliche Planung vorsah, und von den hierfür veranschlagten Haushaltsmitteln im Rechnungsjahr 1955 erst ein geringfügiger Betrag in Anspruch genommen wurde, erklärte die Bundesregierung sich bereit, 1956 einen zusätzlichen Jahresbeitrag für die Stationierung der alliierten Truppen in Höhe von 1.455 Millionen DM zu leisten. Die Bundesrepublik wollte damit zugleich den im NATO-Pakt niedergelegten Grundsatz der gemeinsamen und gegenseitigen Hilfe verwirklichen. Auch für 1957 ist erneut für „gegenseitige militärische Hilfe" ein Beitrag von 1.198 Millionen DM geleistet worden. Daneben leistet die Bundesrepublik einen Beitrag zum NATO-Haushalt und zum Haushalt der Westeuropäischen Union. Ferner ist sie beteiligt an den Kosten der gemeinsamen NATO-Infrastruktur. Der

[1] Vertrag über die wirtschaftliche, soziale und kulturelle Zusammenarbeit und über die kollektive Selbstverteidigung vom 17.3.1948 in der Fassung des am 23.10.1954 in Paris unterzeichneten Protokolls.

[2] Zweimal 400 Millionen DM, viermal 300 Millionen DM und für die letzten sechs Monate sechsmal 200 Millionen DM.

Beitrag zu den Kosten des Unterhalts der von den Paktpartnern in der Bundesrepublik stationierten Streitkräfte stellt allerdings nicht die Gesamtleistung dar, welche die deutsche Volkswirtschaft im Zusammenhang mit der Stationierung ausländischer Truppen zu erbringen hat. Vielmehr sind darüber hinaus als Folge der Weitergeltung des Truppen- und Finanzvertrages zunächst die bisherigen geldwerten Leistungen weiter zu erbringen. Dazu gehören die Unterhaltung der Behörden der deutschen Verwaltung der Verteidigungslasten, zusätzliche Vergütungen für in Anspruch genommene Vermögenswerte der Länder mit Grundsteuern, öffentlichen Gebühren und Abgaben, Bau, Instandsetzung und Instandhaltung der zivilen und militärisch genutzten Verkehrsmittel und Anlagen, Freistellung der Streitkräfte von der Haftung für Schäden an Vermögenswerten der Länder, Erwerb und Räumung von Liegenschaften einschließlich der Folgemaßnahmen.

Bis Ende des Rechnungsjahres 1957 erreichten die von der Bundesrepublik seit 1950 für die ausländischen Truppen erbrachten Leistungen (einschließlich der Besatzungsfolgekosten) insgesamt 43,9 Milliarden DM. Einschließlich der vorher (1945 bis 1949) von den Ländern getragenen Besatzungskosten ergibt sich eine *Gesamtsumme von 66,7 Milliarden RM/DM*.

Die Aufstellung der eigenen Streitkräfte hat mit dem Jahre 1956 begonnen und nach Inkrafttreten der gesetzlichen Grundlagen der Wehrverfassung erhebliche Fortschritte gemacht. 1955 wurde zunächst ein Teilbetrag der eingeplanten Haushaltsmittel, 1956 wurden rund 3,4 Milliarden DM, 1957 rund 5,4 Milliarden DM und 1958 rund 8 Milliarden DM verbraucht.

*

Die sozialen Leistungen bilden im Bundeshaushalt neben den Verteidigungslasten einen mehr oder weniger starren Ausgabenblock. In seiner Höhe ist er kaum zu beeinflussen, da er gesetzliche Verpflichtungen umfaßt, die zu erfüllen sind.

Der Ausgleich der durch den Krieg entstandenen Schäden und Vermögensverluste konnte nicht gleich nach der Rückkehr stabiler Verhältnisse in einem Wurf vorgenommen werden. Ihr Umfang war so erheblich, daß zunächst nur die Maßnahmen getroffen wurden, bei denen ein Hinausschieben aus sozialen Gründen nicht verantwortet werden konnte. Sie waren darauf

Tabelle 10

VERTEIDIGUNGSLASTEN DES BUNDES SEIT 1953

Millionen DM

	1953 Ist	1954 Ist	1955 Ist	1956 Ist	1957 Ist	1958 Ist
Deutsche Verteidigungsstreitkräfte[1] ...	—	—	95	3.405	5.405	7.974
Besatzungskosten und Auftragsausgaben	5.216	5.368	1.088	182[3]	189	199
Stationierungskosten[2]	—	—	2.066	1.688	1.149	191
Verwendung des Überhangs an Besatzungs- und Stationierungskosten	—	—	2.376	1.703	388	105
Besatzungs- und Stationierungs-Folgekosten........................	305	525	479	351	417	355
Insgesamt	5.522	5.892	6.105	7.329	7.547	8.824
Nachrichtlich:						
Rückstellung des Überhangs an Besatzungskosten	1.863	2.157	—	—	—	—

[1] Einschließlich des NATO-Beitrags. — [2] Ab 1957: Gegenseitige militärische Hilfe. — [3] Besatzungskosten Berlin(West).

Quelle: Statistisches Bundesamt.

ausgerichtet, die individuellen Schäden durch laufende Zahlungen zum Unterhalt, durch Entschädigungs- und Versorgungsleistungen soweit zu beheben, daß die Geschädigten in der Lage waren, sich aus eigener Kraft eine neue Existenzgrundlage aufzubauen und sich in den Wirtschaftsprozeß einzugliedern. Zu den vielgestaltigen Maßnahmen dieser Jahre gehörten die Kriegsfolgenhilfe, die Umsiedlung der Heimatvertriebenen in Länder der Bundesrepublik mit günstigen wirtschaftlichen Voraussetzungen, die Versorgung der Kriegsopfer, Versorgung der verdrängten Angehörigen des öffentlichen Dienstes und der früheren Wehrmacht, sowie der Lastenausgleich.

Die Kriegsfolgenhilfe umfaßt die Fürsorgemaßnahmen für die Heimatvertriebenen, Evakuierten, Zugewanderten aus der sogenannten DDR, Ausländer und Staatenlosen, Angehörigen von Kriegsgefangenen und Vermißten, Heimkehrer und Kriegsbeschädigten und -hinterbliebenen. Hinzu kommen vielgestaltige Einzelmaßnahmen und die Einrichtung und Unterhaltung von Grenzdurchgangs- und Notaufnahmelagern für die erste Unterbringung der Bedürftigen. Sie wird von den Fürsorgeverbänden der Länder und Gemeinden im Rahmen der allgemeinen Fürsorge durchgeführt. Hingegen trägt der Bund den überwiegenden Teil der Kosten (1950: 75%, ab 1951: 85%, ab 1955 pauschale Zahlungen).

Der Erfolg der eingeleiteten Maßnahmen, insbesondere auch der Regelung des Lastenausgleichs, zeigte sich bald. Die Zahl der Empfänger von Kriegsfolgenhilfe ging von Jahr zu Jahr zurück (1949: 728.310, 1955: 305.000). Der gesamte Aufwand hat daher bei verbesserten Leistungen an die Empfänger in den Jahren 1949 bis 1955 sich nicht mehr wesentlich erhöht. Die Entwicklung führte dazu, daß die Leistungen des Bundes an die Länder ab 1955 pauschaliert und allmählich reduziert wurden[1].

Tabelle 11

KRIEGSFOLGENHILFE

Millionen DM

1950:	615,8	1955:	736,9
1951:	534,2	1956:	782,1
1952:	624,5	1957:	728,3
1953:	709,6	1958:	739,7
1954:	707,9	1959:	669,5

Quelle: Bundesministerium der Finanzen.

Diese Kriegsfolgelasten werden voraussichtlich bis zum Jahre 1968 abgetragen sein. Ab 1969 werden weitere Zahlungen des Bundes nicht mehr geleistet.

Die *Versorgung der Kriegsopfer* als Bundesaufgabe wurde im Bundesversorgungsgesetz vom 20.12.1950 geregelt. Bis dahin waren diese Versorgungslasten von den Ländern auf Grund besonderer Ländergesetze getragen worden. Bis zum Jahre 1954 hat die Zahl der Versorgungsberechtigten bis auf 4.342.971 ständig zugenommen. Von da ab ist sie infolge der natürlichen Entwicklung von Jahr zu Jahr zurückgegangen und hat am 31.3.1958: 3.711.888 Versorgungsberechtigte betragen. Davon waren 1.473.801 Kriegsbeschädigte, 1.170.232 Witwen, 786.090 Waisen, 281.765 Eltern. Der Kreis der Empfänger der vollen Ausgleichsrente, das heißt der Personen, die ausschlielich auf diese Versorgungsrenten angewiesen sind, wurde durch die vielseitigen Maßnahmen zur Eingliederung der Schwerbeschädigten in den Wirtschaftsprozeß und infolge der

Tabelle 12

KRIEGSOPFER-VERSORGUNG

Millionen DM

1950:	2.230,5	1955:	3.445,7
1951:	3.028,1	1956:	3.938,0
1952:	3.039,5	1957:	3.596,0[1]
1953:	2.985,9	1958:	3.453,5
1954:	2.894,2	1959:	3.336,4

[1] Ohne Erstattungen nach § 90 BVG an die Rentenversicherungen (1956: 432 Millionen DM).

Quelle: Bundesministerium der Finanzen.

[1] Die Fürsorgeleistungen für Flüchtlinge aus der „Zone" und die Leistungen für Kriegsbeschädigte und -hinterbliebene wurden nicht pauschaliert, da ihre Höhe noch größeren Schwankungen unterliegt.

Erhöhung der Renten aus der Sozialversicherung kleiner. Trotzdem erfordert die Versorgung der Kriegsopfer erhebliche Mittel.

Da in der Zwischenzeit die Leistungen durch sechs Novellen zum Bundesversorgungsgesetz, zuletzt 1957, erheblich verbessert worden sind, hat die Abnahme der Versorgungsberechtigten seit 1954 keine wesentliche Entlastung für den Bundeshaushalt ergeben.

Auch für die *Versorgung der 131er* (Verdrängte Angehörige des öffentlichen Dienstes und Berufssoldaten der früheren Wehrmacht) sind bisher in jedem Jahre größere Ausgaben geleistet worden. Die Renten sind den Änderungen der Beamtenversorgung laufend angepaßt und entsprechend erhöht worden. In den Jahren 1953 bis 1956 haben sie im Jahresdurchschnitt etwa 1,1 Milliarden DM betragen. In den folgenden Jahren sind sie weiter gestiegen.

Tabelle 13
VERSORGUNG NACH ARTIKEL 131 GG
Millionen DM

1950:	385,0	1955:	1.138,5
1951:	543,9	1956:	1.260,8
1952:	787,9	1957:	1.476,6
1953:	958,5	1958:	1.541,1
1954:	1.075,1	1959:	1.512,9

Quelle: Bundesministerium der Finanzen.

Die *Entschädigungen an Kriegsgefangene* wurden erst 1954 geregelt[1]. Sie werden voll vom Bund getragen. Nur bei den zusätzlichen Leistungen, wie Aufbaudarlehen, Darlehen zur Wohnraum- und Hausratbeschaffung, sind die Länder mit einer Interessenquote von 20% beteiligt. Der Bundeshaushalt hat im Rechnungsjahr 1954: 48,0, 1955: 192,9, 1956: 617,8, 1957: 331,4 und 1958: 81,6 Millionen DM verausgabt. Für 1959 sind noch 77.0 Millionen DM veranschlagt.

*

Neben diesen sozialen Kriegsfolgelasten hat der Bund in den ersten Jahren für die *Arbeitslosenhilfe*, das heißt die Unterstützung der langfristig Arbeitslosen, recht erhebliche Leistungen aufgebracht, solange die wirtschaftlichen Grundlagen noch nicht so gefestigt waren, daß die Unterbringung dieser Personen möglich war. Verschiedene Maßnahmen zur Beseitigung der strukturellen Arbeitslosigkeit, insbesondere die Umsiedlung der Arbeitslosen in die Industriegebiete, die Schaffung neuer Arbeitsmöglichkeiten in den Notstandsgebieten und die Maßnahmen zur Eingliederung im Rahmen des Lastenausgleichs, haben dazu beigetragen, die Notstände zu beheben.

Die günstige Wirtschaftsentwicklung hat die Zahl der Arbeitslosen seit 1955 sehr stark absinken lassen, und damit auch die Zahl der Empfänger

[1] Gesetz vom 30.1.1954/27.4.1955.

von Arbeitslosenhilfe. Im Jahre 1950 betrug sie (durchschnittlich) 919.217, im Jahre 1957: 193.627. Auch 1958 hat sie weiter abgenommen. Diese Entwicklung ergab für den Bundeshaushalt eine wesentliche Entlastung, die bei Anhalten der Vollbeschäftigung auch künftig bestehen bleiben wird. Die Abnahme des Aufwands wäre noch stärker gewesen, wenn nicht inzwischen die Leistungen wiederholt angehoben worden wären.

Tabelle 14
ARBEITSLOSENHILFE
Millionen DM

1950:	996,6	1955:	680,6
1951:	1.233,1	1956:	468,8
1952:	1.172,4	1957:	411,3
1953:	1.169,2	1958:	369,8
1954:	1.024,4	1959:	368,4

Quelle: Bundesministerium der Finanzen.

Die Zahl der Empfänger von *Arbeitslosengeld*, das auf Grund der Versicherungspflicht aus den Beitragseinnahmen der Bundesanstalt für Arbeitsvermittlung und Arbeitslosenversicherung geleistet wird, also nicht den Bundeshaushalt belastet, hat im Durchschnitt der Jahre 1950 bis 1957 sich nicht wesentlich geändert. Seit 1954 zeigte sie allerdings vorübergehend eine rückläufige Tendenz. Im Jahre 1957 wurden durchschnittlich 453.092 Unterstützungsempfänger gezählt. Die Aufwendungen für Arbeitslosengeld haben infolgedessen bei weitem nicht so stark abgenommen wie die für Arbeitslosenhilfe. 1957 betrugen sie 1.146 Millionen DM gegenüber 890 Millionen DM im Jahre 1956.

*

Tabelle 15
ZUSCHÜSSE ZUR SOZIALVERSICHERUNG
Millionen DM

1950:	700,2	1955:	2.963,2
1951:	1.374,3	1956:	3.459,3
1952:	1.730,5	1957:	4.669,7
1953:	2.641,6	1958:	5.126,9
1954:	2.612,9	1959:	5.207,5

Quelle: Bundesministerium der Finanzen.

Zu *Zuschüssen an die Sozialversicherung* ist der Bund nach Artikel 120 GG verpflichtet. Dies war auch früher der Fall. Das Reich, nach dem Kriege zunächst die Länder, trugen die Grundbeträge der Invalidenversicherung und der knappschaftlichen Rentenversicherung. Diese Lasten wurden 1950 auf den Bund übergeleitet. In den folgenden Jahren mußte der Bund weitere zusätzliche Leistungen aufbringen, die sich aus der Anpassung der Renten an die höheren Lebenshaltungskosten ergaben[1].

[1] Rentenzulagegesetz vom 10.8.1951, Grundbetrags-Erhöhungsgesetz vom 17.4.1953, Fremdrenten- und Auslandsrentengesetz vom 7.8.1953, Renten-Mehrbetragsgesetz vom 23.11.1954 und andere.

Tabelle 16

DIE EINNAHMEN UND AUSGABEN DER SOZIALEN SELBSTVERWALTUNGEN
(Renten-, Unfall-, Kranken- und Arbeitslosenversicherung, Familienausgleichskassen)
Millionen DM

Einnahmen- bzw. Ausgabenart	Kalenderjahr						
	1951[1]	1952[1]	1953[2]	1954[2]	1955[2]	1956[2]	1957[2]
A. Einnahmen							
1. Beiträge							
a) der Versicherten ..	4.124	4.645	5.480	5.919	6.759	7.612	9.053
b) der Arbeitgeber	4.452	5.020	5.863	6.220	7.397	7.993	9.795
2. Staatsbeteiligungen	1.076	1.589	2.349	2.485	2.756	3.216	4.658
3. Vermögenserträgnisse....	99	176	228	345	466	657	826
4. Erstattungen des Bundes[3]...	346	529	505	424	321	525	76
5. Sonstige Einnahmen ...	90	72	61	84	123	214	176
6. Einnahmen[4] insgesamt:....	10.187	12.031	14.486	15.477	17.822	20.217	24.584
B. Ausgaben							
1. Sachleistungen[5]	2.423	2.929	3.348	3.581	4.023	4.396	5.075
2. Barleistungen .	5.972	7.250	8.401	8.747	10.251	11.918	16.663
3. Verwaltungskosten	369	434	525	582	641	730	818
4. Sonstige Ausgaben[6]	67	199	94	103	118	181	139
5. Ausgaben[4] insgesamt:....	8.831	10.812	12.368	13.013	15.033	17.225	22.695
C. Überschuß (+) ..	+1.356	+1.219	+2.118	+2.464	+2.789	+2.992	+1.889

[1] Ohne Berlin(West). — [2] Einschließlich von Berlin(West). — [3] Kosten- und Rentenerstattungen im Rahmen der Arbeitslosenhilfe und Kriegsopferversorgung. — [4] Von Doppelzählungen (Verrechnungsverkehr der Versicherungsträger untereinander) bereinigt. — [5] Einschließlich der Aufwendungen in der wertschaffenden Arbeitslosenhilfe und für Maßnahmen zur Verhütung und Beendigung der Arbeitslosigkeit sowie Kosten der Arbeitsvermittlung und Berufsberatung. — [6] Einschließlich der Aufwendungen für Unfallverhütung.

Quelle: Bundesministerium für Arbeit und Sozialordnung.

Die Bundeszuschüsse sind von 1950 bis 1957 um mehr als das Sechsfache gestiegen. In den letzten Rechnungsjahren deckten sie etwa 36 bis 38% der Gesamtleistungen der gesetzlichen Rentenversicherung.

Eine Änderung brachte im Jahre 1957 die *Rentenreform*[1]. Unter Fortfall der bisherigen Zuschüsse und Erstattungen ist die Leistung des Bundes in bestimmter Höhe festgelegt. In den folgenden Jahren wird sie sich nur entsprechend der Änderung der allgemeinen Bemessungsgrundlage für die Zugangsrenten verändern. In Zukunft wird die Alterssicherung allein aus Beiträgen finanziert, während der Bundeszuschuß für die Invaliditätssicherung verwendet wird. Der Bund trägt nach dem neuen Recht weder bestimmte Rentenanteile und bestimmte Erstattungen, noch ist er mit einem Prozentsatz an den Ausgaben der Rentenversicherung beteiligt. Bundeshaushalt und Gewährung von Leistungen der Träger der Rentenversicherung werden somit in Zukunft sich nicht mehr gegenseitig beeinflussen. Aus der Neuregelung hat sich für 1957 eine Mehrbelastung des Bundes von rund 1,2 Milliarden DM ergeben. Im Bundeshaushalt 1959 ist ein Zuschuß von insgesamt 5,21 Milliarden DM vorgesehen. Davon entfallen auf die Rentenversicherung der Arbeiter 3.067 Millionen DM, auf die Rentenversicherung der Angestellten 767 Millionen DM, auf die knappschaftliche Rentenversicherung 763 Millionen DM und auf sonstige Leistungen 900 Millionen DM.

Die Leistungen der Rentenversicherungen wurden durch die Rentenreform angehoben und werden auch künftig zunehmen, da die Alterslast größer wird. Für 1959 hat die Bundesregierung einer Anpassung der Altrenten mit 6,1% (ab 1.1.1959) zugestimmt. Durch die Reform wird sich aber die Finanzlage der sozialen Rentenversicherungen insofern grundlegend ändern, als die Mehrleistungen der Versicherungsträger voraussichtlich später eine Abnahme der Überschüsse zur Folge haben. Zwar stehen den erhöhten Ausgaben neben höheren Bundeszuschüssen auch höhere Einnahmen gegenüber, die sich aus der Anhebung der Versicherungsbeiträge und aus künftigen Lohnerhöhungen ergeben werden. Die bisher in jedem Jahre entstandenen Überschüsse werden sich insgesamt aber nicht mehr wesentlich erhöhen. Bis Ende 1958 betrugen sie bei der Rentenversicherung schätzungsweise 12,4 Milliarden DM und waren ein starker Faktor der Kapitalbildung.

[1] Rentenversicherungs-Neuregelungsgesetze vom 23.2.1957/21.5.1957, für die Unfallversicherung vom 27.7.1957.

Auch bei den übrigen Versicherungsträgern — Arbeitslosenversicherung, Krankenversicherung und andere — werden sich Änderungen ihrer Finanzlage ergeben. Die kürzlich in der Krankenversicherung eingeführte Lohnfortzahlung im Krankheitsfall hat bereits zu Mehrausgaben geführt, deren weitere Gestaltung noch nicht abzusehen ist.

Faßt man die *Sozialleistungen des Bundes* zusammen und stellt sie den Haushaltsausgaben im engeren Sinne (ohne durchlaufende Posten) gegenüber, so wird ersichtlich, eine wie große Hypothek auf dem Bundeshaushalt lastet. Der Anteil der Sozialleistungen hat in den Jahren 1950 bis 1959 durchschnittlich 37% der Haushaltsausgaben betragen.

Tabelle 17
SOZIALLEISTUNGEN DES BUNDES

Rechnungsjahr	Millionen DM	In % der Haushaltsausgaben im engeren Sinn
1950	5.055,8	*40,8*
1951	6.876,6	*36,5*
1952	7.641,0	*35,9*
1953	8.857,3	*37,8*
1954	8.777,9	*36,2*
1955	9.813,9	*42,6*
1956	10.904,8	*38,5*
1957	11.823,8	*36,5*
1958 (Soll)	11.694,4	*34,0*
1959 (Soll)	11.749,8	*31,2*

Quelle: Bundesministerium der Finanzen.

Die *öffentliche Soziallast*, das sind die Gesamtaufwendungen der öffentlichen Körperschaften, des Lastenausgleichfonds und der Rentenversicherungsträger für soziale Sicherung, hat im Jahre 1957 fast 30 Milliarden DM betragen und wird bis 1959 um weitere 2 Milliarden DM zugenommen haben. Vergleicht man diese Summen mit der Abgabenbelastung der deutschen Wirtschaft und der einzelnen Einkommenbezieher durch Steuern und Beiträge, so hat die Soziallast in den letzten Jahren rund 42% des Aufkommens an Steuern und Beiträgen erfordert. In Prozenten des Bruttosozialprodukts betrug der Anteil der Sozialleistungen rund 13%. Im Vergleich zur Vorkriegszeit (1938: 6%) hat er sich mehr als verdoppelt. Damit dürfte aber die obere Belastungsgrenze erreicht sein. Die weitere Entwicklung der öffentlichen Soziallasten wird daher bei sinkenden Zuwachsraten des Sozialprodukts einer ständigen Beobachtung bedürfen, damit von dieser Seite her die Wirtschaftsentwicklung nicht ungünstig beeinflußt wird. Soziallast und Volkseinkommen müssen in einem wirtschaftlich vertretbaren Verhältnis zueinander stehen, wenn nicht die Gesamtleistung der Wirtschaft gehemmt werden soll. Im internationalen Sozialvergleich gehört die Bundesrepublik zu den am stärksten belasteten Ländern.

Die *Finanzhilfe* (Bundeshilfe) *Berlin* wurde bereits in einem anderen Zusammenhang erwähnt. Finanzwirtschaftlich fällt sie nicht sehr stark ins Gewicht. Ihr Anteil beträgt 1959 nur 2,8% der Haushaltsausgaben. Ihre politische Bedeutung ist wesentlich größer, da sie einen unschätzbaren Beitrag zur Stärkung der Stellung Berlins als eines Außenpostens der Bundesrepublik darstellt.

Der Lastenausgleich

Ein Sonderproblem war der Ausgleich der Kriegsverluste der Vertriebenen und Kriegssachgeschädigten, der sogenannte *Lastenausgleich*. Dieses Problem wurde nach der Währungsreform sofort in Angriff genommen. Seine Lösung gestaltete sich aber sehr schwierig. Möglicherweise wäre der Ausgleich leichter und auch schneller verwirklicht worden, wenn man ihn in Verbindung mit der Währungsreform durchgeführt hätte. Zunächst wurde für die sozial am härtesten Betroffenen im *Soforthilfegesetz* vom 18.8.1949 eine vorläufige Regelung getroffen, um durch Gewährung besonderer Leistungen — Unterhaltshilfe, Hausratshilfe — und Förderungsdarlehen für den Wohnungsbau die dringlichsten sozialen Notstände zu mildern und die Eingliederung der Vertriebenen in den Wirtschaftsprozeß zu erleichtern. Um diese Aufgaben zu erfüllen, wurden dem Soforthilfefonds besondere Abgaben (allgemeine Soforthilfeabgabe, Soforthilfe-Sonderabgabe, Umstellungsgrundschulden) überlassen. Bis zur endgültigen gesetzlichen Regelung des Lastenausgleichs durch das Gesetz vom 14.8.1952 konnten auf diese Weise die schwersten sozialen Schäden behoben werden. Von 1949 bis 1952 (31.8.) wurden durch die Soforthilfe bereits 6,2 Milliarden DM verteilt.

Durch das *Lastenausgleichsgesetz*, das am 1.9.1952 in Kraft trat, erhielt der Lastenausgleich seine endgültige Grundlage. Sie wurde in der Folgezeit nach den Erfahrungen der Praxis weiter verbessert. Die Entwicklung ist nunmehr durch das Achte Änderungsgesetz vom 26.7.1957 vorläufig abgeschlossen. Die bisherige Eingliederungsphase wird durch die beginnende Auszahlung der Hauptentschädigung abgelöst, die bis 1975 beendet sein soll.

Der Lastenausgleichfonds wird als Sondervermögen des Bundes verwaltet. An sich hätte es nahegelegen, seine Leistungen über den Bundeshaushalt zu erfüllen. Die Einnahmen und Ausgaben des Fonds' sind aber nicht Bestandteil des Bundeshaushalts, sondern sie werden nach einem besonderen Wirtschaftsplan bewirtschaftet. Die für Zwecke des Lastenausgleichs gebundenen Abgaben berühren den Haushalt nur durchlaufend.

Tabelle 18

DIE EINNAHMEN UND AUSGABEN DES LASTENAUSGLEICHFONDS' (SOFORTHILFEFONDS')

1948 BIS 1958

Millionen DM

Art der Einnahmen bzw. Ausgaben	Soforthilfe (20.6.48 bis 31.8.51)	Lastenausgleich[1] Rechnungsjahr						
		1952[2]	1953	1954	1955	1956	1957	1958
A. Einnahmen[3]								
Abgaben	6.272	1.210	2.038	2.254	2.754	2.186	2.036	2.215
Zuschüsse von Bund und Ländern.........	—	187	733	782	1.021	1.148	1.268	1.108
Einnahmen aus der Vorfinanzierung	193	—	657	127	550	10	—	495
Sonstige Einnahmen ..	298	69	131	182	220	284	351	415
Einnahmen insgesamt:	6.763	1.466	3.558	3.345	4.545	3.628	3.655	4.233
B. Ausgaben								
Renten, Entschädigungen, Beihilfen[4]								
Hauptentschädigung ..	—	—	—	—	—	1	110	288
Kriegsschadenrente ...	2.153	387	680	823	857	940	963	1.089
Hausratentschädigung .	556	234	924	1.034	1.026	820	1.146	1.206
Ausbildungshilfe	103	53	89	99	96	101	82	76
Sparerentschädigung .	—	—	448	468	178	180	160	243
Sonstige Beihilfen ...	78	—	25	—	—	—	—	—
Darlehen und Zuschüsse für Investitionszwecke[4]								
Wohnraumhilfe[5]	2.369	580	618	566	491	446	337	223
Flüchtlingssiedlung[6] ..	210	53	72	69	125	98	114	24
Aufbaudarlehen	410	45	446	1.050	996	932	783	777[a]
Arbeitsplatzdarlehen ..	66	56	61	57	31	8	—	—
Heimförderung	71	19	15	15	12	8	7	7
Übrige Ausgaben[7]	198	4	24	41	93	213	204	152
Ausgaben insgesamt: .	6.214	1.431	3.404	4.221	3.906	3.746	3.906	4.085
C. Abschluß								
Mehreinnahmen (+), Mehrausgaben (—) ...	+549	+35	+154	—876	+639	—118	—251	—148
Bestand am Ende des Rechnungsjahres[8]	549	673	885	—125	520	433	132	250

[1] Einschließlich von Berlin (West). — [2] Rumpfrechnungsjahr (1.9.1952 bis 31.3.1953). — [3] Nur Bareinnahmen. — [4] Einschließlich der entsprechenden Posten des Härtefonds'. — [5] Einschließlich des Wohnungsbaus aus Umstellungsgrundschulden; Förderung des Wohnungsbaus für Umsiedler. — [6] Einschließlich der Darlehen nach § 46 Absatz 2 des Bundes-Vertriebenengesetzes (BFVG). — [7] Verwaltung, Kosten der Vorfinanzierung, Kursstützung und andere. — [8] Einschließlich der Forderungen am Ende des Rechnungsjahres. — [a] Einschließlich der Liquiditätskredite für die gewerbliche Wirtschaft.

Quelle: Bundesausgleichsamt.

Diese haushaltsrechtliche Konstruktion hat dem Ausgleichfonds eine größere Beweglichkeit und Anpassungsmöglichkeit an die besonderen Verhältnisse seiner Aufgaben gegeben. An eigenen Einnahmen fließen ihm die Ausgleichsabgaben — Vermögensabgabe, Hypotheken- und Kreditgewinnabgabe — zu. Darüber hinaus leisten Bund und Länder aus ihren Haushalten für die Durchführung der Aufgaben sowie zum Ausgleich für ersparte Fürsorgekosten Zuschüsse.

Im Lastenausgleichsgesetz sind die früher vom Soforthilfefonds erbrachten Leistungen wesentlich stärker ausgebaut worden. Die Hausrathilfe konnte bereits weitgehend abgewickelt werden. Durch verschiedene Sondergesetze wurde dem Lastenausgleichfonds auch die Durchführung des Währungsausgleichs und der Altsparer-Entschädigung übertragen. Besonders die Eingliederung der Vertriebenen ist durch Darlehen und Zuschüsse gefördert worden. Neben der Wohnraumhilfe, die durch Darlehensgewährung an die Länder durchgeführt wurde, hatten in den Jahren 1954 bis 1956 die Aufbaudarlehen einen beträchtlichen Anteil an den Gesamtausgaben. Die Leistungen des Lastenausgleichs in diesen Jahren waren erheblich. Wenn auch nur ein Teil der erlittenen Schäden wieder ausgeglichen werden konnte, sind die Zahlungen doch für den Einzelnen eine wesentliche Beihilfe gewesen, die ihm die Eingliederung in Beruf und Wirtschaft erleichterte. Ihre Bedeutung erhellt aus der Tatsache, daß etwa 60% der Leistungen an die Vertriebenen und Flüchtlinge geflossen sind. Die durchschnittlichen

Tabelle 19

LEISTUNGEN AUS DEM LASTENAUSGLEICHFONDS (SOFORTHILFEFONDS)

Stand: 31.12.1958	Millionen DM	%
Förderung des Wohnungsbaues	8.490	*28,4*
Renten	7.935	*26,5*
Hausratentschädigung	6.630	*22,1*
Gewerbliche Wirtschaft	1.645	*5,5*
Währungsausgleich und Altsparer-Entschädigung	1.666	*5,6*
Landwirtschaft	1.483	*4,9*
Sonstige Förderungsmaßnahmen	1.215	*4,1*
Übrige Ausgaben	878	*2,9*
Insgesamt	29.942	*100*

Quelle: Bundesministerium der Finanzen.

Jahresleistungen des Lastenausgleichs, die ursprünglich mit 2,5 Milliarden DM angenommen waren, konnten in den letzten Jahren erhöht werden und erreichten im Durchschnitt rund 4 Milliarden DM. Bis zum 31.12.1958 sind vom Lastenausgleichfonds insgesamt rund 24 Milliarden DM verteilt worden. Einschließlich der vom Soforthilfefonds verausgabten Summen ergibt sich bereits eine Gesamtleistung von rund 30 Milliarden DM.

Das Aufkommen an Lastenausgleichsabgaben und Abgaben des Soforthilfefonds' hat von 1952 bis 1958 rund 20 Milliarden DM (einschließlich 401 Millionen DM restlicher Umstellungs-Grundschulden) betragen. Diese Mittel reichten allerdings nicht aus, um alle Leistungen zu erfüllen. Bund und Länder haben daher ergänzend aus eigenen Mitteln Zuschüsse geleistet. Sie werden sich künftig weiter erhöhen, da nach dem Achten Änderungsgesetz erheblich höhere Leistungen vom Lastenausgleich zu erbringen sind. Bisher erreichten die Zuschüsse von Bund und Ländern insgesamt 6,1 Milliarden DM. Ferner sind vom Lastenausgleich zur Vorfinanzierung seiner Aufgaben in einzelnen Jahren Anleihen aufgenommen worden.

Wiedergutmachung und Bereinigung der Kriegsfolgen

Ein weiterer Schwerpunkt des Bundeshaushalts und auch der Haushalte der Länder sind die *Wiedergutmachungs- und Entschädigungsleistungen.* Sie haben sich aus den Kriegsfolgen ergeben und werden auch künftig schwierige Finanzierungsprobleme auslösen, da sie sich in ihrer vollen Höhe noch nicht übersehen lassen.

Vor der Regelung durch Bundesgesetz im Jahre 1953 waren bereits von einzelnen Ländern nach landesrechtlichen Vorschriften Entschädigungen an die Opfer der nationalsozialistischen Verfolgung geleistet worden. Ihr Gewicht im Rahmen der Finanzwirtschaft war in den ersten Jahren nur unbedeutend[1]. Die bundeseinheitliche Regelung der Wiedergutmachung fand 1953 im „Bundesergänzungsgesetz" ihren ersten Niederschlag. Dieses Gesetz wurde 1956 in seinen entschädigungsrechtlichen Ausmaßen erheblich erweitert und als „*Bundesentschädigungsgesetz*" (BEG) neu gefaßt. Die Gesamthöhe der künftigen Wiedergutmachungsleistungen — sogenannte individuelle Wiedergutmachung — wird nach vorsichtigen Schätzungen mit rund 17 Milliarden DM angenommen. Die Leistungen sollen bis zum Ende des Rechnungsjahres 1962 (31.3.1963) erfüllt sein. Der kurze Zeitraum,

[1] 1949: 141,5 Millionen DM, 1950: 147,4 Millionen DM, 1951: 124,5 Millionen DM, 1952: 355,7 Millionen DM.

der für die Erfüllung zur Verfügung steht, zeigt, daß für die kommenden Haushaltsjahre größere Belastungen zu erwarten sind, wenn das Schlußdatum eingehalten wird. Bereits 1956 sind im Vergleich zu früheren Rechnungsjahren die Leistungen wesentlich erhöht worden. Der Bundeshaushalt verausgabte 1956: 565 Millionen DM, 1957: 893 Millionen DM und 1958: 808 Millionen DM. Für 1959 sind 1.300 Millionen DM veranschlagt. Einschließlich der von den Ländern aufzubringenden Mittel[1] haben die Leistungen im Rechnungsjahr 1957 insgesamt 1.677 Millionen DM betragen. Ein erheblicher Teil der Leistungen — man schätzt ihn auf etwa 60% — geht an Entschädigungsberechtigte im Ausland.

Zu den Ersatzleistungen an das Ausland gehört auch die *Wiedergutmachung an Israel*, die bereits im September 1952 in einem besonderen Abkommen geregelt wurde. Es sieht eine Gesamtleistung von 3,5 Milliarden DM vor und wird bis zum Jahre 1965 erfüllt sein. Bis einschließlich 1958 sind vom Bundeshaushalt rund 1,6 Milliarden DM durch Warenlieferungen und Zahlungen aufgewandt worden.

Tabelle 20

WIEDERGUTMACHUNG UND ENTSCHÄDIGUNGEN

Millionen DM

Rechnungsjahr	Wiedergutmachung nach dem BEG[1]	Sonstige Ersatzleistungen und Entschädigungen[2]
1952	—	90,2
1953	—	257,1
1954	24,2	365,1
1955	131,4	356,6
1956	564,9	397,2
1957	892,6	384,2
1958	808,0	381,7
1959	1.300,0	653,5

[1] Bundesanteil. — [2] Unter anderen Wiedergutmachung an Israel, Leistungen nach dem Kriegsgefangenengesetz, Rückerstattung feststellbarer Vermögenswerte.

Quelle: Bundesministerium der Finanzen.

Weitere Verpflichtungen gegenüber dem Ausland sind in einer Reihe von *Sonderabkommen*, zum Teil im Zusammenhang mit dem Londoner Schuldenabkommen, mit der Schweiz, den Niederlanden, Österreich, Portugal, Belgien, Dänemark, Jugoslawien und Irland geregelt worden[2].

Ursprünglich war beabsichtigt, die gesamten, bisher noch nicht in Einzelgesetzen (zum Beispiel Wiedergutmachung, Lastenausgleich) und Verträgen

[1] Vergleiche Seite 431. — [2] Schweizer Clearing-Milliarde, Abgeltung niederländischer Ansprüche auf Restitution von Aktien, Dänische Flüchtlingshilfe, Rückerstattungen von Vermögenswerten, äußere Restitution und andere.

geregelten Kriegsfolgen und Kriegsschäden in einem Schlußgesetz abschließend zu bereinigen. Damit sollte zugleich die Liquidation des Krieges beendet werden, um für die künftige Finanzplanung und Steuerpolitik übersehbare Verhältnisse zu schaffen. Es setzte sich aber schließlich die Erkenntnis durch, daß dies noch nicht möglich sei und einzelne Entschädigungsprobleme, wie zum Beispiel die Frage der Reparations- und Demontageschäden und die Regelung der Schäden loyaler Rückerstattungs- und Regreßpflichtiger, erst später gelöst werden könnten.

Eine Regelung der Ansprüche gegen das Deutsche Reich und seine Sondervermögen (Reichsbahn und Reichspost), gegen das ehemalige Land Preußen und das Unternehmen „Reichsautobahn" ist nunmehr aber durch das *Allgemeine Kriegsfolgengesetz* erfolgt, das vom Bundestag am 29.8.1957 verabschiedet wurde und am 1.1.1958 in Kraft getreten ist. Infolge der Höhe der Verbindlichkeiten — der Betrag der verbrieften Forderungen wird mit 392 Milliarden RM und der nichtverbrieften Forderungen mit 200 bis 400 Milliarden RM geschätzt — stand von vornherein fest, daß ihre volle Entschädigung oder eine Entschädigung im Verhältnis 10 : 1 finanziell nicht tragbar war, da sie die Leistungsfähigkeit der Bundesrepublik bei weitem überstiegen hätte. Daher mußte unter den Ansprüchen eine Auswahl getroffen werden. Die Masse der Ansprüche ist unter Vorbehalt späterer Einzelregelungen und Erhöhung der Leistungen, die jetzt vorgesehen sind, nunmehr grundsätzlich erloschen. Das Gesetz berücksichtigt nur die verbrieften Schuldforderungen, die den Charakter einer Kapitalanlage tragen. Diese werden rückwirkend vom 1.4.1955 im Verhältnis 10 : 1 durch Ausgabe von Ablösungs-Schuldverschreibungen oder Schuldbucheintragungen umgestellt, mit 4% verzinst und ab 1960 durch Auslosung mit 2% getilgt; Kleinbeträge werden teilweise sogleich bar ausgezahlt. Neben diesen Ablösungsansprüchen werden folgende Ansprüche „erfüllt": Ansprüche persönlicher Art wie Renten- und Versorgungsansprüche, die zur Aufrechterhaltung der Existenz notwendig sind, Verwaltungsschulden wie dingliche Ansprüche, Schadenersatzansprüche, Nachkriegsansprüche aus der Zeit nach dem 31.7.1945, Verträge aus Grundstücksübereignungen. Es liegt auf der Hand, daß diese Regelung gewisse, aber unvermeidbare soziale Härten zur Folge hat. Um diese zu beseitigen und auch Härten auszugleichen, die dadurch entstehen, daß einzelne Entschädigungsansprüche erst später endgültig geregelt werden, sind besondere Härtebeihilfen an natürliche Personen vorgesehen. Diese entsprechen den Leistungen des Lastenausgleichfonds' (Unterhaltsbeihilfen, Ausbildungsbeihilfen, Hausrathilfe und

Aufbaudarlehen). Ferner sind als Übergangshilfen für die Reparations- und Demontagegeschädigten wirtschaftsfördernde Maßnahmen in Form von Darlehen für volkswirtschaftlich wichtige Wiederaufbau- und Ausbauvorhaben vorgesehen. Für Leistungen nach dem Kriegsfolgengesetz sind im Bundeshaushalt 1959: 231 Millionen DM veranschlagt, davon 111 Millionen DM für Verzinsung der Ablösungsschuld, 70 Millionen DM für die zu erfüllenden Ansprüche und 50 Millionen DM für wirtschaftsfördernde Darlehen.

Wohnungsbau und wirtschaftsfördernde Maßnahmen

Neben den direkten Maßnahmen zur Behebung der sozialen Notstände hatten die allgemeinen wirtschaftlichen Förderungsmaßnahmen des Bundes die Aufgabe, den fortschreitenden Gesundungsprozeß zu unterstützen. Insbesondere war die Beseitigung der nach Kriegsende herrschenden Wohnungsnot, die durch den ständigen Flüchtlingsstrom verschärft wurde, eine der dringlichsten Aufgaben und mit eine der Voraussetzungen für die Stabilisierung der Verhältnisse. Sie war zugleich aber auch ein Sozialproblem erster Ordnung, das nur durch besondere steuerpolitische Maßnahmen und durch Bereitstellen größerer Finanzierungsmittel von seiten der öffentlichen Haushalte gelöst werden konnte. Der Kapitalmarkt war in diesen Jahren noch nicht in der Lage, die Finanzierung dieser Aufgaben allein durchzuführen. Die Bundesregierung leitete deshalb schon bald nach der Währungsreform ein umfassendes *Wohnungsprogramm* in die Wege. Der anfängliche Fehlbedarf an Wohnungen konnte dadurch erheblich gemindert werden. Beseitigt wurde er noch nicht; denn er betrug Ende 1955 noch über drei Millionen Wohnungen. Somit mußte auch in den folgenden Jahren diese Aufgabe als vordringlich in den Haushaltsplanungen berücksichtigt werden. Das Zweite Wohnungsbaugesetz vom 27.6.1956 bildet die Grundlage für die weitere Durchführung der Wohnungsbauförderung (unter anderem auch durch stärkere Förderung von Familienheimen) und ihre erweiterte Finanzierung durch öffentliche Mittel (Zins- und Tilgungsbeihilfen, Vor- und Zwischenfinanzierungen, Mietbeihilfen usw.). Das Endziel der Bundesregierung ist aber die freie Wohnungswirtschaft. Sie wird deshalb bestrebt sein, die öffentlichen Maßnahmen Schritt für Schritt abzubauen und neue Wege der Finanzierung zu finden, um den Wohnungsbau dann wieder in die Marktwirtschaft zu überführen.

Vom Bundeshaushalt sind von 1950 bis Ende 1958 insgesamt für Wohnungsbau und Siedlung rund 8 Milliarden DM verausgabt worden. Für 1959 sind weitere 1,8 Milliarden DM veranschlagt. Daneben wurden, wie bereits erwähnt, auch vom Lastenausgleich, von den Ländern und von den Gemeinden erhebliche Förderungsdarlehen gegeben. Alle diese Mittel sind meist über die Länderhaushalte ihrer Bestimmung zugeführt worden. Die Summe der von den öffentlichen Haushalten für die Finanzierung des Wohnungsbaues bereitgestellten Mittel hat bis Ende 1957 mehr als 21 Milliarden DM erreicht. Der Gesamtaufwand für den Wohnungsbau einschließlich der Kapitalmarktmittel und sonstigen Mittel, unter anderem der Eigenmittel der Bauherren, betrug 54 Milliarden DM. Die öffentlichen Mittel deckten somit im Durchschnitt der Jahre mehr als ein Drittel des Aufwandes. In den ersten Jahren war ihr Anteil höher (1950: 44%). Später ist er zurückgegangen (1956: 27%), da Kapitalmarktmittel in größerem Umfange verfügbar waren.

*

Vielseitig waren auch die übrigen *wirtschaftsfördernden Maßnahmen* des Bundes. Ihr finanzielles Gewicht hat besonders seit 1955 zugenommen und ihre Struktur sich wesentlich geändert. Während der Bund in den ersten Jahren sich vornehmlich auf *Subventionen* beschränkte (zum Beispiel die Subventionen zur Verbilligung von Konsumbrot in den Jahren 1950 bis 1952), sind später auch Förderungsdarlehen gegeben worden, die aus volkswirtschaftlichen Gründen notwendig erschienen (zum Beispiel Darlehen für den Wiederaufbau der Handelsflotte und zum Ausbau der Häfen).

Im Jahre 1950 wurden ferner umfangreiche *Sanierungsprogramme* für die von der Not besonders betroffenen Gebiete eingeleitet. Sie zielten darauf ab, diesen Gebieten durch strukturverbessernde Maßnahmen — Straßenbauten zur Verkehrserschließung, für gewerbliche Investitionen, Frachthilfen, Ausbau der Energieversorgung — und steuerliche Erleichterungen zu helfen. Insbesondere die Zonenrandgebiete, die durch die Grenzziehung besonders stark betroffen sind, wurden in diesen Programmen, die 1955 zu einem einheitlichen Förderungsprogramm zusammengefaßt wurden, berücksichtigt. Der Sanierungsfonds des Bundes diente der Spitzenfinanzierung dieser Aufgaben. Der Hauptteil der Finanzierungsmittel stammte aus anderen öffentlichen und privaten Quellen (unter anderem Mittel der Länderhaushalte und der Bundesanstalt für Arbeitsvermittlung und Arbeitslosenversicherung).

Das Landwirtschaftsgesetz vom 5.9.1955 soll die natürlichen und wirtschaftlichen Wettbewerbsnachteile der Landwirtschaft ausgleichen, die

Produktivität steigern und die sozialen Verhältnisse bessern. Auf Grund des „Grünen Berichts", der nach diesem Gesetz zu erstatten ist, werden vom Bundeshaushalt seit 1955 zur *Förderung der Landwirtschaft* erhebliche Mittel für Subventionen (unter anderem Verbilligung von Handelsdünger, Saatgut, Zuschüsse zum Auszahlungspreis der Milch), für Zinsverbilligung und andere strukturelle Maßnahmen (unter anderem Wasserversorgung, Flurbereinigung, Ausbau der Wirtschaftswege) bereitgestellt. Im Rechnungsjahr 1956 sind zur Durchführung des „*Grünen Planes*" insgesamt 616 Millionen DM bewilligt und 430 Millionen DM verausgabt worden. Diese Mittel sind von den Ländern aus eigenen Haushaltsmitteln ihrem Kräfteverhältnis entsprechend und auch aus ERP-Mitteln verstärkt worden. In den Rechnungsjahren 1957 und 1958 sind die Bundesmittel nochmals erhöht worden; verausgabt wurden 1.134 beziehungsweise 1.121 Millionen DM. Einschließlich der bereits früher aus dem Agrarhaushalt des Bundes gegebenen Zuschüsse und Darlehen hat die Förderung der Landwirtschaft damit eine Höhe erreicht, die eine erhebliche Dauerbelastung des Bundeshaushalts darstellt.

*

Auch die *Bundesbahn* mußte in den letzten Rechnungsjahren aus Bundesmitteln gestützt werden; denn sie war bisher nicht in der Lage, ihre Betriebsrechnung auszugleichen und die notwendige Erneuerung der Anlagen auszuführen. Seit der Währungsreform haben sich bei der Bundesbahn erhebliche Fehlbeträge ergeben. Zum Teil waren diese Fehlbeträge auch durch die betriebsfremden Lasten, unter anderem durch Zahlung der Versorgung für verdrängte Beamte der früheren Reichsbahn, mitentstanden. Diese Lasten sind seit 1957 zum Teil vom Bundeshaushalt übernommen worden. Insgesamt sind die für die Bundesbahn aus Bundesmitteln getragenen Ausgaben (Liquidationshilfen, Betriebsmittel und Investitions-Darlehen, Ankauf von Schatzanweisungen) von 1952 bis 1958 auf rund 4 Milliarden DM angewachsen; ohne Berücksichtigung der Steuerstundungen, die zur Erhaltung der Zahlungsfähigkeit der Bundesbahn gewährt worden sind. Die Fehlbeträge der Bundesbahn sind gegen die in den letzten Jahren entstandenen Forderungen des Bundes aufgerechnet worden. Im Rechnungsjahr 1959 sind im Bundeshaushalt Mittel in Höhe von 865 Millionen DM für die Bundesbahn vorgesehen, darunter 145 Millionen DM zur Finanzierung von Anlagen (nach dem Verkehrsfinanzgesetz), 134 Millionen DM für Liquiditätshilfe, 260 Millionen DM für Investitionsdarlehen. Für den Teilausgleich von betriebsfremden Lasten sind 291 Millionen DM eingeplant. Die am

1.2.1958 vorgenommene Erhöhung der Tarife hat infolge des Verkehrsrückgangs die Erwartungen nicht erfüllt.

Neben diesen, ihrer Höhe nach finanzwirtschaftlich bedeutsamen Förderungsmaßnahmen sind auch *andere* einmalige oder laufende *Maßnahmen* mit Bundesmitteln finanziert worden, wenn die Lage es erforderte und Notstände eintraten, deren Beseitigung von allgemein volkswirtschaftlichem Interesse war. Zu erwähnen sind die Darlehen und Zuschüsse an Schleswig-Holstein und Niedersachsen zur Steigerung ihrer Wirtschaftskraft, für den Aufbau Helgolands, Hilfsmaßnahmen zum Ausgleich von Ernte- und Hochwasserschäden und Aufwendungen für die Luftfahrt.

Europäische Gemeinschaft und internationale Organisationen

In diesem Zusammenhang müssen auch die *Beiträge für die europäischen wirtschaftlichen Zusammenschlüsse* hervorgehoben werden, durch welche die Bundesrepublik an der europäischen Integration beteiligt ist. Im Haushaltsplan 1959 sind folgende Beiträge vorgesehen:

Europäische Wirtschaftskommission (ECE)	0,59	Millionen	DM
Organisation für europäische wirtschaftliche Zusammenarbeit (OEEC) mit: Europäischer Zahlungsunion (EZU) [seit Dezember 1958: Europäischem Währungs-Abkommen (EWA)], Europäischer Produktivitätszentrale (EPZ), Europäischer Kernenergie-Agentur, Europäischer Gesellschaft für die Aufbereitung bestrahlter Kernbrennstoffe (EUROCHEMIC)	4,85	,,	,,
Europarat	2,55	,,	,,
Europäische Wirtschaftsgemeinschaft (EWG)	289,84	,,	,,
Europäische Atomgemeinschaft (EAG)	58,26	,,	,,

Die *finanziellen Leistungen der Bundesrepublik an das Ausland* und Förderungshilfen an Entwicklungsländer haben in den letzten Jahren erheblich an Bedeutung gewonnen. Sie werden vielfach unterschätzt, weil die Mittel zum Teil über die verschiedenen internationalen und oben genannten europäischen Organisationen geleitet werden, zum Teil auch als künftige Leistungen, wie zum Beispiel Übernahme von Bürgschaften bei Kapitalanlagen deutscher Unternehmen im Ausland, zunächst nicht sichtbar sind.

Nach dem Stand vom 31.7.1958 haben die effektiven Leistungen an das Ausland (ohne Vorauszahlungen für Rüstungskäufe) mehr als 15 Milliarden DM betragen. Davon waren 9,3 Milliarden DM Haushaltsmittel (einschließlich der ERP-Mittel) und 6,4 Milliarden DM Kredite der Bundesbank.

Von diesen Beträgen entfielen auf

Haushaltsmittel

Internationale Organisationen (Weltbank, Welt-Währungsfonds, Finance Corporation, Europäische Investitionsbank, EZU usw.)	1.220 Millionen DM
Wirtschafts- und Entwicklungshilfe (Umschuldungsmaßnahmen, Exportfinanzierung usw.)	774 „ „
Wiedergutmachung (Israel, BEG)	5.444 „ „
Londoner Schuldenabkommen	1.686 „ „
Sonstiges (Jugoslawien und andere)	133 „ „

Deutsche Bundesbank

Kredite an Weltbank	1.324 Millionen DM
Kredite an EZU	4.045 „ „
Konsolidierungskredite	278 „ „
Devisenkonto bei der Bank von England	794 „ „

Daneben hat der Bund 7.550 Millionen DM Bürgschaften im Ausfuhrgeschäft übernommen. 85 bis 90% davon entfallen auf Entwicklungsländer.

Schulden der öffentlichen Verwaltung

Die Bundesregierung war bestrebt, ihren Zahlungsverpflichtungen aus der Vergangenheit auch dem Ausland gegenüber wieder nachzukommen und den Komplex der deutschen Auslandsschulden zu bereinigen. Die abschließende Regelung dieser Fragen erfolgte durch das *Londoner Schuldenabkommen*. Es wurde nach der Londoner Konferenz am 27.3.1953 unterzeichnet und trat am 16.9.1953 in Kraft. Durch dieses Abkommen wurden die Vorkriegsverbindlichkeiten der öffentlichen und privaten Hand sowie die Verbindlichkeiten aus der wirtschaftlichen Nachkriegshilfe der Besatzungsmächte endgültig auf rund 14 Milliarden DM festgesetzt. Von den Verbindlichkeiten entfallen auf den Bund rund 10 Milliarden DM. Nach dem Abkommen waren bis 1958 entweder nur Zinsen oder nur Tilgungsbeträge auf die einzelnen Schuldenkategorien zu zahlen; erst ab 1958 hat die kombinierte Zahlung von Zinsen und Tilgungen eingesetzt. Bis Ende 1958 betrugen die Gesamtleistungen (Zinsen und Tilgungen, Nebenkosten) auf die nach dem Londoner Abkommen geregelten Vor- und Nachkriegsschulden 4,6 Milliarden DM. Davon entfallen auf die öffentlichen Verpflichtungen 3,3 und auf private Verpflichtungen 1,4 Milliarden DM.

Tabelle 21

ZINSEN UND TILGUNGEN AUF AUSLANDSSCHULDEN[1]
Millionen DM
1953 bis 1958

	Zinsen[2]	Tilgungen	Nebenkosten	Gesamtleistungen
Öffentliche Vorkriegsverpflichtungen........	660	671	28	1.359
Private Vorkriegsverpflichtungen........	246	1.096	17	1.359
Öffentliche Nachkriegsverpflichtungen........	667	1.232	—	1.899
Zusammen:	1.573	2.999	45	4.617

[1] Durch das Londoner Abkommen geregelte Schulden. — [2] Einschließlich der Zinsen auf den inländischen Besitz an Auslandsanleihen.

Quelle: Deutsche Bundesbank.

Die *Gesamtverschuldung der öffentlichen Verwaltung* betrug am 31.3.1958 rund 47 Milliarden DM. Davon entfallen auf Inlandsschulden 37,5 und auf Auslandsschulden 9,5 Milliarden DM. Von der Inlandsverschuldung waren jedoch nur 14,8 Milliarden DM Neuschulden aus Kreditmarktmitteln und aus öffentlichen Sondermitteln. Der größere Teil mit 22,7 Milliarden DM waren Altschulden, insbesondere Ausgleichsforderungen aus der Währungsumstellung.

Die inländische *Neuverschuldung des Bundes* war mit 1,7 Milliarden DM am 31.3.1958 gering. Der Bund hat auf die Aufnahme neuer Anleihen in den letzten Jahren verzichtet; denn die Unterbringung der in den Haushaltsplänen veranschlagten Anleihen war am Kapitalmarkt nicht möglich und auch infolge verzögerter Verteidigungsausgaben nicht nötig. Durch diesen Verzicht konnte der Kapitalmarkt sich entwickeln und auf die künftigen Aufgaben vorbereiten. Größere Anleihen hat der Bund bisher nur in den Jahren 1952 und 1953 aufgenommen; sie sind aber bis Ende 1957 getilgt worden. Die Verschuldung aus öffentlichen Sondermitteln — Schuldbuchforderungen der Rentenversicherungsträger und der Bundesanstalt für Arbeitsvermittlung und Arbeitslosenversicherung (BAfAVuAV) — entstand 1953 und 1954, um teilweise die Renten der Kriegsopferversorgung und die Arbeitslosenhilfe zu decken.

Tabelle 22

DEUTSCHE AUSLANDSSCHULDEN NACH DEM LONDONER ABKOMMEN VON 1953
Stand: 31. 12. 1958 / Nominalbeträge in Millionen DM

	Insgesamt ausstehende Verpflichtungen	Geschätzte Auslandsverschuldung nach Absetzung der im Inland befindlichen Bonds
I. Öffentliche Vorkriegsverpflichtungen		
a) des Bundes		
Young	1.206	534
Dawes	406	165
Sonstige [1]	1.305	1.167
Zusammen	2.917	1.866
b) der Länder und Gemeinden	269	180
II. Private Vorkriegsverpflichtungen		
Anleihen	792	656
Sonstige	324	324
Zusammen	1.116	980
III. Öffentliche Nachkriegsverpflichtungen (Nachkriegswirtschaftshilfe) davon:		
Vereinigtes Königreich	1.235	1.235
Frankreich	35	35
Dänemark	—	—
USA		
Allgemeine Wirtschaftshilfe	4.153	4.153
STEG-Abkommen	281	281
Zusammen	5.704	5.704
Auslandsschulden insgesamt	10.006	8.730

[1] Kreuger-Anleihe, Preußen-Anleihe, Koka-Schuldverschreibungen, Mixed-Claims, Verpflichtungen gegenüber der BIZ, deutsch-schweizerisches Abkommen (Clearing-Milliarde) und andere.

Quelle: Deutsche Bundesbank.

Auch die *Neuverschuldung der Länder auf dem Kreditmarkt* ist relativ klein geblieben. Ihre innere Neuverschuldung im öffentlichen Bereich, das heißt die Verschuldung der Länder gegenüber dem Bund und dem Lastenausgleichfonds, die seit 1950 von Jahr zu Jahr angewachsen ist, entstand vorwiegend aus den über die Länderhaushalte geleiteten Krediten für den Wohnungsbau. Ein erheblicher Teil der Gesamtverschuldung der Länder sind Altschulden aus Ausgleichsforderungen. Von ihnen sind nunmehr die Ausgleichsforderungen der Landeszentralbanken in Höhe von 2,6 Milliarden DM nach Errichtung der Deutschen Bundesbank auf den Bund übergegangen. Die Gemeinden haben dagegen nur geringe Altschulden und Auslandsschulden. Ihre Neuverschuldung aus Mitteln des Kreditmarktes hat sich seit 1953 jedoch verdreifacht. Damit ist nur die reguläre öffentliche Verschuldung ihrer Höhe nach gekennzeichnet. Es darf nicht übersehen werden, daß auch die oben schon erwähnten schuldähnlichen Verpflichtungen aus der Wiedergutmachung, der Kriegsfolgen-Schlußgesetzgebung und aus dem Lastenausgleich laufende Belastungen darstellen. Sie sind ihrer Größenordnung nach höher als die reguläre Verschuldung der öffentlichen Verwaltung aus der Vor- und Nachkriegszeit.

Tabelle 23

SCHULDENDIENST DES BUNDES

Millionen DM

Rechnungs-jahr	Insgesamt	Darunter:			
		Verzinsung	Tilgung	Rückkauf von Schuld-urkunden	Inanspruch-nahme aus Sicherheits-leistungen *
1950	148,9	150,7	—	—	— 1,8
1951	254,6	212,2	48,1	—	— 5,7
1952	257,0	212,7	48,1	—	— 3,7
1953	876,4	353,9	329,4	195,7[1]	— 2,6
1954	939,3	438,9	191,2	257,4[2]	— 3,1
1955	642,2	368,2	207,7	23,2	—11,6
1956	1.078,7	385,5	295,3	218,0[3]	125,2
1957	1.188,3	463,1	559,0	5,9	105,7
1958	1.141,2	717,3[4]	214,7[5]	1,9	126,2
1959 (Soll)	2.240,2	771,7[4]	1.187,6[5]	20,9	220,0

[1] Darunter: 185 Millionen DM Schuldbuchforderungen der Versicherungsträger. — [2] Darunter: 255 Millionen DM Bundesanleihe 1953 aus dem ERP-Vermögen. — [3] Darunter: 120 Millionen DM Auslandsschuldtitel. — [4] Darunter 1958: 67,9; 1959: 93,0 Millionen DM Verzinsung der Ablösungsschuld gemäß dem Kriegsfolgengesetz. — [5] Darunter 1958: 7,7; 1959: 18,0 Millionen DM Tilgung der Ablösungsschuld gemäß dem Kriegsfolgengesetz. — * Rückeinnahmen. Quelle: Bundesministerium der Finanzen.

Tabelle 24 SCHULDENSTAND DER ÖFFENTLICHEN VERWALTUNG

Millionen DM [1]

	Inlandschulden						
	Altschulden aus Kreditmarktmitteln [2]	Neuschulden aus		zusammen	Schulden bei Gebietskörperschaften [4]	insgesamt	Auslandschulden
		Kreditmarktmitteln	öffentl. Sondermitteln [3]				
Bund							
31. 3. 1953	7.621	1.671		9.292		9.292	1.551
31. 3. 1954	7.650	1.587	188	9.425	—	9.425	8.352
31. 3. 1955	7.862	1.683	1.155	10.699	—	10.699	9.432
31. 3. 1956	7.924	1.278	1.145	10.347	—	10.347	9.539
31. 3. 1957 [9]	10.570	1.146	1.132	12.848	—	12.848	9.430
31. 3. 1958	10.519	483	1.193	12.195	—	12.195	9.241
Lastenausgleich							
31. 3. 1953	— [5]						
31. 3. 1954	—	238	—	238	217 [6]	454	—
31. 3. 1955	1.712	730	—	2.442	225	2.667	—
31. 3. 1956	2.087	806	—	2.893	525	3.418	—
31. 3. 1957	2.275	805	—	3.080	535	3.615	—
31. 3. 1958	2.329	643	—	2.972	510	3.482	—
Länder, Hansestädte, Berlin							
31. 3. 1953	12.600	1.067	430	14.097	4.761 [7]	18.858	211
31. 3. 1954	12.547	1.721	705	14.973	6.022	20.995	193
31. 3. 1955	12.567	1.592	909	15.068	7.299	22.367	188
31. 3. 1956	12.604	2.042	974	15.620	8.411	24.031	203
31. 3. 1957 [9]	9.923	2.632	1.052	13.607	9.249 [10]	22.856	179
31. 3. 1958	9.774	3.696	1.064	14.534	10.841	25.374	181
Gemeinden und Gemeindeverbände							
31. 3. 1953	230	1.526	255	2.010	522	2.532	—
31. 3. 1954	102	2.373	318	2.793	731	3.524	—
31. 3. 1955	79	3.346	471	3.897	995	4.892	117
31. 3. 1956	71	4.257	721	5.049	1.188	6.237	142
31. 3. 1957	59	5.124	922	6.106	1.438	7.544	108
31. 3. 1958	48	6.634	1.072	7.754	1.677	9.430	116
Öffentliche Verwaltung insgesamt							
31. 3. 1953	20.450	4.264	685	25.399	5.283	— [8]	1.763
31. 3. 1954	20.298	5.919	1.211	27.428	6.970	—	8.545
31. 3. 1955	22.220	7.352	2.535	32.106	8.519	—	9.737
31. 3. 1956	22.686	8.383	2.840	33.909	10.123	—	9.884
31. 3. 1957	22.827	9.707	3.106	35.641	11.222	—	9.717
31. 3. 1958	22.670	11.456	3.328	37.454	13.027	—	9.538

Anmerkungen siehe Seite 477.

Der *Schuldendienst des Bundes* hat in den letzten Jahren, insbesondere nach Abschluß des Londoner Abkommens, erheblich zugenommen. Im Rechnungsjahr 1958 wurden für Verzinsung und Tilgung 932 Millionen DM verausgabt; einschließlich des Rückkaufs von Schuldurkunden und der Inanspruchnahme von Sicherheitsleistungen waren 1.141 Millionen DM erforderlich. Für 1959 sind rund 2,2 Milliarden DM veranschlagt; davon entfallen auf Auslandschulden rund 1,1 Milliarden DM.

Haushalt und Notenbank

Die Verflechtung zwischen Haushalt und Wirtschaft ist im Vergleich mit der Vorkriegszeit außerordentlich eng geworden. So konnte es auch nicht ausbleiben, daß die Haushaltsentwicklung tiefe Rückwirkungen auf den Konjunkturverlauf zeitigte. Im Jahre 1955 traten Überhitzungen der Konjunktur, insbesondere im Investitionsbereich, ein. Ferner steigerte die Nachfrage des Auslandes sich erheblich, und damit trat neben die Binnenkonjunktur auch eine Exportkonjunktur. Damals waren die retardierenden Wirkungen der Haushaltsüberschüsse insofern ein ausgleichender Faktor, als sie die Zuflüsse an Devisen, die im Umtausch in Deutsche Mark als neue Kaufkraft über das Zentralbanksystem der Wirtschaft zuflossen, in etwa kompensierten. Der Konjunkturverlauf konnte dadurch gedämpft werden.

Diese Wechselwirkungen haben sich im Jahre 1956 gewandelt. Der Devisenstrom hat weiter angehalten, die Überschußbildung im öffentlichen Bereich aber ab September nachgelassen. 1957 gingen sogar zeitweilig expansive Wirkungen von den Haushalten aus. Die Zentralbank konnte aber

[1] Abweichungen in den Summen durch Runden der Zahlen. — [2] Ausgleichsforderungen und sonstige Altschulden. — [3] Unter anderem Kredite der Bundesanstalt für AV. u. AV., der Träger der Sozialversicherung, ERP-Kredite. — [4] Verschuldung der Gebietskörperschaften untereinander (einschließlich der Altschulden). — [5] Deckungsforderungen der Geldinstitute, Versicherungsunternehmen und Bausparkassen. — [6] Schulden beim Bund. — [7] Schulden beim Bund und Lastenausgleichfonds. — [8] Wegen Doppelzählungen nicht summiert. — [9] Beim Bund einschließlich, bei den Ländern und Hansestädten ohne die gemäß dem Bundesbankgesetz mit Wirkung vom 1.7.1957 auf den Bund übergegangenen Schulden der Länder und Hansestädte aus den Ausgleichsforderungen der Landeszentralbanken. — [10] Ohne die zinsfreien Schuldverschreibungen des Landes Berlin(West) anläßlich der Geldausstattung von Groß-Berlin, die gemäß Bundesbankgesetz mit Wirkung vom 1.1.1957 erloschen sind.

Quelle: Statistisches Bundesamt.

im Wege der Offenmarktpolitik diese Wirkungen durch erhöhte Abgabe von Geldmarkttiteln ausgleichen und damit der übermäßigen Ausdehnung des Umlaufs von Mitteln entgegenwirken. Der Umfang dieser Maßnahmen der Zentralbank reichte an die bisherige Stillegung von Geld aus Haushalts-Überschüssen heran. Bis Ende August 1957 stieg der gesamte Umlauf an Schatzwechseln und unverzinslichen Schatzanweisungen aus dem Umtausch von Ausgleichsforderungen auf 5,6 Milliarden DM. Mit diesem Betrag waren zunächst die Möglichkeiten der Zentralbank, auf diesem Wege überflüssige Kaufkraft dem Markt zu entziehen, erschöpft, da der Bestand ihrer Ausgleichsforderungen in etwa die gleiche Höhe hatte. Die Offenmarktpolitik konnte dann aber fortgesetzt werden, weil nach Inkrafttreten des Gesetzes über die Bundesnotenbank auch die den bisher selbständigen Landeszentralbanken zustehenden Ausgleichsforderungen auf die Deutsche Bundesbank übergingen. Insoweit hat bereits das *Gesetz über die Deutsche Bundesbank vom 26.7.1957* günstige Wirkungen auf die Geldmarktpolitik ausgelöst, deren zentrale Gestaltung aus gesamtwirtschaftlichen Gründen eine der Voraussetzungen für die weitere Wahrung der finanziellen Stabilität ist und bleiben wird.

Durch das Gesetz wurde infolge der Verschmelzung der Landeszentralbanken mit der Bank deutscher Länder zur „*Deutschen Bundesbank*" das Zentralbanksystem abgelöst. Zugleich wurde die im Grundgesetz verankerte Bestimmung des Artikels 88, der die Errichtung einer Währungs- und Notenbank vorschreibt, erfüllt. An die Stelle des bisher zweistufigen Systems ist nunmehr eine Einheitsbank getreten. Die Landeszentralbanken sind „Hauptverwaltungen der Bundesbank" geworden. Ihre Vorstände bleiben aber im Rahmen der eigenen Zuständigkeit neben dem Zentralbankrat und dem Direktorium der Bundesbank deren Organe. Somit sind trotz der zentralen Regelung gewisse Elemente des früheren Systems beibehalten. Dem Zentralbankrat als oberstem Organ der Deutschen Bundesbank sind aber wesentlich weitergehende Befugnisse eingeräumt worden. Neben seiner Zuständigkeit für die Kredit- und Währungspolitik kann er nunmehr die Geschäftspolitik durch allgemeine Richtlinien einheitlich ausrichten. Zu den Obliegenheiten der Bundesbank gehören neben den zentralen Aufgaben, dem Geschäftsverkehr mit dem Ausland und den Offenmarktgeschäften, vornehmlich auch die Geschäfte mit dem Bund und seinen Sondervermögen (insbesondere Bundesbahn und Bundespost). Die Hauptverwaltungen nehmen demgegenüber die Geschäfte mit dem Land wahr, in dem sie ihren Sitz haben, sowie die regionalen Kreditgeschäfte. Die Mitwirkung der Bundesregierung bei der

Bestellung der Mitglieder des Zentralbankrates ist verstärkt worden. Die Präsidenten der Landeszentralbanken werden auf Vorschlag des Bundesrates, die Mitglieder des Direktoriums der Bundesbank auf Vorschlag der Bundesregierung durch den Bundespräsidenten ernannt. Das Direktorium der Bundesbank ist nunmehr ein kollegiales Organ, während früher der Präsident der Bank deutscher Länder allein verantwortlich war.

Die Deutsche Bundesbank ist bei der Ausübung der ihr gesetzlich zustehenden Befugnisse von den Weisungen der Bundesregierung unabhängig. Sie soll aber deren Wirtschaftspolitik unterstützen, soweit dies unter Wahrung ihrer Aufgaben geschehen kann. Die Mitglieder der Bundesregierung sind berechtigt, ohne Stimmrecht an den Beratungen des Zentralbankrats teilzunehmen und Anträge zu stellen. Ihre währungspolitischen Befugnisse (Notenausgabe, Diskont-, Kredit- und Offenmarktpolitik, Mindestreservepolitik, Einlagenpolitik) und ihr Geschäftskreis als Bank der Banken ist im Gesetz eingehend festgelegt. Zur direkten Kreditgewährung an die Wirtschaft ist die Bundesbank nicht berechtigt, also nur mittelbar über die Kreditinstitute mit ihr verbunden. Dem Bund, den Sondervermögen des Bundes und den Ländern kann sie im Rahmen des gesetzlich festgelegten Kreditplafonds Kassenkredite gewähren (unter anderem an den Bund 3 Milliarden DM). Für den Bund sind besondere Plafondbestimmungen für die Erfüllung seiner Verpflichtungen gegenüber dem Welt-Währungsfonds, dem Europäischen Fonds und der Internationalen Bank für Wiederaufbau und Entwicklung getroffen. Die öffentlichen Verwaltungen sind demgegenüber verpflichtet, ihre Kassenmittel bei der Bundesbank anzulegen. Nach dem früheren Verfahren waren die Länder bei der Einlage beziehungsweise Anlage ihrer Kassenmittel nur unvollständig an ihre Zentralbank gebunden. Die angeführten Bestimmungen bedeuten demgegenüber einen wesentlichen Fortschritt, weil dadurch die währungspolitischen Möglichkeiten der Bank erheblich erweitert worden sind. Währungspolitisch bedeutsam sind auch die Bestimmungen über die Mobilisierung der Ausgleichsforderungen für Geschäfte am offenen Markt. Bisher wurden Offenmarkt-Operationen mit dem Ziel, kontraktiv auf den Geldmarkt einzuwirken, auf Grund von besonderen befristeten Vereinbarungen mit dem Bundesfinanzministerium durchgeführt. Nunmehr hat die Bank einen Anspruch darauf und kann den Umtausch ihrer Ausgleichsforderungen verlangen. Der Betrag der „Mobilisierungspapiere" kann auf Antrag der Bank über den gesetzlich normierten Höchstbetrag (4 Milliarden DM) hinaus bis zum Nennbetrag ihrer Ausgleichsforderungen — das sind einschließlich der Ausgleichsforderungen der Landeszentralbanken, die an die Deutsche Bundesbank übergegangen sind, rund 8,8 Milliarden DM — festgesetzt werden. Inzwischen hat die Bundesregierung der einstweiligen Erhöhung auf den vollen Betrag der Ausgleichsforderungen zugestimmt, da die Nachfrage nach diesen Papieren weiter gestiegen ist. Ende August 1958 belief der Betrag der von der Bundesbank abgegebenen Geldmarktpapiere (Schatzwechsel oder Schatzanweisungen) sich auf rund 7 Milliarden DM. Bis Ende des Jahres 1958 ist dieser Betrag wieder auf 4,4 Milliarden DM zurückgegangen; bis Ende März 1959 stieg er sodann auf 4,9 Milliarden DM.

Zusammenfassung

Der enge Zusammenhang zwischen Wirtschaft und öffentlichen Finanzen zwingt dazu, die Entwicklung ständig zu beobachten, um einer auftretenden Divergenz zwischen Leistungsfähigkeit und Finanzbedarf zu begegnen. Die Aufrechterhaltung der Stabilität der Währung wird übergeordneter, leitender Grundsatz der Finanzpolitik bleiben. Durch ihn werden die Möglichkeiten einer Erfüllung der Wünsche auf Bewilligung von Ausgaben oder Steuererleichterungen begrenzt.

In den vergangenen Jahren konnte diese Grundlinie der Finanzpolitik eingehalten werden. Das Festhalten am Grundsatz „Keine Ausgaben ohne Deckung" wird aber größere Schwierigkeiten bereiten, wenn an die Leistungsfähigkeit des Bundeshaushalts in den nächsten Jahren neue Anforderungen gestellt werden. Deshalb wird die Finanzplanung stärker als bisher rationalisiert werden. Neue Ausgaben werden sehr eingehend auf ihre finanziellen Auswirkungen zu prüfen sein. Bundes- und Länderfinanzen sind trotz ihrer rechtlichen Unabhängigkeit in vielen Aufgabenbereichen sachlich miteinander verflochten. Diese Prüfung, ob neue Ausgaben geleistet werden können, wird daher beide Ebenen der staatlichen Verwaltung berücksichtigen müssen.

Der Überblick hat gezeigt, wie stark die Nachkriegsprobleme die Entwicklung der öffentlichen Finanzen überschattet haben. Wann diese Nachkriegslasten einmal nicht mehr das Gesamtbild der Finanzen entscheidend bestimmen werden, läßt sich noch nicht übersehen. Grundsätzlich wird es das Ziel der Finanzpolitik bleiben, die Ausgaben so niedrig wie möglich zu halten, um zugleich Steuererhöhungen zu vermeiden. Damit leistet sie einen wesentlichen Beitrag zur Stabilität der volkswirtschaftlichen Entwicklung und bessert die innere Festigkeit und Ausgewogenheit der Gesellschaftsordnung.

Schüler-Lotsendienst

Die TELLKAMPF-Schule in Hannover

Die Jugendherberge Malente in der Holsteinischen Schweiz

Das ALBERT-SCHWEITZER-Kinderheim in Berlin-Steglitz

Wohin geht die Fahrt?

DAS VERKEHRSWESEN IN DER BUNDESREPUBLIK

I. ALLGEMEINE ÜBERSICHT

Die ersten Jahre des Wiederaufbaus

Bei Kriegsende war das deutsche Verkehrswesen in allen seinen Teilgebieten weitgehend zerstört. Die Ströme des Güter- und Personenverkehrs waren versiegt. Eisenbahn, Binnenschiffahrt und Straßenverkehr waren in großen Teilen des Landes so nachhaltig getroffen, daß nicht nur die verkehrsabhängige Wirtschaft lahmgelegt, sondern auch die Versorgung der Bevölkerung mit dem Notwendigsten gefährdet war. Die deutschen Seehäfen zeigten ein Bild trostloser Zerstörung. Von der ehemals großen Deutschen Handelsflotte war nur ein unbedeutender Rest geblieben. Der deutsche Luftverkehr war tot.

Zunächst konzentrierten sich alle Bemühungen darauf, den binnenländischen Verkehr wieder in Gang zu setzen. Nach Überwindung großer Anlauf- und Versorgungsschwierigkeiten nahmen regionale Verkehrsbehörden: Eisenbahndirektionen, Wasserstraßendirektionen, Straßenbau- und Verkehrsverwaltungen ihre Arbeit nach und nach wieder auf. An ihre Seite traten neue Länderbehörden, die den Wiederaufbau des Verkehrs und die Beseitigung der Kriegszerstörungen in ihrem Zuständigkeitsbereich tatkräftig förderten, um der Wirtschaft die nötigen Transportmöglichkeiten zu schaffen. Das gleiche gilt für die Städte und Gemeinden, deren Neuaufbau auf das Wiedererstehen leistungsfähiger Verkehrswege und Verkehrsmittel angewiesen war. Besondere Hervorhebung verdienen dabei die erfolgreichen Bemühungen der Hansestädte um den Wiederaufbau der deutschen Seehäfen, den sie zunächst vollständig und auch später zum Teil aus eigener Kraft vollbrachten.

Die Steuerung des Verkehrs durch eine zentrale Stelle fehlte; vielmehr vollzog sich der Aufbau in den einzelnen Besatzungszonen nach unterschiedlichen Prinzipien. Eine erste Zusammenfassung der Verwaltungsstellen erfolgte am 1. 10. 1946 mit der Bildung des „*Verwaltungsrates für Verkehr*" in Bielefeld. Er wurde im Herbst 1947 in die „*Verwaltung für Verkehr im Vereinigten Wirtschaftsgebiet*" in Offenbach übergeführt. Der Aufbau schritt in der sogenannten „Bizone" schneller voran als in der Französischen Zone. Dem Beitritt dieser Zone folgte im Jahre 1949 unmittelbar die Gründung der Bundesrepublik.

Grundlagen für die Arbeit des Bundesverkehrsministeriums

Die Zuständigkeiten des Bundes auf dem Verkehrsgebiet sind im Grundgesetz festgelegt worden. Sie regeln die gesetzgeberischen Aufgaben des Bundes gegenüber den Verkehrsträgern, die Eigentumsverhältnisse und die darauf beruhenden Verpflichtungen zum Bau und zur Erhaltung der Verkehrswege sowie die Einrichtung einer bundeseigenen Verkehrsverwaltung mit einem eigenen Unterbau der Verwaltung. Als das Bundesverkehrsministerium 1949 seine Tätigkeit aufnahm, waren die Folgen des Krieges noch nicht überwunden. Der Wiederaufbau hat daher noch einige Jahre im Vordergrund aller verkehrspolitischen Sorge und Mühe gestanden.

Das Ziel konnte jedoch nicht sein, lediglich den Zustand wiederherzustellen, der vor dem Kriege bestanden hatte. Der Verkehr steht, von den starken Impulsen des technischen Fortschrittes angetrieben, in ständiger Wechselwirkung mit den übrigen sich schnell entfaltenden Teilen der Wirtschaft. Daher war es unumgänglich, im Inlandverkehr Neues zu planen und zu beginnen. Verkehrswege und Verkehrseinrichtungen, die 1939 noch als ausreichend gelten konnten, bedurften über die Beseitigung der Kriegsschäden hinaus eines großzügigen, dem neuzeitlichen Stand der Technik und den wirtschaftlichen Erfordernissen entsprechenden Ausbaus und einer planvollen Weiterentwicklung.

Voraussetzung dafür bildete die schon im Herbst 1949 begonnene Arbeit an einer neuen Rechtsordnung für das Verkehrswesen in der Bundesrepublik. Eine Reihe grundlegender Ordnungsgesetze wurde in den ersten Regierungsjahren geschaffen, um die Rechtsverhältnisse der einzelnen Verkehrszweige den geänderten politischen und wirtschaftlichen Bedingungen anzupassen und die einzelnen Verkehrsgebiete gegeneinander abzugrenzen. Auf dieser Grundlage entwickelte sich folgerichtig die spätere verkehrspolitische Konzeption der Bundesregierung. Ihr Ziel ist es, alle Verkehrsbereiche unter Erhaltung der bestehenden Werte mit möglichst großem volkswirtschaftlichen Nutzen und geringem Kostenaufwand zu ordnen, in den Wettbewerbsbedingungen anzugleichen und zu einer möglichst harmonischen Zusammenarbeit zu führen. Entsprechend den weltweiten und völkerverbindenden Funktionen des modernen Verkehrs sah die Bundesregierung ferner eine wichtige Aufgabe darin, die internationalen Verkehrsbeziehungen zu festigen und auszubauen. Sie hat sich mit gutem Erfolg um eine fruchtbare Mitarbeit in den bestehenden internationalen Organisationen bemüht und

Tabelle 1

IST-AUSGABEN DES BUNDES FÜR BAU UND UNTERHALTUNG VON VERKEHRSWEGEN[1]

Millionen DM

Jahr	Binnen- und Seewasserstraßen	Bundesfernstraßen	Binnen- und Seewasserstraßen	Bundesfernstraßen
	im Kalenderjahr		im Rechnungsjahr	
1950	.	.	165,4	206,0
1951	212,8	183,2	210,0	210,0
1952	223,3	233,3	230,9	243,4
1953	257,5	305,5	250,1	304,2
1954	248,9	287,2	246,3	296,9
1955	263,7	423,2	263,1	479,7
1956	260,4	665,5	266,3	686,7
1957	277,3	682,6	312,4	725,2
1958	364,0	1.009,5	...	...

[1] Einschließlich wasserwirtschaftlicher und ähnlicher Aufwendungen.

Quelle: Bundesministerium für Verkehr.

Tabelle 2

BEFÖRDERTE GÜTER

Millionen t

Jahr	Bundesbahn[1]	Binnenschiffahrt[2]	Straßenfernverkehr[3]	Seeverkehr	Insgesamt
1950	229.347	71.855	32.900	25.814	359.916
1951	254.933	88.111	41.800	33.143	417.987
1952	262.371	95.270	50.600	37.807	446.048
1953	246.799	101.381	55.900	37.530	441.610
1954	252.288	109.385	61.125	43.941	466.739
1955	282.830	124.612	70.479	52.995	530.880
1956	299.324	135.920	74.866	59.920	570.030
1957	302.944	142.331	76.917	60.970	583.162

[1] Ohne Kraftverkehr. — [2] Die Binnenflotte verfügte am 1.1.1950 erst wieder über 62 % des entsprechenden Vorkriegsumfangs (in Tragfähigkeits-t). Über die Flottenentwicklung seit 1950 siehe Seite 503. — [3] 1950 bis 1953 auf Grund der Ergebnisse von Repräsentativerhebungen 1950 und 1952 geschätzt.

Quelle: Bundesministerium für Verkehr.

GÜTERVERKEHR* NACH VERKEHRSTRÄGERN

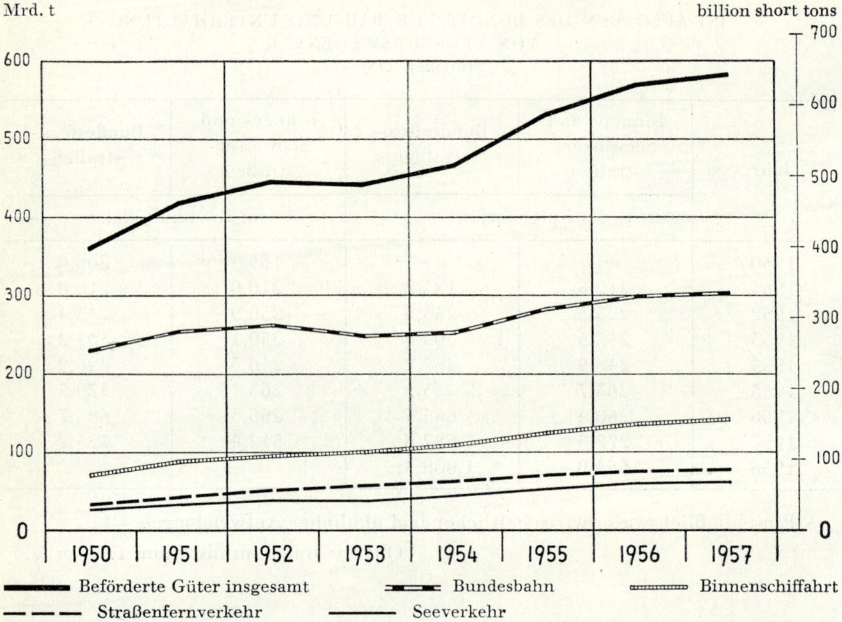

* Bundesrepublik Deutschland (ohne Saarland).

Quelle: Statistisches Bundesamt.

durch zahlreiche zwei- und mehrseitige Abkommen die zwischenstaatliche Zusammenarbeit auf den einzelnen Verkehrsgebieten gefördert.

Die zehnjährige Aufbauarbeit des Bundes hat auf allen Gebieten des Verkehrs zu befriedigenden Leistungen geführt und damit entscheidend zum Wiederaufstieg der Wirtschaft und zur Verbesserung der Lebenshaltung beigetragen. Die Darstellungen der Seiten 483 und 484 zeigen die wachsenden Aufwendungen des Bundes für den Bau und die Unterhaltung von Verkehrswegen sowie die Entwicklung im Gütertransport und Personenverkehr.

II. DIE EISENBAHNEN

Am Ende des Krieges ruhte der Eisenbahnverkehr in Deutschland fast vollständig. Im Bundesgebiet waren ganz oder teilweise vernichtet rund 4.300 km Eisenbahngleise, 16.900 Weichen, 2.300 Stellwerke, 3.150 Eisenbahnbrücken, zahlreiche Bahnhöfe, Güterböden, Ausbesserungswerke, Betriebswerke und Betriebseinrichtungen und nicht zuletzt ein erheblicher Teil des rollenden Materials.

Schon kurz nach dem Zusammenbruch regten sich die ersten Hände, um Ordnung in das Chaos zu bringen und den Eisenbahnbetrieb wenigstens behelfsmäßig in Gang zu setzen. In harter und mühevoller Arbeit ist es trotz dem damaligen Materialmangel und der überaus eng begrenzten finanziellen Mittel in verhältnismäßig kurzer Zeit gelungen, die Verkehrsanlagen und Fahrzeuge wieder instandzusetzen. Zunächst wurde ein regionaler Notverkehr eingerichtet und dieser nach und nach weiter entwickelt.

Heute hat die *Deutsche Bundesbahn* die Kriegsschäden weitgehend beseitigt. Sie verfügt über ein Streckennetz von rund 30.450 km, zu dem ab 1.1.1957 rund 550 km der Saarbahnen hinzugekommen sind. Neben der Deutschen Bundesbahn bestehen etwa 240 nicht-bundeseigene Eisenbahnunternehmen mit einem Streckennetz von rund 6.400 km.

Die Deutsche Bundesbahn ist das größte deutsche Verkehrsunternehmen, das sowohl Personen als auch Güter befördert. Im Netz der Deutschen Bundesbahn verkehren täglich etwa 23.000 Reisezüge und 13.000 Güterzüge, also 36.000 Züge. Der Anteil der Deutschen Bundesbahn am statistisch erfaßten Güterverkehr der Bundesrepublik (beförderte Mengen in Tonnen) betrug im Jahre 1957 rund 52%, am Personenverkehr knapp 50%[1].

Ungeachtet ihrer eindrucksvollen Aufbauleistungen hat die Deutsche Bundesbahn mit erheblichen finanziellen Schwierigkeiten zu kämpfen. Die Einnahmen bei dem für die finanzielle Lage der Deutschen Bundesbahn entscheidenden Güterverkehr sind in den letzten Jahren hinter den Beförderungsleistungen nicht unerheblich zurückgeblieben. Der Güterverkehr der Deutschen Bundesbahn hat sich zwar erhöht; er hat aber nicht im gleichen Maße wie der Güterverkehr auf der Straße und auf den Binnenwasserwegen an der volkswirtschaftlichen Aufwärtsentwicklung teilgenommen. Die Deutsche Bundesbahn schloß im Jahre 1957 mit einem Defizit von 684 Millionen DM ab. In ähnlicher Lage befinden sich fast alle europäischen Eisenbahnen.

Einige der wesentlichen Gründe für die finanziellen Schwierigkeiten der Deutschen Bundesbahn sollen im Nachfolgenden dargestellt werden. Das Tarifsystem der früheren Staatseisenbahnen und auch der Deutschen Bundesbahn ist seit jeher bewußt in den Dienst staats-, wirtschafts- und

[1] Wegen der Aufteilung der Verkehrs*leistungen* (tkm) des binnenländischen Güterverkehrs auf Schiene, Straße und Binnenwasserstraße siehe Seite 483.

sozialpolitischer Zielsetzungen gestellt worden. Über den Transportkosten liegenden Tarifsätzen bei wertvollen Gütern und in den verkehrsstarken Gebieten stehen unter den vollen Selbstkosten liegende Transportentgelte zum Beispiel in wirtschaftsschwachen Randgebieten gegenüber. Eigenwirtschaftliche und kostenmäßige Überlegungen sind in der Vergangenheit nur insoweit berücksichtigt worden, als die Eisenbahnen gehalten waren, aus ihren Einnahmen im ganzen zu einem Ausgleich ihrer Rechnung zu gelangen. Dieses System lief störungsfrei, bis mit der Entwicklung des Kraftwagenverkehrs der tarifliche Ausgleich für die gemeinwirtschaftlichen Leistungen der Eisenbahnen immer schwieriger wurde. Bisher haben Bundesregierung, Bundestag und zum Teil auch die Wirtschaft die Auffassung vertreten, daß an dem gemeinwirtschaftlichen Prinzip bei der Bundesbahn festgehalten werden müsse.

Als ein diesem Prinzip verpflichtetes Sondervermögen des Bundes — mit eigener Wirtschafts- und Rechnungsführung —, aber als ein durch Kriegsschäden und langjährigen Substanzverzehr (zeitbedingte Unterlassung von Unterhaltungs-, Erneuerungs- und Modernisierungsmaßnahmen) geschwächter Betrieb stand die Bundesbahn im Wettbewerb mit den überwiegend privatwirtschaftlich orientierten Verkehrsunternehmen der Binnenschiffahrt und der Straße. Außerdem war sie noch durch soziale Kriegsfolgen, wie etwa die Versorgung verdrängter Eisenbahner, besonders belastet. Schließlich konnte sie als gemeinwirtschaftlich orientierte Anstalt im Gegensatz zu weiten Kreisen der übrigen Wirtschaft ihren Investitionsbedarf auch nicht über den Preis decken.

Diese Umstände haben die Bundesregierung zu verschiedenen Hilfsmaßnahmen veranlaßt, die für die wirtschaftliche und finanzielle Lage der Deutschen Bundesbahn unmittelbar oder mittelbar von Einfluß gewesen sind:

Die neue rechtliche Ordnung der Binnenschiffahrt und des Straßenverkehrs dient gleichzeitig der sinnvollen Koordinierung der binnenländischen Verkehrsträger, an der auch die Bundesbahn lebhaft interessiert ist.

Durch das Verkehrsfinanzgesetz 1955 ist der Straßenverkehr in höherem Grade als bisher zu den von ihm verursachten Wegekosten herangezogen worden. Die Erhöhung der Kraftfahrzeugsteuer für schwere Nutzkraftfahrzeuge und der Mineralölsteuer hat die sehr unterschiedlichen Voraussetzungen für den Wettbewerb zwischen der Schiene und der Straße einander wesentlich angenähert.

Die Eindämmung des Werkfernverkehrs durch eine Erhöhung der Beförderungssteuer ist vorwiegend dem gewerblichen Güterfernverkehr zugute gekommen. In manchen Verkehrsrelationen, bei einigen Güterarten und bei Transporten, die über

Anschlußgleise abgewickelt werden können, war diese Maßnahme aber auch für die Bundesbahn förderlich.

Aus den Erträgen, die durch die Steuererhöhungen im Verkehrsfinanzgesetz 1955 erzielt werden, insbesondere aus dem Aufkommen der Beförderungssteuer, erhält die Deutsche Bundesbahn für einen Zeitraum von zehn Jahren zur Finanzierung von Verkehrsanlagen und rollendem Material 145 Millionen DM jährlich. Um der Bundesbahn gleich die Möglichkeit zu geben, größere Aufträge zu finanzieren, hat das Gesetz den Bundesminister der Finanzen ermächtigt, Bürgschaftsleistungen bis zu 750 Millionen DM zu übernehmen. In diesem Zusammenhang sei erwähnt, daß auch die nichtbundeseigenen Eisenbahnen eine Finanzierungshilfe auf Grund des Verkehrsfinanzgesetzes 1955 erhalten. Die Bundesregierung wird ihnen zehn Jahre lang jährlich Mittel bis zur Höhe von 10 Millionen DM gewähren, die ebenfalls zur Verbesserung der Verkehrsanlagen und zur Beschaffung von rollendem Material verwendet werden sollen.

Der Bund hat der Deutschen Bundesbahn bis zum Jahre 1956 an Darlehen, Liquiditäts- und Kassenhilfen sowie für belassene Beförderungssteuer 3.070 Millionen DM gewährt.

Außerdem sind der Bundesbahn bis zum 31.12.1956 Darlehen aus dem ERP-Sondervermögen in Höhe von 410 Millionen DM zu Rationalisierungszwecken und zur Finanzierung von Aufträgen an die Berliner Wirtschaft zugeflossen.

Die Bundesregierung hat ferner am 30.1.1957[1] beschlossen, die in den Jahresabschlüssen der Deutschen Bundesbahn bis 31.12.1956 ausgewiesenen Verluste zu decken. Dies geschah durch Verrechnung der in diesen Jahren aufgelaufenen betriebsfremden Lasten mit Forderungen des Bundes gegen die Deutsche Bundesbahn. Die Verluste belaufen sich auf rund 1.972 Millionen DM, während der von der Bundesregierung anerkannte Teil der betriebsfremden Lasten der vergangenen Jahre rund 1.992 Millionen DM beträgt. Damit sind die bis zum Ende des Jahres 1956 entstandenen Verluste bereinigt, die Bilanzen ausgeglichen. Tatsächlich waren also die Verluste der Deutschen Bundesbahn wesentlich dadurch verursacht worden, daß sie in den vergangenen Jahren die (im wesentlichen aus Leistungen für das Personal entstandenen) betriebsfremden Lasten vorübergehend selbst tragen mußte.

Ferner hat die Bundesregierung am 30.1.1957 beschlossen, vom Jahre 1958 an folgende einseitige, der Deutschen Bundesbahn auferlegte betriebsfremde Lasten zu erstatten:

die Versorgungs- und Übergangsbezüge für verdrängte Reichsbedienstete und volksdeutsche Bedienstete fremder Staatsbahnen;
die Übergangs- und Versorgungsbezüge der Eisenbahner aus Berlin(West);

[1] Gemäß § 33 Abs. 2 des Bundesbahngesetzes.

den Mehraufwand durch vorzeitige Gewährung von Versorgungsbezügen an Kriegsversehrte und Kriegshinterbliebene des Ersten und Zweiten Weltkrieges;
den Anteil der Deutschen Bundesbahn an der Zinsverpflichtung des Bundes für die Ausgleichsforderung der Bank deutscher Länder.

Die Abnahme dieses Teils der betriebsfremden Lasten war bereits in dem verkehrspolitischen Gesamtplan des Bundesministeriums für Verkehr vom 12.12.1953 vorgesehen. Ihre Höhe wird im Rechnungsjahr 1958 sich auf über 305 Millionen DM belaufen. Für das Jahr 1957 ist ein Teilausgleich dieser Lasten in Höhe von rund 200 Millionen DM erfolgt.

*

Ergänzend zu den Maßnahmen der Bundesregierung laufen die Bemühungen des Vorstandes der Deutschen Bundesbahn, den Betrieb *zu rationalisieren und zu modernisieren.*

In der Zeit von Anfang 1953 bis Ende 1957 wurden zweiundvierzig Betriebs-, Maschinen- und Verkehrsämter, zehn Ausbesserungswerke und mehr als fünfhundert Dienststellen aufgehoben und in entsprechendem Umfange Personal eingespart. Für die nächsten vier Jahre ist die Aufhebung weiterer neun oder zehn Ausbesserungswerke vorgesehen. Nach Abschluß dieser Maßnahmen wird die Zahl der Ausbesserungswerke von dreiundvierzig auf fünfundzwanzig und die Zahl der Werkstättenarbeiter von 47.000 auf 31.000 abgesunken sein. Durch die Zusammenfassung der Fahrzeugunterhaltung in den verbleibenden Werken sind bereits jetzt jährlich mehr als 100 Millionen DM erspart worden.

Die Deutsche Bundesbahn hat zehn Nebenstrecken ganz oder zum Teil stillgelegt, bei fünfundvierzig Nebenbahnen den Reiseverkehr ganz oder teilweise auf die Straße verlagert und für den auf der Schiene verbleibenden Güterverkehr eine vereinfachte Betriebsweise eingeführt. Diese Maßnahmen ersparen schon jetzt jährlich 84 Millionen DM an Kosten. Für andere vierundvierzig Nebenbahnen ist die gänzliche oder teilweise Stillegung und für zweiundzwanzig weitere Nebenbahnen die Verlegung des Reiseverkehrs auf die Straße eingeleitet.

Nach Abschluß dieser Maßnahmen werden — die Genehmigung der Aufsichtsbehörde vorausgesetzt — insgesamt rund 900 km Nebenbahnstrecken (also etwa 10% des Nebenbahnnetzes der Deutschen Bundesbahn) entweder gänzlich oder teilweise stillgelegt sein.

Die Deutsche Bundesbahn hat in der Nachkriegszeit bereits 1.500 Streckenkilometer elektrifiziert und dadurch gegenüber dem Dampfbetrieb jährlich

200 Millionen DM eingespart. Insgesamt werden jetzt bereits rund 3.200 Streckenkilometer (das sind mehr als 10% des Bundesbahnnetzes) elektrisch betrieben.

Bis Ende 1957 hat die Bundesbahn für etwa 42 Millionen DM moderne Gleisbaumaschinen aller Art angeschafft und durch deren Einsatz — nach Abzug der Verzinsung und Amortisation — Ersparnisse von 70 Millionen DM erzielt. Bis Ende 1957 wurden etwa 12.000 km Gleise durchgehend geschweißt. Die Unterhaltungskosten dieser durchgehend geschweißten Gleise konnten um 4 Millionen DM jährlich gesenkt werden.

Seit Kriegsende hat die Bundesbahn 567 alte (meist mechanische) Stellwerke durch nur 306 moderne Gleisbildstellwerke ersetzt. Der Aufwand dafür in Höhe von 138 Millionen DM wird durch die erzielten Ersparnisse in verhältnismäßig kurzer Zeit ausgeglichen werden.

Die Bundesbahn hat sich ständig bemüht, ihren Personalstand dem jeweiligen Verkehrsumfang anzupassen. So hat sie allein in den Jahren 1953 bis 1955 ihren Personalstand um 34.000 Personen dadurch vermindert, daß sie durch Pensionierung oder Invalidität ausgeschiedene sowie verstorbene Arbeitskräfte nicht wieder ersetzt hat. Wegen des Verkehrsrückganges hat sie seit April 1958 den Personalstand abermals um 10.000 Köpfe gesenkt und bis Mitte des Jahres 1959 weitere 6.000 Personen eingespart.

Insgesamt hat die Bundesbahn von 1950 bis 1957 in Bahnanlagen und Fahrzeugen 10,2 Milliarden DM investiert.

III. STRASSENVERKEHR UND STRASSENBAU

Der Straßenverkehr

Die Motorisierung des Straßenverkehrs hat im Gebiet der Bundesrepublik seit dem Kriege erstaunliche Fortschritte gemacht. Die Zahl der Kraftfahrzeuge nahm von rund 1,4 Millionen im Jahre 1949 auf rund 6,6 Millionen im Jahre 1958 zu. Der Bestand hat sich somit fast verfünffacht. Dabei sind die rund 1,9 Millionen Mopeds, die dank ihrer technischen Entwicklung nunmehr als vollwertige Kraftfahrzeuge angesehen werden können, nicht berücksichtigt.

Die motorisierten Fahrzeuge haben in einem Maße zugenommen, daß nicht mehr von einer Fortentwicklung der Verhältnisse des Jahres 1949

Tabelle 3

DIE ENTWICKLUNG
DES BESTANDES AN KRAFTFAHRZEUGEN UND KRAFTFAHRZEUGANHÄNGERN*
1.000

Stichtag 1. Juli	Krafträder[1]	Personenkraftwagen[2]	Kraftomnibusse[3]	Lastkraftwagen	Zugmaschinen	Sonderfahrzeuge[4]	Kraftfahrzeuge insgesamt	Kraftfahrzeuganhänger
	1	2	3	4	5	6	7	8
1950[5]	914	518	14	358	132	14	1.950	214
1951[5]	1.181	685	17	414	181	17	2.495	232
1952	1.582	904	20	495	256	20	3.275	271
1953	2.005	1.129	22	555	318	25	4.054	305
1954	2.301	1.397	25	572	376	28	4.700	321
1955	2.433	1.666	26	564	463	33	5.184	325
1956	2.448	2.033	27	576	553	36	5.673	332
1957	2.388	2.456	28	595	630	39	6.137	345
1958	2.178	2.940	29	603	707	42	6.499	339

* Bundesrepublik (ohne Saarland). Einschließlich aus steuerlichen oder sonstigen Gründen vorübergehend abgemeldeten Fahrzeuge. — [1] Einschließlich der Kraftroller. — [2] Einschließlich der Krankenkraftwagen und Kombinationskraftwagen. — [3] Einschließlich der Obusse. — [4] Einschließlich der Kraftstoffkesselwagen. — [5] Ohne die vorübergehend abgemeldeten Fahrzeuge.

Quelle: Bundesministerium für Verkehr.

gesprochen werden kann. Wir stehen vielmehr mitten in einem Strukturwandel des Straßenverkehrs. Es sind dadurch ähnliche Verhältnisse eingetreten, wie wir sie aus hoch motorisierten anderen Ländern kennen. In Deutschland stand für diese Entwicklung im Gegensatz zu vergleichbaren anderen Ländern aber nur ein Zeitraum von wenigen Jahren zur Verfügung. Daraus mußten sich ganz besondere Schwierigkeiten ergeben, und zwar nicht nur für den Gesetzgeber, für Verkehrsverwaltung und Polizei, für Justiz und Straßenbau, sondern vor allem auch für die Menschen auf der Straße.

Um den *Grad der Motorisierung* mit dem anderer Länder zu vergleichen, wird im allgemeinen eine Relation zwischen Einwohnerzahl und Bestand an Kraftfahrzeugen oder Personenkraftwagen hergestellt. Danach ergibt sich folgendes Bild:

Tabelle 4

GRAD DER MOTORISIERUNG

Land	Stichtag	Einwohner je Kraftfahrzeug	Einwohner je Personenkraftwagen
Bundesrepublik	1. 7.1958	8	17
Frankreich	1. 1.1958	5	10
Vereinigtes Königreich	30. 9.1957	7	12
Italien	31.12.1957	10	40
USA	31.12.1957	3	3

Quelle: Bundesministerium für Verkehr.

Die *Verkehrsdichte* wird jedoch erst ersichtlich, wenn man den Bestand an Kraftfahrzeugen mit der Gebietsfläche und der Länge des verfügbaren Straßennetzes vergleicht, wie die folgende Übersicht zeigt:

Tabelle 5

VERKEHRSDICHTE

Land	Kraftfahrzeuge[1] auf einen Quadratkilometer Gebietsfläche	Kraftfahrzeuge[1] je Kilometer befestigte Straßen
Bundesrepublik	27	26
Frankreich	15	13
Vereinigtes Königreich	29	24
Italien	17	29
USA	9	12

[1] Ohne Mopeds.

Quelle: Bundesministerium für Verkehr.

Charakteristisch für die deutschen Verhältnisse ist die starke Mischung des Verkehrs. Sie erschwert nicht nur seine glatte Abwicklung, sondern sie wirkt sich auch nachteilig auf die Verkehrssicherheit aus.

Obwohl die wachsende Motorisierung als ein erfreuliches Zeichen des wirtschaftlichen Aufschwunges und als zunehmender Wohlstand begrüßt wird, ist es im Interesse der Allgemeinheit erforderlich, diese Entwicklung in geordnete Bahnen zu lenken. Der Bundesminister für Verkehr sieht es deshalb als vordringliche Aufgabe an, den reibungslosen und flüssigen

Ablauf des Verkehrs auf dem nicht überall ausreichenden Straßennetz zu gewährleisten, den verkehrs- und wirtschaftspolitisch notwendigen Ausgleich zwischen den einzelnen Verkehrsträgern herbeizuführen, und vor allem: den Menschen auf der Straße vor den Gefahren des Verkehrs und vor vermeidbaren Belästigungen zu schützen.

Dieser Zielsetzung dienten insbesondere eine umfassende Neuordnung und Fortbildung des Straßenverkehrsrechts sowie eine große Anzahl neuer Vorschriften zur Hebung der Verkehrssicherheit. Gute Erfolge wurden vor allem durch die am 1.9.1957 in Kraft getretene Einführung der Geschwindigkeitsbeschränkung (50 Kilometer in der Stunde) innerhalb geschlossener Ortschaften erzielt.

Abgesehen von diesen gesetzlichen Maßnahmen werden alle Bemühungen gefördert, die auf eine Verbesserung der Verkehrssicherheit und eine wirksame Erziehung der Verkehrsteilnehmer gerichtet sind.

Straßenbau

Die wachsende Kaufkraft immer größerer Bevölkerungskreise, verbunden mit steuerlichen Erleichterungen, begünstigte die seit 1949 anhaltende starke Motorisierungswelle. Die öffentlichen Träger der Baulast für den Straßenbau — Bund, Länder und Gemeinden — müssen den Straßenbau in der Bundesrepublik aus Steuermitteln finanzieren. Es liegt auf der Hand, daß sie dieser Entwicklung nicht folgen konnten, zumal in den ersten Jahren die Investitionen im Straßenbau zwangsläufig hinter den vordringlicheren Ausgaben für Wohnungsbau, Schulen, Produktionsstätten und soziale Einrichtungen zurückstehen mußten. Außerdem verschlangen die Beseitigung der Kriegsschäden und die lange vernachlässigten Arbeiten zur Erhaltung und Wiederherstellung des vorhandenen Straßennetzes einen erheblichen Anteil der verfügbaren Ansätze in den Haushalten. Der Krieg hatte besonders umfangreiche Zerstörungen an den Brückenbauwerken im Zuge der Bundesautobahnen und Bundesstraßen angerichtet. Insgesamt 1.508 Brücken mit einer lichten Weite von mehr als fünf Metern waren zerstört worden. Inzwischen konnten sie bis auf wenige Brücken wieder aufgebaut werden. Allein dafür hat die Bundesregierung rund 400 Millionen DM aufgebracht. Angesichts dieser vordringlichen großen Wiederaufbauleistungen lag eine Weiterführung des Neubaues von Autobahnen (bis auf die Beseitigung einiger kleiner besonders störender Lücken im Netz der Autobahnen) zunächst außerhalb der finanziellen Möglichkeiten.

Erst nach der Verabschiedung des Verkehrsfinanzgesetzes 1955, das neue zweckgebundene Mittel für den Bau von Autobahnen erschloß, konnte ein großzügiger und planvoller Neubau begonnen werden. Durch den im Jahre 1957 gesetzlich verankerten „*Ausbauplan für die Bundesfernstraßen*" ist der Bau von rund 2.000 km neuer Autobahnen festgelegt worden. Die Finanzierung der Ersten Baustufe ist durch das Verkehrsfinanzgesetz gesichert. Auf sie entfallen 664 km, die bis 1961 fertiggestellt werden sollen. Schon nach Vollendung dieser Ersten Baustufe werden wichtige und im Hinblick auf das europäische Straßennetz bedeutsame Fernverkehrs-Verbindungen hergestellt sein. Dazu gehört vor allem die große Nord-Süd-Strecke von Hamburg über Frankfurt am Main nach Basel, mit der das alte „HAFRABA-Vorhaben" verwirklicht wird.

Gleichzeitig wird in Erfüllung des Vertrages zwischen der Bundesrepublik und Dänemark der Ausbau der „Vogelfluglinie" — der über Fehmarn verlaufenden kürzesten Verbindung zwischen der Bundesrepublik, den dänischen Inseln und Skandinavien — betrieben. Ihre Vollendung ist bis 1963 vorgesehen. Der Ausbau der Europastraße 3, in deren Verlauf der in Bau befindliche große Straßentunnel unter dem Nord-Ostsee-Kanal bei Rendsburg liegt, und der Europastraße 4 ist deshalb mit Vorrang in Angriff genommen worden. 1959 wird mit den Bauarbeiten an der Fehmarnsund-Hochbrücke begonnen.

Bis zum Jahre 1963 wird auch die wichtige neue Autobahnverbindung von Frankfurt am Main über Würzburg nach Nürnberg bis auf ein kurzes Stück fertig werden. Sie wird für den Verkehr nach dem Süd-Osten, also besonders den Reiseverkehr nach Österreich und Italien, eine große Entlastung für die bisherige Bundesautobahn bedeuten.

Für den internationalen Verkehr sind ferner der Bau der Strecke Köln—Aachen bis 1961 im Anschluß an die belgischen Fernstraßen und die neue Verbindung von Oberhausen nach Emmerich im Anschluß an das holländische Straßennetz von großer Bedeutung. Die Verbindung nach den Niederlanden erhält besonderen Verkehrswert dadurch, daß auch der Ruhrschnellweg in Oberhausen angeschlossen wird. Auch Saarland soll bis 1961 durch eine Autobahn an das Bundesgebiet angeschlossen werden.

Für das Ruhrgebiet und den von Köln in den Raum Hamm—Bielefeld gehenden Fernverkehr hat schließlich die neue südliche Autobahn-Tangente von Remscheid nach Kamen ganz erhebliche Bedeutung. Diese sehr teure und technisch schwierige Strecke wird voraussichtlich bis zum Herbst 1961 fertiggestellt sein.

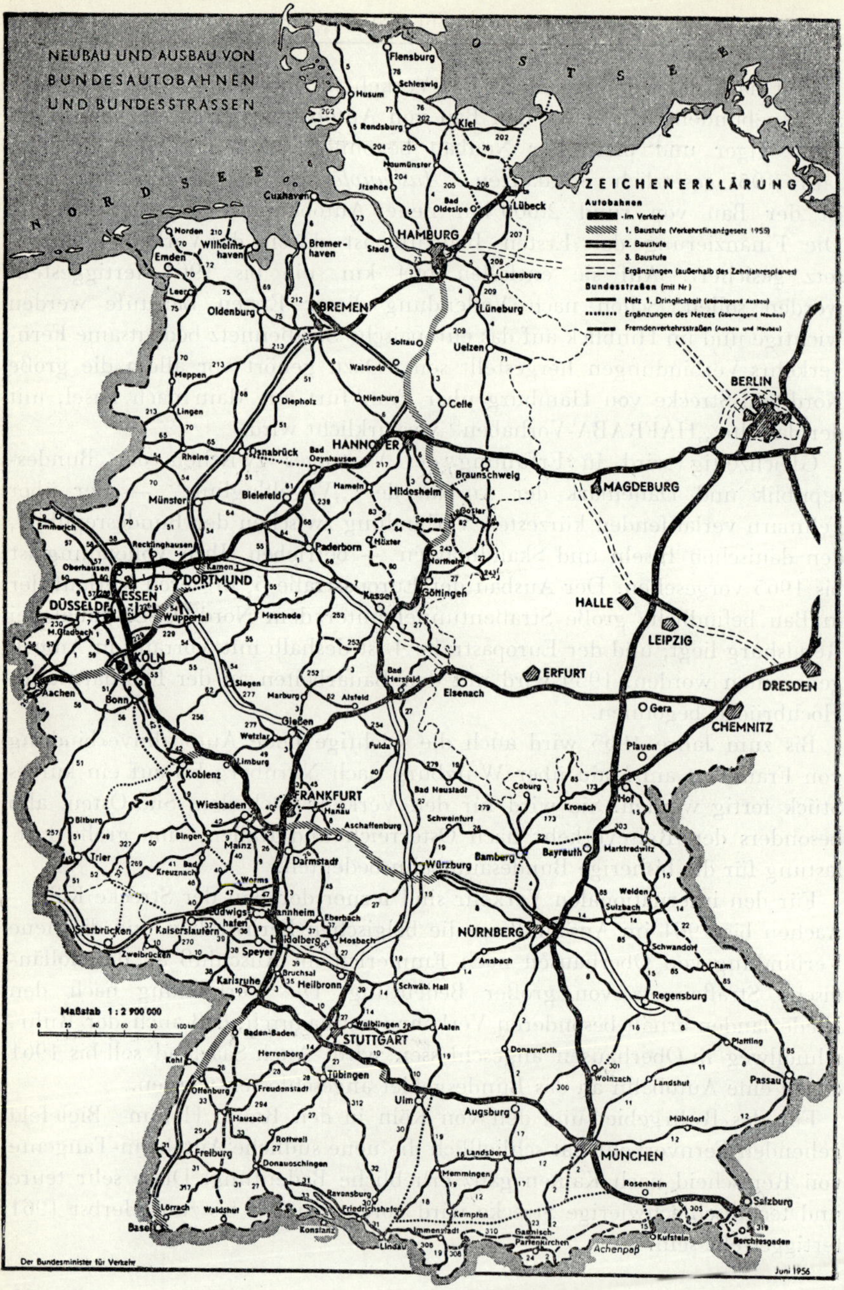
NEUBAU UND AUSBAU VON
BUNDESAUTOBAHNEN
UND BUNDESSTRASSEN
NORDSEE
OSTSEE
ZEICHENERKLÄRUNG
Autobahnen
-im Verkehr
1. Baustufe (Verkehrsfinanzgesetz 1955)
2. Baustufe
3. Baustufe
Ergänzungen (außerhalb des Zehnjahresplanes)
Bundesstraßen (mit Nr)
Netz 1. Dringlichkeit (überwiegend Ausbau)
Ergänzungen des Netzes (überwiegend Neubau)
Fremdenverkehrsstraßen (Ausbau und Neubau)
Flensburg
Husum
Schleswig
Rendsburg
Kiel
Neumünster
Itzehoe
Cuxhaven
Lübeck
Bad Oldesloe
HAMBURG
Wilhelmshaven
Bremerhaven
Norden
Emden
Leer
Stade
Lauenburg
Lüneburg
Oldenburg
BREMEN
Soltau
Uelzen
Walsrode
Meppen
Lingen
Diepholz
Nienburg
Celle
BERLIN
Osnabrück
Rheine
Bad Oeynhausen
HANNOVER
Braunschweig
Münster
Bielefeld
Hameln
Hildesheim
MAGDEBURG
Emmerich
Recklinghausen
Paderborn
Höxter
Seesen
Goslar
Oberhausen
DORTMUND
Kamen
Northeim
ESSEN
DÜSSELDF.
Wuppertal
Kassel
Göttingen
HALLE
M.Gladbach
Meschede
LEIPZIG
KÖLN
Bad Hersfeld
ERFURT
Aachen
Bonn
Siegen
Marburg
Alsfeld
Eisenach
DRESDEN
Gießen
Gera
CHEMNITZ
Wetzlar
Fulda
Plauen
Limburg
Koblenz
Bad Neustadt
Coburg
Kronach
Hof
FRANKFURT
Hanau
Wiesbaden
Aschaffenburg
Schweinfurt
Bitburg
Bingen
Mainz
Bayreuth
Marktredwitz
Trier
Bad Kreuznach
Darmstadt
Bamberg
Würzburg
Worms
Weiden
Ludwigshafen
Mannheim
Eberbach
Sulzbach
Saarbrücken
Kaiserslautern
Heidelberg
Mosbach
NÜRNBERG
Zweibrücken
Speyer
Ansbach
Schwandorf
Bruchsal
Cham
Karlsruhe
Heilbronn
Schwäb. Hall
Regensburg
Maßstab 1 : 2 900 000
Baden-Baden
Waiblingen
STUTTGART
Aalen
Plattling
Kehl
Herrenberg
Donauwörth
Tübingen
Wolnzach
Landshut
Passau
Offenburg
Freudenstadt
Ulm
Hausach
Augsburg
Mühldorf
Rottweil
Freiburg
Donaueschingen
Landsberg
MÜNCHEN
Memmingen
Rosenheim
Ravensburg
Friedrichshafen
Kempten
Salzburg
Lörrach
Waldshut
Basel
Konstanz
Lindau
Immenstadt
Garmisch-Partenkirchen
Kufstein
Berchtesgaden
Achenpaß
Der Bundesminister für Verkehr
Juni 1956

Von den im Ausbauplan vorgesehenen *Autobahnstrecken* sind seit Inkrafttreten des Verkehrsfinanzgesetzes rund 295 km gebaut worden. Außerdem befinden sich zur Zeit rund 266 km der Ersten Baustufe und rund 111 km der Zweiten Baustufe, zusammen also rund 377 km, im Bau.

Der Ausbauplan sieht außerdem den Ausbau des sogenannten *Grundnetzes der Bundesstraßen* vor. Insgesamt sollen rund 10.650 km Bundesstraßen — das sind rund 48% des Gesamtnetzes — in einer Weise ausgebaut werden, daß sie den zunehmenden Verkehrsanforderungen der nächsten zwanzig Jahre, also etwa einer Verdreifachung des heutigen Verkehrs, gerecht werden. Als Grundlage für die Ermittlung dieses Grundnetzes dienen die regelmäßig durchgeführten Straßenverkehrs-Zählungen. Sie geben einen klaren Überblick über den Verkehrswert und die Verkehrsbelastung der westdeutschen Bundesfernstraßen. Laut Ausbauplan sollen innerhalb des Grundnetzes 8.060 km Bundesstraßen (rund 76%) vollständig um- und ausgebaut werden. Hierin sind 515 km Ortsdurchfahrten in Gemeinden mit weniger als 9.000 Einwohnern enthalten. Außerdem sollen rund 1.050 km Bundesstraßen neu gebaut werden. Weitere 3.150 km kommen als Ortsumgehungen bei 1.114 Gemeinden hinzu. In gleichem Zusammenhang werden auf den vorhandenen Straßen alle rutschgefährlichen Pflasterstrecken beseitigt, frostempfindliche Strecken frostsicher ausgebaut, 242 höhengleiche Bahnübergänge beseitigt und 410 Kreuzungen dieser Art durch den Bau von Ortsumgehungen für den Fernverkehr ausgeschaltet. Schließlich sollen aus Gründen erhöhter Verkehrssicherheit 5.300 km Rad- und Mopedwege an Bundesstraßen gebaut werden. Darüber hinaus ist der Ausbau von Fremdenverkehrsstraßen vorgesehen, die vor allem im Interesse des Ausländerverkehrs landschaftlich besonders reizvolle Ausflugsgebiete erschließen sollen.

Die *Europastraßen* besitzen in Westdeutschland eine Gesamtlänge von rund 5.650 km, die etwa je zur Hälfte auf Bundesautobahnen und Bundesstraßen entfallen. Sie sind im Ausbauplan dieser Straßenkategorien vollständig mit erfaßt. Sobald der Plan durchgeführt sein wird, werden also auch die betreffenden E-Straßen gemäß der Genfer ECE-Konvention von 1950 ausgebaut sein.

Zur Durchführung des Gesetzes über den Ausbau der Bundesfernstraßen hat der Bundesminister für Verkehr ein Vierjahres-Programm für die Bundesfernstraßen vorgelegt. Es umfaßt die Rechnungsjahre 1959 bis 1962 und schließt einen Finanzbedarf von 8,0 bis 8,3 Milliarden DM ein. Darin sind als wichtigste Posten die Anforderungen für die Bundesstraßen mit rund 3,9 Milliarden DM und für die Bundesautobahnen mit rund 3 Milliarden DM enthalten. Mit Hilfe eines neuen Straßenbau-Finanzierungs-Gesetzes soll die noch bestehende Finanzierungslücke geschlossen werden.

Die Gesamtkosten des Ausbauplanes betragen 22,4 Milliarden DM. Die Bundesrepublik steht mit ihren Aufwendungen für den Straßenbau heute an erster Stelle unter allen europäischen Staaten. Die gesamten Ausgaben von Bund, Ländern, Gemeinden und Gemeindeverbänden für den Straßenbau beliefen sich

1950 auf 969 Millionen DM,
1954 auf 1.880 Millionen DM,
1957 auf 3.600 Millionen DM und betrugen
1958 über 4.000 Millionen DM.

Diese Zahlen umfassen das jährliche Straßenbauvolumen und geben demnach die effektiven Leistungen in diesem Sektor wieder. Nach Angaben der International Road Federation stand damit die Bundesrepublik 1957 an dritter Stelle hinter den USA und Kanada, 1958 an zweiter Stelle hinter den USA vor Kanada mit Bezug auf die Höhe der Ausgaben für den Straßenbau. Der durch die USA aufgewandte Betrag ist nominell rund zehnmal so hoch wie in der Bundesrepublik; diese liegt, bezogen auf den Quadratkilometer Fläche, aber mit den Ausgaben für den Straßenbau sogar vor den USA an erster Stelle.

Nach dem Stand vom 31.3.1959 beträgt die Gesamtlänge der Autobahnen in Westdeutschland 2.399 km gegenüber einer Länge von 2.116 km am 1.4.1950. Das Straßennetz der Bundesrepublik umfaßt außerdem 24.395 km Bundesstraßen, 56.700 km Landstraßen I. Ordnung und 48.672 km Landstraßen II. Ordnung. Das sind zusammen 132.166 km klassifizierte Straßen. Über die Gesamtlänge der Gemeindestraßen im Bundesgebiet liegen bisher noch keine genauen Zahlen vor. Sie werden auf rund 120.000 km geschätzt.

IV. DER AUSBAU DER WASSERSTRASSEN

Von den 1.270 über Wasserstraßen des Bundesgebietes führenden Brücken waren nach dem Kriege 968 zerstört, darunter sämtliche Rheinbrücken. Die Kanäle und Flüsse mußten von 370.000 t Stahl zertrümmerter oder beschädigter Brückenkonstruktionen, von 400.000 cbm Beton- und Mauerwerktrümmern und von 4.000 Wracks geräumt werden. Diese Arbeiten waren bis 1952 zum größten Teil abgeschlossen. Gleichzeitig damit begann

JUGEND

In der PESTALOZZI-Schule
zu Idstein (Taunus)

Im „Haus für alle“ in Baumholder (Rheinland-Pfalz) kann jeder Besucher seinen Neigungen in der Freizeit nachgehen

Im Schuldorf
Bergstraße: Kinder
unterrichten Kinder

Sozialfürsorge der
Farbenfabriken BAYER:

Altersheim —

— Poliklinik —

— Werkssiedlung

die Wasser- und Schiffahrtsverwaltung des Bundes mit dem planvollen Wiederaufbau. Die zerstörten Brücken wurden wieder hergestellt, die Wasserbauanlagen sowie die beschädigten Uferbefestigungen und Kanaldämme instandgesetzt. Außerdem waren die während des Krieges überall vernachlässigten Unterhaltungsarbeiten nachzuholen. Erst dann konnten neue Aufgaben in Angriff genommen werden.

Die günstige wirtschaftliche Entwicklung in der Bundesrepublik wirkte sich auch in einem stetig anwachsenden *Verkehr auf den Wasserstraßen* aus. Er hat den Vorkriegsstand überschritten und in den Jahren 1956 und 1957 Höchstwerte erreicht. Einzelne Wasserstraßen im Binnenbereich erreichen die Grenze ihrer Leistungsfähigkeit. Die zunehmende Motorisierung der Binnenschiffahrt zwang zu einer Verstärkung der Unterhaltungsarbeiten an den schiffbaren Flüssen und Kanälen. Insbesondere machten die größere durchschnittliche Fahrgeschwindigkeit der Motorgüterschiffe und die dadurch bedingten mechanischen Angriffe auf die Uferböschungen und die Sohle der Fahrrinnen eine Anpassung der Wasserstraßen an die veränderten Verkehrsverhältnisse notwendig. Im Küstenbereich nahmen die Abmessungen der Seeschiffe weiter zu. Besonders die anhaltende Tendenz zur Vergrößerung ihrer Tauchtiefen kennzeichnet hier die wichtigsten wasserbaulichen Aufgaben. Neben dem Bestreben, die vorhandenen Tiefen des Fahrwassers aller von Seeschiffen befahrenen Wasserstraßen zu erhalten, mußte Vorsorge getroffen werden, die Fahrrinnen in den Zufahrten zu den Seehäfen noch weiter zu vertiefen.

Nach dem Kriege wurden nur diejenigen großen Bauvorhaben wieder aufgenommen, die bereits begonnen oder geplant und durch den Krieg unterbrochen waren. Dabei handelt es sich grundsätzlich um Wasserstraßen, die verkehrspolitisch besonders wichtig sind. Um die zur Verfügung stehenden Mittel volkswirtschaftlich möglichst wirkungsvoll zu verwenden, wurden sie im wesentlichen für Baumaßnahmen im Rahmen eines Schwerpunktprogramms eingesetzt. Dazu gehört vor allem der Anschluß der deutschen Seehäfen durch Wasserstraßen, die für 2,50 m Abladetiefe — also das 1.000-t-Schiff — ausgebaut sind, an das mitteldeutsche Fluß- und Kanalnetz. Es handelt sich insbesondere um den Ausbau des Dortmund-Ems-Kanals, die Fertigstellung der Kanalisierung der Mittelweser, die Errichtung einer Staustufe mit Schleuse und Wehr bei Geesthacht an der Elbe, die Fortsetzung der Kanalisierung des Neckars bis Stuttgart sowie die Fortsetzung der Kanalisierung des Mains zwischen Würzburg und Bamberg und die Niederwasser-Regulierung der Donau bis Regensburg im Zuge der Rhein-Main-

Donau-Großschiffahrtsstraße. Ferner wurde mit der im Oktober 1956 vertraglich zwischen Deutschland, Frankreich und Luxemburg vereinbarten Schiffbarmachung der Mosel begonnen.

Durch die gezielte Investitionspolitik der Bundesregierung konnten die genannten Bauvorhaben teilweise schon weit vorangetrieben werden. Die Arbeiten zur Erweiterung des Dortmund-Ems-Kanals sind im wesentlichen durchgeführt, so daß noch im Jahre 1959 der Verkehr mit 2,50 m tief gehenden Fahrzeugen aufgenommen werden kann. An der Mittelweser ist die letzte der sieben Staustufen zwischen Minden und Bremen im Bau. Auch sie wird voraussichtlich im Jahre 1960 fertiggestellt sein. Am Neckar wurde am 31. 3. 1958 der neue Stuttgarter Hafen eröffnet. Nach einer Gesamtbauzeit von siebenunddreißig Jahren hat damit die Kanalisierung des Neckars einen vorläufigen Abschluß gefunden. Auch bei der Fortsetzung der Kanalisierung des Mains konnten die Arbeiten so weit gefördert werden, daß im Jahre 1959 die Stadt Schweinfurt an die Großschiffahrtsstraße angeschlossen und 1961 voraussichtlich Bamberg erreicht sein wird. An der Donau waren die Arbeiten zur Niedrigwasser-Regulierung bereits so erfolgreich, daß der Hafen Regensburg sich zum größten deutschen Donauhafen entwickeln konnte.

Neben der Entwicklung der Binnenwasserstraßen wurde der Ausbau der *Wasserstraßen im Küstenbereich* tatkräftig in Angriff genommen, um den immer größer werdenden Frachtschiffen des Weltverkehrs weiterhin den Zugang zu den deutschen Seehäfen zu ermöglichen. Zu diesem Zweck wird die Zufahrt nach Emden von 7 m auf 8 m bei Niedrigwasser verbessert. Die Fahrwasser der Außenweser unterhalb Bremerhavens und der Elbe zwischen Hamburg und Cuxhaven sollen durchgehend auf 11 m unter Niedrigwasser vertieft werden. In Wilhelmshaven wurde eine neue private Anlage für den Ölumschlag in Betrieb genommen. Ihre Zufahrt von der See her ist auf 12 m unter Niedrigwasser tief ausgebaggert.

Am Nord-Ostsee-Kanal, der nach der Zahl der verkehrenden Schiffe der am stärksten befahrene Seekanal der Welt ist, wird die planmäßige Fahrwassertiefe von 11 m durch Baggerungen wieder hergestellt. Die deutschen *Seehäfen* konnten im Jahre 1957 wiederum eine Umschlagsleistung von 61,3 Millionen Gütertonnen aufweisen.

Zugleich mit dem Ausbau der Wasserstraßen für die Schiffahrt wurde der Energiewirtschaft die Möglichkeit geboten, das an den Staustufen vorhandene Gefälle für die Anlage von *Wasserkraftwerken* auszunutzen. Dabei wurden in den letzten zehn Jahren nach dem Kriege an Elbe, Weser, Neckar, Main und Donau insgesamt vierundzwanzig Wasserkraftwerke mit einer mittleren Jahreserzeugung von 1.630 Millionen Kilowattstunden (kWh) errichtet. Darunter befindet sich das zur Zeit größte Laufwasser-Kraftwerk Mitteleuropas an der Donau bei Jochenstein. Es erzeugt allein 960 Millionen Kilowattstunden. Weitere siebzehn Kraftwerke mit zusammen rund einer Milliarde Kilowattstunden sind an Donau, Mosel und Weser geplant beziehungsweise im Bau.

Die entscheidende Bedeutung der großen Wasserläufe für die Brauch-, Kühl- und Trinkwasserversorgung von Industrie und Siedlungen, für Landwirtschaft, Fischerei, Abwasseraufnahme, Sport und Volkserholung darf ebenfalls nicht unerwähnt bleiben.

Über den Haushalt des Bundesministers für Verkehr wurden von 1949 bis 1957 für Investitionen und Unterhaltungsarbeiten an den Bundeswasserstraßen insgesamt 2.123 Millionen DM ausgegeben. In einem neuen Vierjahres-Programm für den Ausbau der Bundeswasserstraßen im Binnen- und Küstenbereich sind für die Jahre 1959 bis 1962 Investitionen des Bundes in Höhe von rund 575 Millionen DM vorgesehen. Davon entfallen jährlich rund 90 Millionen DM auf Maßnahmen im Binnenbereich, während für den Küstenbereich rund 54 Millionen DM vorgesehen sind.

V. DIE BINNENSCHIFFAHRT

Rund ein Viertel des Güterschiffraums der Binnenflotte war nach dem Zusammenbruch endgültig verloren, ein weiteres Viertel fahruntauglich. Ein ähnliches Bild bot der Schlepperbestand. Einen weiteren Aderlaß bedeuteten die Forderungen ausländischer Staaten auf Herausgabe von Binnenschiffen, die zwar unter ausländischer Flagge fuhren, aber wirtschaftliches Eigentum deutscher Schiffahrtsunternehmer waren.

Bis zur Währungsreform waren nur behelfsmäßige Reparaturen der Flotte möglich. Erst 1949 konnte eine planmäßige Erneuerung einsetzen. Dabei waren die Fortschritte der Schiffbautechnik, die zu erwartenden gesteigerten Anforderungen an die Transportleistung und der Wettbewerb der modernen Flotten der Nachbarländer zu beachten. Andererseits sollten bei einem Verkehrsrückgang nicht allzu große Reserven ungenutzt liegen bleiben. Als Lösung ergaben sich die *verstärkte Motorisierung* der Flotte und die *Entwicklung bestimmter Schiffstypen*.

Die fahrfähige Flotte mit einer Tragfähigkeit von 2,7 Millionen t hat seit Anfang 1949 sich alljährlich im Durchschnitt um 200.000 t vermehrt. Sie umfaßte Anfang 1959 rund 4,6 Millionen t gegenüber 4,8 Millionen t als

Bestand des der Bundesrepublik entsprechenden Gebietes im Jahre 1938. Die Wiederherstellung der Kapazität der Flotte geschah in den ersten Jahren im wesentlichen durch die Instandsetzung und den Umbau des kriegsbeschädigten Raums, später zunehmend durch Neubauten.

Die Entwicklung des Frachtraumes erhält ihren besonderen Akzent durch den bevorzugten Neubau von Motor-Güterschiffen und die Motorisierung von Schleppkähnen. Von 1949 bis 1958 wurden über 840.000 t Frachtraum neu gebaut, davon 775.000 t Motorschiffsraum. Durch den Umbau von Schleppkähnen wurden weitere 640.000 t Motorschiffstonnage gewonnen. Damit stieg der Grad der Motorisierung, der Anfang 1949 nur 15,3% betrug, bis Ende 1958 auf 43,7% an. Die Kapazität der heutigen Flotte hat raummäßig noch nicht den Bestand von 1938 erreicht. Trotzdem liegt sie über der Leistungsfähigkeit des der Bundesrepublik entsprechenden Gebietes des Deutschen Reiches von 1938. Ein annäherndes Bild dieses Anstiegs vermitteln die nachstehenden Zahlen:

Eine Tonne Tragfähigkeit leistete im Durchschnitt jährlich:

1913	2.486 tkm	1953..........	4.021 tkm
1928	2.226 tkm	1954..........	4.142 tkm
1936	2.664 tkm	1955..........	4.490 tkm
1949	2.372 tkm	1956..........	4.805 tkm
1951	4.031 tkm	1957..........	4.845 tkm
1952	4.035 tkm		

Berücksichtigt man, daß durch strukturelle Wandlungen des Verkehrs heute mehr Leerfahrten als früher notwendig sind, so kann man, vor allem dank der Motorisierung, von einer Verdopplung der Durchschnittsleistungen des einzelnen Schiffes in den letzten fünfundvierzig Jahren sprechen.

Auch Neubau und Modernisierung der Schleppkraft wurden nicht vernachlässigt. Schlepper mit zusammen 39.000 PS wurden neu gebaut. Der Anteil der Motorschlepper beläuft mit 221.000 PS sich auf mehr als zwei Drittel der in der Binnenflotte insgesamt vorhandenen Schleppkraft von 320.000 PS.

Ohne Kredithilfen der öffentlichen Hand und steuerliche Förderungsmaßnahmen, an denen die Binnenschiffahrt wie die übrige private Wirtschaft teilnehmen konnte, wäre ein Neuaufbau der Flotte in dem erstrebten Umfang nicht möglich gewesen.

Der Zustand der Wasserstraßen und der Flotte ermöglichten der Binnenschiffahrt in den ersten Nachkriegsjahren geringe und nur langsam steigende

Transportleistungen. Sie blieben weit hinter denen der anderen Binnenverkehrsträger zurück. Zudem waren der deutschen Binnenschiffahrt bis zum Ende des Jahres 1949 Fahrten im grenzüberschreitenden Verkehr nicht erlaubt. Ab 1950 setzte eine anhaltende Aufwärtsbewegung ein. Die deutsche und die ausländischen Flaggen nahmen an ihr gleichmäßig teil. Die Durchführung der Ausbaumaßnahmen an den deutschen Wasserstraßen gestattete der Binnenschiffahrt einen nach modernen Gesichtspunkten eingerichteten Verkehr. Sie konnte sich dabei im Jahre 1957 an der Gesamtverkehrsleistung von 114,3 Milliarden Tonnenkilometern mit 29,5% beteiligen. Im gleichen Jahr entfielen auf den Güterverkehr der Eisenbahnen 54,6% und auf den der Straße 15,9%.

VI. DIE DEUTSCHE FLAGGE AUF DEN WELTMEEREN

Von der deutschen Vorkriegs-Handelsflotte von über 4 Millionen BRT war nach der Kapitulation nur ein Rest von 118.000 BRT übriggeblieben. Noch im Herbst 1949 verfügte die Bundesrepublik über nur 248.000 BRT. Die Lage der deutschen Seeschiffahrt nach dem Zweiten Weltkrieg unterschied sich grundlegend von der nach dem Jahre 1918. Damals bestand kein Verbot der Seeschiffahrt und des Baues von Handelsschiffen. Werften, Entwicklungs-, Forschungs- und Lehrwerkstätten waren vollständig erhalten geblieben. Unmittelbar nach Kriegsschluß konnte daher mit dem Wiederaufbau der Handelsflotte begonnen werden. 1945 dagegen verbot das Potsdamer Abkommen zunächst jeglichen Bau von Seeschiffen. Die Kontrollrats-Direktive Nr. 37 gestattete später nur Ersatzbauten für die verbliebene Restflotte. Die Größe des einzelnen Schiffes blieb auf 1.500 BRT, die Geschwindigkeit auf 12 Knoten beschränkt. Nach langen mühevollen Verhandlungen mit den Alliierten erreichte die Bundesregierung schrittweise den Abbau aller Beschränkungen.

Der erste Erfolg wurde bereits im November 1949 mit dem Petersberg-Abkommen erzielt, durch das die Fesseln im Schiffbau und in der Schiffahrt wenigstens gelockert wurden. Durch das Abkommen über die Industriekontrollen vom 3.4.1951 wurden die Beschränkungen, die der deutschen Handelsflotte hinderlich waren, nahezu völlig beseitigt.

Der Weg für den Wiederaufbau war damit endlich frei. Die Bundesrepublik konnte sich eine Handelsflotte schaffen, die ihren Wirtschaftsbedürfnissen entspricht. Aber noch waren nicht alle Schwierigkeiten überwunden. Die Großwerften Westdeutschlands waren zum größten Teil zerstört oder demontiert. Die Reeder hatten mit ihrer Flotte nahezu ihr gesamtes Sachvermögen verloren. Darum war es die nächste Aufgabe, den Wiederaufbau der Handelsschiffahrt finanziell zu ermöglichen. Das war umso schwieriger, als die Flotte mit Rücksicht auf die Verhältnisse auf dem Weltmarkt privatwirtschaftlich aufgebaut werden mußte. Ein Schritt auf diesem Wege ist das Gesetz über Darlehen zum Bau und Erwerb von Handelsschiffen vom 27.9.1950. Bis zum 31.3.1959 hat der Bund auf Grund dieses Gesetzes aus Haushaltsmitteln 475 Millionen DM für Darlehen bereitgestellt. Darüber hinaus sind bis zu diesem Zeitpunkt aus ERP-Gegenwertmitteln sowie aus ERP-Rückflüssen 387 Millionen DM für Darlehen zur Verfügung gestellt worden. Aus Mitteln zur Arbeitsbeschaffung sind dem Schiffbau 23,5 Millionen DM zugeflossen. Zur Vorfinanzierung weiterer Investitionen hat das Bundesverkehrsministerium den Banken, die sich mit der Finanziernug des Schiffbaus befassen, einen Zentralbank-Rediskontkredit verschafft.

Endlich haben die Steuerpolitik und die Steuergesetzgebung des Bundes den Wiederaufbau der Handelsflotte lebhaft begünstigt. Die Möglichkeiten der Abschreibung, die das Einkommensteuergesetz dem Reeder bis Mitte 1958 bot, gestatteten in erhöhtem Maße die Finanzierung mit Eigenmitteln. Besonders trugen aber steuerbegünstigte Darlehen und Zuschüsse nach § 7d Absatz 2 des Einkommensteuergesetzes mit einem Gesamtbetrag von rund 1,5 Milliarden DM wesentlich zum Wiederaufbau der deutschen Seeschiffahrt bei. Insgesamt sind mit wesentlicher Unterstützung der Bundesregierung in der Zeit vom 1.9.1949 bis zum 31.12.1957 nahezu 5 Milliarden DM in die wiedererstandene deutsche Handelsflotte investiert worden.

*

Die Erfolge dieser Aufbau- und Finanzierungspolitik sind nicht ausgeblieben. Durch Neubauten, Ankäufe im Ausland und Instandsetzung gehobener Wracks stieg der Bestand der Handelsflotte von 248.000 BRT am 1.9.1949 auf 740.000 BRT am 1.1.1951. Am 1.1.1952 waren bereits wieder 1.160.000 BRT unter der Bundesflagge in Fahrt.

Am 1.1.1959 schließlich betrug die Tonnage an Seeschiffen 4.664.260 BRT. Davon sind mit Hilfe des Bundes rund 2.300.000 BRT gebaut oder aus dem Ausland erworben und weitere 515.000 BRT außerhalb der Schiffbauprogramme unter Ausnutzung des § 7d des Einkommensteuergesetzes in Dienst gestellt worden.

BESTAND DER DEUTSCHEN HANDELSFLOTTE AM 1. JANUAR 1959

Seeschiffe (über 50 m³ = 17,65 Reg. Tons Brutto-Raumgehalt)	Anzahl	BRT
1. Frachtschiffe		
a) Trockenladungsschiffe	2.459	3.715.288
b) Tanker	104	509.815
c) Kombinierte Fracht-Fahrgastschiffe	20	174.463
2. Fahr-, Förde- und Bäderschiffe	125	33.189
Handelsflotte insgesamt:	2.708	4.442.755
Dazu:		
3. Frachtschiffe ohne Antrieb	28	10.389
4. Seefischerei-Fahrzeuge	881	167.308
5. Andere nicht eigentlichen Handelszwecken dienende Fahrzeuge	359	53.808
Seeschiffe insgesamt:	3.976	4.664.260

Quelle: Bundesministerium für Verkehr.

Nicht nur den Werften hat der Wiederaufbau Aufträge gebracht. Er hat darüber hinaus die gesamte Wirtschaft des Bundesgebietes stark belebt; denn etwa die Hälfte aller investierten Mittel kommt den Zulieferungsindustrien des Binnenlandes und ihren Beschäftigten zugute.

Am 23.2.1951 trat das Flaggenrechtsgesetz in Kraft. Von diesem Tage an führen die Seeschiffe der Bundesrepublik die Bundesflagge „Schwarz-Rot-Gold". Sie ist damit wieder auf den Weltmeeren und in den großen Häfen des Weltverkehrs erschienen.

Im Laufe der Jahre begann die wachsende deutsche Handelsflotte ihre alten Verkehrsgebiete gegen oft recht schwere ausländische Konkurrenz zurückzugewinnen. Bis Mitte 1949 war nur der Linienverkehr nach Dänemark, Schweden, Finnland, Großbritannien, Holland und Belgien wiederaufgenommen. Die weiteren Monate des Jahres 1949 brachten die Wiederaufnahme der Dienste nach Spanien, Portugal und der Levante. 1950 folgten Dienste nach Westindien, Kuba/Mexiko, der Ostküste Nordamerikas und dem Golf von Mexiko, 1951 nach Nordbrasilien, dem Persischen Golf und Pakistan, den Kanarischen Inseln, West- und Südafrika, der Ostküste Südamerikas, Kanada und den Großen Seen, 1952 nach Indien, Anfang 1953 nach der Westküste Südamerikas. Mit dem fortschreitenden Ausbau der Flotte wurden weitere Dienste des Linienverkehrs, wie nach der Westküste

Nordamerikas, nach dem Fernen Osten und Australien, mit deutschen Schiffen aufgenommen. Heute befährt die deutsche Handelsflotte wieder alle Weltmeere.

Deutsche Reeder haben in den letzten Jahren auch die Zusammenarbeit mit ausländischen Reedern wieder aufnehmen können und sind Mitglieder zahlreicher Schiffahrtskonferenzen geworden, in denen die internationale Linienschiffahrt der einzelnen überseeischen Verkehrsrichtungen sich zusammenschließt. Der Verband Deutscher Reeder gehört der International Chamber of Shipping an. Damit ist er wieder vollberechtigtes Mitglied einer internationalen Organisation, in der fast alle Reedervereinigungen der Welt zusammengeschlossen sind.

*

Die verkehrspolitische Lage der deutschen *Seehäfen* hat durch den Ausgang des Zweiten Weltkrieges einen grundlegenden Wandel erfahren. Durch den quer durch Europa gezogenen Eisernen Vorhang haben die Hafenplätze weitgehend ihre Verbindungen zu wichtigen Teilen des Hinterlandes verloren. Neben den schweren Zerstörungen durch den Luftkrieg ist dieser Verlust die wesentliche Ursache dafür, daß der Verkehr der deutschen Seehäfen während der Nachkriegsjahre sich nicht gleich günstig hat entwickeln können wie der europäischer Wettbewerbshäfen. Die deutschen Seehäfen sind im Vergleich zu den Häfen an der Rheinmündung ständig in der Entwicklung des Verkehrs zurückgeblieben. Sie erreichten im Jahre 1955 nur etwa 110% des Vorkriegsstandes[1], während die niederländischen Seehäfen zirka 168% erzielen konnten.

Aus diesem Zurückbleiben ergab sich die Aufgabe, die politisch bedingten Nachteile für die deutschen Seehäfen nach Möglichkeit auszugleichen und ihre Entwicklung durch geeignete Maßnahmen zu fördern. Diese Aufgabe betrachtet die Bundesregierung nicht nur als eine deutsche, sondern als eine gesamteuropäische. Diesen Standpunkt hat sie immer wieder in Verhandlungen mit westeuropäischen Ländern vertreten.

Die Grundlagen der Tarifpolitik der Seehäfen sind in einer Entscheidung des Bundesministers für Verkehr vom 16.5.1951 festgelegt. Sie regelt sowohl das Wettbewerbsverhältnis der deutschen Seehäfen gegenüber den Häfen an der Rheinmündung als auch der deutschen Seehäfen untereinander.

Eine weitere wichtige Aufgabe des Bundesverkehrsministeriums wird sein, die Verkehrsstellung der deutschen Seehäfen in dem kommenden Gemein-

[1] Durchschnitt der Jahre 1936/38.

samen Markt zu sichern. Durch die Aufstellung von Grundsätzen für den Verkehr, für das Zollwesen, den Handel, das Steuerwesen usw. werden nicht nur für binnenländische Verkehrstreibende neue Voraussetzungen geschaffen, sondern auch für die deutschen Seehäfenplätze, die im Gemeinsamen Markt im Gegensatz zu ihrer Lage im deutschen Reichsgebiet sich in einer Randlage befinden werden.

VII. DER LUFTVERKEHR

Nach 1945 war Deutschland jede Betätigung auf dem Gebiet der Luftfahrt durch die Besatzungsmächte untersagt worden.

Noch im Zeitraum der Errichtung der Bundesrepublik oblagen sämtliche Zuständigkeiten in Angelegenheiten der Luftfahrt den Alliierten. Diese hatten hierfür ein „Ziviles Alliiertes Luftamt" gebildet. Nach allmählicher Lockerung der Verbote wurde am 5.5.1955 die deutsche Lufthoheit wieder hergestellt. Bereits am 6.8.1954 war die *Deutsche Lufthansa AG.* wiedergegründet worden. Sie ging aus der „Aktiengesellschaft für Luftverkehrsbedarf" hervor, die am 6.1.1953 — genau 27 Jahre nach Gründung der alten Lufthansa — ins Leben gerufen wurde.

Der Start der Deutschen Lufthansa war nicht leicht. Sie mußte aus dem Nichts neu anfangen und stieß auf die schärfste Konkurrenz wohlausgebauter alter Luftverkehrsunternehmen, die in Erfahrung und Organisation teilweise einen Vorsprung von über zehn Jahren hatten.

Angesichts dieser Lage mußte die Deutsche Lufthansa in ihrer Planung sehr vorsichtig vorgehen. Sie hatte einen alten guten Ruf zu verteidigen. Daher war sie, um jedes Risiko auszuschalten, genötigt, zwar modernstes, aber nur in jeder Hinsicht erprobtes Fluggerät zum Aufbau zu verwenden. Auf Grund der Planung des Streckennetzes ergab sich die Notwendigkeit, vorerst je ein Muster für die Mittelstrecken und für den Langstreckendienst auszuwählen. Die Wahl fiel auf die bewährte zweimotorige Convair 340 der Consolidated Vultee Aircraft Company und die viermotorige Super-Constellation 1049 der Firma Lockheed. Von jedem Muster wurden zunächst vier Flugzeuge bestellt.

Am 15.5.1955 flog die Deutsche Lufthansa nach London, Paris und Madrid. Am 8.6.1955 startete erstmals eine Super-Constellation der Lufthansa über den Nordatlantik über Shannon nach New York. Im Oktober 1955 wurde die Spanienstrecke bis Lissabon weitergeführt. Für den innerdeutschen Zubringerverkehr wurden zusätzlich zwei DC 3 in Dienst gestellt.

Die Deutsche Lufthansa beförderte 1956 in ihrem ersten vollen Betriebsjahr 229.670 Passagiere, 1.990 t Fracht und 1.050 t Post. Gegenüber den acht Monaten des Jahres 1955 betrug die Zahl der Fluggäste das 3,1fache. Die Fracht erhöhte sich um das 3,6fache und die Postbeförderung um das 2,9fache. Der Sommerflugplan 1956 brachte bereits eine beträchtliche Erweiterung mit der Eröffnung neuer Strecken über Montreal nach Chikago und über Paris nach New York. Insgesamt unterhielt die Lufthansa vom 22.4.1956 an elf wöchentliche Verbindungen über den Nordatlantik in beiden Richtungen. Mit der Indienststellung von vier weiteren Super-Constellation wurde im August und September 1956 die Aufnahme des Verkehrs nach Südamerika (Rio de Janeiro, São Paulo, Buenos Aires) und nach dem Mittleren Osten (Istanbul, Beirut, Damaskus, Bagdad, Teheran) ermöglicht.

Heute befliegt die Deutsche Lufthansa ein Liniennetz von fast doppelter Äquatorlänge. Ihre Flugzeuge legen in jeder Woche nahezu eine halbe Million Flugkilometer zurück. Hierbei werden fünfunddreißig Städte in vierundzwanzig Staaten Europas, Asiens, Afrikas sowie Nord- und Südamerikas planmäßig angeflogen.

Diese Leistungen werden erbracht mit einer Flotte von zwölf Langstreckenflugzeugen der Muster Lockheed L 1649 A „Super Star" und L 1049 E „Super-Constellation", neun Mittelstreckenflugzeugen des Musters Convair 440 „Metropolitan" und drei Kurzstreckenflugzeugen des Musters Douglas DC 3. Auf reinen Frachtstrecken wurde ferner ein Flugzeug vom Muster DC 4 eingesetzt.

Für den kommenden Düsenluftverkehr hat die Lufthansa vier Flugzeuge vom Muster Boeing 707 „Intercontinental" in Auftrag gegeben, deren Lieferung für das Jahr 1960 vorgesehen ist. Ferner wurden für 1958/59 neun Vickers „Viscount" 814 bestellt. Sie werden den Mittelstreckendienst erheblich verstärken.

Im innerdeutschen Verkehr, der sich noch immer auf das Bundesgebiet (ohne Berlin) beschränken muß, verdichtete die Lufthansa ihre Verbindungen zwischen den nunmehr sämtlich angeflogenen neun Flughäfen im Bundesgebiet. Bei wöchentlich 300 Flügen bietet sie hier 13.000 Plätze an.

Auf dem europäischen Kontinent wurden nach Frankreich, dem Vereinigten Königreich, Spanien, Portugal, Irland, Dänemark, Österreich und der Schweiz nunmehr auch Belgien und Italien in das Liniennetz einbezogen. Luftverkehrsverbindungen zwischen zwanzig europäischen Flughäfen waren damit hergestellt. Abgesehen von der Verwendung schnelleren Fluggeräts konnten die Reisezeiten durch eine geschickte Gestaltung des Flugplans und eine Verbesserung der Linienanschlüsse beträchtlich verkürzt werden.

Wie in den Vorjahren lag auch 1958 das Schwergewicht auf den *interkontinentalen Flugstrecken.* Diese entsprechen der strukturellen Eigenart des Luftverkehrs am meisten und sind daher auch ökonomisch besonders aussichtsreich. Auf der im Vordergrund stehenden Luftbrücke über den Nordatlantik ermöglichte die Indienststellung von vier „Super-Star"-Flugzeugen in den Spitzen-Reisezeiten des Sommers 1958 die Durchführung von wöchentlich fünfzehn Flügen zwischen der Bundesrepublik und Nordamerika. Zwölf davon führten nach New York und drei über Montreal nach Chikago. Im Sommer 1957 hatten auf dieser wichtigen Ader des Weltverkehrs wöchentlich nur neun Kurse bestanden. Auch der Verkehr über den Südatlantik wurde durch einen dritten Wochenflug verstärkt. Durch die Verlängerung des Dienstes bis Santiago de Chile wurde die Verbindung erneuert, die zwischen Deutschland und der Küste des Pazifik bereits von der alten Lufthansa vor dem Zweiten Weltkrieg hergestellt worden war. Die Fluglinien nach dem Mittleren Osten erfuhren durch günstigere Flugplanzeiten ebenfalls weitere Verbesserungen. Neu wurde mit Beginn des Winterflugplans 1958/59 Kairo angeflogen.

Auch auf den deutschen *Verkehrsflughäfen* war ein kräftiger Aufschwung zu verzeichnen. In dem Zeitraum von September 1957 bis August 1958 gestaltete sich der gewerbliche Luftverkehr auf den Verkehrsflughäfen der Bundesrepublik und von Berlin(West) gegenüber dem entsprechenden ein Jahr zurückliegenden Zeitraum folgendermaßen:

Tabelle 7

GEWERBLICHER LUFTVERKEHR

	1956/57	1957/58	Zu- (+) bzw. Abnahme (—) 1957/58 gegenüber 1956/57 in %
Bewegungen (Starts und Landungen)	224.661	250.137	+ *11,3*
Fluggäste (Einsteiger und Aussteiger) ...	3.818.731	4.572.302	+ *19,7*
Luftfracht in t (Versand und Empfang) .	66.978	51.392	— *23,3*
Luftpost in t (Versand und Empfang) ...	12.655	13.748	+ *8,6*

Quelle: Bundesministerium für Verkehr.

Das ständige Anwachsen des Luftverkehrs und die Fortschritte der Luftfahrttechnik brachten einen weiteren Ausbau der Verkehrsflughäfen mit sich. So wurden Rollbahnen und Abfertigungs-Vorfelder verstärkt, erneuert und erweitert, Flugzeughallen, Empfangs- und Frachtgebäude vergrößert und ortsfeste Anlagen zur Flugsicherung ergänzt. Die Verlängerung der Startbahnen mehrerer Flughäfen wurde vorbereitet.

Im kommenden Jahr wird auch in der Bundesrepublik der planmäßige Luftverkehr mit strahlgetriebenen Großflugzeugen für interkontinentale Dienste sowie auf Mittelstrecken einsetzen. Die Vorbereitungen auf dem Gebiet der Bodenorganisation wurden mit Nachdruck vorangetrieben. Mit den vielfältigen Problemen, die sich aus der Einführung der Strahlflugzeuge in der Zivilluftfahrt ergeben, befaßten sich unter anderem der vom Bundesminister für Verkehr berufene Luftfahrtbeirat sowie die Arbeitsgemeinschaft Deutscher Verkehrsflughäfen. Sie berücksichtigten dabei die von der Internationalen Zivilluftfahrt-Organisation gegebenen Richtlinien und Empfehlungen für den Düsen-Luftverkehr. Der erste Absprunghafen für die interkontinentalen Düsenverkehrsflugzeuge wird in der Bundesrepublik der Verkehrsflughafen Frankfurt am Main sein. Auf ihm werden auch umfangreiche Wartungsbauten vorbereitet, die dort bei Umkehrflügen von Düsenflugzeugen der Deutschen Lufthansa benötigt werden. Der Ausbau eines weiteren Flughafens zur Aufnahme interkontinentaler Düsenverkehrsflugzeuge ist in Nordrhein-Westfalen vorgesehen.

Die Gesamtzahl der Landeplätze zur Ausübung des Motorflugsports, der Durchführung von Reiseflügen und der gewerblichen Betätigung unter Verwendung von Kleinflugzeugen wurde gegenüber dem Vorjahr erheblich vermehrt. Die Anlage zahlreicher weiterer Landeplätze wurde eingeleitet.

Der deutschen Zivilluftfahrt stehen in der Bundesrepublik (außer Berlin [West]) nunmehr neun Verkehrsflughäfen, neunzig Landeplätze und etwa fünfhundertfünfzig Segelfluggelände zur Verfügung.

DER NACHRICHTENVERKEHR

I. DAS POSTWESEN

Nach den Einschränkungen der Jahre 1945 bis 1948 sind Inanspruchnahme und Leistungen aller Postdienstzweige erheblich angestiegen. Hierfür ein Beispiel:

Im Jahre 1950 wurden 4,2 Milliarden Briefsendungen befördert; 1958 waren es 7,7 Milliarden. Die daraus folgende immer stärkere Belastung aller Posteinrichtungen zwang die Deutsche Bundespost, ihren Betrieb diesen Anforderungen anzupassen — sei es durch organisatorische Vereinfachungen und Verbesserungen oder durch den Einsatz technischer Mittel. Der Zwang zur Rationalisierung ergab sich aber auch aus der zunehmenden Verknappung der Arbeitskräfte.

Im *Postbeförderungsdienst* ist der Aufbau eines modernen Bahnpostwagen-Parks abgeschlossen. Der Bestand an Bahnpostwagen belief sich in den ersten Nachkriegsjahren auf 1.000; heute beträgt er 1.800. Weit über ein Drittel davon sind Neubauten. Die übrigen wurden dem Entwicklungsstand der Technik durch Umbau angepaßt. Um den Dienstablauf zu rationalisieren, ist das Verfahren bei der Übernahme und Übergabe der Postsendungen während des Beförderungslaufs weitgehend vereinfacht worden. Die Verkürzung der Fahrzeiten bei der Deutschen Bundesbahn führte dazu, die Bahnposten über weite Strecken ohne Personal- und Wagenwechsel durchlaufen zu lassen. Ein Gewinn an Arbeitszeit und eine bessere Ausnutzung des Wagenparks waren die Folge. Die Verkürzung der Haltezeiten machte den Einsatz technischer Mittel zur Beschleunigung des Austauschs der Ladung an den Bahnpostwagen erforderlich. Hierfür sind Rollenplatten und Hubwagen entwickelt worden, mit denen die Post innerhalb von Sekunden aus dem Bahnpostwagen heraus- und in den Wagen hineingefahren werden kann.

Im Nah- und Zubringerverkehr wird die Beförderung von Postsachen, soweit wirtschaftlich und lohnend, von der Schiene auf die Straße umgestellt. Der — vielfach durch Wegfall von Dampfzügen der Deutschen Bundesbahn auf Nebenstrecken verursachte — Einsatz von Kraftfahrzeugen im Nahverkehr führte zu günstigerer Beförderung und damit zu besseren Laufzeiten.

Das Schwergewicht der Beförderung, insbesondere im Fernverkehr, liegt jedoch weiterhin auf der Schiene. Die Bahn befördert nach wie vor 90% aller Postsendungen. Zur Beschleunigung, Erleichterung und Verbilligung des Umschlags werden in zunehmendem Maße Behälter verwendet.

Um dem wachsenden Anfall von Sendungen im *Briefverteildienst* mit einem Mindestmaß an Kräften begegnen zu können, wurden die Briefverteilstellen kleinerer Ämter zu zentralen Verteilstellen bei verkehrsgünstig gelegenen Postämtern zusammengefaßt. Infolge der großen Zahl der hier zur Bearbeitung anfallenden Sendungen wird eine feinere Verteilarbeit möglich. Sie führt zur Entlastung der Bahnposten und der Briefdurchgangsämter und verbessert die Betriebsgüte. Bisher sind rund 800 kleine Briefverteilstellen aufgehoben oder in ihrer Arbeit erheblich eingeschränkt worden. Die Zentralisierung des Briefverteildienstes bildet aber auch die Voraussetzung für eine möglichst weitgehende maschinelle Bearbeitung der Briefsendungen. Endziel dieser Entwicklung ist die automatische Briefverteilung.

Das System der *Briefzustellung* befindet sich in der Umstellung nach modernen und wirtschaftlichen Gesichtspunkten. Zu diesem Zweck wird die Einrichtung von Hausbriefkästen durch Werbung und Mitfinanzierung gefördert. In die Aktion sind 255 Städte, das heißt fast alle Städte mit mehr als 20.000 Einwohnern, einbezogen. Ein größerer Teil ist bereits zu mehr als 90% mit Hausbriefkästen ausgestattet. Die Verwendung von Mopeds und Kleinkraftfahrzeugen im Orts- und Landzustelldienst unterstützt diese Umstellung.

Technische Neuerungen setzen auch im *Schalterverkehr* sich immer mehr durch, so die Maschinen für die Annahme von Postanweisungen und Zahlkarten, die sogenannten „stummen Postämter“ mit Wertzeichengeber, Münzwechsler, Fernsprecher und Briefkasten und die Hand-Schalter-Wertzeichengeber für den Schalterbeamten.

*

Im *Postreisedienst* nahm die Zahl der Fahrgäste seit 1956 nicht mehr so stark zu wie in den vorangegangenen Jahren. 1958 ist sie sogar leicht zurückgegangen. Diese auch bei den anderen Verkehrsträgern zu beobachtende Entwicklung findet ihre Erklärung darin, daß der Ausbau des Netzes der Kraftpostlinien in ländlichen Gebieten im wesentlichen abgeschlossen ist und die sprunghafte Zunahme der privaten Kraftfahrzeuge zu einer teilweise sehr spürbaren Umschichtung von den öffentlichen Verkehrsmitteln auf den individuellen Verkehr geführt hat.

Dementsprechend hat der Schwerpunkt der Aufgaben im Kraftpostdienst, der in den ersten Jahren des Wiederaufbaus mehr bei der reibungslosen Anpassung an die schnelle Zunahme des Verkehrsvolumens lag, sich jetzt auf die verstärkte Rationalisierung des Fahrbetriebs und seiner Hilfseinrichtungen, zum Beispiel auf die Fahrzeugauslastung, die Einführung von Fahrscheindruckern usw., verlagert. Hand in Hand mit der innerbetrieblichen Rationalisierung geht die weitere Ausgestaltung der Zusammenarbeit mit den anderen Verkehrsträgern, insbesondere mit der Deutschen Bundesbahn. Auf Grund eines am 1.1.1956 in Kraft getretenen umfassenden Abkommens mit der Deutschen Bundesbahn sind wirksame Maßnahmen zur gegenseitigen Unterstützung und Ergänzung getroffen worden. Ein gemeinsames Omnibus-Kursbuch, das den Reisenden über sämtliche Kraftpost- und Bahnbuslinien innerhalb des Bundesgebiets Auskunft gibt, wurde erstmals für den Sommerfahrplan 1957 herausgegeben. Als weitere Maßnahmen sind zu nennen: die Zusammenlegung von Haltestellen, die gegenseitige Anerkennung von Fahrausweisen, die durchgehende Abfertigung und ein gemeinsamer Fahrplan-Aushang.

Tabelle 1
POSTREISEDIENST

Jahr	Anzahl der Kraftpostlinien	Streckenlänge km	Gefahrene Kilometer 1.000	Beförderte Personen 1.000
1950	1.427	37.118	87.473	134.530
1953	1.665	45.342	134.426	237.881
1956	1.778	48.895	170.488	342.041
1957	1.798	49.947	177.022	354.386
1958	1.761	48.735	175.448	333.762

Quelle: Bundesministerium für das Post- und Fernmeldewesen.

In demselben Maße, wie das *Kraftfahrzeug* in der Nachkriegszeit sich entwickelte und auf allen Gebieten des Lebens Eingang fand, wurde es auch für den Postdienst nutzbar gemacht. Mit einem Wagenpark von nahezu 25.000 Kraftfahrzeugen und über 4.500 Anhängern ist die Deutsche Bundespost heute wieder der größte zivile Kraftfahrzeughalter Europas. Für die Unterhaltung der Fahrzeuge ist eine weitverzweigte technische Organisation geschaffen worden. Ihre Betriebsanlagen sind der neuesten Entwicklung auf dem Gebiet moderner Technik der Erhaltung von Kraftfahrzeugen angepaßt und mit modernen technischen Einrichtungen und Geräten ausgestattet.

*

Luftbrief- und Luftpaketdienst besteht mit allen Ländern der Welt. Der vermehrte Anfall von Luftpostsendungen und die ständige Verdichtung des Weltflugnetzes gestatten es, in zunehmendem Umfang unmittelbare Luftbrief- und Luftpaketposten auch nach weit entfernten kleineren Ländern und Gebieten einzurichten. Die Übermittlungsdauer vieler Luftpostsendungen ließ sich dadurch wesentlich verkürzen. Mit dem weiteren Ausbau des Flugnetzes der Deutschen Lufthansa wird ihr in ständig steigendem Umfang Luftpost zur Beförderung übergeben, so daß heute ein erheblicher Prozentsatz der Luftpostsendungen den Weg über die nationale Fluggesellschaft nimmt.

Tabelle 2
LUFTPOSTDIENST

Jahr	Verkehrsvolumen in Tonnen insgesamt	davon nach dem Ausland
1950	820	279
1955	2.896	965
1956	4.029	1.736
1957	4.487	1.974
1958	rund 4.865	rund 2.754

Quelle: Bundesministerium für das Post- und Fernmeldewesen.

Die Entwicklung des *Postscheckdienstes* veranschaulicht die nachstehende Tabelle. Nach der Eingliederung der Postverwaltung von Saarland wurde das Postscheckamt Saarbrücken dreizehntes Postscheckamt der Deutschen Bundespost.

Tabelle 3
POSTSCHECKDIENST

Jahr	Zahl der Postscheckkonten Millionen	Gesamtumsatz Millionen DM	Zahl der Buchungen Millionen
1950[1]	0,983	163.600	502,9
1955[1]	1,144	251.764	682,9
1956	1,570	361.315	898,6
1957	1,667	403.840	941,7
1958	1,779	442.582	978,5

[1] Ohne Berlin(West).

Quelle: Bundesministerium für das Post- und Fernmeldewesen.

Das Gesamtguthaben im *Postsparkassendienst* hat sich laufend erhöht.

Tabelle 4
POSTSPARKASSENDIENST

Jahr	Zahl der Postsparkonten Millionen	Guthaben Millionen DM
1950	2,371	141,9
1953	4,834	653,9
1956	7,841	1.456,6
1957	8,679	1.821,9
1958	9,450	2.284,8

Quelle: Bundesministerium für das Post- und Fernmeldewesen.

*

Auf dem Gebiet des *internationalen* Postverkehrs ist die Deutsche Bundespost sowohl an den Arbeiten des Weltpostvereins als auch an der europäischen Zusammenarbeit im Postwesen maßgeblich beteiligt. Die Bundesrepublik Deutschland ist den Verträgen des Weltpostvereins im Jahre 1955 wieder beigetreten. Als vollgültiges Mitglied des Weltpostvereins nahm die Deutsche Bundespost erstmals am Weltpostkongreß in Ottawa (1957) teil. Hier wurde sie in die Vollzugs- und Verbindungskommission des Weltpostvereins gewählt. Diese hat als permanentes Organ des Weltpostvereins den Auftrag, in der Zeit zwischen den Kongressen die Arbeiten des Weltpostvereins durchzuführen. Sie wurde ferner Mitglied der vom Kongreß ins Leben gerufenen Beratenden Kommission für postalische Studien und übernahm im Lenkungsausschuß dieser Kommission wichtige Aufgaben.

II. DAS FERNMELDEWESEN

Die durch den Krieg verursachten Zerstörungen im deutschen Fernmeldenetz und die durch die Nachkriegsereignisse bedingten Schwierigkeiten konnten in Jahren intensiver Aufbauarbeit beseitigt werden. Mit dem Aufblühen des deutschen Wirtschaftslebens nahm die Nachfrage nach Fernmeldeeinrichtungen stark zu. Allerdings setzte die Knappheit der Mittel den Planungen immer sehr enge Grenzen. Es war kaum möglich, mit der steigenden Nachfrage Schritt zu halten. Die für den Betrieb notwendigen Vorräte im Leitungsnetz und den technischen Einrichtungen konnten noch nicht geschaffen werden. Auch in den nächsten Jahren wird die Nachfrage nach *Fernsprechanschlüssen* weiter anhalten. In der Bundesrepublik Deutschland kommen auf 100 Einwohner erst 8,75 Sprechstellen gegenüber 14,25 im vergleichbaren Vereinigten Königreich.

Die Entwicklung nach dem Kriege durfte sich nicht darauf beschränken, das Zerstörte wieder zu erstellen. Die umfangreichen neuen Erkenntnisse der technischen Entwicklung mußten dabei mit verwertet werden. So wurden bei der Umstellung der Handvermittlungsstellen auf Wähldienst neue Vermittlungseinrichtungen verwendet, die auch den Anforderungen des Selbstwähl-Ferndienstes genügen und bei höherer Betriebsgüte weniger Wartungsaufwand erfordern. Ende 1958 waren noch rund 260 Handvermittlungsstellen mit 35.000 bis 40.000 Hauptanschlüssen vorhanden. Das bedeutet, daß nur noch etwa 1,5% der Hauptanschlüsse in der Bundesrepublik Deutschland an Handvermittlungsstellen angeschlossen waren. Allerdings ist ein Viertel der Einrichtungen in den Wählvermittlungsstellen bereits seit fünfundzwanzig Jahren und länger in Betrieb und bedarf dringend der Erneuerung. Um auch Nicht-Teilnehmern die Möglichkeiten des Fernsprechers weitgehend zu erschließen, wurden in großem Umfang Münzfernsprecher für den Ortsverkehr und auch zahlreiche Münzfernsprecher für den Selbstwählferndienst aufgestellt.

Der *Selbstwähl-Ferndienst* mit seiner günstigen Tarifgestaltung und seiner guten Ertragslage wurde mit den zur Verfügung gestellten Mitteln weiter ausgebaut. Ende 1958 wurden bereits 71,5% der Ferngespräche von den Teilnehmern selbst gewählt. Der Selbstwähl-Ferndienst hat schon die Grenzen der Bundesrepublik überschritten. Nachdem in einigen Grenzverkehrsbeziehungen gute Erfahrungen gesammelt worden waren, wurde 1958 der Selbstwähl-Ferndienst zwischen dem Knotenamtsbereich Düsseldorf und den Ortsnetzen Brüssel, Antwerpen und weiteren 60 Ortsnetzen in Belgien sowie zwischen rund 400 deutschen Ortsnetzen und dem Großherzogtum Luxemburg aufgenommen.

Der größte Teil der noch handvermittelten Ferngespräche wird im Sofortverkehr abgewickelt; das heißt: der Anmelder kann gleich auf die Herstellung seiner Verbindung warten. Mit Belgien, Frankreich, den Niederlanden, Österreich und der Schweiz besteht ein halbautomatischer Dienst. Dabei wählt die Fernplatzbeamtin im Abgangsamt die gewünschte Verbindung selbst. Die Ausdehnung des halbautomatischen Dienstes als Vorstufe für den Selbstwähl-Ferndienst auf Großbritannien, Italien,

NACHRICHTENVERKEHR *

(Monatsdurchschnitt der Kalenderjahre)

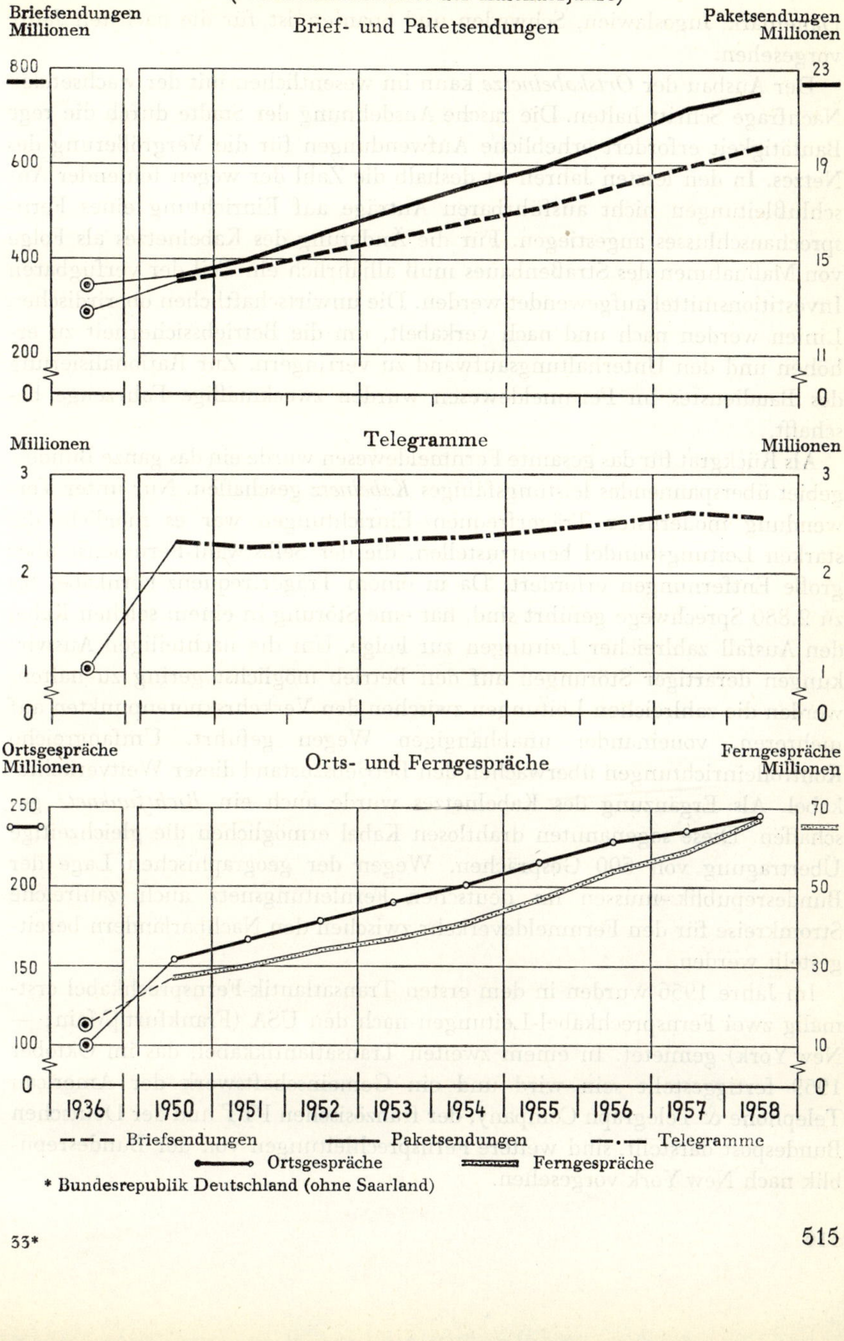

* Bundesrepublik Deutschland (ohne Saarland)

Dänemark, Jugoslawien, Schweden und Spanien ist für die nächsten Jahre vorgesehen.

Der Ausbau der *Ortskabelnetze* kann im wesentlichen mit der wachsenden Nachfrage Schritt halten. Die rasche Ausdehnung der Städte durch die rege Bautätigkeit erfordert erhebliche Aufwendungen für die Vergrößerung des Netzes. In den letzten Jahren ist deshalb die Zahl der wegen fehlender Anschlußleitungen nicht ausführbaren Anträge auf Einrichtung eines Fernsprechanschlusses angestiegen. Für die Änderung des Kabelnetzes als Folge von Maßnahmen des Straßenbaues muß alljährlich ein Teil der verfügbaren Investitionsmittel aufgewendet werden. Die unwirtschaftlichen oberirdischen Linien werden nach und nach verkabelt, um die Betriebssicherheit zu erhöhen und den Unterhaltungsaufwand zu verringern. Zur Rationalisierung des Baudienstes im Fernmeldewesen wurden zweckmäßige Fahrzeuge beschafft.

Als Rückgrat für das gesamte Fernmeldewesen wurde ein das ganze Bundesgebiet überspannendes leistungsfähiges *Kabelnetz* geschaffen. Nur unter Verwendung modernster Trägerfrequenz-Einrichtungen war es möglich, die starken Leitungsbündel bereitzustellen, die der Selbstwähl-Ferndienst über große Entfernungen erfordert. Da in einem Trägerfrequenz-Fernkabel bis zu 2.880 Sprechwege geführt sind, hat eine Störung in einem solchen Kabel den Ausfall zahlreicher Leitungen zur Folge. Um die nachteiligen Auswirkungen derartiger Störungen auf den Betrieb möglichst gering zu halten, werden die zahlreichen Leitungen zwischen den Verkehrsknotenpunkten auf mehreren, voneinander unabhängigen Wegen geführt. Umfangreiche Kontrolleinrichtungen überwachen den Betriebszustand dieser Weitverkehrskabel. Als Ergänzung des Kabelnetzes wurde auch ein *Richtfunknetz* geschaffen. Diese sogenannten drahtlosen Kabel ermöglichen die gleichzeitige Übertragung von 600 Gesprächen. Wegen der geographischen Lage der Bundesrepublik müssen im deutschen Fernleitungsnetz auch zahlreiche Stromkreise für den Fernmeldeverkehr zwischen den Nachbarländern bereitgestellt werden.

Im Jahre 1956 wurden in dem ersten Transatlantik-Fernsprechkabel erstmalig zwei Fernsprechkabel-Leitungen nach den USA (Frankfurt [Main] — New York) gemietet. In einem zweiten Transatlantikkabel, das im Oktober 1959 fertiggestellt sein wird und ein Gemeinschaftswerk der American Telephone & Telegraph Company, der französischen PTT und der Deutschen Bundespost darstellt, sind weitere Fernsprechleitungen von der Bundesrepublik nach New York vorgesehen.

Der *Telegraphendienst* wurde wesentlich umgestaltet. Die einzelnen Telegraphenstellen sind jetzt an ein besonderes Telegraphen-Wählnetz angeschlossen. Jede Telegraphenstelle kann die Telegraphenstelle des Bestimmungsortes unmittelbar anwählen und das Telegramm sogleich übermitteln. Dadurch ist das früher übliche, zeitraubende und arbeitsaufwendige Umtelegraphieren bei den beteiligten Zwischenämtern weggefallen. Nach den guten Erfahrungen im Inland wurde für den Verkehr mit den benachbarten Ländern ein europäisches Telegraphen-Wählnetz geschaffen, an das neben fünfundsiebzig Telegraphenstellen in der Bundesrepublik zahlreiche Telegraphenstellen in Belgien, Dänemark, Frankreich, Luxemburg, den Niederlanden, Österreich und der Schweiz angeschlossen sind. Die an dieses Netz angeschlossenen Telegraphenstellen können sich gegenseitig ebenfalls anwählen und die Telegramme unmittelbar übermitteln.

*

Der *Telexdienst* (öffentlicher Fernschreibdienst) hat mit dem wirtschaftlichen Aufschwung in der Bundesrepublik sehr stark zugenommen. Ende 1958 bestanden in der Bundesrepublik rund 27.000 Telexanschlüsse; das sind mehr als im übrigen Europa zusammen. Die Telexverbindungen nach Belgien, Dänemark, den Niederlanden, Österreich, Schweden und der Schweiz können von einem großen Teil der deutschen Telexteilnehmer bereits selbst gewählt werden. Die Telexverbindungen nach vielen weiteren Ländern werden von den hierfür besonders ausgestatteten Telexämtern Hamburg und Frankfurt (Main) vermittelt. Von der Bundesrepublik bestehen wieder nach allen wirtschaftlich bedeutenden Ländern Fernsprech- und Telegraphiermöglichkeiten. Auch ein Bildtelegraphendienst besteht mit fast allen Ländern der Erde, die über entsprechende Geräte verfügen.

*

Mit dem Kriegsende ruhte der deutsche *Funkverkehr* völlig. In den letzten Jahren wurden wieder umfangreiche und leistungsfähige Anlagen erstellt. Das Funkwesen hat sich dabei einige völlig neue Anwendungsgebiete erschlossen. Richtfunkverbindungen dienen nicht nur der Übermittlung zahlreicher Ferngespräche, sondern auch der Übertragung von Rundfunk- und Fernsehprogrammen. Im deutschen Richtfunknetz, das 109 Richtfunkstellen umfaßt, sind 680.000 km Fernsprechwege, 1.300 km Rundfunk-Übertragungsleitungen und 5.820 km Fernseh-Übertragungswege vorhanden.

Von den Funksende- und Funkempfangsstellen in der Bundesrepublik bestehen wieder zahlreiche Fernsprech- und Telegraphie-Funkverbindungen nach europäischen und außereuropäischen Ländern.

Der *Seefunkdienst* mit Schiffen in der Ostsee wird von Kiel-Radio und mit Schiffen auf allen übrigen Meeren von Norddeich wahrgenommen. Ende 1958 bestanden auf deutschen Schiffen 2.403 Seefunkstellen. Seit dem 1. 7. 1958 besteht über die Küstenfunkstellen Elbe-Weser-Radio, Kiel-Radio, Hamburg-Radio und Helgoland-Radio ein internationaler UKW-Sprech-Seefunkdienst, in den am 8. 9. 1958 auch Norddeich-Radio einbezogen wurde.

Ein weiterer Funkdienst auf Ultrakurzwelle für deutsche Schiffe auf dem Rhein besteht in den Bereichen Duisburg, Köln, Koblenz, Frankfurt (Main), Mannheim und Offenburg. Die achtundachtzig Teilnehmer dieses Dienstes führten im Jahre 1958: 122.374 Gespräche.

Am internationalen *UKW-Rheinfunkdienst*, der seit Mitte 1958 im Bereich Duisburg besteht, nehmen einundzwanzig niederländische Schiffe teil. In den Bereichen Hamburg/Cuxhaven, Bremen/Bremerhaven und Kiel besteht ein Hafenfunkdienst, dessen hundertfünfundachtzig Teilnehmer 1958: 234.746 Gespräche führten.

Auf der Strecke Dortmund-Karlsruhe dienen die Anlagen für den deutschen Rheinfunk auch dem Autostraßen- und Stadtfunk. Fünf Sprechstellen dieses Dienstes sind in Fernzügen der Deutschen Bundesbahn untergebracht und ermöglichen ebenso wie die übrigen in Kraftfahrzeugen die Führung von Ferngesprächen mit allen Fernsprechteilnehmern des öffentlichen Netzes. In den Städten Aachen, Berlin, Hamburg, Hannover, Köln und München besteht ebenfalls ein Stadtfunkdienst mit insgesamt siebenundsiebzig Teilnehmern. Im Jahre 1958 wurden 474.160 gebührenpflichtige Funkgespräche geführt.

Die Zahl der Rundfunkteilnehmer (einschließlich Saarlands) liegt bereits über 15,3 Millionen, und die Zahl der Fernsehteilnehmer hat 2,3 Millionen erreicht. Über Rundfunk und Fernsehen ist in besonderen Kapiteln gehandelt.

Vierundfünfzig Drahtfunk-Netzgruppen mit 555 Drahtfunk-Verstärkerstellen versorgen im Bundesgebiet 115.000 Drahtfunkteilnehmer. In Berlin-(West) sind über 12.000 Drahtfunkteilnehmer vorhanden. Für die Rundfunk- und Fernsehteilnehmer wurden 1958: 135.000 Störungsmeldungen vom Funkstörungsmeßdienst der Deutschen Bundespost bearbeitet.

Ende 1958 waren in der Bundesrepublik 5.368 Amateurfunkstellen genehmigt.

*

Die Bundesrepublik ist seit 1952 wieder Mitglied des Internationalen Fernmeldevereins, und Vertreter der Deutschen Bundespost haben seither bei zahlreichen Tagungen der Internationalen Beratenden Ausschüsse für den Fernsprech-, Telegraphen- und Funkdienst mitgearbeitet. Mit der Intensivierung der Beziehungen zwischen den einzelnen Völkern und dem Ausbau des Nachrichtenwesens ergeben sich zahlreiche Fragen und Probleme, die auf internationaler Basis gelöst werden müssen.

Die Deutsche Bundespost ist bestrebt, leistungsfähige Fernmeldeeinrichtungen bereitzustellen, die allen Anforderungen gerecht werden. Es ist in den vergangenen Jahren mit erheblichen Anstrengungen gelungen, das deutsche Fernmeldewesen so auszubauen, daß es wieder einen internationalen Ruf genießt. Von vielen Ländern wird es als Vorbild für den Ausbau des eigenen Fernmeldewesens genommen.

DEUTSCHLAND — REISELAND

Als ein Land von vielfältigem Reiz für Touristen, mit hochentwickeltem Wirtschaftsleben und Verkehrswesen, war Deutschland von jeher eines der bedeutendsten Reiseländer Europas. Seine Heilbäder und Kurorte, Sommerfrischen und Wintersportplätze wurden alljährlich nicht nur von Millionen Deutschen, sondern auch von Touristen aus aller Welt aufgesucht. Der Fremdenverkehr war bis 1939 in Deutschland ein blühender Wirtschaftszweig. Mit dem Zweiten Weltkrieg kam er zum Erliegen und ging im Chaos von 1945 vollends unter.

Als Deutschland an den wirtschaftlichen Wiederaufbau ging, mußten dabei auch die bedeutenden in der Fremdenverkehrswirtschaft investierten Werte berücksichtigt werden, von denen früher Hunderttausende gelebt hatten. Für den internationalen Reiseverkehr Deutschlands galt dies schon aus materiellen Gründen; denn der Ausländer-Fremdenverkehr ist als ,,unsichtbare Ausfuhr" in hervorragendem Maße geeignet, die durch eine passive Handelsbilanz verursachten Lücken in der Zahlungsbilanz zu verringern. Diesen Bestrebungen kamen zwei Tatsachen entgegen. Einmal setzt ein modernes Wirtschaftsleben einen flüssigen Reiseverkehr voraus. Zum andern war in der durch die Kriegszeit in Mitleidenschaft gezogenen Bevölkerung aller Länder ein sehr starkes Erholungsbedürfnis aufgestaut, das mit zunehmender Konsolidierung der wirtschaftlichen Verhältnisse nach Befriedigung verlangte.

Zunächst galt es, die organisatorischen Voraussetzungen im deutschen Fremdenverkehr zu schaffen. Die *Landesverkehrsverbände* und der *Bund Deutscher Verkehrsverbände* erstanden wieder. Das Hotelgewerbe schloß sich zunächst in einer Arbeitsgemeinschaft zusammen, aus der später der *Deutsche Hotel- und Gaststättenverband* (DEHOGA) hervorging. Der *Deutsche Bäderverband* wurde neu gegründet, ebenso das *Deutsche Reisebüro* (DER), das die Tradition des ehemaligen Mitteleuropäischen Reisebüros (MER) fortsetzt. Diese Organisationen schufen zusammen mit anderen wichtigen Trägern des Fremdenverkehrs, wie der *Deutschen Bundesbahn*, der *Deutschen Bundespost*, der *Arbeitsgemeinschaft kommunaler Spitzenverbände*, dem *Deutschen Industrie- und Handelstag* und der *Vereinigung öffentlicher Verkehrsbetriebe*, im Sommer 1948 die *Deutsche Zentrale für Fremdenverkehr* (ZFV) als Spitzenorganisation des deutschen Fremdenverkehrs. Ihr traten später außerdem der *Deutsche Reisebüro-Verband* (DRV), die *Deutsche Schlafwagen- und Speisewagen-Gesellschaft* und die *Deutsche Lufthansa* bei. Seit 1949 werden die Angelegenheiten des Fremdenverkehrs zentral im Bundesministerium für Verkehr bearbeitet.

In den ersten Jahren des organisatorischen Wiederaufbaus trat der Fremdenverkehr selbst noch sehr wenig in Erscheinung. Ein großer Teil des erhalten gebliebenen Unterkunftsraumes war beschlagnahmt oder durch Belegung mit Flüchtlingen und Evakuierten oder andere Verwendung zweckentfremdet, fiel also für den Reiseverkehr aus. Für den Einzelnen aber

FREMDENVERKEHR[1]
1.000 Personen beziehungsweise 1.000 Übernachtungen

Zeitraum	Fremdenmeldungen insgesamt	Fremdenmeldungen darunter Ausländer	Fremdenübernachtungen insgesamt	Fremdenübernachtungen darunter Ausländer
Sommerhalbjahr				
1949[2 3]	4.354	179	16.004	420
1950[2]	7.159	712	25.765	1.549
1951	9.576	1.157	34.706	2.359
1952	10.856	1.620	40.443	3.188
1953	12.341	2.089	46.601	4.000
1954	13.197	2.576	50.164	4.886
1955	14.781	3.076	57.537	5.777
1956	16.496	3.316	67.626	6.350
1957[4]	17.484	3.566	75.380	6.933
1958[4]	17.988	3.679	79.585	7.220
Winterhalbjahr				
1949/50[2]	4.360	248	11.683	586
1950/51[2]	5.305	403	14.406	925
1951/52	6.201	519	17.015	1.215
1952/53	6.543	600	18.252	1.356
1953/54	7.018	699	20.285	1.541
1954/55	7.482	818	21.765	1.757
1955/56	8.164	939	24.597	2.010
1956/57[4]	9.047	1.007	28.535	2.222
1957/58[4]	9.431	1.067	30.891	2.411

[1] Bundesrepublik (ohne Saarland).

[2] Ohne Rheinland-Pfalz.

[3] April und Mai ohne Niedersachsen, Hessen, Württemberg-Baden und Württemberg-Hohenzollern; Juni ohne Hessen, Württemberg-Baden und Württemberg-Hohenzollern; Juli ohne Hessen und Württemberg-Hohenzollern.

[4] Einschließlich von Saarland.

Quelle: Statistisches Bundesamt.

hatte die Notwendigkeit der Sicherung der Existenz, der Wiederbeschaffung von verlorenem Wohnraum, Hausrat und Bekleidung, den Vorrang vor der Erholungsreise. Erst mit der Rückkehr geordneter Verhältnisse nach der Währungsreform und durch die großzügige Hilfe des Marshall-Plans kam der Fremdenverkehr wieder in Gang. Zahlenmäßig läßt sich diese Zeit nicht belegen; denn eine einheitliche Fremdenverkehrsstatistik, wie sie früher für das Deutsche Reich bestand, fehlte in den ersten Jahren. Die ersten brauchbaren Ergebnisse erbrachte die Statistik für das Sommerhalbjahr 1949.

Der Fremdenverkehr in der Bundesrepublik befindet sich nach stürmischem Wiederanstieg im Sommer 1950 noch in kräftiger Aufwärts-Entwicklung. Sie hat sich bis in die Gegenwart Jahr um Jahr fortgesetzt, wenn auch die jährlichen Zunahmen, entsprechend der wachsenden Befriedigung des Reisebedürfnisses der Bevölkerung, naturgemäß allmählich geringer werden. Unter den ausländischen Besuchern stellen seit jeher die Nordamerikaner das größte Kontigent. Die Niederländer folgen ihnen dichtauf.

Auch der Fremdenverkehr in Berlin(West) ist trotz der besonders schwierigen Lage, in der die Reichshauptstadt sich befindet, wieder im Anstieg. Die Zahl der Fremdenübernachtungen erhöhte sich in den Jahren von 1949

ÜBERNACHTUNGEN VON AUSLÄNDERN[1]
IN GEWERBLICHEN BEHERBERGUNGSBETRIEBEN
1.000 Personen

Herkunftsland	1950[2]	1952	1954	1956	1958[3]
USA	410,7	763,4	982,2	1.293,4	1.506,3
Niederlande	199,7	459,0	772,2	1.209,7	1.370,3
Vereinigtes Königreich	302,5	366,0	548,0	773,6	968,2
Belgien-Luxemburg	163,3	353,7	527,0	675,0	712,0
Frankreich	169,8	371,7	521,7	637,7	704,7
Schweiz	232,9	438,2	556,7	638,7	687,3
Schweden	109,4	331,6	576,7	656,7	617,7
Dänemark	138,5	335,4	537,1	589,0	605,3
Italien	149,7	206,0	248,3	321,0	464,6
Österreich	126,3	223,5	324,1	394,9	445,2
Sonstige	297,6	633,0	945,5	1.291,7	1.668,2
Insgesamt	2.300,4	4.481,5	6.539,5	8.481,5	9.749,8

[1] Bundesrepublik (ohne Saarland).
[2] Ohne Rheinland-Pfalz und für Januar bis März ohne Schleswig-Holstein.
[3] Einschließlich von Saarland.

Quelle: Statistisches Bundesamt.

bis 1958 von 409.550 auf 1.189.786, der Anteil der Ausländer von 17.602 auf 328.907.

Der Devisenertrag aus dem Ausländer-Fremdenverkehr als Zeichen seiner wirtschaftlichen Bedeutung ist recht beachtlich.

DEVISENEINNAHMEN[1] AUS DEM FREMDENVERKEHR VON AUSLÄNDERN
(ohne Einnahmen aus dem Transport)

Jahr	DM	Jahr	DM
1949	rund 82.000.000	1954	713.409.000
1950	rund 164.000.000	1955	951.875.000
1951	228.933.877	1956	1.278.456.000
1952	430.398.317	1957	1.490.903.000
1953	510.054.000	1958	1.906.204.000[2]

[1] Bundesrepublik (ohne Saarland), einschließlich von Berlin(West).

[2] Ab Juli 1958 einschließlich der Barauszahlungen an ausländische Reisende zu Lasten von DM-Ausländer-Konten.

Quelle: Statistisches Bundesamt.

Ebenso läßt die Entwicklung der Beherbergungskapazität eine weitgehende Konsolidierung des Hotel- und Gaststättenwesens erkennen. Zu der eigenen Initiative der Hoteliers und der organisatorischen Hilfe des Deutschen Hotel- und Gaststättenverbandes (DEHOGA) trat die Förderung durch das Bundeswirtschaftsministerium und die Wirtschaftsministerien der Länder. Dadurch konnte das Hotelgewerbe seinen Wiederaufbau tatkräftig in Angriff nehmen.

Von den rund 485.000 Fremdenbetten, die Westdeutschland in der Vorkriegszeit besaß, waren 1949 rund 306.000 vorhanden. Davon standen allerdings nur etwa 40% des Vorkriegsstandes für den Fremdenverkehr zur Verfügung. Der Rest war durch andere Verwendung zweckentfremdet.

Die Ausnutzung der Beherbergungsbetriebe entsprach der Zunahme des in- und ausländischen Fremdenverkehrs. Die Großstädte sind im allgemeinen gleichbleibend ausgelastet. Alle anderen Gruppen von Fremdenverkehrs-Gemeinden sind dagegen sehr stark den jahreszeitlichen Schwankungen unterworfen. So sind zum Beispiel die Seebäder und viele Luftkurorte im Juli und August ausverkauft, in der Vor- und Nachsaison dagegen nur mangelhaft ausgenutzt. Der Reiseverkehr muß also stärker als bisher über den Zeitraum der sommerlichen Hochsaison ausgedehnt werden. Diesem Ziel dienen

BEHERBERGUNGSKAPAZITÄT[1]
Anzahl der Fremdenbetten in gewerblichen Beherbergungsbetrieben
Stand jeweils 1. April

Land	1951	1952	1953	1954	1955	1956	1957	1958
Bayern	95.277	108.997	120.373	133.650	145.542	156.111	168.318	176.536
Baden-Württemberg	66.306	71.089	76.596	83.689	89.572	95.934	102.366	105.784
Nordrhein-Westfalen	48.190	53.561	58.929	65.924	72.051	78.463	86.426	91.111
Hessen	28.788	32.380	39.221	44.158	47.452	52.444	58.729	63.051
Rheinland-Pfalz ...	30.919	33.164	37.420	40.131	40.249	43.391	45.327	47.038
Schleswig-Holstein ..	28.851	32.691	36.419	38.992	42.469	44.028	43.874	46.881
Niedersachsen ...	24.796	26.112	29.265	31.970	34.345	77.270	82.642	86.480
Hamburg .	6.713	7.692	8.102	8.665	9.379	10.157	10.864	11.769
Bremen ...	1.747	1.798	2.033	2.183	2.382	2.670	3.139	3.098
Bundesrepublik	331.587	367.484	408.358	449.362	483.441	560.468	601.685	631.748

[1] Bundesrepublik (ohne Saarland).

Quelle: Statistisches Bundesamt.

die Bemühungen zur Reform der Ordnung der Schulferien, die freilich bisher nicht erfolgreich verliefen, und zur Schaffung besonderer Vergünstigungen für Reisen im Frühjahr und Herbst.

Trotz der erfreulichen Entwicklung der letzten Jahre sind die gesteckten Ziele noch nicht erreicht. Es gilt vor allem, auch das Erholungsbedürfnis der wirtschaftlich schwachen Volkskreise zu befriedigen. Diese Aufgabe will die „*Gemeinschaft für Sozialtouristik und Reisesparen*" (GESOREI) durch Reisesparen und Durchführung besonders preisgünstiger Reisen erreichen. Sie ist vom Deutschen Reisebüroverband, dem Deutschen Hotel- und Gaststättenverband, der Deutschen Zentrale für Fremdenverkehr, dem Bund Deutscher Verkehrsverbände, der Bundesbahn und der Deutschen Verkehrs-Kreditbank gegründet worden. In der GESOREI wirken auch die Deutsche Angestellten-Gewerkschaft, der Deutsche Beamtenbund und die Bundesvereinigung der deutschen Arbeitgeberverbände mit. Neben dieser Gemeinschaft, die sich an alle Bevölkerungskreise wendet, gründete der Deutsche Gewerkschaftsbund

FREMDENÜBERNACHTUNGEN IN AUSGEWÄHLTEN BERICHTSORTEN

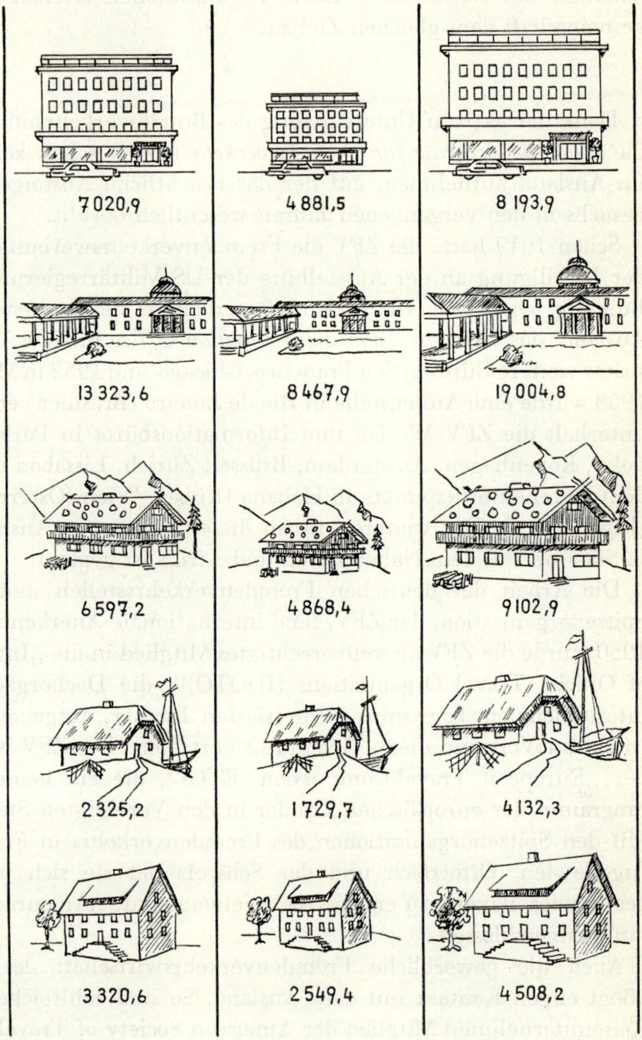

Anzahl der ausgewählten Berichtsorte — 1.000 Übernachtungen	Sommerhalbjahr 1937	Sommerhalbjahr 1951	Sommerhalbjahr 1958
35 Großstädte	7 020,9	4 881,5	8 193,9
79 Heilbäder	13 323,6	8 467,9	19 004,8
69 Luftkurorte	6 597,2	4 868,4	9 102,9
19 Seebäder	2 325,2	1 729,7	4 132,3
Sonstige Berichtsorte	3 320,6	2 549,4	4 508,2

Dem Schaubild liegen 300 ausgewählte Berichtsorte in den Sommerhalbjahren 1937, 1951 und 1958 zugrunde.

in Zusammenarbeit mit den Konsumgenossenschaften und der Gesellschaft „Naturfreunde“ die „*Deutsche Feriengemeinschaft*“ (DFG). Sie fördert ebenfalls das Reisesparen. Beide Organisationen streben in einer Arbeitsgemeinschaft dem gleichen Ziel zu.

*

Dank der aktiven Unterstützung des Bundesverkehrsministeriums konnte die *Deutsche Zentrale für Fremdenverkehr* (*ZFV*) schon zeitig die Werbung im Ausland aufnehmen, auf der das beachtliche Ansteigen des Ausländerbesuchs in den vergangenen Jahren wesentlich beruht.

Schon 1949 hatte die ZFV die Fremdenverkehrswerbung in den USA mit der Beteiligung an der Ausstellung der US-Militärregierung im Rockefeller Building begonnen. Am 15.2.1950 errichtete sie ihr erstes Werbebüro im Ausland, das *German Tourist Information Office* in New York. Ihm folgten später weitere Büros in San Francisco, Chicago und 1952 in Montreal (Kanada). 1958 wurde eine Außenstelle in Rio de Janeiro (Brasilien) eröffnet. In Europa unterhält die ZFV Werbe- und Informationsbüros in Paris, London, Stockholm, Kopenhagen, Amsterdam, Brüssel, Zürich, Lissabon und Rom. Außerdem bestehen Stützpunkte in Habana (Kuba), Wien (Österreich) und Zagreb (Jugoslawien). Der weitere Ausbau dieses Netzes von Auslandsvertretungen in Südamerika, dem Nahen Osten und Afrika ist geplant.

Die Arbeit der deutschen Fremdenverkehrsstellen und besonders ihrer Spitzenorganisation, der ZFV, fand internationale Anerkennung. Im Oktober 1950 wurde die ZFV als vollberechtigtes Mitglied in die „International Union of Official Travel Organisations (IUOTO)“, die Dachorganisation aller am internationalen Tourismus interessierten Länder, aufgenommen. Seit 1957 ist sie im Vorstand dieses Gremiums vertreten. Die ZFV ist ferner Mitglied der „European Travel Commission (ETC)“, die ein gemeinsames Werbeprogramm der europäischen Länder in den Vereinigten Staaten durchführt. Mit den Spitzenorganisationen des Fremdenverkehrs in Frankreich, Italien, Jugoslawien, Österreich und der Schweiz hat sie sich unter Beteiligung des Landes Bayern zu einer Arbeitsgemeinschaft „Alpenraumwerbung“ zusammengeschlossen.

Auch die gewerbliche Fremdenverkehrswirtschaft der Bundesrepublik pflegt engen Kontakt mit dem Ausland. So sind zahlreiche Reisebüros und Reiseunternehmen Mitglied der American Society of Travel Agents (ASTA), der wichtigsten amerikanischen Reisebürovereinigung, und der Fédération Internationale des Agences de Voyages (FIAV). In fünfzehn deutschen Städten

bestehen Skål-Clubs. Sie pflegen die private Geselligkeit und den Gedankenaustausch der Fremdenverkehrsfachleute. Über das Nationalkomitee der Deutschen Skål-Clubs e. V. sind sie der Association Internationale des Skål-Clubs (AISC) angeschlossen.

*

Der 1951 erfolgte Übergang der Paßhoheit von den Besatzungsmächten an die Regierung der Bundesrepublik bedeutete eine wesentliche Erleichterung für den Ausländer-Fremdenverkehr. Seit 1953 hat die Bundesrepublik Deutschland im Zuge der fortschreitenden Liberalisierung des Verkehrs den Visumzwang für viele Staaten völlig aufgehoben, ohne auf dem Prinzip der Gegenseitigkeit zu bestehen. Außerdem ist für die Angehörigen einiger Länder der Paßzwang fortgefallen. Im Verkehr mit Belgien, Frankreich, Italien, Luxemburg, den Niederlanden, Österreich, der Schweiz und Liechtenstein genügt der einfache Personalausweis.

*

Die mit Tatkraft und Energie aufgebaute Werbung kann nur Erfolg haben, wenn den Besuchern etwas geboten wird. Der Wiederaufbau des Hotel- und Gaststättengewerbes hat Deutschlands Ruf als ein gastliches Reiseland erneut gefestigt. Die Deutsche Bundesbahn ist trotz allen finanziellen Schwierigkeiten bestrebt, die Eisenbahnen modern und komfortabel auszubauen. Schnelltriebwagen, Gliedertriebzüge mit Dieselantrieb, neuartige Einbett-Schlafwagen, neue, besonders schnelle F-Züge, modernste Trans-Europ-Express-(TEE-)Einheiten, Aussichtstriebwagen, Ausbau der elektrischen Zugführung auf großen Durchgangsstrecken, grundsätzlich nur je sechs gepolsterte Abteilsitze in den modernen Wagen beider Klassen, Vermehrung der Zahl der festen Menus bei den gemeinsamen Mahlzeiten in den Speisewagen, Wirtschaftsbetrieb in fast allen Eilzügen und auf sämtlichen wichtigen Bahnhöfen: das sind Errungenschaften, die im Wettbewerb mit dem Ausland bestehen können. Ferien-Expreßzüge mit komfortablen, gepolsterten Sitz-Liegewagen der zweiten Klasse, die mit bedeutend ermäßigten Fahrpreisen gefahren werden, ermöglichen auch dem Ferienreisenden mit schmalem Geldbeutel eine angenehme Fahrt in den Urlaub.

Ein weitverzweigter Kraftverkehr mit modernen Fernreise-Omnibussen und der fahrplanmäßige Verkehr mit Kraftautobussen der Bundesbahn und der Bundespost ergänzen den Schienenverkehr auf einem dichten Netz gepflegter Fernstraßen und Autobahnen. Das Liniennetz der Deutschen Touring-Gesellschaft ist in den EUROPABUS-Verkehr eingegliedert. Zur

Betreuung der Autoreisenden wurden bei den Zollämtern der wichtigsten Grenzübergangsstellen Touristik-Auskunftstellen des Allgemeinen Deutschen Automobil-Clubs und der Deutschen Verkehrs-Kredit-Bank eröffnet. Auf den Autobahnen findet man Streckentelephon, Tankstellen und Rasthäuser in regelmäßigen Abständen.

Auf den Flüssen Rhein, Mosel, Main, Neckar und Weser sowie auf den Gewässern in und um Berlin fahren wieder weiße Dampfer und Motorboote für den Personenverkehr, auf dem Rhein auch Schnelldampfer mit Funksprechanlage. Auf den bayerischen Seen und auf dem Bodensee verkehren Dampfer, Motorschiffe und Autofähren. Diese vermitteln auch den Verkehr mit der Schweiz. Camping-Plätze aller Art mit Abstellraum für Kraftfahrzeuge sind an vielen Erholungsorten vorhanden. Am Welt-Luftverkehr, dem Deutschland zunächst ausschließlich durch ein dichtes Netz ausländischer Luftverkehrsgesellschaften angeschlossen war, nimmt die Bundesrepublik seit dem 1.4.1955 wieder mit der Deutschen Lufthansa teil. Sie befliegt neben einem engmaschigen deutschen und europäischen Netz, das alle wichtigen Städte verbindet, Strecken nach Nord- und Südamerika, Afrika und dem Nahen und Mittleren Osten. Ähnliches ist vom Übersee-Schiffsverkehr zu sagen. Norddeutscher Lloyd, Hapag, Hamburg-Süd und andere Reedereien haben mit modernisierten Schiffen und vielen Neubauten wieder erheblichen Anteil am internationalen Personenverkehr auf See.

Wer heute Deutschland besucht, wird die Erfahrung machen, daß es sich in diesem Lande angenehm reisen läßt und die Bundesrepublik im Kreis der europäischen Touristenländer ihren guten Platz hat.

SOZIALES LEBEN

SOZIALE LAGE UND SOZIALE HILFEN

Nach dem Grundgesetz ist die Bundesrepublik ein „*sozialer Rechtsstaat*". Erste Pflicht des Staates ist es danach, die Würde des Menschen zu achten und zu schützen, also dem einzelnen den Weg zu einem menschenwürdigen Leben freizumachen, soweit er das nicht selbst zu leisten vermag. Diesem Auftrag haben Bundestag und Bundesregierung in den vergangenen zehn Jahren gedient. Das deutsche Sozialwesen, nach Krieg und Zusammenbruch vor schwerste Aufgaben gestellt, hat die vielseitigen Probleme im wesentlichen gemeistert. Zunächst mußte für Millionen bedrohte Existenzen rasch und wirksam die unmittelbare Not behoben, dann in steigendem Maße ein System der sozialen Hilfen wiederhergestellt und ausgebaut werden, das dem wachsenden Bedürfnis nach sozialer Sicherheit Rechnung tragen konnte. Diese Maßnahmen hatten den starken Wandlungen der Bevölkerungsstruktur zu entsprechen, die ein Jahrhundert ständig ansteigender Industrialisierung, die anhaltende Landflucht und die tiefgreifende Umschichtung infolge des Einströmens von mehr als zwölf Millionen Vertriebener, Flüchtlinge und Zugewanderter nach 1945 verursacht hatten. Die Bundesrepublik ist einen Weg gegangen, der, ohne dem einzelnen die letzte Verantwortung für die Gestaltung seines Lebens abzunehmen, entscheidend zur Schaffung gesunder sozialer Verhältnisse beigetragen hat.

Um einen Überblick über die soziale Lage zu gewinnen, müssen zunächst die Wandlungen in der Struktur der Bevölkerung dargelegt, die Entwicklung und das System der sozialen Hilfen in Deutschland geschildert und sodann ein Überblick über die heutigen Sozialleistungen in der Bundesrepublik gegeben werden. In kurzen, das Wesentliche herausgreifenden Ausführungen soll vor allem deutlich gemacht werden, in welcher Weise Deutschland versucht, die sozialen Nöte der Nachkriegszeit zu beheben. Dabei kann teilweise an Feststellungen angeknüpft werden, die in anderen Abschnitten dieses Buches getroffen sind; so über die Bevölkerungsbewegung (Seite 22—27), die Kriegsopfer (Seite 35—40), über Vertriebene und Flüchtlinge, Verschleppte und heimatlose Ausländer (Seite 41—82), über den Arbeitsmarkt (Seite 305—314), über Jugendfragen (Seite 632—650). Die Fragen der Betriebsverfassung, des Arbeitsvertragswesens, der Tarif- und Lohnpolitik und des Arbeitsschutzes werden im nachfolgenden Abschnitt behandelt.

Wandlungen der sozialen Struktur

Deutschland war vor hundertzwanzig Jahren noch fast ein reiner Agrarstaat. Diese vorindustrielle Zeit ist gekennzeichnet durch den allmählichen Verfall der alten ständischen Ordnung infolge der durch Emanzipation, Bauernbefreiung und Gewerbefreiheit gesteigerten Freiheit des Individuums. Die liberale Wirtschaftsgesinnung führte zu einer raschen Veränderung der Produktionsverhältnisse. In ihrer Folge geriet die bisher zunft- und schollengebundene Bevölkerung in Bewegung. Die Zahl der Fabrikarbeiter stieg zunächst langsam — von 1802 bis 1867 von 300.000 auf zwei Millionen —, dann immer rascher — von 1867 bis 1882 auf sechs Millionen — an. Die *Industrialisierung* setzte zwar teilweise später ein als in England und Frankreich, holte aber im Zeichen der aufkommenden Gewerbefreiheit rasch auf. Sie begann mit der Textilindustrie und setzte sich allmählich auch in anderen Gewerbezweigen durch. Zu größeren räumlichen Konzentrationen kam es erst mit der Schaffung der Montanindustrie im Ruhrgebiet, in Oberschlesien und im Saarland. Während hier die Kohle die Konzentration bestimmte, orientierten andere Industrien sich nach billiger Wasser- und Arbeitskraft.

Die Arbeitsbedingungen in diesen Anfangszeiten der modernen Industrie stellten an den Arbeiter harte Anforderungen. Er war zwar von Bindungen frei, stand aber, schlecht bezahlt, den besonderen Notlagen, wie Unfall, Krankheit oder Arbeitslosigkeit sie ihm täglich bringen konnten, ungeschützt gegenüber. Aus der wachsenden Bevölkerung strömten immer größere Massen Arbeitsuchender, vor allem aus den agrarischen Provinzen Preußens, in die Industriegebiete, während zwischen 1830 und 1870 allein nach überseeischen Ländern noch 2,5 Millionen deutscher Menschen ausgewandert waren. Aus dem ständischen Gefüge der Landwirtschaft und des Handwerks herausgelöst, bildeten sie eine Masse, die erst allmählich als Arbeiter zu politischem Bewußtsein erwachte. Zunächst — teilweise christliche — Arbeitervereine, dann die politische und die gewerkschaftliche Arbeiterbewegung haben den Arbeiter aus seiner Isolierung herausgeführt und ihn zu einer immer stärkeren Kraft in der damaligen sozialen und politischen Auseinandersetzung der Nation werden lassen. Die unmittelbaren Folgen dieser Umschichtung waren einerseits ein unaufhaltsamer Rückgang des Anteils der landwirtschaftlichen Bevölkerung (1882: 42,2%, 1950: 23,2% der Erwerbspersonen) und ein Rückgang des Anteils der Selbständigen an der Gesamtbevölkerung. Andererseits ergab sich nach Überwindung der anfänglichen Mißhelligkeiten mit dem Aufstieg der deutschen Industrie eine langsame, aber ständige Steigerung des Einkommens der breiten Massen.

Erster Weltkrieg und Inflation haben das bis dahin bei allen Stammesverschiedenheiten immer noch weithin einheitliche Bild des Volksgefüges gewandelt: die einst staatstragenden Schichten des Mittelstandes verarmten und vermochten ihre gesellschaftlich führende Stellung nicht mehr zu halten. Die Folgen des Zweiten Weltkrieges brachten erneut tiefgreifende Wandlungen. Die Kriegsverluste, verbunden mit einem allgemeinen Absinken der Geburtenzahl, aber auch die höhere Lebenserwartung des Einzelnen, ergaben eine erhebliche Steigerung des Durchschnittsalters der Bevölkerung. Eine breite *Nivellierung* hat den Abstand der übrigen Volksschichten zur Fabrikarbeiterschicht vermindert, diese aber auch weitgehend entproletarisiert und vor allem aus qualifizierten Facharbeitern und Angestellten allmählich einen neuen Mittelstand geschaffen.

*

Noch einschneidender für die Bevölkerungsstruktur wirkte sich die enorme Völkerwanderung aus, zu der nach dem Zusammenbruch 1945 die Deutschen in den Ostgebieten durch *Flucht und Vertreibung* genötigt wurden. Ihre Zahl beträgt in der Bundesrepublik rund neun Millionen — sowie 3,2 Millionen aus der sogenannten DDR in die Bundesrepublik Zugewanderte. Der Millionenzustrom hat das deutsche Volk in dem Augenblick schwerster Not vor soziale Aufgaben von bis dahin nicht gekannter Größe gestellt. Wir können heute feststellen, daß es diese Bewährungsprobe bestanden hat. Die Jahre nach dem Zweiten Weltkrieg haben aber das *soziale Gefüge* des deutschen Volkes in einer Weise gewandelt, wie es seit den Tagen der Völkerwanderung nicht mehr der Fall war. Die Eingliederung dieser Millionen Menschen aus den deutschen Ostprovinzen und den ganz oder teilweise deutsch besiedelten Gebieten innerhalb und außerhalb der Reichsgrenzen mußte das historisch gewordene Bild der deutschen Stämme entscheidend ändern. Von Gebieten geschlossener Abstammung und eines einheitlichen religiösen Bekenntnisses kann nun kaum mehr gesprochen werden. Dies umso weniger, als die Suche nach dem geeignetsten Arbeitsplatz die Zuwanderer vielfach nicht am Platze ihrer ersten Zuweisung beließ.

Für die ganze weitere Entwicklung der sozialen Situation in der Bundesrepublik ist es von wesentlicher Bedeutung, daß der *Flüchtlingsstrom* bis zum heutigen Tage *nicht aufgehört* hat. Die politische Entwicklung in der sogenannten DDR läßt diesen Strom seit mehr als zehn Jahren ständig weiterfließen. 1958 sind rund 204.000 Personen in die Bundesrepublik geflohen. Dazu kommen die sogenannten *Aussiedler*, denen in den letzten Jahren die

Übersiedlung aus Sowjetrußland, Polen und Rumänien in die Bundesrepublik ermöglicht wurde (1958 allein 130.000 Personen). Der Flüchtlingszustrom ist damit für eine noch nicht absehbare Zeit ein von der jeweiligen politischen Lage abhängiges Problem ohne Ende. Seine Unüberschaubarkeit macht schon die Schwierigkeiten deutlich, welche die Eingliederung so großer Gruppen in die dicht besiedelte Bundesrepublik notwendig hervorrufen muß. Daß diese Aufgabe im wesentlichen gemeistert worden ist, und daß diese zusätzlichen Menschenmassen nicht proletarisiert wurden, sondern als wertvolle Kräfte in ihrer neuen Heimat aufgenommen worden sind, wird auf lange Sicht wohl als die wesentlichste soziale Leistung der Bundesrepublik anzusehen sein. Damit, daß das Entstehen gefährlicher politischer Sprengkörper in den Flüchtlingsmassen vermieden wurde, hat Deutschland zugleich einen wichtigen Beitrag zur friedlichen Entwicklung in Europa geleistet. Am wirtschaftlichen Wiederaufbau haben diese Menschen, die in schwerer Notzeit hier Halt und Zuflucht suchten und fanden, bedeutsamen Anteil.

Welches Ergebnis die sozialen Umschichtungen in Deutschland auf die Dauer haben werden, ist heute noch nicht voll zu übersehen. Ob die Vermischung der deutschen Stämme, die Auflösung der Geschlossenheit der Landbevölkerung, die Loslösung von althergebrachten Vorstellungen dem Volk zum Segen gereichen werden, kann nur die Zukunft zeigen. Offensichtlich ist aber heute schon, daß das Hereinströmen von Millionen, die gewillt sind, sich mit aller Kraft die Grundlagen für ein neues Leben zu schaffen, zu einer starken Aktivierung weiter Landstriche und einer erneuten Intensivierung der Industrialisierung geführt hat, für die aus dem Strom der Vertriebenen und Flüchtlinge ein großer Erfahrungsschatz zur Verfügung steht.

Der Weg der deutschen Sozialpolitik

Von *Sozialpolitik* im Sinne umfassender staatlicher Maßnahmen zur Behebung von Notständen in der Arbeiterschaft kann man in Deutschland etwa seit 1880 sprechen. Mit der „Kaiserlichen Botschaft" vom 17.11.1881 hat BISMARCK den Aufbau der deutschen Sozialversicherung eingeleitet. Soziales Wirken in den älteren Formen des Armenwesens und der Wohlfahrtspflege reicht aber viele Jahrhunderte weiter zurück in eine Zeit, in der vom modernen Staat noch keine Rede sein konnte. Im *Mittelalter* waren soziale Leistungen in erster Linie Angelegenheit der Kirche, vor allem der Klöster. Hunderte von Spitälern, teils fromme Stiftungen, teils Einrichtungen der erstarkenden Städte, zeugen noch heute von der Opferbereitschaft

vergangener Generationen. Wenn auch die Reformation die Hilfe für die Armen in stärkerem Maße zur Aufgabe der Obrigkeit machte, so hielt sich die öffentliche Gewalt doch noch lange zurück. Nach der Katastrophe des Dreißigjährigen Krieges fanden die Gedanken tätiger Nächstenliebe erst allmählich unter dem Einfluß von Pietismus und Aufklärung wieder Gestalt. Wie primitiv man damals noch vorging, zeigen die „Zuchthäuser" des Achtzehnten Jahrhunderts, die ohne Differenzierung ebenso der Unterbringung von Kranken und Siechen wie von Irren und Fallsüchtigen, Verbrechern und Waisenkindern dienten. Erst AUGUST HERMANN FRANCKE hat zu Beginn des Achtzehnten Jahrhunderts in seinem Halleschen Waisenhaus die Notwendigkeit besonderer Behandlung verschiedenartiger Notstände erkannt und durchgesetzt. Die *Armenfürsorge* blieb noch Jahrhunderte Angelegenheit der örtlichen Stellen und der Mildtätigkeit der Bürgerschaft. Massennotständen in und nach Kriegszeiten und Hungerjahren waren diese Bemühungen in keiner Weise gewachsen.

Ein wirkliches Interesse des Staates an der Behebung sozialer Notstände zeigte sich erst, als mit der Zusammenballung proletarisierter Arbeitermassen die Gefährdung der politischen Ordnung wuchs und der Gesundheitszustand der Arbeiterschaft ihre Tauglichkeit zum Militärdienst herabsetzte. Aus christlich-sozialer Haltung erstrebten weitsichtige Männer eine *Erneuerung des gesellschaftlichen und sozialen Lebens*. Auf katholischer Seite hat der Mainzer Bischof FREIHERR WILHELM VON KETTELER als Erster die sozialen Forderungen der Kirche formuliert und die ständisch-gewerkschaftlichen Bestrebungen entscheidend gefördert. Der „Gesellenvater" ADOLF KOLPING war Bahnbrecher im Zusammenschluß der vielfach alleinstehenden jugendlichen Handwerker und Arbeiter zu Gesellenvereinen (Kolping-Familien). Auf evangelischer Seite wirkten ADOLF STÖCKER und FRIEDRICH NAUMANN für eine Besserung der Verhältnisse, jener als Schöpfer der Berliner Stadtmission, dieser vor allem durch eine Gewissensschärfung unter den Gebildeten. Auch in der Praxis versuchten die Kräfte freier christlicher Liebestätigkeit gegen die schwersten Nöte anzugehen. Das Neunzehnte Jahrhundert wurde die Zeit der Gründung zahlreicher großzügiger *Anstalten* und Rettungshäuser. Alte und Sieche, Krüppel und Geisteskranke, gefährdete Jugendliche und Waisen fanden hier Stätten, in denen ihnen Hilfe geboten und ihrem Leben ein Sinn gegeben werden konnte. Besondere Beispiele dafür sind das Wirken JOHANN HINRICH WICHERNS im „Rauhen Hause" in Hamburg und die VON BODELSCHWINGHschen Anstalten in Bethel bei Bielefeld, bis heute die größte deutsche Heimstätte für geistig und körperlich Schwache.

Den mannigfachen Notlagen, in die der Einzelne durch die Lösung der ständischen Bindungen und die wachsende Industrialisierung gekommen war, konnte aber durch die Bemühungen der freien Liebestätigkeit allein nicht wirksam begegnet werden. Jetzt ging es nicht mehr um die Behebung besonderer Einzelnotstände, sondern um die Existenzsicherung eines neu entstehenden Standes gegen die Gefahren der Krankheit, des Alters und der Invalidität, denen der einzelne Arbeiter bisher weitgehend ungeschützt gegenüberstand. Wohl war BISMARCKs Anliegen in erster Linie der politische Schutz des Reiches gegen soziale Erschütterungen und die Absicht, die Arbeiterschaft Einflüssen zu entziehen, die er für verderblich hielt. Die Schaffung der deutschen *Sozialversicherung* bleibt trotzdem eine Tat, die sich weit über die Grenzen des Reiches hinaus ausgewirkt hat. BISMARCKs Mitarbeiter knüpften dabei sowohl an genossenschaftliche Vorbilder wie an die wissenschaftlichen Vorarbeiten der im „Verein für Socialpolitik" zusammengeschlossenen, damals als „Kathedersozialisten" diskriminierten Sozialpolitiker an.

Das allmähliche Werden des deutschen Sozialrechts in den vergangenen achtzig Jahren hat dazu geführt, daß seine einzelnen Zweige heute nicht in dem Maße aufeinander abgestimmt sind und deshalb auch nicht ein so geschlossenes System darstellen, wie es später von anderen Nationen, die auf diesen Erfahrungen aufbauten, entwickelt werden konnte. Die Lösungen für die Teilgebiete der deutschen sozialen Hilfen sind jeweils Ausdruck ihrer Zeit, die nicht aus einer einheitlichen sozialen oder politischen Sicht oder von einem einheitlichen Menschenbild aus gesehen wurden, sondern die Auffassungen und Probleme der Epochen ihrer Entstehung widerspiegeln. So ist in der ersten Periode der deutschen Sozialversicherung 1883 die Krankenversicherung, 1884 die Unfallversicherung, 1889 die Invaliden- und Altersversicherung geschaffen worden. 1911 wurde die Angestelltenversicherung geschaffen und zugleich der gesamte Komplex der Sozialversicherung in dem einheitlichen Gesetzgebungswerk der *Reichsversicherungsordnung* zusammengefaßt. Das im wesentlichen im letzten Jahrhundert entstandene soziale Recht der Bergleute wurde in den Jahren 1923 bis 1926 in dem Reichsknappschaftsgesetz neu geordnet. 1927 folgte das Gesetz über die Arbeitsvermittlung und Arbeitslosenversicherung. Trotz ständiger Weiterentwicklung der einzelnen Zweige durch zahlreiche Ergänzungen überschneiden sie sich vielfach und tragen damit zu einer gewissen Unübersichtlichkeit des deutschen Sozialsystems bei, die in den letzten Jahren den Ruf nach einer Sozialreform immer dringlicher werden ließ.

Bei diesen Regelungen der Sozialversicherung war das Versicherungsprinzip, wenn auch in sozialer Modifizierung, beibehalten worden. Der *Versorgung der Kriegsopfer* hingegen, deren umfassende Regelung der Erste Weltkrieg erforderlich gemacht hatte, lag die Absicht zugrunde, von Staats wegen die Folgen von Gesundheitsschäden der Opfer des Krieges und ihrer Hinterbliebenen nach Möglichkeit zu mildern. Diese deutsche Kriegsopferversorgung wurde 1950 im Bundesversorgungsgesetz ausgebaut und zusammenfassend geregelt. Ihre Aufgabe ist es, sich der Opfer des Krieges und ihrer Hinterbliebenen in allen Lebenslagen anzunehmen und ihnen zu helfen, die Folgen der Schädigung oder des Verlustes des Ernährers nach Möglichkeit zu überwinden. Sie bemüht sich insbesondere um die soziale und wirtschaftliche Wiedereingliederung der Betroffenen.

*

Neben der Sozialversicherung und Versorgung ging die Entwicklung des *Armenwesens* und der *Wohlfahrtspflege* ihre eigenen Wege weiter, um sich der sozial Ungesicherten anzunehmen. Bis zur Zeit des Ersten Weltkrieges löste die Armenfürsorge sich nicht vom Leitbild des Armen, dem man mehr oder weniger die Schuld an seiner Lage zuschrieb. Die Inanspruchnahme von Armenunterstützung wurde als diskriminierend angesehen und führte zum Beispiel zum Entzug des Wahlrechts. Die Gemeinden, als Ortsarmenverband Träger der zunächst im Heimatrecht begründeten Unterstützungspflicht, leisteten selten mehr als das zur Fristung eines dürftigen Lebens unbedingt Notwendige; die Hilfe für Ortsfremde mußte erst allmählich vom Staat erzwungen werden. Soweit die Hilfe nicht genügte, verwies man den Armen an die Familiengemeinschaft oder die kirchliche Liebestätigkeit. Das „Elberfelder System" zeigt in seiner ehrenamtlichen Mitwirkung einzelner Bürger bei der Durchführung der Armenpflege aber auch verantwortungsbewußten Bürgersinn. Erst um die Jahrhundertwende setzte sich mit dem „Straßburger System" eine behördliche Zentralisierung und das Übergewicht geschulter, hauptamtlicher Kräfte durch.

Ein grundsätzlicher Wandel entstand hier erst, als deutlich wurde, daß die zumeist unverschuldeten Massennotstände im Gefolge des Krieges und der Inflation mit den bisherigen Methoden nicht behoben werden konnten, und als sich auch im staatlichen Bereich ein gesteigertes soziales Verantwortungsbewußtsein durchsetzte. Es ist das Verdienst der Weimarer Republik, in der Notzeit nach 1920 eine Reihe bedeutsamer und zukunftsträchtiger sozialer Gesetzgebungswerke geschaffen zu haben. An die Stelle des Armenwesens trat eine modern gestaltete *öffentliche Fürsorge*, die in der Fürsorgepflichtverordnung und in den Reichsgrundsätzen über Voraussetzung, Art und Maß der öffentlichen Fürsorge, beide von 1924, ihren Ausdruck fand. Im Gegensatz zur Sozialversicherung wird die Fürsorge von den Grundsätzen der Hilfsbedürftigkeit, der individuellen Hilfe und der Subsidiarität beherrscht. Nur dem Bedürftigen wird Hilfe gewährt. Sie richtet sich in Art und Höhe nach den besonderen Verhältnissen des Einzelfalles und greift nur ein, wenn der Bedürftige nicht von anderer, sei es privater oder öffentlicher, Seite Hilfe erhält. Fürsorgeleistungen werden sowohl zum laufenden Lebensunterhalt — hier in Anlehnung an von den einzelnen Ländern festgesetzte Richtsätze —, wie individuell in besonderen Notlagen gewährt. Sie können in dieser „offenen" Form oder durch Unterbringung in geeigneten Heimen oder Anstalten erfolgen. Durch eine gehobene Fürsorge für bestimmte Gruppen Bedürftiger wurde noch eine gewisse soziale Differenzierung anerkannt. Träger der Leistungen sind die einzelnen Stadt- und Landkreise mit ihren Fürsorge- oder Wohlfahrtsämtern, für gewisse Sonderhilfen, zum Beispiel die Tuberkulosehilfe, die überörtlichen Landesfürsorgeverbände.

Die Regelung der Fürsorge hat in ihrer Anpassungsfähigkeit an die persönlichen und örtlichen Verhältnisse sich im allgemeinen bewährt. Allerdings trägt die Notwendigkeit der Offenlegung der persönlichen Verhältnisse und der gewisse Ermessensspielraum, der den Fürsorgebehörden bei der Gewährung der Leistungen gegeben ist, dazu die in der Praxis allerdings stark zurückgetretene Verpflichtung zur Rückerstattung erhaltener Fürsorgeleistungen, nicht zur Beliebtheit der Fürsorge bei. Eine gewisse Schwierigkeit für die Verwirklichung des Gleichheitsgrundsatzes in der Fürsorge liegt in der unterschiedlichen Leistungsfähigkeit, manchmal auch Leistungsbereitschaft, der einzelnen Kommunen. Um das Fürsorgewesen modernen Erkenntnissen anzupassen, bereitet die Bundesregierung zur Zeit eine *Neuordnung des Fürsorgerechts* vor. Danach wird man wohl künftig nicht mehr von „Fürsorge", sondern von „*Sozialhilfe*" sprechen. Die Neuregelung wird jedoch keinen revolutionären Wandel des Fürsorgerechts bringen, sondern eine Weiterentwicklung. Sie wird vor allem der Tatsache Rechnung tragen, daß der Kreis derjenigen, die der Fürsorgeunterstützung zum notwendigen Lebensunterhalt bedürfen, durch die Ausweitung anderer sozialer Hilfen, besonders der Rentenversicherung, erheblich eingeschränkt worden ist. Das neue „*Sozialhilferecht*" wird als der Fürsorge angemessenes Gebiet vor allem die Individualhilfen in besonderen Lebenslagen ausgestalten. Solche Notlagen, in denen auch bisher Hilfe geboten wurde, für die aber nun besondere

Methoden der Hilfe festgelegt werden sollen, sind zum Beispiel die Hilfe für Kranke, Alte, Pflegebedürftige, Gefährdete und für werdende Mütter.

Neben der allgemeinen Fürsorge sind in Deutschland gewisse *Formen der Sonderfürsorge* entwickelt worden, so die Tuberkulosehilfe, die Hilfe für körperlich und geistig Behinderte, für Straffällige (Strafgefangene und Strafentlassene), für Nicht-Seßhafte, für Trinker und andere Süchtige. Bestimmungen hierüber sind teilweise in Sondergesetzen oder Richtlinien des Bundes und der Länder, teilweise in den allgemeinen Bestimmungen des Fürsorge-, Jugendwohlfahrts- oder Gesundheitsrechts enthalten.

Die *öffentliche Jugendhilfe* ist in Deutschland zusammenfassend erstmals 1924 im *Reichsjugendwohlfahrtsgesetz* geregelt worden, einem der fortschrittlichsten Gesetze aus der Zeit der Weimarer Republik. Nach ihm hat jedes Kind ein Recht auf Erziehung zur leiblichen, seelischen und gesellschaftlichen Tüchtigkeit. Die Erziehung Minderjähriger soll in erster Linie in der Hand der Eltern oder der sonstigen Erziehungsberechtigten liegen. Nur wenn der Anspruch auf Erziehung von der Familie nicht erfüllt wird, tritt an ihre Stelle eine öffentliche Erziehung entweder in der Form der mit den Eltern vereinbarten freiwilligen öffentlichen Erziehung oder, wenn Verwahrlosung droht, in derjenigen der gerichtlich angeordneten Fürsorgeerziehung. Als zentrale Stelle für die öffentliche Jugendwohlfahrt ist in jedem Stadt- und Landkreis ein *Jugendamt* eingerichtet, dem allgemein die Aufgaben der Förderung der Kinder und Jugendlichen der verschiedenen Altersgruppen, im einzelnen zum Beispiel der Schutz der Pflegekinder und die Amtsvormundschaft über uneheliche Kinder obliegen. Das Jugendamt hat ferner bei der Durchführung der Schutzaufsicht und der Fürsorgeerziehung, bei der Jugendgerichtshilfe und den Aufgaben nach dem Gesetz zum Schutz der Jugend in der Öffentlichkeit sowie bei der Bekämpfung jugendgefährdender Schriften mitzuwirken. Zu seinen Pflichtaufgaben gehört auch die Förderung der gesunden Jugend durch geeignete Einrichtungen wie Kindergärten, Kindertagesstätten, Jugendhorte und Jugendhäuser. Die Jugendämter und die in den Ländern eingerichteten Landesjugendämter haben sich teilweise zu zentralen Beratungsstellen in allen Jugendfragen entwickelt. Sie führen ihre Aufgaben in enger Zusammenarbeit mit den Jugendverbänden und den Organisationen durch, die sich die Fürsorge und Förderung der Jugend zur besonderen Aufgabe gemacht haben. Ihre Spitzenverbände sind auf Bundesebene in der „*Arbeitsgemeinschaft für Jugendpflege und Jugendfürsorge*" zusammengeschlossen.

Tabelle 1 ERZIEHUNGS- UND AUSBILDUNGSBEIHILFEN

Lfd. Nr.	Leistungsträger	Rechnungsjahr 1952		Rechnungsjahr 1957	
		Mill. DM	%	Mill. DM	%
1.	*Fürsorge*	36,2	*33,2*	107,7	*52,1*
	davon				
	a) Allgemeine Fürsorge ..	22,7	*20,8*	16,5	*7,9*
	b) Soziale Fürsorge für Kriegsopfer	13,5	*12,4*	91,2	*44,2*
2.	*Lastenausgleich*	67,5	*62,0*	84,3	*40,8*
3.	*Arbeitsverwaltung*	5,2	*4,8*	14,8	*7,1*
	Insgesamt	108,9	*100*	206,8	*100*

Jugendfragen sind auch in zahlreichen anderen Sozialgesetzen angesprochen. Eine besondere Rolle spielen dabei die *Beihilfen zur Berufsausbildung* für solche junge Menschen, denen ohne sie eine angemessene Ausbildung versagt bleiben müßte. Im Lastenausgleichs- und im Versorgungsrecht für Kriegsversehrte und Hinterbliebene, in der Fürsorge und im Rahmen der Berufsförderungsmaßnahmen der Arbeitsverwaltung, in den Sondergesetzen für Evakuierte, Spätheimkehrer und anderen finden sich derartige Förderungsmöglichkeiten[1]. Für die Förderung von begabten und bedürftigen Studenten an wissenschaftlichen Hochschulen werden gemeinsam von Bund und Ländern nach dem sogenannten „Honnefer Modell" erhebliche Beträge zur Verfügung gestellt. Sie werden im Einzelfall durch die Selbstverwaltung der Hochschulen bewilligt. Die Förderung der Studierenden an den sogenannten nicht-wissenschaftlichen Hochschulen führen die Länder nach ähnlichen Grundsätzen durch.

*

Die geschilderten sozialen Hilfen sind in ihren wesentlichen Grundlagen schon vor 1933 entwickelt worden. Die Folgen des Nationalsozialismus waren auch für die soziale Arbeit tief einschneidend. In besonderem Maße wurden dadurch die freie Wohlfahrtspflege und die Sozialwissenschaft betroffen. Zahlreiche Sozialwissenschaftler haben damals den Weg der Emigration gehen müssen. Was sich ereignete, war weniger ein Abbau der Leistungen an sich, als ihre Denaturierung zu politischen Zwecken. So hat auch die NS-Volkswohlfahrt als die soziale Massenorganisation dieser Zeit trotz den außerordentlichen Mitteln, die ihr durch die unter politischem Zwang

[1] Vergleiche hierzu Tabelle 1.

stehenden Sammlungen zugeführt wurden, die soziale Arbeit nicht gefördert, sondern in erster Linie als Instrument politischer Machtausübung im sozialen Raum gewirkt. Den Machthabern kam es vor allem darauf an, die Einrichtungen zu beseitigen oder an sich zu ziehen, die ihnen verdächtig erschienen, Menschen in einer dem Regime unerwünschten Weise unmittelbar anzusprechen, oder geeignet, ihnen persönliche, pflegerische oder erzieherische Hilfe angedeihen zu lassen. Vor allem der Einfluß der christlichen Liebeswerke bis herab zum Kindergarten sollte gebrochen werden. Viele, die sich bemühten, derartige Einrichtungen vor dem Zugriff zu retten, haben das mit scharfen Maßnahmen büßen müssen. Wenn es trotzdem gelang, einen erheblichen Teil der Einrichtungen der freien Wohlfahrtspflege durchzuhalten, so ist das ein besonderes Verdienst einzelner Persönlichkeiten im Bereich der freien und öffentlichen Sozialarbeit, die ihre Aufgabe mit Mut und Geschick wahrnahmen.

*

Der *Zusammenbruch* (1945) hat im sozialen Bereich zunächst allgemein eine kaum vorstellbare Notlage geschaffen. Die Städte waren weithin zerstört, die Wirtschaft lag darnieder, Millionen waren nur mit Trümmerbeseitigung und Aufräumungsarbeiten beschäftigt, die Familien vielfach ohne Hilfe des noch kriegsgefangenen Ernährers, die Flüchtlinge in improvisierten, primitiven Lagern ohne Rücksicht, ob Arbeitsmöglichkeit bestand, zusammengedrängt. Die zumeist vom nationalsozialistischen Staat ganz in seinen Machtbereich gezwungenen Träger der Sozialversicherungen waren aktionsunfähig. Der Not war in der Zeit äußerster Lebensmittelknappheit und einer drohenden Hungerkatastrophe zunächst auch nicht nur mit finanziellen Hilfen beizukommen. Die einzelnen Städte, Landkreise und Gemeinden haben damals von unten her mit der Beseitigung der schlimmsten Kriegsschäden und der Wiederherstellung einer gewissen öffentlichen Ordnung begonnen und auf sozialem Gebiet zumeist mit den herkömmlichen Mitteln der öffentlichen Fürsorge die größte Not aufzufangen versucht. Sie haben hier Wesentliches geleistet. Die großen Schwierigkeiten, vor allem der Flüchtlingsnot, hätten sie aber wohl nicht gemeistert, wären ihnen nicht die Verbände und Einrichtungen der freien Wohlfahrtspflege, insbesondere die christlichen und humanitären Liebeswerke, beigesprungen. Diese konnten ein erfreuliches Verständnis und eine nach den furchtbaren Erlebnissen der nationalsozialistischen Zeit überraschend warmherzige Bereitschaft vor allem christlicher Kreise des Auslands aktivieren und damit tatkräftige und rasch wirksame Hilfe vermitteln. Nur so konnte es gelingen, die einströmenden Millionen vertriebener Familien, deren Ernährer sich zumeist noch in Kriegsgefangenschaft befanden, vor Hungersnot und Elend zu bewahren. Die gezwungenermaßen meist sehr kümmerliche Unterbringung, oft jahrelang in Massen- und Notquartieren und in Lagern, in denen manche noch heute auf die Fertigstellung der für sie vorgesehenen Wohnungen warten müssen, hat an diese Menschen sehr schwere Anforderungen gestellt. Gesetzliche Hilfsmaßnahmen konnten zwischen 1946 und 1949 auch auf dem Gebiet der Sozialpolitik zunächst nur in dem den einzelnen Ländern von den Besatzungsmächten eingeräumten engen Rahmen und ohne einheitliche Ausrichtung eingeleitet werden. Die Besatzungsmächte, anfänglich noch im Kontrollrat geeint, waren zwar bereit, gewisse dringliche Maßnahmen auf dem Arbeitsmarkt zu dekretieren, um die Wirtschaft allmählich wieder in Gang zu bringen. Sie taten zunächst aber wenig zur Neuordnung der Sozialversicherung und nichts zum Wiederaufbau der zerschlagenen Kriegsopferversorgung. Alle Notleidenden, auch Vertriebene, Flüchtlinge, Kriegsbeschädigte und Hinterbliebenen, waren damit auf die sehr bescheidenen Sätze der allgemeinen Fürsorge angewiesen. Die gehobene Fürsorge wurde abgeschafft, die Gewährung höherer als der Fürsorge-Mindestsätze an Kriegsopfer ausdrücklich verboten. Nur die Organisationen der freien Wohlfahrtspflege konnten die kaum zum nötigsten Unterhalt ausreichenden Leistungen aus in- und ausländischen Hilfen bescheiden aufstocken. Die Währungsumstellung von 1948 hat auch ihre Arbeit schwer getroffen und ihre Mittel dezimiert.

Die sozialen Leistungen der Bundesrepublik[1]

Wohl selten ist ein Staat im Augenblick einer solchen Notlage seiner Bürger ins Leben gerufen worden wie die Bundesrepublik Deutschland 1949. Daß trotzdem in wenigen Jahren eine wachsende Gesundung der deutschen Wirtschaft erreicht werden konnte, ist außer dem nimmermüden Fleiß, mit dem alle Schichten an den Wiederaufbau des zerstörten Landes herangingen, und einer mutigen Wirtschaftspolitik vor allem den überlegten Maßnahmen zuzuschreiben, durch welche die schweren sozialen Notstände allmählich gemindert oder behoben wurden. Die zunächst bescheidene finanzielle Kraft der Bundesrepublik erlaubte es nicht, alle Probleme, die einer Lösung harrten, zugleich anzupacken. Die Bundesregierung war sich darüber klar, daß es in erster Linie darauf ankam, die Wirtschaft in Gang zu setzen, der Bevölkerung allmählich Vertrauen in ihre Leistungsfähigkeit und in eine

[1] Vergleiche Tabelle 2 auf Seite 541.

Tabelle 2
DIE ÖFFENTLICHEN SOZIALLEISTUNGEN IN DER BUNDESREPUBLIK[1]

Jahr: 1957	Millionen DM					
Soziale Einrichtungen	Gesamteinnahmen	Davon unter anderem Beiträge	Gesamtausgaben	Davon unter anderem: Sachleistungen	Barleistungen	Verwaltungskosten
1	2	3	4	5	6	7
1. *Sozialversicherung*						
a) Krankenversicherung...	6.253	5.072	6.483	3.974	2.110	379
b) Arbeitslosenversicherung	1.558	1.342	1.404	372	857	56
c) Unfallversicherung	1.511	1.439	1.470	248	1.051	104
d) Rentenversicherung der Arbeiter	9.854	6.468	8.385	342	7.167	171
e) Rentenversicherung der Angestellten[2]	4.239	3.227	3.893	112	3.506	67
f) Knappschaftliche Rentenversicherung	1.687	742	1.647	27	1.487	27
2. *Familienbeihilfen* Aufwendungen nach den Kindergeldgesetzen und dem Mutterschutzgesetz ..	638	558	569	—	554	14
3. *Arbeitslosenhilfe (-fürsorge)* .	417	—	417	47	315	17
4. *Öffentliche Fürsorge*	1.368	—	1.368	562	806	—
5. *Lastenausgleich*	2.039	—	2.039	—	2.039	—
6. *Kriegsopferversorgung*	3.853	—	3.853	191	3.435	180
Insgesamt	33.417	18.848	31.528	5.875	23.327	1.015

[1] Ohne Saarland, jedoch einschließlich von Berlin(West). — [2] Einschließlich der Altersversorgung für das Deutsche Handwerk.

Quelle: Bundesministerium für Arbeit und Sozialordnung (Arbeits- und Sozialstatist. Mitteilungen 1959, Heft 2).

gewisse Stabilität der Entwicklung zu vermitteln und damit der erheblichen Arbeitslosigkeit zu begegnen. Auf sozialem Gebiet mußte zunächst versucht werden, die dringendsten Notstände durch Übergangs- und Sofortmaßnahmen zu beheben.

Nach Artikel 120 des Grundgesetzes obliegt es dem Bund, die gesamten äußeren und inneren *Kriegsfolgelasten* zu tragen. Die ersten Bemühungen galten deshalb einerseits dem Wiederaufbau der dringendsten sozialen Hilfen, insbesondere der Wiederherstellung eines bundeseinheitlichen Sozialversicherungs- und Versorgungsrechts, andererseits der Aufbringung und

Verteilung der sozialen Kriegslasten im Rahmen der sogenannten Kriegsfolgenhilfe, vor allem der außerordentlich hohen Aufwendungen für die Vertriebenen und Flüchtlinge. Es ist ein Verdienst dieser Anfangszeit, daß die Bundesregierung damals ohne Rücksicht auf die schwere finanzielle Belastung Regelungen traf, die den zahllosen notleidenden Vertriebenen wirksam über die erste Not hinweggeholfen und damit entscheidend zu ihrer Eingliederung beigetragen haben. Unter den sozialpolitischen Maßnahmen im engeren Sinn standen weiter im Vordergrund Wiedergutmachungsleistungen für die Opfer des Nationalsozialismus' und Hilfen für die aus der Gefangenschaft heimkehrenden Soldaten. Als eine ihrer dringlichsten Aufgaben haben Bundesregierung und Bundestag sodann die Vereinheitlichung und Neuordnung der Versorgung der Kriegsopfer und Hinterbliebenen angesehen. Das Bundesversorgungsgesetz von 1950 hat die Versorgung der Kriegsopfer unter Weiterbildung des Reichsversorgungsrechts von 1920 auf neue Grundlagen gestellt und ist seither wiederholt ergänzt worden. Seine Neugestaltung in Anpassung an die geänderten Verhältnisse wird zur Zeit vorbereitet.

*

Es war verständlich, daß die schweren Erlebnisse des Zusammenbruchs und der plötzliche Wegfall aller finanziellen und sozialen Sicherungen das Streben der gesamten Bevölkerung nach *Sicherheit* außerordentlich steigern mußten. Man wollte nicht nur abhängig sein von karitativen Leistungen der freien Wohlfahrtspflege und den in Art und Höhe nicht voll überseh- und berechenbaren Leistungen der öffentlichen Fürsorge. Mit steigendem Nachdruck drang man auf die Gewährung von Rechtsansprüchen. Dies galt auch für die Vertriebenen und Flüchtlinge, die naturgemäß in besonderem Maße an einem Ausgleich ihrer schweren Opfer interessiert waren. Als Vorstufe des *Lastenausgleichs* wurde durch das Soforthilfegesetz von 1949 zunächst die Behebung der dringendsten Notstände in Angriff genommen. Das endgültige Lastenausgleichsgesetz kam nach jahrelangen Bemühungen 1952 zustande und stellt ein völlig neuartiges System sozialer Hilfe und der Übernahme von Schäden und Lasten eines Volksteils durch die Gesamtheit dar. Gleichzeitig wurde den heimatlosen Ausländern im Bundesgebiet eine Rechtsstellung zugebilligt, die über die in der Internationalen Flüchtlingskonvention vorgesehene erheblich hinausgeht. Die Rechtsstellung der deutschen *Vertriebenen und Flüchtlinge* wurde 1953 durch das *Bundesvertriebenengesetz* geregelt.

*

Die Bemühungen um die Gewährung eines vertretbaren Ausgleichs an die durch den Krieg besonders hart Betroffenen haben im Bewußtsein der Öffentlichkeit das Verständnis für die Möglichkeit des Ausgleichs auch anderer Lasten geweckt. Diese Erkenntnis verband sich mit dem Anliegen der Bundesregierung, die Sozialpolitik stärker auf die *Förderung der Familie* auszurichten. Dieses Anliegen hat in der Schaffung eines besonderen Bundesministeriums für Familien- und Jugendfragen seinen Ausdruck gefunden. Da dem deutschen Leistungslohn die Berücksichtigung des Familienstandes fremd ist, bedeutete die Erziehung und Ausbildung eine größeren Kinderzahl für die Familie mit normalem Verdienst in der Regel eine großes wirtschaftliches Opfer. Hier brachte das *Kindergeldgesetz* von 1954 einen Wandel im Sinne eines gewissen Familienlastenausgleichs: Familien mit drei oder mehr Kindern erhalten danach für das dritte und jedes weitere Kind ein Kindergeld in Höhe von monatlich jetzt 40,— DM. Die Durchführung liegt in der Hand besonderer Familienausgleichskassen, die bei den Berufsgenossenschaften eingerichtet sind. Auch in der Sozialversicherung, der Versorgung und der öffentlichen Fürsorge wurden die Leistungen für die Familie verstärkt. Als weitere Schritte zur Festigung der Familie sind steuerliche Erleichterungen für Familien mit Kindern, die Förderung eines familiengerechten Wohnungsbaus, Fahrpreisermäßigungen für kinderreiche Familien in öffentlichen Verkehrsmitteln, nicht zuletzt die großzügige öffentliche Hilfe für das auf Anregung der verstorbenen Gattin des Bundespräsidenten, Frau ELLY HEUSS-KNAPP, geschaffene Müttergenesungswerk sowie die Einrichtung von Familienferienheimen zu nennen.

*

In diesen Jahren wuchs bei allen Beteiligten die Erkenntnis, daß durch laufende Änderungen und Ergänzungen der Bestimmungen über die sozialen Hilfen keine befriedigenden Ergebnisse herbeigeführt werden können, daß vielmehr nur eine gründliche *Sozialreform* unsere in nahezu einem Jahrhundert entstandenen Sozialgesetze wirksam aufeinander abzustimmen vermöge. Insbesondere sollten dadurch die vielfachen Überschneidungen beseitigt, die Inanspruchnahme verschiedener Sozialleistungen durch dieselbe Person auf das gebotene Maß eingeschränkt und die Leistungen der jeweiligen wirtschaftlichen Entwicklung angepaßt werden. Die deutsche Öffentlichkeit und die Fachkreise haben sich dieser Aufgabe in zahlreichen Äußerungen von Sachverständigenausschüssen, Denkschriften und Vorschlägen angenommen, wobei die Meinungen teilweise erheblich auseinandergingen. An der Vorbereitung der Neuordnung hat besonders der zur Beratung der Bundesregierung eingesetzte Beirat für die Neuordnung sozialer Leistungen mitgewirkt. Von Bedeutung waren ferner das im Auftrag des Bundeskanzlers gefertigte Gutachten der Professoren ACHINGER, HÖFFNER, MUTHESIUS und NEUNDÖRFER sowie vor allem W. SCHREIBERS Vorschlag der „dynamischen Rente" und die von der SPD in ihrem „Sozialplan" (1952) und im Entwurf zum Renten-Neuordnungsgesetz vorgeschlagene „Lohnwert-Rente". Für die Neuordnung des Rechts der Fürsorge und der Jugendhilfe hat der seit fünfundsiebzig Jahren als Fachgremium bewährte „Deutsche Verein für öffentliche und private Fürsorge" wertvolle Vorarbeit geleistet.

Als erster Teil der Sozialreform wurde 1957 die *Rentenversicherung der Arbeiter und Angestellten* sowie die *Knappschaftsversicherung* neu geordnet. Von besonderer Bedeutung auch für die noch ausstehenden Regelungen ist dabei, daß die Höhe der Renten nunmehr an die Entwicklung des Lohnniveaus angepaßt wird, so daß dem Rentenempfänger eine Leistung gesichert bleibt, die dem Anwachsen des Sozialprodukts entspricht und sich dem Wandel der Kaufkraft anpaßt. Durch die Sozialreform sollen besonders auch die Maßnahmen der „Rehabilitation" und der vorbeugenden Gesundheitsfürsorge ausgebaut werden. Im übrigen wurde das System der sozialen Altershilfen in den letzten Jahren durch den Ausbau der gesetzlichen Altershilfe für das Handwerk und durch die Einrichtung einer Altershilfe für selbständige Landwirte erweitert. Als nächste Schritte sind die Reform der Unfallversicherung, der Krankenversicherung und der Kriegsopferversorgung vorgesehen. Außerdem wird, wie dargelegt, eine Neuordnung des Rechts der öffentlichen Fürsorge und der Jugendhilfe vorbereitet.

Die Bemühungen um eine Reform der sozialen Hilfen haben die Frage nach den Grenzen dessen, was mit sozialen Leistungen erreicht werden kann und soll, also der *Grenzen des Sozialstaatsprinzips*, erneut aufgeworfen. Die führenden politischen Kräfte der Bundesrepublik sind sich darüber einig, daß der in der Verfassung verankerte Grundsatz des sozialen Rechtsstaats und die besonderen sozialen Aufgaben, die der Bundesrepublik gestellt sind, es notwendig machen, eine Sicherung der Existenz des einzelnen auch im Falle der Not zu gewährleisten, ohne daß daraus ein allgemeiner Anspruch auf Versorgung durch die Allgemeinheit erwachsen darf. Das Leitbild der sozialen Ordnung soll in der Bundesrepublik auch weiterhin die selbstverantwortliche Persönlichkeit sein. Die Allgemeinheit soll dann eintreten, wenn die Vorleistung, das Verhalten oder die besondere Lage des einzelnen den sozialen Aufwand rechtfertigen. Dem Arbeitsfähigen und dem schuldlos in Not Geratenen soll dabei ohne Kleinlichkeit geholfen werden.

Im übrigen soll aber von Leistungen abgesehen werden, die zu einem nivellierenden Versorgungsstaat führen müßten. Bei diesen Feststellungen darf nicht außer Betracht bleiben, daß im anderen Teil Deutschlands, in der sogenannten DDR, das kommunistische Regime auf sozialem Gebiet Maßstäbe zu entwickeln trachtet, denen in erster Linie die Tendenz zur Steigerung der Arbeitsleistung innewohnt. Diese Maßstäbe können deshalb mit den Auffassungen eines sozialen Rechtsstaats, wie ihn die Bundesrepublik darstellt, in keiner Weise verglichen werden. Schon um des Wohles der Deutschen in der sogenannten DDR willen besteht aller Grund, auch die dortige sozialpolitische Entwicklung aufs Aufmerksamste zu beobachten.

Die freie Wohlfahrtspflege

Die freie Wohlfahrtspflege spielt im deutschen Sozialwesen eine hervorragende Rolle. Sie umfaßt das nicht von Staat und Kommunen getragene Wirken karitativer Kräfte, die als Träger verschiedenartigster Einrichtungen und in der unmittelbaren Hilfe von Mensch zu Mensch tätig sind. Die freie Wohlfahrtspflege ist vor allem aus der Jahrhunderte alten Liebestätigkeit der Kirchen herausgewachsen und deshalb zum großen Teil bis heute konfessionell ausgerichtet geblieben. Seit der Zeit der Aufklärung haben aber auch verschiedene kirchlich nicht gebundene Gruppen aus humanitären Gründen derartige Aufgaben sich zur Pflicht gemacht. Diese Liebeswerke sind zum erheblichen Teil aus örtlichen Schöpfungen hilfsbereiter Persönlichkeiten hervorgegangen. Im Laufe der Zeit haben die einzelnen Einrichtungen sich zu größeren Verbänden zusammengeschlossen, die wichtige Partner der Sozialarbeit des Staates und der Kommunen geworden sind. *Spitzenverbände der freien Wohlfahrtspflege* sind heute: Innere Mission und Hilfswerk der evangelischen Kirchen in Deutschland, Deutscher Caritasverband, Deutsches Rotes Kreuz, Arbeiterwohlfahrt, Deutscher Paritätischer Wohlfahrtsverband und Zentralwohlfahrtsstelle der Juden in Deutschland.

Die *Tätigkeit* und die *Arbeitsweise der freien Wohlfahrtspflege* ist eine außerordentlich vielseitige. Sie unterscheidet sich insofern von der öffentlichen Sozialarbeit, als sie vor allem solche Aufgaben aufgreift und durchführt, die ihrem Wesen nach eine besondere persönliche Verbindung mit dem einzelnen Notleidenden erfordert. Von Anfang an hat die freie Wohlfahrtspflege deshalb in erster Linie die Schaffung von Anstalten und Heimen für solche Menschen sich angelegen sein lassen, die ohne besondere Wartung und Pflege nicht zu leben oder sich zu entfalten vermögen. Sie verfügt in der Bundesrepublik über rund 9.000 Anstalten und Heime mit etwa 700.000 Betten und Plätzen. In den letzten Jahrzehnten haben die großen Wohlfahrtsverbände auch ein weitverzweigtes Netz von Bezirksstellen und Mitarbeitern aufgebaut, mit denen sie den einzelnen Notständen nachgehen. Der Arbeitsbereich der freien Wohlfahrtspflege umfaßt praktisch alle Gebiete menschlicher Not und Hilfsbedürftigkeit. Zu ihren Betreuten gehören ebenso Säuglinge, Kinder und Jugendliche wie Alte, Gebrechliche, Kranke und Krüppel, Obdachlose und Gefährdete, Süchtige und Straffällige. Noch schwer getroffen von den Rückschlägen und Anfeindungen in der Zeit des Nationalsozialismus und von den Schäden des Krieges, haben die freien Wohlfahrtsorganisationen unmittelbar nach dem Ende des Zweiten Weltkrieges erstaunliche Kräfte entfaltet. Vor allem auf den Gebieten der Vertriebenen- und Flüchtlingshilfe, der Versehrten-, Gefangenen- und Heimkehrerbetreuung, der Hilfe für politisch Verfolgte, für heimatlose Ausländer, für Spätheimkehrer und Umsiedler, nicht zuletzt auch durch den Aufbau eines umfassenden Suchdienstes für Vermißte haben sie hohe Verdienste erworben und sich damit ein bleibendes Denkmal im Bewußtsein des Volkes gesetzt.

Die *Einrichtungen*, welche die freie Wohlfahrtspflege trägt und unterhält, sind sehr mannigfaltig: Krankenhäuser der verschiedensten Art (mit rund 210.000 = 38,6% der Krankenbetten in der Bundesrepublik), Heilstätten und Heime für Suchtkranke, Erholungsheime, Anstalten für Gebrechliche und Behinderte, Erziehungs- und Jugendwohnheime (mit rund 200.000 Betten), Alterswohn- und Alterspflegeheime (rund 110.000 Betten), Wohnheime der verschiedensten Art, Flüchtlings-, Übernachtungs- und Bahnhofsheime, Einrichtungen für Nichtseßhafte und Auffangstellen für Strafentlassene. Daneben bestehen als „halboffene" Einrichtungen: Kindergärten, Kinderhorte und Kindertagesstätten (mit etwa 650.000 Plätzen), Wärm- und Nähstuben, Notstandsküchen, Werkstätten für Behinderte, in der „offenen" Fürsorge vor allem Pflegestationen der Gemeinden, Einrichtungen der Trinker-, Gefährdeten- und Auswandererfürsorge sowie Beratungsstellen verschiedener Art. Diese Verbände haben bei ihrer Arbeit auf vielen Gebieten neue Methoden entwickelt und erprobt und dadurch auch für die öffentliche Wohlfahrtspflege beispielhaft gewirkt. Der Dienst, der hier geleistet wird, und der den für die öffentliche soziale Hilfe verantwortlichen Stellen eine unentbehrliche Stütze zur Durchführung der im Einzelfall notwendigen Maßnahmen ist, wäre nicht möglich, wenn nicht auch heute noch der freien Wohlfahrtspflege Kräfte zur Verfügung ständen, die selbstlos die Hilfe am Nächsten zu ihrem Beruf oder zur ehrenamtlichen Aufgabe machen. Diakonisse und Ordensschwester verkörpern im besonderen Maße diesen karitativen pflegerischen oder sozialpädagogischen Dienst, in dem in immer wieder neuen Formen hilfsbereite Menschen ein befriedigendes Wirken in tätiger Nächstenliebe finden. Solche freiwillige Helfer wirken in jüngster Zeit insbesondere auch in den Einrichtungen der Familienfürsorge, der Mütter-, Ehe- und Erziehungsberatungsstellen sowie im Außendienst der Verbände, so besonders in der Nachbarschaftshilfe und der Hauspflege.

Die freie Wohlfahrtspflege wäre nicht in der Lage, ihre Aufgaben durchzuführen, wenn nicht Bund, Länder und Kommunen diese Organisationen großzügig fördern würden. Das geschieht ebenso für die verschiedenen Wirkungsbereiche in Stadt und Land wie auf Bundesebene für die Spitzenverbände. Für die Inanspruchnahme der Anstalten und Heime durch die Sozialversicherung, die Versorgung, die öffentliche Fürsorge oder Jugendhilfe werden im Einzelfall Pflegegelder bezahlt. Nach dem Krieg hat überdies die öffentliche Hand zum Beispiel aus Mitteln des Bundesministeriums des Innern, des Bundesjugendplans und des Lastenausgleichfonds' durch Zuschüsse und Darlehen die Wiedererstellung und den Neubau zahlreicher Heime der freien Wohlfahrtsverbände ermöglicht. Dies hat wesentlich dazu beigetragen, daß die Zahl der Einrichtungen gegenüber der Vorkriegszeit erheblich angewachsen ist. Bundesregierung und Länder haben von Anfang an besonderen Wert darauf gelegt, daß die Verbände durch die öffentliche Förderung in ihrer Entscheidungsfreiheit und in der Gestaltung ihres Aufgabenbereichs in keiner Weise eingeschränkt werden. Nur in einem selbstverantwortlichen, allein von den religiösen oder sittlichen Überzeugungen gelenkten Wirken können sie die Kräfte entfalten, die zur Durchführung ihrer sozialen und karitativen Aufgaben am Mitmenschen nötig sind.

Soziale Ausbildung und sozialer Beruf

Der im Dienste der Sozialarbeit Tätige, neuerdings gern „*Sozialarbeiter*" genannt, bietet in Deutschland weder der Ausbildung noch seinem Wirken und seiner Stellung im öffentlichen Leben nach ein einheitliches Bild. Man unterscheidet heute einmal die pflegerischen, wohlfahrtspflegerischen und sozialpädagogischen Fachkräfte im engeren Sinne. Sie stellen den theoretischen und praktisch gut ausgebildeten Kern der Sozialarbeit dar. In den verschiedenen Zweigen der Wohlfahrtspflege, der Jugendhilfe und der öffentlichen Gesundheitsfürsorge vor allem im Außendienst liegt ihnen der persönliche Kontakt mit den zu betreuenden Menschen ob. Auf der andern Seite steht der zahlenmäßig größere Kreis der Beamten und Angestellten mit

Verwaltungsvorbildung, denen überwiegend der Innendienst, die Büroarbeit in den verschiedenen Zweigen der Fürsorge, der Versorgung und der Sozialversicherung aufgetragen ist. Der soziale Beruf hat in Deutschland seinen Ursprung in den pflegerischen Berufen, deren Leitbild noch heute Ordensschwester und Diakonisse verkörpern. Die soziale Ausbildung gewann in Deutschland um die Jahrhundertwende, vor allem unter dem Einfluß von ALICE SALOMON, Gestalt. Sie entwickelte sich nicht im Rahmen der Hochschulen, sondern in staatlich anerkannten *Wohlfahrtsschulen*, höheren Fachschulen für Sozialarbeit. Damals wurden sie zumeist „Soziale Frauenschulen" genannt. Inzwischen haben längst auch zahlreiche junge Männer diesem Beruf sich zugewandt. Heute bestehen achtunddreißig solcher Wohlfahrtsschulen. Nach einem in der Regel dreijährigen Lehrgang, einer praktischen Ausbildungszeit und nach Ableistung einer staatlichen Prüfung führen sie zur staatlichen Anerkennung als Wohlfahrtspfleger. Daneben bestehen außer Krankenpflege- und Schwesternschulen besondere Ausbildungsstätten für sozialpädagogische Kräfte wie Kindergärtnerinnen und Jugendhortnerinnen, Jugendpfleger und Heimerzieher. Die Schaffung einer Akademie für Sozial- und Jugendarbeit, die im Anschluß an eine Universität der Ausbildung besonders qualifizierter Kräfte dienen und die Verbindung zu den sozialen Wissenschaften herstellen soll, ist ein dringendes Anliegen. Der Aus- und Fortbildung der aus der Verwaltung stammenden Kräfte, die im sozialen Bereich tätig sind, nehmen sich die Länder, die Träger der Sozialversicherung, die kommunalen Spitzenverbände und der Deutsche Verein für öffentliche und private Fürsorge sowie die Berufsorganisationen der weiblichen und männlichen Sozialarbeiter an. Die Anerkennung als Weg zu einer selbständigen Laufbahn des gehobenen Dienstes (Fürsorgeinspektor) hat die wohlfahrtspflegerische Ausbildung erst in einzelnen Ländern erreicht. Sie wird jedoch allgemein erstrebt und ist die Vorbedingung dafür, daß der soziale Beruf, der im öffentlichen Dienst auf die Dauer nicht ausschließlich auf selbstloser karitativer Haltung aufgebaut werden kann, Anerkennung findet und Anziehungskraft ausübt. Beides ist Voraussetzung dafür, daß die sozialen Aufgaben der Gegenwart sachgemäß durchgeführt werden und hierzu die notwendige Zahl fachlich und menschlich geeigneter Kräfte zur Verfügung steht. Erst dann wird dem Bemühen des Parlaments und der Regierungen in Bund und Ländern, der Träger der sozialen Hilfen und der Kräfte der freien Wohlfahrtspflege um die Verbesserung der Leistungen und der Methoden der Sozialarbeit und um die Verwirklichung des sozialen Rechtsstaats ein Erfolg auf lange Sicht beschieden sein.

ARBEITSRECHT

In der deutschen Sozialpolitik nimmt das Arbeitsrecht auf Grund seiner Bedeutung für die arbeitende Bevölkerung und wegen seiner großen Tradition und geschichtlichen Bewährung eine zentrale Stellung ein. Auf den überkommenen Fundamenten wurde nach Bereinigung des Rechtsgebietes von nationalsozialistischem Gedankengut seit Errichtung der Bundesrepublik tatkräftig und mit Mut zu neuen Lösungen weitergebaut. Neuartig für deutsche Verhältnisse und im internationalen Vergleich ist vor allem das Recht der Mitbestimmung der Arbeitnehmer im Betrieb.

I. GRUNDGEDANKEN DER ARBEITSVERFASSUNG

Das Arbeitsrecht bildet einen wesentlichen Teil der sozialen Ordnung in der Bundesrepublik. Wichtigstes Anliegen des Arbeitsrechts ist der Schutz des Arbeitnehmers. Die Schutzbedürftigkeit des Arbeitnehmers ergibt sich aus seiner Einordnung in einen fremden Lebensbereich (Betrieb) und aus der Befugnis des Arbeitgebers, den Einsatz der Arbeitskraft des Arbeitnehmers sachlich, zeitlich und örtlich zu bestimmen. Staatliche Rechtssätze schützen daher den Arbeitnehmer vor einer übermäßigen Ausnutzung seiner Arbeitskraft, insbesondere durch zu lange Arbeitszeiten (*Arbeitsschutzrecht*). Sie sichern die wirtschaftliche Stellung des auf seinen Arbeitsverdienst angewiesenen Arbeitnehmers (*Lohnschutz*). Sie begrenzen oft zwingend die *Rechte des Arbeitgebers*, wie sie andererseits auch dessen *Pflichten* gesetzlich festlegen. Schließlich erleichtern sie durch die Errichtung einer besonderen *Arbeitsgerichtsbarkeit* die Durchsetzung der Rechtsansprüche des Arbeitnehmers. Die Rechtsprechung hat ferner zum Schutze des Arbeitnehmers aus dem Arbeitsverhältnis eine allgemeine *Fürsorgepflicht des Arbeitgebers* gegenüber dem Arbeitnehmer hergeleitet und weitgehende Rechtsfolgen daraus gezogen.

Im geltenden Arbeitsrecht der Bundesrepublik Deutschland ist der Arbeitnehmer aber nicht nur Objekt eines so weit gespannten Schutzes. Vielmehr gestaltet er seine rechtliche und soziale Stellung entscheidend eigenverantwortlich mit. Auf der *überbetrieblichen Ebene* sind heute die Sozialpartner, das sind die Gewerkschaften und die Vereinigungen der Arbeitgeber, wesentlich an der Ordnung der Arbeit beteiligt. In den zwischen ihnen vereinbarten Tarifverträgen regeln sie innerhalb des Rahmens der staatlichen

Sozialgesetzgebung die sozialen Angelegenheiten ihrer Verbandsmitglieder, insbesondere die Arbeitsbedingungen sowie betriebliche und betriebsverfassungsrechtliche Fragen. Darüber hinaus stellen sie die Beisitzer bei den überall paritätisch besetzten Arbeits- und Sozialbehörden und üben maßgebenden Einfluß auf die sozialrechtliche Gesetzgebung aus. Auf der *betrieblichen Ebene* sind den Arbeitnehmern in allen größeren Betrieben Beteiligungsrechte in den sozialen und personellen Angelegenheiten der Belegschaft sowie auch in wirtschaftlichen Fragen des Betriebes und des Unternehmens eingeräumt. Zur Ausübung dieser Rechte sind in den Betrieben Betriebsräte gebildet worden.

Das derzeitige Arbeitsrecht in der Bundesrepublik ist somit durch eine Hinwendung vom einseitig *staatlichen Arbeitsschutzrecht* zur *Arbeitsverfassung* gekennzeichnet. Träger der Arbeitsverfassung sind neben dem Staat (Bund und Länder), die Sozialpartner (Gewerkschaften und Vereinigungen der Arbeitgeber), die betrieblichen Partner (Arbeitgeber und Betriebsrat) und die Parteien des Arbeitsvertrags (Arbeitgeber und Arbeitnehmer). Den einzelnen Trägern der Arbeitsverfassung sind bestimmte Aufgaben und Zuständigkeiten zugeordnet: Der Staat gestaltet weiterhin durch Gesetze und Rechtsverordnungen das eigentliche Arbeitsschutzrecht (Betriebsschutz, Arbeitszeitschutz, Mutterschutz, Schwerbeschädigtenschutz, Heimarbeiterschutz und anderes mehr). Auch in der besonderen Gerichtsbarkeit für Arbeitssachen hat der Staat einen wichtigen Bestandteil der Arbeitsverfassung in eigener Hand behalten. Darüber hinaus hat der Staat es sich aber lediglich vorbehalten, durch die Schaffung wichtiger Gesetze (wie das Tarifvertragsgesetz vom 9.4.1949, das Kündigungsschutzgesetz vom 10.8.1951 und das Betriebsverfassungsgesetz vom 11.10.1952) den rechtlichen Rahmen abzustecken. Innerhalb dieses Rahmens und insbesondere für die inhaltliche Gestaltung der Arbeitsverhältnisse (Lohn, Urlaub und sonstige Arbeitsbedingungen) hat der Staat den anderen Trägern der Arbeitsverfassung und hier wiederum vor allem den überbetrieblichen Sozialpartnern volle Freiheit gelassen, ihre Angelegenheiten in eigener Verantwortung zu regeln. Der Staat hat damit den autonomen Trägern der Arbeitsverfassung wichtige Teile seiner eigenen Ordnungsaufgabe überlassen. Das gilt besonders für den Bund, der nach Artikel 74 Ziffer 12 des Grundgesetzes auf dem Gebiete des gesamten Arbeitsrechts die Befugnis zur konkurrierenden Gesetzgebung inne hat. Nicht zu Unrecht kann daher gesagt werden, die geltende Arbeitsverfassung in der Bundesrepublik Deutschland werde von dem Prinzip der *sozialen Selbstverwaltung* beherrscht.

Die überragende Stellung der überbetrieblichen Sozialpartner innerhalb der Arbeitsverfassung läßt es zweckmäßig erscheinen, sie an die Spitze der nachfolgenden Übersicht über die Organisation, die Aufgaben und die Zuständigkeiten der einzelnen Träger der Arbeitsverfassung zu stellen.

II. DIE SOZIALPARTNER

A. Organisations- und Betätigungsfreiheit

1. Auf Grund des Artikels 9 Absatz 3 des Grundgesetzes haben alle Arbeitnehmer und Arbeitgeber das Recht, zur Wahrung und Förderung ihrer Arbeits- und Wirtschaftsbedingungen Organisationen zu bilden und nach ihrer eigenen Wahl und ohne vorherige Genehmigung solchen Organisationen beizutreten. Diese sogenannte Koalitionsfreiheit gilt auch für die Angehörigen des öffentlichen Dienstes.

2. Für die Bildung von Organisationen der Arbeitgeber und Arbeitnehmer ist eine staatliche Genehmigung nicht erforderlich; ebenso wenig ist eine bestimmte Rechtsform vorgeschrieben. Die großen deutschen Gewerkschaften haben sich als nicht-rechtsfähige Vereine konstituiert, sie besitzen daher keine eigene Rechtspersönlichkeit. Die Arbeitgebervereinigungen bestehen dagegen auf regionaler Ebene zumeist als rechtsfähige Vereine. Die Organisationen haben auch das Recht, Zentralverbände (Spitzenverbände) zu bilden und sich internationalen Organisationen anzuschließen.

3. Zur Betätigungsfreiheit gehört vor allem das in § 2 des Tarifvertragsgesetzes vom 9.4.1949 niedergelegte Recht, Verhandlungen zum Abschluß von Gesamtvereinbarungen (Tarifverträgen) zu führen und derartige Vereinbarungen abzuschließen. Die Betätigung der Sozialpartner beschränkt sich jedoch nicht auf die Vereinbarung von Tarifverträgen; vielmehr werden die Sozialpartner auch an der sozialpolitischen Gesetzgebung, insbesondere bei der Ausarbeitung von Gesetzentwürfen, beteiligt. Ferner haben sie vom Gesetz ein Mitwirkungsrecht zugewiesen erhalten: bei der Bildung und Besetzung der Gerichte für Arbeitssachen und der Sozialgerichte, bei der Bildung der Tarifausschüsse, die maßgeblich bei der Erklärung von Tarifverträgen für allgemeinverbindlich mitwirken, bei der Besetzung der Organe der Bundesanstalt für Arbeitsvermittlung und Arbeitslosenversicherung sowie der Träger der Sozialversicherung usw. Die Gewerkschaften sind außerdem in gewissem Umfang an der Bildung und Betätigung der Arbeitnehmer-Vertretungen in den Betrieben und der Aufsichtsräte in den Unternehmen beteiligt.

4. *Die Gewerkschaften*

Nach 1945 wurden die Gewerkschaften mit besonderer Förderung des Alliierten Kontrollrats neu gegründet. Sie setzten sich zum Ziel, auf ihrem Tätigkeitsfeld, der Vertretung von Interessen der Arbeitnehmer, beim Aufbau der Demokratie als *parteipolitisch und religiös neutrale Verbände* mitzuwirken. Über ihren Aufbau, ihre Arbeit und ihre Bestrebungen unterrichtet ein eigener Beitrag (Seite 605—609).

5. *Die Bundesvereinigung der Deutschen Arbeitgeberverbände*

Die Bundesvereinigung der Deutschen Arbeitgeberverbände (BDA) ist die *sozialpolitische Spitzenvertretung der Unternehmerschaft* in der Bundesrepublik. Sie ist damit auf allen Arbeitsgebieten Partner der Gewerkschaften. Insbesondere sind ihre Verbände jeweils die Vertragspartner der entsprechenden Gewerkschaften beim Abschluß von Tarifverträgen. Als einzige Organisation auf der Unternehmerseite umfaßt die Bundesvereinigung der Deutschen Arbeitgeberverbände die sozialpolitischen Verbände *aller* Wirtschaftszweige der Bundesrepublik, also der Industrie, des Handels, des Handwerks, der Banken, der Versicherungen, der Landwirtschaft und des Verkehrs.

Nach dem Zusammenbruch im Jahre 1945 war zunächst ein organisatorischer Zusammenschluß der Arbeitgeber über die kleinste regionale oder regional-fachliche Ebene hinaus untersagt. Im Zuge der Entwicklung bildeten sich jedoch verhältnismäßig schnell organisatorische Zusammenschlüsse der Arbeitgeberverbände, und zwar sowohl der einen Erwerbszweig umfassenden Arbeitgeberverbände einzelner Branchen, wie etwa der Metallindustrie oder der Chemie, als auch regionale Zusammenschlüsse auf gemischt-gewerblicher Basis bis hin zu den Organisationen auf der Landes- und der Zonenebene.

Im Juli 1948 schufen diese Organisationen für die Britische und Amerikanische Besatzungszone das „Zentrale Sekretariat der Arbeitgeber des Vereinigten Wirtschaftsgebiets" als eine Art Austauschstelle für Erfahrungen und losen organisatorischen Zusammenschluß. Die Notwendigkeit der Neugründung von organisatorisch geschlossenen Arbeitgeberverbänden wurde auch von seiten der Gewerkschaften anerkannt, insbesondere nachdem durch das Tarifvertragsgesetz die Tariffreiheit wiederhergestellt worden war; denn die Tarifpartnerschaft erfordert naturgemäß Organisationen der Arbeitgeber- und der Arbeitnehmerseite.

Am 28. 1. 1949 wurde das „Zentralsekretariat der Arbeitgeber des Vereinigten Wirtschaftsgebietes" übergeführt in die „Sozialpolitische Arbeitsgemeinschaft der Arbeitgeber des Vereinigten Wirtschaftsgebietes", die im April des gleichen Jahres den Namen „Vereinigung der Arbeitgeberverbände" erhielt und nach dem Anschluß der Arbeitgeberorganisationen der Französischen Zone im November 1950 ihren jetzigen Namen annahm.

Oberstes Organ der Bundesvereinigung ist die Mitgliederversammlung, die aus Vertretern der angeschlossenen Organisationen entsprechend der Zahl der in den Betrieben eines Mitgliederverbandes beschäftigten Arbeitnehmer besteht. Der Vorstand der BDA setzt sich zusammen aus den Vorsitzenden der Mitgliedsverbände, die das Recht haben, weitere Persönlichkeiten in den Vorstand zu berufen. Er beschließt die Richtlinien für die Arbeit der BDA und ist für alle Angelegenheiten zuständig, soweit nicht andere Organe vorgesehen sind. Der Vorstand wählt den Präsidenten und die Vizepräsidenten, die durch die Mitgliederversammlung zu bestätigen sind. Außerdem wählt der Vorstand die weiteren Präsidialmitglieder der BDA. Das Präsidium prüft die Beschlüsse des Vorstandes und überwacht ihre Durchführung.

Mitgliedsverbände der Bundesvereinigung können sein: die fachlichen Zusammenschlüsse privater Arbeitgeber und Vereinigungen, die sozialpolitische Aufgaben zu erfüllen haben, und die überfachlichen sozialpolitischen Landeszusammenschlüsse privater Arbeitgeber. Aufgaben siehe Seite 602—605.

B. Tarifrecht

1. Das bedeutsamste Gestaltungsmittel, mit dem die Sozialpartner sich an der Ordnung der Arbeit in den einzelnen Wirtschaftszweigen beteiligen, ist der Tarifvertrag. Die gesetzliche Rechtsgrundlage für den Abschluß von Tarifverträgen bildet das *Tarifvertragsgesetz vom 9.4.1949* in der Fassung des Änderungsgesetzes vom 11.1.1952.

Der Tarifvertrag regelt einmal die Rechte und Pflichten der Parteien des Tarifvertrags untereinander (obligatorische Bestimmungen). Durch den Abschluß des Tarifvertrages ergibt sich für die Parteien des Tarifvertrags die Verpflichtung, den Arbeitsfrieden zu wahren, das heißt keine Kampfmaßnahmen zur Änderung der tariflich vereinbarten Regelungen einzuleiten (*Friedenspflicht*); sowie die Pflicht, die Mitglieder zur Einhaltung der Bestimmungen des Tarifvertrags anzuhalten (*Einwirkungspflicht*). Den Kern des Tarifvertrages bilden aber die *normativen Bestimmungen*, die den Inhalt, den Abschluß und die Beendigung von Arbeitsverhältnissen sowie betriebliche und betriebsverfassungsrechtliche Fragen regeln. Die tariflichen Normen haben *gesetzesähnlichen Charakter*, da sie wie Gesetzesvorschriften gegenüber den tarifgebundenen Arbeitgebern und Arbeitnehmern Geltung beanspruchen. Die Tarifnormen enthalten grundsätzlich nur *Mindestbestimmungen*. Eine Besserstellung der Arbeitnehmer durch vertragliche Vereinbarung ist daher zulässig (*Günstigkeitsprinzip*).

2. Die Sozialpartner haben von ihrer Tarifautonomie reichlich Gebrauch gemacht. Tarifverträge gibt es heute in der Bundesrepublik in nahezu allen

Bereichen, in denen Arbeitnehmer beschäftigt werden. Das gilt auch für den öffentlichen Dienst, soweit es sich nicht um Beamte handelt, deren Rechtsstellung durch die gesetzgebenden Körperschaften festgesetzt wird. Seit dem Inkrafttreten des Tarifvertragsgesetzes vom 9.4.1949 wurden insgesamt etwa 28.000 Tarifverträge vereinbart. Meist handelt es sich um getrennte Tarifverträge für den Lohn einerseits (*Lohntarifverträge*) und für die übrigen Arbeitsbedingungen wie Urlaub, Krankheitsbezahlung, Akkordbedingungen, Arbeitszeitzuschläge usw. andererseits (*Mantel- oder Rahmentarifverträge*).

Auf der Grundlage der Tarifverträge haben die Löhne und Gehälter in der Bundesrepublik sich nominal und real erheblich aufwärts entwickelt.

Tabelle 1

DURCHSCHNITTLICHE BRUTTOSTUNDENVERDIENSTE[1] DER INDUSTRIEARBEITER[2] IM BUNDESGEBIET[3]

	März	Februar								Zunahme 1959 gegenüber 1950 in %
	1950[4]	1953[4]	1954[4]	1955[4]	1956[4]	1957[4]	1957[5]	1958[5]	1959[5]	
	Pfennige									
Alle männlichen Arbeiter	132,8	176,9	180,9	190,5	208,1	223,5	229,3	248,3	257,4	*+93,8*
Alle weiblichen Arbeiter	85,4	110,3	114,3	120,3	131,1	144,2	140,8	153,5	163,9	*+91,9*
Alle Arbeiter ...	121,4	159,7	162,7	171,8	186,5	202,7	209,7	226,9	237,1	*+95,3*

[1] Einschließlich des Baugewerbes. — [2] Alter Berichtskreis ohne, neuer Berichtskreis einschließlich von Bergbau und Energiewirtschaft. — [3] Ohne Saarland und Berlin. — [4] Alter Berichtskreis. — [5] Neuer Berichtskreis. Quelle: Statistisches Bundesamt.

3. Grundsätzlich erfolgt die überbetriebliche Regelung der Arbeitsbedingungen in freier Vereinbarung zwischen den Sozialpartnern durch Tarifverträge. Der Staat (Bund und Länder) greift nur in zwei Ausnahmen helfend ein, und dann auch nur unter ganz genau normierten Voraussetzungen und unter Mitwirkung der Sozialpartner. Der Bundesminister für Arbeit und Sozialordnung und die Obersten Arbeitsbehörden der Länder können nämlich auf Antrag eines der Sozialpartner Tarifverträge im Einvernehmen mit einem aus Vertretern der Sozialpartner bestehenden Tarifausschusses für *allgemeinverbindlich* erklären. Voraussetzung ist, daß die tarifgebundenen Arbeitgeber wenigstens 50% der unter den Geltungsbereich des Tarifvertrages fallenden

Arbeitnehmer beschäftigen *und* die Allgemeinverbindlich-Erklärung im öffentlichen Interesse geboten erscheint. Von diesem Erfordernis kann abgesehen werden, wenn die Erklärung der Allgemeinverbindlichkeit zur Behebung eines sozialen Notstandes notwendig erscheint. Vom Inkrafttreten des Tarifvertragsgesetzes vom 9.4.1949 bis zum Jahre 1958 wurden vom Bundesminister für Arbeit und Sozialordnung und den Obersten Arbeitsbehörden der Länder etwa 1.200 Tarifverträge für allgemeinverbindlich erklärt.

Ferner kann der Bundesminister für Arbeit und Sozialordnung im Einvernehmen mit den Sozialpartnern nach dem *Gesetz über die Festsetzung von Mindestarbeitsbedingungen* vom 11.1.1952 Mindest-Arbeitsbedingungen zur Regelung von Entgelten und sonstigen Arbeitsbedingungen erlassen, wenn keine tarifliche Regelung besteht. Weitere Voraussetzungen für den Erlaß einer solchen staatlichen Regelung sind, daß für den betreffenden Wirtschaftszweig keine Arbeitnehmer- und Arbeitgeberverbände bestehen oder zwar bestehen, aber nur eine Minderheit der Arbeitnehmer oder Arbeitgeber erfassen, daß ferner die Festsetzung aus sozialen Gründen geboten erscheint und eine Regelung der Arbeitsbedingungen durch die Erklärung der Allgemeinverbindlichkeit von Tarifverträgen nicht erfolgt ist.

Aus dieser Aufzählung der Voraussetzungen wird der völlig subsidiäre Charakter der gesetzlichen Regelung vom 11.1.1952 deutlich. Das Gesetz hat insbesondere wegen der vollen Ausnutzung der Tarifautonomie durch die Sozialpartner bisher keine Bedeutung erlangt.

C. Schlichtungsrecht

Streitigkeiten unter den Sozialpartnern über die Schaffung neuer oder über die Änderung beziehungsweise Ergänzung laufender Tarifverträge können das allgemeine Wohl stark berühren. Daher liegen Schlichtungsverfahren für den Fall, daß die Sozialpartnern sich nicht zu einigen vermögen, im Interesse der Beteiligten und der Allgemeinheit.

Das *Gesetz betreffend Ausgleichs- und Schiedsverfahren in Arbeitsstreitigkeiten vom 20.8.1946* (*Kontrollratsgesetz Nr. 35*) gibt den Parteien eines Tarifvertrags die Möglichkeit, die Schlichtung selbst zu regeln. Im Jahre 1950 schufen die Spitzenverbände der Arbeitgeber und der Arbeitnehmer gemeinsam ein Muster einer Schlichtungsvereinbarung, das den Parteien von Tarifverträgen zur Übernahme empfohlen wurde (sogenannte Hattenheimer Vereinbarung vom 12.1.1950). In der Folgezeit sind zahlreiche Schlichtungsvereinbarungen zwischen den Tarifvertragsparteien geschlossen worden. Eine staatliche Zwangsschlichtung, wie sie in Deutschland in den Jahren zwischen 1918 und 1933 bestand, gibt es in der Bundesrepublik nicht mehr.

D. Arbeitskämpfe

Falls die Sozialpartner bei den Verhandlungen zum Abschluß eines Tarifvertrages keine Einigung erzielen und auch ein Schlichtungsverfahren ergebnislos bleibt, haben sie — anders als in der nationalsozialistischen Zeit — nunmehr wieder die Möglichkeit, ihre Ziele mit Hilfe *kollektiver Kampfmittel* durchzusetzen. Das kollektive Kampfmittel der Arbeitnehmer und ihrer Organisationen ist der *Streik*, das der Arbeitgeber die *Aussperrung*.

1. Im Grundgesetz ist das Recht des Arbeitskampfes nicht ausdrücklich verfassungsrechtlich garantiert. Andererseits ist der Arbeitskampf durch das Grundgesetz auch nicht verboten. Seine Zulässigkeit ergibt sich insbesondere aus der historischen Entwicklung der Organisationen der Arbeitnehmer und Arbeitgeber, aus den Grundsätzen des freiheitlichen Rechtsstaates und aus der allgemeinen Entfaltungsfreiheit. Grundsätzlich bestehen danach *Streik- und Aussperrungsfreiheit*.

Tabelle 2

UMFANG DER STREIKBEWEGUNG

(Bundesrepublik ohne Saarland und Berlin[West], 1951 bis 1958)

Jahr	Durch Streiks verlorene Arbeitstage	Beschäftigte Arbeitnehmer 1.000	Verlorene Arbeitstage je 100 Beschäftigte
1951	1.592.892	14.556	10,9
1952	442.877	14.995	3,0
1953	1.488.218	15.583	9,6
1954	1.586.523	16.286	9,7
1955	846.647	17.176	4,9
1956	263.884	18.056	1,5
1957	2.320.927	18.611	12,5
1958	779.911	18.840	4,1

Quelle: Bundesministerium für Arbeit und Sozialordnung.

Unzulässig sind jedoch insbesondere Arbeitskämpfe, die gegen die in einem Tarifvertrag enthaltene Friedenspflicht verstoßen oder andere Ziele verfolgen als eine tarifliche Regelung der Arbeitsbedingungen. Ebenso ist die Zulässigkeit des Streiks und der Aussperrung im öffentlichen Dienst aus Gründen des allgemeinen Wohls Einschränkungen unterworfen.

2. Die Arbeitnehmer der Bundesrepublik haben von der Streikfreiheit bisher einen verhältnismäßig geringen Gebrauch gemacht. Die Zahl der verlorenen Arbeitstage je hundert Beschäftigte liegt beträchtlich unter den entsprechenden Zahlen anderer bedeutender Industrieländer.

III. DER BETRIEB UND DAS RECHT ZUR MITBESTIMMUNG

Der Betrieb ist ein weiteres wichtiges Feld sozialer Selbstverwaltung. Die Arbeitnehmerschaft strebt nach Erreichung der politischen Anerkennung und der Koalitionsfreiheit auf überbetrieblicher Ebene auch eine Partnerschaft in den Betrieben an. Es sind bereits Ansätze vorhanden, innerhalb des Betriebes das Arbeitsverhältnis immer mehr zu einem Rechtsverhältnis umzugestalten, das einen gesellschaft- und mitgliedschaftähnlichen Status besitzt. In diesem Zusammenhang kommt der *Betriebszugehörigkeit* immer größere Bedeutung zu. Die Anfänge dieser Entwicklung haben sich bereits in mehreren Gesetzen über das Recht der Betriebsverfassung niedergeschlagen.

1. Für die private Wirtschaft gilt das *Betriebsverfassungsgesetz vom 11.10. 1952*. Danach sind in allen Betrieben mit mehr als fünf wahlberechtigten Arbeitnehmern *Betriebsräte* zu bilden. Arbeitgeber und Betriebsrat haben vertrauensvoll zusammenzuarbeiten. Sie sollen im Zusammenwirken mit den im Betriebe vertretenen Gewerkschaften und der Arbeitgebervereinigung unter Berücksichtigung des Gemeinwohls das Wohl des Betriebes und der Arbeitnehmer fördern. Sie haben alles zu tun, um den Arbeitsfrieden zu erhalten. Arbeitskämpfe auf betrieblicher Ebene sowie jede politische Betätigung innerhalb des Betriebes sind verboten — wenn auch die kommunistische Infiltration immer wieder versucht hat, über solche Mittel Einfluß zu gewinnen.

Die Zuständigkeiten des Betriebsrats erstrecken sich vor allem auf soziale und personelle Angelegenheiten der Arbeitnehmerschaft, aber in gewissem Umfange auch auf wirtschaftliche Fragen des Betriebes und des Unternehmens. In den *sozialen Angelegenheiten* hat der Betriebsrat insbesondere ein Mitbestimmungsrecht über Beginn und Ende der täglichen Arbeitszeit und der Pausen, über Zeit und Ort der Auszahlung des Arbeitsentgelts, Aufstellung des Urlaubsplanes, Durchführung der Berufsausbildung, Regelung der Sätze des Akkord- und Stücklohns, Verwaltung der Wohlfahrtseinrichtungen usw. Kommt es in diesen Fragen nicht zu einer Einigung mit dem Arbeitgeber, so entscheidet eine paritätisch besetzte Einigungsstelle verbindlich. In den *personellen Angelegenheiten* ist der Betriebsrat insbesondere bei der Einstellung, Eingruppierung und Versetzung von Arbeitnehmern beteiligt.

Zur Mitwirkung in den *wirtschaftlichen Angelegenheiten* sind in Unternehmen mit mehr als hundert Arbeitnehmern *Wirtschaftsausschüsse* gebildet. Sie sind über Fabrikations- und Arbeitsmethoden, über Produktionsprogramme, die wirtschaftliche Lage des Unternehmens, die Produktions- und Absatzlage und über sonstige Vorgänge zu unterrichten, welche die Interessen der Arbeitnehmer wesentlich berühren. In Aktiengesellschaften und Kommanditgesellschaften auf Aktien besteht der Aufsichtsrat zu einem Drittel aus Vertretern der Arbeitnehmer.

Ein noch weitergehendes Recht der Arbeitnehmer zur Mitbestimmung in der Wirtschaft wurde geschaffen für die Großunternehmen des Bergbaus und der Eisen und Stahl erzeugenden Industrie. Hier wird auf Grund des *Gesetzes vom 21.5.1951* der Aufsichtsrat sogar paritätisch aus Vertretern der Arbeitnehmerseite und aus Vertretern der Anteilseigner gebildet. Damit nicht bei Abstimmungen Stimmengleichheit erzielt wird, gehört dem Aufsichtsrat zusätzlich ein Mitglied an, das vom Vertrauen der beiden Seiten getragen wird. Dem Vorstand der unter das Gesetz vom 21.5.1951 fallenden Montanunternehmen muß ein *Arbeitsdirektor* angehören. Er darf nicht gegen die Stimmen der Arbeitnehmervertreter im Aufsichtsrat bestellt werden. Dem Arbeitsdirektor obliegt insbesondere die soziale und personelle Betreuung der Arbeitnehmerschaft. Dieses „erweiterte Mitbestimmungsrecht" in der Montanwirtschaft hat im Ausland größte Beachtung gefunden. Es ist auch von erheblicher politischer Bedeutung.

2. In den öffentlichen Verwaltungen und Betrieben des Bundes sind die Rechte zur Beteiligung der Bediensteten (Beamte, Angestellte und Arbeiter) im *Personalvertretungsgesetz vom 5.8.1955* geregelt. Sie entsprechen im wesentlichen den für die Arbeitnehmer der privaten Wirtschaft nach dem Betriebsverfassungsgesetz vom 11.10.1952 geltenden Mitbestimmungs- und Mitwirkungsrechten. Einschränkungen ergeben sich vor allem aus der Besonderheit des öffentlichen Dienstes (Ausübung hoheitlicher Funktionen, Sicherstellung der öffentlichen Daseinsvorsorge).

IV. DAS ARBEITSVERHÄLTNIS

Trotz einer Fülle staatlicher Gesetze und trotz den vielen Vereinbarungen der Sozial- und Betriebspartner, die Rechtsnormen setzen, bleibt das Arbeitsverhältnis, das unmittelbare rechtliche Band zwischen dem einzelnen Arbeitgeber und Arbeitnehmer, ein wichtiger und unentbehrlicher Ordnungsfaktor des Arbeitslebens. Erst das in freier Entschließung zwischen Arbeitgeber und Arbeitnehmer begründete Arbeitsverhältnis ermöglicht, daß die vom Staat und von den autonomen Trägern der Arbeitsverfassung gesetzten Normen schützend, ordnend und inhaltsgestaltend einwirken können.

A. Begründung des Arbeitsverhältnisses

Das Arbeitsverhältnis wird durch Vereinbarung zwischen Arbeitnehmer und Arbeitgeber begründet. Der Grundsatz der Vertragsfreiheit, der das gesamte bürgerliche Recht beherrscht, gilt auch für die Begründung von Arbeitsverhältnissen. Das heißt: es bleibt den Beteiligten überlassen, ob sie ein Arbeitsverhältnis miteinander eingehen wollen. Als Ausnahme von diesem Grundsatz besteht ein öffentlich-rechtlicher Abschlußzwang nach dem *Schwerbeschädigtengesetz vom 16.6.1953* zugunsten der Schwerbeschädigten. Die Arbeitgeber sind danach verpflichtet, bei mehr als sieben Arbeitsplätzen wenigstens 8% Schwerbeschädigte zu beschäftigen.

B. Inhalt des Arbeitsverhältnisses

1. Grundsätzlich sind der Arbeitgeber und der Arbeitnehmer auch hinsichtlich der Gestaltung des Vertragsinhalts frei. Doch gerade der Inhalt des Arbeitsverhältnisses ist das hauptsächliche Feld der Einwirkung der zwingenden Vorschriften der Gesetze, der Normen der Tarifverträge und der Betriebsvereinbarungen, der öffentlich-rechtlichen Vorschriften über den Arbeitsschutz und der von der Rechtsprechung entwickelten Rechtsgrundsätze. Im Ergebnis wird daher die Freiheit der inhaltlichen Gestaltung des Arbeitsverhältnisses — wenigstens für die Parteien des Arbeitsvertrages — doch sehr eingeschränkt.

2. Die wesentlichsten Pflichten aus dem Arbeitsverhältnis für den Arbeitnehmer sind: *Die Dienstpflicht, die Gehorsamspflicht und die Treuepflicht.*

Der Arbeitnehmer ist auf Grund des Arbeitsverhältnisses zur Leistung der vereinbarten Arbeit verpflichtet. Art und Umfang der Arbeit, insbesondere auch die Arbeitszeit, richten sich nach den zwingenden Gesetzesvorschriften, den Normen der Tarifverträge und der Betriebsvereinbarungen sowie nach den vertraglichen Abmachungen. Im Rahmen der Leistungspflicht bestimmt der Arbeitgeber kraft seines Weisungsrechts die auszuführenden Arbeiten. Erfindungen, die ein Arbeitnehmer im Zusammenhang mit seiner Arbeitsleistung macht, stehen unter dem Schutz des *Gesetzes über Arbeitnehmer-Erfindungen vom 25.7.1957.* Danach hat der Arbeitnehmer, sofern der Arbeitgeber seine Erfindung verwertet, einen Anspruch auf angemessene Vergütung, und ihm allein steht auch die Ehre des Erfinders zu.

Aus dem Arbeitsverhältnis folgt für den Arbeitnehmer ferner eine Gehorsams- und Treuepflicht. Der Arbeitnehmer hat im Rahmen der bestehenden gesetzlichen, tariflichen und vertraglichen Grenzen den Arbeitsanweisungen des Arbeitgebers nachzukommen. Die Treuepflicht gebietet dem Arbeitnehmer neben der eigentlichen Arbeitsleistung, auch Schaden von dem Arbeitgeber abzuwenden und das Betriebsinteresse zu fördern.

3. Die Hauptpflichten des Arbeitgebers aus dem Arbeitsverhältnis sind die *Entlohnungs-, Fürsorge- und Urlaubspflicht.*

a) Der Arbeitgeber ist verpflichtet, dem Arbeitnehmer den vereinbarten *Lohn* zu zahlen. Höhe und Art des Lohnes ergeben sich aus dem jeweiligen Tarifvertrag oder, sofern übertariflicher Lohn gezahlt wird, aus der vertraglichen Einzelabrede. Fällt die Arbeit wegen eines gesetzlichen Feiertages aus, so ist — sofern der Feiertag nicht auf einen Sonntag fällt — der Lohn in Höhe des regelmäßigen Arbeitsverdienstes weiterzuzahlen. Diese Regelung gilt kraft zwingender Vorschriften des *Gesetzes über die Lohnzahlung an Feiertagen vom 2.8.1951.* Die Bezahlung von *Mehrarbeit* (sogenannte Überstunden) ist ebenfalls durch zwingende Bestimmungen der Arbeitsordnung vom 30.4.1938 gewährleistet.

Das tarifliche Lohnsystem in der Bundesrepublik ist grundsätzlich auf den Leistungslohn abgestellt. Dieses Prinzip wird aber durch tarifliche Sozialzulagen (tarifliche Zuschläge für Verheiratete und Kinder) abgeschwächt. Selbständig neben dem Lohnanspruch auf Grund tariflicher oder vertraglicher Vereinbarungen hat der Arbeitnehmer nach dem *Kindergeldgesetz vom 3. 11. 1954* einen Anspruch auf Kindergeld für das dritte und jedes weitere Kind (vergleiche auch Seite 593). Dieser Anspruch ist aber vom Lohnanspruch zu unterscheiden. Er ist ein öffentlich-rechtlicher Anspruch und nicht gegen den Arbeitgeber, sondern gegen die zuständige Familienausgleichskasse gerichtet.

In der Bundesrepublik ist es üblich, bei besonderen Gelegenheiten (zum Beispiel Weihnachten, bei Geschäftsjubiläen) neben dem festen tariflichen

Lehrlings-Erholungsheim der DAIMLER-BENZ A.-G. (Untertürkheim) bei Wiesensteig

links oben:
In einer Werksbücherei

FRITZ-TARNOW-Jugendwohnheim in Frankfurt am Main

Im Lehrlings-Erholungsheim der DAIMLER-BENZ A.-G. (Untertürkheim) bei Wiesensteig

ALLTAG IN DEUTSCHLAND

Bei der Blumenfrau

Was gibt es heute billig zu kaufen?

In der Mensa einer Universität

Essenausgabe in einer Werkskantine

oder vertraglichen Lohn *Gratifikationen* zu gewähren. Es handelt sich hier meist um sogenannte freiwillige soziale Leistungen des Arbeitgebers. Der Arbeitnehmer gewinnt auf solche Leistungen nur dann einen Rechtsanspruch, wenn sie der Arbeitgeber mehrmals vorbehaltlos gewährt hat oder auf Grund des Prinzips der Gleichbehandlung aller Arbeitnehmer im Betriebe zur Zahlung verpflichtet ist.

Der Lohn muß, weil er die wirtschaftliche Existenzgrundlage des Arbeitnehmers bildet, dem Arbeitnehmer auch im Krankheitsfalle weitgehend erhalten bleiben. Ferner muß sichergestellt werden, daß der Lohn — wenigstens zum Teil — dem Arbeitnehmer auch wirklich zufließt. Daher erhalten alle krankenversicherungspflichtigen *Arbeiter* vom Arbeitgeber für die Dauer der Arbeitsunfähigkeit, längstens bis zu sechs Wochen, einen Zuschuß in Höhe des Differenzbetrages zwischen 90% des Netto-Arbeitsentgelts und dem gesetzlichen Krankengeld (65 bis 75% des Grundlohnes). Die *Angestellten* behalten im Krankheitsfalle nach dem Bürgerlichen Gesetzbuch für die Dauer von sechs Wochen ihren vollen Gehaltsanspruch. — Ferner sorgt der gesetzliche Pfändungsschutz dafür, daß allen Arbeitnehmern ein gewisser Teil des Arbeitseinkommens, der nach Familienstand und Einkommen gestaffelt ist, pfändungsfrei und damit zur Bestreitung des notwendigen Lebensunterhaltes erhalten bleibt.

b) Aus dem Arbeitsverhältnis ergibt sich, weil es eine soziale Gemeinschaft zwischen den Beteiligten schafft, eine *Fürsorgepflicht* des Arbeitgebers für die Person des Arbeitnehmers, die neben dem öffentlich-rechtlichen Arbeitsschutz besteht. Die Rechtsprechung hat aus dieser Grundpflicht des Arbeitgebers zahlreiche Einzelpflichten hergeleitet. Insbesondere ist der Arbeitgeber verpflichtet, das Eigentum des Arbeitnehmers, wie Fahrräder, Arbeitskleidung usw., zu schützen, die Rechte des Arbeitnehmers aus der Sozialversicherung wahrzunehmen und überhaupt auf das Leben und die Gesundheit des Arbeitnehmers Rücksicht zu nehmen. Aus der Fürsorgepflicht läßt sich auch die weitere Verpflichtung des Arbeitgebers herleiten, die Arbeitnehmer vor allem bei der Gewährung zusätzlicher sozialer Leistungen gleich zu behandeln.

c) Der Arbeitgeber ist zur Gewährung von *Urlaub* unter Weiterzahlung des Lohnes während der Urlaubszeit verpflichtet. Ein Bundes-Urlaubsgesetz besteht in der Bundesrepublik bisher nicht. Der Urlaub ist aber in den Ländern durch Verfassungsbestimmungen und Ländergesetze geregelt. Nach diesen Bestimmungen beträgt der Mindesturlaub für Erwachsene zwölf Arbeitstage im Jahr. Diese gesetzliche Regelung wird ergänzt durch die tariflichen Vorschriften. Diese Bestimmungen sehen einen Urlaub für Arbeiter vor, der je nach Betriebszugehörigkeit, Berufsjahren oder Alter oder einer Kombination dieser Steigerungsmerkmale in einigen Tarifen bis zu achtundzwanzig Tagen ansteigt. Überwiegend beträgt er achtzehn Tage und bei einem großen Teil aller Arbeitertarife mehr als achtzehn Tage. Bei Angestellten liegen die Sätze etwas höher. Im öffentlichen Dienst liegt der Urlaub bei Arbeitern zwischen vierzehn und vierundzwanzig Arbeitstagen, bei Angestellten im öffentlichen Dienst zwischen sechzehn bis sechsunddreißig Arbeitstagen im Jahr.

Eine Erhöhung des Urlaubs für schwere oder gesundheitsgefährliche Arbeiten ist in Bayern und Schleswig-Holstein durch Gesetz, im übrigen vielfach durch Tarifverträge vorgesehen. Der Zusatzurlaub beträgt drei bis sechs Arbeitstage. Für Arbeitnehmer in Tuberkulose- oder sonstigen Infektionsabteilungen oder Laboratorien mit Infektionsmaterial oder im Röntgen- und Radiumdienst sind sechs bis zehn zusätzliche Urlaubstage je nach Lebensalter vorgesehen. Die Erhöhung des Urlaubs für Personen mit verantwortlicher oder leitender Tätigkeit richtet sich nach den Arbeitsverträgen oder den in Betracht kommenden Angestelltentarifen.

Schwerbeschädigte haben Anspruch auf zusätzlichen Jahresurlaub von mindestens sechs Arbeitstagen. Für Verfolgte des Nationalsozialismus' sehen die meisten Länderurlaubsgesetze einen Zusatzurlaub vor. Er beträgt in Baden zwei, Niedersachsen drei bis sechs, in den übrigen Ländern sechs Arbeitstage. Mehrere Tarifverträge enthalten außerdem Bestimmungen über Zusatzurlaub in Höhe von drei Tagen für Beschädigte mit Erwerbsminderung (25 bis 40%).

Die Heimarbeiter werden von den meisten Ländergesetzen unter dem Begriff der arbeitnehmer-ähnlichen Personen miterfaßt. Außerdem bestehen tarifliche Urlaubsregelungen für Heimarbeiter.

C. Beendigung des Arbeitsverhältnisses

Der praktisch wichtigste Fall der Beendigung des Arbeitsverhältnisses ist die Kündigung. Sozialpolitische Gründe gebieten es, jedem Arbeitnehmer seinen Arbeitsplatz nach Möglichkeit zu erhalten oder ihn zumindest durch Einräumung von Kündigungsfristen vor dem sofortigen Verlust des Arbeitsplatzes zu schützen. Diesem Zweck dienen in der Bundesrepublik die verschiedenen zwingenden gesetzlichen oder tariflichen Kündigungsfristen, sowie die Beteiligung des Betriebsrats und der besondere Kündigungsschutz bei Kündigung des Arbeitsverhältnisses durch den Arbeitgeber. Insgesamt hat der Kündigungsschutz in der Bundesrepublik seine weiteste Ausdehnung und eine gewisse Vervollkommnung erreicht.

1. In der gewerblichen Wirtschaft besteht für den Arbeiter grundsätzlich, soweit nichts anderes vereinbart ist, eine vierzehntägige Kündigungsfrist. Die tariflichen Regelungen bleiben von dieser gesetzlichen Kündigungsfrist unberührt. Für Angestellte sind die Kündigungsfristen auf sechs Wochen bemessen. Sie können durch Vereinbarung gekürzt werden, jedoch höchstens bis auf einen Monat. Die Kündigung ist zulässig entweder zum Schluß eines Monats oder zum Schluß eines Kalendervierteljahres. Verlängerte Kündigungsfristen bestehen für schwerbeschädigte Arbeiter (vier Wochen) und für Angestellte mit längerer Betriebszugehörigkeit (Ausdehnung der Kündigungsfrist bis auf sechs Monate). Besonders lange Kündigungsfristen (bis zu sechs Monaten) gelten auch zum Schutze der älteren Angestellten.

2. In Betrieben mit einem Betriebsrat ist dieser vor jeder Kündigung eines Belegschaftsmitgliedes zu hören. Seiner Zustimmung zu der Kündigung bedarf es nicht; außer, wenn durch Tarifvertrag oder Betriebsvereinbarung etwas anderes vereinbart worden ist.

3. Nach dem neuen *Kündigungsschutzgesetz* ist die Kündigung gegenüber einem Arbeitnehmer, der länger als sechs Monate dem Betrieb angehört und das zwanzigste Lebensjahr vollendet hat, unwirksam, wenn sie *sozial ungerechtfertigt* ist. Die Bestimmung gilt nicht für Betriebe mit fünf oder weniger Beschäftigten. Die Frage, ob die Kündigung sozial gerechtfertigt ist, kann durch das Arbeitsgericht nachgeprüft werden.

Ein besonderer Kündigungsschutz besteht für Schwerbeschädigte (Zustimmung der Hauptfürsorgestelle ist erforderlich) sowie für politisch Verfolgte des nationalsozialistischen Regimes (Ländergesetze Württemberg-Baden, Rheinland-Pfalz, Baden und Berlin). Eine Kündigung von Mitgliedern eines Betriebsrats ist unzulässig, sofern nicht ein Grund zur fristlosen Entlassung gegeben ist.

V. DER STAAT (BUND UND LÄNDER)

Wenn bei der Darstellung der Organisation, der Aufgaben und der Zuständigkeiten der verschiedenen Träger der Arbeitsverfassung der Staat an letzter Stelle steht, so bedeutet dies nicht, daß in der Bundesrepublik die Sorge des Staates um eine gerechte und soziale Ordnung gering ist. Vielmehr soll nur zum Ausdruck kommen, daß der Staat bewußt den Sozial-, Betriebs-

und Arbeitsvertragspartnern weitesten Spielraum zur sozialen Selbstverwaltung gelassen hat. Er setzt nur den rechtlichen Rahmen für ihr Betätigungsfeld und greift lediglich helfend und regelnd dort ein, wo es zwingend erforderlich erscheint. Der *Arbeitsschutz* und die *Arbeitsgerichtsbarkeit* sind indessen von jeher traditionelle staatliche Aufgabenbereiche gewesen und es bis heute auch geblieben.

A. Arbeitsschutz

Kein Staatswesen kann darauf verzichten, den schaffenden Menschen gegen die Gefahren für Leben und Gesundheit, die bei der Berufsarbeit entstehen, weitgehend zu schützen. Dies gilt für die Bundesrepublik in besonderem Maße, weil sich aus den Grundrechten des Grundgesetzes ein verfassungsmäßiger Schutz der Arbeitskraft ergibt.

Zum Arbeitsschutz-Recht gehören alle Rechtsnormen, die ausschließlich öffentlich-rechtliche Pflichten für den Betriebsunternehmer gegenüber dem Staat begründen, um den Schutz des Arbeitnehmers vor den ihn bedrohenden Gefahren bei der Arbeit sicherzustellen. Von diesen Pflichten kann niemals der Arbeitnehmer, sondern ebenfalls nur der Staat selbst den Arbeitgeber freistellen. Seinem Inhalt nach gliedert sich das Arbeitsschutzrecht in zwei Hauptgruppen: den *Betriebsschutz* und den *sozialen Arbeitsschutz*. Während der Betriebsschutz den gesamten technischen Arbeitsschutz umfaßt, gehört zum sozialen Arbeitsschutz vor allem der Schutz der Arbeitszeit einschließlich der Sonntagsruhe und des Ladenschlusses sowie der besondere Schutz der Frauen und Jugendlichen.

1. Betriebsschutz

Der Betriebsschutz gewährt den Arbeitnehmern einen dreifachen Schutz: Schutz des Lebens (Unfallverhütung), Schutz der Gesundheit (Gewerbehygiene) und Schutz der Sittlichkeit. Der Betriebsschutz beruht hauptsächlich auf der Gewerbeordnung vom 21.6.1869 (mit zahlreichen späteren Änderungen) und den Vorschriften der Berufsgenossenschaften über Unfallverhütung, zum Teil auch auf Sondergesetzen (insbesondere für Bergleute und Seeleute). Wegen der Verschiedenheit der einzelnen Gewerbezweige und wegen des ständigen Fortschritts der Technik ist die gesetzliche Regelung des Betriebsschutzes möglichst beweglich gestaltet. Die Gesetze bezeichnen deshalb meist nur den Rahmen der Pflichten des Arbeitgebers und ermächtigen andere Stellen, die Rahmenbestimmungen durch Verordnungen oder Einzelverfügungen auszufüllen. Der Betriebsschutz wird durch Betriebsbesichtigungen der zuständigen Überwachungsorgane laufend kontrolliert.

2. Der soziale Arbeitsschutz

a) Eine der Hauptaufgaben des sozialen Arbeitsschutzes liegt in der Beschränkung der Arbeitsdauer. Die zulässige Höchstdauer der Arbeitszeit ist gesetzlich festgelegt. Die gegenwärtigen gesetzlichen Grundlagen des Schutzes der Arbeitszeit bilden *die Arbeitszeitordnung vom 30.4.1938*, *die Gewerbeordnung* mit ihren Bestimmungen über die Sonntagsruhe und einige Sondergesetze für einzelne Berufsgruppen (Land- und Forstwirtschaft, See- und Luftfahrt, Bäckereien, Krankenanstalten usw.). Für Kinder und Jugendliche gilt noch das *Jugendschutzgesetz vom 30.4.1938* sowie in Niedersachsen das *Jugendarbeitsschutzgesetz vom 9.12.1948*.

Die derzeit zulässige Höchst-Arbeitszeit beträgt acht Stunden täglich und achtundvierzig Stunden wöchentlich. Der Acht-Stunden-Tag gilt jedoch nicht schematisch. In zahlreichen Fällen ist aus wirtschaftspolitischen Gründen eine andere Verteilung oder eine Verlängerung der Arbeitszeit gestattet. So kann zum Beispiel der an einzelnen Tagen regelmäßig eintretende Ausfall an Arbeitsstunden (freier Samstagnachmittag) durch Mehrarbeit an den übrigen Tagen der gleichen sowie der vorhergehenden oder der folgenden Woche ausgeglichen werden. Ferner ist Mehrarbeit auf Grund eines Tarifvertrages, einer behördlichen Genehmigung oder in begrenztem Umfang auch aus eigenem Recht des Arbeitgebers gestattet. Die Höchstgrenze der so verlängerten Arbeitszeit beträgt jedoch grundsätzlich zehn Stunden täglich. Bei einer über acht Stunden täglich hinausgehenden Arbeitszeit (Mehrarbeit) hat der Arbeitnehmer kraft Gesetzes einen Anspruch auf einen Mehrarbeits-Zuschlag. Fehlt es an einer vertraglichen oder tariflichen Regelung, so beträgt dieser Zuschlag 25% des Stundenlohnes.

Die Bestimmungen über die Dauer der Arbeitszeit, insbesondere über die wöchentliche Höchstarbeitszeit von achtundvierzig Stunden, haben für die Masse der Arbeitnehmer an Bedeutung verloren, weil auf Grund tariflicher Vereinbarungen gegenwärtig bereits der weitaus überwiegende Teil aller Arbeitnehmer weniger als achtundvierzig Stunden in der Woche arbeitet. Dagegen sind gerade die Sondervorschriften für einzelne Berufszweige nach wie vor sehr wichtig. Insbesondere die Verkaufszeiten des Einzelhandels (Ladenschluß) bilden eine bedeutsame Ergänzung der Bestimmungen über die Arbeitszeit. Der Ladenschluß ist durch das *Gesetz über den Ladenschluß vom 28.11.1956* bundeseinheitlich geregelt. Grundsätzlich müssen danach die Verkaufsstellen von 18.30 Uhr bis 7 Uhr sowie an Sonn- und Feiertagen geschlossen sein; jedoch besteht eine Anzahl von Ausnahmen. Für das Bäckerei- und Konditoreigewerbe, für das Verkehrsgewerbe, für Apotheken, Krankenanstalten und für die Seeschiffahrt gelten weitere wichtige Sonderregelungen.

3. Sonderschutz für Frauen, Jugendliche und Heimarbeiter

a) Sonderschutz für Frauen

Die Frauen genießen mit Rücksicht auf ihre geringeren körperlichen Kräfte, ihre biologischen Aufgaben und ihre große Anfälligkeit gegenüber den gewerblichen Giften einen stärkeren sozialen Arbeitsschutz als die männlichen Arbeitnehmer. Der Sonderschutz der Frauen ist vor allem in der Gewerbeordnung, in der Arbeitszeitordnung vom 30.4.1938, in der Freizeitanordnung des früheren Reichsarbeitsministers vom 22.10.1943, in dem Gesetz zum Schutze der erwerbstätigen Mutter vom 24.1.1952 (Mutterschutzgesetz), in dem Seemannsgesetz vom 26.7.1957 sowie in den entsprechenden Gesetzen der Länder Nordrhein-Westfalen, Niedersachsen, Bremen und Hamburg über den Hausarbeitstag geregelt.

Der *Sonder-Betriebsschutz für Frauen* ist insbesondere durch Beschäftigungsverbote gekennzeichnet. Danach dürfen Frauen nicht in Bergwerken, Salinen, Kokereien, Betrieben der Eisenindustrie usw. beschäftigt werden. Der *Sonder-Arbeitsschutz für Frauen* sieht unter anderem eine Begrenzung der Höchstarbeitszeit bei an sich zulässiger Verlängerung der Arbeitszeit, ausgedehnte Ruhepausen und ein grundsätzliches Verbot der Nachtarbeit in der Zeit von 20.00 Uhr bis 6.00 Uhr vor. Bedeutsam sind auch die gesetzlichen Regelungen über den *Hausarbeitstag*. Die Freizeitanordnung des früheren Reichsarbeitsministers gibt Frauen mit eigenem Hausstand für jeden Monat Anspruch auf einen freien Wochentag. Die Freizeitanordnung ist zum Teil durch landesrechtliche Vorschriften ersetzt, die sämtlich Bezahlung des Hausarbeitstages vorsehen.

Der *Mutterschutz* nach dem Gesetz vom 24. 1. 1952 enthält Beschäftigungsverbote für werdende und stillende Mütter mit anstrengender oder gesundheitsgefährdender Arbeit. Für einen Zeitraum von sechs Wochen vor und sechs Wochen nach der Niederkunft sind die Mütter von der Arbeit freizustellen. Ihr Unterhalt ist durch Zahlung von Wochengeld durch die Krankenkassen sowie durch die Weiterzahlung des Arbeitsentgelts gesichert. Eine

Kündigung des Arbeitsverhältnisses gegenüber einer Frau während der Schwangerschaft und bis zum Ablauf von vier Monaten nach der Niederkunft ist grundsätzlich unzulässig.

b) Sonderschutz für Jugendliche

Kinder und Jugendliche genießen ähnlich wie die Frauen wegen ihrer geringeren Kraft, oft auch wegen ihrer geringeren Erfahrung und im Interesse ihrer Ausbildung und Entwicklung, einen stärkeren Schutz als die erwachsenen männlichen Arbeitnehmer. Der Arbeitsschutz für Kinder und Jugendliche ist im *Jugendschutzgesetz* sowie in zahlreichen auf Grund dieses Gesetzes erlassenen Rechtsverordnungen geregelt. In Niedersachsen ist das Jugendschutzgesetz durch ein Landesgesetz vom 9. 12. 1948 ersetzt und in zahlreichen Punkten verbessert worden.

Die Grundgedanken des Jugendschutzes sind ein Verbot der Kinderarbeit. Schutz der Jugendlichen vor übermäßiger Beanspruchung (Begrenzung der Arbeitszeit, Verbot der Nachtarbeit) und die Sicherstellung der für die berufliche Weiterbildung sowie für die geistige und körperliche Entwicklung des Jugendlichen notwendigen Freizeit. Eine völlige Neuordnung und Erweiterung des Jugendschutzes in der Bundesrepublik wird gegenwärtig vorbereitet und beschäftigt bereits die gesetzgebenden Körperschaften.

c) Sonderschutz für Heimarbeiter

Heimarbeit wird in allen Gegenden der Bundesrepublik Deutschland und in den verschiedensten Wirtschaftszweigen ausgeübt. Vor allem wird Heimarbeit vergeben in der Textil- und Bekleidungsindustrie, in der Spielwaren- und Instrumentenherstellung, in der Korb- und Stuhlflechterei, in der Papier- und Bürstenverarbeitung, in der Zigarrenherstellung usw. Zur Zeit werden in der Bundesrepublik etwa 200.000 Heimarbeiter, darunter rund 85% Frauen, beschäftigt.

Die Heimarbeit ist durch das *Heimarbeitsgesetz vom 14. 3. 1951* geregelt. Der Zweck dieses Gesetzes ist es, die in Heimarbeit Beschäftigten vor den ihnen wegen der besonderen Eigenart der Heimarbeit drohenden Gefahren zu schützen und ihnen eine angemessene Vergütung für ihre Arbeitsleistung zu sichern. Der Sonderschutz war erforderlich, weil die in Heimarbeit Beschäftigten keine eigentlichen Arbeitnehmer sind und deshalb für sie das allgemeine Arbeitsschutzrecht und auch das sonstige Arbeitsrecht nicht ohne weiteres gelten.

Im einzelnen gewährt das Heimarbeitsgesetz einen *allgemeinen Schutz* durch zwingende Vorschriften über Listenführung der in Heimarbeit

Beschäftigten, über das Anzeigen bei erstmaliger Vergebung von Heimarbeit, über die Offenlegung von Entgeltverzeichnissen und über die Ausstellung von Entgeltbüchern. Das Heimarbeitsgesetz enthält ferner einen *Arbeitszeitschutz* durch Regelungen über die zeitliche Verteilung der Arbeitsmenge und einen *Gefahrenschutz*. Hier kann die Bundesregierung vor allem Heimarbeit einschränken oder verbieten, die mit erheblichen Gefahren für das Leben und die Gesundheit der Beschäftigten verbunden ist. Bedeutsam ist schließlich auch der den Heimarbeitern gewährte *Entgelts- und Kündigungsschutz*.

4. Verwirklichung des Arbeitsschutzes

Alle arbeitsschutzrechtlichen Gesetze und Rechtsverordnungen enthalten Vorschriften über die Einhaltung und Durchsetzung des Arbeitsschutzes in den Betrieben. Staatliche Aufsichtsorgane (Gewerbeaufsichtsämter, die Behörden der Ordnungsverwaltung und die Berufsgenossenschaften) üben in den Betrieben eine kontrollierende, beratende und anordnende Tätigkeit aus. Zur Durchsetzung und Beachtung der Vorschriften des Arbeitsschutzes sind den Aufsichtsbehörden eine Reihe von Zwangsmitteln an die Hand gegeben. Außerdem wird die Beachtung der Vorschriften durch Kriminalstrafe oder Geldbuße gesichert.

B. Arbeitsgerichtsbarkeit

1. Die Gewährung von Rechtsschutz durch die Errichtung und Unterhaltung einer Gerichtsbarkeit ist eine staatliche Aufgabe. In der Bundesrepublik besteht eine besondere Arbeitsgerichtsbarkeit, die organisatorisch von der ordentlichen Gerichtsbarkeit getrennt ist. Die Rechtsgrundlage für die Rechtsprechung der besonderen Gerichte für Arbeitssachen bildet das *Arbeitsgerichtsgesetz vom 3.9.1953*. Aufgabe der Gerichte für Arbeitssachen ist es, Rechtsstreitigkeiten aus den Arbeitsverhältnissen und Gesamtvereinbarungen sowie Streitigkeiten aus der Betriebsverfassung gütlich auszugleichen oder durch Richterspruch zu entscheiden.

2. Gerichte für Arbeitssachen sind: die Arbeitsgerichte, die Landesarbeitsgerichte und das Bundesarbeitsgericht. Die Arbeitsgerichte und Landesarbeitsgerichte sind Gerichte der Länder. Sie unterstehen verwaltungsmäßig den obersten Arbeitsbehörden der Länder. Diese haben bei allen wesentlichen Maßnahmen das Einverständnis der Landes-Justizverwaltungen

herbeizuführen. Nur die oberste Instanz, das Bundesarbeitsgericht, ist ein Gericht des Bundes. Es wird durch das Bundesministerium für Arbeit und Sozialordnung im Einverständnis mit dem Bundesministerium der Justiz betreut.

Alle Rechtsstreitigkeiten werden in erster Instanz von den Arbeitsgerichten entschieden. Das Landesarbeitsgericht ist Berufungs-, das Bundesarbeitsgericht Revisionsgericht. Aufgabe der Rechtsprechung des Bundesarbeitsgerichts ist es vor allem, an Hand der zu entscheidenden Rechtssachen das Arbeitsrecht fortzubilden und auf die Rechtsprechung der unteren Gerichte vereinheitlichend zu wirken.

Die Gerichte für Arbeitssachen sind mit Berufs- und Laienrichtern besetzt. Die Beisitzer werden für die Arbeits- und Landesarbeitsgerichte von den obersten Arbeitsbehörden der Länder, für das Bundesarbeitsgericht von dem Bundesministerium für Arbeit und Sozialordnung auf Grund der von den Sozialpartnern eingereichten Vorschlagslisten bestellt.

3. Die Gerichte für Arbeitssachen entscheiden im *Urteilsverfahren* über bürgerliche Rechtsstreitigkeiten zwischen den Sozialpartnern, unter anderem aus Tarifverträgen und aus unerlaubten Handlungen, soweit es sich insbesondere um Maßnahmen des Arbeitskampfes handelt. Weiter entscheiden sie über Streitigkeiten zwischen Arbeitnehmern und Arbeitgebern aus Arbeitsverhältnissen und unerlaubten Handlungen, die mit dem Arbeitsverhältnis im Zusammenhang stehen. Sie entscheiden ferner im *Beschlußverfahren* über Streitigkeiten, die sich aus der Durchführung des Betriebsverfassungsgesetzes ergeben, und über die Tariffähigkeit von Vereinigungen. Die Gerichte für Arbeitssachen werden dagegen nicht auf dem Gebiet der Schlichtung tätig.

4. Ein wesentliches Ziel des arbeitsgerichtlichen Verfahrens in allen Instanzen ist die *gütliche Einigung* der rechtsuchenden Parteien. Daher ist eine besondere Güteverhandlung für das erstinstanzliche Verfahren zwingend vorgeschrieben. Da vor den Gerichten für Arbeitssachen meist um die wirtschaftliche Existenzgrundlage der Arbeitnehmer gestritten wird, ist das Verfahren in allen Rechtszügen zu beschleunigen. Zur *Beschleunigung des Verfahrens* sind bestimmte in der Zivilprozeßordnung festgelegte Fristen für das arbeitsgerichtliche Verfahren abgekürzt. Um den Arbeitnehmern die Durchsetzung ihrer Ansprüche zu erleichtern, sind ferner die Gebühren im Verfahren vor den Gerichten für Arbeitssachen gegenüber dem Verfahren vor den ordentlichen Gerichten wesentlich niedriger (*Prinzip der Billigkeit* des arbeitsgerichtlichen Verfahrens).

SOZIALE SICHERUNG

I. GRUNDGEDANKE

Auf wohl keinem Gebiet der Sozialgesetzgebung ist der Deutsche Bundestag in den zehn Jahren seines Bestehens so lebhaft und schöpferisch tätig gewesen wie auf dem der sozialen Sicherung. Mehrere hundert Gesetze und Verordnungen wurden erlassen, um den Schutz der Bevölkerung gegen die Wechselfälle des Arbeitslebens, insbesondere gegen Einkommenslosigkeit, auszubauen und den Wandlungen der wirtschaftlichen und gesellschaftlichen Verhältnisse anzupassen.

In der Vorkriegszeit umfaßte die soziale Sicherung im wesentlichen die verschiedenen Zweige der Sozialversicherung — also Krankenversicherung, Unfallversicherung, Rentenversicherung für Arbeiter, Angestellte und Beschäftigte des Bergbaus (Knappschaftsversicherung) — und die Arbeitslosenversicherung, ferner die Kriegsopferversorgung und die öffentliche Fürsorge. Diese herkömmlichen Formen waren und blieben das eigentliche Fundament sozialer Sicherheit in Deutschland. Auf ihren organisatorischen Wiederaufbau, die Wiederherstellung der Selbstverwaltung bei den Versicherungsträgern, die Wiedereinführung der Sozialgerichtsbarkeit und besonders die Verbesserung der Leistungen dieser Sicherungseinrichtungen, richtete sich die Aktivität des Gesetzgebers mit besonderem Nachdruck.

Daneben mußten Sonderformen der sozialen Sicherung geschaffen werden, wenn man mit den neuartigen und umfangreichen Notständen fertig werden wollte, die der Krieg hinterlassen hatte. Zu ihnen gehörten der Lastenausgleich, die Fürsorge für Vertriebene, Flüchtlinge aus der sogenannten DDR und Evakuierte, für Heimkehrer aus der Kriegsgefangenschaft und für Besatzungsgeschädigte.

Wandlungen der Sozialstruktur

Während diese zeitbedingten Sonderformen sozialer Sicherung zur Überwindung der Kriegsfolgen den Gesetzgeber in der Ersten Legislaturperiode noch sehr intensiv beschäftigten, konnte schon der Zweite Bundestag, auf der Grundlage einer erfolgreichen Wirtschafts- und Finanzpolitik, sich wieder auf eine Normalisierung der allgemeinen Lebensordnung einstellen. Mehr und mehr konzentrierte sich dann seine sozialpolitische Arbeit auf eine Modernisierung der bewährten Versicherungsformen, insbesondere auf die Neuregelung der Rentenversicherung. Diese wurde als erster Abschnitt der von der Bundesregierung eingeleiteten Sozialreform verstanden. Als weitere Schritte auf dem Wege zu einem neuen System der sozialen Sicherung sind die Neuregelung des Rechts der sozialen Krankenversicherung und der Unfallversicherung in Vorbereitung.

Anders als die vielfältigen Änderungsgesetze aus der Zeit des Ersten Bundestages, die kurzfristig die augenfällige und schlimmste Not unter den Sozialrentnern zu bekämpfen hatten, sollen die neuen Bestrebungen für die Reform der sozialen Sicherheit den langfristigen Strukturwandlungen von Wirtschaft und Gesellschaft seit der Schaffung der deutschen Sozialversicherung vor über siebzig Jahren Rechnung tragen. Zu diesen Strukturänderungen gehören vor allem die Wandlung der Familiengemeinschaft von der Groß- zur Kleinfamilie, die abnehmende Bedeutung des Besitzes und Vermögens als Grundlage für die Sicherung gegen Einkommensausfall, die Verschiebung von der ländlichen zur städtischen Lebens- und Arbeitsweise und schließlich die gewaltige Zunahme der abhängig beschäftigten Arbeitnehmer bei gleichzeitig wachsender Unsicherheit der selbständig Erwerbstätigen.

Zwang und Freiheit

Die Fülle der gesetzgeberischen Arbeit beim Neuaufbau der sozialen Sicherung in Deutschland stand vorwiegend unter ökonomischen und gesellschaftspolitischen Aspekten. Insgesamt mußte der ständig wachsende Sozialaufwand mit der wirtschaftlichen Leistungsfähigkeit der Bundesrepublik in Einklang gehalten werden. Zum anderen war zu fragen nach dem optimalen Verhältnis zwischen öffentlicher Sicherung und individueller Selbsthilfe, also zwischen Zwang und Freiheit in der Sozialpolitik. Dieses Verhältnis war ständig in dem Maße zu überprüfen, wie der wirtschaftliche Aufschwung sich vollzog und die Möglichkeiten privater Daseinsvorsorge sich erweiterten. Da die ökonomischen und gesellschaftlichen Grunddaten im Industriezeitalter sich dauernd verändern, stand auch die soziale Sicherung unter der Notwendigkeit ständiger Anpassung. Ihre Geschichte ist nicht nur die Geschichte ihrer Expansion, sondern auch die ihrer Revision; die permanente Revisionsbedürftigkeit gehört zu ihren Wesensmerkmalen.

Substitute für das Arbeitseinkommen

Ausgangspunkt aller gesetzgeberischen Aktivität auf diesem Gebiet war die Erkenntnis, daß die große und wachsende Mehrzahl aller Erwerbstätigen ihren Lebensunterhalt allein aus dem Arbeitseinkommen bestreitet. Jede

Unterbrechung der Beschäftigung ist daher in der Regel gleichbedeutend mit einem Ausfall der Unterhaltsmittel für den Arbeitenden und für seine Familie.

Die Sicherung für den Fall, daß Menschen unfreiwillig aus der Beschäftigung ausscheiden oder diese zeitweilig unterbrechen müssen, blieb daher eine der wichtigsten Aufgaben der Sozialpolitik. Die häufigsten Fälle einer erzwungenen Unterbrechung oder Aufgabe der Tätigkeit sind: Arbeitslosigkeit, Krankheit, Mutterschaft, Arbeitsunfall, vorzeitige Invalidität und Alter. Außerdem sind die Hinterbliebenen für den Todesfall des Ernährers zu sichern.

Gegen diese auch international anerkannten Standard-Risiken des modernen Arbeitsleben wurden verschiedene Sicherungseinrichtungen geschaffen, deren Entstehung an anderer Stelle dieses Buches dargestellt worden ist. Sie unterscheiden sich je nach ihrer Zwecksetzung im Aufbau, dem Verfahren der Finanzierung und hinsichtlich des von ihnen geschützten Personenkreises.

Sicherung der Selbständigen

Während die soziale Sicherung nach der früheren Systematik fast ausschließlich für abhängig Beschäftigte Geltung hatte, zeigte sich in neuerer Zeit immer deutlicher, daß die Bedingungen der modernen Arbeitswelt auch selbständig Erwerbstätige, insbesondere wenn sie allein oder nur mit Familienangehörigen tätig sind, zur Aufrechterhaltung ihres Lebensstandards zunehmend auf die Verwertung ihrer Arbeitskraft verweisen. Die Ursache dafür ist, daß die Arbeitseinkommen der Tendenz nach stärker ansteigen als die Besitzeinkommen. Bei einem Ausfall des Arbeitseinkommens gewähren in diesen Fällen die selbständige Existenz und das mit ihr verbundene Vermögen noch keine ausreichende soziale Sicherheit, insbesondere für den Fall der Invalidität und des Alters. Aus diesen Gründen gewinnt ein geregelter Ausgleich zwischen dem im Arbeitsprozeß stehenden Bevölkerungsteil und demjenigen, der nicht mehr arbeitsfähig ist, auch für den Personenkreis der selbständig Erwerbstätigen zunehmend an Bedeutung. Als Folge dieser Entwicklung wurden 1938 die Altersversorgung für das Handwerk und im Jahre 1957 die Altershilfe für Landwirte eingeführt. Gegenwärtig bemühen sich weitere Berufsgruppen um eine Alterssicherung. Die Bundesregierung hat dabei gesetzgeberische Hilfe zugesagt, wenn diese gewünscht wird.

Versicherung im Vordergrund

Typisch für die soziale Sicherung in Deutschland ist das Vorherrschen des Versicherungsgedankens. Die Bundesrepublik ist nicht den Weg einer allgemeinen Versorgung der Staatsbürger zur Abdeckung der wichtigsten sozialen Risiken gegangen. Da die Wechselfälle des Arbeitslebens mit Gewißheit vorhersehbar sind — wie beim Alter — oder erfahrungsgemäß im Durchschnitt in mehr oder minder großem Umfange regelmäßig wiederkehren, hat man zur Abwendung ihrer Folgen die Form der Versicherung beibehalten. Die Zugehörigkeit zur Gemeinschaft der Versicherten kann jedoch nicht in jedem Fall der Einsicht des Einzelnen überlassen bleiben und ist daher für die Masse der Bevölkerung obligatorisch kraft Gesetzes geregelt. Hierin äußert sich das Prinzip der Solidarität als ein tragender Gedanke der deutschen sozialen Sicherung, die von Anfang an weitgehend als organisierte Selbsthilfe der betroffenen Personenkreise verstanden worden ist.

II. DIE SOZIALVERSICHERUNG

Trotz den zahlreichen Änderungen des Sozialrechts während der letzten zehn Jahre hat sich nichts daran geändert, daß die Sozialversicherung, in der eingangs genannten Gliederung, die wichtigste Grundlage der sozialen Sicherheit in Deutschland darstellt. In dieser Sozialversicherung sind grundsätzlich alle Arbeitnehmer versicherungspflichtig, die gegen Entgelt beschäftigt werden. Angestellte sind jedoch bei einem Einkommen von mehr als 660 DM im Monat von der Krankenversicherungspflicht und bei einem Einkommen von mehr als 1.250 DM im Monat von der Renten-(und Arbeitslosen-)versicherung befreit.

Diese *Einkommensgrenzen* für die Versicherungspflicht unterliegen den Anpassungen, von denen vorher die Rede gewesen ist; sie werden von Zeit zu Zeit gesetzlich den veränderten Umständen angepaßt, wobei man sich bemüht, die Notwendigkeit der öffentlichen Sicherung innerhalb der Gesellschaft jeweils sinnvoll abzugrenzen. Ob eine Sicherung durch Gesetz notwendig ist, wird dabei verständlicherweise für den Fall der Krankheit anders beurteilt als für die Fälle der Arbeitslosigkeit, der Invalidität und des Alters, bei denen die Versicherungspflicht nicht beschränkt ist.

In der Krankenversicherung und in den Rentenversicherungen für Arbeiter und Angestellte ist unter bestimmten Voraussetzungen eine *freiwillige Weiterversicherung* möglich. Die Selbstversicherung, also der freiwillige Beitritt, wurde in der Rentenversicherung durch die neuere Gesetzgebung beseitigt, in der Krankenversicherung ist sie beschränkt zugelassen.

Umfang der Versicherung

Mehr als 80% der Gesamtbevölkerung werden durch die gesetzliche Krankenversicherung erfaßt, nämlich etwa sechsundzwanzig Millionen Versicherte mit rund siebzehn Millionen Familienangehörigen. Kaum geringer ist der Personenkreis, den die beiden Zweige der gesetzlichen Rentenversicherung, die Arbeiter- und die Angestelltenversicherung, umfassen, wenn man die freiwillig Versicherten hinzurechnet. Auch in der Unfallversicherung sind rund sechsundzwanzig Millionen Personen pflichtversichert, also weit mehr als die Zahl der unselbständig Erwerbstätigen, die 1959 bei rund zwanzig Millionen liegt. Hinzu kommen die Sicherungseinrichtungen für die Selbständigen. Die Altersversorgung für das Handwerk erfaßt alle selbständigen Handwerker, soweit sie nicht einen Vertrag über eine Lebensversicherung abgeschlossen haben, der von der Versicherungspflicht befreit; das dürfte etwa für die Hälfte aller Handwerker zutreffen. Die Zahl der sozialversicherten Handwerker liegt bei 750.000. In die Altershilfe für Landwirte sind nahezu eine Million selbständige Landwirte einbezogen, deren landwirtschaftliches Unternehmen eine Existenzgrundlage bildet. Zieht man in Betracht, daß für einige weitere Gruppen von Selbständigen regional begrenzte Sicherungseinrichtungen bestehen; ferner, daß ein großer Teil der übrigen Selbständigen freiwillig Beiträge zur Sozialversicherung leistet, so wird deutlich, daß fast die gesamte Bevölkerung der Bundesrepublik von diesem Hauptsystem der sozialen Sicherung erfaßt worden ist.

1. *Die Leistungen*

a) Krankheit

Seit fünfundsiebzig Jahren ist das Recht der gesetzlichen Krankenversicherung in seinen Grundzügen unangetastet geblieben. Es hat sich trotz zwei Weltkriegen und zweimaligem Währungsverfall als brauchbar erwiesen und wird auch heute noch, nach allgemeiner Auffassung, seiner Aufgabe im wesentlichen gerecht. Gleichwohl ist eine Reform in Vorbereitung. Sie soll aber das Bestehende nicht völlig verändern, sondern es nur an die Forderungen der Gegenwart anpassen. Am Versicherungsprinzip wird festgehalten; die Einführung eines nationalen Gesundheitsdienstes ist nicht vorgesehen.

Tabelle 1

DIE SOZIALE KRANKENVERSICHERUNG[1]

	1953	1954	1955	1956	1957
Zahl der Kassen	2.056	2.058	2.071	2.075	2.066
Zahl der Mitglieder in 1.000 (die darin enthaltene Zahl der Rentner ist für die Jahre 1953—1956 geschätzt worden)...	23.400	24.300	24.900	25.700	25.750
Arbeitsunfähigkeitsfälle der Mitglieder (ohne Rentner) in 1.000	8.937,0	8.808,3	10.295,8	10.905,4	13.892,2
Arbeitsunfähigkeitstage der Mitglieder (ohne Rentner) in 1.000	212.657,9	212.552,1	237.447,9	248.991,3	302.500,6
Reineinnahmen in Millionen DM	3.915,8	4.215,7	4.616,8	5.238,4	6.256,4
darunter:					
Beiträge	3.841,1	4.122,0	4.509,8	5.117,3	6.023,3
Kapitalerträge	22,4	25,4	30,6	39,9	44,6
Reinausgaben in Millionen DM...	3.845,2	4.098,1	4.626,9	5.247,2	6.487,0
darunter für:					
ärztliche Behandlung (einschl. von Zahnbehandlung und Vertrauensärztlicher Tätigkeit)	1.014,4	1.134,3	1.309,0	1.445,0	1.618,7
Arzneien und Heilmittel (einschl. von Zahnersatz).....	746,4	769,8	842,7	938,5	1.095,4
Krankenhauspflege, Kuraufenthalt, Anstaltspflege	711,1	756,4	825,8	940,3	1.094,0
Krankengeld	761,6	772,6	938,2	1.082,2	1.674,8
Wochenhilfe	171,2	193,4	209,1	236,1	280,1
Sterbegeld	67,6	69,0	76,9	94,5	126,5

[1] Alle Zahlen beziehen sich auf die Bundesrepublik (ohne Saarland) mit Berlin (West). Quelle: Bundesministerium für Arbeit und Sozialordnung.

Krankenpflege

Nach dem derzeitigen Recht erhält der Versicherte im Falle der Krankheit die sogenannte Krankenpflege. Sie endet, wenn der Kranke während der Krankheit aus der Versicherung ausscheidet, sechsundzwanzig Wochen nach dem Ausscheiden. Die Krankenpflege umfaßt ärztliche Behandlung sowie Versorgung mit Arzneien und kleineren Heilmitteln. Die ärztliche Versorgung soll ausreichend und zweckmäßig sein. Sie darf aber das Maß des Notwendigen nicht überschreiten. Darüber hinaus können durch Beschluß der Selbstverwaltungsorgane der Krankenkassen besondere Leistungen gewährt werden, so Fürsorge für Genesende, Hilfsmittel gegen Verunstaltung oder Verkrüppelung und Maßnahmen zur Krankheitsverhütung. Dieses Recht der Krankenpflege beruht also auf dem Sachleistungsprinzip: außer einer geringfügigen Arzneikostengebühr hat der Versicherte im Krankheitsfall über seinen Krankenkassenbeitrag hinaus gegenwärtig keine weiteren Kosten aufzubringen.

Krankengeld

Bei Arbeitsunfähigkeit, die vom behandelnden Arzt festgestellt und vom Vertrauensarzt kontrolliert wird, erhält der Versicherte Krankengeld für die Dauer von sechsundzwanzig Wochen. Diese gesetzliche Höchstdauer ist jedoch in vielen Fällen durch Satzungsbeschluß bis zu einem Jahr verlängert worden. Das Krankengeld beträgt in den ersten sechs Wochen 65% des Entgelts des Versicherten (bis zur Höhe von 22 DM täglich) und erhöht sich für den ersten Angehörigen um 4%, für den zweiten und dritten Angehörigen um je 3%. Angestellte haben auf Grund gesetzlicher Vorschriften außerhalb des Rechts der Sozialversicherung einen Anspruch auf Fortzahlung ihres Gehaltes für sechs Wochen. Der Anspruch richtet sich gegen ihren Arbeitgeber. Arbeiter erhalten in dieser Zeit einen Zuschuß des Arbeitgebers zum Krankengeld bis zur Höhe von 90% des Nettoarbeitsentgelts. Von der siebten Woche ab fällt dieser Arbeitgeberzuschuß weg; das Krankengeld vermindert sich dann auf 50%, kann jedoch von der Krankenkasse, wenn ihre Finanzlage es erlaubt, bis auf 75% erhöht werden.

Krankenhauspflege

An Stelle von Krankenpflege und Krankengeld kann Krankenhauspflege gewährt werden, die wirtschaftlich durch ein Hausgeld ergänzt wird. Dieses

ALLTAG
IN DEUTSCHLAND

In der Kinderklinik der Universität Bonn

Arbeiter des Volkswagenwerks bei einer Betriebsversammlung

Ein Umtrunk in der Arbeitspause

Studenten im Hörsaal

ALLTAG IN DEUTSCHLAND

Die Hopfenbäuerin

Bauersfrau aus dem Westerwald

Jung beim Wein

Hausgeld beträgt 25% des Krankengeldes. Es erhöht sich auf $66^2/_3$%, wenn der Versicherte einen Angehörigen zu unterhalten hat, und um weitere 10% für jeden weiteren Angehörigen. Die Krankenkasse kann das Hausgeld für den Versicherten mit einem oder mit zwei Angehörigen bis zu 80% des Krankengeldes erhöhen. Es darf aber den Betrag des Krankengeldes nicht überschreiten.

Wochenhilfe

Bei Schwangerschaft wird Frauen, die in einem Arbeitsverhältnis stehen, Wochenhilfe gewährt. Sie besteht aus Hebammenhilfe, Arzneien, kleineren Heilmitteln, ärztlicher Behandlung, einem Beitrag zu den Entbindungskosten, einem Stillgeld und einem laufenden Wochengeld. Das Wochengeld entspricht dem durchschnittlichen Arbeitsentgelt der letzten dreizehn Wochen und wird gezahlt für sechs Wochen vor und sechs Wochen nach der Niederkunft.

Sterbegeld

Beim Tode eines Versicherten wird ein Sterbegeld gewährt. Es beträgt grundsätzlich das Zwanzigfache des auf den Kalendertag berechneten Versichertenentgelts, mindestens jedoch 100 DM. Es kann bis zum Vierzigfachen des auf den Kalendertag berechneten Entgelts erhöht werden; auch kann ein Mindestbetrag von 150 DM festgesetzt werden.

Familienhilfe

Ein wichtiger Bereich der gesetzlichen Krankenversicherung sind die Leistungen für Familienangehörige. Sie bestehen aus Familien-Krankenpflege, Familien-Wochenhilfe und Familien-Sterbegeld. Familien-Krankenpflege wird dem Versicherten für den Ehegatten und die Kinder gewährt, falls sie unterhaltsberechtigt sind. Auch die Familien-Wochenhilfe folgt den Grundsätzen des Rechts der Versicherten, allerdings bei vermindertem Wochengeld. Das Familien-Sterbegeld beträgt die Hälfte des Mitglieder-Sterbegeldes.

Leistungsverbesserungen

Grundzüge der geplanten Neuordnung des Rechts der sozialen Krankenversicherung sind wichtige Leistungsverbesserungen, so die Einführung ärztlicher Vorsorgeuntersuchungen zum Zwecke der Früherkennung von Krankheiten und der vorbeugenden Gesundheitspflege. Auch soll die bisherige zeitliche Begrenzung der Krankenhauspflege, die immer wieder zu sozialen Härten bei langdauernden Krankheiten geführt hat, aufgehoben werden. Das gleiche gilt für die Begrenzung der Zahlung von Krankengeld auf die ersten sechs Wochen der Arbeitsunfähigkeit. Sie hatte zur Folge, daß eine wirksame wirtschaftliche Hilfe gerade dann fehlte, wenn sie am notwendigsten war. Daher soll künftig für die gesamte Leistungsdauer Krankengeld in gleicher Höhe gezahlt werden. Weiter sollen im Interesse einer möglichst umfassenden Krankheitsfürsorge auch für Familienangehörige künftig die Leistungen der Familienhilfe in gleichem Umfange gewährt werden wie für die Versicherten.

Selbstbeteiligung

Zur Finanzierung dieser Mehrleistungen, zur Verhütung des Mißbrauchs der gesetzlichen Krankenversicherung und zur Verhinderung eines weiteren unbegründeten Ansteigens der Aufwendungen der gesetzlichen Krankenversicherung ist eine maßvolle Selbstbeteiligung bei der ärztlichen Behandlung, der Versorgung mit Arzneimitteln und bei der Krankenhauspflege vorgeschlagen worden, während die Opposition jede Art von Selbstbeteiligung ablehnt. Die Zulassung der Ärzte im Rahmen der gesetzlichen Krankenversicherung soll neugeordnet werden, ebenso das Honorarsystem und der Vertrauensärztliche Dienst. Es wird damit gerechnet, daß die Neuregelung des Rechts der sozialen Krankenversicherung noch in der laufenden Dritten Legislaturperiode des Deutschen Bundestages zum Abschluß gebracht werden kann.

b) Arbeitsunfälle und Berufskrankheiten

Die wichtigste Aufgabe der *Unfallversicherung* ist die Verhütung, zumindest aber die Verminderung, von Unfällen und Berufskrankheiten durch vorbeugende Maßnahmen. Auch gehört es zu ihren Bestrebungen, Unfallverletzungen zu heilen oder doch eine Verschlimmerung ihrer gesundheitlichen Folgen zu verhüten. Die Träger der Unfallversicherung haben für eine wirksame erste Hilfe bei Verletzungen zu sorgen. Sie sind verpflichtet, Vorschriften darüber zu erlassen, welche Maßnahmen die Unternehmer zur Verhütung von Unfällen in ihren Betrieben zu treffen haben. Die Durchführung der Unfallverhütung wird durch technische Aufsichtsbeamte überwacht; sie kann durch Ordnungsstrafen erzwungen werden.

Arbeits- und Wegeunfälle, Berufskrankheiten

Die Unfallversicherung gewährt Leistungen bei Arbeitsunfällen und Berufskrankheiten. Als Arbeitsunfälle gelten auch Unfälle bei besonderen Ausnahmesituationen (Feuerwehr, Lebensretter und anderes mehr) sowie Unfälle auf einem mit der Tätigkeit in dem Unternehmen zusammenhängenden Weg nach und von der Arbeits- oder Ausbildungsstätte und schließlich Unfälle bei einer mit der Tätigkeit in dem Unternehmen zusammenhängenden Verwahrung, Beförderung, Instandhaltung und Erneuerung des Arbeitsgeräts, auch wenn es vom Versicherten gestellt wird. Welche Krankheiten als Berufskrankheiten anerkannt sind, ergibt sich aus einem im Laufe der Zeit erheblich erweiterten gesetzlichen Katalog.

Die Entschädigungen

Durch ihre Entschädigungsleistungen erfüllt die Unfallversicherung gleichzeitig die Funktion, privatrechtliche Ansprüche eines verletzten Arbeitnehmers gegen seinen Unternehmer auf Haftung abzulösen. Der Schadensersatz geschieht durch Sach- und Geldleistungen. Die Sachleistungen bestehen aus Krankenbehandlung (ärztliche Behandlung, Versorgung mit Arzneien, Pflege), Berufsfürsorge und Wiederherstellung oder Erneuerung eines beschädigten Körperersatz-Stückes.

Krankengeld und Unfallrenten

Bei Arbeitsunfähigkeit des Verletzten ist ihm ein Krankengeld und während der Dauer einer Pflege in einer Heilanstalt ein Tagegeld und seiner Familie ein Familiengeld zu zahlen. Weiter wird eine *Rente* gewährt, wenn die Erwerbsfähigkeit des Verletzten um mindestens 20% über die dreizehnte Woche nach dem Unfall hinaus gemindert ist. Bei völliger Erwerbsunfähigkeit wird dem Verletzten eine Rente in Höhe von zwei Dritteln des Jahres-Arbeitsverdienstes, mindestens jedoch 90 DM monatlich, gewährt, bei teilweiser Erwerbsunfähigkeit entsprechend dem Maß der Einbuße an Erwerbsfähigkeit ein Teil der Vollrente. Die Witwenrente beträgt jährlich ein Fünftel des Jahres-Arbeitsverdienstes des Verstorbenen, bei Witwen über

c) *Invalidität und Alter*

Wie schon erwähnt worden ist, hat die Bundesrepublik als ersten Abschnitt der von ihr geplanten Sozialreform die Rentenversicherung für Arbeiter und Angestellte bereits einer völligen Neuregelung unterzogen. Diese sogenannte Rentenreform von 1957 ist die wichtigste Entscheidung des Deutschen Bundestages auf dem Gebiete der sozialen Sicherung gewesen. Sie hat nicht nur die Rentenleistungen bei Invalidität und Alter im Normalfall des versicherten Arbeitslebens bedeutend verbessert, sondern auch ein ganz neues System geschaffen, um die Entwicklung von Sozialleistungen und Arbeitseinkommen miteinander im Einklang zu halten.

Aufgaben der Rentenversicherung

Zu den Aufgaben der Rentenversicherung der Arbeiter und der Angestellten sowie der knappschaftlichen Rentenversicherung (für Beschäftigte des Bergbaues) gehören die Erhaltung, Besserung und Wiederherstellung der Erwerbsfähigkeit der Versicherten, die Gewährung von Renten wegen allgemeiner beziehungsweise knappschaftlicher Berufsunfähigkeit oder wegen Erwerbsunfähigkeit und die Gewährung von Altersruhegeld an Versicherte; ferner die Gewährung von Renten an Hinterbliebene verstorbener Versicherter und schließlich die Förderung von Maßnahmen zur Hebung der gesundheitlichen Verhältnisse in der versicherten Bevölkerung.

Vorsorge und „Rehabilitation"

Der Gesetzgeber hat ausdrücklich nicht die Rentenleistungen, die natürlich das Hauptgewicht des Finanzaufwandes ausmachen, in den Vordergrund gestellt; sondern er hat die Maßnahmen zur Erhaltung, Besserung und Wiederherstellung der Erwerbsfähigkeit an erster Stelle genannt. Diese Leistungen können von den Trägern der Rentenversicherungen gewährt werden, wenn die Erwerbsfähigkeit eines Versicherten durch Krankheit oder andere Gebrechen gefährdet oder gemindert ist, und wenn die berechtigte Aussicht besteht, daß sie erhalten, wesentlich gebessert oder wieder hergestellt werden kann. Die Maßnahmen, die allgemein unter dem Begriff „Rehabilitation" zusammengefaßt werden, beruhen auf dem Gedanken, daß eine gesundheitliche und berufliche Förderung sowohl für den einzelnen Versicherten als auch für die Volkswirtschaft sinnvoller und vorteilhafter ist als eine dauernde Rentenleistung. Die Rehabilitation umfaßt Heilbehandlung,

Berufsförderung und soziale Betreuung. Alle Maßnahmen dürfen nur mit Zustimmung des Versicherten durchgeführt werden.

Renten bei Berufs- und Erwerbsunfähigkeit

Bei den Rentenleistungen wird zwischen Renten wegen Berufsunfähigkeit und wegen Erwerbsunfähigkeit unterschieden. Ist die Erwerbsfähigkeit eines Versicherten infolge von Krankheit oder anderen Gebrechen oder Schwäche seiner körperlichen oder geistigen Kräfte auf weniger als die Hälfte derjenigen eines körperlich und geistig gesunden Versicherten ähnlicher Ausbildung und von gleichwertigen Kenntnissen und Fähigkeiten abgesunken, so erhält er eine Rente wegen Berufsunfähigkeit. Kann der Versicherte infolge von Krankheit oder anderen Gebrechen oder von Schwäche seiner körperlichen oder geistigen Kräfte auf nicht absehbare Zeit eine Erwerbstätigkeit in gewisser Regelmäßigkeit nicht mehr ausüben oder nicht mehr als nur geringfügige Einkünfte durch Erwerbstätigkeit erzielen, so erhält er Rente wegen Erwerbsunfähigkeit.

Für die Versicherten der knappschaftlichen Rentenversicherung gibt es außerdem die Bergmannsrente. Sie wird gewährt, wenn verminderte bergmännische Berufsfähigkeit vorliegt und das fünfzigste Lebensjahr vollendet ist und ferner eine Wartezeit von fünfundzwanzig Jahren mit mindestens fünfzehnjähriger Hauerarbeit unter Tage zurückgelegt ist. In allen Fällen ist eine Wartezeit von fünf Jahren zu erfüllen.

Altersruhegeld

Das Altersruhegeld beziehungsweise Knappschaftsruhegeld erhält der Versicherte, der das fünfundsechzigste Lebensjahr vollendet und eine Wartezeit von fünfzehn Jahren erfüllt hat. Frauen können das Altersruhegeld bereits mit sechzig Jahren erhalten, wenn sie in den vorausgegangenen zwanzig Jahren überwiegend eine rentenversicherungspflichtige Beschäftigung ausgeübt haben und eine solche nicht mehr ausüben. Männliche Versicherte erhalten das Altersruhegeld mit sechzig Jahren für die Dauer ihrer Arbeitslosigkeit, wenn sie seit mindestens einem Jahr ununterbrochen arbeitslos sind.

Die Rentenhöhe

Für die Höhe der Rente sind vier Faktoren maßgebend. Das sind: der Steigerungssatz je anrechnungsfähiges Versicherungsjahr, die Versicherungs-

Tabelle 3 DIE RENTENVERSICHERUNGEN DER ARBEITER UND DER ANGESTELLTEN

		1953	1954	1955	1956	1957	1958
Zahl der Versicherungsträger	Arb.	19	19	19	19	19	19
	Ang.	18	2	2	2	2	2
Zahl der laufenden Renten am Jahresende	Arb.	4.501.065	4.535.987	4.541.674	4.904.941	4.912.803	5.154.207
	Ang.	1.400.236	1.442.843	1.524.206	1.573.150	1.633.495	1.756.946
davon:							
Renten an Versicherte	Arb.	2.444.434	2.513.155	2.554.019	2.593.291	2.632.220	2.858.624
	Ang.	656.024	689.212	746.223	782.517	811.999	899.364
Witwenrent.	Arb.	1.056.908	1.095.189	1.153.506	1.572.545	1.621.022	1.715.579
	Ang.	474.811	495.530	529.069	558.073	579.206	621.631
Waisenrent.	Arb.	999.723	927.643	834.149	739.105	659.561	580.004
	Ang.	269.401	258.101	248.914	232.560	242.290	235.951
Reineinnahmen in Millionen DM[1]							
	Arb.	5.145	5.495	6.308	7.391	9.854	10.910
	Ang.	2.264	2.400	2.878	3.298	4.243	5.105
darunter:							
Beiträge	Arb.	3.273	3.531	4.324	4.975	6.467	7.264
	Ang.	1.605	1.701	2.049	2.329	3.226	3.610
Zahlungen des Bundes	Arb.	1.760	1.823	1.794	2.128	3.016	3.163
	Ang.	614	609	694	790	845	804
Vermögenserträgnisse	Arb.	84	135	185	281	363	429
	Ang.	43	76	111	162	164	172
Reinausgaben in Millionen DM[1]							
	Arb.	4.257	4.296	4.817	5.807	8.385	10.295
	Ang.	1.732	1.831	2.192	2.604	3.897	4.820
darunter für:							
Renten	Arb.	3.539	3.563	4.018	4.911	7.136	8.074
	Ang.	1.489	1.571	1.917	2.279	3.499	4.130
Beiträge zur Krankenversicherung der Rentner	Arb.	313	317	317	334	557	737
	Ang.	96	99	104	114	172	317
Heilverfahr.	Arb.	248	243	269	296	373	462
	Ang.	88	93	86	106	119	143

[1] In der Rentenversicherung der Arbeiter ab 1954, in der Rentenversicherung der Angestellten ab 1957 vorläufige Zahlen.

Quelle: Bundesministerium für Arbeit und Sozialordnung.

Tabelle 4
DIE KNAPPSCHAFTLICHE RENTENVERSICHERUNG

	1953	1954	1955	1956	1957
Zahl der Versicherungsträger	7	7	7	7	7
Zahl der Versicherten am Jahresende	667.291	661.623	669.036	688.077	702.649
Zahl der laufenden Renten am Jahresende	624.021	639.033	649.624	668.180	646.742
davon:					
Renten an Versicherte	342.396	354.638	363.778	374.268	365.025
Witwenrenten	204.188	211.408	217.082	229.706	225.013
Waisenrenten	77.437	72.987	68.764	64.206	56.704
Reineinnahmen[1] *in Millionen DM*...	1.074,9	1.121,5	1.368,3	1.578,5	1.686,6
darunter:					
Beiträge	687,4	702,4	769,3	863,7[2]	959,4[3]
Zahlungen d. Bundes	310,1	330,4	475,2	547,5	520,3
Vermögenserträgnis.	6,5	7,6	10,3	15,0	25,3
Reinausgaben in Millionen DM...	1.009,5	1.061,1	1.274,0	1.436,2	1.646,6
darunter für:					
Renten	898,8	945,5	1.144,6	1.264,7	1.479,2
Beiträge zur Krankenversicherung der Rentner	65,8	68,8	76,9	88,3	99,5
Heilverfahren	15,5	18,4	21,4	24,1	30,7

[1] Ab 1956 vorläufige Zahlen. — [2] Davon 183,8 Millionen DM vom Bund getragen. — [3] Davon 217,6 Millionen DM vom Bund getragen.

Quelle: Bundesministerium für Arbeit und Sozialordnung.

Witwen- und Waisenrenten

Auch die Hinterbliebenen-Renten der Invaliden- und Alterssicherung sind einer völligen Neuordnung unterzogen worden. Beim Tode des Versicherten erhält seine Witwe eine Witwenrente in Höhe von sechs Zehnteln der Rente, die dem Versicherten zugestanden hätte, wenn er berufsunfähig gewesen wäre. Hat die Witwe das 45. Lebensjahr vollendet, oder ist sie berufsunfähig, oder hat sie ein Kind zu erziehen, so berechnet sich die Rente nach der Erwerbsunfähigkeitsrente des Versicherten. Ein Witwer erhält die gleichen Leistungen, wenn die Versicherte den Unterhalt ihrer Familie überwiegend bestritten hat. Die Waisenrente beträgt bei Halbwaisen ein Zehntel, bei Vollwaisen ein Fünftel der Erwerbsunfähigkeitsrente des Versicherten zuzüglich des Kinderzuschusses.

Abfindungen, Beitragserstattungen

Heiratet eine Witwe oder ein Witwer wieder, so wird als Abfindung das Fünffache des Jahresbetrages der bisherigen Rente gewährt. Heiratet eine Versicherte, so werden ihr die von ihr nach dem 20. 6. 1948, dem Datum der Währungsreform, entrichteten Beiträge erstattet. Das gleiche gilt für den Fall, daß ein Versicherter nicht zur freiwilligen Weiterversicherung berechtigt ist.

Altersgeld für Selbständige

Die Altersversorgung für das Handwerk, die im Rahmen der Angestelltenversicherung abgewickelt wird, gewährt die gleichen Leistungen wie dieser Versicherungszweig. Schließlich gibt es seit 1957 die schon erwähnte Altershilfe für Landwirte. Danach erhalten Altersgeld alle ehemaligen hauptberuflichen Landwirte, wenn sie fünfundsechzig Jahre alt sind, fünfzehn Jahre Beiträge entrichtet und den Betrieb abgegeben haben.

2. *Die Finanzierung*

Wie werden nun die Mittel aufgebracht, die zur Finanzierung der Leistungen der Sozialversicherung erforderlich sind? Es handelt sich immerhin um ein Leistungsvolumen der Kranken-, Unfall- und Rentenversicherung von insgesamt rund 22 Milliarden DM (1957).

Die Beiträge

Mit Ausnahme der Rentenversicherungen, die Staatszuschüsse erhalten, wird die Sozialversicherung ausschließlich aus Beiträgen der Versicherten und der Arbeitgeber finanziert. In der *Unfallversicherung* sind allein die Arbeitgeber beitragspflichtig; die Finanzierungsmittel werden hier auf dem Wege der Umlage erhoben. Die Beitragshöhe bemißt sich nach den versicherten Arbeitsentgelten, jedoch abgestuft nach Gefahrenklassen, in die die einzelnen Betriebe eingeordnet werden. Bei den gewerblichen Berufsgenossenschaften, den Trägern der gewerblichen Unfallversicherung, belief sich der durchschnittliche Beitragssatz 1956 auf 1% der Arbeitsverdienste, im Bergbau dagegen auf 7%. Die landwirtschaftlichen Berufsgenossenschaften erheben ihre Beiträge nach Maßgabe des Einheitswertes oder des Arbeitsbedarfs der einzelnen Betriebe.

In den beiden anderen Zweigen der Sozialversicherung, wie auch in der Arbeitslosenversicherung, werden die Beiträge von Arbeitnehmern und Arbeitgebern je zur Hälfte gemeinsam aufgebracht.

In den *Rentenversicherungen* der Arbeiter und der Angestellten beläuft sich der Beitrag seit der Rentenreform auf je 7% des Entgelts für Versicherte und Arbeitgeber, in der knappschaftlichen Rentenversicherung auf 8,5% für die Versicherten und 15% für die Arbeitgeber. Die Staatszuschüsse zu den Ausgaben der Rentenversicherungen sind sehr beträchtlich. Bei den Knappschaften decken sie die jeweilige Differenz zwischen den Einnahmen und den Ausgaben, bei den Rentenversicherungen der Arbeiter und der Angestellten (einschließlich der Handwerkerversorgung) stehen sie in einem festen Verhältnis zur allgemeinen Bemessungsgrundlage und unterliegen daher jährlichen Änderungen. Insgesamt hat die Bundesrepublik 1958 einen Staatszuschuß zu den gesetzlichen Rentenversicherungen in Höhe von rund 4,5 Milliarden aufgebracht. Im gleichen Zeitraum betrugen die Gesamtausgaben für Renten rund 13,7 Milliarden DM[1].

In der *Krankenversicherung* sind die Beiträge unterschiedlich. Ihre Festsetzung obliegt den Organen der Selbstverwaltung. 1959 liegt der durchschnittliche Beitragssatz bei etwas mehr als 8,5%. Auch in der Krankenversicherung zahlen Arbeitgeber und Versicherte je die Hälfte. Zur knappschaftlichen Krankenversicherung leistet der Bund einen Zuschuß in Höhe von 1% der Arbeitsentgelte.

Freiwillig Versicherte tragen wie in der Rentenversicherung so auch in der Krankenversicherung den Beitrag allein. Der Krankenversicherungsbeitrag für Rentner und für Arbeitslose ist um ein Drittel niedriger als der Beitrag für die übrigen Versicherten. Er wird von dem Träger der Rentenversicherung beziehungsweise der Arbeitslosenversicherung gezahlt.

Grenzen der Beitragsbemessung

Bei der Beurteilung der Beitragshöhe muß jedoch berücksichtigt werden, daß die Beiträge nicht in allen Fällen vom vollen Entgelt des Versicherten, sondern nur bis zu folgenden Grenzen der Beitragsbemessung berechnet werden:

[1] Vergleiche die Tabellen 3 und 4.

660 DM in der Krankenversicherung,
750 DM in der Arbeitslosenversicherung,
800 DM in den Rentenversicherungen der Arbeiter und Angestellten,
1.000 DM in der knappschaftlichen Rentenversicherung.

Die Grenze der Beitragsbemessung erhöht sich in den Rentenversicherungen in bestimmten Intervallen mit der allgemeinen Bemessungsgrundlage.

Beitragssteigerungen

Es gehört zu den Grundsätzen, auf deren Beachtung die Bundesrepublik bei der sozialpolitischen Gesetzgebung Wert legt, daß Gesetzesänderungen in Zukunft nach Möglichkeit keine weiteren Beitragssteigerungen nach sich ziehen sollen. Für soziale Zwecke werden vom Lohn oder Gehalt gegenwärtig rund 30% einbehalten, in manchen Fällen, so im Bergbau, erheblich mehr. Diese Grenze der direkten Sozialbelastung des Lohnes — die indirekte ist ebenfalls beträchtlich, wenn auch schwer zu ermitteln — bedeutet nach allgemeiner Auffassung eine Obergrenze, die nicht ohne Not überschritten werden sollte. Die Bundesregierung steht auf dem Standpunkt, daß nach Abschluß der Sozialreform eine in der Regel ausreichende Höhe der Sozialleistungen erreicht sein wird. Die zusätzliche Sicherung, die darüber hinaus erwünscht ist, sollte nicht mehr Sache der Gesetzgebung, sondern der privaten Entscheidung sein. Die Bundesregierung hält sich nicht für berechtigt, in noch größerem Ausmaß, als es bisher schon geschehen ist, in die Verwendung der Arbeitseinkommen einzugreifen. Im Gegensatz hierzu verweist die sozialdemokratische Opposition darauf, daß die relative Entlastung des Bundes von Sozialausgaben zu einem Teil zu der hohen direkten Sozialbelastung der Löhne geführt habe. Sie führt für dieses Argument an, daß der Anteil der Sozialausgaben an den Gesamtausgaben des Bundes trotz absoluter Steigerung relativ von 38% (1950) auf 27% (1958) zurückgegangen sei.

3. *Der soziale Ausgleich*

Bei allen Veränderungen, denen die Sozialversicherung in den letzten Jahren unterworfen war und in Zukunft noch ausgesetzt sein wird, ist Wert darauf gelegt worden, ihr das Kennzeichen des sozialen Ausgleichs zu erhalten. Dieser soziale Ausgleich, eine besondere Eigentümlichkeit des Finanzierungsverfahrens in der Sozialversicherung, beruht auf dem Gedanken der Solidarität. Er ist von Anfang an ein erklärtes Ziel der Sozialversicherung gewesen, ohne das sie ihre spezifischen Sicherungsaufgaben nicht erfüllen könnte. Der Ausgleich ist in verschiedener Hinsicht gegeben:

Die Krankenversicherung zum Beispiel gewährt allen Versicherten die gleichen Sachleistungen nach Qualität und Dauer, obwohl der eine Versicherte unter Umständen ein Mehrfaches an Beiträgen zahlt als der andere. Neben diesem Ausgleich nach der Einkommenshöhe besteht auch ein Ausgleich nach dem Familienstand. Der kinderreiche und daher die Versicherung weit mehr beanspruchende Versicherte zahlt die gleichen Beiträge wie ein Alleinstehender. Auch in den Rentenversicherungen vollzieht sich trotz der lohngerechten Bemessung der Beiträge und der Renten ein sozialer Ausgleich; zum Beispiel hinsichtlich des Kinderzuschusses, der rückwirkenden Höherbewertung von Naturallohn-Bestandteilen, der Rentengewährung an sechzigjährige Versicherte, der Leistungen an Hinterbliebene, sowie hinsichtlich der Maßnahmen zur Rehabilitation. In allen Fällen wird eine indirekte Einkommenübertragung zugunsten der Bezieher niedriger Einkommen mit Rücksicht auf die Familiengröße oder andere Tatbestände, und damit ein Ausgleich sozialer Belastungen innerhalb der Gemeinschaft der Versicherten vorgenommen. Dieser Ausgleich unterscheidet in der Bundesrepublik nach wie vor die Sozialversicherung von der Privatversicherung.

4. Die Institutionen

Es gibt auch organisatorisch keine Einheitsversicherung in der Bundesrepublik. Die Aufgaben der hier behandelten drei Versicherungszweige der Sozialversicherung werden von Institutionen, sogenannten Trägern, durchgeführt, die regional oder fachlich dezentralisiert sind.

Krankenversicherung

So wird die Krankenversicherung über finanziell und organisatorisch selbständige Krankenkassen abgewickelt. Man unterscheidet unter den rund zweitausend Kassen der Bundesrepublik Ortskrankenkassen, Landkrankenkassen, Betriebskrankenkassen, Innungskrankenkassen, die See-Krankenkasse, Knappschaftskrankenkassen sowie Ersatzkrankenkassen. Die Kassen unterstehen der Selbstverwaltung durch einen Vorstand und eine Vertreterversammlung. Diese Organe der Selbstverwaltung gehen aus Sozialwahlen hervor und setzen sich paritätisch aus Vertretern der Arbeitgeber und der Versicherten zusammen. Zur Wahrnehmung gemeinsamer Interessen sind die Kassen zu Verbänden auf Landes- und Bundesebene zusammengeschlossen. Die Vergütung für die freiberuflich tätigen und nach bestimmten Grundsätzen zugelassenen Kassenärzte wird zwischen den Verbänden der Krankenkassen und den Kassenärztlichen Vereinigungen vertraglich vereinbart.

Unfallversicherung, Rentenversicherung

In der Unfallversicherung gibt es fünfundneunzig Berufsgenossenschaften und andere Versicherungsträger. In den Rentenversicherungen der Arbeiter und Angestellten sind siebzehn Landesversicherungsanstalten sowie die Bundesbahn-Versicherungsanstalt und die Seekasse Träger der Rentenversicherung der Arbeiter. Dazu kommt die Bundesversicherungsanstalt für Angestellte, die außer den Angestellten auch die selbständigen Handwerker umfaßt. Die Rentenversicherung der Bergleute wird von Knappschaften durchgeführt. Die Selbstverwaltungsorgane, Vorstand und Vertreterversammlung, sind wie in der Krankenversicherung so auch in der Unfall- und in der Rentenversicherung paritätisch von Arbeitgebern und Arbeitnehmern besetzt. Nur bei den Knappschaften für den Bergbau bestehen die Organe zu einem Drittel aus Arbeitgebern und zu zwei Dritteln aus Arbeitnehmern.

Die Altershilfe für Landwirte schließlich wird von achtzehn landwirtschaftlichen Alterskassen durchgeführt. Sie sind als selbständige Körperschaften bei den landwirtschaftlichen Berufsgenossenschaften errichtet worden und werden von den gleichen Organen unter Ausschluß der Arbeitnehmer verwaltet.

III. SONSTIGE FORMEN SOZIALER SICHERUNG

Außerhalb der Sozialversicherung, die Hilfe und Schutz gewährt bei Krankheit, Unfällen, Invalidität, Alter oder Tod des Ernährers, ist neben der Arbeitslosenversicherung neuerdings die Gewährung von Kindergeld eine der ständigen Formen sozialer Sicherung. Mehr oder weniger zeitbedingt dagegen sind, wie eingangs betont, die Kriegsopferversorgung (siehe Seite 35), der Lastenausgleich, die Wiedergutmachung und ähnliche Maßnahmen. Sie werden bei normaler politischer und wirtschaftlicher Weiterentwicklung eines Tages auslaufen.

1. Ausgleich der Familienlasten

Erst spät ist die Bundesrepublik dem Beispiel anderer Länder gefolgt und hat die Gewährung von allgemeinen Kinderbeihilfen eingeführt. Dabei setzte sich der Gedanke durch, daß die Familien mit mehreren Kindern gegenüber Ledigen oder kinderlos Verheirateten wirtschaftlich benachteiligt sind, und daß diese Benachteiligung ungerecht ist; denn die Familien mit mehreren Kindern stellen die Generation der zukünftigen Erwerbstätigen und gewährleisten dadurch auch die Altersversorgung der Kinderlosen. In gewissem Ausmaß wird daher eine Umschichtung der Einkommen von den Kinderlosen zu den Familien mit mehreren Kindern für notwendig und gerechtfertigt gehalten. Eine solche Umschichtung erfolgt zwar schon auf dem Wege der Steuerermäßigung bei zunehmender Kinderzahl; aber diese steuerliche Entlastung ist entweder überhaupt nicht oder nur ungenügend wirksam, weil die Bezieher geringer Einkommen von der Lohn- und Einkommensteuer ganz oder teilweise befreit sind.

Kindergelder

Der Gesetzgeber hat daher Ende 1954 beschlossen, einen besonderen Ausgleich der Familienlasten über die Gewährung von Kindergeldern durchzuführen. Nach dem Kindergeldgesetz erhalten Familien für jedes dritte und weitere Kind unabhängig vom Einkommen der Eltern ein Kindergeld von 40 DM monatlich. Berechtigung zum Bezug von Kindergeld besteht bei Kindern bis zum achtzehnten Lebensjahr, beziehungsweise bis zum fünfundzwanzigsten Lebensjahr, wenn die Kinder für einen Beruf ausgebildet werden oder wegen Gebrechlichkeit außerstande sind, sich selbst zu unterhalten.

Als Träger der Kindergeldzahlung wurden Familienausgleichskassen bei den Berufsgenossenschaften der Unfallversicherung errichtet. Die Mittel für die Kindergeldzahlung werden aufgebracht durch Beiträge der Unternehmer im Wege einer Umlage, die nach der Lohnsumme berechnet wird. Den landwirtschaftlichen Familienausgleichskassen werden zwei Drittel ihrer Aufwendungen von den gewerblichen Kassen erstattet. Der Beitrag beträgt im Durchschnitt etwa 1% der Lohnsumme. Die Aufwendungen für das Kindergeld beliefen sich 1958 auf rund 550 Millionen DM.

2. *Kriegsfolgenhilfe*

Lastenausgleich

Unter den nicht-ständigen Formen der sozialen Sicherung nimmt der Lastenausgleich eine besondere Stellung ein. Es handelt sich dabei um eine Vermögensübertragung von den Bevölkerungskreisen, die keine Verluste

Tabelle 5
IN OFFENER FÜRSORGE* LAUFEND UNTERSTÜTZTE VERTRIEBENE, ZUGEWANDERTE UND EVAKUIERTE

Laufend unterstützte Parteien und Personen	Rechnungsjahr (1.4. bis 31.3.)			
	1954[1]	1955[1]	1956[2]	1957[2]
Parteien insgesamt	610.956	592.612	534.175	510.735
darunter:				
Vertriebene	133.024	124.741	113.610	116.220
Zugewanderte	24.693	22.267	18.110	21.710
Evakuierte	29.748	26.793	.	.
Personen insgesamt	966.879	902.360	796.540	761.715
darunter:				
Vertriebene	223.288	198.962	171.675	174.885
Zugewanderte	42.191	37.331	30.315	35.695
Evakuierte	48.824	41.749	.	.

* Einschließlich der Tbc-Hilfe. — [1] Auf Grund der Vierteljahresstatistik der öffentlichen Fürsorge am 30.9. Unterstützte, Zugewanderte und Evakuierte einschließlich der Mehrfachzählungen. — [2] Auf Grund der 10-Prozent-Zusatzstatistik; nur den ganzen Monat September über Unterstützte.

Quelle: Statistisches Bundesamt.

durch den Krieg erlitten haben, zugunsten der Flüchtlinge, Vertriebenen und Kriegssachgeschädigten. Die Mittel für diesen Ausgleich werden innerhalb eines Zeitraumes von dreißig Jahren aufgebracht und von den Lastenausgleichsämtern verwaltet.

Über die Leistungen des Lastenausgleichs ist oben Seite 61 ff. eingehend berichtet. Die laufenden Leistungen für Unterhaltshilfen und Ausbildungsbeihilfen betrugen 1957 insgesamt 943 Millionen DM.

Vertriebenenhilfe

Über den Lastenausgleich hinaus kommen nach dem Bundesvertriebenengesetz für Vertriebene, Sowjetzonenflüchtlinge und Evakuierte verschiedene Maßnahmen der Wiedereingliederung in Betracht, wie die Umsiedlung zur sinnvollen regionalen Verteilung, die Wiedereingliederung von Landwirten, die bevorzugte Berücksichtigung bei gewerblicher Erlaubnis, Vergebung öffentlicher Aufträge, Zulassung von Ärzten usw. Schließlich enthalten das Notaufnahmegesetz und das Bundesevakuiertengesetz besondere Bestim-

Tabelle 6

FÜRSORGEAUFWAND* FÜR VERTRIEBENE, ZUGEWANDERTE UND EVAKUIERTE
1.000 DM

Aufwand der offenen und geschlossenen Fürsorge[1]	Rechnungsjahr (1. 4. bis 31. 3.)			
	1954	1955	1956	1957
Offene Fürsorge insgesamt	660.438	646.465	691.209	723.016
darunter:				
Vertriebene	150.111	148.846	.	.
Zugewanderte	43.646	30.838	37.910	40.290
Evakuierte	31.805	29.452	.	.
Geschlossene Fürsorge insgesamt	532.566	525.622	589.064	619.314
darunter:				
Vertriebene	130.775	117.985	.	.
Zugewanderte	23.446	21.656	25.434	26.930
Evakuierte	21.655	18.837	.	.

* Einschließlich der Tbc-Hilfe. — [1] Gesamtaufwand und Aufwand für Zugewanderte 1955—1957 auf Grund der Jahresstatistik der öffentlichen Fürsorge, Aufwand für Vertriebene und Evakuierte 1954 und 1955 sowie für Zugewanderte 1954 nach dem Vorrangprinzip schätzungsweise errechnet. Aufwand für Zugewanderte 1956 und 1957 ohne soziale Fürsorge gemäß dem Bundesvertriebenen-Gesetz (BVG).

Quelle: Statistisches Bundesamt.

mungen über die Rückführung und Betreuung von Personen, die aus der sogenannten DDR geflüchtet oder während des Krieges evakuiert worden sind. Auch darüber ist auf Seite 62—66 und 74 f. nachzulesen.

Kriegsgefangene, politisch Verfolgte

Frühere Kriegsgefangene erhalten nach dem Heimkehrergesetz ein Entlassungsgeld von 200 DM, eine Übergangshilfe und gegebenenfalls Arbeitslosengeld. Weitere Vergünstigungen beziehen sich auf die Wohnraumbeschaffung, das Wiederaufleben eines früheren Arbeitsverhältnisses und den Kündigungsschutz. Dazu kommen, ebenso wie bei den Vertriebenen, bestimmte Vergünstigungen in der Sozialversicherung. Spätheimkehrer und politische Flüchtlinge aus der sogenannten DDR haben Anspruch auf eine Entschädigung sowie auf Darlehen und Beihilfen.

Schließlich wird auch Personen, die Schäden durch Angehörige der Besatzungsmacht erlitten haben, eine bestimmte Ersatzleistung gewährt.

3. Sozialleistungen der Betriebe

Im Rahmen der allgemeinen sozialen Sicherung sind nach wie vor die betrieblichen Sozialleistungen von großer Bedeutung. Von jeher haben die Betriebe der gewerblichen Wirtschaft durch eine Vielzahl von Maßnahmen und Leistungen die öffentliche Sozialpolitik ergänzt oder ihr vorgearbeitet. Man hat geschätzt, daß jährlich über 1,5 Milliarden DM oder 2% der gesamten Lohn- und Gehaltssumme für freiwillige betriebliche Sozialleistungen ausgegeben werden. Diese umfassen gesundheitliche Maßnahmen (Werksärzte, Erholungsheime), Wohnungsbau, Werksverpflegung, Gemeinschaftsräume, Sportanlagen, Urlaubszuschüsse, Kindergärten und vieles andere mehr.

Betriebliche Altersversorgung

Im Vordergrund des allgemeinen Interesses und am engsten mit der öffentlichen Sozialpolitik verbunden ist die betriebliche Altersversorgung. Sie wird in mannigfachen Formen durchgeführt. Natürlicherweise kommt sie in Großbetrieben häufiger vor als in Klein- und Mittelbetrieben. Wegen der relativ langen Wartezeit begünstigt sie diejenigen Arbeitnehmer besonders, die auch aus der Sozialversicherung eine gute Versorgung im Alter zu erwarten haben. Es ergibt sich daher die Möglichkeit, daß die Ruhebezüge aus der öffentlichen und der betrieblichen Altersversorgung unter Umständen höher sind als der voraufgegangene Arbeitsverdienst. Hinzu kommt, daß die Ausgaben für betriebliche Sozialleistungen steuerlich begünstigt sind und deshalb indirekt einen Staatszuschuß erhalten. Auch wird gegen diese Form der sozialen Sicherung eingewendet, daß neben dem Motiv der Fürsorge für die Beschäftigten das der Bindung des Arbeitnehmers an den Betrieb eine Rolle spielt.

Wendung zur Eigentumsbildung

Wegen der außerordentlichen Vielfalt der betrieblichen Sozialleistungen ist es schwer, ein gerechtes Urteil über ihre Notwendigkeit und Zweckmäßigkeit zu finden. Mit zunehmender Vervollkommnung der öffentlichen Sozialleistungen drängt sich freilich die Frage auf, ob nicht mindestens die Barleistungen der Betriebe verstärkt der Aufgabe zugeführt werden sollten, die Eigentumsbildung in Arbeitnehmerhand zu fördern. Das sollte nach wiederholten Erklärungen der Bundesregierung eines der wichtigsten Ziele der modernen Sozialpolitik sein. Andererseits wird anerkannt, daß die stets im Fluß befindlichen und sehr vielseitigen betrieblichen Maßnahmen immer wieder Erfahrungen und Anregungen für die sozialpolitische Gesetzgebung hervorbringen. Daß die betrieblichen Sozialleistungen nach Form und Ausmaß von der Entwicklung der Wirtschaft abhängig sind, liegt auf der Hand. Sie haben in den letzten zehn Jahren einen bis dahin unbekannten Umfang erreicht und sind nunmehr im Begriff, sich auf ein optimales Verhältnis zur öffentlichen sozialen Sicherung einzuspielen.

IV. SOZIALGERICHTE

Nach dem Wiederaufbau der Versicherungsträger und den zahlreichen Gesetzen zur Verbesserung der Sozialleistungen, nach der Wiederherstellung der Selbstverwaltung der Sozialversicherung durch die unmittelbar Beteiligten, die Arbeitgeber und die Arbeitnehmer, ist vom Deutschen Bundestag auch die frühere Sozialgerichtsbarkeit wieder eingeführt worden. Streitigkeiten in Angelegenheit der Sozialversicherung, der Altershilfe für Landwirte, der Arbeitslosenversicherung, der Kriegsopferversorgung und des Kindergeldrechts werden von besonderen Gerichten verhandelt und entschieden. Als solche sind in den Ländern die Sozialgerichte, die Landessozialgerichte und im Bund das Bundessozialgericht tätig geworden.

Neben den Berufsrichtern in den Kammern der Sozialgerichte und den Senaten der Landessozialgerichte und des Bundessozialgerichts wirken ehrenamtliche Beisitzer bei der Urteilsfindung mit. Sie sind von den Gewerkschaften und den Arbeitgeberverbänden sowie anderen einschlägigen Vereinigungen vorgeschlagen. Die Beteiligung dieser ehrenamtlichen Sozialrichter, Landes-Sozialrichter und Bundes-Sozialrichter soll die Verbindung zwischen Rechtsprechung und sozialer Wirklichkeit pflegen und fördern. Das Verfahren vor den Sozialgerichten ist kostenfrei. Es entspricht in seinen Grundsätzen dem Verfahren, wie es in der Verwaltungsgerichtsbarkeit üblich ist, und entscheidet über Klagen, die sich gegen Maßnahmen der Verwaltungsbehörden, insbesondere gegen die Bescheide über die Festsetzung oder Ablehnung von Leistungen, richten.

V. SOZIALE SICHERUNG IM INTERNATIONALEN RAHMEN

Die Bundespolitik hat mit einer Anzahl von ausländischen Regierungen zweiseitige Sozialversicherungs-, Arbeitslosenversicherungs-, Grenzgänger-, Gastarbeitnehmer- und Anwerbungsabkommen geschlossen. Sie ist außerdem Vertragspartner einer Reihe von mehrseitigen Verträgen, die aus der Arbeit internationaler Organisationen hervorgegangen sind. Auf dem Gebiet der sozialen Sicherung handelt es sich insbesondere um den Schutz für solche Personen, die mehr oder weniger lange im Ausland tätig sind. Durch die Abkommen werden die gegenseitigen Ansprüche geregelt und Unterschiede oder Unklarheiten, die sich aus unterschiedlichem Recht ergeben, ausgeglichen. Solche Regelungen schaffen eine wichtige Voraussetzung für die Freizügigkeit der Arbeitskräfte und damit für den wirtschaftlichen Zusammenschluß in Europa.

Mindestnormen sozialer Sicherheit

Von den Übereinkommen und Empfehlungen der Internationalen Arbeitsorganisation, die dazu beitragen sollen, den Schutz der erwerbstätigen Bevölkerung gegen die Wechselfälle des Lebens zu verbessern, hat die Bundesrepublik eine beträchtliche Anzahl ratifiziert. Insbesondere wurde dem Übereinkommen über die Mindestnormen der sozialen Sicherheit mit allen seinen Teilen zugestimmt, einem inhaltreichen Dokument, das Mindestnormen für ärztliche Betreuung, Krankengeld, Leistungen bei Arbeitslosigkeit, bei Alter, Arbeitsunfällen und Berufskrankheiten, Familienleistungen, Leistungen bei Mutterschaft, bei Invalidität und an Hinterbliebene aufstellt. Gemäß den Bestimmungen dieses Übereinkommens muß das ratifizierende Land mindestens drei dieser verschiedenen Sozialleistungsarten gewähren. Die Bundesrepublik Deutschland ist das erste ratifizierende Land, das alle Verpflichtungen aus diesem Übereinkommen übernimmt. Weitere Ratifizierungen sind in Vorbereitung.

Sozialcharta

Im Rahmen des Europarates hat das Sozialkomitee den Entwurf einer europäischen Sozialcharta fertiggestellt. Diese Sozialcharta, die in der Europäischen Menschenrechts-Konvention ihr Gegenstück findet, soll die grundlegenden sozialpolitischen Ziele der Mitgliedstaaten des Europarates umreißen. Als abgeschlossen können auch die Arbeiten an einem Europäischen Kodex für soziale Sicherheit gelten. Dieses Vertragswerk umfaßt die gesamte soziale Sicherheit. Es soll die von der Bundesrepublik bereits ratifizierten beiden vorläufigen europäischen Übereinkommen über die soziale Sicherheit ergänzen.

Frieden und Fortschritt

Die sozialpolitische Zusammenarbeit der Bundesrepublik mit anderen Ländern hat das Netz der sozialen Sicherung über die Gebiete der Vertragspartner ausgedehnt. Sie hat damit die Freizügigkeit gefördert und europäische Wanderbewegungen unterstützt. Darüber hinaus dient sie im Rahmen der Internationalen Arbeitsorganisationen und der europäischen Gremien, die auch sozialpolitisch tätig sind, dem Erfahrungsaustausch, der Entwicklung internationaler Vergleichsmaßstäbe für soziale Leistungen, der Verbesserung des Informationswesens, der Erhöhung des allgemeinen Sozialstandards und mittelbar auch der Stabilisierung friedlicher Verhältnisse auf der Grundlage des sozialen Fortschritts.

DIE ORGANISATION DER UNTERNEHMER UND ARBEITNEHMER

I. DIE ORGANISATION DER GEWERBLICHEN WIRTSCHAFT

Als Reaktion auf das organisierte solidarische Handeln der Arbeitnehmer und den zunehmenden staatlichen Interventionismus in der Wirtschafts- und Sozialpolitik sind die Organisationen der Unternehmer entstanden. Über ihre ursprüngliche abwehrende Aufgabenstellung sind sie jedoch heute hinausgewachsen. Sie leisten in Verantwortung gegenüber dem Ganzen ihren Beitrag zur freien Gestaltung der sozialen und wirtschaftlichen Verhältnisse.

Nach 1945 sind die Organisationen der gewerblichen Wirtschaft nicht als Einheitsorganisation, sondern anknüpfend an die Tradition und aus ihrer Aufgabenstellung in den überkommenen Formen neu gegründet worden. Dies sind die Industrie- und Handelskammern als regionale Interessenvertretung, die Arbeitgeberverbände als sozialpolitische Interessenvertretung, und schließlich die wirtschaftspolitische Interessenvertretung mit der Spitze im Bundesverband der Deutschen Industrie (BDI). Zur Koordinierung der Arbeit der drei Spitzenorganisationen wurde der „Gemeinschaftsausschuß der deutschen gewerblichen Wirtschaft" gebildet.

Die Industrie- und Handelskammern (IHK)

Hervorgegangen aus den Zusammenschlüssen der Kaufmannschaften des mittelalterlichen Hanseraumes sind die Industrie- und Handelskammern die ältesten Organisationen der gewerblichen Wirtschaft in Deutschland. Mit Beginn des 19. Jahrhunderts wurden sie nach französischem Muster umgebildet oder neu gegründet. 1848 wurden sie im Königreich Preußen als Vertretungen der regionalen gewerblichen Interessen gesetzlich anerkannt. 1861 schlossen sie sich zum „Allgemeinen Deutschen Handelstag" zusammen. Die gegen Ende des Ersten Weltkrieges in „Deutscher Industrie- und Handelstag" umbenannte Spitzenorganisation der Industrie- und Handelskammern wurde nach 1933 in die Reichswirtschaftskammer eingegliedert. Im Herbst 1949 erfolgte die Wiedergründung des *Deutschen Industrie- und Handelstages* (*DIHT*) mit Sitz in Bonn, dem heute alle 80 Industrie- und Handelskammern der Bundesrepublik und die IHK West-Berlin angehören. Dem DIHT obliegt es, die Zusammenarbeit zwischen den einzelnen Kammern zu fördern und die Belange der gewerblichen Wirtschaft gegenüber den Instanzen des Bundes zu vertreten.

Oberstes Organ ist die alljährlich mindestens einmal zusammentretende Volltagung, in der jede Kammer Sitz und Stimme hat. Die Richtlinien für die Tätigkeit des Deutschen Industrie- und Handelstages bestimmt der Hauptausschuß, der auch grundsätzliche Stellungnahmen zu beschließen hat. Der Vorstand wird vorwiegend aus den Reihen der Mitglieder des Hauptausschusses gewählt; in seiner Zusammensetzung spiegelt sich die enge Verbindung zu anderen maßgebenden Spitzenorganisationen der gewerblichen Wirtschaft wider.

Der Deutsche Industrie- und Handelstag vertritt eine nach den Grundsätzen der sozialen Marktwirtschaft orientierte Finanz- und Steuerpolitik. Er lehnt ein weiteres Eindringen der öffentlichen Hand in den Bereich der privaten Wirtschaft ab und setzt sich für die Erhaltung eines gesunden Eigentumsbegriffs ein. In besonderem Maße widmet er sich der Förderung der außenwirtschaftlichen Beziehungen; er ist federführend in der Betreuung der zur Zeit bestehenden 26 deutschen Auslandshandelskammern. Als Mitglied der Internationalen Handelskammer zu Paris fördert er im Einvernehmen mit der Deutschen Gruppe maßgeblich die Tätigkeit der internationalen Gremien. Er gehört ferner zu den Initiatoren der Ständigen Konferenz der Industrie- und Handelskammern der sechs Länder der EWG.

Als wesentliche Aufgabe betrachtet der Deutsche Industrie- und Handelstag die Verbesserung der Berufsausbildung in der Bundesrepublik. Die berufliche Förderung der wissenschaftlichen Mitarbeiter der Kammern ist in den vergangenen Jahren ebenso ausgebaut worden, wie Ausbildungsmöglichkeiten für die heranwachsende Generation von Unternehmern geschaffen wurden.

Beim Deutschen Industrie- und Handelstag besteht die Geschäftsstelle der „Juniorenkreise der Deutschen Unternehmerschaft", die zur Zeit hundert Juniorenkreise mit über 7.000 Mitgliedern betreut. Sie ist ihrerseits korporatives Mitglied in der Junior Chamber International. Die deutschen Juniorenkreise sind überwiegend an die Industrie- und Handelskammern angelehnt und befassen sich weiterbildend mit Fragen der Wirtschafts- und Sozialpolitik.

Der Deutsche Industrie- und Handelstag läßt sich ferner die Förderung der Wissenschaften und der Forschung, der Lehre und des Studiums angelegen sein. Daher unterstützt er nachhaltig die Bestrebungen des Stifterverbandes für die Deutsche Wissenschaft e. V.

Der Bundesverband der Deutschen Industrie e. V. (BDI)

Während die Kammern der regionalen Interessenvertretung von Industrie, Handel und Gewerbe dienen, sind die wirtschaftspolitischen Verbände Interessenvertretungen des industriellen Unternehmertums der Bundesrepublik. Der 1919 gegründete Reichsverband der deutschen Industrie war 1934 in die

Reichsgruppe Industrie umgestaltet worden. Als Nachfolgeorganisation wurde 1949 der Ausschuß für Wirtschaftsfragen der industriellen Verbände gegründet. 1950 konstituierte er sich als Bundesverband der Deutschen Industrie (BDI) in der Rechtsform des eingetragenen Vereins. Der BDI ist die Arbeitsgemeinschaft der Wirtschaftsverbände der Industrie, welche die gemeinsamen Belange der im Bundesverband zusammengeschlossenen Industriezweige wahren und fördern soll. Die Mitgliedschaft ist freiwillig. Dem BDI gehören heute 38 Fachverbände an, die von 12 Landesvertretungen betreut werden.

In der Mitgliederversammlung sind die angeschlossenen Fachverbände entsprechend der Zahl der in ihrem Bereich beschäftigten Angestellten und Arbeiter vertreten. Permanente Mitgliedervertretung ist der Hauptausschuß, der die Vorstandsmitglieder wählt und den Vorstand bei der Erarbeitung der wirtschaftspolitischen Richtlinien unterstützt. Daneben bestehen der Vorstand und das Präsidium.

Der Bundesverband beschäftigt sich ausschließlich mit wirtschaftlichen Fragen, wie aus der Zusammensetzung seiner Ausschüsse zu ersehen ist. Es bestehen unter anderen Ausschüsse für Absatzförderung, Außenhandel, Betriebswirtschaft, Geld, Kredit und Währung, Verkehr, Versicherungen, internationale Beziehungen sowie für Industrie und Landwirtschaft. Neuerdings befaßt sich ein Mittelstandsausschuß mit der Lösung der besonderen Fragen der mittelständischen Wirtschaft.

Der Bundesverband hat sich auch besonders um die Förderung des Nachwuchses bemüht. Von der ihm nahestehenden „Gesellschaft zur Förderung des industriellen Führungsnachwuchses“ und dem gleichnamigen Institut werden die „Baden-Badener Unternehmergespräche“ veranstaltet. Als selbständige Rechtspersönlichkeit besteht der „Kulturkreis des Bundesverbandes der Deutschen Industrie“, der durch Stiftungen, Stipendien und Ausstellungen die kulturelle Verpflichtung des Unternehmertums bewußt machen und Anregungen geben will. Zur Förderung der Zusammenarbeit zwischen Wissenschaft und Wirtschaft ist ein gleichnamiger Gesprächskreis eingerichtet worden. Er soll die Tätigkeit des als Gemeinschaftsaktion der gewerblichen Wirtschaft bestehenden „Stifterverbandes für die deutsche Wissenschaft“ unterstützen und ergänzen.

Der BDI bejaht die soziale Marktwirtschaft als eine Wirtschaftsordnung, in der privates Eigentum und die Freiheit der Unternehmerinitiative gesichert sind. Er ist der Überzeugung, daß „erst auf der Grundlage stabiler Währungen unternehmerisches Handeln sich bewähren kann.“ Der Bundesverband unterstützt jedes Bemühen, „durch breite Streuung von frei verfügbarem Einzeleigentum auch die Arbeitnehmer am produktiven Kapital zu beteiligen“.

Die Bundesvereinigung der Deutschen Arbeitgeberverbände (BDA)

Als Nachfolgeorganisation der 1913 gegründeten Vereinigung der Deutschen Arbeitgeberverbände, die 1933 durch den nationalsozialistischen Staat aufgelöst worden war, konnte 1949 die Bundesvereinigung der Deutschen Arbeitgeberverbände (BDA) mit Sitz in Köln gegründet werden[1]. Sie hat die Rechtsform eines eingetragenen Vereins. Die Mitgliedschaft ist freiwillig.

Infolge der Mitbestimmung wurde für den Bereich Kohle, Eisen und Stahl eine Sonderregelung durch Neugründung der Wirtschaftsvereinigung Eisen- und Stahlindustrie getroffen. Sie gehört nicht der BDA an. Dagegen ist der Unternehmensverband Ruhrbergbau, in dem die unter Mitwirkung der Gewerkschaften bestellten Arbeitsdirektoren nicht in den Vorständen und Tarifkommissionen vertreten sind, Mitglied der Bundesvereinigung.

Insgesamt gehören der Bundesvereinigung heute 37 Fachspitzenverbände und 14 Landesverbände mit 866 Unterverbänden an. Sie repräsentieren etwa 90% aller privaten Betriebe aus Industrie (einschließlich des Bergbaus), Handwerk, Landwirtschaft, Groß- und Außenhandel, Einzelhandel und Verkehrsgewerbe. Auf tarifpolitischem Gebiet darf die Selbständigkeit der Mitglieder nicht durch Maßnahmen der Bundesvereinigung und ihrer Organe eingeschränkt werden. Empfehlungen, sofern sie vom Vorstand der BDA einstimmig beschlossen werden, sind jedoch zulässig.

Die *Bundesvereinigung der Deutschen Arbeitgeberverbände* hat die über den Bereich eines Landes oder den eines Wirtschaftszweiges hinausgehenden *sozialpolitischen Belange von grundsätzlicher Bedeutung* zu behandeln. Dazu gehören: Koalitionsrecht, Betriebsräterecht, Arbeitsschutzrecht, Lohn- und Tarifpolitik, Schlichtungswesen, Richtlinien der Arbeitsvermittlung, Arbeitslosenhilfe, Sozialversicherung, Sozialfürsorge, sozialer Wohnungsbau und Lohnsteuerrecht.

Die Grundsätze ihrer Politik hat die BDA in der Schrift „Gedanken zur sozialen Ordnung" (1953) veröffentlicht. Sie bekennt sich zur sozialen Marktwirtschaft und erklärt: „Die Aufgabe der Wirtschaftsordnung liegt in der höchstmöglichen Produktion von Gütern als materielle Voraussetzung für eine angemessene Lebenshaltung des Volkes. Es ist die Aufgabe unserer sozialen Ordnung, ein höchstmögliches Maß an sozialer Gerechtigkeit, Sicherheit und Freiheit zu gewährleisten." Als tragenden Grundsatz der Sozialverfassung erkennt die BDA, „daß sich zwei gleichberechtigte Partner unabhängig voneinander gegenüberstehen". Aus diesem Bekenntnis zu einer

[1] Im einzelnen siehe Seite 552f.

partnerschaftlichen Ordnung der Wirtschaft folgt die Bereitschaft zur „Zusammenarbeit mit den Arbeitnehmern", um dem „wirtschaftlichen und sozialen Frieden" zu dienen, wie es in der Erklärung zum Betriebsverfassungsgesetz 1952 heißt. Die BDA bejaht eine Mitbestimmung der Arbeitnehmer in sozialen und eine Zusammenarbeit von Arbeitgebern und Arbeitnehmern in wirtschaftlichen Fragen. Sie tritt ein für eine Leistungsentlohnung nach objektiven Maßstäben. Bejaht wird eine leistungsorientierte Gewinn- und Ertragsbeteiligung auf freiwilliger und betriebsindividueller Basis und die Förderung der Bildung individuellen Eigentums der Arbeitnehmer. Ziel der betrieblichen Sozialpolitik soll die Hilfe zur Selbsthilfe in Eigenverantwortung sein. Die bewußte Verpflichtung gegenüber dem Ganzen findet ihren besonderen Ausdruck in der Lohnpolitik. Die Entwicklung der Arbeitszeitverkürzung und der Lohnpolitik soll nach dem 1956 vorgelegten Zehn-Punkte-Programm als eine Einheit betrachtet werden und sich an der Entwicklung der Produktivität orientieren. Die Entwicklung des Lohnes und der Arbeitszeit sollen gleichzeitig Raum für Preissenkungen lassen. Nur bei Beachtung dieser Grundsätze hält die Bundesvereinigung eine weitere Hebung des Realeinkommens der Arbeitnehmer, die Wahrung der Interessen der Konsumenten und einen weiteren technischen Fortschritt für gesichert.

In dem Bewußtsein, daß eine gerechte soziale Ordnung die Voraussetzung für eine gesunde Demokratie ist, treten die Arbeitgeberverbände für eine partnerschaftliche Ordnung auch in überbetrieblichen Bereichen ein. So bejahen sie, wie auch die Gewerkschaften, die soziale Autonomie, eine weitgehende soziale Selbstverwaltung und damit eine selbstverantwortliche Schlichtung von Arbeitsstreitigkeiten. Mit den Arbeitnehmern beziehungsweise deren Organisationen verwalten sie gemeinsam die Einrichtungen der Sozialversicherung und wirken in der Sozial- und Arbeitsgerichtsbarkeit mit.

Besondere Bemühungen der Bundesvereinigung gelten der Jugend. Grundlage hierfür ist die Erklärung „Die junge Generation in der sozialen Ordnung" (1954).

Für die praktische Arbeit zur Förderung von begabten Jugendlichen gelten unter anderen die Empfehlungen „Wie helfen wir den jugendlichen Flüchtlingen aus Mitteldeutschland, in der Bundesrepublik eine neue Heimat zu finden?", „Freizeithilfen der Unternehmer für jugendliche Arbeitnehmer" und „Förderung begabter Jugendlicher durch Wirtschaft und Betrieb".

Der Gemeinschaftsausschuß der deutschen gewerblichen Wirtschaft

Schon 1920 wurde ein Zentralausschuß der Unternehmerverbände gebildet zur Koordinierung der Arbeit der Spitzenverbände. Nach 1945 ist der

„Gemeinschaftsausschuß der deutschen gewerblichen Wirtschaft" zur Herbeiführung übereinstimmender Auffassungen in den Spitzenverbänden konstituiert worden. Dem Gemeinschaftsausschuß gehören folgende Institutionen an:

Bundesvereinigung der Deutschen Arbeitgeberverbände — Bundesverband der Deutschen Industrie — Deutscher Industrie- und Handelstag — Zentralverband des Deutschen Handwerks — Gesamtverband des Deutschen Groß- und Außenhandels — Zentralvereinigung Deutscher Handelsvertreters- und Handelsmaklerverbände—Zentralarbeitsgemeinschaft des Straßen- und Verkehrsgewerbes — Gesamtverband der Versicherungswirtschaft — Bundesverband der Versicherungswirtschaft — Bundesverband des privaten Bankgewerbes — Deutscher Hotel- und Gaststättenverband — Verband Deutscher Reeder — Zentralausschuß der Deutschen Binnenschiffahrt.

Der Gemeinschaftsausschuß ist federführend unter anderem für die Stellungnahmen der Unternehmerverbände in der Frage der Schaffung eines Bundeswirtschaftsrates und der überbetrieblichen Zusammenarbeit der Sozialpartner. Sein Sitz ist Köln. Daneben bestehen für zahlreiche andere Aufgabengebiete gemeinsame Ausschüsse der Spitzenverbände.

Das Deutsche Industrieinstitut

Zur wissenschaftlichen Erarbeitung und Auswertung der gemeinsamen Auffassungen und Ziele der industriellen Unternehmerschaft in der Öffentlichkeit wurde 1951 von den industriellen Verbänden der Bundesvereinigung der Deutschen Arbeitgeberverbände und dem Bundesverband der Deutschen Industrie das Deutsche Industrieinstitut in Köln gegründet. Das Institut soll über die Tagesaufgaben hinaus bei der Erarbeitung der Grundlagen für die unternehmerische Konzeption mitwirken.

II. DIE GEWERKSCHAFTEN

Bis 1933 waren die deutschen Gewerkschaften in drei weltanschauliche Richtungen gespalten: Freie Gewerkschaften, Christliche Gewerkschaften und Hirsch-Dunckersche Gewerkvereine. Diese drei großen Gruppen hatten in eigenen Verbänden außer Arbeitern und Angestellten auch Beamte organisiert. Das nationalsozialistische Regime löste 1933 die Gewerkschaften auf, beschlagnahmte ihr Vermögen und unterdrückte jede gewerkschaftliche Tätigkeit.

Als nach dem Zusammenbruch im Mai 1945 die Gewerkschaften ihre Arbeit wieder aufnehmen konnten, erlaubten die Besatzungsmächte zunächst nur die Bildung betrieblicher und örtlicher Organisationen. Regionale Zusammenschlüsse konnten erst später vollzogen werden. Sie erfolgten in den einzelnen Besatzungszonen unterschiedlich und waren 1948 abgeschlossen. Durch den Beschluß der Delegierten von sechzehn Gewerkschaften Westdeutschlands wurde im Oktober 1949 auf dem Gründungskongreß in München der *Deutsche Gewerkschaftsbund* (DGB) ins Leben gerufen. HANS BÖCKLER († 1951) wurde erster Vorsitzender.

In Berlin wurde 1948 unter Führung nichtkommunistischer Gewerkschafter eine Unabhängige Gewerkschaftsorganisation (UGO) mit dem Sitz in Berlin(West) gebildet. Sie schloß sich im Sommer 1950 dem DGB an.

DER DEUTSCHE GEWERKSCHAFTSBUND (DGB) BESTEHT AUS 16 INDUSTRIEGEWERKSCHAFTEN (IG) BZW. GEWERKSCHAFTFEN (GEW):

IG Bau, Steine, Erden	Gew. Holz
— Bergbau	— Kunst
— Chemie, Papier, Keramik	— Leder
— Druck und Papier	IG Metall
Gew. der Eisenbahner Deutschlands	Gew. Nahrung, Genuß, Gaststätten
— Erziehung und Wissenschaft	— Öffentliche Dienste, Transport und Verkehr
— Gartenbau, Land- und Forstwirtschaft	Deutsche Postgewerkschaft
— Handel, Banken und Versicherungen	Gew. Textil, Bekleidung

Bereits 1945 bildete sich als besondere Vertretung der technischen und kaufmännischen Angestellten die *Deutsche Angestellten-Gewerkschaft* (DAG). Wiederholte Bemühungen mit dem Ziel des Zusammenschlusses mit dem DGB blieben ohne Erfolg.

*

Auch in der Sowjetischen Besatzungszone Deutschlands entstand bald nach dem Zusammenbruch eine neue Gewerkschaftsorganisation, die sich *Freier Deutscher Gewerkschaftsbund* (FDGB) nannte. In den Jahren 1946 bis 1948 haben wiederholt Beratungen zwischen Vertretern der westdeutschen Gewerkschaften und der Führung des FDGB stattgefunden, welche die Bildung einer gemeinsamen Organisation zum Ziel hatten. Diese Bestrebungen scheiterten an der Haltung der Gewerkschafter der „Zone". Die Entwicklung des FDGB zeigte, daß er keine freie und unabhängige Organisation und damit auch nicht eine Gewerkschaft im eigentlichen Sinne des Wortes war. Die Führung lag in den Händen der SED, die sich immer mehr des FDGB als eines Instrumentes zur Durchsetzung ihrer politischen und wirtschaftlichen Zwecke bedient.

Der FDGB hat immer wieder versucht, durch kommunistische Beauftragte die westdeutschen Gewerkschaften zu unterwandern. Durch die Wachsamkeit der Gewerkschaften schlugen diese Bestrebungen fehl.

In den Jahren von 1950 bis 1955 ist das gewerkschaftliche Erscheinungsbild in der Bundesrepublik wesentlich vielfältiger geworden. Als Zusammenschlüsse von Arbeitnehmern bildeten sich: Gesamtverband Deutscher Angestellten-Gewerkschaften (GEDAG), Union der leitenden Angestellten (ULA), Gemeinschaft Deutscher Lehrerverbände (GDL) und die Christliche Gewerkschaftsbewegung Deutschlands (CGD). Seit dem Zusammenschluß von Saarland mit dem Bundesgebiet nennt sie sich Christlicher Gewerkschaftsbund Deutschlands (CGD). Ihre Mitgliederzahl beträgt rund 120.000. Gewerkschaftliche Spitzenvereinigung von Beamten, Beamten-Anwärtern und Ruhestandsbeamten auf berufsständischer Basis (ohne Einzelmitglieder) ist der Deutsche Beamtenbund (DBB). Er bemüht sich vor allem darum, die Arbeitsplätze dem Berufsbeamtentum zu erhalten. Träger seiner wirtschaftlichen Aufgaben ist der Deutsche Beamtenwirtschaftsbund (BWB).

Die DAG hat rund 438.100, der DBB 598.000 Mitglieder. Mit den etwa 470.000 im DGB erfaßten Beamten gehören also drei Viertel der gesamten Beamtenschaft gewerkschaftlichen Organisationen an. Von den Angestellten sind 25%, von den Arbeitern rund 40% gewerkschaftlich organisiert (nach dem Stand vom 30.9.1957).

Alle diese gewerkschaftlichen Zusammenschlüsse sind Dachverbände. Der DGB hat neun Landesbezirke. Innerhalb der DAG arbeiten acht Berufsgruppen auf elf Landesverbände in zweiter Ebene verteilt. Sieben angeschlossene Verbände zählt die ULA. Bei der GEDAG sind fünf Arbeitnehmergruppen zusammengefaßt. Der DBB umfaßt zehn Vereinigungen von Bundesbeamten und zehn auf Bundesebene zusammengeschlossene Beamtenvereinigungen. Acht angeschlossene Verbände zählt die GDL. Im CGD schließlich sind zehn Berufsverbände zusammengeschlossen. Am 27.6.1959 haben der Gesamtverband der Christlichen Gewerkschaften Deutschlands (CGD), der Gesamtverband Deutscher Angestelltengewerkschaften (GEDAG) und der Gesamtverband der Christlichen Gewerkschaften öffentlicher Dienste, Bahn und Post sich zu einer Spitzenorganisation aller christlichen Gewerkschaften Deutschlands zusammengeschlossen.

Diesen Zusammenschlüssen und ihren Gliederungen ist in der Organisationsform manches gemeinsam. Im Programmatischen hingegen bestehen starke Unterschiede. Gemeinsam ist die eigene Struktur, finanzielle Selbständigkeit, die Verpflichtung zur Sicherung des sozialen Fortschritts der Mitglieder, zur Hebung des Sozialgefüges, auch durch eine gesunde Familienpolitik. Die Gewerkschaften bemühen sich um die Verbesserung der Arbeits-, Lohn- und Gehaltsbedingungen, die Erhöhung der Realeinkommen und die

Anpassung der Löhne an die Fortschritte der Produktivität. Einige Male haben sie auch die Initiative zu einer „expansiven Lohnpolitik" ergriffen, die eine Änderung der Verteilung des Sozialprodukts oder eine Erhöhung der Lohnquote erzwingen sollte. Vor den Folgen einer übersteigerten Automation in Industrie und Wirtschaft suchen sie ihre Mitglieder zu schützen. Durch Investivlöhne, Investmentsparen, Eigenheime, Betriebsaktien und dergleichen soll die Bildung von Eigentum in Arbeiterhand gefördert werden. Auch die Wirtschaftsunternehmungen der Gewerkschaften und ihre Wohnbautätigkeit verdienen Erwähnung. Die Wege, die zu diesen Zielen beschritten wurden, weichen entsprechend der Verschiedenheit der Programme und geistigen Konzeptionen teilweise stark voneinander ab. An den Vorarbeiten für die sozialpolitische Gesetzgebung des Bundes wirken die Gewerkschaften mit.

Ein wesentlicher Programmpunkt aller Gewerkschaften ist die Bildung ihrer Mitglieder. Auch dabei werden verschiedene Möglichkeiten praktiziert: gewerkschaftseigene Schulen, Teilnahme an kulturellen Veranstaltungen, finanzielle Erleichterungen für den Besuch von Volkshochschulen, Bildungswerken und ähnlichem. Die Kontakte mit den Arbeitnehmerorganisationen im Ausland, vor allem die der Bildung der Internationalen Gewerkschaften folgende Zusammenarbeit, sind hier ebenfalls zu benennen.

*

Dem *Deutschen Gewerkschaftsbund* kommt schon auf Grund der Zahl seiner Mitglieder eine bestimmende Rolle im gewerkschaftlichen Leben zu. Sein Vorsitzender ist derzeit WILLI RICHTER. Die Zahl der Mitglieder beträgt über 6,3 Millionen; davon sind 81,7% Arbeiter, 10,9% Angestellte und 7,4% Beamte. Die IG Metall steht zahlenmäßig mit 1,76 Millionen Mitgliedern an der Spitze vor der Gewerkschaft Öffentliche Dienste, Transport und Verkehr mit 914.000 und der IG Bergbau mit 601.000 Mitgliedern.

Die Grundsätze der Arbeit wurden auf dem Gründungskongreß in München (1949) in einem Grundsatzprogramm festgelegt und auf den DGB-Kongressen in Essen (1951), Berlin (1952), Frankfurt (1954) und Hamburg (1956) ergänzt. Der Frankfurter Kongreß beschloß das Aktionsprogramm der Gewerkschaften, das unter anderem die Fünf-Tage-Woche bei vollem Lohn- und Gehaltsausgleich mit täglich achtstündiger Arbeitszeit, größere soziale Sicherheit und verbesserte Mitbestimmung vorsieht. Auf dem Hamburger Kongreß wurde unter einstimmiger Billigung der Delegierten ein *Manifest zur Wiedervereinigung Deutschlands* angenommen. In einer „Erklärung zur Wiedervereinigung Deutschlands" legten Bundesvorstand und Bundesausschuß am

1.5.1957 die Grundsätze des DGB über Ziel und Weg der Wiedervereinigungsbestrebungen vor der Öffentlichkeit dar. Diese Erklärung fand weitgehende Zustimmung in der Bundesrepublik und der übrigen Freien Welt.

Der DGB und die in ihm vereinten Gewerkschaften streben eine Verbesserung der Arbeits- und Vergütungsbedingungen für Arbeiter, Angestellte und Beamte an. Das Sozialprodukt soll nach den Grundsätzen sozialer Gerechtigkeit neu verteilt und der Lebensstandard der Arbeitnehmer, Rentner und ihrer Familien gesteigert werden. Die Mitbestimmung der Arbeitnehmer und ihrer Gewerkschaften in Wirtschaft und Verwaltung soll rechtlich gesichert und ausgebaut werden.

Neuzeitlich eingerichtete Bundesschulen des DGB und der ihm angeschlossenen Gewerkschaften dienen der gewerkschaftlichen, staatspolitischen und beruflichen *Bildungsarbeit.* Die „*Büchergilde Gutenberg*" sieht ihre Aufgabe darin, gute Literatur weiten Bevölkerungskreisen zugänglich zu machen. Die *Ruhrfestspiele* in Recklinghausen und die mit ihnen verbundenen „*Europäischen Gespräche*" sind ständige Einrichtungen gewerkschaftlicher Kulturarbeit. 1957 wurden die Aufführungen der Ruhrfestspiele von 140.000 Menschen besucht.

Die gewerkschaftlichen Wohnungsbaugenossenschaften haben seit 1945 rund 80.000 Wohnungen gebaut.

*

Die gewerkschaftliche Tätigkeit mußte nach dem Zusammenbruch in einer Zeit größter wirtschaftlicher Not und Depression begonnen werden. Das Haupt-Augenmerk gewerkschaftlicher Arbeit lag in dieser Zeit auf der Erhaltung der wirtschaftlichen Substanz, der Sicherung der Arbeitsplätze und der Abwendung der unheilvollen Demontagepolitik. Mit großem Verantwortungsbewußtsein wurden diese schweren Aufgaben gelöst.

Die in der Verfassung gewährleistete Koalitionsfreiheit gibt den Arbeitnehmern das Recht des Zusammenschlusses zum Zweck ihrer gemeinsamen Interessenvertretung. Dadurch erhält die Gewerkschaft eine bedeutsame Stellung im gesellschaftlichen Leben. Die Grenzen ihres Wirkens liegen da, wo die gesetzgeberischen Funktionen des Staates nach dem Willen des ganzen Volkes beginnen. Die disziplinierte und verantwortungsbewußte Haltung der Arbeitnehmer seit 1945 hat entscheidend dazu beigetragen, daß es zu großen Arbeitskämpfen in diesen vierzehn Jahren kaum gekommen ist — wenn auch einige harte Streiks (zum Beispiel in der schleswig-holsteinischen Metallindustrie und der nordwestdeutschen Textilindustrie) ausgetragen worden sind.

DIE FRAU

Rückblick

Wie in allen hochindustrialisierten Ländern ist auch in der Bundesrepublik die Stellung der Frau in ihren Grundzügen durch die Eingliederung der Frauen in den Arbeitsprozeß außerhalb der Familie gekennzeichnet.

Um die Mitte des vorigen Jahrhunderts bahnte sich in Deutschland die von der sogenannten Frauenbewegung ausgelöste Entwicklung an, die den Frauen den Zugang auch in die geistigen Berufe erschloß. Zu Anfang des Zwanzigsten Jahrhunderts öffneten sich den Frauen — zunächst allerdings nur zögernd — die Hochschulen. Seither hat der Berufsraum entsprechend der Nachfrage von Wirtschaft und Verwaltung, aber auch auf Grund von Eignung und Leistung der Frau, sich immer mehr erweitert. Die inzwischen gesetzlich verankerte Gleichberechtigung hat theoretisch jede Schranke hinsichtlich der Berufsausübung niedergelegt.

Parallel hierzu verlief die Entwicklung im politischen Raum. Als sich den Frauen 1908 die Tore zu den politischen Vereinen und Parteien aufschlossen, war der erste Schritt auch zur staatsbürgerlichen Gleichberechtigung getan. Nach dem Ersten Weltkrieg wurde den Frauen im Jahre 1918 das aktive und passive Wahlrecht zugebilligt.

Bis 1933 entwickelte sich auf dieser Grundlage eine reiche Aktivität. Frauen zogen schon 1919 in die Parlamente, vor allem in den Reichstag, ein. Sie eroberten Plätze in den Vorständen der politischen Parteien und leitende Stellen in der Verwaltung und waren in Sachverständigenausschüssen und sonstigen behördlichen Kommissionen vertreten. Auf vielen Gebieten des öffentlichen Lebens war ihr Einfluß spürbar.

Die Sozialpolitik und Wohlfahrtspflege der damaligen Epoche trug unverkennbar weibliches Gepräge. Das 1911 erlassene und 1923 neugefaßte Hausarbeitsgesetz zum Schutz der Heimarbeiterinnen wurde „lex Behm" genannt zu Ehren seiner Hauptvorkämpferin, einer Gewerkschaftlerin. Durch dieses Gesetz fand erstmalig eine der möglichen Ausbeutung durch skrupellose Arbeitgeber besonders preisgegebene Gruppe von Arbeitnehmern, unter denen sich vorwiegend Frauen, Kinder, Alte und Gebrechliche befanden, wirtschaftlichen und gesundheitlichen Schutz.

Von weittragender Bedeutung wurden weiter die Entwicklungsarbeiten auf fürsorgerischem Gebiet, welche die jetzige Bundestagsabgeordnete und Alterspräsidentin des Bundestages, Dr. MARIE ELISABETH LÜDERS, zusammen mit anderen Frauen als Leiterin der im Ersten Weltkrieg (1916) im damaligen Kriegsamt eingerichteten Frauenarbeitszentrale leistete; sie reichten weit über den zeitbedingten Auftrag hinaus.

Zu dem Reichsjugendwohlfahrtsgesetz von 1922, das gelegentlich als das am besten durchgearbeitete Jugendwohlfahrtsgesetz der Welt bezeichnet wurde, haben in fast allen Parteien überwiegend Frauen die wesentlichen Vorarbeiten geleistet.

Die amtliche Berufsberatung entwickelte sich ebenfalls auf Wegen, die Frauen gewiesen hatten. Neuartige Berufe, wie die der Kindergärtnerin und Jugendleiterin, der Fürsorgerin, der Fabrikpflegerin und der Beamtin der weiblichen Polizei — ebenso wie die hierfür zu schaffenden Ausbildungsstätten — entstanden im wesentlichen auf Grund von Gedanken und Vorschlägen und der nicht nachlassenden Initiative von Frauen.

Diesem staatsbürgerlichen Wirken der Frauen wurde durch den Nationalsozialismus vorläufig ein Ende gesetzt. Die Frauen wurden auf ihre häuslichen Aufgaben zurückverwiesen und konsequent aus der Politik und aus leitenden Stellen der Verwaltung entfernt. „Die Frau gehört ins Haus" wurde wieder zur grundsätzlichen Parole. Die gerade überwundene, früher in Deutschland so ausgeprägte Arbeitsteilung zwischen Mann und Frau — dem Mann die Öffentlichkeit; der Frau die Familie — wurde ideell und praktisch neu unterbaut. Die Einhaltung dieser Linie wurde nur notgedrungen im Krieg unterbrochen, als Frauen in großem Umfang für die eingezogenen Männer einspringen mußten.

Erst nach dem Zusammenbruch (1945) konnten die Frauen in der Öffentlichkeit wieder maßgeblichen Anteil an der Gestaltung der Gesellschaftsordnung nehmen.

Die Folgen sowohl der nationalsozialistischen Herrschaft als auch des Zweiten Weltkrieges geben der gegenwärtigen Situation der Frau in der Bundesrepublik noch heute in gewisser Hinsicht ein besonderes Gepräge. Diese Folgen wirken sich nicht nur in faßbaren Tatsachen, sondern auch in bestimmten Verhaltensweisen aus. Dies sei hier zum allgemeinen Verständnis nur kurz angedeutet; in den folgenden Darstellungen wird jeweils näher darauf einzugehen sein.

Fragen der Bevölkerungsstruktur

Die Bevölkerungsstruktur der Bundesrepublik weist durch die Kriegsverluste einen erheblichen *Frauenüberschuß* auf.

Ende 1957 betrug die weibliche Bevölkerung 27,5 Millionen — das sind 53% der insgesamt 51,8 Millionen umfassenden Bevölkerung. Die Zahl der verheirateten Frauen wurde Anfang 1955 auf 11,1 Millionen geschätzt.

Unter den zwischen 1909 und 1927 Geborenen entfielen am 31.12.1956 auf 1.000 Männer im Durchschnitt 1.301 Frauen. Daher erhöhte sich der Anteil der weiblichen Bevölkerung, die selber für ihre Existenz sorgen mußte, beträchtlich. Besonders sichtbar drücken die Kriegsfolgen sich in der hohen Zahl der Kriegerwitwen (rund 1 Million) und der Frauen von Schwer-Kriegsbeschädigten aus. Die gestiegene Zahl der Ehescheidungen (1950

= 15,9 auf 10.000 Einwohner gegenüber 7,5 im Jahre 1939) deutet auf die ehegefährdenden Erscheinungen der Kriegs- und Nachkriegszeit hin. Die Zahl der Ehescheidungen ist jedoch bis 1957 wieder auf 8,2 zurückgegangen.

Die Geburtenziffer, die bis 1953 rückläufig war, fing 1954 an, wieder zuzunehmen. Im Jahre 1957 war[1] der höchste Stand der Lebendgeborenen seit dem Krieg erreicht (auf 1.000 Einwohner 17 Geburten). Es überwiegen aber Familien mit nur einem Kind und mit zwei Kindern. 1950 erfolgten 84% der Erstgeburten innerhalb der drei ersten Ehejahre; im Jahre 1956 dagegen nur 77%. Die Müttersterblichkeit im Zusammenhang mit der Geburt war 1956 gegenüber 1955 rückläufig, ist aber nach wie vor beträchtlich höher als in anderen Staaten. Die Zahl der unehelichen Geburten, die in der ersten Nachkriegszeit relativ hoch war, ist seither stetig zurückgegangen.

Die Tatsache, daß (nach einer Statistik von 1950) 55,1% der verwitweten und geschiedenen Frauen, die Haushaltsvorstände (von Haushalten mit mehreren Personen) waren, für Kinder unter fünfzehn Jahren zu sorgen hatten, weist auf das schwere Problem der sogenannten „Schlüsselkinder" hin. So werden die Kinder, die tagsüber während der Berufstätigkeit der Mutter sich völlig allein überlassen sind („die den Wohnungsschlüssel bei sich tragen"), bildhaft bezeichnet.

*

Besonders schwer lasten die wirtschaftlichen und familiären Kriegsfolgen auf den *weiblichen Vertriebenen*, die unter den schwierigsten Umständen in ganz neuartigen Verhältnissen eine Existenz für sich allein oder auch für ihre Kinder aufbauen mußten (am 13. 9. 1950 waren zum Beispiel 44,7% der weiblichen Vertriebenen ledig und 14,9% verwitwet oder geschieden). Viele von ihnen, die in ihrer Heimat einem anspruchsvollen Haushalt vorgestanden hatten, mußten sich jetzt als ungelernte Arbeiterin, als Hausgehilfin oder als Magd auf dem Lande durchschlagen — je nachdem, wohin der Flüchtlingsstrom sie trieb. Dies erhärten statistische Nachweisungen über die berufliche Eingliederung der Vertriebenen im Jahre 1954/55. Nur 6% der Frauen, die im Zeitpunkt der Vertreibung sogenannte mithelfende Familienangehörige im Familienbetrieb waren, sind als solche wieder tätig; 15% von ihnen sind als Arbeiterinnen beschäftigt. Nur 12% der Frauen, die vor der Vertreibung selbständig waren, arbeiten auch jetzt wieder als Selbständige. Von den früher als Angestellte tätigen sind 11% jetzt Arbeiterinnen.

[1] Mit Ausnahme von 1949.

Das Schulwesen

Schulbildung und Schulformen für die Mädchen in der Bundesrepublik entsprechen grundsätzlich denen der Knaben. Mit der Absolvierung der achtklassigen Volksschule ist zur Zeit in der Regel noch die allgemeine Schulpflicht erfüllt. Die Kinder verlassen infolgedessen die Volksschule meistens schon im Alter von vierzehn Jahren. Eine Vielzahl erst vierzehnjähriger Mädchen tritt somit schon in das Erwerbsleben ein: 1950 wurden 89.000 weibliche Erwerbspersonen unter fünfzehn Jahren gezählt. Davon waren nur 34,4% im elterlichen Betrieb (Landwirtschaft, Gewerbebetrieb und ähnlichen) tätig; 65,6% arbeiteten in einem fremden Betrieb.

Der in der Bundesrepublik angestrebten *Schulreform* mit neun beziehungsweise zehn Pflicht-Schuljahren kommt für die Mädchen ganz besondere Bedeutung zu, weil die gesunde körperliche, geistige und seelische Entwicklung der künftigen Frau weithin von der Lebensführung in diesen entscheidenden Jahren abhängt.

An die Volksschule schließt sich für die Jugendlichen, die keine höhere Schule oder Berufsfachschule besuchen, der Besuch einer Pflicht-Berufsschule bis zum vollendeten achtzehnten Lebensjahr an. Bei den Mädchen nimmt

Tabelle 1

SCHÜLER IN ALLGEMEINBILDENDEN SCHULEN IM MAI 1957[1]
NACH SCHULART UND GESCHLECHT

Schulart	Schüler in allgemeinbildenden Schulen		
	insgesamt	darunter Mädchen	
	1.000		% aller Schüler vorstehender Schulart
Volksschulen[2]	4.774,8	2.349,5	*49,2*
Sonderschulen	104,9	41,5	*39,5*
Mittelschulen[2]	337,6	180,9	*53,6*
Höhere Schulen[2]	806,3	324,2	*40,2*
Allgemeinbildende Schulen zusammen	6.023,6	2.896,0	*48,1*

1 Bundesrepublik Deutschland (ohne Saarland). — Bayern: Stand 1. 10. 1956.

2 Einschließlich der entsprechenden Zweige der Schulen mit neu organisiertem Schulaufbau in Hamburg und Bremen und der Freien Waldorfschulen.

Quelle: Statistisches Bundesamt.

innerhalb der Berufsschule die hauswirtschaftliche Bildung einen wesentlichen Raum ein, doch genügt das nach allgemeiner Auffassung nicht als Vorbereitung für die künftige Aufgabe, einen eigenen Haushalt zu führen.

Auf den Mittelschulen überwiegt die Zahl der Mädchen, auf den höheren Schulen die der Knaben.

*

Die aus der Volksschule entlassenen Mädchen stellen überwiegend den Nachwuchs der ungelernten oder angelernten Fabrikarbeiterinnen, der Lehrlinge im Handwerk (zum Beispiel Schneiderin, Putzmacherin, Friseuse), in der Industrie, im Verkauf und Kontor. In ländlichen und kleinstädtischen Gebieten haben auch die hauswirtschaftlichen und ländlich-hauswirtschaftlichen Arbeits- oder Ausbildungsmöglichkeiten noch eine gewisse Bedeutung für diesen Kreis der Jugendlichen behalten. Die sechzehnjährigen Mittelschülerinnen gehen überwiegend in Büroberufe, und zwar mehr auf Grund des Besuchs einer Fachschule oder von Kurzkursen in Stenographie und Schreibmaschine als einer praktischen Lehre. Auch kommt aus diesem Kreis vielfach der Nachwuchs für medizinisch-technische und sonstige technische Hilfsberufe sowie für die sogenannten Frauenberufe auf sozialem, pflegerischem und sozialpädagogischem Gebiet.

Nach Feststellungen der Arbeitsverwaltung hat 1956 mehr als die Hälfte der von der Schule abgehenden Mädchen (aus allen Schularten) mit einer echten Berufsausbildung begonnen. Es ist jedoch nicht zu verkennen, daß die Neigung vieler schulentlassener Mädchen, eine Berufsausbildung durchzumachen, dort zurückgedrängt wird, wo ein großes Angebot an industriellen Arbeitsstellen besteht. Das gleiche gilt hinsichtlich der Bereitschaft, vor Antritt einer sonstigen Ausbildung oder Erwerbstätigkeit in eine hauswirtschaftliche Ausbildung zu gehen. Da die Zulassung zur Ausbildung in den sozialen, sozialpädagogischen und pflegerischen Berufen fast ausnahmslos von dem Nachweis hauswirtschaftlicher Kenntnisse abhängig gemacht wird, ist ein Teil der Schulentlassenen praktisch zu einer solchen Vorbildung gezwungen. Für die Gesamtzahl der heranwachsenden jungen Mädchen spielt aber diese Ausbildung, die in der Regel an öffentlichen oder privaten Haushaltungsschulen — weniger in Privathaushalten — absolviert wird, keine große Rolle.

*

Eine Übersicht darüber, wie viele Schülerinnen mit Hochschulreife ein *akademisches Studium* aufnehmen, liegt — auch schätzungsweise — nicht vor. Nach den Feststellungen der amtlichen Berufsberatung äußern etwa 50% der Abiturientinnen den Wunsch zu studieren. Der Anteil der Studentinnen an der Gesamtzahl der Studierenden nimmt stetig zu. Er betrug im Sommerhalbjahr 1958: 21,3%.

Tabelle 2

DEUTSCHE STUDIERENDE AN DEN HOCHSCHULEN[1] NACH DEM GESCHLECHT

Sommersemester	Deutsche Studierende[2]		
	insgesamt	darunter weiblich	
	Anzahl		% aller Studierenden
1950	102.621	18.052	*17,6*
1951	102.816	17.563	*17,1*
1952	104.722	17.816	*17,0*
1953	106.215	18.147	*17,1*
1954	110.401	19.479	*17,6*
1955	116.278	21.663	*18,6*
1956	122.856	23.772	*19,3*
1957	132.242	26.849	*20,3*
1958	145.142	30.892	*21,3*

[1] Bundesrepublik Deutschland (ohne Saarland). — Ohne lehrerbildende Anstalten und Einrichtungen. — [2] Ohne Beurlaubte. Quelle: Statistisches Bundesamt.

Bemerkenswerterweise hat die Verteilung des Frauenstudiums auf die einzelnen Fachrichtungen sich in den letzten dreißig Jahren kaum geändert; nur treten allmählich die Fachrichtungen Naturwissenschaften (12%) und Wirtschaftswissenschaften (14%) entsprechend der allgemeinen Tendenz mehr hervor. Im übrigen stehen immer noch an erster Stelle die Kulturwissenschaften (43%); erst mit 11% folgen die Rechtswissenschaften. Lehrerin und Ärztin sind gegenwärtig noch die maßgebenden akademischen Frauenberufe. 27,4% der Studentinnen nehmen erst nach einer Zwischenzeit von einem bis drei Jahren und mehr nach der Schulentlassung das Studium auf. Diese Feststellung weist wohl darauf hin, daß viele junge Mädchen vor dem Studium zunächst verdienen müssen. Fast ein Drittel der weiblichen Studierenden war genötigt, neben dem Studium Erwerbsarbeit zu leisten. 6,7% der Studentinnen waren völlig auf eigenes Einkommen angewiesen[1].

Arbeitsmarkt und Berufssituation

Die Zahl der *weiblichen Arbeitnehmer* hat in den Jahren von 1950 bis 1958 sich um 39,5% und seit 1952 um 37,5% erhöht. Nach den Feststellungen der

[1] Die Erhebung datiert vor dem Inkrafttreten des „Honnefer Modells".

Tabelle 3
BESCHÄFTIGTE WEIBLICHE ARBEITNEHMER[1] NACH WIRTSCHAFTSABTEILUNGEN

Wirtschaftsabteilung	Beschäftigte weibliche Arbeitnehmer[1] 30. 9. 1952 Anzahl	30. 9. 1952 %	30. 9. 1958 Anzahl	30. 9. 1958 %	Zu- (+) bzw. Abnahme (—) gegenüber 1952
Landwirtschaft, Tierzucht, Forst- und Jagdwirtschaft, Gärtnerei, Fischerei	362.977	*7,6*	291.718	*4,4*	*—19,6*
Bergbau, Gewinnung und Verarbeitung von Steinen und Erden, Energiewirtschaft	41.115	*0,9*	53.475	*0,8*	*+ 30,1*
Verarbeitendes Gewerbe	1.823.538	*38,2*	2.596.157	*39,5*	*+ 42,4*
Bau-, Ausbau- und Bauhilfsgewerbe	32.279	*0,7*	53.969	*0,8*	*+ 67,2*
Handel, Geld- und Versicherungswesen	748.506	*15,7*	1.319.823	*20,1*	*+ 76,3*
Dienstleistungen	909.406	*19,0*	1.175.992	*17,9*	*+ 29,3*
Verkehrswesen	116.449	*2,4*	141.789	*2,2*	*+ 21,3*
Öffentlicher Dienst und Dienstleistungen im öffentlichen Interesse	744.262	*15,6*	938.731	*14,3*	*+ 26,1*
Insgesamt	4.778.532	*100*	6.571.654	*100*	*+ 37,5*

[1] Bundesrepublik Deutschland (ohne Saarland). — Beschäftigte Arbeiter, Angestellte und Beamte (Beamte soweit durch die Arbeitsstatistik erfaßt).

Quelle: Bundesanstalt für Arbeitsvermittlung und Arbeitslosenversicherung.

Arbeitsverwaltung zeichnet sich deutlich ein *strukturelles Vordringen* der Frauenarbeit ab. Mehr als ein Drittel der gesamten Arbeitnehmerschaft sind Frauen: 6,6 Millionen im September 1958.

Wie überall in den industrialisierten Ländern sind auch in der Bundesrepublik die meisten weiblichen Arbeitskräfte in den gewerblichen sowie in den kaufmännischen und Büro-Berufen tätig. Alle anderen Sparten treten vergleichsweise in den Hintergrund. In der Industrie hat die Erwerbsarbeit der Frauen in den Jahren des Aufschwungs 1950 bis 1957 prozentual wesentlich mehr zugenommen als die der Männer. Der Anteil der weiblichen Beschäftigten betrug[1] 1957 rund 29%. Er wächst weiter, je mehr die Sozial- und Arbeitsstruktur neue Betätigungsmöglichkeiten für weibliche Arbeitskräfte eröffnet. Allerdings sind vier Fünftel aller in der Industrie beschäftigten Frauen zur Zeit nur Hilfsarbeiterinnen. Sie werden meist kurzfristig am Arbeitsplatz angelernt und haben kaum die Möglichkeit, oft aber auch nicht den Wunsch, qualifizierte Facharbeiter zu werden.

Bei einem Mangel an Arbeitskräften ist die Wirtschaft immer mehr zur Beschäftigung auch verheirateter Frauen bereit. Die Zahl der *verheirateten berufstätigen Frauen* hat demzufolge in den letzten Jahren stetig zugenommen. Die erwähnte erhöhte Zahl der Arbeitnehmerinnen seit 1950 rekrutiert sich zu einem großen Teil aus der sogenannten „stillen Reserve" der Ehefrauen. Gegenüber der letzten Statistik aus dem Jahre 1950, die 18,1% der Arbeitnehmerinnen als verheiratet ausweist, dürfte heute deshalb mit einem wesentlich höheren Anteilsatz zu rechnen sein.

Immer mehr junge Ehefrauen bleiben im Einvernehmen mit ihrem Mann zunächst noch im Beruf, um dem neu gegründeten Haushalt eine bessere wirtschaftliche Grundlage zu geben. Obgleich wissenschaftlich noch nicht hinreichend geklärt ist, welcher Zusammenhang zwischen Berufstätigkeit der Frau und Mutterschaft besteht, wird doch vielfach befürchtet, daß durch die Berufstätigkeit der jungen Ehefrauen nicht nur Geburten hinausgezögert werden, sondern daß die Geburtenfreudigkeit überhaupt abnimmt. Die erwähnten Zahlen über die späten Erstgeburten scheinen diese Befürchtungen zu erhärten.

Noch im Jahre 1950 wurde festgestellt, daß die Mehrzahl der Frauen die Berufsarbeit in den ersten vier Jahren nach der Eheschließung aufgibt; aber auch hier läßt sich eine allmähliche grundsätzliche Änderung vermuten. Zweifellos wirkte 1950 nämlich noch die auf Grund früherer gesetzlicher Bestimmungen zulässige Übung nach, daß Frauen, deren Ehemann verdiente, gekündigt wurde, beziehungsweise, daß man sie mit dem Zeitpunkt der Eheschließung automatisch entließ. Dies ist nach dem Inkrafttreten der Gleichberechtigung (vergleiche Seite 620) nicht mehr möglich.

Auch die Zahl verheirateter Frauen nimmt zu, die nach mehrjähriger Arbeitsunterbrechung in eine Berufsarbeit zurückzukehren wünschen, wenn die herangewachsenen Kinder ihrer Obhut und Pflege nicht mehr im bisherigen Maße bedürfen.

[1] Nach den Ergebnissen der Industrie-Berichterstattung.

Es erscheint daher nicht ausgeschlossen, daß sich auch insoweit in der Bundesrepublik ein struktureller Wandel der Frauenarbeit vollziehen wird, als bei der Ehefrau die weitere Ausübung des Berufs zunehmend „üblich" wird.

Es wurde bereits darauf hingewiesen, daß die Kriegsfolgen viele *Mütter* — insbesondere Witwen und Frauen von noch nicht zurückgekommenen Kriegsgefangenen oder von nicht mehr voll arbeitsfähigen Männern — zwangen, einem Broterwerb nachzugehen. Neueste amtliche Gesamtzahlen liegen nicht vor. Örtliche Feststellungen in den letzten Jahren, die zum Teil aus Erhebungen in großstädtischen Volksschulen stammen, ergeben einen Anteil von 25 bis 60 % voll erwerbstätiger Mütter mit Kindern unter vierzehn Jahren.

Die Frage, ob die Berufsarbeit der Mütter unbedingt erforderlich ist, um die Familie zu erhalten, oder ob es sich um Frauen handelt, die mit ihrem Beruf so verwachsen sind, daß sie meinen, ihn nicht aufgeben zu können, oder ob lediglich der Wunsch maßgebend ist, das Familieneinkommen um des vielzitierten „höheren Lebensstandards" willen zu erhöhen, läßt sich auch in der Bundesrepublik nicht beantworten. Es gibt keinen allgemeingültigen Maßstab für die Abgrenzung „notwendig" oder „nicht notwendig", und im übrigen sind alle Aussagen hierzu stark subjektiv gefärbt. Die Tendenz der gesetzlichen sozialen Maßnahmen geht zwar dahin, allmählich zu erreichen, daß Mütter mit der Betreuung bedürftigen Kindern nicht aus wirtschaftlichen Gründen zur Erwerbsarbeit gezwungen sein sollen. Heute noch reicht aber in den Fällen, in denen die Mütter jung verwitwet sind, die Versorgung aus der Hinterbliebenenrente der gesetzlichen Sozialversicherung oder aus den Bezügen der Kriegsopferversorgung sowie die Versorgung der Beamtenwitwen in vielen Fällen nicht aus, um den bisherigen Lebensstandard beizubehalten. Lebensversicherungen wurden durch die Währungsreform im Jahre 1948 so abgewertet, daß sie keine wirtschaftliche Sicherung der Witwen und Kinder mehr boten.

*

Der zunehmende Anteil der Frauen in den gewerblichen und kaufmännischen Berufen geht vor allem *auf Kosten der Hauswirtschaft und der Landwirtschaft.* Zwar waren am 30.9.1958 noch rund 640.000 weibliche Arbeitskräfte in der Hauswirtschaft beschäftigt; aber gegenüber den Vorjahren war eine beträchtliche Abnahme festzustellen. In der Landwirtschaft kann man von einer ausgesprochenen Landflucht sprechen: Nicht nur sank die Zahl der Arbeitnehmerinnen im letzten Jahr um 7 % auf rund 48.000, sondern auch die Töchter der selbständigen Landwirte, die bisher als sogenannte mithelfende Familienangehörige in der elterlichen Landwirtschaft mitarbeiteten, wandern zunehmend in städtische Berufe ab.

Weder in der städtischen noch in der ländlichen Hauswirtschaft wird bisher der Mangel an weiblichen Arbeitskräften trotz allen Bemühungen der zuständigen Stellen auch nur annähernd durch Rationalisierung und moderne arbeitstechnische Hilfen aufgefangen[1]. Dadurch wird die Lage insbesondere in kinderreichen Haushalten vielfach kritisch. Hieraus ist zu erklären, daß hin und wieder in der Öffentlichkeit der Wunsch laut wird, es möge auf gesetzlicher Grundlage ein sogenanntes hauswirtschaftliches *Pflichtjahr* eingeführt werden, das schulentlassene Mädchen in einem städtischen oder bäuerlichen Haushalt abzuleisten hätten. Ein solches Jahr diene gleichzeitig der erforderlichen hauswirtschaftlichen Bildung der Mädchen und ließe sie in ihre künftigen Familienpflichten hineinwachsen.

Die Bundesregierung hat wiederholt erklärt, sie werde diesem Verlangen nicht entsprechen. Ein solches Pflichtjahr widerspricht dem Grundrecht der persönlichen Freiheit. Es würde kein geeignetes Mittel sein, einen echten Nachwuchs für die Hauswirtschaft heranzuziehen. Überlastete Mütter sind in der Regel auch nicht zu einer sinnvollen Ausbildung in der Lage. Bundesregierung und Länderregierungen fördern jedoch ideell und materiell Maßnahmen zur hauswirtschaftlichen Bildung, die dazu dienen können, junge Mädchen auf freiwilliger Basis für diese Berufe zu gewinnen und auszubilden. Ähnliches gilt für die Berufe in der Krankenpflege, bei denen mit der Zunahme der Krankenhäuser sich ebenfalls Kräftemangel zeigt. Bemühungen um eine zeitgemäße Gestaltung des Arbeitsrechts und Arbeitsschutzes dienen dem gleichen Zweck.

*

Das Vordringen der Frauen in *qualifizierte Berufe* hält mit der quantitativen Ausdehnung der Frauenarbeit auch nicht annähernd Schritt. Wie die Statistik der gesetzlichen Kranken- und Angestelltenversicherung am 30.6.1954 auswies, hatten nur 5% der weiblichen — gegenüber 20% der männlichen — Angestellten Gehälter zwischen 500 und 750 DM brutto im Monat. Im sogenannten „höheren Dienst", der in der Regel eine akademische Ausbildung voraussetzt, und dessen unterste Gehaltsgrenze etwa bei 800 DM liegt, sinkt dieser niedrige Anteil noch erheblich. Im Amtsbereich der Bundesverwaltung lag er in dieser Gruppe (Angestellte und Beamte) am 2.10.1958 bei rund 2,3%. Bei den Verwaltungen der Länder und Gemeinden und in der Wirtschaft dürfte er etwa ebenso hoch sein. Nur im Schuldienst ist die Beteiligung der Frauen absolut und relativ hoch; ausgesprochen niedrig dagegen wieder als Schulleiterin und ebenso als Dozentin an den wissenschaftlichen Hochschulen.

Daß die Frauen bisher nur einen so geringen Anteil an den qualifizierten Berufen haben, steht in merkwürdigem Widerspruch zu der Tatsache, daß ihnen die höheren Schulen und die Hochschulen genauso offenstehen wie den Männern, und daß, wie erwähnt, ein hoher Prozentsatz der Mädchen studiert. Wenn auch viele Frauen ihre Ausbildung infolge von Heirat nicht

[1] Nur ein Beispiel für viele: ein Drittel aller Bauernhöfe in der Bundesrepublik hat noch kein fließendes Wasser im Hause.

vollenden oder die Berufstätigkeit nach der Eheschließung aufgeben, zeigt doch das Beispiel des Schuldienstes, daß hierin keinesfalls eine ausreichende Erklärung für den unbefriedigenden Status liegt. Die Beobachtungen weisen vielmehr darauf hin, daß trotz der gesetzlich verankerten Gleichberechtigung den Frauen im Berufsleben noch keineswegs die gleichen Chancen eingeräumt werden wie den Männern.

Über die freiberuflich tätigen Frauen liegen Gesamtstatistiken nicht vor. Frauen finden sich in allen freien Berufen, in denen auch Männer tätig sind. Zahlenmäßig fallen die Ärztinnen am meisten ins Gewicht. Aber auch Rechtsanwältinnen, Wirtschaftsprüferinnen und Steuerberaterinnen sowie Journalistinnen gewinnen mehr und mehr an Boden.

Der Anteil der selbständigen Unternehmerinnen ist in den Jahren 1939 bis 1950 von 6,8 auf 7,6% gestiegen. Diese Zunahme weist darauf hin, daß viele Ehefrauen nach dem Krieg den Betrieb ihres Mannes weitergeführt haben. Sie beweisen damit, daß Frauen in der Lage sind, sich auch in der Wirtschaft durchzusetzen und leitende Funktionen mit Erfolg wahrzunehmen.

Gleichberechtigung

Der gesellschaftliche Strukturwandel, der der Frau einen Wirkungsbereich auch außerhalb der Familie erschloß und sie zu einem wichtigen Faktor im Arbeitsprozeß machte, spiegelt sich in der Bundesrepublik in einer zeitgemäßen Gesetzgebung wider, deren Wurzeln, wie erwähnt, zum Teil schon vor den Ersten Weltkrieg zurückreichen.

Die den Frauen im Jahre 1918 zuerkannte politische *Gleichberechtigung* ist nach Artikel 3 des Grundgesetzes (GG) der Bundesrepublik Deutschland vom 23.5.1949 auf alle Lebensbereiche ausgedehnt.

Die rechtliche Gleichstellung findet nur dort ihre Grenze, wo die biologische oder funktionelle Verschiedenheit von Mann und Frau sinnvollerweise eine gleiche Behandlung nicht angeraten erscheinen läßt. Diesem Wesensunterschied ist zum Beispiel im Bereich des Wehrdienstes insofern Rechnung getragen, als das Grundgesetz verbietet, Frauen zu einem „Dienst mit der Waffe“ zu verwenden; sie dürfen auch nicht zu einer Dienstleistung ohne Waffe im Verband der Streitkräfte durch Gesetz verpflichtet werden.

Wiederholt haben sich aber bei der Gesetzgebung oder bei der Anwendung von Gesetzen nach 1949 Meinungsverschiedenheiten darüber ergeben, wieweit diese Wesensverschiedenheit sich im einzelnen als so grundsätzlich erweist, daß es gerechtfertigt oder notwendig erscheint, von einer rechtlichen

Gleichbehandlung abzusehen. Unter Umständen entwickeln sich hieraus Rechtsstreitigkeiten, die vor dem Bundesverfassungsgericht oder einem Obersten Bundesgericht zum Austrag kommen.

Grundsätzliche Übereinstimmung besteht jedoch darin, daß — unbeschadet des Grundsatzes der Gleichberechtigung — der Andersartigkeit der Frau im Arbeitsleben durch besondere *Arbeitsschutzbestimmungen* Rechnung getragen werden muß. Diese Gesetze reichen teilweise in den Ausgang des vorigen Jahrhunderts zurück. In der staatlichen „Gewerbeaufsicht" sind besondere weibliche Fachkräfte tätig, welche die Durchführung des gesetzlichen Frauen- und Mutterschutzes in den Betrieben zu überwachen haben.

Neben Beschäftigungsverboten oder -beschränkungen für bestimmte Kategorien gefährlicher oder schwerer Arbeiten, neben dem grundsätzlichen Verbot von Nachtarbeit, Vorschriften über Höchstarbeitszeit und Arbeitspausen sowie Bestimmungen über die Gewährung eines „Hausarbeitstages" für Frauen mit eigenem Hausstand, ist ein besonders wichtiger Arbeitsschutz für werdende und stillende Mütter durch das *Mutterschutzgesetz* vom 24. 1. 1952 geschaffen worden.

Unter bestimmten Voraussetzungen genießen schwangere Frauen einen weitgehenden Kündigungsschutz. Grundsätzlich dürfen sie nicht beschäftigt werden, soweit Leben und Gesundheit der werdenden Mutter oder des Kindes gefährdet sind. In den letzten sechs Wochen (bei Hausgehilfinnen vier Wochen) vor der Niederkunft dürfen Frauen nur mit ihrem ausdrücklichen Einverständnis beschäftigt werden. Bestimmte gefährdende Arbeiten sind während der Schwangerschaft ganz verboten beziehungsweise eingeschränkt. Für die Dauer von sechs Wochen — bei stillenden Müttern acht Wochen — nach der Niederkunft gilt ein allgemeines Beschäftigungsverbot. Während dieser Schutzfristen erhalten die Frauen auf Staatskosten ein ihrem letzten Arbeitsentgelt entsprechendes Wochengeld, sofern sie Pflichtmitglied einer Krankenkasse sind. Anderenfalls muß der Arbeitgeber ihnen das Arbeitsentgelt weiter zahlen.

Ein Teil der durch Arbeitsschutz entstehenden finanziellen Belastungen ist dem Arbeitgeber auferlegt. Dieser Schutz beeinträchtigt daher in Zeiten schlechter Arbeitsmarktlage unter Umständen die Einstellung insbesondere jung verheirateter Frauen. Bei der nun schon jahrelang anhaltenden Hochkonjunktur und dem damit zusammenhängenden Mangel an Arbeitskräften ist dagegen zu beobachten, daß die Arbeitgeber über die Schutzvorschriften hinaus bemüht sind, die Arbeitsplätze durch Berücksichtigung der physischen und psychischen Besonderheiten der Frau möglichst attraktiv zu gestalten und sich auch auf Teilzeitarbeit für Mütter einzustellen. Aber gerade die Mütter, die auf Verdienst angewiesen sind, zeigen wegen des zu geringen Arbeitsentgeltes wenig Neigung, Halbtagsarbeit anzunehmen.

Eine besondere soziale Errungenschaft für die Frauen bedeutet die Bestimmung aus dem Jahre 1957, daß ihnen das Altersruhegeld der gesetzlichen Sozialversicherung schon mit sechzig Jahren — anstatt üblicherweise mit fünfundsechzig Jahren — gezahlt werden kann.

*

Bei der Entwicklung eines den Zeitverhältnissen angepaßten *Arbeitsrechts* mußte mehrmals das Bundesarbeitsgericht in Anspruch genommen werden. In mehreren Urteilen wurde im Jahre 1955 ausgesprochen, daß der Grundsatz der Gleichberechtigung auch den Grundsatz der *Lohngleichheit* für Mann und Frau *bei gleicher Arbeit* umfaßt, und daß der Lohn nur nach der zu leistenden Arbeit bestimmt werden darf, unabhängig davon, ob die Arbeit von einem Mann oder einer Frau erbracht wird. Der Tendenz dieser Urteile entspricht es, daß der Bundestag im Jahre 1955 die Konvention Nr. 100 der Internationalen Arbeitsorganisation verabschiedet hat. In ihr verpflichten die Mitgliedstaaten sich, dafür zu sorgen, daß in ihrem Lande Männer und Frauen gleich entlohnt werden.

*

Einen wesentlichen Schritt auf dem Wege zur Anpassung der Gesetzgebung an die neuartige Stellung der Frau in der Gesellschaft bedeutet das *Gesetz über die Gleichberechtigung von Mann und Frau auf dem Gebiet des bürgerlichen Rechts* vom 18.6.1957, das am 1.7.1958 in Kraft getreten ist. Dieses Gesetz ändert die entsprechenden Bestimmungen des bis dahin geltenden Familienrechts, das stark patriarchalische Züge trug, und hat dem Grundsatz gleicher Rechte und gleicher Verantwortung der Ehepartner zum Durchbruch verholfen. Damit ist der gewandelten Stellung der Frau nunmehr auch im Rahmen der Familie Rechnung getragen.

Alle Angelegenheiten, die ihr eheliches Leben betreffen, müssen von den Ehegatten im gegenseitigen Einvernehmen geregelt werden. Die Ehegatten sind sich gegenseitig — und gemeinschaftlich den Kindern — zum Unterhalt verpflichtet. Sehr wichtig ist, daß die Führung des Haushalts durch die Frau hierbei grundsätzlich einer Erwerbstätigkeit gleichgestellt wird. Auch die sogenannte elterliche Gewalt steht dem Vater und der Mutter gemeinschaftlich zu; allerdings ist bei Meinungsverschiedenheiten dem Vater das Entscheidungsrecht zugebilligt worden. — Es ist nicht ausgeschlossen, daß wegen dieser einschränkenden Bestimmung das Bundesverfassungsgericht angerufen werden wird.

Die den heutigen Verhältnissen angepaßte Rechtsstellung der Ehefrau spiegelt sich auch darin wider, daß die Frau — soweit dies mit ihren Pflichten in Ehe und Familie vereinbar ist — ein Arbeitsverhältnis eingehen kann, ohne, wie bisher, an die Zustimmung ihres Mannes gebunden zu sein. Auch kann sie im Gegensatz zu früher einen eigenen Wohnsitz begründen.

Eine wesentliche Besserstellung der Frau erfolgte auf vermögensrechtlichem Gebiet. Die Verwaltung und Nutznießung des Vermögens der Frau durch den Mann war schon mit der Einführung der Gleichberechtigung gefallen und einer reinen Gütertrennung gewichen. Das neue Gesetz erweitert diese zur sogenannten *Zugewinngemeinschaft*, die es als gesetzlichen Güterstand einführt. Das bedeutet, daß der Zugewinn, den beide Ehegatten während der Ehe erzielt haben, zusammengezählt und in gleichen Hälften unter sie geteilt wird. Somit kommt das wirtschaftliche Ergebnis des gemeinsamen Ehelebens und der gemeinsamen Arbeit auch den Ehefrauen zugute, die ausschließlich im Haushalt tätig waren. Bei Beendigung der Ehe durch den Tod eines Ehegatten erfolgt die Teilung des Zugewinns pauschal durch die Erhöhung des gesetzlichen Erbteils für den Überlebenden. Bei Scheidung kann die Ehefrau ihren Anteil an dem während der Ehe erworbenen Mannesvermögen verlangen, sofern nicht besonders schwerwiegende Gründe dagegen sprechen.

Verbandstätigkeit

Wie überall, wo die Frau den Weg ins öffentliche Leben gefunden hatte, wirkten auch in Deutschland Frauenverbände als Repräsentanten der Frauenbewegung. Von hier aus wurden die die Frauen berührenden wesentlichen Grundsatzfragen in die Öffentlichkeit gebracht und um ihre Klärung gerungen.

Allen diesen Verbänden, die auch innerhalb reicher internationaler Beziehungen standen, wurde durch den Nationalsozialismus die Plattform für ihr Wirken entzogen. Durch Zwangs- oder durch Selbstauflösung stellten sie ihre Arbeit ein, sofern sie nicht als konfessionelle Gruppen im Verborgenen weiterwirken konnten.

Gleich nach dem Zusammenbruch (1945) stellten verantwortungsbewußte Frauen aller sozialen Schichten und politischen Richtungen, insbesondere der älteren Generation, sich zur Verfügung und nahmen die Mitarbeit in der Öffentlichkeit in ihren verschiedenen Formen wieder auf. Sie stießen hierbei um so weniger auf grundsätzliche Hindernisse, als die Zahl der für den Aufbau zur Verfügung stehender Männer zunächst relativ gering war.

Erschwernisse anderer Art machten aber den Aufbau der Frauenverbände nach 1945 außerordentlich mühsam. Die Verbände mußten ohne irgendeine gesicherte finanzielle Grundlage an die Arbeit gehen. Durch die Währungsreform 1948 verloren sie erneut jeden finanziellen Rückhalt. Überdies konnte der Aufbau sich wegen der Zonenteilung zunächst nicht unter einheitlichen Gesichtspunkten vollziehen.

Zu den traditionellen Frauenverbänden, welche die Arbeit nach früherem Vorbild wieder aufnahmen, traten Zusammenschlüsse neuer Art, die deutliche Merkmale der besonderen Zeitumstände trugen. Es waren Vereinigungen mit ausgesprochen politischer — aber überparteilicher — Grundhaltung. Durch ihre strenge Überparteilichkeit verbanden sie sowohl sozialistische Frauen als auch solche, die der alten bürgerlichen Frauenbewegung nahestanden oder in konfessionellen Verbänden mitwirkten; sie sahen in ihren Reihen ebenso Mitglieder der Gewerkschaften wie von außergewerkschaftlichen Berufsverbänden.

Diese Vereinigungen entstanden in spontaner Reaktion auf die Zwangsherrschaft des Nationalsozialismus. Sie gründeten sich auf der Erkenntnis, daß nunmehr notwendigerweise ein möglichst einheitlicher Frauenwille kundzutun sei. Das Spontane dieser Bewegung drückte sich vor allem darin aus, daß derartige Zusammenschlüsse ohne gegenseitige Fühlungnahme oder überhaupt Kenntnis voneinander in allen Teilen des in die vier Besatzungszonen gespaltenen Deutschlands entstanden.

Die meisten dieser Zusammenschlüsse, die sich allmählich in Landesverbänden vereinigten, konnten im Jahr 1949 im „*Deutschen Frauenring*" zusammengefaßt werden — ein Vorgang, der umso bemerkenswerter war, als diesen Vereinigungen die gemeinsame Überlieferung der traditionellen Frauenverbände fehlte. Der „Frauenring" seinerseits hat sich inzwischen mit überkonfessionellen Spitzenverbänden — vorwiegend beruflicher Art — in der „*Arbeitsgemeinschaft überkonfessioneller und überparteilicher Frauenorganisationen*" zusammengefunden. Dieser Arbeitsgemeinschaft auf Bundesebene gehört auch die einzige Frauengewerkschaft der Bundesrepublik, der Verband weiblicher Angestellten, an. Die übrigen gewerkschaftlich organisierten Frauen arbeiten mit den männlichen Gewerkschaftern in den großen Gewerkschaftsverbänden zusammen.

Die vielgestaltigen konfessionellen Verbände haben sich in der „*Arbeitsgemeinschaft der Katholischen Deutschen Frauen*", in der „*Evangelischen Frauenarbeit in Deutschland*" und im „*Jüdischen Frauenbund in Deutschland*" zusammengeschlossen[1].

[1] Da eine Aufzählung auch nur der wesentlichsten Frauenverbände hier zu weit führen würde, sei auf das 1957 vom Informationsdienst für Frauenfragen neu herausgegebene „Handbuch Deutscher Frauenorganisationen" hingewiesen. Es wurde mit Unterstützung des Frauenreferats des Büros des Cultural Attaché der Amerikanischen Botschaft erstellt und gibt eine vollständige Übersicht in deutscher und englischer Sprache.

Eine Anzahl maßgeblicher Frauenverbände, zu denen auch der in Berlin gegründete „*Staatsbürgerinnenverband*“ gehört, sowie die Frauengruppen des DGB und der DAG gründeten im Jahre 1951 den „*Informationsdienst für Frauenfragen*“.

Diesem auf Bundesebene tätigen Verein sind achtzig Bundesorganisationen direkt und indirekt angeschlossen. Er setzt sich zur Aufgabe, „die Entwicklung der staatsbürgerlichen Arbeit der Frau und die damit zusammenhängenden Fragen auf wirtschaftlichem, sozialem, kulturellem und politischem Gebiet zu beobachten, durch statistische Aufnahmen, Einholung von Berichten und Informationen zu verwerten und durch regelmäßige Veröffentlichungen allen Frauen und interessierten Stellen Aufklärung und Material über den Stand dieser Arbeit zu geben“. Er ist durch seine überparteiliche und überkonfessionelle Arbeit, die ihren Niederschlag in den monatlich erscheinenden „*Informationen für die Frau*“ findet, zu einem weit über Deutschlands Grenzen anerkannten Bindeglied zwischen den einzelnen Interessenverbänden geworden und konnte demzufolge neuerdings sein Aufgabengebiet erweitern. Unter dem Namen „*Informationsdienst und Aktionskreis Deutscher Frauenverbände und Frauengruppen gemischter Verbände*“ übernimmt er es jetzt auch, gemeinsame Aktionen der Frauenverbände anzuregen und für ihre Durchführung Sorge zu tragen, sofern sie einstimmig von allen Mitgliederverbänden beschlossen werden. Für solche gemeinsame Aktionen, wie sie zum Beispiel in letzter Zeit im Hinblick auf die Atomgefahr oder bei der Forderung nach weiblichen Mitgliedern im Bundeskabinett für notwendig gehalten wurden, hatte bisher die Plattform gefehlt.

Alle maßgeblichen Frauenorganisationen gehören wieder internationalen Verbänden an — unter den staatsbürgerlichen Verbänden seien hier der *International Council of Women* und die *International Alliance of Women* genannt — und leisten so ihren Beitrag zu dem weltweiten Wirken der Frauen in der Öffentlichkeit.

*

Grundsätzlich unterscheiden die Frauenverbände der Bundesrepublik sich weder in der allgemein staatsbürgerlichen, noch in ihrer den Berufsinteressen dienenden oder in der caritativen Arbeit von den modernen Frauenverbänden in anderen Nationen. Sie erhalten aber ihre besondere Prägung dadurch, daß die Wandlung der Stellung der Frau in Deutschland durch zwei Weltkriege und ihre Folgen sich nicht organisch vollzogen hat. Insbesondere wirkt die Zeit des Nationalsozialismus, wie schon erwähnt, in mehrfacher Hinsicht tiefgreifend auf die Stellung der Frau zurück.

Die junge Frau konnte während des Nationalsozialismus nicht mehr — wie die Generation vor 1933 — organisch in ihre Aufgabe als mitverantwortliche Staatsbürgerin hineinwachsen und dafür vorbereitet werden. Sie wurde vielmehr zwölf Jahre lang unter dem Gesichtspunkt des absoluten staatsbürgerlichen Primates des

Mannes erzogen. Durch die Auflösung der Frauenverbände verlor diese Generation zwischen 1933 und 1945 auch die Verbindung zur alten Frauenbewegung. Den Frauen, die im öffentlichen Leben Pioniere für das neuartige Wirken der Frau in der Öffentlichkeit waren, wurden die Grundlagen für ihr Wirken entzogen. Sie verschwanden als prägende Persönlichkeiten aus dem Blickfeld der Öffentlichkeit. Die nachwachsende weibliche Generation wurde konsequent mit der Blickrichtung auf die traditionelle Arbeitsteilung zwischen Mann und Frau erzogen. Das akademische Studium, soweit es speziell auf gehobene Berufe innerhalb der Verwaltung und der Wirtschaft vorbereitete, bot kaum noch Anreiz für junge Mädchen, weil keine Aussicht auf praktische Verwertung gegeben war.

So fehlten einerseits Antrieb und Möglichkeit, die fruchtbar begonnenen Bemühungen um eine sinnvolle Eingliederung der Frauen in den Arbeitsprozeß in schöpferischer Entwicklung fortzuführen, zum anderen wurde das Verantwortungsgefühl der jungen weiblichen Generation für das aktive Mitwirken in der Öffentlichkeit und für den Einsatz an maßgeblichen Stellen des öffentlichen Lebens künstlich lahmgelegt.

Nach dem Zusammenbruch nahm deshalb die staatsbürgerliche Bildungsarbeit sofort einen breiten Raum ein. Vor allem die amerikanische und die britische Besatzungsmacht unterstützten diese Arbeit ideell und materiell. Sie förderten auch frühzeitig den Kontakt zwischen deutschen Frauen und Frauen ihrer Länder und bereiteten so die Wiederaufnahme deutscher Frauenverbände in die internationalen Organisationen vor.

Frauenverbände in anderen Ländern stehen ebenfalls vor der Frage, wie der jugendliche Nachwuchs zu gewinnen ist. In der Bundesrepublik erhält diese Aufgabe zur Zeit aber ihr besonderes Schwergewicht durch die geschilderte Notwendigkeit, die mangelnde politische Erziehung der Frau in den Jahren 1933 bis 1945 nachzuholen. Ob den Verbänden hier Erfolg beschieden ist, läßt sich nicht etwa nur an der Zahl der jungen Verbandsmitglieder ablesen. Die Tatsache zum Beispiel, daß die Wahlbeteiligung der Frauen wächst, und daß sie bei der Bundestagswahl im Jahre 1957 gegenüber der Wahl 1953 auch in den Jahrgängen zwischen dreißig und fünfzig Jahren zugenommen hat — also bei Jahrgängen, die der Infiltration nationalsozialistischer Gedankengänge in jungen Jahren besonders ausgesetzt waren —, darf der erfolgreichen Arbeit in den Verbänden mit zugeschrieben werden.

Über die Zahl der in Verbänden organisierten Frauen liegen authentische Statistiken nicht vor. Die als Kriegsfolge festzustellende Überbeanspruchung vieler Mütter durch die gleichzeitige Wahrnehmung von Berufs- und Familienpflichten ist zweifellos der Organisationsfreudigkeit vieler Frauen oder zumindest einer zeitraubenden aktiven Mitarbeit in den Verbänden abträglich. Andererseits weisen die Organisationen gerade solche Frauen als besonders aktive und staatspolitisch interessierte Mitglieder auf, die durch ihr persönliches Schicksal von der Notwendigkeit einer Mitarbeit der Frau in der Öffentlichkeit überzeugt wurden.

Gegenüber vielen Frauenorganisationen im Ausland ist in der Bundesrepublik die besondere Situation der Verbände weiter dadurch gekennzeichnet, daß diese — im Zusammenhang mit der Inflation nach dem Ersten und der Währungsreform nach dem Zweiten Weltkrieg — kaum noch Mitglieder haben, die, auf eigenes Vermögen gestützt, größere finanzielle Aufwendungen für die Verbandsarbeit leisten können.

Diese Verarmung der Verbände macht sich etwa bei der Teilnahme an internationalen Frauentagungen im Ausland bemerkbar, für die öffentliche Zuwendungen mit in Anspruch genommen werden müssen. Sie spiegelt sich aber auch in der Tatsache wider, daß es bisher nur wenigen Frauenverbänden gelungen ist, repräsentative Zeitschriften herauszubringen und zu finanzieren. Die Mehrzahl der Frauenverbände beschränkt sich auf die Herausgabe von Mitteilungsblättern an ihre Mitglieder.

Caritative Arbeit

An der caritativen Arbeit auf allen Gebieten des Wohlfahrtswesens nehmen die Frauen als berufstätige oder ehrenamtliche Kräfte hervorragenden Anteil.

In diesem Rahmen soll nur ein Arbeitszweig erwähnt werden, der in neuartiger Weise Kriegsfolgen aufzufangen versucht. Es ist dies das *Müttergenesungswerk*, das sich — aus reiner Fraueninitiative entwickelt — im Jahre 1950 konstituierte. In dieser von der verstorbenen Gattin des Bundespräsidenten HEUSS, Frau ELLY HEUSS-KNAPP, veranlaßten Stiftung sind die Frauengruppen der beiden christlichen Kirchen, des Deutschen Roten Kreuzes, der Arbeiterwohlfahrt und des Deutschen Paritätischen Wohlfahrtsverbandes zusammengefaßt. Soweit wie möglich sollen die infolge ihrer Doppelbelastung in Familie und Beruf erschöpften Mütter durch Erholungskuren körperlich und seelisch gekräftigt werden. Neben der unmittelbaren gesundheitlichen Fürsorge steht eine systematische Betreuung durch lebenserfahrene und psychologisch geschulte Mitarbeiterinnen. Durch diese Hilfe zur Überwindung körperlicher und seelischer Notstände, die vielfach zu Krisen innerhalb der Ehe führen, wird nicht nur der Mutter selber, sondern der ganzen Familie ein wesentlicher Dienst geleistet.

Parlamentsarbeit und sonstige Tätigkeit im öffentlichen Raum

Eine Gegenüberstellung der Bundestagswahlen in den Jahren 1953 und 1957 zeigt, daß die Wahlbeteiligung der Frauen bei der letzten Wahl in allen

Altersgruppen, insbesondere auch in den jüngeren Jahrgängen, zugenommen hat; sie nähert sich mehr und mehr der der Männer. Am höchsten lag sie in der Gruppe der Vierzig- bis Sechzigjährigen.

Im Bundestag und im Durchschnitt aller Länderparlamente sind gegenwärtig rund 10% weibliche Abgeordnete vertreten. Dieser Prozentsatz traf nach einer Umfrage im Jahre 1954 ungefähr auch für kommunale Parlamente zu. In einer ganzen Reihe von Großstädten liegt der Anteil jedoch höher.

Die meisten weiblichen Abgeordneten des Bundestages gehören dem Parlament schon seit 1949 an. Lehrerinnen, Ärztinnen, Juristinnen, Fürsorgerinnen, Verwaltungsbeamte und Angestellte sind die am meisten vertretenen Berufssparten. Über ein Drittel der weiblichen Abgeordneten bezeichnet sich als Hausfrau; die meisten von ihnen waren aber vor ihrer Verheiratung ebenfalls berufstätig.

In die obersten Gremien der Parteien im Bundestag sind von den insgesamt 48 weiblichen Abgeordneten zur Zeit 32 Frauen berufen; 43 gehören den einzelnen Ausschüssen an.

Das Durchschnittsalter der Frauen im Bundestag liegt bei vierundfünfzig Jahren. Frau Dr. Marie Elisabeth Lüders, die 1958 ihr achtzigstes Lebensjahr vollendet hat, ist zur Zeit Alterspräsidentin des Parlaments.

Weibliche Minister — zur Zeit fünf — amtieren bisher nur in einzelnen Bundesländern. Die Forderung der Frauen nach weiblichen Ministern auch in der Bundesregierung ist bisher noch nicht erfüllt worden. Der höchste Rang ist der eines Staatssekretärs im Bundesministerium für Familien- und Jugendfragen. In keinem der Bundesministerien leitet bisher eine Frau eine Abteilung. Die Zahl der Referentinnen und Hilfsreferentinnen hat jedoch seit 1949 langsam zugenommen.

In den Länderregierungen gehören die meisten Frauen im höheren Dienst der Schul- und Medizinalverwaltung an; doch geht die Streuung durchaus über die sogenannten „Frauenberufe“ der Pädagogin und Ärztin hinaus. Neben Juristinnen und Wirtschaftswissenschaftlerinnen haben unter anderem auch schon weibliche Techniker Eingang in die Länderverwaltung gefunden.

Unter den Berufsrichtern befanden sich in der Bundesrepublik am 1.1.1957 2,5% Frauen (288). Ihr Anteil war in der Sozialgerichtsbarkeit mit 4% am höchsten. Als Staatsanwalt waren zwanzig Frauen (1%) tätig. Auch im Bundesverfassungsgericht und an vier oberen Bundesgerichten sind Richterinnen hauptamtlich beschäftigt, darunter eine in der leitenden Stellung eines Senatspräsidenten.

In die höchste diplomatische Laufbahn sind Frauen noch nicht vorgedrungen: keine Diplomatin vertritt die Bundesregierung im Ausland. Lediglich einige Konsulatsleitungen liegen in weiblicher Hand, und mehrere Dienststellen im Ausland beschäftigen Frauen im höheren Verwaltungsdienst. Da das Auswärtige Amt zunehmend auch weibliche Nachwuchskräfte ausbildet, kann allmählich mit einer weiteren Aufschließung des diplomatischen Dienstes für Frauen gerechnet werden.

Das vielgestaltige Bild der Beteiligung der Frauen am öffentlichen Leben rundet sich erst ab, wenn man auch die vielen verschiedenartigen Ausschüsse, Arbeitskreise und sonstigen Gremien von Verwaltung und Selbstverwaltung in die Betrachtung einbezieht, in denen weibliche Mitglieder mitwirken. Die öffentliche Verwaltung steht der Forderung der Frauen nach Beteiligung aufgeschlossener gegenüber als die Wirtschaft. Trotz der beachtlichen Zahl der selbständigen Unternehmerinnen haben Frauen bisher in die Selbstverwaltung der Wirtschaft (zum Beispiel Industrie- und Handelskammern, Handwerkskammern usw.) kaum Eingang gefunden. Am ehesten sind Frauen in den unteren Gremien des Handwerks — etwa als sogenannte Innungsmeisterinnen — vertreten, wenn es sich um einen vorwiegend von Frauen ausgeübten Handwerkszweig, wie zum Beispiel das Damenschneiderhandwerk, handelt.

Im internationalen Raum gehört eine Frau als Deutsche Regierungsvertreterin dem Exekutivrat der UNESCO an. In der Deutschen Delegation der beratenden Versammlung des Europarats sind sechs weibliche Mitglieder, im Europäischen Parlament zwei Frauen vertreten. Mehrere Parlamentarierinnen sind Mitglieder der Europäischen Frauenunion.

Den internationalen Kommissionen der UNO, soweit die Bundesrepublik darin mitarbeitet, sowie der Deutschen UNESCO-Kommission, der Deutschen Gesellschaft für die Vereinten Nationen, dem Deutschen Rat der Europäischen Bewegung und anderen Gremien gehören Frauen als ständige Vertreterinnen ihrer Organisationen oder als hauptamtliche Mitarbeiter an.

Frauenreferat im Bundesministerium des Innern

Eine besondere Initiative zu Gunsten der Frauen ergriff die Bundesregierung, als sie 1950 mit Billigung aller Parteien des Bundestages ein Frauenreferat im Bundesministerium des Innern einrichtete. Es wurde ohne jedes Vorbild ins Leben gerufen. Die wesentlichen Aufgaben ergaben sich aber ohne weiteres aus den Zeitumständen. Es galt zunächst vor allem, den zentralen Frauenorganisationen beim Wiederaufbau Hilfe zu leisten und dafür zu sorgen, daß die Frauen in ihren maßgeblichen Vertretungen bei dem Aufbau der Gesellschaftsordnung zu Gehör kommen. Das Frauenreferat wirkt anregend und koordinierend mit, wo es darum geht, die notwendigen Folgerungen aus der gewandelten Stellung der Frau für Staat und Gesellschaft zu ziehen. Unter diesen Gesichtspunkten ist es an den gesetzgeberischen und Verwaltungsmaßnahmen der Bundesministerien beteiligt; es regt grundsätzliche Forschungen und Untersuchungen an und gibt hierfür finanzielle Beihilfen.

Ausblick

Zunehmend wird versucht, die Öffentlichkeit davon zu überzeugen, daß die aus der veränderten Stellung der Frau sich ergebenden Probleme keine „Interessenfragen der Frau“ sind, sondern zu dem Fragenbereich der gesamten Gesellschaftsordnung gehören und dementsprechend auch von dem Interesse aller Bevölkerungskreise getragen werden müssen.

Folgerungen aus der gewandelten Stellung der Frau sind sowohl auf dem Bildungs- und Erziehungssektor als im Bereich von Wirtschaft, Verwaltung und Politik zu ziehen.

Auf dem Bildungssektor in seinen verschiedenen Bereichen, insbesondere in der Familie, geht es zum Beispiel darum, Erziehung und Bildung in neuer Weise auf die Doppelaufgabe der Frau einzustellen und Vorbereitung und Ausbildung für die beiden Lebensbereiche Familie und Öffentlichkeit in ein ausgewogenes Verhältnis zueinander zu bringen.

Die Familienaufgabe der Frau wird als Schwerpunkt kulturfördernden Wirkens in Deutschland ganz besonders ernst genommen. Die Vorbereitung auf diese Aufgabe soll die innere Bereitschaft des heranwachsenden Mädchens wecken und fördern und einer Abwertung der „nur-Hausfrau“ vorbeugen. Dieser Abwertung muß besonders entgegengewirkt werden, damit die mögliche Freisetzung weiblicher Arbeitskräfte durch die Automation keine destruktiven Folgen für die Familie hat.

Hand in Hand mit diesen Bemühungen geht das Bestreben, die Bereitschaft für eine gute Berufsausbildung zu wecken und der stark eingewurzelten Haltung entgegenzuwirken, die Zeit nach der Schulentlassung brauche als „Wartezeit auf die Ehe“ nur mit einer ungelernten oder angelernten Erwerbstätigkeit, die schnellen Verdienst einbringt, ausgefüllt zu werden. Ganz offensichtlich hat in der Bundesrepublik die Schockwirkung der Kriegszeit, in der deutlich wurde, daß die Ehe der Frau keine wirtschaftliche

Sicherheit garantiert, nachgelassen. Da eine gute Fachausbildung überdies die Voraussetzung ist, um in Schlüsselstellungen zu kommen, von denen aus die Gesellschaftsordnung Inhalt und Formung erfährt, wird diesem Fragenbereich von den Männern und Frauen, die die schöpferische Mitwirkung der Frau für unerläßlich halten, große Aufmerksamkeit zugewandt.

Besondere Maßnahmen sollen dazu dienen, den weiblichen Studierenden an den Hochschulen das Verständnis dafür zu wecken, daß sie als akademisch gebildete Frauen ihre Kräfte und Gaben bei der Lösung der sogenannten Frauenfrage in erster Linie einzusetzen haben; sei es im Beruf, sei es von der Plattform der Familie aus in politischer oder sonst ehrenamtlicher Arbeit.

In der Bundesrepublik ist die verheiratete Frau bisher noch weit weniger als beispielsweise in den USA nebenamtlich in der Öffentlichkeit tätig. Gegenwärtig hat dies zweifellos mit seinen Grund in der erwähnten Überlastung der meisten Frauen, die für ihre Familie zu sorgen haben. Es ist aber nicht zu übersehen, daß hier auch noch sehr stark die Tradition eine Rolle spielt, dies Feld den Männern zu überlassen. Da Berufsausbildung und Berufstätigkeit vor der Ehe neue geistige Kräfte in der Frau und damit das Verlangen wecken, diese Kräfte auch weiterhin einzusetzen, erscheint es im Interesse der Familie unter Umständen sinnvoller, eine zeitlich weniger verpflichtende ehrenamtliche Arbeit als eine volle Berufsarbeit zu wählen. Darum wird auch gerade in diesem Zusammenhang der politischen Bildung der Frau in der Bundesrepublik so große Bedeutung zugemessen.

Den Bemühungen, die Frau zu einer verantwortungsbewußten Partnerin im öffentlichen Raum zu erziehen, entspricht das Bemühen, den geeigneten Frauen die Chancen entsprechender Mitwirkung zu erschließen; sei es durch verantwortliche Mitarbeit in den Parteien oder durch Berufung auf verantwortliche Stellen in Wirtschaft und Verwaltung. Der Wille hierzu lag zum Beispiel der Forderung des Bundestages an die Bundesregierung im Jahre 1950 zu Grunde, in regelmäßigen Abständen einen Bericht über den Anteil der Frauen im öffentlichen Dienst der Bundesverwaltung vorzulegen. Der Bericht wird jährlich erstattet.

Die gekennzeichneten Maßnahmen, an denen amtliche und private Stellen und in entscheidender Weise Frauenverbände und Gewerkschaften mitwirken, dienen dem Zweck, das schöpferische Wirken der Frau in der Familie und in der Öffentlichkeit in echter Partnerschaft mit dem Mann zu ermöglichen.

JUGENDARBEIT, NACHWUCHS, JUGENDPOLITIK

Situation 1945

Von den furchtbaren Auswirkungen des totalen Krieges und des totalen Zusammenbruchs wurde insbesondere die Jugend betroffen wie kaum eine Generation zuvor.

Der Krieg hinterließ in Westdeutschland 1,6 Millionen Waisen und Halbwaisen, zwei Millionen Kinder und Jugendliche, die aus ihrer Heimat vertrieben worden waren, und mehrere Millionen Kinder kriegsversehrter Väter. In den ersten Nachkriegsjahren verloren jährlich rund 80.000 Minderjährige einen Elternteil durch Scheidung. Die Zahl der tuberkulös infizierten Kleinkinder stieg gegenüber der Vorkriegszeit stark an; die Säuglingssterblichkeit lag 1946 um 60% höher als 1938. Etwa 40% der Jugendlichen zeigten neurotische Störungen, die auf Kriegseinwirkungen zurückzuführen waren. 23% der Geschlechtskranken waren Jugendliche. Zu unbeschreiblichem Wohnungselend kamen eine unzureichende Ernährung und Mangel an jeglichen Gebrauchsgütern. Schulen und Jugendheime waren zerstört, es fehlte an Lehrern und ausgebildeten Kräften der Jugendwohlfahrt.

Aus den Kreisen der durch den Krieg Entwurzelten oder einer Familienfürsorge Beraubten rekrutierte sich das Hauptkontingent der vagabundierenden oder beschäftigungslos herumlungernden Jugendlichen, die sich durch Schwarzhandel oder auf sonstige unlautere Weise durchschlugen. In der Britischen Zone schätzte man 1946 ihre Zahl auf achtzig- bis hunderttausend, in der Amerikanischen Zone auf einhundertfünfzigtausend. Kein Wunder, daß die Jugendkriminalität sich in erschreckender Weise erhöhte und die Zahl der in Fürsorgeerziehung eingewiesenen Jugendlichen gegenüber 1939 sich verdoppelte.

Hinter diesen weitgehend meßbaren Notständen aber stand als brennendstes Problem die geistige und seelische Not des jungen Menschen, die mit den Schlagworten Vereinsamung, Hoffnungslosigkeit, Mangel an sittlichen Maßstäben und Mißtrauen gegenüber der Welt der Autoritäten nur angedeutet werden kann.

Aufbau des Verbandslebens

Heute stehen wir einer völlig veränderten Situation gegenüber. Vieles kam mit der fortschreitenden Normalisierung von selbst wieder ins Gleichgewicht, vieles wurde durch private und staatliche Hilfe und durch die Wirksamkeit freier Stellen und Verbände gebessert. Einen wesentlichen Beitrag in dem Bemühen, die Jugend aus dem hoffnungslos scheinenden Chaos des Zusammenbruchs herauszulösen und ihr eine innere und äußere Heimat zu geben, leisteten die *Jugendverbände*.

Schon bald nach dem Zusammenbruch schlossen überall in Westdeutschland junge Menschen sich freiwillig zu Gesinnungsgemeinschaften zusammen. Bereits im Herbst 1946 gab es in den Westzonen 2.000, ein Jahr später 10.000 örtliche Jugendgruppen, die zum Teil auf den Traditionen der Zeit vor HITLER aufbauten. Die Jugendbewegung alter Prägung konnte — der veränderten Problemstellung zufolge — allerdings nicht wieder aufleben. Die Jugendorganisationen trugen ihren Sinn nicht mehr in sich. Ihre Verantwortung lag von Anfang an auf sozialem, kulturellem und erzieherischem Gebiet. An die Stelle der Jugendbewegung trat die Jugendpflege, deren Hauptträger die meist auf weltanschaulicher Grundlage gebildeten großen Jugendverbände wurden.

Die Jugendorganisationen als Zentren positiver Formungskräfte erhielten — bei voller Wahrung ihrer Eigenständigkeit — eine starke Förderung seitens der öffentlichen Hand, insbesondere nach Schaffung des Bundesjugendplanes (über den im weiteren noch ausführlich berichtet werden wird). Die den Jugendverbänden gewährten finanziellen Mittel wirkten sich unter anderem aus auf die Entfaltung ihres Eigenlebens, die staatspolitische und musische Erziehungsarbeit, die Betreuung sozial benachteiligter Gruppen (Heimatvertriebene, jugendliche Flüchtlinge und andere), den Bau von Jugendheimen in den Grenzgebieten zur sogenannten DDR und auf die Belebung und qualitative Steigerung des verbandseigenen Schrifttums.

Heute beträgt die Gesamtauflage der verbandsgebundenen Jugendzeitschriften 1,8 Millionen, die Gesamtauflage aller für die Jugend bestimmten Zeitschriften in der Bundesrepublik über 11 Millionen Exemplare. Von den 600 verschiedenen Titeln entfallen 350 auf Schülerzeitungen von der Jugend für die Jugend, deren Redakteure sich auf Landes- und Bundesebene zur „*Arbeitsgemeinschaft Junge Presse*" zusammengeschlossen haben.

*

Charakteristisch für die neue Form des Jugendlebens nach 1945 ist die überverbandliche Zusammenarbeit. Bereits 1946 wurden in Kreisen und Ländern Jugendringe und Jugendausschüsse gebildet. 1949 erfolgte der Zusammenschluß zum *Deutschen Bundesjugendring* als freiwilliger Arbeitsgemeinschaft. Heute sind im Bundesjugendring die *Landesjugendringe* der elf Länder der Bundesrepublik [Berlin(West)] sowie vierzehn *Jugendorganisationen* mit über 6 Millionen Mitgliedern zusammengeschlossen. Davon entfallen zwei Millionen Mitglieder auf die Deutsche Sportjugend, je eine Million auf den Bund der Deutschen Katholischen Jugend und die Arbeitsgemeinschaft der Evangelischen Jugend Deutschlands, 750.000 auf die Gewerkschaftsjugend, 100.000 auf die Sozialistische Jugend Deutschlands — Die Falken und 150.000 auf die Deutsche Jugend des Ostens. Die letzte ist die überlandsmannschaftliche Vereinigung der Vertriebenenjugend. Weniger stark sind die übrigen, zum Teil sehr aktiven Mitgliedsverbände des Bundesjugendrings: Bund Deutscher Landjugend — Jugend der Deutschen Angestelltengewerkschaft — Naturfreundejugend — Jugend des Deutschen Alpenvereins — Wanderjugend — Deutsche Schreberjugend — Ring Deutscher Pfadfinderbünde — Ring Deutscher Pfadfinderinnen.

Außerhalb des Deutschen Bundesjugendringes bestehen noch zahlreiche beachtenswerte Jugendgemeinschaften, in deren Vielfalt der individualistische Zug der deutschen Nachkriegsjugend sich widerspiegelt. Genannt seien: Jugendrotkreuz — Junge Europäische Föderalisten — Musikalische Jugend — bündische Gruppen. Beliebt sind unverbindliche Neigungsgruppierungen in Foto-, Film- und Jazzklubs.

Die Jugendverbände versuchen, auf immer neuen Wegen auf die nichtorganisierte Jugend auszustrahlen, sei es durch die Veranstaltung von offenen Ausspracheabenden und Jugendforen, die Beteiligung nichtorganisierter Jugendlicher an den Laienspieltagen der Jugend, die Durchführung von Tanztees usw. Der Erfolg läßt sich an den ständig wachsenden Mitgliederzahlen ablesen. Etwa die Hälfte der Jugend in der Bundesrepublik hat sich heute in Jugendverbänden und -gemeinschaften zusammengefunden.

Die deutschen Jugendverbände sind international anerkannt und Mitglieder der entsprechenden Weltorganisationen (YMCA, IUSY, Weltpfadfinderbund und andere). Der Deutsche Bundesjugendring gehört der World Assemblee of Youth (WAY) an.

* * *

Die Arbeit des *Deutschen Bundesjugendringes* wird im Interesse der gesamten Jugend geleistet. Sie dient der Schaffung eines gesunden Jugendlebens, der Festigung der Demokratie in der Bundesrepublik und der Förderung der internationalen Verständigung. In den zehn Jehran seines Bestehens hat der Deutsche Bundesjugendring zu vielen Fragen der Jugendpolitik und des Jugendrechts Stellung genommen, Vorschläge unterbreitet und die Belange der freien Jugendpflege vor Behörden und der Öffentlichkeit vertreten. Hervorgehoben seien etwa die Mitgestaltung des „Inneren Gefüges" der deutschen Wehrverfassung und die Mitarbeit an der Neuregelung der Gesetzgebung über den Jugendarbeitsschutz. Darüber hinaus trat der Bundesjugendring mit zahlreichen Aktionen hervor. Erinnert sei an die Aufrufe an die Jungwähler anläßlich der Bundestagswahlen und die Appelle zur Führung eines fairen Wahlkampfes. In einem — allerdings fruchtlos verlaufenen — Gespräch (17. 3. 1955) mit Angehörigen des Zentralrates der Freien Deutschen Jugend (FDJ) und in zahlreichen Adressen versuchte der Bundesjugendring, die Lage der deutschen Jugend in der sogenannten DDR zu bessern. Einen Schwerpunkt bildete in den letzten Jahren die Vertiefung der deutsch-französischen Verständigung. 1956 wurde das Weltjugendtreffen erstmalig vom Deutschen Bundesjugendring in der Bundesrepublik veranstaltet (6. Ratsversammlung der WAY in Berlin).

*

Nicht unerwähnt bleiben darf der *Ring Politischer Jugend*, in dem sich — über alle weltanschaulichen Schranken hinweg — die Mitglieder der Jungen Union (CDU/CSU), der Jungsozialisten (SPD) und der Jungdemokraten (FDP) zusammengeschlossen haben. Seine Arbeit konzentriert sich auf die politische Erziehung. Von den dreiundzwanzig Abgeordneten unter sechsunddreißig Jahren, die in den Dritten Deutschen Bundestag gewählt wurden, gingen die meisten aus den genannten Nachwuchsorganisationen der Parteien hervor.

Die Aktivität der Jugendverbände hat erheblich mit dazu beigetragen, die deutsche Jugend aus ihrer politischen Lethargie herauszureißen und zu einer wirklichen Anteilnahme am öffentlichen Leben zu führen. Das wurde besonders sinnfällig bei den Bundestagswahlen 1953 und 1957, bei denen ein hoher Prozentsatz der Jungwähler seine Stimme abgab.

Von der Berufsnot der Jugend zum Nachwuchsmangel

Aus den Bemühungen um die gesellschaftliche und berufliche Eingliederung der Jugend entwickelte sich als besonderes Charakteristikum der Nachkriegszeit die *praktische Jugendsozialarbeit.* Bereits 1946 entstanden durch die Initiative einzelner Persönlichkeiten die ersten Einrichtungen, um die wandernden, heimatlosen und alleinstehenden Jugendlichen wieder zu verwurzeln und ihnen eine Heimat zu geben: Kinderdörfer, Jugendhilfsdienste, Jugendsiedlungen und Heimstätten. Diesen Institutionen waren zunächst vorwiegend fürsorgerische Aufgaben gestellt. Nach der Währungsreform jedoch verlagerte das Schwergewicht sich auf die Überwindung der Berufsnot der Jugend. 1949 schlossen alle Träger der praktischen Jugendsozialarbeit in der Bundesrepublik mit Berlin(West) — konfessionelle, interkonfessionelle, sozialistische und kommunale Verbände der Jugendwohlfahrt und Jugendpflege — sich freiwillig zu einer Aktionsgemeinschaft, der *Bundesarbeitsgemeinschaft Jugendaufbauwerk*, zusammen. Ihr Ziel ist, junge Menschen zwischen vierzehn und fünfundzwanzig Jahren durch die Heranführung an einen existenzsichernden Beruf und einen dauerhaften Arbeitsplatz gesellschaftlich einzugliedern und sie auf dieser Grundlage in individueller erzieherischer Anleitung sowie durch ein gruppenpädagogisch gestaltetes Gemeinschaftsleben zu einem sinnvollen Dasein und zu tätiger Mitverantwortung in Gesellschaft und Staat zu führen. Zu diesem Zweck wurde der Bau von pädagogisch zugerüsteten Jugendwohnheimen an den Produktionsstätten mit staatlicher Hilfe[1] in hohem Maße intensiviert. Im Mai 1946 bestanden 20, drei Jahre später 280, 1958 rund 1.525 Heime (mit 120.500 Plätzen). In zehn Jahren ist über eine Million junger Menschen durch die Jugendwohnheime gegangen. Außerdem wurden rund 4.600 berufsfördernde Maßnahmen durchgeführt: Jugendgemeinschaftswerke — gemeinnützige Lehrwerkstätten — Grundausbildungs- und Förderungslehrgänge. Sie dienen zur Überbrückung der vorberuflichen Wartezeit, der Berufsfindung und der Förderung der noch nicht berufs- beziehungsweise betriebsfähigen Schulentlassenen. Im Rahmen der berufsfördernden Maßnahmen wurden rund 152.000 junge Menschen betreut.

Von der Wirtschaft selbst wurden in starkem Umfang neue Lehr- und Anlernstellen geschaffen. In Industrie und Handel stiegen die Ausbildungsplätze um über 100% gegenüber 1946.

Die vielfältigen Hilfsmaßnahmen, verbunden mit dem Aufblühen der deutschen Wirtschaft, bewirkten einen stetigen Rückgang der jugendlichen Arbeitslosen. Ihre Zahl war zu Beginn des Jahres 1955 — trotz starken Schulentlassungsjahrgängen — bereits auf ein Drittel gegenüber 1950 gesunken. Heute kann die objektive Berufsnot der Jugend als beseitigt gelten. An ihre Stelle ist eine Nachwuchsnot getreten, deren Ursache mit in der Abnahme der Abgänger von der Volksschule zu suchen ist.

*

Die Zahl der Ausbildungsverhältnisse beläuft sich zur Zeit auf knapp 1,5 Millionen. Sie geht ebenfalls zurück, vor allem bei den Jugendlichen im

[1] Vergleiche dazu die Tabelle „Bundesjugendplan“ auf Seite 639.

ersten Lehrjahr. Auch durch die zunehmende Ausweitung der Ausbildungsmöglichkeiten für weibliche Jugendliche, deren Anteil 1957 auf fast 35% gestiegen ist, war ein Ausgleich nicht zu erreichen. So ist beim Handwerk der Anteil der weiblichen Jugendlichen auf 18,6% gestiegen. Trotzdem beträgt der Rückgang der Ausbildungsverhältnisse von 1956 auf 1957 insgesamt 7,9%. In Industrie und Handel dagegen hat die Zahl der Lehrlinge und Anlernlinge sich gehalten. Bei ebenfalls starker Erhöhung des weiblichen Anteils entfallen hier 38,2% der Lehrverhältnisse auf gewerblich-industrielle und 55,4% auf kaufmännische Berufe.

Trotz den Aktionen zur berufskundlichen Aufklärung und starker Inanspruchnahme der Berufsberatungsstellen blieben die Berufswünsche einseitig orientiert, wobei oft vordergründige Gesichtspunkte der sozialen Sicherung herausgestellt wurden. Die Jungen bevorzugen Berufe der Metallerzeugung und -verarbeitung, technische Berufe sowie kaufmännische und Verwaltungsberufe. Geringe Neigung besteht für die Berufe Bäcker, Fleischer, Maler, Maurer, Bergmann, Bau- und Möbeltischler. Die Wünsche der Mädchen konzentrieren sich überwiegend auf kaufmännische und Büroberufe. Steigendes Interesse ist für die jahrelang gemiedenen sozialpflegerischen und hauswirtschaftlichen Berufe zu verzeichnen.

Mit dem Umschlag der objektiven Berufsnot der Jugend in eine Nachwuchsnot ist die praktische Jugendsozialarbeit als sozialpädagogische Berufshilfe für die Jugend in eine neue Phase getreten. Ihre Hauptaufgaben werden in der Zukunft auf folgenden Gebieten liegen: Heranführung zusätzlich zu gewinnender Nachwuchskräfte an die Zentren des Wirtschaftslebens und ihre erzieherische Zurüstung; organische Entfaltung der Persönlichkeit und damit der Leistungsfähigkeit der Jugend durch zusätzliche Bildungshilfen berufsvorbereitender und berufsbegleitender Art; Aufbauförderung für aufstiegswillige und begabte werktätige Jugendliche beider Geschlechter in Stadt und Land.

Der Bundesjugendplan

Die gesamte Jugendarbeit in der Bundesrepublik empfing einen besonderen Impuls durch den Bundesjugendplan, den der Bundeskanzler am 18. 12. 1950 verkündete. Damit wurde eine Serie von Maßnahmen eingeleitet, die im Rahmen von neun Bundesjugendplänen sich zu einem *aktiven Jugendprogramm des Bundes* entwickelten. Der Bundesjugendplan ist eine Aktion der Bundesregierung, die im Einvernehmen mit Bundestag und Bundesrat und gemeinsam mit den obersten Jugendbehörden der Länder und den Verbänden der Jugendarbeit durchgeführt wird. Er soll der Jugend helfen, sich körperlich, geistig, sittlich und beruflich in gesunder Weise zu entwickeln, in ihren eigenen Jugendgemeinschaften sich frei zu entfalten und ihre Verantwortung gegenüber Familie, Gesellschaft und Staat zu erfüllen.

Die finanzielle Förderung aus dem Bundesjugendplan ist vor allem Hilfe zur Selbsthilfe der Jugend und der Träger der Jugendarbeit. Sie soll deshalb nicht nur die Durchführung einzelner Maßnahmen ermöglichen, sondern darüber hinaus die Träger auf Dauer in die Lage versetzen, ihre pädagogischen und sozialen Aufgaben aus eigenen Mitteln zu erfüllen.

Aus dem Bundesjugendplan können — unter Beachtung der Zuständigkeit der Länder und Gemeinden — Maßnahmen gefördert werden, die von zentraler Bedeutung sind, oder an deren Durchführung auch ein erhebliches Interesse des Bundes besteht. Hierzu gehören vor allem:

a) die Erziehung und Bildung der Jugend, soweit sie in Ergänzung und außerhalb von Familie, Schule, Beruf und Kirche erfolgt, insbesondere die politische Bildung und die internationale Begegnung der Jugend;

b) die Ausbildung und Fortbildung von hauptberuflichen und ehrenamtlichen Mitarbeitern in der Jugendarbeit;

c) die berufliche und gesellschaftliche Eingliederung von jugendlichen Zuwanderern, insbesondere von jugendlichen Flüchtlingen und Aussiedlern;

d) der Bau, die Einrichtung und die Erhaltung von Stätten der Jugendarbeit, insbesondere von Wohnheimen der Jugendhilfe (einschließlich der Studentenwohnheime), Jugendherbergen, Jugendbildungs-, Jugendfreizeit- und Jugenderholungsstätten;

e) die Jugendarbeit in Notstandsgebieten;

f) die Aufgaben der zentralen Jugendverbände (einschließlich der Studentenverbände) und der sonstigen zentralen Organisationen der Jugendarbeit.

Die Zuwendungen aus dem Bundesjugendplan werden im Rahmen der jährlich vom Deutschen Bundestag bewilligten Haushaltsmittel gegeben. Im Verlauf von neun Bundesjugendplänen (1950 bis 1958) flossen der Jugendarbeit insgesamt 326.600.000 DM aus Mitteln des Bundeshaushalts zu. Sie wurden für folgende Zwecke gegeben:

Die Hilfeleistung des Bundesjugendplanes erstreckt sich außerdem auf Förderung der Ausbildung von Mitarbeitern internationaler Jugendbegegnung,

BUNDESJUGENDPLAN 1950—1958
Millionen DM

Jugendwohnheime	87,2	Studentenwohnheime	13,8
Jugendverbände	40,4	Jugend aus der sogenannten DDR	44,7
Politische Bildung	13,6	Jugendbildung	15,6
Jugendherbergswerk	14,6	Landjugend	8,4
Notstandsgebiete	20,9	Bundesjugendplan Berlin	17,0

Quelle: Bundesministerium des Innern.

Jugendwohlfahrtspflege, Jugendfürsorge, Jugendschutz, Freizeitstätten, Mädchenbildung und Bundesjugendspiele.

Innerhalb der einzelnen Sektoren des Bundesjugendplanes, dessen Mittel fast alljährlich erhöht wurden, haben seit 1950 — entsprechend der Gesamtsituation der Jugend — sich mehrfach die Schwerpunkte verschoben, beziehungsweise neue Gebiete wurden mit einbezogen.

Aus dem Bemühen, zunächst den wirtschaftlichen Lebensraum für die Jugend mit sichern zu helfen, resultierte die bereits geschilderte intensive Unterstützung des *Baues von Jugendwohnheimen* und der *berufsfördernden Maßnahmen.*

Hierzu kam in immer stärkerem Maße die Förderung der Erholung der Jugend und der körperlichen Ertüchtigung. 1951 wurden die Bundesjugendspiele als Nachfolgeveranstaltung der 1922 ins Leben gerufenen Reichsjugendwettkämpfe neu eingeführt. Sie sollen die Jugend anregen, Sport und Turnen zu pflegen. 1951 nahmen 600.000 Jugendliche an den Bundesjugendspielen teil, 1957 über 5 Millionen. Seit 1955 wurde im Rahmen des Bundesjugendplans ein besonderer Titel für Jugenderholung eingesetzt. Im Jahre 1958 haben schätzungsweise 1,2 Millionen junge Menschen ihre Ferien in Heimen und Zeltlagern der Wohlfahrts- und Jugendverbände verbracht.

*

Eine nachdrückliche Förderung erhielt das *Jugendherbergswerk* als Sammelpunkt der gesamten wandernden Jugend. Seine Bedeutung wuchs auch im Zusammenhang mit der aufkommenden Camping-Bewegung, die von den Gesichtspunkten des Jugendschutzes aus zum Teil als problematisch anzusehen war. Nach dem Ende des Zweiten Weltkrieges waren von den 1.200 Jugendherbergen in Westdeutschland nur noch 275 Häuser benutzbar. Im Jahre 1959 stehen in der Bundesrepublik wieder rund 740 Jugendherbergen mit über 69.000 Betten zur Verfügung. Die Übernachtungsziffern in den deutschen

Jugendherbergen nehmen ständig zu. 1948 wurden 1,5 Millionen Übernachtungen gezählt, 1958 mehr als 7 Millionen. Das Jugendherbergswerk hat sich damit als eine wesentliche Brücke von Volk zu Volk erwiesen. Seit 1951 ist das Deutsche Jugendherbergswerk wieder Mitglied des Internationalen Jugendherbergsverbandes.

Politische Bildung

Ein weiteres Schwergewicht des Bundesjugendplans liegt auf der Förderung der *politischen Bildung der Jugend*. Auf die radikale Politisierung unter dem HITLER-Regime war nach dem Zusammenbruch der Rückschlag erfolgt. Weite Kreise der Jugend zeigten eine indifferente, ja sogar radikal antipolitische Haltung. Es stellte sich daher sofort nach Gründung der Bundesrepublik die Aufgabe, die enttäuschten, mißtrauisch und richtungslos gewordenen jungen Menschen für die Mitarbeit am Neubau eines demokratischen Staatsgefüges zu gewinnen und ihnen darüber hinaus die Einsicht in die Notwendigkeit einer engen Zusammenarbeit der europäischen Staaten zu vermitteln. Weit davon entfernt, eine Staatsjugend heranziehen zu wollen, unterstützt die Bundesregierung daher aus Mitteln des Bundesjugendplans alle auf dem Boden der freiheitlichen Demokratie stehenden Verbände, Gruppierungen und Einrichtungen, die sich die staatspolitisch-bildnerische Arbeit an der jungen Generation zur Aufgabe gemacht haben, auch wenn sie in ihrer Gesinnung der Opposition nahestehen.

Für die politische Bildung der Jugend außerhalb der Jugendverbände (und damit im wesentlichen der sogenannten unorganisierten Jugend) wurden in den ersten sieben Bundesjugendplänen (1950 bis 1956) 13,6 Millionen DM, im Achten und Neunten Bundesjugendplan je 4,25 Millionen DM bereitgestellt. Für den Zehnten Bundesjugendplan ist die Erhöhung der Zuwendungen auf fünf Millionen DM vorgesehen. Aus diesen Mitteln wird vor allem die Tätigkeit von dreiundsiebzig sogenannten „Jugendbildungsreferenten“ und vier leitenden sogenannten „Bundestutoren“ bei den freien Verbänden gefördert. Neben diesen Mitteln und Maßnahmen steht die politische Jugendbildung innerhalb der Jugendverbände. Sie ist ebenfalls in steigendem Maße gefördert worden.

Auf diese Weise konnte fast eine Million Jugendliche und Jugendleiter an politischen Bildungsmaßnahmen teilnehmen. Für rund 800.000 Jugendliche wurden internationale Begegnungstreffen, Fahrten und Aufbaulager im In- und Ausland durchgeführt. Hinzu kommen seit 1947 umfangreiche Auslandsprogramme, -stipendien und -praktiken für Schüler und Studenten, für Junglehrer und Jungakademiker, für Jugendleiter, Jungarbeiter und Jungbauern.

In den letzten Jahren wurde der geistigen Auseinandersetzung mit dem dialektischen Materialismus kommunistischer Prägung, der in der sogenannten DDR die Erziehung der Jugend bestimmt, vermehrte Aufmerksamkeit geschenkt. Diese Auseinandersetzung soll dazu dienen, die den Westen bedrohenden Mächte kennenzulernen, und zur verstärkten Besinnung auf die eigene Wertordnung führen. Darüber hinaus soll durch eine Pflege der menschlichen Kontakte zwischen den Deutschen beiderseits der Zonengrenze vermieden werden, daß die durch verschiedenen weltanschaulichen Horizont, verschiedenes Geschichtsbild und verschiedenes Traditionsgefühl schon erschreckend vorgeschrittene geistige Zweiteilung Deutschlands unwiderruflich wird — ein Prozeß, der am Tage der Wiedervereinigung sich verhängnisvoll für Gesamtdeutschland auswirken müßte.

Die Flüchtlinge aus der sogenannten DDR

Zu den Programmpunkten, die innerhalb des Bundesjugendplanes zunehmend an Bedeutung gewannen, gehört die Förderung der *jugendlichen Flüchtlinge aus der sogenannten DDR* und der heimatvertriebenen und nichtdeutschen Jugend in den Flüchtlingslagern.

Bis zur Verkündung des Ersten Bundesjugendplans (1950) waren rund 7,9 Millionen Heimatvertriebene in die Bundesrepublik gekommen. 30% von ihnen waren Jugendliche. Nach dem Zusammenbruch galt die Hauptsorge zunächst der Eingliederung dieses Personenkreises. Diese Aufgabe kann heute weitgehend als gelöst gelten, wenn auch nicht vergessen werden darf, daß noch immer viele Jugendliche aus dem Osten — in den letzten Jahren vor allem junge Umsiedler — und ein kleiner Prozentsatz heimatloser Ausländer in Lagern leben.

Dagegen wuchs die Eingliederung des Flüchtlingsstromes aus der sogenannten DDR sich immer mehr zu einem sozialen, wirtschaftlichen und politischen Problem aus. Als Folge der zunehmenden Einbeziehung Mitteldeutschlands in den Sowjetblock setzte Mitte 1948 eine Ost-West-Wanderung ein, die 1953 ihren Höhepunkt erreichte und bis zum heutigen Tage anhält.

Die Motive der Flucht objektiv zu erhellen, ist sehr schwierig; doch dürften sie bei der Mehrheit zumindest mittelbar in den politischen Verhältnissen der sogenannten DDR zu suchen sein: Spannungen zu dem herrschenden System, der geistige Druck, die Beschneidung der persönlichen Freiheit und seit 1955

ANTRAGSTELLER IM NOTAUFNAHMEVERFAHREN

	1954	1955	1956	1957	1958
Antragsteller insgesamt	184.198	252.870	279.189	261.622	204.092
Davon: Jugendliche (0 bis 25 Jahre) im Familienverband .	52.424	70.075	87.560	82.714	68.681
(in Prozenten)	*(28,4)*	*(27,8)*	*(31,3)*	*(31,6)*	*(33,7)*
Jugendliche alleinstehend ..	37.947	62.487	49.318	53.937	29.576
(in Prozenten)	*(20,7)*	*(24,7)*	*(17,7)*	*(20,6)*	*(14,5)*

auch die verstärkte Anwerbung zur kasernierten Volkspolizei, deren Ablehnung eine Gefährdung nach sich zieht. All diese Gründe veranlassen die Jugendlichen zur Abwanderung. Nur ein geringer Teil gibt wirtschaftliche Gründe an. Puberale Antriebe (zum Beispiel Abenteuerlust) fallen kaum ins Gewicht.

Durch eine Fülle von Gesetzen des Bundes und der Länder wurden Hilfsmöglichkeiten für die Flüchtlinge erschlossen. Das Notaufnahmeverfahren wurde eingeführt, Notaufnahme-, Durchgangs- und Wohnlager wurden geschaffen. Alleinstehende jugendliche Flüchtlinge werden — soweit es sich nicht um Agenten oder Kriminelle handelt — fast ausnahmslos als Vollbürger in die Bundesrepublik aufgenommen, auch wenn die Voraussetzungen für einen Rechtsanspruch auf Aufenthaltserlaubnis nicht gegeben sind. Ein relativ hoher Prozentsatz der politisch anerkannten jugendlichen Flüchtlinge rekrutiert sich aus der jungen Intelligenz (Studenten, Fach- und Oberschüler), die in der sogenannten DDR einer besonderen politischen Pression ausgesetzt ist.

Die Eingliederung der jugendlichen Flüchtlinge in den Arbeitsmarkt gestaltete sich bis 1954 sehr schwierig. Sie mußte überwiegend durch berufsfremde Vermittlung, insbesondere in die Landwirtschaft, gelöst werden. Heute, im Zustand der Vollbeschäftigung und des Nachwuchsmangels, können die meisten jugendlichen Flüchtlinge direkt in ihre Berufe vermittelt werden, wobei die günstige Relation von Gelernten und Ungelernten und der auffallend hohe Anteil der Metall verarbeitenden Berufe sich fördernd auswirken.

Unter den Hilfsmaßnahmen für jugendliche Flüchtlinge nehmen die Ausbildungsbeihilfen für Lehr- und Anlernlinge, für Schüler und Abiturienten, für Praktikanten und Studenten eine hervorragende Stelle ein. Ihre Gewährung war zunächst auf bestimmte Kategorien beschränkt. Ganze Gruppen, wie die Absolventen der Arbeiter- und Bauernfakultäten, zum

Teil Fachschüler, Umschüler und andere, wurden von den Förderungsbestimmungen nicht erfaßt. Darüber hinaus brachten die Vielfalt der möglichen Ausbildungsbeihilfen und der dafür zuständigen Stellen sowie die häufig sehr langwierigen Bewilligungs-Verfahren Unzuträglichkeiten mit sich. Um Lücken zu schließen und eine rasche Hilfe wirksam werden zu lassen, wurde 1956 auf Grund eines interfraktionellen Antrags im Deutschen Bundestag ein Garantiefonds (Vorlage- und Zuschußtitel des Bundeshaushaltsplans) in Höhe von 7,5 Millionen DM geschaffen. Aus dem Garantiefonds können jugendliche Zuwanderer bei Eignung und Neigung für ihre Schul- und Berufsausbildung (einschließlich der Umschulung und Fortbildung) Zuschüsse oder Vorschüsse (bis zum Eintritt des endgültigen gesetzlichen Kostenträgers) erhalten, wenn die ganzheitliche Eingliederung des jungen Menschen gewährleistet scheint. Als jugendliche Zuwanderer gelten: Flüchtlinge aus der sogenannten DDR bzw. Ostberlin, Aussiedler, Verschleppte, Heimkehrer, in Kriegsgefangenschaft usw. Geborene sowie nichtdeutsche Flüchtlinge (zum Beispiel ungarische Jugendliche) unter 25 Jahren.

Von den übrigen Ausbildungshilfen seien erwähnt: Schaffung von Förderklassen und Internatsplätzen für Schüler aus der sogenannten DDR und Aussiedlerkinder — Richtlinien für die Anerkennung von Reifezeugnissen und anderen Bildungsnachweisen aus der sogenannten DDR — Einrichtung von Sonderlehrgängen für Abiturienten und Anfangssemester zum Ausgleich des Bildungsgefälles zwischen Ost und West, insbesondere der erschreckenden Differenzen in den geisteswissenschaftlichen Fächern.

Weit schwieriger als die wirtschaftliche Eingliederung gestalteten sich die soziale Integration und die Assimilierung der jugendlichen Flüchtlinge aus der sogenannten DDR. Das politische Klima der sogenannten DDR, ihre auf Gebundenheit beruhende Gesellschaftsstruktur, die Einflüsse einer zielbewußt gesteuerten kommunistischen Pädagogik und Propaganda sind Faktoren, die den jungen Menschen geprägt haben und vielfach noch latent weiterwirken. Erschwerend kommt hinzu, daß etwa 50% der alleinstehenden jugendlichen Flüchtlinge aus gestörten Familien stammt und auch von dieser Seite her psychische Milieuschädigungen aufweisen dürfte. Es wäre jedoch verfehlt, anzunehmen, daß es sich bei den jugendlichen Flüchtlingen um eine negative Auslese handelt. Die Zahl der vorbestraften Notaufnahme-Antragsteller ist gering. Der Prozentsatz der sozialpädagogischen Fälle liegt nicht wesentlich über dem Bundesdurchschnitt. Der Mehrheit wird normale Begabung, Arbeitsethos und hervorragende politische Aufgeschlossenheit zugesprochen.

Die jugendlichen Flüchtlinge brauchen auf Grund ihrer psychischen Situation erfahrungsgemäß eine Zeit von mindestens acht Monaten der Umstellung. Während dieser Zeit werden sie von sozialpädagogisch geschulten Kräften betreut. Diese Aufgabe wird von den großen Wohlfahrts- und Jugendverbänden wahrgenommen, deren Arbeit mit erheblichen öffentlichen Mitteln unterstützt wird.

Eine wesentliche Aufgabe liegt in der *Herstellung menschlicher Kontakte*. Der an die Kollektivierung seines beruflichen, schulischen und privaten Lebensbereiches gewöhnte junge Flüchtling — die ihm zur Lebensnorm geworden ist, auch wenn er sie als Zwangsmaßnahme abgelehnt hat — sieht sich in der individualistischen Gesellschaft des Westens vor Auswirkungen der neu gewonnenen Freiheit, denen er nicht gewachsen ist. Es ist festgestellt worden, daß nur etwa ein Drittel der alleinstehenden jugendlichen Flüchtlinge zu einer echten Integration gelangt ist — sei es durch die Aufnahme in einen Familienverband oder in eine Betriebsgemeinschaft (vorwiegend in einem handwerklichen oder Kleinbetrieb), sei es durch die Gewinnung einheimischer Freunde. Hier ist ein Problem aufgerissen worden, das die Bewährung der gesamten Gesellschaft erfordert.

Die Landjugend

Zu den Gruppen sozial benachteiligter Jugendlicher gehört auch die bäuerliche Jugend. Ihre Krisensituation als Folgeerscheinung der wirtschaftlichen Strukturwandlung und des damit verbundenen Umbruchs der ländlichen Gesellschaftsordnung rückte in den letzten Jahren mehr und mehr ins Blickfeld. Die Lage der *Landjugend* ist durch Bildungs- und Ausbildungsnot, durch Berufs- und Existenznot gekennzeichnet. Daraus resultiert eine alarmierende Abwanderung der bäuerlichen Nachwuchskräfte. Statistische Unterlagen über die Berufsgliederung der Fünfzehn- bis Vierundzwanzigjährigen zeigen, daß nur 2% in der Landwirtschaft tätig sind. Das ist ein Prozentsatz der in keinem Verhältnis zu der Zahl der erwerbstätigen Bauern in der Bundesrepublik steht.

Die Notwendigkeit der Erhaltung eines gesunden Bauernstandes und der Schaffung von entscheidenden Voraussetzungen für die Eingliederung der deutschen Landwirtschaft in den Gemeinsamen Europäischen Markt — deren Träger die heutige bäuerliche Jugend sein wird — geben der Förderung der Landjugend besondere Bedeutung.

Bereits seit 1950 werden die dem Bundesjugendring angeschlossenen Landjugend-Organisationen aus Mitteln des Bundesjugendplans unterstützt. Auch andere Maßnahmen, wie etwa der Bau von Jugendheimen, Sportplätzen und Schwimmbädern in den Grenzgebieten zur sogenannten DDR sowie die Errichtung von Jugendbüchereien, kamen unmittelbar dem Lande zugute. Im Sechsten Bundesjugendplan (1955) wurde erstmals ein eigener Landjugendplan geschaffen. Er gliederte sich in ein Bildungs- und ein Berufsförderungsprogramm. Ein Teil dieser Aufgaben, nämlich die landwirtschaftlich-fachberuflichen Hilfen, wird heute vom Bundesministerium für Ernährung, Landwirtschaft und Forsten im Rahmen des „Grünen Planes", ein anderer, die Umschulungs-Lehrgänge, von der Bundesanstalt für Arbeitslosenvermittlung und Arbeitslosenversicherung wahrgenommen. Im Herbst und Winter 1957/58 nahmen mit Hilfe des Bundes an rund 3.500 ländlichen Seminaren mehr als 125.000 junge Menschen teil. Die in diesen Seminaren durchgeführten allgemeinbildenden offenen Tages- oder Abendkurse sind bisher am besten zur Wirkung gekommen. Von den beruflichen Hilfen wurden Lehrgänge landtechnischer Richtung bevorzugt. Die Lehrhöfe und Jugendwohnheime auf dem Land haben zur Gewinnung von qualifizierten Nachwuchskräften insbesondere aus den Kreisen der jugendlichen Heimatvertriebenen und Flüchtlinge geführt.

Schrifttum, Musik, Film

Von den vielseitigen Hilfsmaßnahmen des Bundesjugendplanes seien noch die Förderung des guten *Jugendschrifttums*, der *musischen Erziehung* (Jugendmusik, Laienspiel, Tanz und Werken) und der *Jugendfilmarbeit* hervorgehoben. Diese Maßnahmen eines positiven Jugendschutzes dienen dazu, in Verbindung mit den einschlägigen gesetzlichen Bestimmungen die Jugend gegen die schädigenden Einflüsse der „Straße" mit ihren anonymen Mächten — vor allem schlechte Filme und minderwertiges Schrifttum — abzuschirmen. Sie sollen die Entfaltung der Einzelpersönlichkeit fördern und damit einer Fehlentwicklung entgegenwirken, deren Konsequenzen sich in einem Ansteigen der Jugendkriminalität und in den Fehlhandlungen sogenannter „Halbstarker" abzeichnen.

Durch die Förderung von Jugendzeitschriften, fachkundlichem und Bildungsmaterial, von Jugendbuch und Jugendbibliothek gelang es, die Flut der Schmöker und Schundschriften, deren Gesamtauflage 1950/51 rund 93.600.000 betrug, zurückzudrängen. Die „*comic strips*" zeigen seit etwa 1955 eine stark rückläufige Tendenz. Durch den seit 1954 jährlich ausgeschriebenen Jugendbuchpreis erhielt die Produktion von Jugendbüchern einen erheblichen Anreiz. Aktionen in Flüchtlingslagern und Jugendwohnheimen, die Einrichtung von Jugendbüchereien in Grenzgebieten zur sogenannten DDR und die Schaffung von Modellprojekten auf dem Lande (erstmals 1956) trugen nicht nur zur Verbreitung des guten Jugendbuchs bei, sondern halfen auch mit, den geistig-sittlichen Notstand der Jugend zu mindern.

Die Förderung der *musischen Bildungsarbeit* zeigte eindrucksvolle Ergebnisse bei den ,,Festlichen Tagen Junger Musik" 1954 in Passau und bei den ,,Festlichen Tagen Deutscher Jugend" 1957 in Münster. Mit der angestrebten und stellenweise bereits eingeführten Verkürzung der Arbeitszeit und der dadurch ,,wachsenden Freizeit" gewann die musische Bildung als Brücke zu einer sinnvollen Freizeitgestaltung immer mehr an Bedeutung. 1957 wurde aus Mitteln des Bundesjugendplans mit dem Bau der Musischen Bildungsstätte in Remscheid begonnen. In dieser Modelleinrichtung sollen Nachwuchskräfte herangebildet werden, die in der Lage sind, junge Menschen zur Eigenbetätigung anzuregen und schöpferische Kräfte in ihnen zu entfalten.

Die Unterstützung der *Jugendfilmarbeit* beruht auf der Anerkennung des Films als eines eindringlichen Miterziehers der Jugend. Sie verfolgt das Ziel, die Jugend filmkritisch und filmmündig zu machen. Gefördert werden: Filmerziehung — Forschung auf dem Gebiet ,,Jugend und Film" — Herstellung und Vertrieb von Filmen für die Jugendpflege (nicht-gewerbliches Filmwesen). Erstmalig im Zehnten Bundesjugendplan (1959) hat der Bundesminister für Familien- und Jugendfragen den ,,Deutschen Kinderfilmpreis" und ,,Deutschen Jugendfilmpreis" zur Förderung von wertvollen Spielfilmen für Kinder und Jugendliche ausgeschrieben.

*

Neben den geschilderten Aktivitäten wurde im behördlichen und freien Raum — zum Teil mit Hilfe des Bundesjugendplans — eine Fülle von Maßnahmen zur *Intensivierung des Jugendschutzes* entwickelt. In Stichworten seien genannt: Durchführung von Jugendschutzwochen — Einrichtung von ,,Heimen der offenen Tür" als Freizeitstätten für nicht-organisierte Jugendliche — Gewährung von Sonderurlaub an Jugendleiter zur Betreuung von Zeltlagern der Jugend usw. — Einsatz von Schuljugendberatern — Einführung von Fragen der Jugendwohlfahrt in die Lehrerbildung — Errichtung von Erziehungs-Beratungsstellen — Verstärkung der Mittel für Erwachsenenbildung zur Vermittlung moderner entwicklungspsychologischer und pädagogischer Erkenntnisse an Eltern usw. — Einrichtung von offenen und geschlossenen Betreuungsstellen in Gebieten mit besonderer Jugendgefährdung (zum Beispiel bei starken Truppenansammlungen) — Errichtung von Auffangstellen für obdachlose Jugendliche — Überwachung der Durchführung des Jugendarbeitsschutz-Gesetzes durch die Gewerbeaufsichtsämter — Einrichtung berufspädagogischer und berufspsychologischer Beratungsdienste — Schaffung eines Schülerlotsendienstes zur Verminderung der Verkehrsgefährdung — Durchführung von Filmpädagogischen Seminaren, Jugend-Filmveranstaltungen und Filmdiskussionen mit Jugendlichen — Steuerbegünstigung für pädagogisch betreute Sonder-Filmveranstaltungen für die Jugend — Einführung der Filmerziehung an Schulen. Das Wissenschaftliche Institut für Jugendfilmfragen in München wurde 1956 von den obersten Jugendwohlfahrtsbehörden der Länder mit der Ausarbeitung von Richtlinien für die Freigabe von Filmen für die Jugend durch die Freiwillige Filmselbstkontrolle (FSK) betraut. Außerdem wurde eine Prüfung von Film-Werbematerial erreicht, die Vorführung von Werbevorspannen zu nicht jugendfreien Filmen vor Kindern und Jugendlichen verhindert. 1954 wurde die dem Bundesinnenministerium zugeordnete *Bundesprüfstelle für jugendgefährdende Schriften* geschaffen, 1956 im freien Raum das *Deutsche Jugendschriftenwerk* als besondere Form der „literarischen Jugendhilfe“ gegründet. Dieses Gremium hat sich die Beurteilung von Kleinschriften und die Verbreitung für die Jugend geeigneter Hefte zur Aufgabe gemacht. 1957 kam — analog der Freiwilligen Filmselbstkontrolle — die freiwillige „Selbstkontrolle der Illustrierten“ zustande. Die Schutz- und Erziehungsmaßnahmen im Bereich der Justiz seien nur summarisch genannt.

Ausblick

Mit dem Achten Bundesjugendplan ist die Förderungsaktion der Bundesregierung in eine neue Phase getreten. Die Programme der ersten sieben Bundesjugendpläne (1950 bis 1956) dienten dazu, einen entscheidenden Anstoß zur Beseitigung der akuten Notstände der jungen Generation in der Nachkriegszeit zu leisten. Dabei kristallisierten sich die Schwerpunkte: Jugendwohnheime, berufsfördernde Maßnahmen, politische Bildung, Jugendherbergen und vor allem die Hilfe für die jugendlichen Flüchtlinge aus der sogenannten DDR heraus. Nunmehr soll eine Reform im Bereich des Jugendlebens und der Jugendhilfe angebahnt werden. Das Hauptgewicht des Bundesjugendplans liegt dabei auf der Entwicklung von Modellprojekten für die

Freizeitgestaltung in Schwerpunkten der Jugendarbeit, auf der Aus- und Fortbildung von ehrenamtlichen und beruflichen Jugendleitern und auf der Förderung der politischen Bildung.

Jugendgesetzgebung

Bei der Vielschichtigkeit der Jugendprobleme mußte der vorliegende Beitrag sich auf eine Reihe von Schwerpunkten konzentrieren. Schulische und studentische Fragen wurden bewußt ausgeklammert, da sie an anderer Stelle dieses Buches behandelt werden. Es soll jedoch noch hervorgehoben werden, daß die Jugendhilfe des Bundes auch in der *Jugendgesetzgebung* und der Berücksichtigung der Jugendprobleme im Rahmen der Gesamtpolitik zum Ausdruck kommt. Während der Legislaturperiode des Ersten Deutschen Bundestages wurden vier Jugendgesetze verabschiedet, und zwar das *Gesetz zum Schutz der Jugend in der Öffentlichkeit*, das *Gesetz über die Verbreitung jugendgefährdender Schriften*, die *Novelle zum Reichs-Jugendgerichtsgesetz* und die *Novelle zum Reichs-Jugendwohlfahrts-Gesetz*, durch die der Boden für das „Jugendamt neuer Prägung" bereitet werden sollte. Am 1.10.1957 trat die Neufassung des *Gesetzes zum Schutz der Jugend in der Öffentlichkeit*, in der das Jugendschutzalter im allgemeinen auf 18 Jahre erhöht wurde, in Kraft. Alle diese Gesetze sind im Grunde Erziehungsgesetze. Sie sind auf folgenden jugendpolitischen Grundgedanken aufgebaut: Schutz der Jugend vor den Schäden der Zivilisation — Hilfe für die jungen Menschen in den Krisen der Entwicklungsjahre — Erziehung der Erwachsenen zum Jugendschutz — Pflichten des Staates zur Jugendförderung auch außerhalb der Schule — Zusammenarbeit des Staates mit den Jugendgemeinschaften und den freien Organisationen der Jugendhilfe auf der Basis der Gleichberechtigung.

Zu den Jugendgesetzen, deren Verabschiedung in der Legislaturperiode des Dritten Deutschen Bundestages ansteht, gehören ein neuzeitliches Jugendarbeitsschutz-Gesetz und eine grundsätzliche Reform des Jugendwohlfahrts-Gesetzes. Da die Auswirkung der Novelle zum Reichs-Jugendwohlfahrts-Gesetz (1953) vielfach hinter den auf sie gesetzten Erwartungen zurückblieb, wurde im Herbst 1957 von der Arbeitsgemeinschaft für Jugendpflege und Jugendfürsorge und dem Deutschen Verein für öffentliche und private Fürsorge eine Kommission gebildet, die sich eingehend mit einer Neugestaltung des Jugendwohlfahrtsrechts befassen soll. Dabei wird die Prüfung des Jugendwohlfahrtsrechts auf seinen pädagogischen Grundgehalt wesentlich sein. Über eine Reihe von fachlichen Fragen der Jugendfürsorge hinaus ergibt sich besonders das Problem der Neuregelung der Ausbildungsbeihilfen und der damit in engem Zusammenhang stehenden Fragen der Begabtenförderung.

Organisatorische Fragen

Aus dem dritten Teil des Jugendprogramms des Bundes — Maßnahmen im Rahmen der allgemeinen Politik, vor allem der Sozialpolitik — seien einzelne gesetzliche Bestimmungen, welche die Jugend angehen, in Stichworten angedeutet: Jugendsprecher im Betrieb — Berücksichtigung der Lehrlinge im Vertriebenengesetz — Steuerfreiheit für zahlreiche Jugendeinrichtungen — Schutz jugendlicher Arbeiter im Ausland — Devisen-Freibeträge für Jugendfahrten — neue Bestimmungen für Jugendliche im Arbeitsvermittlungsgesetz (AVAVG) und in der Fürsorgepflicht-Verordnung — neuer Jugendstrafvollzug.

Auf Vorschlag der Bundesregierung wurde 1956 ein „*Studienbüro für Jugendfragen*“ gegründet, das seinen Sitz in Bonn hat. Seine Aufgaben sind: sich wissenschaftlich mit den Problemen der Jugendarbeit auseinanderzusetzen, die an Universitäten und Instituten geleisteten Forschungsarbeiten zusammenzufassen und für die Praxis nutzbar zu machen, sowie den auf den Gebieten der Jugendarbeit tätigen Stellen und Organisationen in wissenschaftlichen Fragen zur Seite zu treten und ihnen Anregungen und Material zu vermitteln.

Welche Bedeutung die Bundesregierung den Jugendfragen zumißt, wurde besonders offensichtlich in der ministeriellen Neuordnung nach den Bundestagswahlen 1957. Mit der Regierungsbildung wurde die Arbeitsgruppe Jugend aus dem Bundesministerium des Innern herausgelöst und als Abteilung Jugend dem Familienministerium zugeordnet, das damit zum *Bundesministerium für Familien- und Jugendfragen* erweitert wurde. Die Abteilung Jugend steht gleichgeordnet neben der Abteilung Familienfragen. Ihr Aufgabenbereich umfaßt die Jugendgesetzgebung, den Bundesjugendplan und die Koordinierung der Jugendpolitik der Bundesregierung. Zweck dieser Neuorganisation ist es, die Anliegen der Jugend ihrer Bedeutung entsprechend innerhalb der Bundesregierung stärker zur Geltung kommen zu lassen. Der zuständige Minister formulierte einen Leitgedanken der Jugendpolitik: „Freie Bahn allen aufbauwilligen Kräften im freien Raum im Dienst an der Jugend! Weder Staatsjugend noch Dirigismus, sondern Freiheit in der vielfältigen Jugendarbeit!“ Mit der Neuregelung der Zuständigkeit hat der Bundeskanzler Vorschlägen aus den Kreisen der freien Jugendpflege entsprochen und das Versprechen eingelöst, die Jugendförderung zu einem Schwerpunkt der Regierungspolitik zu machen.

*

Wohl zu keiner Zeit hat man sich mit solcher Gründlichkeit den Kopf über die Probleme der Jugend zerbrochen wie heutzutage. Was ist „Jugend", was sind jugendgemäße Verhaltens- und Ausdrucksweisen heute? Die Jugend hat Millionen Gesichter, und doch lassen bestimmte allgemeingültige Züge sich herausschälen. Nach dem objektiven Sachverhalt ist die junge Generation in der Bundesrepublik sorgsam in die soziale Ordnung eingebettet. Die politische Ausnahmestellung, die der Jugend als „Träger der Nation" im „Dritten Reich" eingeräumt wurde, besteht nicht mehr. Das wird besonders deutlich, wenn man die Lage in der Bundesrepublik mit der in der sogenannten DDR vergleicht, wo die radikale Politisierung der Jugend über den Zusammenbruch hinaus fortgesetzt und ins Extrem gesteigert wurde. Dagegen ist die politische Situation der Jugend in Westdeutschland dadurch gekennzeichnet, daß die eigentlichen Erziehungsmächte — Elternhaus, Schule und Kirche — einen guten Teil des Einflusses zurückgewonnen haben, den sie unter dem HITLER-Regime an den Staat verloren hatten.

Die heutige Jugend ist nicht revolutionär. Mit großer Beweglichkeit paßt sie sich den Daseinsbedingungen in einem hoch zivilisierten und technisierten Wohlstandsstaat an. Sie ist ungewöhnlich lebenstüchtig. In ihren Organisationen und Institutionen praktiziert sie die demokratischen Spielregeln. Sie genügt der Wahlpflicht und — trotz dem Recht auf Wehrdienstverweigerung — der Wehrpflicht. Die sozialen Errungenschaften nimmt sie als selbstverständlich hin, und die Technik ist für sie kein seelisch belastendes Problem. Allen düsteren Prognosen zum Trotz hat sie sich immun gezeigt gegen rechts- und linksradikale Einflüsse. Sie ist tolerant, kritisch und illusionslos, frei von Dogmatik und Militanz. Vagen Idealismus, Pathos und Romantik lehnt sie ab. Doch sind in diesem geistigen Ernüchterungsprozeß auch das Traditionsbewußtsein und das Gefühl für echte geschichtliche Werte verloren gegangen. „Die skeptische Generation" nennt der bekannte Soziologe Professor SCHELSKY seine 1957 erschienene umfangreiche Untersuchung. Darin findet sich auch eine Antwort auf die Frage: Was ist von der heutigen Generation in Zukunft zu erwarten? „Man wird sich auf keine Abenteuer einlassen, sondern immer auf die Karte der Sicherheit setzen. In allem, was man so gern weltgeschichtliches Geschehen nennt, wird diese Jugend eine stille Generation werden, eine Generation, die sich auf das Überleben eingerichtet hat."

DER SPORT

Dem Sport kommt im Leben des Bundesbürgers große Bedeutung zu. Sie wächst in dem Maße, in dem die wöchentliche Arbeitszeit abnimmt und die damit gewonnene Freizeit zunehmend weitere Möglichkeiten sportlicher Betätigung erschließt. Das große Interesse, dessen der Sport in breitesten Volksschichten sich erfreut, wird besonders deutlich, wenn sonntags (oft jetzt auch schon samstags) Zehntausende von Zuschauern von nah und fern in die Stadien zu den großen repräsentativen Fußballspielen eilen, oder wenn Millionen von Hörern und Zuschauern an den Rundfunk- und Fernsehapparaten die Fußballspiele von internationalem Rang oder andere wichtige Sportereignisse miterleben. Die Fußballweltmeisterschaften 1954 in der Schweiz und 1958 in Schweden waren Begebenheiten, die im Bewußtsein der Öffentlichkeit wochenlang alle Ereignisse in Politik, Kultur und Wirtschaft verdrängten und damit in der Bevölkerung einen Widerhall fanden, der seinesgleichen sucht.

Das sportliche Interesse beschränkt sich nicht auf die Teilnahme an spektakulären Ereignissen. Es betätigt sich auch in einem regen Vereinsleben, das bis ins letzte Dorf hinein die sportfreudigen Einwohner beiderlei Geschlechts vereint und damit dem Sport allerorts aktive Teilnehmer und dazu eine große Gemeinde von zahlenden Zuschauern sichert. Im Jahre 1957 wurden 26.116 *Sportvereine* mit insgesamt 4.309.524 Mitgliedern, darunter 933.638 weiblichen, gezählt. Ausgeprägtester Volkssport ist der Fußball. Im Jahre 1958 umfaßte der Deutsche Fußballbund 13.734 Vereine mit 61.779 spielenden Mannschaften und insgesamt 1.773.711 Mitgliedern. Nicht minder eindrucksvoll sind die Zahlen der Zuschauer beim Fußball; man schätzt sie an manchen Wochenenden auf 5 Millionen.

Aber auch andere Sportarten sind sehr verbreitet. So hat der Deutsche Turnerbund jetzt 7.791 Vereine mit 1.342.901 Mitgliedern, darunter 550.703 Turnerinnen. Mit besonderem Glanz wird alle fünf Jahre das Deutsche Turnfest gefeiert, das — wie das Turnen in Deutschland überhaupt — schon an eine ehrwürdige Tradition anknüpfen kann. Die Leichtathletik hat natürlich viele Anhänger, steht sie doch bei den Olympischen Spielen immer wieder im Mittelpunkt des Geschehens. Dasselbe gilt vom Wintersport, der in jedem Jahr viele Tausende Frauen und Männer aller Altersklassen ins Gebirge lockt. Auch Tennis ist viel beliebter und verbreiteter als die derzeitig ungewöhnlich schwache deutsche Position auf internationalen Turnieren ahnen läßt. Die regelmäßig im Hochsommer stattfindenden Internationalen

Deutschen Meisterschaften in Hamburg gehören zu den Spitzenturnieren der Welt. Erwähnt seien noch das Schwimmen und als deutsche Domänen im internationalen Vergleich Reiten und Handball — drei Sportarten, die ebenfalls viele Anhänger haben. Das jährlich veranstaltete Internationale Reitturnier in Aachen ist ein sportlich wie gesellschaftlich im In- und Ausland weithin anerkanntes Ereignis. Der Sport ist somit zu einem sehr beachtlichen Faktor in der Bundesrepublik geworden.

*

Der Staat verzichtet bewußt auf jede Einflußnahme. Alle organisatorischen und fachlichen Entscheidungen überläßt er der sportlichen Selbstverwaltung, deren oberste Dachorganisation der *Deutsche Sportbund* ist. Sein Präsident darf als der berufene Wortführer für den deutschen Sport gelten. In dieser Eigenschaft verhandelt er mit der Bundesregierung und den Länderregierungen und nimmt an internationalen Beratungen teil. Der Deutsche Sportbund wird aus den Landessportbünden und den Sportfachverbänden gebildet. Er ist also regional und fachlich gegliedert. Die Landessportbünde sind die Zusammenschlüsse aller privaten Sportorganisationen und -vereine innerhalb eines regionalen Bezirks, in der Regel eines Bundeslandes. Ihre Vertretung im Deutschen Sportbund spiegelt also den föderativen Aufbau der Bundesrepublik wider. Die *Sportfachverbände* (Spitzenverbände) dagegen sind die das gesamte Bundesgebiet umfassenden Organisationen der einzelnen Sparten. Es gibt ihrer siebenundzwanzig:

Deutscher Amateur-Box-Verband,
Deutscher Athleten-Bund,
Deutscher Badminton Verband,
Deutscher Basketball-Bund,
Deutscher Bob- und Schlittensportverband,
Deutscher Eissport-Verband,
Deutscher Fechter-Bund,
Deutscher Fußball-Bund,
Deutscher Golf-Verband,
Deutscher Handball-Bund,
Deutscher Hockey-Bund,
Deutscher Judo-Bund,
Deutscher Kanu-Verband,
Deutscher Keglerbund,
Deutscher Leichtathletik-Verband,
Bund Deutscher Radfahrer,
Verband der Reit- und Fahrvereine im Bundesgebiet,
Deutscher Rollsport-Bund,
Deutscher Ruderverband
Deutscher Rugby-Verband,
Deutscher Schützenbund,
Deutscher Schwimm-Verband,
Deutscher Segler-Verband,
Deutscher Skiverband,
Deutscher Tennis Bund,
Deutscher Tisch-Tennis-Bund,
Deutscher Turner-Bund.

Mitglieder des Deutschen Sportbundes sind außerdem noch einige andere Organisationen wie zum Beispiel: Deutscher Aero-Club, Deutscher Billard-Bund, Deutscher Schachbund und Verband Deutscher Sportfischer.

Diese Aufzählung vermittelt einen Einblick in die Vielfalt der sportlichen Betätigung. Bedeutung, Mitgliederzahl und Finanzkraft aller dieser Verbände sind natürlich sehr unterschiedlich. Während die großen Vereine der populären Sportarten große Einnahmen aus Mitgliederbeiträgen und Zuschauergeldern haben, sind andere Sparten vielfach auf Unterstützung durch Dritte, vor allem die öffentliche Hand, angewiesen.

Sport wird selbstverständlich auch außerhalb der Sportorganisationen getrieben. Dabei ist vornehmlich an den Schulsport zu denken, aber auch an Wandern, Schwimmen, Rudern, Skilaufen und viele andere Sportzweige, die nicht so sehr an kostspielige Anlagen und Einrichtungen gebunden sind. Zunehmend festigt sich die Überzeugung, daß zum körperlichen und geistigen Wohlbefinden auch noch im vorgeschrittenen Lebensalter irgendein systematisch betriebener Sport gehören sollte.

*

Der Staat und die Gemeinde verwalten den Sport nicht, sie fördern und unterstützen ihn aber nach Kräften. Die Hilfe besteht vor allem in der *Anlage von Spiel- und Sportplätzen.* Sie gilt vornehmlich als Aufgabe der Gemeinden. Es gibt allein zweiunddreißig städtische Stadionanlagen mit einem jeweiligen Fassungsvermögen für mehr als 30.000 Zuschauer. Die Stadien in Stuttgart, Berlin und Frankfurt am Main haben sogar für mehr als 90.000 Zuschauer Platz. Neben diesen Großanlagen, die mehr dem Schaubedürfnis der großstädtischen Bevölkerung dienen, entstehen überall in Stadt und Land Sportplätze, Schwimmanlagen und Turnhallen. Ihre Träger sind meistens die Gemeinden, häufig auch Sportvereine. Der Bau wird vielfach im Zusammenwirken zwischen Gemeinde und Sportverein finanziert. Auch die Länder geben zum Teil erhebliche Zuschüsse, und selbst der Bundeshaushalt enthält seit 1957 einen Betrag von 5 Millionen DM für den Bau von Sportstätten. Nach den Richtlinien des Deutschen Städtetages werden 4 Quadratmeter nutzbare Spielplatzfläche auf den Kopf der Bevölkerung gefordert; ein Ziel, das bisher natürlich erst in wenigen Städten erreicht ist.

Auch für diejenigen Sportarten, die nicht dem Massensport zuzurechnen sind, entstehen neue Anlagen. Es gibt zum Beispiel heute etwa sechzig Ruderregatta-Bahnen und etwa fünfzig größere Golfplätze in der Bundesrepublik. Besonderes Augenmerk gilt außerdem dem Bau von Schwimmanlagen, auch auf dem flachen Land; denn die zunehmende Verschmutzung der Flüsse durch Industrieabwässer läßt das Baden und Schwimmen in ihnen nicht mehr zu.

TURN- UND SPORTSTÄTTEN IM JAHRE 1955[1]

Art	Turn- und Sportstätten Anzahl	Sportfläche 1.000 qm
Turn- und Sporthallen, Gymnastikräume	6.614[2]	1.610[2]
Stadien und Sportplätze	16.885	124.473
Freibäder und Badeanstalten in Naturgewässern	3.097[3]	10.020[3]
Hallenbäder	186	44
Bootshäuser (für mehr als fünf Boote)	863	—
Tennisplätze	4.388	2.902[4]
Rollschuhbahnen	115	95
Kunsteis- und Natureisbahnen	401	11.818
Sprungschanzen	266	—
Rodel- und Bobbahnen	171	—
Sonstige Turn- und Sportstätten[5]	7.283	—

[1] Bundesrepublik Deutschland (ohne Saarland). — [2] Teilweise ohne Nordrhein-Westfalen und Bayern. — [3] Teilweise ohne Hamburg. — [4] Ohne Schleswig-Holstein. — [5] Golfplätze (ohne Hessen), Reitsportanlagen, Radrennbahnen, Kegelbahnen, sportliche Schießstände sowie Regattabahnen. Quelle: Statistisches Bundesamt.

In der Verwaltung der meisten größeren Städte (in weit über hundert Städten) gibt es eine besondere Dienststelle für die Angelegenheiten der Leibesübungen und des Sports, meist als „*Sportamt*“ bezeichnet. Ihre Aufgabe besteht in der Verwaltung der kommunalen Sportanlagen und -einrichtungen, der Betreuung der Vereine und vor allem auch des nicht organisierten Sports, der Einrichtung von sportärztlichen Beratungsstellen und ähnlichen Förderungsmaßnahmen. Diese städtischen Sportämter haben sich in der „Arbeitsgemeinschaft Deutscher Sportämter“ zusammengeschlossen. Sie trägt insbesondere für Erfahrungsaustausch und Erarbeitung statistischen Materials Sorge. Auch die Länderregierungen haben Sportreferenten, die meist bei den Kultusministerien ressortieren. Innerhalb der Bundesregierung ist der Sport mit einem besonderen Referat in der Abteilung für kulturelle Angelegenheiten des Bundes im Bundesministerium des Innern vertreten.

Die finanziellen Aufwendungen der Gemeinden für Zwecke des Sports sind erheblich. Sie betrugen im Rechnungsjahr 1956 rund 110 Millionen DM. Eine beachtliche Geldquelle für den Sport, der daraus jährlich Mittel bis zu 50 Millionen DM erhält, ist auch das Fußballtoto, wenngleich es nicht mehr so reichlich wie in den Anfängen fließt. Der Sport hat aber auch erhebliche Eigeneinnahmen aus Beiträgen der Vereinsmitglieder und aus

Zuschauergeldern. Diese letzten werden mit mindestens 200 Millionen DM jährlich beziffert. In der Masse kommen sie freilich nur einigen wenigen Sportarten zugute.

*

Eine weitere sehr gewichtige Förderung erfährt der Sport dadurch, daß er überall in den Schulen obligatorisch ist. Länder und Gemeinden sorgen für die Bereitstellung von Sportstätten und Sportgerät für die Schuljugend und für die fachliche Ausbildung der Sportlehrer. Besondere Werbekraft geht von den *Bundesjugendspielen* aus. Dieser sportliche Wettbewerb setzt seit dem Jahre 1951 die früheren Reichsjugendwettkämpfe im Gebiet der Bundesrepublik fort. Er wird in enger Zusammenarbeit zwischen der Bundesregierung, den Ländern und den Sportorganisationen durchgeführt und erfaßt die gesamte Schuljugend. Im Jahre 1957 beteiligten sich an den Bundesjugendspielen (Sommer- und Winterspiele) weit über 5 Millionen Jugendliche. Diese hohe Teilnehmerzahl wird dank der Mitwirkung der Schulen erreicht. Die Bundesjugendspiele dürften damit der größte sportliche Wettbewerb in der Welt sein, der nach einer einheitlichen hierfür besonders ausgearbeiteten Ausschreibung abgehalten wird.

*

Seit 1952 hat der Deutsche Sportbund das *Deutsche Sportabzeichen* wieder einheitlich für das Bundesgebiet eingeführt. Es gilt als Auszeichnung für eine fünffach gute sportliche Durchschnittsleistung und will eine Leistungsprüfung auf Herz- und Lungenkraft, auf Spannkraft, auf den Besitz ausreichender Körperfertigkeit, Schnelligkeit und Ausdauer sein. Wie früher wird es entsprechend den Altersklassen in Bronze, Silber oder Gold verliehen. In der gleichen Form ist das Jugendsportabzeichen für Jugendliche zwischen dreizehn und achtzehn Jahren wieder eingeführt worden. Im Jahre 1952 konnten 22.563 Leistungsabzeichen verliehen werden, im Jahre 1956 waren es schon 37.581 Abzeichen.

*

Nicht nur die Schulen, auch die Hochschulen fördern jede Art sportlicher Betätigung. Führendes Organ des Hochschulsports ist der im Jahre 1949 gebildete *Deutsche Hochschulausschuß für Leibesübungen.* Er fungiert als „Arbeitsgemeinschaft der Lehrenden und Lernenden der Deutschen Hochschulen in gemeinsamen Fragen der Leibesübungen". Professoren, Dozenten und Studenten sind in ihm zusammengefaßt. Er führt Lehrgänge für Sportlehrer durch und berät in allen sportwissenschaftlichen Fragen. Mit der

Durchführung des allgemeinen Studentensports sind dagegen die jeweiligen Institute für Leibesübungen an den Hochschulen beauftragt. Die Teilnahme an dem studentischen Sport steht jedem Studenten offen, ist aber keineswegs Pflicht.

Die Hochschulinstitute für Leibesübungen haben nicht nur die Aufgabe, den studentischen Sport zu betreuen. Einigen von ihnen obliegt auch die Ausbildung derjenigen Studenten, die neben einem oder zwei anderen wissenschaftlichen Fächern das Fach Leibeserziehung für das höhere Lehramt wählen.

Eine zentrale Ausbildungsstätte für den Sportlehrernachwuchs ist die *Sporthochschule in Köln*. Sie wurde im Jahre 1947 durch das Land Nordrhein-Westfalen als Nachfolgerin der seit 1920 bestehenden Deutschen Hochschule für Leibesübungen in Berlin gegründet. Ihre Aufgabe ist die Lehre und Forschung auf dem Gebiet der Leibeserziehung. Die Sportstudenten in Köln können nach einer dreijährigen Ausbildung in Theorie und Praxis die Prüfung als Diplomsportlehrer ablegen und nach einer vierjährigen Ausbildung das Staatsexamen in sportlicher Leibeserziehung machen. Daneben gibt es andere Bildungswege mit dem Ziel der Ausbildung zum staatlich geprüften Schulsportlehrer, zum Lehrer im Schulsonderturnen oder zum Schwimmeister. Die Forschung an der Sporthochschule in Köln erstreckt sich auf alle Bereiche der Leibeserziehung, wie die Sportpädagogik, die Sportmedizin, die Soziologie der Leibesübungen und die Geschichte des Sports.

Der Versehrtensport wird als ein Mittel zur Stärkung der Lebensfreude und als Heilmaßnahme für Körperbehinderte besonders gefördert. Schon im Jahre 1955 bestanden in der Bundesrepublik 305 Versehrtensportgruppen. Davon sind ungefähr 139 selbständige Vereine oder Gruppen und 166 Gruppen örtlichen Sportvereinen angeschlossen. Auch um die Beratung dieser Gruppen des Versehrtensports bemüht sich die Sporthochschule in Köln.

*

Die internationalen Beziehungen werden so intensiv wie möglich auf allen Sportgebieten gepflegt. Der jeweilige Leistungsstand wird also stets an internationalen Maßstäben gemessen. Höhepunkte auch der deutschen Sportbegeisterung bringen die Olympischen Spiele. Ihre Vorbereitung liegt in den Händen des *Nationalen Olympischen Komitees*. Seine Aufgaben werden durch die finanzielle Hilfe der Bundesregierung gefördert. Das antike Stadion in Olympia wird zur Zeit in Zusammenarbeit zwischen deutschen

Archäologen und Sportlern in seinem ursprünglichen Zustand wiederhergestellt. Man hofft, daß diese Arbeit bis zum Beginn der Olympischen Spiele im Sommer 1960 beendet ist.

*

Die Alternative: *Breitensport im Dienste der Volksgesundheit oder Förderung von Spitzenleistungen* zur Erzielung international beachtlicher Erfolge beherrscht auch in Deutschland die öffentliche Diskussion. Von ihr wird auch das Problem des Berufsspielertums berührt. Die Bundesrepublik kennt den Berufsspieler im Fußball nicht, wohl aber den Kompromiß des sogenannten Vertragsspielers, dem es gestattet ist, begrenzte Einkünfte aus seinen Fußballspielen zu erzielen. Es wird erstrebt, Breiten- und Spitzensport zu einer Synthese zu vereinigen, indem man die ethischen und volkshygienischen Werte des Sports zu bewahren trachtet und andererseits auch dem Publikumsbedürfnis nach international gültigen Spitzenleistungen Rechnung trägt. Man hofft auf gegenseitige Befruchtung und Ergänzung. Höchstleistungen, die nicht krampfhaft gezüchtet werden, sondern im Spiel organisch wachsen, bauen am ehesten auf einer Sportbewegung auf, die möglichst weite Schichten umfaßt — also in einem sportlich gesunden Volk. Umgekehrt wirken Rekorde anfeuernd und begeisternd und gewinnen immer weitere Kreise für den sportlichen Wettkampf. Es wird viel darauf ankommen, beide Elemente im ausgewogenen Gleichgewicht zu halten, wenn der Sport weiter ein so positiver Bestandteil unseres kulturellen Lebens bleiben soll, als der er bisher mit Recht betrachtet wurde.

DIE KIRCHEN

I. DIE CHRISTLICHEN KIRCHEN

Die Auseinandersetzung mit dem Nationalsozialismus und ihre Folgen

Vor 1945 waren die Kirchen eines der *Zentren des Widerstandes* gegen die totalitäre Gewalt. Sie waren nicht eigentlich eine „Widerstandsbewegung"; denn ihre Ablehnung der Herrschaft des Nationalsozialismus ergab sich nicht vorwiegend aus einer politischen Stellungnahme; sie war vielmehr in ihrer Verkündigung und ihrem Auftrag in der Welt überhaupt begründet. Die christlichen Kirchen waren daher den Gleichschaltungs- und Unterdrückungsmaßnahmen des „Dritten Reiches" gegenüber nur wenig zugänglich.

Der Nationalsozialismus sah von Anfang an in den Kirchen seine grundsätzlichen Gegner. Deshalb versuchte er zunächst, das kirchliche *Organisationsleben* lahmzulegen. Die Organisationen sollten aufgelöst und gleichgeschaltet, ihre führenden Persönlichkeiten als Staatsfeinde gebrandmarkt werden. Gleichzeitig wurde das kirchliche *Schrifttum*, Zeitungen und Vereinsschriften, angegriffen, um den Einfluß der kirchlichen Presse gegen den nationalsozialistischen Ungeist nicht wirksam werden zu lassen.

Der dritte Vorstoß richtete sich gegen den christlichen Charakter der Schulen. Nebenher lief die Bespitzelung der Predigten, der Druck auf die Geistlichen in jeder Form: Verwarnungen und Verweise, Verhöre und Haussuchungen, Schul- und Redeverbot, Ausweisung und Geldstrafen, Schutz- und Untersuchungshaft, Konzentrationslager und Hinrichtungen.

Die Führerschaft der Partei mag zunächst geglaubt haben, daß es möglich sein würde, die Kirche von innen her aufzuspalten und zu überwinden. In die Evangelische Kirche gelang dem Nationalsozialismus ein verhältnismäßig starker Einbruch in der Form der „Deutschen Christen". Durch den Widerstand der „*Bekennenden Kirche*" und die zunehmende Besinnung auf die geistliche Grundlage der Kirche wurde er jedoch im wesentlichen abgefangen. Gegen Ende des „Dritten Reiches" hatte der Nationalsozialismus unter den Amtsträgern der Evangelischen Kirche nur noch wenige Anhänger.

Selbstverständlich sind auch viele Katholiken der Nationalsozialistischen Partei beigetreten, aber kaum einer der führend in der katholischen Arbeit Stehenden. Einige Mitglieder beider Konfessionen haben sich am Anfang der Partei angeschlossen, weil sie auf diese Weise vieles retten zu können glaubten. Die meisten von ihnen haben ihren Irrtum bald erkannt. Gewiß sind auch manche Katholiken unter dem Druck des Regimes aus der Kirche ausgetreten. Obgleich die Katholische Kirche wesentlich geringere Austrittsziffern hatte als die Evangelische, traten im Jahre 1937, dem Höhepunkt dieser staatlich gelenkten Bewegung, 108.000 Katholiken aus. Meistens handelte es sich um solche, die innerlich bereits abseits standen. Andere haben trotz stärkstem Druck den Austritt nicht vollzogen und lieber ihre Stellung und persönliche Sicherheit geopfert.

Die Lehrerschaft hat in ihrer Mehrzahl weiterhin kirchliche Erziehungsarbeit geleistet, obgleich diese besonders den katholischen Lehrern sehr erschwert wurde. Aus dem Gemeinde- und Vereinsleben und vor allem aus dem Klerus wurde schärfster Widerstand gegen das Regime geleistet. Der Widerstand beider Kirchen war innerlich so stark, daß HITLER den letzten Schlag nicht zu führen wagte. Die Pläne des Reichsleiters BORMANN für die Zeit nach dem erwarteten „Endsieg" ließen aber erkennen, daß die Kirchen aus dem Volksleben praktisch ausgeschaltet werden sollten.

*

Nach so vielen Opfern unter Pfarrern und Laien sahen die Kirchen sich 1945 von einem unerhörten Druck befreit, und zugleich wandte sich ihnen eine Welle des Vertrauens aus der ganzen Bevölkerung zu. Als ein sichtbares Beispiel für das Gefühl der Befreiung mag an die Predigt des evangelischen Bischofs von Berlin-Brandenburg D. DIBELIUS auf der ersten Synode nach dem Zusammenbruch erinnert werden. Sie ging über das Wort: „Wenn dich heute oder morgen dein Kind wird fragen: Was ist das?, sollst du ihm sagen: Der Herr hat uns mit mächtiger Hand aus Ägypten, von dem Diensthause, geführt."

Wenn man freilich die seitdem verflossenen vierzehn Jahre in der sogenannten DDR überdenkt, ist offenbar, in welche Nöte die Kirche erneut unter dem Zeichen eines anderen Totalitarismus' geführt worden ist.

Die starke Rückwärtsbewegung zur Kirche nach 1945 beruhte teils auf innerer Umkehr, teils auf Zweckmäßigkeitserwägungen. Seither ist deutlich geworden, daß die Unterdrückung unter HITLER zwar — wie immer bei einer Kirchenverfolgung — zur inneren Stärkung der verbleibenden Gemeinde geführt hat, daß aber die Einbußen zahlenmäßiger Art nicht wieder aufgeholt worden sind, und daß noch viele Deutsche am kirchlichen Leben nicht interessiert sind.

Auch im „Dritten Reich" ist die Zahl der einer Kirche angehörenden Personen aber *niemals unter 94% der Bevölkerung* gesunken. Bei dieser Zahl sind allerdings die Auswirkungen des landesherrlichen Kirchenregiments und des volkskirchlichen Systems zu berücksichtigen. Sie führen vor allem bei der evangelischen Christenheit dazu, daß auch Menschen, die am kirchlichen

Leben gar keinen oder nur einen geringen Anteil nehmen, zumeist *nicht austreten*. Insofern unterscheidet sich die deutsche kirchliche Situation etwa von der amerikanischen sehr wesentlich.

Das unterdrückte kirchliche Vereinsleben war nach 1945 bald wieder lebendig. Leider konnte wegen der entgegenstehenden Bestimmungen der Besatzungsmächte die kirchliche Presse nicht so rasch wieder hergestellt werden. Das innerkirchliche Leben entwickelte sich ebenfalls schnell.

Die Auswirkungen der territorialen Veränderungen in Deutschland auf die Konfessionsgliederung

Vor dem Kriege waren von den rund 69 Millionen Deutschen etwa ein Drittel katholische und zwei Drittel evangelische Christen. Dabei lag das Hauptgewicht des evangelischen Volksteils in den nord- und ostdeutschen Gebieten, während das katholische Element im Westen und Süden überwog.

Die durch die Nachkriegsverhältnisse und die Unterstellung weiter ostdeutscher Gebiete unter sowjetische und polnische Verwaltung bedingte Austreibung und Abwanderung von Millionen deutscher Menschen hat eine

DIE WOHNBEVÖLKERUNG IM BUNDESGEBIET (OHNE SAARLAND) AM 13. 9. 1950[1]
NACH DER RELIGIONSZUGEHÖRIGKEIT
in Prozent

Religionszugehörigkeit	Wohnbevölkerung		
	Insgesamt	darunter	
		Vertriebene	Zugewanderte
	1	2	3
Evangelische Kirche in Deutschland	*50,1*	*17,1*	*4,9*
Freikirchliche Evang. Gemeinden	*1,0*	*19,1*	*3,7*
Römisch-Katholische Kirche	*45,2*	*16,6*	*1,2*
Abendl. romfreie und morgenländ.-kath. Kirchen sowie Angehörige anderer Religionen (außer Juden)	*0,2*	*17,8*	*2,6*
Jüdische Religionsgemeinschaft	*0,0*	*23,6*	*3,2*
Freireligiöse und Freidenker	*3,2*	*7,8*	*6,5*
Ohne Angabe	*0,3*	*12,1*	*6,4*
Insgesamt	*100*	*16,6*	*3,3*

[1] Ergebnisse der letzten Volkszählung. Quelle: Statistisches Bundesamt.

DIE RELIGIONSZUGEHÖRIGKEIT 1950[1]

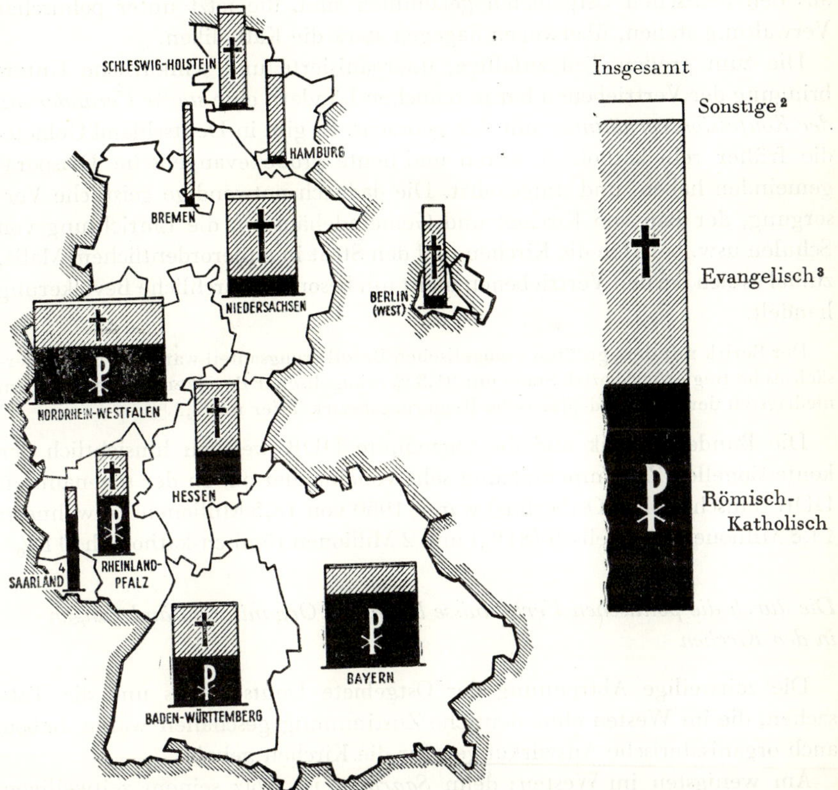

[1] Bundesrepublik Deutschland einschließlich von Saarland und Berlin(West). — [2] Einschließlich von Personen ohne Angabe der Religionszugehörigkeit. — [3] Einschließlich von Angehörigen der romfreien katholischen Kirchen. — [4] Stand: 14.11.1951.
Quelle: Statistisches Bundesamt.

wesentliche Veränderung der Bevölkerungsstruktur und der Konfessionsverhältnisse zur Folge gehabt. Von den seit 1953 durch das Notaufnahmeverfahren der Bundesrepublik gegangenen rund 1,8 Millionen Zugewanderten aus der sogenannten DDR waren von 1953 bis 1958 rund 1,3 Millionen evangelischen und knapp eine halbe Million katholischen Glaubens. Unter den in die Bundesrepublik im Jahre 1958 aufgenommenen Aussiedlern und über das freie Ausland aufgenommenen Vertriebenen, die zu einem großen Teil aus den deutschen Ostgebieten gekommen sind, die jetzt unter polnischer Verwaltung stehen, überwogen dagegen stark die Katholiken.

Die zum großen Teil zufällige, unorganisierte und willkürliche Unterbringung der Vertriebenen hat in manchen Ländern eine *starke Veränderung der Konfessionsverhältnisse* mit sich gebracht. Es gibt in Deutschland Gebiete, die früher rein katholisch waren und heute große evangelische Diasporagemeinden haben, und umgekehrt. Die dadurch notwendige geistliche Versorgung, der Bau von Kirchen und Gemeindehäusern, die Einrichtung von Schulen usw. belasten die Kirchen und den Staat in außerordentlichem Maße, zumal es sich bei den Vertriebenen meist um besonders kirchliche Bevölkerung handelt.

Der Bezirk mit dem größten evangelischen Bevölkerungsanteil war 1950 der niedersächsische Regierungsbezirk Stade mit 91,9 % evangelischer Bevölkerung, der mit dem niedrigsten der rheinland-pfälzische Regierungsbezirk Trier mit 7,9 %.

Die Bundesrepublik und die sogenannte DDR weichen hinsichtlich der konfessionellen Zusammensetzung sehr voneinander ab. In der sogenannten DDR (einschließlich Ostberlins) waren 1950 von 18,3 Millionen Einwohnern 14,8 Millionen evangelisch (81 %) und 2 Millionen römisch-katholisch (11 %).

Die durch die politischen Verhältnisse bedingten Organisationsänderungen in den Kirchen

Die zeitweilige Abtrennung der Ostgebiete Deutschlands und die Tatsachen, die im Westen ohne deutsche Zustimmung geschaffen waren, haben auch organisatorische Auswirkungen für die Kirchen gehabt.

Am wenigsten im Westen; denn *Saarland* ist trotz seinem zeitweiligen Sonderstatus in seinen früheren kirchlichen Gliederungen verblieben.

Im Rahmen eines mit dem Land Nordrhein-Westfalen am 19. 12. 1956 abgeschlossenen Kirchenvertrages wurde aus bisherigen Teilen der Erzbistümer bzw. Bistümer Köln, Münster und Paderborn ein neues Bistum Essen (*Ruhrbistum*) gegründet.

Im Osten sind die evangelischen Kirchenprovinzen Ostpreußen, Danzig-Westpreußen und die frühere unierte Kirche in Polen verschwunden. Von der Kirchenprovinz Pommern ist nur der kleine Teil westlich der Oder mit Greifswald und von der Kirchenprovinz Schlesien die Oberlausitz westlich der Neiße mit Görlitz übrig geblieben. Die Kirchenprovinz Brandenburg hat das gesamte Gebiet der Neumark östlich der Oder verloren.

Die verbliebenen Kirchenprovinzen der Evangelischen Kirche der altpreußischen Union (das heißt der Kirchen in den preußischen Provinzen Berlin-Brandenburg, Pommern, Schlesien, Sachsen, Westfalen und Rheinland) haben sich in einer gegenüber der Vorkriegszeit aufgelockerten Form weiterhin in ihrem alten Verband als Evangelische Kirche der Union zusammengeschlossen.

Auf katholischer Seite haben die Diözesanverhältnisse in juristischer Hinsicht sich nur wenig verändert. Das heißt: hinter der Oder-Neiße-Linie bestehen die Diözesen juristisch weiter; aber sie werden nicht mehr von deutschen Bischöfen verwaltet. Dazu gehören Breslau, Ermland und die Prälatur Schneidemühl. Breslau ist auf den Rest von Görlitz und Neuzelle beschränkt. Obwohl der Erzbischof von Breslau, der Bischof von Ermland und der Prälat der Freien Prälatur Schneidemühl verstorben sind, hat der Heilige Stuhl keine Neubesetzung der Bistümer vorgenommen, sondern sie werden durch Generalvikare polnischer Nationalität verwaltet. Ihnen stehen die in der Bundesrepublik befindlichen Kapitularvikare der alten Bistümer gegenüber.

Auch in der sogenannten DDR besteht kirchenrechtlich die alte kirchliche Verwaltung. Meißen ist nach wie vor Bischofssitz, ebenso Berlin. Der Berliner Bischof hat seinen Sitz in Berlin(West). Der größte Teil seiner Diözese befindet sich in der sogenannten DDR und erstreckt sich teilweise in das Gebiet östlich der Oder-Neiße-Linie.

Der Berliner Weihbischof wohnt im Ostsektor Berlins. Große Teile des Erzbistums Paderborn und der Bistümer Osnabrück, Fulda und Würzburg liegen in der sogenannten DDR. Für das Leben im sächsischen Bereich des Erzbistums Paderborn ist es von großer Bedeutung, daß ein Paderborner Weihbischof seinen Sitz in Magdeburg erhalten hat. Das gleiche gilt von dem zweiten Weihbischof des Bistums Fulda, der in Erfurt seinen Sitz hat.

Das *Reichskonkordat* zwischen dem heiligen Stuhl und dem Deutschen Reich vom 20. 7. 1933 ist nach dem Urteil des Bundesverfassungsgerichts vom 26. 3. 1957 weiter gültig. Die Bundesrepublik ist verpflichtet, die Bestimmungen des Konkordats durchzuführen. Die Bundesrepublik hat jedoch nach dem neuen Verfassungsrecht keine rechtliche Möglichkeit, die Länder zur Durchführung des Konkordats anzuhalten. Frühere Staatskirchenverträge zwischen Evangelischen Landeskirchen und Ländern bestehen fort. Einzelne Länder und Evangelische Landeskirchen haben das evangelische Staatskirchenrecht in Kirchenverträgen in einem, dem neuen partnerschaftlichen Verhältnis von Kirche und Staat entsprechenden, Geist neu geordnet[1].

[1] Staatsverträge von Loccum 1955, Kiel 1957, Detmold 1958.

Die Neuordnung der Evangelischen Kirche

Gegenüber dem losen Deutschen Evangelischen Kirchenbund hatte die 1933 gegründete Deutsche Evangelische Kirche einen wesentlich engeren Zusammenschluß der evangelischen Landeskirchen mit sich gebracht. Dieser wurde jedoch durch die vom Nationalsozialismus inszenierte Gleichschaltung und Gewaltherrschaft entscheidend diskreditiert. Schon während des „Dritten Reiches" hatte der württembergische Landesbischof alle zu einer kirchlichen Zusammenarbeit bereiten Kräfte in einem krichlichen Einigungswerk zusammengefaßt. Kurz nach dem Zusammenbruch trat in der Anstalt der Inneren Mission Treysa in Hessen eine von allen Kirchen beschickte Kirchenversammlung zusammen. Auch die damals noch in Breslau vorhandene evangelische Kirchenleitung Schlesiens war vertreten.

Anfang August 1945 wurde eine vorläufige Ordnung der „*Evangelischen Kirche in Deutschland*" (E.K.D.) festgelegt und ein aus zwölf Theologen und Laien bestehender „Rat" als synodales Leitungsorgan unter Vorsitz des Landesbischofs WURM gewählt.

1948 trat eine weitere Kirchenversammlung in Eisenach zusammen, die eine Verfassung, die *Grundordnung der Evangelischen Kirche in Deutschland*, verabschiedete. Die E.K.D. läßt die Kultus-, Bekenntnis- und Verwaltungsselbständigkeit der Gliedkirchen bestehen. Lediglich in einzelnen bestimmten und ausdrücklich festgelegten Fragen, insbesondere in der Vertretung nach außen und der Versorgung von Auslandsgemeinden, handelt die E.K.D. in eigener Zuständigkeit. Auf der ersten Synode der E.K.D. in Bethel wurde anstelle des wegen seines Alters zurückgetretenen Landesbischofs D. WURM, des Anfang 1953 verstorbenen „großen alten Mannes" der Evangelischen Kirche, der Berliner Bischof D. OTTO DIBELIUS zum Vorsitzenden des Rates und Landesbischof D. HANNS LILJE, Hannover, zum stellvertretenden Vorsitzenden gewählt. Beide wurden auf der Synode in Espelkamp 1955 für weitere sechs Jahre wiedergewählt. Die Kirchenkanzlei hat ihren Sitz in Hannover, Außenstellen in Berlin und Bonn. Das Außenamt ist in Frankfurt am Main.

In den gleichen Jahren war eine stärkere Zusammenfügung der Mehrzahl der lutherischen Gliedkirchen in der „*Vereinigten Ev.-Lutherischen Kirche Deutschlands*" vor sich gegangen. Ihr leitender Bischof ist der niedersächsische Landesbischof D. LILJE. Das lutherische Kirchenamt befindet sich ebenfalls in Hannover; seine Leitung hat — in Personalunion mit der Kirchenkanzlei — Präsident D. BRUNOTTE.

Von den über 40 Millionen evangelischen Kirchengliedern in Gesamtdeutschland gehören etwa 17,5 Millionen zu den zehn Kirchen, welche die Vereinigte Ev.-Lutherische Kirche Deutschlands bilden, 2,5 Millionen zu den übrigen lutherischen Kirchen. Die unierten Kirchen umfassen gut 20 Millionen Glieder. Dabei ist zu bemerken, daß der größte Teil der Gemeinden dieser Kirchen nicht unierten, sondern lutherischen oder reformierten Bekenntnisses, aber dessen ungeachtet in Verwaltungsunionen zusammengefaßt ist. Die beiden reformierten Kirchen umfassen weniger als eine halbe Million Glieder.

Die Evangelische Kirche in Deutschland hat sich von Anfang an bemüht, ihre Funktion als eine *starke Klammer im getrennten Deutschland* wahrzunehmen. Ihre Organe, Rat und Synode, sind aus Gliedern der Kirchen in der Bundesrepublik und der sogenannten DDR nach der zahlenmäßigen Stärke der Kirchen gleichmäßig zusammengesetzt. Die Tagungen der Synode und des Rates haben abwechselnd in Ost und West stattgefunden, die letzte Synode im März 1958 in Ostberlin und in Berlin-Spandau. Anfang 1953 mußte zum erstenmal eine Tagung des Rates, die für München vorgesehen war, nach Berlin(West) verlegt werden, da den Mitgliedern aus der sogenannten DDR die Reisepässe verweigert wurden.

Sämtliche Einrichtungen der Kirche, zum Beispiel die verschiedenen von der Kirche berufenen beratenden Kammern, wie die Jugendkammer, die Kammer für soziale Ordnung und die Kammer für Publizistik, sind für das gesamte deutsche Gebiet tätig. Wo aus Zweckmäßigkeits- oder Rechtsgründen die Einrichtung besonderer Büros für den Osten und Westen erforderlich ist, wie etwa bei der Inneren Mission und dem Evangelischen Hilfswerk, wird die sachliche Arbeit in völliger innerer Gemeinsamkeit und Übereinstimmung geleistet.

Die Zusammenarbeit der Evangelischen Kriche in Deutschland mit den *Freikirchen*, insbesondere den Methodisten und Baptisten, ist seit mehreren Jahren in der „*Arbeitsgemeinschaft christlicher Kirchen in Deutschland*" sichtbar geworden.

Die innere Lage der Kirchen nach 1945

Die Erschütterungen des Kampfes der Kirchen im „Dritten Reich" haben weiterhin nachgewirkt.

Die Kirche war aufgerufen, sich mit den geschaffenen Tatsachen auseinanderzusetzen. Von besonderer Bedeutung ist in diesem Zusammenhang der

Besuch einer Delegation des Weltrates der Kirchen unter Leitung des Bischofs D. BELL von Chichester im Oktober 1945 in Stuttgart gewesen. Er führte zu einer ersten Begegnung mit dem Rat der Evangelischen Kirche in Deutschland. Damals wurde vom Rat die berühmt gewordene *Stuttgarter Schulderklärung* abgegeben. Sie bedeutete nicht, wie man ihr fälschlicherweise unterstellte, die Anerkennung einer Kollektivschuld des deutschen Volkes; aber sie brachte in klarer Weise und in kirchlicher Sprache die *Mitverantwortung* der Christen und der Kirche für das, was in Deutschland und durch Deutsche geschehen war, zum Ausdruck. Von diesem Tage an hat es eine ununterbrochene und vielfältig bewährte *Mitarbeit der Deutschen in den Einrichtungen der Ökumene* gegeben.

Insbesondere haben deutsche Delegationen an den Vollversammlungen des Weltrates der Kirchen in Amsterdam 1948 und Evanston (USA) 1954 (mit der Wahl von Bischof Dr. DIBELIUS zu einem der sechs Präsidenten) und an der Tagung der Bewegung für Glauben und Kirchenverfassung in Lund 1952 teilgenommen. Nicht unerwähnt soll in diesem Zusammenhang auch die Vollversammlung des Lutherischen Weltbundes bleiben, die im Juli 1953 in Hannover stattfand.

Ebenso nehmen die deutschen Katholiken am internationalen katholischen Gemeinschaftsleben wieder teil. Nachdem einmal die Caritas die Brücke der Liebe zum deutschen Volk geschlagen hatte, hat nicht zuletzt durch das Eintreten von Papst PIUS XII. der Deutsche Katholizismus frühzeitig wieder den Anschluß an die internationale katholische Arbeit gefunden.

*

Die starke *Begegnung der evangelischen und katholischen Christen* im Kampf gegen den Nationalsozialismus hat das Verständnis füreinander gestärkt. Gemeinsam hatten sie das Kreuz der Verfolgung zu tragen, gemeinsam in Konzentrationslagern und Gefängnissen gebetet, gemeinsam im Widerstand gegen eine Bewegung gestanden, die das Christentum im deutschen Volke ausrotten wollte. Die theologischen und geschichtlichen Gegensätze der beiden großen Kirchen in Deutschland sind damit freilich nicht überwunden. Deshalb droht gelegentlich wieder die Gefahr einer Verhärtung der konfessionellen Fronten. Naturgemäß haben auch die Verlautbarungen des Heiligen Officiums über die Wiedervereinigung der Kirchen und die darin enthaltenen Weisungen ebenso wie die Dogmatisierung der Himmelfahrt Mariae Auswirkungen gehabt. Diese Auswirkungen zusammen mit unterschiedlichen Ansichten über die Bedeutung des Naturrechts, über die Eheschließung, über das Verhältnis zu den Gewerkschaften, haben jedoch das gefestigte Bewußtsein einer tiefen Verbundenheit und gemeinsamen Verantwortung nicht ernstlich erschüttern können. Die *gemeinsame politische Verantwortung* evangelischer und katholischer Christen wurde seit 1945 in einem bisher in Deutschland nicht bekannten Maße erkannt und in die Tat umgesetzt. Es geht hierbei naturgemäß nicht um Überwindung oder Bagatellisierung konfessioneller Unterschiede, sondern um gemeinsame Wahrnehmung christlicher Verantwortung in der Politik trotz diesen Unterschieden. An den laufenden theologischen Besprechungen nehmen Geistliche beider Konfessionen verantwortlich teil.

*

Die Zeit von 1945 bis heute steht in den Kirchen allgemein im Zeichen einer starken *Aktivierung der Arbeit.*

Insbesondere die Evangelische Kirche hat erkannt, daß die äußere Betriebsamkeit und das Anfassen vieler am Rande des kirchlichen Auftrages liegender Gebiete, wie es vor einem Vierteljahrhundert geübt wurde, kein Kennzeichen inneren kirchlichen Lebens ist.

Die Zeit des Kirchenkampfes hat zwar nicht zu einer breiten Erweckung, aber doch zu einer starken Vertiefung und *Verinnerlichung des Gemeindelebens* geführt. Ernste Bemühungen um die Rückgewinnung verlorengegangener gottesdienstlicher Formen und ihre Einordnung in den Gottesdienst der Gegenwart haben sich in vielfältiger Weise ausgewirkt.

In besonderem Maße ist — von der Jugend ausgehend — das kirchliche Singen gepflegt worden. In beiden Konfessionen gibt es neben den alten bekannten Chören neue hervorragende Jugendchöre. Sie und auch die weltlichen Chöre haben eine äußerst starke Rückbesinnung auf die geistliche Musik erlebt, daneben aber auch junge Komponisten mit moderner geistlicher Musik von großer Bedeutung dem Volke nahegebracht. Es sei nur der Name ERNST PEPPINGs mit seiner außergewöhnlichen Matthäus-Passion genannt.

Die Evangelische Kirche in Deutschland hat im Evangelischen Kirchengesangbuch ein bereits für viele Gliedkirchen eingeführtes einheitliches Gesangbuch geschaffen, das in besonders starkem Maße das Lied der Reformationszeit wieder für den Gottesdienst lebendig macht. Auch mehrere katholische Diözesen haben neue Gesangbücher geschaffen. Dabei ist bemerkenswert, wie stark auch im katholischen Bereich Choräle aus dem protestantischen Bereich aufgenommen sind.

In all diesen Fragen wird eine starke gegenseitige Befruchtung der Kirchen erkennbar.

Beide Kirchen haben nach 1945 die kirchliche studentische Arbeit intensiviert, die schon während der nationalsozialistischen Zeit eine starke Kraft des

Widerstandes gewesen war. Die neuen Verhältnisse geboten neue organisatorische Formen. In der evangelischen Kirche wurde eine „*Evangelische Akademikerschaft*" gegründet. An allen Hochschulen sind besondere Studentengemeinden eingerichtet worden. In der katholischen Arbeit kam es zum Zusammenschluß der kirchlichen Studentenarbeit in der KDSE (*Katholische deutsche Studenteneinigung*). Dazu kommt in beiden Kirchen eine Förderungsarbeit, die darauf abzielt, einen tüchtigen Führungsnachwuchs heranzubilden (*Evangelisches Studienwerk Villigst* und das *Katholische Cusanuswerk*).

Neue Arbeitsformen der Kirche

Die Kirchen beider Konfessionen haben nach 1945 mit großer Tatkraft in ihren Gliederungen und Verbänden die Arbeit verstärkt. Die fast völlige Unterdrückung der christlichen Jugendarbeit unter nationalsozialistischer Herrschaft führte naturgemäß zu einer äußerst starken Intensivierung der Arbeit der Jugend in der Kirche. In vielfältiger Aufgliederung und mannigfachen Formen umfaßt sowohl die evangelische als auch die katholische Jugend einen erheblichen Teil der zur Kirche gehörenden Jugendlichen. Beide Gruppen zusammen stehen in ihrer Stärke mit je fast einer Million Jugendlichen an der Spitze der im Bundesjugendring vereinigten Jugendorganisationen. Keine Jugendbewegung in Deutschland hat ein so verbreitetes Schrifttum wie die katholische.

In der Jugendarbeit ist bei aller Anerkennung der Notwendigkeit jugendlicher Lebensformen in der Tracht und der Gestaltung von Freizeit und Lager eine sehr starke Verinnerlichung und eine Sammlung um die zentralen Fragen der Kirche und des Wortes Gottes festzustellen. Das Verhältnis zwischen Laienführern und geistlichen Führern wird von tiefem Vertrauen getragen.

Auch die übrigen Zweige kirchlichen Lebens haben einen erfreulichen Aufschwung genommen. Sowohl auf katholischer wie evangelischer Seite ist die Männerarbeit stark intensiviert worden. Die Zeitschriften der Männerarbeit beider Kirchen, die zu den größten kirchlichen Zeitschriften überhaupt gehören, zeugen von einer sehr weiträumigen und lebendigen Auseinandersetzung mit den Fragen der Zeit, insbesondere auch im politischen Raum. Das gleiche gilt von der Frauenarbeit.

Die besondere Tradition der *katholischen berufsständischen Arbeit* ist auch heute lebendig. Das Kolpingwerk, die Katholische Arbeiterbewegung und das Katholische Werkvolk sind schnell wieder zur Blüte gelangt. Neuerstanden ist eine Katholische Landjugend- und Landvolkbewegung. Sie erreicht die Stärke des Kolpingwerkes.

Der Familienbund Deutscher Katholiken, eine starke und umfangreiche Mitgliederorganisation, widmet sich familienpolitischer Arbeit und der Pflege des Familiengedankens.

Die Evangelische Kirche, die einer weiträumigen Tradition auf diesem Gebiete entbehrt, ist dabei, auch auf sozialem Gebiet ihrer Öffentlichkeitsaufgabe in stärkerem Maße gerecht zu werden. Die Gründung und erfolgreiche Arbeit der Evangelischen Sozialakademie Friedewald, der evangelischen Aktionsgemeinschaften für Arbeiter- und Familienfragen, der Arbeitsgemeinschaft für den kirchlichen Dienst auf dem Lande und der evangelischen Arbeitsbewegung sind Zeichen für dieses Voranschreiten.

Während die evangelischen Kreise sich im wesentlichen auf den Boden der Einheitsgewerkschaft gestellt haben, hat die 1956 gegründete Christliche Gewerkschaft Deutschlands von Beginn an starke Förderung katholischer Kreise erfahren. Die katholische Arbeiterbewegung hat nach wie vor ihre besonderen, in erster Linie religiösen Aufgaben. Mag sie auch zahlenmäßig nie die Zahlen anderer Gewerkschaften erreichen, so ist doch die innere Geschlossenheit und das Auftreten von mehreren hunderttausend katholischen Arbeitern ein bedeutsames Element im sozialwirtschaftlichen Leben. Die CAJ, die Christliche Arbeiterjugend, wächst ständig und bewußt in die Arbeiterbewegung hinein.

Von besonderer Bedeutung ist das seit 1945 begonnene *Gespräch der Kirche* mit den verschiedensten Berufsständen und die Auseinandersetzung mit den Fragen des politischen, wirtschaftlichen, sozialen und kulturellen Lebens. Ausgehend von der Akademie in Bad Boll haben die „*Evangelischen Akademien*", die es jetzt in fast jeder Gliedkirche gibt, vielseitige und lebendige Arbeit geleistet, indem sie immer neue Gesprächspartner zu einer echten Diskussion auf der Grundlage des Wortes Gottes in ihren Kreis zogen. Industrielle, Arbeiter, Lehrer, Bauern, Journalisten, Beamte, Politiker, Juristen, um nur einige zu nennen, sind die immer stärkstens innerlich beteiligten Besucher der Tagungen der Akademien. Zum Beispiel haben an den Tagungen der Evangelischen Akademie in Hermannsburg, jetzt in Loccum, von 1946 bis 1958: 42.391 Menschen teilgenommen. Es wird sehr viel davon abhängen, ob die Teilnehmer dieser Gespräche, die zum großen Teil den Weg zur Kirche erst wieder zurückfinden müssen, aus der sie anpackenden Diskussion den *Weg in die Gemeinde hinein* gehen.

Inzwischen sind nach dem Vorbild von Stuttgart-Hohenheim, der ersten katholischen Akademie, auch eine Reihe weiterer katholischer Akademien eröffnet worden, die den gleichen Zielen dienen wollen. Es war ein

Kennzeichen des inneren Miteinanders auf dem kirchlichen Gebiet, daß der damalige evangelische Bundestagspräsident, Dr. EHLERS, aufgefordert wurde, auf der ersten Tagung der Katholischen Akademie in Stuttgart einen Vortrag über die gemeinsame Verantwortung der Konfessionen im öffentlichen Raum zu halten.

Aber die Kirchen sind in den vergangenen Jahren in noch weiterem Maße in die Öffentlichkeit hineingegangen. Neben die *Deutschen Katholikentage*, deren achtundsiebzigster 1958 in Berlin abgehalten wurde, sind die *Deutschen Evangelischen Kirchentage* getreten.

Die Katholikentage in Mainz („Tag der Sammlung") 1948, in Bochum („Tag des sozialen Gewissens") 1949, in Passau („Tag religiösen Wachsens") 1950, in Berlin („Tag der Liebe") 1952, in Fulda („Ihr sollt mir Zeugen sein") 1954, in Köln („Kirche, das Zeichen unter den Völkern") 1956 und in Berlin („Unsere Sorge der Mensch, unser Heil der Herr") 1958 sind in ihren Themen von dem Mainzer Satz „Der Christ in der Not der Zeit" bis zu Berlin 1958 ein lebendiges Spiegelbild katholischen kirchlichen Lebens und der Auseinandersetzung mit den Fragen der Zeit. Besonders ist der Bochumer Tag zu nennen, der unter dem Thema „Gerechtigkeit schafft Frieden" der Besinnung über die soziale Verantwortung auch hinsichtlich des Mitbestimmungsrechtes diente.

Das *Zentralkomitee der deutschen Katholiken*, das sich aus dem Zentralkomitee für deutsche Katholikentage entwickelt hat und heute organisatorisch wie zielmäßig und repräsentativ die Laienvertretung des gesamten deutschen Katholizismus darstellt, wird nach wie vor die Katholikentage veranstalten. Es hat aber auch die Aufgabe, ähnlich wie vor 1933 der „Volksverein für das katholische Deutschland", zu allen staatspolitischen, sozial-wirtschaftlichen und kulturpolitischen Fragen Stellung zu nehmen, an der Schulungsarbeit innerhalb des katholischen Volksteiles teilzunehmen, zu gegebener Zeit das wegweisende Wort in den öffentlichen Raum zu sprechen und die Koordination der katholischen Verbände herzustellen. Innerhalb der Katholikenausschüsse gibt es besondere Bildungswerke, die sich an alle Katholiken wenden, aber auch Nichtkatholiken den Zutritt nicht verwehren. Außerdem besitzen die Katholiken heute eine Reihe von Heimvolksbildungsstätten, in denen die besondere Art katholischer Erwachsenenbildung gepflegt wird.

Die Evangelischen Kirchentage haben in Hannover 1949, in Essen 1950, in Berlin 1951, Stuttgart 1952, Hamburg 1953, Leipzig 1954 und Frankfurt 1956 die evangelische Christenheit in einem Maße aufgerufen, wie es früher kaum vorstellbar war. Die Losungsworte waren: „Kirche in Bewegung" (1949),

„Rettet den Menschen" (1950), „Wählt das Leben" (1952), „Werfet Euer Vertrauen nicht weg" (1953), „Seid fröhlich in Hoffnung" (1954) und „Lasset Euch versöhnen mit Gott" (1956). Die regionalen Verantwortungen des Jahres 1957 standen unter dem Wort: „Der Herr ist Gott, der Herr ist Gott". Das Leitwort des für 1959 in München geplanten Kirchentages wird lauten: „Ihr sollt mein Volk sein".

Das Gewicht des Berliner Kirchentages, der im Zeichen der Trennung Deutschlands unter dem Leitwort „Wir sind doch Brüder" stand, lag in der Teilnahme von mehr als 100.000 Gliedern der Kirche aus der sogenannten DDR. Bei den späteren Kirchentagen lag das Gewicht noch mehr auf der lebendigen Aussprache in den Arbeitsgruppen und in der äußerst starken Auswirkung der Gottesdienste, Bibelstunden und volksmissionarischen Veranstaltungen. Es hat sich seitdem gezeigt, daß es im Raum der Kirche möglich ist, *Massen zu versammeln*, und daß sie unter der Wirkung des Wortes Gottes dennoch *nicht Masse bleiben.*

Die Erlebnisse der evangelischen Kirchentage haben nicht nur für die betreffenden Städte, sondern für die Bundesrepublik, für Gesamtdeutschland und darüber hinaus für den ganzen Raum der Oekumene prägende Kraft gehabt.

Bei den katholischen Organisationen ist allgemein das Verhältnis zur Hierarchie stärker geworden. Es liegen festere Bindungen vor, und der Einfluß der Hierarchie, die während des Nationalsozialismus' so starke Verantwortung zu tragen hatte, ist heute größer als früher. Sie ist aber auch sehr darauf bedacht, daß die Initiative der mündig gewordenen Laien und ihre Eigenverantwortung nicht geschmälert werden.

*

Das Gesamtbild der Kirchen in diesen Jahren kann nicht beschrieben werden, wenn nicht der caritativen Arbeit gedacht wird. Die *Caritas* auf katholischer, die *Innere Mission* auf evangelischer Seite hatten eine lange und segensreiche Tradition in ihren Einrichtungen und Anstalten. Trotz zahlreichen Kriegszerstörungen gingen sie an den Wiederaufbau und stellten sich den zahlreichen an sie herantretenden Aufgaben der Nachkriegszeit.

Auf evangelischer Seite wurde das „*Evangelische Hilfswerk*" für die Linderung der aus den Kriegs- und Nachkriegsverhältnissen entstandenen Notlage geschaffen. Ihm und dem die gleichen Aufgaben erfüllenden „*Deutschen Caritas-Verband*" sind in den Jahren nach 1945 aus zahllosen Kirchen des Auslandes Spenden an Lebensmitteln, Bekleidung und Geld in einem Ausmaße zugeflossen, wie es *noch niemals in der Geschichte der Liebestätigkeit* sichtbar geworden ist. Beiden Kirchen, der katholischen insbesondere auch durch die immer erneute Hilfe des Papstes, ist dadurch die Möglichkeit gegeben worden, zahllosen Menschen zu helfen. Man sagt nicht zuviel, wenn man feststellt, daß durch diese Gaben Hunderttausende von Deutschen vor dem Verhungern bewahrt worden sind.

Die Organisationen, die solche Auslandsspenden weiterleiteten, konnten nicht nur Verteilungsstellen ausländischer Gaben sein. Sie haben bis in die letzte Gemeinde hinein auch zur tätigen Hilfe aus den Kräften der Gemeinden selbst aufgerufen und damit eine völlig neue Aktivität in die christliche Liebestätigkeit gebracht. Diese Bereitschaft zur Hilfe hat sich in der Einrichtung zahlreicher Heime, in der Bildung ganz neuer Gemeinden für Vertriebene und in den zahlreichen Wohnungsbauten, die auch christliche Siedlungsgesellschaften errichtet haben, niedergeschlagen. Aus diesem neuen und tieferen Verständnis der caritativen Aufgabe der Kirche ist eine starke innere Belebung der Gemeinden entstanden.

Die traditionellen Werke der Inneren Mission (Diakonische Anstalten, Jugendkammer usw.) und das Evangelische Hilfswerk wurden auf der Synode von Espelkamp 1955 zu einem einheitlichen diakonischen Werk der evangelischen Kirche in Deutschland zusammengeschlossen. Die diakonischen Werke der beiden Kirchen sind mit der staatlichen Wohlfahrtspflege in der Bundesrepublik mannigfach und eng verflochten.

Die kämpfende Kirche im Osten

Die Konsolidierung der wirtschaftlichen Verhältnisse in Westdeutschland hat die Gefahr mit sich gebracht, daß die Kirchen wieder in einen Zustand der Bequemlichkeit und scheinbaren Gesichertheit hineinsinken. In der sowjetisch besetzten Zone Deutschlands ist die Entwicklung einen anderen Weg gegangen; denn nach einer verhältnismäßig kurzen Zeit eines freien und kirchlich bestimmten Wiederaufbaues wurde der *Druck der totalitären Gewalt* stärker und stärker.

Der Kommunismus versuchte besonders die Jugend der Kirche zu entfremden. Er verbot alle Veranstaltungen der Jugend, die nicht rein religiösen Charakter hatten. Glieder der jungen Gemeinden der Kirche wurden unter irgendwelchen Vorwänden oder unter offenem Hinweis auf ihre Zugehörigkeit zur jungen Gemeinde von den Schulen verwiesen. Die einzige zugelassene Zeitschrift für die evangelische Jugend der sogenannten DDR wurde verboten. Als Grund dafür wurde Papiermangel angeführt, obwohl das Papier für die Zeitschrift aus Spenden ausländischer Kirchen für Monate bereitlag.

Jugendliche, Jugendleiter und Pfarrer wurden verhaftet. Die theologischen Fakultäten an den Universitäten der sogenannten DDR waren in Gefahr. Die Einrichtung eines katholischen Priesterseminars in Ostberlin für den Priesternachwuchs der sogenannten DDR wurde verhindert. Studenten, die auf den Universitäten des Westens oder auf der in Berlin eingerichteten Kirchlichen Hochschule studierten, wurde die Einreise und eine Tätigkeit in der sogenannten DDR verweigert.

Durch strengste Zensurmaßnahmen wurde versucht, jede Verbindung der Bevölkerung der sogenannten DDR mit dem geistigen und kirchlichen Leben des Westens auszuschließen. Ebenso bemühten sich die Machthaber des Ostens in ständig verstärktem Maße, die Berührung der Bevölkerung ihrer sogenannten DDR mit den Gemeinden des Westens zu verhindern.

Das Verhältnis zwischen Kirche und Staat drohte schlechter zu werden, als es jemals während der Zeit des Nationalsozialismus gewesen war. Diese Entwicklung wurde am 10.6.1953 unterbrochen. Durch Verhandlungen der Regierung und der Bischöfe der sogenannten DDR wurde an dem genannten Tage erreicht, daß eine Reihe der geschilderten Maßnahmen aufgehoben wurde und eine allgemeine Entspannung des Verhältnisses von Kirche und Staat eintrat. Es unterliegt keinem Zweifel, daß diese Wendung von seiten der sogenannten DDR nicht durch grundsätzliche, sondern durch taktische Erwägungen bestimmt wurde.

Das hervorstechendste Ereignis, das die zeitweilige Änderung des Verhältnisses zwischen Staat und Kirche unterstrich, stellte die Erlaubnis für die Abhaltung des Kirchentages 1954 in Leipzig dar. Die Zahlen der ständigen Teilnehmer wurden auf 50.000 aus dem Osten und auf 10.000 aus dem Westen festgesetzt. Sämtliche Plätze wurden vollständig in Anspruch genommen. An der Schlußkundgebung nahm die ungeheure Zahl von 650.000 Gläubigen teil. Die Regierung der sogenannten DDR hatte mit einem Ereignis von solchem Ausmaß wohl kaum gerechnet.

Im Zuge zeitweiliger Verschärfungen und Entspannungen wurde jedoch von der Regierung der sogenannten DDR der kirchenfeindliche Kurs später wieder konsequent verfolgt. Die Staatsleistungen sind wiederholt gekürzt worden. Den Kirchen ist die Möglichkeit genommen, die Kirchensteuern selbst als Vereinsbeiträge beizutreiben. Die verfassungsmäßigen Rechte der Kirche sind im Zuge einer Rechtsauffassung, nach der die Verfassung sich laufend selbst gegen ihren Wortlaut verändere, beeinträchtigt. Der Kontakt der Christen in der sogenannten DDR mit den Christen in der Bundesrepublik und in der Welt wird durch Erschwerungen des Reiseverkehrs behindert.

„Mit der ganzen grundsätzlichen Radikalität, die es in Europa nur bei den Deutschen gibt, versucht man, wie man das nennt, *das Bewußtsein der Menschen umzubilden*, damit sie sich vom christlichen Glauben loslösen und in die Denkweise des Materialismus' eingehen sollen. Das fängt im Kindergarten an, das setzt sich über die rücksichtslos erzwungene Jugendweihe das ganze Leben hindurch fort" (OTTO DIBELIUS, 1958).

Die Kirchen wissen, daß sie unabhängig von den Grenzen des Eisernen Vorhanges zur Gemeinschaft des Glaubens berufen sind, und tun alles, was in ihren Kräften steht, um diese Gemeinschaft zu erhalten und die Brüder in der sogenannten DDR zu stützen.

So ist das Bild der Kirche in Deutschland 1958 ein getreues Abbild auch der politischen Situation mit allen ihren Schwankungen und Spannungen. Die Kirchen stehen in äußerer und innerer Unabhängigkeit vom Staat in der großen Auseinandersetzung, die ihnen besonders auferlegt ist, zwischen dem dialektischen Materialismus der totalitären Gewalt des Ostens und der Realisierung des Wortes und Gebotes Gottes in ihrem eigenen Leben und dem der Staaten und Völker.

II. DIE JÜDISCHE GEMEINSCHAFT

Die Konsolidierung der jüdischen Gemeinschaft, die sich unmittelbar nach dem Zusammenbruch des nationalsozialistischen Dritten Reiches als schwierig gezeigt hatte, hat in den letzten Jahren erfreuliche Fortschritte gemacht.

Es gibt heute im Gebiet der Bundesrepublik vierundsiebzig jüdische Gemeinden. Sie sind in Landesverbände zusammengeschlossen, deren Sitz sich in den Landeshauptstädten der Länder der Bundesrepublik befindet. Das

Problem der jüdischen „Displaced Persons“ wurde restlos gelöst. Schätzungsweise gibt es in der Bundesrepublik und Berlin etwa 6.000 ehemalige DP's. Sie haben sich zum größten Teil außerordentlich gut eingeordnet und betreiben mit großem Erfolg Geschäfte und Industrien.

Die Zahl der im Gebiet der Bundesrepublik und Berlin lebenden Juden läßt sich schwer übersehen. Die Zahl der Mitglieder der jüdischen Gemeinden in Deutschland beträgt etwa 30.000. Es wird aber angenommen, daß sich außerdem noch etwa 15.000 bis 18.000 zurückgewanderte Juden in Deutschland befinden, die erst nach und nach wieder in die jüdischen Religionsgemeinschaften eintreten. Der Grund dafür ist im wesentlichen darin zu suchen, daß es von den Juden anderer Länder nicht gern gesehen wurde, wenn Juden nach Deutschland zurückkehrten. In den vergangenen Jahren wurde die jüdische Gemeinschaft in Deutschland von den ausländischen jüdischen Gemeinschaften sogar stark bekämpft. Seit einiger Zeit aber hat sich auch das erfreulicherweise sehr geändert. Die positive Haltung der Bundesregierung und der Länderregierungen gegenüber den Juden, die als besonders gut zu bezeichnende Wiedergutmachungsgesetzgebung, die immer deutlicher werdende positive Haltung großer Bevölkerungskreise gegenüber der jüdischen Frage haben wesentlich dazu beigetragen, die Juden in den westlichen Ländern davon zu überzeugen, daß der Wiederaufbau jüdischer Gemeinschaften in Deutschland gerechtfertigt erscheint. Als besonderes Symbol für diese positive Einstellung waren die Reaktionen auf das Buch und das Theaterstück des „Tagebuches der Anne Frank“ und auf den Film „Nacht und Nebel“ zu bemerken. Insbesondere die Haltung der deutschen Jugend gegenüber den Juden wurde im Ausland mit Wohlgefallen vermerkt. Geringfügige Zwischenfälle politisch Unbelehrbarer werden so gewertet wie sie gewertet werden müssen, nämlich nicht als organisierte Aktionen noch vorhandener antisemitischer Gruppen.

Ermutigt durch diese Ereignisse hat der *Zentralrat der Juden in Deutschland* mit Sitz in Düsseldorf als Dachorganisation, der sämtliche Landesverbände angeschlossen sind, seine Aktivität erhöht und seit dem Jahre 1955 mit der Schaffung eines Kultusdezernates die jüdische Kulturarbeit besonders gefördert. Das besondere Augenmerk des Zentralrates und der ihm angeschlossenen Organisationen wird naturgemäß auf den Kultus und die Kultur gelegt. Mit großer Intensität aber widmen die maßgebenden Persönlichkeiten der jüdischen Gemeinschaft in Deutschland sich der Erziehung der jetzt wieder vorhandenen Jugendlichen und Kinder. In Verbindung mit der *Zentralwohlfahrtsstelle der Juden in Deutschland*, die ihren Sitz in Frankfurt am Main hat, wurden die vorhandenen Altersheime wesentlich verbessert und neue Altersheime gegründet. Zwei schöne Jugendferienheime bieten Möglichkeiten der Erholung. Aber auch diese Gelegenheit wird benutzt, diese Jugend der jüdischen Kultur und Tradition immer näher zu bringen. Nach großen Schwierigkeiten ist es gelungen, die erforderliche Anzahl von Lehrern aus dem Ausland zu bekommen und für die Hauptzentren der jüdischen Gemeinden Rabbiner zu gewinnen, welche die kleineren jüdischen Gemeinden mitbetreuen.

Der Lebensstandard der im Bundesgebiet und Berlin lebenden Juden hat sich gegenüber den Nachkriegsjahren wesentlich gebessert. Neben verhältnismäßig großen jüdischen Industriebetrieben gibt es wieder eine Reihe von maßgeblichen Einzelhandelsgeschäften. Die Zahl der jüdischen Anwälte hat sich vermehrt, und ein besonderer Notstand der ersten Nachkriegsjahre, das Fehlen jüdischer Ärzte, ist durch eine erhebliche Rückwanderung, zum geringen Teil auch durch Nachwuchs, so gut wie beseitigt. Es gibt in Deutschland heute wieder viele jüdische Künstler, die begreiflicherweise unmittelbar nach der Schaffung der Demokratie sich noch nicht entschließen konnten, nach Deutschland zu kommen. Bedeutende Künstler haben wieder ihren Wohnsitz in Deutschland genommen; andere kommen jährlich ein bis zweimal zu Gastspielen in die Bundesrepublik und nach Berlin. Es gibt jüdische Richter und an fast allen Universitäten wieder jüdische Professoren.

Nachdem nun auch Düsseldorf eine Synagoge hat, gibt es in allen Landeshauptstädten der Bundesrepublik und in Berlin wieder zum Teil sehenswerte Synagogen. Auch kleinere Städte haben wieder Gotteshäuser, während die Kleinst- und Kleingemeinden sich mit Betsälen begnügen.

Die Zentralwohlfahrtsstelle der Juden hat es neben den bereits erwähnten Aufgaben übernommen, die Sozialbedürftigen zu betreuen. Ihr Hauptaugenmerk richtet sich auf die Jugend und überall dorthin, wo es wieder genügend Kinder gibt, um Kindergärten zu errichten.

In Zusammenwirken mit der Bundesregierung und den Länderregierungen sowie den jüdischen Zentralinstanzen wurde die Pflege der jüdischen Friedhöfe gesichert.

Das Zentralorgan der Juden in Deutschland ist die in Düsseldorf erscheinende „Allgemeine Wochenzeitung der Juden in Deutschland" mit einer monatlichen Beilage, der „Jüdischen Illustrierten". Diese Wochenzeitung hat in den letzten Jahren an Ansehen noch gewonnen, sie ist in der ganzen Welt verbreitet und wird besonders auch von den aus Deutschland ausgewanderten Juden gelesen. Sie ist ein politisches und kulturelles Organ, von dem erfreulicherweise gesagt werden kann, daß es unter seinen Deutschland-Abonnenten eine Vielzahl von nichtjüdischen Lesern hat.

Einige Gemeinden, darunter Frankfurt, Karlsruhe und München, haben sich entschlossen, jüdische Gemeindeblätter herauszugeben.

Der *Jüdische Frauenbund in Deutschland* zählt heute rund 3.000 Mitglieder. Er hat in den letzten Jahren eine starke Aktivität entwickelt. Durch seinen Kontakt mit den jüdischen Frauenorganisationen der westlichen Welt hat er wesentlich dazu beigetragen, daß heute den Juden in Deutschland größeres Verständnis entgegengebracht wird. Der jüdische Frauenbund hat 1956 damit begonnen, zweimonatlich eine kleine Zeitschrift „Die Frau in der Gemeinschaft" herauszubringen

Die Zentralwohlfahrtsstelle der Juden in Deutschland hat die Tradition der früheren Zentralwohlfahrtsstelle aufgenommen und bringt wieder ein sechzehn- bis vierundzwanzigseitiges Blatt „Jüdische Sozialarbeit" heraus. Dieses Blatt liegt, ebenso wie „Die Frau in der Gemeinschaft", der „Allgemeinen Wochenzeitung der Juden in Deutschland" für alle Welt bei. Allmonatlich bringt die Zentralwohlfahrtsstelle der Juden in Deutschland auch eine Kinder- und Jugendzeitschrift heraus.

Die jüdischen Gewerbetreibenden sind in einer *Arbeitsgemeinschaft jüdischer Gewerbetreibender, Industrieller und freier Berufe* zusammengefaßt. In Zusammenarbeit mit einer über das ganze Bundesgebiet verbreiteten Jüdischen Darlehnskasse hat sie wesentlich dazu beigetragen, den zurückgewanderten Juden den Wiederbeginn zu erleichtern.

Alles in allem kann gesagt werden, daß die Konsolidierung der jüdischen Gemeinschaft im Bundesgebiet und Berlin recht erfreuliche Fortschritte gemacht hat. Die in den vergangenen Jahren zeitweise bemerkbare Unruhe unter den jüdischen Mitbürgern wegen der Gefahr neonazistischer Bestrebungen ist, besonders auch durch den Ausgang der Bundestagswahlen des Jahres 1957, zurückgegangen. Sie haben die Bestätigung der beiden großen demokratischen Parteien durch die Bevölkerung der Bundesrepublik erbracht. Es besteht der absolute Eindruck, daß man heute wieder von einer Stabilisierung jüdischen Lebens in Deutschland sprechen kann.

DIE ERNEUERUNG DES RECHTS

Als der Oberste Befehlshaber der alliierten Streitkräfte im Frühjahr 1945 die höchste gesetzgebende und vollziehende Gewalt übernahm, kam in Deutschland auch auf dem Gebiete des Rechtswesens eine Entwicklung zum Abschluß, die ein kaum übersehbares Trümmerfeld hinterließ. Der Verwaltungsapparat des Staates war zerschlagen. Die Gerichtsgebäude waren vielfach zerstört, Akten und Register vernichtet; die gesamte Gerichtsbarkeit stand still. Eine Fülle ungerechter Normen auf allen Gebieten des Rechts, vom Nationalsozialismus zur Erreichung seiner Ziele geschaffen, hatte das sachliche Recht zersetzt. Zahllose Akte staatlicher Willkür harrten der Wiedergutmachung.

Dies war in großen Zügen die Lage, vor die sich die deutschen Juristen gestellt sahen, als es galt, aus dem Chaos des Zusammenbruchs einen Weg zum Aufbau einer neuen Rechtsordnung auf demokratischer Grundlage zu finden. Infolge der politischen Konzeption der Besatzungsmächte, die Wiedererrichtung deutscher Verwaltungsstellen, Gerichte und Gesetzgebungskörperschaften von unten her durchzuführen, fehlte es zunächst an einer einheitlichen Spitze, die sich der Aufgabe einer umfassenden Rechtserneuerung, gleichartig für das gesamte Gebiet Deutschlands nach 1945, hätte unterziehen können. Die Arbeit der ersten Nachkriegsjahre war deshalb durch die Zersplitterung von Gesetzgebung und Rechtsprechung außerordentlich erschwert. Fast schien es, als sei die vollständige *Auflösung der Rechtseinheit* in Deutschland unvermeidlich. In den Jahren 1945 bis 1948 wurden durch Besatzungsmaßnahmen nicht weniger als sechsunddreißig Gesetzgeber konstituiert, deren Zuständigkeit sich in sechs verschiedenen Ebenen abstufte.

Neben dem Alliierten Kontrollrat, den Zonenbefehlshabern und den Militärgouverneuren der einzelnen Länder übten bizonale und zonale Behörden, die neu geschaffenen Länder und in der Britischen Zone vorübergehend sogar die Präsidenten der einzelnen Oberlandesgerichte Gesetzgebungsbefugnisse aus. Jeder dieser Gesetzgeber war selbständig, solange er den durch übergeordnete Stellen gesetzten Rahmen nicht überschritt. Damit mußte die Rechtsentwicklung in jeder Zone, teilweise sogar in einzelnen Ländern, eigene Wege gehen. Gleichwohl gelang es der Einsicht der Verantwortlichen, im Bürgerlichen Recht und im Strafrecht die Rechtseinheit in Westdeutschland im wesentlichen aufrechtzuerhalten. Dagegen schritt die Auflösung des Staats- und Verwaltungsrechts und des Verfahrensrechts unaufhaltsam fort.

*

Mit allen unter den damaligen Verhältnissen zu Gebote stehenden Mitteln und mit wechselndem Erfolg versuchten deutsche Stellen, der Zersplitterung des Rechts entgegenzuwirken. In der Amerikanischen Zone schuf die Initiative der drei süddeutschen Länder und Bremens durch Zusammenfassung der Arbeit ihrer Justizministerien im *Rechtsausschuß des „Länderrats“* in Stuttgart ein Instrument, das zahlreiche, gleichen Zielen dienende Gesetzentwürfe koordinierte und damit die Verkündung einheitlicher Gesetze in dieser Zone sicherstellte. In der Britischen Zone wurde unter Mitwirkung der alliierten Behörden das *Zentraljustizamt* errichtet, das auf dem Gebiete des Zivil- und Strafrechts umfassende Gesetzgebungsbefugnisse erhielt. Es war damit in der Lage, für alle Länder der Britischen Zone gleiches Recht zu schaffen und die vorher teilweise eingetretene Zersplitterung wieder aufzufangen. Eine weitere wichtige Etappe im Ringen um die Erhaltung der Rechtseinheit wurde mit der Konstituierung des Wirtschaftsrats für das Vereinigte Wirtschaftsgebiet, dem die Länder der Britischen und Amerikanischen Zone angehörten, erreicht.

*

Die Rechtsentwicklung in dem von den Sowjets besetzten Gebietsteil Deutschlands trennte sich unter dem politischen Einfluß der Sowjetmacht bald von der Rechtsentwicklung der von den Westmächten besetzten Gebiete und verließ mehr und mehr das Prinzip der Gewaltenteilung.

*

Mit Hilfe des organisatorischen Zusammenschlusses der Britischen und Amerikanischen, schließlich auch der Französischen Zone, der die Grundlage für die Vereinheitlichung des Wirtschafts-, Verkehrs- und Steuerrechts bildete und den Aufbau bizonaler (am Ende trizonaler), für Westdeutschland zuständiger Behörden, insbesondere auch *des Rechtsamts der Verwaltung des Vereinigten Wirtschaftsgebiets*, ermöglichte, konnte auch für die Konstituierung künftiger Bundesorgane wertvolle Vorarbeit geleistet werden. Ein Stamm befähigter Mitarbeiter wurde gewonnen, der später nach seinem Übergang in die Bundesbehörden diese alsbald handlungsfähig machte.

*

Es war ein bedeutsames Kennzeichen dieser ersten Periode, daß dank dem unermüdlichen Einsatz aller an der Gesetzgebung Beteiligten ein in der Öffentlichkeit wenig beachteter *Reinigungsprozeß* sich vollzog. Die Besatzungsmächte hatten nur eine Anzahl von Vorschriften aufgehoben, die offensichtlich auf nationalsozialistischen Vorstellungen beruhten oder den Belangen ihrer Streitkräfte zuwiderliefen. Im übrigen hatten sie das von ihnen angetroffene Recht in seiner Gültigkeit bestätigt. Eine im Besatzungsrecht enthaltene Generalklausel schränkte die Anwendbarkeit früheren Rechts nur insoweit ein, als es eine Privilegierung von Nationalsozialisten zur Folge hatte oder eine Benachteiligung von Personen wegen ihrer Rasse, ihrer Staatsangehörigkeit oder ihres Glaubens vorsah. Mit diesen Maßnahmen war jedoch nur ein erster Schritt zur Bereinigung des geltenden Rechts getan. Soweit es trotz dem Mangel an geeignetem Personal möglich war, wurde von deutscher Seite — teilweise in Zusammenarbeit mit den alliierten Behörden — die *Umgestaltung der überkommenen Rechtsordnung* mit aller Kraft in Angriff genommen.

Dabei zeigte sich, daß die rechtspolitischen Konzeptionen der damaligen Zeit, soweit sie sich auf Nahziele richteten, zu einem erheblichem Teil dem Gedanken der Restauration zuneigen mußten. Man strebte zurück zu dem Rechtszustand der vor-nationalsozialistischen Zeit, um zunächst überhaupt eine Grundlage zu haben, die möglichst bald ein ruhiges und sicheres Arbeiten der Praxis gewährleisten konnte. Die Gesetzgeber wuchsen jedoch verhältnismäßig schnell über dieses ausschließlich an der Vergangenheit orientierte Denken hinaus. Die Verhältnisse des Krieges und der Nachkriegszeit hatten ganz neue Rechtslagen geschaffen, die ohne die Verwendung neuer Begriffe und neuer Methoden nicht gemeistert werden konnten. Neben der *Wiederherstellung altbewährten Rechts* setzten sich deshalb auch *neuartige Rechtsgedanken* durch. Sie hatten ihren Ursprung teilweise in ausländischen Vorbildern; zum Teil waren sie auch aus den unmittelbaren Bedürfnissen des Augenblicks entwickelt. Eine Fülle von Gesetzen entstand, die überwiegend der Liquidation des nationalsozialistischen Erbes dienten.

Es sei hier nur verwiesen auf die Gesetze über die *Wiedergutmachung nationalsozialistischen Unrechts* auf dem Gebiet der Strafrechtspflege und über die Ahndung ungesühnt gebliebener nationalsozialistischer Straftaten; weiter auf die Zusammenfassung des außerordentlich zersplitterten Wirtschaftsstrafrechts in einem *Wirtschaftsstrafgesetz* des Wirtschaftsrates der Verwaltung des Vereinigten Wirtschaftsgebiets, das die Grundsätze des Rechtsstaates in vorbildlicher Weise verwirklichte.

*

Hand in Hand mit der Bereinigung des sachlichen Rechts vollzog sich der *Aufbau der ordentlichen Gerichtsbarkeit.* Während die Gerichte der unteren Stufen schon bald nach dem Zusammenbruch ihre Arbeit wieder aufnehmen konnten, setzte die Tätigkeit der Oberlandesgerichte, deren Wirken gerade damals zur Wahrung der Rechtseinheit in größeren Bezirken wichtig war, infolge Mangels an geeigneten Richterpersönlichkeiten erst geraume Zeit später ein. In der Britischen Zone wurde der Gerichtsaufbau durch die Schaffung eines obersten Revisionsgerichts gekrönt, das die einheitliche Anwendung des gesamten Zivil- und Strafrechts für diese Zone gewährleistete. Die von den Gerichten anzuwendenden Prozeßordnungen wurden — allerdings in den einzelnen Zonen in verschiedener Weise — umgestaltet, um den Erfordernissen eines rechtsstaatlichen Verfahrens zu genügen.

Für den Aufbau der Verwaltungsgerichtsbarkeit ergab sich eine Besonderheit, welche die Gesetzgeber der Zonen und Länder vor eine sehr schwierige Aufgabe stellte. Die Erfahrungen unter der nationalsozialistischen Herrschaft hatten gezeigt, zu welch schwerwiegenden Folgen es führen kann, wenn der Staatsbürger unberechtigten Übergriffen der Staatsgewalt wehrlos ausgeliefert ist. Das im deutschen Verwaltungsrecht seit langem geltende Prinzip, wonach nur wenige genau bezeichnete Akte staatlicher Verwaltung gerichtlich nachgeprüft werden konnten, hatte sich als unzulänglich erwiesen, um die Rechte des einzelnen gegenüber der Obrigkeit in ausreichendem Maße zu sichern. Es mußten deshalb neue Grundlagen für die Verwaltungsgerichtsbarkeit erarbeitet werden, die weit über den Rahmen dessen hinausgingen, was bisher in der deutschen Rechtsordnung verankert war. Dabei wurde in allen Zonen der theoretisch allein in Betracht kommende Weg gewählt, jegliche staatliche Tätigkeit der gerichtlichen Kontrolle zu unterwerfen. Die sogenannte „*Generalklausel im Verwaltungsprozeß*" gibt jetzt dem Bürger die Befugnis, gegenüber jeder ihn beeinträchtigenden Entscheidung einer staatlichen Stelle die Nachprüfung durch ein unabhängiges Gericht zu verlangen.

Angesichts des damals herrschenden Personalmangels war die Sorge berechtigt, ob diese weitreichende Zuständigkeit überhaupt durchführbar sein werde; denn sie stellte die wenigen vorhandenen Gerichte vor Aufgaben, deren Erfüllung von dem einzelnen Richter ein Übermaß an persönlicher Arbeitsleistung forderte. Die weitere Entwicklung hat jedoch dem Gesetzgeber recht gegeben. Es ist inzwischen zu einer Selbstverständlichkeit im Rechtsleben geworden, daß kein Bereich staatlicher Verwaltung, soweit diese sich an den einzelnen Bürger wendet, der Möglichkeit rechtlicher Kontrolle entzogen sein darf.

*

Trotz allen Fortschritten in der Überwindung des nationalsozialistischen Ungeistes blieben die Ergebnisse der Rechtssetzung in den einzelnen

Teilbereichen Westdeutschlands Stückwerk. Erst nach der Konstituierung der Bundesorgane und der Bundesregierung im Herbst 1949 konnte der Aufbau des Rechtswesens nach einem einheitlichen und sorgfältig vorbereiteten Plan in Angriff genommen werden. Die inzwischen in Kraft getretene Verfassung — das Grundgesetz für die Bundesrepublik Deutschland — hatte bereits die Grundsatzfragen entschieden und einen beträchtlichen Teil des Weges für die künftige Gesetzgebung vorgezeichnet. Sie hatte die *Grundrechte des Staatsbürgers* neu belebt und ihn durch eine Reihe unmittelbar geltender Vorschriften gegen ungesetzliche Übergriffe staatlicher Macht geschützt. Zugleich hatte sie die Errichtung des *Bundesverfassungsgerichts* als des Hüters der Verfassung und der *Oberen Bundesgerichte* als Wahrer der Rechtseinheit auf dem Gebiete der Rechtsprechung in den verschiedenen Zweigen der Gerichtsbarkeit vorgesehen. Für die einheitliche Entwicklung des bürgerlichen Rechts, des Strafrechts und des gerichtlichen Verfahrens hatte das Grundgesetz dadurch gesorgt, daß es diese Materien der Gesetzgebungskompetenz des Bundes zuwies.

Die gesetzgeberischen Pläne der Bundesregierung in diesem Bereich mußten danach streben, in der ersten Wahlperiode des Deutschen Bundestages vor allem drei Ziele zu erreichen, die sich bei Übernahme der Regierungsgeschäfte von selbst ergaben. Die durch die Zersplitterung der Gesetzgebung beeinträchtigte *Rechtseinheit* war wiederherzustellen, die *Beseitigung nationalsozialistischer Gedanken* aus der Rechtsordnung zu vollenden und den *Forderungen des Grundgesetzes* durch den Erlaß der notwendigen Durchführungsgesetze Genüge zu leisten.

Den ersten großen Erfolg bedeutete das Gesetz zur Wiederherstellung der Rechtseinheit auf dem Gebiet der Gerichtsverfassung, der bürgerlichen Rechtspflege, des Strafverfahrens und des Kostenrechts. Es brachte für die ordentliche Gerichtsbarkeit wieder ein einheitliches Verfahren und schuf namentlich den *Bundesgerichtshof*, dem die wichtige Aufgabe höchstrichterlicher Rechtsprechung im Zivil- und Strafrecht zufiel. Entsprechende Gesetze für die anderen Zweige der Gerichtsbarkeit (Verwaltungs-, Arbeits- und Sozialgerichtsbarkeit) folgten nach. In Ausführung des Artikels 96 des Grundgesetzes wurden neben dem Bundesgerichtshof, der seinen Sitz in Karlsruhe hat, das *Bundesverwaltungsgericht* (in Berlin) das *Bundesarbeitsgericht*, das *Bundessozialgericht* (beide in Kassel) und der *Bundesfinanzhof* (in München) errichtet. In Berlin wurde außerdem der *Bundesdisziplinarhof* errichtet. Die Schaffung eines Obersten Bundesgerichtes gemäß Artikel 95 GG steht noch aus.

Der Unabhängigkeit der Richter, die im Artikel 97 des Grundgesetzes hervorgehoben wird, soll ein besonderes *Richtergesetz* dienen, das dem Bundestag zur Beschlußfassung vorliegt.

Dem Ziele der Rechtseinheit dient auch die im Juli 1957 vom Parlament verabschiedete Kostenrechtsreform, die das Gerichtskostenwesen auf dem Gebiet der verschiedenen Gerichtsbarkeiten vereinheitlicht und gleichzeitig die bis dahin bestehenden verschiedenartigen Regelungen in den Bundesländern aufhebt.

Im Bereich des *bürgerlichen Rechts*, das durch gesetzgeberische Maßnahmen der nationalsozialistischen Zeit und durch die Rechtszersplitterung der Nachkriegsjahre verhältnismäßig wenig getroffen war, hat die Rechtsvereinheitlichung gute Fortschritte gemacht. Das Ziel, das bewährte Bürgerliche Gesetzbuch wieder zu dem Grundgesetz allen bürgerlichen Rechtsverkehrs zu machen, ist nach der Verabschiedung der Gesetzgebung über die Gleichberechtigung von Mann und Frau fast gänzlich erreicht.

Den gleichen Zielen einer einheitlichen Rechtshandhabung für das Bundesgebiet dient das Gesetz über die Bundesrechtsanwaltsordnung.

*

Wesentlich schwieriger gestalteten sich die Arbeiten auf dem Gebiet des *Strafrechts*. Zur Sicherung der Existenzgrundlage des neuen Staates gegen die Wühlarbeit von Feinden der demokratischen Ordnung mußte eine Lücke, die durch die Gesetzgebung der alliierten Behörden entstanden war, durch wirksame Strafvorschriften gegen Hochverrat, Staatsgefährdung und Landesverrat geschlossen werden[1]. Diese Strafrechtsänderungsgesetze dienen nur dem Ziel, den wirklichen Gegner der staatlichen Grundordnung zu treffen; der politischen Auseinandersetzung im Rahmen dieser Ordnung dagegen legen sie keine Fesseln an. Eines dieser strafrechtlichen Änderungsgesetze dient einer Vereinheitlichung und umfassenden Bereinigung des gesamten Strafrechts. Seine Verabschiedung ermöglichte es, den Text des geltenden Strafgesetzbuches neu bekanntzumachen und damit alle Zweifel an der Fortgeltung alten Strafrechts zu beheben.

Das Dritte Strafrechtsänderungsgesetz regelte einige offen gebliebene Probleme auf dem Gebiete des *Straßenverkehrs*. Das Vierte und letzte Strafrechtsänderungsgesetz brachte die erforderlichen Vorschriften, die aus Anlaß der Aufstellung deutscher *Streitkräfte* im Strafrecht notwendig waren.

Nach diesen notwendigen Änderungen und Ergänzungen entspricht das Strafrecht allen Notwendigkeiten der Gegenwart. Dennoch scheint es

[1] Vergleiche oben Seite 249.

erforderlich, das Strafrecht, das in seinen Grundzügen seit 1874 besteht, gründlich zu überprüfen und den Erkenntnissen der neuzeitlichen Strafrechtswissenschaft anzupassen. Diese Aufgabe bearbeitet die *Kommission für die Strafrechtsreform* unter dem Vorsitz von Dr. h. c. FRITZ NEUMAYER, der von 1953 bis 1956 Bundesjustizminister war. Die Kommission hat die Beratungen über den Entwurf abgeschlossen.

Das *Jugendstrafrecht*, seit 1923 in einem besonderen Jugendgerichtsgesetz kodifiziert, wurde ebenfalls einer Bereinigung unterzogen. Da durch die außergewöhnlichen Verhältnisse des Krieges und der Nachkriegszeit die Jugend in ihrer Entwicklung besonders hart getroffen war, erwiesen sich auf diesem Gebiet weiterreichende Reformen als notwendig.

*

Einen bedeutsamen Meilenstein auf dem Weg zu einem wirklichen Rechtsstaat bildet das *Gesetz über das Bundesverfassungsgericht*, das einen gegenüber allen Verfassungsorganen der Bundesrepublik unabhängigen Staatsgerichtshof konstituiert. Als Hüter der staatlichen Grundordnung soll das Bundesverfassungsgericht die Einhaltung der Vorschriften der Verfassung durch Gesetzgebung, Verwaltung und Rechtsprechung gewährleisten. Die Einführung einer Gerichtsbarkeit, die das ganze Verfassungsleben durchdringt, war ein sehr mutiger und in diesem Umfang in der deutschen Rechtsgeschichte noch nicht gewagter Schritt. Die Schöpfer des Gesetzes waren sich darüber klar, daß das Gericht nur dann seine Aufgabe voll meistern wird, wenn es mit wirklich unabhängigen Richterpersönlichkeiten besetzt ist und die unbestrittene Autorität einer absolut neutralen Instanz gewinnt. Diese Stellung hat das Gericht durch die Objektivität seiner Entscheidungen sich errungen. Es ist das gegebene Instrument, um in den Auseinandersetzungen der Verfassungsorgane des Bundes und der Länder jeden mit dem Grundgesetz nicht zu vereinbarenden Übergriff zu verhindern.

*

Schon kurz nach dem Zusammenbruch haben verschiedene Länder die Initiative ergriffen und Gesetzentwürfe zur *Wiedergutmachung* des unabsehbaren Schadens vorbereitet, den *die nationalsozialistische Willkürherrschaft* ihren Opfern zugefügt hat. Ihrem Erlaß kam der alliierte Gesetzgeber zuvor, indem er kraft Besatzungsrechts die Rückerstattung noch feststellbarer Vermögenswerte an die Berechtigten anordnete.

Die Durchführung dieser Vorschrift ist heute weitgehend abgewickelt. Schwierigkeiten bestehen lediglich noch da, wo dem Staat zugefallene

Vermögenswerte nicht in Natur zurückgegeben, sondern nur durch Gewährung eines entsprechenden Schadenersatzes ausgeglichen werden können.

Auch die Wiedergutmachung von Verfolgungsmaßnahmen gegenüber Angehörigen des Öffentlichen Dienstes ist in vollem Gange. Sie wird bald zu einem erfolgreichen Abschluß kommen. Soweit es die Angehörigen der Justizverwaltung selbst betrifft, ist sie bereits weitgehend abgeschlossen. Die Entschädigung wegen solcher Einbußen, die nicht durch Rückerstattung oder Rehabilition wiedergutgemacht werden können, vor allem wegen unberechtigter Freiheitsentziehung, ist inzwischen durch das *Bundesentschädigungsgesetz* erfolgt.

*

Vieles, was auf dem Gebiet des Rechtswesens in den Jahren seit dem Zusammenbruch geleistet worden ist, konnte in diesem kurzen Überblick nicht oder nur andeutungsweise erwähnt werden. Das große Programm der Vereinheitlichung und Bereinigung der gesamten Rechtsordnung ist im wesentlichen vollendet. Jetzt ist der Weg frei, um auf allen Gebieten des Rechtswesens die Reformen in Angriff zu nehmen, die, wegen der Zeitverhältnisse bisher immer wieder zurückgestellt, nun nicht länger aufgeschoben werden können.

Berlin: Mahnmal für die Opfer des Nationalsozialismus.

KULTUR

DAS KULTURLEBEN

Niemand wird vom deutschen Kulturleben nach 1945 erwarten können, daß es eine problemlose Fortsetzung des Kulturlebens etwa der Weimarer Zeit sei. Der Nationalsozialismus und der Krieg haben auf diesem Feld tiefer eingegriffen und verhängnisvollere Folgen gehabt als etwa im Bereich der Wirtschaft.

Da ist die Emigration (THOMAS MANN, PAUL HINDEMITH . . .). Da ist die Dezimierung des jüdischen Elements, das nicht nur seinen eigenen Beitrag leistete (HUSSERL, WERFEL, REINHARDT . . .), sondern auch als Ferment, als anregender Reiz für das deutsche Kulturleben wichtig war. Da ist schließlich die Spaltung. Die äußere Spaltung schnitt etwa die sächsisch-thüringische Musikkultur (Evangelische Kirchenmusik, Orgel- und Chorpflege, Thomaner, Gewandhaus) vom Musikleben der Bundesrepublik fast völlig ab; die innere Spaltung riß eine Kluft auf zwischen den Dichtern und Schriftstellern des Systems der sogenannten DDR (BERT BRECHT, LUKASZ, HERMLIN . . .) und denen des freien Westens.

Das Kulturleben der Bundesrepublik ist durch diese verschiedenen Blutentnahmen zweifellos begrenzter und „ärmer" als das der Weimarer Republik. Es hat keinen Sinn, vor dieser Tatsache die Augen zu schließen. Der wirtschaftliche Neuaufstieg Deutschlands hat die Welt überrascht und tief beeindruckt: es wäre unbillig, wollte man von der Kultur ähnliches erwarten. So rasch können Dichter, Philosophen und Künstler den seelischen Schock des Zusammenbruchs, der Verwirrungen des Nationalsozialismus', der Mitschuld, der Niederlage, der Zerstörungen, der Spaltung nicht überwinden. Es wäre schlimm, wenn sie „die Ärmel hochkrempelten" und nach dem Vorbild der kommunistischen STALIN-Lyrik flugs Preisgedichte auf das „deutsche Wunder" schrieben oder eine dazu passende optimistische Philosophie erdächten. Der Dichter „verdichtet" das wesentliche Schicksal des Volkes und der Epoche, und ähnliches gilt von jedem Künstler und auch vom Philosophen, zum Teil auch vom Wissenschaftler, so vom Historiker, vom Psychiater, vom Pädagogen. Wenn diese Verdichtung, diese innere Verarbeitung und Neugestaltung recht geschieht, so geschieht sie langsam.

Das muß man wissen, wenn man das deutsche Kulturleben richtig bewerten will. Da gibt es allerdings auch noch das alte Erbe, das sofort nach der

Normalisierung der äußeren Verhältnisse wieder in seine Rechte eintrat: es wird BACH, MOZART, BEETHOVEN, BRAHMS und längst wieder WAGNER musiziert, die Theater führen GOETHE, KLEIST, BÜCHNER, HAUPTMANN auf, SHAKESPEARE, IBSEN, MOLIÈRE, CALDERON; die Neuauflagen der klassischen Dichter erreichen hohe Auflagen, unzählige Bildbände und Reproduktionen halten das Interesse am großen Bestand der bildenden Kunst des Abendlandes wach; in den philosophischen Seminaren studiert und interpretiert man wie eh und je PLATO, KANT und HEGEL; die deutsche Fachwissenschaft setzt ihre kaum unterbrochene Arbeit fort.

Der Ausländer, der eine im Krieg nicht zerstörte lebendige Universitätsstadt wie Tübingen, Erlangen, Heidelberg oder Göttingen besucht, mag weithin in den Vorlesungen, Aufführungen und Buchläden das „*alte Deutschland*" wiederfinden und darüber hinaus gerade an diesen Stätten auch viel neues Leben und echte geistige Unruhe, Studentenbühnen, Problemstücke, Diskussionen. Er wird ferner, wenn er die Großstädte besucht, wieder aufgebaute Theater vorfinden, glänzende Premieren und darin ein Publikum, das allerdings nicht mehr so einheitlich Gesellschaftskleidung trägt wie vor dem Krieg, ausgewogene Programme, gehobene Unterhaltung – das heißt jenen „Kulturbetrieb", der in den Großstädten der Massengesellschaft nun einmal dazugehört. Das also ist „noch" und „wieder" da: das Erbe und der Betrieb. Aber wenn dieser Ausländer genauer prüft, wird er merken, daß in den tieferen Schichten des Kulturlebens nicht alles beim Alten geblieben ist, sondern viel Unruhe und geistige Not anzutreffen ist – und mancherlei neues Leben, mancher bedeutende Ansatz, manches Experiment.

Mit der Trümmer-Kunst ist es allerdings vorbei. Sie hat einige Jahre lang den Vordergrund des Kulturlebens beherrscht in einer Lyrik bald ekstatischer und naturalistischer oder zynischer Färbung, in Schauspielen, sogar in einigen Filmen, vor allem in unzähligen rasch veralteten (und auf schlechtem Papier schlecht und recht gedruckten) Büchern der reflektierenden Besinnung und Kultur-Programmatik. Die Normalisierung des Daseins hat dieser Literatur der Katastrophe und des radikalen Neuanfangs ein Ende gesetzt; nur wenig wird davon übrigbleiben. Auch die vielen Zeitschriften, in denen sich damals, da Bücher zuviel Zeit beansprucht hätten, die Umwertung und Neuwertung der deutschen Vergangenheit, Geschichte und Gegenwart vollzog, sind zum größten Teil verschwunden. Dieselbe Normalisierung hat zwar die alte krisenfeste Literatur und jede Sorte populärer Kunst neu belebt, doch spielt sich das Wichtigste, das Eigentliche gleichsam zwischen der Trümmer-Welt und dem äußeren Wiederaufbau ab.

Das deutsche Bewußtsein ist mit diesem seinem Schicksal noch nicht fertig geworden. Uralte deutsche Sonderprobleme, wie das der Innerlichkeit und der Welt, wie „Geist und Macht", wie das der echten und der falschen Tiefe, beunruhigen die besseren Köpfe. Auch das Verhältnis der Deutschen zu den europäischen Nachbarkulturen, insbesondere zur französischen, ist eine neu gestellte Aufgabe, desgleichen die Abstoßung und Anziehung des Ostens, schließlich die Auseinandersetzung mit dem mächtigen Impuls der amerikanischen Zivilisation. Das alles macht jedes wesentliche deutsche Kulturleben problematisch. Darin liegt sein besonderer Reiz. Darin liegt auch eine Grenze: es gibt wenig große, gültige Aussagen, die das Zeug in sich haben, klassisch oder gar kanonisch zu werden.

Eine weitere Problematik liegt darin, daß geschlossene regionale Kulturprovinzen sich nicht mehr „rein" erhalten lassen. Die schlesische kulturtragende Schicht zum Beispiel hat sich über Westdeutschland verbreitet. Das gilt für die schöpferischen Kräfte, die Dichter und Schriftsteller, es gilt für die disponierenden Köpfe, und es gilt für das Publikum. Die wachen Menschen aus dem Osten bilden in allen Regionalkulturen ein belebendes, anregendes Element; selbst in Bayern, das sich trotz älteren Zuwanderungen vor allem aus Franken und dem Rheinland immer ein wenig für sich gehalten hatte. Damit verschwindet mancher Reiz, aber der Vorgang selbst ist nicht aufzuhalten; er ist ein Stück des deutschen Schicksals. Es gibt eine Gegenbewegung. Man wird in Bayern und anderswo mehr Trachtenfeste, Heimatfeste, Volkskunst und dergleichen antreffen als je; aber nur der oberflächliche Beobachter wird verkennen, daß *die „Integration" der regionalen Kulturen zur deutschen Kultur* Fortschritte macht. Das hat mit der „Kulturhoheit" der Länder nichts zu tun: gehört es doch zu den Pflichten eines bayerischen oder hessischen Kultusministers, auch für die zugewanderten Ostdeutschen zu sorgen, ihnen zum Beispiel den Zugang zu führenden Stellungen im Kulturleben und – ein wichtiges Kapitel – zum Lehramt an der Volksschule und an der höheren Schule in gebührendem Verhältnis zu den einheimischen Kandidaten zu eröffnen. Es wird freilich nur ein geringer Teil des außerordentlichen Schadens, den das deutsche Kulturleben durch den Verlust vor allem Ostpreußens (mit der Universität Königsberg und der für den Katholizismus wichtigen Hochschule Braunsberg) und Schlesiens (mit Breslau) erlitten hat, durch diese Infiltrierung ostdeutscher Kulturträger im Westen wieder wettgemacht.

Dasselbe gilt bis zu einem gewissen, freilich beschränkten Grad auch für die gegenwärtige Abtrennung der mitteldeutschen Gebiete; denn ver-

S
P
O
R
T

W E I N

Schloß Johannisberg, als Benediktinerabtei 1719 erbaut, seit 1816 im Besitz der Fürsten Metternich

Weinlese in der Pfa

Das Türkenfaß in Meersburg am Bodens

Der Weinkeller des Schlosses Johannisberg bei Rüdesheim im Rheingau

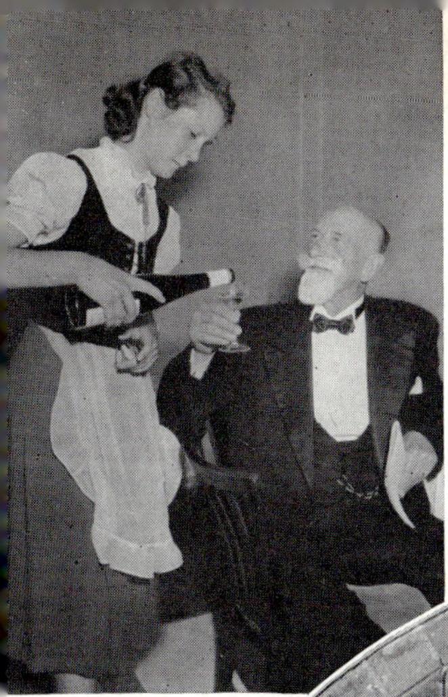

Geschnitztes
Faß der Sekt-
llerei HOEHL,
Eltville

St. Urbanus,
Schutzpatron
der Winzer

W
E
I
N

ıtscher Wein
ı alle Welt

Geisenheim

Ruhrfestspiele
Recklinghausen:
Szene aus
WILLIAM
SHAKESPEARE
„Der Sturm“

HERBERT VON KARAJAN
— als Dirigent

— mit seinen
Schülern

ständlicherweise sind gerade manche besonders aktive Köpfe aus der sogenannten DDR in den Westen übergesiedelt, von den Universitäten Berlin, Greifswald, Leipzig, Jena und Halle an die Freie Universität Berlin oder die westdeutschen Universitäten — zum Vorteil des Westens, zum Nachteil freilich jener Gebiete selbst.

Die Stadt *Berlin* hat auch in dieser Hinsicht eine ganz besondere Bedeutung. Da sie nicht ganz von der sogenannten DDR abzuschnüren ist, da es drüben bekannt wird, was in dieser Stadt geschieht, da sie auch leichter besucht werden kann als der Westen, sichert sie die Verbindung mit den im Ostbereich gebliebenen Kulturträgern. Sie versorgt sie mit Literatur; sie sorgt anderseits dafür, daß der Westen die „Zone" nicht vergißt und kulturell abschreibt. Ohne Berlin wäre die kulturelle Spaltung und Entfremdung viel stärker, als sie es jetzt ist. An sich ist der Eiserne Vorhang auch als Kulturgrenze recht dicht. Schon seit Jahren mußten zum Beispiel die ausübenden Künstler, sogar die Musiker, zwischen dem Auftreten im Westen und dem in der sogenannten DDR sich entscheiden. Im BACH-Jahr, im GOETHE-Jahr und im SCHILLER-Jahr gab es zweierlei Feiern. Nur einige wenige Künstler (wie der Thomaner-Chor) und Wissenschaftler haben so etwas wie ein Privileg der Arbeit in beiden Teilen Deutschlands. (Von den „Sympathisierenden", die dieses Privileg selbst sich nehmen und damit der allgemeinen Mißbilligung verfallen, ist nicht die Rede.) Es findet auch noch ein zum größeren Teil illegaler, zum kleineren Teil legaler Austausch von Büchern und Zeitschriften statt.

Die *Dezimierung des jüdischen Elements* ist besonders am Fall Frankfurt zu studieren, das früher unter den Großstädten den höchsten Anteil jüdischer Mitbürger hatte. Nur ein Bruchteil hat den Nationalsozialismus überlebt, nur wenige Emigranten sind zurückgekommen (so die Professoren HORKHEIMER und ADORNO). Es fehlen aus dieser Gruppe von Bürgern die aktiven Künstler und Wissenschaftler, es fehlen die Mäzene, und es fehlt das starke jüdische Element im Publikum der Theater- und Konzertsäle. Es ist mit Händen zu greifen, wie diese tüchtige Stadt, die ihre geschichtliche Aktivität neubelebt hat, im Geistigen dadurch trotz vielen bedeutenden Leistungen im einzelnen im Durchschnitt doch „provinzieller" geworden ist. Das spricht nicht gegen sie – es ist eine unvermeidliche Konsequenz dieser Seite des deutschen Schicksals. Vergleichbare Erscheinungen lassen in andern Großstädten, vor allem auch in Berlin, sich feststellen.

Die Besatzungsmächte hatten ursprünglich einen starken Einfluß auf die Schule, auf die Publizistik und das Kulturleben ausgeübt. Merkliche Unterschiede zwischen den drei Zonen begannen sich auszubilden. Inzwischen hat sich das ausgeglichen. Übriggeblieben ist vor allem der französische Einfluß auf eine Bildungselite und in ganz Deutschland das, was man „Amerikanismus“ nennt: die Wirkung amerikanischer Vorbilder in der Roman-Literatur, im Erziehungswesen, in den politischen Wissenschaften und in der Soziologie – um nur von der höheren Kultur zu sprechen.

*

Nachdem der Philosoph JASPERS, der so viel für das Selbstverständnis der Deutschen getan hat, im Jahre 1948 von Heidelberg nach Basel übergesiedelt ist, erscheint MARTIN HEIDEGGER in Freiburg als der repräsentativste deutsche Philosoph. Sein Daseinsverständnis („Sorge“) ist in der Krise der Nachkriegszeit und in der Nachbarschaft der Franzosen SARTRE (auch CAMUS) und GABRIEL MARCEL nicht nur herrschende philosophische Richtung, sondern geradezu zur Mode geworden. Die eigentliche Bedeutung der „*Existenzphilosophie*“ für die deutsche Kultur liegt aber wohl darin, daß sie in den mannigfaltigsten Formen von der Fachphilosophie, der Theologie, vom allgemeinen geistigen Bewußtsein, von der Kunst, ja selbst von der Pädagogik aufgenommen, umgedacht, verarbeitet worden ist.

Deutschland ist kulturell gesehen „*dreisprachig*“: christlich, marxistisch und liberal-humanitär. Das existenzphilosophische Denken hat alle drei Sprachen beeinflußt und einander nähergebracht. Der Rationalismus, der angelsächsische Pragmatismus und der amerikanische Behaviorismus sind ebensowenig wie das amerikanische optimistische Grundgefühl in Deutschland sehr verbreitet. (Nur methodisch hat der Positivismus auf einen Teil der Soziologie, auf die „Politischen Wissenschaften“ und die Pädagogik eingewirkt.) Es gibt in Deutschland HEGEL-Nachfolge, Neukantianismus, Logistik und eine Neuscholastik (die an Offenheit und Differenziertheit gewonnen hat); aber als führende Richtung hat sich aus der „Phänomenologie“ die Existenzphilosophie entwickelt. Man darf die deutsche Schule, die als Methode in der philosophischen Tradition steht, freilich nicht mit der publizistischen französischen Form, dem Existentialismus, verwechseln.

Dem Krisenbewußtsein der führenden Philosophie entspricht eine Literatur, die sich im Roman und in der Erzählung viel stärker als im Drama ausspricht. Hierüber wird in einem eigenen Beitrag an anderer Stelle dieses Buches berichtet.

Auf den *Universitäten* wird äußerst fleißig und gründlich gearbeitet. Die Studenten sind politisch wach und kritisch, lassen aber geistig sich durchweg vom Berufsstudium okkupieren. Die Universität empfindet sich trotz ihrem großartig funktionierenden Forschungs- und Lehr-System „in der Krise“: sie will nicht zu einer Fach- und Ausbildungsstätte werden. Ein „*studium generale*“ soll das Fachstudium ergänzen und vertiefen, ein ständiges Gespräch zwischen den Fakultäten wird angeregt und oft geführt. Die mit der gewaltigen Zunahme der Studentenzahl in den letzten Jahren neu auftretenden Fragen hindern die Hochschulen daran, ihre schon lange als dringlich erkannten Grundprobleme zu lösen.

Die wissenschaftliche Forschung im einzelnen wird in einem besonderen Kapitel behandelt. Auch die höhere Schule, gehemmt durch die Sonderentwicklungen in den Besatzungszonen und Ländern, hat noch nicht ihr Gleichgewicht in einem bestimmten System der Fächer und Methoden gefunden. Nicht nur in den Landerziehungsheimen und anderen Privatschulen, auch in der normalen staatlichen und konfessionellen Anstalt wird viel, wenn auch nicht sehr radikal, experimentiert. Die Schulen leiden immer noch unter der Überfüllung der Klassen, dem Mangel an Schulgebäuden, teilweise auch unter dem Lehrermangel. Die pädagogische Diskussion ist lebhaft: *die deutsche Schule ist in Fluß*. Ähnliches gilt von der Volksschule, die trotz allen Anstrengungen noch schwerer mit der Raumnot zu kämpfen hat. In aller Stille bringt die deutsche Lehrerschaft erhebliche Opfer für die Ausbildung und Erziehung der jungen Generation.

*

Es würde schwer sein, für die Bereiche von Theater, Film, Funk und Fernsehen, für das musikalische Leben und die Welt des bildnerischen und architektonischen Schaffens in Deutschland im Rahmen einer allgemeinen Analyse der kulturellen Lage der Bundesrepublik seit dem Ende des Zweiten Weltkrieges mehr auszusagen als unzulässige Verallgemeinerungen. Alle diese Bereiche weisen je nach den Voraussetzungen und tragenden Kräften eine so vielgestaltige Form und so eigentümliche Probleme auf, daß ihre Einzelbetrachtung eigenen Kapiteln vorbehalten bleiben muß.

Ein lebendiger Spiegel des deutschen Kulturlebens sind die Feuilletons der Tageszeitungen und die kulturellen *Zeitschriften*, wie der „Merkur“, die „Neue Rundschau“ und die „Frankfurter Hefte“. Daneben gibt es eine Reihe von wichtigen konfessionellen („Hochland“, „Stimmen der Zeit“, „Furche“) und spezielleren Zeitschriften. Einigermaßen neu ist für Deutschland der Typus der politischen, kulturellen Wochenzeitungen („Rheinischer Merkur“, „Christ und Welt“). Sie tragen viel zur Bewußtseinsbildung sowohl der älteren wie der jungen Generation bei und vermitteln ein Bild von den mannigfachen Strömungen, welche die deutsche Kultur der Gegenwart beherrschen oder beeinflussen.

*

Es wurde beiläufig erwähnt, daß Deutschland kulturell „dreisprachig" sei. Allerdings ist die „marxistische" Geisteswelt in der Zeit nach dem Kriege außer durch solide Beiträge in der Volksbildungsarbeit der Arbeiterbewegung kaum in den Vordergrund getreten. Die Spaltung dieser geistigen Bewegung in den kommunistischen und den sozialistischen Flügel, die Entartung des kommunistischen, die regionale Spaltung – alles das hat die Bedeutung dieser früher so gewichtigen Kulturprovinz sehr vermindert. Man kann den geistigen Einfluß der „Linken" mit dem der französischen Linken nicht vergleichen.

Der Beitrag der humanitären Sprache, die sich aus dem Erbe der deutschen klassischen Zeiten und des deutschen Bürgertums nährt, ist in anderen Zusammenhängen schon geschildert worden. Alles, was über das Kulturleben geäußert worden ist, verteilt sich durchweg auf Beiträge dieser Tradition und Sprache und auf christliche Beiträge, und die Grundauseinandersetzung, die etwa in Frankreich zwischen jenen drei Sprachen sich vollzieht, vollzieht sich in Deutschland vor allem zwischen den verschiedenen Formen des *Humanismus* und dem *Christentum*.

Der geistige Einfluß dieses Christentums ist außerordentlich gewachsen. Die evangelische und die katholische Theologie sind wieder geistige Mächte, die man ernst nimmt, auch auf den Universitäten. Die evangelische Kirche hat ein System von „Evangelischen Akademien" entwickelt, in denen die Sorgen und Probleme der Zeit zwischen Theologen, Fachleuten und Interessierten außerordentlich gründlich und offen durchgearbeitet werden – ein Beitrag zur kulturellen Auseinandersetzung, der nicht mehr wegzudenken ist. Auf katholischer Seite sind entsprechende Einrichtungen geschaffen worden; dort wurde aber auch die Arbeit auf Burg Rothenfels wiederaufgenommen, die, inspiriert von dem bedeutenden katholischen Denker und Erzieher ROMANO GUARDINI, schon vor der nationalsozialistischen Zeit das Bewußtsein der damals jüngeren Generation wesentlich geprägt hat. In religiösen Bildungswerken geschieht eine ähnliche Auseinandersetzung auf örtlicher Basis. Die äußere Aufgabe, zerstörte Kirchen neu zu bauen, fiel in beiden Konfessionen mit günstigen geistigen Bedingungen zusammen: einer Neubesinnung auf das Wesen des Gottesdienstes (katholisch: mit der „liturgischen Bewegung") Die evangelische „Orgel-Bewegung" hat sich durchgesetzt: die Fabrikation romantischer und orchesterkopierender Orgeln der

Jahrhundertwende tritt stark zurück hinter einem werkgerechten und an der Spitzenleistung der Barock-Orgel orientierten Orgelbau; man spielt und fördert eine instrumentgerechte alte und neue Orgelliteratur (HELMUT WALCHA). Auch die intensive Jugendarbeit der beiden Konfessionen ist aus dem Kulturleben Deutschlands nicht fortzudenken, wie im Kapitel über die Kirchen bereits ausgeführt worden ist.

*

Das deutsche Kulturleben, ein reiches vielfältiges Erbe, das von schweren Schicksalen „herausgefordert" wird (um mit TOYNBEE zu sprechen), ist in Fluß. Das deutsche Bewußtsein ist noch nicht fertig mit dem politischen Schicksal. Eine forsche oder forcierte Sekurität einerseits, ein fundamentloser Radikalismus anderseits geben die Grenzen eines breiten Feldes an, in dem sich mit deutscher Gründlichkeit die große *Auseinandersetzung* vollzieht: die Auseinandersetzung der Deutschen mit sich selbst, mit ihrer Geschichte, mit ihrer Schuld und ihren Versäumnissen, mit ihren neuen Aufgaben, mit der drohenden und der lockenden Umwelt, mit den Partnern. Hinter einer allzu glänzenden Fassade und viel Geschäftigkeit und guten Geschäften geschieht hier in einigen Millionen Menschen, deren Kultur für die ganze Welt von einiger Bedeutung ist, ein vielschichtiger Prozeß: die Erneuerung der deutschen Kultur in der höheren Einheit Europa und in der potentiellen Einheit der Einen Welt.

STAAT UND KULTUR

Es liegt im Wesen jedes Bundesstaates, daß seine Glieder an der staatlichen Pflege der Kultur besonders beteiligt sind. Bei Gliedstaaten mit eigener kultureller Tradition wird das auch durch sie getragene Bewußtsein eigener Staatlichkeit Anlaß sein, Selbständigkeit und Wert dieser Kräfte zu respektieren. Je stärker sich im Aufbau des Bundes zentrale Notwendigkeiten durchsetzen, desto eher wird man es für zweckmäßig halten, daß die Gliedstaaten Aufgaben durchführen, die — ohne die bundesstaatlichen Interessen zu beeinträchtigen — in der leichteren Übersicht kleinerer Verwaltungen gelöst werden können. Auf kulturellem Gebiet stehen viele solcher Aufgaben in engem Zusammenhang mit heimatlichen Gemeinschaften, deren Anteilnahme die beste Gewähr für ihre Erfüllung bietet. Schließlich besitzen die Gliedstaaten für einen politisch besonders bedeutungsvollen Bereich des kulturellen Lebens, das Schulwesen, ein durch die Natur der Erziehungsaufgabe gerechtfertigtes Mandat. So wirken historische, politisch-praktische und im Wesen öffentlicher kultureller Arbeit liegende Gesichtspunkte zusammen, um die weitgehende Überlassung der staatlichen kulturpolitischen Zuständigkeit an die Gliedstaaten zu begründen.

Dieser Tendenz ist auch das Grundgesetz der Bundesrepublik Deutschland gefolgt, indem es diese Kompetenz grundsätzlich den Ländern überließ. Das Kaiserreich, die Republik von Weimar und der nationalsozialistische Staat hatten sich zu dem Problem staatlicher Kulturpflege im Bundesstaat sehr verschieden gestellt. Von einem nur sehr lockeren Zusammenhang im Reich von 1871 führte die Entwicklung zu einem wesentlich stärkeren Gewicht zentraler Befugnisse in der Verfassung von 1919. Die zunehmende allgemeine Schwäche der jungen Republik ließ die damals gefundene Lösung nicht zu den erhofften Ergebnissen kommen. Im nationalsozialistischen Staat erweckte die auch im kulturpolitischen Bereich übermäßige Zentralisierung staatlicher Kompetenzen berechtigten Widerspruch. Die damit gemachten sehr ungünstigen Erfahrungen wirkten neben anderen Einflüssen bei der Gründung der Bundesrepublik nach, als die Teilnahme des Bundes an der staatlichen Kulturpflege auf einige wenige Zuständigkeiten beschränkt wurde: konkurrierende, das heißt neben der Kompetenz der Länder bestehende, Zuständigkeit für die Förderung der Forschung, Schutz des deutschen Kulturguts vor Abwanderung, Rahmengesetzgebung für die allgemeinen Rechtsverhältnisse von Presse und Film, Naturschutz und Landschaftspflege.

Die neue Regelung entsprach in den Gebieten mit historischer Staatlichkeit, insbesondere also den süddeutschen Ländern, dem Wunsch nach selbständiger Entwicklung alter staatlicher Kulturpflege von anerkannt hohem Rang. Für die von den Besatzungsmächten gebildeten neuen Länder mußte naturgemäß, obwohl die Voraussetzungen hier in vielfältiger Abstufung anders liegen, die gleiche Regelung vorgesehen werden. Wie als Folge der jahrhundertealten politischen Vielgestaltigkeit Deutschlands ein noch heute fortwirkendes Erbe in der kulturellen Mannigfaltigkeit des Landes erwachsen ist, so haben auch in der Gegenwart und jüngsten Vergangenheit die staatspolitischen Kräfte dauernd in hohem Maße auf die kulturelle Entwicklung eingewirkt. Auch die neuen Länder haben die ihnen zufallenden kulturpolitischen Aufgaben von Anfang an sehr ernst genommen; vielleicht im Lauf der Jahre um so stärker, je mehr in anderen Zweigen der staatlichen Verwaltung das Schwergewicht beim fortschreitenden Ausbau des Bundes auf diesen überging.

Neben dem Zwang zu einer der stürmischen Entwicklung der Forschung angepaßten Wissenschaftspflege rechtfertigt schon der außerordentliche Wert, den eine gleichmäßige, sorgfältige Jugenderziehung und wohlausgebaute Erwachsenenbildung für das Entstehen und die Stärkung echten demokratischen Sinnes und die Bereitschaft zu verantwortlicher Mitarbeit im öffentlichen Leben besitzen, das höchste Interesse aller beteiligten Stellen in Bund und Ländern an diesen Fragen.

*

Der zunächst beabsichtigte Ausschluß des Bundes auch in überregionalen kulturellen Angelegenheiten wurde in zwei Richtungen durchbrochen. Kulturpolitik wird nicht nur innerhalb der deutschen Grenzen getrieben, sondern sie spielt heute mehr als je eine wichtige Rolle im Zusammenhang mit den auswärtigen Beziehungen der Staaten. In diesem Rahmen blieb Kulturpolitik unbestritten Aufgabe des Bundes. Mit der Kulturabteilung des Auswärtigen Amtes arbeiten die Kultusminister der Länder besonders durch ihre Sachverständigen für das Schulwesen beim Wiederaufbau der deutschen Auslandsschulen und anderen Maßnahmen, die der Ausführung der mit anderen Staaten geschlossenen Kulturabkommen dienen, nützlich und verdienstvoll zusammen. Die Schwierigkeiten, die für die Bundesrepublik als Partner völkerrechtlicher Verträge bei deren Erfüllung durch die deutsche Gesetzgebung und Verwaltung im kulturellen Bereich sich ergeben können, sind durch das sogenannte Konkordatsurteil des Bundesverfassungsgerichts vom 26.3.1957 ins Licht gerückt worden.

Im innerdeutschen Bereich hat der Bund die Vorhand in der Behandlung der kulturellen Aufgaben behalten, die im Zusammenhang mit der Teilung Deutschlands und der historisch einzigartigen Lage der Vertriebenen und Flüchtlinge stehen. Um den Zusammenhang mit der Bevölkerung der sogenannten DDR und die geistige und seelische Verbundenheit der in Landsmannschaften zusammengeschlossenen Vertriebenen zu stärken, werden von der Bundesregierung laufend erhebliche Aufwendungen gemacht.

Diese Spezialaufgaben sind schon ihrer Natur nach Bundesaufgaben. Das gleiche gilt von der Betätigung einzelner Fachressorts des Bundes in der Wissenschaftsförderung, soweit sie mit dem Fachgebiet in untrennbarem Zusammenhang steht. Besonders die Bundesministerien für Wirtschaft, Ernährung, Verkehr und für Atomenergie und Wasserwirtschaft finanzieren Maßnahmen zur Förderung der Forschung, zum Teil durch Unterhaltung eigener Institute.

Starke Bedenken der Länder richteten sich zunächst gegen die Einrichtung einer *Abteilung für kulturelle Angelegenheiten des Bundes im Bundesministerium des Innern*, der eine allgemeine Zuständigkeit für die kulturpolitische Arbeit des Bundes zufiel. Gegen sie wirkte die Absicht, das Bedürfnis nach Berücksichtigung überregionaler kultureller Interessen in erster Linie durch eine *von den Ländern selbst getragene Gemeinschaftsarbeit* zu befriedigen. Die entscheidende Frage ist und bleibt dabei, ob diesen kulturellen Erfordernissen (abgesehen von den dem Bund durch Gesetz ausdrücklich zuerkannten Angelegenheiten) unter Ausschluß des Bundes Genüge getan werden kann; oder ob es nicht vielleicht sogar sinnvoll wäre und dem Subsidiaritätsprinzip entsprechen würde, daß der Bund — entsprechend seiner unbestrittenen Kompetenz zur Wahrnehmung gesamtdeutscher kultureller Interessen gegenüber den nicht zur Bundesrepublik gehörenden Teilen Deutschlands und dem Ausland — solche Aufgaben ganz oder in Gemeinschaft mit dem nächstbeteiligten Land erfüllt. Es fehlt nicht an Beispielen dafür, daß derartige Aufgaben auf diesem Wege in befriedigender Weise bewältigt werden konnten. Dennoch ist diese Frage noch heute strittig und vielfach Anlaß zu Erörterungen auch in der Öffentlichkeit gewesen. Der Grund hierfür liegt, abgesehen von den natürlichen allgemeinen Spannungen innerhalb eines Föderativstaates, in der durch das Wesen kulturellen Handelns begründeten *Schwierigkeit, Kulturpolitik in einem Bundesstaat regional zu begrenzen*. Was etwa auf dem Gebiet des Schulwesens als organisatorische Maßnahme der Schulverwaltung eines einzelnen Landes nur für dieses Land rechtlich verbindlich ist, kann schulpolitisch von stärkster

Wirkung für alle Länder des Bundes, also von gesamtstaatlicher Bedeutung sein. Wissenschaft und Kunst vollends entziehen sich ihrer Natur nach jeder regionalen Begrenzung und müssen schlechthin Gegenstand staatlicher kultureller Fürsorge sein, wo immer sie geleistet werden kann. Wesentlich ist hier nur die Frage, wo und wie dem Anspruch der Kultur auf staatliche Förderung praktisch am besten Genüge getan wird. Ist doch staatliche Kulturpflege eine Tätigkeit, die historisch in privatem Mäzenatentum wurzelt und nur schwer in herkömmliche Begriffe der Verwaltungsorganisation einzuordnen ist. Vom Bund gesehen bedeutet dies das Streben nach möglichst enger Zusammenarbeit von Bund und Ländern, um sowohl die besonderen Gesichtspunkte der Nächstbeteiligten im Land wie die der Gesamtheit im Bund rechtzeitig und gleichmäßig zur Geltung kommen zu lassen. Es bedeutet freilich auch die Anerkennung des Grundsatzes, staatliche Kulturpolitik aus möglichst weiter Überschau in möglichst elastischen Formen und ohne zu enge Bindungen an staatliche Verwaltungen zu treiben.

Das Erfordernis, die ganz Deutschland betreffenden zentralen Aufgaben zu lösen, und die Auffassung, welche die Länder über den hierzu gangbaren Weg hatten, führte dazu, daß die Kultusminister der Länder seit 1949 zu einer „*Ständigen Konferenz*" zusammengetreten sind. Sie kann nicht als ein besonderes staatsrechtliches Organ wirksam werden sondern ist ein fester Arbeitskreis unter jährlich wechselndem Vorsitz und mit einem Generalsekretariat. Das Bundesministerium des Innern kann als Gast bei den normalen Tagungen der Konferenz (nicht aber den Arbeiten ihrer drei Fachausschüsse) teilweise vertreten sein. Dies dient überwiegend der Information des Bundes. Bei allem von mancher Seite gezeigten prinzipiellen Mißtrauen und vielerlei Schwierigkeiten im einzelnen hat sich doch längst eine vielfältige sachliche Zusammenarbeit der Länder mit dem Bund in kulturellen Fragen ergeben. Sie hat allerdings noch nicht der Überzeugung zum Siege verhelfen können, daß es auch im Interesse der Länder liegt, wenn auf Seiten des Bundes die von ihnen schon um der besseren Übersicht willen geforderte Zusammenfassung aller kulturpolitischen Aktivitäten auch organisatorischen Niederschlag fände. Eine außerordentlich schwere Belastung aller von Bund und Ländern geleisteten kulturpolitischen Arbeit stellt die Tatsache dar, daß infolge der gegebenen Verhältnisse die aus der Polarität der beiden Partner im kulturellen Bereich erwachsenden Fragen, in der Regel zu Problemen der Finanzverfassung transformiert, die politische Auseinandersetzung beherrschen.

In den öffentlichen Erörterungen der durch diese Verhältnisse bestimmten kulturpolitischen Lage in Deutschland spielt besonders die Kritik an der Schulpolitik der Länder eine Rolle. Dabei ist der Auffassung der Länder unter anderem entgegengehalten worden, daß die nach ihrem System notwendige dauernde Koordinierung abweichender Regelungen kein Ersatz für eine die Bedürfnisse aller Länder rechtzeitig berücksichtigende, in allen Grundfragen allgemein verbindliche Planung sei, sondern nur Korrektur nachträglich festgestellter Ungleichheiten. Die Schwächen, die dieses System hat, haben sich in der Praxis etwa dadurch enthüllt, daß in einigen Ländern im Wechsel politisch verschiedener Parlamente und Regierungen einschneidende Änderungen im Aufbau des Schulwesens erfolgten, die weithin zu Klagen der Erziehungsberechtigten führten. Die Gefahr, die eine von wechselnden Parteikonstellationen getragene, nur auf ein einzelnes Land gerichtete Betrachtungsweise birgt, liegt auf der Hand. Daraus rechtfertigt sich die Überzeugung, daß es notwendig ist, bei allen grundsätzlich bedeutungsvollen Entscheidungen einer Landesregierung in kulturellen Fragen auf das Interesse der im Bund geeinten Gesamtheit zu achten, seine rechtzeitige Berücksichtigung zu empfehlen und den erforderlichen Ausgleich schon im Anfang einer überregional wirkenden Maßnahme vorzunehmen. Diese Überzeugung ist einer der wichtigsten Ausgangspunkte für das Bemühen der Bundesregierung um Einklang von Bund und Ländern in kulturellen Fragen. Sie stützt sich auf die Erkenntnis, daß der Bund nicht ein nur auf politische, soziale und wirtschaftliche Interessen gerichteter Zweckverband ist, sondern ein eigener geistiger Organismus, der ohne Pflege aller Bereiche der Kultur in dem ihnen angemessenen Umfang auch seine anderen Aufgaben auf die Dauer nicht erfüllen könnte. Kein Organismus aber lebt, wenn ihm nicht alle Glieder und Organe in harmonischem Zusammenwirken dienen.

Die Summe der mit den allzu vielen Formen der höheren Schule gemachten ungünstigen Erfahrungen und die davon getragenen Klagen der öffentlichen Meinung gaben zu verschiedenen Reformvorschlägen Veranlassung. Sie gipfelten schließlich in dem mehrfach wiederholten, wenn auch nicht aussichtsreichen Antrag der (föderalistischen) Deutschen Partei im Bundestag, die Kompetenz des Bundes im Grundgesetz auf die „einheitliche Regelung des Erziehungs- und Schulwesens" zu erweitern und demgemäß ein Bundesministerium für Erziehung und Unterricht zu errichten.

Vom Bunde aus werden die Erörterungen über Nutzen und Nachteil der Errichtung eines Bundeskultusministeriums in dem Bewußtsein verfolgt, daß prinzipiell an einer Verstärkung des staatlichen Einflusses auf die Kultur ebensowenig gelegen sein kann wie auch nur an einer Vermehrung der bisher tätigen staatlichen Verwaltungszentralen. Der Bund ist in der glücklichen Lage, auf fast jede Kulturverwaltung verzichten zu können; denn die „Verwaltung" von Kulturfonds bei den Ministerien des Bundes ist nichts anderes als ihre sinnvolle Verausgabung an Stellen, die das empfangene Geld direkt in kulturelle Leistung umsetzen oder es über Verwaltungsorgane weiterleiten. Auch solche Organe „verwalten" im übrigen niemals Kultur, sondern sie fördern Menschen, die kulturelle Leistungen vollbringen, und Einrichtungen, die dieser Arbeit dienen. Das gilt auch für die von der Staatsverwaltung besonders stark umhegte öffentliche Schule, in der das ganze Schwergewicht auf dem frei gestaltenden Schaffen der pädagogischen Persönlichkeit liegt, alle Verwaltung aber nur Hilfe bedeuten darf. Gerade die Entfernung von der notwendig der Einzelheit gewidmeten Tätigkeit einer Landesverwaltung ist es aber, die einer zentralen Stelle im Bund ihr Eigengewicht geben könnte.

*

Das wirklich Wichtige bleibt für das Bildungswesen die gut vorbereitete rechtzeitige verbindliche Planung, die allerdings nicht lediglich der Kulturverwaltung überlassen werden kann. Einen starken Hinweis darauf, durch welche anderen Methoden noch sehr lebendige und gewichtige Kräfte für die Mitarbeit an diesem Problem gewonnen werden können, gibt die im Herbst 1953 erfolgte Gründung des *Deutschen Ausschusses für das Erziehungs- und Bildungswesen.* Die Bemühungen um sein Zustandekommen sind ein gutes Beispiel dafür, daß auch im kulturellen Leben schließlich die Befriedigung des sachlichen Bedürfnisses durch den Mangel eines formellen Rechtssatzes nicht entscheidend gehemmt zu werden braucht. Bund und Länder einigten sich im Jahre 1953 auf die Gründung eines weder beim Bund noch bei den Ländern tätigen, sondern völlig unabhängigen Ausschusses. Seine zunächst zwanzig von Bund und Ländern gleichzeitig und in voller Übereinstimmung berufenen Mitglieder sollen, frei von Aufträgen oder irgendwelchen anderen Bindungen, als Treuhänder der Gesamtheit und ganz aus dem Gewicht ihrer Persönlichkeit für den geistigen Aufbau der Nation durch Ratschläge und Empfehlungen tätig werden. Mit dem Blick auf den Gesamtbereich der deutschen Kultur sollen sie auch dahin wirken, daß grundsätzliche Entscheidungen, insbesondere im Schulwesen, nicht nur aus der Perspektive der parteipolitisch bestimmten Lage eines einzelnen Landes getroffen und Abweichungen nachträglich koordiniert — das heißt durch Kompromisse unter den Verwaltungen ausgeglichen — werden. Mochte für deutsche Verhältnisse der Gedanke neu sein, neben der auch in kulturellen Fragen oft allzu beanspruchten Autorität der staatlichen Behörden das moralische Gewicht einer ganz aus eigener Autorität wirkenden freien Stelle gelten zu lassen — alle bei ihrer Bildung Beteiligten haben doch den Wert einer aus eigener Sachkunde und persönlicher Verantwortung handelnden Instanz anerkannt. Die von dem Deutschen Ausschuß für das Erziehungs- und Bildungswesen inzwischen vorgelegten Empfehlungen und Gutachten zu einzelnen Teilfragen seines Arbeitsbereichs haben erwiesen, daß der mit seiner Gründung beschrittene Weg richtig war. Der dem Ausschuß erteilte Auftrag ist um weitere fünf Jahre verlängert worden.

*

Der Abteilung für kulturelle Angelegenheiten des Bundes im Bundesministerium des Innern kam es zunächst darauf an, die Anerkennung der natürlichen Autorität der Bundesregierung auch in kulturellen Fragen zu erhalten und die Hilfe des Bundes dort zum Tragen zu bringen, wo die Sache es gebieterisch erheischt. Das ist in allen Kreisen des kulturellen Lebens gelungen. Der Begriff „*Kultur*" ist hierbei im weitesten Sinne verstanden. Er umfaßt zum Beispiel auch den Bereich des Sports, dem wesentliche Unterstützung zuteil wird.

Die *Notlage der deutschen wissenschaftlichen Forschung* war besonders in den ersten Jahren des Bestehens der Bundesrepublik so groß, und den Ländern erwuchsen durch den Wiederaufbau der Hochschulen so hohe Ausgaben, daß jede vom Bund geleistete Hilfe willkommen sein mußte. Hier galt es nur, die dem Bund zur Verfügung gestellten Mittel richtig einzusetzen. Eine große Zahl bedeutender überregional wirkender Forschungsstätten war bereits 1949 in dem *Königsteiner Abkommen* der Länder von diesen in eigene gemeinsame Obhut genommen worden, und ihre Zahl vermehrte sich von Jahr zu Jahr. Unter ihnen ragt die für die Entwicklung der Naturwissenschaften besonders wichtige *Max-Planck-Gesellschaft* hervor. Die materielle Fürsorge für die große Zahl von Unternehmungen einzelner Forscher, für den wissenschaftlichen Nachwuchs und das Forschungsmaterial (Bibliotheken, Apparate usw.) war etwa seit der gleichen Zeit zunächst von der erneuerten Notgemeinschaft der Deutschen Wissenschaft, nach deren Vereinigung mit dem nur kurz wirksamen Deutschen Forschungsrat von der als *Deutsche Forschungsgemeinschaft* segensreich tätigen Organisation übernommen worden. Zur Finanzierung der Forschungsgemeinschaft trug der Bund schon vom ersten

Jahre seines Bestehens nach Kräften bei; ein seit 1952 laufendes besonderes „Schwerpunktprogramm" wurde ausschließlich aus relativ hoch bemessenen Bundesmitteln (1955 bereits 15 Millionen DM) finanziert. Nach dem Haushaltsplan für 1959 beläuft sich der Anteil des Bundes an den der Deutschen Forschungsgemeinschaft zur Verfügung gestellten staatlichen Mitteln auf 34 Millionen DM, der der Länder auf 8,5 Millionen DM.

Das Jahr 1957 brachte insofern eine Wende, als die allseits für unerläßlich gehaltene Verstärkung der Maßnahmen zur Förderung der Wissenschaft, über die an anderer Stelle berichtet wird, nicht nur dem Bund eine stärkere Verantwortung aufbürdete, sondern eine sinnvolle Planung forderte. Einer vom Präsidenten der Deutschen Forschungsgemeinschaft in der Öffentlichkeit ausgesprochenen Anregung folgend, wurde ein aus Repräsentanten der Wissenschaft und unabhängigen Persönlichkeiten sowie Vertretern des Bundes und der Länder zusammengesetzter *Wissenschaftsrat* errichtet. An seiner Bildung war der Bund hervorragend beteiligt. Bis die vorgesehenen Empfehlungen vor Aufstellung der Haushaltspläne des Bundes und der Länder durch den Wissenschaftsrat auf Grund seiner Erhebungen gegeben werden können, wird ein zur zusätzlichen Wissenschaftsförderung in den Bundeshaushalt eingesetzter Globalfonds (von zur Zeit 85 Millionen DM) nach den vom Wissenschaftsrat zugeleiteten Plänen verteilt. Die Bildung des Wissenschaftsrats ist vor allem verfassungsmäßig und organisatorisch als ein bedeutsames Zeichen dafür zu werten, daß die Zusammenarbeit zwischen Bund und Ländern im kulturellen Bereich feste Formen anzunehmen beginnt, die zu einer befriedigenden Aufgabenteilung in der Praxis führen. Es lag daher im Zug der Entwicklung, daß im Anschluß an eine umfassende Debatte über kulturpolitische Fragen im Deutschen Bundestag, die mit einer grundlegenden Rede des Bundesinnenministers eingeleitet wurde, das Parlament der Regierung den Auftrag erteilt hat, auf der Grundlage der verfassungsmäßigen Ordnung Verhandlungen mit dem Ziel einer sinnvollen Aufgabenteilung im kulturellen Bereich zwischen Bund und Ländern aufzunehmen. Sie werden, wenn das angestrebte Ziel erreicht werden soll, dazu führen müssen, daß der Bund im Rahmen seiner kulturpolitischen Kompetenz gewisse Lasten übernimmt, welche die Länder bisher getragen haben. Auf diese Weise sollen die Länder in den Stand gesetzt werden, in den Bereichen, in denen es keine Bundeszuständigkeit gibt, ihre Aufgaben besser und ohne Bundeshilfe zu erfüllen. Die Übernahme von zunächst der Hälfte der Kosten für die vom sogenannten Königsteiner Staatsabkommen getragenen wissenschaftlichen Einrichtungen zu Gunsten des dringend erforderlichen Ausbaus von Ingenieurschulen weist die Richtung, in der die Lösung dieser Aufgabe gefunden werden muß.

Die Max-Planck-Gesellschaft erhält schon jetzt einen besonderen Zuschuß des Bundes. Er gestattet ihr die Förderung solcher wichtigen Vorhaben, für welche die von den Ländern bereitgestellten Mittel keine Möglichkeit bieten.

Die zahlreichen Aufgaben, die der Bund in wachsendem Umfang auf kulturellem Gebiet in Angriff genommen hat, können nur durch Beispiele erläutert werden: die nachdrückliche Förderung der wiederauflebenden Erforschung der Probleme des osteuropäischen Raumes; die Errichtung einer für die politische Bildung wichtigen wissenschaftlichen Kommission für Geschichte des Parlamentarismus' und der politischen Parteien; die Förderung des in der Erforschung der nationalsozialistischen Zeit führenden Instituts für Zeitgeschichte; der für die Entwicklung der altgeschichtlichen Wissenschaften wichtige Zusammenschluß in einer eigenen Kommission sowie die Förderung der gegenüber anderen Ländern Europas und der Welt stark zurückgebliebenen Erforschung der Sozialgeschichte und der internationalen Beziehungen in der Neuzeit durch Gründung eigener wissenschaftlicher Kommissionen und Finanzierung ihrer Arbeiten; der organisatorische und finanzielle Wiederaufbau und zum Teil Ausbau der deutschen archäologischen, historischen und kunsthistorischen Institute im Ausland und deren weitere Betreuung; die organisatorische Erneuerung der deutschen Musikwissenschaft; die wirksame Förderung des wissenschaftlichen Films.

Der Bund hat sich überhaupt — wie an anderer Stelle dargestellt wird — die Förderung des Films in zunehmendem Maße angelegen sein lassen. Das gleiche gilt von den Angelegenheiten des Rundfunks und des Fernsehens, deren bundesgesetzliche Regelung zur Zeit Gegenstand lebhafter politischer Erörterungen ist.

Als eine aus gesetzlich anerkannter Bundeskompetenz entspringende Aufgabe sei die Errichtung des *Bundesarchivs* genannt; als Aufgabe von unbezweifelbar gesamtdeutscher Bedeutung die Mitarbeit bei der Gründung der *Deutschen Bibliothek* in Frankfurt am Main. Sie wird vom Bund gemeinsam mit dem Land Hessen, der Stadt Frankfurt und dem Börsenverein des Deutschen Buchhandels laufend finanziell unterstützt.

Die Betreuung der wissenschaftlichen Hochschulen ist alleinige Aufgabe der Länder. Damit ist jeder Einfluß des Bundes auf die für die Studenten im Vordergrund stehende wissenschaftliche Lehre ausgeschlossen. Doch entwickelten sich bald nützliche und erfreuliche Beziehungen zwischen den wichtigsten studentischen Organisationen und der Bundesregierung. Von den sehr nachhaltigen Förderungsmaßnahmen des Bundes für die Studenten ist an anderer Stelle dieses Buches die Rede. Es war sachlich von Wert, in der Zentrale des Bundes eine Stelle zu haben, die dem Gesamtanliegen der Studenten Verständnis und Interesse entgegenbrachte, als es darum ging, so wichtige Dinge wie das Stipendienwesen, die Förderung des Wohnheimbaues und das Austauschverfahren mit dem Ausland von Grund auf zu reformieren und auf eine neue erweiterte Grundlage zu stellen. So wurde es möglich, mit dem sogenannten *„Honnefer Modell" der Studentenförderung* (nach dem Ort einer Hochschultagung im Herbst 1955 so benannt), ein umfassendes Programm der hochschulgerechten Begabtenförderung mit sehr erheblichen Bundesmitteln zu verwirklichen.

Auch Probleme wie die der politischen Bildung an den Hochschulen lassen sich ohne Fühlung mit der zentralen politischen Stelle im Bund offenbar nicht befriedigend lösen. Sie sind für die Haltung der akademisch gebildeten Schichten im demokratischen Staat von hoher Bedeutung. So wurde auch von Professoren wie Studenten in den Erörterungen über die *Reform der Hochschulen* die Beteiligung der Vertreter der Bundesregierung erwartet und begrüßt. Die Honnefer Empfehlungen von 1955 sehen einen von den Ländern zu bildenden Ausschuß zur weiteren Erörterung der Hochschulreform vor. Dieser ist jedoch noch nicht zusammengetreten.

Ein gesamtdeutsches, allen Ländern gemeinsames und deshalb einheitlich zu sehendes Interesse begründet auch die Teilnahme des Bundes an einer Reihe wichtiger kultureller Arbeiten. Hierher gehört die Mithilfe bei der Erhaltung oder Erneuerung kultureller Denkstätten (zum Beispiel das Goethehaus Frankfurt, das Schillerhaus Marbach, das Germanische Nationalmuseum Nürnberg) ebenso wie der Wiederaufbau bedeutender kirchlicher oder profaner, national wertvoller Bauwerke (Aachen, Mainz, Trier, Hildesheim, Osnabrück, Lübeck, Nürnberg und andere). Überall handelt der Bund als Treuhänder der Gesamtheit für Bedürfnisse, für welche die wirtschaftliche Kraft der nächstbeteiligten Länder nicht ausreichte. Er tut es auch in der Überzeugung von der jedem falschen Zentralismus abholden gemeinschaftsbildenden Kraft, welche einer Leistung innewohnt, die von der Gesamtheit des Volkes durch seine höchste politische Repräsentanz im Dienst seiner bedeutendsten kulturellen Werte aus Vergangenheit und Gegenwart vollbracht wird.

So ist auch die Hilfe zu bewerten, die der Bund im Einvernehmen mit den beteiligten Ländern zur Förderung großer künstlerischer Unternehmungen (Bayreuther und Hersfelder Festspiele, Ruhrfestspiele, Kunstausstellungen führender Verbände) und insbesondere der Deutschen Akademie Villa Massimo in Rom nach deren Rückgabe geleistet hat.

Das *Gesetz zum Schutz deutschen Kulturgutes gegen Abwanderung in das Ausland* will erreichen, daß die Erhaltung national besonders bedeutungsvoller Kunst- und anderer Kulturgüter in Deutschland durch Eintragung in amtliche Listen und jeweils notwendige Ausfuhrgenehmigungen gesichert werden soll. Eine inhaltlich gleiche Regelung bestand bereits vor 1933.

Ein verfassungsrechtlicher Streit ist zwischen Bund und Ländern um den ehemals *Preußischen Kulturbesitz* entbrannt. Der Bund strebt eine von Bund und Ländern begründete und zu gleichen Rechten verwaltete öffentliche Stiftung an, zu deren Errichtung bereits ein Bundesgesetz erlassen ist. Die Länder hatten hiergegen so schwerwiegende Bedenken, daß sie den Weg der Klage beim Bundesverfassungsgericht beschritten haben. Es wird in dieser Auseinandersetzung das letzte Wort sprechen.

Mehr allgemeinpolitischen Gesichtspunkten trugen die Bemühungen um Förderung des Ausgleichs von Christentum und Judentum, zur Hebung der allgemeinen politischen Bildung und zu Gunsten des Europagedankens Rechnung. Mit den sich ausweitenden internationalen Beziehungen der Bundesrepublik wuchs auch die Anteilnahme der Bundesregierung an der Pflege des internationalen Kulturaustauschs. Als Beispiele hierfür seien genannt die laufende Mitarbeit in der *Deutschen UNESCO-Kommission*, in der die Bundesregierung, die Ständige Konferenz der Kultusminister, alle großen Kulturorganisationen und frei gewählte Persönlichkeiten aus den verschiedensten Kulturbereichen vereinigt sind, und den in der Bundesrepublik tätigen UNESCO-Instituten. Ferner gehört dazu die Betreuung der deutschen Sektionen internationaler Organisationen wie des Internationalen Musikrats, des Internationalen Museumsrats sowie der deutschen Sektionen für das Theaterwesen und die bildenden Künste. Seit der UNESCO-Hauptversammlung in Montevideo im Herbst 1954 ist die Bundesrepublik auch im Exekutivrat der UNESCO vertreten. Die deutsche Beteiligung an der UNESCO-Arbeit wurde bisher vor allem sichtbar bei der Schulbuchverbesserung wie bei der Erziehung zu internationaler Zusammenarbeit und übernationalem Verstehen. Auch mehreren von der UNESCO angeregten zwischenstaatlichen Abkommen für erleichterten Informationsaustausch auf wissenschaftlichem und kulturellem Gebiet ist die Bundesrepublik beigetreten. Daneben wurden auch die kulturellen Bestrebungen des Europarats, der WEU und der NATO nachdrücklich gefördert.

Chörlein vom Sebalder Pfarrhof in Nürnberg (um 1380)

Muttergottes vor einem Hause (VEIT STOSS, um 1445—1532)

Schreinmadonna aus Westpreußen (um 1390)

Brunnen des Klosters Maulbronn (Baden-Württemberg) das 1146 als Zisterzienserabtei gegründet wurde

DEUTSCHES VOLKSGESICHT

Handwerksmeister vom Bodensee — Bürgerin in Überlinger Tracht

Friesin von der Insel Föhr — Bauer aus dem Gutachtal im Schwarzwald

DEUTSCHES VOLKSGESICHT

Junger Glasmacher aus dem Bayerischen Wald — Mädel aus dem Mühlenbachtal im Schwarzwald

Bergbauern-Tochter aus Oberbayern — Bauer aus dem Odenwald

Professor MAX HARTMANN,
Vizekanzler des Ordens Pour le Mérite

Professor OTTO HAHN, Präsident der
Max-Planck-Gesellschaft

Atom-Forschungsreaktor der Technischen Hochschule München

Elektronen-Synchroton des Physikalischen Instituts der Universität Bonn

Das Kurfürstliche Schloß in Bonn, von 1697–1723 erbaut, seit 1818 Universität

Sichtbarer Ausdruck des wiedererwachten gesamtdeutschen Willens zu kultureller Leistung und Anerkennung dieser Leistung ist das Wiederaufleben des Ordens *Pour le mérite für Wissenschaften und Künste*, der im Jahre 1842 durch König Friedrich Wilhelm IV. gestiftet worden war. Der Orden hat sich am 31.5.1952 als eine freie, sich selbst ergänzende Gemeinschaft von hervorragenden Gelehrten und Künstlern neu bestätigt. Er vereinigt wieder eine große Anzahl von bedeutenden Frauen und Männern des In- und Auslandes. Die jährlichen öffentlichen Kapitelsitzungen in Bonn im Beisein des Bundespräsidenten, der das Protektorat des Ordens übernommen hat, sind Höhepunkte des geistigen Lebens und der kulturellen Repräsentation in der Bundesrepublik.

Über Mittel, Grenzen und Nutzen der auf zwei Ebenen — des Bundes und der Länder — geleisteten deutschen staatlichen Kulturarbeit kann heute nichts abschließend gesagt werden. Auch das sollte ein Zeichen für die Lebenskraft deutschen Kulturwillens sein. Eines Tages wird das, was heute kulturell geplant und versucht, gewünscht und bekämpft wird, Geschichte sein — Geschichte, aber hoffentlich doch auch Baustein für eine bessere Zukunft.

SCHUL- UND BILDUNGSWESEN

I. DAS ALLGEMEINBILDENDE SCHULWESEN

Das Schulwesen in Deutschland hat eine mehr als elfhundertjährige Überlieferung. Vor über zweihundert Jahren wurde in einzelnen deutschen Staaten die Schulpflicht verkündet. In der Mitte des Neunzehnten Jahrhunderts war sie überall durchgeführt.

Das gut ausgebaute allgemeinbildende Schulwesen und die pädagogischen Reformbestrebungen im ersten Drittel des Zwanzigsten Jahrhunderts wurden durch die Herrschaft des Nationalsozialismus' und die Kriegszerstörungen völlig zurückgeworfen. Mit dem Ende des Krieges hatte in Deutschland zunächst alle schulische Tätigkeit aufgehört. Schulen jeder Art wurden durch die Besatzungsmächte geschlossen, die Lehrer entlassen und die Wiederaufnahme der Arbeit von den Vorschriften der Alliierten abhängig gemacht. Damit hatte eine Abwärtsentwicklung vorläufig ihren Abschluß erreicht, die bereits in den Jahren der nationalsozialistischen Herrschaft begonnen und im Kriege zu einem katastrophalen Rückgang des gesamten Erziehungswesens geführt hatte. Zerstörte Schulhäuser, fehlende Lehrkräfte, verkürzter Unterricht, Einsatz von Kindern und Jugendlichen für den totalen Krieg hatten alle erzieherischen Maßnahmen gelähmt. Das Kriegsende führte zu einem völligen Zusammenbruch sowohl der äußeren als auch der inneren Erziehungsfaktoren. Nach Wiedereröffnung der Schulen Ende 1945 galt die erste Sorge der verantwortlichen Stellen der Wiedereinführung eines geordneten Unterrichts.

In mühevoller Arbeit mit überfüllten Klassen, in halb zerstörten Räumen, in Wechselschicht, ohne Lehr- und Lernmittel wurde von den Lehrern Außerordentliches geleistet. Die Lage wurde verschärft durch den Zustrom der Kinder von Vertriebenen und Flüchtlingen, denen über 20% aller Schulkinder angehören. Sie wurde es nicht minder durch die geburtenstarken Jahrgänge seit 1934 und durch den erheblichen Lehrermangel. Nach einer Schätzung aus dem Jahr 1951 waren im Bundesgebiet aus Mangel an Schulraum noch zwei Millionen der eingeschulten Kinder ohne einen zeitlich geordneten Unterricht.

Zugleich führten beim Aufbau des Bildungswesens — je nach den Zonen — die verschiedenartigen bildungspolitischen Einflüsse der Besatzungsmächte zu großen Unterschieden.

*

Das 1949 beschlossene Grundgesetz beließ den *Ländern* die Zuständigkeit für das Schul- und Bildungswesen. Dies entsprach dem Zustand im kaiserlichen Deutschland und — in nicht ganz so entschiedener Form — in der Weimarer Republik. Es gibt deshalb kein Bundesministerium für Unterricht und Erziehung und keine Befugnis des Bundes zur Gesetzgebung auf dem Gebiet des Erziehungswesens. Das Grundgesetz legt im wesentlichen nur die folgenden Grundsätze fest: Das gesamte Schulwesen steht unter der Aufsicht des Staates. Die Erziehungsberechtigten haben über die Teilnahme ihrer Kinder am Religionsunterricht zu bestimmen. Der Religionsunterricht ist an den öffentlichen Schulen — mit Ausnahme der bekenntnisfreien — ordentliches Lehrfach. Das Recht zur Errichtung privater Schulen wird gewährleistet.

Die übrigen Grundsätze des Schulrechts sind in den Länderverfassungen enthalten, das *Schulrecht* selbst in den einzelnen Schulgesetzen der Bundesländer. In allen Ländern wird das Recht auf *gleiche Bildungsmöglichkeiten für alle*, ohne Rücksicht auf wirtschaftliche Lage, gesellschaftliche Stellung, Religion und Rasse anerkannt.

Aus der Einsicht, daß es geboten ist, die allgemeinen Fragen des Schul- und Bildungswesens in Deutschland zu koordinieren, haben die Kultusminister der Länder eine „*Ständige Konferenz*" ins Leben gerufen. Sie unterhält in Bonn ein Generalsekretariat. Von der Konferenz werden die gemeinsamen Probleme erörtert und Empfehlungen verabschiedet, die allerdings die Kultusminister und die Länderparlamente nicht binden. Dieser Zusammenarbeit sind einige Erfolge zu verdanken. Von wesentlicher Bedeutung für eine Vereinheitlichung des Schulwesens in der Bundesrepublik ist besonders ein Abkommen der Ministerpräsidenten aller Länder vom 17. 2. 1955 geworden. Darin sind der gemeinsame Beginn des Schuljahres zu Ostern (mit Ausnahme von Bayern), eine einheitliche Ferienordnung, einheitliche Prädikate, gegenseitige Anerkennung der Lehramts- und Reifeprüfungen, eine Typenbereinigung der Gymnasien sowie eine einheitliche Sprachenfolge in den Gymnasien festgelegt.

Darüber hinaus ist es notwendig, unter Berücksichtigung der veränderten geistigen, sozialen und politischen Verhältnisse unserer Zeit den Gesamtzusammenhang des Deutschen Erziehungs- und Bildungswesens planvoll zu prüfen und entsprechende fachkundige Empfehlungen zu geben. Aus dieser Erkenntnis heraus haben der Bundesminister des Innern und der Präsident der Ständigen Konferenz der Kultusminister der Länder gemeinsam im Herbst 1953 den „*Deutschen Ausschuß für das Erziehungs- und Bildungs-*

wesen" ins Leben gerufen. Seine Mitglieder bilden einen von behördlichen Einflüssen vollkommen unabhängigen Kreis freier Persönlichkeiten. Sie stellen ihre Kenntnisse und Erfahrungen ehrenamtlich zur Verfügung, um die Entwicklung des Deutschen Erziehungs- und Bildungswesens zu beobachten und durch Rat und Empfehlung zu fördern. Aufgabe des Ausschusses ist es, eine *Gesamtkonzeption des deutschen Erziehungs- und Bildungswesens* zu erarbeiten. Eine Reihe von wertvollen Einzelbeiträgen und Vorarbeiten ist abgeschlossen und vorgelegt worden. Die auf fünf Jahre erfolgte Berufung des Ausschusses wurde 1958 um weitere fünf Jahre verlängert.

*

Trotz der Eigenständigkeit des Bildungswesens in den einzelnen Ländern zeigt das deutsche Schulwesen im Grundsätzlichen ein einheitliches Bild.

In jedem Lande ist die oberste Behörde für das Schul- und Erziehungswesen das *Kultusministerium* (in den Stadtstaaten[1] Schulbehörde genannt). An ihrer Spitze steht der dem Landesparlament verantwortliche Kultusminister (-senator). Die Verwaltung der äußeren Schulangelegenheiten (Errichtung und Finanzierung der Schulen) obliegt deren Unterhaltsträgern (Länder, Gemeinden, Gemeindeverbände, Körperschaften öffentlichen oder privaten Rechtes). Die Verteilung der Schullasten ist in den einzelnen Ländern verschieden geregelt. Im allgemeinen tragen die Länder die Personalkosten, die Gemeinden die Sachkosten.

Für den Besuch der Pflichtschulen (Volks- und Berufsschulen) wird seit jeher kein Schulgeld erhoben. Auch bei den weiterführenden Wahlschulen (Real- und höhere Schulen) ist die *Schulgeldfreiheit* heute fast überall durchgeführt. In einigen Ländern besteht außerdem noch Lernmittelfreiheit.

Die gesamten Ausgaben für das allgemeinbildende Schulwesen sind nicht bekannt. Die Ausgaben von Bund, Ländern und Gemeinden (Gemeindeverbänden) für die allgemeinbildenden Schulen, sowie Zuschüsse an Privatschulen und an Schulen von Zweckverbänden mit eigener Rechnungsführung werden jedoch festgestellt, so daß zumindest der Hauptteil dieser Ausgaben genannt werden kann. Im Rechnungsjahr 1956 betrugen die Aufwendungen der öffentlichen Verwaltung für die allgemeinbildenden Schulen 4,2 Milliarden DM. Von diesen entfielen 69% auf die Volks-, Hilfs- und Sonderschulen und 31% auf die Mittel- und höheren Schulen.

Der Schülerzahl nach ist der auf die Mittel- und höheren Schulen entfallende Anteil (rund 18%) geringer. Jedoch abgesehen von dem durch die

[1] Stadtstaaten sind die Hansestädte Hamburg und Bremen sowie Berlin(West).

längere Schulzeit bedingten höheren Aufwand für den einzelnen Schüler erfordert auch der andere Ausbildungsgang dort relativ höhere Aufwendungen als für Volksschulen. Sie beliefen sich im Rechnungsjahr 1955:

für den Schüler der höheren Schule	auf mehr als	1.100 DM
für den Schüler der Mittelschule	auf rund	750 DM
für den Schüler der Volksschule	auf etwa	550 DM

Das allgemeinbildende Schulwesen beanspruchte im Rechnungsjahr 1956 etwa 6,9% aller Ausgaben der öffentlichen Haushalte.

Für die inneren Schulangelegenheiten (Erziehung, Unterricht, Lehrplan, Lehrmethoden usw.) ist das Land zuständig. Dem Kultusministerium steht die Aufsicht zu; es kann die kommunalen Schulträger auftragsweise beteiligen. Die großen Länder haben zwischen dem Ministerium und der Schulaufsichtsbehörde noch mittlere Instanzen in den Kreisen eingeschaltet.

Die Lehrer sind an den öffentlichen Schulen im allgemeinen Beamte, an den staatlich anerkannten Privatschulen Angestellte.

*

Das Schuljahr beginnt zu Ostern (in Bayern im Herbst). Die Schulwoche umfaßt sechs Tage. Die Zahl der Wochenstunden schwankt je nach Alter zwischen achtzehn und dreißig Stunden. Der Unterricht findet vormittags statt. Die Nachmittage sind frei für häusliche Arbeit und außerschulische Tätigkeit. Infolge Raummangels wird jedoch noch in vielen Schulen in Wechselschicht unterrichtet, das heißt eine Klasse benutzt den Raum am Vormittag, eine andere am Nachmittag. Zur Bewertung der Leistungen dienen die Noten 1 = sehr gut bis 6 = ungenügend. Die Ferienordnung wird jeweils für ein Jahr von den Kultusministern bekanntgegeben. Die Gesamtdauer der Ferien beträgt 85 Tage. Im allgemeinen verteilen sie sich auf zwei Wochen zu Ostern, eine Woche zu Pfingsten, fünf bis sechs Wochen im Sommer, eine Woche im Oktober und zwei bis drei Wochen zu Weihnachten.

Das *Verhältnis zwischen Lehrern und Schülern* ist freier und ungezwungener geworden. Es hängt entscheidend von der Persönlichkeit des Lehrers ab. Die körperliche Züchtigung tritt völlig zurück und ist zumeist ausdrücklich verboten. Der Sinn für Selbstzucht und Mitverantwortung im schulischen Leben wird bei den Schülern bewußt geweckt. Die Beteiligung am Schulleben geschieht durch Schülerausschüsse, meist *Schüler-Mitverwaltung* genannt.

Vor Beginn der Schulpflicht können Kinder zwischen dem dritten und sechsten Lebensjahr einen *Kindergarten* besuchen. Diese Einrichtungen werden von Gemeinden, Kirchen, Wohlfahrtsverbänden oder Privatpersonen getragen. Im Kindergarten sollen durch Spielpflege und altersmäßig entwickelnde Erziehung die Selbttätigkeit und der Gemeinschaftssinn des Kindes angeregt werden. Die Hauptaufgabe besteht darin, eine durch die Umwelt der Erwachsenen hervorgerufene Frühreife zu verhindern und berufstätige oder sonst durch Überlastung behinderte Mütter in der Sorge um die rechte Entwicklung des Kindes zu unterstützen.

Besondere Bedeutung haben die Schulkindergärten. Sie sollen solchen Kindern, die zwar das schulpflichtige Alter, aber noch nicht die erforderliche Schulreife erlangt haben, Gelegenheit bieten, in sinnvoll spielender Tätigkeit den Stand zu gewinnen, der für eine Beteiligung am Unterricht in der Schule vorausgesetzt werden muß. Die Kindergärtnerinnen werden an Fachschulen in zweijährigen Lehrgängen ausgebildet.

Die *Schulpflicht* beginnt mit der Vollendung des sechsten Lebensjahres und endet in der Regel mit dem 18. Lebensjahr. Sie gliedert sich in eine acht bis neun Jahre dauernde vollzeitliche Volksschulpflicht und eine anschließende, in der Regel drei Jahre (bis zur Vollendung des 18. Lebensjahres) dauernde Berufsschulpflicht. Die Berufsschule ist eine Teilzeitschule, die neben der Berufsausbildung einhergeht.

In den Volksschulen werden Jungen und Mädchen im allgemeinen gemeinsam unterrichtet. An den weiterführenden Schulen ist die Trennung die Regel. In einigen Privatschulen erfolgt Koedukation aus grundsätzlichen pädagogischen Erwägungen.

Jedes Kind besucht zunächst die Volksschule. Sie ist in den ersten vier Jahren als „*Grundschule*" die Schule, in der alle Kinder gemeinsam unterrichtet und erzogen werden. In dieser Zeit wird der Unterricht nicht in Fächer gegliedert, sondern als Gesamtunterricht erteilt. Er trägt dem kindlichen Charakter Rechnung. Außer dem Lesen, Schreiben und Rechnen lernen die Kinder, sich gestalterisch zu betätigen und in der Heimat zu orientieren. Als besonderes Fach wird nur Religion erteilt.

Nach dem Abschluß der vierten Klasse kann das Kind nach Wahl seiner Erziehungsberechtigten zu einer weiterführenden Schule übergehen oder auf der *Volksschule* verbleiben. Diese endet nach weiteren vier, in einzelnen Ländern fünf Schuljahren. In diesen Jahren versucht die Volksschule, den in ihr verbliebenen Schülern — jetzt etwa 75%, früher 80% — eine Bildung zu vermitteln, welche die Heranwachsenden befähigt, in die handwerkliche, kaufmännische oder industrielle Lehre einzutreten, die Härte des Berufslebens zu bestehen und sich im Leben zu bewähren.

Lebhafte Diskussionen hat die Frage ausgelöst, ob die Volksschulen nach evangelischer und katholischer Konfession getrennt (Bekenntnisschulen) oder Gemeinschaftsschulen (für nur die christlichen oder für alle Bekenntnisse) oder überhaupt bekenntnisfrei sein sollen. Das Ergebnis ist in den einzelnen Ländern unterschiedlich.

Unterricht wird in den Fächern Religion, Deutsch, Rechnen, Heimatkunde (vom fünften Schuljahr ab Erdkunde und Geschichte), Naturkunde, Zeichnen, Singen, Leibesübungen (und für Mädchen Nadelarbeit) erteilt. Von der 5. Klasse ab kann wahlfrei eine Fremdsprache erlernt werden. Vom 5. beziehungsweise 7. Schuljahr ab sind der Volksschule zuweilen Aufbauzüge angegliedert, die in vier Jahren den Bildungsabschluß einer Mittelschule vermitteln.

Der Übergang in die weiterführenden Schulen ist an eine Aufnahmeprüfung gebunden. Sie wird in den Ländern verschieden durchgeführt. In der Regel wird sie von Lehrern der Volksschule und der weiterführenden Schule gemeinsam abgenommen. Die weiterführenden Schulen sind fast allgemein Gemeinschaftsschulen.

Die *Mittelschule* — auch Realschule genannt — baut auf der Grundschule auf. Sie führt in sechs Jahren zu einer gehobenen Allgemeinbildung als Voraussetzung zur Ausbildung für die mittleren Berufe in Verwaltung, Handel, Gewerbe, Hauswirtschaft und Technik. Als Fächer treten besonders Sozialkunde, Mathematik und Naturwissenschaften hervor. Als Pflichtfach wird von der 5. Klasse (das ist das erste Schuljahr der Mittelschule) ab die erste Fremdsprache unterrichtet, als Wahlfach von der 7. Klasse ab eine zweite. Neben der sechsjährigen Mittelschule gibt es in einzelnen Ländern die drei- oder vierjährige Mittelschule, die an das entsprechende Volksschuljahr anschließt. Auch dort erfolgt also der Bildungsabschluß jeweils nach dem 10. Schuljahr. Zur Zeit besuchen etwa 9% aller gleichaltrigen Kinder die Mittelschule.

Die *höhere Schule* (Gymnasium genannt) ist der Ort der allgemein geistigen Grundbildung für die qualifizierten Berufe. Sie führt in neun Jahren zur Hochschulreife. Zur Zeit besuchen etwa 16% aller gleichaltrigen Schüler eine höhere Schule. Das Gymnasium wird in drei Zügen — mit den charakteristischen Fächern als Bildungsschwerpunkt — geführt, als „*Altsprachliches Gymnasium*" (Latein und Griechisch), als „*Neusprachliches Gymnasium*" (Englisch, Französisch, Latein) oder als „*Mathematisch-Naturwissenschaftliches Gymnasium*" (Mathematik und Naturwissenschaften). Die letzten beiden Typen gibt es auch in Kurzform. Sie setzen den Abschluß der Volksschule voraus und führen in sechs Jahren zur Reifeprüfung (sogenannte *Aufbauschulen*). *Abendgymnasien* vermitteln in dreijährigen Abendkursen begabten jungen Berufstätigen die Hochschulreife.

DAS ALLGEMEINBILDENDE SCHULWESEN

1.000

Gegenstand/Gebiet	Mai 1950	Mai 1953	Mai 1956	Mai 1957
SCHULEN				
Bundesgebiet (ohne Saarland)				
Volksschulen	28,50	29,17	29,55	29,69
Hilfsschulen	0,46	0,59	0,67	0,69
Sonderschulen	0,28	0,33	0,34	0,32
Mittelschulen	0,58	0,73	0,83	0,85
Höhere Schulen	1,45	1,54	1,59	1,60
Schulen mit neuorganisiertem Aufbau	0,53	0,48	0,49	0,51
Zusammen	31,79	32,85	33,48	33,66
Berlin (West)	0,44	0,49	0,49	0,49
Insgesamt	32,23	33,33	33,97	34,15
SCHÜLER				
Bundesgebiet (ohne Saarland)				
Volksschulen	6.125,2	5.140,7	4.574,2	4.560,0
davon: Jungen	3.107,3	2.604,4	2.320,2	2.316,5
Mädchen	3.017,9	2.536,3	2.254,0	2.243,5
Hilfsschulen	65,2	76,6	76,3	79,9
davon: Jungen	39,8	46,2	45,7	47,5
Mädchen	25,4	30,3	30,7	32,4
Sonderschulen	24,4	28,5	27,5	25,0
davon: Jungen	15,1	18,0	17,3	15,9
Mädchen	9,3	10,5	10,2	9,1
Mittelschulen	196,1	290,3	314,5	311,3
davon: Jungen	89,9	133,8	145,1	144,2
Mädchen	106,1	156,5	169,4	167,1
Höhere Schulen	604,4	728,1	767,5	760,1
davon: Jungen	360,4	434,9	460,5	456,7
Mädchen	244,1	293,2	307,0	303,4
Schulen mit neu organisiertem Aufbau	280,1	299,2	293,4	287,2
davon: Jungen	143,3	153,2	150,1	146,7
Mädchen	136,8	145,9	143,3	140,5
Zusammen	7.295,4	6.563,3	6.053,4	6.023,6
davon: Jungen	3.755,8	3.390,6	3.138,8	3.127,6
Mädchen	3.539,7	3.172,7	2.914,6	2.896,0
Berlin (West)	286,2	272,4	236,1	223,9
davon: Jungen	146,0	139,6	121,6	115,1
Mädchen	140,2	132,9	114,6	108,8
Insgesamt	7.581,6	6.835,7	6.289,5	6.247,5
davon: Jungen	3.901,7	3.530,2	3.260,4	3.242,7
Mädchen	3.679,9	3.305,6	3.029,2	3.004,8

DAS ALLGEMEINBILDENDE SCHULWESEN (Fortsetzung)
1.000

Gegenstand/Gebiet	Mai 1950	Mai 1953	Mai 1956	Mai 1957
HAUPTAMTLICHE LEHRKRÄFTE				
Bundesgebiet (ohne Saarland)				
Volksschulen	125,8	127,2	124,8	125,0
Hilfsschulen	2,1	3,0	3,3	3,4
Sonderschulen	1,1	1,4	1,5	1,5
Mittelschulen	6,0	9,3	11,7	12,2
Höhere Schulen	27,9	32,7	36,8	37,9
Schulen mit neu organisiertem Aufbau	7,7	9,4	10,0	10,1
Zusammen	170,7	183,1	188,2	190,1
Berlin (West)	8,4	9,0	8,4	8,3
Insgesamt	179,1	192,1	196,5	198,5
SCHÜLER JE LEHRKRAFT				
Bundesgebiet (ohne Saarland)				
Volksschulen	49	40	37	36
Hilfsschulen	31	25	23	23
Sonderschulen	22	20	18	17
Mittelschulen	33	31	27	25
Höhere Schulen	22	22	21	20
Schulen mit neu organisiertem Aufbau	36	32	29	24
Zusammen	43	36	32	32
Berlin (West)	34	30	32	31

Das Absinken der Schülerzahl ist darauf zurückzuführen, daß seit etwa 1948/49 die zahlenmäßig schwachen Geburtsjahrgänge schulpflichtig geworden sind.

Quelle: Statistisches Bundesamt.

Als Oberstufe der höheren Schule gibt es für *Mädchen* einen besonderen Typ, die sogenannte „*Frauenoberschule*". Sie bevorzugt solche Fächer, die für das praktische Leben der Frau von Bedeutung sind. Als weitere Sonderform der Oberstufe einer höheren Schule — zum Teil aber auch als berufsbildende Schule angesehen — wird zur Zeit die „*Wirtschaftsoberschule*" in einigen Ländern erprobt. Sie unterrichtet als charakteristische Fächer Wirtschafts- und Sozialkunde. Bei Besuch dieser beiden Schultypen gewährt der Abschluß jedoch nicht die volle Hochschulreife, sondern berechtigt nur zum Studium in bestimmten Fächern.

Die höhere Schule stellt erhebliche Anforderungen an die geistigen Fähigkeiten und den Leistungswillen ihrer Schüler. Ein großer Teil von ihnen muß sie daher wegen unzureichender Leistungen vorzeitig wieder verlassen. Zahlreiche Schüler verlassen sie aber auch nach dem 10. Schuljahr (also nach der „Untersekunda", dem 6. Jahr der höheren Schule) mit einem Abschluß, der dem der Mittelschule entspricht, um sich einer praktischen Betätiguug zu widmen.

Da das Abitur auf der einen Seite als Prüfung für den Zugang zur Hochschule gilt, auf der anderen Seite, vielfach ohne wirkliche Notwendigkeit, zur Vorbedingung für den Eintritt in zahlreiche Berufslaufbahnen gemacht wird, liegt das Bildungsziel der höheren Schule nicht eindeutig fest. Darum ist gerade sie ein Schwerpunkt der Erörterungen, die um eine *Reform des Bildungswesens* kreisen.

Neben den genannten allgemeinbildenden Schulen gibt es ein ausgebautes *Hilfs- und Sonderschulwesen.* Durch diese Schulen wird körperlich, geistig und sozial benachteiligten aber doch bildungsfähigen Kindern eine ihren Anlagen entsprechende Allgemeinbildung vermittelt. Die Sonderschulen für Blinde, Taubstumme und Krüppel sind häufig mit Internaten verbunden. Das Ziel der Sonderschule besteht darin, das behinderte Kind soweit zu fördern, daß es später sein Leben selbständig führen kann.

Eine von dem bisher geschilderten Schulaufbau abweichende Organisation ist in den *Stadtstaaten* geschaffen worden. An Stelle der Volks-, Mittel- und höheren Schule besteht dort die sogenannte *Einheitsschule.* Sie verfügt über eine einheitliche Grundstufe und eine in den praktischen, den technischen und den wissenschaftlichen Zweig gegliederte Oberstufe.

Als weitere Sonderform ist im Lande Niedersachsen in verschiedenen Volksschulen versuchsweise der sogenannte *differenzierte Mittelbau* eingeführt worden. Hier wird, um jeder Begabung gerecht werden zu können, ein Teil des Unterrichts gemeinsam erteilt, der andere Teil in Kursen, an denen die Schüler je nach Neigung und Begabung teilnehmen können.

Einen eigenen Aufbau für die dreizehn Schuljahre besitzen auch die privaten Landerziehungsheime, Waldorf-Schulen und Hermann Lietz-Schulen.

Etwa 12% der Schüler der mittleren und höheren Schulen suchen nach Absolvierung der Grundschule eine *Privatschule* auf. Solche Schulen bedürfen der Genehmigung des Staates und unterstehen seiner Aufsicht. Sie haben meist Lehrpläne, welche an die der öffentlichen Schulen angeglichen sind; vielfach sind sie auch mit Internaten verbunden. Ihr großer pädagogischer Wert liegt darin, daß sie, von besonderen Bildungsidealen ausgehend, pädagogisches Neuland erforschen und erproben können. Viele von ihnen

SCHEMA DES ALLGEMEINBILDENDEN SCHULWESENS

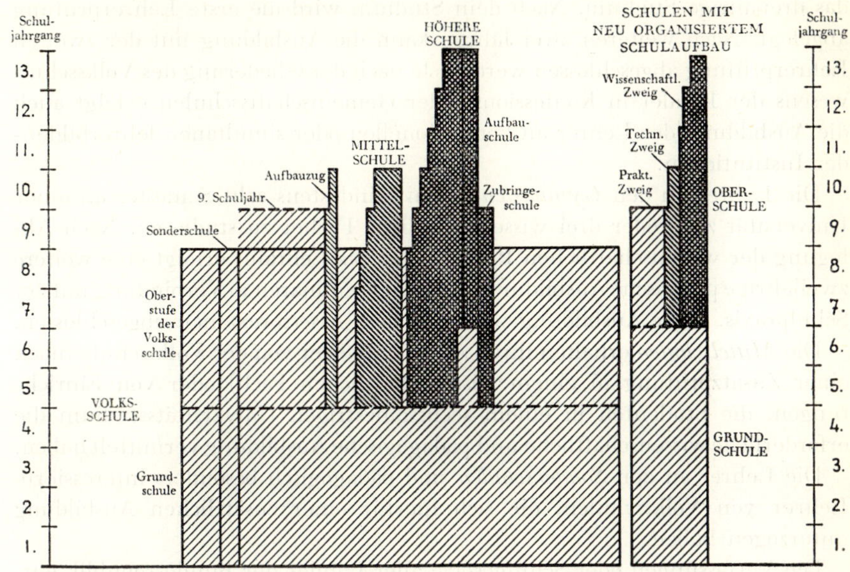

Quelle: Statistisches Bundesamt.

(wie die Schule in Salem, die Jesuitenschule in St. Blasien oder das Evangelische Pädagogium in Bad Godesberg) besitzen einen hervorragenden Ruf.

*

Alle allgemeinbildenden Schulen sehen die Vermittlung von umfassendem *Wissen* nicht als ihre einzige Aufgabe an; sie erstreben vielmehr die *Bildung* ihrer Schüler. Das heißt: sie wollen sie zu freien, selbständigen, leistungsfähigen und verantwortungsbewußten jungen Menschen erziehen. Dazu sollen unter anderem Arbeitsunterricht, Arbeit in Gruppen und Arbeitsgemeinschaften, Wandern, Landheimaufenthalte und Schüleraustausch beitragen.

An allen Schulen unterrichten *Lehrer*, die an Hochschulen und Universitäten ausgebildert worden sind. Voraussetzung dieser Ausbildung ist gegenwärtig grundsätzlich das Abitur.

An über fünfzig Pädagogischen Hochschulen, Akademien und Instituten und etwa zwanzig sonstigen lehrerbildenden Einrichtungen des Bundesgebietes werden zur Zeit fast 18.000 Lehrkräfte in zwei- bis dreijährigem Studium ausgebildet; darunter über 14.300 für das Volksschullehramt und über 2.300 für Lehrämter an berufsbildenden Schulen. Allgemeines Ziel ist das dreijährige Studium. Nach dem Studium wird die erste Lehrerprüfung abgelegt. Nach weiteren zwei Jahren kann die Ausbildung mit der zweiten Lehrerprüfung abgeschlossen werden. Je nach der Gliederung des Volksschulwesens der Länder in Konfessions- oder Gemeinschaftsschulen erfolgt auch die Ausbildung der Lehrer an konfessionellen oder simultanen lehrerbildenden Institutionen.

Die Lehrer an den *Gymnasien* haben mindestens acht Semester an einer Universität zwei oder drei wissenschaftliche Fächer zu studieren. Nach Ablegung der wissenschaftlichen Prüfung für das Lehramt erfolgt eine weitere zweijährige praktische Ausbildung an Studienseminaren in Verbindung mit der Schulpraxis. Diese Ausbildung wird mit dem Assessorexamen abgeschlossen.

Die *Mittelschulen* erhalten ihre Lehrer entweder von der Volksschule (nach einer Zusatzprüfung in einem wissenschaftlichen Fach) oder von Einrichtungen, die Studenten in einem sechssemestrigen Universitätsstudium die erforderliche wissenschaftliche und pädagogische Ausbildung vermittelt haben.

Die Lehrer an den *Sonderschulen* sind pädagogisch besonders interessierte Lehrer von Volksschulen, die sich hierfür einer zusätzlichen Ausbildung unterzogen haben.

Die Verfassungen oder Schulgesetze aller Länder der Bundesrepublik enthalten Bestimmungen über die Mitwirkung der Erziehungsberechtigten am Schulwesen. Zum Teil beziehen sie sich allgemein auf die Erfüllung der Erziehungsaufgabe, zum Teil sprechen sie von der Gestaltung des Schulwesens oder des Schullebens. Diese Mitwirkung der Eltern — in der Klasse oder in der Schule — erfolgt durch „*Elternbeiräte*". An ihren Zusammenkünften können die Lehrer beratend teilnehmen. In anderen Ländern sind es „*Klassen- und Schulpflegschaften*", die aus Lehrern und Eltern bestehen. Über die Einzelschule hinaus sind diese Einrichtungen auf Orts- und Landesebene zusammengefaßt.

Die Elternbeiräte und Schulpflegschaften sehen ihre Aufgabe darin, in der Aussprache mit den Lehrern und in der Mitwirkung bei der Gestaltung des Schullebens eine gute Verbindung zwischen Schule und Elternhaus herzustellen.

Daneben haben sich konfessionelle, nach Schularten differenzierte und völlig freie Zusammenschlüsse der Elternschaft gebildet, die jeweils besondere Bildungsanliegen zu vertreten wünschen (zum Beispiel Erhaltung der Konfessionsschule oder Ausbau des Mittelschulwesens und anderes mehr). Auch erscheinen mehrere Elternzeitungen und -zeitschriften. Sie werden meist von Lehrern herausgegeben und sind für bestimmte Schularten bestimmt.

Der beschriebene Aufbau des deutschen Schulwesens unterliegt im Zusammenhang mit der schon erwähnten lebhaften Kritik der Diskussion über eine *Neugestaltung des deutschen Bildungswesens*. Es geht hierbei vor allem um die Lösung folgender Fragen:

Soll das deutsche allgemeinbildende Schulwesen die überlieferte *Dreigliedrigkeit* behalten oder in eine differenzierte *Einheitsschule* umgewandelt werden? Fällt die Entscheidung für die Dreigliedrigkeit, müssen bessere Übergangsmöglichkeiten zwischen den einzelnen Schulformen geschaffen werden, damit allen Begabungen Gerechtigkeit widerfährt. Entscheidet man sich für eine Art von Einheitsschule, sind Zeitpunkt und Umfang der Differenzierung problematisch, damit nicht die sich früh zeigenden Begabungen in ihrer Entfaltung behindert werden.

Als zweiter Problemkreis wird die *Verlängerung der Schulpflicht* erörtert. Sollen die dafür vorgeschlagenen zwei Jahre der Volksschule als Jahre der Berufsfindung zugewiesen werden oder den berufsbildenden Schulen? Diese müßten in dieser Zeit dann stärker als bisher eine berufsbezogene Allgemeinbildung vermitteln.

Weitere Bemühungen richten sich auf die *Einschränkung der Stoffülle*, besonders an den Gymnasien. Durch die Behandlung des Exemplarischen soll in allen Gebieten die bildende Wirkung des Unterrichtes vertieft werden.

Schließlich tritt als neues Problem die sich ausbreitende Fünf-Tage-Woche in der Industrie auf. Wie kann dieser Entwicklung von Seiten der Schule entsprochen werden, ohne die Unterrichtszeit zu verkürzen, die Bildungswirkung zu vermindern und den Leistungsstand absinken zu lassen?

Welche Entscheidungen in diesen Fragen auch getroffen werden, entscheidend für den Bildungserfolg ist zunächst, daß es gelingt, in hinreichendem Ausmaß einen qualifizierten *Nachwuchs für den Lehrerberuf* zu gewinnen. Trotz den starken Bemühungen der Länder um die Lehrerbildung fehlen nach einer Schätzung immer noch etwa 7.000 Lehrer an den allgemeinbildenden und berufsbildenden Schulen.

Entscheidend ist ferner, daß die Not an Schulräumen behoben wird, damit jede Klasse einen eigenen Raum besitzt und die Klassenstärke pädagogischen Erkenntnissen entspricht. Nur dann ist der pädagogischen Arbeit des Lehrers ein echter Bildungserfolg möglich. Obschon von 1948 bis 1955 über 24.000 Klassenräume mit einem Aufwand von 3,5 Milliarden DM errichtet wurden und seitdem jährlich nochmals eine Milliarde für diesen Zweck ausgegeben worden ist, fehlen heute noch schätzungsweise 22.000 Klassenräume in den allgemeinbildenden und berufsbildenden Schulen.

II. DAS BERUFSBILDENDE SCHULWESEN

Auf dem allgemeinbildenden Schulwesen baut sich in Deutschland das berufsbildende auf. Hierbei sind die Berufsschulen, die Berufsfachschulen und die Fachschulen zu unterscheiden.

Die *Berufsschule* begleitet als Pflichtschule den Jugendlichen nach Verlassen der Volksschule drei Jahre lang beziehungsweise bis zum Abschluß der Lehrzeit. Ihr Besuch ist Pflicht, einerlei ob der Jugendliche sich in der praktischen Berufsausbildung in einem Lehr- oder Anlernverhältnis, in praktischer Berufsausübung in einem sonstigen Arbeitsverhältnis befindet, oder ob er erwerbslos ist. Während der Lehrling in der praktischen Berufsausbildung planmäßig in den Kenntnissen und Fertigkeiten angeleitet und unterwiesen wird, die zur Ausübung des Berufes erforderlich sind, erhält er in der Berufsschule einen berufstheoretischen Unterricht (Fachkunde, Fachrechnen, Fachzeichnen). Darüber hinaus vermittelt die Berufsschule eine berufsbezogene Allgemeinbildung (Deutsch, Sozialkunde, Religion) und bemüht sich, soziale Gesinnung bei den Schülern zu wecken.

Um ihrer spezifischen Aufgabe gerecht zu werden, faßt die Berufsschule die Schüler mit gleichen oder verwandten Berufen in gewerblichen, kaufmännischen, landwirtschaftlichen, hauswirtschaftlichen und bergmännischen Fachklassen zusammen und paßt ihren Unterricht den speziellen beruflichen Erfordernissen an. Häufig besitzt die Berufsschule auch Werkstätten, Übungsküchen und dergleichen mehr.

Die Differenzierung ist am stärksten in den Großstädten. Die kleinen Gemeinden haben sich in der Regel auf Kreisebene und in Zweckverbänden vereinigt, um fachlich durchgegliederte Berufsschulen errichten zu können. Ungeachtet dieser notwendigen Aufgliederung ist man bemüht, eine zu starke Spezialisierung zu vermeiden, indem man den Unterricht als Grundausbildung erteilt, aus der sich die spätere Ausbildung für einen Spezialberuf entwickeln läßt (sogenannter „Wurzelberuf").

Da die Berufsschule die praktische Berufsausbildung begleitet, kann sie nur eine Teilzeitschule sein. An einem oder an zwei Wochentagen werden insgesamt fünf bis zwölf Stunden Unterricht erteilt. Eltern und Arbeitgeber sind dafür verantwortlich, daß ihre Kinder beziehungsweise Lehrlinge am Unterricht in der Berufsschule teilnehmen.

Liegt ein Lehr- oder Anlernverhältnis vor, so findet die Berufsausbildung ihren Abschluß durch eine Prüfung vor der Handwerks-, Industrie- und Handels- oder der Landwirtschaftskammer. In den Prüfungsausschüssen prüfen die Vertreter der Kammern und der Berufsschulen gemeinsam. Das Zeugnis besteht in einem Gesellen- beziehungsweise Gehilfenbrief.

*

Neben der Berufsschule gibt es die *Berufsfachschule*. Unter dieser Bezeichnung werden Schulen verstanden, deren Unterricht nicht lediglich eine Berufsausbildung begleitet, sondern sie selbst vermittelt. In ein- oder mehrjährigen Lehrgängen mit voller wöchentlicher Stundenzahl geben sie entweder eine vollständige, mit Gesellen- oder gleichwertiger Prüfung abschließende gewerbliche oder sonstige (zum Beispiel haushaltspflegerische) Berufsausbildung oder aber eine Grundausbildung für kaufmännische oder Büroberufe. Bei dieser Schulart überwiegen die Fachrichtungen Handel, Verwaltung, Haushaltung, Kinder- und Körperpflege. Das hat zur Folge, daß die meisten Schüler dieser Schulart Mädchen sind. Als Vorbildung kommt bei den Berufsfachschulen in der Regel der Abschluß der Volksschule, aber auch verhältnismäßig stark der der Mittelschule in Betracht. Nur für einige Frauenberufe wird der Abschluß der höheren Schule vorausgesetzt.

Die *Handelsschulen* bereiten je nach der Vorbildung ihrer Schüler in einer ein- bis dreijährigen Ausbildungszeit für kaufmännische und Büroberufe vor. Für ihre Absolventen genügt in der Regel eine kurze anschließende Lehrzeit oder praktische Tätigkeit bis zur vollen Berufsbefähigung.

Eine starke Gruppe stellen die Berufsfachschulen dar, die auf typische *Frauenberufe* vorbereiten, zum Beispiel Frauenarbeitsschulen, Haushaltungsschulen, Schulen für Kinderpflege und Körperpflege. Zu dieser Gruppe gehören auch die Lehranstalten für medizinisch-technische Assistentinnen, deren Ausbildung in schulisch-systematischer Form mit gleichzeitiger praktischer Betätigung erfolgt.

Zur Gruppe der gewerblichen Berufsfachschulen gehören die für Feinmechanik, Edelmetallgewerbe, Kunstgewerbe, Gebrauchsgraphik und ähnliche. Diese Schulen bereiten auf Berufe vor, die weniger durch die arbeitsteilige industrielle Produktionsform geprägt sind als durch die qualifizierte Werkstückarbeit. Die praktische und theoretische Ausbildung ist hier nach drei bis dreieinhalb Jahren mit der Gesellenprüfung abgeschlossen.

Einige Berufsfachschulen schließlich befassen sich mit der Ausbildung für künstlerische Berufe. Dazu gehören zum Beispiel die Schauspiel-, Ballett-, Musik- und Kunstschulen.

Durch den Besuch der Berufsfachschule kann die Berufsschulpflicht ganz oder teilweise abgegolten werden.

*

Jenseits der Schulpflicht liegt der Besuch der *Fachschulen.* Sie dienen der freiwilligen Vervollkommnung der Berufsausbildung. Ihr Besuch setzt daher in der Regel eine längere praktische Berufsausübung voraus. Sie entsprechen der Vielfalt der Berufe, wie sie für die Struktur des modernen Wirtschaftslebens charakteristisch ist. Die Fachschulstatistik unterscheidet rund fünfzig verschiedene Fachrichtungen. Die wichtigsten Schultypen sind die Landwirtschafts-, Landfrauen-, Gartenbau-, Forst-, Meister-, Bau-, Berg-, Ingenieur-, Seefahrts-, Frauenfach- und Wohlfahrtspflegeschulen sowie Schulen für Kinder- und Krankenpflege. Bei dieser Schulart treten Schulen für die Berufe des Handels, des Verkehrs und der Verwaltung stark zurück; denn die Ausbildung des Nachwuchses dieser Berufe erfolgt vorwiegend über die Berufsfachschulen.

Alle Fachschulen haben das Ziel, ihre Schüler für verantwortungsvolle Stellen im wirtschaftlichen und sozialen Berufsleben vorzubilden. Darum wird neben der Fachausbildung der *Vertiefung der Allgemeinbildung* Raum gegeben.

Infolge der Verschiedenartigkeit der Ausbildungsziele der Fachschulen beziehungsweise ihrer einzelnen Lehrgänge schwankt die Ausbildungsdauer zwischen einem und acht Halbjahren. Die überwiegende Mehrzahl der Fachschüler besucht die Fachschulen bis zu vier Halbjahren. Nur ein Viertel der Fachschüler besucht Lehrgänge, die fünf und mehr Halbjahre umfassen. Es sind dies insbesondere die Ingenieur- und Bauschulen sowie die ihnen entsprechenden Einrichtungen. Gerade sie erfahren zur Zeit einen starken Ausbau, um den Mangel an technischem Nachwuchs zu beheben; denn dieser besteht weniger bei den akademisch gebildeten Diplomingenieuren als vielmehr bei den Absolventen der Ingenieurschulen.

Die Fachschulen, insbesondere die zuletzt genannten höheren Fachschulen, werden vor allem von den Ländern, von Städten, Körperschaften öffentlichen Rechts oder Verbänden unterhalten.

Auch Bundeswehr und Bundesgrenzschutz unterhalten Fachschulen besonderer Art. Durch Vertiefung und Erweiterung des allgemeinbildenden Wissens (berufsbezogene Allgemeinbildung) sollen sie der beruflichen Weiterbildung ihrer Angehörigen dienen und damit die Voraussetzungen für den Übertritt in andere Berufe nach Beendigung der Dienstzeit schaffen.

*

Um auch solchen Begabungen, die sich erst später zeigen, und tüchtigen Praktikern im Berufsleben einen bildungsmäßigen und beruflichen Aufstieg zu ermöglichen, wird derzeit eine Reihe von Versuchen unternommen. Unter dem Sammelbegriff des *zweiten Bildungsweges* werden diese in der

DAS BERUFSBILDENDE SCHULWESEN
IN DER BUNDESREPUBLIK DEUTSCHLAND EINSCHLIESSLICH VON BERLIN(WEST)

Gegenstand	1950[1]	November 1953	November 1956	November 1957
SCHULEN				
Berufsschulen	6.767	5.612	3.782	3.289
Berufsfachschulen	875	1.093	1.307	1.419
Fachschulen	1.410	1.796	1.947	1.955
Insgesamt	9.052	8.501	7.036	6.663
SCHÜLER (Angaben in 1.000)				
Berufsschulen	1.699,2	2.127,0	2.269,3	2.094,4
davon: Jungen	992,9	1.203,7	1.272,7	1.175,7
Mädchen	706,3	923,3	996,5	918,7
Berufsfachschulen	88,2	129,5	155,6	157,8
davon: Jungen	23,2	35,3	44,1	43,1
Mädchen	64,9	94,2	111,5	114,7
Fachschulen	112,5	134,1	159,1	154,7
davon: Jungen	75,8	90,1	105,0	100,0
Mädchen	34,0	44,0	54,1	54,7
Insgesamt	1.899,9	2.390,6	2.584,0	2.406,9
davon: Jungen	1.094,7	1.329,0	1.421,9	1.318,8
Mädchen	805,2	1.061,6	1.162,1	1.088,1
HAUPTAMTLICHE LEHRKRÄFTE				
Berufsschulen	15,6	19,4	22,2	22,8
Berufsfachschulen	4,0	5,6	6,6	7,0
Fachschulen	6,8	7,8	8,5	8,6
Insgesamt	26,4	32,8	37,2	38,3
SCHÜLER JE LEHRKRAFT				
Berufsschulen	109	110	102	92
Berufsfachschulen	22	23	24	23
Fachschulen	17	17	19	18
Insgesamt	72	73	70	63

[1] Spätherbst; Hessen und Bayern: Frühjahr 1950.

Das Absinken der Zahl der Berufsschulen ist darauf zurückzuführen, daß zahlreiche kleine Berufsschulen zu größeren, stärker gegliederten Berufsschulen zusammengestellt worden sind.

Quelle: Statistisches Bundesamt.

Öffentlichkeit diskutiert. Innerhalb des berufsbildenden Schulwesens soll unter stärkerer Berücksichtigung einer berufsbezogenen Allgemeinbildung eine *Stufenfolge von Abschlüssen der Berufsbildung* geschaffen werden. Jede Stufe soll jeweils einen Übergang in einen praktischen Beruf gestatten oder einen Aufstieg in die nächsthöhere Stufe der Ausbildung bis hin zum Hochschulabschluß ermöglichen. Es bestehen schon verschiedene Einrichtungen, die auch einem begabten Arbeiter erlauben, die Hochschulreife zu gewinnen.

Wegen der außerordentlichen Veränderungen in der Arbeitswelt ist man bestrebt, das gesamte berufsbildende Schulwesen erheblich auszubauen. Kenntnisse, Fähigkeiten und Fertigkeiten der Schüler sollen gesteigert, Zuverlässigkeit, geistige Wendigkeit und Weltverständnis auf diese Weise erzielt werden.

*

Die Ausbildung der an den berufsbildenden Schulen tätigen *Lehrer* unterlag in den letzten Jahrzehnten Veränderungen. Sie sind bedingt durch die wachsende Bedeutung dieser Schulen und durch die höheren Anforderungen, die daher an die Lehrkräfte gestellt werden. Art und Dauer der Ausbildung sind unterschiedlich bei den Lehrern für die kaufmännischen, die gewerblichen und die landwirtschaftlichen Berufs- und Berufsfachschulen sowie für die Fachschulen. In mehreren Ländern erfolgt die Ausbildung schon an wissenschaftlichen Hochschulen oder doch in Verbindung mit ihnen; zum Teil aber auch an berufspädagogischen Instituten beziehungsweise Staatsinstituten für den landwirtschaftlichen Unterricht. Voraussetzung für die Zulassung zum Studium ist in der Regel neben der Hochschulreife eine praktische Tätigkeit. Die Studiendauer beträgt für die Diplom-Handelslehrer acht, für die Gewerbelehrer und Landwirtschaftslehrer acht beziehungsweise sechs Semester. Die Dauer der Ausbildung der landwirtschaftlichen Berufsschullehrer ist zwar kürzer; doch wird dafür eine längere praktische Tätigkeit vorausgesetzt. Das Studium schließt mit einer ersten Staatsprüfung oder einer Hochschulprüfung ab. Daran schließt sich im Gegensatz zu früher ein im allgemeinen zweijähriger Vorbereitungsdienst. Im Anschluß daran ist eine zweite, pädagogische Staatsprüfung abzulegen. Einige an den berufsbildenden Schulen vertretene Lehrer-Kategorien, wie Diplom-Handelslehrer, Landwirtschaftslehrer (Diplom-Landwirte), erhalten ihre Ausbildung schon seit Jahrzehnten an den wissenschaftlichen Hochschulen. Dozenten an Ingenieurschulen, zum großen Teil Diplom-Ingenieure, müssen vor ihrer Berufung an Stelle des Vorbereitungsdienstes und der zweiten Staatsprüfung eine langjährige praktische Tätigkeit nach der Hochschulprüfung nachweisen.

III. DIE ERWACHSENENBILDUNG

In der modernen, rasch sich wandelnden Welt kann auch eine ausgedehnte Schulzeit den Menschen nicht so bilden, daß er in den vielfältigen Bezügen des beruflichen, wirtschaftlichen, sozialen und politischen Lebens seinen Standort zu bestimmen und zu wahren vermag. Ihm im Bereich der Bildung als Helfer beratend und mahnend zur Seite zu stehen, zu eigener Entscheidung aufzurufen, jedoch nicht zu gängeln und zu bevormunden, ist Sache der Einrichtungen der Erwachsenenbildung. Sie alle sind dadurch gekennzeichnet, daß sie *keine Berechtigung voraussetzen und keine Berechtigung verleihen*.

Um Erwachsenenbildung in diesem Sinne bemühen sich Rundfunk, Fernsehen, Theater und Film. In besonderer Weise dienen ihr aber die *Volkshochschulen* und entsprechenden Einrichtungen sowie die *Volksbüchereien*. Gegenüber den anderen Formen der Erwachsenenbildung besitzen diese beiden ein ausgeprägtes Bewußtsein ihrer pädagogischen Aufgabe.

Zwar werden in den Einrichtungen der Erwachsenenbildung auch beruflich anwendbare Kenntnise wie Stenographie, Maschinenschreiben oder Fremdsprachen vermittelt. Sie stellen aber nicht das wesentliche Ziel der Erwachsenenbildung dar, und die betreffenden Kurse müssen in die Gesamtaufgabe der Erwachsenenbildung eingegliedert sein. Diese besteht darin, dem Menschen in der verwirrenden Lage der Gegenwart die Hilfen anzubieten, die er braucht, um mit den Problemen der Welt fertig zu werden, in die er gestellt ist.

Es ist wesentlich, daß es sich dabei nur um ein Angebot von Möglichkeiten handelt, von denen die Erwachsenen in aller Freiheit Gebrauch zu machen vermögen. Gerade in der *Freiwilligkeit* liegen die großen pädagogischen Möglichkeiten der Erwachsenenbildung.

Weiterhin will die Erwachsenenbildung den Menschen davor bewahren, ein bloßer Konsument der Industrie von Kulturgütern zu werden, die so reichlich sich anbietet. Deshalb stärkt sie seinen *Willen zur Eigenständigkeit und zur Selbstverantwortung*. Die Erwachsenenbildung vermittelt also keine Schulungskurse, bei denen den Teilnehmern bestimmte Überzeugungen eingedrillt werden. Vielmehr wird versucht, durch Vermittlung von Sachwissen und durch Arbeitsformen, die es ermöglichen, einer Frage selbständig gegenüberzutreten, die Kräfte wachzurufen, welche die Bewältigung der vom Leben und von der Umwelt gestellten Probleme ermöglichen. Bei der Erwachsenenbildung stehen deswegen mehr Arbeitsgemeinschaften und Übungen als Vorträge im Vordergrund.

Die Bedeutung der Erwachsenenbildung wurde nach 1945 sofort in ihrer geistigen und politischen Tragweite erkannt. Anregungen des Auslands

(Skandinavien, Vereinigtes Königreich) wie die Überlieferung der Deutschen Erwachsenenbildung aus der Zeit vor 1933 wurden dabei aufgenommen.

Soweit Einrichtungen und Maßnahmen der Erwachsenenbildung von überregionaler Bedeutung sind, werden sie durch die Bundesregierung gefördert.

Den weitesten Kreis dieser Einrichtungen der Volksbildung stellen in Deutschland die *Volkshochschulen* dar. Bei ihnen handelt es sich in der Mehrzahl um Abendschulen (zur Zeit elfhundert), die ihre Kurse ein oder mehrere Semester lang durchführen. Vereinzelt sind mit diesen Abendvolkshochschulen auch Abendgymnasien verbunden.

Demgegenüber vereinigen die *Heimvolkshochschulen* — als Stätten gemeinsamen Lebens und Wohnens — ihre Hörer für eine oder mehrere Wochen zu ganztägiger Arbeit. Hier besteht auch die Möglichkeit, in Gemeinschaft die Weiterbildung bestimmter Gruppen, zum Beispiel Landbewohner, Arbeiter usw., intensiv zu pflegen. Zur Zeit bestehen etwa dreißig derartige Heimvolkshochschulen in der Bundesrepublik. Sie wollen als Keimzellen einer gesunden gesellschaftlichen Ordnung wirken. Darum finden die von so vielen Seiten unternommenen Bestrebungen um die politische Bildung, vor allem der jungen Generation, auch hier eine gegebene Heimstätte.

Volkshochschulen müssen ihrer Bildungswirkung wegen frei sein, und zwar in der Wahl ihrer Leitung, ihrer Dozenten, ihrer Lehrer und Lehrplangestaltung. Sie dienen in Selbstverantwortung und Selbstverwaltung dem Bildungsbedürfnis und dem Lebensinteresse ihrer Teilnehmer. Diese Freiheit wird ihnen gewährt, obschon sie stets der öffentlichen Finanzierungshilfe bedürfen. Träger der Volkshochschulen sind in Süddeutschland meist Vereine, in Norddeutschland meist Gemeinden (Gemeindeverbände).

Die Volkshochschulen sind in Landesverbänden zusammengeschlossen, diese wiederum im Bundesgebiet im *Deutschen Volkshochschulverband*. Von seiner zentralen pädagogischen Arbeitsstelle aus wird der Versuch unternommen, die an den einzelnen Volkshochschulen gewonnenen Erfahrungen und die Ergebnisse eigener Untersuchungen und Forschungen für die Arbeit aller Volkshochschulen auszuwerten und bereitzustellen. Insbesondere bemüht man sich um die Koordinierung der Arbeitsvorhaben in den Volkshochschulen und Landesverbänden, um die Erarbeitung neuer methodischer Grundsätze und die Ausbildung der Mitarbeiter. Diese müssen Einsicht in die Dynamik unserer gesellschaftlichen Entwicklung gewinnen und Arbeitsunterlagen erhalten.

Die Volkshochschulen sind zwar Stätten der Erwachsenenbildung, doch werden sie besonders gern von jungen Menschen unter fünfundzwanzig

Jahren besucht. Dieses Interesse der jungen Generation läßt für die zukünftige Entwicklung der Erwachsenenbildung hoffen.

Im Bildungswerk „*Arbeit und Leben*“ haben Volkshochschulen und der Deutsche Gewerkschaftsbund sich zu einer Arbeitsgemeinschaft zusammengeschlossen. Ihr Ziel ist, die mitbürgerliche und politische Bildung der Arbeitnehmer zu fördern. Ferner wollen sie ihre Angehörigen auf die Wahrnehmung von öffentlichen Aufgaben vorbereiten.

Neben den geschilderten Volkshochschulen sehen die *kirchlichen Einrichtungen* der Erwachsenenbildung es als ihre besondere Aufgabe an, ihre Gesprächspartner auf dem Boden christlicher Ordnungsvorstellungen an der Auseinandersetzung mit dem Geist der Zeit teilnehmen zu lassen.

Im evangelischen Bereich arbeiten *achtzehn Evangelische Akademien*, die zumeist von Landeskirchen getragen sind. Sie verfolgen das Ziel, mit den verschiedenen Gruppen unseres Volkes ins Gespräch zu kommen, um die menschlichen Probleme, die bei ihrer alltäglichen Berufsarbeit oder im Zusammenwirken der Interessengruppen auftreten, zu erörtern und Brücken des Verständnisses zu schlagen.

Einzelne Akademien haben größere Arbeitsstäbe entwickelt, um den Kontakt mit den Personen, die bei den Tagungen erfaßt werden, und ihren einzelnen Lebensgebieten besser halten zu können. So entstanden die Evangelische Aktionsgemeinschaft für Arbeitnehmerfragen, die Evangelische Studiengemeinschaft, die Wirtschaftsgilde, der Politische Club Tutzing und verschiedenartige Freundeskreise der Evangelischen Akademien.

Im katholischen Bereich besteht eine „*Bundesarbeitsgemeinschaft für katholische Erwachsenenbildung*“. In ihr sind alle eigens der Erwachsenenbildung dienenden Einrichtungen wie auch die darin tätigen katholischen Vereine und Verbände vertreten. Auch hier handelt es sich zunächst um die Akademien, die zentralen Bildungsstätten in den Diözesen. Neben den Tagungen in ihren Heimen unterhalten sie ein ausgedehntes Vortragswerk mit anschließenden Aussprachen in zahlreichen Orten. Daneben wirken die kirchlichen sozialen Bildungseinrichtungen, die in ihrer Arbeit Wert auf längere Kurse für alle im sozialen Leben wichtigen Gruppen legen, sowie die Landvolkhochschulen und zahlreiche örtliche Bildungswerke verschiedener Art. Um eine Orientierung in der konkreten — vorwiegend vom Beruf her bestimmten — Lebenssituation bemühen sich vor allem die verschiedenen katholischen Verbände Katholische Arbeiterbewegung und Kolpingfamilie.

Die Einrichtungen der Erwachsenenbildung haben sich im Bewußtsein der Öffentlichkeit einen festen Platz erworben. Problematisch ist noch die *finanzielle Sicherung* ihrer Arbeit, die durch die Einnahmen aus den Hörergebühren nicht gewährleistet ist. Man erstrebt eine Regelung auf gesetzlicher Grundlage, die bisher jedoch nur in wenigen Ländern erreicht werden konnte. Ebenso verfügen fast alle Volkshochschulen — mit Ausnahme der Heimvolkshochschulen — noch nicht über eigene Räume mit entsprechenden Einrichtungen und Lehrmittelsammlungen.

Ebenso wichtig sind für die Erwachsenenbildung die *Volksbüchereien*. Auch sie dienen dem Willen zur Selbstbildung und wollen die Orientierung im Leben erleichtern, Verständnis für die Werte der Kultur vertiefen und die Berufsbildung heben. Nach der letzten, jedoch bereits von der Entwicklung überholten Erhebung bestanden in der Bundesrepublik etwa 7.000 kommunale öffentliche Büchereien mit einem Bestand von über 7 Millionen Büchern. Sie sind im *Deutschen Büchereiverband* organisiert.

Neben den Gemeinden sind vor allem die Kirchen Träger des Volksbüchereiwesens. Ihre Büchereien werden fachlich gefördert und in der Öffentlichkeit vertreten durch die kirchlichen Büchereiverbände, die sich in einer Arbeitsgemeinschaft zusammengeschlossen haben. Sie führen eine schon über hundert Jahre alte Tradition fort. Im *Deutschen Verband Evangelischer Büchereien* sind etwa 3.400 Büchereien zusammengeschlossen. Im katholischen Bereich umschließen der Borromäusverein und der St. Michaelsbund über 7.600 Büchereien mit mehr als 6,3 Millionen Büchern.

Die kommunalen öffentlichen Büchereien — insbesondere die ländlichen — werden in ihrer Arbeit auf Landesebene beraten durch die staatlichen Büchereistellen, die kirchlichen Büchereien durch die Zentralen ihrer Verbände und diözesane Fachstellen. Die von den Ländern und Gemeinden getragene *Einkaufszentrale für Büchereien* hat viel zur Rationalisierung der Büchereiverwaltung beigetragen. Staatliche und kirchliche Büchereischulen dienen der Ausbildung hauptamtlicher Volksbibliothekare, die nicht nur Techniker der Anschaffung und des Verleihs von Büchern sein sollen, sondern vielmehr in ihrem Umgang mit den Entleihern eine volksbildnerische Aufgabe zu erfüllen haben. Durch den Ausbau von Autobüchereien, die die einzelnen Ortschaften eines Landkreises aufsuchen, soll auch die Landbevölkerung in eine engere Berührung mit den Büchern gebracht werden. Als den Volksbüchereien verwandte und ihnen an Einfluß auf die Bildungswelt gleichkommende Einrichtungen — zum Teil allerdings mit anderer Buchauswahl — sind die zahlreichen Werks- und Betriebsbüchereien zu nennen, daneben auch noch die Krankenhaus- und Gefängnisbüchereien. Als Sondereinrichtungen werden auch Musik- und Blindenbüchereien unterhalten.

DIE WISSENSCHAFT

Vorbemerkung

„Wissenschaft" manifestiert sich in Forschung, Lehre und Studium. In Deutschland umfaßt der gleiche Begriff sowohl den geisteswissenschaftlichen als auch den naturwissenschaftlichen Bereich. Stätten der Wissenschaft sind die wissenschaftlichen Hochschulen und zahlreiche außerhalb des Hochschulbereichs stehende reine Forschungsinstitute. Bei dieser Komplexheit ist es nicht verwunderlich, daß der Begriff „*Wissenschaft*" im internationalen Gespräch oft Mißverständnissen ausgesetzt ist.

Nach dem Zusammenbruch von 1945 waren die Pflegestätten der Wissenschaft zum größten Teil dem totalen Krieg zum Opfer gefallen. Von den wissenschaftlichen Hochschulen im späteren Bundesgebiet und in Berlin (West) waren nur noch sechs voll, sechs zu 45 bis 75%, acht bis zu 30% benutzbar, die restlichen beinahe völlig zerstört. Die vierzig Institute der „Kaiser-Wilhelm-Gesellschaft" (jetzt „Max-Planck-Gesellschaft"), die zahlreichen freien und wirtschaftsnahen Forschungsstätten, die wissenschaftlichen werkseigenen Laboratorien der Industrie waren in noch größerem Ausmaß der Vernichtung durch den Luftkrieg anheimgefallen.

Trotz dieser hoffnungslosen Situation, trotz der politischen und geistigen Spaltung des Landes fanden sich starke Kräfte in der Verpflichtung, das geistige Leben in Anlehnung an eine gute Tradition neu zu gestalten und der deutschen Wissenschaft wieder Ansehen zu verschaffen. Angesichts des Mangels an geistiger Substanz, Gebäuden, Büchern und Geräten, in einem Augenblick tiefster Erschöpfung und Niedergeschlagenheit, brachten die aus alten und neuen Kräften gemischten Lehrkörper der Hochschulen den Mut auf, die Tore dem aus dem Kriege heimkehrenden Nachwuchs wieder zu öffnen. Das wissenschaftliche Leben konnte sich — zwar stockend zunächst — doch von Jahr zu Jahr freier und kräftiger entfalten.

Glücklicherweise standen diese Bemühungen unter dem Zeichen verständnisvoller und wirkungsbereiter Hilfe des Auslands. Besonders auf die USA, auf Namen wie CARNEGIE und ROCKEFELLER, das Austauschprogramm der Amerikanischen Hochkommission und das FULBRIGHT-Abkommen muß in diesem Zusammenhang hingewiesen werden.

Vom Sommer 1948 ab bildeten sich wieder die traditionellen — dabei den veränderten Ansprüchen angepaßten — Institutionen und Organisationen des wissenschaftlichen Lebens. So die „Studienstiftung des Deutschen Volkes" (1948), der „Deutsche Akademische Austauschdienst" (1950) und die „Alexander von Humboldt-Stiftung" (1953). Die Rektoren der wissenschaftlichen Hochschulen vereinigten sich 1949 zur „Westdeutschen Rektorenkonferenz", die der Bundesrepublik verbliebenen vier Wissenschaftlichen Akademien traten erneut zusammen, und die früheren Kaiser-Wilhelm-Institute wurden 1953 in die „Max-Planck-Gesellschaft" eingegliedert. 1949 entstand auch wieder die „Deutsche Forschungsgemeinschaft", in den beiden ersten Jahren unter dem einstigen Gründungsnamen „Notgemeinschaft der Deutschen Wissenschaft", als Selbsthilfe der deutschen Wissenschaftler. Im gleichen Jahr fand ein Kreis führender Köpfe der Wirtschaft sich zur Wiedergründung des „Stifterverbandes für die Deutsche Wissenschaft" zusammen.

Neu konstituierte sich 1958 der „Wissenschaftsrat" mit dem Ziel der Koordinierung aller Maßnahmen für Forschung, Lehre und Studium in der Bundesrepublik.

I. LEHRE UND FORSCHUNG

Die wissenschaftlichen Hochschulen in Deutschland dienen zugleich der Lehre und der Forschung, wobei die Verteilung der Mittel schwer feststellbar ist. Diese Hochschulen haben also die Vorbildung für den akademischen Beruf einerseits und die Tätigkeit des Suchens und Experimentierens andererseits als Aufgabe.

Einschließlich von Berlin(West) verfügt die Bundesrepublik über neunzehn Universitäten, acht Technische Hochschulen und sieben kleinere, meist nur eine Fakultät umfassende Hochschulen. Die Freie Universität Berlin und die Universitäten Mainz und Saarbrücken sind erst nach 1945 gegründet worden.

Allen diesen Hochschulen gemeinsam ist die *Rektoratsverfassung* mit dem Recht auf Selbstverwaltung. Ihre wichtigsten Formen sind die Promotion, die Habilitation (Verleihung der Lehrberechtigung) und die Selbstergänzung des Lehrkörpers (Vorschlagsrecht gegenüber dem Ministerium).

Eine Anzahl von anderen Bildungsanstalten, wie die Kirchlichen Hochschulen und die Pädagogischen Akademien, haben weniger wissenschaftliche Aufgaben oder geringere korporative Selbständigkeit.

An den Universitäten führt der Weg zur Berufung auf einen Lehrstuhl in der Regel über die Habilitation. Die Technischen Hochschulen berufen sehr oft Gelehrte aus der Industrie. Im Wintersemester 1952/53 waren etwa 2.200 Hochschullehrer Inhaber eines Lehrstuhls.

Die wissenschaftlichen Hochschulen sind staatliche Einrichtungen mit dem Recht der akademischen Selbstverwaltung. Als Institutionen für freie

DIE WISSENSCHAFTLICHEN HOCHSCHULEN IM BUNDESGEBIET MIT BERLIN(WEST)

Universitäten:
- Berlin (Freie Universität)
- Bonn
- Düsseldorf (Medizinische Akademie)
- Erlangen
- Frankfurt
- Freiburg
- Gießen
- Göttingen
- Hamburg
- Heidelberg
- Kiel
- Köln
- Mainz
- Marburg
- München
- Münster
- Saarbrücken
- Tübingen
- Würzburg

Technische Hochschulen:
- Aachen
- Berlin (Technische Universität)
- Braunschweig
- Darmstadt
- Hannover
- Karlsruhe
- München
- Stuttgart

Sonstige wissenschaftliche Hochschulen:
- Deutsche Hochschule für Politik Berlin
- Bergakademie Clausthal
- Tierärztliche Hochschule Hannover
- Landwirtschaftliche Hochschule Hohenheim
- Wirtschaftshochschule Mannheim
- Wirtschaftshochschule Nürnberg
- Hochschule für Sozialwissenschaften Wilhelmshaven

Forschung und freie Lehre sind sie durch die Verfassungen des Bundes und der Länder geschützt. Nach dem Grundgesetz obliegt Einrichtung und Unterhaltung der Hochschulen den Ländern, in denen sie ihren Sitz haben. Die Aufsicht führt der Kultusminister.

Der Siegeszug der Natur-, Wirtschafts- und Gesellschaftswissenschaften in den letzten Jahrzehnten und die rasch wachsenden Studentenzahlen bedrohen die klassische Gestalt der Deutschen Hochschule, die WILHELM VON HUMBOLDT 1809 mit der Gründung der Berliner Universität geschaffen hat. Die spezialisierte Fachausbildung widerspricht der Idee des umfassend gebildeten Akademikers. Die Verlagerung von Forschungsstätten aus den Hochschulen und die Überlastung der Professoren im Lehrbetrieb verletzen das Prinzip der Einheit von Forschung und Lehre. Mit Recht warnen daher nicht nur die Professoren, sondern auch die Sprecher von Wirtschaft und Staat vor dieser Entwicklung. Zur Bewältigung der Aufgaben, welche die moderne Gesellschaft stellt, bedarf es erst recht eines allseitig gebildeten Menschen von hohem sittlichem Wert. Gefordert wird die Wiederbesinnung auf die eigentlichen Bildungsaufgaben der Hochschulen und die staatsbürgerliche Verantwortung des Einzelnen.

Zur Wahrnehmung gemeinsamer hochschulpolitischer Anliegen haben die wissenschaftlichen Hochschulen[1] sich zur „*Westdeutschen Rektorenkonferenz*" (WRK) mit Sitz in Bad Godesberg zusammengeschlossen. Die Rektorenkonferenz widmet sich vorsorglich auch den Problemen, welche die Gesamtheit der westdeutschen Hochschulen im Falle der Wiedervereinigung Deutschlands zu lösen haben wird, sowie den seit 1947 immer enger gestalteten Beziehungen zu den Hochschulen Westeuropas. Die Konferenz hat keine Verwaltungsaufgaben. Zweimal jährlich vereinigt sie die Rektoren aller einunddreißig wissenschaftlichen Hochschulen der Bundesrepublik und von Berlin(West) zu Plenarsitzungen.

*

Am 5.9.1957 wurde zwischen der Bundesregierung und den Länderregierungen ein Verwaltungsabkommen über die Errichtung des „*Wissenschaftsrates*" abgeschlossen. Die Gründung dieser Institution war die Folge der seit langem sehr lebhaft erörterten Frage, ob nicht die Bedürfnisse der wissenschaftlichen Forschung eine zentrale Einrichtung verlangen, die alle Maßnahmen zur Förderung der Forschung planend lenkt und koordiniert. Von besonderer Bedeutung ist die Erkenntnis der in der Wissenschaft durch den Krieg und die Nachkriegszeit bedingten Rückständigkeiten.

Der Wissenschaftsrat hat die Aufgabe:

a) einen Gesamtplan für die Förderung der Wissenschaft zu erstellen,
b) jährlich ein Dringlichkeitsprogramm aufzustellen,
c) Empfehlungen für die Verwendung derjenigen Mittel auszuarbeiten, die in den Haushaltsplänen des Bundes und der Länder für die Förderung der Wissenschaft verfügbar sind.

Der Wissenschaftsrat besteht aus neununddreißig Mitgliedern, und zwar zweiundzwanzig Wissenschaftlern oder Persönlichkeiten des öffentlichen Lebens und siebzehn Vertretern der Bundes- und Länderregierungen. Sein Sitz ist Berlin, wo auch die Zusammenkünfte der Vollversammlung stattfinden. Eine Geschäftsstelle ist vorläufig in Köln eingerichtet worden. Die konstituierende Sitzung des Wissenschaftsrats, in welcher der Bundespräsident den Vorsitz führte, fand am 6.2.1958 in Bonn statt.

*

[1] Mit Ausnahme der Hochschule für Sozialwissenschaften in Wilhelmshaven.

Von den „*Wissenschaftlichen Akademien*" sind im Gebiet der Bundesrepublik drei (Göttingen, Heidelberg und München) verblieben. Eine vierte ist 1946 in Mainz gegründet worden. Mit Ausnahme von München unterhalten sie keine eigenen Forschungsstätten, fördern aber eine große Zahl langfristiger wissenschaftlicher Gemeinschaftsunternehmungen und publizieren in Sitzungsberichten und Abhandlungen Ergebnisse der Forschung. Die wissenschaftlichen Akademien sind Mittelpunkte geistigen Austausches unter den Gelehrten. Ihnen kommt eine hohe traditionelle Bedeutung zu. Sie sind nach den Ideen von LEIBNIZ gegründet und organisiert worden. Ihre Grundlage war der universale Wissenschaftsbegriff der Aufklärung. Heute haben sie die Aufgabe, die Einheit der wissenschaftlichen Forschung gegenüber dem wachsenden Spezialistentum erneut bewußt werden zu lassen.

*

In der „*Max-Planck-Gesellschaft zur Förderung der Wissenschaften*", der Nachfolgerin der Kaiser-Wilhelm-Gesellschaft, sind einundvierzig Forschungsinstitute von hohem Rang zusammengefaßt. Sie dienen vorwiegend der Grundlagenforschung auf naturwissenschaftlichem Gebiet und sind von den Hochschulen unabhängig. Ihre Finanzierung erfolgte bis 1956 ausschließlich durch die Länder und die Wirtschaft. Seit diesem Zeitpunkt werden der Max-Planck-Gesellschaft auch Sondermittel des Bundes zugewiesen.

*

Aus dem freien Zusammenschluß der wissenschaftlichen Hochschulen, der Wissenschaftlichen Akademien, der Max-Planck-Gesellschaft und anderer zentraler wissenschaftlicher Institutionen ist die „*Deutsche Forschungsgemeinschaft*" (DFG) entstanden. Sie stellt damit eine organisatorische Zusammenfassung der wissenschaftlichen Kräfte und Einrichtungen dar, die eine gemeinsame Willensbildung der deutschen Wissenschaft ermöglicht und eine gemeinsame Vertretung gegenüber den staatlichen Stellen und zur Zusammenarbeit mit dem Ausland erlaubt. Ihre Mitglieder geben sich selbst die Satzung und wählen ihre Organe. Durch die Kommissionen ihres Senats, dem nur Gelehrte angehören, übt sie in wichtigen Wissenschaftsfragen eine den Staat und die Öffentlichkeit beratende Funktion aus. Die Mittel zur Förderung der Forschung erhält sie vom Bund, von den Ländern und (über den Stifterverband für die Deutsche Wissenschaft) von der Wirtschaft[1]. Auf Grund eines sorgfältigen Prüfungsverfahrens entscheidet der

[1] Der „*Stifterverband für die Deutsche Wissenschaft*" ist eine Gemeinschaftsaktion der Gewerblichen Wirtschaft zur Förderung wissenschaftlicher Forschung, Lehre und Ausbildung. Sein Sitz ist Essen.

Hauptausschuß, in dem die Vertreter der Regierungen und des Stifterverbandes Sitz und Stimme haben, über die Verteilung dieser Mittel. Senat und Hauptausschuß stellen gemeinsame Programme der Forschungsförderung auf vernachlässigten und entwicklungsfähigen Gebieten der Wissenschaft auf. So garantiert der finanzierende Staat selbst die Freiheit der Forschung und damit eine einheitliche selbstverwaltende Forschungspolitik.

Trotz der spürbaren Vermehrung der Zuwendungen, die den Forschungsstätten entweder direkt von Bund und Ländern oder indirekt durch Förderungsorganisationen wie die Deutsche Forschungsgemeinschaft zugehen, hält die Forschung mit den Anforderungen nicht Schritt, welche die moderne und rasch fortschreitende Wissenschaft an sie stellt. Die apparative Ausstattung muß verbessert, veraltete Institute müssen erneuert oder ausgebaut werden. Insgesamt zählt man in der Bundesrepublik etwa 2.500 Forschungsstätten aller Art. Hierzu kommen etwa 150 betriebseigene Forschungseinrichtungen der Wirtschaft. Der wissenschaftliche Nachwuchs, der auf zahlreichen Gebieten schon nicht mehr ausreicht, wird nur zu oft von der höheren Bezahlung in der Wirtschaft des In- und Auslandes angezogen.

II. WISSENSCHAFTLICHER NACHWUCHS

Im Sommersemester 1958 zählten die wissenschaftlichen Hochschulen (einschließlich der Philosophisch-Theologischen und Kirchlichen Hochschulen) in der Bundesrepublik mit Berlin(West) einschließlich der Beurlaubten 164.472 deutsche und 14.221 ausländische Studierende.

DIE FACHRICHTUNGEN DER STUDIERENDEN[1] AN DEN WISSENSCHAFTLICHEN HOCHSCHULEN IM SOMMERSEMESTER 1958

Fachrichtung	Studierende insgesamt	Studierende Ausländer
Theologie	6.732	317
Allgemeine, Zahn- und Tier-Medizin, Pharmazie	27.527	4.361
Rechts- und Wirtschaftswissenschaften	43.728	1.123
Kulturwissenschaften	34.682	1.889
Naturwissenschaften	25.192	1.442
Land-, Forstwirtschaft, Gartenbau	2.177	330
Technische Fachrichtungen	32.438	4.362
Insgesamt	172.476	13.824

[1] Ohne Beurlaubte.

Quelle: Statistisches Bundesamt.

Die Zahl der Ausländer hat vom Wintersemester 1956/57 bis zum Sommersemester 1958 um mehr als 50% zugenommen. 32% der ausländischen Studierenden widmen sich einer technischen Ausbildung.

Von den deutschen Studierenden gehören 51% den Fakultäten der Geistes- und Gesellschaftswissenschaften an, 18% den technischen Disziplinen. 16% studieren Naturwissenschaften, und 15% belegen Allgemeine, Zahn- und Tiermedizin und Pharmazie. Die Zahl der Studierenden der Wirtschafts- und Sozialwissenschaften stieg von 1949 bis 1958 von 8.420 auf 18.511. Sie hat also in zehn Jahren sich mehr als verdoppelt.

*

In den vergangenen Jahren war ein großer Teil der Studierenden durch Werkarbeit gehindert, ausschließlich dem Studium nachzugehen: 11% mußten ihr Studium ganz und 25% zum Teil mit Werkarbeit finanzieren. Seit 1957 hat der Bund mit der Förderung nach dem sogenannten „*Honnefer Modell*" eingegriffen. In den Haushalten 1957 und 1958 standen je 30 beziehungsweise 35 Millionen DM für Stipendien und Darlehen zum Hochschulstudium für geeignete und zugleich bedürftige Studenten zur Verfügung; 1959 werden es 41 Millionen DM sein. Die Auslese obliegt der Hochschule.

Abgesehen von diesen staatlichen Mitteln werden zum Beispiel durch das „Evangelische Studienwerk Villigst", das „Katholische Cusanuswerk", die „Friedrich-Ebert-Stiftung", und die Stiftung „Mitbestimmung" weitere deutsche Studenten gefördert. Viele erhalten Sozialbeihilfen nach dem Lastenausgleichsgesetz, Bundesversorgungsgesetz usw. Insgesamt werden etwa 35% der deutschen Studenten in ihrem Studium wirtschaftlich gefördert.

Die Mittel für Stipendien und Darlehen werden über das „*Deutsche Studentenwerk*" den örtlichen Studentenwerken an den Hochschulen zugeleitet. Die Studentenwerke helfen darüber hinaus mit ihrer Krankenfürsorge, mit Mensen, Wohnheimen, Werkstätten und Arbeitsvermittlungen dem akademischen Nachwuchs.

*

Der hochbegabten Studenten nimmt sich schon seit Jahren die „*Studienstiftung des deutschen Volkes*" an. Sie ist eine überregionale Organisation, der Mittel von Bund, Ländern, Gemeinden und über den Stifterverband für die Deutsche Wissenschaft von der freien Wirtschaft zufließen. Nach einem strengen Auswahlverfahren vergibt sie Stipendien, die vom Tage der Aufnahme bis zum Studienabschluß gewährt werden. 1958 wurden von der Studienstiftung des deutschen Volkes an rund 1.750 Stipendiaten etwa 4,2 Millionen DM verteilt.

Im Leben der Studierenden und der Hochschulen spielt die studentische *Selbstverwaltung* eine wichtige Rolle. Jährlich wählt die Studentenschaft ihre Vertretungsorgane, den „*Allgemeinen Studentenausschuß*" (ASTA), an vielen Hochschulen auch Studentenparlamente. Die ASTA stellen sich vor allem soziale Aufgaben. Sie arbeiten als Vertreter der Studentenschaft mit der akademischen Selbstverwaltung zusammen. Die örtlichen Studentenschaften sind im „Verband Deutscher Studentenschaften" zusammengeschlossen. An den Hochschulen gibt es traditionelle studentische Verbindungen (Korporationen) und freie Zusammenschlüsse in klubähnlichen Vereinigungen, Wohngemeinschaften, evangelische und katholische Studentengemeinden und politische Studentengruppen.

Im Dienste des Kontaktes der akademischen Jugend mit dem Ausland steht der „*Deutsche Akademische Austauschdienst*". Hier werden auch die vom Ausland angebotenen Stipendien vermittelt. Durch eigene Ausschüsse trifft er die Auswahl unter den Bewerbern. Die Zuteilung der Stipendien, die Ausländern von deutschen Hochschulen zur Verfügung gestellt werden, erfolgt ebenfalls zum großen Teil über diese Stelle. Sie nimmt sich auch des Professorenaustausches an.

Der „*Alexander von Humboldt-Stiftung*" ist die Aufgabe übertragen, ausländischen Akademikern Studienaufenthalte an deutschen Forschungsinstituten finanziell zu ermöglichen. Die 185 Stipendiaten kommen derzeit aus zweiundvierzig Ländern.

Die spezielle Funktion, deutschen Studenten, wissenschaftlichen Nachwuchskräften und Professoren Studienmöglichkeiten in den USA zu vermitteln, erfüllt seit einigen Jahren die „*Fulbright-Kommission*".

III. AUFWENDUNGEN FÜR DIE WISSENSCHAFT

Die Aufwendungen *des Staates* — das heißt von Bund und Ländern — für Wissenschaft und Forschung waren 1958 mit rund 1.250 Millionen DM (1957: rund 1.000 Millionen DM) angesetzt. Den weitaus größten Teil dieser Finanzmittel bringen die Länder hauptsächlich zur Finanzierung der wissenschaftlichen Hochschulen auf. 1958 waren es einschließlich der Kosten des Königsteiner Abkommens rund 880 Millionen DM (1957: rund 745 Millionen DM). Neben dem Aufwand des Bundes in Höhe von rund 340 Millionen DM im Jahre 1958 (1957 rund 260 Millionen DM) für wissenschaftliche Zwecke wurden für Forschungs- und Entwicklungsvorhaben der Bundesministerien für Verteidigung und für Atomenergie 1958 rund 450 Millionen DM ausgegeben. Der größte Anteil der Ausgaben des Bundes für Wissenschaftsförderung liegt beim Bundesminister des Innern. Sie betreffen die Studentenförderung nach dem „Honnefer Modell" und mit weiteren 85 Millionen DM die zusätzliche Förderung dringender Aufgaben der Wissenschaft. Diese Mittel werden ihr nach den Empfehlungen des Wissenschaftsrates zur Verfügung gestellt.

Die Aufwendungen der Gewerblichen *Wirtschaft* für die freie Wissenschaftsförderung, das heißt also für die Förderung von Forschung, Lehre und Studium an Hochschulen und Instituten (Mäcenatentum), betrugen im Jahre 1957 nach Angaben des Stifterverbandes für die Deutsche Wissenschaft rund 50 Millionen DM. Für die wirtschaftseigene Forschung wurde ein Aufwand von rund 950 Millionen DM ermittelt.

Betrachtet man einen größeren Zeitraum, nämlich die Jahre vom Zeitpunkt der Währungsreform bis zum März 1958, so haben Staat und Wirtschaft für die Finanzierung wissenschaftlicher Bedürfnisse rund 6 Milliarden DM aufgebracht. In der gleichen Zeit hat die Gewerbliche Wirtschaft zusätzlich etwa 4 Milliarden DM für ihre eigene Forschung in Betrieben und Verbänden ausgewiesen. Es muß noch einmal erwähnt werden, daß der größte Teil (rund 4,6 Milliarden DM) der allgemeinen staatlichen Mittel von den Bundesländern für deren wissenschaftliche Einrichtungen (vornehmlich Hochschulen) eingesetzt werden.

Die erste der von der Deutschen Forschungsgemeinschaft herausgegebenen Denkschriften zur Lage der angewandten Forschung hat allein für die sieben darin behandelten Gebiete einen zusätzlichen einmaligen Minimalbedarf von rund 25 Millionen DM errechnet. Seither hat die Deutsche Forschungsgemeinschaft einen zweiten Band über angewandte Forschung und eine Denkschrift über das Fachgebiet der Chemie herausgegeben. Denkschriften über Biologie, Physik und Landwirtschaft werden das Bild der Lage wissenschaftlicher Disziplinen ergänzen und die Erfordernisse deutlicher machen.

Das Interesse und die wachsende Spendenfreudigkeit der Wirtschaft für die Förderung der Wissenschaft wird durch die Tätigkeit des „*Stifterverbandes für die Deutsche Wissenschaft*" geweckt. Er war 1921 als „Stifterverband der Notgemeinschaft der Deutschen Wissenschaft" gegründet worden. Der Stifterverband hat der Wissenschaft allein von 1950 bis 1958 über 80 Millionen DM zuweisen können, wobei der größte Teil seiner freien Mittel der Deutschen Forschungsgemeinschaft und der Max-Planck-Gesellschaft zugewendet wurden. Darüber hinaus hat er mit den übrigen freien Mitteln sich besonders um die Förderung der Geisteswissenschaften sowie des wissenschaftlichen Nachwuchses verdient gemacht.

DIE LITERATUR

Unter die Blütezeiten der Dichtung wird man die Jahre seit 1945 wohl nirgends in unserer Welt zu zählen wagen. Offensichtlich liegt die Literatur weithin in einer Flaute. Es fehlt nicht an Talenten, aber an stilbildender Führung; was als ihr Gefolge denkbar wäre, wirkt unschlüssig und verwirrt. Vernünftigerweise sucht man für solche Situationen nicht nach Gründen; es sei denn man bleibe sich bewußt, wieviel oder wie wenig man damit erklärt.

Wir Deutsche glauben stärker betroffen zu sein als andere und die Gründe dafür sehr genau zu kennen. Hinter uns liegt ein furchtbares Tief unserer Geschichte; eine *Diktatur*, die mit ausdauernder Perfektion freiheitlich gesonnene Menschen jagte, zu Tausenden tötete oder über die Grenzen trieb, die Intelligenz ächtete und die geistige Landschaft durch ihren einfältigen Fanatismus verödete; liegt ein *Krieg*, der Menschenleben millionenfach vergeudete, unseren Wohlstand aufzehrte und das Land in einem vordem kaum denkbaren Maße verwüstete. Als die Deutschen aus diesen Abgründen des Krieges und der Diktatur wieder auftauchten, hatten sie – frei, aber vom Nötigsten entblößt – zu lernen, wie komplex und empfindlich dieses Gebilde „literarisches Leben“ sich erweist, wenn man seinen gestörten Mechanismus ohne das zureichende Instrumentarium an Papierfabriken, graphischen Betrieben, Buchbindereien und buchhändlerischen Organisationen wieder in Gang zu bringen versucht. Zugleich sahen ihre Dichter und Schriftsteller sich vor der Aufgabe, die verratene Wahrhaftigkeit zunächst einmal in *ihrem* Bereich wiederherzustellen und dem unter dem Zugriff der Gewalt und unter den Schrecken eines totalen Krieges verwandelten, verzweifelten, verlorenen Menschen *seine* Sprache zu schaffen.

Wandlung hieß denn auch die von DOLF STERNBERGER noch 1945 gegründete Zeitschrift einer neuen Gesinnung. Ihr folgte in den nächsten Jahren eine lange Reihe dichterischer Dokumente ernstester Verantwortung; darunter die im Kerker niedergeschriebenen Moabiter Sonette von ALBRECHT HAUSHOFER, der 1944 als eines der unzähligen Opfer des mißglückten Aufstandes gegen den Tyrannen hingerichtet worden war; von RUDOLF HAGELSTANGE Venezianisches Credo (1946), von MARIE LUISE VON KASCHNITZ Totentanz (1947), und Nekyia, Berichte eines Überlebenden (1947) von HANS ERICH NOSSACK. Gleichzeitig erschienen die ersten Romane einer neuen Aktualität: Das unauslöschliche Siegel (1946) der hochbegabten ELISABETH LANGGÄSSER († 1950), die in diesem Werk aus Glaube und Gnade eine kühne Architektur über die erste Hälfte unseres Jahrhunderts wölbte; Der Kranz der Engel (1946) der repräsentativen katholischen Dichterin GERTRUD VON LE FORT; Das gute Recht (1946), darin KASIMIR EDSCHMID die Atmosphäre des untergegangenen Reichs an den Tagesnöten eines nonkonformistischen Schriftstellers zu dokumentieren sucht, und HERMANN KASACKs Stadt hinter dem Strom (1947), ein weckendes und weithin wirkendes Symbol neu erkannter menschlicher Existenz. Schon kehrten damals neuere und neueste Romanwerke aus der deutschsprachigen Fremde und Emigration zu uns zurück: so FRANZ WERFELS (1941 in USA geschriebener) Lourdes-Roman Das Lied der Bernadette, HERMAN HESSEs Alterswerk Das Glasperlenspiel (1943 in der Schweiz erschienen) und HERMANN BROCHs Tod des Vergil (zuerst 1945 bei Pantheon Books in New York). Zu diesen, nach Art und Wert gewiß sehr unterschiedlichen Dichtungen traten: THOMAS MANNs grandioses Epos der deutschen Seele im Doktor Faustus (Frankfurt 1947), seit 1949 in rascher Folge die Bücher GOTTFRIED BENNs und ERNST JÜNGERS, seit 1950 die Werke des mächtigsten Anregers der Epoche, FRANZ KAFKA, in einer ersten in Deutschland erscheinenden Gesamtausgabe. Das Ganze wirkte wie eine neue Ernte, die sehr lebendige Diskussion über *Glasperlenspiel*, *Doktor Faustus* und die rätselvolle Erscheinung KAFKAs wie ein schon wieder aufgelebtes, bewegtes literarisches Leben.

Wer sich nicht täuschen ließ, mochte wie ein namhafter französischer Germanist noch 1952 entscheiden: die deutschen Schriftsteller der Nachkriegszeit, die Erwähnung verdienten, seien in Wahrheit Schriftsteller der Vorkriegszeit. Er hatte damit (selbst zu diesem Zeitpunkt) nicht einfach Unrecht; nur übersah er, wie tief Deutschland auch im Geistig-Seelischen verletzt, wieviel also einer neu beginnenden Generation im Vorhinein aufgegeben war. Zweierlei zum mindesten: sich mit einer beängstigenden, beschämenden, verhaßten Vergangenheit auszusöhnen und die Isolierung in einer einigen Welt zu überwinden. Das erste war das bedeutend Schwierigere. Mit dem (poetologischen) Rückgriff auf den Expressionismus, der sich nach dem Ersten Weltkrieg aus einer existenziell ähnlichen Situation entwickelt hatte, war es nicht getan. Auch nicht schon mit den schönen, sorgfältigen Ausgaben, in denen man das dichterische Erbe der schnöde Unterdrückten, schließlich Vergessenen wieder lebendig werden ließ. ELSE LASKER-SCHÜLER und GERTRUD KOLMAR, ERNST BARLACH, WALTER BENJAMIN, HERMANN BROCH, THEODOR DÄUBLER, OSKAR LOERKE, ROBERT MUSIL, JOSEPH ROTH, EUGEN GOTTLOB WINKLER und andere kehrten so zu uns zurück. Eine beeindruckende Reihe des verübten Frevels und des Versuchs seiner Wiedergutmachung, zugleich aber auch ein Anfang der großen Bereinigung, die unausweichlich vor dem Neubeginn unserer Literatur lag, aber doch nicht Sache der Literatur allein, sondern der ganz allgemeinen Bereitschaft des deutschen Gewissens war.

Was indessen eine aus allem Vertrauen geworfene junge Generation aus den deutschen Dichtungen der ersten Jahrhunderthälfte immer gewann; sie hatte es (und das war ihre weitere Aufgabe) nachzuprüfen am Gang der zeitgenössischen *Weltliteratur*, von der sie so lange ausgeschlossen war. Literarische Neugierde kann schwerlich jemals drängender gewesen sein als bei uns in jenem Jahr 1948, in dem unsere wiederhergestellte Währung endlich die lang verschlossenen Tore zu unserer angestammten geistigen Welt wieder öffnete. Der Durchlaß war zunächst nur schmal, nur eben ein Spalt, aber er genügte, wieder zu beleben, was nur durch das Machtwort der Gewalt abgebrochen worden war: Zeitschriften und Bücher des freien Westens strömten herein; persönliche und gruppenweise Fühlungnahme mit den geistigen Nachbarn wurden wieder möglich und setzten sich in Betrachtungen und Diskussionen unserer Zeitschriften und Zeitungen fort. Aus der Beschäftigung mit den neuen und zu neuer Wirkung gelangten älteren fremden Dichtern entstanden die für die Heranbildung eines größeren Kreises von Literaturfreunden so wichtigen Übersetzungen von Werken der ELIOT und POUND, HEMINGWAY und FAULKNER, BECKETT und DYLAN THOMAS, von PROUST, SARTRE, CAMUS, LAUTRÉAMONT, MALLARMÉ, SAINT-JOHN PERSE und GARCIA LORCA.

Auch diese (keineswegs vollständige) Reihe hatte, genau wie die Ausgaben der Expressionisten, gerade erst zu erscheinen begonnen, als die ersten eigenen jungen Kräfte sich zeigten. Nicht im *Drama*! Hier waren wir von Anfang an auf Vorkriegsbegabungen wie CARL ZUCKMAYER (Des Teufels General) und die fortwirkende genialische Dramaturgie BERTOLT BRECHTS angewiesen; haben wir auch heute noch – nachdem uns der vielversprechende WOLFGANG BORCHERT (Draußen vor der Tür) durch einen frühen Tod (1946) genommen wurde – an erfolgreichem jungen deutschsprachigen Theater nur die beiden sehr begabten Schweizer MAX FRISCH und FRIEDRICH DÜRRENMATT.

Dagegen erweist sich der *Essay*, der eigentlich nie eine brillierende deutsche Gattung war, mit HANS EGON HOLTHUSEN, ALBRECHT FABRI, MAX BENSE, FRIEDRICH GEORG JÜNGER und anderen als ein überraschend reich und zukunftsträchtig bestelltes Feld. Das mag ganz allgemein im Zug der neuen europäischen Literatur liegen, die dem Essay zwischen und in den alten Gattungen (wie im Roman) etwas wirkungsvolleren Raum zugesteht und ihn gelegentlich geradezu zur „eigentümlichen Form experimenteller

Literatur" erklärt. Zugleich erscheint er, fast überraschend, in nächster Nähe der Lyrik angesiedelt. Die *Lyrik* aber war seit je die bevorzugte deutsche Form und ist es heute wieder, – so sehr sie sich inzwischen verwandelt zu haben scheint; von GOTTFRIED BENNS († 1956) hochintellektueller Laboratoriumskunst bis zu WILHELM LEHMANNS magischer Naturlyrik (Entzückter Staub) zieht sich eine fast unübersehbare Reihe junger lyrischer Talente, von denen nur einige der schon zu Namen gekommenen – INGEBORG BACHMANN, PAUL CELAN, MARIE LUISE VON KASCHNITZ, KARL KROLOW, HEINZ PIONTEK, WOLF DIETRICH SCHNURRE – hier genannt seien. Einen genaueren Einblick in die lyrischen Bemühungen des Jahrhunderts geben die Anthologien: *Ergriffenes Dasein.* Deutsche Lyrik 1900–1950 (1953); *De Profundis.* Deutsche Lyrik in dieser Zeit. Anthologie aus zwölf Jahren (1947); auf das lyrische Experiment konzentriert: *Transit.* Lyrikbuch der Jahrhundertmitte (herausgegeben von WALTER HÖLLERER, 1956) und die aggressiv fortschrittliche Poetik *Mein Gedicht ist mein Messer.* Lyriker zu ihren Gedichten (herausgegeben von HANS BENDER, 1955).

Während in der Lyrik, die auf Bedeutung Anspruch machen darf, — abgesehen von den der Tradition stärker verpflichteten FRIEDRICH GEORG JÜNGER und WERNER BERGENGRUEN — das fortschrittliche (experimentierende) Element sich fast völlig durchgesetzt hat, bildet es im *Roman* und in der *Erzählung* nur eine Art Spitze, die stetig und ohne Sprünge in eine breitere, traditionsnähere Produktion übergeht. Danach dürfte man, ohne doch schon damit zu werten, die gegenwärtige Situation der Epik in zwei Stufen sehen. In der ersten etwa: ERNST KREUDER (Die Unauffindbaren), HEINRICH BÖLL (Wo warst du, Adam?), MAX FRISCH (Stiller), HANS ERICH NOSSACK (Der jüngere Bruder), ALFRED ANDERSCH (Sansibar oder der letzte Grund); im Übergang: ERNST SCHNABEL (Ich und die Könige), WOLFGANG KOEPPEN (Tauben im Gras), HEINRICH SCHIRMBECK (Ärgert dich dein rechtes Auge); in der zweiten GEORG JÜNGER, WERNER HELWIG (Raubfischer in Hellas), KASIMIR EDSCHMID (Drei Häuser am Meer), STEFAN ANDRES (Die Hochzeit der Feinde), HORST LANGE (Verlöschende Feuer) und GERD GAISER (Schlußball).

Ein solcher Aufbau ist für jede Literatur erwünscht; er ist es im Besonderen für unsere. Wir wären noch zufriedener, wenn die soeben entworfene Pyramide breiter im Traditionellen ruhte, – zahlreicher wäre in den Talenten, die aus der Tradition zu schaffen sich entschlössen, und welthaltiger in ihren Hervorbringungen. An dem einen wie dem anderen fehlt es unserer Literatur (noch immer), vielleicht eben deshalb an der dichteren Atmosphäre literarischen

Lebens. Es zu beleben wurde manches seit unserem Neubeginn getan: Akademien wurden begründet, für Sprache und Dichtung in Darmstadt, für Wissenschaft und Literatur in Mainz, für die Künste in München und in Hamburg. Wir haben Literaturpreise in Fülle und an anspruchsvollen Zeitschriften — Die neue Rundschau, Merkur, Hochland, Wort und Wahrheit, Neue deutsche Hefte, Akzente und andere — soviel, wie der Deutsche, der nie ein großer Zeitschriftenleser gewesen ist, zu tragen sich bereit findet. Im Übrigen ist unser literarisches Leben, obwohl uns neben anderem noch die Hauptstadt fehlt, keineswegs verödet! Dafür strömt aus allen Teilen der Welt zuviel an Literatur bei uns zusammen und schließt auch uns zu spürbar ein in das weite geistige Spannungsfeld eines neuen Weltzustandes, in dem der Anteil der Anderen immer weniger als fremd empfunden wird. In dieser Einsicht nehmen wir aus der Aufgeschlossenheit unserer Verleger und der Aufnahmebereitschaft einer neuen Generation die Gewißheit eines wachsenden deutschen Beitrags zur Literatur der Welt.

VERLAGSWESEN, BIBLIOTHEKEN, ARCHIVE

I. VERLAGSWESEN UND BUCHHANDEL

Das deutsche Verlagswesen mußte nach 1945 in einem doppelten Sinn in Westdeutschland neu aufgebaut werden. Zu den Trümmern des Krieges kam die Abtrennung des alten buchhändlerischen Zentrums Leipzig durch den Eisernen Vorhang. Trotzdem gelang dem Verlagswesen und dem Buchhandel der Bundesrepublik in den vergangenen Jahren eine Buchproduktion, die an die freiheitlichen Tendenzen der Zeit vor 1933 anknüpft und in ihrer Fülle den differenzierten Wünschen der in- und ausländischen Leserschaft entspricht. Mit den 16.690 Titeln, die 1958 in der Bundesrepublik einschließlich von Berlin(West) erschienen, steht die Bundesrepublik in der internationalen Buchproduktion an vierter Stelle hinter der Sowjetunion, Japan und dem Vereinigten Königreich. 1.935 Verlage waren an der Buchproduktion des Jahres 1955 beteiligt; darunter allerdings 1.277 Firmen, die unter sechs Titeln herausbrachten.

Deutschland gehört zu den traditionellen großen Ausfuhrländern für das Buch. Aus äußerst bescheidenen Anfängen war es möglich, im Lauf der Nachkriegsjahre einen Buchexport zu entwickeln, der im Vergleich mit den Ergebnissen anderer großer Nationen sehr beachtlich ist. 1958 wurden ,,Waren des Buchhandels und Erzeugnisse des graphischen Gewerbes“ im Werte von 216,4 Millionen DM ausgeführt.

Die Bundesrepublik Deutschland ist zugleich aber auch lebhaft am ausländischen Buch interessiert; einmal in der Form von Einfuhren des fremdsprachigen Buches und zum anderen durch Übernahme von Übersetzungen. ,,Waren des Buchhandels und Erzeugnisse des graphischen Gewerbes“ wurden im Jahre 1958 im Werte von 74,7 Millionen DM importiert. Mit den 1.514 Titeln, die 1957 aus fremden Sprachen ins Deutsche übersetzt wurden, nimmt Deutschland einen hervorragenden Platz unter den Nationen ein, die sich der Pflege des internationalen Schrifttums widmen.

Rund 40% aller Verlagshäuser sind in Berlin(West), München, Stuttgart, Hamburg und Frankfurt am Main ansässig. Die wichtigsten Zentren des vertreibenden Buchhandels, insbesondere des Sortimentbuchhandels, sind Berlin(West), Hamburg, München, Stuttgart, Frankfurt am Main, Köln und Hannover. Mit den 4.103 Firmen des vertreibenden Buchhandels verfügt der Buchhandel der Bundesrepublik in 996 Orten über ein dichtes und wirkungsvolles Verteilernetz.

Organisatorisches Zentrum des Buchhandels ist Frankfurt am Main mit dem Sitz des „*Börsenvereins des Deutschen Buchhandels e.V.*", der neben dem Goethe-Haus im „Haus des deutschen Buchhandels" beheimatet ist. Unter seinem Namen findet alljährlich die internationale *Frankfurter Buchmesse* statt, die 1958 von 1.485, darunter 807 ausländischen, Verlagshäusern beschickt war. Mit über 60.000 Titeln bot sie einen Überblick über die Buchproduktion nahezu aller Gebiete der westlichen und östlichen Welt. Höhepunkt dieser Buchmesse ist die alljährliche Verleihung des „*Friedenspreises des deutschen Buchhandels*". Er wird jeweils an eine Persönlichkeit verliehen, die ungeachtet ihrer Nationalität durch ihre literarische und geistige Arbeit und durch ihr Wirken Großes für den Friedensgedanken getan hat. Die bisherigen Preisträger waren MAX TAU, ALBERT SCHWEITZER, ROMANO GUARDINI, MARTIN BUBER, CARL J. BURCKHARDT, HERMANN HESSE, REINHOLD SCHNEIDER, THORNTON WILDER und KARL JASPERS. Der zehnte Preisträger (1958) ist THEODOR HEUSS.

Deutschland ist das Ursprungsland der *Buchgemeinschaften*. Von ihnen bestehen über zwanzig mit einer Mitgliederzahl von etwa vier Millionen. Für die neuere Entwicklung des Buchmarktes sind die zahlreichen *Taschenbuchreihen* charakteristisch. Sie bieten erstklassige belletristische Bücher und allgemein verständliche wissenschaftliche Werke aller Kategorien zu niedrigen Preisen an und setzen sie in großen Mengen ab.

Als Archiv des deutschen Buchhandels ist die *Deutsche Bibliothek* in Frankfurt am Main anzusehen. Sie wurde 1947 durch den freien deutschen Buchhandel und die Stadt Frankfurt gegründet. Seit Mitte 1952 arbeitet sie als Stiftung des öffentlichen Rechts, nunmehr auch mit finanzieller Unterstützung des Bundes und des Landes Hessen. Die von ihr redaktionell betreute „*Deutsche Bibliographie*" stellt die deutsche Nationalbibliographie dar.

II. BIBLIOTHEKEN

Das deutsche Bibliothekswesen ist durch eine Trennung in *wissenschaftliche Bibliotheken* und *Volksbüchereien* gekennzeichnet. Sie wurde durch das raschere Wachsen der Volksbüchereien zwischen den beiden Weltkriegen vertieft und konnte trotz vielen Bemühungen bis heute nicht überwunden werden. Nur von den wissenschaftlichen Bibliotheken soll hier gesprochen werden; die Volksbüchereien sind als Teil der Erwachsenenbildung dort behandelt. Die Vielgestaltigkeit der deutschen Bibliotheken ist gerade dort besonders groß, wo sie der Wissenschaft dienen. Eine universale Sammelaufgabe haben vor allem die Universitäts- und Landesbibliotheken, die meist zugleich auch Sammelstätten für die gesamte Literatur des Landes darstellen. Neben ihnen gewinnen die Bibliotheken der Technischen Hochschulen, die den Charakter einer bloßen Fachbibliothek längst weitgehend abgelegt haben, immer mehr an Bedeutung. Den Landesbibliotheken sind nach ihrer Funktion die Bibliotheken einzelner größerer Städte gleichzuachten. Durch sie werden entsprechend der heutigen Geltung der Städte die Zufälligkeiten in etwa ausgeglichen, die bei der Entstehung der Landesbibliotheken obgewaltet haben.

Neben diesen *Universalbibliotheken* steht die fast unübersehbare Reihe der meist jüngeren, aber darum nicht weniger wichtigen wissenschaftlichen *Fachbibliotheken:* die Seminar- und Institutsbibliotheken der Universitäten, die Bibliotheken der Fachhochschulen, der wissenschaftlichen Forschungsinstitute und gelehrten Gesellschaften, die staatlichen Behörden- und Verwaltungsbibliotheken, die Bibliotheken der großen industriellen und wirtschaftlichen Unternehmungen und Gesellschaften, denen allen die Beschränkung ihrer Sammelaufgabe auf ein bestimmtes Fachgebiet und meist die Beschränkung der Zugänglichkeit auf einen bestimmten Personenkreis eigentümlich sind. Eine besondere Stellung nimmt die *Deutsche Bibliothek* in Frankfurt a. M. ein. Nach Art der Deutschen Bücherei in Leipzig bemüht sie sich, das gesamte deutschsprachige Schrifttum im In- und Ausland einschließlich der im Inland erscheinenden fremdsprachlichen Literatur zu erfassen und bibliographisch zu erschließen („*Deutsche Bibliographie*"; vergleiche die vorhergehende Seite).

Die schweren Verluste der Kriegsjahre sind heute schon wieder weitgehend aufgeholt. Die vielfach während des Krieges ausgelagerten Bestände sind meist zurückgeführt. Die zerstörten Gebäude sind, um nur von den Universitäts- und Landesbibliotheken zu sprechen, durch Neubauten (Münster, Gießen und andere) oder durch Um- und Ausbauten (Hamburg, München, Göttingen und andere) ersetzt worden. Andere Neubauten sind erst in der Ausführung oder Planung begriffen (Bonn, Frankfurt am Main). Völlige Neugründungen nach dem Zweiten Weltkrieg sind die Bibliotheken der Freien Universität in Berlin-Dahlem sowie der Universitäten Mainz und Saarbrücken.

Um die Ergänzung der Bestände an ausländischer Literatur und insbesondere die Schließung der Kriegslücken, vor allem an Zeitschriften, hat die Deutsche Forschungsgemeinschaft sich die größten Verdienste erworben. Durch ein wohldurchdachtes System von *Sonder-Sammelgebieten* soll mit ihrer Hilfe erreicht werden, daß die wichtigste ausländische Literatur wenigstens in einem Exemplar in der Bundesrepublik vorhanden ist. Der schnelle Nachweis der vorhandenen Monographien wird durch den von der Universitätsbibliothek Köln laufend geführten und veröffentlichten *Zentralkatalog der Auslandsliteratur* (ZKA) erreicht. Eine analoge Aufgabe für die Zeitschriften soll durch das *Gesamtverzeichnis der ausländischen Zeitschriften* (GAZ) gelöst werden, dessen Druck in der Westdeutschen Bibliothek in Marburg vorbereitet wird.

Schmerzlich fühlbar für die westdeutschen Bibliotheken ist der Ausfall der Preußischen Staatsbibliothek in Berlin. Ihre Aufgabe als Zentralbibliothek insbesondere im Leihverkehr übernimmt mehr und mehr die Westdeutsche Bibliothek in Marburg. Sie verwaltet nicht nur einen großen Teil des ehemaligen Besitzes der Staatsbibliothek treuhänderisch, sondern sie wird auch für diese zentrale Aufgabe systematisch ausgebaut. Eine ähnliche zentrale Stellung für die Technischen Hochschulen ist der Bibliothek der Technischen Hochschule Hannover zugedacht.

*

Der ehemalige deutsche Gesamtkatalog, der mit dem vierzehnten Band sein Erscheinen eingestellt hat, wird durch ein Netz regionaler *Zentralkataloge* in Köln, Hamburg, Göttingen, Frankfurt, Stuttgart und München ersetzt. Sie weisen heute schon wenigstens in einem Katalog in Zettelform die wesentlichsten Bestände der von ihnen erfaßten Länder nach. Der altbewährte deutsche *Leihverkehr* ist in neuer Form wieder aufgelebt. Im Interesse einer gleichmäßigen Ausnutzung der Bestände aller Bibliotheken vollzieht er sich heute in regionalen Bereichen, die denen der Zentralkataloge entsprechen. Gegenseitige Aushilfe und planvolle Zusammenarbeit charakterisieren das deutsche Bibliothekswesen heute mehr als je zuvor.

Der 1948 wieder gegründete *Verein Deutscher Bibliothekare* gehört zusammen mit dem *Verein der Diplombibliothekare an wissenschaftlichen Bibliotheken* dem Internationalen Verband der Bibliothekar-Vereine (IFLA) an. Ihr gemeinsames Organ ist die 1954 ins Leben gerufene *Zeitschrift für Bibliothekswesen und Bibliographie*. Der Verein Deutscher Bibliothekare veröffentlicht außerdem in regelmäßigen Abständen das durch seinen statistischen Teil besonders wertvolle *Jahrbuch der deutschen Bibliotheken*.

III. ARCHIVE

Wert und Bedeutung von Archiven sind im öffentlichen Bewußtsein nach 1945 besonders hervorgetreten. Damals wäre zu Beweiszwecken und zur Erhellung der Zeitgeschichte ein funktionierendes Archivwesen unerläßlich gewesen. Die meisten deutschen Archive waren jedoch auseinandergerissen, häufig durch Zerstörung gemindert oder wegen ihrer Auslagerung zunächst unbenutzbar.

Charakteristisch für das deutsche Archivwesen ist seit jeher seine dezentralisierte Organisation. Trotz manchen Ansätzen konnte eine über den Länderarchiven stehende, diese zusammenfassende zentrale Archivverwaltung nicht verwirklicht werden. Von den Archivverwaltungen der Länder kam denen Preußens und Bayerns eine gewisse Vorrangstellung zu. Daneben gewann das erst 1919 begründete Reichsarchiv wachsend auch an repräsentativem Gewicht. Die preußische Archivverwaltung ist zerschlagen; ihre Bestände sind zerstreut. Die bayerische Archivverwaltung hingegen hat organisatorisch, wenn auch in ihren Beständen nicht ganz ungeschmälert, die Wirren des Krieges und der Nachkriegszeit überstanden.

Für die wissenschaftliche Forschung ist von besonderem Interesse, wie viele der in den Archiven aufbewahrten *Quellen zur deutschen Geschichte* den Krieg überdauert haben. Eine erste Bestandsaufnahme der Kriegsverluste an Archivalien und der Schäden an Gebäuden und Einrichtungen ergab — im ganzen gesehen —, trotz schweren Verlusten im einzelnen, eine größere Bewahrung der archivalischen Substanz, als nach der Schwere der in den deutschen Städten angerichteten Zerstörungen zu erhoffen war. Stärkere Verluste an Archivalien hatten von den Länderarchiven nur Hannover, Düsseldorf, Darmstadt, München und Würzburg zu beklagen. Daß noch größere Einbußen vermieden wurden, war den im allgemeinen rechtzeitig durchgeführten Sicherungsmaßnahmen zu verdanken.

Die Bestände des Reichsarchivs in Potsdam sowie des Preußischen Geheimen Staatsarchivs in Berlin-Dahlem waren überwiegend nach Mitteldeutschland ausgelagert worden. Nach der Besetzung durch sowjetische Truppen wurden sie daher in dem bald aufgebauten Zentralarchiv Potsdam und seiner Zweigstelle in Merseburg zusammengefaßt.

In verhältnismäßig kurzer Zeit haben nach dem Krieg die westdeutschen Länderarchive ihre Bestände der Forschung wieder zugänglich machen können, neue Organisationsformen gefunden und auch den Kontakt der verschiedenen Archivverwaltungen in den gemeinsamen fachlichen Fragen sicherzustellen vermocht.

Mit der Bildung einer halbjährlich zusammentretenden Konferenz der Archivreferenten des Bundes und der Länder, der Begründung des „*Vereins deutscher Archivare*“, der sich in der Fachzeitschrift „Der Archivar“ ein Mitteilungsorgan schuf, und der Errichtung der Archivschule in Marburg, welche die Tradition des früheren Instituts für Archivwissenschaft in Berlin-Dahlem fortsetzt, ist der organisatorische Aufbau nach dem Krieg zu einem gewissen Abschluß gelangt. Die bayerische Archivverwaltung unterhält weiter ihre Archivschule in München und führt die Herausgabe der alten „Archivalischen Zeitschrift“ fort.

*

Mit der Konstituierung der Bundesrepublik im September 1949 ergab sich die Notwendigkeit, ein eigenes *Bundesarchiv* zu errichten. Seine Gründung wurde im Jahre 1950 von der Bundesregierung beschlossen. 1952 nahm es seine Tätigkeit auf. Die neuen fachlichen Probleme des Archivwesens, welche die Entwicklung des deutschen Archivwesens in Zukunft bestimmen, werden im Bundesarchiv zunächst sichtbar.

Die Errichtung eines Bundesarchivs war aus zwei Gründen notwendig. Es hatte künftig die archivwürdigen Akten der zentralen Behörden der Bundesverwaltung aufzunehmen und sie der Verwaltung und der historischen Forschung nutzbar zu machen. Zum anderen obliegt ihm die *Sicherung der noch vorhandenen archivalischen Überlieferung des Deutschen Reiches*, für deren Verwahrung keines der Länderarchive eine Zuständigkeit besaß oder beanspruchen konnte. So mußte das Bundesarchiv die Nachfolge des 1919 gegründeten Reichsarchivs antreten; dazu aber auch die der zentralen Archiveinrichtungen des nicht mehr bestehenden Landes Preußen, soweit diese nicht auf die Archive der Nachfolgeländer übergehen konnten. Es galt zunächst, eine Bestandsaufnahme der archivalischen Überlieferung zentraler Reichs- und preußischer Herkunft vorzunehmen. Die in den mitteldeutschen Raum verlagerten Archivalien des Reichsarchivs und des Preußischen Geheimen Staatsarchivs blieben leider unerreichbar. Aber zahlreich waren die Stellen auf westdeutschem Boden, wohin während des Krieges Zentralbehörden ihre laufenden, nunmehr herrenlos gewordenen Akten verlagert hatten. Größtenteils waren es Trümmer der einstigen Registraturen, versprengte Reste, doch auch einige geschlossene Ministerialregistraturen, die im Bundesarchiv geborgen werden konnten.

Größer waren die Aktenbestände von Reichsbehörden, welche die Siegermächte bei der Besetzung Deutschlands an den verschiedensten Stellen aufgefunden, beschlagnahmt und außer Landes gebracht hatten. Sie zurückzugewinnen war und ist noch ein dringendes Anliegen des Bundesarchivs. Die langen Bemühungen darum beginnen langsam ihre Früchte zu tragen. Ein größerer Teil der Akten des Auswärtigen Amtes ist bereits aus dem Vereinigten Königreich in die Bundesrepublik zurückgekehrt, und wichtige Akten der Reichskanzlei sowie einige weitere kleine Rückgaben von Akten sind in das Bundesarchiv gelangt. Jetzt ist mit einem stetigen Zurückfließen des beschlagnahmten deutschen archivalischen Schriftgutes aus westalliierter Hand zu rechnen.

Unversehrt in ihren Beständen blieb die Abteilung Frankfurt des ehemaligen Reichsarchivs. Sie verwahrt die archivalische Restüberlieferung der zentralen Gewalten des alten Deutschen Reiches bis 1806 — der größte Teil liegt in Wien — und der Einrichtungen des Deutschen Bundes (1815—1866). Nach dem Zusammenbruch hatten das Land Hessen und die Stadt Frankfurt am Main die Sorge für diese Abteilung übernommen. 1953 konnte sie auf das Bundesarchiv übergehen. Dabei blieb, wie früher, die Stadt Frankfurt Unterhaltsträger für Räumlichkeiten und Sachausgaben. Als weitere auswärtige Abteilung wurde im darauf folgenden Jahre das bisher vom Land Nordrhein-Westfalen unterhaltene Personenstandsarchiv II in Kornelimünster bei Aachen dem Bundesarchiv angegliedert. Es führt seitdem auf Grund erweiterter Zuständigkeit die Bezeichnung „*Bundesarchiv Abt. Zentralnachweisstelle*". Diese Abteilung ist zur Aufnahme und Verwaltung solchen militärischen Schriftgutes bestimmt, das dem Nachweis der militärischen Dienstverhältnisse der ehemaligen Wehrmachtsangehörigen (Heer und Luftwaffe) dient. Es hat insbesondere für die Abwicklung von Ansprüchen aus früheren Dienstverhältnissen der Wehrmacht Bedeutung.

Das *Militärarchiv* (MA) ist die jüngst begründete Abteilung des Bundesarchivs. Es nimmt eine gewisse Sonderstellung ein, sowohl was das Mitspracherecht des Verteidigungsressorts auf die personelle Besetzung betrifft, als auch hinsichtlich seiner Zuständigkeit. Das Militärarchiv ist ein sogenanntes Ganzheits-Archiv, das im Gegensatz zu den übrigen Abteilungen des Bundesarchivs nicht nur die Akten der obersten Führungsstellen in sich aufnimmt, sondern auch die der Truppen bis hinab zur letzten Einheit.

Wie das Militärarchiv eine besondere Sparte bildet, so wird man künftig möglicherweise auch für die Archivalien der technischen, Verkehrs- und wirtschaftlichen Verwaltungen eigene Sparten innerhalb einer Bundes-Archivverwaltung ins Auge fassen müssen.

In der Gegenwart stehen für das Bundesarchiv Probleme zur Lösung an, die einerseits den *durch die Kriegsschäden entstandenen Verlust archivalischer*

Überlieferung betreffen, andererseits sich auf die künftige Sicherung des historisch wertvollen Materials aus der ungeheuren Papierflut der modernen Verwaltung beziehen. Während für die Vergangenheit große Lücken klaffen, drohen uns die Aktenmassen der Gegenwart zu ersticken. Der eigentliche Schnittpunkt dieser gegensätzlichen Tendenz sind die Jahre 1945/49. Was vor dieser Zeit liegt, ist wegen der Kriegsverluste quellenmäßig äußerst dürftig belegt und bedarf der subtilen Erforschung dessen, ,,was eigentlich gewesen" (RANKE). Deshalb hat das Bundesarchiv ganz neue Wege beschritten, archivalische Überlieferung der Forschung zugänglich zu machen, indem es in Form von archivalischen Dokumentationen, das heißt Befragungen von Zeugen des Zeitgeschehens, eine neue Gattung historischer Quellen schuf. Auch die bisher als historische Quellen von seiten der Archive wenig beachteten technischen Errungenschaften Film, Ton und Bild erweisen sich in immer stärkerem Maße als ein von einem modernen Zentralarchiv zu beachtendes Gebiet der historischen Forschung. Über eine Million Meter an Filmen bilden schon heute im Bundesarchiv eine unschätzbare Quelle für das Zeitgeschehen der letzten Jahrzehnte.

Erheblich schwieriger ist die Frage, was aus der Fülle der *Aktenproduktion der modernen Verwaltung* als historisch bedeutungsvoll sich zur Übernahme in das Archiv anbietet. Das ist nicht nur eine Frage, die das Zentralarchiv der Bundesrepublik allein angeht, sondern alle Archive, auch die der Länder, berührt. Die staatlichen Archive müssen heute bereits Einfluß nehmen auf die Entstehung des Schriftgutes bei den Behörden, das einmal Quelle für die Geschichtsforschung der Zukunft sein wird. So sind die staatlichen Archive sowohl des Bundes wie der Länder heute anders als früher in ein nahes Verhältnis zur Verwaltung gerückt, der zu dienen ihre vornehmste Aufgabe ist.

Schließlich steckt hinter alle dem auch ein technisches *Raumproblem*. Alle staatlichen Archive der Bundesrepublik stehen unter dem Druck, Massen von Archivalien übernehmen zu sollen, die ihre Aufnahmefähigkeit überschreiten. Die Beseitigung von Kriegsschäden an Gebäuden reicht nicht aus, um dieses Ansturmes Herr zu werden. Zwei Länderarchive haben in den letzten Jahren Neubauten erhalten (Koblenz, Wolfenbüttel). Für die zweckmäßige Unterbringung des Bundesarchivs als des zentralen Archivs der Bundesrepublik ist jetzt eine befriedigende Lösung gefunden worden. Der Druck der Massen ist jedoch kein nur von der bautechnischen Seite her zu lösendes Problem. Es wirft Fragen auf, die stärkstens die *archivalische Methodik* berühren. Der letzte ,,Deutsche Archivtag" hat diese erstmals vor dem Forum der deutschen Archivare zur Diskussion gestellt.

DIE MUSIK

Auch eine Darstellung des heutigen Musiklebens im Bundesgebiet muß von dem Zusammenbruch ausgehen. Im Jahr 1945 waren Organisationen und Kontrakte aufgelöst, Konzertsäle und Theatergebäude in Schutt und Asche gesunken. Um die *Oper* in Deutschland aufbauen zu können, mußten zunächst die Ensembles wiedergewonnen werden. Die Mitglieder der Orchester, der Theaterchöre fanden sich allmählich zusammen, Engagements wurden getätigt, so daß langsam wieder spielfähige Ensembles bereitstanden.

Die zweite Sorge war die Beschaffung von Räumlichkeiten, in denen Opernaufführungen möglich waren. 1945 standen nur noch wenige große Opernhäuser zur Verfügung, wie in München das Prinzregententheater oder die Häuser in Stuttgart und Nürnberg. Diese wurden teilweise nun von den Besatzungsbehörden beschlagnahmt. Da an einen Wiederaufbau der zerstörten Operngebäude zunächst nicht zu denken war, suchte man nach Ausweichmöglichkeiten, schuf Behelfsbühnen und versuchte, sich in Sälen und früheren Kinos einzurichten. Neuerstellt wurden bis jetzt folgende Opernhäuser: 1948 Pforzheim; 1949 Bonn, Hagen, Oberhausen; 1950 Bielefeld, Bremen, Dortmund, Duisburg, Essen, Hannover, Kaiserslautern, Osnabrück; 1952 Bremerhaven, Krefeld, Wilhelmshaven; 1953 Kiel; 1954 Karlsruhe, Remscheid; 1955 Hamburg; 1956 Augsburg, Düsseldorf, Münster, Wuppertal-Barmen; 1957 Köln, Mannheim.

Einige Operntheater spielen aber immer noch behelfsmäßig, teilweise unter räumlich beengten Verhältnissen. Immerhin werden heute im Bundesgebiet wieder etwa sechzig stehende Opernensembles gezählt, bei denen Solisten und Chormitglieder sich im festen Engagementsverhältnis mit Verträgen von mehrjähriger, ganzjähriger oder mindestens achtmonatiger Dauer befinden und die Orchester im Dienstverhältnis des Staates oder der Städte stehen. Die Zuschüsse, ohne welche die Theater nicht arbeiten können, werden von den Ländern und den Stadtgemeinden getragen. Deutschland ist das Land der Oper. Die so oft totgesagte Oper lebt.

Die im Ausland am meisten beachteten *Opernfestspiele* sind die von Bayreuth und München. Die Bayreuther Bühnenfestspiele haben insbesondere durch die neuen Inszenierungsideen von WOLFGANG und WIELAND WAGNER, der beiden Enkel RICHARD WAGNERS, internationale Beachtung wiedergewonnen. München bewahrt seine Tradition, die in erster Linie an die Namen MOZART, WAGNER und RICHARD STRAUSS geknüpft ist.

Der Wiederaufbau der Opernensembles und -orchester ermöglichte die Durchführung des geregelten Spielplanes mit seinen Repertoire-Opern. Er gab ferner die Möglichkeit, zeitgenössisches Schaffen zu fördern. Mit Jahren Verspätung kamen HINDEMITHS Oper „Mathis der Maler" und ALBAN BERGS „Lulu", die in der Schweiz uraufgeführt worden waren, nach Deutschland. An Ur- und Erstaufführungen deutscher Werke, die im Bundesgebiet oder in West-Berlin selbst stattfanden, seien genannt: BLACHERS „Preußisches Märchen", BLACHER-EGKS „Abstrakte Oper Nr. 1", EGKS „Columbus" (szenische Neufassung) und „Revisor", FORTNERS „Bluthochzeit", HARTMANNS „Simplicius Simplicissimus" (Neufassung), HENZES „Boulevard Solitude" und „König Hirsch", HINDEMITHS „Harmonie der Welt", KAMINSKIS „Spiel vom König Aphelius", KLEBES „Räuber", KRENEKS „Pallas Athene weint", REUTTERS „Don Juan und Faust" und die „Witwe von Ephesus"[1]. Besonders bemerkenswert ist eine verstärkte Pflege des Balletts, für das neue Werke von BLACHER, EGK, FORTNER, HENZE und REUTTER geschaffen worden sind.

*

Die Städte, die über ein Operntheater verfügen, aber auch viele andere Gemeinden, veranstalten *Sinfoniekonzerte*. Sie stehen im Mittelpunkt des städtischen Konzertlebens. Auch staatliche Sinfonieorchester widmen sich dieser Seite des musikalischen Lebens. Die Programme stützen sich in erster Linie auf die bedeutenden Werke der sinfonischen Literatur aller Zeiten und Völker. Neue Musik pflegt dosiert, aber in erfreulichem Maße, eingeschoben zu werden. Da die Städte in der Regel über Oratorienchöre verfügen, werden in gewissen Abständen große Chorwerke aufgeführt: BACHS Passionen und Kantaten, BEETHOVENS IX. Sinfonie, ORFFS „Carmina Burana" usw. Es verdient erwähnt zu werden, daß Werke, die in der nationalsozialistischen Zeit als „entartete Kunst" gebrandmarkt waren, heute vom breiten Publikum oft ohne Widerstreben aufgenommen werden.

Die zeitgenössische sinfonische Musik besitzt in Deutschland eine hervorragende Bedeutung. Mit Sinfonien, sinfonischen Werken und Solokonzerten mit Orchester hervorgetreten sind unter anderem KARL AMADEUS HARTMANN (sechs Sinfonien), JOHANN NEPOMUK DAVID (sechs Sinfonien), EDUARD ERDMANN (vier Sinfonien), HANS WERNER HENZE (drei Sinfonien), ferner WALTER ABENDROTH, BORIS BLACHER, WOLFGANG FORTNER, GERHARD

[1] Zwei deutsche Werke wurden im Ausland uraufgeführt: SCHÖNBERGS „Moses und Aron" (Zürich) und EGKS „Irische Legende" (Salzburg).

Frommel, Hermann Heiss, Hugo Hermann, Ernst Pepping, Hermann Reutter, Wilfried Zillig.

Die Berliner Philharmoniker, die Münchner Philharmoniker und die Bamberger Symphoniker (früher Prag) sind ausschließlich Konzertorchester. Sie sind international bekannt. Der ständige Dirigent der Berliner Philharmoniker war Wilhelm Furtwängler; er stand dem Orchester seit dem Tode von Artur Niekisch vor. Sein Nachfolger ist Herbert von Karajan. Die einzelnen Rundfunkorchester haben sich auch im Konzertleben durch ihre hohe Qualität einen hervorragenden Platz erobert.

*

Die Zahl der *Solistenkonzerte* ist im allgemeinen stark zurückgegangen. Das Interesse des musikliebenden Publikums an Konzerten von Solisten, die nicht durch einen international bekannten Namen eine starke Suggestionskraft ausüben, ist fast ganz verschwunden. Das trifft besonders die Liederabende, die kaum mehr begegnen. Es gilt auch für die Konzerte von Kammermusikvereinigungen. Einen gewissen Ausgleich hat der Rundfunk geschaffen, der die Musik ins Haus trägt und die Zweige (Lied, Kammermusik) weiterpflegt, die im Konzertsaal heute nicht mehr wie früher beheimatet sind.

*

Der *Rundfunk* besitzt im Musikleben der Bundesrepublik nicht nur organisatorisch, sondern auch künstlerisch eine Stellung ersten Ranges. Alle acht Sendeanstalten und der Sender Freies Berlin senden eigene Programme. Die Mittel, die dem Funk zur Verfügung stehen, erlauben ihm eine musikalische Tätigkeit von umspannender Breite. Sie reicht vom historischen Konzert alter Musik bis zur Uraufführung von neuer Musik, von dem großen Sinfoniekonzert bis zur Unterhaltungsmusik, von der Kirchenmusik bis zum Jazz. Die genannten neun Sender verfügen über eigene Orchester — teils auch über Chöre — von hoher Qualität, die von Dirigenten mit ersten Namen geleitet werden, greifen darüber hinaus aber auch auf Gastdirigenten zurück. Ganz besondere Verdienste erwarb sich der Funk um die Pflege der *Neuen Musik*, die er durch Aufführung ständig fördert. Komponisten erhalten durch Kompositionsaufträge neue Anregungen und materielle Hilfe. Aufführungen wie die von Orffs Oper „Die Kluge“ im Fernsehen erweisen, daß man auch in dieser Sparte des Funks die musikalischen Belange mit künstlerischem Verantwortungsgefühl pflegen wird. In Verbindung mit dem Funk stehen drei Veranstaltungsreihen, die internationalen Rang besitzen: die von Karl

Amadeus Hartmann in München organisierten Musica-Viva-Konzerte, die Sendefolge „Das neue Werk" des Norddeutschen Rundfunks in Hamburg und die Sendereihe „Musik der Zeit" des Westdeutschen Rundfunks in Köln. Der Initiative des Norddeutschen Rundfunks ist die konzertmäßige Welturaufführung der Oper „Moses und Aron" von Arnold Schönberg zu danken.

*

Zum Bild des Musiklebens gehören die an Zahl immer mehr anwachsenden *Musikfeste*, die in großen und kleinen Städten veranstaltet werden, im Frühling beginnen und — ohne abzureißen — bis in den Spätsommer hineingehen. Sie werden zum Teil an historischen Stätten veranstaltet und haben damit eine Beziehung zur Tradition. Andere gehen auf die Initiative einzelner Künstler oder Organisatoren zurück. Die folgende Aufzählung will weder vollständig sein noch mit der Reihenfolge eine Wertung verbinden. Veranstaltungen großen Stils sind die Berliner Festwochen mit internationalen Operngastspielen und Uraufführungen in Oper, Ballett und Konzert. Internationalen Charakter haben auch die Maifestspiele in Wiesbaden durch Engagements ausländischer Opernensembles. Nach dem Krieg wurden die Internationale Orgelwoche in Nürnberg und die Lemgoer Orgeltage begonnen, bei denen Interpreten an der Orgel aus verschiedenen Ländern in alter und neuer Musik zu hören sind. Mit dem Beethoven-Fest ehrt die Stadt Bonn ihren größten Sohn. Das Mozart-Fest in Würzburg ist eine Veranstaltung, bei der die Musik in den Zauber der Architektur des 18. Jahrhunderts und der Main-Landschaft hineingestellt wird. Ähnlich bringen die Festspiele in Schwetzingen klassische und moderne Werke in Konzert und Oper in dem historischen Rokoko-Theater des Schlosses. In Herford fand 1953 ein Heinrich Schütz-Fest statt. Die Lübecker Musiktage, veranstaltet vom Lübecker Sing- und Spielkreis, bringen alte und neue Musik. Das „Kleine Musikfest" in Lüdenscheid wurde 1953 als Händel-Fest gefeiert. Hitzacker hat seine „Sommerlichen Musiktage", Ansbach seine Bach-Tage, Nürnberg die „Woche des Gegenwartstheaters". Traditionsreich sind die „Niederrheinischen Musikfeste". „Musiktage" gibt es alljährlich in Kassel, Tübingen, Trossingen und Weiden (Oberpfalz). Stuttgart hat seine „Woche der leichten Musik"; Heilbronn hat Kirchenmusiktage; Bayreuth veranstaltet das Internationale Jugend-Festspieltreffen.

Das Bild bedarf einer Ergänzung durch die *Feste zeitgenössischer Musik*, durch die das Bundesgebiet bereits in wenigen Jahren nach dem Krieg zum internationalen Forum wurde. Die traditionsreichen Donaueschinger Musiktage für zeitgenössische Tonkunst werden unter dem Protektorat des Südwestfunks weitergeführt. In Frankfurt am Main findet jährlich die Internationale Woche für Neue Musik statt. Der Westdeutsche Rundfunk veranstaltet das Neue Musikfest in Köln, der Südfunk in Stuttgart hielt 1954 zum vierten Male „Tage zeitgenössischer Musik" ab. „Wege zur Neuen Musik" heißt das zeitgenössische Musikfest in Bremen, Braunschweig hat „Festliche Tage Neuer Kammermusik". In diesem Zusammenhang sei nicht vergessen die Tätigkeit der Sektion Deutschland der Internationalen Gesellschaft für Neue Musik. Eine in der Auswirkung bedeutende, nach außen wenig in Erscheinung tretende Kleinarbeit wird in den Arbeitsgemeinschaften für Neue Musik geleistet, die sich in zahlreichen Städten bildeten. Als Beispiel sei das Studio für Neue Musik in München genannt.

Von einer wiederum ganz anderen Seite will dieses Bild ergänzt sein durch den Hinweis auf einige der wichtigsten *Fachtagungen.* Die Deutsche Musikmesse in Düsseldorf sei zuerst genannt. Sie ist eine große Überschau über die technischen Leistungen der Musik in Verbindung mit der Industrie (Radio, Schallplatte, Instrumentenbau). Weiteren Ruf erlangten die Internationalen Ferienkurse für Neue Musik in Schloß Kranichstein bei Darmstadt. Sie stehen seit ihrer Gründung (1946) unter Leitung von WOLFGANG STEINECKE und sind die Hohe Schule der modernen Musik. In Verbindung mit den Lehrgängen wird jährlich der Kranichsteiner Musikpreis verteilt. Zu der jährlichen Haupttagung des Instituts für neue Musik und Musikerziehung, dessen Ehrenpräsident HANS MERSMANN ist, treffen sich über tausend Fachleute. Ihr Anliegen ist die Verbindung der neuen Musik mit der Musikerziehung. 1955 fand die erste Bundesschulmusikwoche in Mainz statt, 1957 die zweite in Hamburg.

Zum achten Mal wurde 1953 die Arbeitswoche für neue Komposition in Barsbüttel abgehalten. Sie steht unter der Leitung von JENS ROHWER und WILHELM KELLER und dient der gemeinsamen Aussprache über Fragen der modernen Kompositionstechnik. In Heidenheim finden jährlich die von HELMUT BORNFELD geleiteten Arbeitstage für Neue Kirchenmusik statt. Sehr aktiv ist die deutsche Gruppe der Jeunesses musicales. Den Interessen der musikalischen Jugend dienen die Internationalen Arbeitsgemeinschaften und Sommerkurse für Musik des Instituts für Musikerziehung auf Schloß Weikersheim und die Bad Mergentheimer Jugendmusikwochen. Gemeinsam von allen Sendern wird jährlich in München ein internationaler Leistungswettbewerb für Solisten veranstaltet. Den Interessen des musizierenden Laien dient der Arbeitskreis für Hausmusik e.V., der Sing- und Musizierwochen organisiert. Den jährlichen Abschluß bilden die Kasseler Musiktage.

In besonders hohem Maße ist in Deutschland der *Laie* an der Musikpflege beteiligt. Versuchen wir auch hier eine Gruppierung. Es gibt die Jugendmusikbewegung, die aus der alten Jugendbewegung herausgewachsen ist. Ein weites Aufgabenfeld des Laien ist der Chorgesang in den Kirchen beider Konfessionen. Die Kirchenmusik erfuhr in den vergangenen zwanzig Jahren eine weitgehende Reorganisation. Sie wird auf evangelischer Seite an erster Stelle vertreten durch die Namen der Komponisten HELMUT BORNFELD, JOHANN NEPOMUK DAVID, HUGO DISTLER, JOHANNES DRIESSLER, ERNST PEPPING, GÜNTHER RAPHAEL, SIEGFRIED REDA und KURT THOMAS. Auf katholischer Seite sind vor allem JOSEPH AHRENS, JOSEPH HAAS, HEINRICH LEMACHER und HERMANN SCHROEDER zu nennen. Eine umfangreiche Literatur im engen Anschluß an den Stil der Neuen Musik ist entstanden.

Eine Welt für sich ist die *Chormusik* mit den beiden Hauptgruppen der gemischten Chöre und Männerchöre. Auch hier ist festzustellen, daß sich die Gegenwart einen neuen musikalischen Stil geschaffen hat. Er knüpft an die Harmonik und Polyphonie der Neuen Musik an und verbindet mit ihr Elemente der älteren Musik des 16. bis 18. Jahrhunderts.

Von interner, aber darum um so größerer Bedeutung für das deutsche Musikleben sind Veranstaltungen wie das Chormusikfest des Verbandes gemischter Chöre Deutschlands (heute: Verband deutscher Oratorien- und Kammerchöre), das als viertes Fest nach dem Krieg in Essen stattfand und zahlreiche bemerkenswerte Uraufführungen brachte, die Deutsche Sängerbundeswoche (1953 als siebtes Fest in Gelsenkirchen) oder die Evangelische Kirchenmusikwoche in Nürnberg. Die wichtigsten Sängerfeste nach dem Krieg fanden in Mainz und Stuttgart (Deutscher Sängerbund) und in Mainz, Frankfurt a. M. und Hannover (Deutscher Allgemeiner Sängerbund) statt. In diesem Zusammenhang sei noch hingewiesen auf die Deutschen Sängerbundeswochen in Mönchen-Gladbach 1950 und in Gelsenkirchen 1953, auf die Festlichen Tage Junger Musik 1954 in Passau, die Festlichen Tage Deutscher Jugend 1957 in Münster (Westfalen), die alljährlich stattfindende Neue Chormusik-Woche in Ludwigsburg und die Bundessängerfeste der Landesbünde. Um besondere Verdienste in der Pflege der Chormusik und des deutschen Volksliedes von staatlicher Seite zu würdigen, hat der Bundespräsident auf Anregung der Arbeitsgemeinschaft deutscher Chorverbände in Anknüpfung an eine preußische Tradition die „ZELTER-Plakette" gestiftet. Sie kann an Chorvereinigungen verliehen werden, sofern sie auf ein mindestens 100jähriges Bestehen zurückblicken. Viele hundert Vereinigungen haben bisher diese Auszeichnung erfahren.

Ein weites Feld des Laienmusizierens umfaßt die Liebhaber-Orchester, ferner die Volksinstrumente Akkordeon, Zither, Mandoline usw.

Einen wesentlichen Anteil am musikalischen Leben in Deutschland haben die *Musikverlage* des Bundesgebietes. An der Spitze stehen die Verlage B. SCHOTT's Söhne in Mainz und der BÄRENREITER-Verlag in Kassel. In alphabetischer Reihenfolge seien ferner aufgezählt, ohne vollständig zu sein: die Verlage BOTE UND BOCK in Berlin, BREITKOPF UND HÄRTEL in Wiesbaden, CARL MERSEBURGER in Darmstadt, MÖSELER (früher KALLMEYER) in Wolfenbüttel und VANDENHOEK UND RUPRECHT in Göttingen. Das Buch über Musik hat sich auch heute wieder einen hervorragenden Platz in Deutschland erobert. Die Steigerung der technischen Entwicklung und die wachsende Kaufkraft zeichnen sich auch in der Schallplattenindustrie ab, die nach dem Krieg vor einem völligen Neubeginn stand. Erwähnt seien die Deutsche Grammophon-Gesellschaft und die Firma Telefunken in Hamburg. Der Instrumentenbau in Deutschland führt alte Traditionen erfolgreich fort.

Abschließend sei der Tätigkeit der deutschen *Musikwissenschaft* gedacht, die, einst in der Welt führend, ihre frühere Geltung zurückzugewinnen strebt. Die „Gesellschaft für Musikforschung" hat zwei internationale musikwissenschaftliche Kongresse (1953 in Bamberg) einberufen. In Köln fand 1958 der Kongreß der Internationalen Gesellschaft für Musikwissenschaft statt. Die Ausgabe älterer Musikwerke, das „Erbe deutscher Musik", kann seit 1953 fortgeführt werden. Eine besondere Aktivität verrät der Plan neuer großer Gesamtausgaben (BÄRENREITER-Verlag). Zunächst sind neue wissenschaftliche Gesamtausgaben der Werke von BACH, HÄNDEL, LASSO und MOZART mit Unterstützung der Bundesregierung begonnen worden. Gesamt- oder Teil-Ausgaben der Werke von GLUCK, TELEMANN, SPOHR und JOHANN WALTER sind im Erscheinen. Eine neue BEETHOVEN-Gesamtausgabe wird im HENLE-Verlag, eine REGER-Gesamtausgabe bei BREITKOPF UND HÄRTEL vorbereitet. Eine besondere Leistung stellt die allgemeine Enzyklopädie „Musik in Geschichte und Gegenwart" dar, deren Herausgeber FRIEDRICH BLUME ist. Als musikwissenschaftliche Zeitschriften erscheinen im Bundesgebiet „Die Musikforschung" und das „Archiv für Musikwissenschaft". Die übrigen Musikzeitschriften („Musica", „Neue Zeitschrift für Musik" usw.) dienen den Aufgaben des allgemeinen Musiklebens oder sind, wie viele andere Publikationen, Organe der Fachorganisationen oder haben Spezialgebiete.

Die internationale Verflechtung des deutschen Musiklebens läßt nichts mehr von den überwundenen Schwierigkeiten spüren. Zahlreiche Künstler des Auslandes besuchen heute wieder regelmäßig Deutschland, und viele Deutsche konzertieren draußen. Diese glückliche Entwicklung zeigt sich auch in dem Echo, das Werke neuer Musik des Auslandes in Deutschland und deutsche Werke jenseits der Grenze finden.

BILDENDE KUNST, ARCHITEKTUR, MUSEEN

I. BILDENDE KUNST

Das Jahr 1945 ist als die ,,Stunde Null" der deutschen Kunst bezeichnet worden, weil es für viele Maler und Bildhauer Befreiung und Neubeginn bedeutete. Es beendete eine unerträgliche Bevormundung durch die staatlich gelenkte Kunstpolitik, die den schöpferischen Kräften Ausstellungsverbote und Atelierüberwachungen auferlegt hatte, und es gab das Signal, aus der erzwungenen Isolierung und Provinzialisierung herauszutreten, um wieder mit der Kunst der Freien Welt Kontakt aufzunehmen. Aber nicht für alle Künstler gilt diese Situation. Manche der älteren hatten ihre bildnerischen Aufgaben im Verborgenen unbeirrt weiter erfüllt. Sie brauchten nicht sich neu zu orientieren oder zu lernen, von ihrer künstlerischen Freiheit Gebrauch zu machen. Außerdem kamen nach 1945 die Jungen zum Zuge, die vorher noch nicht hervorgetreten waren. Der scharfe Einschnitt in die Entwicklung der bildenden Kunst hat also mehrere Generationen in verschiedenem Maße getroffen.

Seit 1945 gibt es in der Bundesrepublik für Künstler keine ,,Vorschriften" mehr. Selbstverständlich sind auch die ehemaligen Nutznießer der NS-Kunstdiktatur keinerlei Einschränkungen unterworfen. Es besteht nur kein Interesse an pseudo-altmeisterlicher Produktion. Die Öffentlichkeit hat dieses Problem, fern jedem Rachegedanken, durch mangelnde Nachfrage erledigt.

In den Jahren, die auf die Befreiung der Kunst folgten, haben Maler, Graphiker und Bildhauer sich vor allem wieder mit der Entwicklung der Künste in den fremden Ländern vertraut gemacht. Zahlreiche Gastausstellungen aus vielen Teilen der Erde sind zu uns gekommen. Es ist heute schon selbstverständlich, daß die Ausstellungsprogramme der Museen, Kunstvereine und Privatgalerien nach internationalen Maßstäben zusammengestellt werden. Nachdem die Beschränkung der Auslandsreisen aufgehoben war, setzte eine lebhafte Wanderung in die Kunstmetropolen ein, um an Ort und Stelle Anschauungsunterricht zu erhalten. Viele deutsche Künstler arbeiten heute auch wieder im Lande ihrer Wahl, sei es in Frankreich, Italien oder Spanien.

*

Mit eigenen Beiträgen traten die deutschen Maler und Bildhauer erst später hervor. Der Eifer, mit dem manche von ihnen sich nach dem Kriege um neue Formen und moderne Ausdrucksmittel bemühten, mag auf den ersten Blick konjunkturbedingt erscheinen. Aber es ist nur allzu gut verständlich, daß sie die schlimmen Folgen der Vereinsamung und Entgeistigung so schnell wie möglich wettzumachen versuchten, um wie früher am internationalen Gespräch der Kunst teilnehmen zu können. In späteren Jahren wird dieser Aufbruch in die Freiheit der modernen Kunst nach dunklen Jahren der Unterdrückung, dieses allgemein erwachte Interesse für die künstlerischen und kulturellen Probleme der benachbarten Völker, als ebenso ergreifendes Phänomen der Kunstgeschichte bewertet werden wie die künstlerische Revolution in den beiden ersten Jahrzehnten nach 1900.

*

Zur Neuorientierung gehören auch die vielen *Ausstellungen*, die eine Wiederbegegnung mit dem lang entbehrten Besitz an historischer Kunst, Querschnitte durch ganze Epochen, Gedächtnisausstellungen und nicht zuletzt die Bekanntschaft mit jungen Künstlern vermittelten. Schon heute ist es rückblickend nicht mehr möglich, sämtliche Veranstaltungen von Rang aufzuzählen, um die Breite des Interesses zu demonstrieren; doch seien wenigstens aus dem Bereich der alten Kunst die Ausstellungen „Romanische Kunst“ (Köln 1947), „Gotische Kunst“ (Köln 1948), „Zurückgekehrte Meisterwerke aus dem Besitz der Berliner Museen“ (Wiesbaden 1948), die „Ars Sacra“ (München 1950), „Westphalia Sacra“ (Münster i.W. 1951), „Ein Jahrtausend deutscher Kunst“ (Wiesbaden 1952), „Ostasiatische Kunst und Chinoiserie“ (Köln 1953), „Hundert Jahre amerikanische Malerei“ (Frankfurt 1953), „Aufgang der Neuzeit“ (Nürnberg) und „Werdendes Abendland“ (Essen) hervorgehoben.

Von größerer Bedeutung für die zeitgenössische Kunst waren die Retrospektiven in die Anfänge der modernen Bewegung. Hier sei auf die Ausstellung des „Deutschen Werkbundes“ (Köln 1949), den „Blauen Reiter“ (München 1949), die „Maler vom Bauhaus“ (München 1950), die „Documenta“ (Kassel 1955), die „Brücke“ (Essen 1958), „Dada“ (Düsseldorf 1958) und auf die zahlreichen Einzelausstellungen bedeutender moderner Meister hingewiesen, zum Beispiel der Maler Willi Baumeister, Adolf Hoelzel, Paul Klee, Wassily Kandinsky, E. L. Kirchner, August Macke, Franz Marc, Edvard Munch und Pablo Picasso. Ebenso fanden Ausstellungen wesentlicher Bildhauer statt, darunter Wilhelm Lehmbruck, Hans Arp und der nahazu vergessene Richard Haizmann. Nicht minder verdienstvoll waren die Ausstellungen, die Kurt Schwitters wieder in seinem Heimatland bekanntmachten und den Maler-Zeichner Wols (Otto Alfred Wolfgang

SCHULZE, 1913—1951) überhaupt erst in Deutschland vorstellten. Die Veranstaltungen für die großen Meister anderer Länder können nicht einmal genannt werden, weil ihre Zahl schon zu groß ist. Dabei ist der Nachholbedarf heute noch nicht befriedigt.

Seit mehreren Jahren gehen auch Ausstellungen bedeutender deutscher Künstler durch offizielle Vermittlung oder Privatinitiative in das Ausland. In fast allen Weltstädten, selbst in Südamerika, Australien, Neuseeland, Südafrika und Fernost, haben seither Übersichten über unser künstlerisches Schaffen stattgefunden. Einzelausstellungen deutscher Künstler sind keine Seltenheit mehr.

*

Der Wiederaufbau der *Museen* und die Neugründung von öffentlichen *Kunstsammlungen* beziehungsweise Ausstellungsgebäuden (Museum der Stadt Leverkusen in Schloß Morsbroich, Villa Hügel bei Essen, Museum der Stadt Krefeld im von L. MIES VAN DER ROHE erbauten Haus Lange), auch in mittleren und kleinen Städten, machte auf die Dauer die Wiederbegegnungs-Ausstellungen überflüssig. Die Tendenz der Museen geht heute dahin, den Kunstwerken wieder ihren dauernden und wohlvertrauten Ort zu geben, anstatt sie heimatlos herumreisen zu lassen. Bis auf wenige Ausnahmen sind alle bekannten öffentlichen Kunstsammlungen wieder ständig ausgestellt. Einige Museen wie das Wallraf-Richartz-Museum in Köln und die Pinakothek in München haben neue oder wiederhergestellte Gebäude bezogen; andere Häuser, zum Beispiel für das Folkwang-Museum in Essen, befinden sich im Ausbau. Fast alle Museen haben auch Abteilungen für zeitgenössische Kunst. Besonders rühmenswert sind die modernen Sammlungen von Berlin, Essen, Hamburg, Köln, Mannheim, München und Stuttgart. Die deutschen Künstler und Kunstfreunde vermissen jedoch noch ein überregionales Museum des Zwanzigsten Jahrhunderts, wie es die USA, England, Frankreich, Italien und die Niederlande schon längst besitzen.

Außer den Museen, deren Tätigkeit sich stark auf Ausstellungswesen verlagert hat, beschäftigen sich die *Kunstgesellschaften*, *Kunstvereine* und die Informationshäuser anderer Länder (zum Beispiel der USA, Großbritanniens, Frankreichs, Italiens, Belgiens) mit der Organisation von Kunstausstellungen, die oft durch mehrere Städte wandern. Eine wichtige Rolle spielen ferner die privaten Galerien in den Großstädten. Man findet sie im ganzen Lande, da es in Deutschland kein alleiniges und beherrschendes Kunstzentrum gibt. Von den Kunstvereinen und ähnlichen Unternehmungen sind die KESTNER-Gesellschaft in Hannover und die Kunstvereine in Düsseldorf, Freiburg i. Br.,

Hamburg, Frankfurt, Köln, Stuttgart, Münster, Bremen usw. und ebenso die „Gesellschaft der Freunde junger Kunst" (München, Baden-Baden, Düsseldorf) mit ihrem Leihdienst hervorzuheben.

*

Die soziale Lage der Künstler hat in den letzten Jahren viele Probleme aufgegeben. Der Bundespräsident selbst rief die „*Deutsche Künstlerhilfe*" ins Leben. Man ist sich jedoch darüber im klaren, daß staaliches Mäzenatentum nur eine allgemeine soziale Unterstützungsmaßnahme sein könnte, nicht aber eine echte Förderung der Elite. Die große Zahl von Kunstpreisen, die in Deutschland von Ländern, Landschaftsverbänden, Städten und anderen Organisationen regelmäßig verteilt werden, verrät zwar einerseits den guten Willen zur Anerkennung und Unterstützung der Künstler, bewirkt aber andererseits auch eine zu weite Streuung der verfügbaren Gelder. Über die Bestimmungen und Verteilungen der Kunstpreise in den Jahren 1946 bis 1956 hat der „Deutsche Kunstrat e.V." eine aufschlußreiche Druckschrift veröffentlicht.

Zahlreiche Künstler bekleiden ein künstlerisches Lehramt an Hochschulen, Werkkunstschulen oder Höheren Lehranstalten. Viele arbeiten auch in der Gebrauchs- und Werbekunst. Nur wenige müssen ihren Lebensunterhalt durch berufsfremde Arbeiten verdienen. Die Situation auf dem Kunstmarkt ist heute selbst für Künstler der „abstrakten" Richtung, die erfahrungsgemäß weniger populär ist, recht günstig. Die beste Lösung ihrer wirtschaftlichen Probleme sehen die Künstler allerdings darin, als berufene zeitgenössische Formgestalter an den großen öffentlichen Aufgaben beteiligt zu werden. Zahlreiche Ansätze hierzu sind bereits vorhanden, sowohl in kirchlichen wie staatlichen oder städtischen Bauten, nicht zuletzt auch in denen privater Unternehmungen.

Vielfältig sind die Bemühungen, Künstler und Auftraggeber miteinander in Kontakt zu bringen. Eine der bedeutendsten war die vom Bundespräsidenten ins Leben gerufene „*Dankspende des Deutschen Volkes*" für empfangene Auslandshilfe in den Jahren der Not. Hierfür sind moderne Kunstwerke gekauft oder bestellt worden (Graphik, Gemälde, Skulpturen, Altarleuchter, Glasgemälde usw.). Als Käufer von Kunstwerken treten neben der Bundesregierung auch die Landesregierungen und -parlamente auf, nicht zuletzt die Kommunen, die sich vor allem der ortsansässigen Künstler annehmen. Der Ausschuß für Kulturpolitik und Publizistik des Deutschen Bundestages, der Kulturausschuß des Deutschen Städtetages und der „Kulturkreis im

Bundesverband der Deutschen Industrie e.V.“ treten in mannigfachen Unternehmungen für die bildende Kunst der Gegenwart ein. Insbesondere hat sich der „Kulturkreis“ der Industrie durch seine „Museumsspende“, seine Stipendien an aussichtsvolle Künstler, die eigene Sammlung moderner deutscher Graphik und die regelmäßigen Ausstellungen der „Ars Viva“ große Verdienste erworben. Die Gewerkschaften haben sich in den Ruhrfestspielen zu Recklinghausen mit den zugehörigen, thematisch geistvollen und aufschlußreichen Kunstausstellungen ebenfalls erfolgreich an der Förderung der neuen Kunst beteiligt.

Privates Mäzenatentum ist an manchen Orten wieder erwacht. Es entstanden junge Sammlungen moderner Kunst, deren Namen heute schon zu viele geworden sind, um sie alle nennen zu können. Bekannt wurden vor allem die Sammlungen Dr. HAUBRICH (Expressionisten) und Dr. DOMNICK (abstrakte Malerei), die in den Museen von Köln beziehungsweise Stuttgart ausgestellt sind, ferner die Darmstädter Sammlung STRÖHER, die auch durch Preise die zeitgenössischen Künstler unterstützt. Maler, Bildhauer und Graphiker haben sich in zahlreichen Verbänden organisiert. Diese sind entweder berufsständische Vertretungen (Landesberufsverbände bildender Künstler, Zentrale in München) oder Zusammenschlüsse gleichgesinnter Künstler. Der „Deutsche Künstlerbund“ wurde 1950 in Berlin wieder gegründet und stellt jährlich einmal aus (bisher Berlin, Köln, Hamburg, Frankfurt, Hannover, Düsseldorf, Essen). Sein Präsident ist der Bildhauer KARL HARTUNG. Daneben bestehen kleinere Gruppen, Sezessionen und regionale Vereinigungen. Die Künstlerinnen sind in der GEDOK vereinigt, deren Sitz Hamburg ist. Ein „Bund deutscher Gebrauchsgraphiker“ wird von München aus geleitet. Die Beziehungen zur Kunst und zu den Künstlern des Auslands pflegt die „Deutsche Sektion der Internationalen Gesellschaft der bildenden Künste“.

*
* *

Von den *Malern* der expressionistischen Generation sind nur noch wenige am Werk. Als Väter der modernen Kunst in Deutschland haben sie jedoch weitgehend die Arbeit einer breiten Nachfolge beeinflußt. KARL SCHMIDT-ROTTLUFF (*1884) hat von allen „Brücke“-Mitgliedern seinen kraftvollen und einfachen Stil am unbeirrtesten beibehalten. MAX PECHSTEIN (1881 bis 1955) ließ dagegen in den letzten Jahrzehnten nach. ERICH HECKEL (*1883), der zweite noch lebende Meister der „Brücke“, hat sich in eine romantische, oft phantastische Welt zurückgezogen.

Tod und Emigration haben die Reihen der alten Avantgarde des Expressionismus' sehr gelichtet. EMIL NOLDE (1867—1956) trat nach dem Kriege noch einmal in offenbar ungebrochener Schaffenskraft hervor. Sein Werk gehört in seinen Höhepunkten zu den großen malerischen Leistungen des 20. Jahrhunderts. MAX BECKMANN (1884—1950) und ERNST LUDWIG KIRCHNER (1880—1938), die stärksten Exponenten der deutschen Ausdruckskunst, sind im Ausland gestorben. Aus der älteren Generation hat der Meister surrealistischer Malerei, MAX ERNST (*1891), internationalen Ruhm erlangt, den die Heimat dem ausgewanderten Maler 1957 durch Verleihung des Großen Kunstpreises von Nordrhein-Westfalen bestätigt hat.

Der Nachexpressionismus, der in die Jahre nach dem Ersten Weltkrieg zu datieren ist und sich in „Magischem Realismus" und „Neuer Sachlichkeit" äußerte, wird noch von einigen Interpreten sinngemäß, wenn auch ohne die Frische der Gründungszeit präsentiert. Selbständige Künstlerpersönlichkeiten wie KARL HOFER (1878—1955) lassen sich jedoch nicht durch solche Stilbezeichnungen erfassen. In dem weiten Feld, das von der extremen Ausdruckssteigerung bis zur sachlichen Wiedergabe reicht, sind ferner WILHELM SCHMURR (*1878), XAVER FUHR (*1898), OTTO DIX (*1891), MAX UNOLD (*1885), FRIEDRICH AHLERS-HESTERMANN (*1883), HANS PURRMANN (*1880), MAX KAUS (*1891), HEINRICH GRAF LUCKNER (*1891), MARIA CASPAR-FILSER (*1878) und IDA KERKOVIUS (*1879) neben unzähligen Nachfolgern tätig. Die in Ausdruck und Form gemäßigte, spätexpressionistische Malerei scheint die oft festgestellte Vorliebe der Deutschen für Ausdruckskunst zu bestätigen. Neue Talente, die der in die Breite verlaufenden Richtung wieder frische Stoßkraft verleihen könnten, sind seit dem Kriege nicht aufgetreten. Dagegen hat eine ganze Reihe älterer Maler dieser Richtung, wie zum Beispiel HANS MEYBODEN (*1901), ERNST WEIERS (*1909), KURT SOHNS (*1907) und CARL CRODEL (*1894) erst nach Kriegsende ihre eigentliche Entfaltungsmöglichkeit gehabt.

*

Die gegenstandslose Malerei hatte in Deutschland ihre Initiatoren in WASSILY KANDINSKY (1866—1944), der fast drei Jahrzehnte in unserem Lande gelebt hat, sowie in FRANZ MARC (1880—1916) und mit Einschränkungen auch in AUGUST MACKE (1887—1914). Den nationalsozialistischen Machthabern war sie ebenso ein Dorn im Auge wie der gegenständliche Expressionismus. Die Kontinuität ihrer Entwicklung wurde daher durch staatliche Verbote empfindlich gestört. Sogar ältere Maler der abstrakten

Richtung, wie Willi Baumeister (1889—1955), Max Ackermann (*1887), Otto Ritschl (*1885), Carl Buchheister (*1890) und Curt Lahs (*1893) kamen verhältnismäßig spät zum Zuge. Ihre hauptsächliche Wirkung hatten sie erst nach dem Kriege.

Die fruchtbarste und schöpferischste Persönlichkeit dieser ersten Generation ungegenständlicher Maler ist zweifellos Willi Baumeister gewesen. Um ihn hatte sich in Süddeutschland eine Schüler- und Freundesgruppe gebildet, aus der auch Gerhard Fietz (*1910), der sich mittlerweile zu freierer Formensprache entwickelt hat, hervorgegangen ist. Eine Künstlergemeinschaft mit ausgeprägtem Profil sammelte sich in der Münchener ZEN-Gruppe, der Fritz Winter (*1905), ein Bauhausschüler und der erfolgreichste unter den „Abstrakten", sowie Rolf Cavael (*1898), Rupprecht Geiger (*1909) und Fred Thieler (*1916) angehören. Georg Muche (*1895) kehrte von der gegenstandslosen Kunst zu figurativen Kompositionen zurück. Abstrakte kalligraphische Formen bestimmen vor allem das Werk von Julius Bissier (*1893).

Ungegenständliche Malerei im Sinne Mondrians, die sich also auf eine mathematische Denkweise gründet, gibt es in Deutschland kaum. Georg Meistermann (*1911) näherte sich in den letzten Jahren einem dekorativen Konstruktivismus, der jedoch nicht die gleiche zähe Konsequenz hat wie die geometrische Malerei des an der Ulmer Hochschule lehrenden Vordemberge-Gildewart (*1889). Andere Vertreter konstruktivistischer Malerei sind Otto Ritschl, Fritz Levedag (1899—1951), Hildegard Stromberger (*1904), Joachim Albrecht (*1916) und Heinrich Siepmann (*1904).

Bei den meisten gegenstandslosen Malern herrschen die expressiven Formen vor. Ernst Wilhelm Nay (*1902) verwendet intensive, leidenschaftlich bewegte Farben, die trotz gelegentlich dekorativ wirkenden Kompositionen für seinen „abstrakten Expressionismus" zeugen. Fritz Winter bevorzugt dunklere Töne, aus denen Farben sparsam, aber kräftig hervorleuchten. Theodor Werner (*1886), der nach 1945 auftrat, konnte mit seinen harmonischen Bildern die Aufmerksamkeit der internationalen Kritik auf sich ziehen. Ebenfalls ist Joseph Fassbender (*1903) in den letzten Jahren die verdiente Anerkennung zuteil geworden. Seine Formerfindungen waren in ihrem grüblerischen Reichtum nicht immer leicht zugänglich. Heute ist seine Palette heller, seine Formensprache einfacher geworden, ohne darüber an Originalität einzubüßen. Fassbenders Wandbild „Sternzeichen" im Bonner Ernst-Moritz-Arndt-Gymnasium ist eine der großen Leistungen moderner Monumentalmalerei. Der aus Südamerika zurückgekehrte Maler

Hann Trier (*1915) hat sowohl durch die eigentümlich „strickende“ Handschrift seiner Malerei, wie durch technisch hervorragende Farbradierungen Beachtung im In- und Ausland gefunden.

*

Bei den jüngeren Malern ist der Kontakt zum vorangegangenen Expressionismus nicht mehr unmittelbar zu spüren. Emil Schumacher (*1912), Heinz Trökes (*1913), Thomas Grochowiak (*1914), K. O. Götz (*1914), Bernhard Schultze (*1915), Karl F. Dahmen (*1917), Hans Platschek (*1922) und viele andere zeigen in ihren Bildern eine Formenwelt, die nicht mehr auf einer national begrenzten Tradition basiert, sondern aus der Gemeinschaft der internationalen Malerei von heute erwächst.

Zwischen den beiden Polen eines inhaltlich gebundenen Expressionismus und der rigorosen Abwendung vom Gegenstand läßt sich das Schaffen zahlreicher Maler in verschiedenen Stufungen einordnen. Willi Müller-Hufschmid (*1890), Rolf Müller-Landau (1903—1956), Ernst Weil (*1919), Carl Barth (*1896), Gustav Deppe (*1913), Gerhard Kadow (*1909), Hubert Berke (*1908), Arnold Fiedler (*1900), Hans Kuhn (*1905), Herbert Spangenberg (*1907), Marielouise Rogister (*1901) und Ernst Geitlinger (*1895) wären hier zu nennen, ferner Hans Jaenisch (*1907), Alexander Camaro (*1901) und Werner Heldt (1904—1954), die aber mehr zum Figurativen tendieren. Die Stellung zwischen den „Fronten“ ist für viele der um 1900 Geborenen bezeichnend. Manche haben aus dieser zwiespältigen Situation das Beste gemacht und einen persönlichen Stil erlangt, beispielsweise der Poet unter den figürlichen Malern, Werner Gilles (*1894), oder der andere moderne Italien-Deutsche Eduard Bargheer (*1901), dessen Begabung in der Landschaft und im Aquarell liegt. Vincent Weber (*1902), Wolf Hoffmann (*1898), Peter Herkenrath (*1900), Friedrich Vordemberge (*1897), Rudi Baerwind (*1910), Peter Janssen (*1906) und Ferdinand Lammeyer (*1899) streben über die Vereinfachung und Reduktion der Form zur sachlichen Mitteilung zurück.

Nach dem letzten Weltkrieg erschien auch eine späte surrealistische Renaissance, die wesentlich von Max Ernst beeinflußt wurde. Heinz Trökes war vorübergehend dabei engagiert. Am beharrlichsten ergehen Richard Oelze (*1900), Mac Zimmermann (*1912), Hans Thiemann (*1910) und Edgar Ende (*1901) sich in den Gefilden einer surrealen Phantasie.

*

Es ist für die deutsche Kunst bezeichnend, daß eine ganze Anzahl von Künstlern sich nur als Graphiker (Druckgraphik, Handzeichnung) betätigt. HAP GRIESHABER (*1909), ein hervorragender Holzschneider und Pädagoge, hat den überdimensionalen Holzschnitt zum „Tafelbild" erhoben und einen eigenwilligen kraftvollen Stil entwickelt. GOTTFRIED DIEHL (1896—1955) und OTTO COESTER (*1902) sind ebenfalls im wesentlichen Graphiker. Der eine leistete Besonderes in der Lithographie, der andere ist durch seine subtilen gegenstandslosen Radierungen bekannt geworden. Der schon erwähnte J. FASSBENDER ist ein Meister der Monotypie. Mit montierten und geschnittenen Metalldruckstöcken arbeitet der geistvolle Schwabe ROLF NESCH (*1893), der in Norwegen lebt. HEINZ BATTKE (*1909) hat sich als phantastischer Zeichner einen Namen gemacht. Vom Nachwuchs ist WOLFGANG V. SCHEMM (*1920) durch witzige Zeichnungen aufgefallen.

*

Seit kurzem treten überhaupt die jüngsten Maler, die zwischen 1920 und 1930 geboren sind, mehr und mehr in den Vordergrund. Die meisten bekennen sich zum „abstrakten Expressionismus" oder zur jungen internationalen „informellen Kunst". Für viele ist WOLS (1913—1951) das Vorbild. Man kann daher von einer „Tachisten"-Gruppe sprechen, wenn auch kein organisierter Zusammenhang besteht, und dazu etwa folgende Maler rechnen: HERBERT KAUFMANN, PETER BRÜNING (*1929), WINFRIED GAUL (*1928), OTTO GREIS (*1913), GERHARD HOEHME (*1920) und HEINZ KREUTZ (*1923). EGON NEUBAUER (*1920), KLAUS BENDIXEN (*1924) und GERHARD WIND (*1928) bevorzugen konstruktive Lösungen, die RUDOLF MAUKE (*1924) zugunsten freierer Formen aufgegeben hat.

Bei KLAUS J. FISCHER (*1930) und MANFRED BLUTH (*1926) bestehen Beziehungen zum Surrealismus. K. R. SONDERBORG (*1923) schreibt eine Art abstrakter Schnellschrift, die zur Routine werden könnte; doch ist er einer der wenigen jüngeren Maler, die schon einen eigenen Beitrag zu liefern vermochten. Wenn bei den Fünfzigjährigen vielfach noch die Frage nach der Selbständigkeit unbeantwortet bleiben muß, so kann man selbstverständlich von den Jüngsten keine reifen und originalen Lösungen bildnerischer Aufgaben erwarten. Es sieht jedoch so aus, als würden sie schneller und ungehinderter zur eigenen Klärung kommen als die ältere Generation, da ihnen die Freiheit des Lernens und Schaffens gegeben ist.

*

* *

Ein Überblick über die *Plastik* in Deutschland zeigt, daß die größere Zahl der Bildhauer figürlich arbeitet. Die zahlreichen Experimente, die es in anderen Ländern gibt, wird man hier noch selten antreffen. Archaisierung und Klassizismus sind für viele Bildhauer der älteren Generation immer noch die bestimmenden retrospektiven Ideale. GEORG KOLBE (1877—1947), ERNST BARLACH (1870—1938) und WILHELM LEHMBRUCK (1881—1919) markieren in etwa die Grenzen, in denen sich viele Bildhauer älterer Jahrgänge bewegen, zum Beispiel KARL ALBIKER (*1878) und RICHARD SCHEIBE (*1879). Ihnen stehen als Antipoden einer neuen Formgestaltung KARL HARTUNG (*1908), BERNHARD HEILIGER (*1915) und vor allem der kühne Stahlplastiker HANS UHLMANN (*1900) gegenüber. Die Werke der letzten stehen in mehr oder weniger enger Beziehung zu der plastischen Kunst von HENRY MOORE, HANS ARP und ALEXANDER CALDER, womit nur ihre allgemeine Richtung angedeutet sei. GERHARD MARCKS (*1889), der ehemalige Bauhaus-Meister, wird bei uns, aber auch im Ausland, vielfach als der repräsentative deutsche Bildhauer der Gegenwart angesehen. MARCKS hält sich von allen Experimenten fern und kultiviert einen gleichmäßigen, zeitlos zu nennenden Stil. EWALD MATARÉ, der ebenfalls weithin berühmt geworden ist, hat gleich MARCKS ein großes graphisches Werk geschaffen. Seine plastische Formensprache unterscheidet sich von der des archaisierenden MARCKS' durch Aufnahme vieler Einflüsse, Experimentierfreude und entschiedenere Hinwendung zur Abstraktion. Beide Künstler haben mehrere Bauskulpturen und Denkmäler geschaffen. LUDWIG GIES (*1887) arbeitet vielfach auch als Glasfenster-Entwerfer; PHILIPP HARTH (*1887) und HANS RUWOLDT (*1891) spezialisierten sich auf kraftvolle Tierdarstellungen, ebenso die impressionistisch modellierende RENÉE SINTENIS (*1888). EMY ROEDER (*1890), die vom Expressionismus kommt, leistete während der letzten Jahre Bedeutendes in der Porträtplastik. EDWIN SCHARFF (1887—1955) widmete sich zuletzt monumentalen Entwürfen. Die Generation der Fünfzigjährigen, HANS METTEL (*1903), ALEXANDER GONDA (*1905), PAUL DIERKES (*1907), abstrahiert durch Ausscheidung des Unwesentlichen zugunsten der wesentlichen Form, ohne jedoch den Entschluß zur gegenstandslosen Plastik zu forcieren. Für den keramischen Plastiker ARNO LEHMANN (*1905) ist die stilistische Situation dieselbe.

HEINRICH KIRCHNER (*1907), TONI STADLER (*1888), HANS WIMMER (*1907), GEORG BRENNINGER (*1909), ANTON HILLER (*1893), GERHARD SCHREITER und PRISKA V. MARTIN (*1912) sind vortreffliche Bronzeplastiker mit vorwiegend archaisierenden Formen. KURT LEHMANN (*1905) bevorzugt bei gleicher Stilhaltung die Steinbildhauerei. L. G. SCHRIEBER (*1907) vollbringt seine besten Leistungen in der glatt gedrechselten Holzskulptur. JOSEF JAEKEL (*1907) hat sich auf metallgetriebene dekorative Plastik spezialisiert. Abseits der üblichen Produktion sind die roh behauenen Feldsteine und grob geschmiedeten Eisenfiguren des Grafen BYLANDT-RHEYDT (*1905). Die ungegenständliche Raumplastik des jungen NORBERT KRICKE wird aus Stahlstangen und Drähten komponiert. H.-A. SCHUMANN (*1919) strebt zur ,,organischen Abstraktion", für die er meist Stein und Hartholz benutzt. HANS STEINBRENNERS (*1928) holzgeschnitzte Raumformen stehen unter dem Einfluß HENRY MOORE's. Originelle figurative Plastik mit einer Tendenz zum Spielerischen haben FRITZ KOENIG (*1924) und HELMUT ROGGE (*1924) beigetragen. Andere jüngere Bildhauer wie HARALD KIRCHNER (*1930), OTTO H. HAJEK (*1927), GUIDO JENDRITZKO (*1925) und ERNST HERMANNS (*1914) entschieden sich für gegenstandslose Formen, zu denen sich neuerdings auch WILHELM LOTH (*1920) nach einigem Zögern bekennt. THEO BECHTELER (*1903) gestaltet seine eigenwilligen vegetabilischen Plastiken in weichem Zinn.

II. ARCHITEKTUR

Für die *Architekten* bedeuteten die ersten Jahre nach 1945 weitgehend Improvisation zur Behebung größter Raumnot. Planung und Ausführung waren darauf abgestellt, daß Arbeitskräfte und Material kaum zur Verfügung standen. Bauten aus dieser Zeit sind so zu betrachten und tragen oft den Stempel der ,,Selbsthilfe" (Flüchtlingssiedlungen, Notkirchen usw.).

Erst nach der Währungsreform (1948) konnte man wieder allmählich vom tastenden Beginn einer ,,Baukunst" sprechen. Von den großen Architekten und Lehrern der zwanziger Jahre waren nicht mehr allzu viele übrig geblieben. LUDWIG MIES VAN DER ROHE (*1886) und WALTER GROPIUS (*1893) waren ausgewandert und wirken erfolgreich als Baumeister und Lehrer in den USA. ERNST MAY war über Rußland nach Afrika gegangen und kehrte erst vor einigen Jahren zurück. Um die anderen war es zum Teil still geworden: (PAUL BONATZ 1877—1958, WILHELM KREIS 1873—1955, RICHARD RIEMERSCHMID 1868—1958, BRUNO PAUL *1874, HUGO HÄRING 1882—1958) oder sie starben in den Nachkriegsjahren: (HEINRICH TESSENOW 1876—1950, FRITZ SCHUMACHER 1869—1948). Dagegen hörte man bald wieder von OTTO BARTNING (1880—1959), PAUL SCHMITTHENNER (*1884), DOMINIKUS BÖHM (1880—1956), HANS SCHAROUN (*1893), WILHELM RIPHAHN (*1889), OTTO

Ernst Schweizer, Wassili Luckhardt (*1889), Hans Luckhardt (1890 bis 1954), Richard Döcker (*1894) und Max Taut (*1884).

Die Schüler dieser Meister vor dem Dritten Reich und mit ihnen die Generation der Jahrgänge 1900 bis 1912 kamen nun meist erstmalig zum richtigen eigenen Wirken, nachdem sie in den Dreißiger Jahren vielfach anonym in großen Büros, bei Baufirmen oder militärischen Organisationen Arbeit gefunden hatten. Viele von ihnen besetzten die verwaisten Lehrstühle der Hochschulen, und heute lehrt eine neue Generation ausgezeichneter Architekten.

Im Städtebau war wohl die schwerste Aufgabe zu bewältigen. Die fruchtbarsten Lösungen zeigen sich da, wo Architekten-Persönlichkeiten am Werk sind oder waren: Hillebrecht in Hannover, Hebebrand und May in Hamburg, Jensen in Kiel, Guther in Ulm, Leitl in Rheydt, Scharoun in Berlin, Schwarz in Köln, Bangert in Kassel.

Es war natürlich, daß auch beim Bauen selbst Gedankengut, Erkenntnisse und Leistungen der Zeit vor Hitler aufgegriffen wurden. Dazu orientierte man sich im Ausland, besonders in nordischen Ländern und der Schweiz, wo es keinen Stillstand oder gar Rückfall gegeben hatte. Nicht unwesentlich trug auch der Austausch von internationalen Zeitschriften dazu bei, daß in verhältnismäßig kurzer Zeit der Spuk des Dritten Reiches vergessen war. Man versuchte allenthalben wieder, zu einer sachlichen, ehrlichen Lösung zu kommen und den künstlerischen Ausdruck von der Aufgabe und dem Material her zu finden. Der große Bedarf auf allen Gebieten und die Verarmung durch den verlorenen Krieg ließen im allgemeinen übermäßig phantasievolle Lösungen ausfallen und erlaubten nicht die Anwendung allzu kostbaren Materials. Das bedeutet, besonders auch für den Bau von Kirchen und Festräumen, eine gewisse Nüchternheit, der aber trotzdem die Festlichkeit nicht mangelt. In letzter Zeit beginnt man wieder, im Material wählerischer zu sein; auch die Heranziehung namhafter Künstler wird häufiger.

*

Im evangelischen *Kirchenbau* hatte Otto Bartning besonders durch seine Stahl- und Sternkirchen bereits lange Zeit die Führung. So war er auch nach 1945 in das große Aufbauprogramm der evangelischen Kirche eingeschaltet. Nach zahlreichen Notkirchen in allen Teilen Deutschlands entstanden unter anderen von ihm die evangelische Kirche in Bad Godesberg und die Gustav-Adolf-Kirche in Berlin (in Zusammenarbeit mit Otto Dörzbach und Werry Roth). Weitere bedeutsame evangelische Kirchen jüngerer Architekten sind die Ludwigs-Kirche in Freiburg von HORST LINDE, die Matthäus-Kirche in Pforzheim von EGON EIERMANN, die Christus-Kirche in Düren von HELMUT HENTRICH und HUBERT PETSCHNIGG, zwei Kirchen der Gemeinde Christi in Frankfurt und München von WALTER SCHULZ.

Im katholischen Kirchenbau war neben DOMINIKUS BÖHM noch von früher her RUDOLF SCHWARZ bekannt, der schon 1933 mit der Fronleichnams-Kirche in Aachen wohl den entscheidenden Schritt zum neuen katholischen Kirchenbau getan hatte. Von ihm (unter teilweiser Mitarbeit von JOSEF BERNARD und KARL WIMMENAUER) stammen auch jetzt wieder eine Reihe neuer Kirchen, unter anderen „St. Marien" in Köln-Kalk, „St. Michael" in Frankfurt, „St. Josef" in Köln, „Maria Königin" in Saarbrücken, Pfarrkirche in Düren. Daneben wurden andere Kirchenbauten sehr beachtet, wie „St. Bonifatius" in Dortmund von EMIL STEFFANN, „St. Paulus" in Velbert und „St. Albert" in Saarbrücken von GOTTFRIED BÖHM, „Allerheiligen" und „Maria Hilf" in Frankfurt von ALOIS GIEFER und HERMANN MÄCKLER, die Pfarrkirche in Dellrat und Köln-Rad von FRITZ SCHALLER, „St. Rochus" in Düsseldorf von SCHNEIDER-ESSLEBEN, „St. Alfons" in Würzburg und „St. Kilian" in Schweinfurt von HANS SCHÄDEL, „St. Pius" in Köln von KARL BAND. Darüber hinaus wirkten als Kirchenbaumeister ALFONS LEITL (Trier), JOSEF LEHMBROCK (Düsseldorf), RUDOLF STEINBACH (Aachen), H. T. R. MAUERER, GUSTAV GSÄNGER, O. A. GULBRANSON (München).

Beim Wiederaufbau zerstörter *Theater* tat WERNER KALMORGEN (Hannover) sich hervor. Der Neubau der Hamburger Staatsoper und des Mannheimer Staatstheaters wurden von GERHARD WEBER vorbildlich gelöst. Das Stadttheater Münster von DAILMANN, V. HAUSEN, RAWE und RUHNAU erfreut durch seine Heiterkeit und absolut unkonventionelle Lösung. Als letztes großes modernes Theater wurde die Kölner Oper von WILHELM RIPHAHN geschaffen. Für das Kasseler Staatstheater hatten HANS SCHAROUN und HERMANN MATTERN einen ungewöhnlichen Entwurf gemacht, der leider nicht zur Ausführung kam. Nach dem freundlichen Rundfunkhaus in Hannover von FRIEDRICH WILHELM KRÄMER, DIETER ÖSTERLEN und GERT LICHTENHAHN entstand in Frankfurt ein akustisch und künstlerisch gleich guter Sendesaal von GERHARD WEBER. Im Kölner Rundfunkhaus war P. F. SCHNEIDER ebenfalls bemüht, die überaus komplizierte Technik eines solchen Bauwerks mit den künstlerischen Anforderungen in Einklang zu bringen. Besonders gelungen ist auch die Berliner Musikakademie von PAUL BAUMGARTEN sowie der Kölner Gürzenich von RUDOLF SCHWARZ und KARL BAND — das letzte Bauwerk besonders durch seine glückliche Verbindung von Alt und Neu. Nach der Schwarzwaldhalle in Karlsruhe von ERICH SCHELLING und der Westfalenhalle in Dortmund von W. HÖTCHER entstand kürzlich die viel besichtigte Liederhalle in Stuttgart von ABEL und GUTBROD und zuletzt die Kongreßhalle in Wiesbaden von H. ROSSKOTTEN. Als eines der ersten neuen Museen ist das Walraff-Richartz-Museum von RUDOLF SCHWARZ zu nennen, über dessen architektonischen Ausdruck und seine Zweckmäßigkeit man sich zur Zeit noch nicht einig ist.

Die Bundesbaudirektion und andere staatliche und städtische Behörden schufen teils in Zusammenarbeit mit freien Architekten teils allein große *öffentliche Bauten*. Erwähnt seien in Bonn das Bundeshaus mit HANS SCHWIPPERT, in Wiesbaden das Statistische Bundesamt mit PAUL SCHÄFFER-HEYROTHSBERGE und die Landespfandbriefanstalt mit V. BRANCA und WICHTENDAL, die Oberfinanzdirektion in Frankfurt mit HANS KÖHLER, das Arbeitsamt Hannover mit DIETER ÖSTERLEN, Landrats-, Zoll- und Finanzämter in Süddeutschland mit HORST LINDE. Im Ausland entstand das Deutsche Haus in Paris mit JOHANNES KRAHN und die Deutsche Botschaft in Stockholm mit GODBER NISSEN. Zusammen mit amerikanischen Architekten schufen OTTO APEL und EBERHARD BRANDEL vorbildliche Konsulate in Frankfurt und Bremen. In Godesberg erstellte JOHANNES KRAHN Gebäude für die französische Botschaft.

Bei den Bauten für *Universitäten und Hochschulen* fallen besonders die von HORST LINDE und HANS MÜLLER geplanten Institute der Freiburger Universität auf. Auch in Frankfurt entstanden unter FERDINAND KRAMER viel beachtete Bauten, wie das Biologische Institut und das Amerika-Institut. In Berlin bauten SOBOTKA und MÜLLER die Freie Universität und WILLI KREUER die amerikanische Gedenkbibliothek. In Aachen planten HANS SCHWIPPERT und RUDOLF STEINBACH. Von STEINBACH seien das Institut für Rationalisierung und das Hörsaalgebäude genannt. Einen schönen Bau erstellte THEODOR PABST mit der Evangelischen Akademie im Taunus.

Neben den Ländern und Gemeinden, die zum Teil eigene Richtlinien für den neuen *Schulbau* herausgaben und sich bei den verschiedensten Schulsystemen experimentierfreudig zeigten, taten sich besonders hervor: RUDOLF HILLEBRECHT und WERNER DIERSCHKE mit Gymnasien, Berufs- und Volksschulen in Hannover, PAUL SEITZ mit Elementarschulen in Leverkusen und Hamburg, JOHANNES KRAHN mit französischen Schulen in Baden-Baden und Saarburg, GÜNTHER WILHELM mit einer Schule in Zupfenhausen, ALBRECHT LANGE und HANS MITZLAFF mit einer technischen Schule in Buchen, HANS DETLEF RÖSIGER und GÜNTHER SEEMANN mit einer Handelsschule in Weinheim, ADOLF BAYER mit verschiedenen Schulen in Offenbach,

GUSTAV HASSENPFLUG mit einer Schule in Hamburg, PETER PÖLZIG mit einer Schule in Oberhausen und FRIEDRICH LINDAU mit einer Gewerbeschule in Springe. WERNER HEBEBRAND, WALTER FREIWALD und WALTER SCHLEMPP bauten eine Gewerkschaftsschule in Lohr.

Für den Krankenhausbau bahnten neue Wege: WERNER HEBEBRAND, BENNO SCHACHNER, GUSTAV HASSENPFLUG, PETER PÖLZIG, OTTO BARTNING und andere. Erwähnt seien das städtische Krankenhaus Mahrl von WERNER HEBEBRAND und WALTER SCHLEMPP, das Röntgen-Institut in Osnabrück von EMANUEL LINDNER, die Tuberkulose-Station in Offenbach von ADOLF BAYER und das Kinderkrankenhaus in Lörrach von ROLF DIETSCHE.

*

Den größten und wohl auch wichtigsten Raum nehmen die neu erstandenen, zumeist öffentlichen *Wohnbauten* ein, die zahlenmäßig hauptsächlich von gemeinnützigen Baugesellschaften erstellt wurden. Neben den sogenannten „Schubladenentwürfen" gibt es eine ganze Reihe von guten Siedlungen und Wohnblocks; zumeist allerdings nur da, wo freie Architekten eingeschaltet waren oder ein Mann wie ERNST MAY an der Spitze steht, der umfangreiche Siedlungen in Hamburg und Bremen im Rahmen einer Gesellschaft baute. Aus der Vielzahl der übrigen seien einige wenige besonders hervorgehoben: die Wohnbauten für bei den Amerikanern angestellte Deutsche in Godesberg und Mehlem von OTTO APEL, RUDOLF LETOCHA, WILLIAM ROHRER, FRANZ MOCKEN und SEP RUF, die Siedlung „Alter Teichweg" in Hamburg von HERBERT SPROTTE und PETER NEWE, gute Wohnblocks in Frankfurt von MAX MEID und HELMUT ROMEICK sowie von WERNER HEBEBRAND und WALTER SCHLEMPP, die Grindelberg-Hochhäuser der Arbeitsgemeinschaft der Architekten HERMKES, HOPP, JÄGER, LODDERS, SANDER, STREB, TRAUTWEIN und ZESS in Hamburg; das Appartementhaus „Klufterhöh" in Godesberg von EUGEN BLANCK und WALTER KRATZ, die Henkel-Siedlung in Düsseldorf-Holthausen von ERNST PETERSEN und WALTER KÖNGETER. Darüber hinaus gibt es gute Lösungen von WERNER GABRIEL (Stuttgart), von GEORG W. BARNERT (Augsburg), von WILHELM SCHLECHTENDAHL (Nürnberg), von SEP RUF (München), von WILHELM RIPHAHN (Köln), von ALEXANDER HUNECKE (Berlin). Besonders gelungen sind die Einfamilien-Reihenhäuser in Darmstadt und Wiesbaden von RAINER SCHELL, die Einzelhausgruppen in Hamburg von BERNHARD HERMKES, in Hannover von PETER HÜBODDER. Darüber hinaus entstand eine große Zahl sehr guter Einfamilienhäuser der verschiedensten Architekten.

Eine wichtige Bedeutung kommt in Deutschland auch dem Bau von Alters- und Ledigenheimen, Caritas- und Kolpinghäusern, Kindergärten und Jugendherbergen zu. Hier seien einige Namen von Architekten genannt, deren Arbeiten Beachtung fanden: WERNER WIRSING (München), ERNST BREITLING (Tübingen), WERNER DÜTTMANN (Berlin), ALOIS STROHMAYER (Augsburg), THEODOR KELTER (Köln), ALOIS GIEFER und HERMANN MÄCKLER (Frankfurt), ERNST NEUFERT (Darmstadt), FRITZ RAICHARD (Offenbach), HEINRICH LAUTERBACH (Kassel), HUBERT HOFFMANN (Berlin).

*

Daß auch die Bauten für *Wirtschaft*, *Gewerbe und Verkehr* im Rahmen des gesamten Wiederaufbaus besonders in den Großstädten sehr zahlreich sind, liegt auf der Hand. Hier können nur einige wenige hervorgehoben werden: das Bürohaus der Höchster Farbwerke von GERHARD WEBER, die Industrie- und Handelskammer in Köln von KARL HELL und die in Stuttgart von ROLF GUTBROD und ROLF GUTBIER, die Maxburg in München von THEODOR PABST und SEP RUF, die Geschäftshäuser Pfeiffer und Schmidt in Braunschweig von FERDINAND KRAMER, Defaka in Kiel von GODBER NISSEN, das AEG-Hochhaus in Frankfurt von ADOLF ASSMANN und HANS BARTOLMESS, der Bienenkorb in Frankfurt von JOHANNES KRAHN, das Messe-Hotel und das Verwaltungsgebäude der Kali-Chemie in Hannover von ERNST ZINSSER (das letztgenannte mit FRIEDER RUHN, Goldschmied), die Bayerische Staatsbank von SEP RUF, das Haus der Glasindustrie in Düsseldorf von BERNHARD PFAU, die Garagenhochhäuser in Düsseldorf von PAUL SCHNEIDER-ESSLEBEN und in Frankfurt von MAX MEID und HELMUT ROMEICK; ein Autobahn-Rasthof bei Hannover von DIETER ÖSTERLEN und Autobahntankstellen von GEORG WELLHAUSEN und ERNST NEUFERT. Von FRITZ LEONARD sind ganz ausgezeichnet auch einige Brücken (Köln-Deutz und andere) und vor allem der Fernsehturm bei Stuttgart. HERMANN BLOMEYER baute Fährhäuser am Bodensee.

Als gute Industriebauer haben einen Namen: EGON EIERMANN und ROBERT HILGERS (Karlsruhe), RUDOLF LODDERS (Hamburg), ERNST NEUFERT (Darmstadt), PAUL STOHRER (Stuttgart), EMANUEL LINDNER (Osnabrück), FRIEDRICH WILHELM KRÄMER (Braunschweig), GEORG LEOWALD (Düsseldorf). Auch auf dem Gebiet der Messebauten gibt es gute Einzelleistungen, so in Hannover die Messehallen von ERNST FRIEDRICH BROCKMANN, den Hösch-Pavillon von GEORG LEOWALD, in Hamburg den Phillippsturm, das Pflanzenhaus und den Buchgarten von BERNHARD HERMKES, das Rosenhof-Restaurant von JOACHIM MATTHÄI und ERICH SCHMARJE, den Berlin-Pavillon in Hannover von den Brüdern LUCKHARDT und den in München von EDUARD LUDWIG. Die jüngsten bemerkenswerten Bauten entstanden auf der Interbau in Berlin, wo die prominenten ausländischen Kollegen und eine große Zahl Berliner und westdeutscher Architekten Beiträge zum sozialen Wohnungsbau vom Einfamilienhaus bis zum Hochhaus zeigen; dazu zwei Kirchen, eine Kongreßhalle, einen Kindergarten und eine Bücherei.

III. ANGEWANDTE KUNST; NACHWUCHS; KUNSTKRITIK

Von den *angewandten Künsten* haben Werbegraphik, Ausstellungsarchitektur und Plakatkunst sich am stärksten gewandelt. Auf diesem Gebiet, in dem die Kunst unmittelbar und in größter Verbreitung den „Verbraucher" erreicht, waren veraltetete Methoden zu überwinden. Man würde freilich die Situation zu günstig beurteilen, wenn man von einer vollständigen Wandlung zu künstlerisch befriedigenden und werbepsychologisch erfolgreichen Plakaten usw. sprechen würde. Altes und Neues stehen sich auch hier gegenüber, und die Qualitätsunterschiede sind womöglich noch krasser als in der „freien" Kunst. Das Kunsthandwerk ist in seiner Bindung an die Tradition, die Volkskunst, Landschaft und handwerkliche Technik den Neuerungen ziemlich verschlossen. Keramiker wie RICHARD BAMPI (*1896), KURT DERKUM (*1904), STEPHAN ERDÖS (1906—1956), HUBERT GRIEMERT (*1905) und WILHELM MÜHLENDYCK (*1885) bilden formschöne Gefäße im modernen Stil. In der Goldschmiedekunst haben ELISABETH TRESKOW (*1898), HEIN WIMMER, HERMANN GRETSCH, FRITZ SCHWERDT, EMIL LETTRÉ (1877—1954) und HANNS RHEINDORFF durch persönliche Technik oder Formgebung neue Wege beschritten. TH. A. WINDE und FRITZ BERNUTH sind für ihre Holzarbeiten, FRIDA SCHOY durch repräsentative Buchbinderarbeiten, HEINZ LÖFFELHARDT und TRUDE PETRI durch ihre Porzellanentwürfe bekannt. Die Bildteppiche von WOTY WERNER (*1903), ELISABETH JAEGER-KADOW (*1906) und JOHANNA SCHÜTZ-WOLFF gehörten eigentlich wegen ihrer künstlerischen „Zweckfreiheit" zur Malerei. In der industriellen Produktion werden seit Jahren bedeutende Formgestalter beschäftigt: WILHELM WAGENFELD (*1900) für Gläser und Bestecke, MARGRET HILDEBRAND (*1917) und TEA ERNST für Stoffe und Tapeten, GERHARD KADOW für Porzellanmanufakturen. Die Reihe dieser Namen könnte noch beträchtlich erweitert werden, da auch mehrere „freie" Künstler gelegentlich „angewandte" Kunst produzieren. Der „*Deutsche Kunstrat e. V.*", ein Zusammenschluß freier und kompetenter Persönlichkeiten, widmet sich der Förderung der künstlerischen Qualität und der Verbreitung moderner Kunst im In- und Ausland sowie der Veranstaltung von Ausstellungen fremder Kunst in Deutschland.

Um die gute Form und ihre Verbreitung kümmert sich in Westdeutschland außer dem „*Rat für Formgebung*“ insbesondere der „*Deutsche Werkbund*“, der 1934 aufgelöst worden war, nach dem Kriege aber neu gegründet werden konnte. Sein Programm hat sich gegenüber der ursprünglichen Tendenz von 1907 insofern geändert, als er nicht mehr die „ästhetische Veredelung einer ‚gesicherten Lebensform‘“, sondern „Sinn und Gestalt des Daseins im heutigen Deutschland zu erkennen, zu wollen und zu bilden“ anstrebt (Erstes Werkbundtreffen in Rheydt, 1947). Der Leiter des neuen „Deutschen Werkbundes“ ist HANS SCHWIPPERT. Dem Werkbund gehören Künstler, Architekten und Produzenten an. Der „Rat für Formgebung“ ist 1952 vom Bundesminister für Wirtschaft ins Leben gerufen worden. Aus der Industrie hervorgegangen ist der „Arbeitskreis für industrielle Formgebung“. Die Hochschule für Gestaltung in Ulm — Geschwister-Scholl-Stiftung — und das ihr angegliederte Institut für Produktform haben sich zur Aufgabe gemacht, dazu beizutragen, daß Zivilisation und Kultur in Einklang gebracht werden. Sie lehren mit diesem Ziele Produktform, Architektur, Stadtbau, Visuelle Kommunikation und Information.

Ein wichtiges, viel umstrittenes Gebiet ist die *Erziehung des künstlerischen Nachwuchses*. Neben den Kunstakademien des alten Typs, wie sie in Berlin, Düsseldorf, Frankfurt, Nürnberg, Stuttgart und München bestehen, wirken sogenannte Werkkunstschulen (die Bezeichnungen differieren hin und wieder, betreffen aber alle den gleichen Schultyp) in Kassel, Köln, Essen, Offenbach, Trier, Wiesbaden, Krefeld und vielen anderen Orten. Dem „Bauhaus“ vergleichbar, fassen sie eine gestalterische Gemeinschaft von Kunst, Handwerk und Industrieform unter einem Dach zusammen. Sie unterscheiden sich also von den Akademien oder Hochschulen durch Einbeziehung angewandter oder handwerklicher Lehrthemen. Ein dritter Typus ist die Meisterschule für Kunsthandwerk als Nachfolgerin der Kunstgewerbeschule des Neunzehnten Jahrhunderts. Sie legt den Akzent auf das Handwerkliche. Als einzige Akademie hat die Westberliner Hochschule für bildende Künste eine größere Anzahl moderner Künstler für pädagogische Aufgaben gewonnen. Die Hamburger Hochschule unternahm in vergangenen Jahren das Experiment, „abstrakte“ Maler von Rang (F. WINTER, E. W. NAY, G. MEISTERMANN, J. FASSBENDER, G. FIETZ, R. CAVAEL, H. TRIER und H. TRÖKES) semesterweise als Gastprofessoren zu gewinnen.

*

Die *Kunstkritiker* sind in der deutschen Sektion der „Association Internationale des Critiques d'Art" (AICA) zusammengeschlossen. Die AICA ist keine berufsständische Organisation, sondern in ihrer Struktur dem PEN-Club verwandt; das heißt, sie wählt ihre Mitglieder unter bewährten Publizisten aus. Eine deutsche Sektion der „Association Internationale des Arts plastiques" ist neuerdings auch gegründet worden, um den Künstlern die Beteiligung am internationalen Gespräch über ihre Berufsprobleme zu erleichtern.

Von den früher bekannten *Kunstzeitschriften* sind viele verschwunden. Der zeitgenössischen Kunst widmet sich, wenn auch nicht ausschließlich, „Die Kunst und das Schöne Heim" (München). „Das Kunstwerk" (Krefeld/Baden-Baden) bringt vorwiegend Beiträge zur Moderne. Die „Zeitschrift für Kunstwissenschaft" (Berlin) dient der Publikation längerer kunsthistorischer Studien. Die „Kunstchronik" (München) erfüllt informatorische und rezensorische Aufgaben. „Das Münster" (München) bringt christliche Kunst aller Epochen. „Die Weltkunst" (München) ist das Organ des Kunsthandels. Architektur und Formgestaltung behandeln unter anderem die Zeitschriften „Bauen und Wohnen" (München), „Baukunst und Werkform" (Nürnberg), „Architektur und Werkform" (Stuttgart), „Bauwelt" (Berlin), „Die Innenarchitektur" (Essen). „Pflanze und Garten" (Darmstadt) vertritt die Garten- und Landschaftsgestaltung. Die Werbegraphik hat in „Gebrauchsgraphik" (München) und „Graphik" (Stuttgart) ihre Foren. Das Mitteilungsblatt des „Deutschen Werkbundes" ist „Werk und Zeit" (Düsseldorf). Allgemeine kulturpolitische Fragen kommen in der „Kulturarbeit" (Köln) und im „Magnum" (Köln) zu Wort.

IV. MUSEEN

Nach den Angaben des Statistischen Jahrbuches deutscher Gemeinden sind von 395 deutschen Museen, die vor dem Kriege bestanden haben, 108 total und 149 teilweise zerstört worden. Die Gebäude von 76 Museen waren 1955/56 bereits vollständig, 55 teilweise im Wiederaufbau begriffen oder hatten Neubauten Platz gemacht. Seither sind Planung und Aufbau vielerorts tatkräftig gefördert worden. Dieser Überblick erläutert, wie schwer die Kriegsfolgen auf die Konservierung der Sammlungen sich haben auswirken müssen. Der Substanzverlust selbst ist glücklicherweise geringer. An Totalverlusten waren 37 zu beklagen, während in 201 Museen Teile der Sammlungen verloren gingen.

Daß es gelang, in Städten, die vom Bombenkrieg hart betroffen waren, hohe Prozentsätze des beweglichen Kunstbesitzes in den Kirchen und Museen zu erhalten (zum Beispiel in Nürnberg mehr als 98%), ist auf die sorgsame, zum Teil vorsorgliche Bergungsarbeit der Museen zurückzuführen. Im einzelnen ist der Erfolg einer zentralen Unterbringung und der Verteilung auf gestreute auswärtige Bergungsorte verschieden gewesen. So hat Nürnberg unter der Burg seine kostbarsten Schätze in klimatisierten „Zellen" bewahren können, während Berlin bei und nach der Einnahme der Stadt in den Flaktürmen schwere Einbußen hat hinnehmen müssen. Köln hat aus fränkischen Schlössern und Klöstern seine Sammlungen wohlbehalten zurückholen können. Das Schicksal wertvollster Bestände aus der Bremer Kunsthalle, die in der Mark Brandenburg ausgelagert waren, ist dagegen nach wie vor ungewiß, zum Teil infolge von Plünderungen besiegelt.

Neubau, Neuordnung und Aufstellung begannen frühzeitig. Vor der Währungsreform hatte man in den mehr oder weniger zufälligen Bergungsorten unter der Schirmherrschaft der Besatzungsmächte die ersten Begegnungen mit den lang entbehrten Originalen herbeigeführt. Nach 1948 setzte die planmäßige Rückführung und museale Arbeit ein. Dabei verdient die Rundreise bedeutender Werke aus den ehemals Preußischen Museen in Berlin durch die USA erwähnt zu werden. Unbeschadet der vielfach aufgetretenen beklagenswerten Schäden an den Bildern hat doch die Vorstellung deutscher Museumsbestände im Auslande für die deutsche Kunst und für die Sammeltätigkeit der deutschen Museen im Neunzehnten Jahrhundert internationales Verständnis und Interesse erweckt.

Die zeitbedingte Beweglichkeit der Museumsschätze hat nach zwei Richtungen eine Neuorientierung herbeigeführt: in der Ausstellungstechnik und in der Organisation der Museen selbst. Ein international beachtetes Beispiel für neuzeitliche Ausstellungstechnik bot die *documenta* in Kassel (1955). Dort hatte die Leitung sich den Rohbau des Museums Fridericianum zunutze gemacht, um in diesem Gehäuse mit Hilfe von beweglichen Untergliederungen, zeltartigen Vorhängen und einfallsreichen Lichteffekten die europäische Kunst des 20. Jahrhunderts einem breiten Publikum vorzuführen. Ähnliche Erfolge sind mit Wanderausstellungen zu Ehren zeitgenössischer Meister (PICASSO, KOKOSCHKA, LEHMBRUCK, NOLDE) oder bedeutenden Ausstellungen historischer Kunst (Ars sacra in München, Werdendes Abendland an Rhein und Ruhr in der Villa Hügel zu Essen) erzielt worden. Mit diesen Veranstaltungen wurden weiteste Besucherkreise angesprochen, wie sie die „feste" Museumsordnung von einst nie hätte erzielen können. Damit stellte die deutsche Museums- und Ausstellungspolitik der Nachkriegszeit sich an die Seite der Bemühungen in den Nachbarländern, wo die Museen seit längerem mit Erfolg in ähnlichem Sinne arbeiten.

Die auf Blickpunkte, Heraushebung bedeutender Einzelwerke und lebendige Anschaulichkeit bedachte Ausstellungspraxis ist nicht ohne Einfluß auf die Bestandsaufnahme der Museen geblieben. Die überfüllten Säle der

Fachsammlungen gehören der Vergangenheit an. Man scheidet bei den Neuaufstellungen zwischen Schau-, Lehr- und Studiensammlungen. Die Aufnahmefähigkeit des Betrachters wird in Rechnung gestellt, Vollständigkeit nicht angestrebt. Dabei unterscheidet das Museum sich von zeitlich begrenzten Ausstellungen durch Beständigkeit, Dauerhaftigkeit der Werkstoffe und Exaktheit. Es dient der Belehrung und Erziehung ebenso wie der ästhetischen Freude und der gehobenen Unterhaltung. Um dieser Funktion gerecht zu werden, ist das neuzeitliche Museum darum bemüht, seiner architektonischen Gestalt nüchterne Zweckdienlichkeit zu geben. Hierin unterscheidet es sich durchaus von den historisierenden oder äußerlicher Repräsentation gewidmeten Monumentalbauten des Neunzehnten Jahrhunderts. Auch wo man Neuaufstellungen in bestehenden Bauten vornahm, ist das Prinzip der Auswahl, der sparsamen Hängung, der künstlerischen Führung sichtbar.

Als Beispiele seien wenige Museen genannt: Ehemalige Staatliche Museen, Berlin-Dahlem; Landesmuseum Bonn; Landesmuseum Darmstadt; Museum für Kunst und Gewerbe, Hamburg; Museum in Hamburg-Altona; Bayerisches Nationalmuseum, München; Germanisches Nationalmuseum, Nürnberg. Für den Wiederaufbau der Pinakotheken in München hat zwar die Pietät vor LEO VON KLENZE den Ausschlag gegeben, doch wiederholt die innere Gliederung keineswegs den früheren Grundriß. Radikaler entschied man sich in Köln, wo das Wallraf-Richartz-Museum zwar an der alten Stelle, aber in einer Gestalt aufgebaut wurde, die jeden historisierenden Zusammenhang zurückweist und sich damit begnügt, als Gehäuse der inneren Funktion sich zu behaupten.

Andernorts hat die Not des Gebäudeverlustes zu großartigen architektonischen Wirkungen geführt. Die Denkmäler wurden in einen Zusammenklang mit hochwertiger echter Architektur gebracht, die mit einem Schlage die Fragwürdigkeit der imitierten ,,Stil"-räume in den älteren historischen Museen erweist. Beispiele sind Schloß Cappenberg (Westf.) mit den Beständen des Museums zu Dortmund; Schloß Gottorf mit den Beständen des Schleswig-Holsteinischen Landesmuseums zu Kiel; Feste Marienberg in Würzburg, wohin das Luitpoldmuseum zog und zu einem der schönsten deutschen Museen umgestaltet wurde. Auch in anderen privaten oder öffentlichen Schlössern hat sich ein lebhafter Besuch entwickelt, der in gleicher Weise der Architektur wie den Sammlungen gilt. Als Beispiele mögen stehen: Schloß Arolsen; Maihingen im Ries; Schloß Pommersfelden; Schloß Neuenstein und Weikersheim; neuerdings Schloß Aschach.

Die Idee des Museumsdorfes oder des Freilichtmuseums, in Holland und den skandinavischen Ländern zu hoher Blüte geführt, ist in Deutschland nicht weiter verfolgt worden. Das Museumsdorf in Cloppenburg (Oldenburg) ist wieder fast vollständig und erfreut in seiner Verbindung von Vorgeschichte und Volkskunde sich regen Zuspruchs.

Den ersten Neubau eines kulturgeschichtlichen Museums in Deutschland seit 1913 führt Bremen durch. In Verbindung mit Gut Riensberg und einem alten Park werden die Sammlungen des Focke-Museums in einem Areal untergebracht werden, dessen Besonderheit in der Einheit aus Garten, historischer Baugruppe und Neubau bestehen wird. Auch das Landesmuseum in Münster/Westfalen bereitet einen Wettbewerb für einen Neubau vor.

In zunehmendem Maße wenden die Museen, insbesondere auch die technischen und naturwissenschaftlichen Museen (Deutsches Museum in München; Übersee-Museum in Bremen, mit 253.735 Besuchern im Jahre 1956 die meistbesuchten Sammlungen in Deutschland) ihre Arbeit den Kindern und Jugendlichen zu. Sie bemühen sich sowohl um verstärkte Berücksichtigung in den Lehrplänen der Schulen (Lehrerkurse, Unterrichtsräume) als auch um die Bereitstellung ihrer Sammlungen für die zu erwartende verlängerte Freizeit. Die aktuelle Bedeutung der Museen trat in einer Ausstellung des Stadtmuseums München 1957 in Erscheinung: „Keine Angst vor der Freizeit."

Bund und Länder haben in den letzten Jahren gemeinsam Mittel aufgebracht, um die Erhaltung zweier national wertvoller Kunstwerke für den deutschen Museumsbesitz zu sichern: den Echternacher Codex im Germanischen Nationalmuseum zu Nürnberg und die Madonna des Sandro Botticelli in der Gemäldegalerie zu Berlin-Dahlem.

Das Gesetz über die Stiftung Preußischer Kulturbesitz (1957) bezeugt ebenfalls, daß nach langjähriger treuhänderischer Verwaltung durch die preußischen Nachfolgeländer die Einheit des Berliner Museumsbesitzes als gemeinsame kulturelle Verpflichtung bejaht worden ist.

Überregionale wissenschaftliche Anerkennung genießen das Römisch-Germanische Museum in Mainz, das Museum König in Bonn, das Deutsche Museum in München und das Germanische Nationalmuseum in Nürnberg. Sie werden von den Ländern aus dem „Königsteiner Abkommen" mitfinanziert. Maßgeblich für diese Förderung ist, daß mit der volksbildenden Arbeit dieser Sammlungen eine Forschungstätigkeit verbunden ist, die bis in die Gründerjahre des deutschen Museumswesens überhaupt zurückreicht.

DAS THEATER

Französisches Theater wird in Paris gemacht, englisches in London und amerikanisches in New York. Wer aber vom deutschen Theater spricht, meint nicht Berlin oder Bonn, sondern eine abwechslungsreiche Theaterlandschaft mit mehreren Kristallisationspunkten.

Diese den ausländischen Besucher erstaunende Erscheinung hat eine lange Geschichte. Sie beginnt mit dem Repräsentationsbedürfnis und den künstlerischen Ambitionen der deutschen Fürstenhöfe im Siebzehnten Jahrhundert, die ihre eigenen Opern errichteten, denen später Schauspielhäuser folgten. So bewirkte der Partikularismus in Deutschland die Bildung vieler verschiedener Zentren der Kunst. Den Höfen wollte es der Bürgerstolz in den aufblühenden Städten gegen Ende des Achtzehnten Jahrhunderts gleich tun. Die kühne Idee des ,,*Nationaltheaters*“ gewann in Berlin, Hamburg oder Mannheim Gestalt.

Ein reiches Theaterleben entfaltete sich an zahlreichen Orten im Neunzehnten Jahrhundert. Neben ständigen Bühnen wurde der Gedanke der *Festspiele* erstmalig verwirklicht – von RICHARD WAGNER in Bayreuth, allerdings zunächst nur für die Oper und nur für sein eigenes Werk. Aber der Gedanke wirkte weiter bis zu den vielen Festspiel-Neugründungen während der letzten vierzig Jahre, die allerdings nach dem Zweiten Weltkrieg fast schon ein Übermaß erreicht haben.

Eine geschichtlich bedeutsame Tat war die Übernahme der höfischen Bühnen in Deutschland nach der Novemberrevolution 1918 durch den jungen Staat. In den fünfzehn Jahren der Weimarer Republik feierte die *Gegenwartskunst* in all ihrer schillernden Vielfältigkeit glanzvolle Triumphe. Die Virtuosität der Leistungen blieb dem Theater in Deutschland auch noch von 1933 bis 1945 erhalten – trotz schweren Verlusten durch die Emigration jüdischer und einiger aus politischen Gründen verfemter Künstler.

Die Säulen des deutschen Thaters, Ensemble und Repertoire, wurden sogar noch verstärkt. Und der im Leben erfolglose Widerstand gegen die Herrschaft der Gewalt suchte und fand auf der Bühne einen Weg, den Geist der Freiheit in Metapher und Gleichnis zu verkünden. Das Theater als Hort des Widerstandsgeistes? Ja, das gab es! Er konnte sich an Klassiker-Aufführungen entzünden, wenn Antigone ausrief: ,,Nicht mitzuhassen, mitzulieben bin ich da“, wenn Marquis Posa in SCHILLERS ,,Don Carlos“ Gedankenfreiheit forderte oder Kaiser Rudolf II. in GRILLPARZERS ,,Bruderzwist in Habsburg“ einen heimlichen, unsichtbar zu tragenden Orden für Tapferkeit des Herzens verlieh, und er konnte sich tarnen hinter bewußt

„unheroischen", zeitgenössischen Komödien, die in irgendeinem historischen Gewand die damalige Gegenwart verspotteten.

*

Einer ganz neuen Situation stand das deutsche Theater 1945 gegenüber. Beschränkung und Bereicherung, Substanz-Verlust und -Gewinn wurden zu schöpferischen Impulsen. 60% der Gebäude waren zerstört oder schwer beschädigt. Im Bundesgebiet und Berlin(West) ist der größte Teil davon während der letzten acht bis zehn Jahre wieder errichtet worden oder befindet sich zur Zeit im Bau.

Damals waren Geld und Material für derartige Wiederherstellungen nicht vorhanden. Man spielte in behelfsmäßigen Räumen und, da auch die Mittel für Dekorationen und Kostüme fehlten, in skizzenhaft andeutenden Ausstattungen. Doch aus diesem scheinbaren Mangel wuchs ein Stil, der das Pathos und den sogenannten „Staatsnaturalismus" überwand. Die Szene wurde wieder transparent für die Welt hinter den Dingen. Die sichtbaren Erscheinungen der Bühne wollten keine Vortäuschung und keine künstliche Überhöhung der Wirklichkeit mehr darstellen, sondern Chiffren, wesenhafte Zeichen für das Inbild sein.

Während die Materialnot zu schöpferischen Auswegen zwang, erforderte die formal oft neuartige Dramatik des Auslands, die uns seit 1945 überflutete, einen unkonventionellen Darstellungsstil. Die kosmischen Revuen WILDERs mit ihren formsprengenden Elementen, die ironischen Traumgebilde von GIRAUDOUX oder die anachronistischen Tragödien von ANOUILH, die imaginäre Welt PIRANDELLOs oder KAFKAs, die ihre Wiederauferstehung im Theater lange nach dem Tode der Dichter feierte, erhielten in den deutschen Aufführungen visionäre Akzente. Ein magischer Realismus setzte sich durch, der nun nicht nur für zeitgenössische Werke Anwendung findet, sondern längst auch die Wiedergaben aus dem klassischen Repertoire beeinflußt.

Dieser Fülle an dramatischen Gestaltungen unseres Daseins, die insbesondere aus Frankreich und Amerika in Deutschland eintrafen, stand eine anfangs *spärliche Dramen-Produktion* im eigenen Land gegenüber. Leider sprangen die Schubladen nicht wie erwartet auf, gefüllt bis zum Rand mit in der Zeit der Unterdrückung geschriebenen Manuskripten. Sie waren leer. Diese Enttäuschung, die uns gleich nach dem Kriege überfiel, ist Jahre hindurch permanent geblieben. Der Schock der Kriegs- und Nachkriegsjahre verhinderte zunächst eine bezwingende und gültige Darstellung der jüngsten Vergangenheit. Das politische Agitationsstück aber kann eine dichterische

Übersetzung der Schicksale unserer Zeit, die über das Tagesinteresse hinauszugehen vermag, nicht ersetzen. Und auch diese Gattung, die oft gerade durch ihre eilfertige Aktualität und ihren Reportage-Charakter ein schnelles, wenn auch flüchtiges Interesse findet, fehlte damals bei uns. Und das zeitlose Drama? Die Zeit schien es erstickt zu haben. Erst allmählich – etwa seit der Krieg ein Jahrzehnt vergangen ist – zeichnet sich eine junge Dramatiker-Generation mit beachtenswerten Leistungen ab.

Viel gespielt werden seit Kriegsende drei deutsche Dramatiker, denen man nach zwölf Jahren Verbot ihren einstigen Wert und Rang wieder zuerkannt hat. Aus den zwanziger Jahren reichen CARL ZUCKMAYER und FERDINAND BRUCKNER zu uns herüber. ZUCKMAYER hat in seinen Nachkriegsdramen Gegenwartsprobleme angesprochen und sich dazu einer hautnahen Nachzeichnung der Wirklichkeit bedient, die in „Des Teufels General" um so erstaunlicher ist, als er die dargestellte Zeit nicht in Deutschland, sondern in den USA verbracht hat. Daß ZUCKMAYER keine Angst vor heißen Eisen besitzt, bewies er in der Darstellung eines Atombomben-Verrats aus Friedensliebe in dem Drama „Das kalte Licht".

BRUCKNER dagegen, der in seinen Jugendwerken aggressive Diagramme der seelischen Krankheiten des Jahrzehnts nach dem Ersten Weltkrieg lieferte, schrieb seit seiner Rückkehr aus der Emigration nach Berlin (1950) psychologisch differenzierte szenische Studien individueller Vorgänge in einem herb durchgeistigten Klassizismus, der unsere allgemeine Situation nur wie in einem leicht verhangenen Spiegel auffängt. Durch seinen Tod am 5. 12. 1958 verlor das deutsche Theater einen profilierten Dramatiker.

Zu dieser Generation der mit jugendlichem Elan tätigen Altmeister der deutschen Gegenwartsdramatik gehörte auch der 1956 verstorbene BERTOLT BRECHT. Während seine umstrittenen Theorien des „epischen Theaters" und des „Verfremdungs"-Effektes mehr diskutiert als angewendet werden, spielt man sein Werk auf beiden Seiten des Eisernen Vorhangs. Auch die ideologische Verbohrtheit des mit dem Kommunismus paktierenden Autors hat seinen mit dialektischer Schärfe geätzten Stücken den Weg auf die Bühnen der Bundesrepublik nicht versperren können.

Neben diesen Altmeistern erleben auch die schon vor längerer Zeit gestorbenen Dramatiker der zwanziger Jahre eine posthume Renaissance. Man spielt wieder WALTER HASENCLEVER und BRUNO FRANK, CARL STERNHEIM und vor allem GEORG KAISER, dessen Kritik an der geistigen Wurzel ansetzt. Wie sehr GERHART HAUPTMANNS Mitleidsdramatik von zeitloser Aktualität ist, erweisen Inszenierungen gerade auch seiner naturalistischen

Tragödien. Daß FRANK WEDEKIND wieder entdeckt wird, ist nicht verwunderlich angesichts der häufig bei seinem Bänkelsänger- und Moritaten-Stil anknüpfenden Gegenwarts-Dramatik. Als eine „Wiedergutmachung“ an dem 1938 verfemt gestorbenen Bildhauer und Schriftsteller ERNST BARLACH könnte man die Neuaufführungen seiner schwerblütigen, mit Gedanken befrachteten Tragödien an einer Reihe deutscher Theater betrachten. Aber es ist mehr. Wenn auch die Resonanz beim Publikum nicht allzu groß zu sein scheint, so läuft doch eine direkte Linie von diesen Werken zu einer symbolträchtigen lebenden Literatur.

*

Und wie sieht nun die Produktion der deutschen *Nachwuchs-Dramatiker* aus? Man darf heute wohl anders als noch vor zehn bis zwölf Jahren sagen: hoffnungsvoll! Damals gelang eigentlich nur einem einzigen jüngeren Schriftsteller ein dichterischer Wurf. Der so früh verstorbene WOLFGANG BORCHERT schrieb mit seiner ursprünglich für den Funk gedachten tragischen Heimkehrer-Ballade „Draußen vor der Tür“ Schmerz und Verzweiflung, die Frage nach der Verantwortung und die Anklage wider eine herz- und gewissenlose Gesellschaft sich von der Seele.

Schlimm waren die Folgen. Unzählige Heimkehrer-Stücke entstanden in der gleichen Un-Form und mit der gleichen Neigung zu rhetorischen Tiraden, denen aber die dichterische Kraft kühn hingewischter Skizzen und bannender Visionen völlig fehlte. Erst als die deutschen Dramatiker sich von diesem gefährlichen, weil unwiederholbaren Vorbild lösten, konnten sie originelle Werke schreiben. Einigen davon mag vielleicht eine Lebensdauer über unsere unmittelbare Gegenwart hinaus beschieden sein.

Bei aller Skepsis gegen *Literaturpreise* muß doch anerkennend vermerkt werden, daß einige von ihnen, wie der Dramatikerpreis des Deutschen Bühnenvereins, der Gerhart-Hauptmann-Preis der Westberliner Freien Volksbühne oder die dramatischen Wettbewerbe einzelner Bühnen, insbesondere des Mannheimer Nationaltheaters, auf den Dramatiker-Nachwuchs nachdrücklich hingewiesen und ihn gefördert haben. Vor allem der Gerhart-Hauptmann-Preis, der aus den Spenden der Volksbühnen-Mitglieder dotiert wird, macht es sich zur Aufgabe, noch nicht oder erst wenig gespielte Autoren zu entdecken. CLAUS HUBALEK, dessen 1954 uraufgeführte Satire „Der Hauptmann und sein Held“ Bühne, Funk und Film erobert hat, GERT WEYMANN, dessen „Generationen“-Tragödie auch im Ausland gespielt worden ist, oder THEODOR SCHÜBEL, der sein Schauspiel „Der Kürassier Sebastian und sein Sohn“ abseits des Theaterbetriebes geschrieben hat, sind als Hauptmann-Preisträger erstmalig an die Öffentlichkeit getreten. Außer ihnen verdienen nachdrückliche Erwähnung LEOPOLD AHLSEN, der besonders erfolgreich mit einem im griechischen Widerstandskampf spielenden Drama der Menschlichkeit „Philemon und Baukis" hervorgetreten ist, und KARL WITTLINGER, der die Tragödie des heimatlos gewordenen Heimkehrers – ohne Pathos – in einem geistreichen, tragikomischen Zweipersonen-Stück „Kennen Sie die Milchstraße?" behandelt. RICHARD HEY geht mit aggressiver Brillanz gegen die Zeiterscheinungen an. Aber seine symbolträchtigen Dramen, wie „Thymian und Drachentod" oder „Der Fisch mit dem goldenen Dolch", sind in abstrakten Ländern angesiedelt und verlieren dadurch manchmal die für eine Zeitkritik doch wohl notwendige unmittelbare Wirkung. Noch viele andere Dramatiker haben sich in den letzten Jahren an den deutschen Theatern durchgesetzt. Oft gelangen sie, wie WOLFGANG HILDESHEIMER, der noch vor der Uraufführung seines klugen Turandot-Dramas „Der Drachenthron" 1954 mit dem Hörspielpreis der Kriegsblinden ausgezeichnet wurde, von der Funkarbeit zum Bühnenstück.

Von der älteren Generation sind noch HANS-HENNY JAHNN, dessen surreale und expressionistische Dialogstücke wieder aufgeführt werden, HANS JOSÉ REHFISCH, ein Verfechter der dramatischen Reportage, die nur jetzt und hier wirken und in eine akute Auseinandersetzung eingreifen will, GÜNTHER WEISENBORN, der mit historischen Stoffen auf plakatives Zeittheater zielt, und vor allem ERICH KÄSTNER zu nennen. Dieser Dichter der sogenannten heiteren Muse geht zum Beispiel in seiner 1957 uraufgeführten „Schule der Diktatoren" den Weg über die kabarettistische Satire, um den Zeitgenossen seine unbequemen Wahrheiten zu sagen.

In der Dramatik sind also Substanz-Verlust und -Gewinn ausgewogen.

*

Wie sehen nun die Spielpläne der deutschen Bühnen aus? Die neuesten Erfolgs- oder Diskussions-Stücke des Auslands von JOHN OSBORNE bis zu TENNESSEE WILLIAMS, ARTHUR MILLER bis zu PETER USTINOV, SAMUEL BECKETT bis zu EUGÈNE JONESCO oder von T. S. ELIOT und CHRISTOPHER FRY bis zu ARTHUR ADAMOV werden nicht nur in den großen Städten, sondern auch in der sogenannten Provinz nachgespielt. Der Ehrgeiz, modern und, wie es so schön heißt, „avantgardistisch" zu sein, ist in unseren Landen weit verbreitet. Aber es stecken auch viel aufrichtiges Interesse und viel echte Auseinandersetzung in diesem Bestreben.

Der Hunger nach Novitäten macht sich auch in dem Wettlauf der Theaterleiter nach *Uraufführungen* deutscher oder deutschsprachiger Werke bemerkbar. Besonders den arrivierten Schriftstellern werden die Stücke, auch wenn sie erst im Manuskript und vielleicht sogar noch unfertig vorliegen, aus den Händen gerissen. So ist es ZUCKMAYERS Komödie ,,Der trunkene Herkules" ergangen, die von mehreren Bühnen, ohne daß sie ihnen überhaupt bekannt war, zur Uraufführung angenommen wurde. Ähnliche Erfahrungen machen die Schweizer Dramatiker MAX FRISCH und FRIEDRICH DÜRRENMATT, deren Dramen meist in Deutschland ihre Uraufführung erleben, der Österreicher FRITZ HOCHWÄLDER oder der in der Schweiz lebende ULRICH BECHER, die großes Ansehen in Deutschland genießen.

Ein Überblick über die deutschen Theaterspielpläne der Gegenwart wäre unvollständig, würde man nicht der bedeutenden Rolle gedenken, die nach wie vor die Klassiker in Anspruch nehmen. LESSINGS ,,Minna von Barnhelm", ,,Emilia Galotti" und nicht zuletzt sein großes Epos der Humanität und Toleranz ,,Nathan der Weise" werden in regelmäßigen Abständen ebenso aufgeführt wie GOETHES ,,Götz von Berlichingen", ,,Clavigo", ,,Iphigenie auf Tauris", ,,Egmont", ,,Torquato Tasso" und ,,Faust" (I. und gelegentlich auch II. Teil). FRIEDRICH VON SCHILLERS ,,Räuber", ,,Verschwörung des Fiesco zu Genua", ,,Kabale und Liebe", ,,Don Carlos", ,,Wallenstein", ,,Maria Stuart" ,,,Jungfrau von Orléans", ,,Braut von Messina" und sein ,,Wilhelm Tell" gehören im Jahre 1959, da alle Welt der zweihundertsten Wiederkehr seines Geburtstages gedenkt, wohl zu den meistgespielten Werken überhaupt.

*
* *

Vorherrschender Theatertyp in Deutschland ist immer noch das *subventionierte Repertoire-Theater* mit wechselndem Spielplan. Dabei gibt es in mittleren und kleineren Städten gemischte Betriebe mit Oper, Operette und Schauspiel, während in den Großstädten die staatlichen oder städtischen Schauspiel-Theater gesondert von den Opernbühnen verwaltet werden und oft zwei Häuser für das große Drama und für das intime Kammerspiel umfassen.

Aber das Ensuite-Theater, in dem eine Inszenierung jeweils vier bis acht Wochen hintereinander läuft, gewinnt auch in Deutschland an Boden. Dieser Strukturwandel entspringt nicht einer Nachahmung der Londoner und Pariser Boulevard-Bühnen oder der monate- und jahrelang laufenden Produktionen am Broadway. Die Ursachen einer solchen Entwicklung reichen in tiefere Schichten. Das *Ensemble*, eine noch im Krieg intakte, vom Ausland oft bewunderte Stütze des deutschen Theaters, ist kurz vor Kriegsende von einem lebensbedrohenden Schlag getroffen worden. Nach der Schließung der

Theater im Spätsommer 1944 wurden die letzten „kriegsdienst-verwendungsfähigen" Schauspieler eingezogen, die weiblichen Bühnenangehörigen kriegsdienstverpflichtet, die Ensembles dadurch gesprengt und in alle Winde verstreut. Außerdem ergriff der Flüchtlingsstrom aus den bombardierten Städten auf das Land und von Ost nach West auch die Mitglieder der Theater.

1945 konnte man von Flensburg bis Konstanz in oft ganz entlegenen Städten und an kleinen Provinzbühnen dorthin verschlagene prominente Schauspieler treffen, um die herum Theater arrangiert wurde. Die in über hundertfünfzigjähriger deutscher Tradition geprägte Form des Ensemblespiels schien zerschlagen, und so rasch ließen sich die Scherben nicht wieder zusammenkitten. Gewiß, Ensemblereste fanden sich bald wieder zusammen. Aber gerade die Spitzendarsteller, die sich frei und vielleicht auch lästiger Zügel ledig fühlten, überließen sich nur allzu gern ihrer selbstherrlichen Freizügigkeit. Verluste durch Tod infolge der letzten Kriegs- und der ersten Nachkriegs-Ereignisse, die Rückwanderung vieler an Bühnen der deutschen Hauptstadt Berlin und der Theaterprovinz engagierter Wiener Künstler in ihre Heimat, die Auswanderung anderer in die damals lukrative Schweiz, wohin schon viele von 1933 bis 1945 geflüchtet waren, und nicht zuletzt die wieder erwachte Vagabunden-Lust beraubten die Ensembles vielfach ihrer besten Kräfte.

Film, Funk und Fernsehen holten sich außerdem die Stars der Bühne mehr denn je für ihre Produktionen. Natürlich wollten die von so vielen Seiten begehrten Schauspieler möglichst dort Theater spielen, wo sie dank der technischen Vervielfältigung einer einmaligen Leistung gut verdienten. Dieser verständliche Wunsch förderte den Wandertrieb noch mehr.

Das Publikums-Bedürfnis nach Perfektion, das aus der Bekanntschaft mit den in Film und Schallplatte konservierten oder durch Funk und Fernsehen überall hin ausstrahlenden Darbietungen erster Künstler entstanden ist, kam dieser Wanderfreudigkeit entgegen. Der Schritt zum *Tournee-Theater*, wie es heute in Deutschland blüht, war dann nicht mehr weit. Dem Schauspieler bietet diese Einrichtung die erwünschte Gelegenheit, mit einem umfangreicheren Publikum als dem einer einzigen Stadt in Kontakt zu kommen und den eigenen Gesichtskreis zu erweitern. So kann man heute erstklassige Weltstadt-Aufführungen in Wolfsburg, Marl, Schweinfurt oder Iserlohn von führenden Darstellern erleben, die sich zu einer einmaligen Einstudierung zusammenfanden. Auch an den großen stehenden Bühnen macht sich dieser Zug vom Ensemble- zum Star-Theater und vom Repertoire- zum Ensuite-Theater bemerkbar. Die großen Schauspieler werden nämlich in einer Saison zwischen Berlin und Düsseldorf, Hamburg und Frankfurt oder Köln und München ausgetauscht. Sie sind oft vier bis fünf Monate an der einen und dann noch einige Monate in einer anderen Stadt engagiert oder lassen sich sogar nur noch für Stückverträge verpflichten. Auf diese Weise entsteht eine Mischform des Spielplans zwischen Ensuite und Repertoire. Bestimmte Aufführungen müssen in wenigen Wochen oder Monaten abgespielt werden und sind dann so oft angesetzt, daß dies fast einer Ensuite-Serie gleichkommt.

Die *Verringerung der Zahl an Neueinstudierungen* pro Jahr, die früher an einer subventionierten Bühne oft zehn bis zwölf und mehr betrug, wirkt einem vielfältigen Repertoire entgegen. Sechs bis acht und kaum über zehn Produktionen sind heute an einem Haus üblich. Durch die Vergrößerung des Publikums, Vergrößerung hinsichtlich der absoluten Zahl ebenso wie hinsichtlich der sozialen Schichtung, können die Theater ihre Aufführungen länger spielen und brauchen weniger neue herauszubringen.

*

Ensemble und Repertoire – auch in diesen Ausprägungen der deutschen Theaterform, die nach dem Kriege wesentlichen Veränderungen unterworfen waren, können allem Anschein nach Verlust und Gewinn gegeneinander aufgewogen werden. Wie sieht nun aber die *schauspielerische Qualität* aus?

Ein ausländischer Regisseur stellte einmal die Beobachtung an, daß wir drei verschiedene Darstellungsstile in unserem gegenwärtigen Theater hätten. Die alte Generation komme aus der vitalen Fülle der Schauspielerei, wie MAX REINHARDT sie verlangte. Die junge Generation sei von BERT BRECHTS intellektuell demonstrativem Interpretationsstil geprägt. Und die mittlere Generation scheine zwischen den beiden Extremen unentschieden zu sein. Die armen Regisseure aber müßten so heterogene Kräfte zu einer Einheit binden.

Diese radikal vereinfachende Ansicht hat auf den ersten Blick etwas Bestechendes. Tatsächlich aber ist die *Komödianterie* unvergänglich. Sie feierte an den REINHARDT-Bühnen ebenso Triumphe wie bei OTTO BRAHM und andernorts, wo man am Anfang unseres Jahrhunderts den Naturalismus pflegte. Und Komödianten mit der Lust an der restlosen Verwandlung in die Rolle gibt es auch unter dem jüngsten Nachwuchs. Sogar das anti-emotionelle Theater kann diesem ursprünglichen Gewächs nichts anhaben, und auch das angelsächsische unterbelichtende Spiel des sogenannten *understatement* läßt dem blutvollen Komödianten freie Bahn. Die umgekehrte Richtung, bei der ein Schauspieler nicht in die Rolle schlüpft, sondern diese seinem eigenen Ich anverwandelt, hat es auch immer gegeben.

Eins ist allerdings gewiß: daß der Zug zum rationalistischen und lehrhaften Theater sich verstärkt hat. Der bestimmende Eindruck von der Bühne herab ist nicht der: „Seht her, so ist das Leben", sondern: „Hört zu, das ist falsch daran" oder „So sollte es nicht sein". Nun macht sich natürlich diese Wandlung des Theaterstils auch generationsweise bemerkbar, und da ist dann die oben zitierte Unterscheidung nicht ganz von der Hand zu weisen.

*

Besonders imponierend finden ausländische Besucher immer wieder die Zahlen, die das Theaterwesen der Bundesrepublik umreißen. Sie dürfen daher hier nicht fehlen. Fast zwanzig Millionen Theaterbesucher in einem Jahr, einhundertfünfzig Millionen Mark jährliche Subventionen, wobei die für Opernhäuser gezahlten mitgerechnet sind, etwa einhundertachtzehn subventionierte Bühnen, davon zwanzig staatliche, achtzig städtische und achtzehn Landesbühnen mit Standort in einer mittleren oder kleinen Stadt und Tourneen in die Umgebung, dazu noch rund dreißig Privattheater. Diese Bilanz verrät ein blühendes Theater in Deutschland.

*

Enge Beziehungen zum Theater hat natürlich auch die *Oper*, die im deutschen Kunstleben seit jeher einen bedeutenden Platz eingenommen hat, Ihre Darstellung ist jedoch dem Abschnitt „Musik" vorbehalten. Vornehmlich CARL ORFF (* 1895) sucht in seinen der Sprache auf besondere Weise verbundenen Werken („Carmina burana", 1936; Musik zu SHAKESPEARES „Sommernachtstraum", letzte Fassung 1952; „Die Bernauerin", 1947) neue Wege. Auch BORIS BLACHER (* 1903), WERNER EGK (* 1901), dieser insbesondere in seiner „Irischen Legende", 1955, und schließlich GOTTFRIED VON EINEM (* 1918; „Dantons Tod", 1947) haben einen wachen Sinn für das auf der Bühne Wirksame. In neuerer Zeit sind vielfältige Bemühungen in Richtung einer „*Funkoper*" zu erkennen, die auf alles Sichtbare verzichten muß.

*

* *

Großes Interesse findet im Ausland eine soziale Einrichtung des deutschen Theaters, die *Altersversorgung der Bühnenkünstler*, die heute jeden an einer Bühne im Bundesgebiet und Westberlin engagierten Künstler erfaßt.

Immer wieder werden in der Deutschen Sektion des Internationalen Theater-Instituts[1], die sich unter Förderung der UNESCO für einen weltweiten geistigen Austausch auf dem Gebiet des Theaters einsetzt, Fragen nach den *Besucher-Organisationen* gestellt. Die größte ist die *Volksbühne*, die ihren 410.000 Mitgliedern in achtundneunzig örtlichen Vereinigungen durch öffentliche Subventionen verbilligte Plätze zu einem Durchschnittspreis von drei Mark zur Verfügung stellt. Bei rund zehn Vorstellungen je Mitglied in der Saison fließen den Theatern aus dieser Quelle jährlich rund zwölf Millionen DM zu. Nicht diese Ausmaße besitzen die *Theatergemeinden*, christlich bestimmte Besucher-Organisationen, die vor allem im Rheinland einen größeren Einfluß besitzen. Ein anderer Weg zu ermäßigten Eintrittskarten sind die schon früher allgemein üblichen örtlichen Abonnements. Einen direkten Spielplan-Einfluß üben die organisierten Besucherschichten fast nirgendwo aus, wohl aber einen beratenden. Außerdem wird die Sicherung, die sie durch feste Abnahme gerade problematischen Werken der Moderne bieten, von den Theatern sehr geschätzt.

*

Wo liegen heute die *Schwerpunkte des deutschen Schauspiel-Theaters*? Die Bühnen der Hauptstadt *Berlin* sind auf dem Wege zu neuer Weltgeltung. Der Intendant BOLESLAW BARLOG leitet die beiden städtisch subventionierten Schauspielhäuser, das 1951 eröffnete, wieder aufgebaute Schiller-Theater und das kleine Schloßpark-Theater. Er hat aus dem Reservoir der ehemaligen Staatstheater ein Ensemble gebildet, mit dessen Reichtum an Charakterschauspielern und vorzüglichen Chargen, mit dessen Ensemblegeist wenige deutsche Bühnen sich messen können. Die alljährlichen SCHILLER-Aufführungen zu Beginn der Berliner Festwochen im Herbst, für deren Regie meistens der Darmstädter Intendant GUSTAV RUDOLF SELLNER nach Berlin kommt, BARLOGs Inszenierungen ganz aus dem Ensemble heraus wie die des „Fuhrmann Henschel" von GERHART HAUPTMANN oder die gegenwartsnahen Wiederausgrabungen von Dramatik der zwanziger Jahre durch den Oberspielleiter HANS LIETZAU, sind einige Pluspunkte dieser Bühnen. Die stärksten schauspielerischen Magneten sind hier die Gäste HERMINE KÖRNER und MARIANNE HOPPE, die junge JOHANNA V. KOCZIAN, MARTIN HELD, der trotz lockenden Filmangeboten dem Theater treu bleibt, WILHELM BORCHERT und KLAUS KAMMER.

Das der Freien Volksbühne gehörende Theater am Kurfürstendamm, das in der Saison 1958/59 von LEONARD STECKEL geleitet wurde, spielt *ensuite*

[1] Berlin-Halensee, Kurfürstendamm 72.

jede seiner Produktionen zwei Monate lang. Dem früheren Direktor, OSCAR FRITZ SCHUH, gelang eine Abschiedsinszenierung von EUGENE O'NEILLS „Fast ein Poet", die doppelt so lange hätte laufen können. Denn hier vereinigte des Ehepaar PAULA WESSELY und ATTILA HÖRBIGER sich zu einzigartigem Spiel. Das war großartiges Schauspielertheater, gebändigt von einem Regisseur, der an die Stelle der Emotion die Demonstration setzen will. Sehr gepflegte Boulevard-Theater, die unternehmungslustige kleine Tribüne und das volkstümliche Hebbel-Theater an der Sektorengrenze sind weitere Akzente im Westberliner Bild.

Berlin ist für den ausländischen Besucher noch aus einem anderen Grunde wichtig: als Klammer zur sogenannten DDR. Obwohl das Ostberliner Theater dem in der sogenannten DDR turmhoch überlegen ist, kann der aufmerksame Beobachter doch auch hier die ganze Öde eines völlig politisierten, zu einem Instrument in der Hand der Machthaber herabgewürdigten Theaters studieren. Die Aushängeschilder drüben aber sind WALTER FELSENSTEINS „Komische Oper", das von BRECHTS Witwe, HELENE WEIGEL, geleitete „Berliner Ensemble", das zwar ideologisch treu auf dem Boden des Marxismus steht, aber in seinem Darstellungsstil meilenweit vom geforderten „sozialistischen Realismus" entfernt ist, und einige vor allem musikalisch hochwertige Aufführungen in der wiederaufgebauten Staatsoper Unter den Linden.

*

Die Hansestadt *Hamburg* hat mit der Verpflichtung des einstigen Berliner Staatstheater-Intendanten GUSTAF GRÜNDGENS, der seit 1955 das dortige Deutsche Schauspielhaus leitet, sich den großen Zauberer gesichert. Er vereinigt in sich die Fähigkeiten eines virtuosen Schauspielers, genialen Regisseurs und diplomatisch geschickten Direktors. Seine Inszenierungen der beiden Teile von GOETHES „Faust", die er als atemberaubendes kosmisches Weltdrama szenisch verwirklicht hat, sind sensationelle Ereignisse der letzten Spielzeiten. Die akute Auseinandersetzung zwischen Forschung und Macht wurde in dem grüblerischen Faust WILL QUADFLIEGS und dem agilen Mephisto von GRÜNDGENS selber personifiziert.

Hamburger Theater ist nicht GRÜNDGENS allein. Durch gediegenes Ensemblespiel und einen abwechselungsreichen Spielplan zeichnet sich das Thalia-Theater aus. Die Kammerspiele zeigen sich entdeckerfreudig und haben in ihrer Direktorin IDA EHRE eine Schauspielerin von intensiver Ausdruckskraft. Das erste deutsche „Theater im Zimmer", von HELMUTH GMELIN 1948 in Hamburg gegründet, pflegt das intime Diskussionsstück von

SHAW bis ANOUILH, Unterhaltungsliteratur mit tieferer Bedeutung, und experimentiert erfolgreich mit älteren Kammerspielen.

*

Der Nachfolger von GRÜNDGENS am Schauspielhaus in *Düsseldorf* ist gleichfalls ein ehemals in Berlin tätiger Regisseur. KARLHEINZ STROUX hat sich viele Berliner in die elegante westdeutsche Stadt geholt und macht mit ihnen ein Theater der großen Namen mit einem geschickt zwischen Tradition und Moderne sich bewegenden Spielplan, von SCHILLER bis zu O'NEILL, von SHAKESPEARE bis zu EZRA POUND. Seine Stars sind der geniale Verwandlungskünstler WERNER KRAUSS, der als „König Lear" Triumphe feierte, der patriarchalische ERNST DEUTSCH, ein unnachahmlich weiser und reifer „Nathan", JOANA MARIA GORVIN und – in einer auch im Ausland gezeigten „Maria Stuart"-Inszenierung – HEIDEMARIE HATHEYER als leidenschaftliche schottische Königin und MARIA WIMMER als kluge Elisabeth.

*

Nicht minder rege ist das Theaterleben in *München*, in dem der eruptive Regisseur und Schauspieler FRITZ KORTNER eine führende Rolle spielt. Anti-Konvention steht auf seinem Panier bei jeder Klassiker-Inszenierung. Das Bayerische Staatsschauspiel hat ihm mehrfach im Residenz-Theater Gelegenheit dazu gegeben. Die Leitung dieser führenden süddeutschen Bühne ist in der Saison 1958/59 von dem ehemaligen Wuppertaler Intendanten HELMUT HENRICHS übernommen worden. Ihre Lebendigkeit verdanken die Münchener Kammerspiele HANS SCHWEIKART, der die Talente eines Komödien-Schriftstellers, eines Dramaturgen mit der Witterung für anregend provokatorische Gegenwartsliteratur, eines wirkungssicheren Regisseurs und umsichtigen Direktors in einer Person vereinigt. Besonders verdienstvoll war unter anderem seine Uraufführung von KÄSTNERS „Schule der Diktatoren" als Vision einer dämonischen Utopie.

*

Die Städtischen Bühnen in *Frankfurt am Main* unter dem Intendanten HARRY BUCKWITZ entwickeln in einem behelfsmäßigen kleinen und dem als „Großes Haus" wiederaufgebauten früheren Schauspielhaus einen vielseitigen Spielplan unter besonderer Berücksichtigung der Zeitgenossen. Der Chefdramaturg Dr. GÜNTHER SKOPNIK und der Oberspielleiter HEINRICH KOCH spüren immer wieder neue und diskussionswerte Bühnenstücke aus Vergangenheit und Gegenwart auf.

*

Auch an den Württembergischen Staatstheatern in *Stuttgart* ist ein Dramaturg, Dr. ROLF BADENHAUSEN, der erste Berater des Intendanten Dr. WALTER ERICH SCHÄFER und zeichnet mitverantwortlich für ein Programm großer Klassiker- und wegweisender Aufführungen des musikalischen Theaters.

*

Ein repräsentatives neues Haus haben die Städtischen Bühnen in *Köln* erhalten. Zu ihrem Intendanten ist Prof. OSCAR FRITZ SCHUH ernannt worden, der 1958 Berlin verließ, um in dem gemischten Betrieb aus Oper und Schauspiel seine kühnen Besetzungspläne in einem größeren finanziellen Rahmen als ihm das Theater am Kurfürstendamm erlaubte, verwirklichen zu können.

*

Neu ist auch der moderne Bau des *Mannheimer* Nationaltheaters mit kleinem und großem Haus unter einem Dach sowie Verwandlungsmöglichkeiten von der Guckkasten- bis zur Raum- und Arenabühne. ERWIN PISCATOR, der „episches Theater" mit westlichen Vorzeichen machen will, hat hier für seine Experimente, die Rampe in raumhaften Szenerien auszulöschen und den Zuschauer direkt anzusprechen, den idealen Rahmen gefunden.

*

Noch viele andere Theater sollte derjenige besuchen, der das deutsche Theater kennen lernen will. Da sind vor allem SELLNERs Darmstädter Landestheater mit seinen mutigen Experimenten und erfrischenden Skandalen, HEINZ HILPERTs „Deutsches Theater" in Göttingen, das von dem einstigen Berliner Intendanten wie eine Enklave Berlins im Westen geführt wird mit atmosphäredichten Inszenierungen, die an HILPERTs Zeit im „Deutschen Theater" in Berlin bis 1944 erinnern, oder HANS SCHALLAS Bochumer Schauspielhaus, das mit seinen ebenso komödiantischen wie angriffsfreudigen Aufführungen von WEDEKIND bis BRECHT und SARTRE im Pariser „Théâtre des Nations" Aufsehen erregte, zu nennen. Aber die Liste der interessanten Bühnen ist damit längst nicht vollständig. Sie müßte noch mindestens Tübingen, Karlsruhe unter dem Intendanten PAUL ROSE, der früher das im Krieg zerstörte traditionsreiche Rose-Theater im Osten Berlins geleitet hat, Baden-Baden, Kassel, Wuppertal, das von Dr. KARL PEMPELFORT geleitete Theater der Stadt Bonn, Hannover, Braunschweig, Bremen und Lübeck enthalten. Ein besonderes Spezifikum der Nachkriegsjahre sind vor

*

allem die vielen experimentierfreudigen Keller- und Zimmerbühnen, die intimen Einraumtheater und Arenabühnen in Kammerspielformat, von denen der Bonner Contrakreis mit Spielfläche in der Mitte und 110 Plätzen besondere Erwähnung verdient.

Festspiele mit Schauspielprogramm haben in Deutschland erst als Nachkriegskinder das Licht der Welt erblickt. Weder Reize der Landschaft noch irgend eine künstlerische Tradition sind die Ursache der 1947 von den Gewerkschaften ins Leben gerufenen *Ruhrfestspiele in Recklinghausen.* Aus der ursprünglichen Begegnung von Künstlern und Bergleuten ist inzwischen ein Festival der geistigen Auseinandersetzung unter dem Motto von Kunst und Arbeit mit dem immer wieder spannenden Thema des Theaters und seiner Wirkungsmöglichkeiten in unserer Zeit geworden. Führende Regisseure inszenieren hier mit eigens zusammengestellten Festspiel-Ensembles Klassiker und Zeitgenossen. Dazu ergeben die Gastspiele deutschsprachiger Bühnen so etwas wie eine Theater-Olympiade, die sich an den arbeitenden Menschen aller Schichten wendet.

Ganz der Schönheit des Ortes sind die seit 1951 alljährlich unter der Schirmherrschaft des Bundespräsidenten veranstalteten Freilicht-Festspiele in der romanischen *Hersfelder* Klosterruine verpflichtet. Intendant JOHANNES KLEIN läßt hier vor den romanischen Bogen und einer herrlichen Naturkulisse bei nahezu idealer Akustik meist klassische Dramen in glanzvollen Besetzungen zur Aufführung gelangen. Den kulturpolitischen Akzent setzt die Nähe zur Zonengrenze.

Ein internationales Rendezvous der Künste in der einstigen Hauptstadt Deutschlands sind die gleichfalls seit 1951 jeweils zum Auftakt der Saison veranstalteten *Berliner Festwochen.* Die einheimischen Ensembles bringen repräsentative Inszenierungen sowie Ur- und Erstaufführungen in dieser Zeit heraus. Bühnen aus dem Bundesgebiet, aus Frankreich, Spanien, Italien, der Schweiz, England, Dänemark oder den USA kommen zu Gast nach Berlin und treten hier in einen künstlerischen Wettbewerb. Dabei bewegt sich das ganze Programm, das Theater, Oper, Ballett, Konzerte, bildende Kunst und Gespräche umfaßt, in einem ausgewogenen Rhythmus zwischen Tradition und Moderne. Diese Harmonie zu finden, im lebendigen Wechsel von Vergangenheit und Gegenwart, Erbe und neuer Gestalt, ist das Bestreben des gesamten Theaters in Deutschland.

RUNDFUNK, FILM, FERNSEHEN

I. DER RUNDFUNK

Bei Kriegsende (1945) war die Bevölkerung allein auf die Sender der Alliierten angewiesen. Die Besatzungsmächte übernahmen schließlich die vorhandenen Einrichtungen. Im Laufe der Zeit wurden auf Grund ihrer Anordnungen geschaffene Rundfunkorganisationen in deutsche Hände überführt und die Besatzungskontrolle schrittweise abgebaut. Die in diesen Jahren entstandene Organisation war an den Grenzen der Besatzungszonen orientiert, die keineswegs immer den stammes- und landschaftsgebundenen Besonderheiten entsprachen. Darüber hinaus bestimmten die unterschiedlichen Vorstellungen der Besatzungsmächte auch die Organisation und die Programmgestaltung. In der Amerikanischen Besatzungszone wurden der Bayerische Rundfunk, der Hessische Rundfunk, der Süddeutsche Rundfunk und Radio Bremen gegründet. In der Französischen Besatzungszone entstanden der Südwestfunk und die Saarländische Rundfunkverwaltung. Nach dem Vorbild der BBC erhielt die Britische Zone im Nordwestdeutschen Rundfunk (NWDR) eine einzige Rundfunkanstalt, die bis zur Errichtung des Senders Freies Berlin auch im Land Berlin Sender betrieb.

Mit Ausnahme der auch auf diesem Gebiet eigenen Entwicklung im Saarland hatten diese Organisationen eine äußerlich gemeinsame Rechtsform: die Anstalt des öffentlichen Rechts. Diese im Selbstverwaltungsrecht entwickelte und in vielen Bereichen bewährte Rechtsform war gewählt worden, um einerseits eine Abhängigkeit des Rundfunks vom Staat zu verhindern und anderseits einem Mißbrauch der technisch bedingten Monopolstellung vorzubeugen. Die festgelegte innere Verfassung, insbesondere die Zusammensetzung der Aufsichtsorgane, sollte die Gewähr dafür bieten, daß die für das öffentliche Leben bedeutsamen Organisationen und Gemeinschaften und mit ihnen die im „freien Raum" wirkenden Kräfte, nicht aber Regierungen, das Gesicht des Rundfunks bestimmten. So bestehen die oft als „Rundfunkparlamente" bezeichneten Rundfunkräte meist aus einer Vielzahl von Vertretern verschiedenster Organisationen. Der Rundfunkrat seinerseits wählt den für die Überwachung der laufenden Tätigkeit der Anstalt verantwortlichen Verwaltungsrat und dieser den Intendanten. Dem Intendanten obliegt die Leitung der gesamten Geschäftsführung einschließlich der Programmgestaltung.

In den Ländern des nord- und westdeutschen Raums gilt inzwischen eine andere Regelung. Der NWDR ist aufgelöst worden. Die Länder Hamburg,

Niedersachsen und Schleswig-Holstein haben den Nordeutschen Rundfunk errichtet, während im Land Nordrhein-Westfalen der Westdeutsche Rundfunk entstanden ist. Alle vier Länder haben den Nord- und Westdeutschen Rundfunkverband gegründet, dem vor allem die Gestaltung des Fernsehprogramms obliegt. Nach den für diese Länder getroffenen Regelungen ist es Sache der Landtage (in Hamburg der Bürgerschaft), die Mitglieder des Rundfunkrats zu berufen. Diese dürfen allerdings nur zu einem Teil den Parlamenten angehören.

Es besteht keine einheitliche Meinung zu der Frage, ob die für die Anstaltsverfassungen gefundenen Formen die mit ihrer Einrichtung verbundenen Erwartungen erfüllt haben. Die Befürworter meinen, das aus allgemeinen, gleichen, unmittelbaren, freien und geheimen Wahlen hervorgegangene Parlament sei der sicherste Garant für die Auswahl der Mitglieder der Auswahlgremien; darüber hinaus sei die Öffentlichkeit durch die verschiedensten Organisationen in besonders ausgewogener Weise repräsentiert. Von anderer Seite wird eingewandt, der Parteienproporz habe sich als unbrauchbares Mittel für die Wahrung der Überparteilichkeit erwiesen. Der Rundfunk sei ein Bestandteil der öffentlichen Ordnung, die zu sichern nicht zur Aufgabe der Legislative gehöre. Auch sei ein Großteil des Volkes nicht organisiert, so daß die Organisationen kein Spiegelbild der breiten Öffentlichkeit darstellten.

Als die Rundfunkanstalten in ihrer jetzigen Form mit Hilfe der damaligen Besatzungsmächte ins Leben traten, war die Bundesrepublik Deutschland noch nicht konstituiert. Die durch das Grundgesetz dem Bund zugewiesenen Aufgaben mußten im Rahmen des Erforderlichen von den Ländern wahrgenommen werden. Es ist deshalb nicht verantwortlich, daß die Belange des Gesamtstaats in dem damals geschaffenen Rundfunksystem nicht berücksichtigt worden sind.

Sehr bald nachdem der Bund ins Leben getreten war, wurden deshalb die ersten Versuche unternommen, den Belangen des Gesamtstaates durch eine Ergänzung der Rundfunk-Organisation Rechnung zu tragen. Die inzwischen in der „Arbeitsgemeinschaft der Öffentlich-rechtlichen Rundfunkanstalten der Bundesrepublik Deutschland" lose zusammengeschlossenen Anstalten übernahmen schließlich die Durchführung von Kurzwellensendungen nach Übersee, die Deutsche Welle, und die Ausstrahlung von Langwellensendungen für ganz Deutschland. Für die Sendungen der Deutschen Welle wird von vielen Seiten ein weiterer Ausbau dringend gefordert. Die Schwierigkeiten liegen nicht zuletzt im Fehlen einer eigenen Organisationsform mit selbständiger Rechtspersönlichkeit. Die Langwellensendungen sind unbestritten nur ein Behelf. Es fehlt an einer Frequenz, auf der ein Sender mit der erforderlichen Sendestärke arbeiten kann, ebenso wie an einer eigenständigen Organisation.

Die wirtschaftlichen Grundlagen der Rundfunkanstalten beruhen in erster Linie auf den Gebühreneinnahmen der Deutschen Bundespost, die durchschnittlich 80% der von den Tonrundfunkteilnehmern im einzelnen Anstaltsbereich aufgebrachten Gebühren an die jeweilige Rundfunkanstalt weiterleitet. Hier erweisen sich die teilweise ganz unsystematisch gezogenen Grenzen einzelner Anstaltsbereiche als besonders hemmend. Neben Rundfunkanstalten, die einen erheblichen Teil ihres Gebührenanteils für Rundfunkzwecke überhaupt nicht verwenden können, stehen Anstalten, deren Gebührenanteil bei weitem nicht ausreicht, um auch die notwendigsten Ausgaben zu decken.

Die in jüngster Zeit technisch möglich gewordene Ausstrahlung eines zweiten Fernsehprogramms hat die Frage auftauchen lassen, von wem dieses Programm gestellt werden soll. Mit den in einem anderen Abschnitt dieses Buchs behandelten Fernsehfragen besteht insofern ein innerer Zusammenhang, als der bundesgesetzlich festgelegte Begriff „Rundfunk“ als Oberbegriff den Ton- wie Fernsehrundfunk umfaßt; das Fernsehen hat sich dementsprechend auch innerhalb der für den Tonrundfunk geschaffenen Organisation entwickelt. Bei den Diskussionen über eine Neuordnung des Rundfunks spielt deshalb auch die Frage des Fernsehens eine wichtige Rolle.

Gegen Ende der Ersten Legislaturperiode wurde der Entwurf eines Rundfunkgesetzes von Abgeordneten mehrerer Fraktionen als Initiativantrag eingebracht, aber wegen des bevorstehenden Ablaufs der Legislaturperiode nicht mehr weiterverfolgt. In der Zweiten Legislaturperiode erarbeitete eine Bund-Länder-Kommission für Rundfunkfragen Entwürfe für einen Staatsvertrag mit mehreren Zusatzverträgen, die zwischen den Ländern und zwischen dem Bund und jedem einzelnen Land abgeschlossen werden sollten. Neben allgemeinen Vorschriften waren selbständige Organisationsformen für Kurzwellen-, Langwellen- und Fernsehsendungen vorgesehen. Es zeigte sich dabei, daß es kaum möglich ist, die Interessen von zehn, später elf gesetzgebenden Körperschaften des Bundes und der Länder sowie der entsprechenden Zahl von Regierungen im erforderlichen Maße aufeinander abzustimmen; auch hätten die Entwürfe jedenfalls im Bundestag die für eine Verabschiedung erforderliche Mehrheit nicht gefunden.

Bald nach Beginn der gegenwärtigen Legislaturperiode beauftragte die Bundesregierung den Bundesminister des Innern damit, dem Kabinett den Entwurf eines Bundesrundfunkgesetzes vorzulegen. Die Schwierigkeiten für das Gesetzgebungsverfahren liegen darin, daß die Länder dem Bund die Gesetzgebungsbefugnis auf weiten Gebieten des Rundfunks bestreiten. Obwohl die Bestimmungen der früheren Weimarer Reichsverfassung[1] von den entsprechenden Vorschriften des Grundgesetzes inhaltlich nicht abweichen, sind die Länder der Auffassung, daß die im Ganzen die Länder mehr begünstigende Grundtendenz des Grundgesetzes auch hier ihren Ausdruck

[1] Artikel 6 Nr. 7 und Artikel 88.

finde. Im übrigen habe der Begriff des Rundfunks einen verfassungsrechtlich zu beachtenden Bedeutungswandel vom Technischen zum Kulturellen erfahren. Da der Großteil der Zuständigkeit für den kulturellen Bereich bei den Ländern liege, sei der Bund mangels einer ausdrücklichen Regelung im Grundgesetz für die Gesetzgebung im Bereich des Rundfunks nicht zuständig. Die wissenschaftlichen Lehrmeinungen sind geteilt; während man in früheren Jahren von einer dem Standpunkt der Länder angenäherten Gesamtmeinung sprechen konnte, neigt die herrschende Meinung seit einigen Jahren wohl zunehmend dem Standpunkt des Bundes zu, der die Gesetzgebungs- und Verwaltungszuständigkeit auf dem Gebiete des Rundfunkwesens seinen Aufgaben entsprechend für sich beansprucht.

Bund und Länder sind sich darüber einig, daß die gegenwärtige Rundfunkorganisation vor allem deshalb nicht befriedigend ist, weil sie den Belangen des Gesamtstaates nicht hinreichend Rechnung trägt. Das Fehlen eines Überseerundfunks, der seine großen Wirkungsmöglichkeiten voll ausnutzen kann, wird als empfindliche Lücke empfunden. Als besonders schmerzlich wird von allen Seiten die Tatsache angesehen, daß für die siebzehn Millionen Deutschen in der sogenannten DDR nur unzureichende Möglichkeiten bestehen, sich über die Verhältnisse im freien Teil des Landes objektiv zu unterrichten. Der Rundfunk ist das einzige Mittel dazu, mit den Deutschen jenseits des Eisernen Vorhangs auf breiter Basis Verbindung zu halten und sie am Geschehen der Freien Welt teilnehmen zu lassen. Die Lösung dieser Fragen im Zusammenhang mit der Organisation eines zweiten Fernsehprogramms gehört zu den wichtigen Aufgaben des Deutschen Bundestages in seiner gegenwärtigen Legislaturperiode. Es ist zu hoffen, daß die Erörterungen zwischen Bund und Ländern bald zu einer alle Teile befriedigenden Lösung führen.

*

Das Bild des deutschen Rundfunks seit 1945 wäre unvollkommen gezeichnet, wenn man nicht auch die technischen Probleme und die Programmfragen kurz ansprechen würde.

Die Rundfunksendeanlagen, die bis Kriegsende im Eigentum der Deutschen Reichspost standen und in reichseigener Verwaltung betrieben wurden, sind im Jahre 1945 in das Eigentum der einzelnen Rundfunkanstalten übergegangen. Diese betreiben auch die Sender, und zwar auf Grund von Sendegenehmigungen des Bundesministeriums für das Post- und Fernmeldewesen. Die der Bundesrepublik Deutschland zugewiesenen Mittelwellen reichen nicht aus, um innerhalb der gegenwärtigen Organisation einen störungsfreien

Empfang zu gewährleisten. Die Deutsche Bundespost und die Rundfunkanstalten haben deshalb sehr bald nach Kriegsende ein dichtes Netz von Ultrakurzwellensendern mit den entsprechenden Verbindungsleitungen errichtet und auf diese Weise die Rundfunkversorgung der Bevölkerung sichergestellt. Dieses System hat sich so sehr bewährt, daß auch andere europäische Länder es übernehmen und die guten Empfangsbedingungen der Ultrakurzwellen auf breiter Basis verwerten möchten. Die Vorteile werden allgemein als so groß anerkannt, daß die hohen Investitionskosten in Kauf genommen werden.

Die verhältnismäßig große Anzahl der Rundfunkanstalten bringt es mit sich, daß die Programme des deutschen Rundfunks recht vielgestaltig sind. Auch strahlt jede Rundfunkanstalt in den Hauptempfangszeiten auf Mittel- und Ultrakurzwelle jeweils verschiedene Programme aus. Die Vielgestaltigkeit der Interessen und des Bildungsgrades der Tonrundfunk-Teilnehmer kann so in besonderem Maße berücksichtigt werden. Einzelne Rundfunkanstalten strahlen zu bestimmten Tageszeiten auch noch ein drittes Programm aus, das sich vor allem an anspruchsvollere Teilnehmer am Tonrundfunk wendet. So ist auf dem Gebiet der Programmgestaltung seit 1945 eine sorgfältige und im allgemeinen erfolgreiche Arbeit geleistet worden. Leider können die Rundfunkteilnehmer nur sehr unzureichend von diesen vielgestaltigen Möglichkeiten der Unterrichtung, Belehrung und Unterhaltung Gebrauch machen. Die Störungsempfindlichkeit der Mittelwellen und die geringe Reichweite der Ultrakurzwellen erlauben keinen weiträumigen Empfang und verweisen den Rundfunkteilnehmer im wesentlichen auf die Sender in der Umgebung des Empfangsgeräts. Die Bundesrepublik erhofft unter diesen Umständen von der nächsten Wellenplan-Konferenz eine angemessene Berücksichtigung ihrer Belange.

Die Teilnehmerdichte spricht dafür, daß der deutsche Rundfunk auch unter den schwierigen Bedingungen der Nachkriegszeit eine von der Bevölkerung anerkannte Arbeit geleistet hat. Als vollendet und allgemein zufriedenstellend kann die Gestaltung des deutschen Rundfunks allerdings erst dann angesehen werden, wenn die oben erwähnten organisatorischen und technischen Maßnahmen getroffen und durchgeführt sind.

Mit der Zahl von 15,593 Millionen Tonrundfunkteilnehmern (Stand: 1.6.1959) dürfte der Sättigungsgrad nahezu erreicht sein.

II. DIE ENTWICKLUNG DES NACHKRIEGSFILMS

Der Film ist eines der größten Unterhaltungsmittel unserer Zeit. Seine wirtschaftliche Rolle ist unbestritten. Er bildet aber zugleich ein Stück nationaler Repräsentanz im kulturellen Bereich und stellt eines der bedeutendsten Instrumente der Volksbeeinflussung im Guten wie im Bösen dar. Alle diese Seiten des komplexen Verhältnisses, in dem Film und Öffentlichkeit zueinander stehen, müssen bei der Darstellung der Verhältnisse im deutschen Filmwesen berücksichtigt werden. Will man die Entwicklung des deutschen Films in der Nachkriegszeit verstehen, so muß man sich zunächst die bis 1945 bestehende Situation auf diesem Gebiet vergegenwärtigen. Vor allem in den zwanziger Jahren hatte der deutsche Film sich Weltgeltung verschafft. Er war ein bedeutender Exportartikel. Natürlich gab es auch damals eine Fülle anspruchsloser Filme. Jedoch haben es Spitzenfilme, wie — um nur einige zu nennen — „Das Cabinet des Dr. Caligari", „Der Golem", „Die Nibelungen", „Geheimnisse einer Seele", „Dr. Mabuse", „Der letzte Mann" und die Masse der guten Unterhaltungsfilme dazu gebracht, daß ein erheblicher Teil des Einspiel-Ergebnisses für deutsche Filme im Ausland lag.

Auf filmwirtschaftlichem Gebiet ist für diese Zeit vor allem die UFA (*Universum Film A.G.*) zu nennen. Auf staatliche Anregung zurückgehend, entwickelte sie sich zu einem der größten Filmkonzerne. Die Stärke der UFA bestand vor allem darin, daß sie alle Sparten der Filmwirtschaft — Atelierbetrieb, Produktion, Verleih und Theater — in sich vereinigte. Durch diese vertikale Verbindung war ein wesentlicher Ausgleich des Risikos gegeben.

In der nationalsozialistischen Zeit ging die Filmwirtschaft durch Ankauf der Gesellschaftsanteile in Reichseigentum über. Während des Krieges wurde sie unter der Dachgesellschaft UFA-Film GmbH. (UFI) zusammengefaßt. In künstlerischer Hinsicht litt der Film in dieser Epoche unter den direkt wie indirekt ausgeübten staatlichen Eingriffen und unter der Abwanderung namhafter Künstler und Regisseure ins Ausland.

*

Nach dem Kriege hatte die Filmwirtschaft zunächst aufgehört zu existieren. Die Besatzungsmächte hatten das reichseigene Filmvermögen, von dem ein Großteil in der Sowjetischen Besatzungszone lag, beschlagnahmt und Treuhändern mit dem Ziel der Reprivatisierung unterstellt. Der Filmmarkt wurde vom ausländischen Film beherrscht. An deutschen Filmen wurden lediglich einige Reprisen zugelassen.

Es galt, eine neue geistige und wirtschaftliche Grundlage zu finden. Beide sind gerade beim Film eng miteinander verknüpft. Vor allem in Not- und Aufbauzeiten besteht die Versuchung, die geistig-künstlerischen Ansprüche beim Film wirtschaftlichen Erwägungen zu opfern.

Der Aufbau ging langsam vor sich. Zunächst war er immer noch behindert durch die Einschränkungen, die sich für Produzenten, Verleih, Theater und Schauspieler durch das von den Besatzungsmächten vorgeschriebene *Lizenzsystem* ergaben. So wurden 1946 ein Spielfilm, 1947 neun, 1948 dreiundzwanzig und 1949 zweiundsechzig Spielfilme produziert. Nach Aufhebung des Lizenzsystems entstand eine neue Schwierigkeit. Da die Besatzungsmächte sich gegen eine Zusammenballung wirtschaftlicher Macht auf dem Gebiete des Films wandten, wurde eine Unzahl von Produktions- und Verleihfirmen gegründet. Sie wurden oft von branchefremden Personen geleitet und waren in härtestem Konkurrenzkampf unter ungünstigen Voraussetzungen nicht in der Lage, die wirtschaftlichen Schwierigkeiten zu überwinden. Im Jahre 1950 entschlossen sich Bund und Länder, in großem Umfang *Filmbürgschaften* zu übernehmen. Diese Bürgschaftsaktion, die bis zum Jahre 1956 durchgeführt wurde, hat die Filmwirtschaft vor dem Ruin bewahrt und es ermöglicht, die Keime eines neuen Wirtschaftsgefüges am Leben zu erhalten. Eine gewisse Stabilisierung wurde erreicht. Trotzdem hatte die Filmwirtschaft noch weiter schwer zu kämpfen.

Das Aufnahmevolumen des deutschen Filmmarktes ist trotz der beachtlichen Zahl der Filmtheater, die von 1.150 (Sitzplätze: 402.000) im Jahre 1945 auf 6.577 (Sitzplätze: 2.739.615) Ende 1957 gestiegen ist, wie das jedes Marktes beschränkt. Durch die *Liberalisierung* des deutschen Marktes für ausländische Filme wurde das Volumen weitgehend von diesen in Anspruch genommen. Der Verleihumsatz betrug beispielsweise im Jahre 1957: 361,2 Millionen DM. Hiervon entfielen auf den deutschen Film nur 172,2 Millionen DM. Der geringe Anteil der deutschen Filme (ohne Reprisen) an den insgesamt gespielten Filmen ergibt sich aus folgender Übersicht:

Verleihangebot	1951/52	1952/53	1953/54	1954/55	1955/56	1956/57	1957/58
insgesamt	440	417	454	484	496	480	553
darunter Ausland.	375	339	350	374	372	363	446

Von den ausländischen Filmen stellen die USA mit über 200 Filmen jährlich (1957/58: 233) den größten Anteil. Es folgen Frankreich mit siebenundsechzig, das Vereinigte Königreich mit neunundvierzig und Italien mit siebenunddreißig Filmen im Jahre 1957/58.

Demgegenüber ist es noch nicht gelungen, aus dem Export deutscher Filme nennenswerte Einnahmen zu erzielen. Die Einnahmen aus dem Export amerikanischer Filme nach Deutschland betrugen zum Beispiel im Jahre 1957: 57 Millionen DM. Hingegen erreichten die Einnahmen für deutsche Filme, die nach den Vereinigten Staaten exportiert wurden, nur 208.000 DM.

Weiter ist die Abspielbasis gegenüber der Vorkriegszeit stark verringert. Zwar hat der Kinobesuch sich wesentlich erhöht. Die Zahl der Kinobesucher stieg von 300 Millionen im Jahre 1946 auf 801 Millionen im Jahre 1957. Das entspricht einem durchschnittlichen Filmbesuch von 15,1 je Kopf der Bevölkerung. Dieser Erhöhung steht jedoch eine beträchtliche Steigerung der Ausgaben gegenüber. So liegen die Herstellungskosten für einen Schwarzweiß-Spielfilm, von wenigen Ausnahmen abgesehen, bei mindestens einer Million DM. Dazu kommt, daß die Einnahmen sich auf wesentlich mehr Betriebe verteilen.

HERSTELLUNG VON SPIELFILMEN

Jahr		Jahr	
1950	82	1955	128
1951	60	1956	123
1952	82	1957	106
1953	104	1958	114
1954	109		

Die deutsche Filmwirtschaft ist auch heute noch nicht saniert. Die Filmproduktion hat sich zwar weiter erhöht (siehe die Tabelle). Die Zunahme ist jedoch weniger ein Zeugnis wirtschaftlicher Stabilisierung als der Ausdruck eines durch die Zersplitterung bedingten scharfen Konkurrenzkampfes. Der sich anbahnende Prozeß der Konzentration, der vor allem durch die Neugründung der UFA gekennzeichnet ist, kann zur Gesundung führen. Die neue UFA ist im Jahre 1956 entstanden, als ein Großteil des ehemaligen reichseigenen Filmvermögens durch ein vor allem aus Banken bestehendes Käufergremium erworben wurde. Bei ihr ist wiederum die vertikale Verbindung durchgeführt, die einleitend bei der früheren UFA erwähnt wurde.

Auch beim Filmexport, der von der Bundesregierung eine finanzielle Förderung erfährt, beginnt ein Aufschwung sich abzuzeichnen. Erfolge wurden vor allem in südamerikanischen Ländern sowie in Belgien und den Niederlanden erzielt. Die steigende Zahl der Gemeinschafts-Produktionen und die Verpflichtung ausländischer Stars für deutsche Filme stellen einen Versuch dar, den deutschen Film wieder in den Weltmarkt einzuführen.

Schon warten jedoch, wie in anderen Ländern, auf die Filmwirtschaft neue Schwierigkeiten. Sie steht in Auseinandersetzung mit dem Fernsehen. Der seit 1957 einsetzende Besucherrückgang um 2% gegenüber dem Vorjahr und von 6% im Ersten Halbjahr 1958 wird vor allem auf diesen Konkurrenten zurückgeführt. Die zwischen der Filmwirtschaft und den Fernsehanstalten sich anbahnenden Gespräche lassen jedoch hoffen, daß die wünschenswerte und für beide tragbare Abgrenzung der Interessen gefunden werden kann.

*

Die Entwicklung des Films als eines kulturellen Faktors ist ebenso wie sein wirtschaftliches Schicksal durch die Cäsur des Jahres 1945 gekennzeichnet. Der schon angedeuteten Versuchung, den wirtschaftlichen Niedergang durch vorbehaltlose Konzessionen an den vermeintlichen Geschmack des Publikums möglichst rasch zu überwinden, wurde durch die geistige Situation der Nachkriegszeit Vorschub geleistet.

Die geistigen Kräfte hatten Mühe, aus der Katastrophe heraus sich neu zu entfalten. Der Kampf um die bloße Existenz, bedingt durch die Not der ersten Nachkriegszeit, ließ kaum eine schöpferische Tätigkeit zu. So war denn auch zunächst der deutsche Nachkriegsfilm im allgemeinen unbefriedigend. Von geringen Ausnahmen abgesehen, war er durch Flucht in die Unwirklichkeit, in den „Klamauk" und die Rührseligkeit gekennzeichnet, die jede künstlerische Intuition vermissen ließen. Der deutsche Film ist auch später und bis in die Gegenwart hinein noch stark im Schablonenhaften stecken geblieben, wofür vor allem die sogenannten Heimatfilme als Beispiel dienen können.

Die Bundesregierung hat den Versuch unternommen, durch die Auszeichnung wertvoller Filme mit dem *Deutschen Filmpreis* einen Ansporn zu schaffen, bei der Produktion von Filmen nicht allein an das Geschäft zu denken, sondern auch dem künstlerischen Wollen und Können Ausdruck zu geben. Der Deutsche Filmpreis wird seit dem Jahre 1951 für Filmwerke und Einzelleistungen auf dem Gebiet des Filmschaffens vergeben. Seit 1955 ist er mit namhaften Geldprämien in Höhe von insgesamt 750.000 DM verbunden. Seit 1953 werden die Auszeichnungen anläßlich der *Internationalen Filmfestspiele in Berlin* verliehen. Diese international anerkannte Veranstaltung wird von der Bundesregierung und dem Senat von Berlin gemeinsam gefördert. Sie ist in jedem Jahr das glanzvollste Ereignis auf dem Gebiet des Films und ein Treffpunkt der Filmschaffenden des In- und Auslandes. Wenngleich der Deutsche Filmpreis bisher in keinem Jahre in vollem Umfang vergeben werden konnte, dürfte doch auf künstlerischem Gebiet der Tiefstand der ersten Nachkriegsjahre überwunden sein. Sicher gibt es nur wenige Filme wie „Nachtwache", „Weg ohne Umkehr", „Der Hauptmann von Köpenick" und „Nachts wenn der Teufel kam". Diese wenigen zeigen jedoch, daß schöpferische Kräfte vorhanden und zu bedeutenden Leistungen befähigt sind, wenn die Voraussetzungen dafür durch den Produzenten geschaffen werden. Eine große Anzahl der ausgezeichneten Filme bezeugt auch die Kraft zur geistigen Auseinandersetzung mit den Zeitproblemen, die im deutschen Film sonst noch wenig geübt wird. Ein Ansatzpunkt für eine Niveausteigerung wird vor allem in der Forderung des Publikums nach dem besseren Film liegen. Durch die Arbeit der Filmklubs und der Landesfilmdienste, die ebenfalls durch die Bundesregierung gefördert werden, ist das Verständnis für den guten Film in breiten Kreisen geweckt und verstärkt worden.

Der Verbreitung des guten Films dient schließlich in wirkungsvoller Weise die Senkung der Vergnügungssteuer auf Grund von Prädikaten, die von der *Filmbewertungsstelle* in Wiesbaden verliehen werden.

Die Entwicklung des deutschen *Kultur- und Dokumentarfilms* in den Nachkriegsjahren zeigt ein etwas günstigeres Ergebnis. Dieser Bereich, in dem der deutsche Film einstmals führend war, lag nach 1945 ebenfalls vollkommen darnieder. Bald setzte jedoch eine Flut von Produktionen ein. Während es in den Jahren 1952 bis 1954 noch jeweils 260 bis 300 Kulturfilme waren, wurden 1955 bis 1958 zwischen 400 und 485 derartiger Filme im Jahr hergestellt. Zunächst war auch hierbei eine Flucht ins Klischee und ein allgemeiner Zug zur minderen Qualität zu beklagen, die den Zuschauer sowohl der Langeweile als auch der Peinlichkeit des falschen Pathos' aussetzten. Die Maßnahmen der Bundesregierung zur Förderung wertvoller Kulturfilme haben hier mehr als bei den Spielfilmen zu einer Qualitätssteigerung geführt. Alljährlich werden bei der *Mannheimer Kultur- und Dokumentarfilmwoche*, der bedeutendsten Veranstaltung für den in- und ausländischen Kulturfilm in der Bundesrepublik, Urkunden über die Auszeichnung besonders wertvoller Kulturfilme durch Geldprämien im Gesamtbetrag von 600.000 DM aus Mitteln zur Filmförderung des Bundesministeriums des Innern überreicht.

Die selbständige Bedeutung, die der Kulturfilm früher einmal für den Zuschauer hatte, wurde noch nicht erreicht. Oft wird der Kulturfilm in den Filmtheatern nur eingesetzt, um durch sein Prädikat eine Senkung der Vergnügungssteuer herbeizuführen. Er hat jedoch wieder Eingang in das Filmtheater gefunden, und das ist schon ein Erfolg.

Das *Wochenschau-Monopol* hatten die Besatzungsmächte bis zu Beginn des Jahres 1950 voll in Anspruch genommen. Die Lichtspieltheater waren verpflichtet, eine Wochenschau vorzuführen, die von den Besatzungsmächten oder in ihrem Auftrag hergestellt worden war. Für die Britische und Amerikanische Besatzungszone war die Wochenschau „Welt im Bild" obligatorisch, während in der französischen Besatzungszone „Blick in die Welt" vertrieben wurde. Das im Dezember 1949 gegründete erste deutsche Wochenschauunternehmen, die „*Neue Deutsche Wochenschau GmbH.*", nahm 1950 die Produktion auf. Diese Wochenschau hat die Aufgabe, den Zuschauer in objektiver Weise mit dem Geschehen der Zeit vertraut zu machen und die Öffentlichkeit über die demokratischen Einrichtungen und die staatliche Entwicklung in Deutschland laufend zu unterrichten. Die NDW GmbH. gibt heute zwei Wochenschau-Ausgaben unter den Titeln „Neue Deutsche Wochenschau (NDW)" und „UFA" heraus. Sie versorgt mit ihren Ausgaben etwa 60% des Lichtspieltheater-Marktes. Die Wochenschau „Blick in die Welt" ist inzwischen als privatwirtschaftlich geführtes Unternehmen tätig und wird im ganzen Bundesgebiet vermietet. Daneben erscheint die dem 20th-Century-Fox-Konzern angegliederte „Fox tönende Wochenschau", die ihren Produktionssitz in München hat.

Die Wochenschau ist diejenige Filmsparte, die vom Inhalt her am meisten von der Konkurrenz des Fernsehens betroffen ist. Die Tagesschau des Fernsehens übertrifft die Wochenschau an Aktualität und beraubt sie daher ihrer eigentlichen Aufgabe. Zwar wünscht auch heute noch ein großer Prozentsatz aller Kinobesucher, die Wochenschau zu sehen. Mit zunehmender Verbreitung des Fernsehens wird die Wochenschau jedoch sich inhaltlich umgestalten müssen, um weiterhin ein wirtschaftlich lohnendes Interesse zu finden.

Die Entwicklung des deutschen Nachkriegsfilms wäre ohne Erwähnung der *Freiwilligen Selbstkontrolle der Filmwirtschaft* (FSK) nicht erschöpfend dargestellt. Sie ist als ein Organ der Selbstverwaltung der Spitzenorganisation der Filmwirtschaft 1949 gegründet worden, nachdem die Besatzungsmächte auf ihre Zensurbefugnisse verzichtet hatten und eine staatliche Zensur durch das Grundgesetz der Bundesrepublik ausgeschlossen worden war. Den Prüfungsausschüssen der Freiwilligen Selbstkontrolle gehören Vertreter der Filmwirtschaft, der Kirchen, der Jugendverbände und Vertrauensleute der öffentlichen Hand, jedoch keine weisungsgebundenen Beamten an. Die Freiwillige Selbstkontrolle übt keine Geschmackszensur aus, sondern begutachtet die Filme nach von ihr selbst aufgestellten Richtlinien und prüft sie außerdem auf ihre Eignung für die Jugend. Ihren Entscheidungen unterwirft sich die Filmwirtschaft freiwillig. So leistet die FSK durch Verhinderung negativer Einflüsse auf sittlichem, religiösem und politischem Gebiet einen wichtigen Beitrag zur Gewährleistung einer unteren Niveaugrenze.

III. DAS FERNSEHEN

Am 22. 3. 1935 wurde in Berlin ein Fernsehprogrammdienst aufgenommen. Es war der erste in der Welt. An drei Abenden in der Woche wurde von 20.30 Uhr bis 22.00 Uhr das Programm ausgestrahlt. Durch Kriegseinwirkungen wurden die Sender zerstört.

Mit den Vorbereitungen für die Wiedereinführung des Fernsehens begann der damalige Nordwestdeutsche Rundfunk etwa Mitte 1950. Zum Teil griff er dabei auf die Erfahrungen zurück, die beim Berliner Fernsehen bis 1943 gesammelt worden waren. Nach zweijähriger Vorbereitungszeit wurde am 25.12.1952 das erste Fernsehprogramm der Bundesrepublik ausgestrahlt.

FERNSEHTEILNAHME

Stichtag	Fernseh-Rundfunk-Genehmigungen
1.4.1953	1.524
1.4.1954	21.722
1.4.1955	126.778
1.4.1956	392.926
1.4.1957	835.120
1.4.1958	1.513.258
1.1.1959	2.129.183

Quelle: Statistisches Bundesamt.

Träger der *Funkhoheit* ist der Bund. Die Rechte und Pflichten des Bundes auf dem Gebiete des Fernmeldewesens werden vom Bundesminister für das Post- und Fernmeldewesen wahrgenommen. Eine gesetzliche Neuordnung ist noch nicht geschaffen. Einheitlich geregelt wurde lediglich die organisatorische Grundform. Die heute bestehenden Rundfunk- und Fernsehanstalten haben die Form von Anstalten des öffentlichen Rechts. Sie obliegen dem einheitlichen Grundsatz, daß niemandem, auch nicht dem Staat, die Möglichkeit gegeben werden soll, die öffentliche Meinungsbildung durch Rundfunk oder Fernsehen zu beeinflussen. Es besteht also Unabhängigkeit auf dem Gebiete der Programmgestaltung.

Sieben Rundfunkanstalten, der Nordwestdeutsche Rundfunkverband (NDR und WDR) in Hamburg und Köln, der Bayerische Rundfunk (BR) in München, der Hessische Rundfunk (HR) in Frankfurt, der Süddeutsche Rundfunk (SDR) in Stuttgart, der Südwestfunk (SWF) in Baden-Baden und der Sender Freies Berlin (SFB) bestreiten seit dem 6. 1. 1954 ein *Gemeinschaftsprogramm „Deutsches Fernsehen"*. Seit 1958 beteiligt sich auch Radio Bremen gelegentlich am Gemeinschaftsprogramm. Die Zahl der Sender hat sich bis zum 1.1.1959 auf 27 Fernsehsender, 69 Umsetzer und 16 Umlenkantennen erhöht.

Um die Übertragung von Fernsehsendungen über weite Strecken hin zu ermöglichen, wurde 1951 mit dem Bau von *Dezimeter-Richtfunkstrecken* begonnen. Der Bau der Richtfunkstrecken wird von der Deutschen Bundespost durchgeführt, in deren Zuständigkeit auch der Betrieb fällt. Sie führen heute von Hamburg über Köln—Frankfurt am Main—Weinbiet—Hornisgrinde—Stuttgart nach München. Auf dieser Strecke bestehen die Abzweigungen Höhenbeck—Berlin(West), Mellendorf—Hannover, Ölberg—Bonn, Hornisgrinde—Baden-Baden. Als weitere Strecken sind Baden-Baden—Basel (Ütliberg), Köln—Lüttich, Köln—Mierlo (Holland), Hamburg-Bremen und Hamburg—Kiel 1956 in Betrieb genommen worden; ebenso die Kabelleitung München—Dillberg—Nürnberg, die Richtfunkstrecken Hamburg—Dänemark, München—Salzburg und Dabo (Frankreich)—Hornisgrinde. Bis auf die Verbindung mit Berlin(West) kann das Fernsehübertragungsnetz innerhalb der Bundesrepublik pausenlos umgeschaltet werden. Bei Übertragungen aus einem Lande anderer Zeilennorm werden Umwandler eingesetzt. Sie setzen die ausländischen Zeilennormen auf die in der Bundesrepublik verwandte Zeilennorm von 625 um und umgekehrt.

Die *Investitionen* für das Fernsehen werden auf 150 Millionen DM geschätzt. Der Anteil der Rundfunkanstalten ist den Einnahmen aus den Rundfunk- und Fernsehgebühren entnommen worden. Die Gebühren für Errichtung und Betrieb eines Fernsehanschlusses betragen monatlich 5 DM zusätzlich zu der Tonrundfunkgebühr von 2 DM.

Die durchschnittlichen *Kosten für eine Programmstunde* bemessen die Rundfunkanstalten (ohne Investitionen und Amortisation) heute mit etwa 35.000 DM. Diese beträchtlichen Erstellungskosten sind mit ein Grund für die vorläufige Programmbegrenzung. Zur Zeit wird (außer dem Werbe-Fernsehen) wöchentlich im Durchschnitt an fünfunddreißig Stunden gesendet. Diese Zahl erhöht sich häufig durch Übertragung von Sonderveranstaltungen (Bundestagsdebatten, Sportereignisse, kulturelle Darbietungen usw.). Die ständige Übertragung aktueller Ereignisse nimmt einen erheblichen Platz ein. Informationssendungen aus Politik, Wirtschaft und Kultur finden um ihres aktuellen und informativen Charakters willen hohes Interesse. Größter Beliebtheit erfreuen sich die Tagesschau, der Internationale Frühschoppen, die Übertragung von Sportereignissen, Fernsehspielen und Quizsendungen.

Die Leitung des Gemeinschaftsprogramms ist durch einen Fernsehvertrag einer „*ständigen Programmkonferenz*" überantwortet worden, in die Fernsehbeauftragte der einzelnen Rundfunkanstalten berufen wurden. Der Vorsitz wird aus der Reihe der Beauftragten gewählt und wechselt von Jahr zu Jahr. Die Anstalten sind am Programm des deutschen Fernsehens prozentual

FERNSEHDICHTE[1]

Fernseh-Rundfunkgenehmigungen auf 10.000 Einwohner

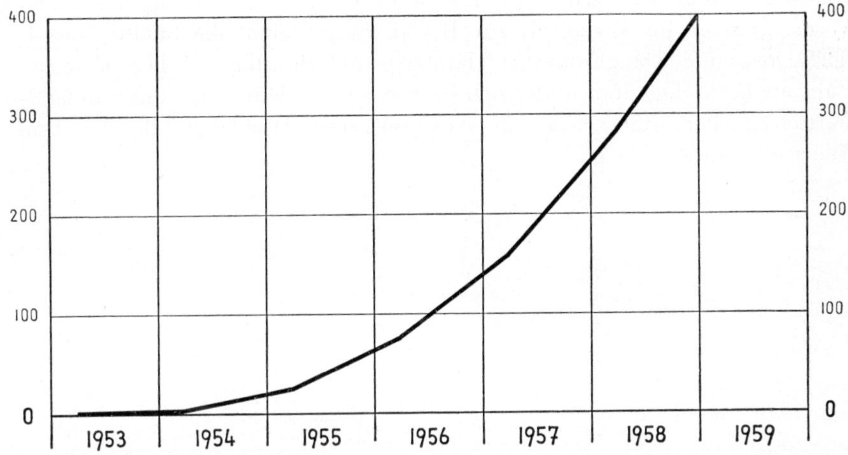

[1] Bundesrepublik Deutschland (ohne Saarland) einschließlich von Berlin(West). — Stand jeweils am 1.4.; 1959 Stand am 1.1. Quelle: Statistisches Bundesamt.

beteiligt. Nach dem festgesetzten Schlüssel bestreitet der NWDR 46% des Programmes der BR 18%, die vier übrigen Anstalten (SFB, SWF, SDR und HR) je 9%. Diese Aufschlüsselung bezieht sich nur auf das Abendprogramm, nicht auf die Gesamtsendezeit.

Alle deutschen Rundfunkanstalten außer Berlin(West) und Bremen senden zusätzlich ein tägliches Regionalprogramm von 30 bis 45 Minuten für den jeweiligen Sendebezirk. Seit November 1956 senden der Bayerische Rundfunk, seit Dezember 1956 der Sender Freies Berlin und seit 1958 auch andere Rundfunkanstalten ein halbstündiges *Werbeprogramm* aus, das sich auf den regionalen Raum dieser Sender beschränkt. Die Aufnahme eines „*zweiten Programms*", das als Hauptprogramm wahlweise neben dem ersten Hauptprogramm empfangen werden kann, wird erwogen. Eine gesetzliche Regelung wird angestrebt.

Für die Übertragung besonderer internationaler Ereignisse haben zwölf europäische Länder sich zur „*Eurovision*" zusammengeschlossen, dem westeuropäischen Austausch von Fernsehsendungen. An diesem Austausch sind achtzig Sender beteiligt.

Die Gesamtzahl der am 1.3.1959 in der Bundesrepublik (ohne Saarland) und in Berlin(West) angemeldeten Fernsehapparate betrug nach dem Ausweis des Bundespostministeriums 2.426.993. Die größte derzeitige Dichte an Fernsehgeräten im Verhältnis zur Bevölkerung weisen die Städte Düsseldorf, Dortmund, Köln, Frankfurt, Hamburg und Münster auf. Die geringste Zahl an Fernsehgeräten findet sich in stadtfernen Gemeinden der rein landwirtschaftlichen Räume, so in Niedersachsen, Westfalen, Bayern und Württemberg.

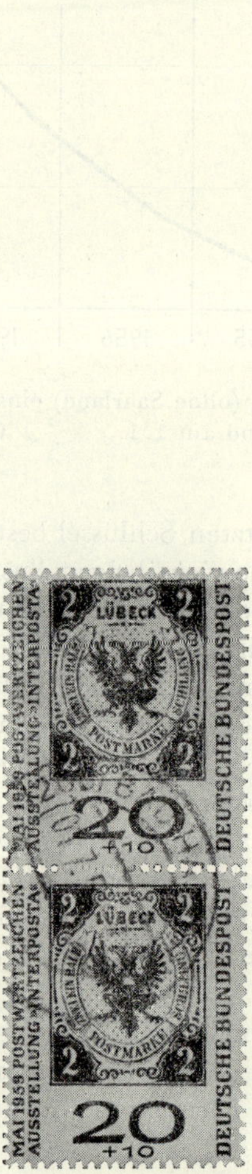

ZEITTAFEL[1]

I. WELTKRIEG BIS ZUM BITTEREN ENDE

> In dieser Zeit, wo Gewalttätigkeit, in Lüge gekleidet, so unheimlich wie noch nie auf dem Throne der Welt sitzt, bleibe ich dennoch überzeugt, daß Wahrheit, Liebe, Friedfertigkeit, Sanftmut und Gütigkeit die Gewalt sind, die über aller Gewalt ist. Ihnen wird die Welt gehören, wenn nur genug Menschen die Gedanken der Liebe, der Wahrheit, der Friedfertigkeit und der Sanftmut rein und stark und streng genug denken und leben. ALBERT SCHWEITZER

15. 3. 1939:
Unter Bruch des Münchner Abkommens läßt ADOLF HITLER die Tschechoslowakei besetzen und proklamiert das „Reichsprotektorat Böhmen und Mähren". Damit löst er eine entschiedene Politik des Widerstandes bei den Westmächten aus.

31. 3. 1939:
Garantie-Erklärung des Vereinigten Königreichs und Frankreichs für Polen.

23. 8. 1939:
Deutsch-sowjetischer Nichtangriffspakt.

1. 9. 1939:
Mit dem Einmarsch der Wehrmacht in Polen beginnt der *Zweite Weltkrieg*.

9. 4. 1940:
Besetzung von Dänemark; Angriff gegen Norwegen, das am 9.6.1940 kapituliert.

10. 5. 1940:
Angriff gegen die Niederlande, Luxemburg, Belgien und Frankreich (25.6.1940 Waffenruhe).

6. 4. 1941:
Feldzug gegen Jugoslawien (Kapitulation 17.4.1941) und Griechenland (21.4. 1941 Waffenruhe).

22. 6. 1941:
Kriegsbeginn gegen die Sowjetunion.

12. 8. 1941:
Der Präsident der USA und Premierminister CHURCHILL . . . hoffen, daß nach der endgültigen Zerstörung der Nazityrannei ein Friede geschaffen wird, der allen Nationen die Möglichkeit gibt, in Sicherheit innerhalb ihrer eigenen Grenzen zu leben, und der Gewähr dafür bietet, daß alle Menschen in allen Ländern der Welt ihr Leben frei von Furcht und Not leben können (*Atlantik-Charta*).

7. 12. 1941:
Japan beginnt den Krieg gegen die USA (*Pearl Harbour*).

[1] Die Texte stellen wörtliche Auszüge aus den betreffenden Verlautbarungen dar, aber nicht immer fortlaufende Satzfolgen.

7. 12. 1941:

„Nacht- und Nebel-Erlaß" (Befehl HITLERS, alle gegen das Reich oder die Besatzungsmacht straffällig gewordenen Personen in den besetzten Gebieten, sofern die Todesstrafe nicht binnen einer Woche ausgesprochen und vollstreckt werden konnte, in Konzentrationslager im Reichsgebiet zu überführen und über ihr Schicksal keine Auskünfte zu geben).

20. 1. 1942:

„Wannsee-Protokoll" (Richtlinien für die *Endlösung der Judenfrage*). Zur Vorgeschichte: HITLER vor dem Reichstag, 30.1.1939: „Vernichtung der jüdischen Rasse in Europa"; GÖRING an HEYDRICH, 31.7.1941: Vorbereitungen gemäß dem Führerbefehl über die physische Totalvernichtung der Juden.

24. 1. 1943:

Die Alliierten geben nach der Konferenz von Casablanca ihre Forderung auf *bedingungslose Kapitulation Deutschlands* bekannt.

31. 1. und 2. 2. 1943:

Kapitulation der Sechsten Armee in Stalingrad.

13. 5. 1943:

Kapitulation der deutschen Verbände in Nordafrika.

30. 10. 1943:

Nach der Außenministerkonferenz von Moskau erklären die Regierungschefs der USA, des Vereinigten Königreichs, der Sowjetunion und Chinas gemeinsam, daß ihr mit der Verpflichtung zur Führung des Krieges gegen ihre Feinde eingegangenes Zusammenwirken zum Zweck der Herbeiführung und Erhaltung von Frieden und Sicherheit fortgeführt werden wird.

1. 12. 1943:

Nach der Konferenz von Teheran erklären die Regierungschefs der USA, des Vereinigten Königreichs und der Sowjetunion:
Hinsichtlich des Friedens sind wir sicher, daß unsere Eintracht ihn zu einem dauernden machen wird. Wir erkennen in vollem Umfange die höchste Verantwortung, die wir und alle Vereinten Nationen tragen, einen Frieden herzustellen, der von dem guten Willen der überwältigenden Massen der Völker der Welt getragen werden und Geißel und Schrecken des Krieges für viele Generationen bannen wird.

6. 6. 1944:

Anglo-amerikanische Landung in der Normandie (die „*Invasion*").

15. 7. 1944:

Schreiben des Feldmarschalls ROMMEL an HITLER:
Die Lage an der Front der Normandie wird von Tag zu Tag schwieriger, sie nähert sich einer schweren Krise.
Die eigenen Verluste sind bei der Härte der Kämpfe, dem außergewöhnlich starken Materialeinsatz des Gegners, vor allem an Artillerie und Panzern, und bei der Wirkung der den Kampfraum unumschränkt beherrschenden feindlichen Luftwaffe derart hoch, daß die Kampfkraft der Divisionen rasch absinkt . . . Wie die Kämpfe gezeigt haben, wird bei dem feindlichen Materialeinsatz auch die

tapferste Truppe Stück für Stück zerschlagen . . . Auf der Feindseite fließen Tag für Tag neue Kräfte und Mengen an Kriegsmaterial der Front zu. Der feindliche Nachschub wird von unserer eigenen Luftwaffe nicht gestört. Der feindliche Druck wird immer stärker.

Ich muß Sie bitten, die Folgerungen aus dieser Lage unverzüglich zu ziehen.

20. 7. 1944:

Attentat der deutschen Widerstandsgruppe auf HITLER.

Sommer 1944:

Der Schatzsekretär der USA, HENRY MORGENTHAU, entwirft einen Plan für die Behandlung Deutschlands nach dem Kriege. Der Plan sieht unter anderem die Vernichtung der gesamten Schwerindustrie, die Schließung der Bergwerke im Ruhrgebiet und die drastische Reduzierung der leichten Industrie vor. Deutschland soll im wesentlichen in einen Agrarstaat mit leichten Zubringerindustrien umgewandelt werden. Im August 1944 erklärt Präsident ROOSEVELT sich entgegen den schweren Bedenken des Außenministers HULL und des Kriegsministers STIMSON für den Plan. Am 15. 9. 1944, auf der Zweiten Konferenz von Quebec, gibt der britische Premierminister CHURCHILL seine Zustimmung, wendet jedoch ein, man dürfe Großbritannien „nicht an eine Leiche ketten". Am 11. 2. 1945 erklären auf der Konferenz von Jalta die Sowjets ihre Übereinstimmung mit den Zielen des MORGENTHAU-Plans.

1. 1. 1945:

ADOLF HITLER im Rundfunk: Dieses Volk und dieser Staat und seine führenden Männer sind unerschütterlich in ihrem Willen und unbeirrbar in ihrer fanatischen Entschlossenheit, den Krieg unter allen Umständen erfolgreich durchzukämpfen, auch unter Inkaufnahme aller durch die Tücken des Schicksals uns auferlegten Rückschläge. Die Welt muß wissen, daß dieser Staat *niemals kapitulieren* wird.

11. 2. 1945:

Konferenz von Jalta (Krimkonferenz): Gemäß dem in gegenseitigem Einvernehmen festgelegten Plan werden die Streitkräfte der Drei Mächte je eine besondere Zone Deutschlands besetzen. Der Plan sieht eine koordinierte Verwaltung und Kontrolle vor . . . Es ist beschlossen worden, daß Frankreich aufgefordert werden soll, eine (vierte) Besatzungszone zu übernehmen.

Es ist nicht unsere Absicht, das deutsche Volk zu vernichten; aber erst nach Auslöschung des Nazitums und des Militarismus' wird für die Deutschen Hoffnung auf ein würdiges Leben und einen Platz in der Gemeinschaft der Nationen bestehen.

15. 3. 1945:

Denkschrift von Reichsminister SPEER:

Wir haben die Verpflichtung, dem *Volk* in den schweren Stunden, die es zu erwarten hat, zu helfen . . .

Wenn der Gegner das Volk und seine Lebensbasis zerstören will, dann soll er dieses Werk selbst durchführen. Wir müssen alles tun, um dem Volk, wenn vielleicht auch in primitivsten Formen, bis zuletzt eine *Lebensbasis* zu erhalten . . .

Es muß sichergestellt werden, daß, wenn der Kampf weiter in das Reichsgebiet vorgetragen wird, niemand berechtigt ist, Industrieanlagen, Kohlenbergwerke, Elektrizitätswerke und andere Versorgungsanlagen sowie Verkehrsanlagen, Binnenschiffahrtsstraßen usw. zu zerstören . . .

Wenn die Gegner . . . zerstören wollen, so soll ihnen diese geschichtliche Schande ausschließlich zufallen.

20. 3. 1945:

Hitlers Zerstörungsbefehl:
Alle militärischen, Verkehrs-, Nachrichten-, Industrie- und Versorgungsanlagen sowie Sachwerte innerhalb des Reichsgebiets, die der Feind für die Fortsetzung seines Kampfes irgendwie sofort oder in absehbarer Zeit sich nutzbar machen kann, sind zu zerstören.

29. 3. 1945:

Zerstörungsbefehl des OKW:
Das Ziel ist, im preisgegebenen Gebiet eine Verkehrswüste zu schaffen.

April 1945:

Direktive JC 1067 des US-Wehrmachtgeneralstabes an den Oberbefehlshaber der Besatzungstruppen der USA, General Eisenhower, über *die grundlegenden Ziele der Militärregierung in Deutschland.* Die Anweisung enthält wesentliche Elemente des Morgenthau-Plans.

30. 4. 1945:

Der „Führer" Adolf Hitler entzieht sich durch Selbstmord der Verantwortung.

1. 5. 1945:

Londoner Abkommen. Grundlegende Bestimmungen über die Organe, mittels derer die Besatzungsmächte ihre Befugnisse in Deutschland ausüben werden.

1. 5. 1945:

Proklamation des Großadmirals Dönitz: Meine erste Aufgabe ist es, deutsche Menschen vor der *Vernichtung durch den bolschewistischen Feind* zu retten. *Nur für dieses Ziel geht der militärische Kampf weiter.* Soweit und solange die Erreichung dieses Zieles durch die Briten und Amerikaner behindert wird, werden wir uns auch gegen sie weiter verteidigen und weiterkämpfen müssen. Die Anglo-Amerikaner setzen dann den Krieg nicht mehr für ihre eigenen Völker, sondern allein für die *Ausbreitung des Bolschewismus in Europa* fort.

2. 5. 1945:

Graf Schwerin von Krosigk, der als Reichsaußenminister fungiert, im Rundfunk: Auf den Straßen des noch unbesetzten Deutschlands zieht ein großer Strom verzweifelten und hungernden Volkes westwärts, verfolgt von Kampfbombern in ihrer Flucht vor einem unbeschreiblichen Terror. Im Osten rückt ein *eiserner Vorhang* unablässig vorwärts, hinter dem die Welt das vor sich gehende Zerstörungswerk nicht erkennen kann. In San Franzisko sind gleichzeitig Beratungen im Gange zur Organisation einer neuen Welt, die dazu bestimmt sein soll, der Menschheit Sicherheit vor einem neuen Krieg zu bringen . . .
Das deutsche Volk, seine gequälten Frauen und Mütter bitten zu Gott, daß der Welt ein neuer Krieg mit all seinen Schrecken erspart bleibe. Mit uns erwarten auch *alle anderen Völker Europas, die von Not und bolschewistischem Terror bedroht sind,* eine neue Ordnung, die diesem Kontinent einen wirklichen und dauerhaften Frieden und Möglichkeiten für ein freies und sicheres Leben bringt. Je mehr des deutschen Ostens in die Hand der Bolschewisten fällt, um so größer wird die Gefahr der Hungersnot in ganz Europa. Ein bolschewisiertes Europa ist der erste

Schritt zur Weltrevolution, nach der die Sowjets seit 25 Jahren streben... Die Menschheit sehnt sich nach einer Lösung der brennenden sozialen Fragen, die in jedem Lande bestehen. Eine solche Lösung kann aber nicht im Bolschewismus gefunden werden. Sie muß sich auf eine gerechte soziale Ordnung gründen, welche die Freiheit und Würde des Einzelnen wahrt. Wir glauben aufrichtig, einen Beitrag zu einer solchen Lösung leisten zu können. Die Welt steht gegenwärtig vor der größten Entscheidung, die sie jemals zu treffen hatte. Die Art der Entscheidung wird Chaos oder Ordnung, Krieg oder Frieden, Leben oder Tod zum Ergebnis haben.

2. 5. 1945:
Von offiziöser englischer Seite wurde bekanntgegeben, daß vorstehende Rede den denkbar schlechtesten Eindruck in englischen Regierungskreisen gemacht habe. Es sei unbegreiflich, daß die deutsche Diplomatie die einfachsten Dinge immer noch nicht begriffen habe und daran festhalte, man könne den *Bolschewismus als Schreckgespenst gegenüber Großbritannien und den Vereinigten Staaten* verwenden (Exchange-Meldung).

7. 5. 1945:
GRAF SCHWERIN VON KROSIGK im Rundfunk:
Die Regierung wurde infolge des Zusammenbruchs aller physischen und materiellen Kräfte gezwungen, das Ende der Feindseligkeiten zu verlangen.
Niemand darf sich hinsichtlich der Strenge der Bedingungen, die uns von unseren Feinden auferlegt werden, Illusionen hingeben.
Gehen wir mit Mut den uns vorgeschriebenen harten Weg und retten wir eines: *unsere nationale Einheit.* Nach der Ehre, die unsere Nation im heldenhaften Kampfe eingelegt hat, seien wir entschlossen, die wir zur Welt der christlichen Zivilisation im Westen gehören, unseren Beitrag zu den ehrenhaften Friedensbestrebungen zu bringen, was den besten Traditionen unserer Nation entspricht.

7.—8. 5. 1945:
Unterzeichnung der *bedingungslosen Kapitulation der Deutschen Wehrmacht* in Reims und Berlin-Karlshorst. Die nationalsozialistische Diktatur in Deutschland ist zu Ende.
Punkt 4 der Kapitulationsurkunde: Diese Kapitulationserklärung stellt kein Präjudiz für an ihre Stelle tretende allgemeine Kapitulationsbestimmungen dar, die durch die Vereinten Nationen oder in deren Namen festgesetzt und Deutschland und die Deutsche Wehrmacht als Ganzes betreffen werden.

9. 5. 1945:
Letzter Bericht des Oberkommandos der Wehrmacht:
Auf Weisung des Großadmirals (DÖNITZ) haben die deutschen Streitkräfte einen Kampf eingestellt, der aussichtslos geworden war.... Jeder Soldat kann nun die Waffen niederlegen und in diesen schwersten Stunden unserer Geschichte stolz zu seiner Arbeit zurückkehren für das ewige Leben des deutschen Volkes. Wir verneigen uns heute ehrfürchtig vor den gefallenen Kameraden. *Die Toten verpflichten uns zu stummem Gehorsam und zur Disziplin gegenüber dem Vaterlande, das aus unzähligen Wunden blutet.*

23. 5. 1945:

Das Alliierte Oberkommando gibt bekannt, daß Großadmiral DÖNITZ und alle Mitglieder der sogenannten ,,Dönitz-Clique", die sich bisher als Deutsche Regierung bezeichnete, als Kriegsgefangene in Gewahrsam genommen wurden.

2. 9. 1945:

Unterzeichnung der Kapitulation Japans nach dem Abwurf der Atombomben auf Hiroshima und Nagasaki.

Kölnischer Kurier

Dienstag, 14. August 1945

Herausgeber: Die britische Besatzungsbehörde / Zweimal wöchentlich

Verlag und Redaktion: Köln, Breite Straße 70. Fernsprech-Sammelnummer 54747. Verbreitungsgebiet: Der gesamte Regierungsbezirk Köln (Stadt und Landkreis Köln, Kreis Bergheim, Kreis Euskirchen, Stadt- und Landkreis Bonn, Kreis Siegburg, Oberbergischer Kreis, Rheinisch-Bergischer Kreis.)

Nummer 23
Verkaufspreis 20 Pf.

Vor dem Ende des Weltkrieges

Letzte Kämpfe

Die alliierten Befehlshaber an allen Fronten des ostasiatischen Kriegsschau-

Japans Kapitulation stündlich zu erwarten

Nach dem Abwurf von zwei Atombomben auf Hiroschima und Nagasaki und

Die Welt atmet auf

Fr. Köln, den 14. August 1945

Die Nachrichten überstürzen sich. Nachrichten voll atemraubender Spannung: Erfindung der Atombombe! Menschliche Wissenschaft dringt ein in die tiefsten Geheimnisse der Natur und legt Kräfte frei, deren Ausmaß bisher nur geahnt werden

Freitag, 17. August 1945

Herausgeber: ...

Verlag und Redaktion: Köln, Breite Straße 70. ... und Landkreis Köln, Kreis Bergheim, Kreis Euskirchen, Stadt- und ...

Die Waffen ruhen überall

... allen Fronten ... einzustellen. ... die amtliche japanische ... klärung ... sind, seitens ... ung und des kaiserlich ... Oberkommandos zu ermächtigen ... festzusetzen. 3. Seine Majestät ist ferner

... hat von General ... Befehl erhalten, sich in einem ... japanischen Flugzeug, das an den Tragflächen grüne Kreuze zeigen muß, nach der Insel Ie in der Nachbarschaft der Insel Okinawa zu begeben, wo sie von einem amerikanischen Flugzeug übernommen und nach Manila gebracht werden sollen.

Schluß mit allen Kriegen!

Feierliche Parlamentseröffnung in England

II. DIE DEUTSCHE STAATSGEWALT IN ALLIIERTER HAND

1945

5. 6. 1945:

Erklärung in Anbetracht der Niederlage Deutschlands und der *Übernahme der obersten Regierungsgewalt hinsichtlich Deutschlands* durch die Regierungen der Vier Mächte.

Feststellung seitens der Regierungen der vier Großmächte über das Kontrollverfahren in Deutschland: Einsetzung des *Alliierten Kontrollrats* mit Sitz in Berlin. Die Entscheidungen ,,über alle Deutschland als Ganzes betreffenden wesentlichen Fragen" müssen *einstimmig* getroffen werden.

Feststellung seitens der Regierungen der vier Großmächte über die *Besatzungszonen in Deutschland*. Gemeinsame Besetzung von Groß-Berlin; Einrichtung der *Komendatura*.

26. 6. 1945:

Gründung der Vereinten Nationen.

1. 7. 1945:

Die von Truppen der USA besetzten Länder Sachsen und Thüringen werden im Austausch für die Besetzung der drei westlichen Sektoren Berlins an die sowjetischen Behörden übergeben.

17. 7.—2. 8. 1945:

Konferenz von Potsdam. Das Potsdamer Abkommen bestimmt, bei der Organisation des deutschen Wirtschaftslebens das Hauptgewicht auf die Entwicklung der Landwirtschaft und der einheimischen für friedliche Zwecke arbeitenden Industrien zu legen. Als Richtschnur hierfür soll dienen, daß der Lebensstandard in Deutschland nicht höher sein dürfe als in dem Durchschnitt aller europäischen Länder, ausschließlich Großbritanniens und der Sowjetunion, aber einschließlich der süd- und osteuropäischen Länder. Deutschland soll die Produktion aller seetüchtigen Schiffe verboten werden. Die Produktion von Metallen, Chemikalien, Maschinen und „anderen Gütern, die für eine Kriegswirtschaft unmittelbar notwendig sind". soll einer strengen Kontrolle unterworfen bzw. demontiert oder zerstört werden. *Reparationen* sollen innerhalb von zwei Jahren in Sachwerten aus Deutschland entnommen werden. Reparationen sind Guthaben, Gold, Schiffe, Fabrikeinrichtungen und laufende Produktion. Kriegsbeute wird nicht zu den Reparationen gerechnet.

9. (IV): Bis auf weiteres wird keine zentrale deutsche Regierung gebildet werden. Jedoch werden einige wichtige zentrale deutsche Verwaltungsabteilungen errichtet werden . . .

30. 8. 1945:

Eine französische Kommission übernimmt die Verwaltung des *Saargebiets.* Am 18. 7. 1946 werden dem Saargebiet 156 Gemeinden der Rheinprovinz eingegliedert. Nach den Wahlen vom 5. 10. 1947 beschließt am 9. 11. 1947 der Saarländische Landtag die wirtschaftliche Angliederung des Gebiets an Frankreich, dessen Ansprüche am 11. 4. 1947 durch Großbritannien und die USA sanktioniert worden waren. Am 10. 1. 1948 übernimmt ein Französischer Hochkommissar die bisherigen Befugnisse der Französischen Militärregierung an der Saar.

Herbst 1945:

Der in Potsdam beschlossene zentrale deutsche Verwaltungsapparat scheitert an einem französischen Veto.

November 1945 bis Oktober 1946:

Nürnberger Prozeß gegen 24 Haupt-Kriegsverbrecher.

6. 11. 1945:

Bildung des *Länderrats* der US-Zone in Stuttgart.

9. 12. 1945:

Der US-Außenminister BYRNES erwägt Zentralisierung von Verkehr und Währung in den drei Westzonen und erteilt dem US-Militärgouverneur entsprechende Weisungen. Das Vereinigte Königreich lehnt ab.

1946

10. 2. 1946:

Die Deutschen stehen deshalb vor einer schweren Aufgabe, weil die Welt meint, der Nazismus sei Deutschland gewesen, das ganze deutsche Volk sei schuldig . . . Es ist nicht das ganze deutsche Volk schuldig, und wir lehnen eine derartige These ab . . . Immer sind es vor 1933 und nach 1933 große Teile der Deutschen gewesen, die gegen HITLER gekämpft und Mut bewiesen und Leid erduldet haben (Dr. KURT SCHUMACHER).

15. 2. 1946:

Einrichtung eines *Zonenbeirates* in Hamburg zur Beratung der Britischen Militärregierung durch eine Vertretung der deutschen Verwaltung, der Parteien und der Gewerkschaften.

Februar 1946:

Frankreich fordert vor Einrichtung einer Zentralverwaltung die Internationalisierung der Ruhr oder völlige Zerstörung ihres Wirtschaftspotentials sowie ständige militärische Besetzung des Rheinlandes.

26. (28.) 3. 1946:

Erster Industrieplan für Deutschland (Ausarbeitung der Potsdamer Beschlüsse durch den Alliierten Kontrollrat). Die Höhe der Industrieproduktion soll etwa 50—55 % der Produktionshöhe von 1938 betragen. Alle darüber hinausgehenden Produktionskapazitäten sollen entweder als Reparationsgüter ins Ausland geliefert oder an Ort und Stelle zerstört werden. Der Plan unterscheidet zwischen völlig *verbotenen* Industrien (darunter neben der Waffen- und Munitionsproduktion auch Seeschiffe, zahlreiche Chemikalien, Funksendeausrüstungen, schwere Traktoren, schwere Werkzeugmaschinen, synthetische Treibstoffe, synthetischer Gummi und Kugel- und Rollager) und Industriezweigen, deren Produktion *eingeschränkt* werden soll. Als wichtigste Industriebeschränkungen werden festgelegt: Stahlkapazität 7,5 Millionen Tonnen jährlich; chemische Grundstoffe 40 % der Kapazität von 1936; Werkzeugmaschinenindustrie 11,4 % der Kapazität von 1938, Elektrofabrikation 50 % von 1938. Die Produktion von Transportmitteln soll beschränkt werden auf 40.000 Personen- und Lastkraftwagen, 4.000 leichte Straßenschlepper und 10.000 Motorräder jährlich; landwirtschaftliche Maschinen 30 % von 1938 usw.

Entsprechend den . . . Grundsätzen wurden die Hauptelemente des Planes unter folgenden Voraussetzungen vereinbart: a) . . ., b) daß Deutschland als einziges Wirtschaftliches Ganzes betrachtet werden wird, c) . . . .

25. 5. 1946:

Der stellvertretende US-Militärgouverneur General CLAY befiehlt die (vorübergehende) Einstellung der Reparationslieferungen an die Sowjetunion wegen Ausbleibens der Gegenleistungen.

2. 6. 1946:

Dr. KURT SCHUMACHER: Aber das ganz überwältigende Gros der jungen Menschen, die mehr oder weniger gezwungen in der Hitler-Jugend waren, die als Soldaten das taten, was ihnen befohlen war, und was sie als ihre Pflicht ansahen, sind im tiefsten Sinn nicht verantwortlich. Sie haben die Knochen hingehalten für ein vermeintliches Ideal . . . — 2. 7. 1946: Die US-Militärregierung nimmt die Jugend durch Generalamnestie von der Anwendung der Entnazifizierungs-Gesetze aus.

15. 6.—15. 7. 1946:

Zweite Außenministerkonferenz in Paris. Der sowjetische Außenminister MOLOTOW widerspricht dem Plan des Zusammenschlusses der vier Besatzungszonen. Der US-Außenminister BYRNES gibt seinen Plan zur Entwaffnung und Besetzung Deutschlands auf 25 (beziehungsweise 40) Jahre bekannt und tritt den sowjetischen

Forderungen (10 Milliarden Dollar Reparationen und Teilnahme an einer internationalen Kontrolle des Ruhrgebiets) entgegen. Ein Kompromißvorschlag der USA und des Vereinigten Königreichs über die Einrichtung alliierter Zentralstellen mit deutschem Vollzugpersonal als Vorstufe einer deutschen Zentralregierung wird von Frankreich abgelehnt.

20. 7. 1946:

Der US-Militärgouverneur General McNarney lädt die Besatzungsmächte ein, „einheitliche Wirtschaftspolitik in allen Zonen“ durchzuführen. Am 1. 8. stimmt das Vereinigte Königreich zu; am 10. 8. lehnt Frankreich ab. Die Sowjetunion antwortet nicht. Am 5. 9. erfolgt die Vereinbarung des Britischen mit dem US-Militärgouverneur über den wirtschaftlichen Zusammenschluß der beiden Zonen. Fünf Zentralstellen für die gemeinsame Verwaltung werden eingerichtet. Am 2. 12. 1946 unterzeichnen die Außenminister James F. Byrnes und Ernest Bevin das Abkommen über die *wirtschaftliche Vereinigung* der US- und Britischen Zone mit Wirkung vom 1. 1. 1947.

6. 9. 1946:

Rede des US-Außenministers James F. Byrnes in Stuttgart über die Notwendigkeit der wirtschaftlichen Einheit Deutschlands und die Belebung seiner wirtschaftlichen Kräfte sowie die Stärkung der deutschen Selbstverantwortung in Politik und Wirtschaft. *Neuer Abschnitt der US-Deutschland-Politik*: „Das amerikanische Volk will dem deutschen Volk helfen, seinen Weg zurückzufinden zu einem ehrenvollen Platz unter den freien und friedliebenden Nationen der Welt.“

5. 9.—11. 9. 1946:

Als erste gemeinsame Einrichtung der „Bizone“ wird ein „Wirtschaftsrat“ in Minden errichtet. (Mit Errichtung der „Verwaltung des Vereinigten Wirtschaftsgebietes“ am 9. 8. 1947 aufgelöst.)

4. 10. 1946:

Interzonenkonferenz der Regierungschefs der Länder und Städte der Britischen und US-Zone in Bremen. Vorschläge zur Bildung eines „Deutschen Länderrats“.

2. 12. 1946:

Verfassung des Freistaates Bayern (und andere, so: 15. 5. 1946 Hamburg, 13. 10. 1946 Bremen, 11. 12. 1946 Hessen).

1947

1. 1. 1947:

Übergang der Wirtschaftsverwaltung der Britischen und der US-Zone von den Alliierten auf den „Verwaltungsrat für Wirtschaft“ (siehe 5. 9. 1946) in Minden.

24. 1. 1947:

Das erste Handelsabkommen der Doppelzone wird mit den Niederlanden abgeschlossen.

25. 2. 1947:

Gesetz Nr. 46 des Kontrollrats über die *Auflösung des Landes Preußen.*

1. 3. 1947:

Die US-Militärregierung überträgt durch Proklamation Nr. 4 den Ländern der US-Zone die legislative, exekutive und richterliche Gewalt.

11. 3. 1947:

Präsident TRUMAN verkündet die Unterstützung der freien Völker im Kampf gegen die kommunistische Bedrohung. Die ,,Truman-Doktrin" wird die Grundlage des Atlantikpaktes.

26. 3. 1947:

Der ehemalige US-Präsident HOOVER fordert den Wiederaufbau der deutschen Produktion. Am 8. 5. 1947 spricht der stellvertretende US-Außenminister DEAN ACHESON sich für den Wiederaufbau Deutschlands als ,,*der großen Werkstatt Europas*" aus.

10. 3.—24. 4. 1947:

Außenministerkonferenz in Moskau. Keine Einigung über die Frage einer deutschen Zentralregierung. Der Sowjetische Außenminister MOLOTOW spricht sich für die Bildung eines deutschen Einheitsstaates unter Übernahme der Weimarer Reichsverfassung aus. Dagegen ist er nicht bereit, die wirtschaftliche Einheit Deutschlands zu verwirklichen. Daher scheitert die Friedensregelung. Am 23. 4. 1947 beschließen die Außenminister die Rückführung aller deutschen Kriegsgefangenen bis zum 31. 12. 1948. Nach dem Mißerfolg der Konferenz beginnen die drei Westmächte mit der Ausarbeitung eines neuen Industrieplans für ihre Besatzungszonen.

29. 5. 1947:

Abkommen zwischen der Britischen und US-Militärregierung über die Einrichtung eines *Wirtschaftsrates für das Vereinigte Wirtschaftsgebiet* mit Sitz in Frankfurt am Main ,,bis zur Errichtung von Regierungs- und Verwaltungsstellen für ganz Deutschland".

5. 6. 1947:

Der US-Außenminister MARSHALL schlägt in einer Rede vor der Harvard-Universität den Zusammenschluß der Völker Europas zu einem gegenseitigen wirtschaftlichen Hilfs- und Wiederaufbauprogramm vor. Die USA seien bereit, die hierzu nötige Wirtschaftshilfe zu leisten. Deutschland soll in das Programm eingeschlossen sein. Auf der am 27. 6. 1947 in Paris zusammentretenden Konferenz der europäischen Länder versagt der Sowjetische Außenminister MOLOTOW schon nach den ersten Verhandlungstagen die Mitarbeit der Sowjetunion und verläßt Paris. Polen und die Tschechoslowakei werden gezwungen, ihre Mitarbeit ebenfalls zu versagen. Der ,,Marshallplan" wird damit praktisch auf Westeuropa begrenzt. Der Schlußbericht der Pariser Konferenz von 16 Nationen über den Marshallplan sieht am 22. 9. 1947 die Teilnahme der drei Besatzungszonen Westdeutschlands an der Durchführung des Planes vor.

6.—8. 6. 1947:

Die einzige Konferenz aller deutschen Länderchefs scheitert mit der Abreise der Ministerpräsidenten der Sowjetzone von München. Innerdeutscher Bruch mit den Länderregierungen der Sowjetzone.

10. 6. 1947:

Gemeinsame Anordnung der US- und Britischen Militärregierung über ,,die Einsetzung eines Wirtschaftsrates, eines Exekutivausschusses und von Direktoren, um die Lösung dringender wirtschaftlicher Probleme und den Aufbau des Wirtschaftslebens durch dem Volke verantwortliche deutsche Stellen zu fördern".

25. 6. 1947:
Konstituierung des von den Landtagen der „Bizone" gewählten Zweizonen-Wirtschaftsrates in Frankfurt als dem obersten Organ des Vereinigten Wirtschaftsgebietes zur Koordinierung der Wirtschaft beider Zonen. (Sogenannter „Erster Wirtschaftsrat"; bis 9. 2. 1948.)

17. 7. 1947:
Neue Richtlinien der US-Regierung an den Militärgouverneur General LUCIUS D. CLAY an Stelle der Anweisungen von 1945: Entwicklung der deutschen Selbstverantwortlichkeit in den Ländern, Beschränkung des Industrieabbaus auf Kriegsindustrie. Allmähliche Erhöhung der Lebenshaltung; wirtschaftliche Unabhängigkeit Deutschlands von Zuschüssen als Ziel.

28. 8. 1947:
Veröffentlichung des „*Zweiten Industrieplans*" (Dreimächtekonferenz: USA, Vereinigtes Königreich, Frankreich in London). Französische Vorbehalte hinsichtlich bestimmter Industriezweige. Die deutsche Industrieproduktion in den Westzonen soll auf 90—95 % des Standes von 1936 gehoben werden. Im einzelnen wird festgelegt (vgl. 28. 3. 1946):
Stahlproduktion 10,7 Millionen Tonnen jährlich; schwere Maschinen 80 % der Vorkriegserzeugung, wovon aber 35 % als Reparationen abgeführt werden sollen; Automobilindustrie 160.000 Personenwagen und 61.500 Lastwagen; chemische Industrie 100 % von 1936 (mit Ausnahme der verbotenen Produkte) usw.
Trotzdem sollen nach diesem Plan (gemäß Liste vom 17. 10. 1947) *noch 918 Industriewerke demontiert* werden, und zwar 338 als sogenannte Kriegsindustrien und 580 als sogenannte überschüssige Betriebe. Davon liegen allein 496 in der Britischen Zone, darunter Walzwerke, Eisenbahnzulieferungswerke, Röhrenwerke, Bergbauzulieferungswerke usw. (US-Zone 186, Französische Zone 236 Werke).

25. 11.—15. 12. 1947:
Außenministerkonferenz in London. Keine Einigung über eine Friedensregelung mit Deutschland. Der US-Außenminister MARSHALL lehnt Reparationen aus der laufenden deutschen Produktion ab.

1948

7. 1. 1948:
Konferenz der Militärgouverneure der Britischen und US-Zone mit den Länderchefs der beiden Zonen über die *Neuorganisation der Zweizonenverwaltung*. Beschlüsse zur Umbildung des Wirtschaftsrates, Schaffung einer zweiten Kammer aus Vertretern der Länder, Errichtung eines Deutschen Obergerichtshofes und einer Zentralbank für das Vereinigte Wirtschaftsgebiet.

9. 2. 1948:
Inkrafttreten der neuen Ordnung der Wirtschaftsverwaltung der „Bizone". Schaffung eines Länderrats neben dem umgebildeten Wirtschaftsrat und eines Verwaltungsrates als Oberleitung der Wirtschaftsverwaltungen: „*Zweiter Wirtschaftsrat*" aus 104 Mitgliedern. Am 2. 3. 1948 wird Dr. HERMANN PÜNDER zum Oberdirektor des Verwaltungsrates gewählt.

6. 3. 1948:

Kommuniqué der Londoner Sechsmächtekonferenz (einschließlich der Beneluxstaaten), die nach dem Scheitern der Londoner Viermächtekonferenz vom Dezember 1947 am 23. 2. 1948 begonnen hatte. Die Westmächte empfehlen Zusammenarbeit der Drei Mächte in Westdeutschland, ein föderatives Regierungssystem für Deutschland und Deutschlands Teilnahme an der internationalen Ruhrkontrolle.

19. 3. 1948:

Die Sowjets verlassen den Alliierten Kontrollrat für Deutschland (angeblich aus Protest gegen die Londoner Beschlüsse vom 6. 3. 1948).

1. 4. 1948:

Beginn der *Blockade von Berlin.* (30. 6. 1948: Errichtung der Luftbrücke nach Berlin[West]. 12. 5. 1949: Ende der Berliner Blockade.)

2. 6. 1948:

Kommuniqué der *Londoner Sechsmächtekonferenz* (nach Wiederaufnahme der Besprechungen am 20. 4. 1948): Anerkennung der Notwendigkeit, ,,dem deutschen Volke die Möglichkeit zu geben, auf der Basis einer freien und demokratischen Regierungsform *die schließliche Wiederherstellung der gegenwärtig nicht bestehenden deutschen Einheit zu erlangen* . . . Das deutsche Volk soll in den verschiedenen Ländern die Freiheit erhalten, für sich die politischen Organisationen und Einrichtungen zu schaffen, um diejenigen staatlichen Aufgaben übernehmen zu können, die mit den Mindesterfordernissen der Besetzung und der Kontrolle vereinbar sind und letzten Endes das deutsche Volk in die Lage versetzen werden, volle Regierungsverantwortung zu übernehmen. Es wird empfohlen, die Ministerpräsidenten der westdeutschen Länder zu ermächtigen, eine *verfassunggebende Versammlung* einzuberufen . . .'' Gleichzeitig werden sehr weitgehende Sicherheitsmaßnahmen beschlossen, darunter die Einrichtung einer militärischen Sicherheits- und einer internationalen Ruhrkontrollbehörde.

20. 6. 1948:

Währungsreform in den drei Westzonen.

Frühsommer 1948:

Die *Marshallplan-Organisation* (*Organization for European Economic Cooperation* = OEEC) wird in Paris gegründet. Das Vereinigte Wirtschaftsgebiet, die Französische Zone und Berlin(West) sind zunächst durch die Besatzungsmächte vertreten.

III. DER WEG ZUR SOUVERÄNITÄT DER BUNDESREPUBLIK

1948

1. 7. 1948:

Die Militärgouverneure übergeben den elf westdeutschen Regierungschefs die „*Frankfurter Dokumente*“. Am 26. 7. 1948 wird mit den Militärgouverneuren über die Grundlagen eines westdeutschen Zusammenschlusses Übereinstimmung erreicht.

10. 8.—23. 8. 1948:

Tagung des vorbereitenden Verfassungsausschusses im Schloß Herrenchiemsee.

1. 9. 1948:

Beginn der Tagung des *Parlamentarischen Rates* in Bonn. Zum Präsidenten wird Dr. KONRAD ADENAUER gewählt.

22. 11. 1948:

Memorandum der westalliierten Verbindungsoffiziere beim Parlamentarischen Rat. Die Alliierten präzisieren ihre Ansichten vor allem hinsichtlich des von ihnen gewünschten *föderativen Staatsaufbaues.*

10. 12. 1948:

Beginn von Verhandlungen über den *Abschluß einer nordatlantischen Allianz* zwischen den Botschaftern der Mächte des Brüsseler Paktes und Kanadas sowie dem State Department in Washington. Vorstufen: 5. 3.—17. 3. 1948: Fünf-Mächte-Konferenz (Frankreich, Vereinigtes Königreich, Beneluxstaaten) zur Bildung einer Westunion und Unterzeichnung des Brüsseler Paktes. 12. 6. 1948: Die VANDENBERG-Resolution über militärische Hilfe der Vereinigten Staaten für regionale Bündnisgruppen und andere kollektive Vereinbarungen im Rahmen der Vereinten Nationen wird vom US-Senat mit 64 : 4 Stimmen gebilligt. 26. 10. 1948: Der Rat des Brüsseler Pakts einigt sich in Paris über die Grundsätze eines atlantischen Defensivpaktes.

Am 4. 4. 1949 wird der „*Nordatlantikpakt*“ in Washington durch die Außenminister von zwölf Staaten unterzeichnet (Belgien, Dänemark, Frankreich, Vereinigtes Königreich, Island, Italien, Kanada, Luxemburg, Niederlande, Norwegen, Portugal, USA). Am 6. 10. 1949 unterzeichnet Präsident TRUMAN den Mutual Defence Assistance Act.

28. 12. 1948:

Londoner Sechs-Mächte-Abkommen über die Einsetzung einer *Internationalen Ruhrbehörde* (*Ruhrstatut*). Die drei Militärgouverneure vertreten Westdeutschland in der Behörde.

1949

17. 1. 1949:

Einrichtung des Alliierten Sicherheitsamtes zur Überwachung der Entmilitarisierung in Westdeutschland.

15. 3. 1949:

Der US-Militärgouverneur General CLAY gibt den Abschluß der negativen Phase der US-Besatzungspolitik in Deutschland und den Beginn einer konstruktiven Politik bekannt.

10. 4. 1949:

Die Außenminister der USA, des Vereinigten Königreichs und Frankreichs beenden ihre *Konferenz in Washington* über Deutschland. Ein Abkommen über die Fusion der drei Westzonen wird beschlossen, der Wortlaut des *Besatzungsstatuts* für Westdeutschland bekanntgegeben. Damit endet das Bestehen der Militärregierungen als solcher. Die Funktion der alliierten Behörden wird aufgeteilt; Kontrollbefugnisse werden von den Hohen Kommissaren und militärische Funktionen von den Oberbefehlshabern ausgeübt. Die Außenminister betonen, es sei das höchste Ziel der Drei alliierten Regierungen, den festen Einbau eines demokratischen deutschen Bundesstaates in den Rahmen eines europäischen Zusammenschlusses zu ermutigen und zu fördern.
Das Washingtoner Abkommen enthält gleichzeitig eine *Revision des Demontageprogramms*. Von der Demontageliste werden 159 Fabriken in den Westzonen ganz oder zum größten Teil abgesetzt. Gerettet werden unter anderem 32 Stahlwerke, 88 Metallbearbeitungsfabriken, 32 chemische Werke usw. Die deutsche Stahlkapazität soll auf 13,3 Millionen Tonnen, die Produktion auf 11,1 Millionen Tonnen pro Jahr erhöht werden. Gleichzeitig werden die Listen der verbotenen und beschränkten Industrien revidiert.

8. 5. 1949:

Der Parlamentarische Rat nimmt das *Grundgesetz* mit 53 gegen 12 Stimmen an. Am 12. 5. 1949 genehmigen es die Militärgouverneure.

10. 5. 1949:

Wahl *Bonns* zur vorläufigen Bundeshauptstadt.

18. 5. 1949:

John McCloy wird Amerikanischer, am 19. 5. A. François-Poncet Französischer, am 1. 6. Sir Brian Robertson Britischer Hochkommissar in Deutschland. Am 20. 6. 1949 wird das Statut der Alliierten Hochkommission unterzeichnet.

23. 5. 1949:

Das Grundgesetz tritt in Kraft.

21. 6. 1949:

Der Rat der Außenminister, der nach der Aufhebung der Blockade von Berlin in Paris tagt, veröffentlicht ein Communiqué über die deutschen Frage.

14. 8. 1949:

Wahlen zum Ersten Bundestag (78,5 % Wahlbeteiligung).

17. 8. 1949:

Der britische Oppositionsführer Churchill fordert Deutschlands Aufnahme in den am 29. 1. 1949 gegründeten *Europarat* (vgl. 31. 3. 1950).

7. 9. 1949:

Bundestag und Bundesrat der Bundesrepublik Deutschland konstituieren sich in Bonn.

12. 9. 1949:

Prof. Dr. Theodor Heuss wird durch die Bundesversammlung zum Bundespräsidenten gewählt.

15. 9. 1949:
Der Bundestag wählt Dr. KONRAD ADENAUER zum Bundeskanzler.

20. 9. 1949:
Der Bundeskanzler gibt die von ihm gebildete Koalitionsregierung aus CDU/CSU, FDP und DP bekannt. Die Führung der Opposition wird von der SPD unter Dr. KURT SCHUMACHER übernommen.

21. 9. 1949:
In Anerkennung der Gründung der Bundesrepublik Deutschland empfängt der aus den drei Hochkommissaren gebildete Rat der Alliierten Hochkommission den Bundeskanzler und Mitglieder seines Kabinetts auf dem Petersberg bei Bonn, dem Sitz der Alliierten Hochkommission. Am gleichen Tage wird das *Besatzungsstatut*, in dem die den Besatzungsbehörden vorbehaltenen Befugnisse festgelegt sind, verkündet.

7. 10. 1949:
Im Gebiet der Sowjetischen Besatzungszone wird ein staatsähnliches Gebilde begründet, das sich als „*Deutsche Demokratische Republik*" bezeichnet. Am gleichen Tage veröffentlicht die Bundesregierung eine Erklärung, in der die Schaffung der Sowjetzonenregierung als rechtswidrig bezeichnet wird, da sie nicht auf freien Wahlen beruhe. Aus den gleichen Gründen erklärt die Alliierte Hochkommission in einem Communiqué vom 10. Oktober, die Sowjetzonenregierung sei nicht befugt, Mitteldeutschland oder Gesamtdeutschland zu vertreten.

10. 11. 1949:
Communiqué der Außenminister der drei Westmächte nach ihrer Besprechung in Paris: Bekräftigung ihrer Politik, der Bundesregierung in der Führung deutscher Staatsgeschäfte weiten Spielraum zu lassen und eine allmähliche Eingliederung des deutschen Volkes in die europäische Gemeinschaft zu befürworten. Am gleichen Tage ermächtigt die Alliierte Hochkommission die Bundesregierung, mit anderen Ländern Handels- und Zahlungsabkommen zu vereinbaren und abzuschließen. Vertreter der Alliierten werden an diesen Verhandlungen als Beobachter teilnehmen.

13. 11. 1949:
Der US-Außenminister DEAN ACHESON trifft in Bonn mit dem Bundespräsidenten und dem Bundeskanzler zusammen.

20. 11. 1949:
Beitritt der Bundesrepublik zur Internationalen Ruhrbehörde (IAR).

22. 11. 1949:
Petersberg-Abkommen auf Grund der Verhandlungen des Bundeskanzlers mit den Hochkommissaren. Rettung wichtigster Industriewerke vor der Demontage. Im Januar 1951 wird der Bundesregierung offiziell von der Alliierten Hochkommission mitgeteilt, daß das Demontageprogramm beendet sei.

15. 12. 1949:
Der Bundeskanzler und der Amerikanische Hochkommissar unterzeichnen ein Abkommen, wonach die Bundesregierung an Stelle der Besatzungsbehörden Empfängerin der *Marshallplan-Hilfe für Westdeutschland* wird. Dieses zweiseitige Abkommen ist der erste Staatsvertrag der Bundesrepublik.

1950

26. 1. 1950:
Die drei Hochkommissare fordern den Bundeskanzler auf, deutsche Generalkonsuln für London, Washington und Paris zu bestellen.

28. 2. 1950:
Der US-Hochkommissar McCloy schlägt *gesamtdeutsche Wahlen* für den 15. 10. 1950 vor.

3. 3. 1950:
Zwölf Wirtschaftskonventionen zwischen Frankreich und dem Saargebiet (siehe 30. 8. 1945) werden durch den französischen Außenminister Robert Schuman und den Ministerpräsidenten des Saargebiets, Johannes Hoffmann, in Paris unterzeichnet. Die Autonomie des Saargebiets wird — vorbehaltlich der Bestimmungen eines Friedensvertrages mit Deutschland — anerkannt. Mit dem gleichen Vorbehalt werden die Saargruben für 50 Jahre an Frankreich verpachtet. Am 5. 5. 1950 protestiert die Bundesregierung in einer Note an die Alliierte Hochkommission gegen die Konventionen und schlägt eine internationale Behörde für die Saar ähnlich der Internationalen Ruhrbehörde vor.

7. 3. 1950:
Bundeskanzler Dr. Adenauer schlägt eine deutsch-französische Union vor.

8. 3. 1950:
Der Rat der OEEC in Washington beschließt die Aufnahme des Vereinigten Königreichs und Deutschlands in die Europäische Zahlungsunion (EZU). Am 19. 9. 1950 unterzeichnet die Bundesrepublik Deutschland in Paris gemeinsam mit den übrigen Mitgliedstaaten der OEEC die Vereinbarung über die Europäische Zahlungsunion. Am 24. 1. 1951 wird sie vom Deutschen Bundestag gebilligt.

16. 3. 1950:
Der britische Oppositionsführer Churchill tritt vor dem Unterhaus für Deutschlands Wiederbewaffnung ein.

22. 3. 1950:
Die Bundesregierung schlägt Wahlen zu einer verfassunggebenden Nationalversammlung in ganz Deutschland vor. Die Behörden der sogenannten DDR lassen den Vorschlag unbeantwortet.

31. 3. 1950:
Der Ministerausschuß des Europarates in Straßburg lädt die Bundesrepublik Deutschland und das Saarland in aller Form ein, dem Rat als außerordentliche Mitglieder beizutreten. Am 7. 8. 1950 wird die Bundesrepublik Mitglied.

2. 4. 1950:
Der Bundeskanzler fordert in einem UP-Interview eine *Sicherheitsgarantie* für die Bundesrepublik.

9. 5. 1950:
Der französische Außenminister Schuman legt den Plan zur Bildung einer westeuropäischen *Montan-Union* vor. Die Verhandlungen über die Montan-Gemeinschaft dauern in Paris vom 20. 6. 1950 bis 19. 4. 1951.

15. 5. 1950:
Communiqué der drei westalliierten Außenminister nach der Londoner Konferenz: Deutschland soll „in fortschreitendem Maße wieder *in die Gemeinschaft der freien Völker Europas eintreten.* Wenn diese Situation voll erreicht ist, soll es von den Kontrollen befreit werden, denen es gegenwärtig noch unterworfen ist, und es soll ihm seine Souveränität in dem größtmöglichen Maße, das mit der Grundlage des Besatzungsstatuts vereinbar ist, zuerkannt werden." Bildung eines Studienausschusses zur Vorbereitung der Überprüfung des Besatzungsstatuts.
Die Außenminister stellen fest, daß „*die friedliche Wiedervereinigung Deutschlands* das Endziel der Politik der Alliierten bleibt", und einigen sich über die Grundsätze, nach denen diese Wiedervereinigung erfolgen soll.

23. 5. 1950:
In gleichlautenden Noten an die Sowjetunion fordern die drei Westmächte die Auflösung der halbmilitärischen Formationen der Volkspolizei der sogenannten DDR.

1. 6. 1950:
Das alliierte Gesetz zur Verhinderung einer deutschen Wiederaufrüstung tritt in Kraft.

8. 6. 1950:
Das Britische und US-Außenministerium erklären, die Regierungen Polens und der sogenannten DDR könnten nicht die endgültige deutsch-polnische Grenze festlegen, da die Entscheidung darüber gemäß dem Potsdamer Abkommen einem Friedensvertrag vorbehalten bleiben müsse. Das US-Außenministerium weist auch darauf hin, daß der mitteldeutschen „Regierung" die demokratische Grundlage fehle, und daß sie nicht im Namen des deutschen Volkes spreche. (Die Erklärung bezieht sich auf das Grenzabkommen vom 6. 6. 1950.) Am 13. 6. 1950 verwahrt sich der Bundestag feierlich gegen die Oder-Neiße-Grenze.

25. 6. 1950:
Ausbruch des Koreakrieges.

11. 8. 1950:
Der britische Oppositionsführer CHURCHILL regt vor dem Europarat in Straßburg die Schaffung einer europäischen Armee unter Beteiligung Deutschlands an. Die weitere Behandlung wird vertagt.

19. 8. 1950:
Der Bundeskanzler fordert *deutsche Verteidigungsgruppen* als Gegengewicht zur Volkspolizei der sogenannten DDR.

5. 9. 1950:
Der US-Hochkommissar McCLOY, der am 22. 7. 1950 erklärt hatte, die Selbstverteidigung könne den Deutschen nicht verwehrt werden, teilt vor der Presse in Washington mit, er habe dem Präsidenten der USA die Teilnahme der Deutschen an der Verteidigung Europas empfohlen.

12. 9.—23. 9. 1950:
New Yorker Konferenz der drei Außenminister DEAN ACHESON, ERNEST BEVIN und ROBERT SCHUMAN unter teilweiser Hinzuziehung der Verteidigungsminister

und der drei Hochkommissare. Besprechungen über den Aufbau *europäischer Streitkräfte unter deutscher Beteiligung.* SCHUMAN und BEVIN sind zunächst gegen einen deutschen Verteidigungsbeitrag; BEVIN gibt jedoch unter Bedingungen nach. *Neue Politik gegenüber der Bundesrepublik* wird angekündigt.
Die Außenminister erklären, daß sie und ihre Regierungen ,,den Wunsch des deutschen Volkes nach *Wiedervereinigung Deutschlands* unter Achtung der Grundfreiheiten teilen . . . Bis zu dieser Wiedervereinigung betrachten die drei Regierungen die Regierung der Bundesrepublik als die *einzige nach Freiheit und Recht konstituierte deutsche Regierung*, die deshalb allein berechtigt ist, als Vertreterin des deutschen Volkes . . . für Deutschland zu sprechen . . .'' Sie kündigen Schritte zur Beendigung des Kriegszustandes mit Deutschland und zur Verstärkung ihrer dort stationierten Streitkräfte an und werden jeden Angriff auf die Bundesrepublik oder auf Berlin(West) als Angriff gegen sich selbst betrachten.

16. 9.—26. 9. 1950:

Der Rat des Atlantikpaktes in New York beschließt die Schaffung einer gemeinsamen Armee mit zentralem Oberkommando. Deutschland soll ,,in die Lage versetzt werden, einen Beitrag zur Verteidigung Westeuropas zu leisten''.

26. 10. 1950:

Regierungserklärung des Ministerpräsidenten PLEVEN vor der Französischen Nationalversammlung: Schaffung einer aus möglichst kleinen nationalen Einheiten bestehenden Europa-Armee unter einem europäischen Verteidigungsminister. Dieser soll der europäischen Versammlung verantwortlich sein. Deutsche Kontingente sollen nach Unterzeichnung des Schumanplans aufgestellt werden. Die Nationalversammlung stimmt der Regierungserklärung mit 343 gegen 225 Stimmen zu (,,*Pleven-Plan*'').

28. 10.—1. 11. 1950:

Der Verteidigungsausschuß der NATO kommt in Washington angesichts des Plevenplans zu keiner Einigung über die Frage der deutschen Beteiligung. Die Frage wird an den Stellvertreterrat verwiesen. Dieser nimmt am 7. 12. 1950 den *Spofford-Plan* an (Kompromiß zwischen dem ursprünglichen amerikanischen Plan und dem Pleven-Plan). Am 13. 12. 1950 billigen Militärausschuß und Stellvertreterrat der NATO in London Empfehlungen an den NATO-Rat zur Schaffung einer atlantischen Armee mit Einschluß deutscher Kontingente. Am 18./19. 12. 1950 faßt der NATO-Rat in Brüssel nach gemeinsamer Tagung mit dem Verteidigungsausschuß den Beschluß zur Schaffung einer europäischen Armee mit deutschen Kontingenten gemäß obigen Empfehlungen. General EISENHOWER wird Oberkommandierender. Aus dem Schluß-Communiqué:
,,Der Rat erzielte auch eine völlige Einigung über die Rolle, die Deutschland bei der gemeinsamen Verteidigung übernehmen könnte. Die deutsche Beteiligung würde die Verteidigung Europas stärken, ohne in irgendeiner Weise den rein defensiven Charakter der NATO zu verändern. Der Rat hat die Regierungen Frankreichs, des Vereinigten Königreichs und der Vereinigten Staaten eingeladen, diese Frage gemeinsam mit der Regierung der Deutschen Bundesrepublik zu prüfen.''

4. 11. 1950:
Die Sowjets schlagen eine neue Viererkonferenz über Deutschland vor.

8. 11. 1950:
Das Bundeskabinett befürwortet vor dem Bundestag einen deutschen Beitrag bei der Verteidigung Westeuropas.

1. 12. 1950:
Der Bundeskanzler fordert die Ablösung des Besatzungsstatuts durch einen Sicherheitsvertrag.

19. 12. 1950:
Außenministerkonferenz der drei westlichen Großmächte in Brüssel. Es wird beschlossen, auf dem Verhandlungswege mit der Regierung der Bundesrepublik das Problem des deutschen Verteidigungsbeitrags zu verfolgen und das Besatzungsstatut durch ein System von Verträgen abzulösen.

1951

1. 1. 1951:
Als erstes Land beendet die Republik Indien den Kriegszustand mit Deutschland.

9. 1. 1951:
Auf dem Petersberg beginnen zwischen Vertretern der Bundesregierung und der Alliierten Hochkommission informatorische Besprechungen technischer Art, um festzustellen, wie Deutschland an der Erhaltung des Friedens und der gemeinsamen Verteidigung Europas teilnehmen kann.

26. 1. 1951:
Frankreich lädt die Bundesrepublik zur gleichberechtigten Teilnahme an der Konferenz über die Europa-Armee ein. Die „*Pleven-Plan-Konferenz*" tritt am 15. 2. 1951 unter Vorsitz von Außenminister Robert Schuman zusammen. Die deutsche Delegation verhandelt in voller Gleichberechtigung.

27. 2 1951:
Die Bundesregierung beantragt die Mitgliedschaft beim Internationalen Währungsfonds und der Weltbank. Die Aufnahme der Bundesrepublik erfolgt am 29. 5. 1952.

5. 3. 1951:
Vertreter der Vier Großmächte treten in Paris zusammen, um unter anderm über ihre Deutschlandpolitik zu beraten (Vorkonferenz zu einer Außenministerkonferenz). Nach 73 unproduktiven Sitzungen werden die Besprechungen am 21. 6. ergebnislos abgebrochen, da keine Einigung über die Tagesordnung zustande kommt. Die Drei Westmächte teilen der Sowjetunion mit, daß eine Fortsetzung der Besprechungen „keinen praktischen Zweck" habe.

6. 3. 1951:
Die Alliierte Hochkommission verkündet die *Erste Revision des Besatzungsstatuts* gemäß den New Yorker Beschlüssen vom 19. 9. 1950.

15. 3. 1951:

Bundeskanzler Dr. ADENAUER übernimmt Aufgaben und Titel eines *Bundesministers des Auswärtigen.*

18. 4. 1951:

Unterzeichnung des *Schumanplans* und der europäischen Deklaration in Paris. In einem Briefwechsel stellen die Bundesregierung und die Französische Regierung fest, daß die *Saarfrage* nur in einem Friedensvertrag einer endgültigen Lösung zugeführt werden kann.

2. 5. 1951:

In Straßburg billigt der Ministerausschuß des *Europarates* die Aufnahme der Bundesrepublik als vollberechtigtes Mitglied. (Der saarländische Innenminister wird als Beobachter zugelassen.)

10. 5.—3. 8. 1951:

Gemäß den Brüsseler Außenminister-Beschlüssen finden Vorbesprechungen zwischen Vertretern der Alliierten Hochkommission und der Bundesrepublik mit dem Ziel statt, Empfehlungen über die Neuregelung der gegenseitigen Beziehungen auf vertraglicher Grundlage auszuarbeiten.

13. 6. 1951:

Die Generalkonsuln der Bundesrepublik in New York, Paris und London werden zu Geschäftsträgern ernannt.

21. 6. 1951:

Die Vollkonferenz der UNESCO in Paris beschließt die Aufnahme der Bundesrepublik.

9. 7. 1951:

Das Vereinigte Königreich *beendet den Kriegszustand* mit Deutschland; die Staaten des Britischen Commonwealth schließen sich diesem Vorgehen an. Frankreich folgt am 13. Juli. Präsident TRUMAN fordert den amerikanischen Kongreß auf, die gesetzliche Grundlage für die Beendigung des Kriegszustandes mit Deutschland zu schaffen; diese Maßnahme tritt am 19. 10. 1951 in Kraft.

14. 9. 1951:

Zum Abschluß ihrer *Konferenz in Washington* geben die Außenminister der USA, des Vereinigten Königreichs und Frankreichs eine Erklärung heraus, wonach ihre Regierungen ,,die Einbeziehung eines demokratischen Deutschlands auf der Grundlage der *Gleichberechtigung* in eine kontinental-europäische Gemeinschaft anstreben", ebenso wie eine völlige Umgestaltung der deutsch-alliierten Beziehungen, unter anderem durch die Ablösung des Besatzungsstatuts durch vertragliche Abmachungen und eine Mitwirkung Westdeutschlands an der Verteidigung des Westens. Sie ,,glauben, die mit der Bundesregierung nunmehr zu treffenden Abmachungen sollten die Grundlage der Beziehungen zwischen ihren Ländern und der Bundesrepublik bilden, bis eine *Friedensregelung mit einem geeinten Deutschland* möglich wird". Die Alliierten Hochkommissare erhalten entsprechende Instruktionen. Es soll keine Einmischung in innerdeutsche Angelegenheiten mehr stattfinden.

Die Alliierten behalten sich einige *Sonderrechte* vor, die sich ,,nur auf die Stationierung bewaffneter Streitkräfte, auf den Schutz dieser Streitkräfte sowie auf

Fragen, die Berlin und Deutschland in seiner Gesamtheit einschließlich der eventuellen Friedensregelung und der friedlichen Wiedervereinigung Deutschlands betreffen, beziehen".

27. 9. 1951:

14-Punkte-Programm der Bundesregierung und des Bundestags zur *Frage gesamtdeutscher Wahlen* unter Überprüfung in allen Teilen Deutschlands durch eine internationale Kommission. Annahme eines Antrags der SPD, in dem *freie Wahlen in ganz Berlin* als erster Schritt auf dem Wege zur Wiedervereinigung Deutschlands und ein Appell an die Vier Besatzungsmächte, gesamtdeutsche Wahlen zu ermöglichen, gefordert werden. Am 2. 12. 1951 schlagen die Westmächte den Vereinten Nationen die Einsetzung einer solchen Kommission vor. Sie wird am 20. 12. 1951 von der Vollversammlung beschlossen.

22. 11. 1951:

Bundeskanzler Dr. ADENAUER trifft mit den Außenministern der drei Westmächte in Paris zu einer Konferenz zusammen. Die Minister stimmen dem Entwurf eines „*Generalvertrages*" zu, der die Grundlage für das an die Stelle des Besatzungsstatuts tretende vertragliche Verhältnis bilden soll.

3. 12. 1951:

Bundeskanzler Dr. ADENAUER trifft zum *Staatsbesuch in London* ein, dem ersten offiziellen Besuch eines deutschen Regierungschefs in England seit 1925. Er wird auch von König GEORG VI. empfangen.

21. 12. 1951:

Aufhebung des Ruhrstatuts.

1952

11. 1. 1952:

Mit 232 gegen 143 Stimmen ratifiziert der Bundestag den Schuman-Plan. Am 16. 6. 1952 ist die Ratifizierung von allen Teilnehmerstaaten vollzogen. Am 25. 7. 1952 erklären die Außenminister in Paris, daß der Vertrag über die Montangemeinschaft in Kraft getreten ist.

26. 2. 1952:

Außenminister SCHUMAN erklärt die Bereitschaft Frankreichs, die Saarfrage noch vor Abschluß eines Friedensvertrags mit Deutschland zu lösen.

29. 2. 1952:

Schreiben der Bundesregierung an den Generalsekretär des Europarats über die nicht gewährten politischen Grundfreiheiten an der Saar. Am 23. 4. 1952 bringt der Deutsche Bundestag in einer Entschließung erneut zum Ausdruck, daß das Saargebiet als deutsches Staatsgebiet zu betrachten sei und sein Schicksal nicht ohne deutsche Zustimmung entschieden werden könne.

10. 3. 1952:

Erste Sowjetnote an die Westmächte über gesamtdeutsche Wahlen, Friedensvertrag usw. 25. 3. 1952: erste Antwortnote der Westmächte. 9. 4. 1952: zweite sowjetische Note. 13. 5. 1952: zweite Antwortnote der Westmächte. 24. 5. 1952: dritte sowjetische Note. 10. 7. 1952: dritte Antwortnote der Westmächte. 23. 8. 1952: vierte sowjetische Note. 23. 9. 1952: vierte Antwortnote der Westmächte.

Freie Wahlen werden als Vorbedingung für die Bildung einer gesamtdeutschen Regierung und die Wiedervereinigung Deutschlands gefordert.

26. 5. 1952:

In Bonn wird der „Vertrag über die Beziehungen zwischen der Bundesrepublik und den drei Mächten" (*Deutschlandvertrag*), der das Besatzungsstatut ablösen und Westdeutschland zum gleichberechtigten Partner innerhalb der Gemeinschaft der freien Völker machen soll, unterzeichnet.

27. 5. 1952:

Der am 9. 5. 1952 paraphierte Vertrag über die Europäische Verteidigungsgemeinschaft (EVG) wird in Paris unterzeichnet.

1. 7. 1952:

Der US-Senat ratifiziert den Deutschlandvertrag. Am 1. 8. 1952 ratifiziert das Britische Unterhaus den Deutschlandvertrag und die gegenseitigen Garantien mit den Ländern der geplanten EVG.

20. 8. 1952:

Tod des Ersten Vorsitzenden der SPD, Dr. KURT SCHUMACHER. Am 27. 9. 1952 wird ERICH OLLENHAUER zum Ersten Vorsitzenden der SPD gewählt.

27. 8. 1952:

Appell der USA an die Sowjetunion, zur Klärung des Schicksals der in den Ostblockländern vermißten 2,5 Millionen Deutschen, Japaner und Italiener beizutragen.

8. 9. 1952:

In Luxemburg eröffnet Bundeskanzler und Außenminister Dr. ADENAUER als erster Präsident die konstituierende Sitzung des Ministerrats der Montanunion. Beschluß, die erweiterte Versammlung der Montangemeinschaft zu bitten, den Entwurf eines Vertrages über die Gründung einer Europäischen Politischen Gemeinschaft auszuarbeiten (Communiqué vom 10. 9. 1952). Am 10. 3. 1953 wird der Entwurf in Straßburg angenommen.

1953

10. 2. 1953:

Die Hohe Behörde der Montanunion eröffnet den gemeinsamen Markt für Kohle, Schrott und Eisenerze in den sechs Ländern. Ab 1. 5. 1953 werden alle Beschränkungen des Stahlhandels innerhalb des gemeinsamen Marktes abgeschafft.

27. 2. 1953:

Londoner Abkommen über die Regelung der deutschen Auslandsschulden. Verbindlichkeiten der Bundesrepublik: rund 13.730.000.000 DM.

2. 3. 1953:

Höhepunkt des Flüchtlingsstromes aus der sogenannten DDR: 6.000 Menschen suchen in Berlin um Asyl nach. Am 4. 3. 1953 verabschiedet der Bundestag das Flüchtlings-Notleistungsgesetz und am 25. 3. 1953 das Bundesvertriebenengesetz.

18. 3. 1953:

Der Bundestag nimmt mit großer Mehrheit das deutsch-israelische Wiedergutmachungsabkommen an. Am 27. 3. tritt es in Kraft.

19. 3. 1953:

Der Bundestag billigt in dritter Lesung die deutsch-alliierten Vertragswerke mit einer Mehrheit von über 60 Stimmen (vgl. 26./27. 5. 1952).

9. 4. 1953:

Gemeinsames Communiqué über die Besprechungen des Bundeskanzlers mit Präsident EISENHOWER in Washington. Das deutsch-amerikanische Kulturabkommen tritt in Kraft. Am 3. 6. 1953 tritt der Freundschafts-, Handels- und Konsularvertrag zwischen Deutschland und den USA von 1923 wieder in Kraft.

17. 6. 1953:

Deutsche Arbeiter erheben sich gegen das Terrorregime in Ost-Berlin und der sogenannten DDR (*Juni-Aufstand*). 22. 6. 1953: Dringender Appell der Bundesregierung an die drei Westmächte um verstärkte Bemühungen zur Wiedervereinigung. Am 1. 7. 1953 verkündet der Bundeskanzler vor dem Bundestag ein sechs Punkte umfassendes Sofortprogramm zur Wiedervereinigung. Die drei Regierungschefs der Westmächte sagen ihre Unterstützung erneut zu und entsprechen am 16. 7. 1953 dem Wunsch der Bundesregierung nach einer Viererkonferenz über die Frage der deutschen Wiedervereinigung. Am 26. 11. 1953 nimmt die Sowjetunion die Einladung zu einer Viererkonferenz über das Deutschland- und Österreichproblem an und schlägt als Tagungsort Berlin vor. Am 10. 12. 1953 bekundet der Bundestag erneut den Willen zur nationalen und staatlichen Einheit. Die Konferenz der Außenminister der vier Großmächte findet vom 25. 1.—18. 2. 1954 in Berlin statt.

29. 7. 1953:

Ende der Legislaturperiode der ersten Bundestags. Am 6. 9. 1953 finden die Wahlen zum Zweiten Bundestag mit einer Wahlbeteiligung von 86,0 % statt. Die Politik der Bundesregierung wird von einer überwältigenden Mehrheit gebilligt: die CDU/CSU erhält 244 von 487 Mandaten. Am 20. 10. 1953 ist die neue Bundesregierung wiederum unter der Führung von Dr. KONRAD ADENAUER gebildet.

29. 9. 1953:

Tod des Regierenden Bürgermeisters von Berlin(West), Professor ERNST REUTER.

22. 11. 1953:

Aufhebung des Interzonenpasses zwischen der Bundesrepublik und der sogenannten DDR.

1954

15. 1. 1954:

Tod des ersten Präsidenten des Bundesverfassungsgerichts, Dr. Dr. h. c. HERMANN HÖPKER-ASCHOFF. Zu seinem Nachfolger wird am 19. 3. 1954 Dr. JOSEF WINTRICH, bisher Präsident des Bayrischen Verfassungsgerichtes in München, gewählt († 19. 10. 1958).

23. 2. 1954:

Der Bundeskanzler erklärt in Berlin, daß die Bundesregierung trotz dem erfolglosen Ausgang der Berliner Konferenz ihre Politik der Wiedervereinigung Deutschlands in Frieden und Freiheit fortsetzen werde. Am 25. 2. 1954 lehnt der Bundestag die Deutschland- und Europapläne der Sowjetunion ab und bekundet seine Entschlossenheit, sich mit allen Kräften für die Wiedervereinigung einzusetzen.

26. 2. 1954:

Der Bundestag billigt die Wehrergänzung des Grundgesetzes. Am 19. 3. wird sie vom Bundesrat angenommen, am 25. 3. von der Alliierten Hochkommission mit der Maßgabe genehmigt, daß die Ergänzung zu Artikel 73 GG bis zum Inkrafttreten der geplanten EVG suspendiert bleibt.

26. 4. 1954:

Beginn der Fernost-Konferenz in Genf.

14. 6. 1954:

Konstituierung des Kuratoriums des „Unteilbaren Deutschlands, Volksbewegung für die Wiedervereinigung" aus 128 führenden Vertretern aller Gebiete des öffentlichen Lebens. Am 18. 7. 1954 wird der ehemalige Reichstagspräsident PAUL LOEBE zum Präsidenten gewählt.

6.—11. 7. 1954:

In Leipzig findet der Evangelische Kirchentag vor 500.000 Teilnehmern zum ersten Male in der sogenannten DDR statt.

17. 7. 1954:

Prof. Dr. THEODOR HEUSS wird in Berlin als Präsident der Bundesrepublik wiedergewählt.

24. 7. 1954:

Die Sowjets schlagen in einer neuen Note an die Westmächte die Einberufung einer Konferenz der großen Vier über Europa vor und lassen am 4. 8. 1954 eine zweite Note zum gleichen Thema folgen. Am 6. 9. 1954 fordern die Westmächte demgegenüber Viermächteverhandlungen über Deutschland und die europäische Sicherheit.

30. 8. 1954:

Mit 319 gegen 164 Stimmen lehnt die französische Nationalversammlung eine weitere Debatte über die EVG und damit die Ratifizierung des Vertrages ab.

28. 9.—3. 10. 1954:

Neun-Mächte-Konferenz in London. Die Außenminister der Westmächte unterzeichnen die „Londoner Akte" (Aufnahme der Bundesrepublik in eine erweiterte Organisation des Brüsseler Paktes und die NATO, Zuerkennung der Souveränität).

21.—23. 10. 1954:

Pariser Neunmächtekonferenz auf der Grundlage der „Londoner Akte". Die Aufnahme der Bundesrepublik und Italiens in die neue Brüsseler Paktorganisation („Westeuropäische Union") wird beschlossen und Einigung über die Beendigung des Besatzungsregimes erzielt. Die neun Mächte stimmen einer Empfehlung zur Aufnahme der Bundesrepublik in die NATO zu.

29. 10. 1954:

Bundestagspräsident Dr. HERMANN EHLERS stirbt. Am 16. 11. 1954 wählt der Bundestag Dr. EUGEN GERSTENMAIER zum Präsidenten.

13. 11.—21. 12. 1954:

Notenwechsel zwischen den Westmächten und der Sowjetunion, ausgelöst durch eine Note der Sowjetregierung an die Französische Regierung. Eine Konferenz über Fragen der europäischen Sicherheit wird von den drei Westmächten abgelehnt

(Moskauer Rumpfkonferenz, 29. 11.—2. 12. 1954, mit Unterzeichnung der „Moskauer Deklaration" durch die Ostblockstaaten. Die Bildung der Zonenarmee wird formell beschlossen). Am 9. 12. erklärt die Sowjetregierung, daß die Wiederbewaffnung Deutschlands eine Wiedervereinigung unmöglich mache.

27. 12. 1954:
Mit 289 gegen 251 Stimmen billigt die französische Nationalversammlung die Aufnahme der Bundesrepublik in die NATO. Am 29. 12. stimmt sie mit 287 gegen 260 Stimmen der deutschen Wiederbewaffnung und der Aufnahme der Bundesrepublik in den erweiterten Brüsseler Pakt zu.

1 9 5 5

15. 1. 1955:
Radio Moskau verbreitet eine Deutschland-Erklärung. Darin wird die *Wiederherstellung der Einheit Deutschlands durch freie Wahlen* mit dem Zusatz vorgeschlagen, daß die Annahme der Pariser Verträge Verhandlungen über die Wiedervereinigung unmöglich machen würde. Zugleich schlägt die Sowjetunion die Normalisierung ihrer Beziehungen zur Bundesrepublik vor.

25. 1. 1955:
Die Sowjetunion gibt bekannt, daß sie den Kriegszustand mit Deutschland als beendet ansieht. Gleichzeitig erklärt sie alle Beschränkungen für hinfällig, denen deutsche Staatsbürger bislang unterworfen gewesen seien, behält sich jedoch die Ausübung ihrer „Rechte und Pflichten" aus den für ganz Deutschland gültigen alliierten Viermächteabkommen weiterhin vor. Die Erklärung bezieht sich ausdrücklich auf beide Teile Deutschlands.

27. 2. 1955:
Der Bundestag ratifiziert in dritter Lesung mit klaren Mehrheiten die Pariser Verträge. Der Deutschlandvertrag wird mit 324 gegen 151 Stimmen, der Beitritt zum Atlantikpakt und zur Westeuropäischen Union mit 314 gegen 157 Stimmen bei zwei Enthaltungen, das Saarabkommen mit 262 gegen 202 Stimmen bei neun Enthaltungen angenommen. Am 24. 3. werden die Verträge durch den Bundespräsidenten unterzeichnet (vgl. 5. 5. 1955).

20. 4. 1955:
Die USA und die Bundesrepublik Deutschland hinterlegen in Bonn die Ratifizierungsurkunden für das *Protokoll über die Beendigung des Besatzungsregimes* und den Vertrag über den Aufenthalt ausländischer Streitkräfte in der Bundesrepublik.

5. 5. 1955:
Das Besatzungsstatut wird durch eine Erklärung seitens der Hohen Kommission beendet, die zugleich mit ihren Unterorganen zu bestehen aufhört.

5. 5. 1955:
Das Vereinigte Königreich, Frankreich und die Bundesrepublik hinterlegen im Belgischen Außenministerium die Ratifizierungsurkunden über die Gründung einer Westeuropäischen Union, die damit in Kraft tritt. Gleichzeitig hinterlegen

das Vereinigte Königreich und Frankreich die Ratifikationsurkunden über den Deutschland- und den Truppenvertrag in Bonn (vgl. 20. 4. 1955). *Damit erhält die Bundesrepublik die Souveränität.*
Das deutsch-französische Abkommen über die Saar tritt mit einem Notenaustausch in Kraft.

9. 5. 1955:
Die Bundesregierung wird als 15. Mitglied in den Nordatlantikpakt (NATO) aufgenommen.

IV. BEMÜHUNGEN UM DIE DEUTSCHE EINHEIT

7. 6. 1955:
Die Regierung der *Sowjetunion* richtet eine Einladung an die Bundesregierung, in Moskau über die Aufnahme diplomatischer, kultureller und wirtschaftlicher Beziehungen zu verhandeln. Vorbereitende Besprechungen finden seit dem 12. 8. 1955 zwischen den Botschaftern beider Mächte in Paris statt. Die Bundesregierung nennt auch die Fragen der Wiedervereinigung und der Kriegsgefangenen als Besprechungsthemen (siehe 8.—14. 9. 1955).

18.—23. 7. 1955:
Genfer Konferenz der Regierungschefs Frankreichs, des Vereinigten Königreichs, der Sowjetunion und der USA. In der Frage der Wiedervereinigung Deutschlands werden keine Fortschritte erzielt; sie soll im Zusammenhang mit dem Problem der europäischen Sicherheit auf einer Konferenz der Außenminister behandelt werden. Diese endet am 26. 10. 1955 ohne positives Ergebnis in der deutschen Frage.

22. 7. 1955:
Beschluß des WEU-Rats, die Dreimonatsfrist für die Vorbereitung der *Saarabstimmung* mit der Verkündung der Gesetze des Saarlandtags vom 8. 7. 1955 (also am 23. 7. 1955) beginnen zu lassen (siehe 23. 10. 1955).

8.—14. 9. 1955:
In Moskau wird die Aufnahme diplomatischer Beziehungen zwischen der *Sowjetunion* und der Bundesrepublik beschlossen. Die Sowjetregierung sagt die Heimkehr der *Kriegsgefangenen* zu. Das Abkommen wird am 23. 9. 1955 vom Bundestag einstimmig gebilligt. Am 7. 10. 1955 trifft der erste Heimkehrertransport ein. Am 20. 12. 1955 besitzt Deutschland zum erstenmal nach vierzehn Jahren wieder diplomatische Beziehungen mit der Sowjetunion.

20. 9. 1955:
Die Sowjetunion erklärt die sogenannte DDR durch einen Vertrag für souverän.

23. 10. 1955:
68 % der saarländischen Wähler lehnen das „europäische Statut" ab. Am 18. 12. 1955 erhalten die drei im „*Heimatbund*" zusammengeschlossenen Parteien (Christlich-Demokratische Union—CDU, Demokratische Partei Saar—DPS, Sozialdemokratische Partei Deutschlands—SPD) 64 % der Stimmen und 33 von 50 Mandaten im Landtag. Am 10. 1. 1956 wird Dr. HUBERT NEY (CDU) zum Ministerpräsidenten gewählt. Am 31. 1. 1956 beschließt der Saarländische Landtag in einer

Grundsatzerklärung die Angliederung von *Saarland* an die Bundesrepublik (siehe 5. 6. 1956).

9. 12. 1955:

Der Bundesminister des Auswärtigen weist auf die Folgen hin, die eine Aufnahme diplomatischer Beziehungen mit der sogenannten DDR durch dritte Staaten für deren Verhältnis zur Bundesrepublik auslösen müßte (siehe 19. 10. 1957).

1 9 5 6

6. 3. 1956:

Die durch die Aufstellung der *Bundeswehr* notwendig gewordene „Zweite Wehrergänzung des Grundgesetzes" wird durch den Bundestag verabschiedet. Am 7. 7. 1956 wird das *Wehrpflichtgesetz* mit 270 gegen 166 Stimmen beschlossen.

5. 6. 1956:

Gemäß der in Luxemburg zwischen der Französischen Regierung und der Bundesregierung getroffenen Vereinbarung wird *Saarland* am 1. 1. 1957 politisch und bis Ende 1959 auch wirtschaftlich der Bundesrepublik angegliedert werden. Am 14. 12. 1956 werden die deutsch-französischen Saarverträge durch den Bundestag einstimmig gebilligt (siehe 5. 7. 1959).

18. 8. 1956:

Das Bundesverfassungsgericht erklärt die *Kommunistische Partei Deutschlands* (KPD) als verfassungswidrig und ordnet ihre Auflösung an.

24. 9. 1956:

Belgisch-deutsches Abkommen über die endgültige Regelung der Grenzprobleme zwischen beiden Ländern.

23. 10. 1956:

Aufstand in Ungarn.

29. 10.—7. 11. 1956:

Bewaffneter Konflikt um den Sueskanal (nach dessen Verstaatlichung am 27. 7. 1956).

1 9 5 7

22. 1. 1957:

Der Bundestag verabschiedet mit 398 gegen 32 Stimmen bei 10 Enthaltungen das Gesetz über die Reform der Rentenversicherung der Arbeiter und Angestellten (*Rentenreform*).

6. 2. 1957:

Der Bundestag bestätigt *Berlin* als Hauptstadt Deutschlands.

25. 3. 1957:

In Rom werden die Vertragswerke über den Gemeinsamen Europäischen Markt (EWG) und die Europäische Atomgemeinschaft (EAG) unterzeichnet. Am 5. 7. 1957 stimmt der Bundestag mit großer Mehrheit zu.

23. 7. 1957:

In Moskau beginnen Handels- und Repatriierungsverhandlungen (siehe 8. 4. 1958).

29. 7. 1957:

Die Regierungen der Drei Westmächte und der Bundesrepublik unterzeichnen in Berlin ein Zwölf-Punkte-Programm zur deutschen Einheit („Berliner Erklärung").

15. 9. 1957:

Bei den Wahlen zum Dritten Bundestag erhält die CDU/CSU 50,2% der gültigen Stimmen. Am 29.10.1957 tritt die dritte Regierung ADENAUER (aus Ministern der CDU, CSU und der DP) ihr Amt an.

3. 10. 1957:

WILLY BRANDT (SPD) wird durch das Berliner Abgeordnetenhaus zum Regierenden Bürgermeister von Berlin(West) gewählt.

4. 10. 1957:

Die Sowjets starten den ersten künstlichen Erdsatelliten. Am 1.2.1958 gelingt den USA der Start des ersten Erdsatelliten. Vom 23.7. bis 5.8.1958 fährt das Atom-U-Boot „Nautilus" der USA-Marine durch die Beringstraße unter dem Polareis des Nordpols in den Nordatlantik.

19. 10. 1957:

Abbruch der diplomatischen Beziehungen der Bundesrepublik zu Jugeslawien als Folge der diplomatischen Anerkennung des Regimes der sogenannten DDR durch Belgrad.

11. 12. 1957:

Durch ein neues Paßgesetz und andere Maßnahmen vertiefen die Behörden der sogenannten DDR die Spaltung Deutschlands.

1958

24. 2. 1958:

Professor WERNER HEISENBERG gibt seine „neue Formel" bekannt (Lösungen für alle Arten von Materie durch Gleichungssysteme).

25. 3. 1958:

Der Bundestag beendet mit einer Entschließung die dreitägige Debatte über die Ausrüstung der Bundeswehr mit Atomwaffen.

8. 4. 1958:

In Moskau wird ein deutsch-sowjetisches Handelsabkommen paraphiert und eine Vereinbarung über die Rückkehr deutscher Staatsangehöriger aus der Sowjetunion getroffen. Die Vertragsunterzeichnung erfolgt in Bonn am 25.4.1958 durch den Ersten Stellvertretenden Ministerpräsidenten der Sowjetunion, ANASTAS MIKOJAN, und den Bundesminister des Auswärtigen.

29. 5. 1958:

General CHARLES DE GAULLE übernimmt die Regierungsbildung in Frankreich. Am 5.10.1958 beginnt die „Fünfte Republik".

29. 6. 1958:

Karl Arnold † (Ministerpräsident von Nordrhein-Westfalen 1947—1956).

2. 7. 1958:

Der Bundestag fordert einstimmig die Einsetzung eines Viermächte-Gremiums zur Vorbereitung der Wiedervereinigung Deutschlands. Die entsprechende Note der Bundesregierung wird den Vier Mächten am 9. 9. 1958 überreicht.

4. 7. 1958:

Bundespräsident Heuss spricht vor den beiden Häusern des USA-Kongresses.

13. 7. 1958:

Umsturz im Irak. Am 15. 7. 1958 landen Streitkräfte der USA in Libanon. Am 4. 9. 1958 wird der Höhepunkt der Fernostkrise (Taiwan und die USA in der Auseinandersetzung mit der Volksrepublik China) erreicht.

Juli 1958:

Der private Reiseverkehr zwischen der sogenannten DDR und der Bundesrepublik ist gegenüber dem Vorjahr um 83,3% gedrosselt: die Behörden der sogenannten DDR stellen 78.000 Reisegenehmigungen gegen 468.000 im Juli 1957 aus.

21. 8. 1958:

Der Rektor der Universität Jena flieht in die Bundesrepublik.

30. 9. 1958:

Mit 327.500 Arbeitslosen (= 1,7% der rund 19,3 Millionen Arbeitskräfte) wird der tiefste Stand seit der Währungsreform erreicht (siehe 30. 6. 1959).

9. 10. 1958:

Papst Pius XII. †. Am 28. 10. 1958 wird der Patriarch von Venedig zum Papst (Johannes XXIII.) gewählt und am 4. 11. 1958 gekrönt.

10. 11. 1958:

Ministerpräsident Chruschtschew fordert die Revision des Potsdamer Abkommens.

14. 11. 1958:

Der bisherige Ministerpräsident von Baden-Württemberg, Dr. Gebhard Müller, wird als Nachfolger von Dr. J. Wintrich zum Präsidenten des Bundesverfassungsgerichts gewählt.

27. 11. 1958:

Die Sowjetunion kündigt ihre Besatzungsverpflichtungen in Deutschland auf und verlangt für Berlin(West) den Status einer „entmilitarisierten Freien Stadt". Die deutsche Antwortnote wird am 5. 1. 1959 übergeben.

7. 12. 1958:

Bei einer Wahlbeteiligung von 93,7% anläßlich der Wahlen zum Abgeordnetenhaus in Berlin(West) erhält die SED 1,9% der abgegebenen gültigen Stimmen (SPD 52,6%, CDU 37,7%).

29. 12. 1958:

Die Europäische Zahlungsunion (EZU) wird aufgelöst. Die Deutsche Mark und die Währungen von neun anderen westeuropäischen Staaten werden frei austauschbar (Europäisches Währungsabkommen = EWA).

1959

10. 1. 1959:

Note der Sowjetregierung an die Teilnehmerstaaten des Krieges gegen Deutschland sowie an die Bundesrepublik und die sogenannte DDR betreffend *Vorschlag eines Friedensvertrags mit Deutschland.*

31. 1. 1959:

Bundespräsident THEODOR HEUSS wird 75 Jahre.

24. 3. 1959:

Mit der Ausgabe von Preußag-Aktien beginnt (über „Volksaktien") die Privatisierung von Teilen des Bundesvermögens. Die Aktien werden von 210.000 Interessenten gezeichnet.

11. 5. 1959:

Eine Deutschland-Konferenz der Außenminister der Vier Mächte beginnt in Genf (nach Vertagung fortgesetzt vom 13. 7. bis 5. 8. 1959). Delegationen aus der Bundesrepublik und der sogenannten DDR werden als Berater hinzugezogen.

30. 6. 1959:

Die Zahl der Arbeitslosen macht mit 255.395 nur noch 1,3% der Zahl der Arbeitsfähigen aus.

1. 7. 1959:

Die Bundesversammlung wählt in Berlin Dr. h. c. HEINRICH LÜBKE (derzeit Bundesminister für Ernährung, Landwirtschaft und Forsten) zum zweiten Präsidenten der Bundesrepublik Deutschland.

5. 7. 1959:

Im Einvernehmen der Bundesregierung mit der Französischen und der Saarländischen Regierung endet die auf höchstens drei Jahre befristete Übergangsfrist für die wirtschaftliche Eingliederung von Saarland.

3. 8. 1959:

Präsident EISENHOWER gibt bekannt, daß Ministerpräsident CHRUSCHTSCHEW im September auf seine Einladung die USA besuchen, und daß er den Besuch erwidern wird.

5. 8. 1959:

Die Genfer Außenministerkonferenz vertagt sich auf unbestimmte Zeit.

VERZEICHNIS DER SCHAUBILDER

DIE MITARBEITER[1]

Dr. Hermann Achenbach im Bundesministerium für Gesamtdeutsche Fragen ⋆ Dr. Manfred Attenberger, Regierungsrat im Bundesministerium des Innern ⋆ Gerhard Bantzer, Ministerialrat im Bundesministerium für Ernährung, Landwirtschaft und Forsten ⋆ Georg M. Bartosch, Pressestellenleiter des Wirtschaftsverbandes der Filmtheater Nordrhein-Westfalen e. V., Düsseldorf ⋆ Walter Büttner im Bundesministerium für Verkehr, Hamburg ⋆ Walter Dirks, Abteilungsleiter im Westdeutschen Rundfunk, Köln ⋆ Dr. Emil Ehrich, Oberregierungsrat bei der Vertretung des Landes Niedersachsen beim Bund, Bonn ⋆ Professor Dr. Hanns W. Eppelsheimer, Direktor der Deutschen Bibliothek, Frankfurt am Main ⋆ Dr. Werner Essen, Ministerialrat im Bundesministerium für Vertriebene, Flüchtlinge und Kriegsgeschädigte ⋆ Dr. Konrad Friesicke, Jugendreferent im Presse- und Informationsamt der Bundesregierung ⋆ Günther Fuchs, Oberregierungsrat im Bundesministerium des Innern ⋆ Dr. Hermann Fuchs, Direktor der Universitätsbibliothek Mainz, Vorsitzender des Vereins Deutscher Bibliothekare ⋆ Dr. Anton Furch, Oberregierungsrat im Bundesministerium für Gesamtdeutsche Fragen ⋆ Dipl. Ing. Alois Giefer, Architekt BDA, Frankfurt am Main ⋆ Dr. Margot Gleue, Pressestelle des Bundesministeriums für Verkehr ⋆ Horst Graebe, Oberregierungsrat im Bundesministerium für Vertriebene, Flüchtlinge und Kriegsgeschädigte ⋆ Dr. Witilo von Griesheim, Pressestelle des Bundesministeriums für Verkehr ⋆ Georg Gronau im Bundesministerium für Vertriebene, Flüchtlinge und Kriegsgeschädigte ⋆ Horst Haase im Presse- und Informationsamt des Landes Berlin ⋆ Karl Ulrich Hagelberg, Ministerialrat im Bundesministerium des Innern ⋆ Carla Herrmann im Presse- und Informationsamt der Bundesregierung ⋆ Professor Dr. Walther Herrmann, Leiter der Volkswirtschaftlichen Abteilung im Bundesverband der Deutschen Industrie, Köln ⋆ Ministerialdirektor Prof. Dr. Paul Egon Hübinger, Leiter der Abteilung für kulturelle Angelegenheiten des Bundes im Bundesministerium des Innern ⋆ Oberregierungsrat Friedrich Hoffmann, Institut für Landeskunde in der Bundesanstalt für Landeskunde und Raumforschung, Bad Godesberg ⋆ Dr. Hans Hoppe, Oberregierungsrat im Bundesministerium der Finanzen ⋆ Dr. Kurt Kaminski, Ministerialrat im Bundesministerium des Innern ⋆ Dr. Dorothea Karsten, Ministerialrätin, Leiterin des Frauenreferats im Bundesministerium des Innern ⋆ Dr. Eduard Kmonitzek, Oberlandforstmeister im Bundesministerium für Ernährung, Landwirtschaft und Forsten ⋆ Rudolf König, Oberregierungsrat im Bundesministerium des Innern ⋆ Franz Lepinski, Leiter der Pressestelle des Deutschen Gewerkschaftsbundes, Düsseldorf ⋆ Dr. Eberhard Lutze, Leitender Regierungsdirektor bei dem Senator für das Bildungswesen, Bremen ⋆ Karl Marx, Hauptschriftleiter der Allgemeinen Wochenzeitung der Juden in Deutschland, Düsseldorf ⋆ Dr. Gerhard Meseck, Ministerialdirigent im Bundesministerium für Ernährung, Landwirtschaft und

[1] Es sind die Funktionen zur Zeit der Abfassung der Beiträge angegeben.

DIE MITARBEITER

Forsten ⋆ Professor Dr. EMIL MEYNEN, Direktor der Bundesanstalt für Landeskunde und Raumforschung, Bad Godesberg ⋆ ALBERT MÜLLER, Pressereferent des Bundesministeriums für Arbeit und Sozialordnung ⋆ Dr. WOLFGANG MÜLLER, Oberarchivrat im Bundesarchiv, Koblenz ⋆ Dr. INGVELDE MÜLLER-KARWEHL, Geschäftsführerin der Deutschen Sektion des Internationalen Theater-Instituts e. V. (ITI), Berlin ⋆ Dr. HERMANN MUNZ, Legationsrat im Auswärtigen Amt ⋆ Dr. KLAUS-EBERHARD MURAWSKI im Bundesministerium für gesamtdeutsche Fragen ⋆ FERDINAND ERNST NORD, Verbandsdirektor des Stifterverbandes für die Deutsche Wissenschaft, Essen-Bredeney ⋆ Dr. DIRK ONCKEN, Legationsrat I. Klasse im Auswärtigen Amt ⋆ Dr. KURT PLÜCK im Bundesministerium für Gesamtdeutsche Fragen ⋆ Oberkirchenrat HANS JÜRG RANKE, Evangelische Kirche in Deutschland, Bonn ⋆ Ministerialrat a. D. Dr. HERBERT RHODE, Braunlage im Harz ⋆ Dr. HEINRICH RÖTTSCHES im Presse- und Informationsamt der Bundesregierung ⋆ Dr. WALTER RÜDIG, Oberregierungsrat im Bundesministerium für Arbeit und Sozialordnung ⋆ Dr. HANS-HELMUT RUETE, Legationsrat I. Klasse im Auswärtigen Amt ⋆ Dr. ALFONS SCHEUBLE, Oberregierungsrat im Bundesministerium für Arbeit und Sozialordnung ⋆ Dr. HANS-GEORG SCHLICKER, Pressereferent des Bundesministeriums für Vertriebene, Flüchtlinge und Kriegsgeschädigte ⋆ CHRISTIAN SCHNEIDER im Bundesministerium für Wohnungsbau ⋆ Hauptmann Dr. WOLFGANG SEIZ im Bundesministerium für Verteidigung ⋆ SIEGFRIED TAUBERT, Börsenverein des Deutschen Buchhandels, Frankfurt am Main ⋆ HANS THIER, Oberregierungsrat im Bundesministerium der Justiz ⋆ PETER TITZHOFF, Deutsche Zentrale für Fremdenverkehr, Frankfurt am Main ⋆ Dr. EDUARD TRIER, Kunstkritiker und Schrifsteller, Köln ⋆ GÜNTER TRIESCH, Referent in der sozialwissenschaftlichen Abteilung des Deutschen Industrieinstituts, Köln ⋆ Dipl.-Volkswirt Dr. HANS-HERBERT WEBER, Regierungsrat im Bundesministerium für Wirtschaft ⋆ HANS-HEINRICH WELCHERT, Referent im Presse- und Informationsamt der Bundesregierung ⋆ ARNOLD WELLER, Ministerialrat im Bundesministerium des Innern ⋆ Reg.-Ass. Dr. OTFRIED WLOTZKE im Bundesministerium für Arbeit und Sozialordnung ⋆ Dr. KARL H. WÖRNER, Dozent der Folkwangschule, Essen-Werden ⋆ Dr. GERHARD WOLFRUM, Oberregierungsrat im Bundesministerium für Vertriebene, Flüchtlinge und Kriegsgeschädigte ⋆ Senatsrat Dr. OTTO WOLKWITZ, Vertretung des Landes Berlin beim Bund, Bonn ⋆ WILHELM WRASMANN, Pressereferent des Bundesbevollmächtigten in Berlin ⋆ Bundesministerium für das Post- und Fernmeldewesen (Gemeinschaftsarbeit).

Soweit in diesem Buch Material der amtlichen Bundesstatistik verwendet wurde, ist es durch das STATISTISCHE BUNDESAMT in Wiesbaden zur Verfügung gestellt worden. Verbindungsreferentin: Regierungsrätin ELSA GRALLERT.

GESAMTREDAKTION: PROFESSOR DR. HELMUT ARNTZ.

REGISTER[1]

[1] Begriffe, die nur der sogenannten DDR eigen sind, stehen in Anführungszeichen. — Römische Zahlen beziehen sich auf die Bildtafeln.

[1] Die Namen der auf den Seiten 766 bis 772 genannten Architekten sind im Register nicht einzeln aufgeführt.

[1] Die Namen der auf den Seiten 756 bis 766 genannten Künstler sind im Register nicht einzeln aufgeführt.

[1] Die Namen der auf den Seiten 736 bis 740 genannten Dichter sind nicht einzeln in das Register aufgenommen.

[1] Die auf den Seiten 749–755 genannten Komponisten sind in das Register nicht einzeln aufgenommen.

[1] Die auf den Seiten 778–791 genannten Autoren, Intendanten usw. sind im Register nicht einzeln verzeichnet.

NACHWEIS ZU DEN BILDTAFELN

Die Aufnahmen stammen von der *Bundesbildstelle* im Presse- und Informationsamt der Bundesregierung, Bonn, Welckerstraße 11, mit folgenden Ausnahmen[1]:

Tafel II l. o. (EISENHOWER mit HEUSS) dpa ⋆ VIII l. o. Archiv des BM für Verteidigung; M. SHAPE; u. USIS ⋆ XVI o. Agfa-Bildarchiv ⋆ XX M. Werksphoto FRIEDRICH KRUPP, Essen; u. Werksphoto Farbenfabriken Bayer AG, Leverkusen (desgleichen XXII o. und u.; XXXVI o., M. und u.; XXXVII l. o.) ⋆ XXIII (6 Bilder) Werksphotos der DEMAG AG, Duisburg; XXVIII (3 Bilder) und XXIX (3 Bilder) Land- und Hauswirtschaftlicher Informationsdienst (AID), Bad Godesberg ⋆ XXX l. o., l. M. und r. u. Hauptverwaltung der Deutschen Bundesbahn, Pressedienst ⋆ XXXI o. HUGO SCHMÖLZ, Köln; l. u. AERO EXPLORATION, Frankfurt am Main (freigegeben unter Nr. 143/56 durch Hess. Min. für Arbeit); r. u. Donaukraftwerk Jochenstein AG, Passau ⋆ XXXII (3 Bilder) Bildarchiv des BM für das Post- und Fernmeldewesen ⋆ XXXVII r. o. und r. u. sowie XXXVIII r. u. Werksphotos der Daimler-Benz AG, Untertürkheim ⋆ XLVI und XLVII (8 Bilder): Aufnahmen von ERNA LENDVAI-DIRKSEN im Besitz der Bundesbildstelle.

[1] l., r., M., o., u. = links, rechts, Mitte, oben, unten.

ABKÜRZUNGSVERZEICHNIS

Soweit möglich, wurden keine Abkürzungen ohne Erklärung verwendet. Es sind erklärt . . . auf Seite . .